Microcomputers & Applications

# Microcomputers & Applications

Ernest S. Colantonio
University of Illinois

D.C. HEATH AND COMPANY
Lexington, Massachusetts Toronto

Acquisitions Editor: Peter Gordon
Developmental Editor: Ann Hall
Production Editor: Laurie Johnson
Editorial Assistant: Katherine Sheehan
Production Coordinator: Michael O'Dea
Photo Researcher: Janet Goldman
Text Permissions Editor: Margaret Roll
Cover Photographs: Dan Nerney/Dot



Published simultaneously in Canada.

Printed in the United States of America.

International Standard Book Number: 0–669–16549–2

Library of Congress Catalog Card Number: 88–83917

10 9 8 7 6 5 4 3 2 1

## Notes to dBASE III Plus Users

Important: Please read this page before using the dBASE III Plus program, a copy of which is being made available to you for use in conjunction with the Textbook pursuant to the terms of this Agreement for educational, training, and/or demonstration purposes. By using the dBASE III Plus program, you show your agreement to the terms of this license.

### EXCLUSIONS OF WARRANTIES AND LIMITATIONS OF LIABILITY

THE COPY OF THE dBASE III PLUS PROGRAM MADE AVAILABLE FOR USE WITH THIS TEXTBOOK IS A LIMITED FUNCTIONALITY VERSION OF dBASE III PLUS, AND IS INTENDED SOLELY FOR EDUCATIONAL, TRAINING, AND DEMONSTRATION PURPOSES. ACCORDINGLY, THIS COPY OF dBASE III PLUS IS PROVIDED "AS IS," WITHOUT WARRANTY OF ANY KIND FROM ASHTON-TATE OR D. C. HEATH. ASHTON-TATE AND D. C. HEATH HEREBY DISCLAIM ALL WARRANTIES OF ANY KIND WITH RESPECT TO THIS LIMITED FUNCTIONALITY COPY OF dBASE III PLUS, INCLUDING WITHOUT LIMITATION THE IMPLIED WARRANTIES OF MERCHANTABILITY AND FITNESS FOR A PARTICULAR PURPOSE. NEITHER ASHTON-TATE NOR D. C. HEATH SHALL BE LIABLE UNDER EXEMPLARY DAMAGES ARISING OUT OF THE USE OF THIS LIMITED FUNCTIONALITY COPY OF dBASE III PLUS, EVEN IF ASHTON-TATE OR D. C. HEATH HAS BEEN APPRISED OF THE LIKELIHOOD OF SUCH DAMAGES OCCURRING. IN NO EVENT WILL ASHTON-TATE'S OR D. C. HEATH'S LIABILITY (WHETHER BASED ON AN ACTION OR CLAIM IN CONTRACT, TORT OR OTHERWISE) ARISING OUT OF THE USE OF THIS LIMITED FUNCTIONALITY COPY OF dBASE III PLUS EXCEED THE AMOUNT PAID FOR THIS TEXTBOOK.

### LIMITED USE SOFTWARE LICENSE AGREEMENT

**Definitions**

The term "Software" as used in this agreement means the Limited Use version of dBASE III Plus which is made available for use in conjunction with this Textbook solely for educational, training and/or demonstration purposes. The term "Software Copies" means the actual copies of all or any portion of the Software, including back-ups, updates, merged or partial copies permitted hereunder.

**Permitted Uses**

You may:

- Load into RAM and use the Software on a single terminal or a single workstation of a computer (or its replacement).
- Install the Software onto a permanent storage device (a hard disk drive).
- Make and maintain up to three back-up copies provided they are used only for back-up purposes, and you keep possession of the back-ups. In addition, all the information appearing on the original disk labels (including copyright notice) must be copied onto the back-up labels.

This license gives you certain limited rights to use the Software and Software Copies for educational, training and/or demonstration purposes. You do not become the owner of and Ashton-Tate retains title to, all the Software and Software Copies. In addition, you agree to use reasonable efforts to protect the Software from unauthorized use, reproduction, distribution or publication.

All rights not specifically granted in this license are reserved by Ashton-Tate.

**Uses Not Permitted**

You may not:

- Make copies of the Software, except as permitted above.
- Rent, lease, sublicense, time-share, lend or transfer the Software, Software Copies or your rights under this license except that transfers may be made with Ashton-Tate's prior written authorization.
- Alter, decompile, disassemble, or reverse-engineer the Software.
- Remove or obscure the Ashton-tate copyright and trademark notices.
- Use the Software or Software Copies outside the United States or Canada.

**Duration**

This agreement is effective from the day you first use the Software. Your license continues for fifty years or until you return to Ashton-Tate the original disks and any back-up copies, whichever comes first.

If you breach this agreement, Ashton-Tate can terminate this license upon notifying you in writing. You will be required to return all Software Copies. Ashton-Tate can also enforce our other legal rights.

**General**

This agreement represents the entire understanding and agreement regarding the Software and Software Copies and supersedes any prior purchase order, communication, advertising or representation.

This license may only be modified in a written amendment signed by an authorized Ashton-Tate officer. If any provision of this agreement shall be unlawful, void, or for any reason unenforceable, it shall be deemend severable from, and shall in no way affect the validity or enforceability of the remaining provisions of this agreement. This agreement will be governed by California law.

## Notes to WordPerfect 4.2 Users

The Limited-Use introductory version of WordPerfect 4.2 (L-WP) is intended to allow one to learn the features of WordPerfect 4.2; however, the L-WP is not intended to allow one to print usable academic or professional documents[1].

Certain limitations *(which should not deter learning WordPerfect through the L-WP)* have been encrypted into the L-WP to guard against productive use, and are as follows:

I. One may work with as large a document on screen as desired, but one may only save to disk a data file no larger than 50,000k (appx. 25-30 regular pages).

II. Data files of any size may be printed through parallel printer port "1" without defining a printer, but font changes and extended ASCII characters are not allowed. Also, "*WPC" will be printed after each paragraph.

III. One will be able to learn all the functions of WordPerfect 4.2's speller and thesaurus by calling up the "readme.wp" file and following the step-by-step directions; however, one cannot use the L-WP speller and thesaurus with any of one's own documents because there are only a limited number of words in the L-WP speller and thesaurus. (The regular speller has 115,000 words, and the regular thesaurus has approximately 150,000 words.)

IV. The help file of L-WP allows the user to retrieve the function-key template, but similar to the speller and the thesaurus described above, space will not allow the full help files on the L-WP disk.

L-WP is designed to be used for introductory, word processing courses, and thus far has been well received in these types of environments. Notwithstanding the broad abilities provided in the L-WP, presumably the L-WP will not satisfactorily substitute for regular WordPerfect 4.2, and therefore the full feature version may be obtained directly from WordPerfect Corporation via the order form, found at the end of this book, at a 75% educational discount.

1. "*WPC" will be automatically printed after each paragraph of text to discourage academic or professional use of the L-WP. *See* paragraph II above.

# Preface

The microcomputer has become standard equipment in most schools, offices, and businesses. A wealth of exceptional software is available to apply this versatile tool to a wide range of tasks. *Microcomputers and Applications* has been written for the novice end-user of microcomputers and application software.

Most end-users are not computer engineers; therefore, we discuss hardware only to help students understand how to use software. Most end-users are not computer programmers; we do not teach programming. Most microcomputer users, however, do work with operating system, word processing, spreadsheet, and data base management software. They may also use communications, networking, graphics, desktop publishing, and accounting software, as well as other more specialized application programs. This text teaches students how to use such software in their everyday lives.

## Text Content and Organization

*Microcomputers and Applications* has been carefully designed for use in any first course in microcomputer application software. It should also be helpful to individuals who want to learn more about using microcomputers.

**Variety** The text emphasizes the most commonly used microcomputer software—operating systems and word processing, spreadsheet, and data base management packages. Its comprehensive coverage also includes many other popular types of application software—from disk backup utilities to expert system shells. Despite this diversity, *Microcomputers and Applications* requires no previous computer skills or mathematical skills beyond basic arithmetic.

**Flexibility** The text can be used in many different courses. Its 16 chapters are divided into six parts that can, with some exceptions, be taught in any order. We recommend covering Part 1, The Microcomputer System (Chapters 1 through 3), first, and then Part 2, Operating Systems (Chapters 4 and 5). After that, Part 3, Word Processing (Chapters 6 and 7); Part 4, Spreadsheets (Chapters 8 and 9); Part 5, Data Base Management (Chapters 10 and 11); and Part 6, Special Applications (Chapters 12 through 16), can be read in any order.

**Computer Skills** The text can be used in courses with or without microcomputer laboratory facilities. Parts 2 through 5 all have both a chapter on general concepts and a chapter that covers the details of using a particular software product. Specifically, the text teaches DOS 4.00, WordPerfect Versions 4.2 and 5.0, WordStar Release 5, Lotus 1-2-3 Release 2.01, SuperCalc 5.0, and dBASE III PLUS. Many other commercial software products are used as examples throughout the text. Instructors may use their own software packages or adopt any of the many software supplements offered by D. C. Heath for *Microcomputers and Applications* (see the section on Software Support).

**Appendixes** The text's six appendixes provide additional material that may be of interest to students and instructors. Appendix A, Data Representation, briefly discusses how computers code numbers and characters. Appendix B, Selecting a System, provides valuable tips for those individuals faced with the daunting task of purchasing hardware and software. Appendix C, Software Installation, briefly summarizes how to set up DOS, WordStar, Lotus 1-2-3, and dBASE III PLUS on a computer. Appendix D, Spreadsheet Details: SuperCalc 5.0, presents an alternative to Chapter 9 for those who do not have access to Lotus 1-2-3. D. C. Heath offers an educational version of SuperCalc 5.0, a powerful new spreadsheet package. Finally Appendix E, Word Processing Details: WordPerfect 5.0, and Appendix F, Word Processing Details: WordPerfect 4.2, present alternatives to Chapter 7. D. C. Heath offers an educational version of WordPerfect 4.2.

## Text Learning Aids

*Microcomputers and Applications* combines a relaxed writing style with an outstanding array of pedagogical features to facilitate understanding and encourage reader enthusiasm.

**Chapter Outline** Each chapter opens with *In This Chapter*, an outline of the chapter's headings.

**Chapter Preview** Students learn more effectively if they are presented with clear learning objectives. Each chapter's *Preview* section introduces the material and provides learning objectives.

**Computer Insights** The *Insight* box in each chapter poses an intriguing question about microcomputers and then answers it with information obtained from computer experts.

**The Real World** Every chapter includes *The Real World*, a selection from a magazine, newspaper, or book about a topic covered in the chapter. This feature is designed to help the reader understand how microcomputers and application software are actually being used in today's world.

**Annotation** Marginal notes throughout each chapter help students quickly locate key topics.

**Readability** The text's engaging writing style ensures that concepts are explained clearly and simply. Editors, course instructors, and reviewers have carefully monitored the reading level to maintain accessibility for students.

**Design and Illustrations** Students prefer a textbook that will hold their interest. We have created a design that is simple, but that effectively presents the material. Current photographs, striking line art, and high-resolution computer screen views are liberally inserted throughout each chapter to help illustrate major topics. Sections of color photographs enhance the presentation of key subjects.

**End-of-Chapter Materials** A carefully graded set of review materials is provided at the end of each chapter. First, the *Summary* briefly reviews the information that parallels the learning objectives stated in the chapter's *Preview*. Next, the *Key Terms* presents all of the chapter's boldfaced glossary terms and their page references.

Twenty short-answer *Review Questions* follow, providing a rote review of the chapter's major topics. The 15 *Multiple Choice* questions provide further opportunity for students to review the chapter. Finally, four special *Projects* encourage students to extend their learning beyond the chapter content. In addition, chapters that cover the details of a specific software product (Chapters 5, 7, 9, and 11, and Appendixes D, E, and F) also include a *Command Summary*, which is a quick reference guide to the software, and 15 *On-line Exercises*, which provide hands-on tasks for students with access to a microcomputer and the software.

**Glossary and Index** A complete glossary, with chapter references, includes clear definitions for the boldfaced terms in the text. In addition, a detailed index provides a handy reference for both student and instructor.

## Software Support

An extensive software supplements package is offered with the text to help both student and instructor. D. C. Heath is pleased to make available to adopters of this text educational versions of WordPerfect 4.2, SuperCalc 5.0, and dBASE III PLUS for use with this text. Your local Heath representative would be happy to supply you with master diskettes of these powerful and popular software packages. You may also call our toll-free number, (800) 235-3565, for quick attention to your software needs. In addition to the three software packages licensed with this text, the *Heath Software Guide Series* and programming supplements are also available.

The *Heath Software Guide Series* includes the following student software laboratory workbooks and programming texts, most available with software:

### Word Processing

Using WordStar 4/5*
Using WordPerfect 5.0*
Using PC-Write*
Using PC-Type+*

### Spreadsheet

Using SuperCalc 5.0*
Using Lotus 1-2-3
Using VP-Planner Plus*
Using PC-Calc+*

### Data Base

Using dBASE III PLUS*
Using PC-File+*

### Expert Systems

Using VP-Expert*

### Communications

Using PC-Dial*

### Operating Systems

Using DOS and OS/2

### Macintosh Software

Using Macintosh Software*

### Programming Texts

Introduction to Structured Microsoft Basic
Programming in Pascal, with Lab
Modula 2

These workbooks and texts provide students with instructions, examples, and exercises to get them started using microcomputers quickly and confidently. Each book begins with an introduction to the microcomputer and a tutorial on DOS or the Macintosh operating system.

*Available with software.

## Supplements

**Instructor's Supplements** In addition to the software support, the supplements designed for instructors include an *Instructor's Guide* with transparency masters, a *Test Item File*, HeathTest Plus (a Computerized Test Generator), and *Transparencies*.

**Instructor's Guide** Prepared by Dr. Paul W. Ross of Millersville University, the *Instructor's Guide* includes the following materials for busy teachers: learning objectives, chapter overviews, annotated lecture outlines, answers to text questions, additional classroom and lecture materials, and transparency masters.

**Test Item File** A *Test Item File* developed by Richard E. Morel includes approximately 2000 test questions: 40% true-false, 30% multiple choice, and 30% fill-in.

**HeathTest Plus** A computerized test generator for microcomputers is also available. Instructors can produce chapter tests, mid-terms, and final exams easily and accurately. Instructors can also edit existing questions or add new ones as desired, or preview questions on screen and add them to a test with a single keystroke.

**Transparencies** The transparency package includes 50 transparencies.

## Acknowledgments

Many people helped make *Microcomputers and Applications* possible. I would like to thank Dr. Robert Hendersen and Nancy Sampson of the University of Illinois Department of Psychology Instructional Computer Laboratory for the use of various microcomputer hardware and software. Dr. Paul W. Ross of Millersville University provided many helpful suggestions throughout the development of this project. In addition to her work as Developmental Editor, Ann Hall helped extensively with the *Insight* and *The Real World* features.

I would like to thank all of my colleagues who reviewed the manuscript:

Professor Harvey Blessing
Essex Community College

Professor Walter Bremer
California Polytechnic University

Professor Frank S. Butash
University of Hartford

Dr. William Engelmeyer
Anne Arundel Community College

Professor Clinton P. Fuelling
Ball State University

Professor C. Brian Honess
University of South Carolina

Professor Susan Karian
Denison University

Professor Gladys Norman
Linn-Benton Community College

Dr. J. Douglas Robertson
Bentley College

Professor Jerry Sitek
Southern Illinois University
at Edwardsville

Professor Karen Watterson
Shoreline Community College

Thanks also to the following software vendors for their continued efforts in their support of students and faculty by making it possible for publishers to offer free educational versions of their software: Ashton-Tate, especially Judith Delaney and Larry Colker; Computer Associates, especially Gershon Blumstein; WordPerfect, especially Mary Hunn.

Finally, my special gratitude and appreciation go to all the people at D. C. Heath who worked long hours and sweated endless details to make this text the best that it could be.

E. S. C.

## About the Author

Ernest S. Colantonio brings combined teaching, technical, and writing skills to this textbook. Currently a professional textbook author, he also develops software tools for the University of Illinois Department of Psychology Instructional Computer Laboratory. Mr. Colantonio received his undergraduate degree in psychology and has completed several semesters of graduate work in computer science at the University of Illinois at Urbana-Champaign. While in graduate school, he also taught introductory courses in computer science for nontechnical majors.

# Brief Contents

# Contents

# Part 2 Operating Systems 113

# Part 1

# THE MICROCOMPUTER SYSTEM

The computer has changed our world. Almost every sector of our economy and every aspect of our society have been affected by computers. It's not just the scientists, engineers, and business people who need to know how to use computers; to some extent, we all do. The simple fact is: If you work with information, sooner or later you'll have to use a computer.

Microcomputers are by far the most numerous and accessible type of computer. These small, relatively inexpensive computers have infiltrated virtually all large corporations, most schools, and many homes. Why? Because they have proven to be extremely useful, versatile, and economical. The key to their power is the tasks they have been programmed to do. These tasks, or **applications,** are the primary focus of this book.

This part of the text sets the stage for your study of microcomputer applications. Chapter 1 presents basic computer concepts. Chapter 2 describes the physical components that make up microcomputer systems. Chapter 3 introduces the instructions, or **software programs,** that make microcomputers work.

# 1

# Computer Concepts

## In This Chapter

## PREVIEW

As this story demonstrates, once you get past the technical terminology of computers, they're really not all that difficult to learn about and use. This chapter sets the stage for your study of microcomputers by discussing why you should learn about computers, how these machines are used, and the various types of computers. Don't be alarmed if you see unfamiliar words. Most of the technical terms in this chapter will be initially defined very briefly or in context. Important terms will be defined again more rigorously in later chapters, after you have read additional background material. You may not wind up teaching people how to use computers or running a computer business, but this text will show you how to effectively use microcomputers in our high-tech information age.

After studying this chapter, you will understand

- why you should study computers.
- some of the ways in which microcomputers are used.
- the elements of a typical microcomputer system.
- the different types of microcomputers.
- the dominant microcomputer standards.
- the various types of other computers.

## WHY STUDY COMPUTERS?

Computers have been getting a lot of attention lately. We hear about them almost every day and we see them all around us. In fact, every time you cash a check, go through a supermarket checkout, or listen to a compact disc player, computers are involved. What can they do for you? Why should you spend the time and effort to learn more about computers? Why did you take this course?

You could simply answer that this course is required by your department or perhaps it is a prerequisite for some other, more advanced course that you want to take. There are, however, more profound reasons why you should know more about computers. A few of them have to do with learning, employment, productivity, capability, and fun.

### Learning

*Better educated*

Computers affect our lives, whether we realize it or not. They are used in banks, offices, stores, factories, schools, government agencies, military installations, and just about any other organization you can think of. Tiny specialized computers are built into many modern appliances, machines, and vehicles. All kinds of advanced equipment from cameras to jet aircraft depend utterly on computer technology. Unless you learn a few fundamental computer concepts, it will be difficult to understand many of today's and tomorrow's technological issues. Just as people had to learn to use the telephone in the early twentieth century, people have to learn to use computers in order to function in our increasingly complex society.

This is especially true for college students, because computer use on campuses has been growing at a phenomenal rate. According to a report in the *Chronicle of Higher Education*, colleges spent $800 million and students spent another $1 billion on microcomputer products in 1987 alone. At many colleges, courses in a wide

**Insight**

## How Small Can Computers Get?

Look in the mirror. What you see is the only restriction on the incredible shrinking computer. Your hands have to fit on the keyboard and you have to be able to see the screen. Simple.

In their infancy, computers were giant Baby Hueys that filled the whole floor of a building. They pumped out heat, regularly blew out their vacuum tubes, clattered and whirred. Some of them had to have their circuits rewired whenever their programs were changed.

Some early microcomputers, such as the Compaq and Kaypro, were about the size of a portable sewing machine and weighed around 25 to 30 pounds. They weren't exactly portable—more like lugable. The person on the go could develop back strain carrying one of these around.

But there was a big market for smaller computers, which prodded manufacturers into producing machines that were about the size of a portable typewriter. These became known as laptop computers.

Laptops have a flat screen like a pocket calculator or a digital watch. They have at least one floppy disk for storing programs and data, and the newer systems have a built-in hard drive capable of storing at least 10 million characters of information. They can be plugged into a wall outlet or they can run for a few hours from an internal, rechargeable battery pack.

Laptops are being improved all the time. Their limited space is being used more efficiently, and their memory and storage are being expanded. If a modem is used with the laptop, files can be moved back and forth from a central computer. This increases the unit's power and flexibility, making it ideal for traveling business people or for journalists filing stories.

range of subjects now require students to use computers (see Figure 1.1). In some cases, faculty members are designing their own ways for students to use computers in their studies. For example, the philosophy department at Carnegie Mellon University in Pittsburgh offers a computerized course to help students learn the principles of symbolic logic at their own pace. Students who already know how to use a computer may find it easier to adapt to these types of courses.[1]

**Figure 1.1 Computers in Education**
Many schools now require students to use computers in some of their subjects.

1. Jack Hayes, "Do Computer Skills Make College Grads More Marketable?," *Family & Home Office Computing,* April, 1988, pp. 26-28.

## Employment

*Competitive job skills*

Since most businesses and other organizations routinely use computers, employers need workers who are at least familiar with them. Knowing how to use a computer certainly won't guarantee you a job, but it can help you to be more competitive in today's labor market. At Northwestern Mutual Life, for example, microcomputers are essential tools. The company has sold more than 2000 computers to its 6000 independent insurance agents. Agents working in the same office generally share computers, so every agent has access to a computer (see Figure 1.2). According to Mark Lichtenberger, a technical planning officer at Northwestern Mutual, "An agent can't do business without a PC (personal computer). Without one, he or she has no access to sales-illustration charts, which are impossible to calculate manually." Some life insurance policies now offered by Northwestern Mutual are so complex that agents need a computer to demonstrate the advantages to potential customers.[2]

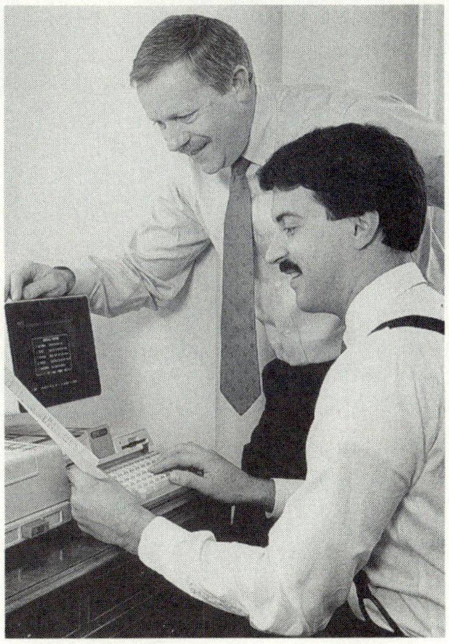

**Figure 1.2 Computers on the Job**
At Northwestern Mutual Life, insurance agents simply can't do business without a microcomputer.

Another indication that students with computer skills do better in the job market comes from an informal survey done by Barbara Kurshan, former director of academic computing at Hollins College, a liberal arts school in Roanoke, Virginia. A cross section of students was questioned, including one hundred who had taken at least two computer courses at Hollins. Kurshan found that 70 percent of the students who had taken computer courses were routinely using computers in their jobs. These individuals generally thought that they got their jobs and were paid more because of their computer experience.[3]

## Productivity

*Increased efficiency*

A compelling reason for learning to use a computer is that it can help you do certain jobs more efficiently. For example, **word processing**, a common computer application (see Figure 1.3), allows you to produce documents, such as letters and

2. Craig Zarley, "PCs an Essential Tool for Insurance Sales," *PC Week*, March 15, 1988, pp. 47-53.
3. Hayes, "Computer Skills," pp. 26-28.

reports, with a computer. Once you learn how to do word processing with a computer, producing documents is easier, faster, and more flexible than with an ordinary typewriter. Since you can correct errors before committing your work to paper, word processing also can produce much cleaner final documents, more efficiently. For example, a study done by R. Haider in 1979 suggests that word processing can eliminate up to 70 percent of the time spent on conventional typing.[4] Besides word processing, many other computer applications can save you a great deal of time and effort in your routine work.

**Figure 1.3 Word Processing On a Microcomputer**
Many people use word processing to increase their personal productivity.

## Capability

*Perform otherwise impossible tasks*

Computers not only let you perform everyday tasks more efficiently, but they also allow you to tackle jobs you otherwise wouldn't be able to do at all. One example is a computer-simulated chemistry lab at the University of Illinois (see Figure 1.4). This lab lets students mix hazardous chemicals and see the results without endangering themselves or the building. Actually, students don't mix real chemicals; they just tell the computer what they would mix. The computer then displays on a screen prerecorded video sequences of the results that would occur if those chemicals were actually combined. Although computer-simulated explosions aren't quite as exciting as the real thing, they are much safer for students and less destructive to equipment and facilities.

4. R. Haider, "New Frontiers in Office Automation," Proceedings of the Infotech State of the Art Conference, Vienna, 1979.

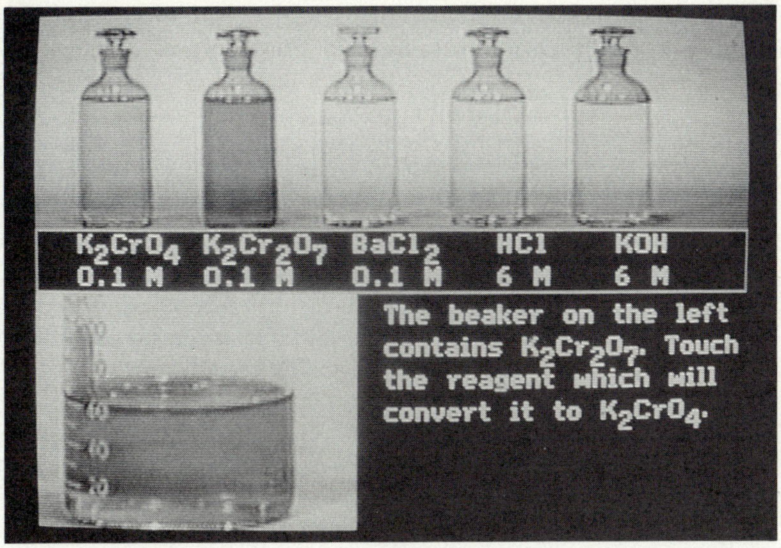


**Figure 1.4 Computer Chemistry Lab**
At the University of Illinois, computers enable students to simulate mixing dangerous chemicals without blowing themselves up.

## Fun

*Entertainment*

Once they learn to use a computer, most people find that they enjoy it. It's fun to work with such an interactive and attentive device. Give the computer the correct command and it will leap into action, often completing the task much more quickly than you thought possible. Some people even seem to get a greater feeling of accomplishment after successfully performing a task with a computer than if they did it by hand. Besides, there are many computer games available—from simulations of traditional board games such as chess and Monopoly, to exciting arcade games such as Pac Man and Dark Castle (see Figure 1.5). The computer opens whole new worlds of information, communication, productivity, and entertainment.

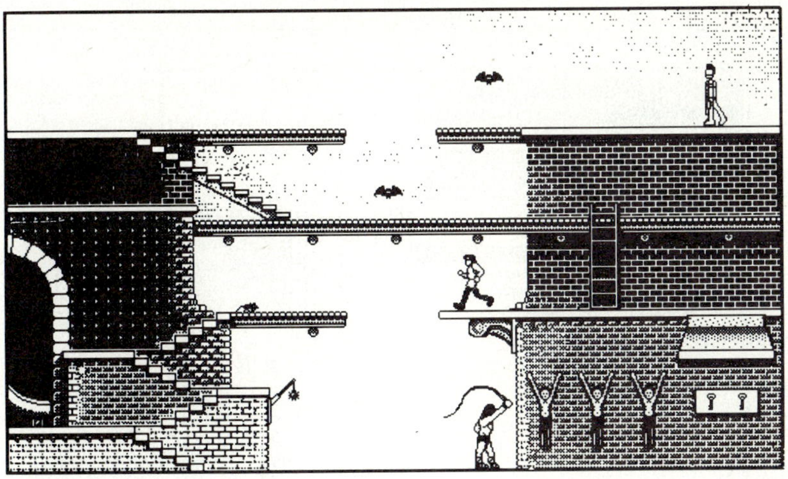

**Figure 1.5 Computer Entertainment**
Microcomputers are often used to play games and to pursue other entertaining activities.

## HOW COMPUTERS ARE USED

Computers are tools; they help people perform many different kinds of tasks. One way to gain an appreciation for computers is to see how some people use them in their daily lives. The sections following in this chapter describe a few specific examples of people using computers to improve their personal productivity, to manage information, to communicate with others, to make presentations, and to help them learn.

## Personal Productivity

*Organizing daily activities*

Dr. Robert Hendersen, the acting head of the Psychology Department at the University of Illinois at Urbana-Champaign, uses microcomputers nearly every day. Dr. Hendersen has an IBM Personal Computer AT in his office on campus and an identical system at home. When he travels to conferences he often takes a small, battery-operated IBM Convertible. Dr. Hendersen probably uses his microcomputers most frequently for word processing. He uses a program called WordPerfect to prepare scientific articles, classroom lectures, student handouts, and research specifications. Many of the graphs and figures Dr. Hendersen includes in his articles and lectures are prepared on his computer with graphics programs such as Energraphics and AutoCAD. He even used AutoCAD to design the landscaping of his yard at home.

Dr. Hendersen also uses his computers for much of his routine correspondence with colleagues. From home with his Personal Computer AT or from a hotel room with his Convertible, Dr. Hendersen can call up and tap into the large computer housed in the Psychology Building on campus. He can read messages sent to him by other faculty members and send them immediate replies. For regular phone correspondence, Dr. Hendersen maintains a list of associates' telephone numbers with a program called SideKick (see Figure 1.6). This same program also provides an on-screen calculator, an appointment calendar, and a notepad for jotting down ideas. Finally, since many psychology classes and research projects require microcomputers, Dr. Hendersen uses his machines to test and demonstrate software that is developed by teaching assistants, research assistants, and other faculty members. In short, the Psychology Department at the University of Illinois would probably be run much less efficiently if Dr. Hendersen didn't use microcomputers.

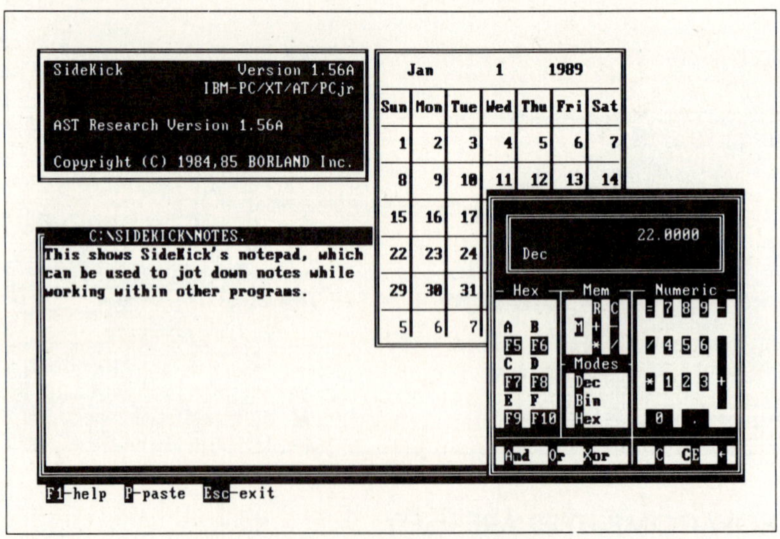


**Figure 1.6 Personal Productivity Software**
SideKick, from Borland International, is one example of personal productivity software. This program provides functions such as a notepad, calculator, calendar, and phone dialer.

## Information Management

*Tracking contacts*

Computers are excellent tools for managing large quantities of information (see Figure 1.7). Just ask Ron Wubker, a partner at Western Freezers, a Fremont, California-based company that sells ice cream machines. Wubker uses an IBM Personal Computer and a program called Prodex to keep track of staff, suppliers, and other contacts. Once he entered the name, address, phone number, and a few brief notes about each of his 200 contacts into the computer, Wubker was able to maintain and retrieve this information much more efficiently than he could with a Rolodex file. The Prodex program allows him to organize his list of contacts by last name, first name, company, or recall date. If he wants to make a call to one of his contacts, Wubker can tell the program to have the computer automatically dial the phone. Instead of taking a card file of contacts with him on business trips, Wubker simply prints out the entire list on paper. It's a lot less frustrating, Wubker claims, than spending half the night in a hotel room reorganizing his card file after accidentally spilling the cards all over the floor.[5]

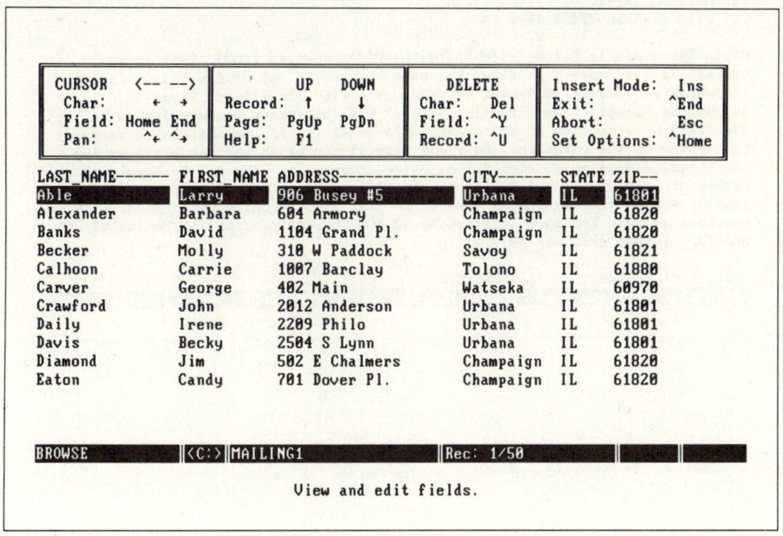


**Figure 1.7 Information Managers**
Microcomputers are frequently used to manage information, such as lists of personal contacts and their addresses and phone numbers.

## Communication

*Interacting with distant colleagues*

The telephone and the computer are two of our most useful tools. Combine them and you end up with a powerful communication system. Many people use their computers together with their telephones to call **on-line information services**. These services allow computer users access to vast quantities of information. They can read the latest news, shop, bank, buy stocks, make travel arrangements, and communicate with other users all over the world. Many information services allow users who share special interests to participate in electronic forums, or **teleconferences**. For example, CompuServe is the largest on-line information service in the world. One of its many special interest groups is MedSIG, the Medical Special Interest Group (see Figure 1.8). MedSIG recently sponsored an on-line conference about an anti-inflammatory drug called Zomax. According to Dr. John Sheppard,

5. Sam Diamond, "People Tracking," *Personal Computing*, December, 1987, pp. 133-139.

a general practitioner in Vermont who operates MedSIG, one of the members of the group started the conference because "he believed people were dying from the drug, and he wanted to see what kinds of experiences other doctors were having after prescribing the drug for their patients." This electronic conference was one of the first organized discussions about problems with the drug Zomax. Other doctors, it seemed, were also having bad results with Zomax. One of the conference participants happened to be a member of the Food and Drug Administration. Eventually, Zomax was withdrawn from the market. The FDA was so impressed with the MedSIG conference that it is investigating ways to use an internal on-line information service.[6]

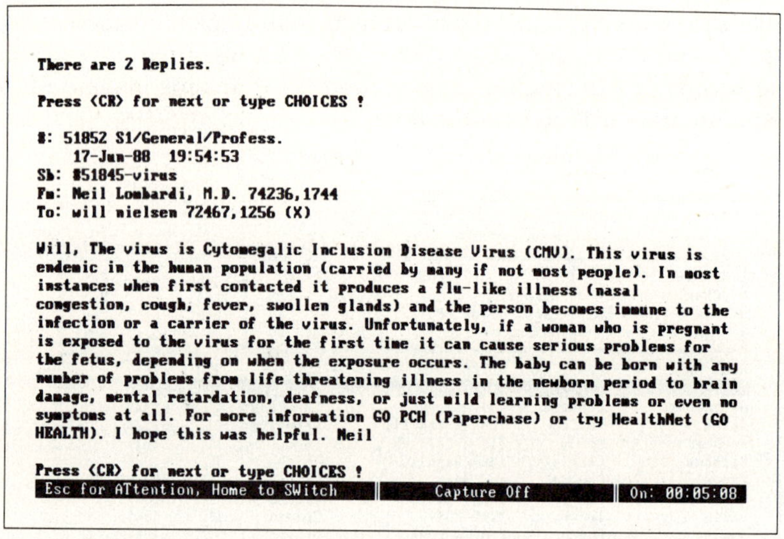


**Figure 1.8 Computer Communications**
Microcomputers are often used to tie into on-line information services and participate in special interest group teleconferences, such as this one on CompuServe's MedSIG.

## Presentation

*Putting on computerized slide shows*

Microcomputers are frequently used to present graphs, charts, and other figures at meetings, lectures, and demonstrations (see Figure 1.9). For example, when U.S. Secretary of the Interior Donald Hodel presented his $5 billion 1989 budget proposal at a press conference, he used a microcomputer to project images on a 20-foot screen. The secretary began his presentation by saying, "To those of you who are cost-conscious and think this looks sophisticated, it's an off-the-shelf technology using a $49.95 software package called Hypercard on the Macintosh II." Hodel went on to describe his department's annual budget proposal for managing park lands, Indian reservations, and wildlife protection programs. Sue Masica, budget analyst for the Department of the Interior, controlled the projected images from the Apple Macintosh II sitting next to the podium. "Budget numbers are always changing at the last minute," said Masica, who had just learned to use the Macintosh three months before. "Hypercard is wonderful in that it gives us the ability to make sure things are correct right up until the last minute. We didn't have to send out to get our slides made. We had complete control of the process right here in the office." As Hodel said to his audience, "We're using a new technique, different from slides. Not only can we show images in sequence, but if a question arises, we can go back

6. Henry Fersko-Weiss, "On-line Contacts," *Personal Computing*, January, 1987, pp. 83-91.

or pick out images to help answer them." Apparently, the presentation was a success. According to *New York Times* correspondent Phil Shabbacoff, who was in the audience, "[Hodel] could push a button and go immediately to a line item that someone was asking about. I had never seen that before. I found his ability to flash those numbers on the screen very impressive."[7]

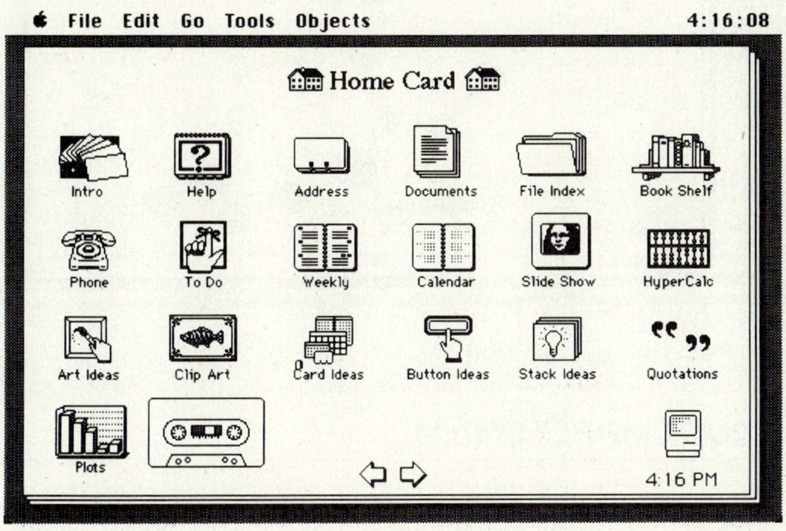


**Figure 1.9 Microcomputer Presentations**
Secretary of the Interior Donald Hodel used an Apple Macintosh II and a program called Hypercard to present his 1989 budget proposal.

## Education

*Learning difficult subjects*

You know by now that microcomputers are widely used in schools. This is especially true at colleges and universities. Drexel University in Philadelphia, for example, made an early commitment to microcomputers. Starting in 1984, all freshmen were required to have access to an Apple Macintosh, and most students bought their own from Drexel at less than half the retail price. Students were enthusiastic, and the program has continued with each incoming freshman class. Today there are more than 12,000 Macintoshes on the Drexel campus.

Many faculty members at Drexel create Macintosh programs to help their students learn difficult subjects. Allan Smith of the chemistry department, for example, developed the Molecular Editor, which students can use to build complex molecules on the screen (see Figure 1.10). Atoms of any element in the periodic table can be combined, manipulated, and analyzed without using expensive laboratory equipment. The Molecular Editor includes an animation of a chemical reaction in three dimensions and ready-made samples of organic molecules, inorganic molecules, and crystals. Undoubtedly, the Molecular Editor has made chemistry more understandable to students at Drexel.[8]

7. Stuart Silverstone, "Hypercard Helps Hodel Present Budget Proposal," *MacWeek*, March 8, 1988, pp. 42-44.
8. Donna Osgood, "The Difference in Higher Education," *Byte*, February, 1987, pp. 165-178.

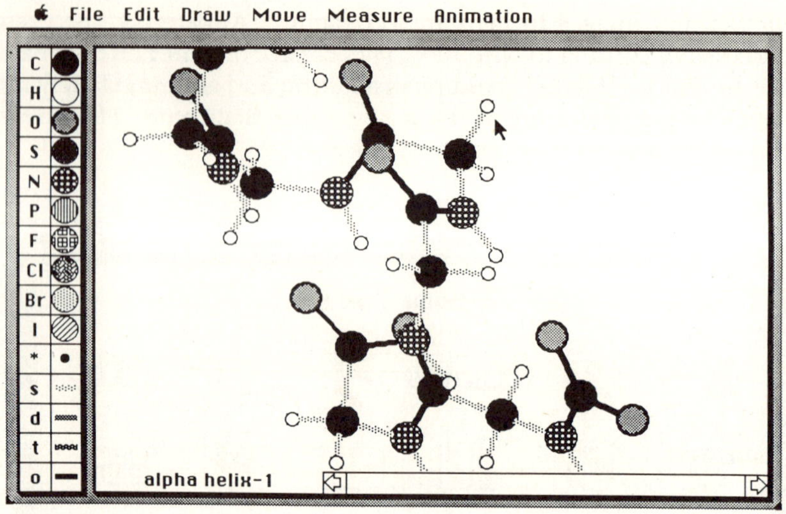


**Figure 1.10 Microcomputers on Campus**
The Molecular Editor was developed by Allan Smith of Drexel University to allow students to build molecules on the Apple Macintosh screen and rotate them in three dimensions.

## A TYPICAL MICROCOMPUTER SYSTEM

Now that you've seen some examples of how microcomputers are used, let's define exactly what we mean by the term **microcomputer** and examine the three basic elements that make up a microcomputer system: hardware, software, and users (see Figure 1.11, p. 13).

### What Is a Microcomputer?

*A small, single-user, inexpensive computer*

Its very name tells us that a microcomputer is a small computer. As you will see, several types of computers are classified as microcomputers. Most people think of a microcomputer as being small enough to fit on a desktop. In addition, although some powerful models can serve several users simultaneously, most microcomputers are used by only one person at a time. For this reason, microcomputers are also often called **personal computers**.

Another characteristic of microcomputers is that their "brain" or **central processing unit (CPU)** consists of a single electronic device known as a **microprocessor**. This device, a marvel of miniature engineering, controls the microcomputer, performs its calculations, and processes information. We'll have more to say about microprocessors and other internal components of microcomputers in the next chapter.

*Same operations as all computers*

One way to define microcomputers is by what they do. We've already discussed some real-life examples of the tasks microcomputers can accomplish. Fundamentally, however, a microcomputer performs the same basic operations as all computers. First, a **program** is needed to tell the computer what to do. This is a set of instructions that controls a computer's operation. The program lets you enter **data**, which can consist of numbers, text, pictures, and even sounds. This data entered into the computer is called **input**. The program instructs the computer to process the data by doing calculations, comparisons, and other manipulations. The final result is **information**, which should be a more organized and useful form of the original input. This information produced by the computer is called **output**. Keep in mind that there is no magic here—a program is needed to tell the computer what to do, and the output information is only as valid as the original input data.

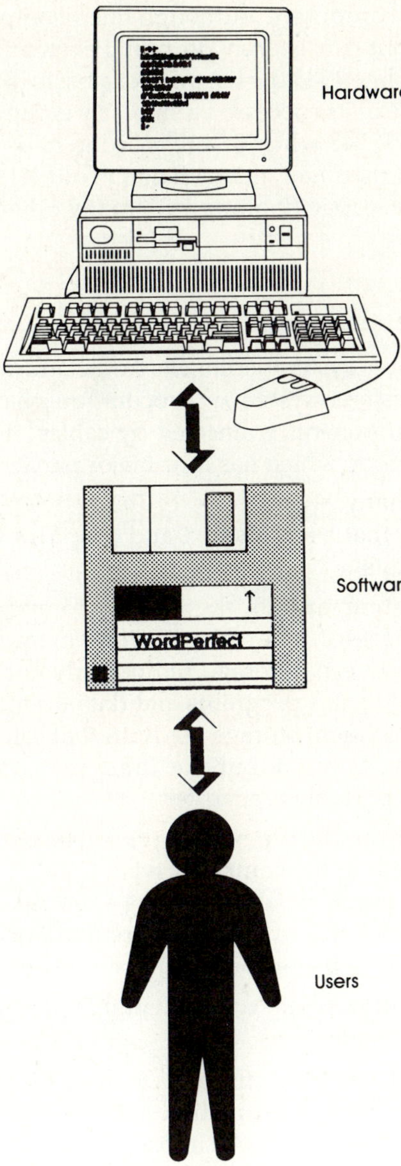


**Figure 1.11 The Microcomputer System**
A microcomputer consists of three basic elements: hardware, software, and users.

Although microcomputers perform the same basic operations as larger computers, they differ in speed and capacity. Larger computers generally can process data faster than microcomputers. They also can internally store more data at a time than microcomputers. These factors make larger computers better for performing lots of extremely complex and time-consuming computations. Microcomputers are also less adept than larger computers at handling several different users or tasks at the same time. On the other hand, microcomputers are superbly adapted to help with many work-a-day tasks like typing papers, figuring taxes, maintaining mailing lists, sending messages, drawing charts, managing finances, and even playing games.

Finally, microcomputers generally fall within a given price range. They can cost as little as $100 or as much as $15,000. Today the average price of a typical microcomputer used in business is around $2500. This is, however, a good deal less than the many thousands or even millions of dollars typical of much more powerful computers. We'll give some specific prices later in this chapter when we describe the various kinds of larger computers. Although microcomputers are by no means cheap, their prices have been consistently dropping even as their capabilities have increased. For example, in late 1983 the list price of a basic IBM Personal Computer XT was $5675. The list price of its successor, a similarly equipped IBM Personal System/2 Model 30, was only $2545 when first released in mid 1987. Even though the newer Model 30 costs less than half as much as the old XT, it still has more than twice the speed and storage capacity, along with many other improvements.

## Hardware

*Physical components*

The **hardware** of a computer system is the electronic and mechanical equipment that makes it work. Like a stereo system, microcomputer hardware generally consists of several distinct components connected by cables. Figure 1.12(a) shows a typical microcomputer system, which has four major parts:

- *Display.* Similar in many ways to an ordinary television, the **display**, or **monitor**, is the screen that presents text and **graphics** (any kind of pictures, drawings, charts, or plots).
- *System Unit.* The **system unit** is the central component that houses the computer's microprocessor, control circuitry, memory, and disk drives. **Memory**, a computer's internal storage, temporarily holds programs and data. A **disk drive** reads and writes programs and data on magnetic disks. A **magnetic disk** is a semipermanent storage medium that can be erased and rewritten over and over again. From the outside, the system unit looks like a shallow box about the size of a portable typewriter.
- *Keyboard.* Descended from the typewriter, the **keyboard** is the primary device for entering text and telling the computer what to do. Many microcomputers also have an auxiliary input device known as a **mouse**. This little box, which is slid across the table top, allows the user to manipulate objects on the display screen and select actions to be performed by pressing one or more buttons.
- *Printer.* The **printer** is an auxiliary component that produces permanent copies of text and graphics on paper.

There are, of course, several common variations to the typical arrangement of these four computer parts. For example, sometimes the system unit and display are joined in a single housing. The Apple Macintosh SE has this arrangement, shown in Figure 1.12(b). In other cases, the system unit and keyboard are combined. As Figure 1.12(c) shows, this arrangement is used in the Toshiba T3100. Finally, you can often mix and match some components from different manufacturers and add devices to expand your system's capabilities. In the next chapter, we'll examine the different microcomputer hardware components in a bit more detail.

## Software

*Instructional components*

By itself, computer hardware is useless. Programs and people are needed to operate the hardware. As we mentioned before, a program is simply a sequence of instructions that tells a computer what to do. **Software** is a general term that refers to any single program or group of programs. In contrast to hardware, which is constructed from physical materials like metal and plastic, software is built from knowledge, planning, and testing. A person who creates programs is called a **programmer**. Programmers use their knowledge of how a computer works to plan sets of instructions that accomplish useful tasks. These instructions are entered into the computer

(a)

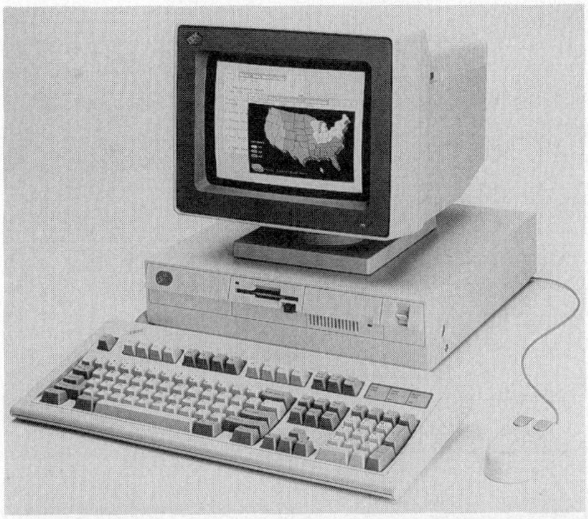

(b)

(c)

**Figure 1.12 Typical Microcomputers**
(a) An IBM Personal System/2 Model 30 with a mouse.
(b) An Apple Macintosh SE.
(c) A Toshiba T3100.

and repeatedly tested and modified until they achieve the desired results. You will recall that programs and data generally are kept on storage media such as magnetic disks, where they can be retrieved and used over and over again. One common type of magnetic disk, the **floppy disk**, is quite inexpensive and can be removed from the computer's disk drive when not in use (see Figure 1.13). Note that the disks themselves aren't the software, they're just the medium on which software and data are stored.

For an analogy, think of a stereo system. The stereo receiver/amplifier, compact disk player, and speakers are the hardware. The receiver/amplifier is like the central processing unit and memory, the compact disk player is like the disk drive, and the speakers are like the display, except they present audio instead of video out-

**Figure 1.13 The Floppy Disk**
The floppy disk is a commonly used medium for storing computer programs and data.

put. The music, which is stored on compact disks, is like software, which is stored on floppy disks. Just as you can amass a huge music collection by buying more compact disks, you can build a bigger software library by purchasing additional programs on floppy disks. The stereo system is of little use without the compact disks, and the compact disks are useless without the stereo system. Similarly, a computer system is useless without software, and software is useless without a computer system on which to run.

*Types of software*

Just as there are different types of hardware, there are also different types of software. We'll have much more to say about software in Chapter 3 and the rest of this book, but for now you should realize that there are three basic categories:

- *System Software.* **System software** handles the many details of managing a computer system. One example of system software is a program that identifies which key you've pressed, determines the character that corresponds to that key, and forms that character on the display screen. Another example is a program that lets you erase the contents of a magnetic disk. Some system software is built into the computer, while other system software comes on magnetic disks and must be purchased separately.
- *Programming Languages.* Computer programs are developed with **programming languages,** which are simply sets of symbols and rules used to direct the operations of a computer. Many different programming languages are in common use, each designed to develop certain types of programs. As we will discuss in Chapter 3, a few of the most popular programming languages are BASIC, Pascal, C, FORTRAN, COBOL, and Ada.
- *Application Software.* **Application software** applies the computer to useful tasks like helping you write letters, figure your taxes, maintain mailing lists, and draw charts. Also called **application packages** or simply **applications,** these programs are the real reason most people buy and use microcomputers. As we said before, a word processor is an application package, one that helps you prepare documents. Other examples of application software include: **spreadsheet packages,** which help you manipulate tables of numbers; **data base management packages,** which help you organize and retrieve large quantities

of information; **communications packages**, which let your computer "talk" to other computers; **graphics packages**, which let you use your computer to produce pictures and charts; **desktop publishing packages**, which allow you to combine the results of word processing and graphics to produce near-typeset-quality documents; and **accounting packages**, which let you manage the finances of a business. We'll have much more to say about these and the many other types of application software in Chapter 3 and Chapters 6 through 16.

### Users

*The human component*

It might seem obvious, but hardware and software don't do anything without users. A **user**, sometimes called an **end user**, is simply a person who runs software on a computer to accomplish some task. Just as there are different kinds of hardware and software, there are also different kinds of users. A beginning user is often called a **novice**. Somewhat unfamiliar with computers, novices need a little extra help to perform some tasks. Many computer programs are developed with the novice in mind. These easy-to-learn programs are sometimes described as **user friendly** because they can be run by people who don't necessarily have a lot of computer experience.

At the other end of the user spectrum are those who have a great deal of computer experience. An **expert**, sometimes called a **power user**, is someone who feels quite at home using computers. While programmers are generally experts, every expert is not necessarily a programmer. A person can become an expert at running particular application programs without knowing how those applications were actually developed in the first place. A race car driver, as an analogy, is certainly an expert automobile user. A good race car driver, however, need not be an auto mechanic or engineer.

## TYPES OF MICROCOMPUTERS

We've described the typical microcomputer system, but in fact there are many different types of microcomputers sold today. An obvious way to classify them is by physical size, or how easy they are to pick up and carry around. Although a few models are difficult to classify, most microcomputers easily fall into one of the following size categories: hand-held, laptop, portable, desktop, and floor model.

### Hand-held Computers

*Pocket powerhouses*

At first glance, the smallest microcomputers resemble large hand-held calculators (see Figure 1.14). Upon closer examination, however, several important differences appear. Typically smaller than a paperback book and weighing less than a pound, a **hand-held computer** has a complete alphabetic keyboard in addition to the number keys you find on ordinary calculators. The screen is usually a one- or two-line **liquid crystal display (LCD)** that can hold anywhere from twelve to sixty-four characters at once. Most LCD screens present black characters against a grey background and are commonly used in watches, clocks, and calculators. Hand-held computers generally have very limited memory capacities and run on built-in rechargeable batteries. Some hand-held computers can be connected to a wide range of optional devices, such as printers, disk drives, and larger display screens. The model shown in Figure 1.14 is a typical hand-held computer. This Tandy PC-6 Pocket Computer sells for about $120, has a twenty four-character LCD, and folds up to around six square inches.

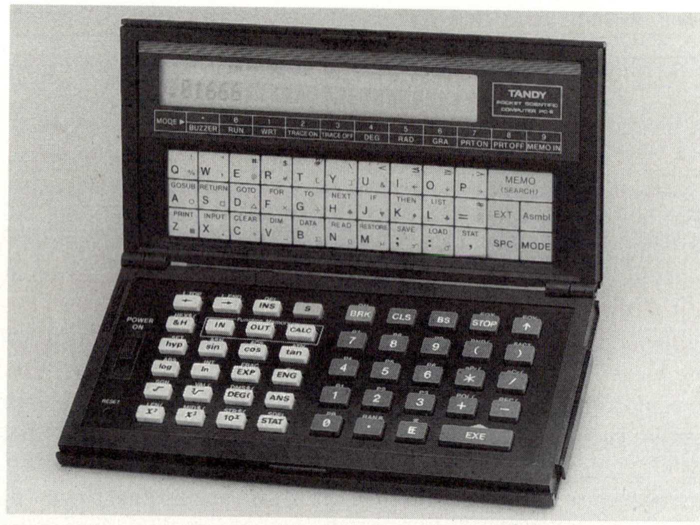


**Figure 1.14 Hand-held Computer**
This is a typical hand-held computer, the Tandy PC-6 Pocket Computer.

Hand-held microcomputers are ideal for on-the-go engineers, business people, and students who need more computing power than pocket calculators provide. Their small screen sizes, tiny keyboards, and minimal memory, however, make hand-held computers inappropriate for the most commonly used application software. They are usually used for simple financial formulas, statistics, engineering math, and games.

## Laptop Computers

*Sleek traveling companions*

The **laptop computer**, also called a **briefcase computer**, is to some people perhaps the most alluring of all types of microcomputers. It's a full-fledged microcomputer crammed into a 4- to 15-pound package smaller than most briefcases (see Figure 1.15). Laptops have an LCD or other type of flat display screen, usually around 5 by 9 inches in size, that normally can accommodate as much text and graphics as larger microcomputer monitors can. The keyboard is pretty much like that of full-size microcomputers, except perhaps without a separate numeric keypad and with fewer special-purpose keys. Many laptops have memory capacities and disk drives similar to that of larger desktop models. Most laptop computers can run on built-in rechargeable batteries, some for as long as twenty hours at a time. The NEC MultiSpeed HD shown in Figure 1.15 is a typical laptop microcomputer. This model is compact enough to fit in a knapsack, weighs a little more than 14 pounds, can run on batteries for almost 2 hours of average use, and offers most of the functionality of a desktop computer.

Laptop computers have become increasingly popular in recent years thanks to the many technological improvements that have been made. Except for their small screens, laptops are in many ways just as good as full-size microcomputers. They are easy to carry and are a boon to travellers who can't do without a computer.

**Figure 1.15 Laptop Computer**
This NEC MultiSpeed HD is a typical laptop microcomputer.

## Portable Computers

*"Lugable" micros*

Of course, hand-held and laptop computers are portable in the sense that they're easily carried about. The term **portable computer,** however, has come to mean a microcomputer that's more or less the size of a small suitcase (see Figure 1.16). These rugged machines, which typically weigh from 20 to 30 pounds, are designed to be moved, but not to be used in transit. Portable computers aren't battery powered, so they can only be used near an electrical socket. For the most part, portable computers are just as capable as comparably priced desktop models. They usually have a small screen, say 5 by 9 inches, that can display as much text and graphics as the larger monitors used with desktop computers can. Many portables can have as much memory as similar desktop computers and are also equipped with disk drives. Basically, a portable computer is a complete microcomputer you can fold up and take with you, just as you would a portable electric typewriter. The Compaq Portable 386 shown in Figure 1.16, for example, is an extremely powerful state-of-the-art microcomputer. Faster and more advanced than most desktop computers, this model from Compaq weighs just over 21 pounds and lists for about $8000.

In general, the portable computers on the market today are as well-designed and useful as their desktop relatives. As long as you don't have to carry one too far and you don't mind the slightly smaller screen, a portable computer may be ideal for taking your work home with you for an evening or away for a weekend.

## Desktop Computers

*Most common microcomputers*

The **desktop computer** is the most common type of microcomputer (see Figure 1.17). It's small enough to fit on top of a table or desk, and that's where it's generally kept, although some users set their system unit on its side on the floor to clear more table space. As we said before, some of these microcomputers have a separate system unit, monitor, and keyboard, while others combine the system unit and monitor, or the system unit and keyboard, into a single housing. Despite the growing popularity of laptop models, desktop computers are still by far the most com-

**Figure 1.16 Portable Computer**
This Compaq Portable 386 is one of the most advanced microcomputers you can buy, even if it does come in a relatively small package.

mon type of microcomputer. The IBM Personal System/2 Model 50 shown in Figure 1.17 is a good example of a typical desktop microcomputer.

## Floor Models

*Stand up computers*

Some microcomputers are specifically designed to stand upright on the floor. A **floor model** is usually a powerful, expensive microcomputer. The system unit of a floor model is often larger than the typical desktop system unit and is designed to accommodate more add-in hardware components. Some floor models are set up to serve several users or are used to coordinate several individual microcomputers connected together. The IBM Personal System/2 Model 80 shown in Figure 1.18, for example, is a powerful floor model microcomputer that can be used alone or connected to other computers in a large information system.

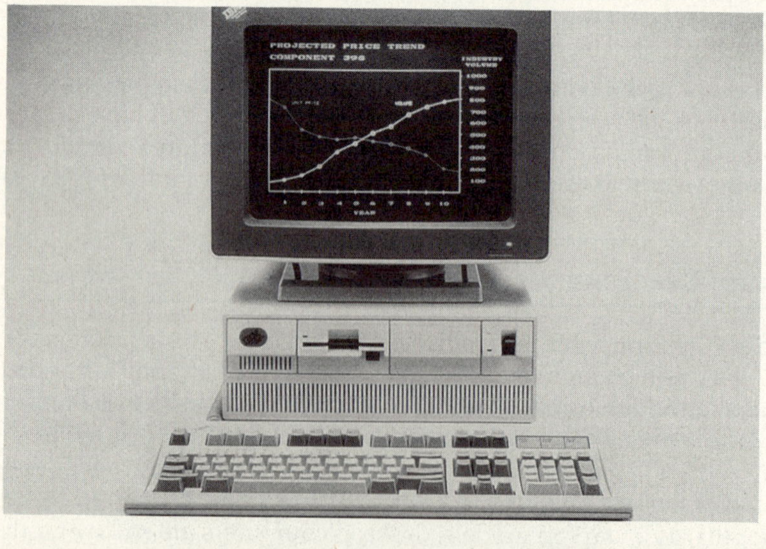


**Figure 1.17 Desktop Computer**
The IBM Personal System/2 Model 50 is a typical desktop microcomputer.

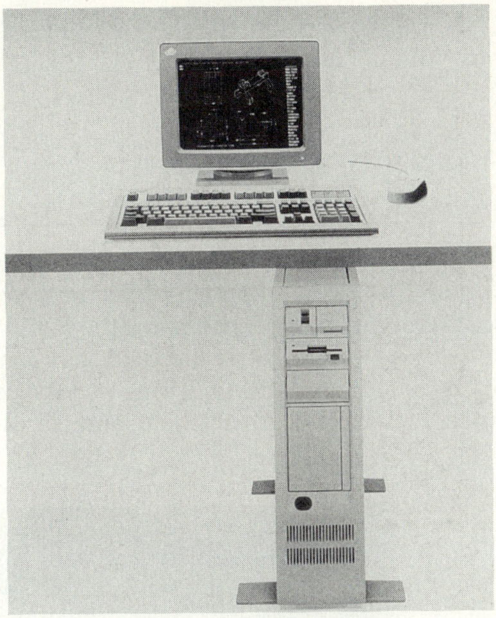

**Figure 1.18 Floor Model**
The IBM Personal System/2 Model 80 is a powerful microcomputer designed to stand upright on the floor. It has more room inside than a desktop model to accommodate more add-in hardware components.

## MICROCOMPUTER STANDARDS

*Agreed-upon conventions*

We've just described how microcomputers can be classified according to their physical size. Perhaps a more meaningful approach is to categorize them by microcomputer standards. A **microcomputer standard** is a generally accepted set of rules by which hardware and software operate. One way to establish a standard is to get a formal agreement between manufacturers on how to develop hardware and software. In most cases, however, standards emerge from the leadership of a few powerful manufacturers. One manufacturer may make a computer, hardware component, or software package that becomes so popular that other manufacturers follow. Even though no formal agreement has been reached, a ***de facto*** standard exists because other manufacturers voluntarily make products that will work together. Today, there are three dominant microcomputer standards: the Apple II, IBM, and the Apple Macintosh.

### Apple II

*Popular early microcomputer*

You've probably heard the rags-to-riches story of how Apple Computer was formed in 1976 by Steven Jobs and Stephen Wozniak, who built their prototype, the Apple I, in a garage for $1300. By the end of 1977, the Apple II had emerged as one of the most popular microcomputers on the market. One of the major reasons for its widespread acceptance was that Apple encouraged many hardware and software manufacturers to develop products that worked with the Apple II. When Dan Bricklin and Bob Frankston developed VisiCalc, the first spreadsheet program, for the Apple II in 1979, microcomputers began to attract serious business users. Even after the introduction of more powerful microcomputers by IBM and Apple itself, the Apple II family of computers remained very popular, especially in homes and schools. Today, the Apple II family of computers still sells well, thanks to continual improvements by Apple and a huge base of available software. The current line of Apple II computers includes the Apple IIe, the Apple IIc, and the Apple IIGS (see Figure 1.19).

## IBM

*Most popular microcomputers ever*

International Business Machines, by far the most successful seller of large, powerful computers, didn't enter the microcomputer market until August of 1981. Its first model, the IBM Personal Computer, quickly became the world's best-selling microcomputer (see Figure 1.20). Although it wasn't especially innovative from an engineering standpoint, the solidly built IBM PC triggered the overwhelming acceptance of microcomputers by business, government, and educational institutions.

**Figure 1.19 The Apple II Family**
Even though there are more powerful machines on the market, the Apple II family remains a very popular microcomputer standard.

(a)

(b)

(c)

IBM's handling of the PC was somewhat unorthodox. The company ignored many of its time-honored traditions and released a machine that primarily consisted of off-the-shelf parts. Furthermore, IBM readily distributed the technical specifications of its new microcomputer. Instead of developing its own system software for the PC, IBM selected Microsoft Corporation to do it. Microsoft was also allowed to sell this system software to anyone who wanted to buy it. These factors, combined with IBM's reputation as one of the biggest and most stable companies in the world,

**Figure 1.20 The Original IBM Personal Computer**
The original IBM Personal Computer was released in August, 1981 and quickly became a runaway best seller.

encouraged many independent hardware and software manufacturers to develop products that worked with the IBM Personal Computer.

Soon companies such as Compaq Computer Corporation developed the first **clones** of the IBM Personal Computer. Also called **IBM-compatibles**, these machines worked just like (or in some ways even better than) the original IBM Personal Computer and usually sold at a lower price. When IBM released its more powerful PC-XT in 1983 and the more advanced PC-AT in 1984, the clone makers followed suit and produced compatibles for these machines as well. Eventually, the clone makers together sold more IBM-compatibles than IBM itself sold. The IBM PC, PC-XT, and PC-AT have each become standards no longer completely controlled by IBM.

IBM-compatible computers offer varying degrees of speed and storage capacity but all are able to use the same software and hardware components as real IBM Personal Computers. The original IBM PC, PC-XT, and PC-AT standards are currently the most popular types of microcomputers in the world, with tens of millions of machines in offices, factories, schools, and homes. Hundreds of companies now sell IBM-compatible microcomputers.

In 1987, IBM introduced its new Personal System/2 line of microcomputers. Today, the IBM PS/2 line is made up of six basic models: the Model 25, the Model 30, the Model 50, the Model 60, the Model 70, and the Model 80 (see Figure 1.21). These computers are different from their predecessors in several important ways. Although they can run virtually all of the previously written IBM PC software, the PS/2 computers have different floppy disk drives. Except for the Models 25 and 30, PS/2 computers cannot use many of the internal hardware components that work with their PC predecessors. The IBM PS/2 Models 50 through 80 have a different underlying circuit design known as the **Micro Channel Architecture**. These Personal System/2 computers offer significantly higher performance than previous computers. A new generation of software is required, however, to take full advantage of the Personal System/2 Models 50, 60, 70, and 80. A few hardware manufacturers, such as Tandy and Dell Computer Corporation, are working on clones of the Personal System/2 computers, which suggests that the IBM Personal System/2 family has spawned a new, slightly different IBM microcomputer standard.

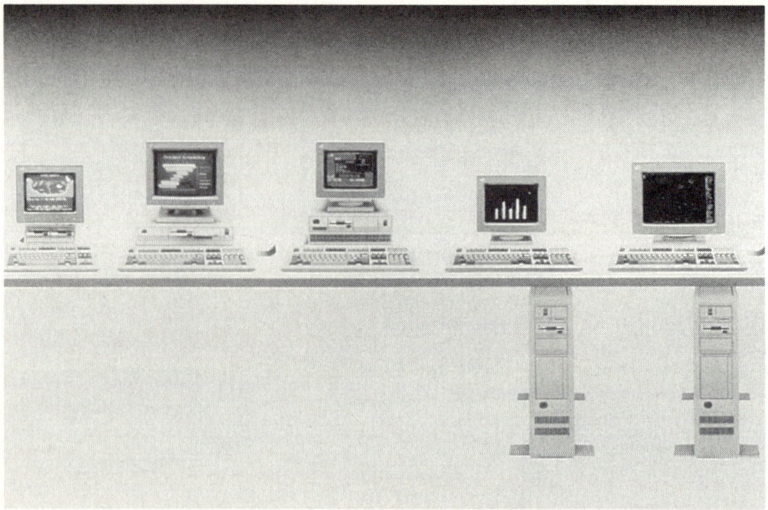

**Figure 1.21 The IBM Personal System/2 Family**
IBM's line of Personal System/2 microcomputers has replaced the earlier IBM PCs, PC-XTs, and PC-ATs.

## Apple Macintosh

*The trend-setting micro of the 80s*

The Apple II was the best-selling microcomputer from 1978 until 1982, when the IBM Personal Computer overwhelmed the market. By mid-1983, after the unenthusiastic reception of Apple's two new models, the Lisa and the Apple III, market analysts began to wonder if Apple would survive as a major microcomputer manufacturer. Amid corporate infighting, Steven Jobs himself took over the division of Apple that was building its last, best hope—the Macintosh. Released in early 1984 amid the ballyhoo of a $20-million advertising scheme, the Apple Macintosh was hailed as "the computer for the rest of us."

Many of the easy-to-use features incorporated into the Apple Lisa and the Macintosh were actually developed by Xerox in the early 1970s at the Palo Alto Research Center. Xerox's 8010 Star Information System was the first commercial computer to use concepts later popularized by the Apple Macintosh. These features included the use of a sharp black-on-white graphics screen, a mouse, menus, windows, and icons. You already know what a mouse is: a device for manipulating objects on the screen and selecting activities to be performed. A **menu** is simply a list of activities you can select to perform. A **window** is a boxed-in area on the screen that shows the activity of a particular software program. Several windows may be on the screen at the same time. Finally, an **icon** is a small pictorial symbol that represents some activity. For example, to erase a disk on a computer that uses icons you might move a little picture of a floppy disk on top of a little picture of a trash can. Apple certainly didn't invent the mouse, menus, windows, and icons. Nevertheless, the Macintosh was the first affordable microcomputer that did a good job of incorporating all of these user-friendly features.

The Apple Macintosh is a **proprietary** system. This means that Apple holds and tightly controls the patents for many of the Macintosh hardware components and the copyrights for the system software. Apple has not licensed these patents and copyrights to other manufacturers, so there are no legal Macintosh clones. This allows Apple to maintain a higher profit margin, but it also means that the Macintosh standard is not nearly as widespread as the IBM-PC standard. Many more IBM and IBM-compatible microcomputers are in use than Apple Macintoshes. Nevertheless, Apple has sold millions of Macintosh computers. There are three basic models: the Macintosh Plus, the Macintosh SE, and the Macintosh II (see Figure 1.22).

**Figure 1.22 The Apple Macintosh Family**
Apple's Macintosh family represents a microcomputer standard totally different from the Apple II and all of the IBM machines.

## OTHER TYPES OF COMPUTERS

*Connected in networks*

This textbook emphasizes microcomputers, but several other types of computers also play very important roles in many businesses and organizations. Nowadays, computers of all types are frequently connected in **networks** to share hardware, software, and data. Although there is considerable overlap between categories, computers can be classified according to their physical size, storage capacity, speed, number of simultaneous users, and cost. At the low end are microcomputers. Continuing up the hierarchy in order of increasing power and cost are workstations, minicomputers, mainframes, and supercomputers, which we will examine in more detail shortly.

Table 1.1 compares specific examples of these various types of computers according to the number of simultaneous users, speed, and cost. Keep in mind, however, that the values in this table are approximations. The actual number of simultaneous users can vary depending on how the system is equipped and set up. The speeds, given in units of **million instructions per second**, or **MIPS**, are also estimates. Theoretically, a computer that operates at 1 MIPS executes one million instructions per second. Many experts downplay the significance of measuring computer performance in MIPS, because different instructions accomplish different tasks on different computers. Nevertheless, MIPS do give some basis for comparing the performance of computers. Finally, the actual cost of a particular computer depends on the exact way in which it is equipped. Despite these qualifications, Table 1.1 should give you some idea of the differences between computers. The microcomputer used for comparison is the IBM Personal System/2 Model 50, shown previously in Figure 1.17.

**Table 1.1 Computer Types**

| Type | Example | Users | Speed (MIPS) | Approx. Cost ($) |
|---|---|---|---|---|
| Microcomputer | IBM PS/2 50 | 1 | 1.6 | 4,000 |
| Workstation | Sun-3/60 | 1 | 3.0 | 12,900 |
| Minicomputer | DEC VAX 8200 | 1 to 30 | 2.0 | 100,000 |
| Mainframe | IBM 3090/600E | 1 to 500 | 73.4 | 10,300,000 |
| Supercomputer | Cray Y-MP | 1 to 500 | 2000.0 | 20,000,000 |

## Workstations

*Powerful, single-user design tools*

A **workstation**, sometimes called a **supermicro**, is a small, yet powerful computer generally used by only one person at a time (see Figure 1.23). Similar to microcomputer floor models with large graphics screens, workstations have been traditionally used by scientists and engineers as tools for drafting, design, and map-making. They are superior to most microcomputers in their ability to perform complex calculations, display sharp and colorful graphics, and communicate with other computers. Ranging in price from around $4000 to $100,000, workstations are also faster than most microcomputers and can typically run several different programs at the same time. Although many workstations use the same microprocessors found in powerful microcomputers, others employ more specialized types of central processing units. Figure 1.23 shows a typical workstation, the Sun-3/60 from Sun Microsystems. This computer, with its sharp 16-inch color screen, can execute around three million instructions per second and costs about $12,900.

## Minicomputers

*Mid-size, multiuser machines*

The term **minicomputer** generally describes medium-sized computers that simultaneously serve several users or control complex equipment (see Figure 1.24). In the past, minicomputers were easier to distinguish from other types of computers than they are today. Powerful microcomputers and workstations approach, and in some cases surpass, the capabilities and speed of some contemporary minicomputers. Powerful minicomputers, sometimes called **superminis**, approach the capabilities of some larger systems. The smallest minicomputers are about the same size as floor model microcomputers, while the largest may be as big as one or two file cabinets. Minicomputer prices range from about $15,000 to $500,000. Most general-purpose minicomputers are set up to serve multiple users, usually fewer than one hundred at the same time.

Minicomputers are commonly used in small businesses and organizations for routine office tasks such as accounting, billing, order entry, inventory, and word processing. More specialized minicomputers are also used to monitor instruments in laboratories and to control automated manufacturing equipment in factories.

**Figure 1.23 Workstation**
The Sun-3/60 is a typical workstation.

Some minicomputers are used to control networks of interconnected computers. A good example of a typical minicomputer is the VAX 8200 from Digital Equipment Corporation, shown in Figure 1.24. This computer can simultaneously serve up to 30 users, runs at about 2 MIPS, and costs around $100,000.

**Figure 1.24 Minicomputer**
Digital Equipment Corporation's VAX 8200 is a good example of a typical minicomputer.

## Mainframes

*Room-size computers that can cost millions*

A **mainframe** is a big, powerful, fast, expensive computer. Mainframes typically serve hundreds of users at the same time, execute many millions of instructions per second, and cost anywhere from $100,000 to $20 million. A mainframe computer may be as small as one or two file cabinets or large enough to fill an entire room. Some mainframes must be kept in carefully controlled environments to keep them cool and as dust free as possible. Mainframe computers are generally used by large businesses and organizations for high-volume data processing, such as the preparation of thousands or even millions of paychecks, bills, orders, and mailing labels. Mainframe computers are also used to maintain huge **data bases** or collections of facts, such as Social Security and income tax records. In addition, large networks of computers often require mainframes to manage the connections and communications. A typical mainframe computer is the IBM 3090/600, shown in Figure 1.25, which operates at around 73.4 MIPS, can serve hundreds of users at the same time, and costs $10.3 million.

## Supercomputers

*The world's fastest calculating machines*

A **supercomputer** is an extremely fast mainframe. These computers typically execute *billions* of instructions per second, can serve hundreds of users simultaneously, and cost between $5 million and $25 million each. Although there are only a few hundred supercomputers operating today in the world, they perform many vital tasks that would be impossible with ordinary mainframes. Supercomputers are used mostly in scientific and military research. There are eleven supercomputers at Los Alamos Scientific Laboratory in New Mexico, for example, where they are used for top-secret weapons research. The National Security Agency in Fort Mead, Maryland, uses supercomputers to crack military codes and manage the flood of intelligence data the agency collects every day. At the University of Illinois, a Cray X-MP supercomputer is used to simulate and display colorful animations of natural phenomenon, from the swirling birth of a tornado to the turbulent activity of a black hole at the center of a galaxy. On the lighter side, Digital Productions, a Hollywood film company, uses a Cray X-MP supercomputer to produce special effects for movies.

**Figure 1.25 Mainframe**
The IBM 3090/600 is a powerful mainframe computer.

Although several companies now produce supercomputers, Cray Research dominates the market. This single company accounts for approximately 60 percent of all supercomputers sold in the world. The Cray Y-MP, introduced in 1988, is a good example of a supercomputer (see Figure 1.26, p. 30). It succeeds the popular Cray X-MP supercomputer and is two to three times as powerful. Under ideal conditions, the eight processing units of the Cray Y-MP work together to execute two billion to four billion instructions per second. This is roughly equivalent to the computing power of 1,250 IBM Personal System/2 Model 50s. The Y-MP can serve hundreds of users at the same time and costs around $20 million.

**Figure 1.26 Supercomputer**

The Cray Y-MP is one of the most powerful supercomputers in the world.

## The Real World

### You're Smarter Than You May Have Thought

There was a lady who sort of thought she might like to find out what computers were all about. But she kept putting it off, because she felt intimidated before she even began her quest. Some of what she had read and heard had led her to believe that she lacked the manual dexterity to interact successfully with a computer.

(On the day she had that thought, she successfully and single-handedly took command of a 4000-pound machine whose proper operation required her to coordinate and synchronize independent activities of her left hand, her right hand, her left foot and her right foot, and to monitor, with eye and ear, various gauges and sounds, while looking over her left shoulder. She backed her car out of her garage.)

She had read just enough computer ads to be able to fret about the apparently incomprehensible vocabulary of bits and bytes and modems not to mention peripherals and programming and other concepts that made "learning computers" sound like an academic enterprise well beyond her mental abilities.

(On *that* day, she utilized the concepts of accounts payable and receivable, cash flow management, double entry bookkeeping, information storage and retrieval, mathematics, and inference. She balanced her checkbook.)

She tentatively set foot in her neighborhood computer store. She felt uncomfortable and out of place in the sleek high-tech environment. She *did* find it impossible to communicate with the young man who was on duty at the store, who looked at her with a mixture of pity and disdain when she apparently failed his initial vocabulary test.

She left the computer store in confusion and mounting despair.

While shopping at the supermarket that very afternoon, she impulsively bought a Commodore VIC-20 computer off the shelf, between the paper towels and the photographic film, took it home, read the manual, hooked it up, plugged it in, turned it on, started enjoying herself, bought a couple of other books to supplement the not-always-great manual, played games, started in on a home bookkeeping system, made a few tentative stabs at learning programming, took a class in programming, wrote programs, bought a larger and more sophisticated computer, helped automate her husband's business, gave lectures on overcoming computer fear, taught classes in computerization, and finally opened her own computer service bureau in the storefront vacated by the bankruptcy of the computer store she had first visited.

Source: John Bear, *Computer Wimp*, Ten Speed Press, Berkeley, California, 1983, pp. 134-136.

## Summary

- *Why you should study computers.* A knowledge of computers may help you to complete your education, to get a job, to increase your productivity, to increase your capabilities, and to have fun.
- *Some of the ways in which microcomputers are used.* Microcomputers are used to increase personal productivity, to manage information, to communicate with others, to make presentations, and to help learn difficult subjects.
- *The elements of a typical microcomputer system.* Hardware (display, system unit, keyboard, and printer), software (system software, programming languages, and application software), and users are the three basic ingredients of a microcomputer system.
- *The different types of microcomputers.* Classified by size, they are hand-held, laptop, portable, desktop, and floor model.
- *The dominant microcomputer standards.* Apple II, IBM-compatible, and Apple Macintosh are the three most widely used microcomputer standards.
- *The various types of other computers.* In addition to microcomputers, there are workstations, minicomputers, mainframes, and supercomputers.

## Key Terms

As an extra review of this chapter, try defining the following terms. If you have trouble with any of them, refer to the page number listed.

accounting package (17)
application software (application package, application) (16)
central processing unit (CPU) (12)
clone (23)
communications package (17)
data (12)
data base (28)
data base management package (17)
*de facto* standard (21)
desktop computer (20)
desktop publishing package (17)
disk drive (14)
display (monitor) (14)
expert (power user) (17)
floor model (21)
floppy disk (14)
graphics (14)
graphics package (17)
hand-held computer (17)
hardware (14)
IBM-compatible (23)
icon (24)
information (12)
input (12)
keyboard (14)
liquid crystal display (LCD) (17)
laptop (briefcase) computer (18)
microcomputer (personal computer) (12)
Micro Channel Architecture (24)
microcomputer standard (21)
microprocessor (12)
million instructions per second (MIPS) (26)
minicomputer (26)
mouse (14)
network (25)
novice (17)
on-line information service (9)
output (12)
personal computer (12)
portable computer (19)
printer (14)
program (12)
programmer (14)
programming language (16)
proprietary (25)
software (14)
spreadsheet package (17)
supercomputer (28)
supermini (26)
system software (16)
system unit (14)
teleconference (9)
user (end user) (17)

magnetic disk (14)
mainframe (27)
menu (24)
memory (14)
user friendly (17)
window (24)
word processing (5)
workstation (supermicro) (26)

## Review Questions

1. Give a specific example of how computers are used in education.
2. Why do employers need workers who are familiar with computers?
3. What common application of computers allows you to produce documents such as letters and reports?
4. List some of the activities you can do with an on-line information service.
5. How are microcomputers often used at meetings, lectures, and demonstrations?
6. What electronic device is the central processing unit of a microcomputer?
7. What is the difference between data and information?
8. In what ways do microcomputers differ from larger computers?
9. What is the average price of a typical microcomputer used in business?
10. List four major microcomputer hardware components.
11. List three basic categories of software.
12. List seven types of application software.
13. What are hand-held microcomputers typically used for?
14. What is the difference between a laptop and a portable microcomputer?
15. What is the most common size of microcomputers?
16. What are the three dominant microcomputer standards?
17. List four features in the Apple Macintosh previously introduced commercially in Xerox's 8010 Star Information System.
18. How are workstations superior to most microcomputers?
19. What is the fastest type of computer?
20. List two common uses of minicomputers.

## Multiple Choice

1. A microcomputer's CPU consists of a single
   (a) display.
   (b) microprocessor.
   (c) keyboard.
   (d) printer.
2. A computer processes data to form
   (a) input.
   (b) programs.
   (c) information.
   (d) hardware.

3. A computer's internal storage, used to temporarily hold programs and data, is called
   (a) a system unit. (b) memory.
   (c) a keyboard. (d) a mouse.

4. What type of software processes keypresses and forms characters on the display screen?
   (a) system software (b) programming language
   (c) application software (d) word processor

5. A spreadsheet program is a type of
   (a) system software. (b) programming language.
   (c) application software. (d) printer software.

6. Which of the following can most likely be operated on batteries?
   (a) laptop (b) portable
   (c) desktop (d) floor model

7. The most common microcomputer size is the
   (a) laptop. (b) portable.
   (c) desktop. (d) floor model.

8. Which of the following is most likely to be a powerful, expensive microcomputer?
   (a) laptop (b) portable
   (c) desktop (d) floor model

9. Which company developed the system software for the IBM Personal Computer and its descendants?
   (a) IBM (b) Apple
   (c) Microsoft (d) Compaq

10. Which of the following is not considered to be a popular microcomputer standard?
    (a) Apple II (b) Sun-3/60
    (c) Apple Macintosh (d) IBM PC

11. Which one of the following commercial computers was the first to incorporate user-friendly features such as a mouse, menus, windows, and icons?
    (a) Apple II (b) IBM Personal Computer
    (c) Xerox 8010 Star Information System (d) Apple Macintosh

12. The Apple Macintosh is a
    (a) Micro Channel Architecture system. (b) proprietary system.
    (c) operating system. (d) mainframe system.

13. What type of computer has been traditionally used by individual scientists and engineers as a tool for drafting, design, and map-making?
    (a) workstations (b) minicomputers
    (c) mainframes (d) supercomputers

14. Mainframe computers are generally used by
    (a) hobbyists.
    (b) students.
    (c) small businesses.
    (d) large businesses.

15. How many instructions can the typical supercomputer execute per second?
    (a) hundreds
    (b) thousands
    (c) millions
    (d) billions

## Projects

1. Why do you want to learn about computers? Write a brief essay specifying the reasons you have for taking this course. How do you think a microcomputer could help you with your studies or work?

2. Does anyone you know use a microcomputer? If not, try to find an article in a magazine or book about a real person who uses a microcomputer in his or her daily life. Write a brief report describing how the computer is used. What kind of microcomputer does the person have and what kind of software? How does using a microcomputer make a difference in the user's life?

3. Find out if there are any computer clubs or users groups in your area. You don't actually have to go to any meetings (unless you want to, of course), but try to learn a little bit about these organizations. How many members do they have, and what kinds of microcomputers do they use?

4. Get a recent issue of a popular computer magazine at a newsstand, bookstore, or library. Find a review of some hardware or software product. Read the article carefully and "review" the review. How helpful do you think this review would be if you were shopping for that particular type of hardware or software?

# 2

# Hardware

## In This Chapter

## PREVIEW

As the Insight on p. 36 indicates, advances in microprocessor technology are a primary reason for the growing role microcomputers now play in our society. Hardware determines the software that can be run, and hence profoundly influences how computers are used. You needn't become a computer engineer, but it is important to have a basic understanding of the hardware components that make up a typical system. In this chapter, we examine the physical parts of a microcomputer and see how they work. We discuss what makes the newest microprocessors so powerful. Memory, disk drives, displays, keyboards, mice, expansion boards, printers, and modems are all covered. Learning about these devices will help you realize what computers can do, given the right software. Once you become familiar with the hardware of microcomputer systems, you can then concentrate on the software that puts it to work.

After studying this chapter, you will understand

- the components inside the system unit.
- the key features that affect a microprocessor's power.
- the difference between RAM and ROM.
- commonly used secondary storage devices.
- the primary input device.
- the basic types of displays.
- how microcomputer systems can be expanded.
- the basic types of printers.
- how computers communicate with modems.
- alternate input and output devices.

## THE MICROCOMPUTER REVEALED

*Inside the system unit*

Let's take the cover off a typical microcomputer and look at its internal structure. Figure 2.1 shows the system unit of an IBM Personal System/2 Model 50 taken apart. Inside we find that there are several major components. We'll briefly examine each of these parts, and then go on to delve into the ones that are most important for understanding how a computer processes data. Afterwards, we'll cover the input, output, and other devices that are commonly connected to the system unit of a microcomputer. The components you see in Figure 2.1 include:

- *Chassis*. The **chassis** is a frame, constructed of metal and high-impact plastic, that houses all of the internal components of a computer. This particular computer also has a plastic *subchassis*, which helps secure the disk drives and extra circuit boards. When all the parts are assembled, the chassis is covered by a plastic case coated on the inside with conductive silver paint to reduce radio frequency emissions.
- *Motherboard*. The **motherboard** or **system board** is the main circuit board of a computer (see Figure 2.2). Among other components, the motherboard holds the computer's CPU, some memory, and much of its control circuitry. Although not all computers are constructed with a motherboard in this fashion, it's a popular arrangement used in most microcomputers.

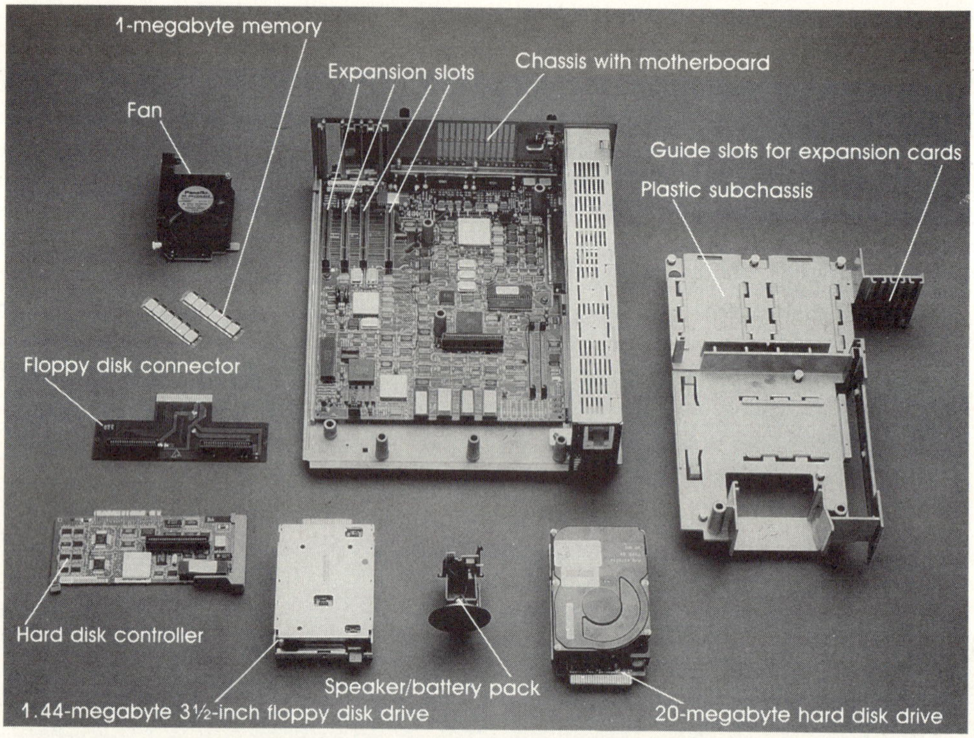


**Figure 2.1 Inside the System Unit** Here are the components of the system units of an IBM PS/2 Model 50.

- *Memory.* In this particular computer, most of the memory, or **primary storage**, is made up of chips mounted on their own small circuit boards that plug into special sockets on the motherboard. Many computers, however, have their memory chips plugged or soldered directly into the motherboard.
- *Power Supply.* The delicate circuits that make up any computer require a refined source of electrical power. The **power supply** plugs into an ordinary outlet, but contains a transformer to lower and regulate the voltage level of the electricity provided to the computer. Relatively large and heavy, the power supply in the IBM Personal System/2 Model 50 extends the entire right-side length of the chassis (see Figure 2.1). The red toggle at the front end is the power switch that turns the computer on and off.

**Insight**

## Do I Need to Learn a Programming Language?

Learning a high-level programming language like BASIC, Pascal, or COBOL can take a lot of time and effort. Don't do it unless you have to.

Most people use their computers for word processing or for keeping track of their finances with spreadsheets. Learning to use a word processor is only a little harder than learning to use a typewriter. The spreadsheet is the computer equivalent of the accountant's ruled pad. A simple knowledge of math and elementary algebra is all that you need to use one.

The need to learn a programming language starts to stir when you get into more advanced spreadsheet use. For example, it becomes tedious to type in long and involved command sequences. The Lotus 1-2-3 spreadsheet program lets you use a special form of notation called macros to record these keystroke sequences. That's very simple programming.

Learning a programming language is more important when you are using a data base, since the tasks involved in producing a report or searching a data base for information can become very involved. Most data base systems have some sort of programming language to help with this. You may want to learn more about programming languages if you will be working heavily with data bases.

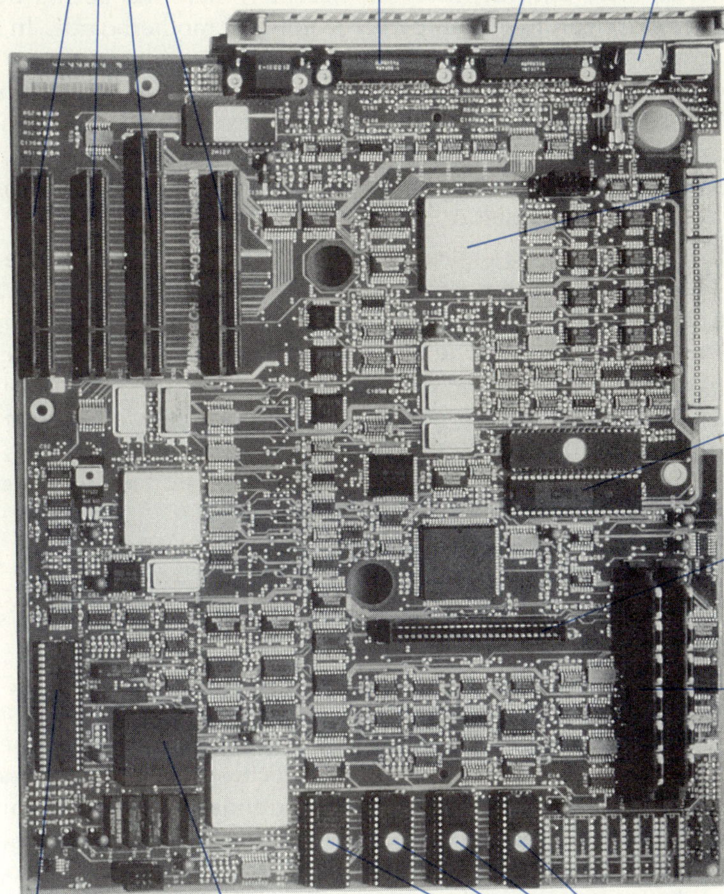


**Figure 2.2 The Motherboard**
Here is the motherboard of an IBM PS/2 Model 50 with its principal components labeled.

- *Expansion Slots.* An **expansion slot** is an internal connector that allows you to plug an additional circuit board into the motherboard. This particular computer has four expansion slots, although some computers come with eight or more. A circuit board that plugs into an expansion slot is called an **expansion board**, **card**, or **adapter**. Such circuit boards make it possible to connect a wide variety of auxiliary peripheral equipment to a computer, thus expanding its capability. We'll have more to say about expansion slots and boards later in this chapter.
- *Disk Drives.* As we said in Chapter 1, a disk drive is a piece of equipment that can read and write programs and data on disks. Most microcomputers now have two basic kinds of disk drives. A **floppy disk drive** works with *floppy disks*, which are inexpensive flexible magnetic disks encased in plastic. Floppy disks can be inserted and removed from their disk drives. This computer also comes with a hard disk drive. Unlike floppy disk drives, a **hard disk drive**, or **fixed disk drive**, usually has its magnetic disks permanently sealed inside. The magnetic disks inside a hard disk drive are rigid, much faster, and have much greater capacity than a floppy disk. We'll have more to say about both floppy and hard disk drives later in this chapter.

- *Device Controllers.* A **device controller** is a set of chips or a circuit board that operates a piece of computer equipment such as a disk drive, display, keyboard, mouse, or printer. Some device controllers are so complex that they are, in actuality, small computers unto themselves. Recently, there has been a trend toward building device controllers onto microcomputer motherboards. In this IBM Personal System/2 Model 50, for example, the device controllers for the display, keyboard, mouse, and floppy disk drives are made up of chips mounted on the motherboard (see Figure 2.2). The *hard disk controller*, on the other hand, is a separate circuit board that plugs into one of the expansion slots. By having the hard disk controller on a removable expansion board, the computer can be easily upgraded later with a faster or higher capacity hard disk.
- *Other Components.* Most computers have various other components inside the system unit. This particular computer, for example, also has a speaker, battery pack, fan, and floppy disk connector. The *speaker* is used for emitting "beeps," musical tones, and other sounds. The *battery pack* is used to maintain power to a few special memory chips that hold the current date, time, and various equipment settings. The *fan* is an important piece of equipment needed to keep the sensitive computer circuits from overheating. In this particular computer, the *floppy disk connector* is needed to plug floppy disk drives into their device controller on the motherboard.

## THE MICROPROCESSOR

*Processing data into information*

As we said in Chapter 1, the brain of a computer is called the *central processing unit*, or *CPU*. The CPU of a microcomputer is a single microprocessor, which is a small processor. What does it process? Data. In the computer world, all data are essentially numbers. Even alphabetic letters, pictures, and sounds are encoded as numbers by computers. Computers process data by performing arithmetic operations, comparing, moving, and copying data from one place to another. In fact, all computers really have only three basic functions: they receive numbers as input, process them in some fashion, and present the results as output. Every component of a computer system performs one or more of these three basic functions. For example, a keyboard is an input device; a display is an output device. The system unit, which contains the microprocessor, control circuitry, and storage devices, performs all three functions.

### Structure

Figure 2.3 shows what a typical microprocessor looks like. This one is an Intel 8088, the CPU used in the original IBM Personal Computer and many other similar microcomputers. It's about two inches long, a half-inch wide, and a quarter of an inch thick. The forty pins sticking out and bent down from the two longer sides are electrical connections that plug into a socket or are soldered into a larger circuit board. In fact, the black rectangle you see is not actually the microprocessor itself, but rather a ceramic or plastic case within which the microprocessor is permanently and completely sealed. The actual microprocessor is an extremely complex integrated circuit chip.

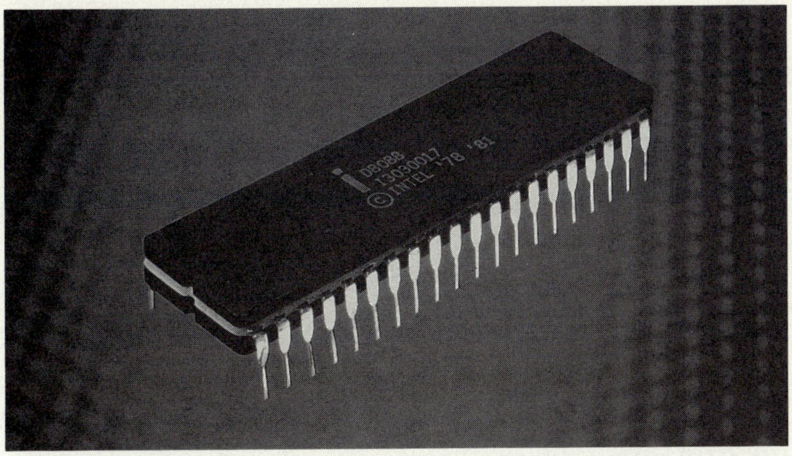


**Figure 2.3 Microprocessor**

The Intel 8088 microprocessor chip is a popular CPU, used in the original IBM Personal Computer and many other similar microcomputers.

*Thousands of circuits on a chip*

An **integrated circuit chip** is a thin slice of semiconductor material, such as pure silicon crystal, impregnated with carefully selected impurities. A **semiconductor** is a substance that conducts electricity poorly at low temperatures, but pretty well at high temperatures. The impurities, such as boron and phosphorus, enhance its ability to transmit electricity. These impurities are laid out into intricate patterns that define the electronic and logical properties of the chip. Amazingly, this design enables a single solid chip to behave as if it were constructed of many extremely tiny electronic circuits known as *gates*. Each one of these gates is like a switch that can be turned off or on. As simple as these off/on gates operate, they can be arranged into complex circuits that are capable of storing, adding, subtracting, multiplying, dividing, and comparing numbers. A microprocessor is an especially complex chip that contains thousands of gates. Table 2.1 examines some of today's most popular microprocessor chips.

**Table 2.1 Popular Microprocessors**

This table presents some of today's most popular microprocessor chips. Each chip is listed along with its register size in bits, its data bus size in bits, its maximum speed in megahertz, its maximum addressable memory, and an example of a computer that uses the chip.

| CHIP | REG. SIZE (BITS) | DATA BUS SIZE (BITS) | MAX. SPEED (MHZ) | MAX. MEMORY (BYTES) | EXAMPLE MICROCOMPUTER |
|---|---|---|---|---|---|
| MOS Technology 6502 | 8 | 8 | 1 | 64K | Apple IIe |
| Intel 8088 | 16 | 8 | 10 | 1M | IBM Personal Computer |
| Intel 8086 | 16 | 16 | 10 | 1M | IBM PS/2 Model 30 |
| Intel 80286 | 16 | 16 | 20 | 16M | IBM PS/2 Model 50 |
| Intel 80386SX | 32 | 16 | 16 | 4G | Compaq Deskpro 386S |
| Intel 80386 | 32 | 32 | 25 | 4G | IBM PS/2 Model 80 |
| Motorola 68000 | 32 | 16 | 12.5 | 16M | Apple Macintosh SE |
| Motorola 68020 | 32 | 32 | 25 | 4G | Apple Macintosh II |
| Motorola 68030 | 32 | 32 | 25 | 4G | Apple Macintosh IIx |

1K (kilobyte) = 1,024 bytes
1M (megabyte) = 1,048,576 bytes
1G (gigabyte) = 1,073,741,824 bytes

Besides the main microprocessor, some microcomputers contain other chips designed to perform certain specialized tasks. Such chips are called **coprocessors** because they work along with the main microprocessor. Coprocessors often help speed up microcomputers by taking over certain types of time-consuming operations. For example, many microcomputers use separate coprocessors for certain complex mathematical calculations, input/output operations, and the display of graphic images. Since they're specialized, coprocessors can do their jobs more efficiently than the general-purpose main microprocessor. Furthermore, the main microprocessor is relieved from having to do these tasks. The result can be a significant increase in overall computer performance.

## Register Size

*Storage compartments inside the CPU*

The power of a particular computer depends upon several characteristics of its CPU. Although there are many ways to evaluate a particular processor's power and some of them can be quite involved, one convenient measure is the size of a computer's registers. A **register** is essentially a storage compartment inside the CPU for temporarily holding numbers that are currently being manipulated. You can think of registers as scratch pads for the computer. The larger the registers, the larger the numbers they can hold. Register size is usually expressed in terms of bits, which we will examine now.

As we said before, computer circuitry is made up of gates that can turn off or on. Electrically, off is represented by the absence of current and on is the presence of some predefined level of current. Numerically, *off* is symbolized by 0 and *on* is symbolized by 1. Because of this, most computers use the binary number system. Instead of the ten digits of our familiar decimal system, there are only two digits in the binary number system: 0 and 1. A single binary digit is called a **bit**, which can only be 0 or 1. Larger numbers are constructed from strings of zeros and ones representing successive powers of two. A commonly used grouping of bits is the **byte**, which consists of eight bits (see Figure 2.4). This is the amount of storage used to hold a number between 0 and 255, or a single character, such as A, b, or $.

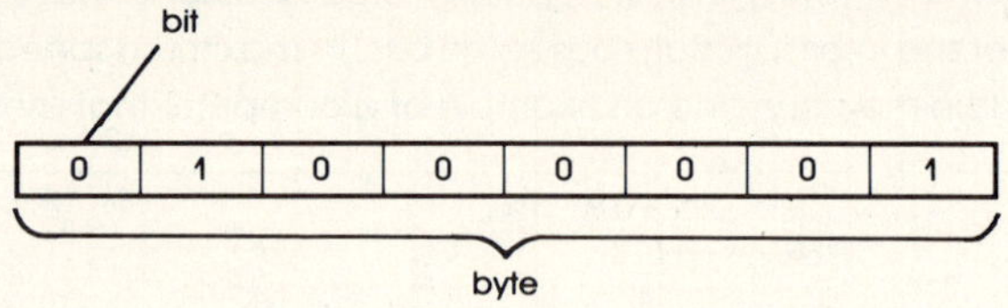


**Figure 2.4 Bits and Bytes**
A bit is a zero or a one. A byte is a group of eight bits. This particular byte holds the number 65 in binary form, which is also the code representing an uppercase A in most computers.

The more bits a computer can work with at a time, the faster and more efficiently it can get the job done. For example, a computer with 32-bit registers can usually process data at least twice as fast as a computer with 16-bit registers. In general, the bigger the register size, the more powerful the computer.

Virtually all of the microprocessors in microcomputers today use 8-bit, 16-bit, or 32-bit registers. The 8-bit microprocessors are the oldest and least powerful of the bunch. They are still used in some low-end Apple, Atari, and Commodore computers. Microprocessors with 16-bit registers are currently the most common. The

Intel 8088 you see in Figure 2.3 is a good example of a 16-bit microprocessor because it's used in so many IBM Personal Computers and similar machines. Finally, 32-bit microprocessors have become increasingly popular since their choice by Apple for the Macintosh line of computers. Other powerful 32-bit microcomputers are also available from several manufacturers, including Compaq, IBM, Tandy, and Zenith.

## Data Bus Size

*Moving data between the CPU and memory*

Register size isn't the only measure of a CPU's ability to process data. Another important factor is the size of the **data bus**. This is the pathway connecting the microprocessor to memory. We said before that the main circuit board of a microcomputer is called the motherboard and is housed inside the system unit. The microprocessor, memory, and various other chips and circuits are all plugged, soldered, or embedded in the motherboard. The main circuit connecting all of these components is called the **bus** (see Figure 2.5). Basically, the bus can be likened to a group of wires that connects the internal and external devices of a computer to the CPU. The wires are divided into three groups: address lines, data lines, and control lines. Address lines carry signals that indicate which memory locations are to be read or written for a particular operation. Data lines, or the data bus, carry program instructions and data from memory to the CPU and back. Control lines convey directives from the CPU to other computer components.

**Figure 2.5 The Bus**
The bus connects the CPU to memory and to input and output device controllers.

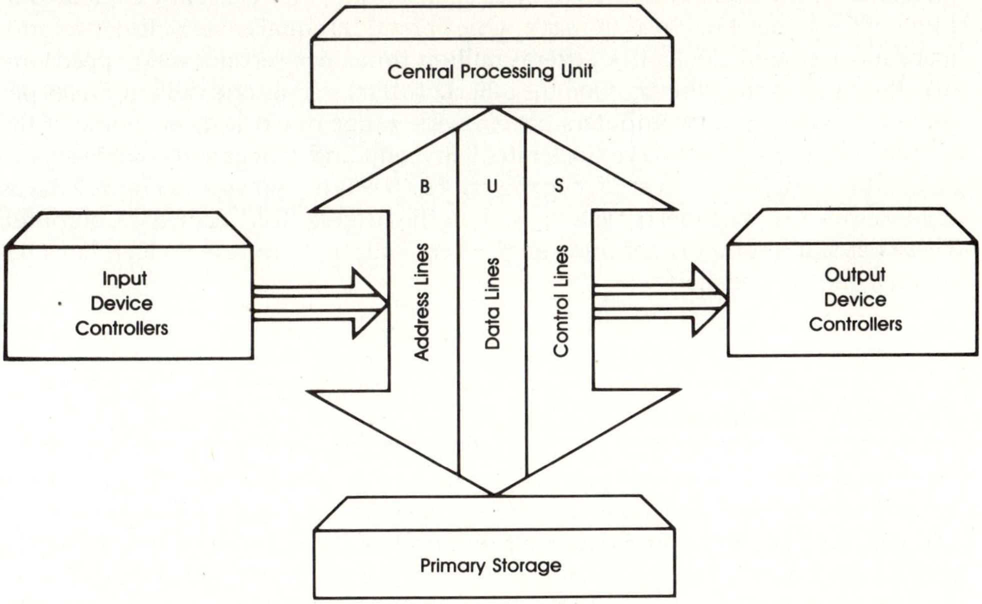


How does the size of the data bus affect computer performance? Basically, it determines how much data can be moved, and thus processed, at a time. Imagine that you had a big jar of jelly beans and you had to move them to another jar. Let's say that you couldn't pour them from one jar to the other and you had to move just eight jelly beans at a time. If there were 1024 jelly beans in the first jar, it would take you 128 transfers to get the job done. On the other hand, if you could move 32 jelly beans at a time it would only take you 32 transfers. In the analogy, you are like the computer, a jelly bean is like a data bit, and the number of jelly beans you can transfer at one time is like the size of the computer's data bus. In general, the larger the data bus, the more powerful the computer.

### Speed

*How fast the system clock ticks*

Another way to evaluate the performance of a particular microprocessor is to look at the speed with which it operates. This speed is dependent upon two factors. The first is the microprocessor design, since manufacturers specify a range of possible speeds for each type of microprocessor they make. The second factor is the speed of the **system clock**. This clock is a crystal that oscillates, or "ticks" at a certain frequency. This frequency is typically several million times per second. The system clock is connected to the microprocessor and other electronic circuits of the computer. It synchronizes the internal operations of these computer components. In some respects, the system clock acts like a musician's metronome by pacing the work of the microprocessor and the devices connected to it.

Since all computer operations require a certain number of clock ticks to be completed, the faster the clock operates, the faster the work gets done. As microcomputers have become more advanced, we have come to expect them to perform more complex tasks faster and faster. So, manufacturers have constantly tried to increase the clock speeds of their microprocessors. Consequently, many modern microcomputers are significantly faster than much bigger computers of the previous decade.

The speed of a system clock, and hence the microprocessor connected to it, is measured by the number of ticks or cycles per second. This is usually expressed in a unit of frequency known as the *hertz*. One hertz (Hz) equals one cycle per second. Since most system clocks tick several million times per second, their speeds are usually given in **megahertz**. One megahertz (MHz) equals one million cycles per second. Today's microcomputers have a wide range of clock rates. Some of the low-end 8-bit computers have clock rates between 1 and 2 megahertz, while expensive 32-bit models can run at 25 megahertz. The 8088 chip you see in Figure 2.3 was used with a 4.77 megahertz system clock in the original IBM Personal Computer. These days, it's common for mid-range microcomputers to run at clock rates between 8 and 12 megahertz.

## PRIMARY STORAGE

*Temporary storage for programs and data*

As we said before, computers process data in the form of numbers. They also need numerically coded instructions to tell them specifically what to do with the data. Ultimately, all programs and data are just numbers. For computers to achieve the speed and efficiency they do, programs and data must be presented to the CPU very rapidly when needed. A good way to do this is to compile programs and data beforehand and hold them temporarily in some quickly accessible storage area. Although a CPU's registers do store numbers, there simply isn't enough room to hold all the data and instructions for a typical task. For example, the Intel 8088 microprocessor has only fourteen 16-bit registers. Clearly, more storage than this is needed.

To solve the problem of program and data storage, computers are given memories. This memory, or primary storage, consists of an array of specialized integrated circuit chips that have the ability to hold numbers. Directly connected to the CPU, primary storage is an essential component of every computer system. The overall performance of a computer depends as much on the speed and amount of its primary storage as it does on the speed and power of its CPU. In general, the total amount of memory a particular computer can have is dependent upon the capabilities of its CPU. Table 2.1, for example, lists the maximum memory that can be used with various microprocessors under ordinary circumstances. In microcomputers, two basic types of primary storage are used: random access memory (RAM) and read-only memory (ROM).

## RAM

*Read-write memory for programs and data*

A computer's memory consists of a sequence of individual storage locations. Each storage location has a unique identifying number. This number is called an **address**, just like the addresses that identify the individual mail boxes in a post office. When a number is placed in storage at a particular address, it is said to be *written* to memory. When a number is looked up in storage, it is said to be *read* from memory. **Random access memory** or **RAM** is storage in which all addresses are equally accessible. In other words, any location can be written to or read from in the same amount of time.

That's the technically correct definition of RAM. RAM, however, has come to mean the memory in a computer that can be freely written to and read from. Sometimes called *read-write memory*, it's the storage that's used by the computer to hold both programs and data as needed. The amount of RAM is another measure of a computer's power. The more RAM a computer has, the more complex the programs it can run and the more data it can have quickly accessible.

As we said before, computers deal with binary numbers, which consist of strings of bits (zeros and ones). A convenient grouping of bits is the byte, which is eight bits long. Since the byte is the smallest unit of storage that can be directly addressed by most computers, memory is measured in bytes. How much memory a computer has is usually expressed in units of 1024 bytes. This number, which is 2 to the 10th power, is somewhat imprecisely called 1 **kilobyte (K)**, because *kilo* is a Greek prefix meaning thousand. When we refer to a computer as having 640K of RAM, we really mean it has 640 times 1024 or 655,360 bytes of memory. Some computers have so much memory that even bigger units are used, such as **megabyte (M)** and **gigabyte (G)**. One megabyte (*mega* stands for million) is equal to 2 to the 20th power, or 1,048,576 bytes; and one gigabyte (*giga* stands for billion) is equal to 2 to the 30th power, or 1,073,741,824 bytes.

The maximum amount of RAM a microcomputer can have is determined by the microprocessor it uses. Today's microcomputers exhibit a wide range of possible memory capacities. For example, while the original Apple II computer could have no more than 64K of RAM, the Apple Macintosh II can theoretically handle up to 4 gigabytes. In reality, memory is also limited by cost and space considerations. Most microcomputers these days have somewhere between 512K and 4 megabytes of RAM. For example, the IBM PS/2 Model 50 comes with 1 megabyte of RAM (see Figure 2.1).

## ROM

*Memory that cannot be altered*

In almost all microcomputers, RAM is used for the temporary storage of programs and data. This is because the most commonly used RAM chips lose their contents when the power is shut off. Most computers have a small set of programs and data that are used very frequently, yet never have to be changed. For these, **read-only memory**, or **ROM**, is used.

ROM is like RAM in that every location has its own address and every address can be read in the same amount of time. The difference is that ROM chips are manufactured with programs and data permanently written in their storage locations. When the power is turned off, ROM chips retain their contents. Hence the programs and data can be read and used, but they cannot be altered. Manufacturers must be very careful to make sure programs and data are correct before they are placed into ROM chips. Despite the extra precautions that must be taken, ROM chips are used because they are simple, inexpensive, fast, and reliable. Most microcomputers contain at least one ROM chip as part of their primary storage. For example, the IBM Personal System/2 Model 50 computer uses four 32K ROM chips to store essential programs and data (see Figure 2.2).

## SECONDARY STORAGE

*Long-lasting storage for programs and data*

In order to do any processing, a computer must have a program and any necessary data in primary storage. But a computer also must have some kind of secondary storage system. **Secondary storage** supplements primary storage by providing a place to keep programs and data when they are not needed at the moment. Although secondary storage generally takes longer to access than primary storage, it is used for the following reasons:

- *Secondary storage is unlimited.* Even though new computers are continually being developed with more and more primary memory, there still isn't enough for users to store all of their programs and data. Secondary storage systems typically involve disks or tapes. Since you can always buy more of these, there's no limit to the amount of secondary storage a computer system can have.
- *Secondary storage is economical.* Although technological advances are steadily reducing the cost of primary storage, secondary storage still costs less.
- *Secondary storage is stable.* The contents of RAM, which makes up most of primary storage, are lost when the power is turned off. The contents of most secondary storage systems remain intact until you direct the computer to change them.
- *Secondary storage is portable.* The programs and data in one computer's RAM cannot be transferred to another computer unless a direct communication link exists between the two computers. Many forms of secondary storage can be easily transported between computers.

### Floppy Disk Drives

*Relatively rugged and inexpensive*

*Floppy disks* or *diskettes* are the most common secondary storage medium used with microcomputers. They are called *floppy* because the disk itself is a circular sheet of thin, flexible plastic. Thinly coated with a magnetic film, floppy disks store binary numbers in the form of tiny magnetic spots arranged in concentric circles.

Microcomputer floppy disks generally come in two sizes: 5.25 inches and 3.5 inches. The 5.25-inch floppies are encased in a square, flexible plastic jacket that leaves the enclosed disk exposed in a couple of places (see Figure 2.6(b)). Because of this exposure, 5.25-inch floppies are usually stored in a protective paper sleeve when they aren't being used. Floppy disks of the 3.5-inch variety look considerably different (see Figure 2.6(a)). Besides being smaller, 3.5-inch floppies are completely enclosed in a square case of rigid plastic. Access to the disk inside is through a sliding metal door that remains closed until the floppy is slipped inside the computer. Currently, the older, 5.25-inch floppies are still more popular, mainly because there is a huge installed base of computers that use them. This situation is gradually changing, however, because newer microcomputers tend to use the 3.5-inch format. Although the 3.5-inch floppies are generally faster, more rugged, more durable, and more compact than the 5.25-inch diskettes, they also cost more.

**Figure 2.6 Floppy Disks**
The two most common types of floppies are:
(a) 3.5-inch diskettes (b) 5.25-inch diskettes

In addition to the two sizes, other differences distinguish floppy disks. All disks, of course, have two sides: a top and a bottom. If only one of these sides is used for storage, that disk is called *single-sided*. Predictably enough, floppy disks that use both sides for storage are called *double-sided*. Variations also exist in the density of the magnetic coating that cover diskettes. The denser the coating, the more bytes a floppy disk can store. *Single-density*, *double-density*, and *high-density* are commonly used terms that reflect how much data can be stored on a particular diskette. To get an idea of the types and storage capacities of the floppy disks used in several popular microcomputers, examine Table 2.2.

**Table 2.2 Popular Floppy Disk Types**

| SIZE (INCHES) | SIDES | DENSITY | CAPACITY (BYTES) | EXAMPLE MICROCOMPUTER |
|---|---|---|---|---|
| 5.25 | single | single | 140K | Apple II |
| 5.25 | double | double | 360K | IBM Personal Computer |
| 5.25 | double | high | 1.20M | IBM Personal Computer AT |
| 3.5 | single | double | 400K | Apple Macintosh |
| 3.5 | double | double | 800K | Apple Macintosh SE |
| 3.5 | double | double | 720K | IBM PS/2 Model 30 |
| 3.5 | double | high | 1.44M | IBM PS/2 Model 50 |

1K (kilobyte) = 1,024 bytes
1M (megabyte) = 1,048,576 bytes

A *floppy disk drive*, or *floppy drive*, is a device that reads and writes the data stored on floppy disks (see Figure 2.7). Most microcomputers have at least one floppy disk drive, and some can even accommodate four. One or two floppy drives are the most common, however, and they're usually enclosed inside the system unit. Some computers, such as the Apple IIe, have external floppy drives in their own separate little cabinets. From the outside, there's an open slot into which you put a single floppy disk at a time. Most 5.25-inch floppy drives also have a door or lever you close after you put a diskette inside. Disk drives for 3.5-inch floppies may only have a slot visible from the outside, or they may have a slot and a button that you can press to eject the disk.

The disk drive operates by spinning the disk under a read-write head mounted on the tip of an access arm (see Figure 2.8). This **read-write head** is a tiny electromagnet that can create or erase minuscule magnetic spots on the disk directly

**Figure 2.7 Floppy Disk Drive**
The floppy disk drive reads and writes programs and data on floppy disks.

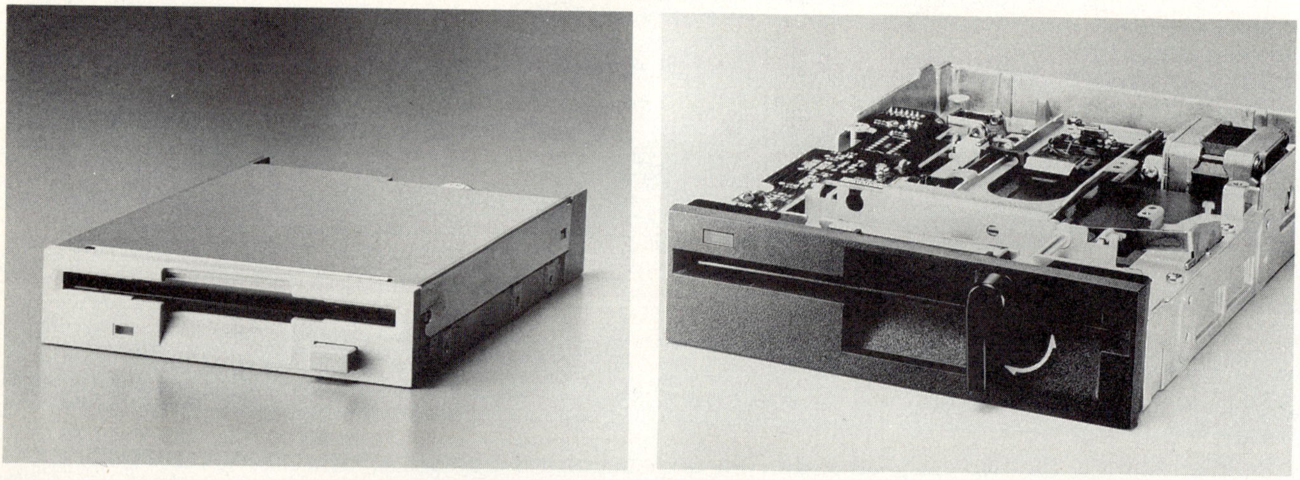

(a) (b)

**Figure 2.8 Inside a Floppy Disk Drive**
This diagram shows the major internal components of a floppy disk drive.

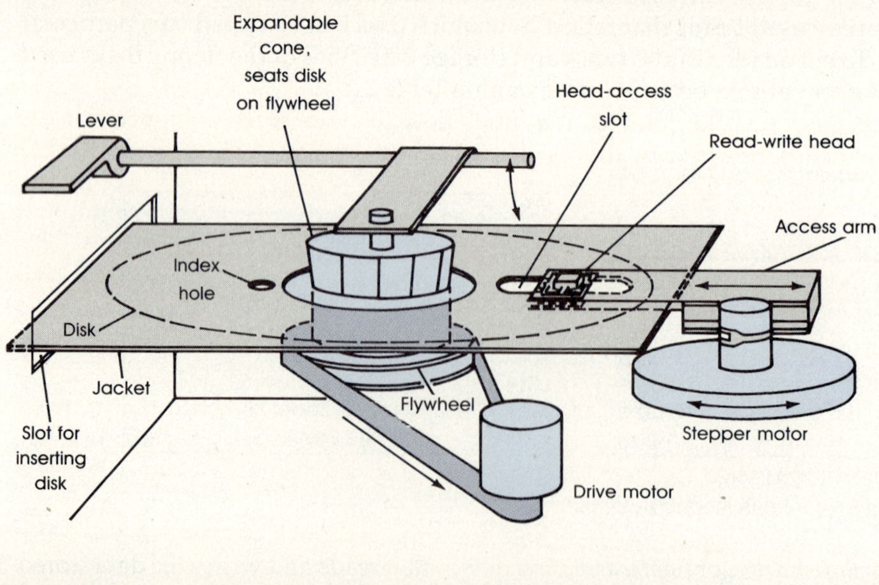

below. The **access arm** is a mechanical extension that can move the read-write head toward or away from the center of the disk. The combination of rotating the disk and moving the access arm enables the read-write head to be placed above any spot on the disk. Double-sided disk drives have forked access arms that hold a read-write head for each of the two disk surfaces.

In general, you must know what kind of floppy disk drive your computer has so that you can select the correct diskettes. Obviously, a 3.5-inch floppy disk drive cannot accommodate 5.25-inch floppy disks, nor can a 5.25-inch drive accept 3.5-inch floppies. Although most double-sided disk drives can use single-sided diskettes, this doesn't utilize the disk drive's full potential. The density of the floppy disk magnetic coating also must be considered. The best approach is to carefully read your computer's user manual so that you understand what kind of floppy disks it requires.

As we said before, floppy disks are the most common form of secondary storage and most microcomputers have at least one floppy drive. There are several reasons for this. First, floppy disk drives are relatively inexpensive. The typical price range is between $80 and $500 for a single disk drive. Second, floppy disk drives are reliable. Like any other mechanical device, floppy drives do occasionally break down, and some models require periodic cleaning and adjustment. But in most cases, floppy disk drives provide years of service without any problems whatsoever. Finally, they are now a very important means for distributing and copying programs and data. Most programs that are purchased come on floppy disks. Because floppies are fairly durable, lightweight, compact, thin, and inexpensive, they can be easily packaged and mailed. People who are using similar computers can very easily trade data with each other. For example, this textbook was written with a microcomputer and the individual chapters were sent to the publisher on floppy disks. Floppy disks are also very easy to reproduce. This makes them an important medium for keeping extra copies of programs and data. Because it's so easy and cheap to make extra or **backup** copies of vital programs and data, computer users are encouraged to do so. This gives them something to fall back on if the original copy is accidentally lost, destroyed, or erased.

## Hard Disk Drives

*Fast, high-capacity storage*

Despite the advantages of floppy disks, many microcomputer users need still more storage. In one sense, floppy disk storage is unlimited because you can always buy more diskettes. But if you have only one floppy disk drive, you can only gain access to the storage of one floppy disk at a time. Perhaps your microcomputer can accommodate additional floppy drives. The upper limit is usually four, however. For very large programs and huge amounts of data, the capacity of even four floppy disks isn't sufficient.

The *hard disk drive* was developed to meet this need for ever increasing amounts of storage (see Figure 2.9). It's a very fast device that can hold much more data than a single floppy disk. Although the basic operating principles of hard disk drives are similar to those of floppy disk drives, there are some important differences. A **hard disk** is a circular platter of rigid aluminum covered with a thin magnetic coating. Just like floppy drives, a hard disk drive has a read-write head mounted on an access arm for each surface of the disk. It's common, however, for hard disk drives to have more than one disk mounted inside on the same spindle, like records stacked on a turntable. Because hard disks are rigid, they can be spun much faster than floppy disks. The movement of the access arms in hard disk drives is much more precisely controlled than in floppy drives. Hard disks are also covered with a very

**Figure 2.9 Hard Disk Drive**
The hard disk drive is a fast, high-capacity secondary storage device.

high quality, dense magnetic coating. These factors combine to make hard disk drives much faster at transferring data than floppy drives, while at the same time providing a much higher storage capacity.

Most hard disk drives consist of hard disks, spinning motors, access arms, and read-write heads completely enclosed in a sealed, airtight housing (see Figure 2.10). This arrangement minimizes vibration and keeps out dust, dirt, smoke, and other contaminants. Hard disks spin so quickly (more than 100 miles per hour), and read-write heads are positioned so closely to disk surfaces (about 20 millionths of an inch), that sharp vibrations and foreign matter such as dust can cause considerable damage. The read-write head can collide with a minute obstruction or actually hit the disk surface itself. This **head crash** can destroy the read-write head and data stored at the point of collision on the disk surface. Fortunately, such disasters are quite rare with the hard disk drives now used in microcomputers. Nevertheless, hard disk drives still tend to be less rugged than floppy disk drives.

**Figure 2.10 Inside a Hard Disk Drive**
This diagram shows the major internal components of a hard disk drive.

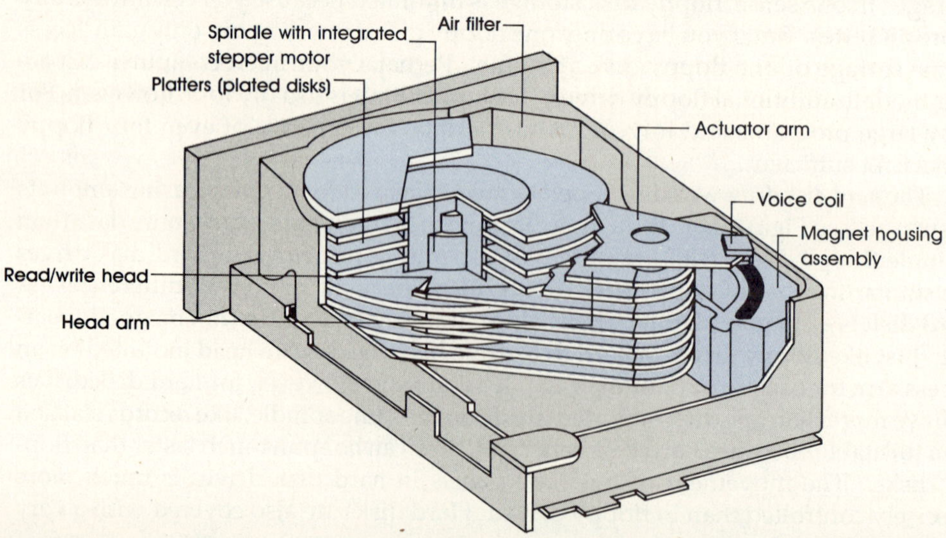

Like floppy drives, hard disk drives are usually enclosed inside the system unit, but they are sometimes found in their own external housings. As we said before, most hard disk drives used with microcomputers have their hard disks permanently sealed inside. This is the reason the term *fixed disk drive* is often used to refer to a hard disk drive. You can't buy additional hard disks to increase the storage capacity of most hard disk drives. Many users find that this isn't a problem because hard disk drives already have such a high capacity. For example, a typical microcomputer hard disk drive can hold at least 20 megabytes and may cost as little as $250. The capacity of this hard disk drive is equal to that of almost 57 floppy disks that hold 360K each. If you still need more storage, you can usually purchase a hard disk drive with an even higher capacity. Some microcomputer hard disk drives can hold hundreds of megabytes. Although most microcomputers seldom have more than a single hard disk drive, it's often possible to connect an additional one.

A microcomputer with one or two floppy disk drives and a hard disk drive has a truly powerful secondary storage system. Most people who have this arrangement store all the programs and data they use daily on the hard disk. This provides faster access and high capacity for those large programs and huge sets of data. The floppy drive is used to copy programs and data to and from the hard disk. Infrequently used programs and data can be copied to floppy disks and taken off the hard disk instead of being completely abandoned. Finally, the floppy disk drive also can be used to make backup copies of important programs and data normally kept on the hard disk.

## Magnetic Tape Drives

*Keeping copies on tape*

In the early days of microcomputers, floppy disk drives were quite expensive and no sane hobbyist would even think of using a hard disk drive for secondary storage. The most common secondary storage device for microcomputers at that time was the cassette tape recorder. Instead of storing music, cassettes were used in early microcomputers to store programs and data in an inexpensive and reliable form. The process of reading and writing data was rather slow, but cassette tape recorders were perfectly adequate for the simple microcomputers of the time. Although they are still used for secondary storage in some very inexpensive microcomputers, cassette tape recorders are rarely seen today in the more powerful systems found in most schools, offices, and homes. They are, however, one example of a class of secondary storage devices that now serves an important specialized function in some modern microcomputers.

A **magnetic tape drive** is a secondary storage device that uses magnetic tape to store programs and data. **Magnetic tape** consists of a long strip of thin plastic covered with a magnetic coating. Just like disks, read-write heads are used to read and write data in the form of magnetic spots on these tapes. Unlike disks, however, magnetic tape is a **sequential access medium**. This means that numbers are recorded one after another along the length of the tape. Consequently, the farther away it is on the tape the longer it takes to reach a number. If the read-write head is positioned at the beginning of the tape and the number you want is at the end of the tape, the computer has to skip through all the numbers that are in between. A familiar example of this is the way songs are recorded on cassette tape. If you want to listen to a song at the end of a tape, you have to push the fast-forward button until you get to it. Disks, on the other hand, are a **direct access medium** because you can go directly to any piece of data on the disk in a very short time.

Although magnetic tape drives have been used with computers for years, they have taken on a specialized function in some modern microcomputer systems.

Their sequential access nature makes them poorly suited to the routine storage of programs and data used daily. Magnetic tape drives, however, work very well as backup systems for hard disk drives. Data can be stored very compactly on magnetic tape, and the sequential reading and writing of data can be done very rapidly. For example, some magnetic tape backup systems can copy in about five minutes the entire contents of a 20-megabyte hard disk onto a tape that looks very much like a cassette tape. Systems such as these can play an important role in preventing the loss of valuable programs and data.

Some microcomputers come with built-in magnetic tape backup systems. In most cases, however, the magnetic tape drive is purchased separately and installed into the system unit or externally connected to the microcomputer with a cable (see Figure 2.11). Tape backup systems are only used with microcomputers that have hard disk drives. In fact, only a minority of hard disk users get magnetic tape backup systems. Most people can get by with keeping extra copies of their programs and data on floppy disks. For some groups of users who need to make periodic backup copies of their entire hard disks, a magnetic tape drive is worth the added expense. Since the tape drive is only used every so often, it can be shared among several microcomputers if it is an external model. This also helps to justify the cost of the tape backup system, which can be anywhere from $300 to several thousand dollars.

**Figure 2.11 Tape Backup System**
Magnetic tape drives, such as this system shown, are now used primarily for making backup copies of hard disks.

## Bernoulli Disk Drives

*Combining the benefits of floppies and hard disks*

Floppy disk and hard disk drives are by far the most commonly used secondary storage devices for microcomputers. They are, almost always, the only types of secondary storage that come as standard equipment with microcomputers. Some companies, however, have developed alternatives to these devices. One such alternative is the **Bernoulli disk drive**, sometimes called the **Bernoulli box** (see Figure 2.12). It's a secondary storage device that, in a sense, combines the advantages of both floppy and hard disk drives.

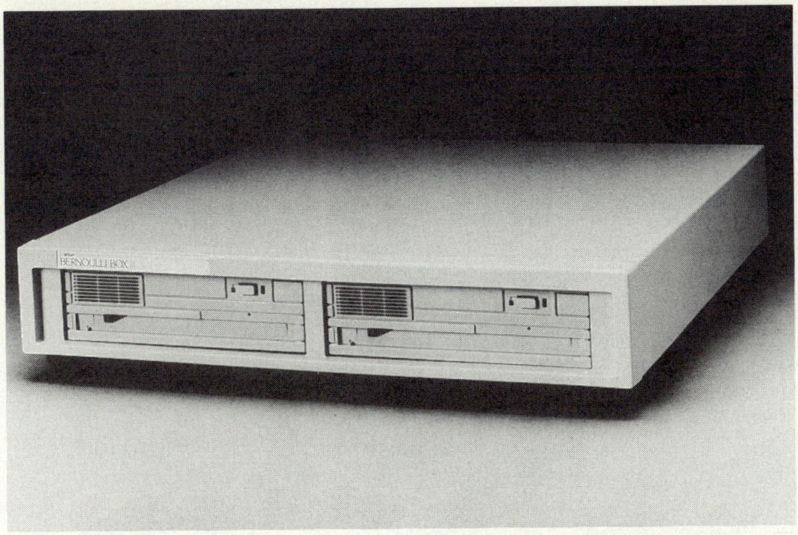


**Figure 2.12 The Bernoulli Box**
The Bernoulli Box combines some of the advantages of both floppy and hard disk drives.

The Bernoulli disk drive is like a high performance, high capacity floppy disk drive (see Figure 2.13). It uses a special type of floppy disk that's sealed inside in a hard plastic case. The disk is spun at about 3000 revolutions per minute. This is fast enough to subject the flexible disk to an aerodynamic effect first described by the Swiss mathematician Daniel Bernoulli in the eighteenth century. Basically, the Bernoulli effect causes the disk to be lifted close to the read-write head and stabilized by the air currents generated when it is rotated at high speeds. If a dust particle gets in the way, or a sharp vibration occurs, the rotation slows and the disk temporarily falls safely away from the read-write head, thus preventing a head crash. The air flow also tends to purge contaminating particles from the disk.

The Bernoulli disk drive is often housed in its own separate cabinet, connected to the microcomputer system unit with a cable. Bernoulli disks generally come in two capacities: 10 and 20 megabytes. This type of secondary storage device operates at about the same speed as a slow hard disk drive, but costs significantly more. Nevertheless, Bernoulli drives offer a distinct advantage: the disks are rugged and removable like floppy disks, yet they have the capacity of hard disks. So, if you need more storage, you can purchase additional disks. Bernoulli disks cost between $40 and $80, but each one can store a large amount of data. Some Bernoulli units have two drives built into one cabinet so you can use two disks at the same time and easily make backup copies. They are a viable alternative to hard disk drives for some users, despite the added expense.

## Optical Disk Drives

*Using lasers to store vast quantities of data*

In the last few years, an entirely new class of secondary storage devices has emerged that is based on light rather than magnetism. The **optical disk drive** uses a laser to read or write data in the form of pits molded into a plastic disk. Currently, two basic types of optical disk drives are commonly used with microcomputers: CD-ROM drives and WORM drives.

**Compact Disk Read-Only Memory**, or **CD-ROM**, is a specialized form of secondary storage that only allows you to read previously recorded data, not record it yourself. CD-ROM drives use compact disks (CDs) that look just like the digital

**Figure 2.13 Inside the Bernoulli Box**
This diagram shows the major internal components of a Bernoulli disk drive.

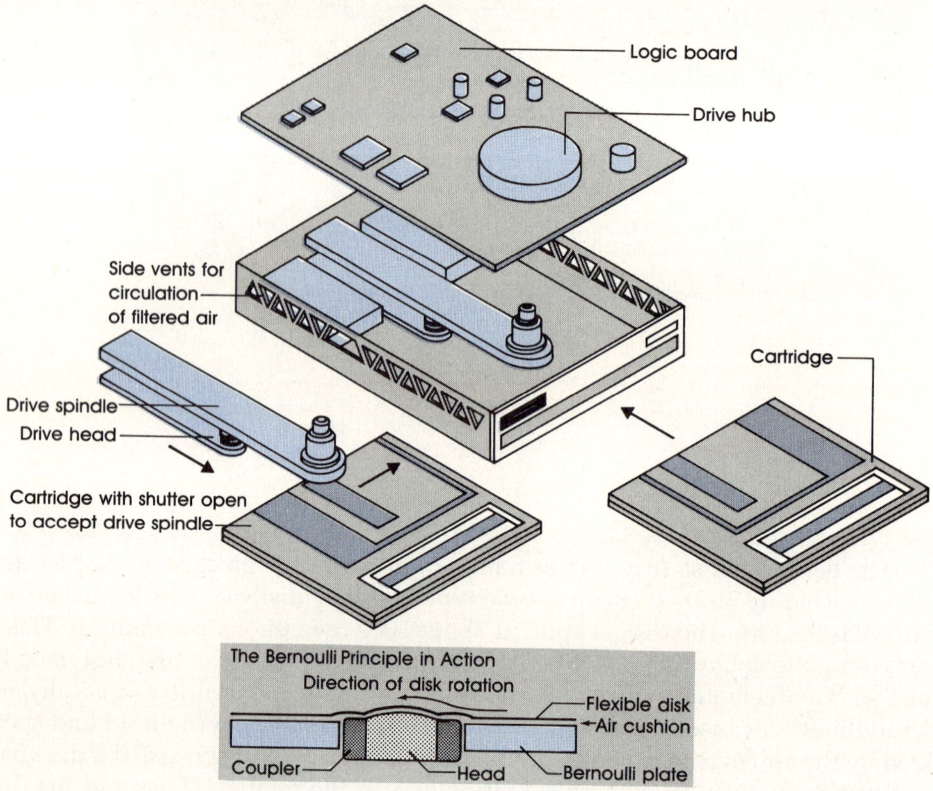


audio disks first introduced by Sony in 1983. When used to store data, these 12-centimeter (4.72-inch) disks of molded plastic can each hold an amazing 550 megabytes—the equivalent of several hundred books. Just like audio CDs, CD-ROM disks can be written only at the factory by special equipment. Since the appearance of the first CD-ROM drives early in 1985, many businesses have published encyclopedias, reference works, professional directories, and other large sets of data on CDs. Some CD-ROM drives can be installed inside a microcomputer's system unit, while other models are housed in their own external cabinets (see Figure 2.14).

**Write Once, Read Many (times),** or **WORM**, is a slightly different type of optical disk storage that allows users to record their own programs and data. Once programs and data have been copied onto a WORM disk, they can be used but never changed or deleted. WORM disks typically hold between 100 and 400 megabytes each. WORM disk drives are similar to CD-ROM drives except that they include a more powerful laser used to record data by melting little depressions in the recording surface. Since these pits are irreversible physical changes in the disk, once data is written on WORM disks it cannot be erased. Despite this limitation and the fact that they are still rather expensive (between $2,000 and $10,000), WORM disk drives can be invaluable to users who need to create huge, permanent collections of data.

**Figure 2.14 CD-ROM Drive**
The CD-ROM drive reads the contents of previously recorded compact disks, each of which can hold around 550 megabytes of programs and data.

## KEYBOARDS AND MICE

*Telling computers what to do*

The primary input device of every microcomputer is a keyboard, used to enter data and tell the computer what to do. Like typewriters, microcomputer keyboards have keys for alphabetic letters, numbers, mathematical symbols, and punctuation marks. These keys are almost always in the same positions on most keyboards. In addition to this basic set of keys, microcomputer keyboards have other, special-purpose keys. Some popular microcomputers, like IBM's Personal System/2 series, come with keyboards that have more than 100 keys (see Figure 2.15), twice that of most typewriters. Different types of computers have distinct keyboard designs for the additional keys. Other differences also exist, such as how the keys feel and sound when they are pressed, and the relative sizes of certain keys. Most modern microcomputers have a detachable keyboard that is connected to the system unit with a coiled cable. This gives you the freedom to alter the position of your keyboard or even type with it in your lap. For more comfort, many keyboards also can be adjusted to lie flat on the table or be tilted a bit toward you.

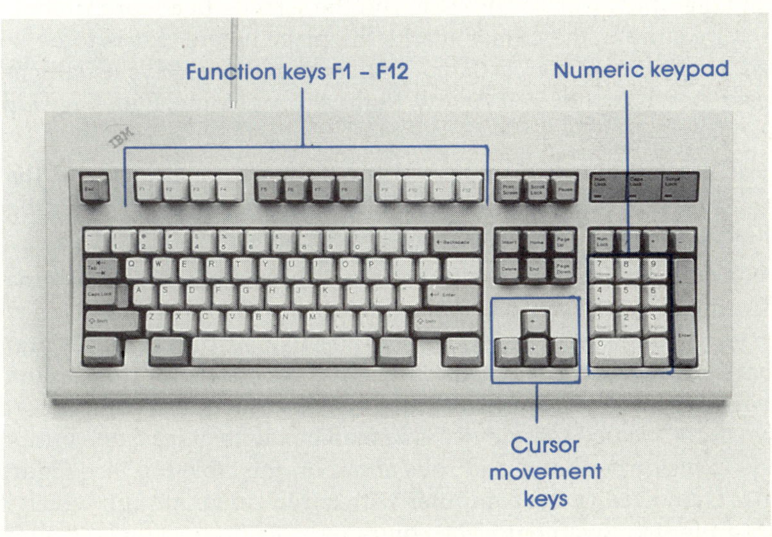


**Figure 2.15 Microcomputer Keyboard**
IBM's Enhanced Keyboard has 101 keys.

Computer keyboards work by constantly scanning themselves to see if any keys are currently depressed. Every key is assigned its own code number. When a key is pressed, its code is sent to the computer. If the computer is busy or if keys are pressed more quickly than the computer can process them, key codes may be temporarily stored by the keyboard in its own memory chips and sent when the computer is ready. As you can imagine, microcomputer keyboards have become rather sophisticated devices. In fact, many keyboards are so complex that they contain their own microprocessor to handle the work of decoding and storing keystrokes. It's important to realize that the keyboard merely passes on key codes to the computer; it is the computer that actually decodes the keypresses and interprets the actions to be taken. Thus, computer programs may assign different meanings to different keys, especially the special-purpose keys we mentioned.

Since special-purpose keys are found on many microcomputer keyboards, let's go into a bit more detail and describe what some of these keys are and what they're typically used for:

- *Enter or Return Key*. Analogous to the carriage return on a typewriter, this key is used to signal the end of an entry. When pressed, it tells the computer to go ahead and process what was just typed.
- *Escape Key*. This key is often used to cancel a previously typed entry or to prematurely end a program.
- *Break Key*. This key is much like the escape key and is used by some programs in a similar fashion.
- *Control Key*. Somewhat like a shift key, the control key is pressed in conjunction with other keys. It's used to control a program's actions by sending certain codes to the computer.
- *Alternate Key*. Very similar to the control key, the alternate key is also pressed in conjunction with other keys. It's used to give an alternate meaning to the keys pressed along with it.
- *Insert Key*. This key is often used to insert a new entry between existing entries.
- *Delete Key*. This key is often used to erase an entry or a single character.
- *Function Keys*. These keys are pressed to activate frequently used operations within a program. They are used differently by different programs. Microcomputers that have function keys typically have between two and twelve of them.
- *Cursor Movement Keys*. Most programs use these keys to let you move the cursor (a little blinking underscore or box) around the screen. In a word processing program, for example, the cursor marks the place where text is to be inserted, deleted, or otherwise manipulated. Cursor movement keys usually include Up Arrow, Down Arrow, Left Arrow, Right Arrow, Home, End, Page Up, and Page Down keys.
- *Numeric Keypad*. This is an array of keys at the right side of a keyboard that resembles the layout of a calculator's keys. It includes the ten digits and other symbols that facilitate the entry of numbers and formulas.

Early microcomputers usually didn't have all these keys. The original Apple Macintosh computer, for example, had a keyboard with only 58 keys. In an effort to keep their microcomputers as easy to use as possible, Apple purposely minimized the number of keys on its keyboards. To help compensate for the elimination of most special-purpose keys, Apple included with its Macintosh computers a little device known as the *mouse*. This device is a small box with at least one button that the user holds in his or her hand and rolls about on the table top (see Figure 2.16). The mouse is connected to the computer with a thin cable through which it sends signals indicating its movement. The computer uses these signals to similarly move a cursor or arrow on the screen. Thanks to clever computer programming, the mouse is quite a versatile tool. It can be used to point the cursor at symbols (also called *icons*) that represent activities to be performed. By pressing a button on the mouse, the user tells the computer to go ahead and complete the activity depicted by the icon at which the cursor is currently pointing. In addition to its use in moving the cursor and selecting options, a mouse also can be used to draw figures. Although Apple certainly didn't invent the mouse, the company did popularize this useful accessory by making it an essential component of the Macintosh computers. Because the mouse has proven so useful, other computer manufacturers have jumped on the bandwagon. Now, most microcomputers can accommodate a mouse as an optional input device, even if they have many special-purpose keys on their keyboards.

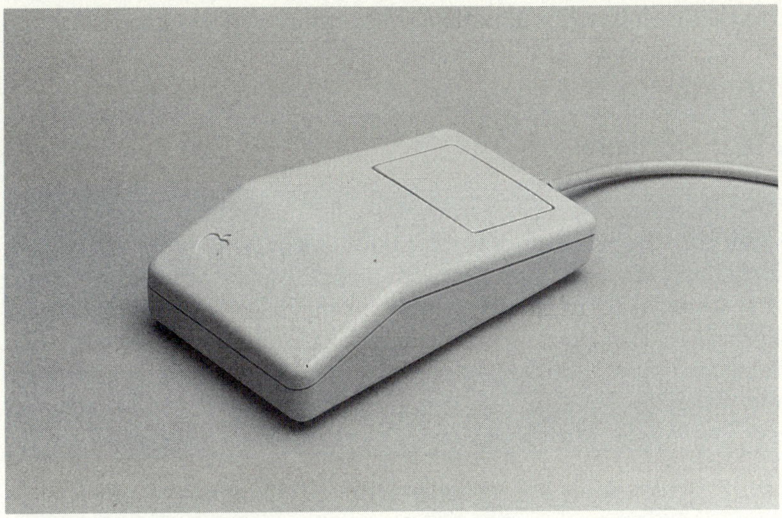

**Figure 2.16 Mouse**
The mouse is the most popular alternate input device, used for pointing, selecting, and drawing.

Incidentally, Apple has abandoned the very simple keyboard of its original Macintosh. Modern Macintoshes are equipped with one of two keyboard designs: the 81-key Apple Keyboard, or the 105-key Extended Keyboard, which is similar to the IBM Enhanced Keyboard shown in Figure 2.15.

## DISPLAYS

As we said in Chapter 1, a computer display, or monitor, is an output device that has a screen on which text and graphic images are presented to the user. Virtually every microcomputer has some type of display. This essential component is used by the computer to echo back the characters you type at the keyboard and to show the results of the programs you run.

*Screen mechanisms*

Most computer displays are similar to ordinary television screens. They consist of a **cathode ray tube**, or **CRT**, that uses an electron gun to paint images on a phosphor-coated glass screen. Screen sizes of CRTs typically range from nine to nineteen inches, measured diagonally. CRT screens are by far the oldest and most commonly used type of computer display.

In addition to CRT screens, several kinds of flat-panel displays are used, primarily with small portable computers. These screens are relatively small, thin, and lightweight. Currently, the most popular and inexpensive of these flat-panel screens is the **liquid crystal display**, or **LCD**. Smaller versions of this type of display have been used in watches, calculators, tiny televisions, and other electronic devices for years. They consist of a thin layer of liquid crystalline substance sandwiched between two sheets of glass. Very thin wires are embedded horizontally in one glass sheet and vertically in the other sheet. When electricity is passed through a wire in each sheet, the crystals at the intersection line up to produce a dark dot. Images are constructed from these tiny dots.

Besides these technological differences, we've mentioned before that some microcomputer models have the display built into the same cabinet as the system unit, while others have a separate display connected to the system unit by a cable. There also are differences in the type of images that displays can present. Most displays fall into one of the following classifications: monochrome text monitors, monochrome graphics monitors, and color graphics monitors.

## Monochrome Text Monitors

*Displaying characters in one color*

A **monochrome text monitor** displays characters such as letters and numbers in a single color (see Figure 2.17). Sometimes these characters include symbols that can be combined to form lines, boxes, bar graphs, and even primitive pictures, but these images are limited. Consequently, microcomputers with monochrome text monitors can only run programs that generate rather simple output. They are completely useless for programs that must display complex graphic images such as drawings, figures, charts, and maps.

**Figure 2.17 Monochrome Text Monitor**
This monochrome (green) text monitor, used with IBM's original line of Personal Computers, can display only 256 different types of characters.

The display color may vary from model to model. Currently, the most common colors for monochrome monitors are green, amber, or white characters on a black background, and black on a white background. Most monochrome monitors can highlight by brightening or dimming text, underlining text, and causing characters to blink.

The characters presented on a monochrome text monitor are arranged into rows and columns. Each character takes up the same amount of space as every other character, so the rows are perfectly aligned horizontally and the columns are perfectly aligned vertically. The most common arrangement is to have 25 lines (or rows) of 80 characters (or columns) each. The characters themselves are made up of little dots. The more dots used per character, the more sharply defined those characters appear. A monitor with sharply defined characters is much more pleasant to work with because eyestrain is minimized. This sharpness, or **resolution**, of a character is expressed in terms of the width and height of the box that contains the character. For example, many monochrome text monitors have a 9 by 14 character box. In other words, every character displayed by these monitors fits into a box that is 9 dots wide and 14 dots high. Other common character resolutions are 8 by 8, 8 by 14, 8 by 16, and 9 by 16.

Monochrome text monitors are the simplest and least expensive type of microcomputer display. Some monochrome text monitors sell for as little as $70. Although they are limited to rather simple output, monochrome text monitors are still used in many microcomputer systems, such as the original IBM Personal Computer shown in Figure 2.17.

## Monochrome Graphics Monitors

*Displaying text and pictures in one color*

**Computer graphics** is the presentation of images such as figures, charts, graphs, maps, diagrams, and other pictures on a display screen. A **monochrome graphics monitor**, therefore, presents such pictures in a single color, usually green, amber, white, or black (see Figure 2.18). It also can display ordinary characters, just like a text monitor. In fact, a monochrome graphics monitor may differ from a monochrome text monitor only in the electronic circuit board that controls it. We'll have more to say about these circuit boards later in this chapter when we discuss the ex-

**Figure 2.18 Monochrome Graphics Monitor**
The monitor built into Apple's Macintosh SE can display graphics as well as text, but only in black and white.

pansion capabilities of microcomputers. For now, let's just say that graphics monitors have the electronic circuitry to allow the computer to individually control every dot on the screen.

Each dot, also called a **pixel** or **pel** (for *picture element*), can be turned on or off to construct images. The effect produced is somewhat like the pictures you see in black and white newspapers, which also are made up of dots. Most monochrome graphics monitors only have the ability to turn pixels on or off, but some also can vary the intensity of each pixel and make them blink, too.

One of the most important factors to consider with graphics monitors is resolution, since this determines not only how sharp characters can be, but also the ultimate definition of pictures produced. The resolution of graphics monitors is given as the total number of horizontal dots by the total number of vertical dots. For example, the Apple Macintosh SE screen you see in Figure 2.18 is a monochrome graphics display with a resolution of 512 by 342 pixels. In other words, there are 342 rows and 512 columns of dots. There are quite a few different screen resolutions used with microcomputer graphics monitors. Some monitors can even use different resolutions at different times. Occasionally, you'll see the terms *low-resolution*, *medium-resolution*, and *high-resolution* used in describing the capabilities of a graphics monitor. No standard values define these terms, but in IBM microcomputers, for example, low-resolution is 160 by 200 pixels, medium-resolution is 320 by 200 pixels, and high-resolution may mean 640 by 200, or more.

## Color Graphics Monitors

*Displaying text and pictures in several colors*

A **color graphics monitor** can present text and pictures in more than one color. It's like a monochrome graphics monitor except that each pixel may be any one of several possible colors. Most color graphics monitors can display different resolutions at different times. The number of different colors that can be displayed on the screen at one time is related to the resolution. In general, the greater the resolution, the fewer the colors that can be displayed at one time. This combination of screen resolution and number of colors that can be used at one time is often called a **video mode**. For example, many color graphics monitors can only display two colors when they are used in their high-resolution video mode. If the color used for the background is black, and the other color used for text or pictures is white, the color graphics monitor may look just like a monochrome graphics monitor. The difference is that the color graphics monitor can vary these two colors, while in the monochrome monitor the background and foreground colors cannot be changed.

The total number of colors you have to choose from in a particular video mode is called the **palette**. On some monitors, the palette can be quite large. For example, the color graphics monitors available for IBM's Personal System/2 microcomputers have a palette that consists of 262,144 colors. On these computers, in the medium-resolution video mode (320 by 200 pixels), you can choose 256 colors out of this palette of 262,144 to be present on the screen at the same time. With monitors such as these, the picture quality can approach that of ordinary color television.

Color graphics monitors are the cream of the crop when it comes to microcomputer displays, but they are significantly more expensive than monochrome text or graphics monitors. Prices can range from $200 up to several thousand dollars. Even so, many computer owners find that the advantages of a color graphics monitor are well worth the cost.

## EXPANDING THE SYSTEM

*Adding optional equipment*

One of the best features microcomputers have to offer is that most of them can be easily expanded and upgraded. This means that additional devices can be connected to a system, and existing devices can be replaced with better models. Microcomputer manufacturers generally encourage other companies to build equipment that can be added to their systems. Consequently, all kinds of devices have been designed to work with microcomputers, so that buyers can start simply and gradually add more capabilities to their systems. With these individually tailored additions, the microcomputer can become an extremely versatile machine, as reflected by its widespread use in not only offices, but also in homes, schools, laboratories, factories, and just about every business imaginable. The hardware components that make this versatility possible are expansion slots, expansion boards, and interfaces.

### Expansion Slots

*Extending the bus*

Previously in this chapter, we said that a computer's *bus* is a group of wires that connects the internal and external components to the CPU. In many microcomputers, the bus is extended to a set of one or more connectors on the motherboard. Each of these connectors, called an *expansion slot*, lets you plug in an additional circuit card known as an *expansion board* (see Figure 2.19). Many of the external devices that can be connected to a microcomputer require an expansion board to control their functions and connect them to the bus. Expansion slots make it easy to expand and upgrade a microcomputer system. In many cases, all you have to do to add a new hardware component is open the system unit's case and simply plug in an expansion board. On some microcomputers, you don't even need a screwdriver to do this.

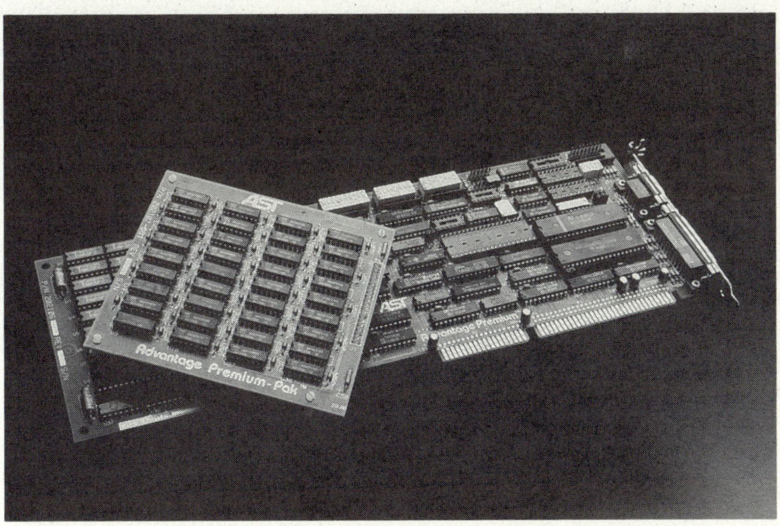


**Figure 2.19 Expansion Board**
This multifunction board combines several different capabilities on a single circuit card. The connector along the bottom edge plugs into an expansion slot on the microcomputer's motherboard.

## Expansion Boards

*Device controllers*

Expansion slots and expansion boards make it possible to add a host of optional hardware components and devices to an existing computer system. Here are a few of the more common types of expansion boards:

- *Additional memory.* Many microcomputers can accommodate more RAM than will fit on the motherboard. In these cases, expansion boards that contain additional memory can be installed to run bigger programs or handle more data.
- *Display adapters.* Some microcomputers have the control circuitry for their displays built onto their motherboards. On quite a few other models, displays must be plugged into a special type of expansion board called a **display adapter**. It's not just the type of monitor, but also the type of display adapter that determines whether your computer can present monochrome text, monochrome graphics, or color graphics.
- *Disk drive controllers.* Some microcomputers also have their floppy and hard disk drives controlled by expansion boards. This is especially true for external disk drives which usually plug into an expansion board via a cable.
- *Real-time clocks.* As we said before, all computers have a system clock which acts as a metronome for the CPU. Most of them also have another type of clock, known as a real-time clock, that is used to keep the date and time-of-day. Some expansion boards contain a real-time clock run by a battery that keeps time even when the computer is turned off.
- *Game Adapters.* There are both computer games and more serious programs that require the use of certain alternate input devices. We'll be discussing these devices, such as joysticks and trackballs, later in this chapter. For now, suffice it to say that on some microcomputers, these devices are controlled by a type of expansion board called a **game adapter**.
- *Network Adapters.* A **local area network** (**LAN**) is an arrangement in which two or more microcomputers are connected by cables for the purpose of sharing programs, data, and hardware devices such as printers and high-capacity hard disks. A **network adapter** is a sophisticated expansion board that's used to connect a microcomputer to a local area network.
- *Multifunction Boards.* Microcomputers only have so many expansion slots. While some computers have as many as eight, other models may have only one. An option like a real-time clock, however, doesn't take up enough space to fill an entire expansion board. So, this prompted the idea of putting several different options on a single expansion board. Thus the **multifunction board** was born (see Figure 2.19). There are now all kinds of multifunction boards sold that include every conceivable combination of add-on options, including memory, real-time clocks, game adapters, display adapters, and serial and parallel interfaces.

## Interfaces

*External connectors*

An **interface** is a connection between a computer's CPU and an external device operated under its control. Such devices, sometimes called *peripherals*, perform input, output, and storage functions. We've already discussed several examples of peripherals: external disk drives, monitors, and keyboards. The three most popular interfaces used to connect peripheral devices to microcomputers are the serial interface, the parallel interface, and the small computer system interface.

### The Serial Interface

A **serial interface** or **serial port** transmits bytes of data, one bit at a time, between a computer and an external device. Each bit in a byte is sent serially, one by one. Serial interfaces are often used to connect computers to graphic input devices such as a mouse. They also are used to connect computers to modems (devices that transmit data over telephone lines, which we'll be discussing later in this chapter). Less frequently, serial interfaces are used to connect computers to printers. The serial interface is reliable and inexpensive, but is limited in speed because it only transmits one bit of data at a time.

*Communicating a bit at a time*

The *RS-232C standard* is one type of serial interface used with many microcomputers. It specifies the functions and voltage levels of 25 wires attached to pins on a standardized plug or holes in a standardized socket. Thanks to this standardization, many external devices and computers from different manufacturers use the RS-232C serial interface.

Some computers have at least one serial interface built into the motherboard that connects to a plug emerging from the back of the system unit. Other computers may have one or more serial interfaces on expansion boards. One or two serial interfaces are often included on multifunction boards.

### The Parallel Interface

A **parallel interface** or **parallel port** transmits data, an entire byte at a time, between a computer and an external device. The eight bits in each byte are sent simultaneously, in parallel, with a single wire carrying each bit. Ten wires are needed to send data in parallel: one for each of the eight bits in a byte, a ground (electrical reference) line, and a control line. Parallel interfaces are most commonly used to connect printers to microcomputers.

*Communicating a byte at a time*

The *Centronics standard* is perhaps the most popular type of parallel interface used with microcomputer printers. It's based on the connector first used in the printers manufactured by Centronics Data Computer Corporation. Subsequently, many printer and microcomputer manufacturers have adopted this standard.

As with serial interfaces, some computers have a parallel interface built onto the motherboard while others provide it on an expansion board.

### The Small Computer System Interface

The **Small Computer System Interface** or **SCSI** (pronounced *scuzzy*) provides high-speed access to peripheral devices. It's most often used to connect hard disk drives and magnetic tape backup systems to microcomputers. Although the SCSI is not as common as the RS-232C and Centronics standard interfaces, it has been gaining popularity lately. Apple uses the SCSI in its Macintosh computers for both internal and external hard disks.

*High-speed connector for disk and tape drives*

## PRINTERS

A printer is a device that prints text and possibly graphics onto paper. Although a printer is not an absolutely essential component of a microcomputer system, most microcomputers have one connected to them. This is because computers are commonly used to produce letters, reports, books, tables, figures, charts, graphs, diagrams, maps, and pictures. Paper output, or *hard copy* as it's also called, is a convenient medium for distributing and communicating this work to others.

*Producing output on paper*

Virtually all printers are connected to microcomputers through a serial or parallel interface. Despite this common bond, there are many types of microcomputer printers. They differ in how they operate, which also affects the type and quality of their output. The four kinds of printers most frequently used with microcomputers are dot-matrix printers, daisy-wheel printers, ink-jet printers, and laser printers. In addition, a special class of paper output devices, called plotters, is also important.

## Dot-Matrix Printers

*The most popular type of printer*

A **dot-matrix printer** is an output device that uses tiny dots to create text and graphics on paper. Just as graphics monitors use pixels to construct characters and pictures on a screen, dot-matrix printers similarly use dots of ink on pages of paper. Inside the dot-matrix printer a *printhead* is moved across the paper from left to right, and sometimes also from right to left. This printhead may contain anywhere from 7 to 27 pins arranged in a vertical column. While most dot-matrix printers use 9 pins, more expensive printers with 18 or 24 pins are also common. As the printhead moves horizontally, it constructs a character by repeatedly striking these pins against an inked ribbon and the paper (see Figure 2.20). Electrical signals cause the appropriate pins to be thrust out at the proper moment to form the successive columns of dots that make up a character's image. Each column of the character is struck in turn against the ribbon and paper until the complete image has been formed. Dot-matrix printers are more frequently used for text, but this printing mechanism allows most models to produce graphics, too.

Dot-matrix printers are by far the most popular type of microcomputer printer. They are reasonably priced, fairly quick, and pretty reliable. Prices range between $150 and $3,000, but the typical cost of an average 9-pin dot-matrix printer is about $500. The speed of a dot-matrix printer depends upon what print mode it is using. The fastest mode is called **draft mode**, in which characters are formed by just a single pass of the print head. Some expensive dot-matrix printers are able to achieve speeds of 400 characters per second in draft mode. Many dot-matrix printers also have a **near letter-quality** or **NLQ** mode. In this mode, the printhead makes two or more passes over each character, slightly shifting its position each time. This tends to fill in the gaps between the dots and makes text appear more like the printing of an electric typewriter. Using NLQ mode may slow some printers down to only 15 characters per second. Generating graphics with a dot-matrix printer also can be time-consuming. Depending upon how dark the images are, it may take several minutes per page to produce graphics on a dot-matrix printer.

## Daisy-Wheel Printers

*True letter-quality printing*

A **daisy-wheel printer** is an output device with solid, raised characters embossed on the ends of little arms arranged like the spokes of a wheel or the petals of a daisy. As the wheel spins, a tiny hammer strikes the back of the proper character when it passes (see Figure 2.21). This impact drives the character pattern, which is embossed in reverse, against an inked ribbon and the paper. Daisy-wheel printers are true **letter-quality** printers because they produce well-defined text just like electric typewriters. Their prices are comparable to those of dot-matrix printers. Unlike dot-matrix printers, however, daisy-wheel printers cannot produce graphics. They also are noisier and slower than dot-matrix printers. The typical daisy-wheel printer can only print about 10 characters per second, and even the most expensive

(a)

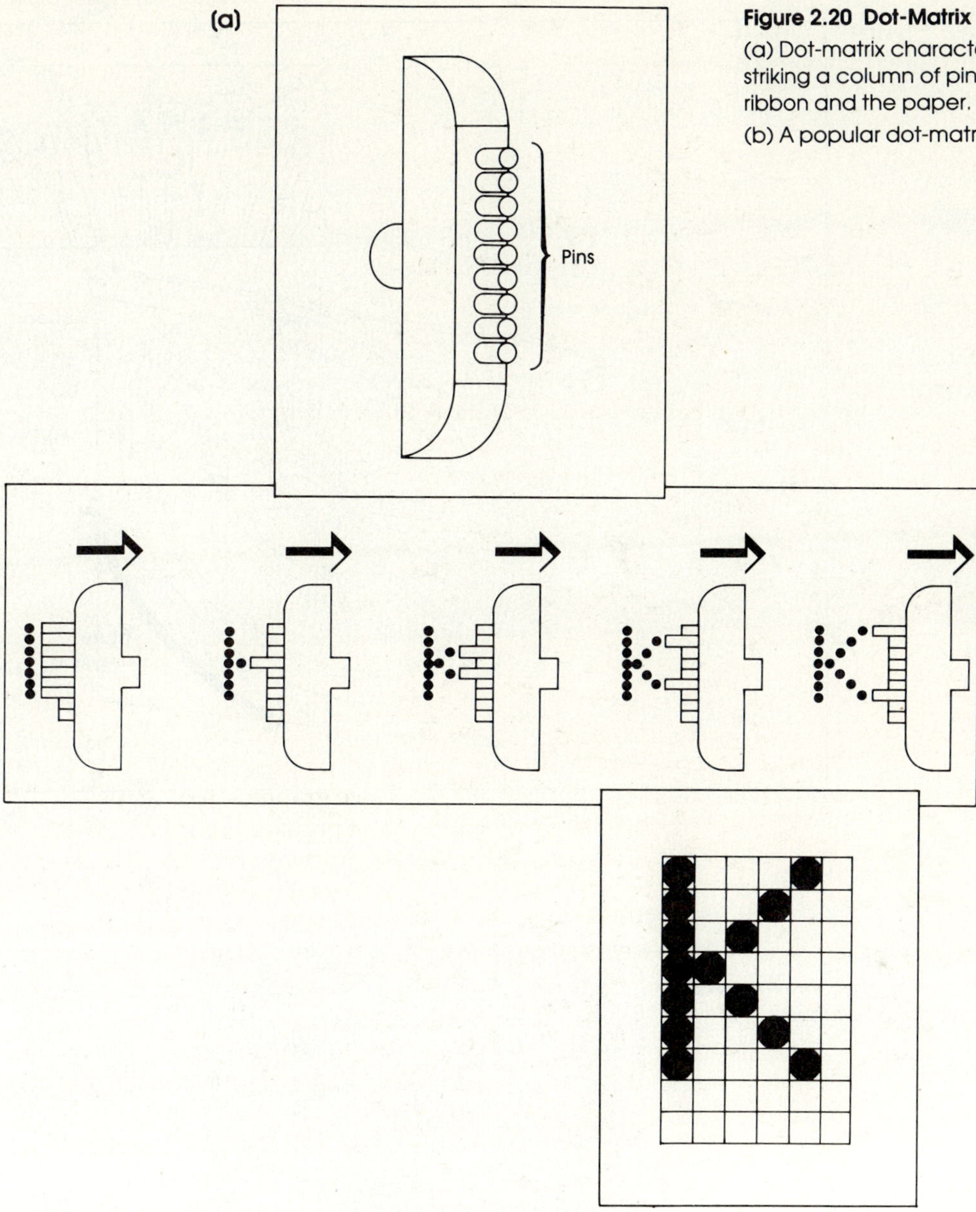


(b)

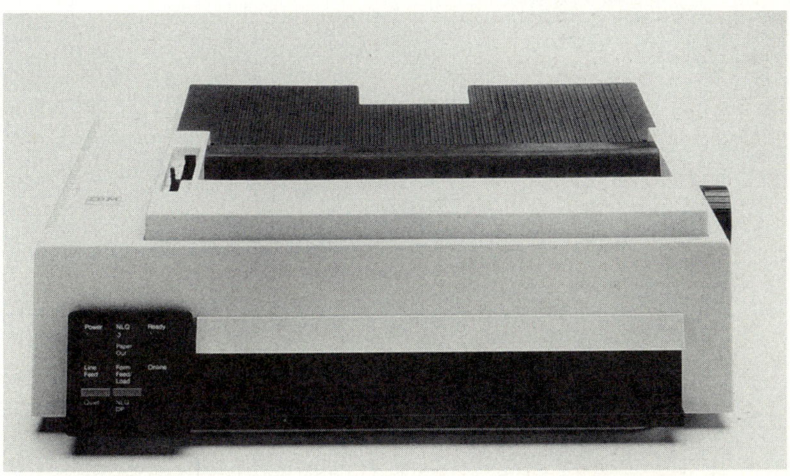

**Figure 2.20 Dot-Matrix Printer**

(a) Dot-matrix characters are formed by striking a column of pins against an inked ribbon and the paper.

(b) A popular dot-matrix printer.

(a)

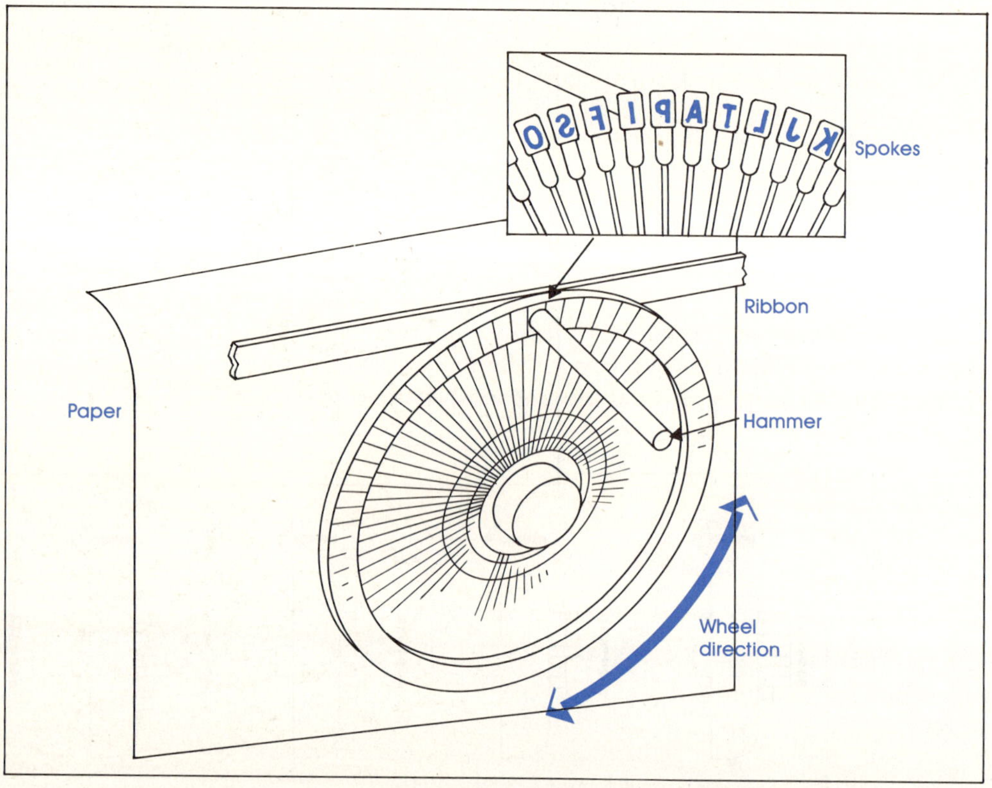


(b)

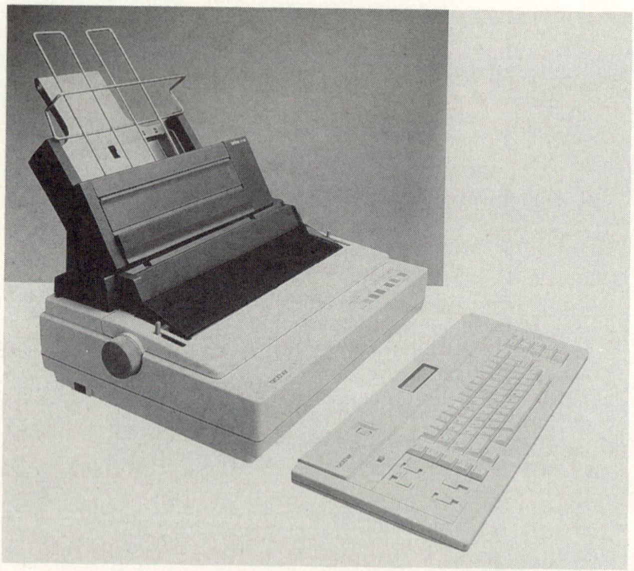

**Figure 2.21 Daisy-Wheel Printer**
(a) The daisy-wheel printing mechanism works somewhat like a typewriter to produce letter-quality text.
(b) A popular daisy-wheel printer.

models generally cannot do better than one hundred characters per second. Daisy-wheel printers are still common, but they are gradually being supplanted by 24-pin dot-matrix printers and laser printers.

## Ink-Jet Printers

*Spray printing*

An **ink-jet printer** has a mechanism that squirts tiny, electrically-charged droplets of ink out of a nozzle and onto the paper (see Figure 2.22). Ink-jet printers are fast, quiet, and can produce high-quality print, but they are slightly more expensive than dot-matrix printers. Some ink-jet printers have a tendency to clog their nozzle with ink and smear characters on paper. Many ink-jet printers, however, have the capability to print in color, a capability most other types of printers lack.

**Figure 2.22 Ink-Jet Printer**

(a) A stream of tiny ink drops are shot out of a nozzle and guided onto the paper by electrically charged deflection plates.

(b) A popular ink-jet printer.

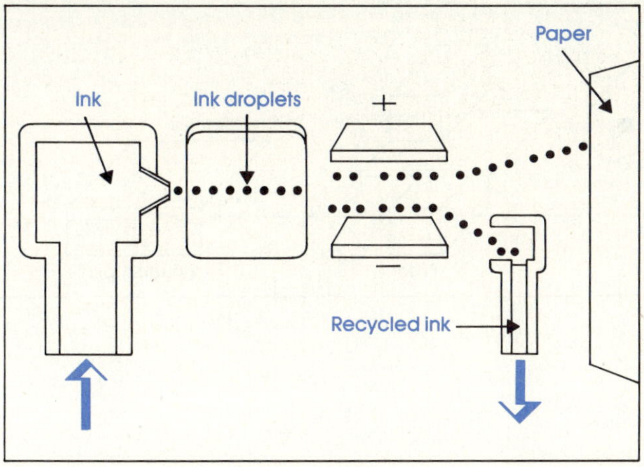

## Laser Printers

*Near-typeset-quality printing*

A **laser printer** is an output device that uses tightly focused beams of light to transfer images to paper (see Figure 2.23). A tiny laser emits pulsating pinpoint bursts of light that are reflected off a special spinning mirror. This mirror reflects light onto a rotating drum. Light striking the drum causes it to become charged with electricity. An ink-like toner is attracted to the drum in these electrically charged spots. When the drum is rolled over a piece of paper, the toner is transferred to the paper and an image is permanently fixed through a combination of heat and pressure. This image transfer process is similar to that found in a standard copy machine. The result is high-quality text and graphics that almost look as if they were typeset.

Laser printers represent a very advanced printing technology. Although the images they produce are made up of dots, these dots are much smaller and more densely packed than the dots created with a dot-matrix printer. The typical microcomputer laser printer is capable of printing at a resolution of 300 dots per inch, both horizontally and vertically. This means 90,000 dots per square inch. Besides printing high-quality images, laser printers are also fast and quiet. The average speed of most laser printers is eight pages per minute. This is equivalent to about 400 characters per second. Because laser printers don't use impact methods like dot-matrix and daisy-wheel printers, they are very quiet by comparison. The major disadvantage of laser printers is their cost. Prices generally start at about $1500. Despite the cost, more and more laser printers are being used with microcomputers every year. They are especially popular in offices where the printer can be shared among several users.

(a)

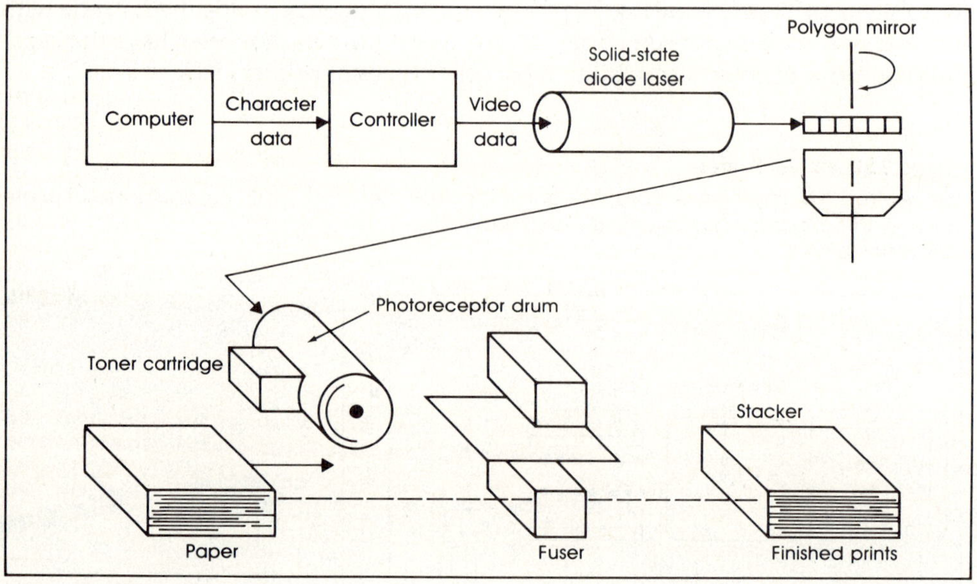


**Figure 2.23 Laser Printer**

(a) A laser printer uses light to transfer images to paper.

(b) A popular laser printer.

(b)

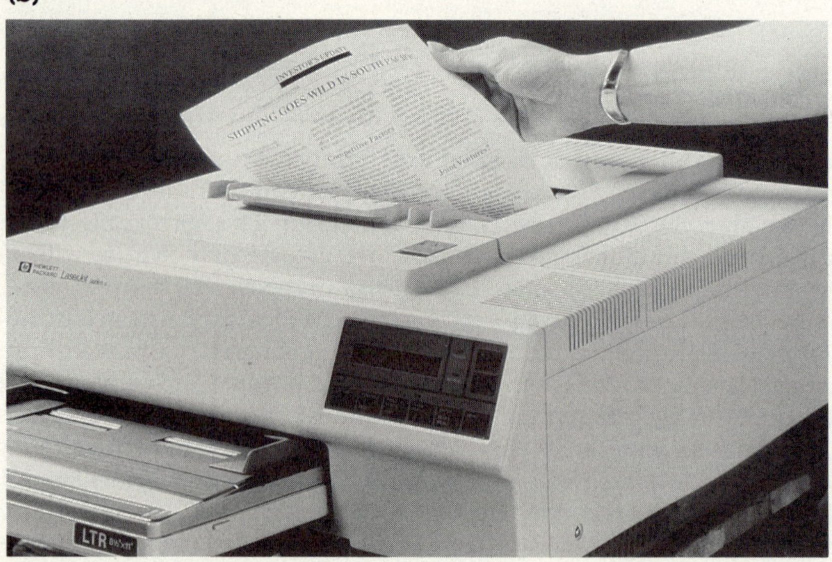

### Plotters

A **plotter** is an output device that uses one or more pens to draw on paper (see Figure 2.24). Plotters are especially well-suited to producing high-quality graphs, charts, diagrams, maps, and blueprints. Although they are much slower than printers, plotters are quiet and can generate extremely accurate, well-defined drawings. Plotters with several pens can even create multicolored drawings. They are, however, inappropriate for producing textual documents such as formal letters, reports, and manuscripts. Consequently, plotters are used much less frequently than printers.

*Computer drawing device*

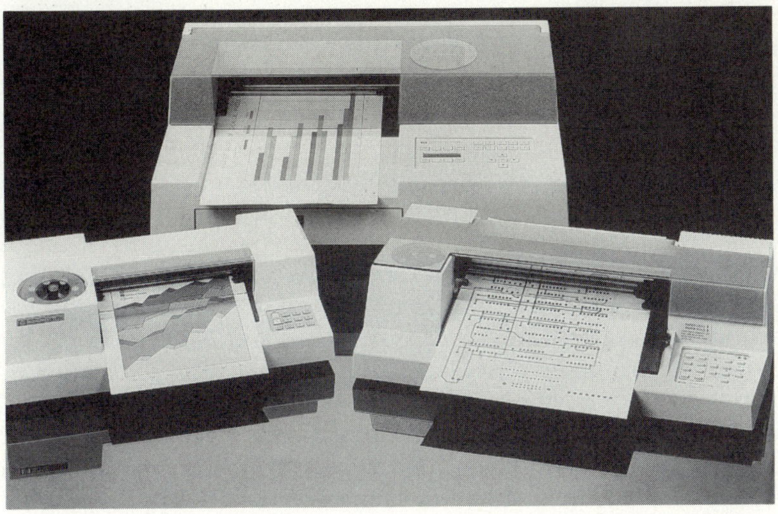

**Figure 2.24 Plotter**
A plotter is a computer output device that draws with one or more pens.

## MODEMS

One of the most useful tasks microcomputers can perform is communicating with other computers. In some cases where the computers are in the same building, this communication takes place through a local area network, which we briefly described when we discussed expansion boards. When the computers are far apart, the connection is often made through telephone lines. Since the telephone system is a world-wide network, it's technically feasible for one computer to communicate with almost any other computer on earth. This opens up a whole range of possibilities as microcomputers tap into huge quantities of data and complex programs that exist only on much larger and more expensive computers. For example, information services have sprung up that cater to microcomputer users. These services allow users to "chat" with one another, post messages, join special interest groups, hold electronic forums, get stock market data, make travel reservations, read the latest news, shop and bank by computer, and gain access to all kinds of compiled data. An individual microcomputer owner can even set up a mini-information service in the form of an electronic bulletin board that can be read by other computer users. Recently, many people are even using microcomputers to **telecommute**, or

*Connecting computers over phone lines*

work at home using a microcomputer that is connected to a computer at their office.

The electronic device that makes all of this possible is the **modem**, which allows a computer to transmit and receive data over telephone lines. Modems are necessary because computers use digital signals while most telephone lines are designed to carry analog signals. *Digital signals* are the discrete low and high voltages that represent zeros and ones. In contrast, *analog signals* are continuous voltage ranges, which in the case of the telephone, are used to represent the sounds of human voices. Digital signals must be converted to analog signals before they can be transmitted over most phone lines. This conversion is called *modulation*. At the other end, where data transmissions are received, the analog signals must be reconverted into digital signals again. This is called *demodulation*. A modem, therefore, is a *mo*dulator/*dem*odulator.

Microcomputer modems are relatively inexpensive options with prices that range from about $80 to $600. An average modem usually costs around $120. The price differential is based mainly on the speed with which modems can transmit and receive data. This speed is usually expressed in terms of **bits per second**, or **bps**. For example, nowadays most microcomputer modems can operate at 1200 bps. This means that they can transfer between 120 and 150 bytes per second. In other words, the contents of a single-spaced typed page can be transmitted in about 20 seconds. Some microcomputer modems operate as slowly as 300 bps, while other high-speed models can transmit and receive at up to 9600 bps. The most popular speeds for microcomputer modems are currently 1200 bps and 2400 bps.

Besides speed, there are other differences that distinguish microcomputer modems. Two basic types of modems are commonly used: internal and external.

An **internal modem** is either built onto the motherboard of a computer or is a circuit board that fits into an expansion slot. It's generally less expensive than an external modem because it needs no separate cabinet or power supply. Internal modems are convenient because they take up no desk space and don't have to be plugged into an electrical socket. A telephone cord is plugged right into the back of the computer or expansion board. The only disadvantages to internal modems are that they require an expansion slot and are specifically designed for particular computers. For example, you can't use an internal modem designed for an IBM Personal System/2 computer in an Apple Macintosh computer.

An **external modem**, or **direct-connect modem**, is built into a box about the size of a paperback book (see Figure 2.25). It plugs right into a phone set or telephone wall jack and usually requires a power supply consisting of an AC adapter that plugs into an electrical socket. The external modem also requires a serial interface to connect it to the computer. So, if your computer has a serial interface already built in, an external modem doesn't take up an expansion slot. It does, however, take up desk space and usually an electrical socket. The major advantage to an external modem is that you can use the same modem with any computer that has a serial interface. External modems generally cost $10 to $30 more than internal modems of comparable speed.

## OTHER PERIPHERALS

*Alternate input and output devices*

Thanks to serial and parallel interfaces and expansion slots, a wide variety of devices can be attached to most microcomputers. Although we couldn't possibly discuss every type of peripheral device on the market, a few are worth mentioning.

**Figure 2.25 External Modem**

Any computer with a serial interface can use a device such as this direct-connect modem to communicate with other computers over ordinary telephone lines.

Courtesy of Hayes Microcomputer Products, Inc.

## Joysticks

*Popular game control*

Anybody who's played video games is familiar with the joystick. Fashioned after the control mechanism used in early airplanes, the **joystick** is a vertical lever that can be tilted forward and backward, left and right, and every direction in between (see Figure 2.26). With computers, joystick movements are used to control a cursor or steer a simulated vehicle. Most computer joysticks also have one or more buttons, often used to fire missiles on the display screen. Although joysticks are mostly used for computer games, they are sometimes used like a mouse.

**Figure 2.26 Joystick**

The joystick is an alternate input device often used for computer games.

## Trackballs

*Mouse alternative*

Basically, a **trackball** is like a mouse turned upside-down. It's a box that contains a protruding ball, often similar to a billiard ball, that can be freely rotated in any direction (see Figure 2.27). Also like a mouse, a trackball generally has one or more buttons, which are mounted beside or in front of the ball on top of the box. When first used with microcomputers, trackballs were primarily intended for game control. Increasingly, however, they are being touted as a stationary alternative to the mouse. A trackball can do everything a mouse can do, yet it takes up less desk space because only the ball is moved, not the whole trackball box. Some optional keyboards on the market even have a trackball built in. Many people find moving a cursor around the screen is easier with a trackball. On the other hand, most people think drawing is easier with a mouse.

**Figure 2.27 Trackball**
The trackball is an alternative to the mouse.

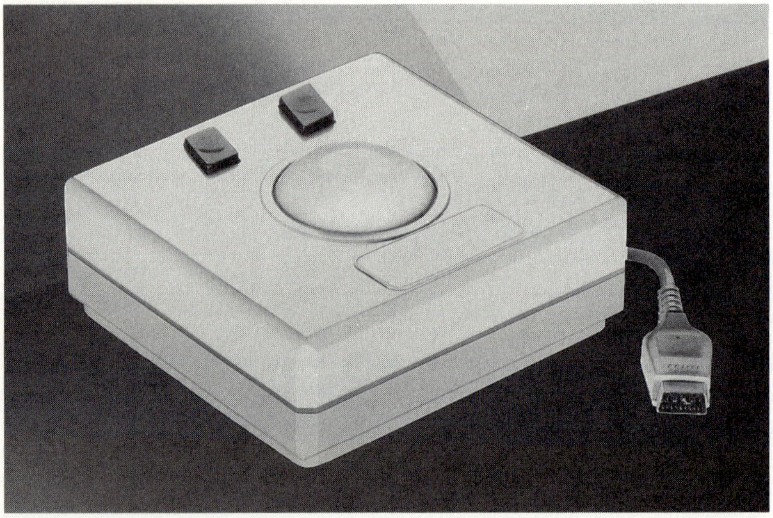

## Light Pens

*Drawing on the screen*

A **light pen** is a rod that's used to point at or draw on a computer display screen (see Figure 2.28). Most light pens have a cord that plugs into the graphics adapter, but some cordless models are also available. The light pen works by detecting where its point is positioned on the screen, then passing this positional data to the computer through the graphics adapter. This information is then handled by computer programs especially designed to work with light pens. Light pens are sometimes used in microcomputer systems that handle order entry in warehouses and in some sophisticated cash registers. They are also used by some computer drawing and design programs.

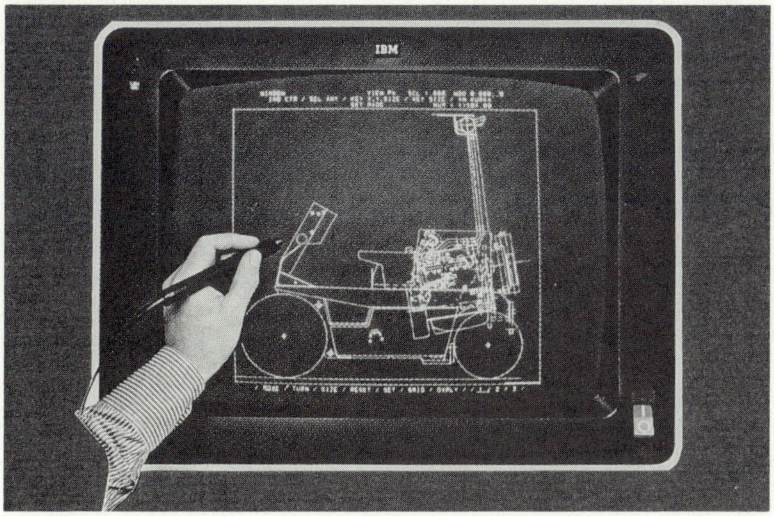


**Figure 2.28 Light Pen**
A light pen lets you draw and manipulate objects right on the display screen.

## Touch-Screens

*Let your fingers do the pointing*

Eliminate the light pen and just use your finger to point, and you have the basic concept of the touch-screen. More precisely, a **touch-screen** is an input device that's built into or fits over a display screen (see Figure 2.29). It uses infrared light beams or an electrically conductive surface to identify the position of your finger as it touches the screen. Touch-screens are simple to use, but they have several drawbacks. Fingers are, after all, rather wide pointers. So, the number of different positions on a screen that can be distinguished by a pointing finger is somewhat limited. Also, having to lift your arm to point at the screen over and over again can become tiresome. Finally, fingerprints tend to accumulate on touch-screens which increases glare and generally looks messy. Despite these problems, touch-screens are being

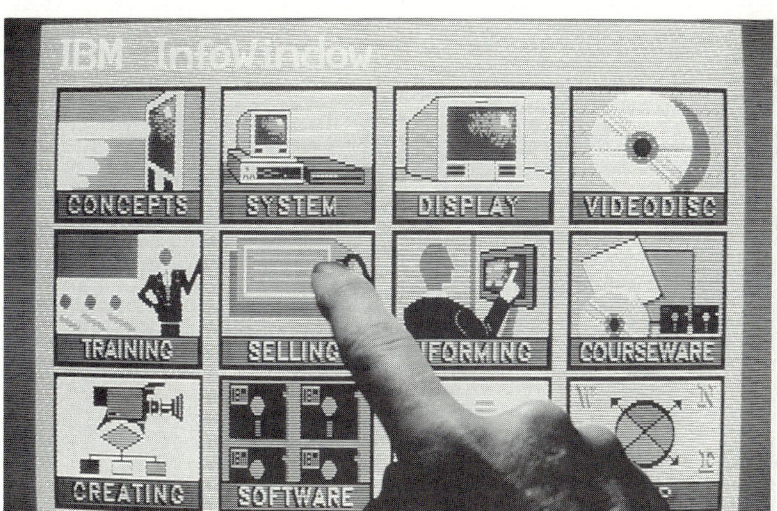


**Figure 2.29 Touch-Screen**
A touch-screen lets you use your fingers to point to objects on the display.

successfully used in specialized situations, such as in shopping center kiosks, public information displays, museums, and automated teller machines.

## Graphics Tablets

*High-resolution input device*

A **graphics tablet**, also called a **digitizer**, is a flat surface on which the user draws with a stylus, pen, or some other pointing device (see Figure 2.30). The tablet senses where it is touched and communicates this positional data to the computer. Some graphics tablets are capable of very high resolutions and can be extremely accurate. Consequently, they are often used in map-making and computer-aided design applications.

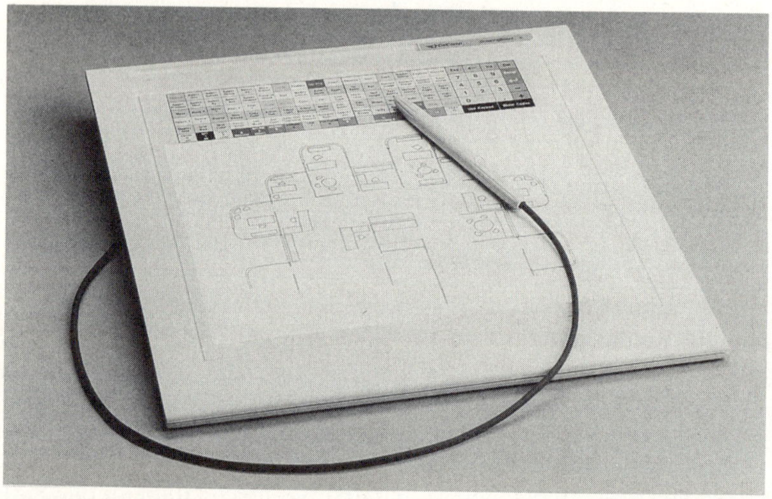

**Figure 2.30 Graphics Tablet**
The graphics tablet is an alternate input device well-suited to drawing and computer-aided design.

## Scanners

*Automatically reading text and graphics*

In many offices, secretaries often must enter previously typed or printed information into computers. In other situations, workers must laboriously enter maps, blueprints, and other figures into computers by hand with graphics tablets. Imagine being able to feed a sheet of paper containing text or graphics into a machine that automatically reads the contents and enters it into the computer for you. A **scanner**, like the one in Figure 2.31, can do just that. These devices, relative newcomers on the microcomputer scene, are becoming increasingly common. Although full-page scanners are rather expensive ($1,000 to $40,000), many organizations and even some individuals find that they save so much time, they are well worth the money. Besides, there are now a number of small, hand-held scanners on the market that perform almost as well as full-page scanners for as little as $200.

## Voice Recognition Systems

*Decoding human speech*

Why can't you just talk to your computer? After all, this would clearly be the most natural method of communication with computers for most people. Unfortunately, technology is not yet sufficiently advanced to make true conversation with comput-

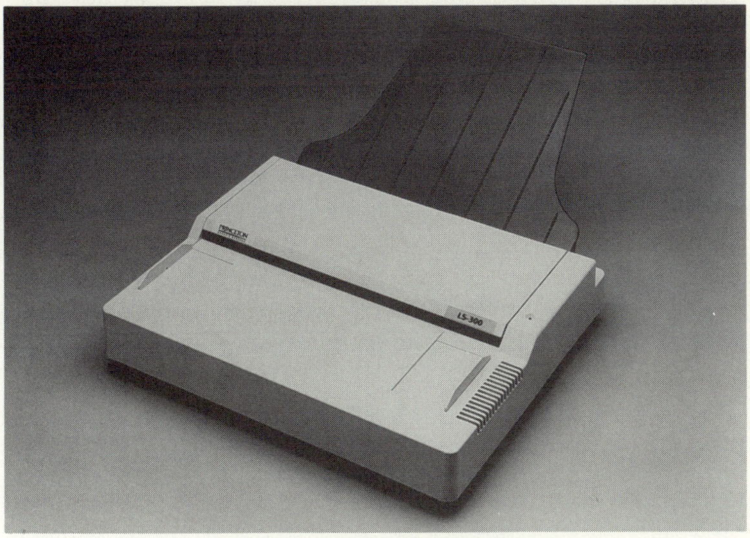

**Figure 2.31 Scanner**
A scanner enables the computer to read text and graphics directly from a source document.

ers possible. Nevertheless, several devices on the market can, in a limited sense, understand some human speech. A **voice recognition system** is an input device that can recognize a finite number of isolated sounds, words, and phrases (see Figure 2.32). Currently, the most advanced microcomputer voice recognition systems have a maximum vocabulary of about 1000 words. Furthermore, most systems must be "trained" by having users initially pronounce every word to be recognized. The voice recognition system analyzes each word's sound waveform, encodes this waveform as a series of numbers, and stores these numbers in memory. Subsequently, it recognizes words by comparing their waveforms as they are spoken with the previously stored waveforms. If a match is found, the word is understood. Most manufacturers of voice recognition systems claim an accuracy rate of better than 90 percent. Unless your voice is distorted by a cold, sore throat, or some other affliction, this means that the system should recognize the words it has been trained to understand nine times out of ten. Although voice recognition systems are expensive, have limited vocabularies, and must be trained, they are being used successfully in several unique applications. For example, some are currently being used to help busy factory workers control their assembly lines, to answer simple phone requests automatically, and to help the physically disabled control appliances in their homes.

## Speech Synthesizers

*Talking computers*

Making computers talk is quite a bit easier than making them listen. Computer-generated voice output has been possible for quite some time and has even become commonplace. A **speech synthesizer** is a device that either mimics human speech or constructs it out of prerecorded sounds. These devices have been crafted onto integrated circuit chips and are now quite inexpensive. Thanks to this technology, we now have talking cash registers, kitchen appliances, automobiles, vending machines, greeting cards, airport trains, video games, and, of course, computers. Microcomputer speech synthesizers typically plug into a serial port or are built onto an expansion board. They may use a speaker inside the microcomputer or require an external one. Speech synthesizers operate by taking text and translating it into spoken words. One of the most useful applications is a microcomputer-controlled reading machine for the blind that scans printed text and pronounces the words aloud.

**Figure 2.32 Voice Recognition System**
This diagram illustrates how voice recognition systems work.

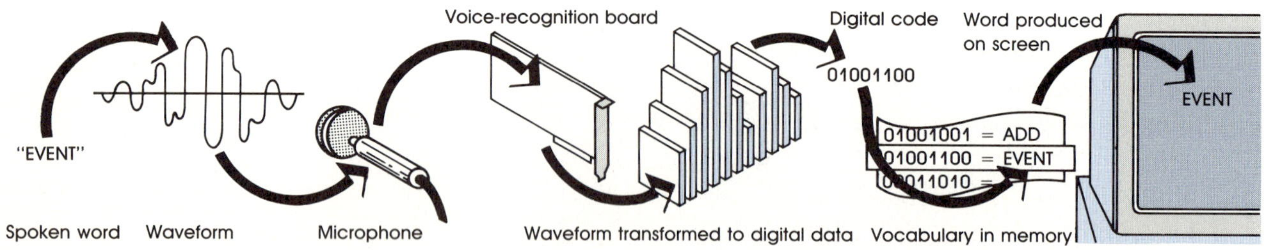


## The Real World

### Changing Chips

A new generation of computer chips is changing the face of the computer industry.

The new chips, such as Motorola's 68030 and Intel's 80386, may make the microcomputer the dominant force in the computer business. Edward M. Esber, Jr., chief executive of PC software supplier Ashton-Tate, believes microcomputers will become "the core of computing—more important than minis or mainframes." Mainframes have ruled the computer roost for roughly 30 years because of their considerable power.

How can tiny components the size of a fingernail have such a hugh impact? Compared with the complex circuitry in larger computers, microprocessor chips have always been considerably cheaper. But they have been less powerful, as well. Now, a new generation of chips has hit the market with astounding impact.

The newest microchips have double the information-processing capacity of their ancestors. This means they can transmit data in 32-bit chunks, the same as Digital Equipment Corp. minicomputers. The main difference is that the new desktop microcomputers using Intel's 80386 chip can cost as little as $5000 and Digital's minicomputers cost $500,000. IBM claims that its PS/2 Model 80 with an 80386 chip, which sells for around $7000, has the processing speed of a 1975 mainframe that cost $3.5 million.

Intel officials speculate that more than 100 computer companies are designing machines that will use the 80386 microchip. They predicted that perhaps 5 million of these computers will be sold annually by 1992.

Source:
"Computers: The New Look", by John W. Verity and Geoff Lewis, *Business Week*, November 30, 1987, pp. 112-123.

## Summary

- *The components inside the system unit.* A typical microcomputer system unit contains a chassis, motherboard, memory, power supply, expansion slots, disk drives, and device controllers.
- *The key features that affect a microprocessor's power.* Important features include its register size, data bus size, and speed.
- *The difference between RAM and ROM.* RAM is used for temporary storage, while ROM holds programs and data that never change.
- *Commonly used secondary storage devices.* The most commonly used devices for secondary storage are floppy disk drives, hard disk drives, magnetic tape drives, Bernoulli disk drives, and optical disk drives.
- *The primary input device.* Every microcomputer has a keyboard as its primary input device, but many also have a mouse.
- *The basic types of displays.* Three types of displays are monochrome text monitors, monochrome graphics monitors, and color graphics monitors.
- *How microcomputer systems can be expanded.* Expansion slots, expansion boards, and interfaces make it possible to add a host of optional hardware components to most microcomputers.
- *The basic types of printers.* Among the types of output devices are dot-matrix, daisy-wheel, ink-jet, and laser printers. Plotters are a special type of output device that draws with pens.
- *How computers communicate with modems.* A computer with a modem can transmit and receive programs and data to similarly equipped computers over ordinary telephone lines.
- *Alternate input and output devices.* Other commonly used peripherals include joysticks, trackballs, light pens, touch-screens, graphics tablets, scanners, voice recognition systems, and speech synthesizers.

## Key Terms

As an extra review of this chapter, try defining the following terms. If you have trouble with any of them, refer to the page number listed.

hard disk drive (fixed disk drive) (37)
head crash (48)
ink-jet printer (65)
integrated circuit chip (39)
interface (60)
internal modem (68)
joystick (69)
kilobyte (K) (43)
laser printer (65)
letter-quality (62)
light pen (70)
liquid crystal display (LCD) (56)
local area network (LAN) (60)
magnetic tape (49)
magnetic tape drive (49)
megabyte (M) (43)
megahertz (MHz) (42)
modem (68)
monochrome graphics monitor (57)
monochrome text monitor (56)
motherboard (system board) (36)
multifunction board (60)
near letter-quality (NLQ) (62)
network adapter (60)
optical disk drive (52)
palette (58)
parallel interface (parallel port) (61)
pixel (pel) (58)
plotter (67)
power supply (37)
primary storage (37)
random access memory (RAM) (43)
read-only memory (ROM) (43)
read-write head (46)
real-time clock (60)
register (40)
resolution (57)
scanner (72)
secondary storage (44)
semiconductor (39)
sequential access medium (49)
serial interface (serial port) (61)
Small Computer System Interface (SCSI) (61)
speech synthesizer (74)
system clock (42)
telecommute (67)
touch-screen (71)
trackball (70)
video mode (58)
voice recognition system (73)
Write Once, Read Many (times) (WORM) (52)

## Review Questions

1. Where is the CPU located on many microcomputers?
2. What are the two basic kinds of magnetic disk drives?
3. What type of material is used to make integrated circuit chips?
4. List the three register sizes used by microcomputer microprocessors.
5. How does the size of the data bus affect computer performance?
6. How is the speed of the system clock related to the operation of a microprocessor?
7. What is the function of primary storage in a computer?
8. RAM and ROM are both used to store programs and data. What is the major difference between these two kinds of memory?
9. Why is secondary storage a necessary supplement to primary storage?
10. What is the most common secondary storage medium used with microcomputers?
11. How do hard disk drives differ from floppy disk drives?
12. What is the primary use for magnetic tape drives in microcomputer systems?

13. In what sense do Bernoulli drives combine the advantages of both floppy and hard disk drives?
14. What are the two basic types of optical disk drives used with microcomputers?
15. List some special-purpose keys found on microcomputer keyboards.
16. What are some uses of a mouse?
17. List the three basic types of microcomputer displays.
18. What hardware components make it possible to expand and upgrade most microcomputers?
19. What type of printer uses tightly focused bursts of light to transfer images to paper?
20. Why are modems needed to enable computers to send data over phone lines?

## Multiple Choice

1. Which of the following computer components is not usually built onto the motherboard?
   (a) CPU (b) memory
   (c) control circuitry (d) monitor
2. Which of the following register sizes describes the most powerful microprocessor?
   (a) 2-bit (b) 8-bit
   (c) 16-bit (d) 32-bit
3. Which of the following microcomputer components synchronizes the internal operations of the microprocessor and other electronic circuits.
   (a) real-time clock (b) system clock
   (c) chassis (d) ROM
4. Which of the following units represents the largest amount of memory?
   (a) byte (b) kilobyte
   (c) gigabyte (d) megabyte
5. What type of memory chip holds programs and data that are used very frequently, yet can never be changed?
   (a) RAM (b) ROM
   (c) CRT (d) LCD
6. What is the most common form of secondary storage?
   (a) floppy disks (b) magnetic tape
   (c) Bernoulli disks (d) WORM disks
7. What type of disk drive uses circular platters of rigid aluminum covered with a thin magnetic coating?
   (a) floppy (b) hard
   (c) CD-ROM (d) Bernoulli
8. Which of the following is a sequential access medium?
   (a) floppy disk (b) hard disk
   (c) magnetic tape (d) CD-ROM

9. Which of the following storage media does not allow you to record your own programs and data?
   (a) floppy disk (b) hard disk
   (c) WORM (d) CD-ROM
10. What is the primary input device of every microcomputer?
   (a) keyboard (b) mouse
   (c) trackball (d) display
11. What type of display mechanism is used by most computer screens?
   (a) CRT (b) LCD
   (c) RAM (d) WORM
12. Which of the following terms describes a screen with the sharpest picture?
   (a) no-resolution (b) low-resolution
   (c) medium-resolution (d) high-resolution
13. A multifunction board plugs into a(n)
   (a) monitor. (b) expansion slot.
   (c) serial interface. (d) display adapter.
14. An external modem plugs into a(n)
   (a) display adapter. (b) parallel interface.
   (c) serial interface. (d) expansion slot.
15. What is the most common type of microcomputer printer?
   (a) dot-matrix (b) daisy-wheel
   (c) ink-jet (d) laser

## Projects

1. Select a microcomputer system that you have access to at home, school, or work. Read the user manual or talk to someone familiar with that particular system's configuration. Try to answer the following questions about the microcomputer:

   What company makes this computer?
   What model is it?
   What kind of microprocessor does it use?
   What is the speed of the system clock?
   How much ROM does this computer have?
   How much RAM does this computer have?
   What is the maximum RAM it can have?
   How many expansion slots are there?
   What expansion boards are currently installed?
   What kind of floppy disk drive(s) does it use?
   If there is a hard disk, what is its capacity?
   What type of display is used?
   If there is a graphics display, what is its resolution?
   What kind of printer, if any, is connected?
   What kind of interfaces does it have?
   List any other peripheral devices it has.

2. To get a better idea of how much data can be held in secondary storage, figure out *approximately* how many bytes of information are in a well-known set of encyclopedias. Assume that each character of text requires one byte of storage.

How many 360K, 5.25-inch floppies would this encyclopedia take up? How many 800K, 3.5-inch floppies? How many megabytes would it require? Would it fit on a single 550-megabyte CD-ROM disk?

3. The length of time it takes to retrieve a piece of data from computer storage is often referred to as *access time*. Frequently, this is expressed in milliseconds, or thousandths of a second. Investigate the typical access times of RAM and ROM, as well as of various secondary storage devices like floppy disks, hard disks, and optical disks. Prepare a table that compares these values.

4. Even if you don't own a computer, you've probably used some kind of keyboard. But have you ever used a mouse? If not, try to experience its use. Perhaps there is an Apple Macintosh computer you can use at home, school, or work. You may be able to try a mouse at a local computer store. After you've tried using one, write a brief report presenting your opinion of this alternate input device. List the advantages and disadvantages of using a mouse versus depending completely on a keyboard. Finally, do you think a trackball would be better than a mouse? In discussing your opinion, describe the situations in which one is superior to the other.

# 3

# Software

## In This Chapter

- Computer Programs
- System Software
    - Operating Systems
    - Utilities
    - Windowing Environments
- Programming Languages
    - Machine Languages
    - Assembly Languages
    - High-level Languages
        - BASIC
        - Pascal
        - C
        - FORTRAN
        - COBOL
        - Ada
    - Fourth Generation Languages
- Application Software
    - Word Processing
    - Spreadsheet
    - Data Base Management
    - Communications and Networking
    - Graphics
    - Desktop Publishing
    - Accounting
    - Other Packages
- The User Interface
    - Commands
    - Prompts
    - Static Menus
    - Pop-up Menus
    - Pull-down Menus
    - Icons, Windows, and Desktops

## PREVIEW

In the previous chapter, we spent a lot of time discussing the various hardware components of a typical microcomputer system. With all the talk of microprocessors, RAM, ROM, disk drives, monitors, expansion slots, printers, and other devices, you might get the impression that hardware is the most important aspect of a computer. This simply isn't so. You must understand hardware to some extent because it determines the ultimate potential of a computer system. But computer hardware by itself is utterly useless. Software is what makes the computer the indispensable helper it has become in our society. People determine the task and run the software; software operates the hardware. For most computer users, software issues far outweigh hardware concerns. This is why software is the major focus of the rest of this book.

After studying this chapter, you will understand

- how programs tell computers what to do.
- how system software helps you use a computer.
- the major types of programming languages.
- the major types of application software.
- the major types of user interfaces.

## COMPUTER PROGRAMS

*Telling computers what to do*

We've already said that a computer *program* is a set of instructions that tells a computer what to do. *Software* is a general term that refers to any single program or group of programs. In contrast with hardware, which is made from physical materials such as metal and plastic, software is constructed solely from knowledge, thinking, planning, and testing. You can't really touch a computer program because it's an expression of the ideas of the people who designed it.

Despite the amazing accomplishments of a well-programmed computer, it's really just a machine. Every computer is only capable of a limited set of simple tasks. Each of these simple tasks is represented by a single instruction, and each instruction is encoded as a number. A computer's **instruction set** consists of all of those simple tasks that it can do when it receives a single instruction. Take the Intel 8088 microprocessor, for example. You may recall that this is the microprocessor used in millions of IBM Personal Computers and similar machines. The 8088 instruction set consists of only about 100 basic instructions. Table 3.1 shows a few of the more commonly used instructions.

To a computer, programs are just lists of numbers, like the code numbers you see in Table 3.1. These numbers represent simple instructions that tell the central processing unit what to do with other numbers. Computers can store and manipulate programs just as they do data. In a sense, programs are data too. Computers can be instructed to perform operations on the very numbers that make up other programs. This is the key to the power of the computer. Starting from a very simple set of instructions, more complex operations can be built; then operations can be put together like building blocks to perform abstract tasks. No one need start from scratch because programs can be permanently stored. Every person who uses computers uses some programs written by others. In fact, most people who use computers don't write any programs at all. Some programs control the various hardware components of a computer. Others help people manage their computer systems. Some even help people write other programs. Finally, there are programs

**Table 3.1 Selected 8088 Instructions**

| INSTRUCTION | NUMERIC CODE | OPERATION |
|---|---|---|
| MOV | 139 | Copies contents of one register to another |
| XCHG | 147 | Exchanges contents of two registers |
| IN | 228 | Inputs a byte from some external device |
| OUT | 230 | Outputs a byte to some external device |
| INC | 64 | Increments (adds 1 to) a register's contents |
| DEC | 72 | Decrements (subtracts 1) from a register |
| ADD | 3 | Adds the contents of two registers |
| SUB | 43 | Subtracts one register's contents from another |
| MUL | 247 | Multiplies contents of two registers |
| CMP | 59 | Compares the contents of two registers |
| JZ | 116 | Jumps to another instruction if result is zero |
| AND | 35 | Logically combines contents of two registers |
| LOOP | 226 | Repeats one or more instructions |
| CALL | 255 | Carries out some other group of instructions |
| RET | 195 | Returns when finished with a CALL instruction |

that help people with their daily activities, such as writing reports, figuring budgets, and maintaining business accounts. All these different types of programs can be divided into three basic categories: system software, programming languages, and application software.

## SYSTEM SOFTWARE

*Handling the details*

Computer systems are complicated equipment. We've seen that they consist of several sophisticated components: microprocessors, memory chips, circuits, displays, keyboards, disk drives, and printers. All of these devices are controlled by programs designed to accomplish very specific tasks. As we said in Chapter 1, the programs that deal most intimately with a computer's hardware are called *system software*.

System software handles the very basic details of managing a computer's hardware and software resources. Some system software is not obvious to the user, such as the programs that interpret keypresses or form characters on the display screen. The user directly invokes other programs to perform "housekeeping" activities, such as erasing a disk or changing a printer from draft mode to near-letter-quality mode. Still other system software is essential to people who develop application programs, allowing them to both write and test the programs. Finally, other system software helps people who aren't necessarily computer experts manage and use their software.

As you can see, a wide variety of programs can be called system software. Although the categories overlap somewhat, there are several different types of system software: operating systems, utilities, and alternative operating environments.

**Insight**

## What Happens When Your Computer Goes Out of Production?

You just spent $1500 on a new computer. You have unpacked it. You have finally figured out how to get it working.

The next morning, the headline is on the front page: Your new computer is being replaced by a newer, more powerful, less expensive model. Your new computer is a dinosaur.

Or, it could be that the manufacturer has stopped producing your model, which means parts are no longer available and service will be difficult. In either case, you are allowed a predictable and understandable childish reaction. Then you have to sit down and think.

Businesses face this sort of problem all the time. It can be especially hard on companies that have a lot of money tied up in hardware and software or on businesses that rely heavily on their computers.

Businesses have a special way of dealing with the financial impact of obsolescence. The cost of major assets such as computers is amortized, or spread out over the useful life of the equipment. This is based on the assumption that after maybe five to seven years, the machine or system will be worn out and will have to be replaced. The way things are changing in the computer field, this useful lifetime may become even shorter.

Both you and business have several ways to handle this problem.

First, you can always hope that parts and service will be available from the manufacturer for two or three years. If the company also goes out of business, you'll have to track down the company that bought up its stock or parts.

The second possibility is to trade in or sell your computer and move your applications and files to another system. This often is the best idea, because the useful life of software is at most three or four years. By then, your needs or the needs of your business may have changed, and you'd have to replace your software anyway.

Finally, you can run the system as long as you can, salvaging parts from other computers. This works well for the business that is upgrading its system and has enough old machines to supply the parts.

### Operating Systems

*Controlling hardware and managing software*

An **operating system** is a set of programs that controls a computer's hardware and manages the use of software. It is the heart and soul of a computer. Besides providing valuable services for other software, it's the main channel through which you tell the computer what to do. An operating system also enables the various parts of a computer to work together. Every general-purpose computer can be run by at least one operating system. This essential software basically determines what you can accomplish with a particular computer and how easy that computer is to use.

Turn on your computer and the operating system is automatically brought into action (see Figure 3.1). It tests and sets up various hardware components and then waits for your command. Do you want to use your word processing program? Just enter the name of your program or perhaps select its symbol with a mouse-controlled pointer. The operating system interprets your command, loads the word processing program from disk into primary storage, and instructs the CPU to run the program. From that point, until you're done with the word processor, the operating system silently works in the background, helping the word processor use hardware devices and other software. When you're finished with your word processing program, control is returned to the operating system. Again, it patiently waits to help you with some other task. Constantly, tirelessly, the operating system works to bridge the gaps between you and your software, and between your software and the computer hardware. Under normal circumstances, the operating system ceases its chores only when the computer is turned off.

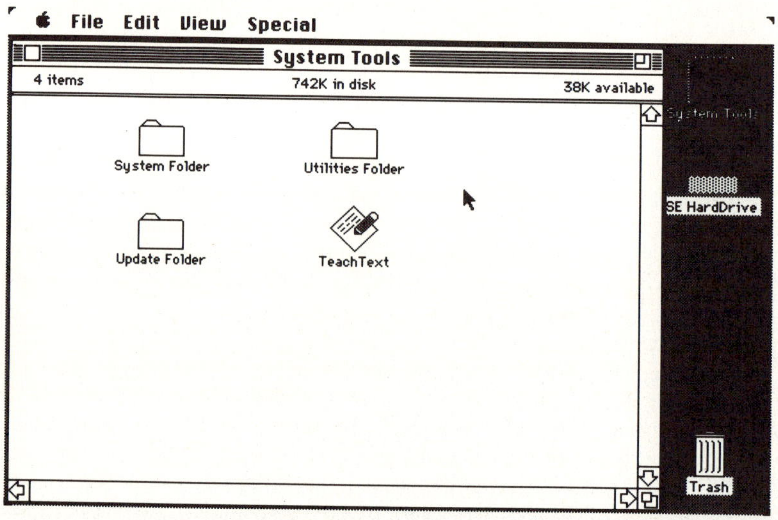


**Figure 3.1 Operating System**
Turn on the computer and the operating system of the Apple Macintosh automatically tests various hardware components and then waits for you to tell it what programs you want to run.

Besides its work with other programs, the operating system provides a set of services that you can use directly to help with certain frequently performed activities. For example, operating systems typically include programs that let you set up new floppy disks, copy programs and data, erase programs and data, display information on your screen, send information to your printer, reset the real-time clock, indicate which disk drive to use, organize your secondary storage, and specify certain hardware settings. To a large extent, the type of work you do with your computer determines how much you will directly interact with the operating system. Some users, especially novices, tend to use operating system services as little as possible. They try to get by with functions that are built into the programs they use. For instance, many word processing programs let you copy, delete, and print documents without having to exit and return to the operating system. Other users, especially computer experts, try to take full advantage of the services provided by the operating system. They can almost tell you what every command does and how you might use it. Most people find that they are somewhere between these two extremes. Every computer user must interact with the operating system to some extent, so learning a few of the basics can help you work much more efficiently. We will have more to say about the specifics of operating systems and present some examples of microcomputer operating systems in Part 2 of this book.

## Utilities

*Small, specific programs*

Despite all the services operating systems provide, computer users always seem to need more programs to help them manage their hardware and software resources. A **utility** is a program that fills some very specific need. Such programs tend to be fairly small and quite limited in scope. Utilities perform all kinds of different but very useful tasks. In one sense, utility programs are like accessories to operating systems. They fill in gaps by doing little jobs not easily accomplished by the operating system's services. Some utility programs come packaged with operating systems, but many are offered by other software producers. Quite often, a programmer develops a utility for his or her own use and offers it free or at a very nominal cost to others. If the utility becomes popular, it might even be the basis for a new software company.

Utility programs, by their very nature, can be somewhat difficult to classify. There are so many different types of utilities that it might seem strange to group them together. Often, if a program performs one or more very specific tasks and doesn't fit into any other particular category, it's called a utility.

Some utilities are designed to help average users in commonly encountered situations. For example, the operating system used with most IBM microcomputers has no provision for letting you recover programs and data you've accidentally erased. As a result, several companies offer programs that, in many cases, can help users who find themselves in such predicaments. Other utility programs enhance the capabilities of certain hardware devices. Some printer utilities, for example, let you change print modes, print mailing labels and envelopes, and even print very wide tables so that they appear sideways across several pages. Keyboard enhancement utilities allow you to customize the way your keyboard works by redefining keys and assigning several keystrokes to certain control and function keys. Some utility programs provide desktop accessories like simulated calculators, calendars, notepads, appointment books, and telephone books (see Figure 3.2). Hardware-related utilities help you diagnose potential problems, as well as maintain, adjust, and even repair devices such as disk drives, displays, and printers. Finally, a whole group of utilities is designed to assist programmers in their development of software. These utilities compare programs, sort and merge programs, help isolate and correct errors, cross reference memory locations, and manage updates of new program versions. In Chapter 16, we'll have more to say about some of the most popular types of utility programs.

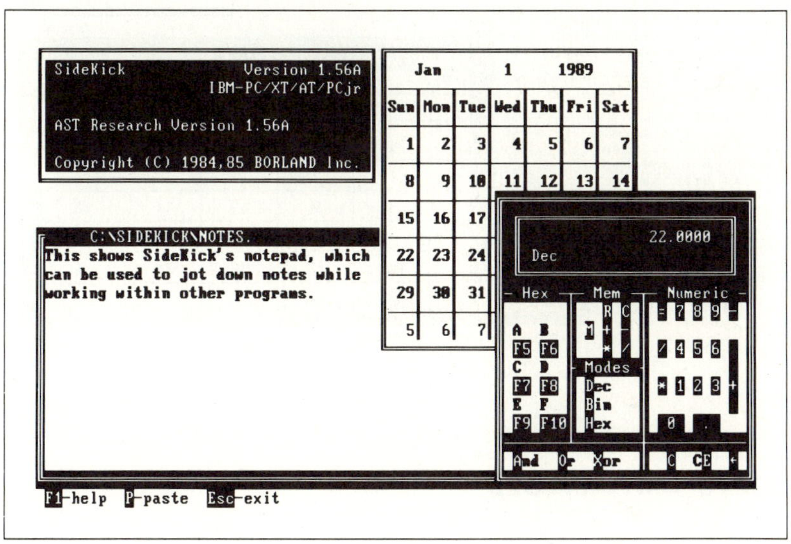


**Figure 3.2 Utility Program**
SideKick is a popular utility program that provides various desktop accessories, including a calculator, calendar, and notepad.

## Windowing Environments

*Making systems easier to use*

Even with extra utilities and the ability to write additional programs, some operating systems still leave much to be desired. Most people find that operating systems such as that of the Apple Macintosh are visually pleasing, intuitively understandable, and easy to use. Other operating systems, such as that of the original IBM Personal Computer and compatible machines, seem inadequate to some people by comparison. So, a few software developers have come up with windowing environments that work along with such operating systems.

A **windowing environment**, sometimes called an **alternate operating environment**, is a type of system software that surrounds a basic operating system with a shell that displays a simulated desktop (see Figure 3.3). This desktop, which appears on the display screen, contains menus and enclosed boxes, called *windows*, that pop up and allow you to select the programs that you want to run. You can even execute several programs seemingly at the same time. These windowing programs are designed to improve the way the operating system interacts with the user, while at the same time give the user more power to do several tasks at once. Basically, windowing environments try to make rather difficult operating systems easier to use. We'll have more to say about windows later in this chapter when we talk about the user interface, and we'll discuss windowing environments in Chapter 16.

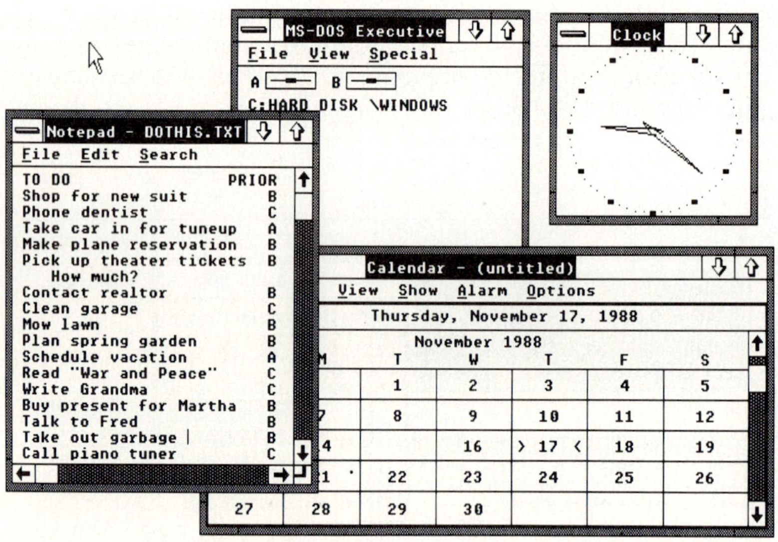


**Figure 3.3 Windowing Environment**
Microsoft Windows is a popular windowing environment for IBM-compatible microcomputers.

## PROGRAMMING LANGUAGES

*Symbols and rules for writing software*

A language, as you know, is a means of communicating. People use spoken and written languages to convey ideas, feelings, and requests to one another. As we said in Chapter 1, a computer *programming language* is a set of symbols and rules used to direct the operations of a computer. As such, programming languages are a very limited, yet precise form of communication. You can't write a love sonnet in a programming language, but you can use a programming language to write a word processing program.

As with human languages, dozens of computer programming languages are in common use. Each one was primarily designed to solve certain kinds of problems. The purpose of every programming language, however, is to create programs that direct the operations of a computer. So, they all have certain types of instructions in common. Although instructions for the computer may be expressed in vastly different ways, all programming languages, in general, perform the following tasks:

- *Input and Output*. These instructions tell the computer to get data from the user or some input device and to present information on a display screen or printer.
- *Calculation*. These instructions direct the computer to perform mathematical operations such as addition, subtraction, multiplication, and division.
- *Comparison*. These instructions tell the computer to examine a number to see if it's less than, greater than, or equal to another number.
- *Data Movement, Storage, and Retrieval*. These instructions direct the computer's use of primary and secondary storage.
- *Transfer of Control*. The normal sequence of computer operation is to execute program instructions in order, one after another. Transfer of control instructions tell the computer to deviate from this sequential processing. So, the computer can be instructed to jump (or *branch*) back to previous instructions or ahead to skip instructions. These are perhaps the most powerful type of instructions because they enable computers to perform different operations given different input. They also let computers repeat sequences of instructions by jumping back and *looping* through those instructions again and again.

Although there are many different programming languages, the most common microcomputer languages can be put into one of four categories. These categories can be ranked by their relative level of abstraction. In other words, low-level languages are not at all abstract because they are similar to the simple numeric codes all computers ultimately use as instructions. High-level languages are much more abstract because they're closer to the languages people use, such as English. Going from lowest to highest, the microcomputer programming language classifications are: machine languages, assembly languages, high-level languages, and fourth generation languages.

## Machine Languages

*Zeros and ones*

The only programming language that can be directly used by a particular computer is its own machine language. A **machine language** program consists of binary numbers that represent the CPU instructions, memory addresses, and data needed to solve a particular problem. So, every machine language is just numbers expressed in binary form. The exact numbers and their arrangement, however, generally differ from one computer model to the next. For example, the machine language of IBM Personal Computers is quite different from the machine language of Apple Macintosh computers. Both machine languages are just binary numbers, but a program in the IBM Personal Computer machine language would not work correctly, if at all, on an Apple Macintosh.

Machine language instructions are basically composed of two parts. The first part is called the **operation code** or **opcode** because it's a numeric code for the operation to be performed. You've already seen examples of some opcodes in decimal form in Table 3.1. In microcomputers, opcodes are basically microprocessor instructions in binary number form. The second part of a machine language instruction is called the **operand**, or the number on which the operation is to be performed. An operand may be a piece of data or a memory address that specifies the location of a piece of data. For example, the following two binary numbers make up a machine language instruction for computers that use the Intel 8088, 8086, 80286, and 80386 microprocessors:

00000101   00001101

ADD   13 (in binary)

This instruction tells the computer to add 13 to the number currently in a special register known as the accumulator.

In the very early days of computers, all programming was done with machine languages. Every instruction, memory location, and data value had to be specified in strings of zeros and ones. This made machine language programming exceedingly tedious, time-consuming, and error-prone. Although computers work perfectly well with binary numbers, people aren't particularly happy, efficient, or accurate when they have to write zeros and ones all day. Consequently, other programming languages have since been developed that are much easier for people to use. Now people write programs using these more abstract languages, enter them into the computer, and run a program that translates the more abstract language into machine language.

No one programs directly in machine languages anymore. It's important to realize, however, that no matter which language is used, programs somehow must be translated into machine language before they can be executed by a computer.

## Assembly Languages

*Abbreviations and symbols*

The next level up from machine languages are assembly languages. An **assembly language** substitutes meaningful abbreviations for the numerically coded instructions of a machine language. You can see some examples of these easy-to-remember abbreviations, called **mnemonics**, in Table 3.1. Even the relatively simple concept of using mnemonics such as ADD instead of 00000101 to represent computer operations makes assembly languages vastly superior to machine languages. In addition to mnemonic abbreviations for CPU instructions, most assembly languages also allow the use of words to represent memory addresses and data values. This **symbolic addressing** lets a programmer call a memory location TOTAL, for example, instead of some meaningless numeric address such as 01001010. Symbolic addressing enables programmers to name and use memory locations like variables in algebraic equations. Furthermore, constant data values can also be named to lend even more meaning to programs. For instance, in several places a program might compare input values against a maximum value to make sure that no outrageous data is entered. Naming that value MAXIMUM instead of expressing it as a number helps make the program easier to understand, check for errors, and update if necessary. Finally, assembly languages generally allow programmers to express numbers in bases other than base two. More familiar or convenient number systems such as decimal (base 10), octal (base 8), and hexadecimal (base 16) can also be used. All of these factors make assembly languages much easier to use than machine languages for programming computers.

Figure 3.4 shows a very simple assembly language program for IBM microcomputers. Like machine languages, assembly languages are specific to particular types of computers. So, this assembly language program won't run on an Apple Macintosh computer. Another similarity between machine and assembly languages is that individual instructions aren't very powerful. In fact, there is generally a one-to-one correspondence between machine language and assembly language instructions. Assembly language is primarily a more convenient way of expressing machine language. Because each individual instruction has a very specific and limited function, it usually takes many, many instructions to get the computer to perform even the simplest tasks.

**Figure 3.4 Assembly Language Program**

This simple assembly language program displays a short message on the screen.

```
;****************************************************************************
;  HELLO Program
;
;  This program writes the message "Hello There!" to the display screen at
;  the current cursor location.
;
;  Author:  Ernest Colantonio           Computer:  IBM Personal Computer
;  Date:    September 25, 1988          Language:  IBM 8088 Macro Assembler
;
;****************************************************************************
;----------------------------------------------------------------------------
stack           SEGMENT PARA STACK 'stack'        ; Set up stack area.
                DB      256 DUP (0)               ; Reserve 256 bytes.
stack           ENDS
;----------------------------------------------------------------------------
data            SEGMENT PARA PUBLIC 'data'        ; Set up data area.
message         DB      'Hello There!'            ; Define message bytes.
n_characters    EQU     12                        ; Number of characters.
data            ENDS
;----------------------------------------------------------------------------
code            SEGMENT PARA PUBLIC 'code'        ; Set up code area.
                ASSUME CS:code, SS:stack, DS:data ; Associate segment registers.

program         PROC    FAR                       ; Program procedure.

start:          PUSH    DS                        ; Initialize stack for
                MOV     AX,0                      ;   return to
                PUSH    AX                        ;   operating system.

                MOV     AX,data                   ; Initialize
                MOV     DS,AX                     ;   the data registers.

                LEA     SI,message                ; Load message address.
                MOV     CX,n_characters           ; Load number of characters.

next_character: MOV     AH,2                      ; Load display output code.
                MOV     DL,[SI]                   ; Load character to display.
                INT     33                        ; Operating system service.
                INC     SI                        ; Increment character pointer.
                LOOP    next_character            ; Do the next character.

                RET                               ; Return from procedure.
program         ENDP                              ; End of procedure.

code            ENDS                              ; End of code area.
;----------------------------------------------------------------------------
                END     start                     ; End of program.
;****************************************************************************
```

Unlike machine languages, assembly languages must be translated before they can direct computer operations. After a program is written in assembly language, it's run through a special program called an **assembler** that translates assembly language instructions into the binary numbers of machine language. Software in assembly language (or any higher-level language) prior to this translation process is often called **source code**. Once the program has been converted to machine language, it may be referred to as **object code**.

As we said, assembly language is a definite improvement over machine language, but it still requires manipulating very low-level computer operations. A good deal of knowledge concerning the inner workings of a particular computer is needed in order to write assembly language programs. The process of developing software with assembly language remains fairly tedious, time-consuming, and error-prone. Nevertheless, assembly language programming is often worth the extra effort in some special situations. Expert programmers who must deal with the unique characteristics of a particular computer usually work in assembly language. Because assembly languages afford a great deal of control over individual computer operations, they are often used for programs that must be extremely fast, efficient, or compact. For these reasons, assembly languages are frequently used to develop system software such as operating systems, utilities, and programming language translators.

## High-level Languages

*Concentrating on the task*

The two main disadvantages of assembly languages are that they are difficult even for experts to use and they are machine-specific. Although assembly languages have their uses, it became apparent that another type of programming language would be needed to help more people develop complex computer software. High-level languages were devised to make programs easier to write and easier to adapt to different computers. A **high-level language** is an abstract programming language that facilitates the expression of complex data processing operations. Such languages are often called *procedure-oriented* or *problem-oriented* because they allow programmers to concentrate on the task to be performed rather than worry about the specific details of how their particular computers operate. Because individual high-level language instructions may correspond to many machine language instructions, powerful programs are much easier to develop. Complex operations can often be expressed in just a few high-level language statements.

Like assembly language programs, high-level language programs must be translated into machine language before they can be run by a computer. Nevertheless, high-level languages are generally *machine-independent*. This means that a program written in a high-level language can easily be adapted to any computer that has the applicable translator program. There are two basic types of translators: compilers and interpreters.

Most high-level languages are translated into machine language by special programs called compilers. A **compiler** is like an assembler, except it translates a particular high-level language instead of an assembly language. Compilers and assemblers translate an entire program all at once, producing a complete machine language program. Another type of high-level language translator, called an **interpreter**, works a little differently. An interpreter translates and runs one program instruction at a time as it's entered into the computer. This interactive environment allows a programmer to test ideas or modify programs and see the results almost instantly. Interpreters often make programming easier and hasten the software development process, but interpreted programs generally run slower than compiled programs once they're finished. Some high-level languages have both compilers and interpreters available for program translation.

High-level languages offer many advantages over assembly languages. In general, high-level languages are much easier to learn and use. Instructions are expressed in words and mathematical symbols, making high-level languages more understandable than assembly languages. Consequently, it's easier to write, correct, and revise programs in high-level languages. Since programmers can ignore most machine-specific details, they can concentrate on problem solving. Thanks to their greater degree of abstraction, high-level languages are much better suited than assembly languages to the development of large, complex programs. Programming errors are easier to avoid when you work with high-level languages, and easier to find and correct when they do occur. Finally, because high-level languages are machine-independent, programs can be used on different types of computers without having to be completely rewritten in different assembly languages. For these reasons, most people use high-level languages instead of assembly languages to program computers.

Many high-level languages are used on microcomputers, but a few clearly stand out as the most popular. These commonly used microcomputer programming languages are BASIC, Pascal, C, FORTRAN, COBOL, and Ada.

## BASIC

*Beginners' language*

**BASIC,** an acronym for Beginners' All-purpose Symbolic Instruction Code, was developed by Dr. John Kemeny and Dr. Thomas Kurtz at Dartmouth College in 1965. It was originally designed as a simple interactive language to teach students about computer programming. Although BASIC was first used on large multiuser computers, it has become the most popular programming language for microcomputers. In fact, BASIC was the first high-level programming language to be adapted for use on microcomputers. William Gates and Paul Allen developed a version of BASIC in 1975 to run on the first commercially available microcomputer, the Altair 8800. With this product, Gates and Allen founded Microsoft Corporation, which has become perhaps the single most important microcomputer software company in the world.

BASIC is a simple language that most people find easy to learn and easy to use. Although BASIC compilers are commonly available, most versions of this language are translated by interpreters. Because BASIC is so simple, it's extremely well suited for use on small computers. BASIC is often included on a disk along with the other system software when you purchase a microcomputer. Some microcomputers, like those from IBM, even have a simple version of BASIC embedded in a ROM chip. Microcomputer users who decide that they want to learn a programming language usually wind up choosing BASIC. Figure 3.5 shows an example BASIC program.

**Figure 3.5 BASIC Program**
This simple BASIC language program displays a table of squares and square roots of the numbers 1 through 20.
(a) Source code of the program.

```
010 REM ***********************************************************************
020 REM  SQUARE Program
030 REM
040 REM  This program prints a table of the squares and square roots of the
050 REM  numbers from 1 to 20.
060 REM
070 REM   Author:  Ernest Colantonio          Computer:  IBM Personal Computer
080 REM   Date:    September 25, 1988         Language:  IBM BASIC
090 REM
100 REM ***********************************************************************

110 LPRINT " N         N Squared      Square Root of N"
120 LPRINT "==========================================="
130 FOR N = 1 TO 20
140    LPRINT N, N*N, SQR (N)
150    NEXT N
160 END

999 REM ***********************************************************************
```

(b) Printed output of the program.

| N | N Squared | Square Root of N |
|---|---|---|
| 1 | 1 | 1 |
| 2 | 4 | 1.414214 |
| 3 | 9 | 1.732051 |
| 4 | 16 | 2 |
| 5 | 25 | 2.236068 |
| 6 | 36 | 2.44949 |
| 7 | 49 | 2.645751 |
| 8 | 64 | 2.828427 |
| 9 | 81 | 3 |
| 10 | 100 | 3.162278 |
| 11 | 121 | 3.316625 |
| 12 | 144 | 3.464102 |
| 13 | 169 | 3.605551 |
| 14 | 196 | 3.741657 |
| 15 | 225 | 3.872984 |
| 16 | 256 | 4 |
| 17 | 289 | 4.123106 |
| 18 | 324 | 4.242641 |
| 19 | 361 | 4.358899 |
| 20 | 400 | 4.472136 |

## Pascal

*Simple, structured language*

**Pascal** is a modern programming language named in honor of the seventeenth-century French philosopher and mathematician Blaise Pascal. It was developed by Swiss computer scientist Niklaus Wirth. Introduced in 1971, Pascal was originally intended as a general-purpose, high-level language for teaching principles of good programming design. Simplicity, elegance, and structure made Pascal immediately popular with computer scientists and students, scientific programmers, and microcomputer users. Although not quite as simple as BASIC, Pascal is a well-designed language that is straightforward and fairly easy to learn. Furthermore, it imposes rules that encourage sound programming habits. Pascal has become an inexpensive, compact, yet powerful alternative to BASIC for small computers.

## C

*Concise, powerful language*

**C** is a concise, yet powerful programming language originally developed at Bell Laboratories by Dennis Ritchie in 1972. Similar in some ways to Pascal, C was intended as an alternative to assembly languages for the development of system software. It can perform many low-level operations normally achievable only with assembly languages. C has become popular with more expert microcomputer programmers who use it to develop software that's compact, efficient, and fast. Consequently, C is now considered the language of choice for programmers who develop system and application software.

## FORTRAN

*Mathematical and scientific language*

**FORTRAN**, a contraction of FORmula TRANslator, was one of the very first high-level computer programming languages. Developed by IBM and introduced in 1957, FORTRAN was designed to fulfill the computational needs of scientists, engineers, and mathematicians. It originally ran on large computer systems but was adapted for use on microcomputers when they became widespread. Because of its facility at expressing complex computations, FORTRAN is still the most widely used programming language in the scientific community.

## COBOL

*Business language*

**COBOL**, which stands for COmmon Business Oriented Language, is also a relatively old programming language. It was introduced in 1960, after having been developed by the Conference On Data Systems Languages (CODASYL), a committee of U.S. government and industry representatives called together by the Department of Defense. COBOL was designed especially for business data processing. Because its use was greatly encouraged by the U.S. government, COBOL has been extensively applied throughout business and industry. It's probably still the single most widely known and used computer language in the world. When businesses started acquiring microcomputers in large numbers, COBOL was inevitably adapted so that existing software could still be used.

## Ada

*Powerful, comprehensive language*

**Ada** is a relatively new high-level programming language, first introduced in 1980. It was named for Countess Augusta Ada Lovelace, a mathematician considered to be the first computer programmer. In 1842, she described how to program Charles Babbage's Analytical Engine, a general-purpose, mechanical computer designed in 1833 but never built. The programming language Ada was commissioned by the

U.S. Department of Defense, the world's largest software consumer. Similar in some ways to Pascal, Ada is a powerful, comprehensive language applicable to a wide range of problems. It is now used on all kinds of computers, by all kinds of organizations (not just the Department of Defense).

## Fourth Generation Languages

*Abstract, yet easy to use*

**Fourth generation languages** or **4GLs** are the most abstract type of programming language. They are also known as *application generators, very high-level languages,* and *nonprocedural languages.* Fourth generation languages are designed to make it as easy as possible for users to tell the computer what to do. They eliminate many of the strict rules characteristic of most high-level programming languages. With a fourth generation language, the user typically concentrates on specifying the necessary input and the desired output instead of giving the computer explicit procedural instructions on how to convert input to output.

Some fourth generation languages are like human languages, such as English, but with very limited vocabularies. Others are like traditional high-level programming languages, such as Pascal, but have fewer rules. Still others guide you through the entire software development process and let you easily design your own data files, menus, output screens, and printed reports. Figure 3.6, for example, shows Clarion Professional Developer, a popular application generator for IBM-compatible microcomputers.

**Figure 3.6 Application Generator**
The main menu of CLARION Professional Developer, a popular application generator for IBM-compatible microcomputers.

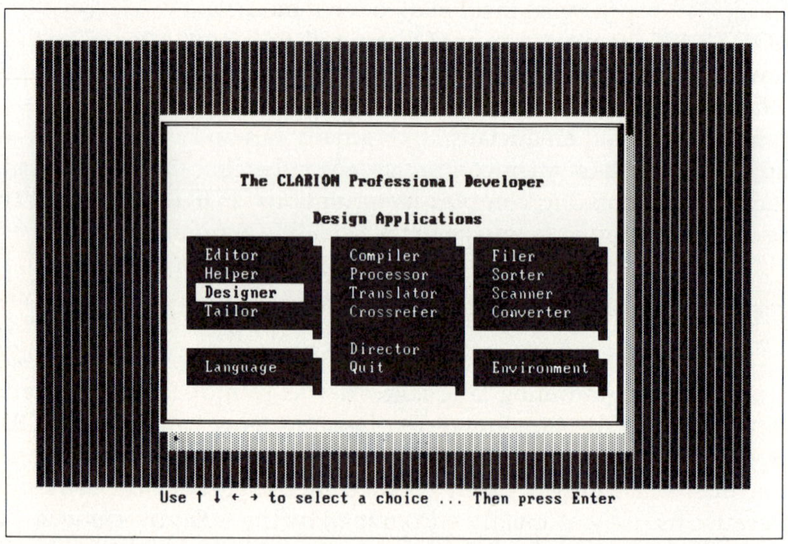


Fourth generation languages are becoming more popular as computer hardware and software systems become more sophisticated. They offer many advantages, especially to users who aren't trained as programmers. Even professional programmers often find fourth generation languages easier to use than traditional high-level programming languages. One particularly important advantage of fourth generation languages is that they can often significantly reduce the time it takes to develop new application software. In some cases, reducing development time can be more important than any other consideration. Some industry experts predict that fourth generation languages will gradually replace conventional high-level programming languages as tools for software development.

For now, however, there are still some disadvantages to fourth generation languages. Most of them are proprietary systems, developed and sold by a single company for a particular type of computer. This means that there is little industry-wide standardization. No fourth generation language has achieved the popularity and versatility of high-level languages such as BASIC and Pascal. Furthermore, fourth generation languages are typically not suitable for the development of system software. In many cases, application programs created with fourth generation languages run slower and use more memory than equivalent programs written in high-level languages. Fourth generation languages are often more expensive and require more memory and disk space than high-level language compilers. Finally, high-level languages are still widely used to develop the great majority of application packages. This means that most programmers and many users are already familiar with conventional high-level languages. They may be hesitant to learn a fourth generation language, even if it would ultimately prove easier to use and cut software development time.

## APPLICATION SOFTWARE

*Performing useful work*

System software deals with the management and effective use of a computer's hardware and software resources. The tasks performed by system software are quite specific and somewhat incidental to what most people really want their computers to do. *Application software* puts computers to practical use. These programs, sometimes called *application packages*, are designed to help people do all kinds of workaday jobs such as writing letters and planning budgets. Application software has been central to the computer revolution. By making computers work for people who perhaps aren't programmers themselves, application packages have become the primary reason why most individuals, businesses, and organizations purchase computers.

Application software is generally bought separately when the computer is purchased. Since the advent of microcomputers, the number of companies developing application software has increased dramatically. Consequently, literally thousands of different programs are on the market. One way to classify application software is by what it does. Three categories stand out as clearly the most prevalent types of microcomputer software: word processing, spreadsheet, and data base management. In addition, communications and networking, graphics, desktop publishing, accounting, and some other packages are also commonly used with microcomputers.

### Word Processing

*Creating documents*

Word processing packages are perhaps the most popular of all types of application software (see Figure 3.7). It's been estimated that more than 90% of all microcomputer owners have at least one word processing program. Simply stated, a word processing package helps you enter, store, modify, format, copy, and print text. Such software gives a microcomputer and printer the power to do much more than an ordinary typewriter. Many of the tedious and time-consuming tasks associated with typing can be done automatically by word processing packages. For example, most word processors can start a new line when you reach the margin, start a new page when you reach the bottom of a page, center titles, copy sections of text, alter line spacing, and even check for spelling errors. You can type, correct, and format your entire document on the computer display screen. Once you're satisfied that everything looks just right, you can print out any number of perfect copies on paper. Not only do word processors make it easy to initially enter and print text, but they allow you to store and update documents as well. We'll have more to say about this amazing tool in Chapters 6 and 7.

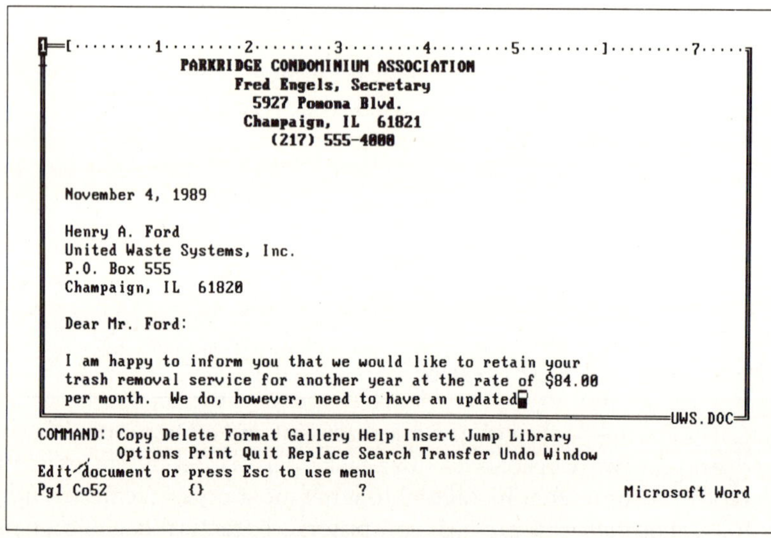


**Figure 3.7 Word Processing Package**
This screen shows Microsoft Word for IBM-compatible microcomputers being used to create a letter.

## Spreadsheet

*Manipulating tables of numbers*

Spreadsheet packages are a relatively new type of application software initially designed especially for microcomputers. In 1978, an MIT graduate named Dan Bricklin, who was enrolled in Harvard Business School, felt that he was spending too much time laboring over the financial worksheets required for his accounting classes. **Worksheets,** also called **spreadsheets,** are basically tables of rows and columns of numerical data. Bricklin had only two choices at the time: perform the many worksheet computations with a pocket calculator, or use the school's mainframe computer. Neither of these alternatives particularly suited Bricklin. Because he couldn't store intermediate results except by writing them down, using a pocket calculator would be too time-consuming and error prone. Gaining access to and programming the school's mainframe would be inconvenient. So Bricklin devised a microcomputer program that could easily manipulate tables of numbers. He and fellow MIT alumni Bob Frankston and Daniel Flystra formed a company called Software Arts in 1979. They sold the first spreadsheet program, called VisiCalc (short for Visible Calculator), which ran on Apple microcomputers. Although VisiCalc is no longer sold, it paved the way for a whole new class of microcomputer software.

The spreadsheet program is an extremely flexible tool that can be applied to a wide range of common problems (see Figure 3.8). Adept at manipulating tables of numbers, spreadsheet software is most often used to handle typical business accounting chores such as cash flow projections, depreciation calculations, balance sheets, and income statements. Spreadsheet programs also can be used to monitor investments, balance checkbooks, and work out home budgets. One of their most valuable features is that they allow users to ask "what if" questions about their data. This is possible because spreadsheet programs can automatically recalculate all entries whenever any single figure is changed. Once a worksheet has been set up, it's easy to try different values just to see what the results would be. The potential uses of spreadsheet programs are almost endless. In addition to the applications we've already mentioned, spreadsheet programs also have been used to create conversion tables, statistical analyses, financial models, and even games. Chapters 8 and 9 will cover spreadsheet packages in more detail.

A2: [W12] 'Expenditures READY

| | A | B | C | D | E | F | G |
|---|---|---|---|---|---|---|---|
| 1 | | January | February | March | April | May | June |
| 2 | Expenditures | | | | | | |
| 3 | Insurance | $247.00 | $247.00 | $247.00 | $247.00 | $247.00 | $247.00 |
| 4 | Snow Plowing | $310.00 | $150.00 | | | | |
| 5 | Merry Maids | $48.00 | $48.00 | $48.00 | $48.00 | $48.00 | $48.00 |
| 6 | Lawn Service | | | | $420.00 | $420.00 | $420.00 |
| 7 | Trash Pickup | $84.00 | $84.00 | $84.00 | $84.00 | $84.00 | $84.00 |
| 8 | Electricity | $95.00 | $97.00 | $178.00 | $160.00 | $201.00 | $94.00 |
| 9 | Tree Care | | | | $160.00 | | |
| 10 | Light Bulbs | | | | $108.00 | $36.00 | |
| 11 | Supplies | $24.00 | $27.00 | $25.00 | $16.00 | $23.00 | $18.00 |
| 12 | TOTALS | $808.00 | $653.00 | $582.00 | $1,243.00 | $1,059.00 | $911.00 |
| 13 | | | | | | | |
| 14 | Income | | | | | | |
| 15 | Condo Fees | $976.00 | $976.00 | $976.00 | $976.00 | $976.00 | $976.00 |
| 16 | | | | | | | |
| 17 | Balance | $168.00 | $491.00 | $885.00 | $618.00 | $535.00 | $600.00 |
| 18 | | | | | | | |
| 19 | | | | | | | |
| 20 | | | | | | | |

30-Aug-88 10:07 AM

**Figure 3.8 Spreadsheet Program**
This screen shows Lotus 1-2-3 being used to create a condominium association's year-end budget.

## Data Base Management

*Organizing information*

One of the major jobs we delegate to computers is that of managing huge quantities of data. Sometimes we don't need computers to actually compute anything—just store, sort, retrieve, print, or in some manner manipulate information. Large computers were doing this long before microcomputers came on the scene. Once microcomputers became so popular, however, it was only natural that they also be put to work managing data bases.

A *data base* is an organized collection of one or more files of interrelated data. A **file** is simply a mass of individual data items kept together in secondary storage. Computer files may contain programs, numerical data, or text. In general, data bases are made up of files containing numbers and text compiled for some specific purpose. For example, data bases are often used to store mailing lists, phone numbers, personnel files, customer accounts, credit records, inventories, bibliographies, and even entire reference works. *Data base management packages* enable people to create, add to, delete from, update, sort, rearrange, select from, print out, and otherwise administer data files (see Figure 3.9). We'll have more to say about these sophisticated information storage and retrieval systems in Chapters 10 and 11.

**Figure 3.9 Data Base Management Package**
Here dBASE III PLUS is being used to maintain a mailing list.

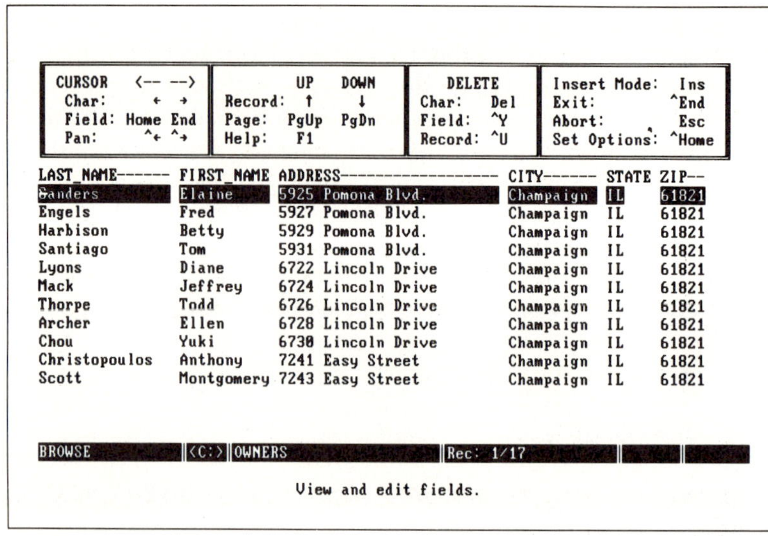


## Communications and Networking

*Connecting computers*

In the previous chapter we saw how modems enable microcomputers to transmit and receive data over telephone lines. Communications software is just as important as hardware in the process of exchanging data and accessing remote computers. Communications packages perform essential tasks such as coordinating the manner and speed in which data are transmitted and received, dialing phone numbers, capturing incoming data in secondary storage, and sending messages, files, and commands over transmission lines (see Figure 3.10).

As we briefly mentioned in Chapter 2, a local area network (LAN) is an arrangement that connects several microcomputers and peripherals together, usually in the same building or in nearby buildings. This allows people to easily exchange data, share files, and take turns using expensive peripherals like laser printers and high-capacity hard disks. Along with special hardware like network adapters and cables, LANs also require network software to control the flow of data and manage the use of peripheral devices. Communications and networking are two far-reaching microcomputer applications about which we'll have more to say in Chapter 12.

## Graphics

*Generating images*

Graphics packages let users create pictures with their computers. (You know what they say about a picture being worth a thousand words.) Computer-generated graphics can transform dull data into eye-catching, informative images. Several different types of graphics application packages are available for microcomputers. Some are used to produce graphs, charts, maps, simulated slide shows, and animated presentations. Others are freehand painting and drawing programs often used to create illustrations (see Figure 3.11). Even more sophisticated packages are used for precise computer-aided design and drafting applications. Chapter 13 covers graphics packages in more detail.

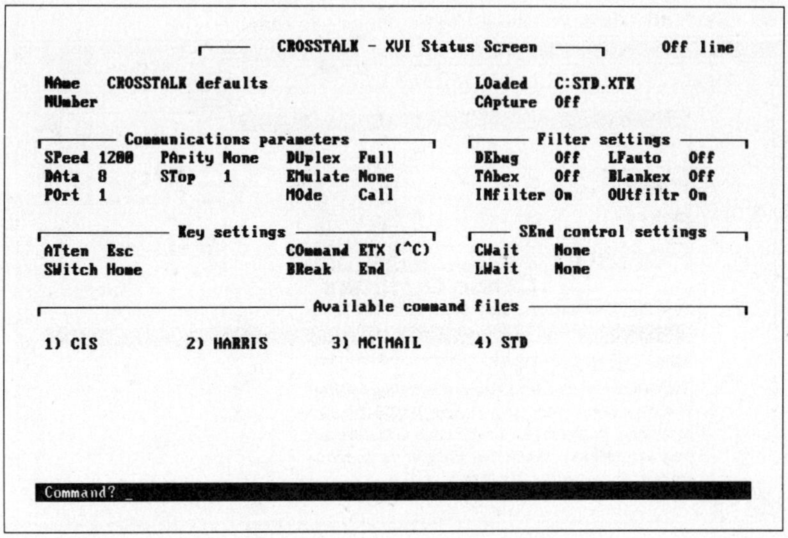


**Figure 3.10 Communications Program**
CROSSTALK XVI is a popular communications program for IBM- compatible microcomputers.

**Figure 3.11 Graphics Program**
Programs such as MacPaint for the Apple Macintosh can be used to create freehand illustrations.

## Desktop Publishing

*Combining text and graphics*

Combine word processing and graphics capabilities with the beautiful output of a laser printer and you have the essence of *desktop publishing*. This type of application package can produce near-typeset-quality printed material complete with illustrations using microcomputers and laser printers at relatively low cost (see Figure 3.12). All kinds of organizations, from small clubs to multinational corporations, are using desktop publishing packages to produce their own newsletters, advertisements, memos, contracts, documents, and even books. Chapter 14 will examine further the recent phenomenon of desktop publishing.

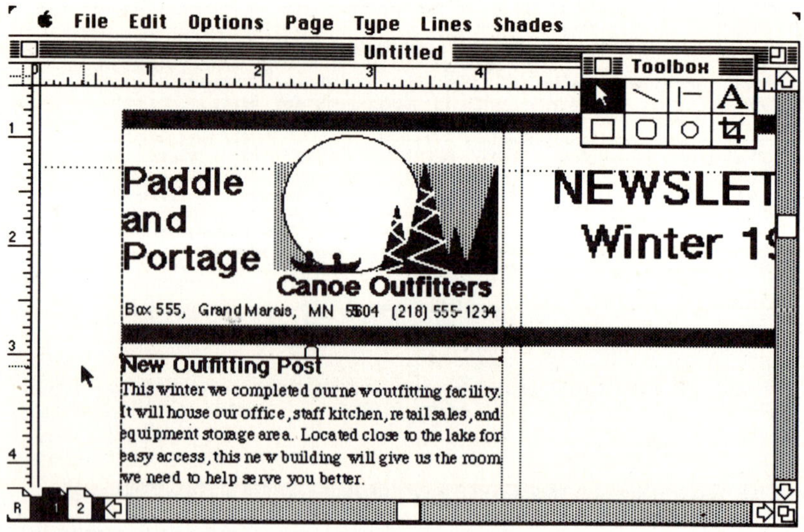


**Figure 3.12 Desktop Publishing**
Programs such as PageMaker let you create documents with both text and pictures.

## Accounting

*Keeping the books*

Despite the widespread acceptance of computers by virtually every segment of our society, they are still used by business most of all. So it's only natural that a large number of microcomputer application packages have been developed especially for business accounting. This software helps boost profits, cut costs, improve cash flow, pay bills, calculate earnings, assemble marketing information, and explore operational alternatives (see Figure 3.13). We'll have more to say about these electronic bookkeepers in Chapter 15.

## Other Packages

*Software sidelights*

In addition to the major types of software we've just discussed, still more packages are often used with microcomputers. These include the following (which will be covered in Chapter 16):

- *Integrated software.* These large programs typically include several different applications in the same packages. For example, a single integrated package might include word processing, spreadsheet, data base management, graphics, and communications capabilities.
- *On-line references.* Imagine having a dictionary, thesaurus, book of quotations, zip code listing, stock market table, or census information in your computer's secondary storage.
- *Statistical and math packages.* These types of software, long available on large computers, have become increasingly popular for use on microcomputers. These packages are especially attractive to business analysts, mathematicians, and engineers, as well as physical, biological, and social scientists.
- *Project management packages.* These applications are used to help managers plan and coordinate huge multitask projects.
- *Personal finance and tax packages.* These applications can do everything from balancing your checkbook to managing your investments and figuring your income taxes.

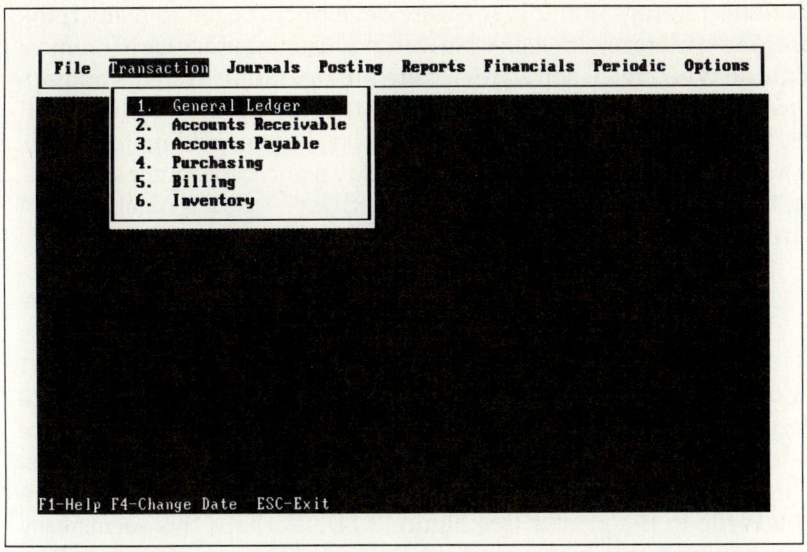


**Figure 3.13 Accounting Package**
This screen shows DAC Easy Accounting, a popular, low-priced accounting package for IBM-compatible microcomputers.

- *Educational packages.* A wide range of topics and skills can be taught with microcomputer software, from the alphabet to experimental physics.
- *Entertainment packages.* Games, simulators, and music-makers are but a few of the many types of entertainment software available for microcomputers.
- *Hypertext packages.* These programs let you store, organize, and present unstructured information.
- *Artificial Intelligence and Expert Systems.* These programs, pioneers on the software frontier, attempt to enable computers to learn, deduce, diagnose, and advise.

## THE USER INTERFACE

*Interacting with software*

System software and application software tell computers what to do. But to perform most tasks with computers, people must tell software what to do. The way people interact with software—how you direct the actions of software and how that software responds to your requests—is often called the **user interface**. Since most people who now use computers are not necessarily technical experts, the user interface has become an increasingly important aspect of software and even hardware design.

In the early days of computers, little attention was paid to making computers easy to use. User interfaces were primarily determined by programmers, who believed that the tasks performed by computers were of paramount importance. How people interacted with software was considered incidental, so whatever was easiest to program became the user interface. Since most computer users were scientists and engineers, and the tasks themselves required little interaction, user interfaces were pretty primitive. People just had to adapt to the software.

Then along came microcomputers. People who programmed them and people who used them were for the most part ordinary folks, not rocket scientists. It became evident that software would have to be easier to use. Instead of designing user interfaces for ease of programming, software developers began to really think about making programs more *user friendly*. Nowadays, user interfaces are foremost in the minds of those who create software. There are operating systems and application packages with sophisticated user interfaces that are almost intuitively understood by most people. Computer software has at last begun to adapt to people.

A wide range of user interfaces is still found in today's microcomputer software, however. Going from primitive to more sophisticated, let's take a look at some of the ways software interacts with people.

## Commands

*Typed directives*

A **command** is a directive that you issue to a program and is perhaps the simplest type of user interface. Commands are quick and efficient, but they require a substantial initial learning and memorization process. For example, the operating system used with most IBM microcomputers requires you to issue the PRINT command to send a text file to the printer (see Figure 3.14). Perhaps this seems easy enough, but there may be many, many commands and their names may not all be so memorable. How do you know when you can print files? Is the printer turned on or even connected? How do you tell the operating system which file to print? If you forget the name of a command or don't know exactly how it operates, you may have to look it up in a reference manual.

Using commands isn't completely negative, however. Once you memorize the commands you need and know how they work, you can often get things done very quickly. The real problem comes when you try to use some other command-driven software. Its commands might be totally different or, worse, similar in name but different in function. For instance, in some word processors you erase the character to the left of the cursor by pressing the backspace key. In other word processors, the delete key does the same job. Little differences like this can be very annoying if you have to use several programs with conflicting commands.

**Figure 3.14 Command**
On an IBM-compatible microcomputer, one way to print the contents of a file is to issue a PRINT command.

```
A>PRINT README.TXT

  A:\README.TXT is currently being printed

A>-
```

## Prompts

*Questions and answers*

One step up from commands are prompts. A **prompt** generally provides information or instructions about how to do something and then waits for your response. For example, a prompt familiar to users of IBM microcomputers is

```
Current date is Tue  1-01-1980
Enter new date (mm-dd-yy):_
```

In some cases, a prompt may take the form of a question. If you issue the ERASE command to tell the IBM Personal Computer operating system to delete every file on a disk, it uses a prompt to confirm this drastic action (see Figure 3.15):

```
Are you sure (Y/N)?_
```

Prompts, generally easy to understand, are occasionally used by most software. But prompts can only be used when software is waiting for some very specific response from you. They can't be used too often, because software has no way of determining when you might want to initiate some action on your own.

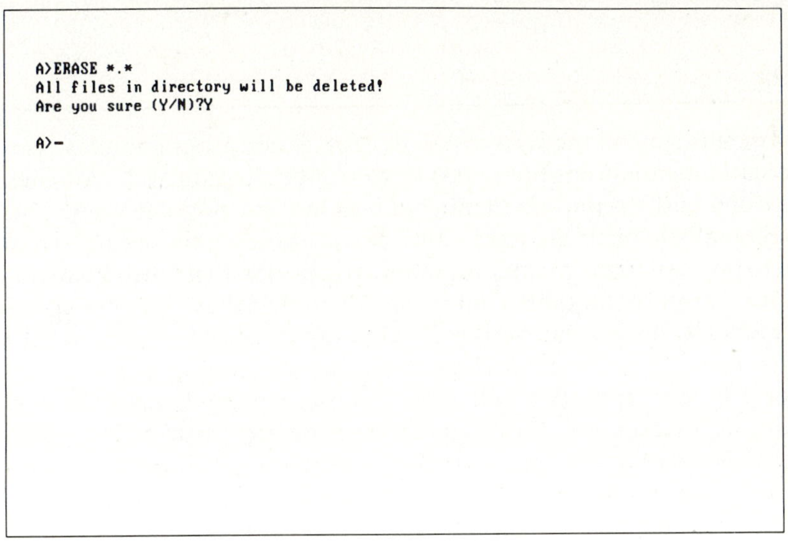


**Figure 3.15 Prompt**
After you issue an ERASE command that will delete all files, the operating system of IBM-compatible microcomputers presents a prompt asking you if you are sure this is what you want to do.

## Static Menus

*Lists of options*

One of the major problems with commands is that they may be difficult to memorize. This deficiency can be addressed through the use of menus. As we said in Chapter 1, a *menu* is a list of available alternatives that's displayed on the screen. A **static menu** is one that remains on the screen in a fixed position (see Figure 3.16). In some respects, menus combine prompts and commands. By providing information about which commands are available and how to invoke them, menus are much easier to use than commands by themselves and much more versatile than individual prompts. Unfortunately, static menus take up valuable screen space, and complex actions may require several levels of submenus. On balance, however, menus are a significant improvement over commands and prompts.

**Figure 3.16 Static Menu**
WordStar 4.0, a popular word processing program for IBM-compatibles, uses static menus to provide information about the available commands and how to invoke them.

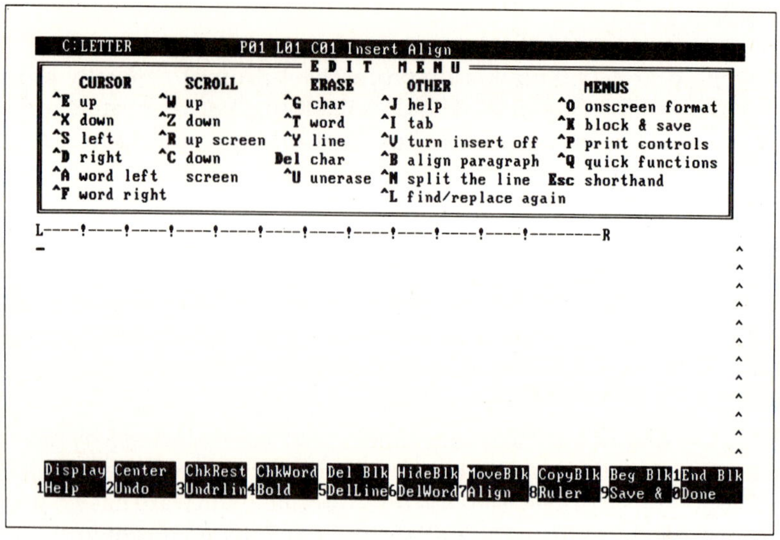


## Pop-up Menus

*Now you see them, now you don't*

In general, static menus stay on the screen in one place. Some programs allow you to remove their static menus from the screen with a special command. An even more flexible type of menu, the **pop-up menu**, has become very popular lately. This type of menu is generally kept off the screen until you issue a special command that causes the menu to pop up. Some clever programs can position their pop-up menus so that information currently on the screen is not covered, if there's empty space. Other programs actually let you move the menu around so you can see what's beneath. Once the menu is up, what you type goes toward selecting an alternative and doesn't appear in the application below. In a sense, you are temporarily disconnected from the normal action of the program when the pop-up menu is in place. When you've made a selection, the pop-up menu automatically disappears, leaving your screen as it was before.

Pop-up menus are a definite improvement over static menus. Their most obvious benefit is that they take up screen space only when in actual use. Pop-up menus are out of sight when you don't need them, thereby reducing clutter and confusion. Another benefit is that certain actions can only be performed when the menu is up on the screen. This helps prevent accidentally invoking some command by inadvertently pressing its keys. Keypresses can have different meanings when a pop-up menu is present, yielding more possible commands. Pop-up menus are often cited as the beginning of truly friendly user interfaces.

A good example of pop-up menus can be found in the extremely successful Lotus 1-2-3 spreadsheet package (see Figure 3.17). To invoke the main menu, you press the / (forward slash) key. A list of words appears that represent actions to be taken. In the Lotus 1-2-3 program, these words are listed horizontally across one or two lines, but the same basic concept has been used in other programs that list options vertically.

A choice is made in one of two ways. The first method involves a brightly lit or colored bar that's used to highlight one of the alternatives. This highlight bar can be moved from one option to the next by pressing arrow keys. Sometimes this highlight bar is called a *cursor* or *pointer*. When it's positioned on top of the desired selection, the Enter key is usually pressed to confirm and execute that alternative.

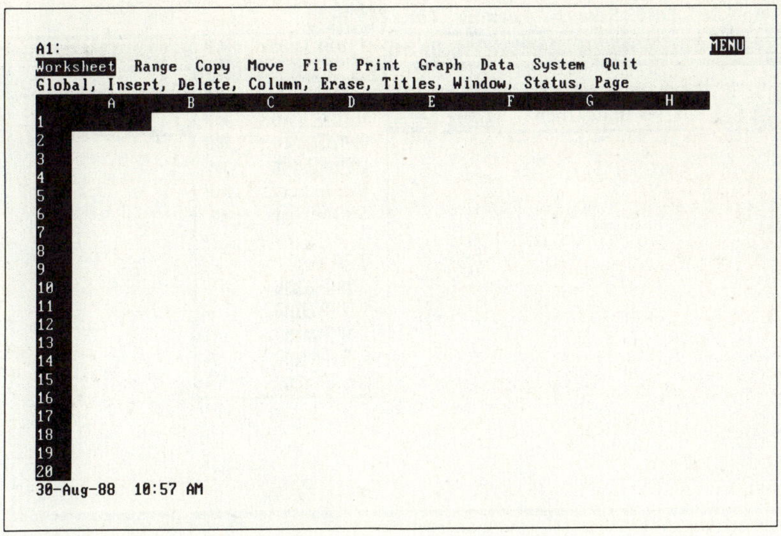


**Figure 3.17 Pop-up Menu**
Lotus 1-2-3 uses a pop-up menu system that you invoke by pressing the / (forward slash) key. The Main Menu then appears at the top of the screen with the Worksheet option highlighted.

The other method of selection is quicker. All the options listed in this type of menu begin with a different letter. To select an option, all you have to do is press the key that matches its first letter. This type of menu is now used in a wide range of different software packages.

## Pull-down Menus

*Mouse-controlled options*

Pop-up menu is a term generally reserved for software that runs on text displays. Although similar, the **pull-down menu** is characteristic of programs that have a graphics user interface. These packages keep the screen in some graphics mode and almost always use a mouse. The mouse controls a little pointer, shaped like an arrow or index finger, so that it can be moved anywhere on the screen. When the pointer is positioned on top of a word or symbol along the top of the screen, a mouse button can be pressed to pull down a menu (see Figure 3.18). Once the menu is on the screen, the pointer is used to drag a highlight bar up or down the list of options. When the desired option is highlighted, the mouse button is released, the menu disappears, and the selected alternative is executed. Most people find it very natural to use a mouse to position a pointer. This can make pull-down menus even easier to use than pop-up menus.

## Icons, Windows, and Desktops

*Graphical interface*

Perhaps the most sophisticated and easiest to use of all types of microcomputer user interfaces is that popularized by the system and application software of the Apple Macintosh. With pull-down menus, icons, and windows, this computer arranges the display screen into a simulated desktop (see Figure 3.19). *Icons*, as we said in Chapter 1, are graphic symbols used to represent hardware devices, programs, data files, and actions to be performed. Computer concepts and devices are represented pictorially as familiar office items. Actions are indicated graphically. For example, instead of typing a command to erase a file, you discard data by using the mouse to drag a file folder over to a trash can. Instead of issuing typewritten commands, the computer is directed by manipulating objects on the screen with a mouse-

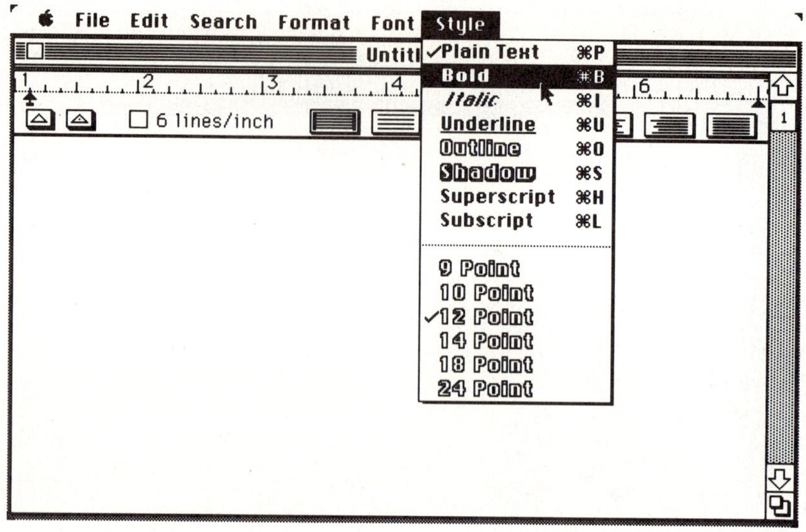


**Figure 3.18 Pull-down Menu**

This screen shows a pull-down menu in MacWrite, a popular word processing program for the Apple Macintosh. The Style menu has been pulled down and the Bold option is currently highlighted.

controlled pointer. The screen becomes a familiar desktop. The contents of storage devices, data files, and documents are displayed inside their own individual windows that pop up on that desktop. System utilities and application software have similar windows displayed while they are running. Windows can be superimposed on the screen just as you can lay several file folders on your desk at the same time. The one on top is currently active.

On computers such as the Apple Macintosh, most software presents the same basic user interface. This means that a person who masters one program can use many of those same skills in running some completely different type of software. The graphical interface has proven so effective, especially for novice users, that it's gradually being adapted to software other than that which runs on the Apple Macintosh. Much system and application software for IBM microcomputers now uses similar concepts.

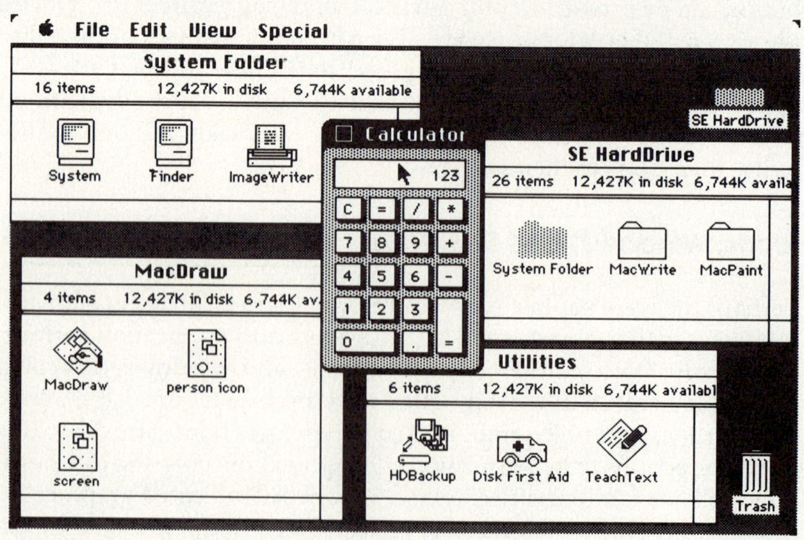


**Figure 3.19 Macintosh Desktop**

This screen shows the Apple Macintosh operating system with several windows open on the desktop.

There are some drawbacks, however, to this sophisticated type of user interface. In general, it takes a great deal of computer power and memory to make such schemes work. User-friendly software is difficult and more expensive to develop. Some people find the cute user interface tiresome once they become experts. Critics argue that after you master a command-oriented system, such as the IBM Personal Computer operating system, you can work faster and more efficiently. Proponents on both sides of the issue have made good points, but what's important is that users now have more options than ever in the way they interact with computers.

## The Real World

### Microsoft's Phenomenon

William H. Gates III is 32 years old and worth $1 billion. He didn't inherit the money and he didn't win the lottery. What Gates did was found one of the world's largest software companies—Microsoft Corp. Consider this: Gates and partner Paul Allen began Microsoft in 1975, after Gates had dropped out of Harvard. In 1986, when the company offered stock to the public, Gates's share was worth roughly $300 million. Two years later the stock had more than quadrupled. He was a billionaire.

Many people believe that Microsoft is the leading software designer in the $35 billion personal computer industry. It supplies programming language translators and applications programs, but it is perhaps best known as the creator of MS-DOS, the operating system chosen by IBM for its personal computer line. After IBM made its choice, Tandy, Compaq, and all the IBM clone-makers followed. By 1986, DOS was being used in 58 percent of the 7.1 million personal computers installed in the United States.

Microsoft's new operating system, OS/2, runs on high-end IBM-compatible machines, enabling them to perform several tasks at once, and making them easier to use.

In many ways, Gates is a typical young computer entrepreneur. He is precocious, shrewd, visionary, and a perfectionist. And he won't take "no" for an answer. When IBM executives balked at buying his Windows software in favor of developing their own, Gates calmly sat down and convinced them to change their minds.

Microsoft is striving to maintain its entrepreneurial spirit as well, with company meetings; flexible hours, and weekly parties.

Source: "The Billion-Dollar Whiz Kid", by Richard Brandt, *Business Week*, April 13, 1987, pp. 68-76.

## Summary

- *How programs tell computers what to do.* Every computer is only capable of a limited set of simple tasks, each represented by a single instruction. A program is a group of instructions that tells a computer what to do.
- *How system software helps you use a computer.* System software handles the details of managing a computer's hardware and software resources, and includes operating systems, utilities, and alternative operating environments.
- *The major types of programming languages.* Arranged from less abstract to more abstract, the major types of programming languages are machine languages, assembly languages, high-level languages, and fourth generation languages.
- *The major types of application software.* Three categories stand out as clearly the most prevalent: word processing, spreadsheet, and data base management. Communications and networking, graphics, desktop publishing, and accounting software packages are also very popular.

- *The major types of user interfaces.* The types of user interfaces, listed from simple to more complex include commands, prompts, static menus, pop-up menus, pull-down menus, and icons, windows, and desktops.

## Key Terms

As an extra review of this chapter, try defining the following terms. If you have trouble with any of them, refer to the page number listed.

Ada (94)
assembler (90)
assembly language (88)
BASIC (91)
C (93)
COBOL (93)
command (102)
compiler (90)
file (97)
FORTRAN (93)
fourth generation languages (4GLs) (94)
high-level language (90)
instruction set (82)
interpreter (91)
machine language (87)
mnemonics (88)
object code (90)
operand (87)
operating system (83)
operation code (opcode) (87)
Pascal (93)
pop-up menu (104)
prompt (103)
pull-down menu (105)
source code (90)
static menu (104)
symbolic addressing (88)
user interface (101)
utility (84)
windowing environment (alternate operating environment) (86)
worksheets (spreadsheets) (96)

## Review Questions

1. What is a group of instructions that tells a computer what to do?
2. How are instructions encoded by computers?
3. List some tasks performed by system software.
4. What software is immediately brought into action when you turn on a computer?
5. What kinds of tasks are performed by utility programs?
6. What are the basic types of instructions included in all programming languages?
7. Explain the distinction between low- and high-level computer programming languages.
8. What is the only programming language that can be directly used by a computer?
9. What advantages do assembly languages have over machine languages?
10. What are some of the disadvantages of using assembly languages?
11. What are the two basic types of programs used to translate high-level language source code into object code?
12. What advantages do high-level languages have over assembly languages?

13. List the most commonly used microcomputer high-level programming languages.
14. What kind of software improves the way an operating system interacts with the user, while often affording the power to do several tasks at once?
15. What kind of software has primarily motivated people to buy computers?
16. What is perhaps the most popular of all types of application packages?
17. List some of the applications of spreadsheet software.
18. What kinds of tasks does a data base management package perform?
19. List some other popular types of microcomputer application software.
20. Briefly describe six of the interaction methods found in the user interfaces of today's microcomputer application software.

## Multiple Choice

1. Every computer is only capable of a limited set of simple tasks, each represented by a single
   (a) bit. (b) byte.
   (c) instruction. (d) operating system.
2. Programs that deal most intimately with a computer's hardware are called
   (a) programming languages. (b) system software.
   (c) application software. (d) user interfaces.
3. Which of the following tasks is usually performed by the operating system?
   (a) setting up new floppy disks (b) drawing pie charts
   (c) creating documents (d) sorting mailing lists
4. A small program that lets you recover accidentally erased files would usually be categorized as a(n)
   (a) application package. (b) operating system.
   (c) data base manager. (d) utility.
5. Which of the following types of instructions is not normally included in a programming language?
   (a) input and output (b) boot up
   (c) calculation (d) comparison
6. Which type of low-level programming language is characterized by the use of mnemonics and symbolic addressing?
   (a) machine language (b) assembly language
   (c) Pascal (d) fourth generation language
7. Which type of programming language is generally machine-independent?
   (a) machine language (b) assembly language
   (c) high-level language (d) system language

8. Which type of programming language translator program translates and runs one program instruction at a time as it's entered into the computer?
   (a) assembler (b) compiler
   (c) interpreter (d) converter
9. Which was the first high-level programming language to be adapted for use on microcomputers?
   (a) BASIC (b) Pascal
   (c) FORTRAN (d) COBOL
10. Which type of programming language generally makes it easiest for the user to tell the computer what to do?
    (a) machine language (b) assembly language
    (c) high-level language (d) fourth generation language
11. Which is probably the most popular of all types of application software?
    (a) word processing (b) spreadsheet
    (c) data base management (d) communications and networking
12. Which type of software is best for manipulating tables of numbers?
    (a) word processing (b) spreadsheet
    (c) data base management (d) accounting
13. Which type of software would you use to store mailing lists, phone numbers, personnel files, inventories, and bibliographies?
    (a) word processing (b) spreadsheet
    (c) data base management (d) on-line references
14. Which is the most primitive type of user interface?
    (a) command (b) static menu
    (c) pull-down menu (d) window
15. Which type of user interface almost always uses a mouse?
    (a) command (b) prompt
    (c) pop-up menu (d) pull-down menu

## Projects

1. A computer program is really just a detailed list of the steps required to accomplish some task. In your own words, write a "program" that describes how to prepare your favorite meal.
2. Investigate a few of the other high-level programming languages also used with microcomputers. Write a short description of each one. Be sure to mention under which circumstances each of these languages is typically used.
3. In this chapter we've tried to mention the most popular types of application software. An almost infinite variety of packages is available for microcomputers, however. Using computer magazines, newspapers, and books, compile a list of some of these other types of applications.

4. One way to see if software is easy to learn and use is to observe how many books are published about it. An operating system that novices find difficult to understand generally spawns a whole school of supplementary books on the subject. Go to a local bookstore and see how many books you can find about the IBM Personal Computer operating system (called PC-DOS or MS-DOS) versus the number you see covering the Apple Macintosh system.

# Part 2

# OPERATING SYSTEMS

An operating system is an essential component of any general- purpose computer, since you cannot use a computer without working with its operating system. It's important to learn about operating systems in general so that you can understand how people tell computers what to do. You must also learn some specifics about any particular operating system you are going to use. In Part 2, we examine microcomputer operating systems. Chapter 4 is a general introduction to operating systems. Chapter 5 describes how to use DOS, the world's most popular microcomputer operating system.

# 4

# Operating System Concepts

## In This Chapter

## PREVIEW

An operating system is the "heart and soul" of a computer. It is the foundation on which all application software rests. The operating system takes care of low-level details, such as interpreting your keypresses, reading data from a disk, and erasing the display screen. Application packages handle more abstract tasks, such as helping you create a document, draw a graph, or compute statistics. The computer user, operating system, and application packages must work together as a team to process data into information.

Many different types of operating systems are used with computers today. Some are specific to a particular computer, while others have been adapted to run on many very different computers. This chapter emphasizes microcomputer operating systems, but sometimes we will mention features mainly found on much larger and more powerful machines. This will help you understand operating systems in general and suggest the capabilities of future microcomputer operating systems.

After studying this chapter, you will understand

- what operating systems do.
- the basic types of computer operating systems.
- the fundamental components of an operating system.
- how people use operating systems.
- several important microcomputer operating systems.

## WHAT OPERATING SYSTEMS DO

*Performing essential chores*

In Chapter 3, we introduced the operating system as a set of programs that controls a computer's hardware and manages the use of software. Operating systems perform several essential chores, which can be divided into three broad categories: controlling hardware, managing software, and interacting with users.

### Control Hardware

*Supervising devices*

Many of the operations of a computer system's internal components and peripheral devices are controlled by built-in electronic circuits. Software, however, controls many other important operations. Operating systems include programs that direct the actions of many hardware devices, including displays, keyboards, printers, real-time clocks, serial and parallel interfaces, and especially disk drives. These programs are extremely valuable to programmers developing application software for computers. They provide a standard, readily accessible method of using the various hardware devices of a computer system, thereby saving programmers a great deal of work. Some of the specific hardware-control tasks performed by operating systems include

- automatically and periodically updating the current time of day based on the ticking of the real-time clock.
- erasing the display screen.
- drawing a dot at a given location on a graphics display.
- given its code, drawing a character on the screen.
- changing background and foreground colors on a color display.

- when a key on the keyboard is pressed, temporarily halting the current program to acknowledge and store the code that identifies that key.
- constantly noting the current location of the mouse and updating the corresponding pointer or cursor on the screen.
- reading and writing data to and from floppy and hard disks.
- sending data through a parallel interface to a printer.
- transmitting and receiving data through a serial interface connected to a modem.
- generating sounds through the computer's speaker.
- automatically testing memory and internal circuits, and reporting problems.

Although these activities may sound simple enough, in actuality they may require many computer instructions each. In order to write programs to perform these tasks, a programmer would have to know a great deal about the low-level internal workings of computer hardware. For maximum efficiency, programs such as these must usually be written in assembly language. If all programmers had to write their own programs in assembly language to do each one of these common tasks, they would require more training and the development of application software would be even more time consuming and expensive.

**Insight**

## What Causes an Operating System to Crash?

It may not be as bad as skidding off a rain-slick road and wrapping your VW around a tree, but an operating system crash can be pretty painful.

You might lose work or miss a deadline, or an entire connected computer network might grind to a halt. When a computer crashes, it usually just stops dead. Nothing seems to revive it, including pounding on the keyboard. Sometimes, random characters glare at you from the screen, or the disk drives keep spinning aimlessly.

Why does this happen? First, remember that an operating system consists of the programs that manage the computer and run application software. The operating system makes its home in the computer's memory. When it's in control, the computer taps into this memory for the step-by-step instructions it needs to work.

One of the most common causes for an operating system crash is that a program inadvertently overwrites an area of memory occupied by the operating system. For example, suppose a poorly written spreadsheet program accidentally stores data in a critical area of memory used by the operating system. This area might contain the program for gaining access to the disk drive. When the application program you're running tries to read or write data to the disk drive, the system crashes.

Obvious programming errors like this are rare because the software is usually tested before it's released.

Unfortunately, however, large programs can become so complex that it's almost impossible to detect every potential bug. This means that if you routinely use a computer, you'll have the displeasure of an operating system crash sooner or later.

In most cases, the only way to revive the system is to restart, or *reboot*, it. Sometimes you can do this by pressing a certain combination of keys, but you may have to turn off the computer and then turn it on again. Any programs you were running will have to be rerun. Worse yet, you'll probably have to reenter any data you were working on at the time of the crash, because rebooting an operating system erases the entire contents of the computer's memory. An operating system crash may also scramble programs and data stored on disk drives. Not a good way to start the day.

### Manage Software

*Governing programs*

Operating systems manage software by controlling how programs are run and what computer resources they can utilize. Among other activities, this includes loading a program from its disk into memory, getting the computer ready to run the program, initiating the program, providing built-in software resources for the program to use, watching for and reporting any grave errors that might occur, and, after the program is finished, preparing the computer to run the next program. In some cases, operating systems must place restrictions on the memory and disk storage to which a particular program has access. This is especially true for operating systems on computers that can run more than one program at a time or serve several users simultaneously. For example, two users or two programs cannot use the same memory locations, disk space, printer, or input device without conflicts occurring. It's the operating system's job to facilitate the execution of programs, while preventing such conflicts.

### Interact with Users

*Processing commands and selections*

The third major function of an operating system is to help average users, not necessarily programmers, put their computers to work. When you first turn on a microcomputer, the operating system is activated and awaits your instruction. You might type a command or use a mouse to select an activity from a menu. In either case, the operating system processes your directive and initiates some program. Some of these programs are part of the operating system itself. They allow users to change settings, examine or print files, check the contents of disks, reorganize disk storage, or otherwise manage their computers. Most of the time, however, users are just interested in running their application software. The operating system is simply the vehicle through which application software is activated. It allows users to see what programs they have stored on their disks and select which one they want to run. In some cases, this selection process can be automated by the operating system for those users who want to run a particular application every time they turn on their computer. Still, just about everyone who uses a computer eventually has some direct interaction with its operating system. Most people who use computers on a regular basis find it worth the effort to become familiar with this essential system software.

## TYPES OF OPERATING SYSTEMS

*Classifying systems*

Several different types of operating systems are in common use; they are classified according to the number of people who can use the system simultaneously, the number of programs (also referred to as *tasks*) that can be run at the same time, and the number of processing units that are being controlled.

### Single-user, Single-tasking

*One person, one program*

The simplest and most common type of operating system accommodates a single user and is **single tasking**. In other words, only a single program is run at a time (see Figure 4.1). That program generally has access to all of the computer's resources, such as memory, disk storage, keyboard input, display output, and printer output. Once initiated, a program usually runs until it's finished or the user stops it. While running, however, the program may be frequently interrupted for very short periods of time by the operating system to handle activities such as updating the time of day and processing keyboard input. On some computers, the operating system's ability to temporarily interrupt processing to handle some critical task has been put to some rather ingenious uses. **Memory-resident** (also called **RAM resident**) programs have been developed for some operating systems that allow the user to temporarily suspend an activity and switch to some other one. For example, one such program that simulates a hand-held calculator may be loaded into memory but not executed when the computer is turned on. By pressing some key combination, the user can activate this calculator. So, if you are using a word processing program and you need to add several numbers, you can activate the calculator, temporarily suspend the word processor, compute your sum, and then deactivate the calculator and return to word processing. It may be possible to have several different memory-resident programs installed and switch among them at will, but the computer is still only running a single program at a time. Most microcomputers have single-user, single-tasking operating systems.

**Figure 4.1 Single-user, Single-tasking Operating System**
The simplest type of operating system lets a single user run a single program at a time.

## Single-user, Multitasking

*One person, several programs*

The majority of microcomputer users probably get along quite well running only a single program at a time. In several instances, however, running a single program at a time doesn't utilize the computer's full potential. For example, most printers print characters much more slowly than computers can send them over the cable. Depending upon the word processor or printing program, you might not be able to use your computer for other tasks while it prints a document. For long documents, this can tie up your computer for quite a while. This and many similar problems can be solved by multitasking operating systems.

**Multitasking** is the ability to run more than one program concurrently, or seemingly at the same time. This is similar to what a juggler does. First one ball is thrown up into the air, then another is caught and thrown up into the air, and so on. The juggler works so quickly that all the balls seem to be in the air at once. A single-user, multitasking operating system can juggle the execution of several programs (see Figure 4.2). The central processing unit very rapidly takes turns attending to each task so that it seems as if the programs are running simultaneously. For programs that use different computer resources, this works very well. For example, a spreadsheet program would probably run just as fast while a document is printing as it would if the printer were idle. Unless the CPU is powerful, however, running several applications that draw on the same computer resources usually results in some decrease in performance. A spreadsheet program would probably run slower, for instance, while a statistics program is also running because both programs involve substantial numeric processing. For this reason, multitasking operating systems are generally implemented on computers with fairly sophisticated CPUs.

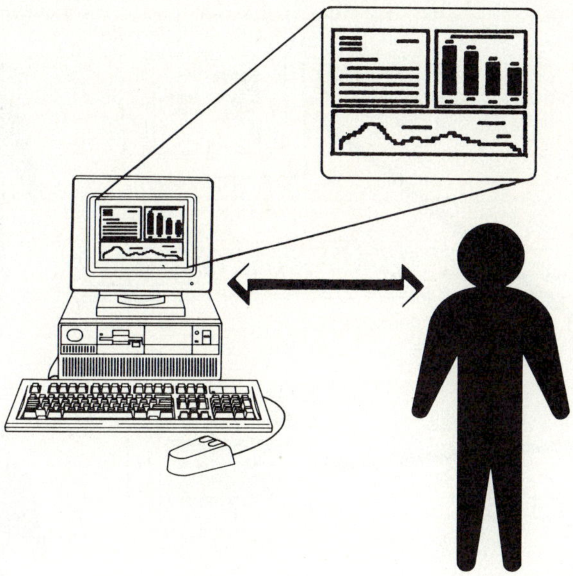

**Figure 4.2 Single-user, Multitasking Operating System**
A multitasking operating system lets you run several programs concurrently.

## Multiuser, Single-tasking

*Several people, one program each*

A single-user, single-tasking operating system under-utilizes the resources of a powerful computer. Single-user, multitasking operating systems are one way to more fully exploit a computer's potential. Another approach is to let several people use the same computer at the same time. Multiuser, single-tasking operating systems let several people each run one program at a time (see Figure 4.3). Each user is equipped with his or her own **terminal**, which is an input/output station consisting of a keyboard and display. The terminal is connected to the central computer. This arrangement is also called **time-sharing**, because the operating system instructs the computer to rapidly switch among users at fixed intervals of time. These intervals, called *time slices*, are so small (typically a few thousandths of a second) that each user gets the illusion of having the computer's complete attention. As long as the CPU isn't saddled with more users than it can handle, its *response time* is quick enough to maintain this illusion. Consequently, time-sharing operating systems are generally implemented on computers with fast, powerful, and sophisticated CPUs. Although they are predominantly found on large computer systems, there are a few multiuser, single-tasking operating systems for some microcomputers.

Besides allowing several users to share the resources of a single computer, multiuser operating systems offer some other benefits, too. The cost per user for expensive hardware devices and software packages is reduced. Multiuser systems enable people to easily share data bases and send messages to one another. This can be especially useful in an office. One disadvantage of multiuser systems, however, is that if the central computer breaks down, everyone's work is brought to a halt.

**Figure 4.3 Multiuser, Single-tasking Operating System**

Also called time-sharing, this type of operating system accommodates several users each running a single program at the same time.

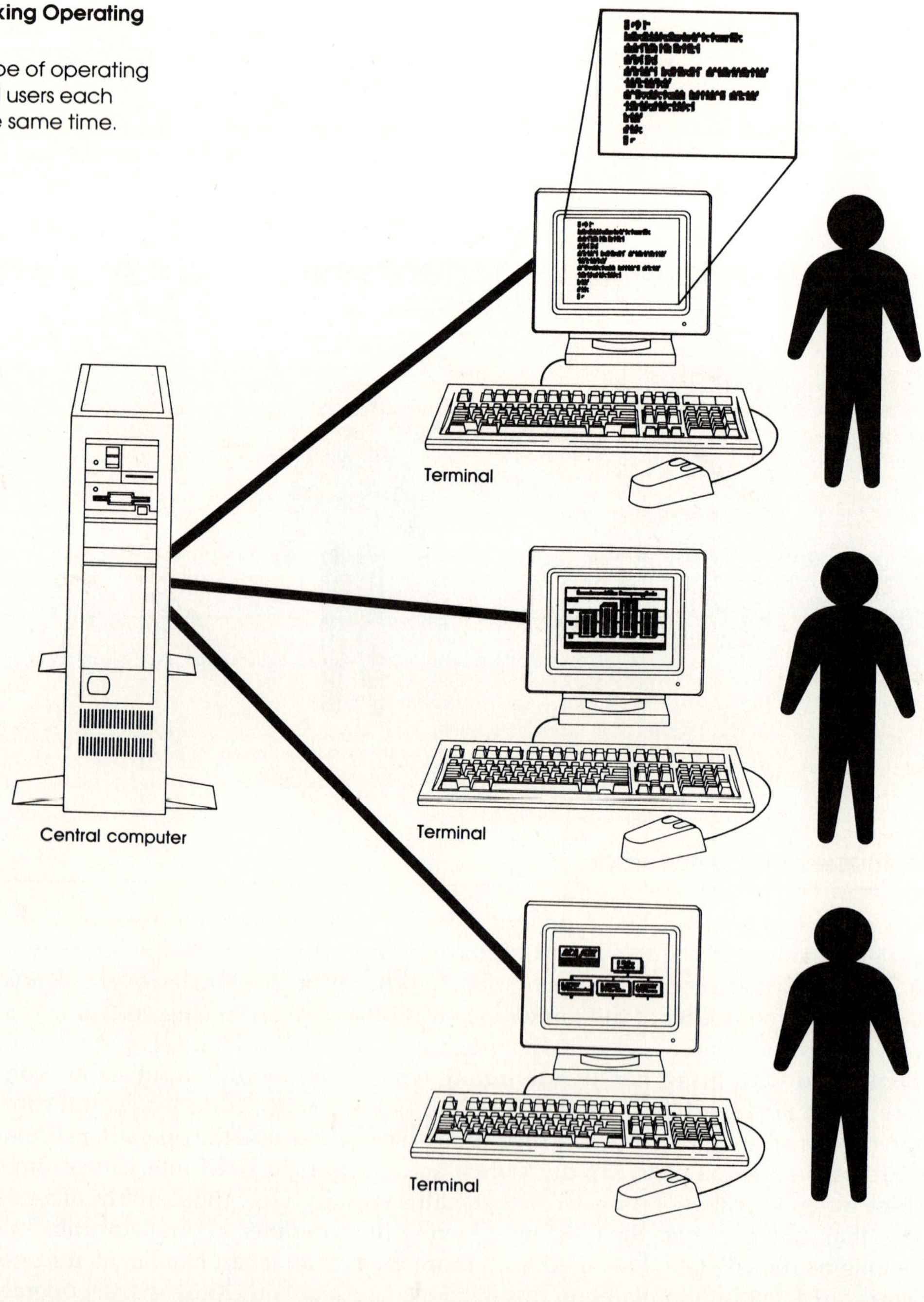

## Multiuser, Multitasking

Some sophisticated operating systems combine the concepts of timesharing and multitasking (see Figure 4.4). This allows several users to each have more than one activity in progress at once. As you can imagine, multiuser, multitasking operating systems are quite sophisticated and generally require powerful computers. Nevertheless, such operating systems are currently available for 16-bit and 32-bit microcomputers. As microcomputer technology advances, it's likely that multiuser, multitasking operating systems will become increasingly popular.

*Several people, several programs*

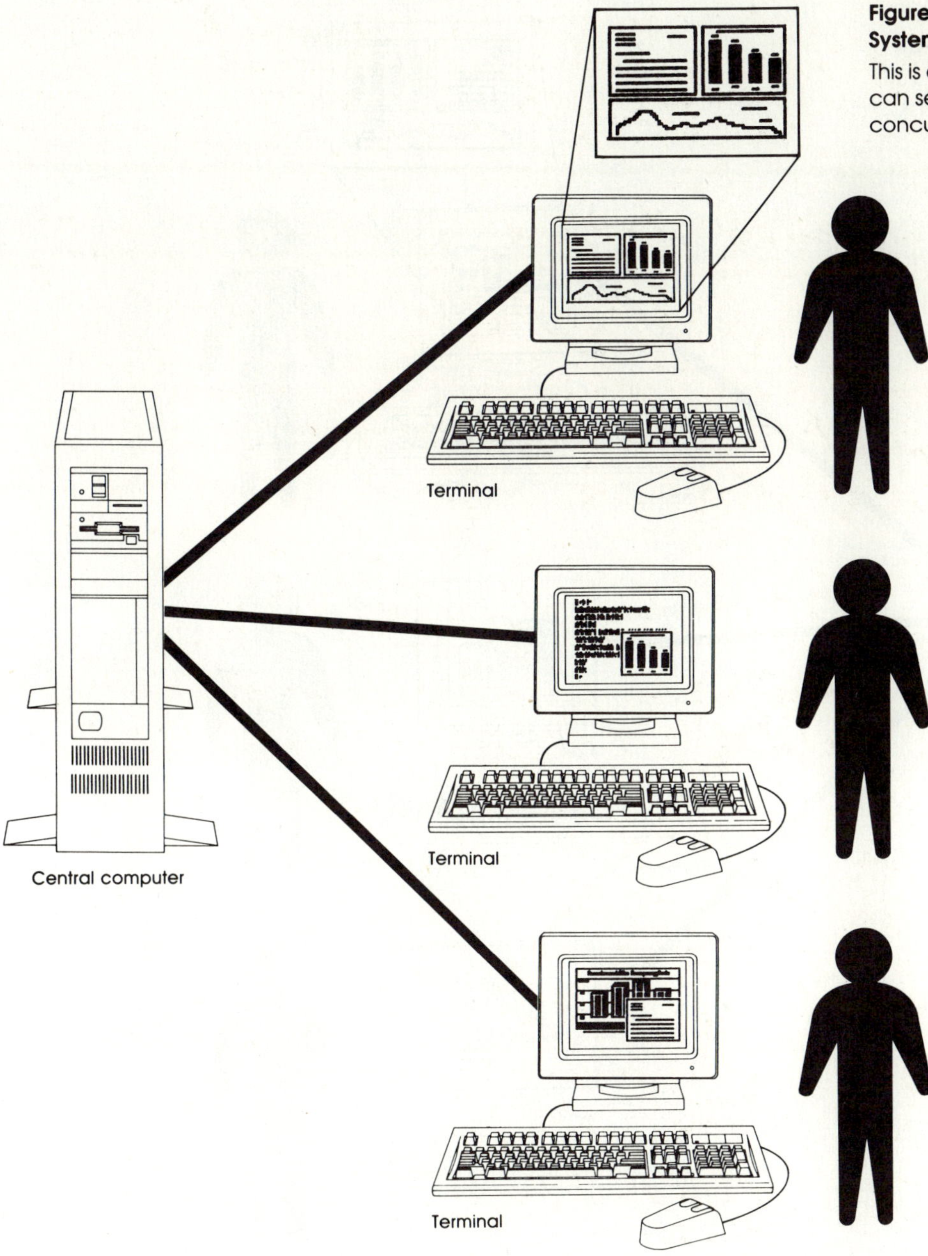


**Figure 4.4 Multiuser, Multitasking Operating System**
This is a sophisticated operating system that can serve several users each running several concurrent programs.

## Multiprocessing

*Several processing units*

Timesharing and multitasking operating systems work by rapidly switching the computer's single CPU between several active users or programs. The primary goal is to get more work done in a given amount of time. Another way computer designers have approached this problem is to construct systems that use more than one processing unit. So, instead of one central processing unit, there may be several equally capable processing units. **Multiprocessing** is the term used to describe such computers and the operating systems that run them (see Figure 4.5). Some multiprocessing systems assign a separate processing unit to each user or program, while

**Figure 4.5 Multiprocessing Operating System**
A true multiprocessing operating system can run only on a computer with several processing units.

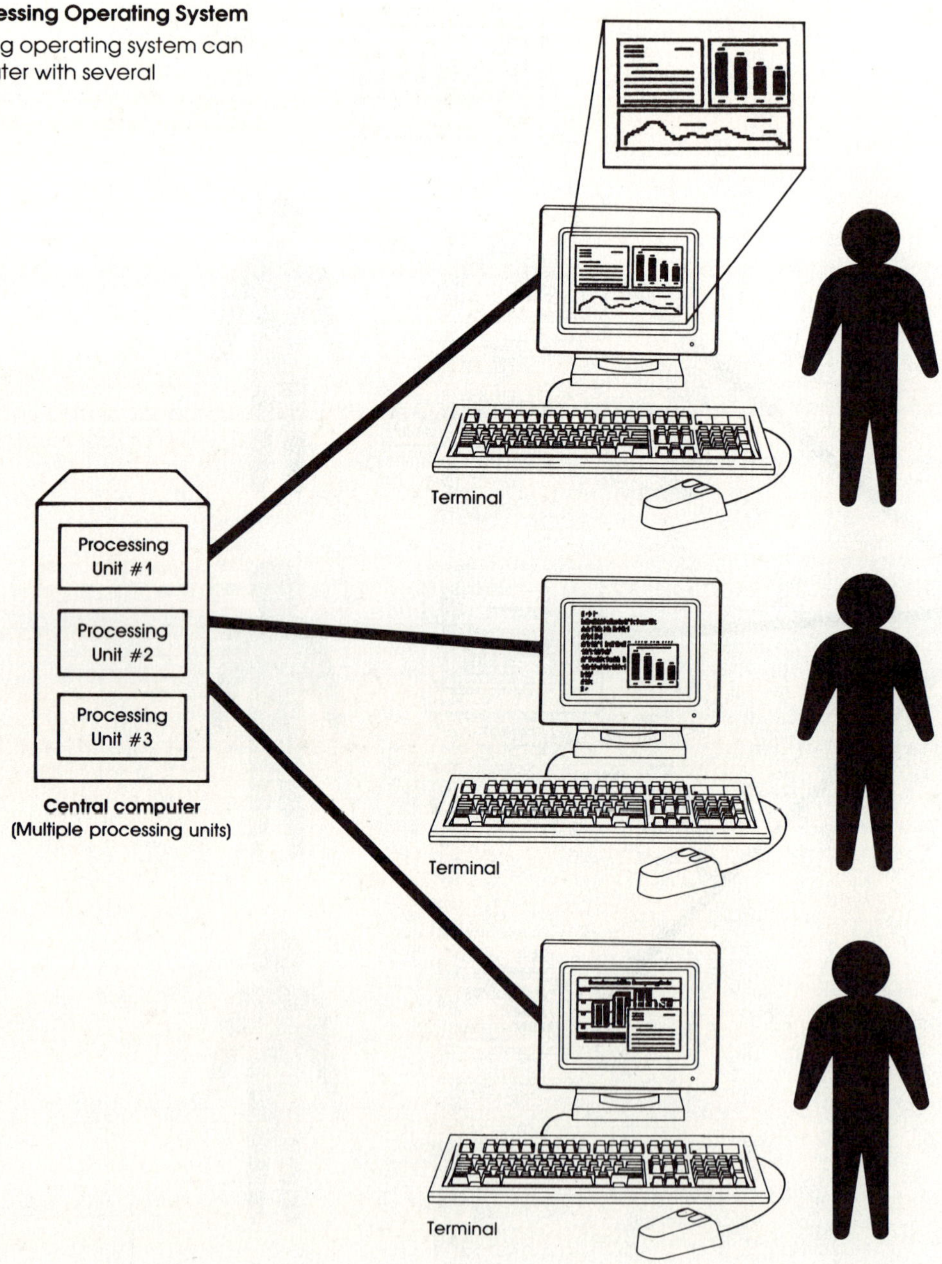

others switch the processing units from user to user or program to program. Unlike timesharing and multitasking operating systems, multiprocessing systems truly serve several users or programs simultaneously. Sometimes programs are broken down into steps that can be accomplished at the same time, and these steps are completed in parallel by the multiprocessing computer. Such *parallel processing* often can perform complex mathematical computations much more quickly than the sequential processing method of computers that have a single CPU. Multiprocessing systems are also generally more reliable than single CPU computers. If one processor fails, multiprocessing computers are usually constructed so that the other processors can automatically take over without the system grinding to a halt.

Multiprocessing operating systems are used primarily on mainframes and supercomputers. There are, however, a few microprocessor-based computers that use multiprocessing. The **Transputer**, for example, is a microprocessor that can be connected with other Transputers to construct a very fast and powerful computer. The T800-20 from INMOS Limited is a 32-bit parallel processing Transputer chip. Many T800-20 chips can be connected together in a box the size of a desktop microcomputer to yield near supercomputer performance. The Atari Abaq is a prototype of a new breed of "personal supercomputers" based on Transputer chips. It uses a new multiprocessing operating system called Helios. Although microcomputer multiprocessing systems are just beginning to appear in the marketplace, their use is expected to increase as Transputer technology advances.

### Networking

*Several stand-alone computers*

A multiprocessing system may have many processing units, but it's still considered a single computer. A networking operating system connects many individual computers (see Figure 4.6). This gives users the advantages of having their own stand-alone computers, while allowing them to share software, data bases, and hardware devices such as disk drives and laser printers. Users can also transmit and receive messages to others on the network. Networking all kinds of computers, especially microcomputers, has become extremely popular lately. Most major microcomputer operating systems either allow networking directly or they can be equipped with additional software that allows individual computers to be connected. Because microcomputer networking is such an important topic, we'll have more to say about it in Chapter 12.

## OPERATING SYSTEM COMPONENTS

*Software layers*

Even simple operating systems are complex software, painstakingly developed by an elite corps of professional programmers. You've seen in this chapter that there are several different classes of operating systems. Most are comprised of several levels or layers of software, each of which performs some specified set of tasks. The innermost layer of an operating system deals with the intimate details of controlling hardware, while the outermost layer handles communication with the computer user. The middle layer performs tasks that help application software deal with both hardware and the user. We call these layers the hardware interface, the application interface, and the user interface (see Figure 4.7).

**Figure 4.6 Networking Operating System**
A networking operating system connects several independent computers.

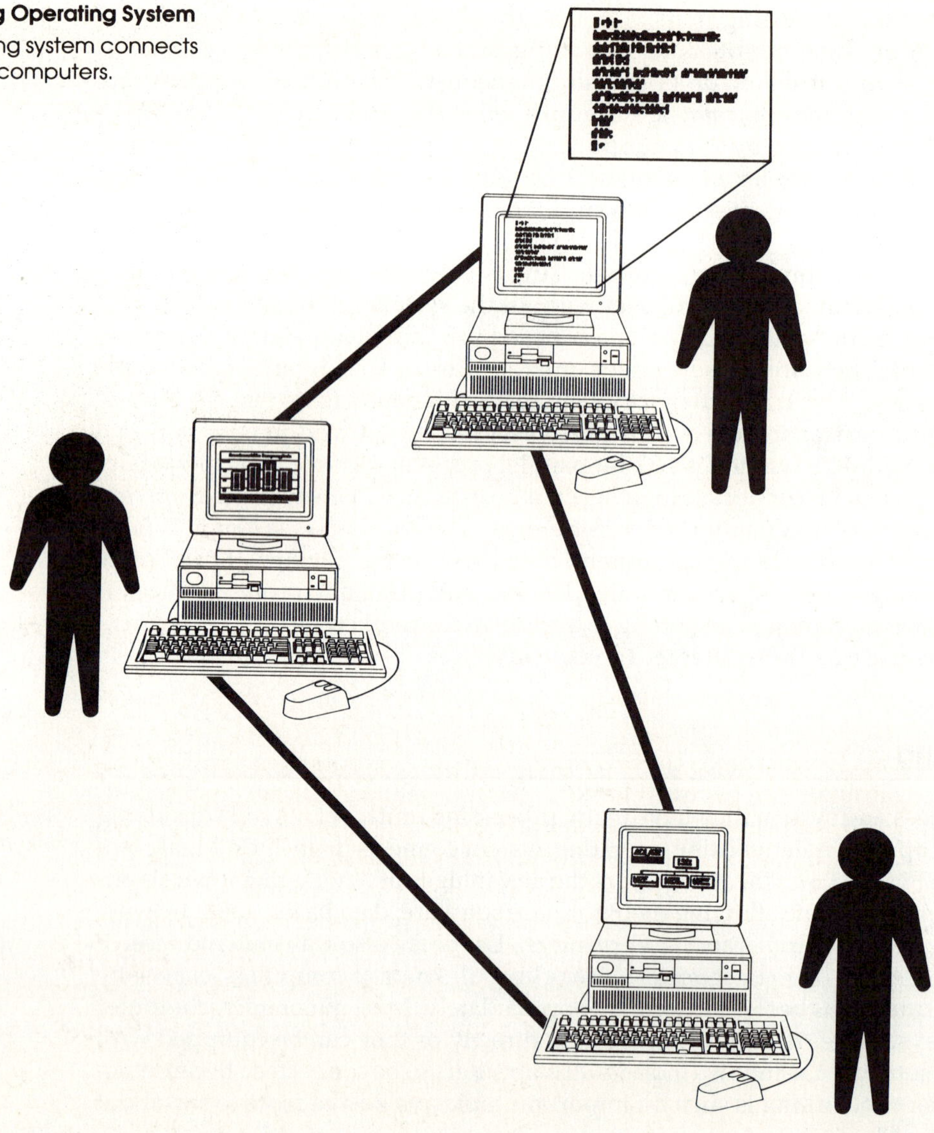

## Hardware Interface

*Controlling the physical components*

The innermost layer of an operating system is the hardware interface. This is the software that controls the physical components, devices, and peripherals of the computer system such as the disk drives, monitor, keyboard, and printer. In many cases, part or all of this software is permanently encoded onto one or more ROM chips installed in the computer. Its job is to accommodate the immediate needs of the computer's hardware so that higher-level software need not be concerned with the details of how this hardware works. On some computers, this hardware interface is called the **BIOS**, or **Basic Input/Output System**.

Fundamentally, the BIOS acts as a connector and translator between the physical components of a computer and the other system software and application packages run on that computer. The BIOS is really software, but because it deals so intimately with computer hardware and is often stored on ROM chips, it's sometimes

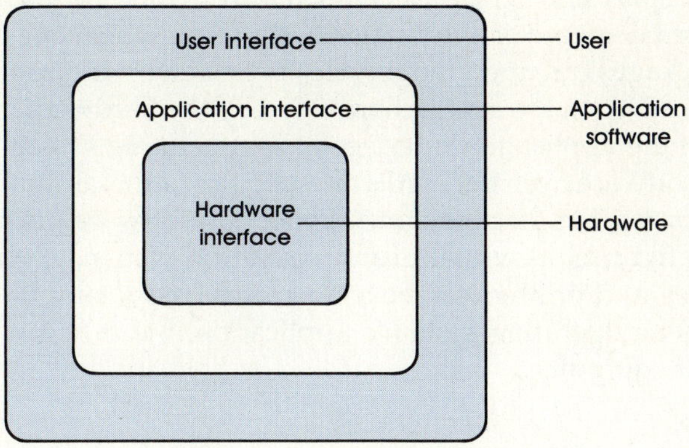


**Figure 4.7 Operating System Layers**
An operating system is made up of three basic layers of software: the hardware interface, the application interface, and the user interface.

called **firmware**. The programs that make up the BIOS perform all kinds of essential activities. Some involve automatically checking components to see if they are working correctly. For example, the BIOS in most microcomputers makes sure that every memory location can be read, checks to see how many and what kind of disk drives are attached, and sends special codes to set up devices such as printers and keyboards. If all the equipment appears functional, the BIOS then loads the rest of the operating system from disk into memory and begins its execution. While the computer is running, programs in the BIOS automatically handle incoming signals from components such as keyboards and modems. These signals, called **interrupts** because they break into the program currently running, tell the CPU that some critical event has occurred, such as a keypress or data transmission. Besides these automatic programs, the BIOS also contains **service programs**, or **system calls**, that can be invoked by other software to perform hardware-related tasks. For example, BIOS services often include programs to erase the display, write a character or draw a dot on the screen, read data from a disk, and send characters to the printer.

## Application Interface

*Working with high-level software*

The services performed by the hardware interface of an operating system are low-level tasks that deal with the physical aspects of computer components. At a higher, more abstract level are the services provided by the application interface of an operating system. These application services perform more complex activities that deal with the computer in a logical, rather than simply physical, fashion. For example, the BIOS provides programs that merely read and write data bytes anywhere on a disk. Most application software, however, cannot deal with data stored randomly on a disk; data must be organized into files. So, the application interface of an operating system provides programs that allow other software to create, write, read, copy, delete, and rename data files in the same fashion no matter which physical storage device is actually being used. Similarly, programs are provided that allow application packages to ignore the particular type of display connected to a computer. While the BIOS may have separate programs for writing a character on a monochrome text display and writing a character on a color graphics display, the application interface takes care of automatically deciding which one to use.

Application packages call upon the services provided by the application interface, which in turn call upon the services provided by the hardware interface. The primary purpose of the application interface of an operating system is to further isolate application software from the hardware specifics of the computer. The practical result of this approach is that the same application software can run on all different computer configurations with the same operating system. A wide variety of monitors, disk drives, and printers can be connected to most computers. Software that effectively uses an operating system's application interface can run on most combinations of this equipment.

## User Interface

*Telling the system what to do*

Unless you're a computer designer or programmer, you probably will never directly use the programs that make up the hardware and application interfaces of an operating system. To be sure, any application packages you run use these programs, but you can probably get along just fine without knowing the details of how they operate. If you use computers at all, however, you'll definitely deal with an operating system's user interface. As we said in Chapter 3, the user interface defines the manner in which people interact with software. The user interface of an operating system specifies how you will tell the computer to run system software and invoke application packages. It also sets the tone for how application packages will interact with users. For example, user-friendly operating systems that have menus, icons, windows, and desktops generally breed application software with similar features (see Figure 4.8).

**Figure 4.8 User-friendly Operating System**
The operating system of the Apple Macintosh microcomputer uses menus, icons, windows, and desktops.

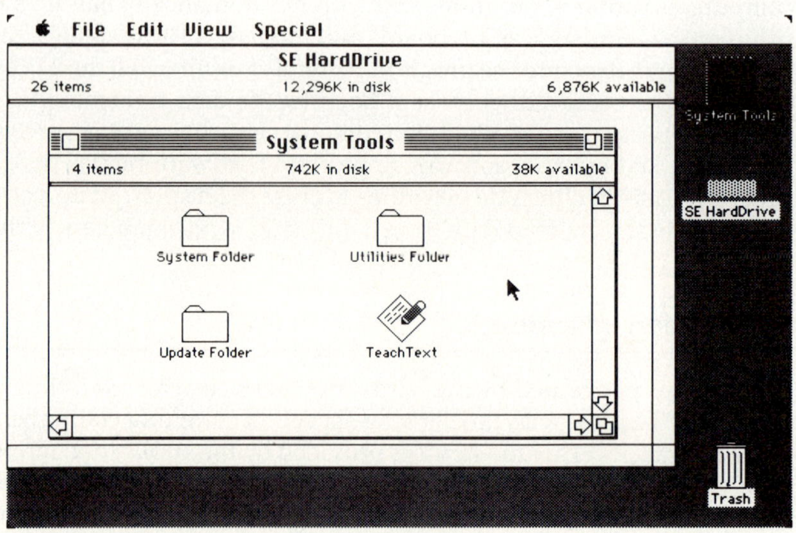


The user interface of an operating system is what actually processes the commands you type or the activities you select with a mouse. It translates your directives into the computer instructions necessary to load and run the programs you choose. While an application package is running, the operating system's user interface generally remains dormant. When you're finished with the package, it regains control and awaits your next command or selection.

## USING OPERATING SYSTEMS

*Managing hardware and software resources*

For most people, learning to use an operating system isn't an end in itself, but rather a means to the ultimate goal of accomplishing useful, educational, or fun activities with a computer. Although an operating system is essential software for every computer, for the average user it can only perform a limited number of specific tasks. You can't write a term paper, balance a budget, maintain a mailing list, or draw a picture with an operating system. Nevertheless, you need an operating system to help you manipulate the software and hardware resources to do these jobs. In the next chapter, we'll look at some of the specific tasks you can perform with one particular operating system. For now, let's concentrate on the general ways in which people use operating systems. For the most part, this consists of running application software, managing secondary storage, controlling computer devices, and programming.

### Running Software

*Loading and starting programs*

Even with an operating system, a computer without other software is of little use to most people. Imagine a hand-held remote control unit for a home video recorder without any blank tapes or prerecorded movies. You may be able to change channels, start recording, stop recording, fast forward, freeze frame, and rewind from the comfort of your favorite couch, but the controller is of little value unless you have a videotape cassette in the machine. The primary purpose of any operating system is to help the user run application software.

#### Application Software

*Programs for useful work*

The most common use of an operating system is to run application software packages. Fortunately, this is the easiest operating system function to learn and use. In fact, it's usually the first operating system procedure most people master. With some operating systems, an application program is normally started by typing its name and pressing the **Enter** or **Return** key. On other computers, a program is executed by positioning an arrow on top of its icon or name on the screen with a mouse and "clicking" the mouse's button once or twice (see Figure 4.9). Once a program is selected, the operating system handles all the details of finding the program on the disk, deciding what memory locations to use, copying the program from disk into memory, preparing the program to be run, and then turning control of the computer over to the program. When the program is finished or terminated by the user, the operating system regains complete control over the computer and waits for the next request.

#### Batch Processing

*Automating a sequence of commands*

A user frequently will run several programs in succession, one after the other. These programs might consist of both application packages and operating system commands and utilities. For example, let's say you first run an operating system utility to put the printer in letter quality mode. Then you use a word processing pack-

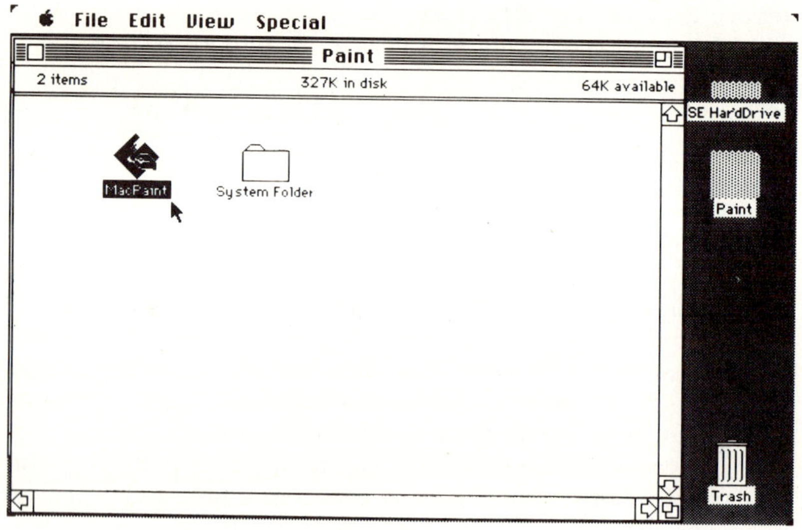


**Figure 4.9 Running an Application Package**
On the Apple Macintosh, a program is started by pointing to its icon and clicking the mouse button twice.

age to update and print certain documents. Finally, you use an operating command to copy the newly updated document files from hard disk to a backup floppy disk. If this exact procedure is followed every day, for instance, it would be nice to somehow automate the sequence of commands. Instead of entering the same sequence of commands every day, you could save time and make it easy for other users who want to follow the same procedure by reducing several commands to just one command.

Many operating systems can do this by **batch processing**. A special type of file, called a **batch file** or **procedure file**, can be created that lists, in the desired order, the separate commands you would otherwise issue directly to the operating system. The batch file is given its own name and saved on a disk along with program and data files. Then, when you want to run that batch of commands, all you have to do is enter a single command: the name of the batch file. Batch processing is a powerful extension of the operating system's ability to run programs. Besides saving time, it can be used to help novice users accurately run complicated sequences of operating system commands. For example, many software developers include batch files on the disks that contain the application packages they sell (see Figure 4.10). These batch files, created by experts, help purchasers by automating the process of installing the new application software on their own computers.

## Managing Storage

*Working with disk files*

Most system software and application programs are stored in files. In addition, virtually all application programs work with data files of some kind. Word processors store documents, spreadsheet programs store worksheets, data base managers store data bases, and graphics programs store pictures, graphs, and charts in files. These program and data files are kept on floppy and hard disks. A primary function of any operating system is to help manage and organize the files kept in secondary storage. To do this, operating systems include small programs that can be run by users to perform common activities such as preparing disks for storage; copying, deleting, renaming, displaying, and printing files; listing the names of files on a disk; switching from one disk drive to another; and organizing files. Although some of these tasks can be done inside certain application packages, it's important to know how to perform them with the operating system. Not every application package can do all of these activities, and you may find that in some instances the services provided by the operating system must be used.

```
echo Copying files to drive %1 . . .
echo █
copy dbase.exe %1
copy dbaseinl.ovl %1
copy dbase.msg %1
if not exist %1config.db copy config.db %1
if not exist %1config.sys copy config.sys %1
:SYS2
echo █
echo Insert the dBASE III PLUS System Disk #2 in drive A.
echo █
pause
if not exist dbase.ovl goto SYS2
echo █
echo Copying files to drive %1 . . .
echo █
copy dbase.ovl %1
copy help.dbs %1
copy assist.hlp %1
if not exist %1dbase.ovl goto ErrDbase
if not exist %1dbase.exe goto ErrDbase
if not exist %1dbase.msg goto ErrDbase
if not exist %1dbaseinl.ovl goto ErrDbase
echo █
echo dBASE III PLUS has been successfully installed.
```

**Figure 4.10 Batch File**

This screen shows part of a batch file included with the dBASE III PLUS data base management package for IBM-compatibles. It helps you install the package on your computer.

## Formatting Disks

*Preparing disks for storage*

One of the most critical jobs done by an operating system is preparing new disks for storage. This activity is necessary because most disks that come from the factory cannot be immediately used by computers. Different operating systems have different methods of storing files on disks, even if they can utilize the same type of disks. For example, both the IBM Personal System/2 and Apple Macintosh computers can use 3.5-inch, double-sided, double-density diskettes, which we discussed in Chapter 2. These computers use different operating systems, however, and require diskettes to be prepared in different ways. This initialization process, called **formatting**, must be completed once before files can be stored on any hard or floppy disk. Some operating systems do this automatically whenever a new, unformatted disk is inserted into a disk drive. Other operating systems require that you explicitly issue a command to set up a new disk. When the same process is applied to erase and reinitialize used disks for storage, it's called **reformatting**. In some ways, formatting a disk is like drawing ruled lines on a blank sheet of paper. The operating system formats disks to set up guidelines and markers delineating how files are to be organized.

## Managing Files

*Erasing, copying, renaming, and printing files*

Once disks are formatted, files can be stored on them. In most cases, new files are created by application programs. Word processors create document files, spreadsheet programs create worksheet files, data base managers create data files, and graphics programs create picture files. After files are created, the operating system can help manage and organize them on disks.

Just as you discard old letters you no longer need, you occasionally may want to erase computer files. Sometimes you may want an extra copy of a file to modify slightly or keep as a backup on another disk. You may want to change the name of an existing file. Perhaps you want to work with a file on a disk drive other than the one the operating system is currently using. Perhaps you want to display the contents of a file on the screen or send it to the printer. Or, you may need a listing of the files currently stored on a particular disk. Operating systems can usually perform all of these activities.

## Organizing Files

*Computer file cabinets*

As you can imagine, people who use computers extensively often generate a large number of files. Before microcomputers were routinely equipped with large-capacity hard disks, this meant that users had to juggle many different diskettes. Organizing files meant physically organizing diskettes by keeping them well labeled and putting them in subdivided boxes, racks, or cabinets. Once hard disks became common, microcomputer operating systems had to be extended to include methods of organizing large numbers of files. Even a modest 20-megabyte hard disk can potentially store thousands of different files. Looking for one particular file among hundreds or thousands is time-consuming and tedious for both users and operating systems.

As a result, most microcomputer operating systems now have **hierarchical** methods of organizing files into groups, allowing you to cluster files into orders or ranks that are subordinate to the one above. These groups of files, sometimes called **subdirectories**, are like file folders that can be nested within one another (see Figure 4.11). Disks can be organized into subdirectories, each of which can contain files and other subdirectories. Operating systems provide commands that create, name, and delete subdirectories. Other commands let you switch the operating system from one subdirectory to another and transfer files among them. Once you're "in" a subdirectory, the files you can directly deal with are generally only those files within it. As the potential capacity of computer storage grows, operating systems and application software must provide increasingly sophisticated methods of organizing and gaining access to files.

**Figure 4.11 Hierarchical File System**
A hierarchical file system lets you group files into different subdirectories on the same disk. Any subdirectory can contain individual files and other subdirectories.

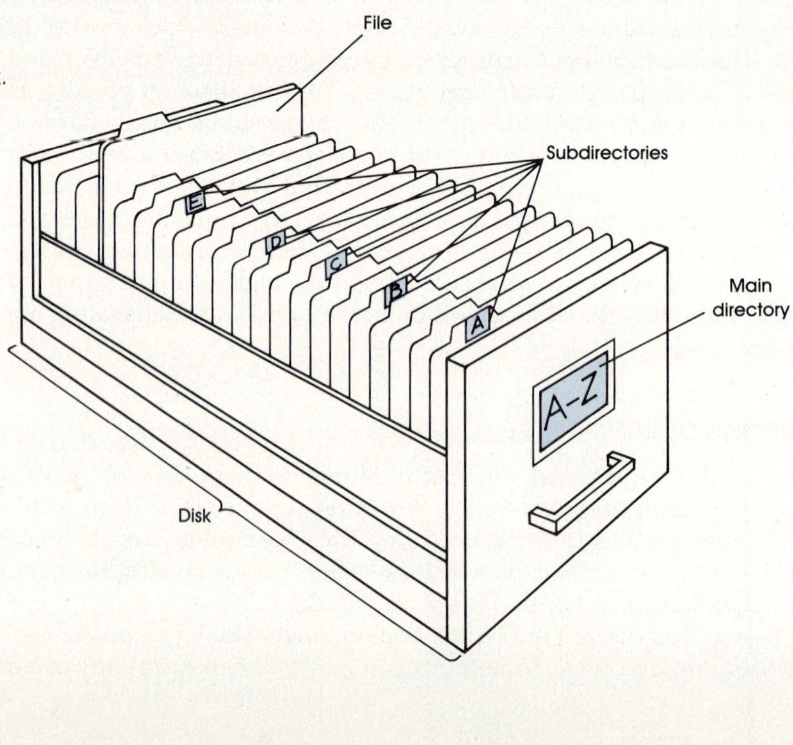

## Controlling Devices

*Managing hardware*

As we said before, most of the components and peripheral devices of a computer system are controlled to some extent by the operating system. Many operating systems also give the user some direct control over hardware. Figure 4.12, for example, shows the Control Panel of the Apple Macintosh operating system, which allows the user to change the operation of the display, keyboard, mouse, real-time clock, memory, and speaker. Most operating systems also allow the user to control the printer and serial interface.

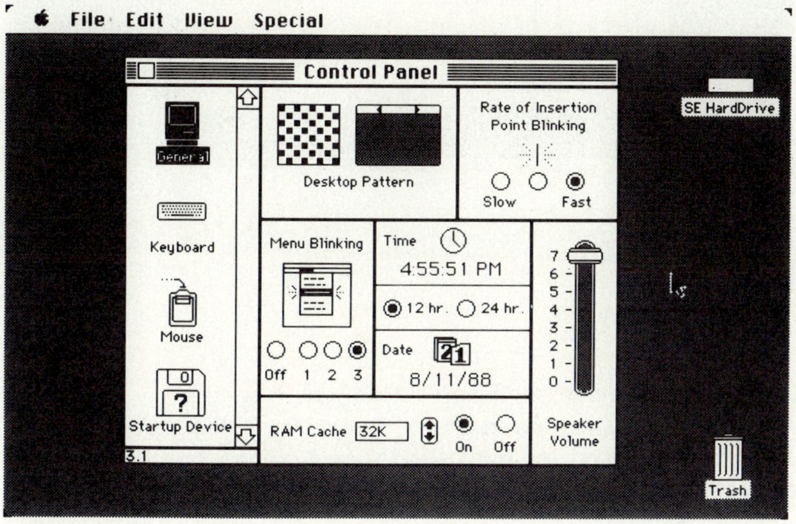


**Figure 4.12 Macintosh Control Panel**
The Macintosh Control Panel lets you change the operation of several hardware devices.

### Display

Many microcomputers have displays that can operate in several different video modes. Some even have two different displays connected. Operating system commands often determine the current video mode and, if two monitors are connected, which one is active. Screen colors and background patterns can be changed on some computers via the operating system. With the Macintosh Control Panel, for example, the user can change the desktop pattern and the blinking rate of menu options and the *insertion point*, which is a type of cursor (see Figure 4.12).

### Keyboard

Some computer keyboards are constructed so that the keys resist slightly and "click" when pressed. On other computers the keys don't physically click, but the operating system generates a simulated click or soft beep whenever a key is pressed. The operating system may have a command that allows the user to shut off and turn on this simulated key-click. In addition, most microcomputer keyboards will automatically repeat a key's code when that key is held down for a certain period of time. Some operating systems allow users to control the rate at which keys repeat and how long a key must be held down before it begins to repeat (see Figure 4.13).

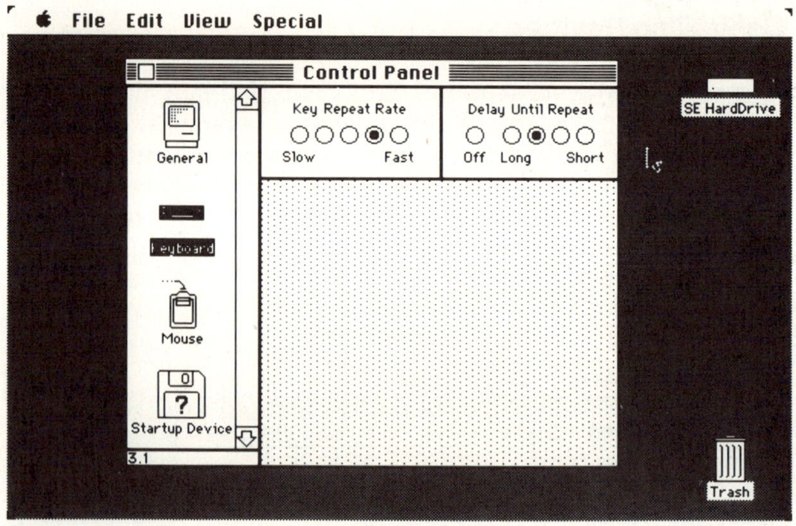


**Figure 4.13 Keyboard Control**
You can select the keyboard repeat rate and how long it takes before a pressed key begins repeating.

## Mouse

For a computer that also uses a mouse, the operating system may have commands that control its function. Users can often set the sensitivity of the mouse buttons and how rapidly the mouse *tracks*, or moves the screen pointer in relation to the physical movement of the mouse on the table top (see Figure 4.14).

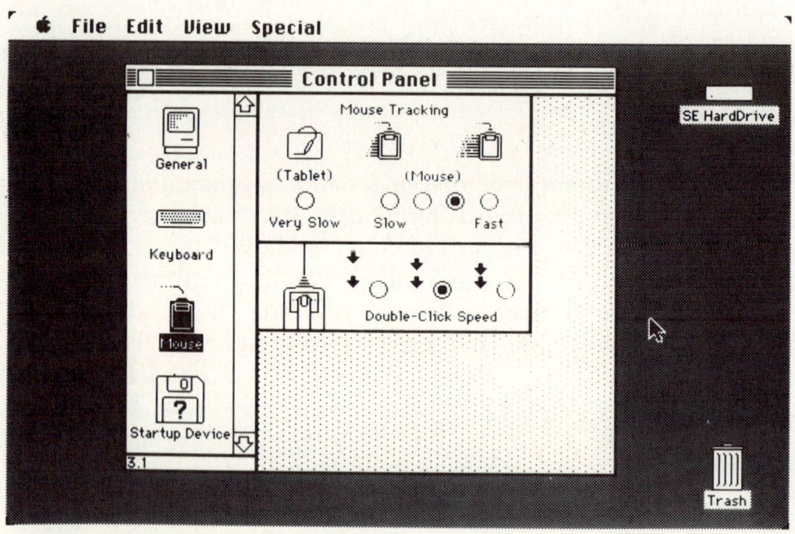


**Figure 4.14 Mouse Control**
You can select the mouse tracking speed and the sensitivity of the mouse button.

## Real-time Clock

Just like ordinary clocks, computer real-time clocks must occasionally be reset so that they accurately report the current date and time. Operating systems include commands that allow you to display the current date and time, as well as change them when the need arises (see Figure 4.12).

## Memory

Some operating systems allow users to control how some RAM is to be used. For example, a **RAM cache** may be used to speed up programs (see Figure 4.12). This is a part of memory specially reserved for applications to hold data that must be frequently retrieved. Instead of going to the disk every time such data is needed, the program saves time by keeping it in the much faster RAM cache. Many operating systems can use a similar concept known as a **RAM disk**. This is an area of memory that is set up to simulate a disk drive. It can be used just like a disk, but since it's really RAM, it operates much more quickly. Operating systems that can have RAM caches and RAM disks often let the user specify how much memory and which particular locations are to be set aside for them.

## Speaker

Most microcomputers have some type of speaker and the circuitry to control it. This speaker may simply be used to emit beeps indicating errors, or it may be part of a sophisticated sound system that can synthesize music and even generate voice output. Many operating systems allow the user to shut off the speaker or set its volume (see Figure 4.12).

## Printer

In addition to having commands to print files, operating systems usually include other commands that control the functions of printers. Printers that have different print modes (such as draft, near-letter-quality, and letter-quality) may be set by an operating system command (see Figure 4.15). Other commands may control how fast to print, which printer to use if more than one is connected, which files are to be printed, and how to terminate printing before a file is completely finished.

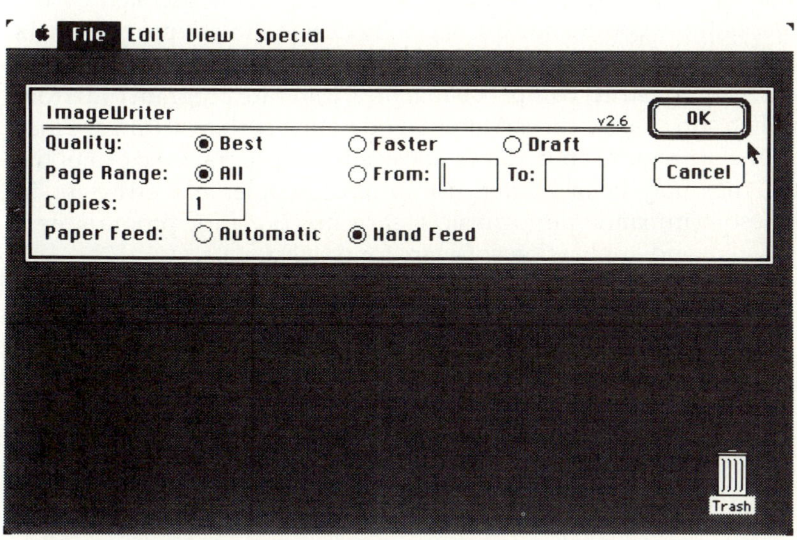


**Figure 4.15 Printer Control**
The operating system of the Apple Macintosh lets you control how your printer works.

### Serial Interface

Computers with serial interfaces connected to modems and other input/output devices often have operating systems that allow users to specify data transmission settings. These choices typically include specifying transmission speed, the method of error checking, the number of data bits sent at a time, and other transmission variables.

## Programming

*Helping programmers create new software*

Most people who use computers have no notion of how to program them. There's nothing wrong with this, of course. After all, most people who drive cars aren't auto mechanics. A great many people do program microcomputers, however, and operating systems usually include features designed to aid software developers. These features include the built-in service programs of the hardware and application interface, along with operating system commands used primarily by programmers. In addition, a wide range of other software is available especially for programmers, including various utilities and languages.

### Services

The small operating system programs that control various hardware devices and perform other common low-level functions are called *services* or *system calls* because software developers can summon them to do certain jobs. Besides saving time and effort, using operating system service calls ensures that software developed with them will work with updated releases of that operating system. System calls are most frequently found in assembly language programs. They are also used directly in high-level language programs to accomplish tasks that may be difficult or even impossible within the confines of those more abstract languages. Operating system services consist of programs to perform activities such as displaying characters, drawing dots and lines, and erasing the screen; determining which keyboard keys have been pressed; reading and writing data on disks; sending data to the printer; and transmitting data over a serial interface.

### Commands

Operating systems may include many esoteric commands rarely invoked by the average user. Most of these commands are specially designed with programmers in mind. For example, some operating systems include commands that compare the contents of files, help construct complex batch files, translate program files from one format to another, and change certain internal operating system settings. Since many of these commands require an in-depth knowledge of programming or of the operating systems, they may be of limited use to most people. Nevertheless, in many instances these commands perform necessary functions for programmers developing both system and application software for the rest of us.

### Utilities

In Chapter 3 we said that utilities are small, special-purpose programs included with operating systems or sold separately. Many such programs are available to help in the process of developing software. For example, operating systems commonly come with programs such as line editors, linkers, and debuggers. A **line editor** is like an extremely primitive word processor that can only work with a single line of text at a time. It's used to create, modify, and display programming language source code and other simple text files. A **linker** is a program used to combine the output files of some programming language translators into a single file that can be run as an executable program. A **debugger** helps detect errors in a program under development by providing ways to monitor and control that program while it runs. Other common utilities designed especially for programmers include programs to cross-reference memory locations, monitor the function of certain hardware components, view the contents of memory and disks, and manage the updates of new software versions.

### Languages

As you know, programmers use programming languages to develop software. Many different programming languages are in common use, and they all require some type of translator program. In most cases, these translators can be classified as either interpreters or compilers. Sometimes a particular language translator is included as an inherent component of a microcomputer or operating system. For example, IBM microcomputers come with a simple BASIC interpreter embedded in a ROM chip and a more advanced BASIC interpreter is included with its most popular operating system. Other programming language translators usually can be purchased from the company that developed the operating system and other software firms.

## IMPORTANT MICROCOMPUTER OPERATING SYSTEMS

*Generic and proprietary systems*

A number of operating systems are commonly used on microcomputers. Some of these are classified as **generic operating systems** because they can be adapted to run on diverse computers. Generic operating systems are typically marketed by software companies that don't have a stake in any one particular brand of computer. **Proprietary operating systems**, on the other hand, usually are developed by a hardware manufacturer or a software firm contracted by a hardware manufacturer. These operating systems are designed specifically for use on computers sold by that hardware manufacturer. Proprietary operating systems are not often licensed by the manufacturer for use on other companies' computers. Both generic and proprietary operating systems are found on microcomputers. Some of the most noteworthy of these operating systems are CP/M, DOS, OS/2, UNIX, ProDOS, and the Apple Macintosh System. Let's briefly examine these operating systems now.

## CP/M

*"Grandfather" of microcomputer operating systems*

**CP/M** stands for *Control Program/Monitor* or *Control Program for Microcomputers.* It was developed in 1973 by Gary Kildall, a software consultant then working for Intel Corporation. The operating system is now sold by Digital Research, a company Kildall founded in 1976. CP/M was the first popular microcomputer operating system sold by an independent software firm. Subsequent microcomputer operating systems have largely replaced CP/M, but it is still used by some loyal devotees. CP/M is noteworthy mainly as the predecessor and early rival of the much more popular DOS, which we will be discussing shortly. Originally designed as a single-user, single-tasking operating system for computers with 8-bit microprocessors such as the Intel 8080 and Zilog Z80 chips, CP/M has been constantly revised and upgraded. There is a version called CP/M-86 that runs on microcomputers that use the 16-bit 8086 family of microprocessors and even a multiuser, multitasking version called MP/M.

CP/M is a relatively simple operating system that can be easily adapted to run on different computers. Kildall isolated all of the machine-specific portions of the operating system and put them into a single BIOS module. No matter which computer the operating system is running on, the remaining parts of the operating system are basically the same. This adaptability coupled with its small size made CP/M the preeminent generic operating system used on many early microcomputers. CP/M has few commands that the user need memorize, but these commands were carefully chosen for their power. Although by today's standards CP/M isn't considered to be particularly user-friendly, it paved the way for the more sophisticated operating systems to come. A large collection of application software packages is still available for machines that run under this "grandfather" of microcomputer operating systems.

## DOS

*World's most popular operating system*

**PC-DOS,** which stands for *Personal Computer Disk Operating System,* was developed in 1981 by Microsoft Corporation for IBM. Microsoft also kept the right to sell the operating system under its own name, **MS-DOS**. Although there are a few very minor differences, PC-DOS and MS-DOS are basically the same operating system. The major distinction is that PC-DOS is sold by IBM for IBM microcomputers, and MS-DOS is sold by Microsoft for IBM-compatible microcomputers. Starting with version 4.0, IBM began calling the operating system *IBM DOS*. Since they are so similar, from now on we'll refer to all of these operating systems generically as **DOS** (see Figure 4.16).

**Figure 4.16 IBM DOS**
This screen shows IBM DOS version 4.00 after the CHKDSK (Check Disk) command has been executed.

```
Current date is Thu 08-11-1988
Enter new date (mm-dd-yy):
Current time is  7:59:51.50p
Enter new time:


IBM DOS Version 4.00
          (C)Copyright International Business Machines Corp 1981, 1988
          (C)Copyright Microsoft Corp 1981-1986

A>chkdsk
Volume Serial Number is 293C-0FF1

   1213952 bytes total disk space
     69632 bytes in 2 hidden files
    884224 bytes in 41 user files
    260096 bytes available on disk

       512 bytes in each allocation unit
      2371 total allocation units on disk
       508 available allocation units on disk

    524288 total bytes memory
    411920 bytes free
```

Since the original IBM Personal Computer was introduced in 1981, DOS has become the dominant operating system for 16-bit computers that use the Intel 8088, 8086, and 80286 chips. At this time, it's also still the most popular operating system for powerful 32-bit microcomputers that use the Intel 80386 microprocessor. More microcomputers use DOS than any other operating system, and there are literally thousands of application packages available that run under it. According to *Forrester's Professional Automation Report*, an estimated 3.3 million copies of DOS were sold in 1988 alone. IBM estimates that around 20,000 different application packages have been developed to run under DOS.

Microsoft did not develop DOS on its own, however. In 1981, it purchased an operating system called QDOS (short for *Quick and Dirty Operating System*) from Seattle Computer Products and revised the system for IBM. IBM offered it as PC-DOS, the standard operating system on its first family of microcomputers. When IBM-compatibles appeared in the marketplace, Microsoft sold the operating system under the MS-DOS label. When IBM and IBM-compatible microcomputers became runaway bestsellers, DOS gained its immense popularity in home, school, and especially business markets.

Conceptually similar in some ways to CP/M, DOS also borrows concepts from the UNIX operating system, which we'll be discussing shortly. Although DOS was originally designed to have the same general "feel" as CP/M, it was equipped with some important improvements. Working together, IBM and Microsoft have continually upgraded DOS since 1981. Today, DOS is a powerful single-user, single-tasking operating system equipped to handle the latest hardware developments. Although it's not particularly easy for novices to fully master, DOS is a fairly straightforward operating system with a huge following of devoted users. Because DOS runs on many different brands of computers, it's not classified as a proprietary operating system. It is, however, basically limited to the Intel 8086 family of microprocessors. For this reason, DOS is not a fully generic operating system either. Nevertheless, because of the continuing popularity of IBM-compatible microcomputers, DOS will likely remain the most widely used operating system for some time.

## OS/2

*Second generation operating system*

IBM and Microsoft joined forces again in 1987. They announced **OS/2**, a single-user, multitasking operating system designed for IBM and IBM-compatible microcomputers that use the Intel 80286 and 80386 microprocessors (see Figure 4.17). OS/2 does not run on IBM and IBM-compatible machines that use the 8088 and 8086 chips. This long-awaited operating system, however, more fully utilizes the power of the 80286 and 80386 chips in ways that DOS never could. OS/2 is a complex operating system that allows programs direct access to almost 16 megabytes of memory and provides true multitasking. Although it requires a new generation of application packages to make full use of this power, OS/2 can run most existing DOS programs in its *DOS Compatibility Box*. This is a special environment that can run a single DOS application at a time. Other applications designed especially for OS/2 can be concurrently run as separate tasks while a DOS program executes in the DOS Compatibility Box.

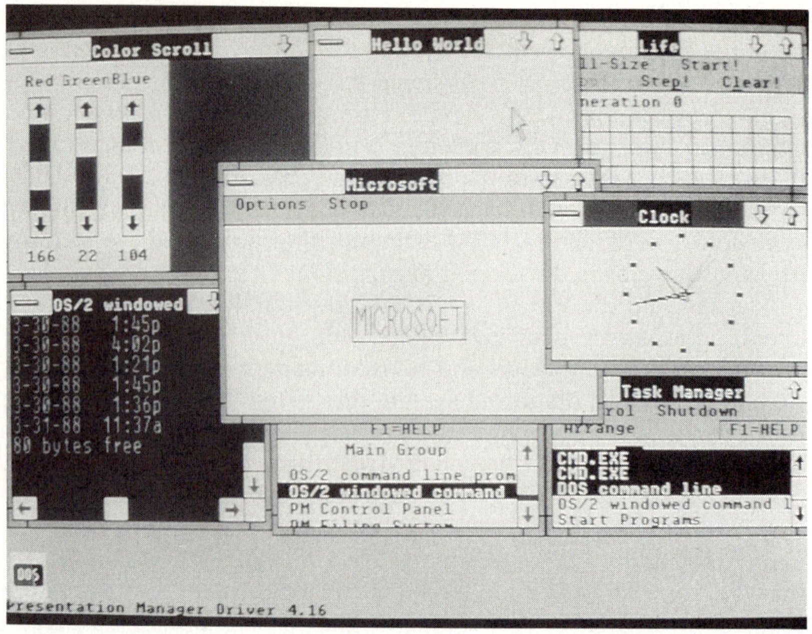


**Figure 4.17 OS/2**
Here you see OS/2, the advanced operating system for high-end IBM and IBM-compatible microcomputers.

At its most basic level, OS/2 appears to be very similar to DOS. It has the same command-oriented user interface and duplicates many of the existing DOS commands. Software applications are run from OS/2 just like they are from DOS: by typing their name and pressing the **Enter** key. The difference is that with a special combination of keypresses you can switch the entire display screen to a different task and begin a new program before the other program is finished. Each of these different *screen groups*, as they are called, can run a single program or a group of programs. OS/2 can maintain as many as sixteen simultaneous screen groups, each running different programs. One special screen group is reserved for the DOS Compatibility Box we mentioned before, which can only run a single DOS program at a time.

The first version of OS/2 was released with only this basic command-oriented user interface. Subsequent versions of OS/2, however, include a graphics-based windowing environment called the *Windows Presentation Manager*. The Presentation Manager is itself a separate screen group that can run multiple programs. Although the simple command-oriented user interface is fine for full-screen programs that do not use graphics, the Windows Presentation Manager is much better for graphics applications.

A disadvantage of OS/2 is that it is a new operating system, so relatively few applications have been written especially for it. It's also more expensive and requires more memory than DOS. However, OS/2 does provide some compatibility with the huge base of existing DOS applications. It also has the potential to run extremely powerful application software. IBM and Microsoft hope that OS/2 will become the standard operating system on 80286 and 80386 computers. The foundations established by OS/2 could carry such microcomputers through to almost the end of this century.

## UNIX

*Popular powerhouse*

**UNIX** is a multiuser, multitasking operating system originally developed at AT&T's Bell Laboratories in the early 1970s. Ken Thompson, a staff member at Bell Labs, led the group which developed the first assembly language version of UNIX in 1969. In 1972 Dr. Dennis Ritchie rewrote the operating system in his new high-level programming language C. At the time, before the advent of microcomputers, UNIX was designed to run on PDP-7 and PDP-11 minicomputers made by Digital Equipment Corporation. Since then, UNIX has been adapted to run on all kinds of computers, large and small. It's perhaps the best example of a truly generic operating system (see Figure 4.18).

```
login: ernie
Password:
You have mail.
$
$ date
Mon Jan 02 09:25:52 CST 1989
$ who
jcd      tty0     Jan 02 08:13
ernie    tty2     Jan 02 09:25
fred     tty4     Jan 02 08:22
ellen    tty5     Jan 02 09:01
vulcan   tty7     Jan 02 07:14
rah      tty8     Jan 02 09:14
$ mail
From vulcan Mon Jan 02 08:01 CST 1989
Call me sometime today about the documentation for STATUS.

?
From ellen Mon Jan 02 09:10 CST 1989
How about lunch today at Garcia's?

? d
$
$ mail ellen
Sounds good.  I haven't had pizza all week!  I'll meet you there at noon.
```

**Figure 4.18 UNIX**
This screen shows part of a typical session with UNIX, a popular operating system for multiuser computers.

At first, UNIX was used internally at Bell Labs. In 1973 it was licensed to nonprofit organizations. This made UNIX available to many educational institutions. By 1975 UNIX had become very popular at colleges and universities. As students and faculty members left school, they took their enthusiasm for UNIX with them. Consequently, UNIX has become increasingly popular with both scientists and business people. Today, about 10 percent of all the computers in the world run some version of UNIX. The market research firm International Data Corporation estimates that 22 percent of computers worldwide will be running UNIX by 1991.

About 95 percent of the UNIX operating system is written in the high-level programming language C. The rest is written in assembly language. As a result, UNIX can be easily adapted to run on almost any computer. This is a major attraction, but UNIX also has many other desirable features. It can accommodate multiple users, each of whom can run several concurrent tasks. UNIX is ideal for software developers because it generally comes with hundreds of utility programs that perform many useful chores and can be easily incorporated into programs being developed. In fact, many UNIX applications can be entirely constructed from this rich set of ready-made, built-in utilities.

Although UNIX is loved and cherished by many computer scientists and software developers, it also has its drawbacks as a microcomputer operating system. Computer novices often find UNIX difficult to learn, but the operating system is so flexible that it can be enhanced to present a more friendly user interface. Perhaps the biggest problem some people have with UNIX is that several different versions are in common use, none of them completely compatible. Even AT&T has a few distinct varieties of UNIX. One popular microcomputer version of UNIX, called XENIX, is sold by Microsoft for IBM and IBM-compatible machines that use the 80286 and 80386 microprocessors. Apple also has a version of UNIX called A/UX for the Macintosh II. Some versions of UNIX were designed primarily for educational and scientific uses, so they may lack features important for business use. Another drawback is that fewer application packages are available for UNIX systems than there are for other popular operating systems such as DOS. Nevertheless, UNIX is an extremely influential operating system whose use is expected to become even more widespread.

## ProDOS

*For the Apple II family*

In 1983 Apple introduced **ProDOS**, a new single-user, single-tasking proprietary operating system for the Apple II family of microcomputers. It's faster and represents a significant improvement over previous Apple II operating systems, such as Apple DOS 3.3. ProDOS offers advanced features such as a hierarchical file system that allows subdirectories, a maximum file size of 16 megabytes, support for high-capacity hard disk drives, and the ability to handle interrupt signals from hardware devices. These capabilities allow software developers to write advanced and highly interactive applications such as word processors, spreadsheets, data base managers, graphics programs, and communications and networking packages.

Although many Apple II owners still use the older Apple DOS 3.3 operating system, ProDOS is now the preferred operating system. Most new Apple II application software runs under ProDOS. Because ProDOS disks are formatted differently than DOS 3.3 disks, there are some incompatibilities between the two operating systems. This means that some programs and data files created under Apple DOS 3.3 won't work under ProDOS. Apple does include a utility to convert programs and data files between the two systems, but some Apple DOS 3.3 programs may not be convertible. Since March of 1984, ProDOS has been the standard operating system shipped with new computers of the Apple II family. Because so many Apple II computers are in current use, ProDOS has become a popular microcomputer operating system.

## Apple Macintosh System

*User-friendly trend setter*

The original Apple Macintosh microcomputer, introduced in 1984, utilized the powerful 32-bit Motorola 68000 microprocessor. This microcomputer, which evolved from the earlier Apple Lisa line, was revolutionary in design and achieved a high degree of user friendliness. Most of this was due to its specially designed operating system, which had little in common with DOS or any other existing microcomputer operating system. The advanced Macintosh operating system had its roots in the Smalltalk programming language developed at Xerox's Palo Alto Research Center in the 1970s and borrowed many easy-to-use features originally included in the Xerox 8010 Star Information System. Early versions of the Macintosh operating system were strictly single-user, single-tasking. More recent versions, however, include an accessory called the **MultiFinder** that adds some multitasking capabilities to the newer Macintosh computers (see Figure 4.19). These include the

Macintosh Plus, the Macintosh SE, the Macintosh II, which has a Motorola 68020 microprocessor, and the Macintosh IIx, which has a 68030 chip.

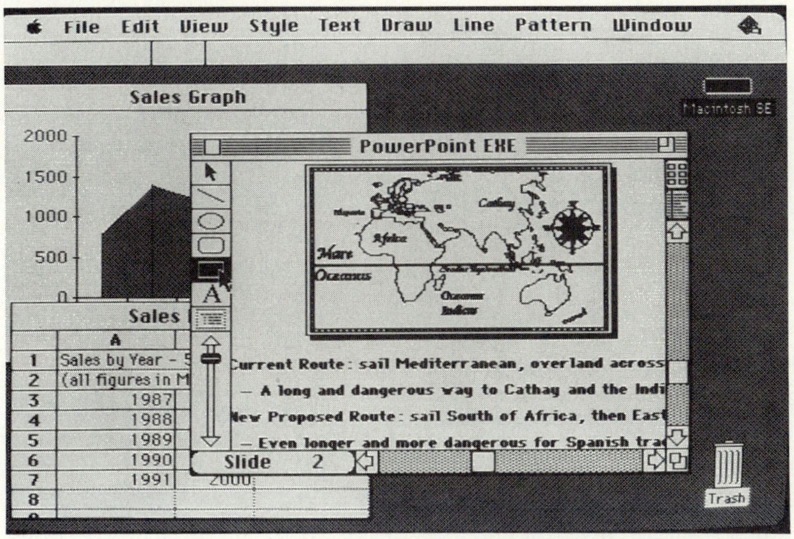


**Figure 4.19 MultiFinder**
The MultiFinder is a multitasking accessory to the Apple Macintosh operating system that lets you switch between several programs on your screen at the same time.

The Macintosh operating system is made up of several levels. At the top level are the MultiFinder and the **Finder**. Both of these are system programs, each stored in its own disk file. They manage the Macintosh "desktop" (see Figure 4.8) by letting you run application programs, set up disks, and organize, copy, and delete files. Older Macintoshes came with just the Finder, which allows you to run only one application program at a time. The newest Macintoshes also include the MultiFinder, which lets you open up several windows with a different program running in each one and lets you rapidly switch between these windows. Although this sounds like multitasking, the current version of the MultiFinder isn't a true multitasking system. Only the program in the currently selected window is fully active. Certain specially designed programs can run in the background, however, and perform unattended, time-consuming tasks such as printing documents and making backup copies of disks.

Below the MultiFinder and the Finder is an accompanying file, called the System file. The System file contains typefaces, graphic images, text messages, and some of the program code that makes up the Macintosh operating system. At the lowest level of the Macintosh operating system is a powerful set of subprograms permanently encoded in a ROM chip that is built into the computer.

The main idea underlying the Macintosh operating system is that the computer should adapt to the user instead of the other way around. It has an exceptional user interface that allows you to perform many tasks quickly and easily. You instruct the computer to perform tasks by using a mouse to manipulate graphic objects on the screen and select options from pull-down menus. These graphic objects, called **icons**, are symbols for files, file folders, actions to be performed, or application programs to be run. For example, to delete a file from a disk, you simply point to the icon representing that file, hold down the mouse button to capture the icon, drag the file icon over to a trash can symbol, and release the mouse button. With little instruction, most users can quickly learn to operate the Macintosh. This friendly operating system encourages experimentation and is just plain fun to use.

The Apple Macintosh and its operating system are a proprietary system. Apple holds and tightly controls the patents for many of the Macintosh hardware components and the copyrights for the system software. Apple has not licensed these patents and copyrights to other manufacturers, so there are no legal Macintosh clones. There are some modified Macintoshes sold by a few companies, but these are just Apple Macintoshes that have been taken apart and reassembled in a different form, for example as a laptop computer. By keeping such tight controls over its microcomputers, Apple can maintain a high profit margin, but this means that the use of the Macintosh operating system is not nearly as widespread as other operating systems, such as DOS and UNIX. Nevertheless, there are still several million Apple Macintoshes currently in use.

## The Real World

### The Lure of UNIX

Gary D. Handler, the executive in charge of computer systems for Shearson, Lehman Brothers' trading floor, is a UNIX convert. After considerable reluctance, he agreed to base his company's computerized trading operations on this much-ballyhooed operating system. Now he believes he's ready for the future.

Operating system software provides basic instructions for a computer's operation. AT&T's UNIX is one of the stars of the operating system market. The 1986 market for UNIX-based computers was valued at $3.7 billion, up 37 percent from 1985, according to industry analysts.

What makes UNIX so popular is that it can run on computers of different sizes and brands, although sometimes slight modifications are necessary. Users can build networks of many kinds of computers. By contrast, property systems, such as those of Digital Equipment Corp. and Apple, run only on machines built by those companies.

The Air Force was so taken by UNIX that it announced a $4.5 billion contract recently for computers that use the operating system. The company that won the contract would provide more than 20,000 mid-size computers, printers, and maintenance to the Air Force, Army, and defense agencies around the world. The contract's goal was to cut costs and increase efficiency by using the UNIX standard for all computer purchases.

Source:
John Wilke, "Digital, Wang Drop Bid for Air Force Contract," *The Boston Globe,* January 6, 1988, p. 57.

## Summary

- *What operating systems do.* Operating systems control hardware, manage software, and interact with users.
- *The basic types of computer operating systems.* The types of operating systems include single-user, single-tasking; single-user, multitasking; multiuser, single-tasking; multiuser, multitasking; multiprocessing; and networking.
- *The fundamental components of an operating system.* An operating system is composed of layers of software including the hardware interface, the application interface, and the user interface.

- *How people use operating systems.* People use operating systems to run application software, manage secondary storage, control computer devices, and to develop programs.
- *Several important microcomputer operating systems.* The major microcomputer operating systems include CP/M, DOS, OS/2, UNIX, ProDOS, and the Apple Macintosh System.

## Key Terms

As an extra review of this chapter, try defining the following terms. If you have trouble with any of them, refer to the page number listed.

batch file (procedure file) (128)
batch processing (128)
BIOS (Basic Input/Output System) (125)
CP/M (135)
debugger (135)
DOS (PC-DOS, MS-DOS) (136)
Finder (141)
firmware (125)
formatting (129)
generic operating system (135)
hierarchical (130)
interrupt (125)
line editor (134)
linker (135)
memory-resident (RAM resident) (118)
MultiFinder (140)
multiprocessing (122)
multitasking (118)
OS/2 (137)
ProDOS (140)
proprietary operating system (135)
RAM cache (133)
RAM disk (133)
reformatting (129)
service program (system call) (125)
single-tasking (117)
subdirectory (130)
terminal (119)
time-sharing (119)
UNIX (139)

## Review Questions

1. List three broad categories of activities performed by operating systems.
2. List five specific hardware-control tasks performed by operating systems.
3. List five specific software-control tasks performed by operating systems.
4. How might you tell an operating system to run a program?
5. What are some factors used in the classification of operating systems?
6. What is the simplest and most common type of operating system?
7. Describe one instance in which multitasking might be useful.
8. What are some advantages of time-sharing operating systems?
9. What kind of operating systems allow users to each run several different programs concurrently?
10. What kind of computers and operating systems serve several users and/or several programs in a truly simultaneous fashion?
11. What is the difference between multiprocessing and networking?
12. What are the basic component layers of an operating system?

13. Where is an operating system's BIOS often stored?
14. What is the difference between the hardware and application interfaces?
15. What is the most common use of an operating system?
16. Why aren't diskettes generally formatted at the factory?
17. Why are hierarchical methods of organizing files into subdirectories used in many operating systems?
18. How do some operating systems allow users to control part of memory to speed up their work?
19. What programmer utility helps detect errors in software under development?
20. What is currently the single most popular microcomputer operating system?

## Multiple Choice

1. Which of the following tasks is not performed by operating systems?
   (a) controlling disk drives (b) loading programs into memory
   (c) processing user commands (d) calculating statistics
2. What is the simplest and most common type of operating system for microcomputers?
   (a) single-user, single-tasking (b) single-user, multitasking
   (c) multiuser, single-tasking (d) multiprocessing
3. Which of the following types of operating systems is also called time-sharing?
   (a) single-user, single-tasking (b) single-user, multitasking
   (c) multiuser, single-tasking (d) multiprocessing
4. Which type of operating system connects many individual, stand-alone computers?
   (a) single-user, single-tasking (b) multiuser, multitasking
   (c) multiprocessing (d) networking
5. What is the innermost layer of an operating system?
   (a) hardware interface (b) application interface
   (c) user interface (d) serial interface
6. Which operating system layer allows software to create, write, read, copy, delete, and rename files in the same fashion no matter which storage device is being used?
   (a) hardware interface (b) application interface
   (c) user interface (d) serial interface
7. Which operating system layer processes commands and menu selections?
   (a) hardware interface (b) application interface
   (c) user interface (d) serial interface
8. What is the most common use of an operating system?
   (a) maintaining mailing lists (b) running application packages
   (c) creating application packages (d) controlling modems

9. What feature do many operating systems provide for automating a sequence of commands?
   (a) menus (b) icons
   (c) batch files (d) utilities

10. Many operating systems help you organize files through the use of
    (a) utilities. (b) menus.
    (c) formatting. (d) subdirectories.

11. Which type of utility helps programmers combine the output of programming language translators into executable programs?
    (a) line editor (b) linker
    (c) debugger (d) system call

12. Which was the first popular generic operating system for microcomputers?
    (a) CP/M (b) DOS
    (c) OS/2 (d) UNIX

13. Which operating system runs on the original IBM Personal Computer?
    (a) ProDOS (b) DOS
    (c) OS/2 (d) Apple Macintosh System

14. Which of the following operating systems is designed especially for IBM and IBM-compatibles that use the Intel 80286 and 80386 microprocessors?
    (a) CP/M (b) DOS
    (c) OS/2 (d) Apple Macintosh System

15. Which of the following is a multiuser, multitasking operating system that has been adapted to run on all kinds of computers, large and small?
    (a) CP/M (b) ProDOS
    (c) OS/2 (d) UNIX

## Projects

1. Several popular microcomputers have a variety of operating systems available for them. For example, an IBM Personal System/2 Model 80 can run DOS, OS/2, CP/M-86, XENIX, and several other less popular systems not mentioned in this chapter. Investigate the various operating systems for a computer such as the IBM PS/2 Model 80. Write a report that enumerates some of the major differences between these operating systems. If you owned such a computer, which operating system would you choose? Why?

2. Most operating systems are constantly upgraded by the manufacturer. It's not uncommon for a new version of a particular operating system to be released every year or so. In most cases, the upgrade is prompted by advancements in computer hardware. Choose one of the operating systems discussed in this chapter and research its history. Write a report that lists each major release and the reason for the upgrade. Computer books and past issues of computer magazines such as *PC Magazine*, *Byte*, *A+*, and *MacWorld* are good sources of information.

3. As microcomputer hardware becomes more advanced, the trend is toward more sophisticated operating systems. Many newer computers either already have multitasking operating systems or have programmers working furiously to develop them. No doubt the expert "power users" will find ample opportu-

nity to apply multitasking to their everyday work, but what about average users? Is it really that helpful to be able to run sixteen different programs at once? Or are single-tasking operating systems already powerful enough for most people? Look through some computer magazines for reviews of multitasking operating systems. Write a report that presents the pros and cons of multitasking operating systems as compared to single-tasking operating systems.

4. Choose one of the specific operating systems we've discussed in this chapter and try to find out more about it. Prepare a report that details the system's most important features. If you can gain access to a computer that runs the system, learn how to use it. Discuss how easy or difficult you found it to use and why.

# 5

# Operating System Details: DOS

## In This Chapter

## PREVIEW

According to *Business Week*, some 10 million IBM and IBM-compatible microcomputers were being used in businesses around the world by the middle of 1987. Joseph R. "Rod" Canion, president of Compaq Computer Corporation, figures that customers have spent $80 billion on IBM PCs, IBM-compatibles, and the hardware and software that work with them. IBM sold approximately 2.7 million microcomputers in 1988. Compaq, the leading "clone" manufacturer and Number 2 business computer maker in the United States, sold around 500,000 that same year. The Number 3 business computer manufacturer is Apple, which makes machines that are not IBM-compatible, unless they are fitted with special equipment. Frederic E. Davis, Editor-in-Chief of *MacUser* magazine, estimates that IBM and IBM-compatibles outnumber Apple Macintoshes in the marketplace by six to one. Clearly, IBM and IBM-compatibles are by far the most popular class of microcomputer. The overwhelming majority of these machines are running DOS.

After the original IBM Personal Computer was unveiled in 1981, DOS quickly became popular in offices, large corporations, and other businesses where IBM has traditionally wielded a great deal of influence. As soon as various hardware manufacturers started selling lower-cost IBM-compatible computers, DOS also began popping up in small businesses, organizations, and institutions as well as schools, libraries, and homes with tight budgets. Because of this "hardware explosion," many software developers began to write application packages to run under DOS. This attracted even more users, who attracted still more software developers. At the same time, hardware manufacturers began to develop expansion boards and peripheral devices to be used with computers that run DOS. Today, a huge body of application software and a multitude of hardware devices are devoted to DOS microcomputers. Despite more advanced operating systems, such as OS/2 and XENIX, designed for high-end IBM and IBM-compatible machines, DOS is still the single most popular microcomputer operating system in the world. For example, in 1987 approximately 75 percent of all microcomputers sold used DOS. This percentage is expected to increase until at least 1991.

The purpose of this chapter is to introduce DOS in more detail. By covering specific features and explaining important commands, we'll not only describe an extremely influential microcomputer operating system, but we'll show you how to use it, too. Keep in mind, however, that we won't attempt to cover all DOS commands or even explain every variation of the commands we do discuss. Instead, we will focus on a subset of the simplest, yet most frequently used features of this powerful operating system.

After studying this chapter, you will understand

- why DOS is such an important operating system.
- why there are different versions of DOS.
- how to boot up DOS.
- how to see what files are on a disk.
- DOS file names.
- DOS keyboard functions.
- how to work from a different disk drive.
- how to check disk and memory status.
- how to format disks.
- how to copy files and disks.
- how to change file names.

## Insight

### Will PC-DOS Be Replaced by Another Operating System?

Watch out, PC-DOS—there are a couple of hounds nipping at your heels.

PC-DOS (or MS-DOS) has been enjoying a fairly safe and secure life as a leader of the operating system pack since the microcomputer population explosion of the 1980s. But time is taking its toll, and the gray hairs are starting to show.

DOS was originally designed to be a single-user, single-tasking operating system, allowing only one program to be run at a time. Today, there are some clever applications packages that seem to let you do two things at once, such as print a file in the background while you're still working with the word processor. DOS doesn't handle this well.

When you want to perform more involved tasks, such as processing a large number of accounting transactions while still working on a spreasheet, DOS is definitely inadequate. In large business, scientific, and engineering applications, these kinds of tasks are almost required today.

More elaborate *multitasking* operating systems can run several programs at the same time. Actually, they switch back and forth between tasks, giving each program a small slice of time. The switching is so fast that it's not apparent to the user.

People who use their IBM-compatible microcomputers for multitasking have two main choices in operating systems today—UNIX and OS/2. UNIX is a very powerful and flexible operating system that was developed by Bell Laboratories and originally ran on minicomputers. OS/2 was developed jointly by Microsoft and IBM. It is a memory-hungry system that runs only on the more powerful IBM-compatible microcomputers that use the Intel 80286 and 80386 processors.

UNIX and OS/2 are being groomed as the operating system leaders of the next generation of powerful microcomputers. But it's unlikely that DOS will just slink off into the woods. DOS has a huge, installed base and many devoted users. For many simple computing needs, it will undoubtedly remain on top.

- how to erase files.
- how to protect floppy disks.
- how to display and print text files.
- how to run an application package.
- how to use subdirectories.
- how to use batch files.
- how to use the DOS Shell.

## DOS VERSIONS

*System upgrades*

Computer hardware and software technology advances very quickly. To remain popular, an operating system such as DOS must be continually upgraded to accommodate new computers and new capabilities that have been added to existing models. For example, IBM has released nine major versions of DOS so far. In each case, bugs have been worked out and improvements have been made to previous versions. The primary driving force behind each new version of DOS, however, has been new hardware capabilities, usually related to floppy or hard disk drives.

It's important to know which version of DOS you are using, because some hardware and software can only be used with more recent releases. Fortunately, each new version of DOS is **upwardly compatible** with previous versions. This means, at least in theory, that every official command that worked with previous versions should work with the new version. In most cases, this is so. However, there always seems to be at least one command that doesn't work quite the same in the new release. Nevertheless, for the most part you don't have to change the way you did things before unless you specifically want to take advantage of the additional capabilities of a new DOS version.

If you don't need these additional capabilities, you don't have to buy the latest version of DOS each time a new release is issued. As long as the version you have works well with your hardware and software, you can continue using it. Keep in mind that although the new DOS version may add certain capabilities, you must pay for the upgrade, and that besides this added expense, new DOS versions typically use more memory and more disk space. In many cases, upgrading is simply not worth it. Unless you're buying a new machine or adding a different disk drive, you may not need the latest DOS version.

DOS versions are denoted by numbers such as 1.00, 2.10, and 4.00. The number to the left of the decimal point reflects a major classification; the numbers to the right represent more minor differences. The larger the number, the more recent the version. This table lists each major IBM DOS version that has been released so far along with the primary reason for the upgrade:

| VERSION | DATE | REASON FOR UPGRADE (NEW CAPABILITIES) |
|---|---|---|
| 1.00 | 8/81 | 5.25" 160K single-sided floppy disk drives |
| 1.10 | 5/82 | 5.25" 320K double-sided floppy disk drives |
| 2.00 | 3/83 | 5.25" 360K floppy, 10M hard disk drives |
| 2.10 | 10/83 | 5.25" 360K half-height floppy drives |
| 3.00 | 8/84 | 5.25" 1.2M floppy, bigger hard disk drives |
| 3.10 | 3/85 | Network disks and file sharing |
| 3.20 | 12/85 | 3.5" 720K floppy disk drives |
| 3.30 | 3/87 | 3.5" 1.44M floppy disk drives |
| 4.00 | 7/88 | Hard disks larger than 35M, DOS Shell |

Throughout this chapter we'll be using IBM DOS 4.00 for all of our examples. Most of what we cover, however, should also apply to DOS 2.00 and newer versions. Versions 1.00 and 1.10 are now considered obsolete. If you use a version of DOS other than 4.00, the screens you see on your computer may be slightly different than the ones shown in this chapter.

## BOOTING UP

*Starting the system*

DOS stands for Disk Operating System. This means that the programs that comprise the operating system are stored on a disk, either hard or floppy. Although many of the BIOS (hardware interface) programs are stored in ROM chips, the higher-level programs of the operating system's application and user interfaces are kept on a disk. Like any program, the operating system must be loaded into the computer's memory before it can start working. We've said, however, that the operating system loads programs into memory and sets up the computer to execute them. If this is so, how does the operating system itself get started? Does it load itself? In a way, yes. Basically, a small program in the ROM BIOS is automatically invoked every time the computer is turned on or reset. After loading itself into memory, this program then loads the rest of the operating system into memory and begins execution. In a sense, the computer pulls itself up by its own bootstraps. So the process of initially loading and executing the operating system is often called **booting up**. In the particular case of IBM and IBM-compatibles, this is also called booting DOS, loading DOS, or simply starting DOS.

## With the Computer Off

*Turning on the power*

Booting up a computer that is off is really very easy. If your computer has a hard disk with DOS installed on it, all you do is turn on the computer. Older IBM microcomputers put the big red power switch on the right side of the system unit toward the rear; the newer Personal System/2 models put the switch right up in front (see Figure 5.1). In most cases, you flip up the switch to turn on the computer. With some microcomputers you also have to turn on the monitor, which usually is controlled by a round knob on the front or a rotating wheel just beneath the front edge.

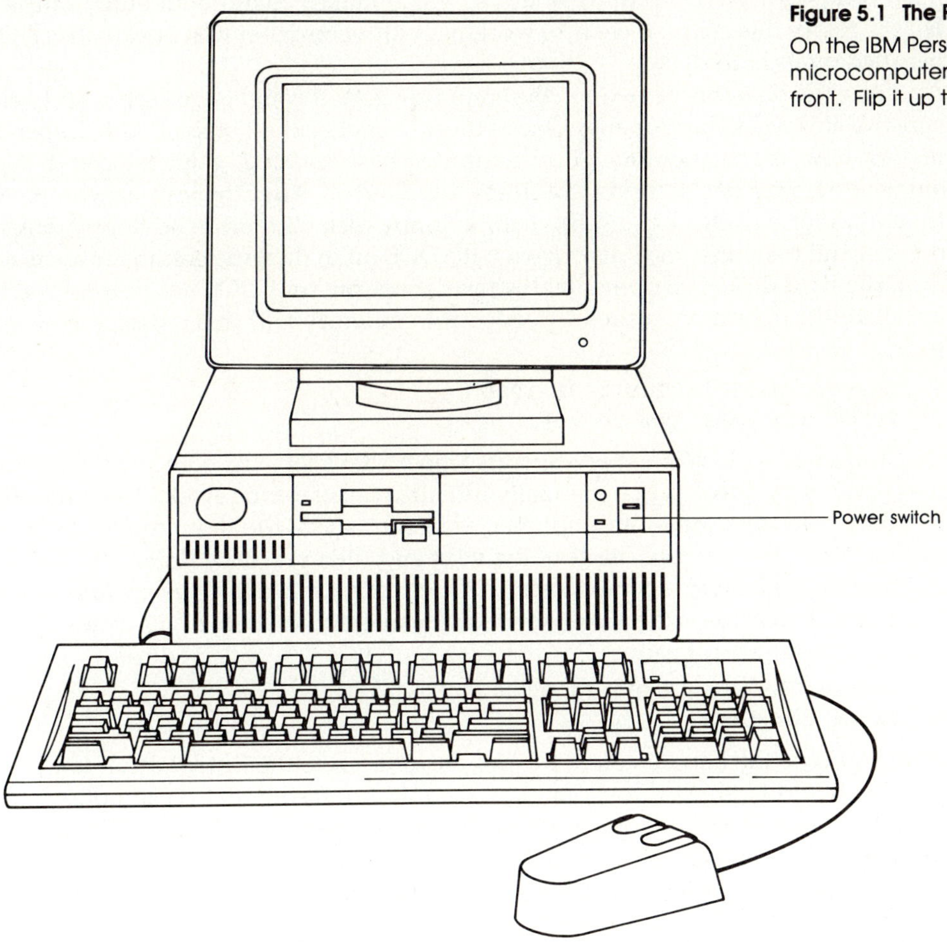


**Figure 5.1 The Power Switch**
On the IBM Personal System/2 microcomputers, the power switch is right up front. Flip it up to turn on the computer.

If your computer does not have a hard disk or if the hard disk doesn't have DOS installed on it, then you must boot up from a floppy disk. On IBM and IBM-compatible computers the disk drives are designated with letters A, B, C, and so on. If there is a hard disk drive, it's designated as C. If the computer has two floppy drives, side by side, the A drive is on the left and the B drive is on the right. If the two floppy drives are arranged vertically, the A drive is usually on top. If there is only one floppy drive, then it is the A drive. To boot up from a floppy disk, you must first insert the DOS disk into drive A and close the door or lever (see Figure 5.2). Then you turn on the computer.

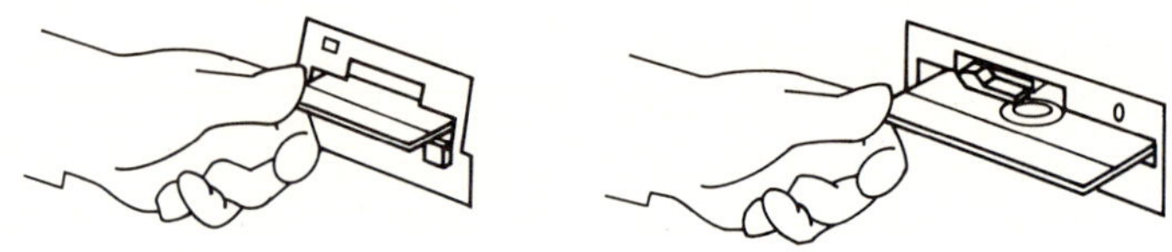

**Figure 5.2 Inserting and Removing Diskettes**
(left) Insert 3.5" diskette with arrow side up and arrow pointing to diskette drive. Press gently on diskette until it "clicks" and drops into place. Remove by pressing eject button on lower right of diskette drive. (right) Insert 5.25" diskette into drive until it "clicks" into place; label must be facing up with write-protect notch on left. Close drive door. Remove by opening drive door and gently pulling out diskette.

In Appendix C we discuss how to install DOS on a hard disk. Nowadays, most microcomputers have a hard disk drive, which makes using them much simpler. For the rest of this chapter, we'll be working with a computer that already has DOS installed on its hard disk.

Once the power is turned on, the computer goes through some self-tests to ensure that it is working properly. One of these tests checks all of the RAM. Depending on how much memory your computer has installed, this test could take anywhere from a few seconds to a couple of minutes. After the tests are complete, the computer will check the A drive for a floppy disk. If there is no floppy disk in drive A and there is a hard disk drive with DOS on it, then the computer boots up from the hard disk. Assuming all the tests check out and DOS has been properly installed, the operating system is loaded into memory and this message may appear:

```
Current date is Tue 1-01-1980
Enter new date (mm-dd-yy): _
```

On computers without a battery-operated clock that keeps the date and time when the power is off, this lets you manually initialize the real-time clock. To set the correct date, you type the month number, a dash or slash, the day number, another dash or slash, the last two digits of the year, and then press the **Enter** key. If your computer has a battery-operated clock, DOS already knows the current date and all you have to do is press the **Enter** key. After you enter the date or just press **Enter**, a message like this appears:

```
Current time is 0:00:36.90
Enter new time: _
```

Here you type the hour, a colon, the minute, and press the **Enter** key. If it's afternoon, you add twelve to the hour as in the military fashion. For example, 2 P.M. would be 14:00. Again, if your computer has a battery-operated clock, DOS already has the correct time and you can just press the **Enter** key without entering a new time. Figure 5.3, for example, shows the screen after booting DOS on a computer with a battery-operated clock.

The C> that you see on the last line is called the **DOS prompt** or **system prompt**. It signifies that drive C is the current **default drive**, or active drive, where DOS will look for programs and data files unless you specify otherwise. If you had booted up from floppy drive A, then the DOS prompt would be A>. The system prompt indicates that DOS is patiently waiting for you to enter a command.

## With the Computer On

*Rebooting the system*

Occasionally something goes wrong in a program and the computer may seem to get stuck. In other cases, you might want to reset your computer to the way it was when you first turned it on. You could, of course, simply turn off the computer and boot up as we've just described. There is, however, another way to *reboot* the computer without shutting it off. DOS has a special combination of keys that you can press to do this. All you have to do is press the three keys marked **Ctrl**, **Alt**, and **Del**, and hold them down at the same time for a moment (see Figure 5.4). In most cases, the computer will clear the screen, beep, and check the disk drive just as it did when you first turned it on. If nothing happens, a serious program error has probably erased a crucial part of DOS from memory and you will have to turn off the computer and boot up again. If all goes well, DOS will again ask you to supply the new date and time, after which it will present the system prompt.

```
Current date is Tue 08-16-1988
Enter new date (mm-dd-yy):
Current time is 10:18:18.32a
Enter new time:


IBM DOS Version 4.00
          (C)Copyright International Business Machines Corp 1981, 1988
          (C)Copyright Microsoft Corp 1981-1986

C>_
```

**Figure 5.3 Booting DOS**
On many systems, you will be asked to supply the date and time after you turn on the computer. If the current date and time are correct, all you have to do is press the **Enter** key.

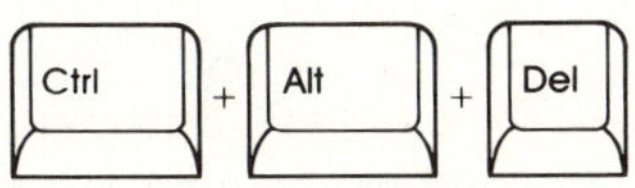


**Figure 5.4 Rebooting DOS**
If the computer is already turned on, you can reboot DOS by pressing these three keys and holding them all down for a moment.

## ISSUING A COMMAND

*Telling DOS what to do*

DOS has a very command-oriented user interface. This means that within DOS, almost everything you do is in the form of a command or a response to a prompt. Some DOS commands are loaded into memory when the computer is booted up and kept there until the power is turned off. These **internal commands**, also called **resident routines**, are kept in memory because they are the most essential or the most frequently used parts of the operating system. For example, one of the simplest and most commonly used DOS internal commands is DIR, which displays a file directory. The remaining DOS commands are called **external commands** or **transient routines**, because they are kept in disk storage and temporarily loaded into memory only when they are needed or specifically requested. CHKDSK, for example, is an external DOS command that displays information about a disk and the memory installed in your computer.

## Listing a Directory of the Default Drive

*Seeing which files you have*

All types of programs and data are stored on disks in files. The DIR command lets you see which files you have on a particular disk or in a particular subdirectory. A subdirectory, you'll recall from Chapter 4, is a separate group of files on a disk. We'll have more to say about subdirectories throughout this chapter.

Besides listing each file's name, the DIR command also shows the file's size in bytes, and the date and time it was created or last changed. All you do is type **DIR** and press the **Enter** key to get a directory of the disk in your default drive. Figure 5.5, for example, shows a directory listing of a hard disk.

**Figure 5.5 Using the DIR Command**
Entering **DIR** by itself gives you a listing of the files on your default disk.

```
C>DIR

 Volume in drive C is HARD DISK
 Volume Serial Number is 124C-5488
 Directory of  C:\

AUTOEXEC BAT        56 08-16-88  10:01a
COMMAND  COM     37637 06-17-88  12:00p
CONFIG   SYS       101 08-16-88   9:48a
DOS          <DIR>     08-16-88   9:42a
        4 File(s)   19812352 bytes free

C>_
```

Incidentally, it doesn't matter whether you type commands in uppercase (capital letters), lowercase (small letters), or a mixture of both. DOS ignores case when processing command names. In this chapter, we'll use uppercase for DOS command names to make them stand out from the rest of the text.

Examine the screen in Figure 5.5. First it reveals the volume label of the disk. This is IBM's terminology for the name of the hard disk, which is simply HARD DISK. Next is the volume serial number, which is just a code number assigned to the disk when it is formatted. Then DOS says that this is a directory of the disk in drive C and it lists the names, sizes, dates, and times of the files. Notice that the first three file names all have two parts. We'll have more to say about this file name format shortly. The last file name in the list, DOS, is the name of a subdirectory. The <DIR> designation next to the name tells you that it is a subdirectory and not an ordinary file. This subdirectory, which we'll look at later, contains the files that make up most of DOS. It was created by the person who set up this hard disk.

Each file name, except for the DOS subdirectory, has a number to its immediate right. This is the size of that file in bytes. A byte, you'll recall, is basically equivalent to a single character. Finally, listed to the right of each file size is the date and then the time at which the file was created or last changed. The first file in the list, for example, is named AUTOEXEC.BAT, occupies 56 bytes, and was created on August 16, 1988 at 10:01 A.M.

At the bottom of the listing, the DIR command tells you that four files are in this directory and there are 19,812,352 "bytes free." This means that 19,812,352 bytes of storage are still left unused on the disk. Since it's important to know what files are on a disk and how much room is left, DIR is one of the most frequently used DOS commands.

## Listing a Directory of Another Drive

*Looking at a different disk*

When you type **DIR** and press the **Enter** key, DOS assumes that you want to check the directory of the disk in the default drive. If you want the directory of a different drive instead, you have to type **DIR** followed by at least one **delimiter** (space, comma, semicolon, equal sign, or tab key) and then the **drive specifier**. This specifier consists of the disk drive letter immediately followed by a colon (:). So, to see which files are on the disk in drive A, you could type **DIR A:** and then press the **Enter** key. The colon after the drive letter tells DOS that the preceding A is a drive letter and not a file name.

This drive specifier is an example of a **parameter**, which is used to designate possible alternate actions. Most DOS commands accept one or more parameters.

## Looking for a Particular File

*Specifying a file name*

Another parameter you can use with the DIR command is a file name. Frequently, you'd like to check if a particular file is on a disk without having to look through the entire directory. The DIR command can easily do this if you give it the name of the file for which you're looking. For instance, to see if the file MEMO.DOC is on the disk in the current default drive, you could type **DIR MEMO.DOC** and then press the **Enter** key. To see if a file of that name is on a disk in some other drive, say drive A, you could type **DIR A:MEMO.DOC** and then press the **Enter** key. If the file is on the disk, DOS will list an abbreviated directory with only that file in it (see Figure 5.6). If, on the other hand, that file is not on the disk, then DOS will say, "File not found."

```
C>DIR A:MEMO.DOC

 Volume in drive A has no label
 Directory of  A:\

MEMO     DOC      3633 11-10-87   2:04p
        1 File(s)      31744 bytes free

C>_
```

**Figure 5.6 Looking for a Particular File**
You can tell the DIR command which file you want to find.

### Listing the Contents of a Subdirectory

*Specifying a subdirectory*

The DIR command can also be used to examine the contents of a subdirectory. All you have to do is type the name of the subdirectory after the DIR. For example, to see the contents of the DOS subdirectory, you would type **DIR DOS** and press the **Enter** key. Figure 5.7 shows the screen after this command finishes. Since 71 files are in this subdirectory but only 25 lines can be shown on the screen, many of the names have moved up and disappeared off the top of the screen. Figure 5.7, therefore, shows only the bottom part of the directory listing.

**Figure 5.7 Looking at the DOS Subdirectory**
This shows the screen after it stops scrolling.

```
GRAPHICS COM      16733 06-17-88  12:00p
GRAPHICS PRO       9413 06-17-88  12:00p
JOIN     EXE      17457 06-17-88  12:00p
LABEL    COM       4490 06-17-88  12:00p
MEM      EXE      20133 06-17-88  12:00p
MORE     COM       2166 06-17-88  12:00p
MORTGAGE BAS       6207 06-17-88  12:00p
NLSFUNC  EXE       6910 06-17-88  12:00p
PCIBMDRV MOS        295 06-17-88  12:00p
PCMSDRV  MOS        961 06-17-88  12:00p
PCMSPDRV MOS        801 06-17-88  12:00p
PRINT    COM      14163 06-17-88  12:00p
RECOVER  COM      10732 06-17-88  12:00p
RESTORE  COM      40030 06-17-88  12:00p
SHELL    CLR       4438 06-17-88  12:00p
SHELL    HLP      66977 06-17-88  12:00p
SHELL    MEU       4588 06-17-88  12:00p
SHELLB   COM       3937 06-17-88  12:00p
SHELLC   EXE     153975 06-17-88  12:00p
SORT     EXE       5914 06-17-88  12:00p
SUBST    EXE      18143 06-17-88  12:00p
TREE     COM       6334 06-17-88  12:00p
        71 File(s)  19812352 bytes free

C>_
```

## DOS FILE NAMES

*The first part is required*

Every file in a particular disk directory must have a unique name so that DOS can distinguish it from other files. You may, however, have files with the same name on different disks or in different subdirectories on the same disk. A file's name may consist of two parts; the first part is required, while the second part is optional. The primary part, called the **filename** by IBM, is from one to eight characters long. It can include any of the characters you see on the keyboard, except for the following, which are considered invalid in filenames:

. " / \ [ ] : | < > + = ; ,

### Extensions

*The second part is optional*

The second part of a file's name is called the **extension**. This optional part is separated from the primary filename by a period and may be up to three characters long. The extension may also consist of any characters except those invalid ones we just mentioned. If a file's name does have an extension, you may be required to specify it along with the primary filename when telling DOS to do something with that file.

Extensions are used to classify files and help you remember what's in them. For example, here are some common DOS file extensions and the types of files they usually designate:

| | |
|---|---|
| COM | DOS external command or an executable program |
| EXE | DOS external command or an executable program |
| BAT | Batch file |
| SYS | System setup file |
| ASM | Assembly language program |
| BAS | BASIC language program |
| PAS | Pascal language program |
| TXT | Text file |
| BAK | Backup copy of some other file |
| DOC | Document file of some word processing programs |
| WKS | Worksheet file of some spreadsheet programs |
| DBF | Data base file of some data base managers |

## File Specifications

*Filename prefixes*

An extension is like a filename suffix, but a filename can have a prefix, too. In fact, you've already seen an example of a filename prefix: the disk drive specifier. Any filename can be prefixed with the designation of the disk drive it's to be found on, for example **A:MEMO.DOC**. Later in this chapter, when we discuss subdirectories further, we'll show how a subdirectory designation can also be used as a filename prefix. The combination of a disk drive specifier, a filename, and an extension is known as a **file specification**.

## Global File Name Characters

*Specifying groups of files*

Some DOS commands can deal with several files at once. For example, the DIR command can not only find a single file on a disk or in a subdirectory, but it also can list a group of files if their names have some characters in common. This is made possible through the use of the DOS **global file name characters**, * and ?. These characters may be included in filenames and extensions to give you greater flexibility in specifying files. The * character is used in a file specification to symbolize any character or group of characters. For instance, ***.DOC** means any file with an extension of DOC. The ? character is used to symbolize any single character. So, **MO?E.COM** means any file that has an extension of COM and a four-letter filename beginning with MO and ending with an E. More than one global file name character may be used in the same file specification, too. For example, **???.*** means any file with at most three characters in its first part (see Figure 5.8).

**Figure 5.8 Looking for a Group of Files**

This command shows all the files in the DOS subdirectory with a primary filename no longer than three characters.

```
C>DIR DOS\???.*

 Volume in drive C is HARD DISK
 Volume Serial Number is 124C-5488
 Directory of  C:\DOS

.            <DIR>      08-16-88   9:42a
..           <DIR>      08-16-88   9:42a
SYS      COM      11472 06-17-88  12:00p
EGA      CPI      49052 06-17-88  12:00p
LCD      CPI      10592 06-17-88  12:00p
MEM      EXE      20133 06-17-88  12:00p
        6 File(s)   19812352 bytes free

C>_
```

## DOS AND THE KEYBOARD

*Special-purpose keys*

In Chapter 2 we introduced some of the special-purpose keys found on many microcomputer keyboards. These include the Enter, Escape, Break, Control, Alternate, Insert, and Delete keys, as well as function keys, cursor movement keys, and numeric keypad keys (see Figure 5.9). Most IBM and IBM-compatible computers have all of these special-purpose keys on their keyboards. You've already learned how to use some of these keys. For example, you know that you must press the Enter key after typing a command to tell DOS to go ahead and process what you've typed. Besides the special-purpose keys, there are several familiar keys just like those found on typewriters, such as Tab, Backspace, Shift, and Caps Lock. These keys generally operate in much the same manner as they do on typewriters. The Backspace key, for instance, is used to go back and type over errors on a line before you press the Enter key. Finally, you've learned that by holding down the Control

**Figure 5.9 The Keyboard**

Here are some of the special keys used by DOS.

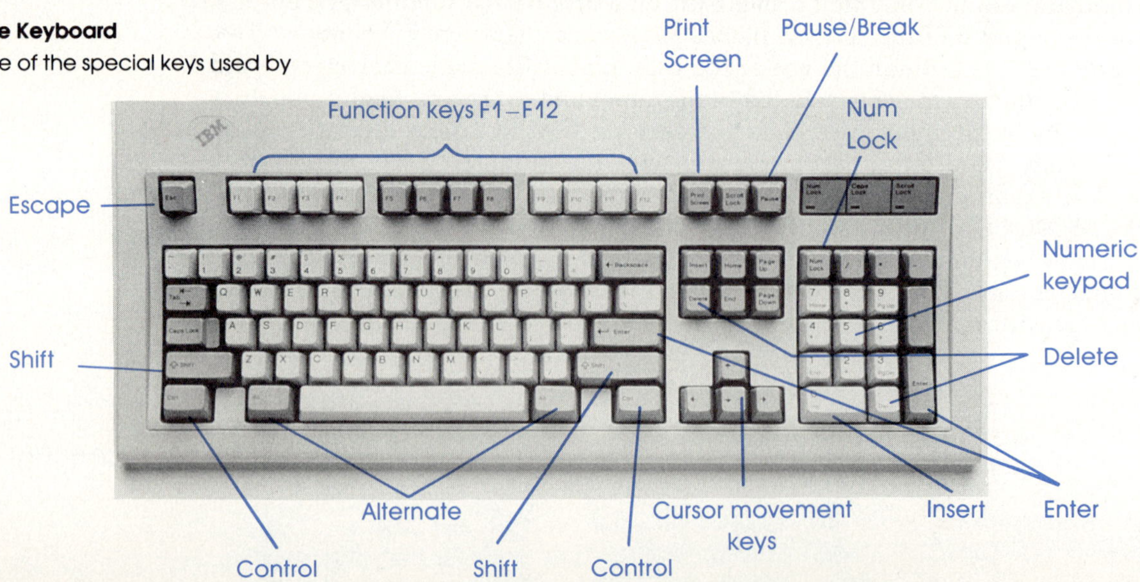

(Ctrl), Alternate (Alt), and Delete (Del) keys at the same time, you can reboot DOS with the power on. Other keypress combinations perform certain functions within DOS, too.

## Cancel a Line

*Starting over*

Most computer users aren't professional typists and it's easy to make mistakes with a keyboard. Fortunately, computers usually make it simple to correct typing errors. If the command you're typing is short and you haven't pressed the Enter key yet, the quickest way to fix a mistake is often to backspace over the erroneous characters and retype them. If the command is long or if you've made several errors and haven't pressed the Enter key yet, you can cancel the entire line you just typed and start over again by pressing the **Escape (Esc)** key. When you press the Escape key, DOS displays a backward slash (\) to signify that the line has been canceled, and it skips down to the next line so you can start over again.

## Pause Screen Scrolling

*Temporary freeze-frame*

Sometimes a DOS command, such as DIR, displays so much text that the beginning part disappears off the top of the screen. This upward movement of text on a display screen is called **scrolling**, because the effect is similar to unrolling a scroll. Although this technique enables computers to display very large text files on relatively small screens, the information may scroll by before you get a chance to read it. It would be nice if you could temporarily stop the screen so that you wouldn't have to take speed reading lessons to use the computer. Fortunately, DOS allows you to pause screen scrolling. On older IBM keyboards, this is accomplished by holding down the **Control (Ctrl)** key and pressing the **Num Lock** key. The newer IBM Enhanced Keyboards have a special key, labelled *Pause*, that performs the same function. Pressing **Ctrl-Num Lock** or the **Pause** key immediately halts the movement of text. To resume scrolling, all you have to do is press any key except a Shift, Lock, Control (Ctrl), or Alternate (Alt) key. You can pause and resume scrolling as many times as you wish.

## Cancel a Command

*Terminating a program*

Once you press the Enter key, DOS proceeds to process whatever command you've typed. If you've made a mistake or don't want to wait for a command to finish, you can cancel a command by holding down the **Control (Ctrl)** key and pressing the **Break** key. For example, let's say that you've entered **DIR** and DOS begins to display a long list of files. If you've seen enough and want to stop the display, you would hold down the **Control** key and press the **Break** key. On older IBM keyboards, the Break key is also labelled *Scroll Lock* and is next to the Num Lock key on the upper-right side of the numeric keypad. On the newer IBM Enhanced Keyboards, the Break key and the Pause key are the same. Note that pressing Ctrl-Break is different from pressing the Escape key. Escape cancels a line typed at the DOS prompt before the Enter key has been pressed, while Ctrl-Break cancels a command after the Enter key has been pressed and the command is already executing.

### Print the Screen

*Reproducing the current screen on paper*

Occasionally there is a sequence of commands or some other information on your display screen that you would like to remember. You could, of course, just write everything down on paper, but DOS has an easier method. If you have a printer connected to your computer, DOS can produce a paper copy of the text currently on your screen. All you have to do is press the **Print Screen** key on Enhanced Keyboards, or hold down one of the shift keys and then press the **PrtSc** key on older IBM PC and AT keyboards.

### Echo to the Printer

*Creating a session transcript*

Printing the screen works well if you just have a single screen of information you want to save. But it isn't very helpful if you want to save the output of a program that scrolls many lines of text across your screen. For example, you may want a paper copy of a directory listing that doesn't fit on a single screen. DOS can easily solve this problem by letting you echo the characters that appear on your screen to your printer. All you have to do is hold down the **Control (Ctrl)** key and press the **Print Screen (PrtSc)** key before you type your command or press the **Enter** key. From that point on, whatever you type and whatever the computer displays will also be sent to the printer. This echoing continues until you press **Ctrl-PrtSc** again. So, you could use this method to get a paper copy of an entire computer session. Or, you could press **Ctrl-PrtSc** and then enter **DIR** to get a paper copy of a long directory listing.

## CHANGING THE DEFAULT DISK DRIVE

*Using a different disk*

IBM and IBM-compatible computers without hard disks boot up off the floppy in drive A, which is the default disk drive. Computers that have a hard disk with DOS installed on it boot up from drive C, which is considered the default drive. You will recall that the current default drive is indicated by the DOS prompt, for example, A> or C>. This means that whenever you enter a command that doesn't explicitly specify a particular disk drive, the current default drive is assumed. For example, when you enter **DIR** by itself, you get the directory of the current default drive. If your computer has more than one disk drive, like most IBM and IBM-compatible computers, you may occasionally want to change your default drive from A or C to another installed drive. This is a common procedure, sometimes called *switching drives*. Let's look at how and why you would change the default disk drive.

If you have a computer with two floppy disk drives, you can change your default drive from A to B simply by typing **B:** and pressing the **Enter** key. If you have a hard disk, you can change your default drive from C to A by typing **A:** and pressing the **Enter** key. As soon as you switch drives, DOS responds with a new prompt that indicates the letter of the new default drive. Being able to change the default drive like this gives you full use of your installed disk drives. Most users find that they switch drives quite frequently.

For example, let's say that your computer has a hard disk drive C and a floppy disk drive A. You've just purchased a new program, which comes on a single floppy disk, and you'd like to try it out before you copy it onto your hard disk. You put the floppy disk into drive A, close the drive door, and enter **A:**. The system switches to drive A and you can run your new program directly from the floppy disk. When you are finished with the program, you can switch back to the hard disk by typing **C:** and then pressing the **Enter** key.

## CHECKING DISK AND MEMORY STATUS

*Seeing how much storage space you have*

You've already seen how one DOS command, DIR, can be used to list information about the files on a disk or in a subdirectory. Another DOS command, CHKDSK, can be used to display further information about a disk and the memory installed in your computer. To check the default drive, simply type **CHKDSK** and press the **Enter** key. Figure 5.10 shows an example of what you might see displayed on the screen.

```
C>CHKDSK

Volume HARD DISK   created 08-16-1988 10:02a
Volume Serial Number is 124C-5488

  21309440 bytes total disk space
     71680 bytes in 3 hidden files
      4096 bytes in 1 directories
   1370112 bytes in 72 user files
     51200 bytes in bad sectors
  19812352 bytes available on disk

      2048 bytes in each allocation unit
     10405 total allocation units on disk
      9674 available allocation units on disk

    524288 total bytes memory
    441168 bytes free

C>_
```

**Figure 5.10 Checking Disk and Memory Status**
The CHKDSK command produces a status report like this, but the actual contents depend on how your system is set up.

This status report supplies several useful items of information. First, it tells you that the total capacity of the hard disk is 21,309,440 bytes (a little more than 20 megabytes). This is roughly equivalent to about 6575 pages of single-spaced typewritten text. *Hidden files* are special files used by DOS and some other programs. They're hidden because they do not appear in the disk directory so that you won't rename, change, or delete them. Next the CHKDSK command tells you how many subdirectories and ordinary user files are on the disk and how much space they occupy. It also says that 51,200 bytes on this disk are in "bad sectors." This means that some of the hard disk is unusable due to manufacturing flaws—a fairly common occurrence with hard disks. The unusable areas were discovered when the disk was formatted and were marked so that DOS doesn't use them. That leaves 19,812,352 bytes of empty space still on the disk.

The CHKDSK command also reveals information about *allocation units*, which relate to how DOS assigns disk space to files. This is technical information that most users don't really need to know. Finally, CHKDSK reports that this particular computer has 524,288 bytes (or 512K) of RAM installed, of which 441,168 bytes are free to be used by application programs. The difference between these latter two figures,

83,120 bytes, is the amount of RAM taken up by the parts of DOS that remain in memory, including the internal commands.

## FORMATTING DISKS

*Preparing a disk for use*

As we said in the last chapter, every new disk must undergo an initial preparation known as formatting before it can be used to store programs and data files. Many manufacturers and retailers will initially format hard disks that are installed in the computers they sell. This initialization for diskettes, however, is not commonly done at the factory, so generally you must format each new floppy you're going to use with your own computer. You also can reformat a previously formatted disk to completely erase all files that are stored on it. But you should be very careful whenever you format a previously used disk. Make sure that it doesn't hold any important files that you want to save. Basically, DOS performs the following procedures when you format a disk:

- Checks the disk for bad or damaged spots that cannot reliably store data and marks these as unusable.
- Completely erases any programs and data that might be on the disk.
- Builds a directory to hold information about the files that eventually will be stored on the disk.
- Marks off the empty space on the disk into equal-sized sections.
- Copies part of the operating system onto the disk if specified to do so.

### Program and Data Diskettes

*Disks without DOS*

The most common and simplest use of the DOS FORMAT command is setting up diskettes that will not be used to boot up the computer. Since the operating system is not installed on these diskettes, they can devote all of their space to holding programs and data files. Again, if you plan to reformat a diskette that has been previously used, you should double-check to make sure that you're willing to discard all files that might be on it.

Let's say that drive C is your default drive and you want to format a new floppy disk in drive A. You type **FORMAT A:** and press the **Enter** key. DOS tells you to insert a new diskette into drive A and press the **Enter** key when you are ready. If the diskette to be formatted is already in drive A, all you have to do is press the **Enter** key again and wait.

The procedure takes about a minute for a 5.25-inch double-sided, double-density diskette, during which DOS displays a percentage that shows how much it has formatted so far. When the formatting procedure is finished, DOS prompts you to supply a volume label. This is your chance to enter a name for the disk. If you don't want to enter a name, you can just press the **Enter** key. The FORMAT command then reports the total number of bytes of disk space and the number of bytes that are available for use. If the diskette has no bad sectors and the operating system is not installed, these two numbers will be the same: 362,496 bytes for a 5.25-inch double-sided, double-density diskette. The FORMAT command also displays information about the disk's allocation units and reports the volume serial number. Finally, the FORMAT command asks you if you want to format another diskette. You type **Y** for yes or **N** for no. When you're done, you get the DOS prompt C> again.

## System Diskettes

*Boot up disks*

A diskette formatted in the manner we've just described can be used to store programs and data files. It cannot, however, be used to boot up the computer because it doesn't have DOS installed on it. If you want to format a DOS diskette that can be used to boot up your computer, you must follow a slightly different procedure. The FORMAT command must be given a special parameter, /S, which tells it to copy the hidden operating system files from the disk in the default drive to the new diskette. So, to tell DOS to prepare the diskette in drive A so that it can boot the computer, you must type **FORMAT A:/S** and press the **Enter** key. The rest of the procedure is the same as we outlined before. Figure 5.11 shows the screen after the FORMAT command is finished.

```
C>FORMAT A:/S
Insert new diskette for drive A:
and press ENTER when ready...

Format complete
System transferred

Volume label (11 characters, ENTER for none)? FLOPPY DISK

    362496 bytes total disk space
    108544 bytes used by system
    253952 bytes available on disk

      1024 bytes in each allocation unit
       248 allocation units available on disk

Volume Serial Number is 2D37-14EA

Format another (Y/N)?N
C>_
```

**Figure 5.11 Formatting a System Diskette**
The /S parameter tells the FORMAT command to prepare a disk on which you can install DOS.

This time the FORMAT command informs you that the system was transferred and that 108,544 bytes were used by the operating system. That leaves 253,952 bytes available on the disk for programs and data files. You can use the DIR command to examine the new diskette, as shown in Figure 5.12. The directory listing shows that COMMAND.COM is the only non-hidden file present. This is a special file containing the program that processes the DOS commands you enter. Besides COMMAND.COM and the DOS hidden files, the new diskette does not contain any of the external commands or other files that come with DOS. So, although you could boot up with this new diskette, and you could execute internal commands such as DIR, you could not use any external commands such as CHKDSK and FORMAT unless you somehow copied their command files also. We'll tell you how to copy files shortly.

## Hard Disks

*Proceed with caution*

The FORMAT command also works for hard disks. Once a hard disk is initially formatted, however, it may be seldom, if ever, formatted again. Since computers with hard disks often have large numbers of important and sometimes irreplaceable files

**Figure 5.12 The Newly Formatted Diskette**
The /S parameter copies the command processor onto the formatted disk.

```
C>DIR A:

 Volume in drive A is FLOPPY DISK
 Volume Serial Number is 2D37-14EA
 Directory of  A:\

COMMAND  COM     37637 06-17-88  12:00p
        1 File(s)     253952 bytes free

C>_
```

on them, you should be extremely cautious with them. Don't attempt formatting a hard disk unless you know exactly what you're doing and you're sure that all files on the hard disk have backup copies. As we said, many computers now come with their hard disks already formatted by the manufacturer or retailer.

## COPYING

*Duplicating files*

One of the reasons computers are so useful is that they make it a simple matter to copy programs and data. Once information is entered into a computer, any number of copies usually can be made very easily and quickly. An important function of any operating system is the duplication of files. DOS provides several methods of copying files. Two of the more popular commands are COPY, which reproduces one or more individual files, and DISKCOPY, which duplicates an entire diskette at once.

### A File to Another Disk

*From one disk to another*

COPY is a versatile DOS command that can be used in various ways. For example, let's say that you have a file named MEMO.DOC on the floppy disk in drive A. To copy it from the disk in drive A to the hard disk drive C, you could enter the following command:

```
COPY A:MEMO.DOC C:MEMO.DOC
```

The specification of the file you want to copy, called the *source*, is the first parameter after the COPY. The specification of the new file you want to produce, called the *target*, is the second parameter. In this particular case, the source and the target have the same name. This is permitted because the copy is to be placed on a different disk.

Copying a file from one disk to a file with the same name on another disk is a common procedure. Consequently, DOS provides a shorter way to specify this action. In many cases, if you omit certain information DOS makes an assumption about what you mean. As we said before, these assumed values are called *defaults*. So, if you don't supply a disk drive specifier in front of a filename, DOS assumes that you mean the current default drive. Similarly, if you don't give a name for the target file, the COPY command assumes that it is to use the same name as the source. This works just fine as long as the source and the target are on different disks or in different subdirectories. Therefore, if drive C is your current default drive, here is another way to copy MEMO.DOC from the disk in drive A to the hard disk:

```
COPY A:MEMO.DOC
```

Like many DOS commands, you should use COPY with some caution. If, for example, there already is a file named MEMO.DOC on the hard disk, entering either one of the two commands we've just described would replace that file with a copy of the file from drive A. So, before copying any files, you should first check the target disk or subdirectory. Make sure you no longer need any files on the target disk or subdirectory with the same names as the copies to be created.

## A File into the Same Directory

*Making a copy with a different name*

You cannot have two files in the same directory with identical names. The COPY command simply will not allow you to duplicate a file in the same directory unless you provide a different name for the target file. So, the COPY command can reproduce a file on the same disk or in the same subdirectory, but the source and the target must have different names.

One common reason for duplicating a file in the same directory is for backup purposes. Let's say that you're going to change an existing file. If that file is especially important, you might want to keep a copy of the original version before you make any alterations. Then if some problem occurs, you will still have the original version intact. So, before you change a file, it might be a good idea to make a copy of it, but with a slightly different name. For example, let's say you were going to somehow change the file MEMO.DOC on your default disk. You could make a backup copy of the original version on the same disk by entering this command:

```
COPY MEMO.DOC MEMO.BAK
```

Because the COPY command allows you to specify different names for the source and the target, you can also copy files on different disks or subdirectories and give them different names.

## A Group of Files

*Using global file name characters*

One of the most useful features of the COPY command is its ability to duplicate several files at once. By using the global file name characters * and ?, you can copy a group of files from one disk or subdirectory to another. For example, you could copy all the files with an extension of DOC from the hard disk to the diskette in drive A with this command:

```
COPY *.DOC A:
```

DOS lists each file it copies. When it's finished, your screen might look like Figure 5.13.

**Figure 5.13 Copying a Group of Files**
This particular COPY command allows you to duplicate all files with an extension of DOC and put them on the disk in drive A.

```
C>COPY *.DOC A:
MEMO.DOC
REPORT.DOC
ARTICLE.DOC
CONTRACT.DOC
        4 File(s) copied

C>_
```

You can also use the COPY command to duplicate every non-hidden file on a disk or in a subdirectory. Instead of entering a separate COPY command for each file, you could simply type **COPY *.* A:** and press the **Enter** key. This would copy every file in the current directory to the disk in drive A.

## An Entire Diskette

*Duplicating floppy disks*

Duplicating every file on a diskette with COPY *.* works well for non-hidden files on the source diskette as long as the target diskette is already formatted. But DOS has a more specific command, DISKCOPY, that lets you make an exact copy of an entire diskette all at once. This command formats the target diskette if necessary and copies all files, hidden or otherwise, exactly as they are on the original source diskette. DISKCOPY may only be used to duplicate floppy disks, not hard disks. Furthermore, it may only be used with certain combinations of diskette drives and diskettes. For examplc, you may not use DISKCOPY to copy a 5.25-inch floppy to a 3.5-inch floppy. In general, you can only use DISKCOPY with two diskettes of the same size and type. Fortunately, you can still use DISKCOPY even if you only have a single floppy drive.

If your computer has two identical floppy drives, you can enter **DISKCOPY A: B:** to copy a diskette from drive A to drive B. If your computer has a single floppy drive and a hard disk drive, you would enter **DISKCOPY A: A:** to duplicate a diskette. The DISKCOPY command tells you when and where to insert your source and target diskettes. You may have to swap the source and target diskettes several times if you're using the DISKCOPY command with only a single drive, but the number of times depends on how much RAM your computer has. For example, if your computer has less than 360K of RAM and you're copying a 360K diskette, the entire contents of the disk will not fit into memory. The computer wouldn't be able to copy the source diskette all at once. When DISKCOPY tells you to do so, you would have to take out the source disk, replace it with the target disk, wait for the contents of memory to be copied to the target disk, and then put the source disk back into the drive. When the copying is finished, DISKCOPY asks you if you want to copy another diskette and you can type **N** for no or **Y** for yes.

DISKCOPY is a useful command for making backup copies of especially important diskettes. In fact, the documentation that comes with many application packages strongly suggests that you use the DISKCOPY command to duplicate all of your original diskettes as soon as you get them. Furthermore, it may say that you should put the originals away for safekeeping and only use your copies on a daily basis. Then if you should accidentally erase some file or if your diskette should become damaged or wear out, you would still have your original diskettes from which to make additional copies.

## CHANGING FILE NAMES

*Renaming files*

When you create a file, either through a DOS command such as COPY or from within an application package such as a word processor, you assign it a name. This name need not be permanent, however. DOS lets you change file names very easily. There are several reasons why you might want to change an existing file name. Perhaps you've thought of a more appropriate name or maybe you would like to shorten a name. You may want to copy a file onto a disk that already contains another file with the same name. In this case, you could change the name of the file already on the disk so that its contents will not be overwritten by the file you want to copy. The RENAME command lets you change the names of one or more files.

Changing the name of a single file is simple. Just type **RENAME** (or its abbreviation **REN**), followed by the file name you want to change, and then the new name that file is to have. For example, to change the name of the file MEMO.DOC to MEMO.BAK, you would enter the following command:

```
RENAME MEMO.DOC MEMO.BAK
```

You could then copy a different version of MEMO.DOC from another disk and still have the original version in the file MEMO.BAK.

The RENAME command also can handle a group of files. By using the global file name characters * and ?, you can rename several files at once. For example, with a single command you could rename every file with an extension of DOC and give it an extension of BAK. All you would have to do is type **RENAME *.DOC *.BAK** and press the **Enter** key. Every file in the current directory with an extension of DOC would then be changed to have an extension of BAK. You could change all the file names back again just as easily, because there is no limit to the number of times you can use RENAME on a file.

## ERASING FILES

*Removing files from disks*

Just as you accumulate old memos, notes, letters, clippings, and other scraps of paper on your desk, disks also can become cluttered with files that are no longer needed. Occasionally, you may have to clean up a disk and discard unnecessary files. Once you erase a file, however, it may be difficult or even impossible to retrieve its contents. In fact, DOS includes no utility for "unerasing" files, although such programs are sold by some independent software developers. Before you erase any file, make sure you no longer need it. DOS makes it very easy to erase files, so you should be careful. Many instances of people losing files can be attributed to accidents or carelessness with the ERASE or DEL command.

To erase a single file, all you have to do is enter **ERASE** or **DEL** (short for DELete), followed by the name of the file you want to discard. For example, to delete the file MEMO.DOC, you could type **ERASE MEMO.DOC** and press the **Enter** key. DOS does not ask for confirmation; if it finds that file in your current directory, the file will be erased without comment and you will be presented with the DOS prompt again.

By using the global file name characters * and ?, you can delete several files with a single ERASE command. Needless to say, even more caution is advised here. If you're careful, however, this feature can save you much time. For example, to delete every file with an extension of DOC, you could type **ERASE *.DOC** and press the **Enter** key. Again, DOS would not ask you if you're sure, it would simply delete the files. The only time the ERASE command will ask for confirmation is if you use a potentially destructive parameter such as *.* or ????????.???. Since these file specifications mean every file on a disk or in a particular subdirectory, DOS will ask, "Are you sure (Y/N)?" before erasing every file (see Figure 5.14).

**Figure 5.14 Erasing All the Files in a Directory**
The *.* designation refers to all the files in the current directory.

```
C>ERASE A:*.*
All files in directory will be deleted!
Are you sure (Y/N)?Y

C>_
```

## WRITE-PROTECTION AND COPY-PROTECTION

*Preventing erasure or modification*

In certain situations, commands such as FORMAT, COPY, DISKCOPY, RENAME, and ERASE won't work. Most diskettes have a feature that prevents them from being altered. This feature, called **write-protection**, is somewhat similar to the tabs on audio and video cassette tapes that you can remove to prevent accidentally recording over material you want to save. Most 5.25-inch diskettes have a small rectangle cut out of one side, called the **write-protect notch** (see Figure 5.15(a)). This notch can be covered with a gummed tab or tape to write-protect the diskette. Files on a diskette protected in this manner can be read but not written or altered as long as the notch remains covered. Some 5.25-inch diskettes, such as the original DOS diskettes, don't have a write-protect notch. These diskettes are permanently write-protected.

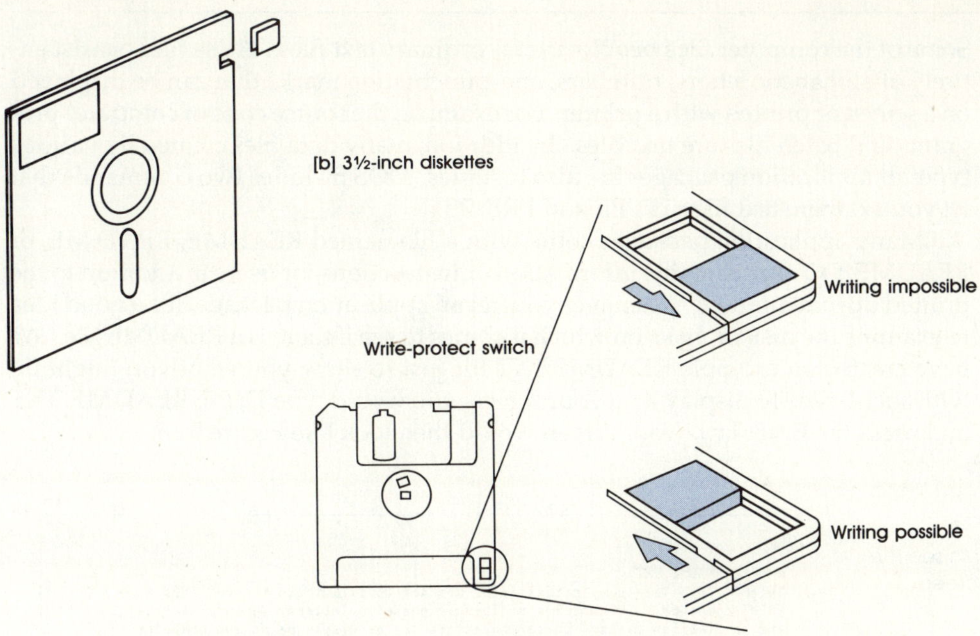


**Figure 5.15 Write-Protecting Diskettes**

The smaller 3.5-inch diskettes also can be write-protected, but the mechanism is slightly different. These diskettes have a **write-protect switch** on the reverse side in the lower right corner (see Figure 5.15(b)). This switch is a tab that can be slid to open or close a little hole in the disk's plastic case. When the hole is open, the diskette is write-protected. When it is closed, files can be written and altered on the diskette. Diskettes that are write-protected cannot be formatted, have files renamed on them, have files copied onto them, or have files erased from them. If you attempt to do so, DOS simply issues a write-protect error message.

With write-protection, you can safeguard programs and data that are stored on diskettes from accidental erasure. Some software developers use **copy-protection** to discourage you from duplicating their packages and illegally selling or giving away copies. Copy-protected diskettes are prepared in a manner that makes it difficult or impossible to copy them with ordinary DOS commands such as COPY and DISKCOPY. Since it is so easy to duplicate diskettes, some manufacturers feel that they must copy-protect their software to prevent widespread distribution to people who don't rightfully pay for it. Unfortunately, copy-protected software is often inconvenient for rightful owners to use or backup. Although manufacturers of most major application packages have since dropped copy-protection from their products, many game programs are still copy-protected.

If you try to use COPY or DISKCOPY on a diskette that is copy-protected, any one of several results might occur. The attempt could simply fail and cause an error message to be displayed. In other cases, the copy procedure might seem to successfully complete, but when you try to run the software it just won't work. Trying to duplicate copy-protected diskettes can be an effort in futility; to spare the user unnecessary frustration, manufacturers should clearly state whether their packages are copy-protected. The safest course is to follow the instructions for using and making backup copies of original diskettes.

## DISPLAYING AND PRINTING TEXT FILES

*Examining file contents*

Some of the computer files people use are ordinary text files. These files consist entirely of alphabetic letters, numbers, and punctuation marks that can be displayed on a screen or printed with a printer. For example, the source code of computer programs and batch files are text files. In addition, many data files created by various types of application packages are also text files. DOS includes two commands that let you examine text files: TYPE and PRINT.

Many application packages come with a file named README, READ.ME, or README.TXT that contains information or instructions for users in addition to the printed documentation. Whenever you get an application package, it's a good idea to examine the disk or disks on which it comes to see if there is a README file. We have created an example README.TXT file just to show you what you might do with such a file. To display it on your screen, you would type **TYPE README.TXT** and press the **Enter** key. Your screen would then look like Figure 5.16.

**Figure 5.16 Displaying a Text File**
The TYPE command allows you to see the contents of a text file on your screen.

```
C>TYPE README.TXT
Hello! This is a sample text file, created to illustrate the DOS TYPE and
PRINT commands. It contains ordinary alphabetic letters, numbers such as 123,
and punctuation marks. These characters can be displayed on any computer
screen and sent to any printer. Text files are usually created with a text
editor or word processing program. They are commonly used for batch files and
programming language source code. Goodbye.

C>-
```

Frequently, README or other text files may be too long to completely fit on a single screen and DOS will scroll the display. In many cases text files contain information that you would like to save on paper. The PRINT command can be used to produce a paper copy of an entire text file. All you would have to do for a paper copy of the README.TXT file is type **PRINT README.TXT** and press the **Enter** key. The first time you use the PRINT command after you turn on your computer, DOS will respond with the somewhat cryptic prompt, *Name of list device [PRN]:*. This allows you to specify which printer to use if you have more than one connected to your computer. The expression "[PRN]" means that unless you indicate otherwise, DOS will send the file to the default printer, which it designates as PRN. If you have only one printer, then this is your default printer. All you have to do here is simply press the **Enter** key. DOS will prompt you in this manner only the first time you use PRINT for any given computer session. Instead of appearing on your screen, the contents of README.TXT then will be sent to your printer.

## RUNNING APPLICATION SOFTWARE

*Executing programs*

Every time you enter a DOS command you are running a program. Internal commands are programs that are kept in memory by DOS, while external commands are programs that are kept on a disk until they are actually used. Application programs are much like external commands, although they are not included with DOS and are generally larger than external commands. Nevertheless, application packages are run in the same manner as external commands.

To run an application package, first you must make sure that the disk containing its files is in one of your drives. The program will either be installed on your hard disk or you must run it off a floppy. If the drive that contains the program's files is not your current default drive, then you should either switch drives or prefix the name of the program with the drive specifier. Otherwise, you simply type the program's file name and press the **Enter** key. This file name will have an extension of EXE, COM, or BAT, but you don't have to type the extension. For example, to run the dBASE III PLUS data base management package, you type **DBASE** and press the **Enter** key. You may have to consult the program's documentation to determine which file name you should enter.

## SUBDIRECTORIES

*Organizing files*

As we said before, a subdirectory is a group of files in a hierarchical file system. Subdirectories, sometimes simply called *directories*, are like nesting file folders. They are invaluable tools for organizing programs and data files on high-capacity storage devices. In addition, subdirectories make it easier for the operating system to locate a particular file because large numbers of files are divided into smaller subgroups. Although subdirectories are almost always found on hard disks, they are occasionally used on floppy disks, too. DOS includes commands that let you create, change, and remove subdirectories.

Every disk has a single main directory, known as the **root directory**. DOS automatically creates a root directory on every disk you format. This is the directory you are in when you first boot up DOS or when you first change your default drive. The root directory itself has no name, but it's represented by a single backslash (\). In some ways, the root directory is like a large room that can contain individual files as well as filing cabinets. These filing cabinets can contain any number of file folders, which can themselves contain other file folders as well as individual files.

Subdirectories help you organize and more quickly find files, but there is another reason for using them, especially on hard disks. DOS limits the number of entries that can be in a root directory. The actual number depends on the type of disk, but it is almost always less than 512. In other words, a hard disk without subdirectories can hold no more than 512 files. Although this might seem like quite a few, hard disks generally have room for thousands of files. In most cases, you simply must use subdirectories to fully utilize the capacity of your hard disk. Unlike the root directory, subdirectories can contain any number of files. The number is limited only by the amount of space available on your disk.

### Making Directories

*Creating new subdirectories*

The best way to organize a hard disk is to minimize the number of individual files in the root directory. Except for a few critical files, the root directory should contain only subdirectories. For example, imagine that you have a new computer with a hard disk. The hard disk is formatted, and DOS has already been installed in its own subdirectory. The root directory contains only three other files, as shown in Figure 5.5. These critical files are AUTOEXEC.BAT, COMMAND.COM, and CONFIG.SYS. We'll discuss AUTOEXEC.BAT later in this chapter when we cover batch files. We've already said that COMMAND.COM is the program that processes your DOS commands. CONFIG.SYS is a special file that DOS looks for in the root directory of the default disk whenever you boot up. It contains commands that set up your system in a certain way, and is usually created when you install DOS or a new application package.

Let's say that you plan to use DOS and three basic application packages: a word processor, a spreadsheet program, and a data base manager. A good way to set up your hard disk is to create three additional subdirectories: one for your word processor, one for your spreadsheet, and one for your data base manager.

The DOS command MKDIR (MaKe DIRectory) or just MD is used to create a new subdirectory. To create a subdirectory, you type **MD** and a name. The rules for naming subdirectories are the same as the rules for making filenames. But subdirectories can themselves contain other subdirectories, so the name of a subdirectory may be prefaced with a **path**. This is a drive specifier followed by a list of subdirectory names, separated by backslashes, that describes the route you would take to arrive at a particular subdirectory. The simplest path is a single backslash \, which represents the root directory of your current default drive.

Let's say that you want to create subdirectories for your three application packages. You could name the subdirectories WP, SS, and DB. The complete paths for these subdirectories would be C:\WP, C:\SS, and C:\DB. But C:\ is your current directory path, so you don't have to specify it. To create the three subdirectories, you would type the following commands, pressing the **Enter** key after each one:

```
MD WP
MD SS
MD DB
```

At this point, if you entered **DIR** to display your hard disk's directory, your screen would look like Figure 5.17.

**Figure 5.17 Creating Subdirectories**
The MD command is used to create new subdirectories.

```
C>MD WP

C>MD SS

C>MD DB

C>DIR

 Volume in drive C is HARD DISK
 Volume Serial Number is 124C-5488
 Directory of  C:\

AUTOEXEC BAT       56 08-16-88  10:01a
COMMAND  COM    37637 06-17-88  12:00p
CONFIG   SYS      101 08-16-88   9:48a
DOS         <DIR>     08-16-88   9:42a
WP          <DIR>     08-16-88   4:55p
SS          <DIR>     08-16-88   4:55p
DB          <DIR>     08-16-88   4:56p
        7 File(s)   19806208 bytes free

C>_
```

As you can see, your root directory now has seven entries: the files AUTOEXEC.BAT, COMMAND.COM, and CONFIG.SYS; and the subdirectories DOS, WP, SS, and DB. Subdirectories are indicated by the <DIR> designation in the listing. Conceptually, the structure of this hard disk is shown in Figure 5.18. In this diagram, the boxes are directories and the names without boxes are files.

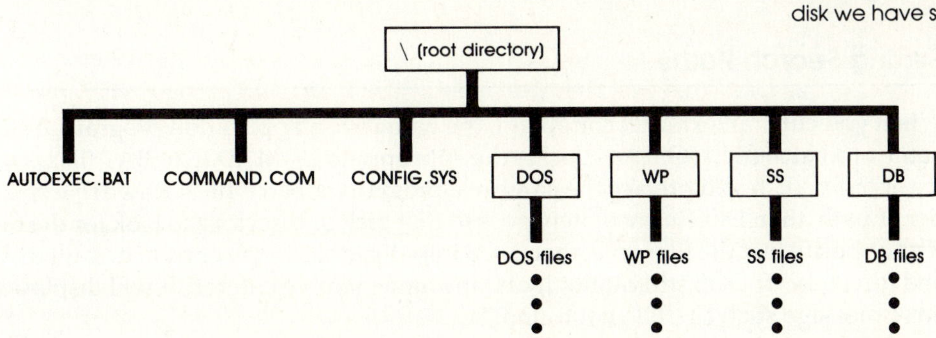


**Figure 5.18 Hard Disk Structure**
This diagram shows the structure of the hard disk we have set up.

## Changing Directories

*Moving into a different directory*

At this point, the root directory is your current default directory. You are still "in" the root directory. Unless you specify otherwise, DOS looks for files only in this directory. To fully utilize subdirectories, you must be able to move in and out of them. You need the ability to change your default directory just as you can change your default drive. The CHDIR (CHange DIRectory) or CD command lets you do this. For example, to change from the root directory to the WP subdirectory, you could type **CD WP** and press the **Enter** key. To change back to the root directory, you would type **CD ** and press the **Enter** key.

Once you are in a subdirectory, you can almost think of it as a separate disk. Many DOS commands that deal with files will operate only on the files in your current directory unless you specify otherwise. For example, to set up your WP directory you need to copy the files from the floppy disks that came with your word processing package. If you are currently in the subdirectory C:\WP, you would put a diskette from the word processing package in drive A and then type **COPY A:*.*** and press the **Enter** key. This command would copy every file on the diskette in drive A to your current directory, C:\WP. You could then repeat the process with any additional diskettes that came with the word processing package. Once you do this, you can take the diskette out of drive A and use your word processing package as long as you remain in your WP subdirectory.

## Removing Directories

*Deleting empty subdirectories*

Just as unneeded files must occasionally be deleted, sometimes subdirectories must be removed, too. You cannot, however, remove a subdirectory with the ERASE (or DEL) command. The DOS command RMDIR (ReMove DIRectory) or RD must be used instead. Before removing a subdirectory, you must first erase every file inside. A subdirectory can only be removed if it is empty. Furthermore, only one subdirectory can be removed at a time. You cannot remove the root directory or your current default directory. You must return to the root directory or be in some unrelated directory before you can remove a subdirectory. So, if you want to remove the WP subdirectory, you would first have to erase all the files inside. If you are already in the WP subdirectory, you would first type **ERASE *.*** and press the **Enter** key. Note that this will only delete the files inside the WP subdirectory; it will not affect the root directory or any other subdirectories on the disk. Then you would return to the root directory by typing **CD ** and pressing the **Enter** key. Finally, you would actually remove the subdirectory entry by entering **RD WP**.

## Setting Search Paths

*Telling DOS which directories to search*

When you enter an external command, the name of an application program, or the name of a batch file, DOS must locate the appropriate COM, EXE, or BAT file before it can proceed. If you preface the name of a program or batch file with a drive specifier or path, then DOS immediately goes to that disk or directory to look for the file. If you specify just the filename, then DOS initially looks in the current default drive and directory. If DOS still cannot locate the name you've entered, it will display an error message such as, "File not found."

Subdirectories would be tedious to use if you had to specify the full path every time you wanted to run a program in a different directory. Fortunately, DOS provides a means by which you can specify one or more paths for it to automatically search whenever it cannot immediately find a COM, EXE, or BAT file. The PATH command lets you do this. For example, let's say that you have all the DOS external command files in your DOS subdirectory. Unless you are in that subdirectory, you cannot use a command such as FORMAT without specifying its path. You can, however, use the PATH command once, say when you first turn on your computer, to tell DOS to look in the DOS subdirectory when it can't find a particular COM, EXE, or BAT file. To do this you would type **PATH C:\DOS** and press the **Enter** key. Instead of entering **C:\DOS\FORMAT A:** to format a diskette from a directory other than the DOS subdirectory, you could simply enter **FORMAT A:** and DOS will look for the file FORMAT.COM in the DOS subdirectory.

The PATH command can also accept just drive specifiers and the root directory designation as well as subdirectory paths. Furthermore, several search paths can be specified, as long as you separate them with semicolons (;). For example, you could tell DOS to automatically search the root directory of drive C, the DOS subdirectory, the WP subdirectory, and drive A, in that order with this command:

```
PATH C:\;C:\DOS;C:\WP;A:
```

Finally, note that the PATH command only sets up search paths for files that can be executed. Even if you use the PATH command, DOS can only find files with COM, EXE, and BAT extensions. Files with other extensions will not be found unless they are in the current directory or unless their paths are also specified. IBM DOS versions 3.30 and 4.00 do include a command that can be used to set up search paths for other kinds of files. This command, called APPEND, is not found in earlier versions of DOS. APPEND is often used in addition to the PATH command. Search paths are specified in the same manner for both commands.

## Displaying Directory Information

Computer users often create many subdirectories on their hard disks. Furthermore, it's common to have much more complicated structures than the simple ones we've described in this section. Since every subdirectory can itself contain any number of subdirectories, users can create very complex directories. Sometimes, they might even forget how their disks are organized or which subdirectory they are currently using. DOS provides several simple methods for providing information about subdirectories and search paths. Some commands can be entered without any parameters and DOS merely reports what the current settings are. For example, if you forget what subdirectory you are currently using, you can simply type **CD** and press the **Enter** key. DOS will respond with the full path of your current default directory. Similarly, if you forget the search paths you've specified, you can type **PATH** or **APPEND** (with DOS 3.30 or 4.00) without any parameters and then press the **Enter** key. DOS will respond with the list of search paths previously specified.

*Seeing the structure of a disk*

Finally, one DOS command can display the structure of your entire disk. The TREE command lists the paths of all subdirectories on the specified disk. For example, let's say that your hard disk is set up like we described earlier with four subdirectories named DOS, WP, SS, and DB. Furthermore, assume the DOS subdirectory contains all of the DOS external command files and the PATH command was used to set the search path to C:\DOS. To display all of your subdirectories, you would type **TREE** and press the **Enter** key. Figure 5.19 shows the listing that would appear on your screen. If you also wanted to see the name of every file in the root directory and all subdirectories, you could use the /F parameter and enter **TREE /F** instead.

```
C>TREE
Directory PATH listing for Volume HARD DISK
Volume Serial Number is 124C-5488
C:.
├───DOS
├───WP
├───SS
└───DB

C>_
```

**Figure 5.19 The TREE Command**
The TREE command displays the subdirectories on your disk.

## BATCH FILES

*Automating commands and programs*

As we said in Chapter 4, a batch file is simply a text file that contains a list of commands or programs to be run. Batch files are usually created with a text editor or word processing program. In DOS, every batch file name must have an extension of BAT. A batch file is generally invoked by typing its filename and pressing the **Enter** key. When this is done, DOS executes each command or program listed in the batch file, one at a time. DOS includes features that enable experienced computer users to construct complex and very helpful batch files. Even if you never actually make your own batch files, you will undoubtedly use some if you work with DOS.

The most commonly used batch file is a special one named AUTOEXEC.BAT. Whenever you boot up your computer, DOS searches the root directory of the current drive for this file. If there is no AUTOEXEC.BAT file present, then DOS simply asks you for the date and the time and then displays its prompt. On the other hand, if AUTOEXEC.BAT is found, then the commands in that batch file are automatically executed. You will not be asked to supply the date and time unless the DATE and TIME commands are present in the AUTOEXEC.BAT file.

Since the AUTOEXEC.BAT file is automatically invoked every time you boot up your computer, it is ideal for executing certain commands and programs you always run when you first turn on your machine. For example, let's say that you have a DOS subdirectory containing all of the external commands. You could put a PATH command in the AUTOEXEC.BAT file to set the search path to C:\DOS so that the external DOS commands can be executed from any directory. This is exactly what was done when DOS was installed for the examples in this chapter. Most DOS users eventually set up their own AUTOEXEC.BAT file or have someone else set one up for them.

### The Real World

## CP/M Crash Lands

There's an interesting story that claims to explain why the IBM Personal Computer was introduced with its own new operating system, DOS, rather than with the 16-bit version of the existing and popular CP/M system. Truth or myth, it makes a fascinating legend.

As the story goes, when IBM came shopping for CP/M, Gary Kildall, the man who created CP/M, intentionally kept IBM's representatives waiting, and fuming, while he flew his plane for hours in the skies overhead. Kildall, we're told, thumbed his nose at IBM as a customer, while Bill Gates, the head of Microsoft, rolled out the red carpet for IBM. Gates donned his rarely worn business suits for meetings with IBM to demonstrate that he was serious about doing business with them.

In the 8-bit computer world, Gates' company, Microsoft, had been dominant in programming languages and Kildall's company, Digital Research, dominated operating systems. IBM was prepared to keep it that way, planning to hire each of them for their specialties. But Kildall played hard to get, even after IBM had Bill Gates plead the case for Kildall's cooperation.

In the end, IBM turned to Microsoft for an operating system as well as programming languages, and Microsoft had to come up with one in very short order. It delivered the goods by picking up an existing but little-known CP/M-like operating system and polishing it to meet IBM's requirements. That operating system became the DOS that nearly every PC user works with.

With DOS as the dominant operating system for the PC family, CP/M's fortunes took a nose dive. Gary Kildall's flight led to a crash landing for his operating system.

Source: *Inside the IBM PC* by Peter Norton, Copyright 1986 by Brady Communications Company, Inc., pp. 269-271.

## THE DOS SHELL

*Using the menu and file system*

Starting with DOS version 4.00, IBM included an enhancement to the operating system's user interface called the *DOS Shell*. This feature allows you to complete common DOS tasks by selecting options from a menu instead of entering commands at the DOS prompt. Novices sometimes find it easier to use the DOS Shell than ordinary DOS commands.

We have not been using the DOS Shell in this chapter so far. It wasn't offered with previous versions of DOS and most people are still using regular DOS commands. Nevertheless, it is worthwhile to take a brief look at this new user interface. If you have DOS 4.00, you might find that you prefer using the DOS Shell.

The DOS Shell is an option; you can choose whether or not to use it. DOS 4.00 can be installed so that the DOS Shell is activated every time you turn on the computer. This is done by putting the DOSSHELL command in the AUTOEXEC.BAT file. If DOS is installed without putting the DOSSHELL command in the AUTOEXEC.BAT file, you can still use the DOS Shell by entering this command yourself. For example, to activate the DOS Shell from the DOS prompt, you simply type **DOSSHELL** and press the **Enter** key.

Figure 5.20 shows the first screen you see in the DOS Shell—the Start Programs screen. From here you can run programs, customize the DOS Shell menus, change the screen colors, and manage your files and subdirectories. For example, several common DOS tasks are available under the heading DOS Utilities. To select this heading, you press the **Down Arrow** key three times to position the reverse-video highlight bar on top of it and then press the **Enter** key.

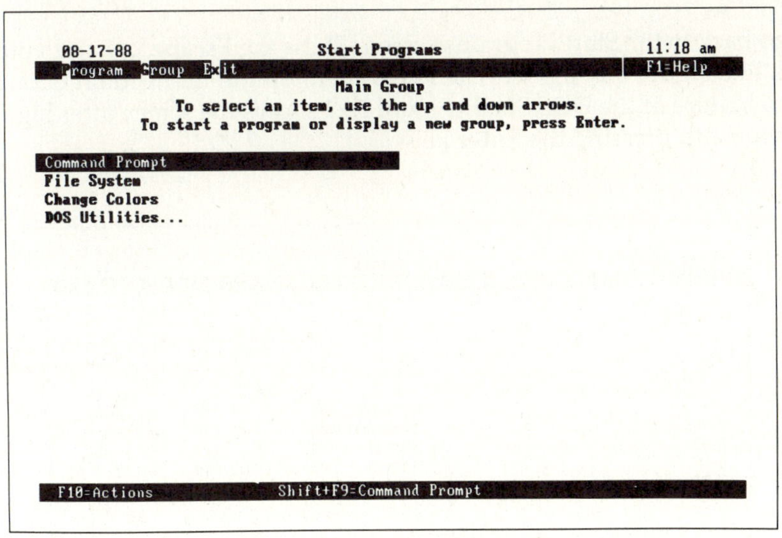


**Figure 5.20 Start Programs Screen**
This is the first screen you see after starting the DOS Shell.

Figure 5.21 shows the new screen that appears—the DOS Utilities menu. The options that appear in this menu correspond to some DOS commands. If you want to copy a diskette, for instance, you would position the highlight bar on the second option in this menu and press the **Enter** key. The DOS Shell would then prompt you for more information about making the copy. Although this menu contains only a few DOS functions, other commands can be added as options, such as CHKDSK, COPY, TYPE, and PRINT.

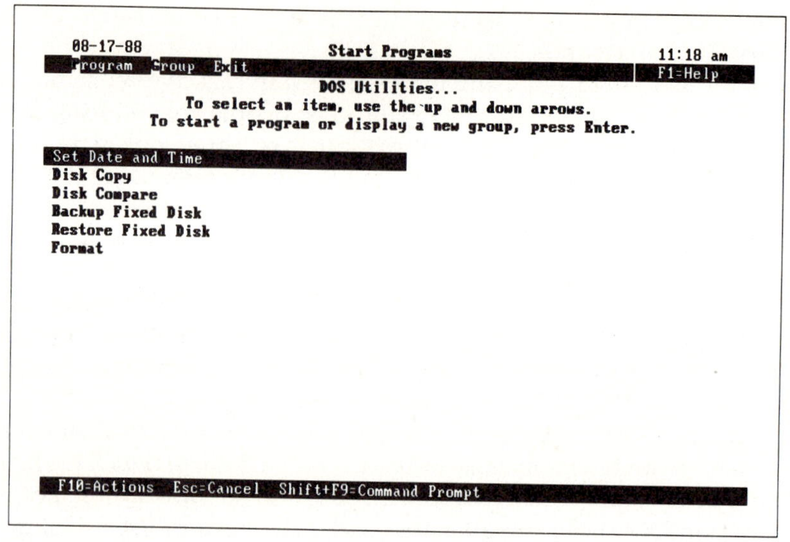


**Figure 5.21 DOS Utilities Menu**
This is the menu you see after selecting the DOS Utilities option from the Start Programs screen.

Now let's go back to the Start Programs screen. Press the **Escape** key and your screen will look like Figure 5.20 again. The File System option in the Main Group is another useful feature of the DOS Shell. Figure 5.22 shows the screen after highlighting this option and pressing the **Enter** key.

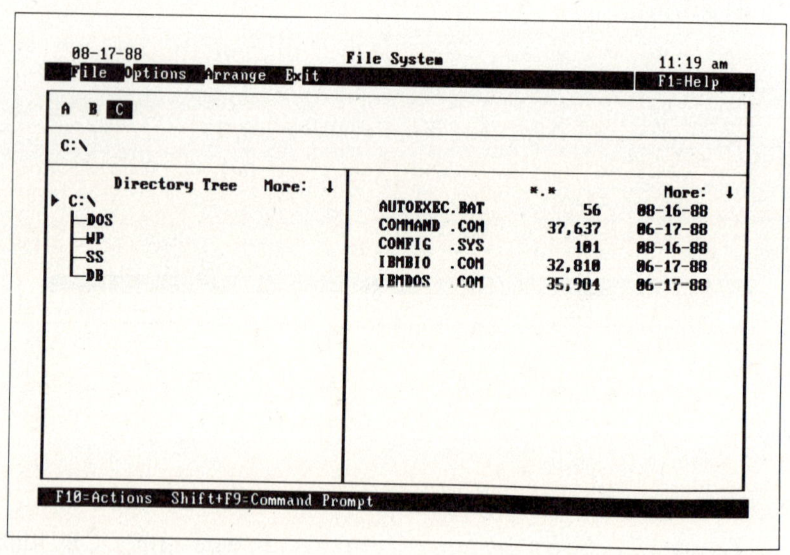


**Figure 5.22 File System Screen**
After you select the File System option from the Start Programs screen, the DOS Shell displays a directory tree of your disk and lists the files in your root directory.

The File System shows your current disk and subdirectory path. The left side of the screen presents a chart that shows the structure of the current disk. The right side of the screen shows the files in the currently selected directory, including the hidden files. Right now, the root directory of hard disk C is depicted. This is the same hard disk that we used before in the section on subdirectories. You should recognize the files AUTOEXEC.BAT, COMMAND.COM, and CONFIG.SYS. The two additional entries, IBMBIO.COM and IBMDOS.COM, are the hidden files of DOS in the root directory of the hard disk.

Changing to another subdirectory and viewing its contents is very easy. For example, let's look at the DOS subdirectory. You press the **Tab** key to move the highlight bar from the disk drive letter to the directory tree chart. Then you press the **Down Arrow** key once to highlight the DOS subdirectory. Figure 5.23 shows the screen you see. The right side lists the files in the DOS subdirectory in alphabetical order. If you press the **Tab** key again, the highlight bar will move to this directory listing. You can execute any program in the subdirectory simply by highlighting it and pressing the **Enter** key.

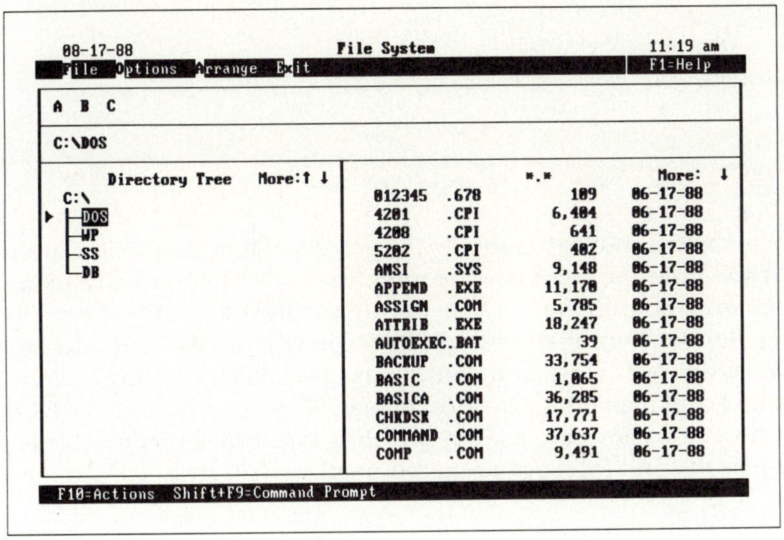


**Figure 5.23 Viewing a Subdirectory**
After you select a subdirectory from the tree, the DOS Shell shows its contents in the box on the right side of your screen.

Some people prefer to use a menu-oriented system like the DOS Shell, while others rather enter commands from the DOS prompt. Fortunately, it's easy to switch back and forth between the DOS prompt and the DOS Shell. For example, to activate the DOS prompt, you hold down the **Shift** key and press the **F9** function key (see Figure 5.24). When you want to return to the DOS Shell from the DOS prompt, you type **EXIT** and press the **Enter** key.

Although we've only briefly introduced the DOS Shell, you should see that it can be an easy system for novices to use. There are many features of the DOS Shell we have not covered. For example, the DOS Shell can be set up to present more attractive screens if your computer has a high-resolution graphics adapter and dis-

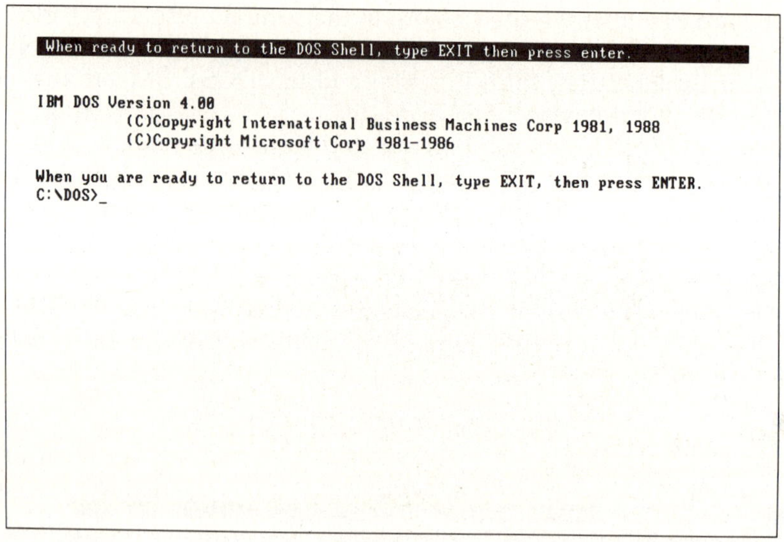


**Figure 5.24 Returning to the DOS Prompt**
Pressing **Shift-F9** returns you to the DOS prompt, where you can use ordinary DOS commands.

play. It can also work with a mouse to simplify the process of selecting options from menus. Unlike DOS from the command prompt, the DOS Shell provides comprehensive help information; all you have to do is press the **F1** function key. The DOS Shell is very flexible since it allows you to create new menus and add any programs you like as options. Existing menus can be modified by adding options, deleting options, and copying options from other menus. So even though the DOS Shell can make it easier for a novice to use the operating system at a very basic level, it also offers complex features for more advanced users.

## Summary

- *Why DOS is such an important operating system.* DOS is the single most popular microcomputer operating system in the world.
- *Why there are different versions of DOS.* DOS is continually upgraded to keep pace with new hardware capabilities, especially related to disk drives.
- *How to boot up DOS.* Turn on your computer with DOS installed on the default disk; if the computer is already on, press **Ctrl-Alt-Del**.
- *How to see what files are on a disk.* Use the DIR (directory) command to examine the contents of disks and subdirectories.
- *DOS file names.* A file name has two parts: the primary part, which is from one to eight characters long, and an optional extension, which is separated from the primary part by a period and can be up to three characters long.
- *DOS keyboard functions.* Press **Esc** to cancel a line. Press **Pause** or **Ctrl-Num Lock** to halt screen scrolling. Press **Ctrl-Break** to cancel a command. Press **Print Screen** or **Shift-PrtSc** to print the current screen. Press **Ctrl-PrtSc** to echo to the printer.

- *How to work from a different disk drive.* Change the default disk drive by entering a drive letter followed by a colon.
- *How to check disk and memory status.* Use the CHKDSK command to display information about a disk and the memory installed in your computer.
- *How to format disks.* Use the FORMAT command, which lets you set up program and data disks as well as DOS boot-up disks.
- *How to copy files and disks.* Duplicate one or more files with the COPY command. Duplicate floppy disks with the DISKCOPY command.
- *How to change file names.* Use the RENAME command to change the names of existing files.
- *How to erase files.* Use the ERASE or DEL command to remove files from disks.
- *How to protect floppy disks.* Diskettes can be write-protected so that files cannot be erased or altered.
- *How to display and print text files.* The TYPE command displays a text file on the screen, while the PRINT command sends it to the printer.
- *How to run an application package.* After making sure its disk is in your default drive, type the program's name and press the **Enter** key.
- *How to use subdirectories.* Use subdirectories to better organize files on your disks, especially hard disks.
- *How to use batch files.* Use batch files to automate frequently used programs and DOS commands.
- *How to use the DOS Shell.* If you have IBM DOS 4.00, you can use the DOS Shell menu and file system by entering **DOSSHELL**.

## Command Summary

The following table summarizes DOS keypresses.

| KEYPRESS | DESCRIPTION |
|---|---|
| Ctrl-Alt-Del | Reboots DOS. |
| Ctrl-Break | Cancels a command. |
| Ctrl-PrtSc | Echos to the printer |
| Enter | Processes a command. |
| Esc | Cancels a line. |
| Pause or Ctrl-Num Lock | Pauses screen scrolling. |
| Print Screen or Shift-PrtSc | Prints the contents of the screen. |

The following table summarizes commonly used DOS commands. All of them are mentioned either in the chapter text or in the On-line Exercises and Projects at the end of this chapter.

| COMMAND | DESCRIPTION |
|---|---|
| APPEND | Specifies the paths to be searched for all files. |
| BACKUP | Backs up a hard disk to floppies. |
| CD or CHDIR | Switches between subdirectories. |
| CHKDSK | Displays a disk and memory status report. |
| CLS | Clears the screen. |
| COPY | Duplicates one or more files. |
| DATE | Prompts you to enter or change the date. |
| DIR | Lists the files on a disk or in a subdirectory. |
| DISKCOPY | Duplicates an entire floppy disk. |
| DOSSHELL | Starts the DOS Shell (IBM DOS 4.00). |
| ERASE or DEL | Removes one or more files from a disk. |
| EXIT | Returns to the DOS Shell from the DOS prompt. |
| FORMAT | Prepares a disk for use. |
| LABEL | Creates or changes a disk's name (volume label). |
| MD or MKDIR | Creates a new subdirectory. |
| PATH | Tells DOS where to search for COM, EXE, and BAT files. |
| PRINT | Sends a text file to the printer. |
| RD or RMDIR | Removes a subdirectory. |
| RENAME or REN | Changes the name of one or more files. |
| RESTORE | Restores files backed up with the BACKUP command. |
| SORT | Accepts input, arranges it in order, and writes it out. |
| TIME | Prompts you to enter or change the time. |
| TREE | Displays the directory structure of a disk. |
| TYPE | Displays a text file on the screen. |
| VER | Displays the DOS version number. |
| VOL | Displays the disk name (volume label). |

## Key Terms

As an extra review of this chapter, try defining the following terms. If you have trouble with any of them, refer to the page number listed.

- booting up (150)
- copy-protection (169)
- default drive (152)
- delimiter (155)
- DOS prompt (system prompt) (152)
- drive specifier (155)
- extension (156)
- external commands (transient routines) (153)
- file specification (157)
- filename (156)
- global file name characters (157)
- internal commands (resident routines) (153)
- parameter (155)
- path (172)
- root directory (171)
- scrolling (159)
- upwardly compatible (149)
- write-protect notch (168)
- write-protect switch (169)
- write-protection (168)

## Review Questions

1. What is the most popular microcomputer operating system?
2. Describe the major reason behind new releases of DOS.
3. If an operating system loads programs into memory and begins their execution, how does DOS start initially?
4. Which key or keys do you press to reboot DOS if your computer is already turned on?

5. Why are internal commands kept in memory?
6. Which command would you enter to list a directory of the current default disk drive?
7. What are the two parts that make up the name of a DOS file?
8. What does the * character mean when it is used in a file specification?
9. Which key or keys would you press to cancel a line you are typing at the DOS prompt before you've pressed the **Enter** key?
10. How do you change the default disk drive?
11. What specifically does the CHKDSK command do?
12. What parameter would you use with the FORMAT command to prepare a diskette with which you could boot up your computer?
13. What is the difference between the COPY command and the DISKCOPY command?
14. What does ERASE *.* do?
15. How do you write-protect a 5.25-inch diskette?
16. Which commands would you use to display and print a text file?
17. How do you run most application packages?
18. What are the commands you use to create, change to, and remove subdirectories?
19. Which command would you use to tell DOS to automatically search certain directories every time you enter the filename of a COM, EXE, or BAT file?
20. What batch file is automatically executed every time you boot up a computer running DOS?

## Multiple Choice

1. The process of initially loading and executing the operating system is called
   (a) formatting. (b) booting up.
   (c) prompting. (d) scrolling.
2. Suppose that after you enter the DIR command, DOS begins to display a long list of file names. After a second or so, you've seen enough and want to cancel the DIR command. Which key(s) do you press?
   (a) Esc (b) Enter
   (c) Ctrl-PrtSc (d) Ctrl-Break
3. What is the usual DOS prompt after you boot up from a hard disk?
   (a) A> (b) B>
   (c) C> (d) D>
4. Which command would you use to find out how much memory is installed in your computer?
   (a) FORMAT (b) CHKDSK
   (c) DISKCOPY (d) DIR

5. Which of the following commands would you use if you wanted to copy a floppy disk, but had only one floppy drive in your computer?
   (a) DISKCOPY A: A: (b) DISKCOPY A: C:
   (c) DISKCOPY (d) COPY *.* A:
6. ERASE *.* deletes every file in your current directory. Which of the following commands does the same thing?
   (a) DEL *.DOC (b) ERASE FILE.*
   (c) DEL ????????.??? (d) COPY A: B:
7. What is the write-protect mechanism on 3.5-inch floppy disks?
   (a) write-protect notch (b) write-protect switch
   (c) write-protect label (d) copy-protect lock
8. What kind of files are usually processed by the TYPE and PRINT commands?
   (a) COM files (b) EXE files
   (c) text files (d) graphics files
9. Every disk has a single main directory known as the
   (a) subdirectory. (b) root directory.
   (c) branch directory. (d) atomic directory.
10. Which of the following paths represents the root directory?
    (a) \ (b) C:\DOS
    (c) C:\ROOT\DIRECTORY (d) A:\WP
11. What must you do before removing a subdirectory?
    (a) Use CD to move into that subdirectory.
    (b) Use MD to make a new subdirectory.
    (c) Erase every file inside.
    (d) Copy every file inside.
12. Which command would you use to see the structure of a disk?
    (a) CHKDSK (b) TREE
    (c) DISKCOPY (d) DIR
13. Which of the following extensions must be part of every batch file?
    (a) BAT (b) COM
    (c) EXE (d) SYS
14. Which batch file is automatically executed every time you boot up a computer running DOS?
    (a) AUTOEXEC.BAT (b) COMMAND.BAT
    (c) CONFIG.BAT (d) DOS.BAT
15. Which version of IBM DOS was the first to include the DOS Shell?
    (a) 1.00 (b) 2.00
    (c) 3.00 (d) 4.00

## On-line Exercises

1. Produce a directory listing of the disk in your default drive. If you have a printer, press **Ctrl-PrtSc** to turn on printer echoing before you issue the directory command so that you can get the listing on paper.

2. On many systems DOS asks you to supply the date and time when you boot up. Two commands, DATE and TIME, tell you the current date and time and let you change these settings. Try the DATE and TIME commands. If you don't want to change the date and time settings, just press the **Enter** key when asked for the new date or time. Notice how DOS automatically figures out and displays the day of the week.
3. Use the * global file name character to produce a directory listing of all the files on your current disk with an EXE extension.
4. Do you know what version of DOS you are using? Type **VER** and press the **Enter** key to find out.
5. DOS versions 3.0 and newer have a command that lets you create, change, or delete a disk's name, or volume label, without having to reformat the disk. If you have DOS 3.0 or newer, use the LABEL command to change the name of a disk. Use the DIR command to see the result. Now change the volume label back to what it was before.
6. Another way to find out the volume label of a disk is to use the VOL command. Put a formatted floppy disk in drive A and enter **VOL A:** to see the volume label of that disk.
7. You can create a text file using just the keyboard and the COPY command. This can be used to make a small batch file. In certain cases DOS can refer to its peripheral devices as if they were files. Several file names have a special meaning to DOS. These are called DOS device names. CON refers to the console, or the keyboard and screen. For example, enter this command:

   ```
   COPY CON TEST.BAT
   ```

   Now type the following lines, pressing the **Enter** key at the end of each one:

   ```
   ECHO This is a batch file to see the date and time
   DATE
   TIME
   ```

   When you are finished, press the **F6** function key and then press the **Enter** key. To use your new batch file, type **TEST** and press the **Enter** key.
8. It is also possible to display a text file on the screen with the COPY command instead of the TYPE command. For example, make sure you have completed Exercise 7 and then enter the following command:

   ```
   COPY TEST.BAT CON
   ```

9. Just as CON is a DOS device name that refers to the keyboard and screen, PRN is a DOS device name that refers to the printer. Use the COPY command to print the TEST.BAT file you created in Exercise 7.
10. The DIR command has two optional parameters that can be useful when looking at disks with many of files on them. The /P parameter will automatically pause scrolling when the screen is full, then wait for you to press a key before continuing. The /W parameter will display the directory in a wide format across the screen, omitting the sizes and creation dates and times so that more file names will fit at once. Try these commands:

    ```
    DIR /P
    DIR /W
    ```

11. As you've noticed by now, DOS does not erase the screen after you finish a command. This helps you see what you've just done, but it can leave the screen looking cluttered. Fortunately, it's easy to erase your screen with CLS, the clear screen command. Try it now.

12. As we said in this chapter, the TREE command can be used with the /F parameter to list all the files in all the subdirectories on a disk. For example, make sure you are in the root directory, and then type **TREE /F** and press the **Enter** key.

13. DOS has a feature called *redirection* that lets you change the destination of a command's output. For example, if you have a printer, enter this command:

    ```
    DIR >PRN
    ```

    The > symbol redirects the output of the DIR command to the printer, symbolized by the device name PRN. This redirection feature can be used with most DOS commands.

14. Redirection can also be used to create a text file. For example, enter this command:

    ```
    DIR >DIRLIST.TXT
    ```

    This time, the output from the DIR command is redirected into a newly created text file named DIRLIST.TXT. To see the results, type **TYPE DIRLIST.TXT** and press the **Enter** key. If you have a printer, make a paper copy of this file with the PRINT command.

15. DOS has several commands that act as *filters* by accepting input, changing that input, and writing the results to an output device. SORT, one of the DOS filter commands, receives information from an input device, arranges the information in numerical or alphabetical order, and then writes the information to an output device. In addition, DOS has a feature similar to redirection called *piping*. This feature, symbolized by the vertical bar ( | ), allows you to channel the input from one program or command into another program. For example, enter this command:

    ```
    DIR | SORT
    ```

    This command pipes the output from DIR into the SORT filter, which alphabetizes the file names and presents them on your screen.

## Projects

1. The DOS BACKUP command allows you to make a back up copy of a single file, a group of files, an entire subdirectory, or an entire disk. In most cases, BACKUP is used to copy all or part of a hard disk to a group of floppy disks. Get four formatted floppy disks that are either blank or don't have any important files on them. If your computer has a hard disk with a DOS subdirectory, enter this command:

    ```
    BACKUP C:\DOS\*.*  A:
    ```

    Follow the directions given by DOS. See how the BACKUP command can use several diskettes. This feature makes it more appropriate than the COPY command for backing lots of files. BACKUP can even be used to back up an entire hard disk, although it would be a tedious job requiring many floppies (around sixty 5.25-inch diskettes for a 20-megabyte hard disk). If you accidentally erased the contents of the DOS subdirectory on your hard disk and wanted to restore the files you backed up, you would enter the following command (but don't do it now):

```
RESTORE A:  C:\DOS\*.*
```

2. This book was written on an IBM Personal Computer AT with a hard disk, running DOS. The word processor used, Microsoft Word, was stored in its own subdirectory named WORD. The PATH command was used so that the program could be used from inside other subdirectories. The entire textbook was stored under a subdirectory named TEXTBOOK. However, because each chapter often consisted of several files (some of them for figures), the TEXTBOOK subdirectory was further divided so that there was a subdirectory for each of the sixteen chapters. These subdirectories were named CHAP01, CHAP02, CHAP03, and so on. List the MD commands and the PATH command you would use to create this structure on a hard disk (the C drive). Give the CD command you would use to go into the subdirectory that contains Chapter 5. Finally, draw a diagram, like the output of the TREE command, that illustrates the relationship between the directories on this hard disk.
3. If you have DOS 4.00, invoke the DOS Shell. Try using the Format and Disk Copy options from the DOS Utilities menu. Then switch to the File System and select the DOS subdirectory. Now try using some of the DOS commands. Use the F1 key to get more information about the DOS Shell. Go back to the Start Programs screen and try changing the screen colors. When you are finished exploring the DOS Shell, return to the DOS prompt.
4. Now that you've seen DOS in more detail and perhaps even used it, what do you think of it? Did you find DOS commands straightforward enough? Would you rather use the DOS prompt or the DOS Shell? Prepare a report that describes your impressions of DOS and list what you feel are its advantages and disadvantages.

# Part 3

# WORD PROCESSING

Next to operating systems, which all microcomputers require, word processing packages are undoubtedly the most used type of software. It has been estimated that more than 90 percent of all microcomputer owners have at least one word processing program. This means that tens of millions of word processing packages are available, ready to produce all kinds of documents. A word processing package is the first application package most novices learn to use. Whether you need to create a brief memo or an entire book, word processing software, along with a microcomputer and printer, can help you do the job faster, easier, and neater. In Part 3, we examine the benefits and techniques of word processing. Chapter 6 is a general introduction to word processing concepts. Chapter 7 describes WordStar 5.0, the newest version of one of the most long-lived and popular microcomputer word processing software packages.

# 6

# Word Processing Concepts

## In This Chapter

## PREVIEW

As we said back in Chapter 3, a word processing package is software that helps you enter, store, modify, format, copy, and print text. Word processing packages are by far the most popular type of application software, since almost every microcomputer user has at least one word processing program. In fact, many people purchase microcomputers solely for their word processing capabilities. The reason is simple. Anyone who routinely produces written material can benefit from a word processing package.

Our economy has been gradually shifting its emphasis from manufacturing industries to service and information industries. There are currently more white-collar workers in the United States than blue-collar workers. Almost everyone, from grade-school students to chief executive officers of multinational corporations, must communicate using the written word. Memos, letters, resumes, reports, proposals, legal briefs, contracts, term papers, theses, articles, and books can all be produced with a word processing package.

Frequently, the first application package mastered by microcomputer users is a word processing package. Even after they learn how to use other types of software, many people find that they still use their word processing packages most often. In this chapter, we'll introduce word processing packages and what they can do. The next chapter will examine a particular microcomputer word processing package in more detail.

After studying this chapter, you will understand

- the basic types of word processing systems.
- the functions every word processing package performs.
- the editing features offered by word processing packages.
- some state-of-the-art word processing features.
- three popular microcomputer word processing packages.

## TYPES OF WORD PROCESSORS

*Machines that produce documents*

In one sense, word processing existed long before the advent of microcomputers. Some people maintain that the first word processor was Gutenburg's movable-type printing press, invented around 1450. Relatively inexpensive mechanical typewriters, which first became popular in the late 1800s, dramatically increased the quantity and quality of routine business communication. Still further improvements were brought about by the electric typewriter, developed during World War II. IBM coined the term *word processing* in 1968 for its line of automated electric typewriters. These machines could store documents on magnetic tapes or cards, which were used to make as many copies as necessary. This significantly reduced repetitive typing. Besides their ability to automatically retype entire documents, machines such as IBM's Magnetic Card Selectric Typewriter also could be used to produce personalized form letters very rapidly. Gradually, typewriters became more and more like computers.

In the meantime, people were using computers to produce documents. Although early computers were poorly suited to word processing, the hardware and software rapidly improved. Soon, documents could be prepared on computer terminals with CRT display screens and well-designed keyboards. The final draft could be stored on a disk and printed after all mistakes were eliminated. Computer word processing had the potential to become much better than typewriting, but computers were still too big and too expensive for most individuals. Finally, microcomputers burst on the scene in the mid-1970s, and programmers began to develop powerful, yet easy-to-use word processing software. Today, some word processing systems cost little more than good electric typewriters. Four basic types of word processors are now in common use: electronic typewriters, dedicated systems, microcomputer systems, and shared systems.

**Insight**

## Have Word Processors Made Typewriters Obsolete?

On one end of the rope are the word processor users, looking smug and confident. One the other end are the typewriter devotees, their heels dug in and grim looks on their faces. This tug of war has been going on for some time now, and it looks like the word processors are winning.

They're winning because their machines have a number of inherent advantages over the typewriter. The biggest, of course, is that word processors allow major editing changes on a document without much effort or cost.

Word processors are like money in the bank for businesses. Studies have shown that an ordinary, single-page business letter can cost more than $20 to produce, excluding the price of the stamp and envelope. This includes the time the executive spends in dictating the letter, as well as the time it takes to type it, make corrections, and retype it. Sometimes the corrections, revisions, and retyping take place over many stages.

Besides their strength in editing, word processors include at least a spell checker and often a thesaurus for looking up synonyms. People who work with word processors generally turn out better products than people who work with typewriters because they are willing to make necessary and beneficial changes.

About the only things that typewriters are used for anymore is to put addresses on envelopes and to fill out forms. But double-bin sheet feeders, with one bin for stationery and the other for envelopes, are attacking this last stronghold of the typewriter. Forms present a more complicated situation. They may be internally generated on a word processor, but if the form originates elsewhere, a typewriter may still be necessary.

### Electronic Typewriters

*Typewriters with CPUs*

An **electronic typewriter** is essentially a typewriter with a built-in microprocessor (see Figure 6.1). More advanced than ordinary electric typewriters, these machines offer many features associated with word processing. Electronic typewriters let users correct, insert, and delete words before the text is committed to paper. Their keyboards usually include special keys to center titles, line up margins, print in boldface and italics, and underscore words. They use various printing mechanisms, including dot-matrix, daisy-wheel, and removable-ball-type elements. Many companies offer interchangeable print elements that can be purchased to equip their electronic typewriters with different typefaces.

**Figure 6.1 Electronic Typewriter**
The electronic typewriter is an electric typewriter with a built-in microprocessor.

Electronic typewriters are really very specialized computers. They have a CPU (the microprocessor), as well as memory (ROM and RAM). Many electronic typewriters also have secondary storage in the form of magnetic tapes, cards, or disks. Each tape, card, or disk can hold one or more pages of text, which can be retrieved to make updates or print additional copies. Most electronic typewriters have an LCD (Liquid Crystal Display) or LED (Light-Emitting Diode) screen similar to those found on calculators. Some models have a small screen that can display only a portion of one line of text; other models are equipped with a larger screen that can hold several complete lines of text. Many of today's electronic typewriters even have built-in dictionaries to detect and correct misspelled words automatically.

Electronic typewriters are well suited to repetitive tasks that don't require extensive editing and revision. These machines are particularly useful to good touch-typists, who find that the advanced features can significantly speed up their work. Electronic typewriters are generally more powerful and more reliable, yet they often cost no more than electric typewriters. For these reasons, electronic typewriters have replaced electric typewriters in many organizations.

## Dedicated Systems

*Specialized microcomputers*

A **dedicated word processor** is a microcomputer system expressly designed and solely used to prepare, store, and print documents. Outwardly, these dedicated systems are similar to ordinary microcomputers (see Figure 6.2). They typically include a system unit, CRT display, keyboard, floppy disk drives, and a letter-quality printer. Some models may include a hard disk drive. A few even have built-in modems or circuit cards that allow them to communicate with other computers and word processors. There are differences, however. The display screen of a dedicated word processor is often tall enough to present an entire 66-line page of text. Furthermore, the keyboard may include a number of special-purpose keys for common word processing functions.

**Figure 6.2 Dedicated Word Processor**
The dedicated word processor is a specialized microcomputer, solely devoted to preparing documents.

Dedicated word processors are single-user systems primarily designed for medium to large offices. They run on built-in word processing software that usually cannot be replaced or supplemented by other application programs. Unlike general-purpose microcomputers, dedicated word processors cannot run software like spreadsheet programs and data base management packages. However, they are complete systems designed purely for effective word processing. Consequently, dedicated word processors are powerful, fast, and generally easy for office personnel to use.

## Microcomputer Systems

*General-purpose microcomputers*

The most popular type of word processor is a general-purpose microcomputer system running a word processing application package such as WordStar, WordPerfect, or Microsoft Word. Figure 6.3 illustrates a typical system. Although an ordinary microcomputer may not be as efficient or quite as easy to use as a dedicated word processor, most people would rather have a computer that can be used to run other software too. In most cases, microcomputer systems are also less expensive than dedicated word processing systems. Today's microcomputers generally have easy-to-read displays and well-designed keyboards. A wide range of word processing packages is on the market, from the very simple to the very sophisticated. Much of this software is easy to learn and easy to use. Furthermore, microcomputers can be equipped with high-quality input and output devices, like page scanners and laser printers. With devices such as these, the combination of word processing, graphics, and desktop publishing software can be used to create near-typeset-quality printed materials at a relatively low cost. So, microcomputer word processing systems are potentially much more versatile and powerful than dedicated word processors.

**Figure 6.3 Microcomputer Word Processor**
The most popular word processing system is a general-purpose microcomputer running a word processing package.

## Shared Systems

*Multiuser word processors*

Word processing also can be done on much larger, multiuser computers. These systems are often called **shared word processors** because they serve several users at once on a time-sharing basis (see Figure 6.4). Since large computers are already used in many offices and businesses for processing all kinds of data, it's often economical to run word processing packages on existing facilities. The same software can be used by different people working at different computer terminals. Expensive peripheral devices like hard disk drives and laser printers can be shared by many users. Nevertheless, shared word processors are perhaps the least common of all

**Figure 6.4 Shared Word Processor**
The shared word processing system consists of a large, time-sharing computer with word processing software that can serve several users at once.

types of word processors. In one sense, word processing "wastes" the time of extremely expensive large computers. These powerful machines are better suited to tasks involving complex calculations on large sets of data, which cannot be done on smaller computers in a reasonable amount of time. Dedicated systems and microcomputer systems generally are much cheaper and easier to use for word processing than large computers. Most organizations, even those that already own big computers, have been purchasing microcomputers in large numbers. Given the popularity of microcomputer word processors, it's likely that shared systems will gradually become even less common.

## BASIC WORD PROCESSING FUNCTIONS

*Preparing documents*

The ultimate purpose of any word processor is the preparation of documents. Different types of word processors approach this task in different ways. For the rest of this chapter we will concentrate on word processing programs for microcomputer systems. But even within this single category of word processors there are many different approaches. Some programs are relatively simple—designed with the novice or occasional user in mind. Other packages are powerful systems that provide more features than most people even learn, let alone routinely use. Perhaps the most apparent difference between various word processing packages involves their user interfaces. Some primarily use commands, while others rely more on menus. Some use the keyboard to perform all operations, while others also employ a mouse. Finally, some are limited to text displays, while others can utilize graphics to produce various typefaces and incorporate figures.

Despite these differences, every word processing package performs five basic functions. In general, word processing packages create, edit, format, print, and manage documents.

### Creating Documents

*New files*

Whenever you run a word processing package, you initially have two choices: either to create a new document or work on an existing one. If you don't specify an existing document, some word processing packages automatically create a new document. Others ask if you want to create a new document or wait for you to select a menu option to do so. In any case, the word processing package opens a new file on a disk to create a new document. At first, this document file is empty and the word processing package simply waits for you to enter text. Most of the screen will be empty—reserved for the material you will type (see Figure 6.5). Depending upon the word processing package, there may also be a menu across the top or bottom of the screen. In addition, there is usually one or more lines of information about your document. The name of the document file may be shown along with the page, line, and column of your current location within the document. Sometimes, a *ruler* or *format line* is also displayed, which shows the margin and tab settings being used.

At the top left of the empty text area is the cursor. On some word processing packages, the cursor is also known as the **insertion point**. The cursor may be a blinking underscore, vertical bar, or box that marks the exact position where text is inserted or some other operation is performed. To create a document, all you do is simply type the words and punctuation. All word processing packages have a feature that makes text entry easy and fast. With this feature, called **word wrap**, whenever you type a word that extends beyond the current right margin, that word is

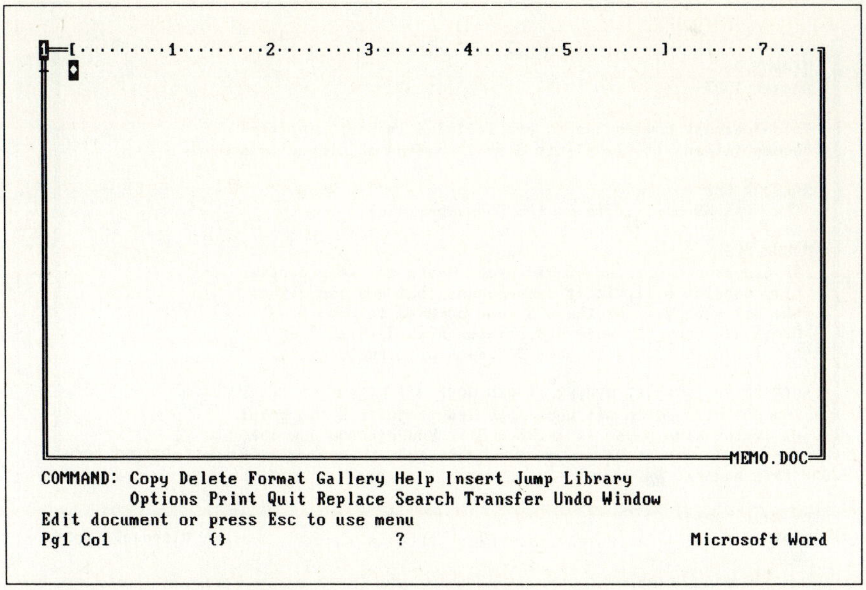


**Figure 6.5 Word Processing Screen**
This shows the screen you see when you start up Microsoft Word, a popular package for IBM-compatibles.

automatically "wrapped around," or moved down to the beginning of the next line. This allows you to type continuously without having to constantly check to see if you're near the end of a line. The carriage return (Enter key) need only be pressed to begin a new paragraph or explicitly start a new line. The word wrap feature is a great boon to typists, because it increases both speed and accuracy.

## Editing Documents

*Updating, correcting, and revising*

Even the best typists make mistakes. In addition, many initially correct documents frequently must be updated, altered, or otherwise revised. Furthermore, word processing packages are extensively used to compose, and not just retype, written material. As any author will tell you, writing is a very dynamic process. Sentences are sometimes changed many times before a document is finished and large portions of text may be repeatedly modified. Word processing packages are superb at performing these editing operations. Most word processing packages enable you to view, insert, delete, overwrite, manipulate, search and replace, and proofread text, as well as undo mistakenly executed operations.

### Viewing the Document

*Moving to different parts of the document*

Most documents are too long to fit entirely on the display screen. Every word processing package therefore must provide some mechanism to view different parts of the document. One common approach is to use special keystrokes to move within the document. Up Arrow and Down Arrow keys can be used to scroll the screen one line at a time, up or down. Page Up and Page Down keys can be used to move more rapidly. There may be a combination of keypresses (such as Control-Home or Control-End) to instantly move to the beginning or end of a document. Sometimes, a command or menu option is available that can be used to jump immediately to a particular page number (see Figure 6.6).

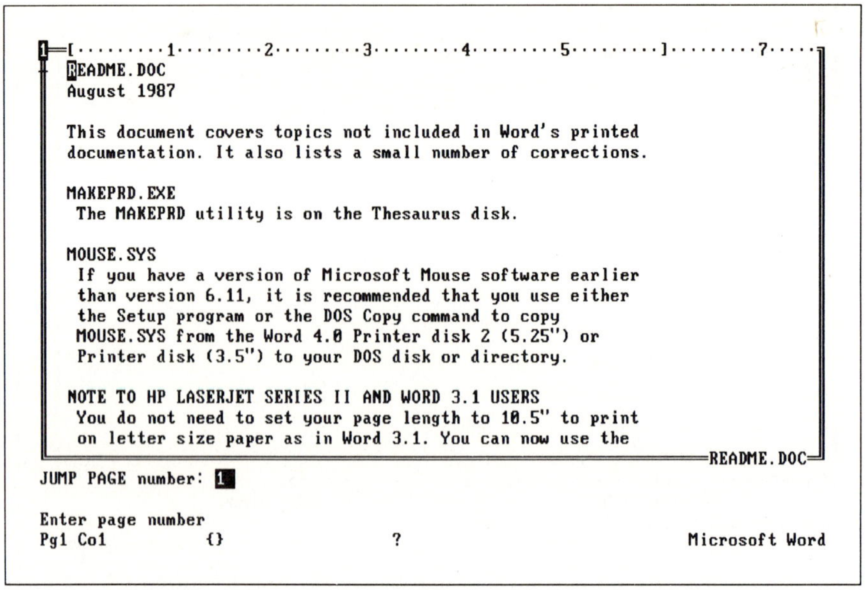


**Figure 6.6 Jumping to a Particular Page**
This screen demonstrates how you jump to a particular page in Microsoft Word.

Word processing packages that have a graphics interface and use a mouse, such as those that run on the Apple Macintosh computers, generally operate slightly differently. Besides the insertion point, these word processing packages also have a dark pointer that can be moved anywhere on the screen with the mouse. A **scroll bar** is used to allow movement within a document (see Figure 6.7). This is a thin vertical rectangle outside the text area with an arrow pointing up at the top and an arrow pointing down at the bottom. Within this bar is a lighter square box containing the current page number. Movement within the document can be accomplished in several ways. For example, to move up one line at a time, position the mouse-directed pointer on the up arrow and press the mouse button. To move more rapidly, position the pointer on the square box, hold down the mouse button, and drag the box up or down, as little or as much as you like.

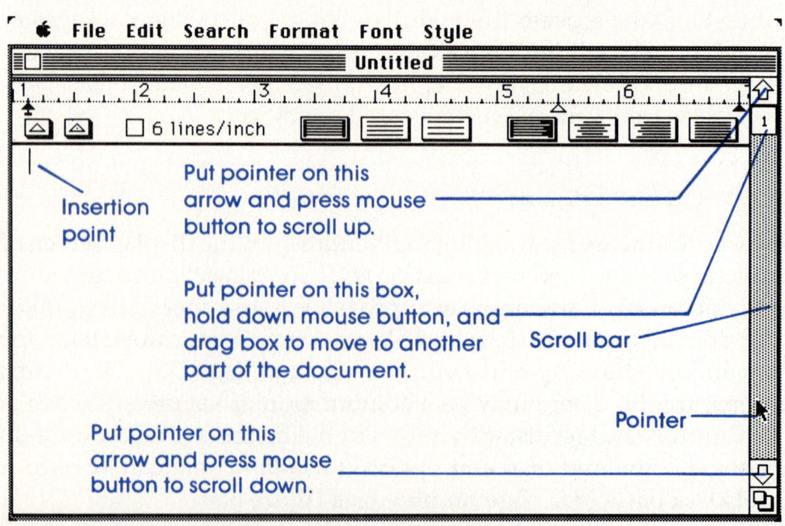


**Figure 6.7 MacWrite Scroll Bar**
Word processing software for the Apple Macintosh, such as the popular MacWrite program, generally has a scroll bar that lets you move about and view different parts of a document.

## Inserting Text

*Adding new material*

Inserting new material into existing text is a frequently used editing feature. Anything from a single character to many pages may be inserted anywhere in a document. This process is usually quite straightforward. Many word processing packages have two typing modes: insert and overwrite. When the program is in **insert mode**, all characters typed at the current cursor location simply push aside any text to the right. The opposite of insert mode is **overwrite mode**. In this state, characters typed at the current cursor location replace existing characters. Many word processing packages use insert mode by default, but allow the user to switch to overwrite mode by pressing a special key, executing a command, or selecting a menu option. To insert new material into existing text, all you have to do is make sure the program is in insert mode, move the cursor to the desired position, and simply type the characters to be inserted.

Word processing packages that use a mouse and a graphics interface often have a somewhat different procedure for inserting text. When the mouse-controlled pointer is moved into the text area on the screen, it changes shape from a dark arrow to a little I-beam (see Figure 6.8). To move the insertion point, relocate the I-beam with the mouse and click the mouse button. In this manner, you can move the insertion point anywhere within text you've already typed. Any characters you then type will be inserted into the document at the new position you've selected.

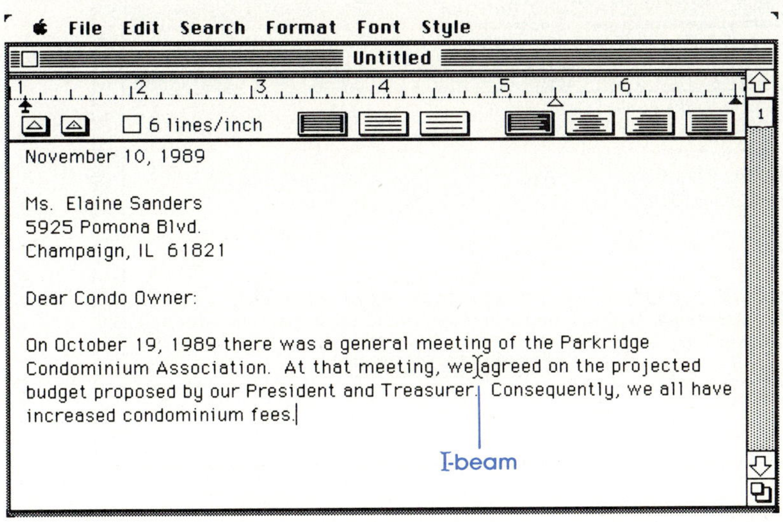


**Figure 6.8 I-Beam Insertion Point**
In MacWrite, the insertion point changes to resemble an I-beam when you attempt to insert new text into existing text.

## Deleting Text

*Removing unwanted material*

Deleting unwanted text is another common editing procedure. Usually, there are several different ways to erase text. The simplest involve the use of the Backspace or Delete keys. Some computers have both of these keys. The Backspace key generally is used to delete the character to the immediate left of the current cursor location. The Delete key is often used to erase the character at the current cursor location. Unfortunately, this convention isn't standardized. Some systems have only a Delete key and use it like a Backspace key. Other systems have both keys, but use the Delete key to erase characters to the left and the Backspace key to simply move the cursor to the left.

For erasing entire words, lines, sentences, and paragraphs, most word processing packages have additional operations. Some have special keypresses or commands that will delete the word, line, sentence, or paragraph where the cursor is currently located. Another approach is to allow a segment of text, from a single character to an entire document, to be *marked* or *selected* in some fashion. For example, with some word processing packages you move the cursor to the first character to be deleted and press a combination of keys or a single function key to mark the beginning of the selected segment. Then you move the cursor to the last character of the segment of text to be deleted and perhaps press another function key. The text in between will be highlighted in some fashion so that it stands out from the rest of the document (see Figure 6.9). This text may be in dark letters against a light background, light letters against a dark background, or another color. To remove the highlighted block of text, you simply press the Delete key, a function key, or perhaps some special combination of keystrokes. The deleted portion disappears, and the surrounding text closes up the gap. Word processing packages with a graphics interface use a similar approach, except that text generally is selected with the mouse.

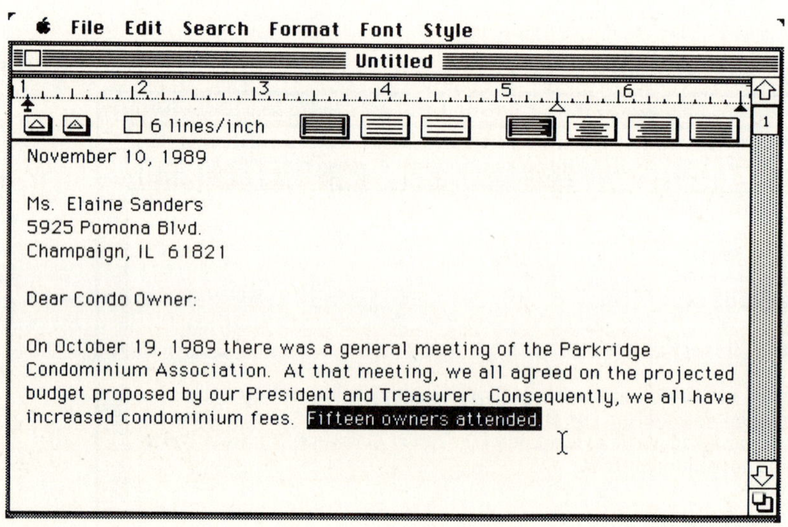


**Figure 6.9 Selecting Text**
In MacWrite, a segment of text is selected before it can be deleted, moved, or copied. The selection appears in reverse video highlighting.

## Overwriting Errors

*Changing existing characters*

Small errors often can be corrected by changing existing characters, instead of deleting and inserting. With word processing packages that have an overwrite mode, this can be done by simply moving the cursor to the desired place, switching to overwrite mode, and typing new characters over the old ones.

## Manipulating Text

*Moving and copying text*

It's often useful to be able to move an existing section of text from one place to another, an operation called **cut-and-paste**, or to reproduce text in another location, which is known as **copy-and-paste**. Most word processing packages offer these operations. In both cases, you select and mark a segment of text as if you were going to delete it. Instead of deleting, however, you use a cut or copy operation. This may be done through a keystroke combination, command, or menu selection. Cutting removes the text from its original location, while copying merely reproduces it. You can then move the cursor or insertion point to the location where you want to put the segment of text. Finally, you perform the paste operation by pressing a combination of keys, issuing a command, or choosing a menu option (see Figure 6.10). The segment of text that was cut or copied is then pasted into the document at the selected location. So, a cut-and-paste operation removes text from its original location, while a copy-and-paste operation simply reproduces it in a different location. Many word processing packages let you do cut-and-paste and copy-and-paste operations between different documents as well as within a single document.

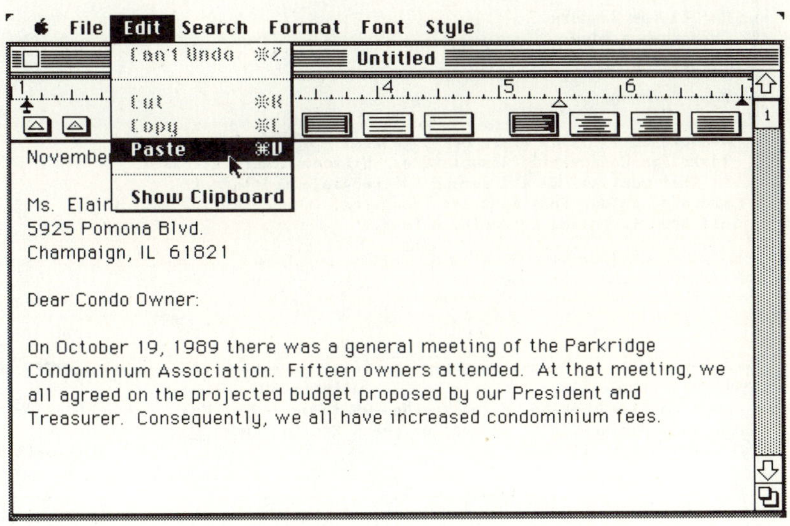


**Figure 6.10 Pasting in MacWrite**
After a segment of text has been cut or copied, the Paste option from the Edit menu is used to insert it into the document.

## The Search and Replace Feature

*Finding text and making changes*

People are not very good at finding needles in haystacks. Computers, on the other hand, are ideally suited to this type of task. Most word processing packages can quickly scan through a document to find a particular word or phrase. This **search** feature can be very useful if you want to locate a name or topic, for example, within a long document. It's even more useful if you need to look at every occurrence of that word or phrase within the document. This is just the kind of repetitive, boring task that computers can do much more quickly and accurately than people. Typically, you press a keystroke combination, execute a command, or select a menu option to initiate the search, or *find* operation, as some word processing packages call it. Then you type the word or phrase you want to locate and execute the operation. The word processing package advances the screen if necessary, moves the cursor to the beginning of the next occurrence of the word or phrase, and perhaps asks you if you want to search again.

Often you will want to find all instances of a word or phrase so that you can change them. For example, perhaps you've consistently misspelled someone's name throughout an entire document. You could, of course, use the search feature and correct each mistake, one by one. However, word processing packages generally have a **replace** feature that can do this automatically. It works like the search feature, but it goes one step further by allowing you to specify the word or phrase to be substituted for each item found. Many word processing packages can also be told to search and replace, but ask for your approval each time an item is located (see Figure 6.11). This way, you can change some of the words, but not all of them. Search and replace operations are good examples of powerful word processing features that can save a great deal of time, as well as increase the accuracy of document preparation.

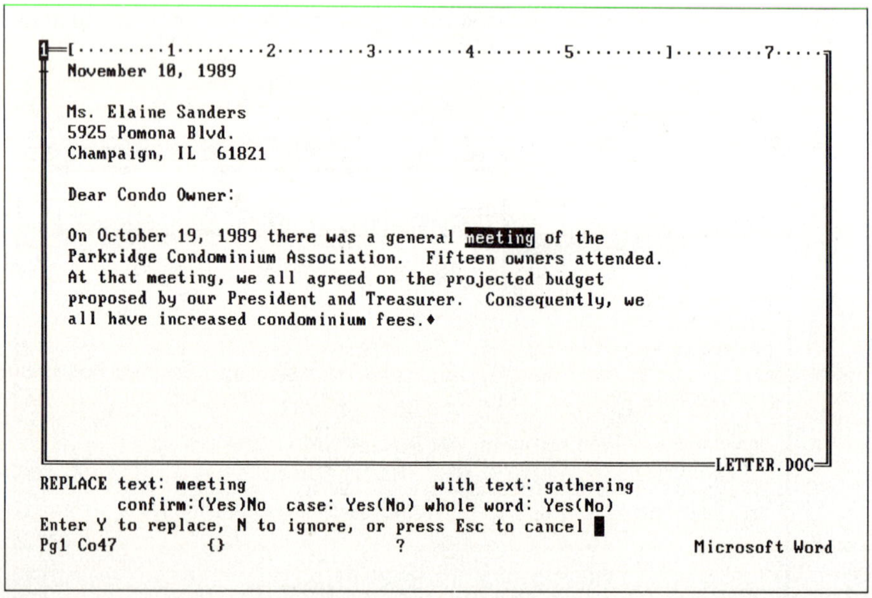


**Figure 6.11 Replacing in Microsoft Word**
In Microsoft Word, you can have the program ask for confirmation before it replaces a word it has found.

## Undoing Mistakes

*Canceling the previous command*

Errors, of course, aren't limited to text entry. In word processing, sometimes a command or menu selection is mistakenly executed. For a potentially disastrous error like the accidental deletion of an entire paragraph, fixing the mistake can be very discouraging indeed. Fortunately, most word processing packages have an **undo** feature (see Figure 6.12). This is an operation that simply undoes whatever you just did. If you just deleted a sentence by mistake, for instance, invoking the undo feature would recover that sentence. The undo feature is usually executed by pressing a certain combination of keys, entering a command, or choosing a menu option.

In addition to an undo feature, many word processing packages automatically create a backup copy of the document on which you are working. This leaves your original version intact in case you perform a destructive action that cannot be fixed with the undo command. Then if you have an accident, you can start all over again without losing any of the original text. Some word processing packages even periodically save your document on a disk as you work in case of an electrical power failure. Then if you make a big mistake, you may be able to retrieve the document as it was when it was last saved, avoiding having to start all over from scratch.

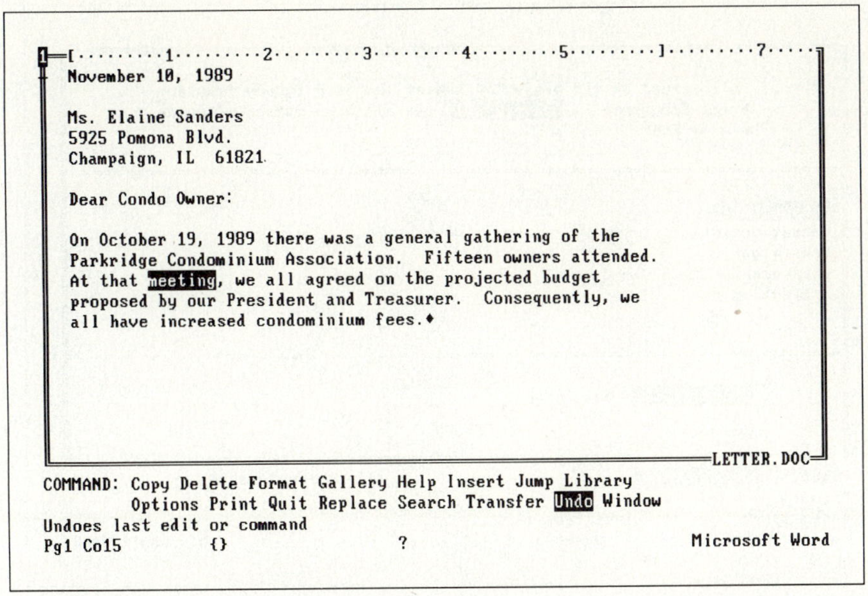


**Figure 6.12 The Undo Feature of Microsoft Word**

You can cancel your previous command by selecting the Undo option of the Microsoft Word command menu.

## Proofreading Aids

*Checking spelling*

Careful proofreading is required for most written work, but it seems that no matter how careful you are or how many times you go over your text, errors still slip by. Nowadays, word processing packages can help with some of this proofreading. The most common automatic proofreading feature is a **built-in dictionary** or **spelling checker**, as it's also called. There are two basic ways to use most spelling checkers. The first method lets you look up a particular word if you're not sure of its spelling. Typically, you would mark the word and then invoke the spelling checker by pressing a combination of keys, executing a command, or choosing a menu option. If the word is incorrectly spelled, the word processing package will say so and perhaps suggest some possible alternatives. The other, more common method of using a built-in dictionary is to check the entire document for spelling errors all at once. Spelling checkers use an ingenious procedure to look up every single word in the entire document. Each word not found in the internal dictionary is presented to you (see Figure 6.13). Then you may simply leave the word alone, correct it yourself, have the computer automatically correct it, or choose from a list of possible corrections.

Today's built-in dictionaries are very good; some contain more than 100,000 words. Nevertheless, there will always be some correct words not found in the dictionary. These may include proper names, jargon, slang, and technical terms, as well as certain variations of correct words such as some plurals and possessives. Many word processing packages allow you to add words to the built-in dictionary or even create your own "user dictionaries" for specific types of documents. Although spelling checkers can eliminate many typographical errors, they still cannot identify correctly spelled words used in incorrect places. For example, if you accidentally type *on* instead of *of*, a spelling checker will not help with this error. Still, most writers find that a spelling checker is a great benefit that can significantly reduce the drudgery of proofreading.

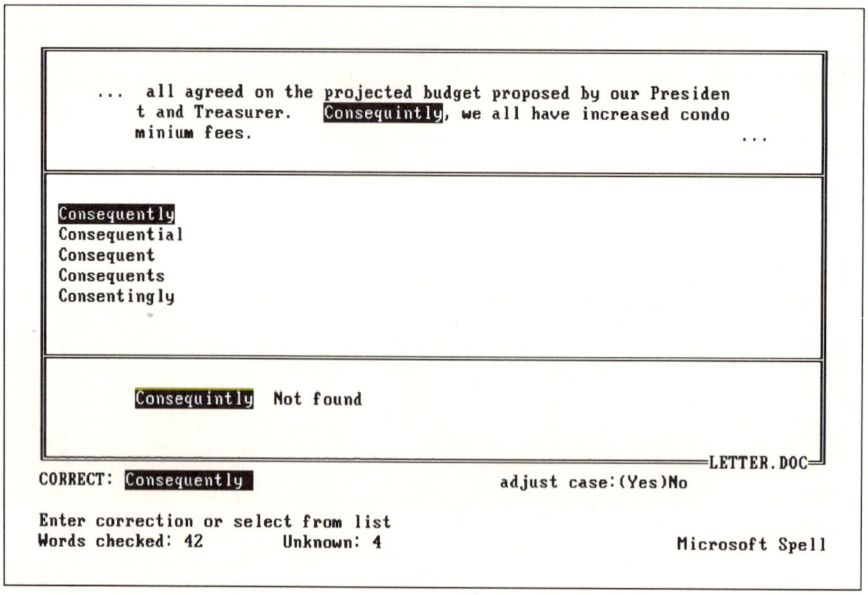


**Figure 6.13 Microsoft Word Spelling Checker**
In Microsoft Word, you can have your document automatically proofread for spelling errors.

## Formatting Documents

*Controlling the final appearance*

Formatting a document basically involves arranging the appearance of the text to be printed. There are several different levels of formatting and many features for controlling the appearance of text. Although different word processing packages often use different terminology, document formatting has three basic levels: character, paragraph, and page formatting.

### Character Formatting

*Varying the appearance of letters and words*

**Character formatting** allows you to vary the way individual letters or words are presented. Many word processing packages let you underline, double underline, boldface, italicize, cross out, and add superscript and subscript to selected words or parts of words within a document. In the typewriter tradition, many word processing packages also let you choose between standard *pica* (10 characters to the horizontal inch) and *elite* (12 characters to the horizontal inch) type. Word processing packages that use a graphics interface usually give you an even wider selection of various type fonts, styles, and sizes, and let you mix any combination of these within the same document. A **font** or **typeface** is a set of letters, numbers, punctuation marks, and other symbols with a consistent appearance. This appearance may be slightly altered by varying the font's style, such as boldface or italic. The vertical size of characters usually is specified in points. (A **point** is a typographical measure equal to 1/72 of an inch.) Figure 6.14, for example, shows some of the character formats available with most word processing programs that run on Apple Macintosh computers.

Generally, to switch character formats you either press some special combination of keys or select a menu option before typing. Many word processing packages also let you change the format of words after you've already typed them. This is usually done by marking the text to be changed, and pressing a keystroke combination or choosing a menu option.

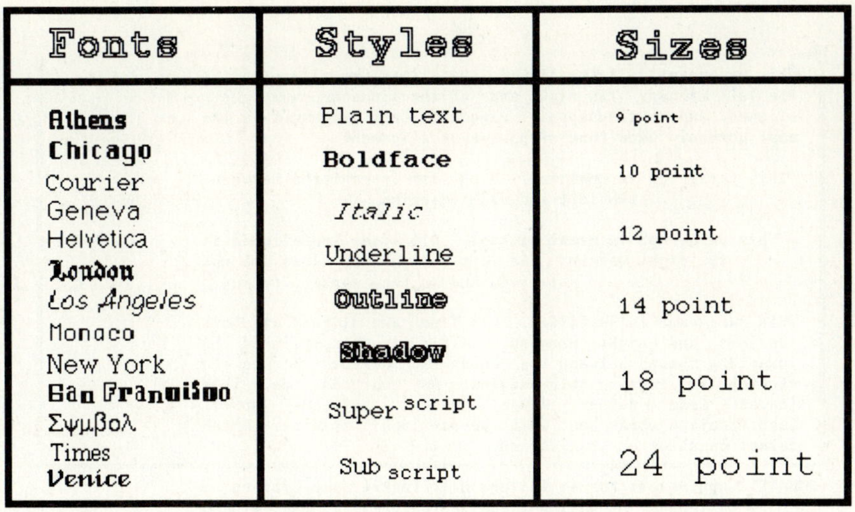


**Figure 6.14 MacWrite Character Formats**
This screen shows the character formatting options available with MacWrite.

## Paragraph Formatting

*Arranging blocks of text*

**Paragraph formatting** allows you to alter the appearance of individual blocks of text. This usually involves controlling the alignment, indentation, and spacing of a paragraph. All of these features may be controlled with keystrokes, commands, or menu selections.

*Alignment* refers to how the words are lined up within a paragraph. There are four basic alignment variations: left, centered, right, and justified (see Figure 6.15). Left alignment is perhaps the most familiar; text is even along the left margin, while the right margin is uneven, or "ragged." Centered alignment puts each line in the middle, equally positioned between the left and right margins. Right alignment is the opposite of left alignment. **Justified** alignment essentially combines both left and right alignment to create a block look; spaces are inserted here and there so that every line is flush to both the left and right margins. The paragraphs you see in this typeset book, for example, are justified.

*Indentation* refers to how many spaces, if any, a paragraph is to be set in from the left or right margin. Again, there are several common variations. Most paragraphs simply have their first line indented, or pushed in several spaces to the right. Others have their first line pulled out to the left from the rest of the paragraph. This is often called a *hanging indent* or an *outdent* (see Figure 6.16). Sometimes you want all the lines of a paragraph indented to create an inset block for some special text, like a long quotation, for example. Most word processing packages let you perform all these types of paragraph indentation.

*Spacing* refers to the distance between the lines of text within a paragraph or the distance between paragraphs. For example, single-spacing leaves no blank lines between adjacent lines of text. Double-spacing leaves one blank line between lines of text; triple-spacing leaves two blank lines, and so on.

**Figure 6.15 Paragraph Alignment**

This screen demonstrates left, centered, right, and justified paragraph alignment in Microsoft Word.

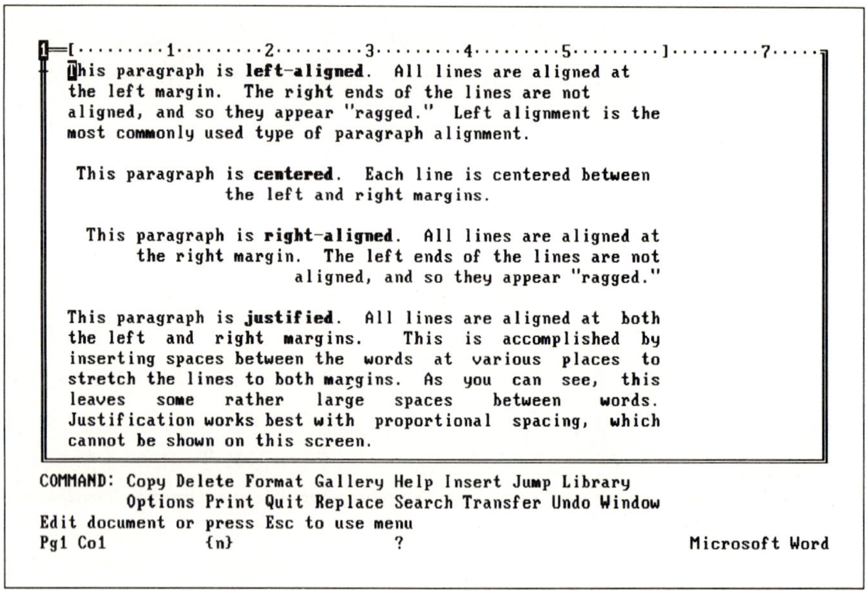


**Figure 6.16 Hanging Indent**

The hanging indent is one type of paragraph formatting.

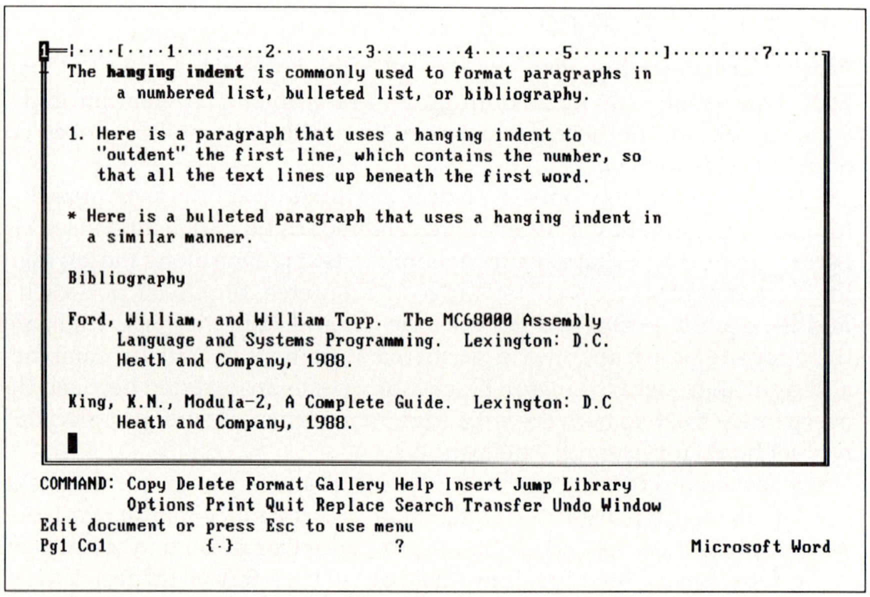


## Page Formatting

*Organizing pages*

**Page formatting** allows you to specify the general organization of an entire page of text. This can involve setting the left and right margins as well as any tab stops. The number of lines to appear on each page can be specified, along with the position and format of page numbers (see Figure 6.17). Many word processing packages let you have the same title (often called a **running head**) printed at the top or bottom of every page.

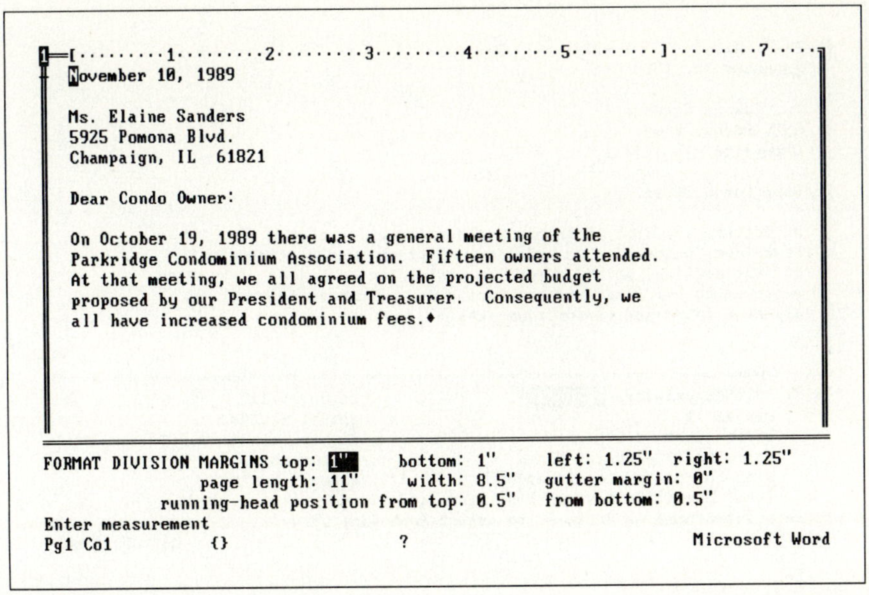


**Figure 6.17 Page Formatting**
This screen shows how you specify page formatting options with Microsoft Word.

Many different format options are offered by today's word processing packages, and we've described only a few of them. Fortunately, you don't have to specify all of these settings every time you work on a document. Virtually all word processing packages are preprogrammed with default settings for most format options. These defaults are sensible settings that will work fine for most documents. The word processing package automatically puts these default settings into effect unless you specifically change them. For example, a word processing package might assume that you want ordinary pica type, single-spacing, one-inch margins on all four sides, and a page number at the bottom center of each page. If you want double-spacing instead, you are free to change just this setting and leave all of the other default format settings the same. Once the format options are set, they will automatically be performed by the word processing package, freeing you to concentrate on what you are writing.

## Printing Documents

*Producing hard copy*

The basic purpose of every word processor is to produce documents on paper. So, an essential component of any system is a printer. The word processing software takes charge of the printer and translates the document you see on the screen to pages formatted on paper. Most word processing packages provide facilities to help you control various aspects of this printing process (see Figure 6.18).

### Printing Parts of a Document

*Printing selections*

Most of the time, you print an entire document when you are finished working on it. In addition, word processing packages usually let you print just a single page or several selected pages from a document.

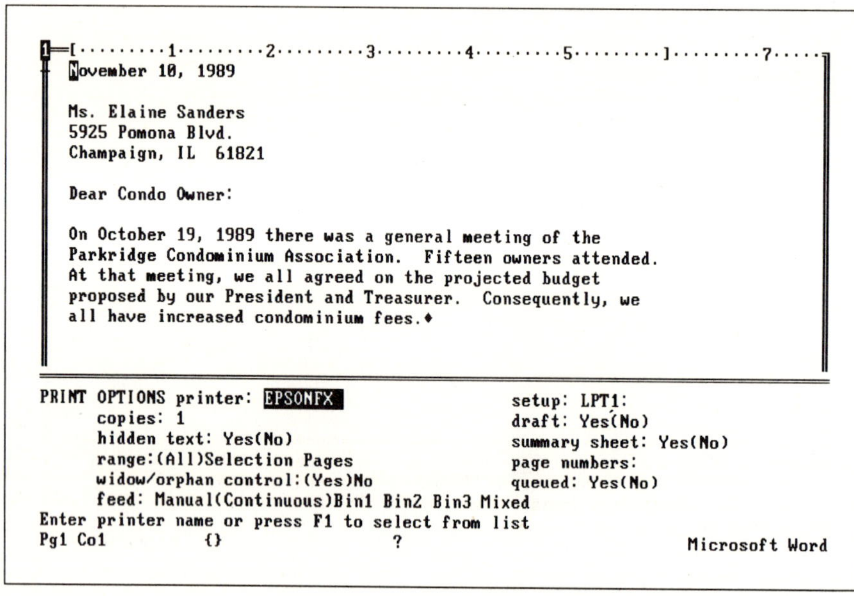

```
[·········1·········2·········3·········4·········5·········]·········7·····
November 10, 1989

Ms. Elaine Sanders
5925 Pomona Blvd.
Champaign, IL  61821

Dear Condo Owner:

On October 19, 1989 there was a general meeting of the
Parkridge Condominium Association.  Fifteen owners attended.
At that meeting, we all agreed on the projected budget
proposed by our President and Treasurer.  Consequently, we
all have increased condominium fees.♦

PRINT OPTIONS printer: EPSONFX                        setup: LPT1:
     copies: 1                                        draft: Yes(No)
     hidden text: Yes(No)                             summary sheet: Yes(No)
     range:(All)Selection Pages                       page numbers:
     widow/orphan control:(Yes)No                     queued: Yes(No)
     feed: Manual(Continuous)Bin1 Bin2 Bin3 Mixed
Enter printer name or press F1 to select from list
Pg1 Co1          {}                 ?                           Microsoft Word
```

**Figure 6.18 Printing Documents**
Word processing packages like Microsoft Word provide several options that control how a document is printed.

## Printing Copies

*Producing more than one*

Sometimes you need several copies of the same document. Instead of waiting until each copy is finished and then initiating another print operation, most word processing packages let you print several copies of a document with a single command.

## Paper Feed

*Feeding in the blank pages*

Many printers can use single sheets of paper, like preprinted letterheads, as well as continuous fan-fold computer paper. Some can even print on envelopes, gummed labels, and checks. *Sheet feeders* or paper trays can be attached to many printers so that you can put a whole stack of blank pages in the printer at once. This way, single sheets can be fed into the printer automatically. If you're going to use single sheet paper and your printer doesn't have a sheet feeder or paper tray, then you will have to feed in each blank page by hand. In these cases, the word processing package must be told to pause between pages, so that a new sheet can be manually inserted each time.

## Print Quality

*Specifying the print mode*

Many word processing systems offer several possible print modes. Dot-matrix printers may have a draft mode for quick, lower-quality output; a medium-quality mode that is a bit slower but easier to read; and a true letter-quality mode for final versions. Other printers, like daisy-wheel printers and laser printers, always produce letter-quality output. Some word processing packages and printers can use **proportional spacing**, which allots different amounts of space for different characters. For example, a proportionally spaced *i* takes up less space than a *w*. Proportional spacing makes the print look more like it was professionally typeset and works better for justified text. Although it ultimately depends on your printer, most word processing packages give you some control over print quality features.

### Printer Selection

*Specifying the printer*

Sometimes, two printers can be connected to the same computer. For example, you might have an inexpensive dot-matrix printer for everyday use and a laser printer for special projects. Many word processing packages can accommodate two printers by letting you select which one to use to print a particular document.

### Print Spooling

*Printing while editing*

**Print spooling**, also called **print buffering**, gives you the ability to print one document while you work on another. Once you initiate it, the printing proceeds in the background, while you are free to use the word processing package for something else. This is possible because most printers operate much more slowly than computers can send them data. Word processing packages that have print spooling can save you a great deal of time if you frequently print long documents.

### Print Queuing

*Printing several documents*

A *queue* is a first-come-first-served line, like a line you might stand in to buy movie tickets. **Print queuing** is the ability to specify a list of documents to be printed. Some word processing packages have this capability, which works especially well with print spooling.

## Managing Documents

*Organizing your files*

One of the most important advantages word processing packages have over ordinary typewriters is that they can store documents in disk files. Even after a document is printed, it's usually saved in secondary storage. Besides providing a compact method of keeping documents, disk storage allows you to quickly retrieve, view, and extract material from existing documents. Word processing packages help you organize your documents by offering several file management facilities (see Figure 6.19). You can save documents in their own disk files, load existing documents from their disk files into memory, combine, delete, copy, rename, and display directories of document files. Although some of these operations can also be performed with the operating system, it is often easier and quicker to use the word processing program.

# STATE-OF-THE-ART FEATURES

*Additional capabilities*

All word processing packages let you view, create, edit, format, print, and manage documents. Most of the features we mentioned in the previous sections are fairly common in today's word processing software. There are, however, products on the market that offer even more features. With the constantly changing microcomputer software industry, new versions of existing packages are released almost every year. Programs seem to get bigger and faster, while incorporating even greater capabilities. In many cases these can simplify your job, if you take the time to master advanced features. In addition to the basic functions we've already discussed, many word processing packages also include more advanced features. Let's examine several of them now.

**Figure 6.19 Managing Documents with Microsoft Word**

Most word processing packages have options for loading, saving, merging, deleting, copying, and renaming document files.

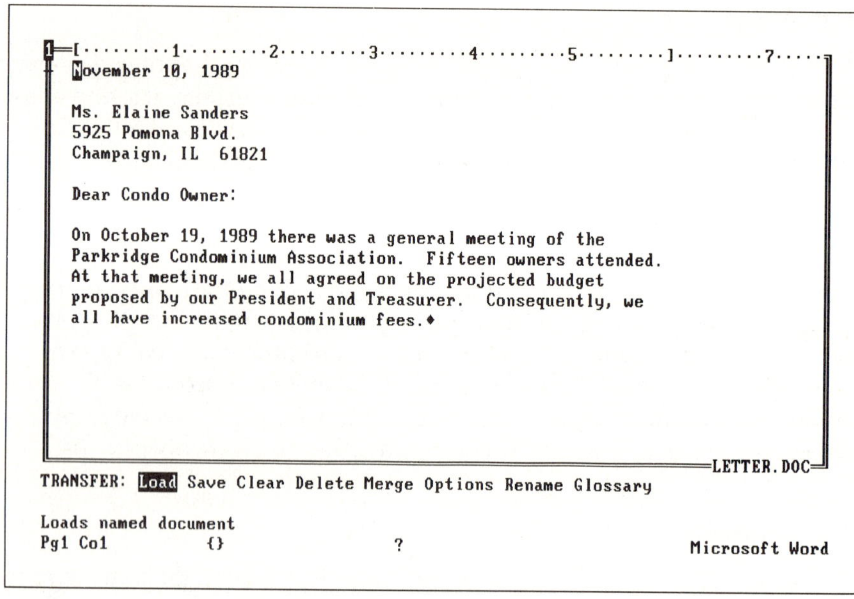


## On-line Help

*Instant reference manual*

The more complex and powerful a program, the more difficult it is for users to remember the options and how to invoke them. Because of this, many software packages provide **on-line help**. This is a way for you to find out how to perform some operation from within a program, without having to look it up in the printed reference manual. It's called *on-line* because the information is presented to you on your computer screen. In many cases the help is **context-sensitive**. This means that when you invoke the help facility, it will display information specifically relevant to whatever you are currently doing inside the program. For example, with Microsoft Word for IBM microcomputers, you can get on-line help by holding down the Alternate key and pressing H. If you are typing text at the time you do this, Word will display information about editing, as shown in Figure 6.20.

## Style Sheets

*Formatting instructions*

As we said before, word processing packages generally have a set of default options for formatting documents, which will be used automatically unless you specify otherwise. Perhaps these conventions work well in many situations, but certain documents may require a completely different set of formatting guidelines. A **style sheet** is a collection of formatting instructions for setting margins, indentations, and so on that can be saved in a file and applied to different documents (see Figure 6.21). Instead of respecifying each formatting instruction every time you create or edit a particular type of document, you can simply tell the word processing package to use an existing style sheet. All of the formatting instructions saved in the style sheet will then be applied to your document. Once you have created a style sheet, formatting a document becomes much faster and easier than specifying each option individually. If you were writing a book, for example, you might create a style sheet that specifies the format for all chapters. This style sheet would contain the margin settings, line spacing, paragraph indentation, page length, page numbering scheme, and running head. Every time you begin a new chapter, you would simply apply the style sheet by pressing certain keys or selecting a menu option. Besides saving you a great deal of time, using the style sheet ensures that every chapter will have the same format.

## Automatic Paragraph Reformatting

*Keeping paragraphs aligned*

Virtually all word processing packages can automatically wrap words and align paragraphs as you enter text. But what happens if you go back and delete some words, change the paragraph alignment, or reset the margins? With some word

```
EDITING                                               Screen 1 of 7

TO:                           DO THIS:

Enter or insert text          Use direction keys to position highlight where
                              you want text to begin, then type

Erase mistakes                Press Backspace key






 Tutorial: Entering Text
 Manual: Chapter 3, "Getting Started"

HELP: Resume Next Previous
      Basics Index Tutorial
Returns to location or menu where Help was requested
P32 D2 Co1        {}              ?                          Microsoft Word
```

**Figure 6.20 On-line Help**
This screen shows the context-sensitive on-line help facility of Microsoft Word.

```
1=|···[·····1·········2·········3·········4·········5·····]···6·········7·····
 1   NL Paragraph 2                                NUMBERED LIST
        PS (roman a) 10/12. Flush left, Left indent 0.4" (first line indent
        -0.4"), right indent 0.4", space before 1 li, space after 1 li
        (keep in one column).
 2   TI Paragraph 3                                TITLE
        Modern i 14/12 Bold. Centered.
 3   SH Paragraph 7                                SUBHEAD
        Modern i 12 Bold Underlined. Flush left.
 4   LE Paragraph 1                                LIST ENTRY
        PS (roman a) 10/12. Flush left, Left indent 1" (first line indent -
        1"), right indent 0.4", space after 2 li (keep in one column). Tabs
        at: 1" (left flush).
 5   SP Paragraph Standard                         STANDARD PARAGRAPH
        PS (roman a) 10/12. Flush left.
 6   RH Paragraph Running Head                     RUNNING HEAD
        PS (roman a) 10/12 Italic. Centered.
 7   L1 Paragraph 4                                LEFT SIDE-BY-SIDE
        PS (roman a) 10/12. Flush left, right indent 3.25". Place side by
        side.
                                                             SAMPLE.STY
COMMAND: Copy Delete Exit Format Help
         Insert Name Print Transfer Undo
Select style or press ESC to use menu
GALLERY          {}              ?                           Microsoft Word
```

**Figure 6.21 Microsoft Word Style Sheet**
This screen shows a Microsoft Word style sheet, which contains formatting specifications that can be named, stored, and applied to a document with a few keystrokes.

processing packages, you must then go back and *reformat* each paragraph you changed. This might involve moving the cursor to each paragraph and then pressing some keystroke combination or invoking some command to realign the words. Automatic paragraph reformatting is a handy feature that saves you from doing this. Many of today's word processing packages will immediately reformat text if you delete or insert words, change the paragraph alignment or indentation, or change the margins or page length.

## Thesauruses

*Instant synonyms*

If you've ever used a thesaurus to find synonyms or antonyms, you know how helpful a reference it can be. Many word processing packages now include a built-in thesaurus to help users find alternate terms as they work on their documents (see Figure 6.22). Similar in some ways to a spelling checker, a built-in thesaurus can save you a significant amount of time. Instead of looking up a word in a thick book, all you have to do is position the cursor on the word and press some keystroke combination. The thesaurus lists synonyms of the selected word right on your screen. Pick a new word from the list, and it will instantly replace the old word. A typical word processing package's built-in thesaurus contains more than 200,000 synonyms.

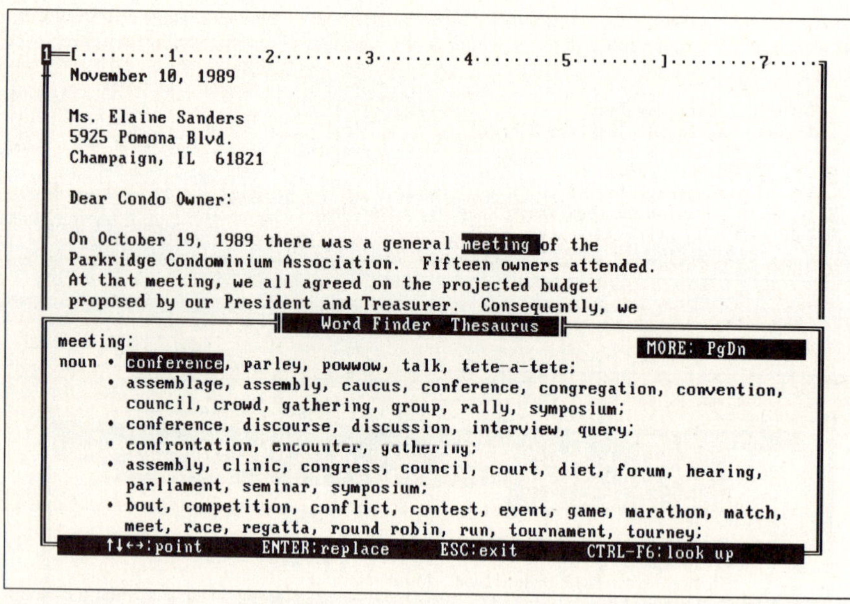


**Figure 6.22 Built-in Thesaurus**
This screens shows the built-in thesaurus of Microsoft Word being used to find synonyms.

## Grammar and Style Checkers

*Evaluating documents*

Some computer programs are designed to check the grammar and writing style of documents (see Figure 6.23). However, they are not yet commonly included with popular word processing packages and typically are purchased separately. Although they can help correct obvious grammar and style errors, no computer program is about to replace English teachers. Languages like English are just too irregular and inconsistent to be easily checked by an inflexible computer program. Nevertheless, grammar and style checkers can be useful in some instances. They are generally good at compiling statistics about a document, such as word counts, the average sentence length, and the average word length. These programs also are sometimes used to estimate the reading level of documents, expressed as a school year grade.

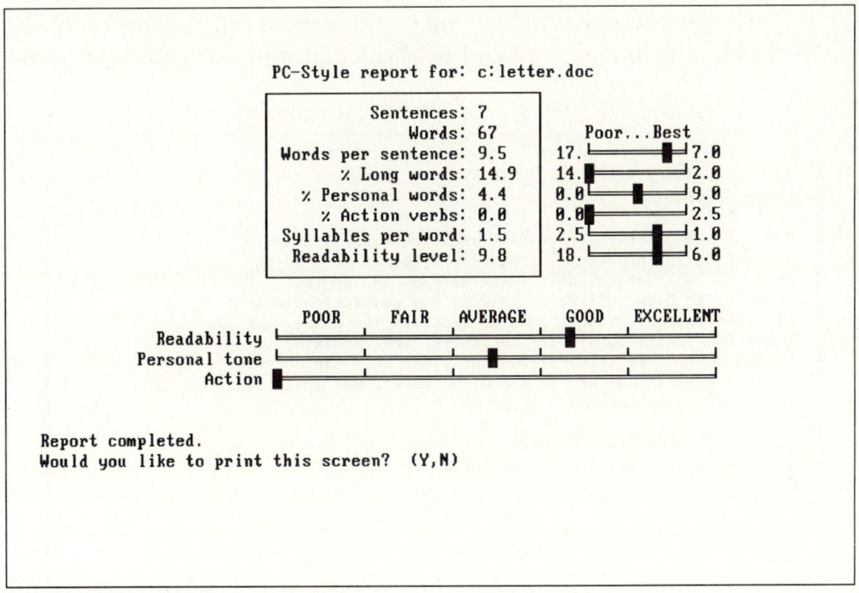


**Figure 6.23 Style Checker**
Buttonware's PC-Style is a stand-alone program used to analyze the writing style of a document.

## Table of Contents and Index Generation

*Automating tedious chores*

Book authors know the tedium of compiling a table of contents or an index. Fortunately, many word processing packages can help automate the process. Basically, this involves designating table of contents or index entries as you go along. Items are marked by special keystroke combinations or characters that are stored in the document but not printed. When a document is finished, a special command or menu option is executed to find all the marked entries and automatically create the table of contents or index, complete with the correct final page numbers (see Figure 6.24). Table of contents and index generation are somewhat specialized features, but they can be of great benefit to authors of books, pamphlets, and long articles.

## Outline Processing

*Organizing text in a document*

Most of us are taught in school that it's best to create an outline before writing an essay, term paper, or report. Outlining helps to organize your thoughts and ensure that you cover all the relevant topics in the correct order. Many word processing packages now include built-in facilities that help you use outlines to structure your work (see Figure 6.25). You create an outline by typing headings and assigning levels to these headings. This outline then becomes the foundation for your document. Headings can be reordered, renumbered, and moved in or out to different levels. Text is inserted beneath each outline heading. You can collapse this text to view just your headings, or expand headings to also display the text beneath them. Many writers find that using an outline processor helps them better develop and organize their text.

## Math Functions

*Performing calculations*

Many documents contain numbers. These may be individual figures or entire tables of values. Let's say you need to do some mathematical calculations on these numbers. You could, of course, use a hand-held calculator or exit your word pro-

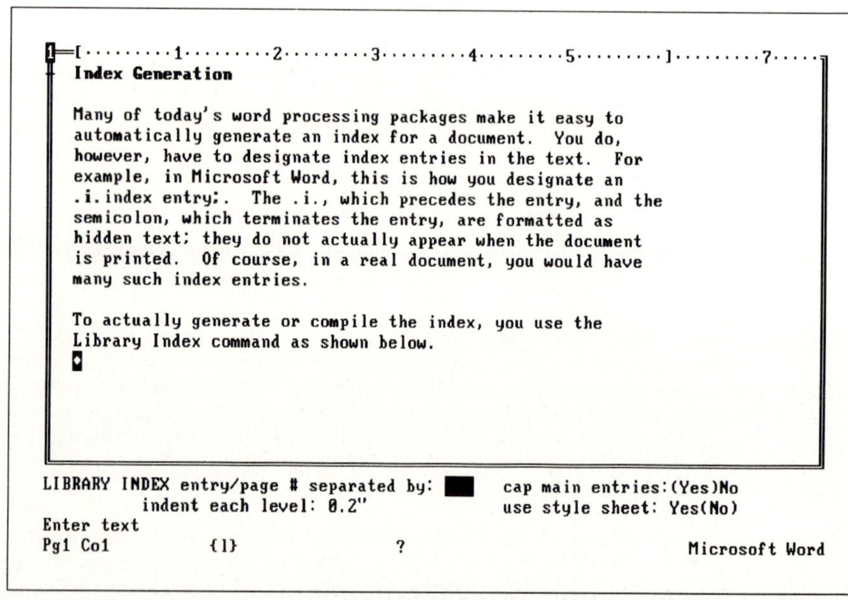


**Figure 6.24 Index Generation**
Microsoft Word lets you easily create an index by first designating index entries in your document, and then using the Library Index command to compile the index.

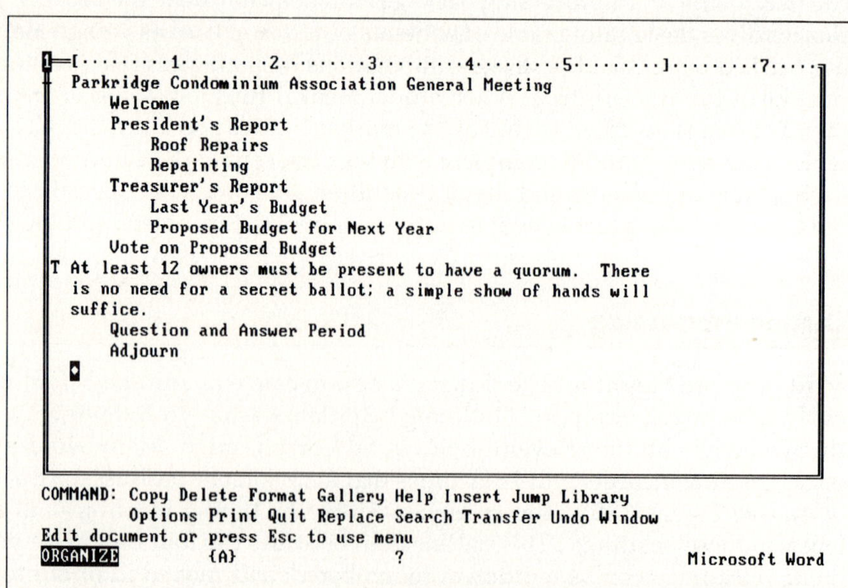


**Figure 6.25 Outline Processing**
Like many advanced word processing packages, Microsoft Word includes a built-in outlining facility to help you organize the development and presentation of information.

cessing package to use a spreadsheet program. It would be much more convenient, however, to be able to do your calculations within your word processing package. Many word processing packages have this ability (see Figure 6.26). They can add, subtract, multiply, and divide numbers, as well as compute percentages. A few can even calculate logarithms, square roots, and trigonometric functions like sines, cosines, and tangents. You can use a word processing package's built-in calculator to compute a single sum or perform complex calculations on entire columns of numbers. Word processing packages can't compete with spreadsheet programs when it comes to extensive number handling, but they can provide a quick and easy method of doing occasional calculations within a document.

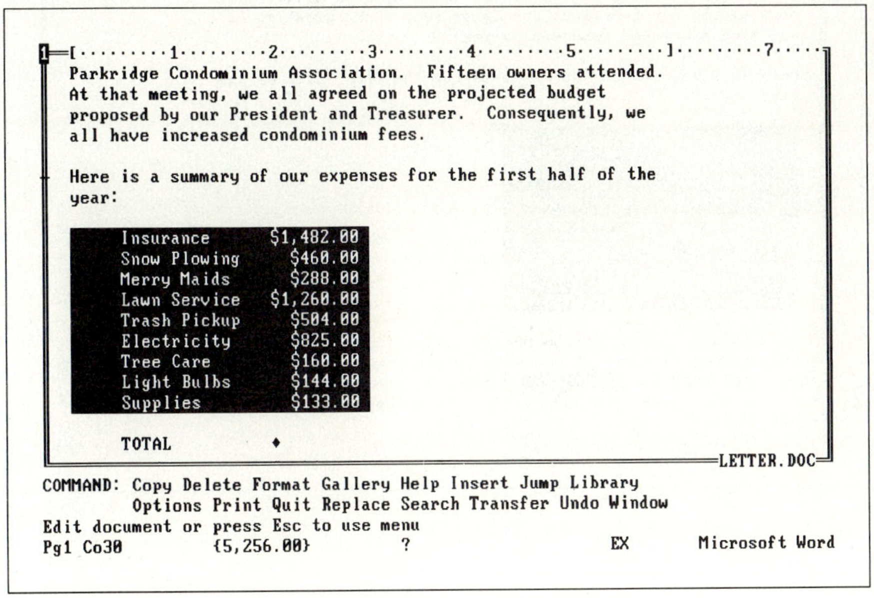


**Figure 6.26 Math Functions**
Many word processing packages, such as Microsoft Word, have a built-in calculator that you can use to add, subtract, multiply, and divide numbers, as well as calculate percentages, within a document.

## Sorting

*Alphabetizing text*

**Sorting** is arranging items in some particular order. When numbers are sorted, they are arranged into either ascending or descending order. When words are sorted, they are usually arranged alphabetically. Many word processing packages can sort numbers, words, lines of text, outline headings, and even entire paragraphs (see Figure 6.27). This can be very handy for documents that contain tables and lists. For example, you might have a mailing list of names and addresses that you want to sort by last name or perhaps by zip code. Although huge tables and lists are best left to data base management systems, word processing packages with sorting capabilities can effectively handle smaller tables and lists that are inside documents along with other text.

## Mail-Merge

*Generating form letters*

Speaking of mailing lists, a common use of word processing is to create form letters. This process, often called **mail-merge**, involves combining a master document with a data file (see Figure 6.28). The master document contains the main body of text along with instructions for merging the data file. The data file contains the variable information that will be used to "fill in the blanks" of the master document. For example, a form letter would be the master document, and a separate list of names and addresses would be the data file. Besides personalized letters, mail-merge is also used for invoices, contracts, and reports. Many word processing packages, especially those designed for business use, have at least some mail-merge capabilities.

**Figure 6.27 Sorting with Microsoft Word**
Many word processing packages let you alphabetize text and rearrange numbers into numerical order.

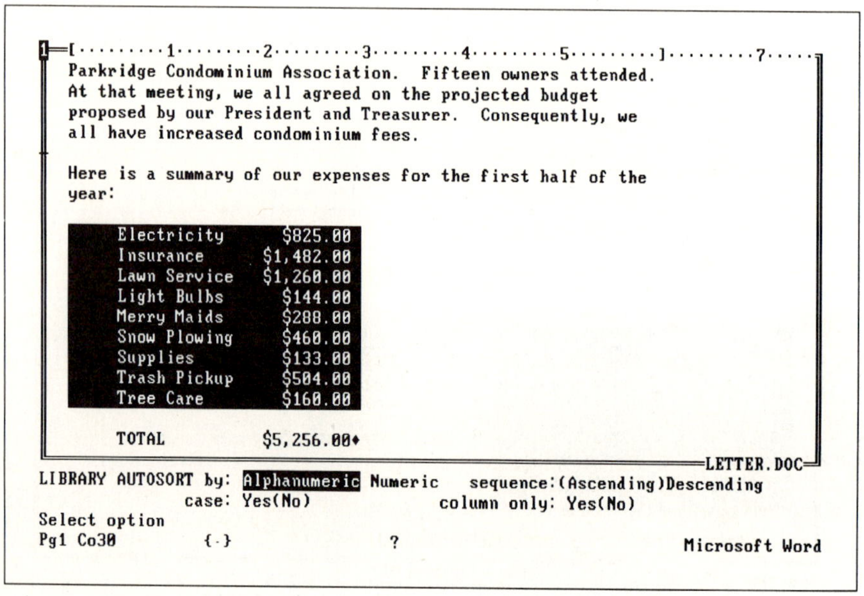


**Figure 6.28 Mail-Merge Facility**
Most word processors have a mail-merge facility that you can use to generate form letters automatically. A master document that contains the letter is combined with a data file that contains the names and addresses.

(a) An example master document.

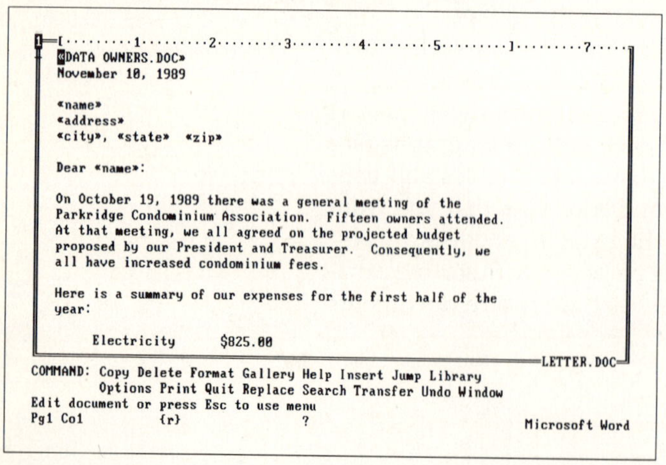


(b) An example data file.

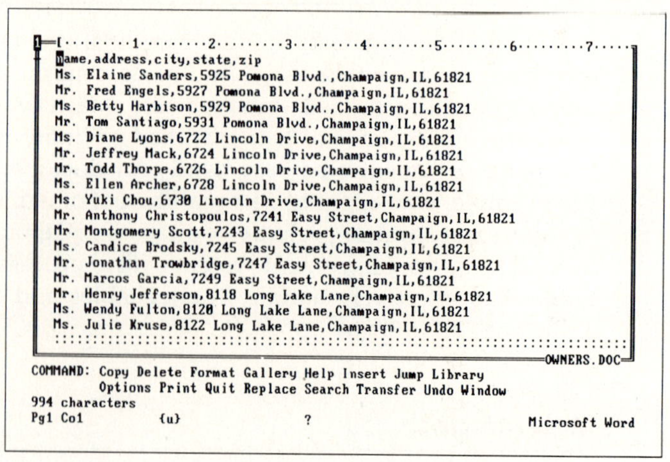

## Keyboard Macros

*Abbreviating commands and entries*

Many word processing operations are invoked by pressing some combination of keys or entering commands. This is especially true for word processing packages that don't use pull-down menus and a mouse. Some common operations may be done over and over again in the same document. Besides repeatedly entering commands, users often find themselves retyping the same long word, name, title, or phrase. A **keyboard macro** is a timesaving feature that lets you abbreviate a sequence of commands or a line of text. In essence, a keyboard macro is a shorthand way to record a series of keystrokes and "play" them back at any time. Long commands and text sequences can be assigned to single keystroke combinations. For example, let's say that you are writing a report about IBM and you frequently have to type "International Business Machines Corporation." A word processing package might let you assign this entire name to a keystroke combination like Alt-I. Then instead of typing "International Business Machines Corporation," all you would have to do is press the **Alternate** key and the **I** key at the same time. The word processing package would instantly generate the whole name, saving you from typing 42 characters. Once they learn how to use them, many people find that keyboard macros can eliminate much repetitive typing and really speed up their work.

## Multiple Windows

*Two or more views on the screen*

One advantage of working with a typewriter and paper is that you can look at previous pages or material from other documents while you type. In fact, you can cover your entire desk with various pages and look at all of them at the same time. Although you can't do this with a word processing package, some programs let you split your screen into two or more separate windows (see Figure 6.29). You can look at different parts of the same document in different windows, or view different documents in different windows. In some cases, you can control the relative sizes and positions of the windows on the screen. It's easy to switch between windows,

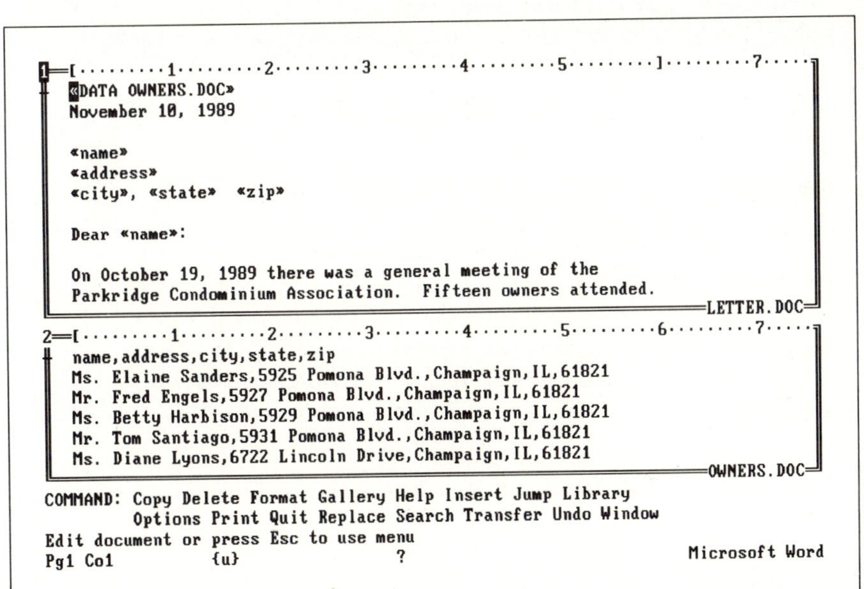


**Figure 6.29 Multiple Windows in Microsoft Word**

This screen shows how you can use multiple windows in Microsoft Word to see two different documents or two different sections of the same document at the same time. You switch from one window to the other by pressing the F1 key.

move about, and edit material in different places or different documents. Generally, you can even cut-and-paste and copy-and-paste text between windows. Computer screens aren't as big as desktops, but multiple windows can help you reference and edit text in more than one place at the same time.

## Snaking and Parallel Columns

*Arranging text in columns*

Many newspapers, newsletters, and magazines print text in two or more vertical columns on each page. **Snaking (newspaper-style) columns** have text continue from the bottom of one column to the top of the next column to the right. **Parallel columns** look similar, but don't continue text across columns; if text is continued, it's continued on another page. While some word processing packages can only print columns on paper, more advanced software can also display them on the screen. The ability to work with columns is a somewhat specialized feature, but organizations that produce newspapers, newsletters, or magazines often find it helpful.

## What-You-See-Is-What-You-Get

*Simulating printouts on the screen*

**What-you-see-is-what-you-get** or **WYSIWYG** (pronounced "wizzywig") is a useful word processing feature, even if it has one of the most unusual names in computer jargon. Basically, it means that a document will appear on paper exactly as it appears on the screen. Most WYSIWYG word processing packages use a graphics interface to represent the appearance of printed documents (see Figure 6.30). Many such systems can display full pages on the screen, complete with different character formats, text columns, ruled lines, and graphic pictures. Perhaps the best examples of true WYSIWYG word processing packages are those that run on Apple Macintosh computers, although there are several IBM-compatible packages with this feature, too.

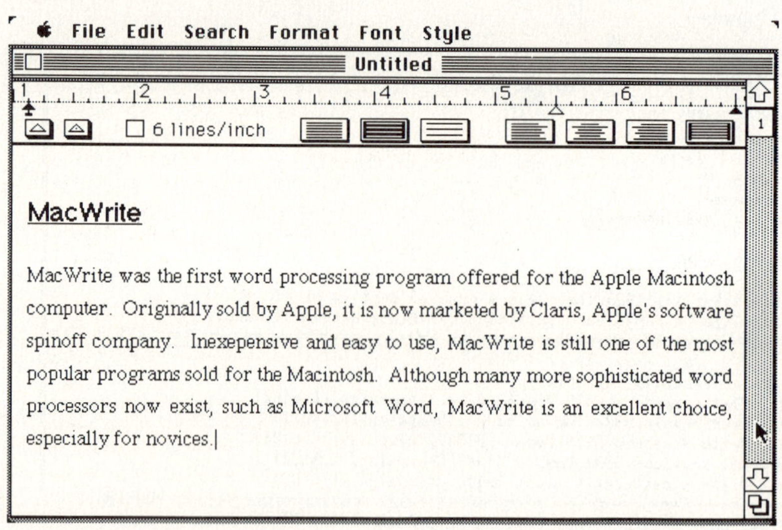


**Figure 6.30 What-You-See-Is-What-You-Get**
Most word processing packages for the Apple Macintosh are true WYSIWYG software. The screen accurately represents how the document will look when it is printed.

## Graphics

*Incorporating images*

As we just mentioned, many WYSIWYG word processing packages can display and print pictures inside documents. This graphics capability is a feature that first became common in Apple Macintosh word processing packages. Now several word processing packages for IBM-compatible microcomputers can also handle graphics (see Figure 6.31). The pictures that can be included in documents may come from any one of a number of sources. Some application packages, such as spreadsheet programs, produce graphics in the form of charts and graphs. Other packages produce maps. Sometimes a page scanner or video camera is used to copy a photograph, drawing, or some other figure on paper. Finally, images may be produced with a mouse or graphics tablet used in conjunction with a freehand painting or drawing program. Word processing packages with graphics ability can incorporate pictures from any of these sources into documents. A few word processing packages even give you limited drawing capabilities themselves.

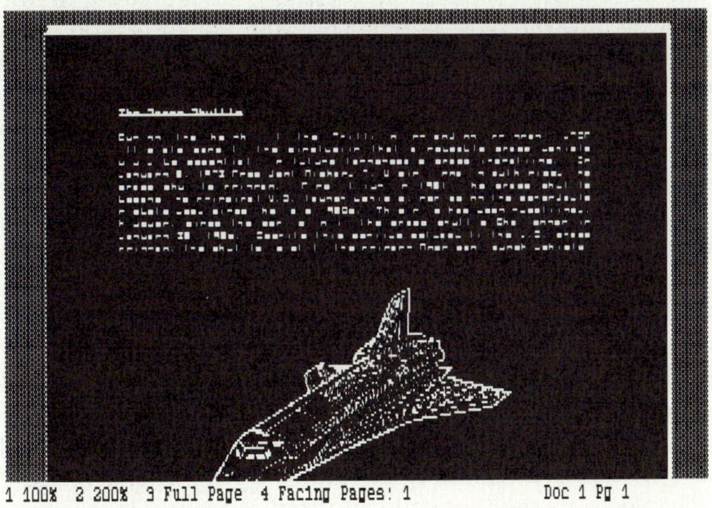


**Figure 6.31 Graphics in WordPerfect Documents**
Many advanced word processing packages for IBM-compatibles, such as WordPerfect, can now incorporate graphics into documents.

## Desktop Publishing

*Typesetting features*

The most advanced word processing packages often use a graphics interface, mouse, and WYSIWYG display to let you create snaking and parallel columns and incorporate graphics with text (see Figure 6.31). As we said in Chapter 1, these features are characteristics of desktop publishing. In general, however, desktop publishing packages are separate programs that combine the output from a word processing package along with graphics to produce near-typeset-quality material on a laser printer. For people with relatively simple desktop publishing needs, an advanced word processing package may be sufficient. However, desktop publishing has become a very significant microcomputer application. True desktop publishing systems go well beyond the features offered by even advanced word processing packages. Desktop publishing has been described as "complicated and expensive, but worth it." We'll have much more to say about this important topic in Chapter 14.

## POPULAR MICROCOMPUTER WORD PROCESSING PACKAGES

*Widely used, powerful applications*

There are probably more microcomputer word processing packages than any other single type of application software, and, for some reason, software developers keep releasing more of them. It's unlikely that you'll find much consensus among users as to which package is the "best." Everybody seems to have his or her own particular favorite. So, it is impossible to come up with a comprehensive list of all the popular microcomputer word processing packages. Three packages stand out from the others, however, even if only by a little bit: WordStar, WordPerfect, and Microsoft Word are all popular, powerful word processing packages with versions that run on a number of different computers.

### WordStar

*Word processing veteran*

WordStar, from MicroPro International Corporation, is one of the best-known, most long-lived microcomputer application packages. Originally introduced in mid-1979, WordStar became the most popular program for early 8-bit microcomputers running under the CP/M operating system. Soon Apple II computers, equipped with CP/M circuit boards, also began running WordStar. Finally, when the IBM Personal Computer became a hit, MicroPro released a version of WordStar to run under PC and MS-DOS. It has been estimated that more than three million copies of WordStar have been sold so far. Many people consider WordStar the standard against which many other word processing packages are compared.

WordStar is an interesting phenomenon. Despite its immense popularity, reviewers and critics have berated it as poorly designed, old-fashioned, difficult to use, and slow. However, the most recent version (Release 5) of this venerable package is much faster, much easier to use, and offers many advanced word processing features (see Figure 6.32). These include pull-down menus, context-sensitive on-line help, automatic paragraph reformatting, mail-merge, a spelling checker, a thesaurus, table-of-contents and index generation, an undo command, keyboard macros, character formatting, multiple windows, proportional spacing, and math functions. Thanks to its millions of loyal users, WordStar is still one of the most popular of all word processing packages.

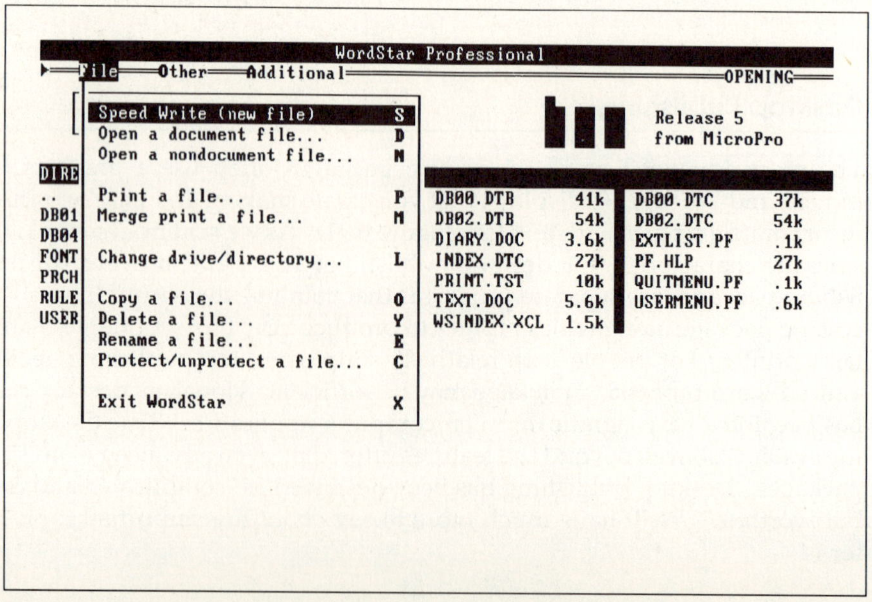


**Figure 6.32 WordStar**
This screen shows WordStar Release 5, the latest version of one of the most popular microcomputer programs.

## The Real World

### On Word Processing

John D. MacDonald, author of *Condominium* and the Travis McGee detective novels:

For over two and a half years I've been writing my novels using the WordStar word processing program. The hardware is immaterial. I am a very picky kind of writer insofar as word choice is concerned. My theory is to work like hell to make things look as if they were done very swiftly and easily. And I like to turn in very clean manuscripts.

When you're trying to produce the "effortless" manuscript, finding exactly the right word for each situation is crucial. I used to sit staring at the damned sheet of paper, *knowing* there was a precise word available if only I could think of it. Sometimes—often—I would settle for the almost right word. (Sam Clemens said the difference between the right word and the almost right word is the difference between lightning and a lightning bug.) Then, during one of the endless rereadings, I would dredge up the word I'd been looking for, but because there was *already* another one in the sentence, almost as descriptive, I would tend to leave the weaker word in rather than mark up the page or retype.

Now I merely leave a blank, just big enough so it catches the eye. And when I reread, sooner or later I can come up with the word I was reaching for and fit it into the blank—with no clue that I hesitated for even a moment.

The second best part of word processing is the ability to tone down the purple prose, or delete the Gee Mom parts of it.

The third best aspect is the revision-on-demand advantage. When Knopf asked for a detailed revision of *One More Sunday*, I was able to provide in eight days of intense effort, eight twelve-hour days, what would have taken me six weeks the way I used to work. And I believe the revision (those changes that I agreed with) is better than the original version.

Source: *Digital Deli* by The Lunch Group & Guests, edited by Steve Ditlea, Copyright 1984 by Steve Ditlea, Workman Publishing Company, Inc., New York, p. 163.

### WordPerfect

According to sales figures from retail computer stores, WordPerfect, from WordPerfect Corporation, is today's best-selling word processing package. Some industry experts estimate that WordPerfect has captured about 30 percent of the market, significantly more than other popular word processing packages like WordStar and Microsoft Word. Since its introduction in October 1982, WordPerfect has won the highest praise from both reviewers and users alike. A rich set of powerful new features seems to be added with every release. Versions have been developed to run on many different machines, including IBM, Apple II, Apple Macintosh, Commodore Amiga, Atari ST, and Digital MicroVAX computers.

*Best-selling package*

The current version of WordPerfect includes many of the advanced word processing features we've discussed in this chapter (see Figure 6.31). Although it's not a true WYSIWYG word processing package on IBM machines, WordPerfect does offer a preview mode that lets you see what pages containing text and graphics look like before they are printed. Even for everyday use, most people find that WordPerfect is powerful, easy to use, and fast.

### Microsoft Word

Microsoft Word is a state-of-the-art word processing package for both IBM-compatible and Apple Macintosh computers. First introduced in April 1983, Word became the program of choice for many people with laser printers. The Macintosh version is a true WYSIWYG word processing package; on IBM-compatibles, Word can be

*Graphics interface*

set up to more closely resemble WYSIWYG than most other word processing packages. Word is often used with a graphics display and a mouse. Like WordPerfect, Microsoft Word includes many of the advanced features we've discussed in this chapter (see Figure 6.29). However, some people feel that Word is slightly more difficult to learn, a little slower, and not quite as easy to use as WordPerfect.

Word occupies a unique niche as the word processing package most often used in desktop publishing systems. Its graphics interface, along with advanced printing capabilities make Word ideal for this purpose. Word works with a wide range of printers and is especially adept at driving laser printers. Backed by the most influential microcomputer software producer, Microsoft Word most likely will remain one of the leading word processing packages for a long time to come.

## Summary

- *The basic types of word processing systems.* Electronic typewriters, dedicated systems, microcomputer systems, and shared systems are the types of word processors in common use.
- *The functions every word processing package performs.* Word processing packages let you create, edit, format, print, and manage documents.
- *The editing features offered by word processing packages.* Editing features allow you to view a document, insert text, delete text, overwrite errors, move text, copy text, search and replace words and phrases, undo mistakes, and check spelling.
- *Some state-of-the-art word processing features.* Most leading word processing packages offer on-line help, style sheets, automatic paragraph reformatting, a built-in thesaurus, table of contents and index generation, outline processing, math functions, sorting capability, a mail-merge facility, keyboard macros, multiple windows, snaking and parallel columns, and some ability to incorporate graphics. Some packages are WYSIWYG and can perform simple desktop publishing tasks. Grammar and style checkers are available as separate programs.
- *Three popular microcomputer word processing packages.* WordStar, WordPerfect, and Microsoft Word are all popular, powerful word processing packages available for a number of different microcomputers.

## Key Terms

As an extra review of this chapter, try defining the following terms. If you have trouble with any of them, refer to the page number listed.

built-in dictionary (spelling checker) (203)
character formatting (204)
context-sensitive (210)
copy-and-paste (201)
cut-and-paste (200)
dedicated word processor (193)
electronic typewriter (192)
font (typeface) (204)
insert mode (199)
insertion point (196)
justified (205)
keyboard macro (217)
mail-merge (215)
on-line help (210)
overwrite mode (199)
page formatting (206)
paragraph formatting (205)
parallel columns (218)
point (204)
print queuing (209)
print spooling (print buffering) (209)
proportional spacing (208)
replace (202)

running head (206)
scroll bar (198)
search (201)
shared word processor (195)
snaking (newspaper-style) columns (218)
sorting (215)
style sheet (210)
undo (202)
what-you-see-is-what-you-get (WYSIWYG) (218)
word wrap (196)

## Review Questions

1. Who can benefit from using a word processing package?
2. What distinguished the very first word processors from electric typewriters?
3. For what sorts of tasks are electronic typewriters well-suited?
4. What is the major difference between a dedicated word processor and a microcomputer-based word processing system?
5. What is the least common type of word processor?
6. List the five basic functions every word processing package performs.
7. Which word processing feature relieves you from having to press the carriage return at the end of every line?
8. What is the difference between cut-and-paste and copy-and-paste operations?
9. What editing feature might you use to correct a consistently misspelled name throughout a document?
10. Which operation is used to cancel the effect of the previously executed command?
11. What kinds of correctly spelled words might not be found by a spelling checker?
12. What are some of the ways in which you can format characters?
13. What kind of paragraph alignment is used in this book?
14. What kind of spacing allots different amounts of space for different characters?
15. How do word processing packages help you manage documents?
16. What kind of on-line help displays information specifically relevant to what you are currently doing inside a program?
17. Why might paragraphs have to be reformatted?
18. What timesaving feature lets you record a series of keystrokes and play them back at any time?
19. What word processing features are generally considered to be characteristics of desktop publishing?
20. List three popular microcomputer word processing packages that run on more than one particular computer.

## Multiple Choice

1. Which of the following types of word processors would probably cost the least?
   (a) electronic typewriter (b) dedicated system
   (c) microcomputer system (d) shared system
2. Which is the most popular type of word processor?
   (a) electronic typewriter (b) dedicated system
   (c) microcomputer system (d) shared system
3. Which is a task not normally performed with word processing software?
   (a) creating a document (b) editing a document
   (c) formatting a document (d) compiling source code
4. The word processing feature that eliminates having to press the Enter key at the end of every line is called
   (a) justification. (b) word wrap.
   (c) indentation. (d) mail-merge.
5. Many word processing packages with a graphics interface let you move up or down in a document through the use of a(n)
   (a) cursor. (b) insertion point.
   (c) ruler line. (d) scroll bar.
6. Which typing mode would you use to add a new word between two existing words?
   (a) insert (b) overwrite
   (c) justify (d) word wrap
7. In many cases, the simplest way to remove the last few characters you've typed is with the
   (a) Up Arrow key. (b) Page Down key.
   (c) Backspace key. (d) Alternate key.
8. Which operation involves moving an existing segment of text from one place to another?
   (a) cut-and-paste (b) copy-and-paste
   (c) search and replace (d) global delete
9. Which feature would you use to change every occurrence of *Jerry* to *Geri* in an entire document?
   (a) cut-and-paste (b) copy-and-paste
   (c) search and replace (d) global delete
10. Which of the following words in a document would probably be presented to you as a possible error by a spelling checker?
    (a) the (b) brown
    (c) dog (d) Ernie
11. Which of the following is an example of character formatting?
    (a) justification (b) boldface
    (c) indentation (d) spacing
12. What feature would you look for in a word processing package if you wanted to be able to print one document while editing another?
    (a) letter-quality mode (b) print spooling
    (c) print qucuing (d) proportional printing

13. Which feature would you use to create form letters?
    (a) style sheet (b) WYSIWYG
    (c) mail-merge (d) keyboard macro
14. Which feature lets you record a series of keystrokes and "play" them back at any time?
    (a) style sheet (b) WYSIWYG
    (c) mail-merge (d) keyboard macro
15. Which of the following word processing packages first appeared on the market?
    (a) MacWrite (b) WordStar
    (c) WordPerfect (d) Microsoft Word

## Projects

1. In this chapter we have briefly described many of the basic and advanced features offered by today's word processing packages. Try to find five other features we have not discussed and write a paragraph about each of these. Periodicals like *PC Magazine*, *PC World*, *BYTE*, *Mac World*, and *Mac User* may be your best sources of information.
2. As we have said, many popular microcomputer word processing packages are on the market. We've only briefly discussed three of them in this chapter. Choose three others and write a paragraph or two about each one. Again, computer magazines are a good place to look for information. Try to find issues that contain product reviews of word processing packages.
3. Do you think that you could use a word processing package for school or work? Specifically, for what tasks would you use one? Based on the descriptions we've given and the research you have done on word processing packages for the previous question, which package would you choose? Why?
4. Once you have learned how to use a word processing package, in most cases you can prepare documents much faster than on a typewriter. But can a word processing package help you improve the quality of your writing? How do you think using a word processing package would affect the way you write? What features would you like to see included in the word processing package of the future?

# 7

# Word Processing Details: WordStar

## In This Chapter

## PREVIEW

WordStar is a software classic. First released in 1979, it was one of the first microcomputer application packages to achieve widespread popularity. Many people believe that WordStar was the first true word processing program for microcomputers. MicroPro International Corporation, the company that developed WordStar, estimates that more than 3 million copies have been sold since 1979. Despite its early lead in the market, however, by the mid-1980s WordStar had fallen behind more sophisticated software packages, such as WordPerfect and Microsoft Word. Then, in February 1987, MicroPro International introduced WordStar Professional Release 4. In its first year, the package sold 243,000 copies, 40 percent of which were upgrades purchased by previous WordStar owners. Release 4 included much needed features and improvements. Although WordStar did not regain its lead in the market, the new release proved that the word processing veteran was still in the race. In August 1988, MicroPro International introduced WordStar Professional Release 5. This latest version adds a host of new features and boasts a much friendlier user interface, while remaining generally compatible with previous versions. According to most reviews, WordStar Release 5 is a strong product in a very competitive market, even if it doesn't quite match the current leaders, WordPerfect and Microsoft Word.

After studying this chapter, you will understand

- how to start WordStar.
- how to use the WordStar menus.
- how to create a new document.
- how to edit a new or existing document.
- how to format characters, paragraphs, and pages.
- how to print a document.
- how to manage document files.
- some additional features included in WordStar.

## WORKING WITH WordStar

*Powerful word processing package*

In this chapter, we take a closer look at WordStar Professional Release 5, a powerful word processing package from MicroPro International Corporation for IBM and IBM-compatible microcomputers.

Like many powerful application packages, WordStar must first be installed on your system before you can use the program on a regular basis. If your computer has a hard disk, this process typically involves creating a subdirectory on the hard disk, copying files from the original diskettes to this subdirectory, and then running an installation program. Appendix C describes this installation procedure in more detail. For the examples in this chapter, WordStar Professional Release 5 has been installed on a hard disk in a subdirectory named WS5.

Once WordStar has been installed, running it is easy. First, you change to the WS5 subdirectory by typing **CD C:\WS5** and pressing the **Enter** key. To start WordStar, you then type **WS** and press the **Enter** key. The copyright notice shown in Figure 7.1 then appears on the screen for a few moments.

**Figure 7.1 WordStar Copyright Screen**
This screen appears for a moment after you start WordStar.

```
WordStar Professional Release 5.00 #American 085
Copyright (C) 1983, 1988 MicroPro International Corporation.
All rights reserved

IBM PC Compatible
Draft Printer


MailMerge, TelMerge, and MailList copyright (C) 1983, 1988.
MicroPro International Corporation.  All rights reserved

Thesaurus, speller and hyphenation technology copyright (C)
1986, 1988 Microlytics, UFO Systems, Xerox Corporation.
All rights reserved
```

**Insight**

## How Has WordStar Influenced Other Software Packages?

There's nothing like your first car. Whether it's a junk pile on wheels or a Maserati—you'll compare every other car you own with it.

That's basically what happened in the development of word processing software, only that first car was WordStar. Appearing in the late 1970s, WordStar was the first adequate word processing package available for commercial and business use on CP/M-based machines.

WordStar was developed to run with almost any keyboard or display. That meant WordStar designers couldn't count on a standard set of function or cursor-control keys. All the keyboards in use were capable of generating the ASCII code sequences, however. The ASCII code is a standard set of internal codes assigned to various symbols and key combinations that can be created with a computer terminal.

WordStar designers took advantage of that fact. For example, pressing **CONTROL-T** with WordStar deletes a word to the right of the cursor, and **CONTROL-D** moves the cursor to the right. No cursor keys are needed. If cursor keys are present, as they are with IBM-compatible microcomputers, either the right arrow key or CONTROL-D will move the cursor to the right.

The people who developed other software were so accustomed to WordStar and its control key sequences that they used the same ideas on their own products. Two good examples are Turbo Pascal from Borland International and the dBASE III PLUS data base system from Ashton-Tate.

The internal editors on both these systems use the WordStar control key conventions. This means that anyone familiar with WordStar doesn't have to learn a new set of key commands to use these packages. The systems can be operated with only minor additional training.

## WordStar MENUS

*Selecting options from pull-down menus*

After the initial copyright notice disappears, WordStar displays its Opening screen with a list of files in your current directory (see Figure 7.2). In our case, the current directory is the WS5 subdirectory containing all the files that make up the WordStar package. The double line near the top of the screen is called a **menu bar**; it contains the names of pull-down menus. The Opening screen has three pull-down menus, File, Other, and Additional. Each pull-down menu is a list of word processing tasks and the key or keys you press to perform each one. To activate a pull-down menu, you press the first letter of its name. For example, press **F** to activate the File menu. Your screen now looks like Figure 7.3. To select an option from a menu, you press the key or keys listed to its right, or use the **Up Arrow** or **Down Arrow** key to

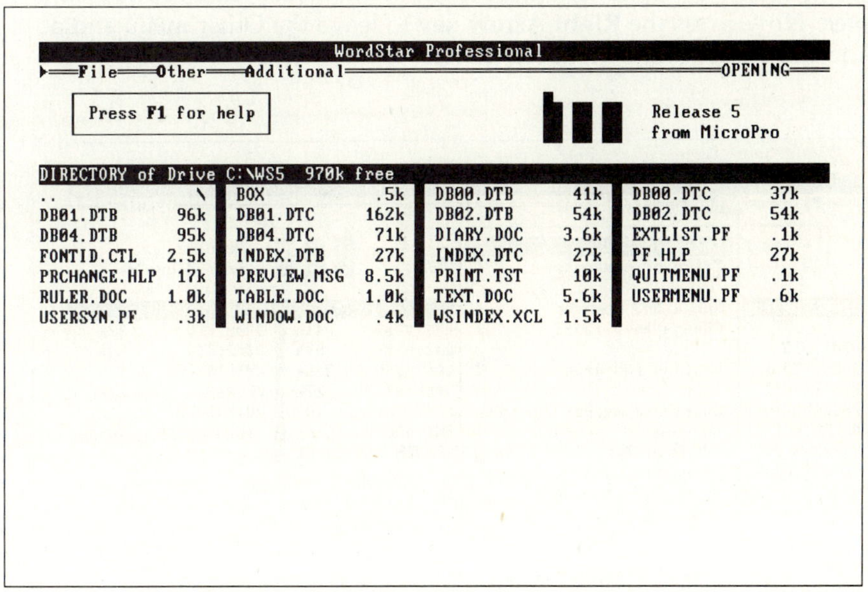


**Figure 7.2 Opening Screen**
WordStar's Opening screen has a menu bar and list of files in the current directory.

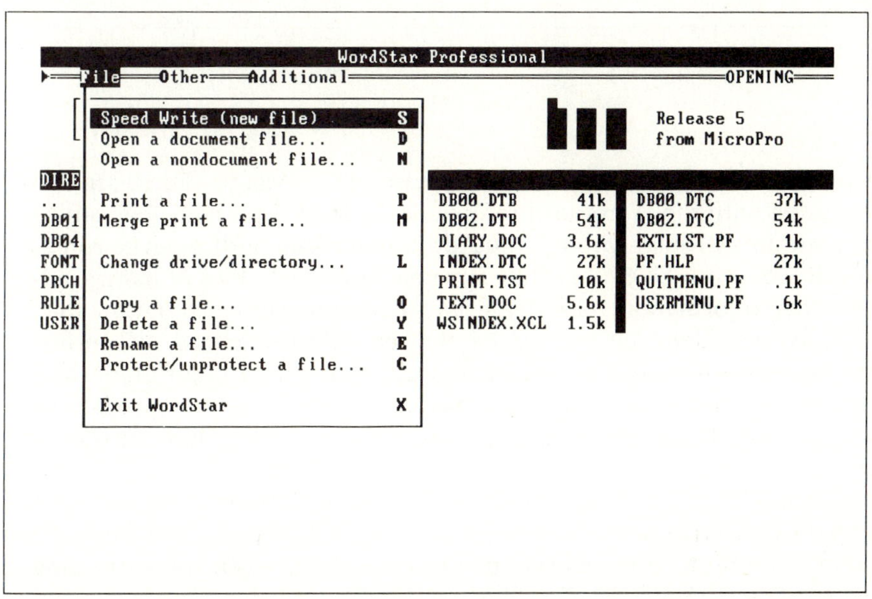


**Figure 7.3 File Menu**
The File menu of the Opening screen lets you open, print, and organize your documents.

highlight the option and then press the **Enter** key. For instance, to exit WordStar and return to DOS, you press **X**. You could also perform the same action by pressing the **Up Arrow** once and then pressing the **Enter** key.

As you can see, the File menu contains options for working with files while running WordStar. We'll have more to say about these options later in this chapter. Now, let's look at the other two menus in the Opening screen. First, press the **Escape** key, which makes the current pull-down menu disappear. Then press **O** to invoke the Other menu. Another way to leave the File menu and display the Other menu would be to press the **Right Arrow** key once.

The Other menu, shown in Figure 7.4, is a list of miscellaneous commands that perform tasks such as generating an index or table of contents, temporarily suspending WordStar to run a DOS command like FORMAT, changing the type of menus that appear on the screen, showing how memory is being used, and working with keyboard macros. We'll have more to say about most of these options later in this chapter. Now, press the **Right Arrow** key to leave the Other menu and activate the Additional menu, shown in Figure 7.5.

**Figure 7.4 Other Menu**
The Other menu of the Opening screen contains a few miscellaneous WordStar features.

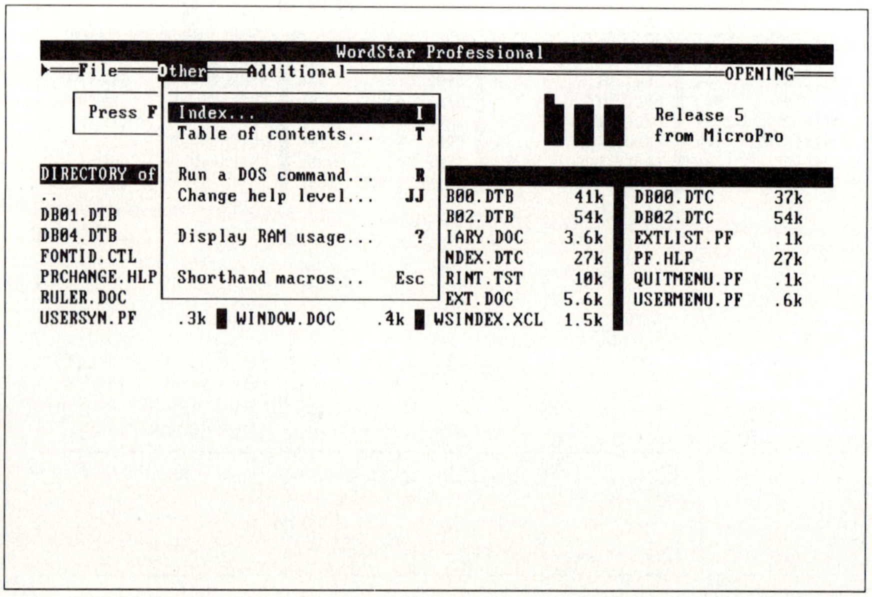


This menu contains only two options: MailList and TelMerge. These are two programs included with the WordStar Professional Release 5 package that can be invoked from within WordStar through the Additional menu or that can be run as stand-alone software from DOS. MailList lets you create data files of names, addresses, and other information. TelMerge is a communications program that, provided you have a modem, lets you send and receive electronic mail, call on-line information services such as CompuServe, call mainframe computers, and exchanges messages and files with other microcomputer users. Although MailList and TelMerge are both handy programs, we won't be discussing them further in this chapter.

The three menus, File, Other, and Additional, contain all the options you have available from the Opening screen. Some of these options, however, have their own menu bars. For example, a different list of menus is available when you are editing

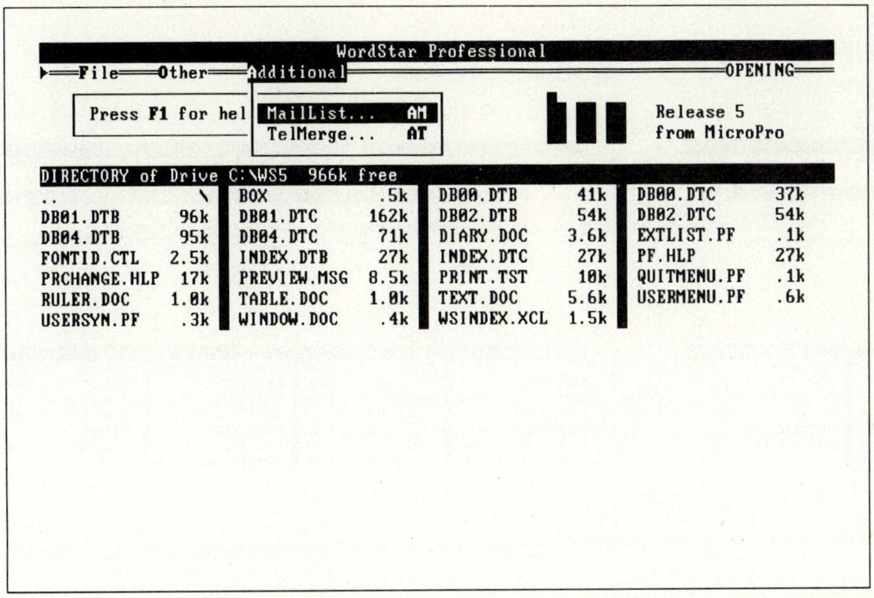


**Figure 7.5 Additional Menu**
The additional menu of the Opening screen lets you run MailList, for creating mailing lists, and TelMerge, for communicating with other computers.

a document, as we will see shortly. This pull-down menu system, new with WordStar Release 5, is an easy-to-use, yet powerful way to perform word processing tasks.

## CREATING DOCUMENTS

*A sample letter*

Before you can edit, format, print, or save a document, you must create it. To illustrate word processing with WordStar, let's create a sample document. This particular document will be a letter from the secretary of a condominium association to the unit owners.

### Opening a Document

*Choosing a file name*

To create this letter, first you tell WordStar to open a document and choose a new file name. Bring up the File menu from the Opening screen, then press **D** to open a document file. WordStar prompts you for a file name, as shown in Figure 7.6(a). A document is identified by the name of the file in which it's stored. The rules for naming WordStar document files are the same as the rules for all DOS files, which we discussed in Chapter 5: the filename is one to eight characters long and it may be followed by an optional extension of up to three characters. So, you could name your document **LETTER.DOC** simply by typing this and pressing the **Enter** key. Although WordStar doesn't require you to use an extension of .DOC to identify your file as a document file, many people do this. If there is no file in the current directory named LETTER.DOC, WordStar displays the screen shown in Figure 7.6(b). Here you press **Y** for yes to tell WordStar to create a new document named LETTER.DOC.

**Figure 7.6 Opening a New Document File**

(a) Here you specify a name for your document.

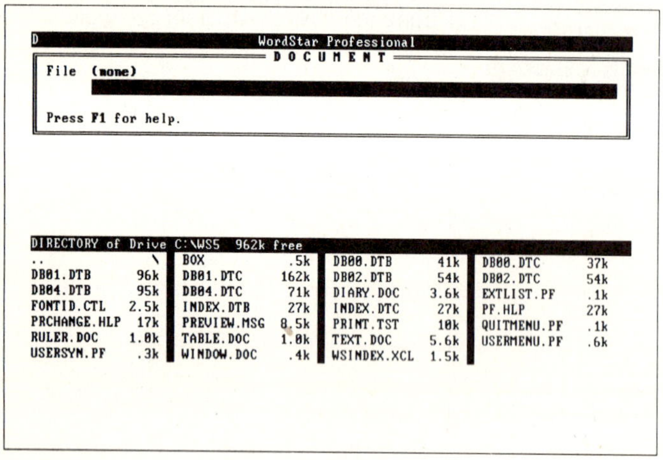


(b) If that document doesn't already exist, WordStar can create it.

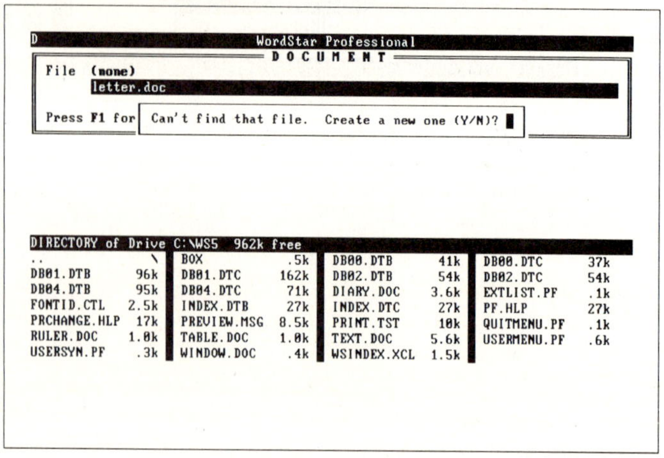


## The Edit Screen

*Where you enter and edit text*

After you name your new file, WordStar displays the Edit screen, shown in Figure 7.7. The top line of this screen is called the **status line**. At the left side, the status line shows the current disk drive and file name of the document on which you are working. Toward the middle, the status line displays the page number, line number, column number, and distance in inches from the left margin of the current cursor location. The Insert indicator tells you that WordStar's insert mode is turned on, the Align indicator tells you that automatic paragraph reformatting is turned on, and the RgtJust indicator tells you that text will be automatically justified to both the left and right margins. Beneath the status line is the Edit menu bar, about which we'll have more to say when we discuss editing documents.

**Figure 7.7 Edit Screen**

Here you enter and edit the text of your document.

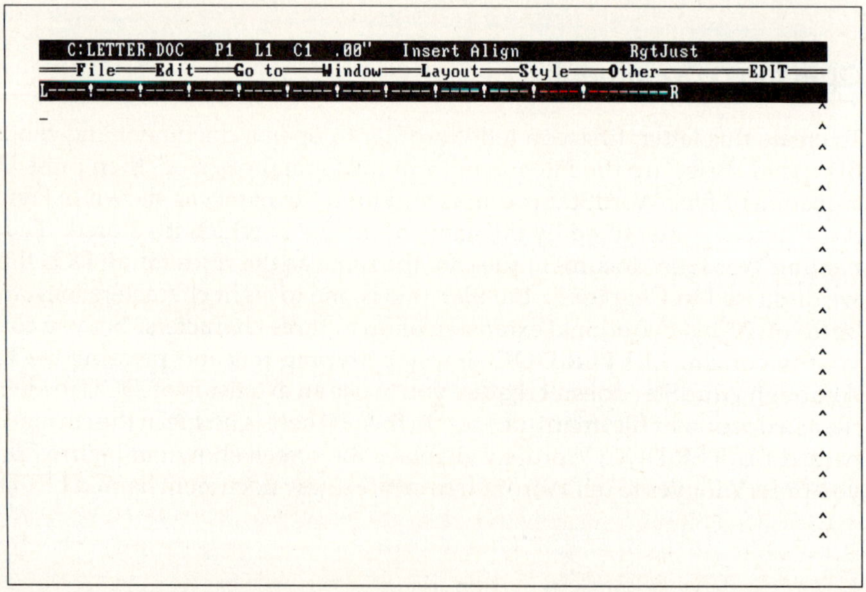

Below the Edit menu bar and just above the blank text area is a line of dashes and exclamation points. This is the **ruler line**, which shows you the positions of the left margin (the L), the tab stops (the ! characters), and the right margin (the R). By default, WordStar sets up a line length of 65 characters. The left margin is at column 1, the right margin is at column 65, and a tab stop is placed at every fifth column, beginning at column 6. Along the right edge of the screen is the **flag column**. This column contains a special character for each line, called a **flag**, that WordStar displays to tell you something about that line. For example, each ^ flag that you see in Figure 7.7 indicates that the file ends on or above that line. Since no text is in the document yet, every line on the screen indicates the end of the file. The empty space in the center of the screen is where you type your document.

## Typing Text

*Automatic word wrap*

Once you open a document, WordStar initially places the cursor in the first column of the first line of the first page. To create a new document, you simply type the words and punctuation. WordStar has automatic word wrap, so that whenever you type a word that extends into the right margin, WordStar moves that word down to the next line. If you explicitly want to begin a new line or start a new paragraph, just press the **Enter** key. Figure 7.8 shows the Edit screen after some of the text of LETTER.DOC has been typed.

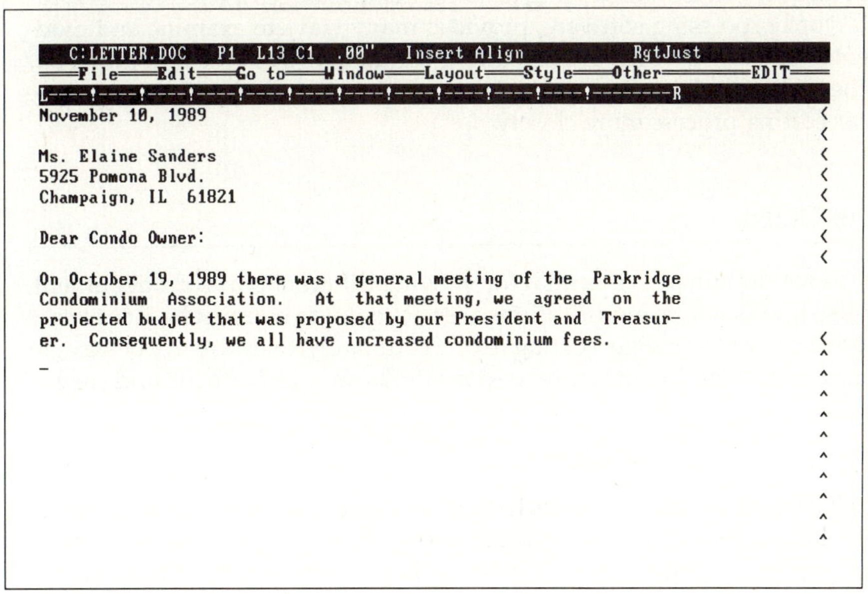

```
   C:LETTER.DOC    P1  L13 C1   .00"    Insert Align            RgtJust
====File====Edit====Go to====Window====Layout====Style====Other========EDIT==
L----!----!----!----!----!----!----!----!----!----!----!--------R
November 10, 1989                                                          <
                                                                           <
Ms. Elaine Sanders                                                         <
5925 Pomona Blvd.                                                          <
Champaign, IL  61821                                                       <
                                                                           <
Dear Condo Owner:                                                          <
                                                                           <
On October 19, 1989 there was a general meeting of the  Parkridge
Condominium  Association.    At  that meeting, we  agreed  on  the
projected budjet that was proposed by our President and  Treasur-
er.  Consequently, we all have increased condominium fees.                 <
_                                                                          ^
```

**Figure 7.8 Edit Screen with LETTER.DOC**
Some of the text of the LETTER.DOC document has been entered.

Examine this figure carefully. Since justification is turned on, each full line is aligned to both the left and right columns. Whenever a word wrap is performed, WordStar automatically fills out the previous line, if it doesn't end exactly at the right margin, by inserting extra spaces here and there between words. These extra blanks are called **soft spaces**. The blanks you type with the space bar are called **hard spaces**. WordStar inserts and deletes soft spaces as needed when it aligns and indents paragraphs. Hard spaces, on the other hand, can only be inserted and deleted explicitly by you.

**Auto-hyphenation** is also exhibited in Figure 7.8. This word processing feature can hyphenate words at the ends of lines when necessary. For example, the word *Treasurer* was automatically hyphenated by WordStar as it wrapped the word to the next line. The hyphen that breaks up the word *Treasurer* is a **soft hyphen** because it was added by WordStar. If text is later inserted or deleted, or if the margins are changed, this soft hyphen could disappear when the text is automatically reformatted. If you want a hyphen to stay in the text unless you explicitly erase it, you must insert a **hard hyphen** by pressing the - key. Like word wrap and justification, auto-hyphenation can be turned off if you like.

WordStar also has hard and soft returns. A **hard return**, which begins a new line, is only inserted into a document when you press the Enter key. But a **soft return**, which also begins a new line, is inserted by WordStar whenever a word wrap is performed. Like soft spaces and soft hyphens, soft returns can be automatically added and removed by WordStar if margins or indentation are changed. A line that ends in a hard return has a < character in the flag column, while a soft return is indicated by a blank in the flag column, as Figure 7.8 shows.

## EDITING DOCUMENTS

*Viewing and changing files*

To edit a document, you look at existing text and make changes if necessary. WordStar, like all word processing software, provides many ways to examine and modify documents. You can choose various editing commands from the Edit menu bar or invoke them directly by pressing special combinations of keys. Let's examine the WordStar editing process more closely.

### Moving the Cursor

*Going places*

Learning to move the cursor is essential for viewing different parts of a document. The cursor also marks where modifications are to occur, so you must be able to precisely move the cursor to change existing text. Fortunately, there are many ways to move the cursor. The most commonly used methods are quick, direct, and easy.

#### Arrow Keys and the Cursor Diamond

*Up, down, left, and right*

All IBM and IBM-compatible keyboards have at least one set of arrow keys. In many programs, including WordStar, the simplest way to move the cursor is to press an arrow key. Pressing and releasing the **Up Arrow** key once moves the cursor up one line, while the **Down Arrow** key moves the cursor to the line directly below. The **Left Arrow** key moves the cursor backward, and the **Right Arrow** key moves the cursor forward. Pressing an arrow key for more than a second without releasing it causes it to automatically repeat, so that you can move the cursor more rapidly. Finally, holding down the **Control** (Ctrl) key and pressing the **Left Arrow** key moves the cursor to the beginning of the word to the left. Similarly, holding down the **Control** key and pressing the **Right Arrow** key moves the cursor to the beginning of the word to the immediate right.

Although pressing the arrow keys is probably the most frequently used method, there are alternate methods of performing the same cursor movement operations.

For example, to move the cursor up one line, you could hold down the **Control** key and press the **E** key. So, Ctrl-E is equivalent to the Up Arrow key.

The original version of WordStar was developed before the IBM Personal Computer was introduced in 1981. In those early days, most microcomputer keyboards had fewer keys than are now common. Virtually all had a Control key, but many had no arrow keys or other special keys like Page Up (PgUp), Page Down (PgDn), Home, and End. So, early versions of WordStar used the Control key in combination with some ordinary letter keys to move the cursor. This arrangement, called the **cursor diamond** (see Figure 7.9), has been preserved in more recent versions of WordStar for the convenience of people who upgraded from earlier releases. In addition, some people, especially touch typists, prefer using the cursor diamond to arrow keys because they don't have to move their hands from the "home" keys (ASDF and JKL;) to move the cursor.

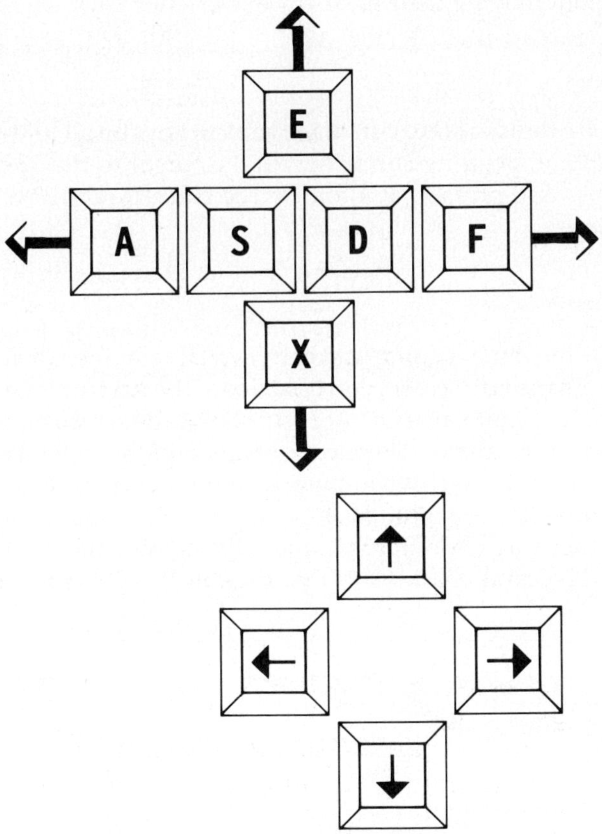


**Figure 7.9 The WordStar Cursor Diamond**
WordStar maintains some cursor movement commands that were developed before arrow keys were common on microcomputer keyboards.

| To Move the Cursor | Press |
|---|---|
| Up one line | Ctrl-E or ↑ |
| Down one line | Ctrl-X or ↓ |
| Left one character | Ctrl-S or ← |
| Right one character | Ctrl-D or → |
| Left one word | Ctrl-A or Ctrl- ← |
| Right one word | Ctrl-F or Ctrl- → |

## Scrolling and Paging

*Moving within long documents*

Most documents are too long to completely fit on the display at once. Scrolling and paging commands let you change what part of your document is displayed on the screen. One simple way to scroll the screen is to press the Up Arrow or Down Arrow key even after the cursor reaches the top or bottom edge of the text area. If there are more lines above or below, WordStar scrolls the screen and moves the cursor to the next line.

Paging is like scrolling an entire screenful at a time. The easiest way to do this is with the Page Up and Page Down keys. If your document extends above the top of the screen, pressing the **Page Up** key displays the previous screen and moves the cursor there. Pressing the **Page Down** key has the opposite effect. WordStar also lets you perform the same actions by holding down the **Control** key and pressing **R** or **C**. So, Ctrl-R moves up to the previous screen and Ctrl-C moves down to the next screen. Again, some users prefer the control commands because they can execute them without moving their hands from the letter keys.

## Home and End

*Top and bottom of the screen*

Home and End are the two other cursor movement keys on all IBM-compatible keyboards. In WordStar, pressing **Home** moves the cursor to the upper-left corner of the current screen, and pressing **End** moves the cursor to the lower-right corner of the current screen.

## The Go To Menu

*More ways to move the cursor*

Still more cursor movement commands are available in the Go To menu. To pull down a menu from the Edit screen, you hold down the **Alternate** (Alt) key and press the first letter of the menu name. Figure 7.10 shows the screen after pressing **Alt-G** to pull down the Go To menu. These commands rapidly move the cursor within a document. For example, to move to the end of your current document, you could press the **Up Arrow** key to highlight the Go to File End option and then press the **Enter** key. Another way to do this is to press the combination of keys listed to the option's right. The carat character (^) you see in WordStar menus is a common

**Figure 7.10 Go To Menu**
The Go To menu lets you quickly move to different parts of your document.

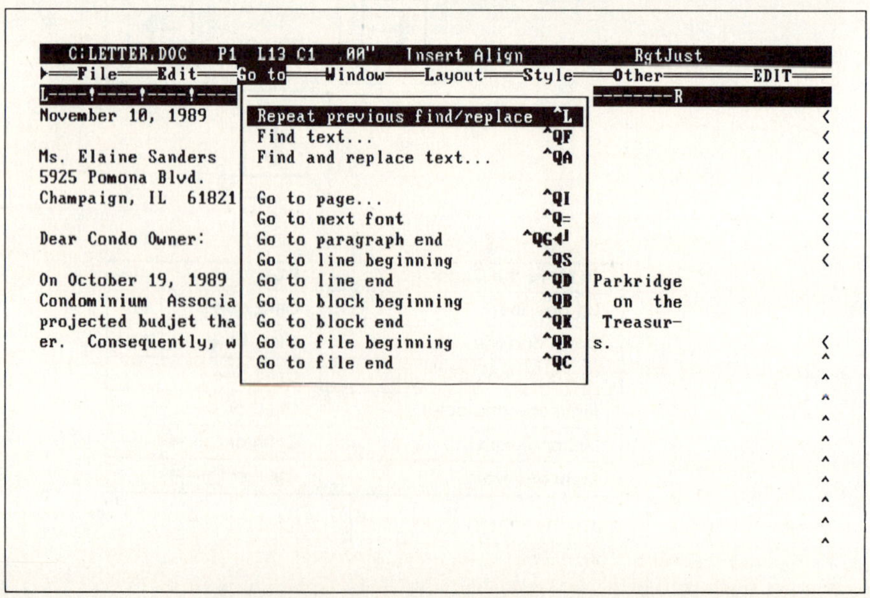

shorthand notation that means "hold down the Control key." For example, to move the cursor to the end of the document file, you could also hold down the **Control** key and type **QC**. In fact, you can use Control key commands such as Ctrl-QC directly from the Edit screen without having to pull down any menus.

## Inserting and Overwriting

*Adding new text*

WordStar, like most word processing software, has two basic typing modes: insert and overwrite. By default, WordStar has insert mode turned on when you open a document. This means that to insert new material into a document, you just move the cursor to the location where you want the insertion to occur, then simply type. For example, you can move the cursor just past the end of the last sentence of the document in Figure 7.8 and insert the rest of the letter (see Figure 7.11). The new characters you type push any existing characters to the right. When insert mode is turned on, the word *Insert* is displayed near the middle of the status line at the top of the screen.

```
   C:LETTER.DOC    P1  L22 C1  .00"   Insert Align          RgtJust
═══File═══Edit═══Go to═══Window═══Layout═══Style═══Other═══════════EDIT═══
L----!----!----!----!----!----!----!----!----!----!----!--------R
November 10, 1989                                                      <
                                                                       <
Ms. Elaine Sanders                                                     <
5925 Pomona Blvd.                                                      <
Champaign, IL  61821                                                   <
                                                                       <
Dear Condo Owner:                                                      <
                                                                       <
On October 19, 1989 there was a general meeting of the  Parkridge
Condominium  Association.   At  that meeting, we  agreed  on  the
projected budjet that was proposed by our President and  Treasur-
er.   Consequently, we all have increased condominium fees.   The
monthly fee for your unit is now $69.53.  If you have not already
sent  this amount for the month of November, we would  appreciate
it if you could send the balance as soon as possible.                  <
                                                                       <
Sincerely,                                                             <
                                                                       <
                                                                       <
David Franklin                                                         <
Secretary                                                              <
_                                                                      ^
```

**Figure 7.11 Inserting the Rest of the Letter**
This screen shows the completed LETTER.DOC document.

To switch typing modes, you simply press the Insert key. If insert mode is already on, WordStar changes to overwrite mode; if overwrite mode is turned on, pressing the Insert key switches back to insert mode. When you change to overwrite mode, WordStar erases the *Insert* indicator in the status line. When overwrite mode is turned on, characters you type replace existing characters in the same positions. Although overwrite mode is handy for correcting small mistakes, insert mode is necessary for adding new material to existing text.

## Deleting Text

*Erasing characters, words, and lines*

One of the most common editing operations is deleting text. WordStar has commands for erasing individual characters, words, and lines. In WordStar Release 5, as with most word processing packages, the Backspace key erases the character to the left of the cursor and the Delete key erases the character at the current cursor position. WordStar versions before Release 4, however, had the Delete key erase the character to the left of the cursor and the Backspace key move the cursor to the left without erasing anything.

WordStar also makes it easy to erase an entire word or line of text. To delete a word, place the cursor on the first character in the word and press **Ctrl-T**. To delete a line, place the cursor anywhere in that line and press **Ctrl-Y**. If you forget these commands, you can look them up or execute them from the Edit menu. Press **Alt-E** to pull down the Edit menu, which is shown in Figure 7.12. The Delete Word option is the same as pressing Ctrl-T, and the Delete Line option is the same as pressing Ctrl-Y. WordStar has several other commands for deleting text, but Backspace, Delete, Ctrl-T, and Ctrl-Y are the most frequently used.

**Figure 7.12 Edit Menu**
The Edit menu contains commands that let you easily manipulate text.

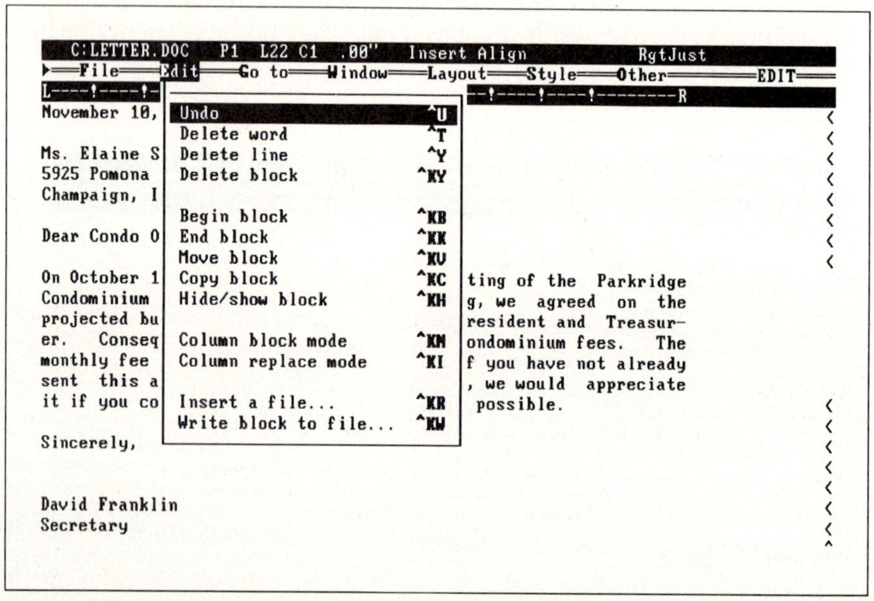


## Working with Blocks of Text

*Sections of characters*

Besides individual characters, words, and lines, most word processing packages let you specify and manipulate other sections of text. In WordStar, a **block** is a piece of text that can be any size—from a single character to an entire document. Once a block is designated, it can be deleted, copied, or moved.

### Marking a Block

*Highlighting a section of text*

The first step in working with a block of text is to mark where it begins and ends. One way to mark the beginning of a block is to move the cursor to the first character in that block, hold down the **Control** key, and then type **KB**. The other way is to pull down the Edit menu with **Alt-E** and select the Begin Block option (see Figure 7.12). When you do either of these, WordStar displays its begin block marker <B> on the screen to the left of the cursor. This marker isn't actually inserted into your document; WordStar just temporarily displays it to show where the block begins.

Marking the end of a block is similarly done. First move the cursor to the character just past the end of the block. Then you can press **Ctrl-KK**, or pull down the Edit menu with **Alt-E** and select the End Block option. In either case, WordStar displays its end block marker <K> on the screen. If there is already a begin block marker on the screen, WordStar turns off both block markers and simply highlights the marked block in reverse video (dark characters against a light background—see Figure 7.13).

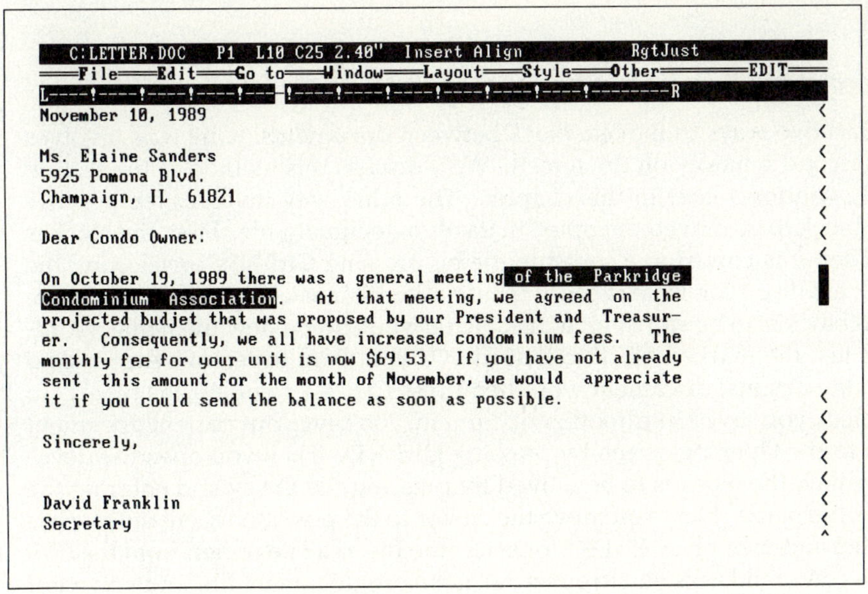
C:LETTER.DOC P1 L10 C25 2.40" Insert Align RgtJust
File Edit Go to Window Layout Style Other EDIT
November 10, 1989

Ms. Elaine Sanders
5925 Pomona Blvd.
Champaign, IL 61821

Dear Condo Owner:

On October 19, 1989 there was a general meeting of the Parkridge Condominium Association. At that meeting, we agreed on the projected budjet that was proposed by our President and Treasurer. Consequently, we all have increased condominium fees. The monthly fee for your unit is now $69.53. If you have not already sent this amount for the month of November, we would appreciate it if you could send the balance as soon as possible.

Sincerely,

David Franklin
Secretary

**Figure 7.13 Marked Block**
This screen shows a marked block on the screen in reverse video (dark characters against a light background).

WordStar lets you mark only one block at a time in the same window. You can extend the end of a marked block by advancing the cursor and pressing Ctrl-KK. Similarly, you can also move the cursor and remark the beginning of a block. You can even start by marking the end first and then the beginning, if you like. But what if you want to "unmark" a block? To shut off, or *hide*, a marked block you can press Ctrl-KH or select the Hide/show Block from the Edit menu. The block will still be marked, but the reverse video highlighting is turned off. Pressing Ctrl-KH turns the highlighting back on again. To actually remove a block marker from your document, you need to put the cursor just past the existing marker and enter the same marker command again.

## Deleting a Block

*Removing a section of text*

Using a block is a handy way to delete several words, several lines, or some other irregular portion of text. Examine Figure 7.13 again. Let's say that you want to delete the phrase "of the Parkridge Condominium Association" from the end of the first sentence. Once this block is marked, there are two ways to delete it. You can either press **Ctrl-KY** or pull down the Edit menu and select the Delete Block option.

## Copying a Block

*Duplicating a section of text*

Reproducing a block of text is as easy as deleting it. First you mark the block and move the cursor to the location where you want the new copy to begin. Then you can either press **Ctrl-KC** or pull down the Edit menu and select the Copy Block option to copy the marked block and "paste" it at the current cursor position.

### Moving a Block

*Relocating a section of text*

WordStar's cut-and-paste operation is similar to copying, except the original is also deleted. First you mark the block and place the cursor where the block is to go. Then you can either press **Ctrl-KV** or pull down the Edit menu and select the Move Block option to move the marked block from its former location to the current cursor position.

### Copying and Moving between Documents

*Cutting and pasting in different files*

WordStar has two ways to move a block between documents. One way involves opening a second window on the screen. We'll discuss this method in the section on multiple windows later in this chapter. The other way involves temporarily saving the block to be moved or copied in its own document file. First, the block is marked. Then it is copied to a separate file by pressing **Ctrl-KW** or selecting the Write Block to File option from the Edit menu. WordStar asks for a file name where the marked block is to be stored on a disk. After you enter a new file name, WordStar copies just the marked block to that file. If you want to remove the marked block from the original document, you then press **Ctrl-KY** to delete the block. To insert the block you saved into another document, you save your current document and return to the Opening screen by pressing **Ctrl-KD**. Then you open the document into which the block is to be moved by pressing the **D** key and entering the document's file name. Next you move the cursor to the position where the block is to be inserted and then press **Ctrl-KR** or select the Insert a File option from the Edit menu. This command asks you to enter the name of a document file, and you enter the name you chose when you saved the block from the other document. Finally, WordStar inserts the contents of that file into the document you are editing at the current cursor position.

## Searching and Replacing

*Finding and substituting text*

The letter to condominium owners we've been using as an example document is quite short; it wouldn't be difficult to find and fix a consistent error throughout the entire document. With longer documents, however, manually searching and replacing can be tedious. WordStar, like most word processing packages, has commands that can automatically seek out and substitute text.

Sometimes you don't want to replace anything, but just want to see where a certain word or phrase is mentioned. WordStar's Find Text command from the Go To menu (see Figure 7.10) can quickly locate any piece of text up to 65 characters long. Let's say that you want to find every reference to the word *President* in a document. First you move the cursor to the beginning of the document. Then you press **Ctrl-QF** or select the Find Text option from the Go To menu. WordStar presents a box on the screen where you fill in the word or phrase you want to find. In this case, you type **President** and press the **Enter** key (see Figure 7.14). You can also specify one or more options that give you more control over the way the search will proceed. You can, for example, tell WordStar to search backward from the current cursor location or ignore the case (uppercase or lowercase) of characters while searching. If you don't need any of these options, you can just press the **Enter** key again. WordStar advances the cursor to the next location of the word *President*. If it can't find *President*, WordStar tells you so, asks that you press the **Escape** key, and leaves the cursor at the end of the document.

If the word you want to find is repeated throughout the document, you can tell WordStar to find the next occurrence without having to redo the Find Text com-

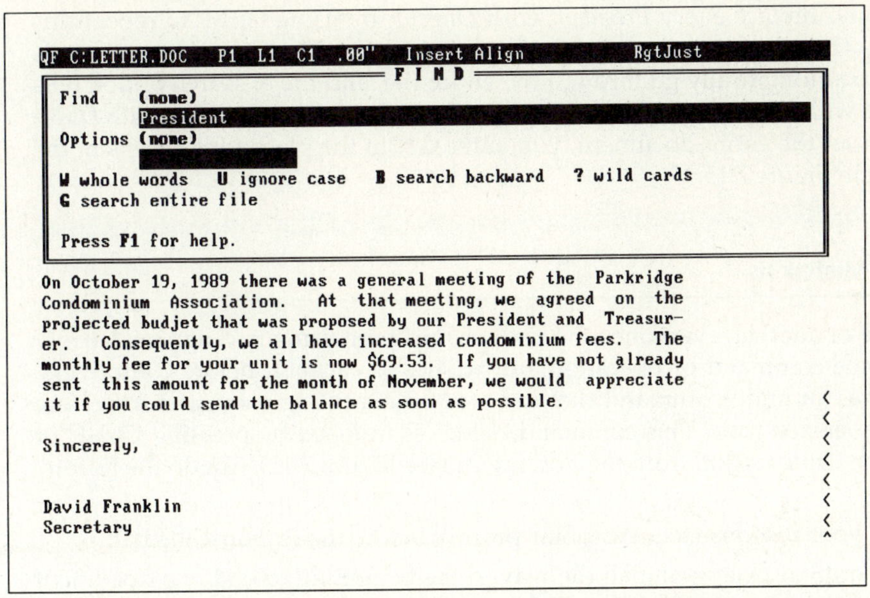

```
QF C:LETTER.DOC    P1  L1  C1  .00"  Insert Align          RgtJust
                          F I N D
 Find    (none)
         President
 Options (none)

 W whole words  U ignore case   B search backward   ? wild cards
 G search entire file

 Press F1 for help.
On October 19, 1989 there was a general meeting of the  Parkridge
Condominium  Association.   At  that meeting, we  agreed  on  the
projected budjet that was proposed by our President and  Treasur-
er.   Consequently, we all have increased condominium fees.   The
monthly fee for your unit is now $69.53.  If you have not already
sent  this amount for the month of November, we would  appreciate
it if you could send the balance as soon as possible.           <
                                                                <
Sincerely,                                                      <
                                                                <
                                                                <
David Franklin                                                  <
Secretary                                                       ^
```

**Figure 7.14 Find Text Command**
The Find Text command lets you search your document for specific words or phrases.

mand and retype the word. Pressing **Ctrl-L** automatically repeats the previous search and advances the cursor to the next location of the word.

To search and replace, you use a different command. Let's say that you want to change *President* to *Director*. First, press **Ctrl-QA** or select the Find and Replace Text command from the Go To menu. A box appears on the screen; here you enter the word or phrase to be found and its replacement (see Figure 7.15). You can also specify any of the find and replace options displayed at the bottom of the box. If you don't need any of these options and just press the **Enter** key, WordStar advances the cursor to the next occurrence of *President*. A message in the upper-right corner of the screen then asks if you want to replace the text. If you type **Y** for yes, WordStar replaces *President* with *Director*.

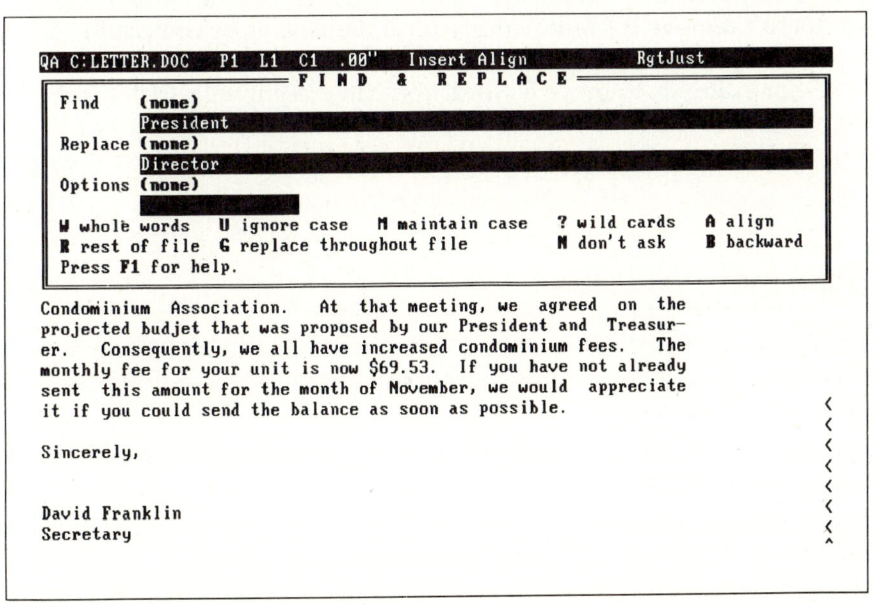

```
QA C:LETTER.DOC    P1  L1  C1  .00"  Insert Align          RgtJust
                     F I N D   &   R E P L A C E
 Find    (none)
         President
 Replace (none)
         Director
 Options (none)

 W whole words  U ignore case  M maintain case   ? wild cards   A align
 R rest of file  G replace throughout file       N don't ask    B backward
 Press F1 for help.
Condominium  Association.   At  that meeting, we  agreed  on  the
projected budjet that was proposed by our President and  Treasur-
er.   Consequently, we all have increased condominium fees.   The
monthly fee for your unit is now $69.53.  If you have not already
sent  this amount for the month of November, we would  appreciate
it if you could send the balance as soon as possible.           <
                                                                <
Sincerely,                                                      <
                                                                <
                                                                <
David Franklin                                                  <
Secretary                                                       ^
```

**Figure 7.15 Finding and Replacing Text**
The Find and Replace command lets you make substitutions for specific words or phrases.

You could replace every *President* with *Director* by using Ctrl-L to repeat this procedure. There is, however, a quicker and easier way. The G search option tells WordStar to automatically go through the entire file, and the N search option tells it to replace without asking. So, to automatically replace every *President* with *Director* throughout the entire document, you enter **GN** in the place for Options in the box shown in Figure 7.15.

## Undoing Mistakes

*Restoring deletions*

At one time or another, everyone who uses a word processing package mistakenly initiates some command or operation, but wishes to cancel it before completion. WordStar has an undo command that can stop an executing command or restore accidentally erased text. This command, which is invoked by pressing **Ctrl-U** or selecting the Undo option from the Edit menu (see Figure 7.12), can do the following:

- Cancel your response to a WordStar prompt before the response is final.
- Stop WordStar from going all the way to the beginning or end of a document after you've pressed Ctrl-QR or Ctrl-QC.
- Halt a find or a find-and-replace operation.
- Cancel a spelling check.
- Halt printing.
- Restore the most recently deleted text item.

This last action is the most common use of the Undo command. Whenever you erase text, be it a single character or an entire block, WordStar temporarily stores this text in a special area of memory. If you press **Ctrl-U**, WordStar inserts this stored text into your document at the current cursor location. So, if you accidentally erase some text and haven't moved the cursor, pressing Ctrl-U puts the text back where it was before the erasure. If you do move the cursor, you can still restore the text, but in a different place.WordStar's undo command is a handy feature, but it only brings back the most recently removed text. Every time you erase something, WordStar discards the text saved from the previous erase command and replaces it with the text most recently erased. Pressing Ctrl-U copies this text to the current cursor location, but doesn't remove it from memory until the next erase command. So, you can use the combination of an erase and undo as another way to move and duplicate text. For example, to move a word, you can erase it with **Ctrl-T**, move the cursor to where you want the word, and press **Ctrl-U** to restore the word in a new location. To duplicate the word, you can simply insert it again by pressing **Ctrl-U**.

## Checking Spelling

*Proofreading*

WordStar, like many word processing packages, includes a dictionary that can help you find and correct misspellings and typographical errors. There are three ways to use WordStar's spelling checker:

- You can check the spelling of a single word before you enter it into your document by pressing **Ctrl-QO**.
- You can check the spelling of a single word already in your document by putting the cursor on that word and pressing **Ctrl-QN**.

- You can check the spelling of all the words at once, from the current cursor location to the end of your document by pressing **Ctrl-QL**.

The last two methods are also listed in the Other menu of the Edit screen.

As an example, let's check the spelling of the letter you see in Figure 7.11. First, you put the cursor at the beginning of the document, if it's not there already. Then you press **Ctrl-QL** or select the Check Document Spelling option from the Other menu to begin checking each word in the document, one by one. When it finds the first word it can't recognize, WordStar displays the Spelling Check Menu, presents the unknown word, and suggests possible replacements. As you can see from Figure 7.16(a), the first unknown word in this letter is *Blvd.* This word isn't misspelled, just an abbreviation not found in the dictionary. WordStar gives you one suggestion on what the word might be. At this point you can tell WordStar to ignore the word or put it into your personal dictionary. The personal dictionary feature allows you to compile your own list of names or technical terms not normally found in ordinary dictionaries. Any word you add to your personal dictionary will be recognized in the future and not singled out as a potential misspelling. If you choose not to add *Blvd.* to your personal dictionary, you type **I** to tell WordStar to ignore this word and continue checking the rest of the words. Similarly, WordStar goes on to question the word *Parkridge.* Since this word is correct, just not in the dictionary, you press **I** again to tell WordStar to just ignore it too. Finally, WordStar comes to the word *budjet.* This word really is misspelled, and WordStar suggests five possible corrections (see Figure 7.16(b)). Obviously, *budget* is the correct choice. To automatically replace an error with a suggested correction, simply type the number of the correction. In this case *budget* is numbered with 1, so you type **1** to have WordStar replace *budjet* with *budget*. WordStar then checks the rest of the words in the letter, finds them to be correct, and leaves the cursor at the bottom of the document.

**Figure 7.16 Checking Spelling**

(a) "Blvd." is the first term questioned by the WordStar spelling checker.

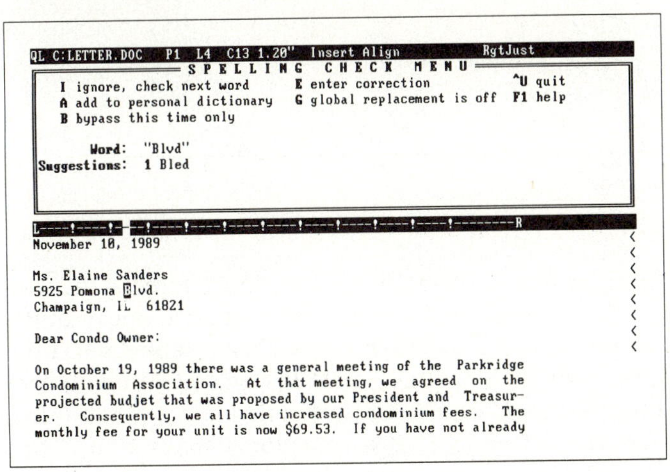


(b) The word "budjet" really is misspelled and WordStar suggests some possible corrections.

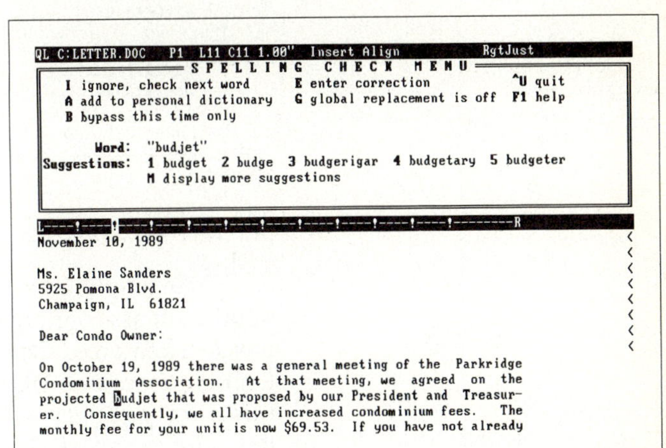

## FORMATTING DOCUMENTS

*Specifying document appearance*

Formatting a document involves specifying how it will look when it is eventually printed. True what-you-see-is-what-you-get (WYSIWYG) word processing software has an exact correspondence between the screen and the printed page. WordStar is not a true WYSIWYG word processing package; some formatting specifications show up on the display screen, but others only become evident when the document viewed with the Advanced Page Preview feature (which we will discuss later in this chapter) or is committed to paper. WordStar has three basic levels of formatting: character, paragraph, and page.

### Character Formatting

*Boldface, underlining, italics*

WordStar has several options that let you change the appearance of characters in a document with boldface, underlining, italics, and so on. These options are listed in the Style menu, shown in Figure 7.17.

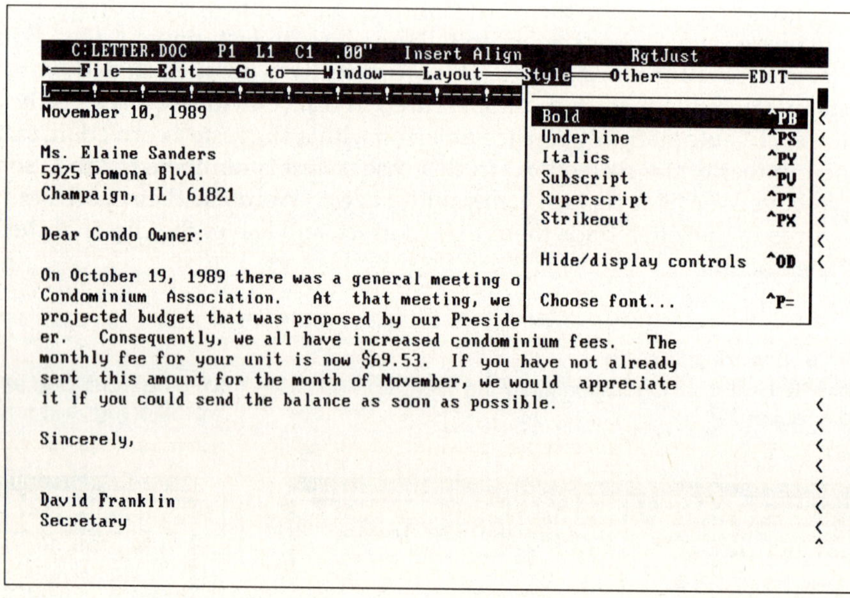


**Figure 7.17 Style Menu**
The Style menu contains several character formatting options.

For example, let's say that you want to underline the word *increased* in the condominium association letter. First you move the cursor to the first character in the word. Then press **Ctrl-PS** or pull down the Style menu with **Alt-S** and select the Underline option. WordStar inserts a ^S symbol before the word to show where underlining begins. Monochrome monitors display underlined text as underlined, but color monitors show underlined text in a different color (usually blue). You have to turn off underlining after the word *increased* or it will remain on for the rest of the document. Move the cursor to the space just past the last character to be underlined and press **Ctrl-PS** again. Now just the text between the two ^S symbols is highlighted (see Figure 7.18). The ^S symbols are not actually part of the text of your document; when you print the document the ^S symbols won't be printed, but the word between them will be underlined.

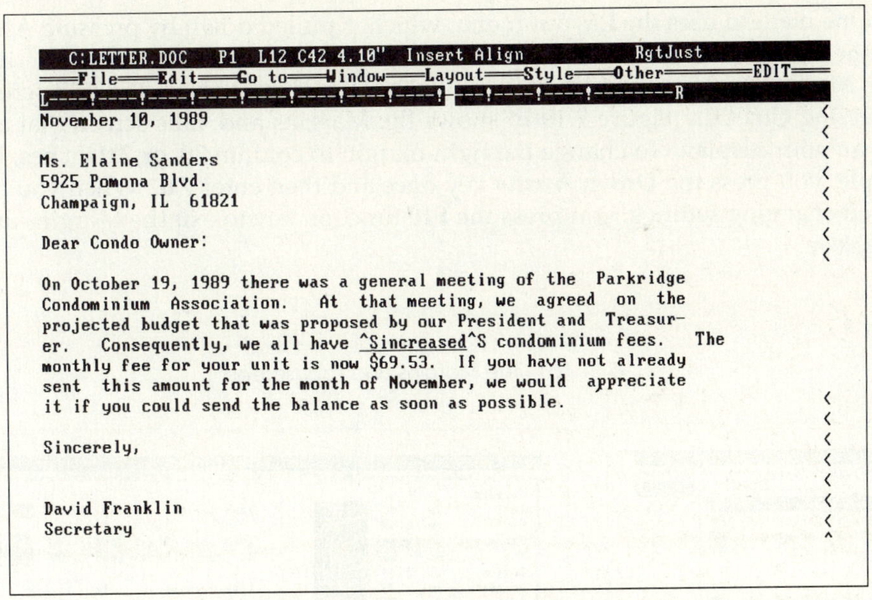

```
 C:LETTER.DOC    P1  L12 C42 4.10"  Insert Align          RgtJust
===File===Edit===Go to===Window===Layout===Style===Other===========EDIT===
L----!----!----!----!----!----!----!----!----!----!----!---------R
November 10, 1989                                                       <
                                                                        <
Ms. Elaine Sanders                                                      <
5925 Pomona Blvd.                                                       <
Champaign, IL  61821                                                    <
                                                                        <
Dear Condo Owner:                                                       <
                                                                        <
On October 19, 1989 there was a general meeting of the  Parkridge
Condominium  Association.   At  that meeting, we  agreed  on  the
projected budget that was proposed by our President and  Treasur-
er.   Consequently, we all have ^Sincreased^S condominium fees.   The
monthly fee for your unit is now $69.53.  If you have not already
sent  this amount for the month of November, we would  appreciate
it if you could send the balance as soon as possible.                   <
                                                                        <
Sincerely,                                                              <
                                                                        <
                                                                        <
David Franklin                                                          <
Secretary                                                               ^
```

**Figure 7.18 Underlining**

The word "increased" has been underlined, as indicated by the ^S symbol before and after it.

Boldface and underlining are the two most commonly used character formats, but WordStar also provides the other options you see in the Style menu of Figure 7.17. These options, which work on most dot-matrix printers, include

- *Subscript*. Smaller, lowered characters like $_{\text{this}}$.
- *Superscript*. Smaller, raised characters like $^{\text{this}}$.
- *Strikeout*. Crossed out characters like ~~this~~.
- *Italics*. Italicized characters like *this*.

The Hide/Display Controls option of the Style menu allows you to turn off or on the display of character format symbols such as the ^S that appears before and after underlined text. The Choose Font option allows you to select different typefaces, styles, and sizes of characters for use with hard copy output devices, such as laser printers, equipped with a number of fonts. These fonts, however, do not appear on the display screen.

## Paragraph Formatting

*Controlling sections of text*

Like most word processing packages, WordStar has a number of features for controlling the appearance of paragraphs and other sections of text. Some common formatting operations involve changing margins, aligning paragraphs, setting tab stops, turning word wrap on or off, turning justification on or off, indenting paragraphs, setting line spacing, and centering text.

### Margins

*Document edges*

WordStar initially sets the left and right margins of a document at columns 1 and 65, respectively. In other words, since the default width of a character in WordStar is 0.01 inch, the right margin is at 0.0 inches and the left margin at 6.5 inches. These margins act as text boundaries and are shown in the ruler line as L for the left margin and R for the right margin. There are several ways to change margins in Word-

Star. One method uses the Layout menu, which is pulled down by pressing **Alt-L** from the Edit screen (see Figure 7.19(a)). Then you select the first option in this menu, Margins and Tabs, which also can be invoked directly from the Edit screen by pressing **Ctrl-OL**. Figure 7.19(b) shows the Margins and Tabs screen that appears on your display. To change the right margin to column 70, or 7.0 inches, for example, you press the **Down Arrow** key once and then enter **7.0**. When you are finished changing settings, you press the **F10** function key to exit the Margins and Tabs screen.

**Figure 7.19 Changing Margins**

(a) The Layout menu.

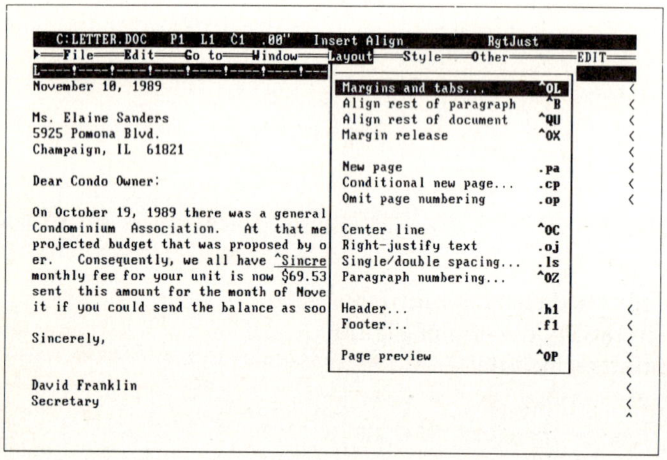


(b) The Margins and Tabs screen.

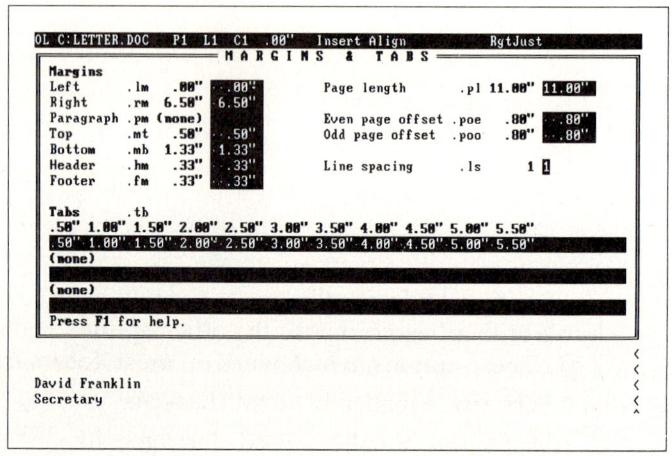


Figure 7.20 shows the results of changing the right margin to 7.0 inches. The ruler line extends 5 characters farther to the right, and the characters .RM 7.00" appear in the first line of the document. This expression is a special kind of WordStar command known as a **dot command**. This particular dot command was automatically created and inserted at the beginning of your document when you changed the Margins and Tabs screen. You can also enter a dot command directly into your document without using a menu. This type of command consists of a period (or dot) followed by a two-character command code and any other information that goes with it. A dot command must be entered on its own line and must begin in column 1. When a dot command is entered, a period appears in the flag column for that line. As Figure 7.20 shows, the dot command to change the right margin to 7.0 inches is .RM 7.0". Similarly, the left margin dot command is .LM followed by the number of inches. Although you can see dot commands on the screen and they are stored with the text when you save a document, they don't appear on paper when the document is printed. Dot commands perform a number of different functions in WordStar, generally related to formatting printed pages. We'll see other examples of dot commands throughout the rest of this chapter.

## Aligning Paragraphs

*Reformatting*

Whichever method you use to change margins, WordStar simply modifies the ruler line. Even though WordStar aligns any new text you type to the new margin settings, it does not automatically align or *reformat* existing text. You must explicitly

```
 C:LETTER.DOC   P1  L1  C1  .00"  Insert Align           RgtJust
===File===Edit===Go to===Window===Layout===Style===Other==========EDIT===
L----!----!----!----!----!----!----!----!----!----!-------------R
.RM 7.00"                                                              .
November 10, 1989                                                      <
                                                                       <
Ms. Elaine Sanders                                                     <
5925 Pomona Blvd.                                                      <
Champaign, IL  61821                                                   <
                                                                       <
Dear Condo Owner:                                                      <
                                                                       <
On October 19, 1989 there was a general meeting of the  Parkridge
Condominium  Association.   At  that meeting, we  agreed  on  the
projected budget that was proposed by our President and  Treasur-
er.   Consequently, we all have ^Sincreased^S condominium fees.   The
monthly fee for your unit is now $69.53.  If you have not already
sent  this amount for the month of November, we would  appreciate
it if you could send the balance as soon as possible.                  <
                                                                       <
Sincerely,                                                             <
                                                                       <
                                                                       <
David Franklin                                                         <
Secretary                                                              <
```

**Figure 7.20 The .RM Dot Command**

WordStar inserts a .RM dot command when you change the right margin from the Margins and Tabs screen. You can also enter this dot command directly.

align paragraphs whenever you make certain changes. This procedure must be done to existing text when you change margins, justification, or line spacing. To align a paragraph, move the cursor to its first line and press **Ctrl-B** or select the Align Rest of Paragraph option from the Layout menu (see Figure 7.19(a)). WordStar rearranges the words to fill out lines to the right margin and aligns them exactly if justification is turned on. To align more than one paragraph, or even an entire document, press **Ctrl-QU** or select the Align Rest of Document option from the Layout menu. This command aligns every paragraph from the current cursor location to the end of the document.

## Tab Stops

*Using the Tab key*

Computer keyboards, just like typewriters, have at least one Tab key. When this key is pressed, the cursor advances immediately to some preset location. By default, WordStar initially sets tab stops at every fifth column, starting with column 6. These tab stops are shown in the ruler line as exclamation points (!). To move the cursor to the next tab stop, just press the **Tab** key. If insert mode is turned on, pressing the Tab key pushes any existing characters to the right; if overwrite mode is turned on, the Tab key just moves the cursor over existing text.

To change the current tab settings, you press **Ctrl-OL** or select the Margins and Tabs option from the Layout menu (see Figure 7.19(a)). This activates the Margins and Tabs screen shown before in Figure 7.19(b). Press the **Down Arrow** key until the cursor moves to the tab stop entries at the bottom of the box. To change a particular tab setting, you move the cursor to it and enter a new number of inches. When you are finished changing tab settings, you press **F10** to exit the Margins and Tabs screen. The ruler line is updated accordingly.

## Word Wrap

*Turning word wrap off or on*

As we said before, word wrap is a common word processing feature that lets you type without having to press the Enter key at the end of every line. WordStar keeps track of what you type and automatically wraps words down to the next line whenever you go beyond the right margin. By default, WordStar initially has the word wrap feature turned on. Even though word wrap is a great benefit, sometimes it is advantageous to turn off this feature. For example, typing tables or columns of information generally is much easier without word wrap. Fortunately, WordStar lets you turn word wrap off and on. When it is turned off, you can continue typing past the right margin all the way to column 255.

There are two ways to turn word wrap off and on. If word wrap is on, you can turn it off by pressing **Ctrl-OW**; you can turn it back on by pressing **Ctrl-OW** again. The other way to turn word wrap off and on is with the .AW dot command. Entering **.AW off** on its own line beginning in column 1 turns off word wrap, and entering **.AW on** turns it back on again. This dot command allows you to permanently turn off word wrap for selected sections of text.

## Justification

*Turning justification off or on*

When a document is justified, text is aligned exactly to both the left and right margins. If necessary, spaces are automatically inserted here and there to give the text a block look. By default, WordStar initially has the justification feature turned on. The justified text can look professionally typeset when it is produced by a printer that can do proportional spacing and microjustification. As we said in the previous chapter, proportional spacing allots different amounts of space for different characters. **Microjustification** spreads the white space of a line between words and letters so that no large gaps appear. The combination of justification, proportional spacing, and microjustification produces text that looks like the typeset material in this book.

For computer printers that cannot do proportional spacing and microjustification, it's often better to turn off justification. The resulting text will have a ragged right margin similar to typewritten text. WordStar lets you turn justification off and on like word wrap with either a Control key command or a dot command. To turn off justification, press **Ctrl-OJ**; to turn it back on, press **Ctrl-OJ** again. The dot command for justification is .OJ followed by *off* or *on*. Remember: if you want to change the justification of existing text, you have to go back and realign the paragraphs with Ctrl-B or Ctrl-QU after you turn justification off or on.

## Indenting

*Leaving space on the left*

Indented text is spaced in evenly from the regular left margin. WordStar provides several different methods for you to choose from according to your particular situation. If you only need to indent a line a few spaces, you can simply use the **Space Bar** to move the cursor over before typing. An even easier method is to press the **Tab** key, provided tab stops are set where you want them. These two simple methods work well for infrequent indenting, but WordStar has still other ways to indent whole blocks of text and automatically indent the first line of every paragraph.

One way to indent an entire paragraph is with the temporary indent command Ctrl-OG. This is handy for blocking off long quotations or other sections of text that must be indented. Pressing **Ctrl-OG** automatically indents your text to the next tab stop; all you have to do is type. Words are wrapped to the tab stop instead of the left margin. While the temporary indent command is active, the left edge of your text is marked by a V in the ruler line. The indenting stops when you press the **Enter** key or press **Ctrl-B** to align the paragraph.

Another way to indent an entire paragraph is to change the left margin with the left margin dot command. Type .LM followed by a number of inches larger than that of your current left margin. Then type your paragraph. When the paragraph is complete, use another .LM command to change the left margin back to its original value. Temporarily changing the left margin like this is probably the best way to indent a large number of lines or even several paragraphs.

In many documents, only the first line of most paragraphs is indented. Although it's probably not that much trouble to press the Tab key every time you begin a new paragraph, you can tell WordStar to do this automatically with the paragraph margin dot command. For example, if you enter **.PM 0.5"** and the left margin is at 0.0", the first line of every paragraph will be automatically indented 0.5 inch. With word wrap turned on, you press **Enter** only to begin a new paragraph. Each time you do this, WordStar indents the next line you type to the currently set paragraph margin.

By setting the paragraph margin to a column less than the left margin, you can even do hanging indents. For example, if your left margin is set at 0.5 inch and you enter **.PM 0.0"**, then the first line of every subsequent paragraph will be "outdented" (protrude to the left) 4 spaces. In other words, each paragraph's first line will begin at column 1, but the remaining lines will start at column 5.

## Line Spacing

*Spacing between lines*

Most typewriters have a little lever that controls the space that is left between lines when you press the carriage return. Word processing packages give you similar control over line spacing. By default, WordStar initially sets line spacing to 1. In other words, lines are automatically single spaced. This means that no blank lines are left between successive lines of text whenever a word wrap occurs or whenever you press the Enter key. Double spacing leaves one blank line between successive lines of text, triple spacing leaves two blank lines, and so on. WordStar lets you set line spacing to any whole number value from 1 to 9.

Line spacing can be set in two ways with WordStar. One way is to press **Ctrl-OS** or select the Single/double Spacing option from the Layout menu (see Figure 7.19(a) again). This brings up the Margins and Tabs screen you see in Figure 7.19(b), where you can change the Line Spacing setting displayed at the middle-right side of the screen. The other way to set line spacing is to use the **.LS** dot command directly. For example, to change to double spacing, you can move the cursor to the beginning of the document and enter **.LS 2** on its own line starting at column 1. Remember that if you want to change the line spacing of existing text, you must use Ctrl-B or Ctrl-OU to realign paragraphs after setting the line spacing with Ctrl-OS or .LS.

## Centering Text

*Placing text in the center*

Many documents require that certain headings or other text be centered between the left and right margins. To do this manually, you have to count the number of characters in the heading, subtract it from the line length, divide the result by two, and then press the space bar that many times before typing the heading. Another method is to go to the center of the line and backspace once for every two characters in the heading. Fortunately, word processing packages generally have commands that let you avoid all this and automatically center text.

To center a line of text with WordStar, first move the cursor to any character on the line to be centered. Then press **Ctrl-OC** or select the Center Line option from the Layout menu; WordStar centers all the characters on that line between the current left and right margins. If you insert or delete characters deleted from that line later, you must recenter the line again. To "uncenter" a heading, move the cursor to the first column on that line and press **Ctrl-T**. This deletes all the leading blanks and moves the text back to the left margin.

## Page Formatting

*Laying out pages*

Page formatting generally refers to features that affect entire pages of text. WordStar has several commands that let you specify how pages are laid out. These commands control line height, page length, top and bottom margins, page breaks, page offset, page numbering, and headers and footers.

### Line Height

*Distance between lines*

In WordStar, the distance between lines of printed text is called **line height**. This is not the same as line spacing. Line height is measured from the bottom of one line to the bottom of the next line below. Line spacing is one plus the number of blank lines left between successive lines of text. In practice, line height is seldom changed. WordStar's default line height, which is expressed in 48ths of an inch, is 8. This yields 6 lines of text per vertical inch, which is the standard line height of most typewriters. To change this line height, you use the .LH dot command followed by the number of 48ths of an inch for the new line height. For example, to change the line height to 16/48 (three lines per inch), you would enter **.LH 16**.

### Page Length

*Paper size*

Standard letter-size paper is 8 1/2 inches wide and 11 inches long. Given a standard line height of 6 lines per inch, the number of lines on letter-size paper is 6 times 11, or 66. WordStar's default page length is 11 inches or 66 lines, but this can be changed with the Margins and Tabs option of the Layout menu or the .PL dot command. For example, if you're using legal-size paper (8 1/2-x-14 inches) in your printer, you would enter **.PL 14"** for a page length of 14 inches (or 84 lines at 6 lines per inch).

### Top and Bottom Margins

*Leaving space top and bottom*

Most documents are printed with some blank space at the top and bottom of every page. By default, WordStar leaves a 0.5-inch top margin (3 blank lines) and a 1.33-inch bottom margin (8 blank lines). These top and bottom margins can be changed, however, with two dot commands. For example, to change the top margin to 1 inch (6 blank lines), you would enter **.MT 1"**. Similarly, the dot command for the bottom margin is **.MB**.

### Page Breaks

*Starting a new page*

The actual number of lines of text printed on a page depends on the various factors we've been discussing. For example, WordStar's default page format has a line height of 8/48ths of an inch, a page length of 11 inches, a top margin of 0.33 inch, and a bottom margin of 1.33 inches. That leaves 66 minus 3 and minus 8, or 55, as the number of lines of text actually printed on a page.

As you type text with WordStar, the word wrap feature automatically starts new lines. Similarly, assuming the default page format settings, WordStar automatically starts a new page by inserting a page break after every 55 lines you type. A **page break** is simply a division between two pages. It is symbolized on the screen by a horizontal line ending with a P in the flag column (see Figure 7.21). This line is not actually printed on paper, it just shows you where a new page will begin.

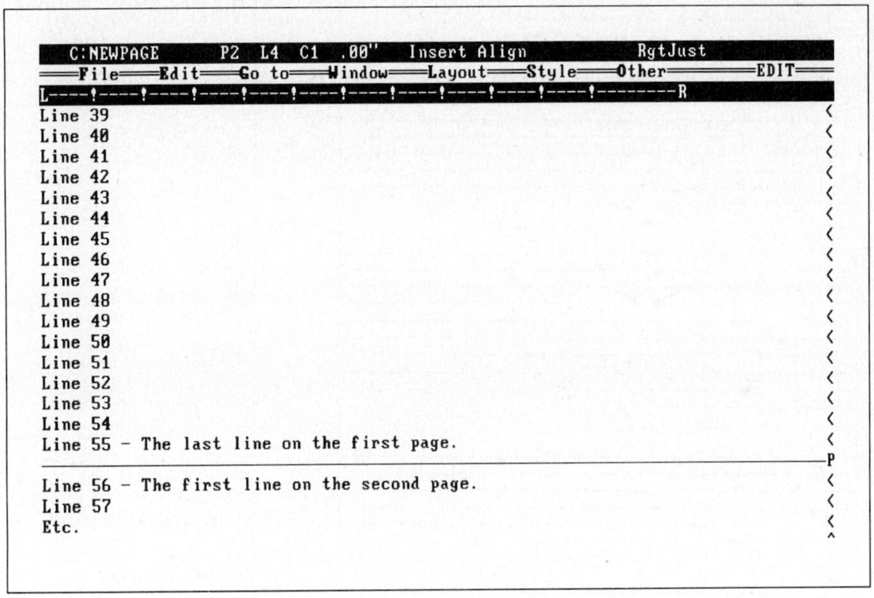


**Figure 7.21 Automatic Page Break**
WordStar's default settings generate an automatic page break into your document every 55 lines.

Although WordStar's automatic page break feature is nice for typing long sections of text, there are often times when you want to begin a new page at some point other than every 55 lines. In these cases a page break can be *forced* by using the New Page option from the Layout menu or the .PA dot command. By typing **.PA** in column 1 and pressing the **Enter** key, you can begin a new page at any point within a document. A forced page break can be removed from a document by deleting it with **Ctrl-Y**.

## Page Offset

*Space to the left of the margin*

As we said before, by default WordStar initially sets the left margin at 0.0 inch (column 1) and the right margin at 6.5 inch (column 65). But these are not usually the exact page positions where the text is actually printed (see Figure 7.22). WordStar *offsets* text a little to the right of the edge of the paper. This offset, known as the **page offset**, is initially set to 0.8 inch or 8 spaces by default. To determine exactly where your text will print on the page, you need to add the page offset to the left margin. For example, if the page offset is 0.8 inch and the left margin is 0.0 inch, text will begin printing on the paper just past an 0.8-inch space, or in column 9. You use the .PO dot command to change the page offset. For instance, if you want a page offset of 1 inch, you enter **.PO 1"** on its own line beginning in column 1 at the top of your document.

**Figure 7.22 WordStar Default Page Layout**

This diagram illustrates the way WordStar sets up a page, unless you specify otherwise.

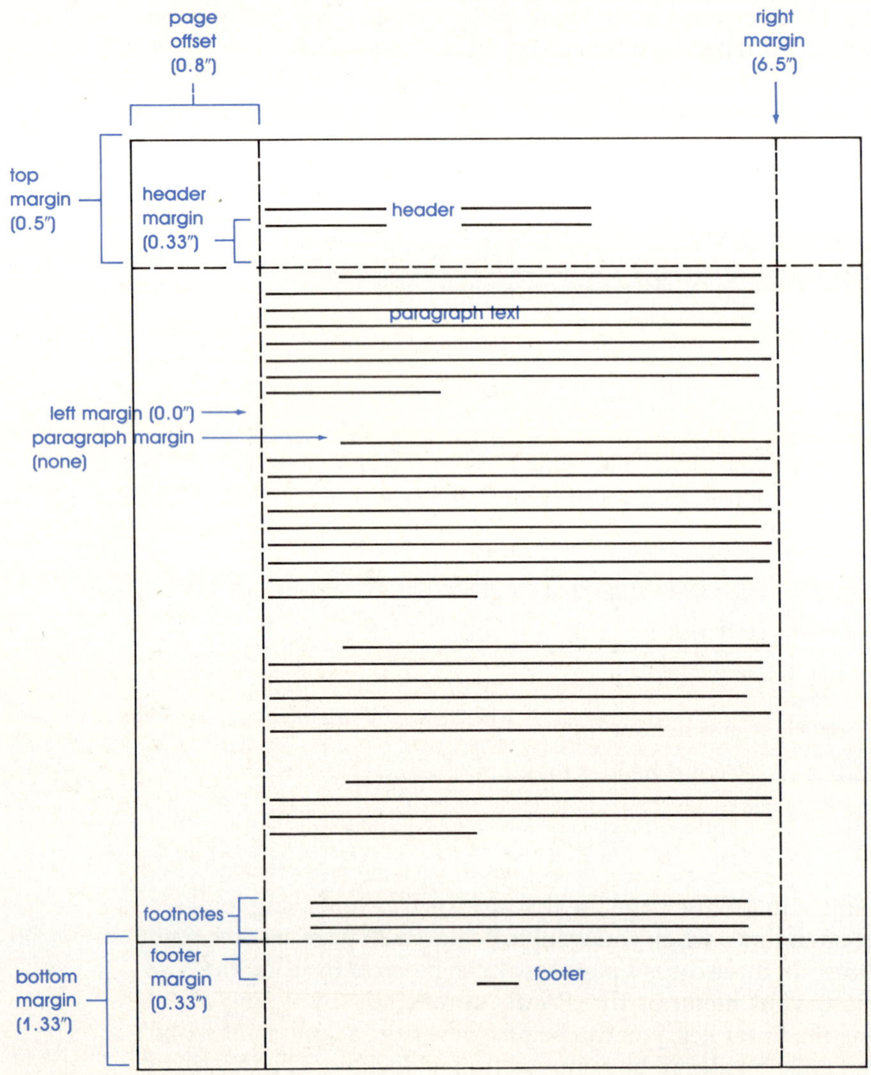


## Page Numbering

*Controlling page numbers*

WordStar automatically keeps track of page numbers while you edit a document and displays the current page number preceded by the letter P in the status line. As we said before, page breaks show where one page ends and the next page begins. By default, WordStar prints the correct page number on each page and centers it 1 inch from the bottom. Here are four dot commands that control the printing of page numbers:

.PC The .PC command sets the position where page numbers will be printed. For example, to print page numbers 4 inches from the left margin, you enter **.PC 4.0"**. To center page numbers between the current margins, enter **.PC0**.

.OP The .OP command omits the page number from the current page and subsequent pages. It is the same as selecting the Omit Page Numbering option from the Layout menu (see Figure 7.19(a)). This command is useful in many documents, such as letters, which must omit page numbers.

.PG The .PG command turns page numbering back on after a previous .OP command.

.PN Using the .PN command changes the page number that will be printed on a page. This is handy for printing a document that is split between two or more files. Suppose that your first file is 20 pages long. To print the next file with page numbers beginning at 21, you would enter **.PN 21** at the top of the second file.

### Headers and Footers

*Text in the top and bottom margins*

In WordStar, a **header** is one or more lines of text printed in the top margin of every page. A **footer** is like a header, except it is printed in the bottom margin of every page. WordStar allows you to define up to three lines of text each for a header and footer. If you don't define a footer, WordStar automatically prints a centered, one-line footer with just the page number.

Each line of a header or footer is defined separately with its own dot command. The dot command is typed in column 1, followed by the text of that header or footer. From that point on, every printed page will have that header or footer line. Here are the dot commands for headers and footers:

| | |
|---|---|
| .HE or .H1 | First header line. |
| .H2 | Second header line. |
| .H3 | Third header line. |
| .FO or .F1 | First footer line. |
| .F2 | Second footer line. |
| .F3 | Third footer line. |

For example, to print the title "The Great American Novel" at the top of every page, you would enter the following dot command, starting in column 1 at the beginning of your document:

```
.HE The Great American Novel
```

## PRINTING DOCUMENTS

*Getting a hard copy*

With all you've learned about WordStar so far, you would have little trouble creating, editing, and formatting most documents. The next step, of course, is printing. Let's print the condominium association letter we've been using as an example.

Once the text is formatted, proofread, and corrected if necessary, it must be saved before printing. You can do this by pressing **Ctrl-KD** or selecting the Save File, Go to Opening Screen option from the File menu. Both of these actions save the current document in its disk file and return to the Opening screen. At this point, it's a good idea to check your printer to make sure it's turned on and connected to your computer. From the Opening screen, you pull down the File menu (see Figure 7.3) and press **P** to select the Print a File option. After you do this, the Print screen appears on your display, as shown in Figure 7.23. This screen lets you change various default print options that control how your document will be printed. In most cases, the default print options will be adequate, so all you have to do to begin printing is press the **F10** function key. When WordStar is finished printing, it returns to the Opening screen.

**Figure 7.23 Print Screen**
Here you specify the document to be printed along with various other printing options.

```
P                         WordStar Professional
                                 P R I N T
  File   letter.doc
         letter.doc

  Page numbers  All       A                      Pause between pages N  N
  All/even/odd pages      All      A             Use form feeds      Y  Y
  Printer name            DRAFT    DRAFT         Nondocument         N  N
                                                 Number of copies    1  1
  Redirect output to      (none)

  Press F1 for help.
DIRECTORY of Drive C:\WS5  1018k free
..               \   BOX             .5k  DB00.DTB        41k  DB00.DTC        37k
DB01.DTB       96k   DB01.DTC       162k  DB02.DTB        54k  DB02.DTC        54k
DB04.DTB       95k   DB04.DTC        71k  DIARY.DOC      3.6k  EXTLIST.PF      .1k
FONTID.CTL    2.5k   INDEX.DTB       27k  INDEX.DTC       27k  LETTER.BAK      .8k
LETTER.DOC     .8k   NEWPAGE         .8k  PF.HLP          27k  PRCHANGE.HLP    17k
PREVIEW.MSG   8.5k   PRINT.TST       10k  QUITMENU.PF     .1k  RULER.DOC      1.0k
TABLE.DOC     1.0k   TEXT.DOC       5.6k  USERMENU.PF     .6k  USERSYN.PF      .3k
WINDOW.DOC     .4k   WSINDEX.XCL    1.5k
```

## MANAGING DOCUMENTS

*Organizing files*

A document is almost always kept in a disk file even after it is printed. Consequently, document files tend to accumulate on disks. WordStar has several commands that let you maintain and organize your documents. Some of these commands are available through the File menu of the Opening screen, while others are in the File menu of the Edit screen (see Figure 7.24). Basically, WordStar allows you to save, open, rename, copy, delete, and protect document files, as well as change disk drives and directories.

### Saving Files

*Keeping documents on disks*

The ability to save documents in disk files is one of the most important and useful attributes of a word processing package. Documents are saved so that they may be edited, revised, printed, or included in some other document later. In addition, periodically saving your document while you enter or edit it helps prevent a total loss of your work in the event of a power failure or some other accident. Then even if some disaster does occur, you'll at least have the latest saved version of your document.

WordStar's save commands are in the File menu of the Edit screen shown in Figure 7.24. There are five variations:

*Save File, Resume Editing.* This is what you use to periodically save your document as you work on it. Pressing **Ctrl-KS** without pulling down the File menu accomplishes the same result.

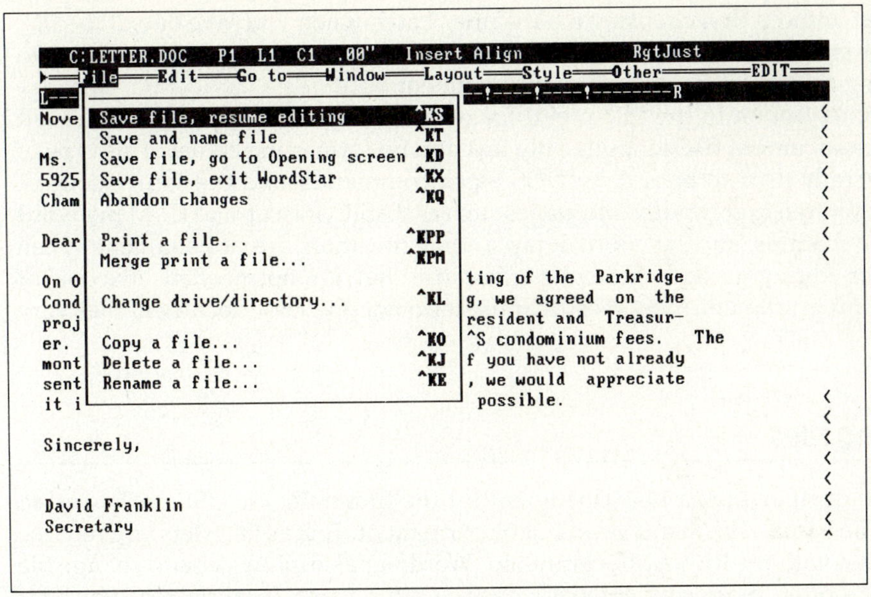


**Figure 7.24 File Menu of Edit Screen**
The File menu of the Edit screen lets you save, abandon, print, and organize your documents.

*Save and Name File.* This option allows you to choose a different name for your document file before you save it, leaving the original file intact. It is useful for saving a different version of a document, or, if your disk is full, saving the file on another disk. The same action may be performed by pressing **Ctrl-KT** directly from the Edit screen.

*Save File, Go to Opening Screen.* This option is used to save the document and return to the Opening screen to print it, or perhaps do some other WordStar activity. Pressing **Ctrl-KD** achieves the same result.

*Save File, Exit WordStar.* This option immediately ends your work with WordStar by saving the document, exiting the program, and returning to the DOS prompt. The same action may be performed by pressing **Ctrl-KX**.

*Abandon Changes.* This option tells WordStar not to save the document; simply return to the Opening screen. It is handy for just viewing a document without changing it. Pressing **Ctrl-KQ** achieves the same result.

## Opening Files

*Loading existing documents*

You've already learned how to open a new document: simply pull down the File menu from the Opening screen (see Figure 7.3), type **D**, and then enter a name for the file. Opening an existing document file is almost exactly the same. To continue working on a file that's already been created, you again select the Open a Document File option from the File menu, but this time enter the name of the existing file. If the file is in your current directory, its name will be listed in the Opening screen beneath the menu bar, and you can enter just the filename and extension. If the document is stored on a disk in some other drive or in some other subdirectory, you should enter the full file specification. WordStar then loads the file from disk into memory and displays it on the Edit screen.

Two other options for opening files are also listed in the File menu of the Opening screen (see Figure 7.3). The Speed Write option allows you to go directly to the

Edit screen without first choosing a file name. Later, when you save or exit the file, you are prompted for a file name. The Speed Write option is handy if you want to start typing right away and name your document later.

The other option in the File menu for opening files is Open a Nondocument File. A **nondocument file** contains only text and no formatting codes. This type of file is generally used to hold data, DOS batch commands, and the source code of programs written in computer languages such as BASIC, Pascal, and C. Many word processing features, such as word wrap and justification, are not available when entering or editing a nondocument file because they are not needed. Except for computer programmers, most WordStar users do not open nondocument files very often.

## Renaming Files

*Changing file names*

When you open or save a new document for the first time, WordStar asks you to supply a file name. This name need not be permanent. Just as DOS lets you rename existing files with the RENAME command, WordStar also allows you to change file names. It's often more convenient to change a file name from within WordStar rather than exit WordStar, change the file name, and then restart WordStar.

WordStar lets you rename a file from either the File menu of the Opening screen (see Figure 7.3) or the File menu of the Edit screen (see Figure 7.24). From either menu you select the Rename a File option and WordStar presents a screen in which you specify the current name of a file and the new name you want it to have. Figure 7.25, for example, shows how you would fill in the Rename screen to change the name of the file LETTER.DOC to SANDERS.DOC.

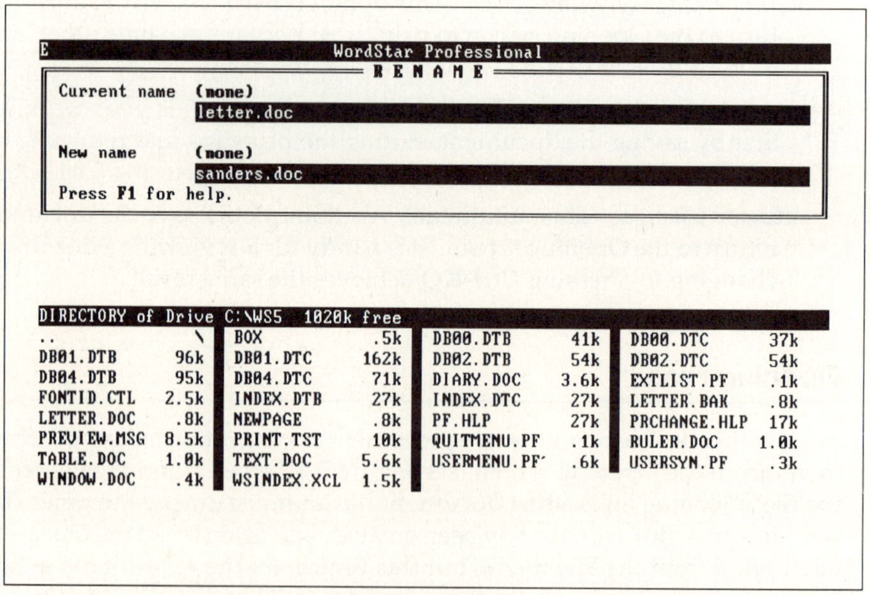


**Figure 7.25 Renaming a File**
When you rename a file, you must specify the current name and the new name.

## Copying Files

*Duplicating documents*

Sometimes you want to reproduce an existing document so that you can make a slightly different version. In other cases, you might want to copy a document from one disk or directory to another for backup purposes. Although you can use the DOS COPY command, there are also file copy commands you can use from within WordStar.

As in renaming, WordStar lets you copy a file from File menus of both the Opening and Edit screens. The program presents a screen similar to the one in Figure 7.25, where you enter the name of the file to be copied and the name of the new copy.

## Deleting Files

*Discarding documents*

WordStar also duplicates the DOS ERASE (or DEL) command. Again, you can delete a file from the File menu of either the Opening screen or the Edit screen. You cannot, however, delete the file you are currently editing from the Edit screen. After you select the Delete a File option and enter the name of the file you want to delete, WordStar asks you if you are sure you want to do this before it actually removes the file.

## Protecting Files

*Preventing changes*

Almost everyone who uses a computer accidentally changes or deletes a needed file at some time or other. In addition, microcomputers often are shared by several people at different times, or they are connected to a local area network and share disk space with other computers. On occasion, a user may accidentally or even maliciously change or delete some other user's file. For these reasons, WordStar has a command that lets you protect a file. Once a file is protected, it cannot be modified or deleted until it is explicitly "unprotected" later.

To protect a file, you select the Protect/unprotect a File option from the File menu of the Opening screen (see Figure 7.3). WordStar presents a screen where you enter the name of the file you want to protect. After you enter the name, WordStar states whether or not the file is currently protected and asks if you want to change this.

Once a file is protected, it cannot be deleted from DOS or from within WordStar. When you edit a protected file, WordStar allows you to perform only those actions that do not modify the file in any way. For example, if you try to insert or delete characters from a protected file, WordStar merely "beeps." If you want to change or delete a protected file, first you must "unprotect" it. This is done by again selecting the Protect/unprotect a File option from the File menu of the Opening screen. After you enter the name of the file, WordStar tells you that it is currently protected and allows you to change it back to being unprotected again.

## Changing the Drive or Directory

*Using a different disk or directory*

In WordStar, the **logged** drive or directory is the one you're currently working in, that is, the default disk drive and directory. Unless you specify otherwise, WordStar looks for and stores files on the current logged disk drive and directory. Initially, the logged drive and directory is the one you are in when you start WordStar. The full disk drive and directory path is displayed in the directory listing beneath the menu bar of the Opening screen (see Figure 7.3), and the disk drive letter is shown in the status line of the Edit screen (see Figure 7.7).

You might want to change the logged drive or directory to work with a document on another disk or in another subdirectory. This can be done by selecting the Change Drive/Directory option in the File menu of either the Opening screen or the Edit screen. After you invoke this command, WordStar presents a screen in which you can specify the new drive and directory path. WordStar then changes the logged disk drive and directory and displays the new directory listing in the Opening screen beneath the menu bar.

## ADDITIONAL FEATURES

*Handy options*

WordStar Release 5 has many features associated with state-of-the-art word processing packages. Some of these features are used quite often, others only in special situations. Besides the features we've already discussed, the most recent version of WordStar includes on-line help, a thesaurus, table of contents and index generation, math functions, sorting, mail-merge, keyboard macros, multiple windows, and Advanced Page Preview. Let's briefly examine each of these.

### On-line Help

*Instant reference manual*

Thanks to the pull-down menu system introduced with Release 5, WordStar is now relatively easy to learn and use. In addition, Wordstar is usually very clear when it prompts you for information like file names. Yet still more help is available from within Wordstar itself. You can get context-sensitive, on-line help for most commands simply by pressing the F1 function key. Figure 7.26, for example, shows the help message that appears on your screen when you press F1 while viewing the File menu from the Edit screen. Since the Save File, Resume Editing option was highlighted when you pressed F1, the help message refers specifically to this command.

**Figure 7.26 Help Screen**
Pressing F1 displays a help screen about the currently selected option.

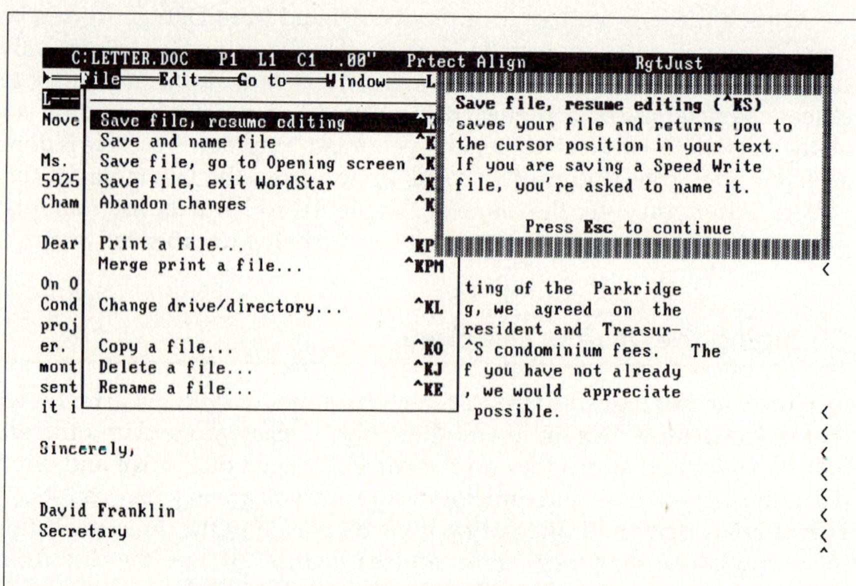

Besides presenting help screens, the help command also allows you to change the **help level**. This is a number that determines which menus and prompts are displayed. Changing the help level lets you display WordStar's *classic menus* instead of the newer pull-down menus; WordStar veterans may prefer the old-style menus used in previous releases of the program. For example, to turn off the pull-down menus and turn on the classic menus, you select the Change Help Level option from the Other menu of either the Opening screen or Edit screen. Then you choose help level 3, which turns on all of the classic menus. Figure 7.27 shows the result, an Edit menu like the one used in WordStar Release 4.

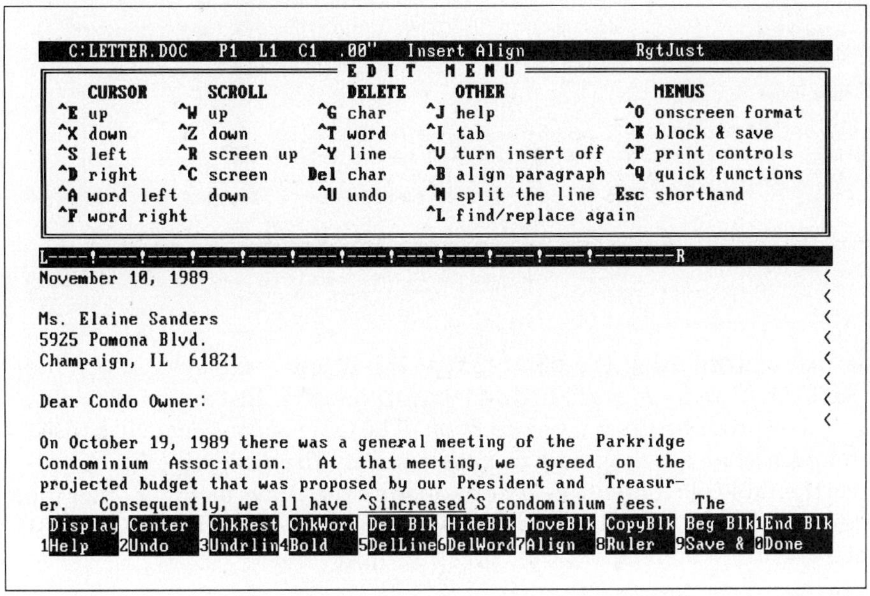


**Figure 7.27 Classic Menus**
WordStar can be set up to present menus like those that appeared in previous releases.

## Thesaurus

*Finding synonyms*

WordStar Release 5 has a built-in thesaurus that makes it very easy to look up synonyms while you work on a document. This particular thesaurus contains around 220,000 synonyms.

Suppose that you want to see synonyms of the word *meeting* in the condominium association letter we've been working on. First, you move the cursor anywhere within *meeting* and then select the Thesaurus option from the Other menu or press **Ctrl-QJ**. Figure 7.28 shows the result. At this point, you can replace *meeting* with one of the synonyms by moving the cursor to that synonym and pressing the **Enter** key, or you can simply press the **Escape** key to resume editing and leave *meeting* intact. You can also have the thesaurus display synonyms of these synonyms, look up another word you enter, or even display a brief definition of any of these words.

## Table of Contents Generation

Producing a table of contents can be a tedious chore for authors of long documents like books. WordStar has commands that can help with this task.

**Figure 7.28 Thesaurus**
WordStar's thesaurus is handy for finding synonyms.

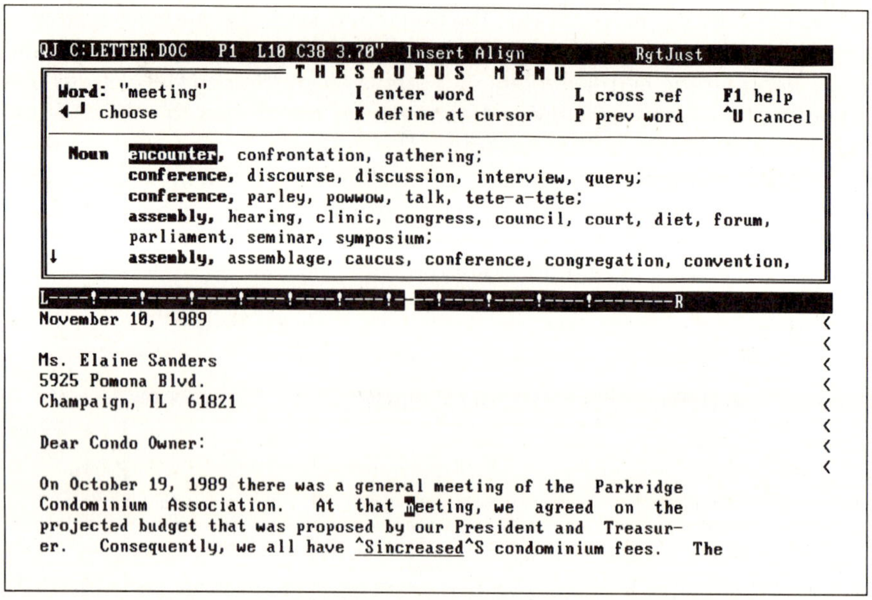


*Indicating the titles*

Suppose that you are using WordStar to type this chapter into a document file named CHAP07.DOC and you want to do a table of contents. Just assume that this one chapter will be produced as if it were a book. The table of contents will consist of an entry for each heading along with its page number. To create this table of contents, first use the Table of Contents Entry option from the Other menu or enter the **.TC** dot command directly to put each entry in your text. For example, the very first table of contents entry would be:

```
.TC Working with WordStar ........................ #
```

The # symbol tells WordStar to substitute the actual page number when the table of contents is generated. This entry is placed in the document directly above the chapter section entitled *Working with WordStar*. A similar dot command entry is inserted into the document before each heading in the chapter. When all the dot command entries are made, the document is saved and you return to the Opening screen. To actually produce the table of contents, select the Table of Contents option from the Other menu (see Figure 7.4). The Table of Contents screen then appears where you specify the name of the file that contains the .TC commands, which in this case would be CHAP07.DOC, and the range of pages for which you want to create the table of contents. WordStar searches through the document for each .TC dot command entry and its actual page number. Omitting the .TC, WordStar copies each entry and page number to a new document file entitled CHAP07.TOC. This file contains the table of contents for CHAP07.DOC and you can print or edit it as necessary.

## Index Generation

Producing an index by hand is even more tedious than doing a table of contents. Fortunately, WordStar has powerful methods for automatically creating an alphabetical list of topics, words, and phrases along with their page numbers.

*Indicating the entries*

One way involves marking each word or phrase to appear in the index. This is done by pressing **Ctrl-PK** at the beginning and end of each word or phrase you want to include in the index. You can also type the **.IX** dot command followed by a word or phrase to create an index entry that doesn't appear in the text exactly as you want it to appear in the index. When all the index entries are marked or created, you save the document and return to the Opening screen. To generate the index, select the Index option from the Other menu (see Figure 7.4). WordStar then presents a screen where you specify the name of the file containing the index entries, say CHAP07.DOC. A separate document file is then created with the index and named with an extension of .IDX. For example, if the file containing the index entries is CHAP07.DOC, then the index file would be named CHAP07.IDX. This file can then be printed or edited.

## Math Functions

*Calculating with WordStar*

WordStar includes two handy features for doing math while editing a document. The first feature is a built-in calculator that lets you enter a problem and then evaluates it. For example, let's say that you need to solve the following expression: (126.5 + 347.8) ÷ 3. To use WordStar's calculator while editing, select the Calculator option from the Other menu or press **Ctrl-QM**. This invokes the Math Menu as shown in Figure 7.29. Simply type **(126.5+347.8)/3** and press the **Enter** key. WordStar calculates the answer and displays it in the upper right corner beside the heading *Last Result*.

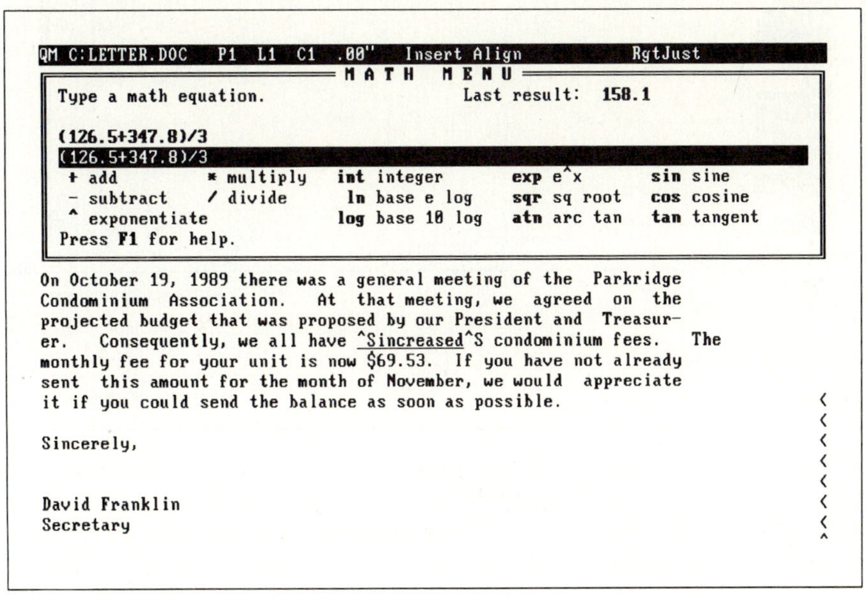


**Figure 7.29 Math Menu**
WordStar's Math menu is like a built-in calculator.

The other math function WordStar can perform is adding the numbers in a marked block of text. Let's say that you have a column of numbers in your document that need to be totaled. First mark a block containing the column with **Ctrl-KB** and **Ctrl-KK**. Then you choose the Block Math option from the Other menu or press **Ctrl-KM**. WordStar adds all the numbers in the block and displays the total at the top of the screen. You press the **Escape** key to resume editing. To insert the result just computed in your document at the current cursor location, press the **Escape** key again, and then press the **Equal Sign** key (=).

## Sorting

*Rearranging lines of text*

As we said in Chapter 6, sorting is arranging items in some particular order. WordStar Release 5 makes it very easy to sort lines of text into alphabetic or numeric order. For example, suppose you have lines of text or numbers that you want sorted. These may be names, addresses, zip codes, or simply individual words that you want to alphabetize. First, you mark them as a block by pressing **Ctrl-KB** before the first line and **Ctrl-KK** after the last line. Then you press **Ctrl-KZ** to execute the sort command. As Figure 7.30 shows, WordStar asks you to specify whether you want to sort the lines into ascending (A to Z) or descending (Z to A) order. After you press **A** for ascending or **D** for descending, WordStar rearranges the lines in the specified order.

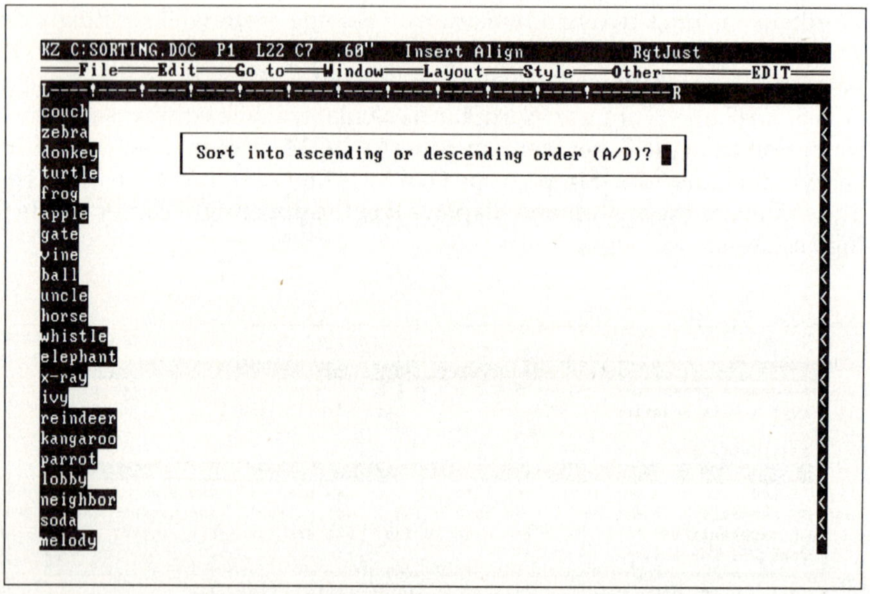


**Figure 7.30 Sorting**
Lines of text must be marked as a block before they can be sorted into ascending or descending order.

## Mail-Merge

*Creating form letters*

Mail-merge is the ability to combine a document with a data file to print form letters or other personalized text. This capability is very useful to businesses and organizations that frequently send letters or bills to various individuals. WordStar's mail-merge facility is quite good and relatively easy to use. To show you how it works, let's make our condominium association document into a form letter.

The first step is to create a data file containing the variable information. In our example, this variable data consists of the names and addresses of the condominium unit owners. The data file must be a nondocument file. As we said before, this is a file that contains only text; no formatting codes are found in nondocument files. To create a nondocument file, you pull down the File menu from the Opening screen and press **N**. WordStar prompts you for a file name and you enter one different from any already in your current directory. For a file of data about unit owners, you might enter a name such as **OWNERS.DTA**. Editing a nondocument file is similar to editing a document, except that you don't use character, paragraph, and page formatting. Suppose there are just four owners. The data file consists of one line of text for each owner. Each item of information is separated from the previous item by a comma. You terminate each line by pressing the **Enter** key. For our example, the data file looks like this:

```
Ms. Elaine Sanders,5925 Pomona Blvd.,Champaign,IL,61821
Mr. Fred Engels,5927 Pomona Blvd.,Champaign,IL,61821
Ms. Betty Harbison,5929 Pomona Blvd.,Champaign,IL,61821
Mr. Tom Santiago,5931 Pomona Blvd.,Champaign,IL,61821
```

After you enter these lines, you press **Ctrl-KD** to save the file and return to the Opening screen.

Once the data file is finished, you can create the **master document**. This is the text of the form letter along with some special commands. In our case, we can simply modify the condominium association letter to include a centered letterhead in boldface and the commands to merge the names and addresses. Figure 7.31 shows how the letter looks after it has been modified. It is saved with Ctrl-KT to give it a different name, FORM.DOC. This leaves the original LETTER.DOC document intact.

```
   C:FORM.DOC       P1  L1  C1             Insert Align             RgtJust
══File══Edit══Go to══Window══Layout══Style══Other═══════════EDIT══
L----!----!----!----!----!----!----!----!----!----!----!--------R
.DF OWNERS.DTA                                                          :
.RV name,address,city,state,zip                                         :
.OP                                                                     .
                 ^BPARKRIDGE CONDOMINIUM ASSOCIATION                    <
                          2935 Ridge Road                               <
                        Champaign, IL  61821^B                          <
                                                                        <
                                                                        <
November 10, 1989                                                       <
                                                                        <
&name&                                                                  <
&address&                                                               <
&city&, &state&  &zip&                                                  <
                                                                        <
Dear Condo Owner:                                                       <
                                                                        <
On October 19, 1989 there was a general meeting of the  Parkridge
Condominium  Association.   At  that meeting, we  agreed  on  the
projected budget that was proposed by our President and  Treasur-
er.   Consequently, we all have ^Sincreased^S condominium fees.   The
monthly fee for your unit is now $69.53.  If you have not already
sent  this amount for the month of November, we would  appreciate
```

**Figure 7.31 Mail-Merge Master Document**

The master document includes special dot commands and the names of data items, which will be replaced by actual data when the pages are printed.

Examine Figure 7.31 more closely. The dot command .DF OWNERS.DTA tells WordStar that the data file for this master document is named OWNERS.DTA. The .RV dot command that follows lists the names of the data items for each person. You are free to choose any names you wish for these items; the names don't really matter, but their relative positions are very important. Each item name must correspond to the item in the same position in the data file. The first item is *name*, the second item is *address*, the third item is *city*, the fourth item is *state*, and the fifth item is *zip*. After the data file and data items are identified in this manner, you use the name of each item, enclosed in ampersands (&), in the document. For example, instead of typing an actual name, like Elaine Sanders, you enter **&name&**. When the letter is printed, WordStar substitutes items from the data file for the item names in the document.

The .OP dot command, as we mentioned earlier in this chapter, shuts off page numbering, which normally isn't used in one-page letters like ours. Although it doesn't appear on the screen, a .PA dot command has been entered at the end of the document to tell WordStar to start a new page before printing the next letter.

The final step in the mail-merge process is to actually print the letters. After the master document has been created and saved, you return to the Opening screen, pull down the File menu, and press **M** to invoke the Merge Print a File option. WordStar presents a screen similar to Figure 7.23. Here you specify the name of the master document to be merge printed and press the **F10** key. WordStar then prints four letters—each one with a different name and address from the data file.

## Keyboard Macros

*Shorthand characters*

WordStar has a keyboard macro feature called *shorthand* that allows you to replace a series of keystrokes with a two-keypress code: the Escape key followed by a letter or number. In essence, you can "record" a sequence of keystrokes and "replay" them at any time. These keystrokes may include menu commands, dot commands, and ordinary text. For example, suppose you are working on a document in which you must frequently type *Parkridge Condominium Association*. WordStar lets you assign this whole phrase to a shorthand character, say A. Once you do this, instead of typing *Parkridge Condominium Association* over and over, simply press the **Escape** key and then type **A**. WordStar automatically inserts the entire phrase at the current cursor location.

To define a shorthand character, press the **Escape** key and then press **Question Mark (?)**. WordStar asks you for the character to be defined, as shown in Figure 7.32. For the example we've just described, you would type **A**. WordStar then presents a screen where you specify a description and definition for your keyboard macro. The description is optional; it is an explanation of what your shorthand character does. The definition consists of the keystrokes that will be activated when you press Escape followed by the shorthand character. Below the box in Figure 7.32, five shorthand characters are already described and defined. For example, the first shorthand character in this list is C. Its description is *Center* and its definition is *^OC*. In other words, pressing Escape and then C centers a line of text, just like pressing Ctrl-OC.

Descriptions are especially handy for keyboard macros that include commands. In our example, a description isn't really necessary, so you can just press the **Enter** key to leave it blank. Then you specify the definition of the macro by entering **Parkridge Condominium Association**. Your new shorthand character and its definition are inserted into the list on the screen. Press the **F10** key when you are finished entering the description and definition. WordStar then asks if you want to store the changes you've made on your disk. If you type **N** for no, the new keyboard macro is only in effect until you exit WordStar. If you type **Y** for yes, your shorthand character definition is saved in a file on your disk and it will be in effect whenever you use WordStar.

## Multiple Windows

*Two views*

WordStar Release 5 lets you have two windows on your screen to look at two different documents or two parts of the same document at the same time. For example, suppose you are editing LETTER.DOC and you want to see FORM.DOC. To open a new window, pull down the Window menu and select the Open/switch Between

Windows option (see Figure 7.33(a)). You can also do this by pressing **Ctrl-OK**. Then you specify the name of the second file, which in our case is FORM.DOC. The screen splits in half, with LETTER.DOC above and FORM.DOC below (see Figure 7.33(b)).

You can switch between these windows and edit text in either one. To move the cursor from LETTER.DOC to FORM.DOC, select the Open/switch Between Windows option or press Ctrl-OK again. Now you can work on FORM.DOC while LETTER.DOC remains in the window above. As shown in Figure 7.33(a), you can

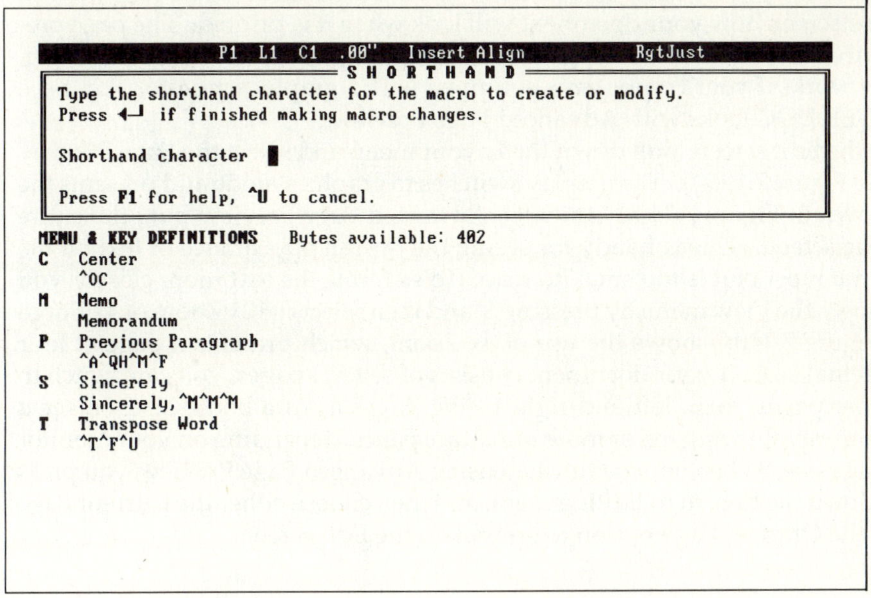


**Figure 7.32 Shorthand Screen**

Here is where you specify the shorthand character that will name your keyboard macro.

**Figure 7.33 Multiple Windows**

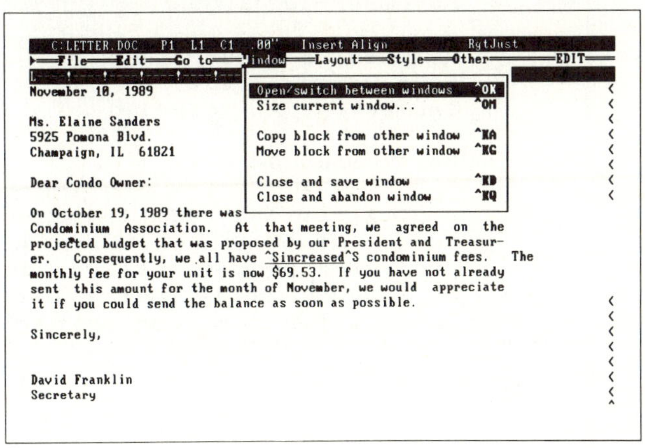


(a) The Window menu.

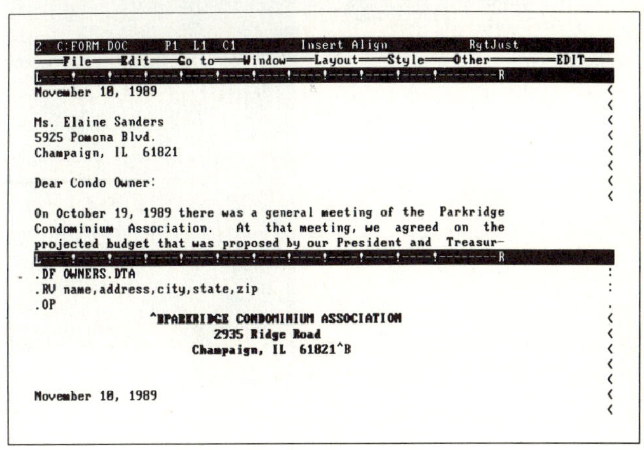


(b) The screen is split into two windows, with FORM.DOC on top and LETTER.DOC on the bottom.

also change the size of your current window, and move and copy a block from one window to the other. To close a window, you first move the cursor to that window, pull down the Window menu, and select the Close and Save Window option or the Close and Abandon Window option.

## Advanced Page Preview

*Depicting the printout on your screen*

WordStar Release 5 includes a feature called Advanced Page Preview that lets you see on your screen how your document will look when it is printed. The page preview feature fairly accurately depicts character, paragraph, and page formatting, but it only works if your computer is equipped with a graphics monitor. Let's see how LETTER.DOC looks with Advanced Page Preview.

From the Edit screen, pull down the Layout menu and select the Page Preview option (see Figure 7.19(a)). The display switches to graphics mode and presents the screen shown in Figure 7.34(a). Initially, Advanced Page Preview puts the entire page on the screen. This is handy for seeing the overall appearance of text on the page, even if most of it is too small to read. To examine the text more closely, you can pull down the View menu by pressing **V** and then select the 2x Zoom or 4x Zoom option. Figure 7.34(b) shows the use of 4x Zoom, which presents a page at four times its actual size. If your document consists of several pages, you can switch to see different pages, view left and right facing pages as in a book, or even see a *thumbnail display* showing ten or more miniature pages, depending on your monitor and the page size. When you are finished using Advanced Page Preview, you press **R** to pull down the Return to Editing menu and then choose either the Current Page option or the Original Page option to go back to the Edit screen.

**Figure 7.34 Advanced Page Preview**

(a) The Whole Page view. (b) The 4x Zoom view.

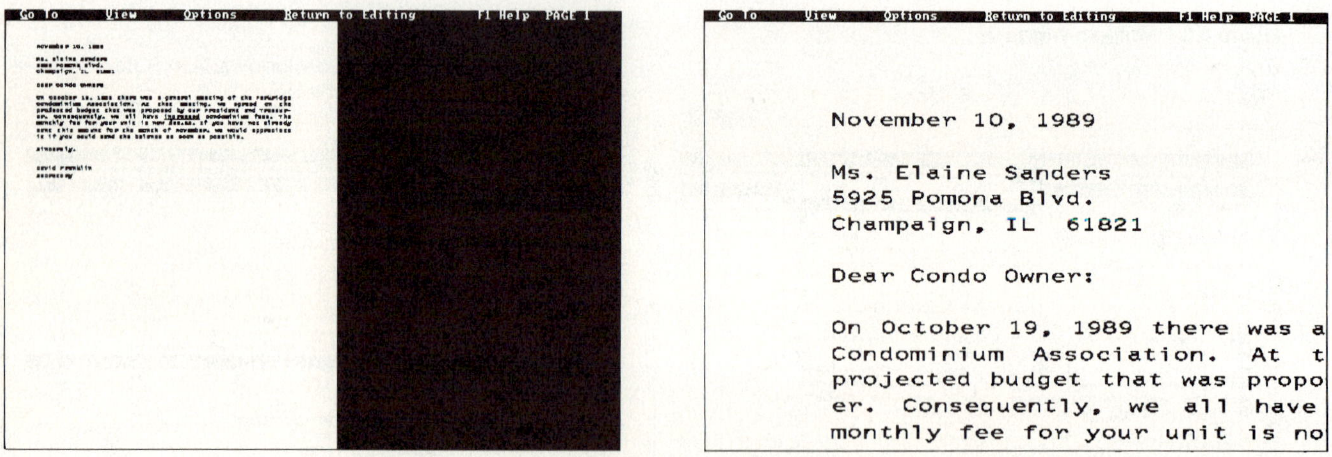

## The Real World

### Why I Use WordStar

Barbara Robertson, editor and research director of the *Whole Earth Software Catalog*:

WordStar was the first word processor I used, and though I've tried and tested several others in the last four years, I still use it. WordStar stays out of my way and never interferes with my work. Programs that make me stop, pay attention, change modes and take three or more steps before I can edit, use boldface, or save or print a document waste my time and irritate me.

WordStar is predictable and I trust it. I've never lost a document. No, there's no little gauge on the screen to tell me how much disk space I have left. On the other hand, if I run out of space I can, without leaving the document, check the disk directory and erase an old file to make room.

Hard to learn? Maybe. But it's easy to use, and once you learn the commands, they're hard to forget.

Source: Brand, Stewart, Editor in Chief, *Whole Earth Software Catalog*, Garden City, N.Y., Quantum Press/Doubleday, 1984, p. 56.

## Summary

- *How to start WordStar.* After WordStar has been installed, you switch to the proper subdirectory and enter **WS**.
- *To use the WordStar menus.* WordStar Release 5 includes pull-down menus that are activated by pressing the first letter of the menu's name. In the Edit screen, you must hold down the Alternate key and then press the first letter. An option is selected by highlighting it and pressing **Enter**, or pressing the key(s) listed to the option's right.
- *How to create a new document.* Select the File menu from the Opening screen, press **D** to open a document file, specify a file name, and begin typing.
- *How to edit a new or existing document.* You can move the cursor anywhere within the document and insert, overwrite, delete, mark, copy, move, find, replace, and check the spelling of text.
- *How to format characters, paragraphs, and pages.* From the Style menu you can select character formats such as boldface, underlining, italics, and so on. Using other menus and commands, you can also change margins, align paragraphs, set tab stops, turn word wrap and justification on or off, indent paragraphs, set line spacing, and center text. WordStar lets you control page layouts by specifying line height, page length, top and bottom margins, page breaks, page offset, page numbering, headers, and footers.
- *How to print a document.* First save the document in a disk file, return to the Opening screen, pull down the File menu, and select the Print a File option.
- *How to manage document files.* From the File menu, you can save, open, rename, copy, delete, and protect document files, as well as change disk drives and directories.
- *Some additional features included in WordStar.* Release 5 also lets you get on-line help, use a built-in thesaurus, generate a table of contents and an index, perform calculations, sort text, create form letters, create keyboard macros, use two windows, and display page previews.

## Command Summary

The following table summarizes commonly used WordStar Release 5 keypresses and commands.

| KEYPRESS/COMMAND | DESCRIPTION |
|---|---|
| | From the Opening Screen |
| F1 | Display help screen. |
| F | Pull down the File menu. |
| O | Pull down the Other menu. |
| A | Pull down the Additional menu. |
| | From the Opening Screen File Menu |
| S | Speed write (open a new document without specifying a name). |
| D | Open a document file. |
| N | Open a nondocument file. |
| P | Print a file. |
| M | Merge print a file. |
| L | Change drive and directory. |
| O | Copy a file. |
| Y | Delete a file. |
| E | Rename a file. |
| C | Protect or unprotect a file. |
| X | Exit WordStar and return to DOS. |
| | From the Opening Screen Other Menu |
| I | Generate an index file. |
| T | Generate a table of contents file. |
| R | Temporarily suspend WordStar to run a DOS command. |
| JJ | Change help level. |
| ? | Describe the use of memory. |
| Escape | Shorthand (keyboard macros) menu. |
| | From the Edit Screen |
| F1 | Display help screen. |
| Alt-F | Pull down the File menu. |
| Alt-E | Pull down the Edit menu. |
| Alt-G | Pull down the Go To menu. |
| Alt-W | Pull down the Window menu. |
| Alt-L | Pull down the Layout menu. |
| Alt-S | Pull down the Style menu. |
| Alt-O | Pull down the Other menu. |
| | Menu/Prompt Screen Actions |
| F1 | Display help screen. |
| Ctrl-U | Cancel (no answers). |
| Escape | Exit a menu; activate shorthand menu. |
| F10 | Exit a screen after answering prompts. |

| KEYPRESS/COMMAND | DESCRIPTION |
|---|---|
| | Cursor Movement |
| Up Arrow | Up one line. |
| Down Arrow | Down one line. |
| Left Arrow | Left one space. |
| Right Arrow | Right one space. |
| Ctrl-Left Arrow | Left one word. |
| Ctrl-Right Arrow | Right one word. |
| Tab | Advance to next tab stop. |
| Home | Top of current screen. |
| End | Bottom of current screen. |
| Page Up | Up one screen. |
| Page Down | Down one screen. |
| Ctrl-QR | Beginning of file. |
| Ctrl-QC | End of file. |
| | Find and Replace |
| Ctrl-QF | Find text. |
| Ctrl-QA | Find and replace text. |
| Ctrl-L | Repeat previous find or replace operation. |
| | Insert/Delete Operations |
| Enter | Insert a hard return. |
| Insert | Turn insert typing mode on or off. |
| Backspace | Delete character to the left of the cursor. |
| Delete | Delete character at the cursor. |
| Ctrl-T | Delete word at the cursor. |
| Ctrl-Y | Delete line at the cursor. |
| Ctrl-KR | Insert a file while editing. |
| Ctrl-U | Undo (restore deleted text). |
| Ctrl-KY | Delete a block. |
| Ctrl-KJ | Delete a file. |
| | Text Alignment |
| Ctrl-B | Align rest of paragraph. |
| Ctrl-QU | Align rest of document. |
| Ctrl-OA | Turn auto-align off or on. |
| Ctrl-OH | Turn auto-hyphenation off or on. |
| Ctrl-OJ | Turn justification off or on. |
| Ctrl-OW | Turn word wrap off or on. |
| .AW | Turn word wrap off or on. |
| | Block Operations |
| Ctrl-KB | Mark block beginning. |
| Ctrl-KK | Mark block end. |
| Ctrl-KC | Copy block. |
| Ctrl-KA | Copy block from other window. |
| Ctrl-KY | Delete block. |
| Ctrl-KH | Hide or show block. |
| Ctrl-KV | Move block. |
| Ctrl-KG | Move block from other window. |
| Ctrl-KZ | Sort lines in marked block. |
| Ctrl-KM | Sum numbers in marked block. |
| Ctrl-KW | Write marked block to file. |

| KEYPRESS/COMMAND | DESCRIPTION |
|---|---|
| | File Operations from Edit Screen |
| Ctrl-KT | Save and name file. |
| Ctrl-KD | Save file, go to Opening screen. |
| Ctrl-KX | Save file, exit WordStar. |
| Ctrl-KQ | Abandon file changes, go to Opening screen. |
| Ctrl-KPP | Print a file. |
| Ctrl-KPM | Merge print a file. |
| Ctrl-KL | Change drive and directory. |
| Ctrl-KO | Copy a file. |
| Ctrl-KJ | Delete a file. |
| Ctrl-KE | Rename a file. |
| | Character Formatting |
| Ctrl-PB | Turn boldface on and off. |
| Ctrl-PS | Turn underlining on and off. |
| Ctrl-PY | Turn italics on and off. |
| Ctrl-PV | Turn subscripting on and off. |
| Ctrl-PT | Turn superscripting on and off. |
| Ctrl-PX | Turn strikeout on and off. |
| Ctrl-P= | Choose a font. |
| Ctrl-OD | Hide or display character format symbols. |
| | Paragraph and Page Formatting |
| Ctrl-OL | Set margins and tabs. |
| Ctrl-OC | Center line. |
| Ctrl-OP | Page preview. |
| Ctrl-OG | Temporarily indent for paragraph. |
| Ctrl-OS | Set line spacing. |
| .HE or .H1 | First header line. |
| .H2 | Second header line. |
| .H3 | Third header line. |
| .FO or .F1 | First footer line. |
| .F2 | Second footer line. |
| .F3 | Third footer line. |
| .PA | Start new page. |
| .RM | Set right margin. |
| .LM | Set left margin. |
| .PM | Set paragraph margin. |
| .LS | Set line spacing. |
| .LH | Set line height. |
| .PL | Set page length. |
| .MT | Set top margin. |
| .MB | Set bottom margin. |
| .PO | Set page offset. |
| .PC | Set page number position. |
| .OP | Omit page numbers. |
| .PG | Turn on page numbering. |
| .PN | Change page number. |
| | Spelling Checker and Thesaurus |
| Ctrl-QL | Check spelling of rest of document. |
| Ctrl-QN | Check spelling of word at cursor. |
| Ctrl-QO | Check spelling of a word you enter. |
| Ctrl-QJ | Look up word in thesaurus. |

| KEYPRESS/COMMAND | DESCRIPTION |
|---|---|
| | Table of Contents and Index Generation |
| .TC | Table of contents entry. |
| .IX | Index entry. |
| Ctrl-PK | Turn index entry on and off. |

| | |
|---|---|
| | Math Functions |
| Ctrl-QM | On-screen calculator. |
| Ctrl-KM | Sum numbers in marked block. |

| | |
|---|---|
| | Mail-Merge |
| .DF | Specify data file name for mail-merge. |
| .RV | Read variables from data file. |

| | |
|---|---|
| | Window Operations |
| Ctrl-OK | Open a new window; switch to other window. |
| Ctrl-OM | Change size of current window. |
| Ctrl-KA | Copy block from other window. |
| Ctrl-KG | Move block from other window. |
| Ctrl-KD | Close and save window. |
| Ctrl-KQ | Close and abandon window. |

## Key Terms

As an extra review of this chapter, try defining the following terms. If you have trouble with any of them, refer to the page number listed.

auto-hyphenation (234)
block (238)
cursor diamond (235)
dot command (246)
flag (233)
flag column (233)
footer (253)
hard hyphen (234)
hard return (234)
hard space (233)
header (253)
help level (259)
line height (250)
logged (257)
master document (263)
menu bar (229)
microjustification (248)
nondocument file (256)
page break (251)
page offset (251)
ruler line (233)
soft hyphen (234)
soft return (234)
soft space (233)
status line (232)

## Review Questions

1. After you have changed to the WordStar subdirectory, what command do you enter at the DOS prompt to start WordStar?
2. Which menus are available from WordStar's Opening screen?
3. Which Opening screen menu do you use to open a new document?
4. When WordStar performs a word wrap, is a hard return or a soft return inserted into the document?
5. What does the ruler line show?

6. List two different ways to remove a single character from a document.
7. Once a block is marked, how do you move it to a different location within a document?
8. Which WordStar command would you use to retrieve text removed by a previous erase operation?
9. How would you check the spelling of every word in a document?
10. Which Edit screen menu lists the most commonly used character formatting options?
11. Which dot commands are used to set the left and right margins?
12. Which WordStar command would you use to realign a single paragraph after changing margins?
13. What is the easiest way to center a heading in WordStar?
14. How do you tell WordStar to begin a new page?
15. If you are writing a single-page letter, how do you tell WordStar not to print a page number?
16. How do you tell WordStar to print a document?
17. How do you save the document you are editing and return to the Opening screen?
18. How can you change to WordStar's classic menus?
19. How do you look up a word with WordStar's thesaurus?
20. What are the two types of files needed to print mail-merge letters?

## Multiple Choice

1. To pull down a menu from the Edit screen you hold down the Alternate key and
   (a) press the first letter of the menu's name. (b) press the last letter of the menu's name.
   (c) press the appropriate function key. (d) press the mouse button.
2. Which keys would you press to reformat an entire document after changing its margins?
   (a) Ctrl-A (b) Ctrl-B
   (c) Ctrl-QU (d) F10
3. One or more lines of text printed in the top margin of every page is called a
   (a) page offset. (b) flag.
   (c) header. (d) footer.
4. Which type of file would you use to hold mail-merge data, DOS batch commands, or programming language source code?
   (a) document (b) nondocument
   (c) .IDX (d) .TOC
5. Which command would you use to keep a file from being modified or deleted?
   (a) Protect/Unprotect a File (b) Abandon Changes
   (c) Save File, Exit WordStar (d) Save and Name File

6. Which command would you use if you wanted to edit files on a disk in a drive or directory different than your WordStar subdirectory?
   (a) TelMerge
   (b) Open/Switch Between Windows
   (c) Change Drive/Directory
   (d) Page Preview
7. Which key is pressed to get context-sensitive, on-line help in most menus and screens?
   (a) F1
   (b) F10
   (c) Escape
   (d) Page Up
8. Before you can look up a word with the thesaurus, you must
   (a) check the spelling of your document.
   (b) mark the word as a block of text.
   (c) move the cursor anywhere within the word.
   (d) load the thesaurus as a nondocument file.
9. Which command would you use to create an index entry for an item that doesn't appear in your document exactly the way you want it to appear in the index?
   (a) .TC
   (b) Ctrl-PK
   (c) .IX
   (d) .OP
10. The block math feature, which is invoked by pressing Ctrl-KM, is used to
    (a) evaluate expressions in a block of text.
    (b) add up the numbers in a block of text.
    (c) display the on-screen calculator.
    (d) merge two blocks of text.
11. Before you can sort lines of text by pressing Ctrl-KZ, you must first
    (a) mark them as a block.
    (b) move them to a different window.
    (c) copy them to their own disk file.
    (d) insert them with the Undo command.
12. Which of the following dot commands is used in a mail-merge master document to indicate the name of the corresponding data file?
    (a) .OP
    (b) .PA
    (c) .RV
    (d) .DF
13. In WordStar, a shorthand character is the same as a
    (a) print control.
    (b) keyboard macro.
    (c) pull-down menu.
    (d) dot command.
14. Which option would you use to look at two different documents on your screen at the same time?
    (a) Open/Switch Between Windows
    (b) Open a Nondocument File
    (c) Page Preview
    (d) TelMerge
15. If your computer has a graphics monitor, which WordStar Release 5 feature would you use to see how your document will look when it is printed?
    (a) Open/Switch Between Windows
    (b) Open a Nondocument File
    (c) Page Preview
    (d) TelMerge

## On-line Exercises

1. If you are not already running WordStar, change to the proper disk drive directory and enter **WS**. Open a document file and name it MEMO.DOC. Type the following text, pressing the **Enter** key only once after the last line:

```
The next meeting of the Parkridge Condominium Association
Board of Managers will be held at 7:00 P.M. on November 19,
1989 in Room 217 of Champaign Federal Savings.  This is an
important meeting, so please try to attend.
```

2. Move the cursor to the top of the document and type the following lines, pressing **Enter** after each one:

```
To:  Board of Managers
From:  David Franklin, Secretary
Re:  Next meeting
```

3. Press the **Enter** key again to leave a blank line before the paragraph. Move the cursor to the top of the document, type **M E M O**, and press **Enter**. Boldface, underline, and center this title.

4. Move the cursor to the last line of the memo and delete it by pressing **Ctrl-Y**. Restore the text you've deleted with the Undo command.

5. Mark *Parkridge Condominium Association* as a block of text and copy it in front of the *Board of Managers* after the *To:*.

6. Move the cursor to the top of the file. Use the find and replace command to change *Managers* to *Directors* throughout the entire document.

7. Set the right margin position to 6 inches, move the cursor to the beginning of the document, and reformat all of the text.

8. Turn off justification and auto-hyphenation, and reformat all of the text.

9. Insert the appropriate dot command to turn off page numbering for this one-page memo.

10. Save the document in its disk file and return to the Opening screen.

11. If your computer is equipped with a printer, make sure it is turned on and on-line, and print this memo.

12. Return to the Opening screen and protect MEMO.DOC so that it cannot be changed. Now open MEMO.DOC and try to insert or delete text. What happens? Return to the Opening screen and try to delete this file. What happens? When you are finished exploring the protect feature, unprotect MEMO.DOC.

13. Pull down a menu from the Opening screen and try WordStar's on-line help facility. Select a different option and try it again. Now open MEMO.DOC and invoke the help facility from the Edit screen. Pull down a menu, highlight an option we haven't discussed in this chapter, and learn more about it with WordStar's help feature.

14. With MEMO.DOC displayed on your memo screen, highlight a word and invoke WordStar's thesaurus. Try using the options that appear in the Thesaurus screen to see additional synonyms and brief definitions of these words.

15. If your computer is equipped with a graphics monitor, use the page preview feature to examine MEMO.DOC. Does the screen view accurately depict the actual printout? Try the 2x Zoom and 4x Zoom options from the View menu. You can shift the display to see other parts of your document by pressing the arrow keys.

## Projects

1. Use WordStar to print your academic schedule for this semester. List the days, times, classes, buildings, rooms, and instructors.
2. Look in a newspaper or placement office listing for job ads. Select a position in line with your experience and goals. Use WordStar to prepare a resume and cover letter for this job. Be sure to use underlining and boldface where appropriate.
3. Use WordStar to create a quick reference guide to WordStar. List the menu commands, dot commands, and other keystrokes you think are especially important to remember. Feel free to use WordStar's on-line help facility to get information about the various commands.
4. Use WordStar to create a mail-merge form letter to be sent to the following software companies requesting information about the word processing packages they sell.

   WordStar
   MicroPro International Corporation
   33 San Pablo Ave.
   San Rafael, CA 94903

   Microsoft Word
   Microsoft Corporation
   N.E. 36th Way
   Redmond, WA 98073

   Wordperfect
   Wordperfect Corporation
   288 W. Center St.
   Orem, UT 84057

# Part 4

# SPREADSHEETS

Spreadsheet packages hold a special place in the history of microcomputers. The very first one, called VisiCalc, was originally conceived by Harvard graduate student Dan Bricklin for the Apple II computer in 1978. Before VisiCalc, microcomputers were toys. After VisiCalc, microcomputers became business and personal productivity tools. VisiCalc has probably sold more Apple IIs than any ad campaign.

In August 1981, IBM introduced its original Personal Computer. VisiCalc and other spreadsheet packages were quickly adapted to run on this new machine. but they weren't substantially upgraded to take full advantage of its power. Mitch Kapor, founder of Lotus Development Corporation, knew what to do. He and Jonathan Sachs developed 1-2-3, a powerful package designed especially for the IBM PC. With its excellent spreadsheet, graphics, and data management functions, 1-2-3 eventually became the best-selling application package of all time. The combination of IBM hardware and software like 1-2-3 really made the business world take notice. Software and hardware go hand-in-hand; Like VisiCalc and the Apple II, many organizations and individuals bought IBM PCs just so they could run Lotus 1-2-3. So, spreadsheet packages have significantly helped spur the microcomputer revolution.

Part 4 examines these versatile software tools. Chapter 8 introduces microcomputer spreadsheet packages in general and Chapter 9 covers one particular spreadsheet package, Lotus 1-2-3, in specific detail.

# 8

# Spreadsheet Concepts

## In This Chapter

## PREVIEW

In many ways, a spreadsheet package is like a word processing package, but whereas word processing software helps you work with words, spreadsheet software helps you work with numbers. You can enter, edit, format, calculate, copy, move, rearrange, print, and, in some cases, even graph data. Before spreadsheet software, you had to be a programmer to make use of a computer's numerical abilities. Now almost anyone can easily perform all kinds of "number crunching." Even for experienced programmers, using spreadsheet programs often proves to be faster, simpler, and more convenient than writing specialized software to solve numerical problems.

The real advantage of a spreadsheet package is its ability to instantly recalculate figures when any related figures are changed. Besides making it easy to correct, update, and revise data, this ability also lets you try out "what-if" situations. For example, let's say you're figuring your income taxes with a spreadsheet package. After you're finished, you wonder "What if I get that raise?" All you have to do is enter a new income figure and your taxes are automatically recalculated. This chapter will examine some of the features of spreadsheet packages.

After studying this chapter, you will understand

- the general structure of a worksheet.
- the data that can be entered into a worksheet.
- how data can be manipulated in a worksheet.
- how to format the contents of a worksheet.
- how formula results are calculated in a worksheet.
- how to print a worksheet.
- how to save and retrieve worksheets in disk files.
- additional spreadsheet program features.
- which popular spreadsheet programs are currently on the market.

## WORKSHEET STRUCTURE

*Tables of numbers and labels*

In Chapter 1, we said that a spreadsheet package is a type of application software that lets you manipulate tables of numbers. In Chapter 3, we said that these tables are called spreadsheets or worksheets. Figure 8.1 shows a typical handwritten worksheet. The numbers and labels are clearly organized into rows and columns. Some of the numbers are obtained from outside sources. For example, all of the expenditures in Figure 8.1 come from bills or receipts. Other numbers, such as the totals and balances, are calculated from various figures inside the worksheet. Accountants previously used handwritten worksheets for all kinds of documents, including income statements, balance sheets, and financial projections. Today they use spreadsheet packages. Even people who aren't accountants commonly use spreadsheet packages to draw up budgets, monitor investments, and balance checkbooks.

**Figure 8.1 Handwritten Spreadsheet**

Spreadsheets such as this budget for Parkridge Condominium Association have long been used by accountants and others who work with tables of numbers.

*Parkridge Condominium Association*

| | Jan | Feb | March | April | May | June | TOTAL |
|---|---|---|---|---|---|---|---|
| Expenditures | | | | | | | |
| Insurance | 247 00 | 247 00 | 247 00 | 247 00 | 247 00 | 247 00 | 1482 00 |
| Snow Plowing | 310 00 | 150 00 | | | | | 460 00 |
| Merry Maids | 48 00 | 48 00 | 48 00 | 48 00 | 48 00 | 48 00 | 288 00 |
| Lawn Service | | | | 420 00 | 420 00 | 420 00 | 1260 00 |
| Trash Pickup | 84 00 | 84 00 | 84 00 | 84 00 | 84 00 | 84 00 | 504 00 |
| Electricity | 95 00 | 97 00 | 178 00 | 160 00 | 201 00 | 94 00 | 825 00 |
| Tree Care | | | | 160 00 | | | 160 00 |
| Light Bulbs | | | | 108 00 | 36 00 | | 144 00 |
| Supplies | 24 00 | 27 00 | 25 00 | 16 00 | 23 00 | 18 00 | 133 00 |
| TOTALS | 808 00 | 653 00 | 582 00 | 1243 00 | 1059 00 | 911 00 | 5256 00 |
| | | | | | | | |
| INCOME | | | | | | | |
| Condo Fees | 976 00 | 976 00 | 976 00 | 976 00 | 976 00 | 976 00 | 5856 00 |
| | | | | | | | |
| BALANCE | 168 00 | 491 00 | 885 00 | 618 00 | 535 00 | 600 00 | 600 00 |

## Insight

# How Do Businesses Use Spreadsheet Packages?

To understand how real businesses use spreadsheets, let's create a company with a problem.

Imagine that you've just been named president of ChowDown Inc., a large food-processing company with a number of plants scattered around the country. Each plant is accountable for managing its own budget. Overall sales goals are set at corporate headquarters in Moneybags, Mississippi. On the basis of these goals, each plant works up its own production plan for the coming year.

Part of the production plan requires setting up a detailed budget for each plant. In turn, each plant's many departments have to set up their own budgets. There may be as many as 10 to 12 separate departments in each plant, such as quality control, shipping, accounting, product manufacturing, and so on. And each department has expenses for items such as salaries, training, and maintenance.

The budget-building process begins with developing an hourly labor estimate and a cost estimate for each specific line item in the department budget. Not only must budget totals be developed for each line item, but a plan also has to be developed to show how the funds will be spent on a monthly basis. The various departmental budgets then are combined into the plant-wide budget.

If a plant budget exceeds the goals you and your executives set, the plant and department budgets must be revised. Because the process is so complex, even the smallest revision involves many people and major recalculations. Without a computer, this budget-building process can take an agonizing five to six weeks.

You, in your infinite wisdom, have looked at this problem and gone out and bought a computer system. Now, with a microcomputer and a spreadsheet program, the budgets for all departments are structured in a similar manner. A single spreadsheet design is used for all departments. The budget for the entire plant is generated through the program's ability to merge the data from different spreadsheets into a single document.

Because of spreadsheets, changes are easier to make. The budget-building process now takes less than two weeks, and there are substantial savings in cost, and frayed tempers, as well.

## Rows and Columns of Cells

*Cell addresses*

A worksheet consists of rows and columns of cells. A **cell** is simply the small box at the intersection of a row and a column (see Figure 8.2(top)). Each cell in a worksheet is identified by its own unique **cell address**. This is a designation that specifies the cell's exact location within the worksheet. The spreadsheet program in Figure 8.2(top) denotes columns with letters (*A, B, C,* and so on) and rows with numbers (*1, 2, 3,* etc.). In this case, the address of the upper-left cell is A1. Some spreadsheet programs denote columns and rows slightly differently, with both rows and columns numbered. Figure 8.2(bottom) shows just such a spreadsheet program. In this case, the address of the upper-left cell is R1C1 (Row 1, Column 1). A few spreadsheet programs let you choose either of these two methods of specifying cell addresses.

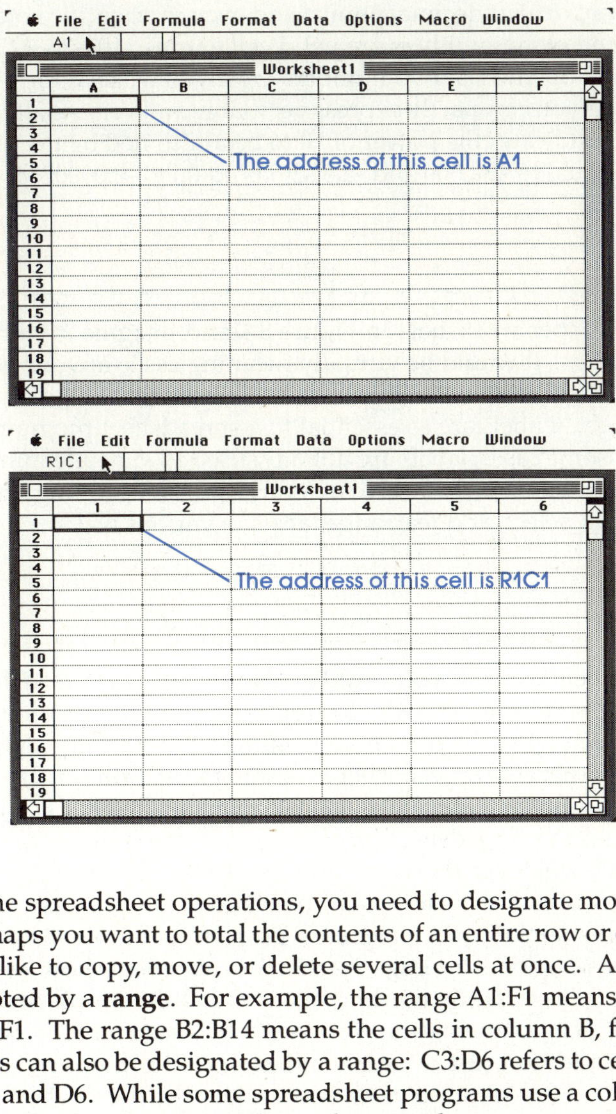


**Figure 8.2 Cell Addresses**

(top) Most spreadsheet programs label columns with letters and rows with numbers.
(bottom) A few programs let you number both the columns and rows.

For some spreadsheet operations, you need to designate more than one cell at a time. Perhaps you want to total the contents of an entire row or column, or maybe you would like to copy, move, or delete several cells at once. A series of adjacent cells is denoted by a **range**. For example, the range A1:F1 means the cells in row 1, from A1 to F1. The range B2:B14 means the cells in column B, from B2 to B14. A block of cells can also be designated by a range: C3:D6 refers to cells C3, C4, C5, C6, D3, D4, D5, and D6. While some spreadsheet programs use a colon to separate the two corner cells of a range, as we have shown, other programs use two dots (..) instead, like this: A1..F1. Whichever way they are expressed, ranges are a very convenient means to denote any contiguous portion of a worksheet, from two adjacent cells to an entire worksheet.

The screens you see in Figure 8.2 show only 15 columns and 6 rows, but worksheets can be much larger than this. Just as a word processing program lets you scroll the screen to work on large documents, spreadsheet programs let you do the same to work on truly massive worksheets. Spreadsheet programs not only let you scroll up and down, but also left and right. Many popular spreadsheet programs can address more than 200 columns and more than 8,000 rows. The actual number of cells that can be used, however, depends on the amount of memory installed in the computer.

## Numbers

A worksheet cell is a place where you can put a piece of data. Three different types of data can be entered into a cell: numbers, labels, and formulas.

*Quantities*

Numbers, of course, are quantities. They may be expressed as positive or negative values, with or without decimal points, and even in scientific notation. For example, all of the following numbers are valid cell entries: 10, -22, 1234, 0.5, -11.23, 4.32E+5, and -2.54E-5. The last two numbers are given in scientific notation. This type of notation lets you compactly express very large and very small numbers. The portion after the *E* indicates the power of 10 to be multiplied by the part before the *E*. So, 4.32E+5 is equal to 432,000 and -2.54E-5 is equal to -0.0000254.

## Labels

*Headings, titles, and notes*

Look again at the paper worksheet in Figure 8.1 and imagine it without any row and column headings. It would be virtually meaningless to anyone but the person who created it. A **label** is a heading, title, or other note that helps explain the contents of a worksheet. Labels are as essential to a spreadsheet program as numbers and formulas. In some cases, labels are not only used to annotate numbers, but are manipulated as textual data themselves. Many spreadsheet programs can be instructed to examine, select, and rearrange labels in various ways.

## Formulas

*Computing and manipulating data*

If numbers and labels were all you could enter into cells, a spreadsheet program would be nothing but a primitive way to store data. You need formulas to tell the spreadsheet program what to do with your numbers and labels. A **formula** is an expression that instructs the spreadsheet program to perform calculations or other manipulations on numbers, labels, and the contents of cells. For example, the formula A1+B1 tells the spreadsheet program to add the contents of cell A1 to the contents of cell B1, whatever those contents might be. The resulting sum is displayed in the cell containing the formula (see Figure 8.3).

Formulas make spreadsheet programs powerful, flexible, and easy to use. Anyone with a basic understanding of arithmetic can learn how to construct all kinds of formulas. The notation used in formulas is quite simple and is similar to that used in traditional mathematics. You've already seen that the plus sign (+) is used to symbolize addition, just as you would expect. The minus sign (-) represents subtraction, the asterisk (*) represents multiplication, and the forward slash (/) represents division. Besides these basic arithmetic operators, most spreadsheet programs also have symbols for raising a number to a power (exponentiation), combining text labels, and comparing numerical quantities. Figure 8.4 shows examples of some simple spreadsheet formulas.

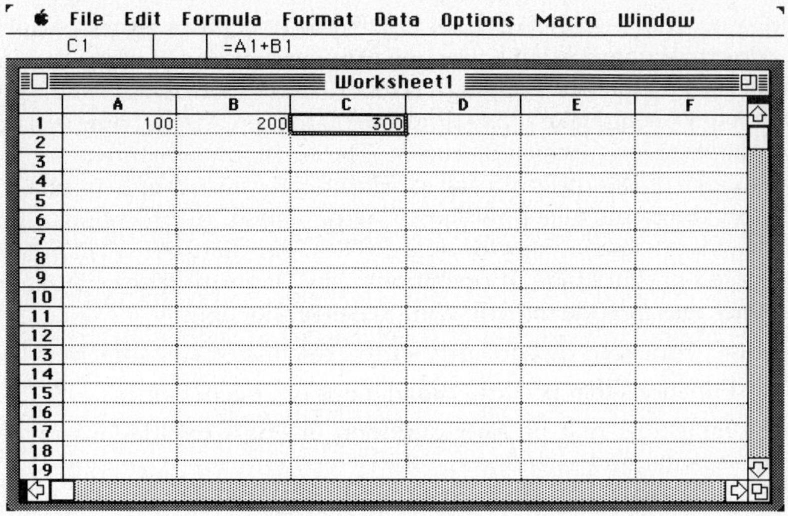


**Figure 8.3 The Formula A1+B1**

Cell C1 contains the formula =A1+B1, which adds the current contents of cells A1 and B1, and displays the result in cell C1. The equal sign (=) in front of the formula is required by this particular spreadsheet program (Microsoft Excel for the Apple Macintosh) to distinguish formulas from text labels.

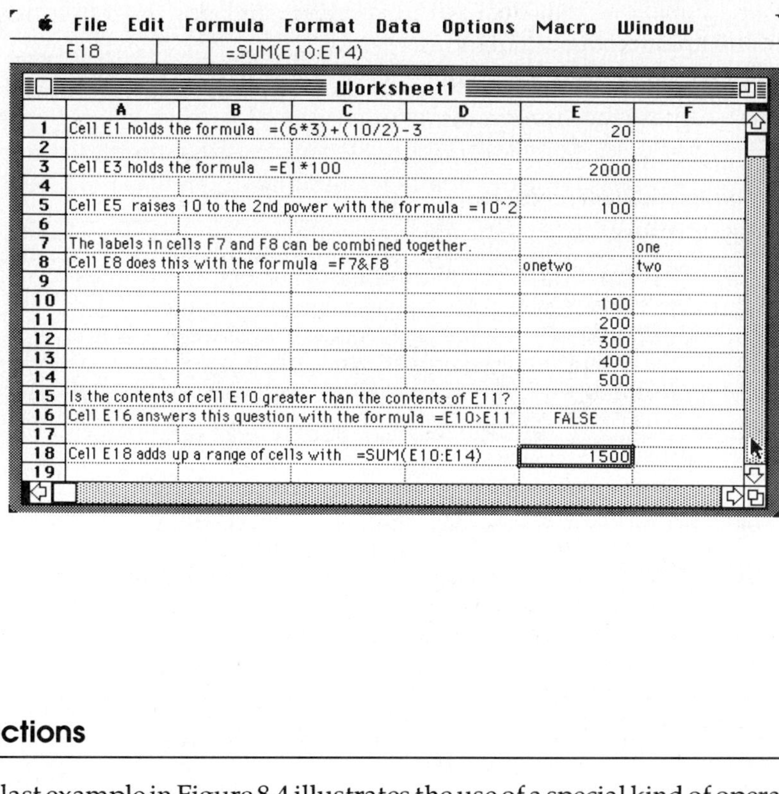


**Figure 8.4 Spreadsheet Formulas**

This screen displays several examples of the types of formulas that can be used in a worksheet.

## Functions

*Computational shortcuts*

The last example in Figure 8.4 illustrates the use of a special kind of operation known as a **function**. This is a ready-made procedure that performs tedious, complex, or often-used computations or other manipulations. A function is like a shortcut that allows you to do a complex operation without having to specify how the individual steps are done. The SUM function in the last example of Figure 8.4 is probably the most frequently used spreadsheet function. It adds the contents of a given range of cells. All you have to do is supply the range of cells to be totaled, and the SUM function does the rest. In this particular example, using SUM is more convenient than entering the formula E10+E11+E12+E13+E14. Some operations are practically impossible to perform without using a function. For example, what if you had to add up the contents of 1,000 cells, A1 through A1000? Typing A1+A2+A3 and so on all the way up to A1000 would take a long time, even if the spreadsheet program would accept a formula that long (which it won't). The SUM function, however, makes adding the contents of 1000 cells as easy as adding the contents of two cells.

Spreadsheet programs generally have a wide variety of predefined, built-in functions that you can use in your formulas. These functions are often organized into groups based on the kinds of operations they perform. For example, most spreadsheet packages include the following types of functions:

- *Mathematical.* Functions that do fairly simple calculations on numerical values.
- *Statistical.* Functions that perform calculations on lists of values.
- *Financial.* Functions that perform common business calculations involving loans, investments, and cash flows.
- *Text.* Functions that manipulate labels and parts of labels.
- *Logical.* Functions that allow you to compare values in cells and perform different actions based on the results of those comparisons.
- *Date and Time.* Functions that return dates and times in various formats.
- *Trigonometric.* Functions that deal with angles and triangles.
- *Logarithmic.* Functions that deal with exponents and powers, often used in scientific and engineering calculations.

Table 8.1 provides some common examples of these types of functions, which are included in many spreadsheet programs.

**Table 8.1 Common Spreadsheet Functions**

| MATHEMATICAL FUNCTIONS | |
|---|---|
| ABS | Computes the absolute value of a number. |
| INT | Returns the integer (whole number) part of a number. |
| MOD | Computes the remainder (modulus) of a division operation. |
| RAND | Gives a random number between 0 and 1. |
| ROUND | Rounds a value to a given number of decimal places. |
| SQRT | Computes the square root of a number. |

| STATISTICAL FUNCTIONS | |
|---|---|
| AVG | Computes the average of a list of values. |
| COUNT | Computes the number of entries in a list of values. |
| MAX | Returns the largest value in a list of values. |
| MIN | Returns the smallest value in a list of values. |
| STD | Computes the standard deviation of a list of values. |
| SUM | Computes the sum of a list of values. |
| VAR | Computes the variance of a list of values. |

| FINANCIAL FUNCTIONS | |
|---|---|
| FV | Computes the future value of an investment. |
| IRR | Computes the internal rate of return of an investment. |
| NPV | Computes the net present value of an investment. |
| PMT | Computes the payment on a loan per payment period. |
| PV | Computes the present value of an investment. |
| RATE | Computes the rate of return of an investment. |
| TERM | Computes the number of loan payments. |

| TEXT FUNCTIONS | |
|---|---|
| MID | Extracts characters from the middle of a text label. |
| LENGTH | Computes the number of characters in a text label. |
| REPEAT | Duplicates a sequence of characters within a text label. |

| LOGICAL FUNCTIONS | |
|---|---|
| IF | Returns one number if a condition is true, another if false. |
| ISERR | Returns TRUE (the number 1) if a calculation error occurred. |

| DATE AND TIME FUNCTIONS | |
|---|---|
| DATE | Returns a code number representing the given date. |
| TIME | Returns a code number representing the given time of day. |
| NOW | Returns a code number representing the current date and time. |

| TRIGONOMETRIC FUNCTIONS | |
|---|---|
| COS | Computes the cosine of an angle. |
| SIN | Computes the sine of an angle. |
| TAN | Computes the tangent of an angle. |
| PI | Returns the value of pi (approximately 3.1415926). |

| LOGARITHMIC FUNCTIONS | |
|---|---|
| EXP | Computes the value of the constant e raised to a given power. |
| LN | Computes the natural (base e) logarithm of a value. |
| LOG | Computes the base 10 logarithm of a value. |

## ENTERING AND EDITING DATA

*Cell entries*

The numbers, labels, and formulas manipulated by a spreadsheet program don't just miraculously appear; one way or another, these entries must be entered into the microcomputer, usually by being typed in at a keyboard. Although many spreadsheet packages can bring in data generated by other programs, such as word processors and data base managers, most worksheets are created by entering items directly. Once data is entered, various editing features can be used to modify, insert, delete, select, copy, and move items.

### Moving the Cell Pointer

*Where you enter data and commands*

Just as word processors have a cursor to indicate where you can enter text, spreadsheet programs have a **cell pointer** that marks the location where you can enter data or initiate commands. The cell marked by the cell pointer is often called the **current cell** or **active cell**, and is shown on the screen as darkly outlined, brightly lit, or otherwise highlighted. For example, in Figure 8.2(top) the active cell is A1; in Figure 8.3 the active cell is C1; and in Figure 8.4 the active cell is E18. This particular spreadsheet package, Microsoft Excel for the Apple Macintosh computer, outlines the active cell with a dark box and also indicates its address in the upper left just below the File pull-down menu heading.

Moving a spreadsheet's cell pointer is somewhat similar to moving a word processor's cursor. On computers without a mouse, the simplest way to move the cell pointer is with the arrow keys. Pressing the Down Arrow key, for example, moves the cell pointer to the cell directly below the current cell. To scroll the worksheet to a cell not currently on the screen, you simply move the cell pointer "past the edge." The worksheet shifts accordingly, and the screen displays a new row or column. Besides the arrow keys, there usually are other keys that move the cell pointer more rapidly and scroll the worksheet if necessary. In Lotus 1-2-3 for IBM-compatible computers, for example, the Home key returns the cell pointer to cell A1, the Page Down key moves the cell pointer down one whole screen, and holding down the Control key and pressing the Right Arrow key moves the cell pointer one screen to the right.

Spreadsheet programs that use a mouse make it even easier to move the cell pointer. All you do is move the mouse pointer to the cell you want and then press the mouse button. To move to a cell not currently on the screen, you must first use the up-down or left-right scroll bar to shift the screen. These work just like a typical Macintosh word processor's scroll bar, which we described in Chapter 6 (see Figure 6.5). In Figure 8.4, for example, the black mouse pointer near the lower right corner of the screen is inside the up-down scroll bar. Even with a mouse, programs such as Microsoft Excel for the Macintosh also let you use arrow keys (present on newer Macintosh keyboards) or other keypress combinations to move the cell pointer.

## Typing Entries

*Control panel*

When you begin a spreadsheet program, the cell pointer is generally put in cell A1 and you can immediately enter data. You can, of course, move the cell pointer to any other cell before typing. In some spreadsheet packages, like Lotus 1-2-3 for IBM-compatibles, the characters you type appear at the top of the screen, above the worksheet in a place called the *control panel*. Your entry isn't actually put into the cell until you press the Enter key or move the cell pointer. Other spreadsheet packages, like Microsoft Excel for the Macintosh, immediately show the characters you type both in the active cell and above the worksheet in the control panel. In general, you must either press the Enter key or move the cell pointer to another cell when you are finished typing to finalize your entry.

### Numbers

*Values*

A number is the simplest kind of data to enter; you just type the number and press the Enter key or move the cell pointer. Most spreadsheet programs assume your entry is a number if it begins with one of the following characters:

0 1 2 3 4 5 6 7 8 9 . + - $ (

### Labels

*Text*

Labels are almost as simple as numbers. Any entry that begins with a character not used in numbers or formulas is assumed to be a label. For example, if you type the word *Expenditures* into a cell, it will be immediately recognized as a label. In some cases, you may need to enter a label that begins with a digit or another character normally associated with numbers or formulas. Let's say that you want to head a column with the label *1989 Expenditures.* While some spreadsheet packages are clever enough to recognize this as a label, others might require you to begin this entry with a special *label prefix* character, like a quotation mark (' or "), to distinguish it from a number.

Sometimes you need to use labels that are too long to fit in a single cell because the default width of a column of cells is usually only 9 or 10 characters. We'll discuss later how you can change cell column widths, but often this isn't necessary for long labels. Spreadsheet packages generally allow long labels to overlap into adjacent cells, provided these cells are empty. For example, the notes you see at the left side of the worksheet in Figure 8.4 are long labels all entered into cells in column A. These long labels can be fully displayed because the adjoining cells in columns B, C, and D are all empty. Keep in mind, however, that even though parts of the labels are displayed in columns B, C, and D, the labels are really stored only in cells from column A. The cells in columns B, C, and D are still empty.

### Formulas

*Expressions*

Formulas are expressions that may include numbers, mathematical operators like + and *, cell addresses like A1 and F16, functions like SUM, and even labels enclosed in quotation marks. Consequently, formulas are not as easy for spreadsheet programs to identify as numbers and labels. Most programs either require a formula to begin the way a number does, or to begin with some special character. As you can see from Figure 8.4, Microsoft Excel requires that every formula begin with an equal sign (=). Lotus 1-2-3, on the other hand, is a bit more flexible; formulas can begin with any of the following characters:

```
0 1 2 3 4 5 6 7 8 9 . + - ( @ # $
```

Lotus 1-2-3 formulas that start with a cell address must be preceded by a plus sign (+), like this: +A1+B1.

## Modifying Cells

*Retyping and editing cell contents*

We have said that a number, label, or formula isn't actually entered into a cell until you press the Enter key or move the cell pointer to another cell. If you make a mistake and you haven't yet pressed the Enter key or moved the cell pointer, you can use the backspace key to erase characters you've just typed. Then you can correctly retype the entry. Some spreadsheet packages are more flexible than this, also allowing you to go back and insert or delete characters before you finish an entry.

Once you press the Enter key or move on to another cell, the procedure for going back and modifying an entry is slightly different. The simplest way to change the existing contents of a cell is to move the cell pointer to that cell and re-enter the whole number, label, or formula. In addition, spreadsheet programs generally let you edit the existing contents of a cell by inserting, deleting, or overwriting selected characters. This is especially handy for modifying long labels or formulas you don't want to completely retype.

## Inserting Rows and Columns

*Making room for more data*

Sometimes when entering data into a worksheet you forget an entire row or column. In other cases, worksheets may be periodically updated by adding a new row or column. Fortunately, you don't have to re-enter the entire worksheet whenever a new row or column must be added. Spreadsheet programs have insert commands that let you shift existing rows down and shift existing columns to the right. These commands make room for new rows and columns to be inserted into an existing worksheet.

Suppose that you are converting the paper worksheet in Figure 8.1 to a computerized version with a spreadsheet program like Microsoft Excel. Only after you have begun entering the formulas for totaling expenditures do you discover that you forgot the row for electricity bills. There's no need to get upset, because adding the missing row is quite simple. First move the mouse pointer to the left side of the screen on top of the row number where you want the new row to be inserted, and then press the mouse button (see Figure 8.5(a)). This selects the entire row 8 and highlights it in reverse video. In this particular spreadsheet program, you then pull down the Edit menu and select the Insert command. Figure 8.5(b) shows how the spreadsheet program moves the cells down to reveal a new blank row 8. Not only are the rows shifted down, but any formulas that refer to cells in the shifted rows are automatically adjusted to reflect the new row numbers. At this point, you can simply enter the *Electricity* label in cell A8, the electricity bill values in cells B8 through G8, and the formula =SUM(B8:G8) to compute the row total in column H8.

**Figure 8.5 Inserting a Row**

(a) First select the place where the new row is to be inserted.

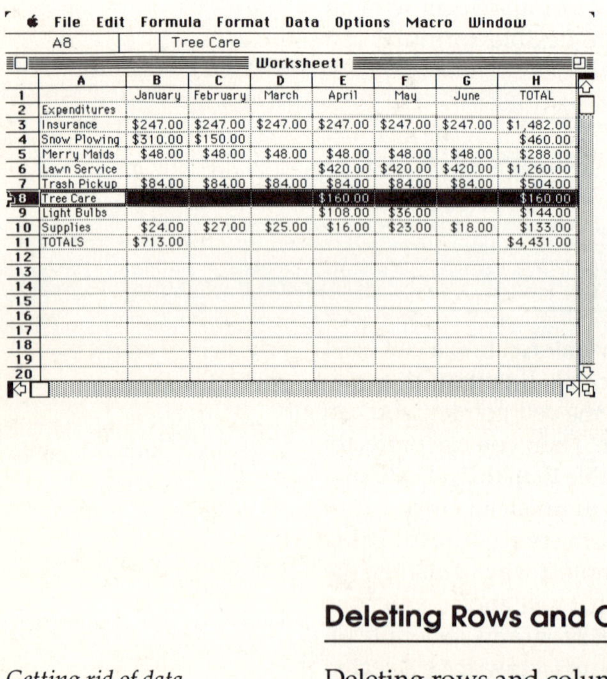


(b) Then select the Insert option from the Edit menu, and the new row appears.

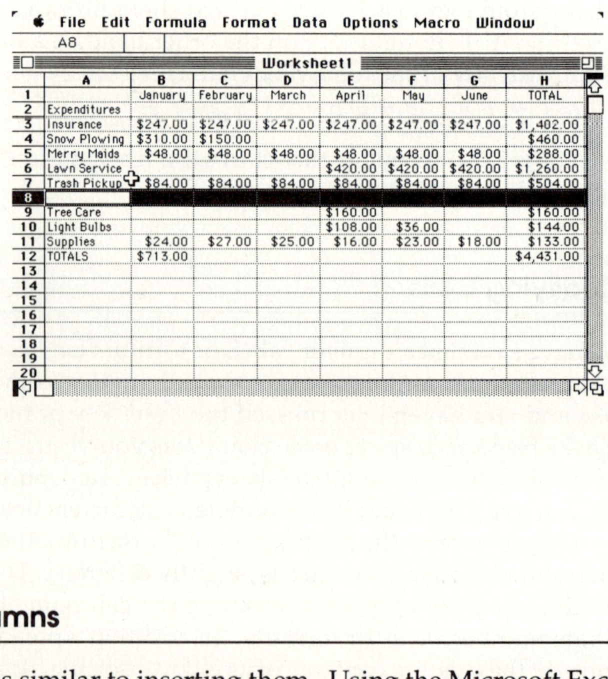


## Deleting Rows and Columns

*Getting rid of data*

Deleting rows and columns is similar to inserting them. Using the Microsoft Excel worksheet example from the previous section, let's say that you want to delete column G, with the expenditures for June. First you move the mouse pointer to the box containing the G just above the first row, and then press the mouse button. This selects column G and highlights it in reverse video (see Figure 8.6(a)). Next you pull down the Edit menu and select the Delete option. The previous contents of all the cells in column G are deleted, and the cells that were in column H are shifted to the left (see Figure 8.6(b)). Again, formulas are automatically adjusted to reflect this deletion. For example, before the deletion the formula total in the *Insurance* row in cell H3 was =SUM(B3:G3). After deleting column G, the spreadsheet program automatically changes this formula, now in cell G3, to =SUM(B3:F3).

**Figure 8.6 Deleting a Column**

(a) First select the column.

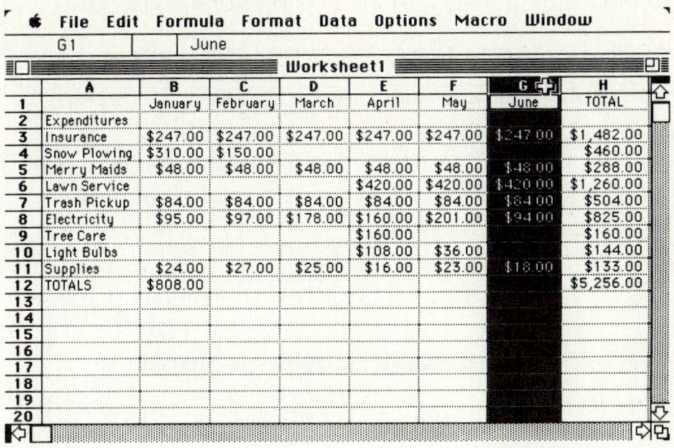


(b) Then select the Delete option from the Edit menu, and the column disappears.

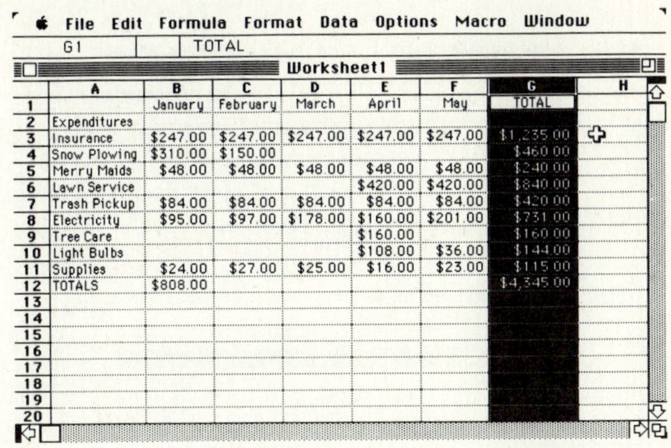


## Selecting Ranges

*Blocks of adjacent cells*

As we said before, a range designates a block of cells. This may be a single cell, like A1:A1; part of a row, like A1:H1; part of a column, like A1:A20; a rectangle of cells, like A1:C10; or even an entire worksheet. As one of its more powerful features, a spreadsheet program allows you to perform certain operations on ranges as well as on single cells. This can significantly speed up your work and decrease the amount of time you spend typing repetitive entries. For example, you can designate a range and then in one step fill that entire range of cells with a particular number, label, or formula.

Many different spreadsheet commands work with ranges. Some spreadsheet packages have commands that prompt you for a range, and, in response, you enter a range designation like, A1:C10. You may also be able to select a range in a manner similar to highlighting a block of text with a word processing program. For instance, suppose that you now want to add the condominium fee income figures to the worksheet we've been using as an example. As you can see from Figure 8.1, the condominium fees are exactly the same for each month. Why type the same number six times when you only have to do so once? First enter **976** into cell B15, then select cells B15 through G15 like this: hold down the mouse button, move to cell G15, and then release the mouse button. The range B15:G15 is then selected and highlighted as shown in Figure 8.7(a). Now all you do is pull down the Edit menu and select the Fill Right command. Cells C15 through G15 are filled with the contents of cell B15, the first cell in the range. As you can see from Figure 8.7(b), now cells B15 through G15 all contain $976.00, and you only had to enter 976 once.

## Copying and Moving Data

*Manipulating ranges*

We've just described one way to copy data—replicating the contents of a single cell across part of a row or column. Most spreadsheet programs provide additional commands for both copying and moving the contents of a range of cells. These commands are very similar to the copy-and-paste and cut-and-paste operations

**Figure**
**8.7 Filling a Range**

(a) First select the range of cells to be filled.

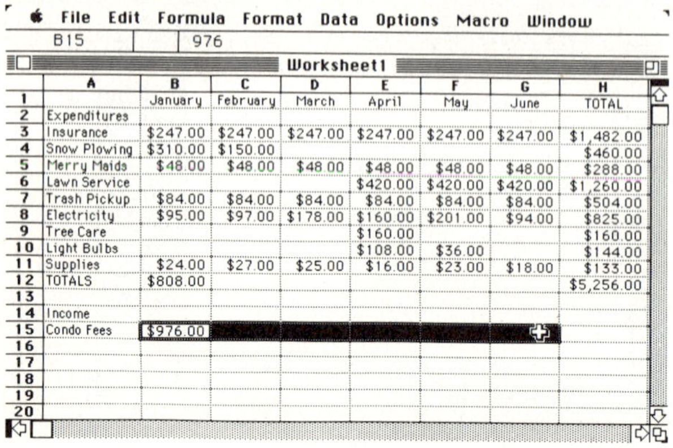


| | A | B | C | D | E | F | G | H |
|---|---|---|---|---|---|---|---|---|
| 1 | | January | February | March | April | May | June | TOTAL |
| 2 | Expenditures | | | | | | | |
| 3 | Insurance | $247.00 | $247.00 | $247.00 | $247.00 | $247.00 | $247.00 | $1,482.00 |
| 4 | Snow Plowing | $310.00 | $150.00 | | | | | $460.00 |
| 5 | Merry Maids | $48.00 | $48.00 | $48.00 | $48.00 | $48.00 | $48.00 | $288.00 |
| 6 | Lawn Service | | | | $420.00 | $420.00 | $420.00 | $1,260.00 |
| 7 | Trash Pickup | $84.00 | $84.00 | $84.00 | $84.00 | $84.00 | $84.00 | $504.00 |
| 8 | Electricity | $95.00 | $97.00 | $178.00 | $160.00 | $201.00 | $94.00 | $825.00 |
| 9 | Tree Care | | | | $160.00 | | | $160.00 |
| 10 | Light Bulbs | | | | $108.00 | $36.00 | | $144.00 |
| 11 | Supplies | $24.00 | $27.00 | $25.00 | $16.00 | $23.00 | $18.00 | $133.00 |
| 12 | TOTALS | $808.00 | | | | | | $5,256.00 |
| 13 | | | | | | | | |
| 14 | Income | | | | | | | |
| 15 | Condo Fees | $976.00 | | | | | | |
| 16 | | | | | | | | |
| 17 | | | | | | | | |
| 18 | | | | | | | | |
| 19 | | | | | | | | |
| 20 | | | | | | | | |

(b) Then select the Fill Right command from the Edit menu, and the range is filled with the contents of the first cell.

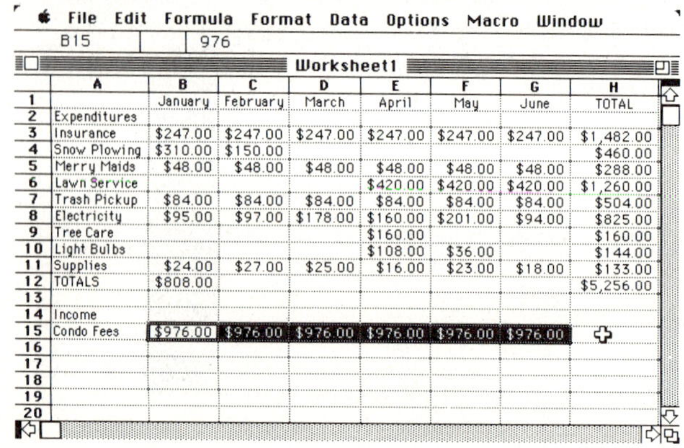


| | A | B | C | D | E | F | G | H |
|---|---|---|---|---|---|---|---|---|
| 1 | | January | February | March | April | May | June | TOTAL |
| 2 | Expenditures | | | | | | | |
| 3 | Insurance | $247.00 | $247.00 | $247.00 | $247.00 | $247.00 | $247.00 | $1,482.00 |
| 4 | Snow Plowing | $310.00 | $150.00 | | | | | $460.00 |
| 5 | Merry Maids | $48.00 | $48.00 | $48.00 | $48.00 | $48.00 | $48.00 | $288.00 |
| 6 | Lawn Service | | | | $420.00 | $420.00 | $420.00 | $1,260.00 |
| 7 | Trash Pickup | $84.00 | $84.00 | $84.00 | $84.00 | $84.00 | $84.00 | $504.00 |
| 8 | Electricity | $95.00 | $97.00 | $178.00 | $160.00 | $201.00 | $94.00 | $825.00 |
| 9 | Tree Care | | | | $160.00 | | | $160.00 |
| 10 | Light Bulbs | | | | $108.00 | $36.00 | | $144.00 |
| 11 | Supplies | $24.00 | $27.00 | $25.00 | $16.00 | $23.00 | $18.00 | $133.00 |
| 12 | TOTALS | $808.00 | | | | | | $5,256.00 |
| 13 | | | | | | | | |
| 14 | Income | | | | | | | |
| 15 | Condo Fees | $976.00 | $976.00 | $976.00 | $976.00 | $976.00 | $976.00 | |
| 16 | | | | | | | | |
| 17 | | | | | | | | |
| 18 | | | | | | | | |
| 19 | | | | | | | | |
| 20 | | | | | | | | |

found in word processing software. For example, with a spreadsheet program like Microsoft Excel, you first select and mark a range. If you want to copy the range, you then choose the Copy command from the Edit menu; if you want to move the range, you choose the Cut command. Then you simply move the cell pointer to the position where the range is to go and select the Paste command from the Edit menu. The selected range is then copied or moved to the new location.

Whenever you insert, delete, move, or copy cells, spreadsheet programs automatically adjust any cell references in formulas to account for any changes of position. For example, let's say you have the formula A1+A2 in cell A3 and you move or copy cells A1, A2, and A3 to cells B1, B2, and B3, respectively. The spreadsheet program automatically changes the formula A1+A2 to B1+B2 when it is moved or copied to cell B3, because the A1 and A2 in the formula are assumed to be relative cell references. A **relative cell reference** is a cell address that pertains to a cell's position rather than to the cell itself. For example, the spreadsheet program assumes that the A1 in the formula A1+A2 refers to the cell located two cells above the formula. In fact, most spreadsheet packages assume all cell references are relative unless you specify otherwise.

In certain situations, however, you would not want relative cell references. For example, you may use a constant value, like the current interest rate, in several different formulas in several different places. But you need only store the interest rate once, in one single cell. If you are going to move or copy cells containing formulas that reference this interest rate, you should not use relative cell references in your formulas for the cell containing the interest rate. Instead, you should use an **absolute cell reference** for the cell containing the interest rate. This is a cell address that does not change when you move or copy it. With many spreadsheet programs, you indicate an absolute cell reference by preceding the column and row designations with a dollar sign. For instance, suppose you have the formula $A$1+A2 in cell A3. The $A$1 is an absolute reference that always means the current contents of cell A1, but the A2 is a relative cell reference that means the cell directly above the formula. Now if you move or copy the formula in A3 to B3, cell B3 will contain the formula $A$1+B2.

Two dollar signs are used in the preceding example because many spreadsheet programs also let you have mixed cell references. A **mixed cell reference** is half-relative and half-absolute, in which either a row or a column is absolute, but not both. For example, $A1 is a mixed cell reference that always means column A, but the row might vary depending upon where this reference is copied or moved. Similarly, A$1 is a mixed cell reference that keeps the row constant.

## FORMATTING DATA

*Different formats for different uses*

Chapters 6 and 7 described how word processing software lets you format text in various ways to improve its appearance both on the screen and in the final printed document. Spreadsheet programs provide similar capabilities to make your worksheets easier to use and read.

### Numeric Formats

*How values are presented*

Spreadsheet programs are, first and foremost, number processors. You would expect them to be able to display and print numbers in a variety of ways. While spreadsheet programs are perhaps most often used for manipulating monetary values, they are also used for scientific, engineering, and mathematical data processing. These different uses generally require different formats for the display of numbers in worksheets. For example, the numbers you see in the worksheets presented so far in this chapter are all in **fixed currency format**. This means that there are two places to the right of the decimal point, thousands are separated by commas, and each number is preceded by a dollar sign—for example, $1,523.25. Negative currency values are enclosed in parentheses instead of being preceded by a minus sign—for example, ($1523.25). Clearly, this format wouldn't be appropriate for a worksheet displaying a table of sines and cosines.

Different spreadsheet programs have slightly different procedures for specifying the formats of numbers. You may have to execute a format command, select a particular type of numeric format, and then designate the range of cells to have this format. Or you may first select the range and then choose the particular format to apply to the numbers and formula results in those cells. Microsoft Excel, for example, takes the latter approach. First you select the range of cells you want to format, highlighting it as we previously described. Then you pull down the Format menu and choose the Number option. You are presented with a menu of available numeric formats. This particular spreadsheet program offers several possible numeric formats, illustrated and described in Figure 8.8. As you can see, spreadsheet packages are quite flexible in the way they can display numbers.

### Column Widths

*Making room for cell entries*

For any numeric format you may choose, you must make sure that numbers and formula results will completely fit into their cells. Unlike labels, numeric values cannot simply extend into empty adjacent cells. A number too long to fit into a cell will not be displayed. When this happens, spreadsheet programs usually fill the cell with asterisks (*) or pound signs (#) to indicate that a formatted entry is too long to fit. Most spreadsheet programs initially set the default width of all cells to 9 or 10 characters, but, for some long numbers, this isn't wide enough. Besides, long labels will only be overlapped into adjacent cells when those adjacent cells are empty. If the cell to the immediate right is occupied, labels will be cut off instead of continued.

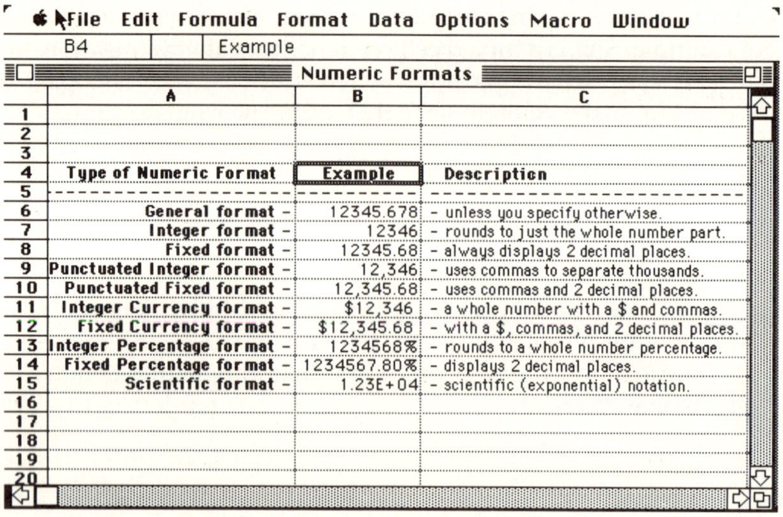


**Figure 8.8 Numeric Formats**
This worksheet displays various types of numeric formats.

Fortunately, spreadsheet programs make it very easy to change column widths. You can usually set a new default width for every column in the worksheet or individually set the widths of particular columns. Some spreadsheet packages let you set column widths to any value from 1 to 240 characters, so you can tailor your column widths for the best possible worksheet appearance. For example, the worksheets in Figures 8.2, 8.3, and 8.4 simply use Microsoft Excel's default column width of 10. Figure 8.8, on the other hand, shows a worksheet in which columns A, B, and C have been appropriately widened. With this particular spreadsheet program, all you have to do to change a column width is move the cell pointer to that column, pull down the Format menu, select the Column Width option, and enter a new column width.

Column widths can be decreased, of course, as well as increased. In fact, some spreadsheet programs even let you set the width of a column to 0 characters. How can you display a column that is 0 characters wide? You can't. This is one way in which some spreadsheet packages let you "hide" data. A **hidden column** is one that exists and contains data, but is not displayed or printed. Suppose you are preparing a budget for the personnel department that must contain detailed information about salaries and benefits. You might want to display the results of this forecast without revealing sensitive data about individual employees. By hiding the column that contains the salary figures, you can keep them secret, yet still use these figures in formulas. Some spreadsheet programs let you hide columns by setting their widths to 0, whereas others may have a special command for hiding columns.

## Alignment

*Justifying cell contents*

The alignment of labels and numeric values within their cells is another simple, but important factor in the appearance of a worksheet. There are three types of alignment: left-justified, centered, and right-justified. By default, all numbers and formula results are right-justified and all labels are left-justified within their cells, but it's easy to change this. You can set the alignment of a single cell, an entire row, an entire column, or a whole range of cells. Some spreadsheet programs also let you reset the default alignment to be used for all cells. Figure 8.8 illustrates all three types of alignment. The titles in columns A and B are centered within their respective cells. The rest of columns A and B are right-justified, and all of column C, including the title, is left-justified.

## Displaying Formulas

*Checking cell contents*

Appearances can be deceiving. Sometimes what you enter into a cell isn't what is actually displayed in the worksheet. Some numeric formats cause values to be rounded before they are displayed. For example, 12345.678 is the actual number that was entered into cells B6 through B15 in Figure 8.8. Besides, when you enter a formula into a cell, the spreadsheet program normally evaluates the formula and displays its result, not the formula itself. If you want to see the true contents of a cell, you have to move the cell pointer to that cell and look above the worksheet in the control panel. Figure 8.4 illustrates this nicely. The cell pointer is at cell E18, which contains the formula =SUM(E10:E14). But the worksheet only shows 1500, the result of evaluating this formula. The actual formula is displayed above the worksheet in the control panel, where the contents of the active cell are displayed.

In most cases, this is exactly what you want. When you print the final version of a worksheet, you want to see formatted numbers and formula results. After all, these formats and computations are what you wanted the worksheet to show you. Nevertheless, sometimes it helps to see the actual numbers and formulas in the cells that contain them. This is especially true if your worksheet has several formulas that reference each other. It's easier to check their accuracy if you can see them all on the screen at once. Fortunately, spreadsheet programs usually provide a means by which you can display the actual numbers and formulas down in the worksheet portion of the screen. With Microsoft Excel, for example, you simply pull down the Options menu, select the Display option, and turn on the Formulas switch. Figure 8.9 demonstrates this feature using the Parkridge Condominium Association budget we introduced in Figure 8.1.

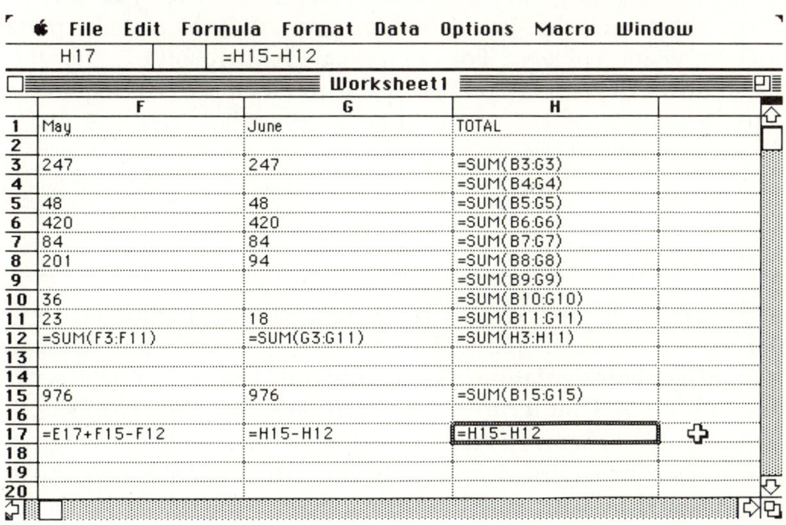


**Figure 8.9 Displaying Formulas**
This screen shows part of the condominium association budget with the Display Formulas option turned on. Instead of showing formula results and formatted values, the spreadsheet program displays formulas and numbers exactly as they were entered.

## CALCULATING RESULTS

*How formulas are evaluated*

People use spreadsheet programs to perform calculations. The ease-of-use, power, and flexibility of these programs can make them superior to other methods of calculation. In fact, spreadsheet packages are generally so easy to use that you often don't even need to think about how they function. Nevertheless, most people who regularly use spreadsheet packages find it helpful to understand in principle how these programs evaluate formula results.

### Automatic Recalculation

*Recomputing the entire worksheet*

As we have said, one of the great advantages of using a spreadsheet package is that you can change existing figures to try out "what if" scenarios. Many spreadsheet programs immediately update the entire worksheet whenever you change the contents of a single cell. This feature is called **automatic recalculation**. If your worksheet is small or doesn't have many formulas, automatic recalculation works quite nicely. The worksheet is updated so quickly that you aren't even aware of the time it takes to do so. Unfortunately, it can take several seconds to several minutes to recalculate every cell in a large or very complex worksheet. In the meantime, all you can do is wait until the worksheet is recalculated. Although this might not seem like a very long time, it can become tiresome to have to wait after every minor editing change. There are, however, two solutions to this problem: manual recalculation and smart recalculation.

### Manual Recalculation

*Recomputing only on demand*

Most spreadsheet packages that use automatic recalculation have a way to shut off this feature, and, alternatively, allow **manual recalculation**. This feature causes the formulas in a worksheet to be recalculated only when you explicitly tell the program to do so. When manual recalculation is turned on, you can enter values and formulas into your worksheet without having to wait for the spreadsheet program to update every cell after each entry. This can indeed save you a lot of time and frustration when editing large or complex worksheets. After you are finished editing, you can simply tell the spreadsheet program to recalculate by pressing a special key or combination of keys. For example, with Microsoft Excel for the Macintosh, you hold down the Apple Command key and then press the equal sign key to manually recalculate. Lotus 1-2-3 for IBM-compatibles has you press the F9 function key to recalculate a worksheet.

### Smart Recalculation

*Recomputing only affected cells*

Although most spreadsheet packages have a manual recalculation feature, some programs don't have automatic recalculation as we've described it. Instead they use **smart** or **intelligent recalculation**. While this type of recalculation is performed automatically, unless you shut it off, it doesn't update the entire worksheet every time you change a cell. When you enter new data or change the existing contents of a cell, a spreadsheet program with smart recalculation updates only those cells, if any, that are affected by your entry. This is a good compromise between automatic and manual recalculation that can save time, yet always keep your worksheet updated.

## Order of Recalculation

*Which formulas to calculate first?*

So far, we've discussed *when* worksheet cells are recalculated, but not *how* this is done. Specifically, in what order are cells recalculated? Since the average microcomputer can only do one calculation at a time, a spreadsheet program must begin recalculating with a single cell and then proceed throughout the worksheet in some particular order. Early spreadsheet programs like VisiCalc gave you a choice between two methods: column-wise and row-wise recalculation. **Column-wise recalculation** begins with cell A1 and proceeds down column A, goes on to cell B1 and proceeds down column B, and so on. **Row-wise recalculation** also starts at cell A1, but then proceeds to go across row 1, then row 2, and so on. The problem with both of these methods is that they can lead to incorrect results if you're not careful about how you set up your worksheet. For example, let's say you are using column-wise recalculation with the following simple worksheet:

| Cell | Actual Contents |
|---|---|
| A1 | 100+A3 |
| A2 | 200 |
| A3 | 100+A2 |

As soon as you finish entering this worksheet, the formulas are calculated for the first time and this is the result:

| Cell | Displayed Result |
|---|---|
| A1 | 100 |
| A2 | 200 |
| A3 | 300 |

Already there is a problem. Cell A1 is supposed to contain 100 plus the value in cell A3. It should contain 400, but it only contains 100. Since the cells were evaluated in the order A1, A2, and then A3, there was nothing in cell A3 when cell A1 was originally evaluated. That's why A1 only contains 100. Now suppose you change the contents of cell A2 to 222. With either column-wise or row-wise recalculation, here are the results:

| Cell | Displayed Result |
|---|---|
| A1 | 400 |
| A2 | 222 |
| A3 | 322 |

This is *still* not right. Cell A1 should contain 422. It now contains 400 because the program added 100 to the formula result of 300 left in cell A3 after the previous example. Clearly, in some instances there can be a problem with both column-wise and row-wise recalculation.

The way that most modern spreadsheet packages solve this problem is to use **natural recalculation**. This method recalculates a cell only after evaluating any cells on which it depends. For example, natural recalculation would evaluate our worksheet example in this order: A2, A3, and then A1. The results would then be computed correctly. Although natural recalculation is best for most worksheets, some spreadsheet programs also allow you to set the recalculation order to column-wise or row-wise. This lets you create worksheets in which you have explicit control of the order of recalculation.

## Circular References

*Formulas that "chase their own tails"*

As you've just seen, formulas can reference cells that contain other formulas. In the previous example, cell A1 contains a formula that refers to cell A3, but A3 also contains a formula. Although this might seem unusual and perhaps even a bit confusing, it's really quite common for worksheets to contain formulas that reference other formulas. As long as natural recalculation is being used, there is seldom a problem. One potential problem, however, can occur. A **circular reference** occurs when a formula in a cell is either directly or indirectly dependent on the value in that very same cell. The most obvious example is when you use a formula that references the same cell in which it is stored. This is a direct circular reference. For instance, if you enter the formula 100+A1 in cell A1, the spreadsheet program cannot evaluate it. Every time the program tries to evaluate the formula in A1, the value in cell A1 changes. No matter how many times it tries, the program cannot compute a final result for this formula. Usually you would get some kind of error message telling you that this particular circular reference cannot be resolved.

## Iterative Recalculation

*Recomputing repeatedly*

Certain *indirect* circular references, however, can be eventually resolved. An absolute final answer may not be reached, but an approximate result can often be obtained by recomputing the formulas a number of times. This method is called **iterative recalculation**, or simply **iteration**, and it can be used to solve certain types of problems. For example, just about everyone knows what a square root is, but do you know how to calculate one? There is seldom the need to do so by hand anymore because most calculators, spreadsheet packages, and programming languages have built-in functions to compute square roots. Before these handy tools, people simply looked up square roots in a table published in a reference book. So although you'll probably never have to know how to compute a square root, we'll show you an interesting way to do it with a spreadsheet program without using the built-in SQRT (square root) function.

One method to compute the square root of a number is to repeatedly make better and better estimates until you finally arrive at the correct answer. Figure 8.10 shows a worksheet that simulates this process. The formula in cell A3 displays the current result of the formula in cell A4, and the formula in A4 uses the current result of the formula in cell A3. This is an indirect circular reference. Each time these formulas are recalculated, the result in cell A4 gets closer to the true square root of the number in cell A1. After several iterations, the final answer is obtained and the worksheet stops recalculating.

By default, most spreadsheet packages recalculate formulas only once when you change a cell. In other words, iterative recalculation is initially turned off. Since indirect circular references (as in our square root example) are relatively uncommon, having iterative recalculation initially turned off is appropriate for most worksheets. To use iterative recalculation for specific cases, you must explicitly turn it on. You also must specify the maximum number of iterations that will be performed each time recalculation occurs. This tells the spreadsheet program when to stop if it encounters a set of formulas that never reaches a final result. With Microsoft Excel, for example, you pull down the Options menu, select the Calculation option, and turn on the iteration switch. The default number of maximum iterations is 100, but this can be changed if necessary.

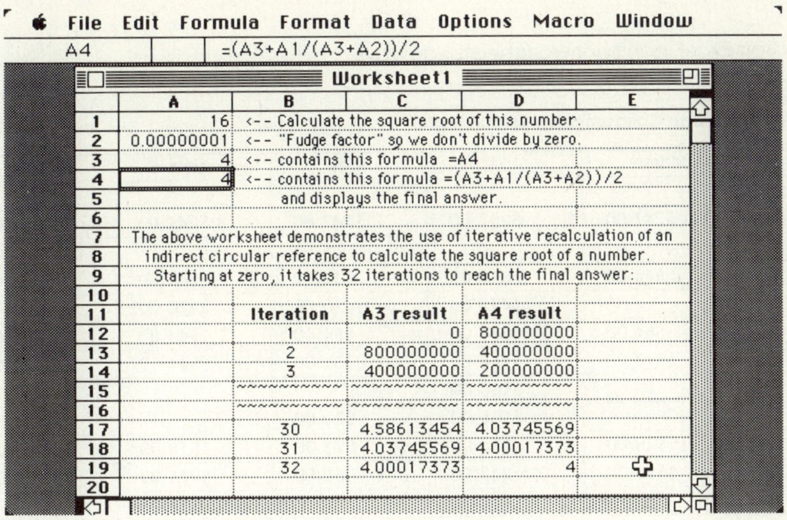


**Figure 8.10 Iterative Recalculation**
This worksheet shows how iterative recalculation can be used to compute a square root.

## PRINTING

*Producing a finished report*

Worksheets, like documents produced with word processing packages, are usually printed with spreadsheet programs that make it easy to produce attractive reports. Many worksheets can be printed in just one or two steps, if you use the spreadsheet program's default print settings. On the other hand, you can play a more active role in designing page layouts by explicitly setting print formatting options like margins, page length, headers, footers, forced page breaks, and page numbering. You often can tell the spreadsheet program to print row numbers, column labels (A, B, C, etc.), and grid lines. Depending upon the capabilities of your printer, some spreadsheet programs can use various type fonts, styles, and sizes. Even more useful, some spreadsheet programs can print a very wide worksheet sideways on a page and continue it across several pages if necessary. For example, Figure 8.11 shows the completed condominium association budget printed sideways on a page with Microsoft Excel. This was done by pulling down the File menu and selecting the Page Setup option to set the page orientation and margins, and to turn off the display of row and column labels. Then the File menu was pulled down again, and this time the Print option was selected to actually print the worksheet.

## SAVING AND RETRIEVING WORKSHEETS

*Keeping and revising your work*

Most worksheets, like most documents, are saved on a disk even after they are printed. This allows you to go back and make updates or changes without having to re-enter the entire worksheet and provides a compact and efficient way to keep important worksheets.

Typically, to save a worksheet you simply execute a File Save command or select the Save option from a File menu. The first time you save a worksheet, you may be required to enter a new name for its file. Otherwise, it may be given a default name like UNTITLED1 or WORKSHEET1. Once a worksheet has been named, it will be saved under that name unless you specifically elect to rename it.

**Figure 8.11 Printing Sideways**
Some spreadsheet programs, such as Microsoft Excel, can print worksheets sideways, across the length of one or more pages.

**Parkridge Condominium Association**

| | January | February | March | April | May | June | TOTAL |
|---|---|---|---|---|---|---|---|
| Expenditures | | | | | | | |
| Insurance | $247.00 | $247.00 | $247.00 | $247.00 | $247.00 | $247.00 | $1,482.00 |
| Snow Plowing | $310.00 | $150.00 | | | | | $460.00 |
| Merry Maids | $48.00 | $48.00 | $48.00 | $48.00 | $48.00 | $48.00 | $288.00 |
| Lawn Service | | | | $420.00 | $420.00 | $420.00 | $1,260.00 |
| Trash Pickup | $84.00 | $84.00 | $84.00 | $84.00 | $84.00 | $84.00 | $504.00 |
| Electricity | $95.00 | $97.00 | $178.00 | $160.00 | $201.00 | $94.00 | $825.00 |
| Tree Care | | | | $160.00 | | | $160.00 |
| Light Bulbs | | | | $108.00 | $36.00 | | $144.00 |
| Supplies | $24.00 | $27.00 | $25.00 | $16.00 | $23.00 | $18.00 | $133.00 |
| TOTALS | $808.00 | $653.00 | $582.00 | $1,243.00 | $1,059.00 | $911.00 | $5,256.00 |
| | | | | | | | |
| Income | | | | | | | |
| Condo Fees | $976.00 | $976.00 | $976.00 | $976.00 | $976.00 | $976.00 | $5,856.00 |
| | | | | | | | |
| Balance | $168.00 | $491.00 | $885.00 | $618.00 | $535.00 | $600.00 | $600.00 |

Before you can change or update an existing worksheet, you must retrieve it from disk and load it into memory while running your spreadsheet program. This procedure is as easy as saving a file. You execute a File Retrieve command or perhaps select the Open option from a File menu. In either case, you'll probably be offered a list of names of worksheet files in your current disk drive directory. Simply choose a name from this list or perhaps enter a different disk drive directory and file name; the worksheet will be read from disk and loaded into your spreadsheet program. You can then edit, format, print, and save the worksheet again.

## ADDITIONAL SPREADSHEET FEATURES

*More capabilities*

So far, we've covered the basics of using spreadsheet packages. Most programs have many more features described in menus, commands, and reference manuals. With every new release, spreadsheet programs get even more powerful, flexible, and easy to use. Let's look at some other important spreadsheet features. Many of them began as advanced capabilities, but are now considered standard spreadsheet features.

### Graphing

*Charting your numbers*

Ever since the introduction of Lotus 1-2-3, the ability to display and print graphs has been a virtual requirement of sophisticated spreadsheet packages. Since bar graphs, pie charts, scatterplots, and line graphs often can communicate information much better than tables of numbers, business people and educators are fond of using visual aids to enhance their ideas. Spreadsheet programs with graphics capabilities make it easy for people who aren't necessarily graphic artists to produce polished graphs both on the display screen and the printed page. These graphs then can be inserted into documents or photocopied onto transparency pages for use with overhead projectors.

As an example, let's produce a couple of graphs from our condominium association budget. First, we'll make a bar graph showing the monthly balance, or money in the bank, for the first half of the year. With Microsoft Excel, all you have to do is select the range of cells to graph (in this case A17:G17), pull down the File menu, select the New option, and choose the Chart option. Excel automatically determines that a bar graph is the most appropriate way to display this data and it uses default settings to produce the reasonable chart you see in Figure 8.12.

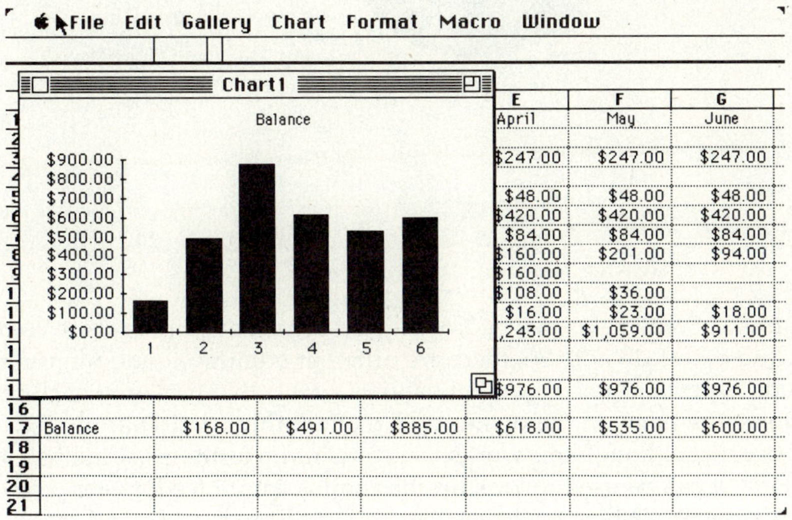


**Figure 8.12 Bar Graph**
This screen shows how Microsoft Excel can create a bar graph of the monthly balances of the Parkridge Condominium Association budget worksheet.

With a little experimentation, you can add titles, axis labels, legends, and other niceties to your graphs. You can often control the print quality as well as use different fonts, styles, and sizes for your text. Figure 8.13 shows another type of graph easily made from the expenditures totals of the condominium association budget worksheet.

## Data Management

*Maintaining tables of data*

One of the reasons spreadsheet programs are so popular is that people generally understand them and feel comfortable using them. The tabular arrangement of numbers, text labels, and formulas is well suited to a wide range of common tasks. It often makes sense to organize labels and numbers into rows and columns, even if you don't use any formulas. Consequently, many people use spreadsheet packages to store tables of data like mailing lists, price lists, and inventories. Spreadsheet programs typically include several functions to help you create, maintain, search, and rearrange tables of data.

As an example, let's return to the Parkridge Condominium Association. This organization includes several different buildings, each of which has a few different

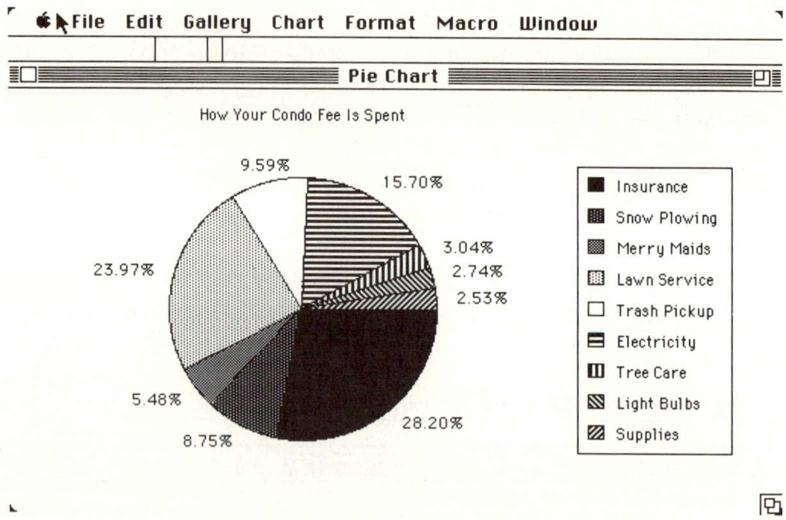


**Figure 8.13 Pie Chart**
Here is a pie chart of the Parkridge Condominium Association budget that has been printed with Microsoft Excel.

types of units. Some have two bedrooms and some have three, some come with garages, and others do not. So, there are different monthly condominium fees for the various kinds of units. Figure 8.14 shows a table that lists each condominium unit address, the name of the owner, and the monthly condominium fee for that unit. Notice that although this worksheet contains no formulas, it can still be quite useful. First, it can be used to look up the condominium fee for each unit or each owner. Many spreadsheet packages have a Data Search command that can scan through rows until it finds a cell that contains a specified entry. In addition, the worksheet can be rearranged with a Data Sort command to order rows on the basis of the contents of one or more cells. The worksheet in Figure 8.14, for instance, can be sorted by each apartment's address, by the name of the owner, or even by the condominium fee. Although spreadsheet programs cannot match the power and flexibility of full-fledged data base management packages, they can provide an easy way to organize small and uncomplicated tables of data.

## Macros

*Recording and replaying your keystrokes*

Creating worksheets often involves the repetitive typing of certain entries and commands. To help you avoid some of this tedium, many spreadsheet programs let you define and use macros. This capability is very similar in concept to the keyboard macro facilities found in some word processing packages. With a macro, you can store a sequence of keystrokes and replay this sequence later by pressing a single combination of keys or making a menu selection. For example, if you must frequently enter the names of the months across a single row, as in several of the worksheets in this chapter, you can automate this process with a macro. With some spreadsheet programs you must type the keystrokes for a macro into cells in an unused part of the worksheet. Other programs let you store macro definitions in a separate file so that you can use them in any worksheet. Special words or phrases are used to symbolize the pressing of certain keys. For example, with Lotus 1-2-3 you type {right} to symbolize pressing the Right Arrow key. Other spreadsheet packages make the process of initially defining a macro easier by providing a **learn**

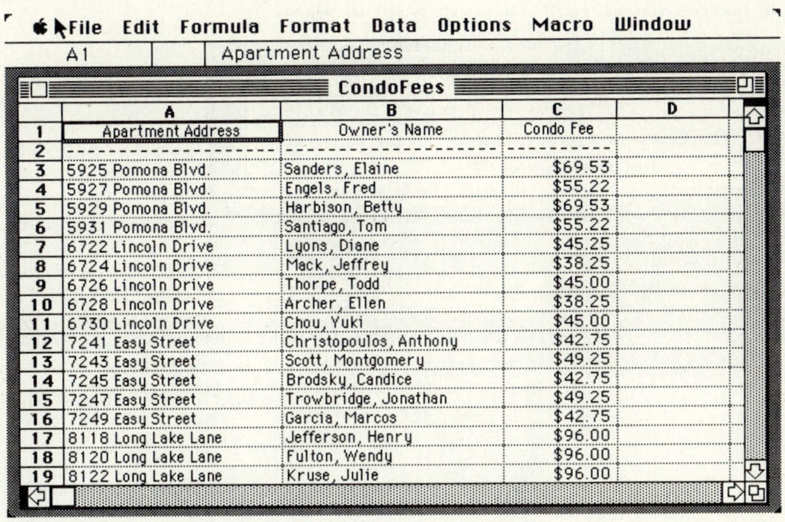


**Figure 8.14 Spreadsheet Data Management**
Spreadsheet programs can be used to maintain simple data tables, such as this information about the Parkridge Condominium Association units, owners, and condominium fees.

**mode**. Once you put the spreadsheet program into learn mode, every keystroke you make is recorded until you exit that mode. These keystrokes then become the macro that you can "play back" later. Once you define the macro, you have to name it and choose a keystroke combination that will replay it.

Macros are one of the most sophisticated features offered by spreadsheet programs. In addition to reducing repetitive typing, macros can execute command sequences and formulas that are complicated or difficult to remember. Some spreadsheet packages even let you create macros that can compare values, make decisions, and perform different actions based on these decisions. This makes the macro facility almost as powerful as a full-fledged programming language. With these sophisticated macros, worksheets can display messages on the screen, prompt you for input, store your responses in specified cells, and proceed to calculate formula results. Interactive worksheets can be created to walk you through every step of solving a particular problem.

## Templates

*Filling in the blanks*

The condominium association budget we have used as an example throughout this chapter is a special-purpose worksheet. Its sole objective is to generate a budget for the Parkridge Condominium Association. The square root worksheet in Figure 8.10, on the other hand, is a general-purpose worksheet. All you have to do is change the number in cell A1, and this worksheet will compute the square root of any number. A general-purpose worksheet like this one, in which you fill in the blanks or change selected entries, is called a **template** or sometimes a **form**. Templates are worksheets that contain text labels, formulas, and perhaps some constant numbers; you must supply the variables. Figure 8.15 illustrates another template to compute the monthly payment on a loan, given the principal, interest rate, and term. Initially, the cells that are supposed to contain these given values are empty, as you see in Figure 8.15(above); they will be filled by whoever uses this template. The error message in cell A4, the result of a division by zero in the PMT (payment) function,

**Figure 8.15 Loan Payment Template**

Above is the empty template.

Below values have been entered for the amount of the loan, annual interest rate, and term of the loan. The monthly payment was calculated by the worksheet.

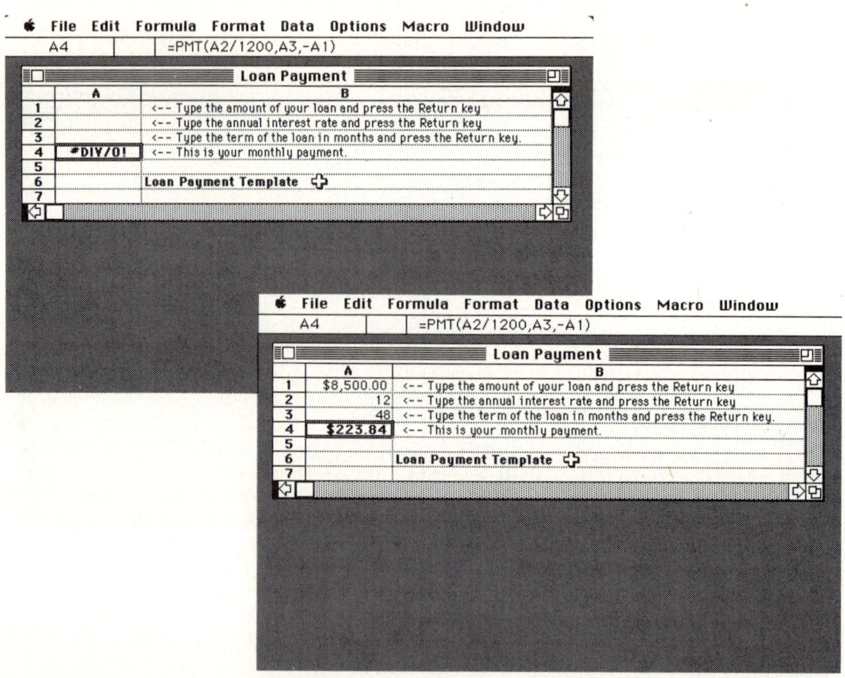


will disappear when actual values are entered into cells A1, A2, and A3. For example, let's say that you are thinking of buying a new car. All you have to do is enter the amount you need to borrow (the principal) in cell A1, the annual interest rate in cell A2, and the term of the loan (how many monthly payments you must make) in cell A3. This template has been prefabricated by the author to compute the monthly payment and display it in cell A4. Figure 8.15(below) shows what the template looks like after some hypothetical values are entered into cells A1, A2, and A3. Templates are a way for novices to use ready-made worksheets designed by experts. They often may be obtained from colleagues, copied from computer magazines, or purchased from software development firms.

## Protecting Cells

*Helping prevent accidents*

Worksheets that are designed to be templates generally contain labels, formulas, and constant numbers that should not be changed. The creator of the template carefully designed and tested it to ensure that it works correctly. The best way to keep it working correctly is to prevent a user from accidentally changing cells that should remain unchanged. One way to do this is to hide the cells, as we described earlier in the chapter. Another way is to protect the cells that should not be changed. A **protected** or **locked cell** is one that cannot be altered, deleted, or moved unless it is first *unprotected*. Typically, you can protect one or more cells by selecting those cells and executing a Protect command. In addition, there is usually a command to protect all the cells in a worksheet. To unlock cells, you need to execute an Unprotect command. For even more security, some spreadsheet programs let you choose a password when you initially protect all the cells in a worksheet. This protection cannot be turned off later unless you first reenter the correct password.

## Multiple Windows

*Opening new vistas*

With spreadsheet programs, you can easily create worksheets too large to entirely fit on your screen at once. Comparing cells in two distant portions of a large worksheet can be very frustrating if you must keep scrolling the screen back and forth or up and down. And what if you want to look at two different worksheets at the same time? Fortunately, many spreadsheet programs offer a solution to these problems. Multiple windows can be created to simultaneously view different parts of the same worksheet or completely different worksheets. Although you can only edit one worksheet at a time, you can usually cut-and-paste or copy-and-paste data from one window to another. Often spreadsheet programs allow only two windows on the screen at a time. You simply execute a Window command and indicate whether the screen is to be split vertically or horizontally. A special key or combination of keys is pressed to switch from one window to the other. Spreadsheet packages with graphics interfaces, such as those that run on Apple Macintoshes, often allow you to create any number of windows on your screen. Windows can be resized and moved anywhere on the screen. To switch from one window to another, you simply move the mouse pointer to any visible portion of the desired window and press the mouse button. The selected window then becomes active and is moved to the forefront. Figure 8.16 shows how Microsoft Excel for the Macintosh can present several different worksheet windows on the screen at the same time.

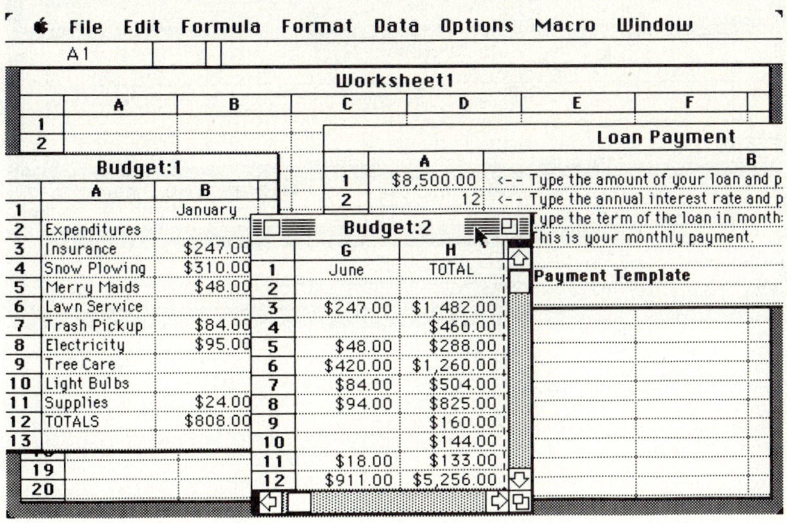


**Figure 8.16 Multiple Windows**
Spreadsheet programs such as Microsoft Excel let you open as many windows on your screen as you like. These windows can be loaded with different views of the same worksheet, or of entirely different worksheets.

## Merging Worksheets

*Copying data from one worksheet to another*

Even spreadsheet programs that do not support multiple windows have ways to copy data from one worksheet to another. This is usually called **merging** or **combining** worksheets. One way to do this is to execute a Combine command that prompts you for the name of a worksheet file and perhaps a range of cells to be copied. Data is then copied from this file into your current worksheet with the upper-left corner at the current cell pointer position. Other spreadsheet packages use a temporary storage area known as a **clipboard**. You first select a range of cells in the source worksheet and copy the data there to the clipboard. Then you exit the source worksheet and load the target worksheet. Finally, you move the cell pointer to the desired position and copy data from the clipboard into the target worksheet.

Spreadsheet programs can offer several options for merging worksheets. For example, the contents of the selected cells in the source worksheet may be simply copied, overwriting the contents of corresponding cells in the target worksheet. Alternatively, the contents of the selected cells from the source worksheet may be added to the corresponding cells in the target worksheet. Figure 8.17 illustrates this type of merge. Using the add option, the contents of Worksheet 1 were merged with the contents of Worksheet 2 to produce what you see in Worksheet 3. Besides allowing you to add, some spreadsheet programs also let you subtract, multiply, or divide cell contents when merging worksheets. Although merging is generally used to combine numeric values from one worksheet with another, some spreadsheet programs also allow you to transfer formulas, labels, and cell format settings such as for numeric display and alignment.

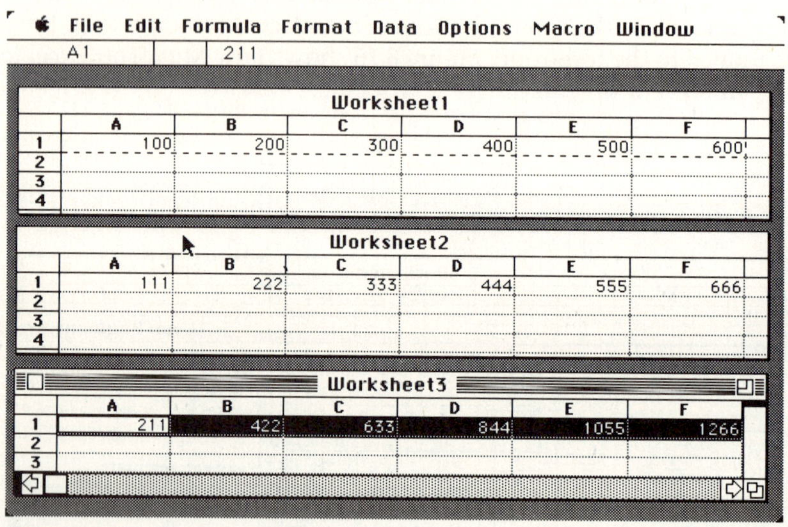


**Figure 8.17 Add Merging Two Worksheets** Worksheet 3 was created by merging Worksheets 1 and 2, and adding their contents.

## Linking Worksheets

*Connecting cells in different files*

In this chapter, you have seen many instances in which one cell in a worksheet was dependent on the value of one or more other cells. Figure 8.15, for example, shows how the value displayed in cell A4 is dependent on the values in cells A1 through A3. You could say that the value displayed in cell A4 is *linked* to the values currently in cells A1, A2, and A3. Whenever you change any of the values in A1, A2, or A3, the value in A4 also changes. Note, however, that this dependent relationship between cells only exists within this one particular worksheet. There are situations in which it would be nice if cells in *different* worksheets could be linked. This would allow you to have values in one worksheet dependent on the values of certain cells in another worksheet. Some spreadsheet programs allow you to link worksheets in this manner.

Figure 8.18 illustrates the linking of two worksheets. The Parkridge Condominium Association budget was modified to link the monthly income cells to the sum of the individual condominium fees, stored in the worksheet of Figure 8.14. This allows the fees to be kept in just one place: the table of units, owners, and condominium fees in the Condominium Fees worksheet. Instead of our inserting an actual number in the Budget worksheet for each month's condominium fees, the sum is obtained directly from the Condominium Fees worksheet. If condominium fees ever have to be increased, they need only be changed in one place: the Condominium Fees worksheet. By permanently linking related worksheets, it's much easier to make revisions and still keep your numbers accurate.

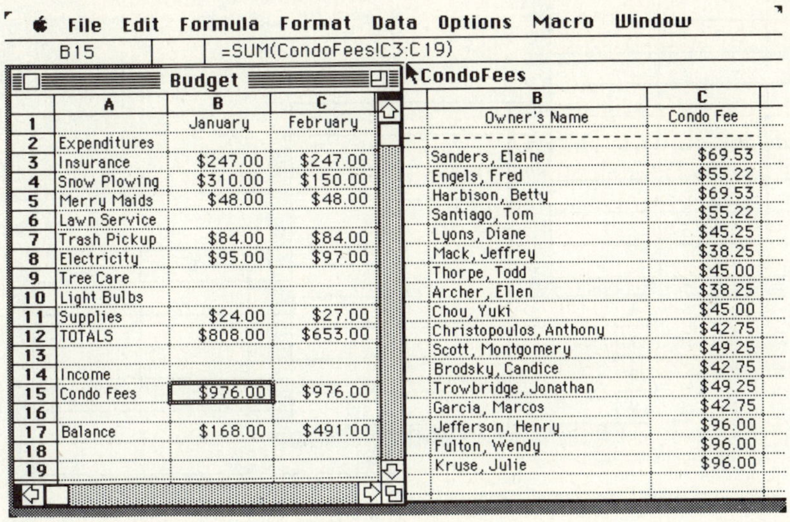


**Figure 8.18 Linking Worksheets**
The Parkridge Condominium Association Budget worksheet has been linked to the CondoFees worksheet. The sum of the condominium fees is computed from the CondoFees worksheet and inserted into cell B15 of the Budget worksheet.

## Multidimensional Spreadsheets

*Stacks of worksheets*

**Multidimensional spreadsheet** programs carry linking to its logical extreme: they allow every cell in a worksheet to be connected to corresponding cells in other worksheets. Although some multidimensional spreadsheet programs provide as many as eight dimensions, three-dimensional spreadsheets are the most common. A third dimension creates a kind of "super-worksheet" that is like a stack of conventional worksheets. Perhaps the easiest way to envision a three-dimensional worksheet is as a sequence of pages, each of which is a table of rows and columns (see Figure 8.19). So, the address of the fourth cell in the third row of the second page of a three-dimensional worksheet would be 2D3. How might you use a three-dimensional worksheet? For instance, let's say that the Parkridge Condominium Association has been in existence for several years. Every year a budget is prepared and the surplus balance from the previous year is carried over. If a three-dimensional worksheet is used, each year's budget could be put on a different page. Although relatively few spreadsheet programs with multidimensional capabilities are currently on the market, some computer-industry experts expect this advanced feature to become increasingly common.

## Moving Data Between Applications

*Transferring data from one program to another*

In addition to being able to transfer data between worksheets, many spreadsheet programs also can work with other application programs. For example, worksheet files often can be loaded into a word processing or data base management package. Data often can be loaded into a worksheet from text files created by word processing or data base management software. Some spreadsheet programs can even load worksheet files from other spreadsheet programs. Microsoft Excel, for example, can

**Figure 8.19 Multidimensional Worksheet**
A three-dimensional worksheet is like a sequence of individual worksheet pages in which all corresponding cells are connected.

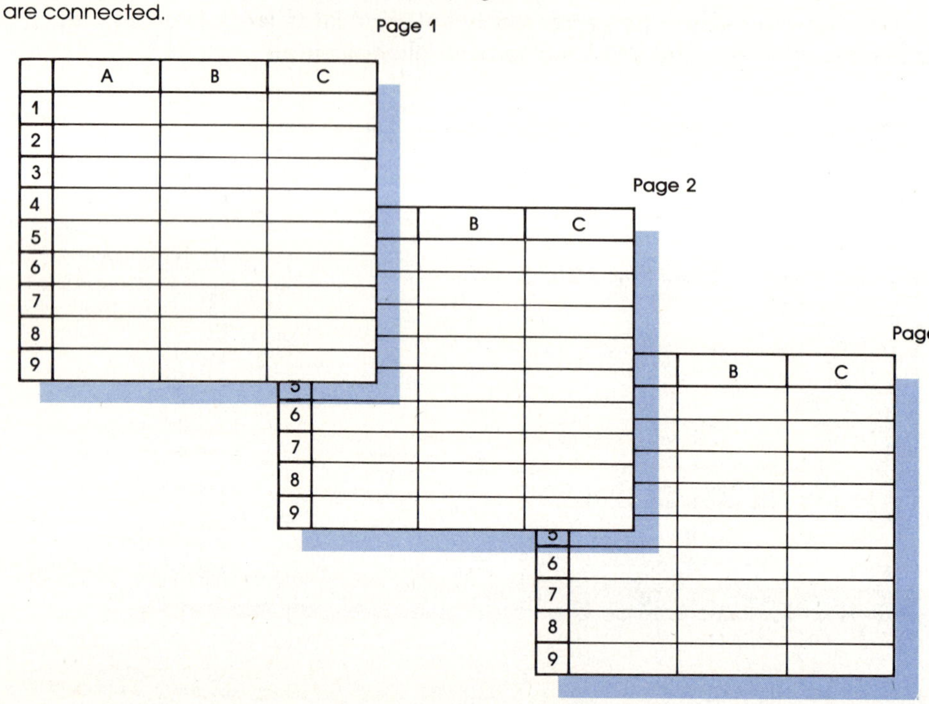


directly load worksheets created by Lotus 1-2-3, and save worksheets in files that can be directly loaded into 1-2-3. Many graphics programs and desktop publishing packages can accept graphs and charts created by popular spreadsheet programs. Although you may have to experiment a little and perhaps reformat some entries, it's usually possible to perform at least some transfers of data and graphics between a spreadsheet program and other types of application software.

## POPULAR SPREADSHEET PROGRAMS

*Leading contenders*

Early in microcomputer history, there were only a few really popular spreadsheet packages. The Apple II world was dominated by VisiCalc and the IBM-compatible world was dominated by Lotus 1-2-3. When the Apple Macintosh came along in 1984, some spreadsheet programs were developed to run on it, but there was no single package as popular as VisiCalc was on Apple IIs or 1-2-3 was on IBM-compatibles. Today, VisiCalc is no longer sold and there are many popular spreadsheet programs. Besides Lotus 1-2-3, SuperCalc and Microsoft Excel are among the most noteworthy.

### Lotus 1-2-3

*All-time best seller*

As you may already know, Lotus 1-2-3 has become almost synonymous with the word *spreadsheet*. It is probably the best-selling application software package of all time. Ever since 1-2-3 was introduced in 1982, it has been the spreadsheet program against which all others are compared. This program not only has one of the most powerful spreadsheets in the business, it also includes graphics and data management capabilities. These three major components give 1-2-3 its name. Lotus 1-2-3 is still by far the most popular spreadsheet program for IBM-compatibles. It has an especially loyal following in corporate and business markets. Although Lotus had not yet released a version of 1-2-3 for Apple Macintosh computers at the time of this book's printing, it has announced its intention to do so. It will be interesting to see how 1-2-3 fares in the Macintosh arena.

## SuperCalc

*Spreadsheet veteran*

SuperCalc is a veteran spreadsheet package. It's one of the few programs that was originally released *before* Lotus 1-2-3, yet still survives. Now sold by Computer Associates International, SuperCalc began as a spreadsheet program for computers running under the CP/M operating system, including Apple II computers equipped with a CP/M circuit board. When IBM introduced its Personal Computer, SuperCalc was adapted to run on it. Soon, SuperCalc 2 and SuperCalc 3 were introduced. SuperCalc 2 had improved formatting and macro capabilities, while SuperCalc 3 included graphics and data management. The latest incarnation is SuperCalc 5, a powerful, well-designed program for IBM-compatibles that can easily hold its own against the likes of Lotus 1-2-3. Although not as popular as 1-2-3, SuperCalc 5 is a fine product with a substantial following of fiercely loyal users.

## Microsoft Excel

*For both Macintoshes and IBM-compatibles*

Microsoft Excel is a flexible package that has become the top-selling spreadsheet program for the Apple Macintosh. When Microsoft introduced an IBM-compatible version of Excel in 1987, *PC Magazine* declared it to be "unquestionably the most powerful PC spreadsheet you can buy." It has a graphics interface that makes extensive use of pull-down menus, windows, and a mouse. Like Lotus 1-2-3, Excel also offers data management, but its graphics abilities are more advanced and easier to use. Microsoft, arguably the leading microcomputer software developer, certainly has the technical know-how and marketing savvy so that Excel can be a strong competitor of the entrenched Lotus 1-2-3.

### The Real World

### What the Numbers Know

Stewart Brand, Editor in Chief of *Whole Earth Software Catalog*:

"Spreadsheet programs have given me this peculiar vision of civilization. What I find new and wonderful about computerized spreadsheets is that you can have a vast array of meaningful numbers, and *all the numbers know about each other*. Change any one of them, and they all adjust immediately. They're positively ecological in that. The same goes for economies. Increasingly, all the numbers in the world know about each other. The value of your stock knows about the amount of change in my pocket as well as the turns of war in the Sudan and the quality of growing seasons in Colombia. The change in my pocket is ever alert to what you're deciding not to buy this week."

"Computers are in the thick of that. A study I keep waiting for is a productivity analysis of what personal computers have done for the national economy in the last couple years—without any government intervention or even policy (except the decades of military research that invented the field in the first place—and the defending of patent rights). Some say that half of all IBM PCs are running just 1-2-3. Numbers—clever, quick, knowledgeable—boiling the stupidity out of countless business decisions."

Source: *Whole Earth Software Catalog* by Stewart Brand, Editor in Chief. Copyright 1984 by Point (Foundation), Quantum Press/Doubleday, p. 65.

## Summary

- *The general structure of a worksheet.* A worksheet is a table of rows and columns of cells.
- *The data that can be entered into a worksheet.* Numbers, text labels, and formulas are the three types of data that can be entered into a worksheet. Formulas can contain ready-made procedures called functions.
- *How data can be manipulated in a worksheet.* New data is simply entered into cells. Existing data can be easily modified. Rows and columns can be inserted and deleted. Ranges of cells can be selected and data can be moved and copied.
- *How to format the contents of a worksheet.* Spreadsheet programs let you specify numeric formats, column widths, the type of alignment, and whether formulas or formula results are to be displayed.
- *How formula results are calculated in a worksheet.* Most spreadsheet programs offer automatic or smart recalculation, but they also have a manual recalculation feature. Natural recalculation is the method most often used to ensure results are calculated in the correct order. Circular references must usually be avoided, but they are sometimes purposely used with iterative recalculation.
- *How to print a worksheet.* Simply select the page formatting options and execute the Print command.
- *How to save and retrieve worksheets in disk files.* Execute the File Save command to store a worksheet; use the File Retrieve or Open command to load an existing worksheet.
- *Additional spreadsheet program features.* Many spreadsheet packages also allow you to produce graphs, manage data tables, create macros, create templates, protect cells, use multiple windows, merge worksheets, link worksheets, create multidimensional worksheets, and move worksheet data between applications.
- *Which popular spreadsheet programs are currently on the market.* Three of the most noteworthy spreadsheet programs are Lotus 1-2-3, SuperCalc, and Microsoft Excel.

## Key Terms

As an extra review of this chapter, try defining the following terms. If you have trouble with any of them, refer to the page number listed.

absolute cell reference (290)
automatic recalculation (294)
cell (281)
cell address (281)
cell pointer (285)
circular reference (296)
clipboard (303)
column-wise recalculation (295)
current cell (active cell) (285)
fixed currency format (291)
formula (282)
function (283)
hidden column (292)
iterative recalculation (iteration) (296)
label (282)
learn mode (300)
manual recalculation (294)
merging (combining) (303)
mixed cell reference (291)
multidimensional spreadsheet (305)
natural recalculation (295)
protected cell (locked cell) (302)
range (281)
relative cell reference (290)
row-wise recalculation (295)
smart recalculation (intelligent recalculation) (294)
template (form) (301)
worksheet (279)

## Review Questions

1. What is the main function of spreadsheet programs?
2. What is the cell address of the tenth column of the sixth row in a worksheet?
3. Why are labels used in worksheets?
4. Write a formula that adds the contents of the first five cells in column B.
5. Give an example of a computation that would be impossible without using a function.
6. How is the active cell typically indicated on the screen?
7. Why would you use an absolute cell reference in a formula?
8. Which numeric format would you use if you had extremely large or small values?
9. Why might you specify a column width to be 0?
10. What are the three types of alignment for labels and numeric values?
11. Why might you shut off automatic or smart recalculation?
12. What is one way to resolve certain indirect circular references?
13. Why are most worksheets saved in disk files?
14. How are worksheets used as simple data managers?
15. Why might you create a spreadsheet macro?
16. What is a good reason to protect one or more cells?
17. Besides simply copying data, what other operations are sometimes offered by spreadsheet programs that can merge worksheets?
18. What advanced feature lets you make a cell in one worksheet dependent on values in another worksheet?
19. What is a three-dimensional worksheet?
20. What is the single most popular spreadsheet program?

## Multiple Choice

1. The intersection of a row and a column in a worksheet is called a
   (a) macro. (b) cell.
   (c) formula. (d) function.
2. The range C3:D6 refers to which of the following sets of cells?
   (a) C3, C4, C5, C6, D3, D4, D5, and D6 (b) C3, C4, C5, and C6
   (c) D3, D4, D5, and D6 (d) A1, B2, C3, and D6
3. Which is not a basic type of data that can be entered into a worksheet cell?
   (a) number (b) label
   (c) formula (d) pointer

4. Which of the following Microsoft Excel formulas adds the contents of cells A1, A2, A3, A4, and A5?
   (a) =COUNT(A1:A5) (b) =AVG(A1:A5)
   (c) =SUM(A1:A5) (d) =A1+A5
5. Unless you specify otherwise, most spreadsheet packages assume all cell addresses are
   (a) macros. (b) relative cell references.
   (c) absolute cell references. (d) mixed cell references.
6. If you want numbers in a worksheet to be preceded by dollar signs and to have two places to the right of the decimal point, you should use
   (a) general format. (b) integer format.
   (c) scientific format. (d) fixed currency format.
7. A hidden column may be one with a width of
   (a) 0. (b) 10.
   (c) 100. (d) 1000.
8. A spreadsheet program that immediately updates the entire worksheet whenever you change the contents of a cell is using
   (a) automatic recalculation. (b) manual recalculation.
   (c) smart recalculation. (d) intelligent recalculation.
9. Which of the following recalculation methods is used by most modern spreadsheet packages?
   (a) row-wise recalculation (b) column-wise recalculation
   (c) natural recalculation (d) circular recalculation
10. Before you can change or update an existing worksheet, you must
    (a) perform iterative recalculation. (b) print a report.
    (c) retrieve its file from disk and load it into memory. (d) create a macro.
11. Which spreadsheet feature allows you to store a long sequence of keystrokes and replay it later by pressing a single combination of keys or selecting a menu option?
    (a) formula (b) macro
    (c) function (d) clipboard
12. A general-purpose worksheet that lets you perform a task by simply filling in the blanks is called a
    (a) formula. (b) macro.
    (c) function. (d) template.
13. Worksheets are often merged to
    (a) make larger worksheets. (b) add the contents of corresponding cells.
    (c) save disk space. (d) use three dimensions.
14. A three-dimensional worksheet can be envisioned as a
    (a) stack of conventional worksheet pages. (b) pie chart.
    (c) circular reference. (d) macro template.

15. Which of the following spreadsheet packages was first developed for the Apple Macintosh?
    (a) Lotus 1-2-3
    (b) SuperCalc 5
    (c) Microsoft Excel
    (d) PC-Calc+

## Projects

1. In this chapter we have briefly described many of the basic and advanced features offered by today's spreadsheet programs. Try to find a few other features we have not mentioned and write a paragraph describing each of these. Periodicals like *PC Magazine*, *BYTE*, *MacWorld*, *Mac User*, and *InfoWorld* may be your best sources of information.
2. Although there aren't as many spreadsheet packages on the market as word processors, there are more than just the three products we've discussed in this chapter. Research three other popular spreadsheet programs and write a paragraph or two about each one. Again, computer magazines and newspapers are a good source of information. Try to find issues that contain product reviews of spreadsheet programs.
3. Do you think that you would use a spreadsheet package at school, work, or home? Specifically, for what tasks would you use one? Based on the descriptions we've given and the research you have done for the previous question, which spreadsheet package would you choose? Why?
4. Spreadsheet programs are an extremely popular type of application package, especially in the business community. Consequently, many add-on software products have been introduced that are designed to enhance the use of spreadsheet packages like Lotus 1-2-3. For example, many ready-made templates are sold to help you with common accounting chores and figuring your income taxes. There are products that add more ease and power to spreadsheet graphics and data management capabilities. For people who never want to leave the comfortable confines of their favorite spreadsheet package, there are even products that make spreadsheet programs behave like simple word processors, complete with spelling checkers. Research two or three of these add-on products and write a paragraph about each one. Do you think they are truly useful, or are they merely trying to capitalize on the current popularity of the spreadsheet package they claim to "enhance?" Again, computer magazines and newspapers are probably your best sources of information.

# 9

# Spreadsheet Details: Lotus 1-2-3

## In This Chapter

- Working with 1-2-3
  - Starting 1-2-3 with the Lotus Access System
  - Starting 1-2-3 Directly
- The 1-2-3 Screen
  - The Blank Worksheet
  - Menus
  - Help
- Entering and Editing Data
  - Moving the Cell Pointer
  - Typing Entries
    - Numbers
    - Labels
    - Formulas
  - Editing Cells
  - Inserting and Deleting Rows and Columns
  - Moving and Copying Data
- Formatting Data
  - Numeric Formats
  - Column Widths
  - Alignment
  - Displaying Formulas
- Calculating Results
  - Formulas and Operators
  - Order of Operations
  - Recalculation
- Printing the Worksheet
- Saving and Retrieving Worksheets
- Additional Features
  - Graphing
  - Data Management
  - Macros
  - Templates
  - Hiding and Protecting Cells
  - Split-Screen Windows
  - Combining Worksheets
  - Translating Data between Applications

## PREVIEW

If you could learn only one spreadsheet program, which would it be? For IBM-compatible microcomputers, the choice is clear: Lotus 1-2-3. It may no longer be the fastest, most powerful, easiest-to-use, most feature-packed spreadsheet on the market, but 1-2-3 is close enough for a great majority of people. This program, without a doubt the best-selling spreadsheet, is probably the world's single most popular application package. Millions of copies are sold every year. More than 3 million copies of Lotus 1-2-3 were sold in the second quarter of 1987 alone. Lotus Development Corporation, the company that sells 1-2-3, rivals Microsoft Corporation for being the world's leading software developer. Consequently, 1-2-3, with its massive installed base, is the spreadsheet against which all others are measured, and it will continue to be a force to contend with for the foreseeable future. Learning at least a little about using 1-2-3 is almost a prerequisite for computer literacy.

After studying this chapter, you will understand

- how to start 1-2-3.
- the various components of the 1-2-3 display screen.
- how to enter new data into a worksheet and change existing data.
- how to control the appearance of a worksheet.
- the way in which 1-2-3 calculates formula results.
- how to print a worksheet.
- how to save and retrieve a worksheet.
- some additional features included in Lotus 1-2-3.

## WORKING WITH 1-2-3

*On a hard disk, in subdirectory \123*

As you might expect, there have been several releases of Lotus 1-2-3 since its introduction in 1982. A great deal of similarity exists between the versions, especially in the way you use the program. For the examples in this chapter, we'll be using Lotus 1-2-3 Release 2.01 for IBM and IBM-compatible microcomputers. Nevertheless, much of what we cover also applies to other 1-2-3 releases.

When you purchase 1-2-3, you get several manuals, diskettes, and quick reference guides. The manuals include a small guide to setting up 1-2-3, a tutorial booklet, and a reference manual. In Appendix C we discuss the contents of the 1-2-3 diskettes and how to install the package on your computer. For the examples in this chapter, Lotus 1-2-3 has been installed on a hard disk in a subdirectory named 123.

### Starting 1-2-3 with the Lotus Access System

*Programs included with the 1-2-3 package*

The **Lotus Access System** is a program called *Lotus* that lets you start 1-2-3 or any of the other programs that come with the package, including:

- *PrintGraph*, which lets you print your 1-2-3 graphs.
- *Translate*, which lets you transfer data between 1-2-3 and other application packages.
- *Install*, which lets you set up 1-2-3 to use a printer and display graphs.
- *View*, which is an onscreen tutorial program that helps you learn about 1-2-3.

**Insight**

## Lotus 1-2-3 and IBM Sales

Never has one spreasheet done so much for one company.

Of all the microcomputer spreadsheets ever developed, experts say that Lotus 1-2-3 has boosted IBM sales more than any other computer applications product.

The reason goes back into the dim mists of computer history. People who used VisiCalc, the first spreadsheet package, found that it had serious limitations. One problem was that to execute a series of commands, the same sequence of keystrokes had to be entered over and over. A second problem was that VisiCalc has only a limited capability for presenting graphics. In the days of the early CP/M-based machines and the Apple II series of computers, however, this was not a serious drawback.

Then along came the IBM PC and its various compatible machines. They were the Boy Wonders of the computer world, with up to 16 times as much memory and 15 times the speed of the CP/M machines they were replacing. The IBM PC also had a screen-graphics capability that exceeded anything seen before, except in specialized graphics terminals and mainframe computers.

Lotus Development Corporation saw the gap between the primitive but sound ideas of VisiCalc and the IBM PC. The resulting package, Lotus 1-2-3, took the business world by storm.

The graphics capabilities of Lotus 1-2-3 support a whole range of graphs, such as pie charts, line charts, and bar graphs. Frequently used keystroke sequences can be stored as part of the spreadsheet and called on as necessary with a single keystroke.

Lotus 1-2-3 is the most widely sold and imitated spreadsheet package ever designed, and may, in itself, be reason enough to buy a microcomputer.

Let's assume the computer is already turned on and you have booted DOS. Furthermore, let's assume the computer has 1-2-3 installed on a hard disk in a subdirectory named 123. First, you must switch to the 123 subdirectory by entering **CD \123**. Then, type **LOTUS** and press the **Enter** key to start the Lotus program. Figure 9.1 shows what appears on your screen. At this point, you simply press the **Enter** key to run 1-2-3.

### Starting 1-2-3 Directly

*Bypassing the Lotus Access System*

The Lotus Access System makes it easy to switch back and forth between 1-2-3 and the other programs that come with the package. You can also run each of these programs directly and simply not use the Lotus Access System. For example, to run 1-2-3 from a hard disk, you first switch to the 123 subdirectory by entering **CD \123**. Then you type **123** and press **Enter** to actually start the 1-2-3 program. It doesn't matter whether you use the Lotus Access System or start 1-2-3 directly. Either way, 1-2-3 briefly displays the copyright screen you see in Figure 9.2.

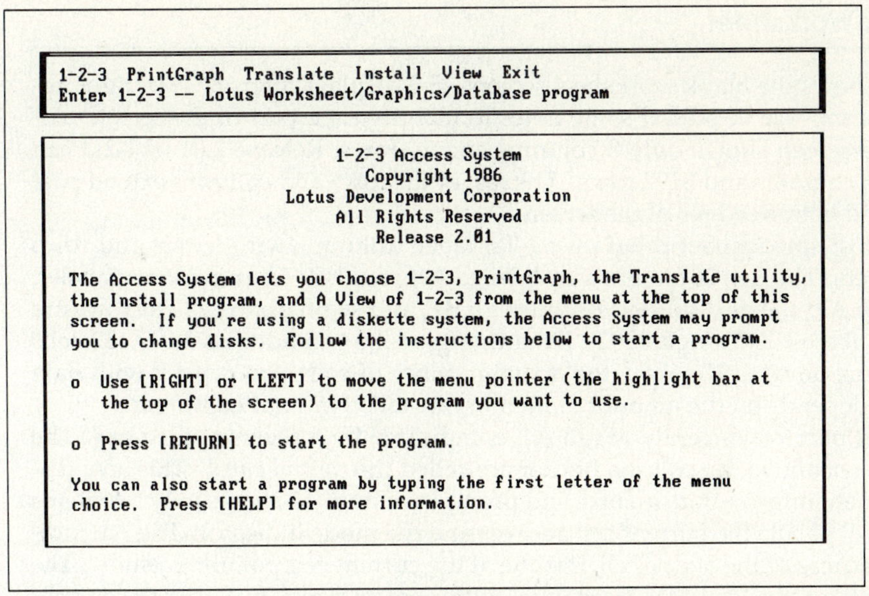


**Figure 9.1 The Lotus Access System**

This is the screen you see when you enter **LOTUS** from the DOS prompt.

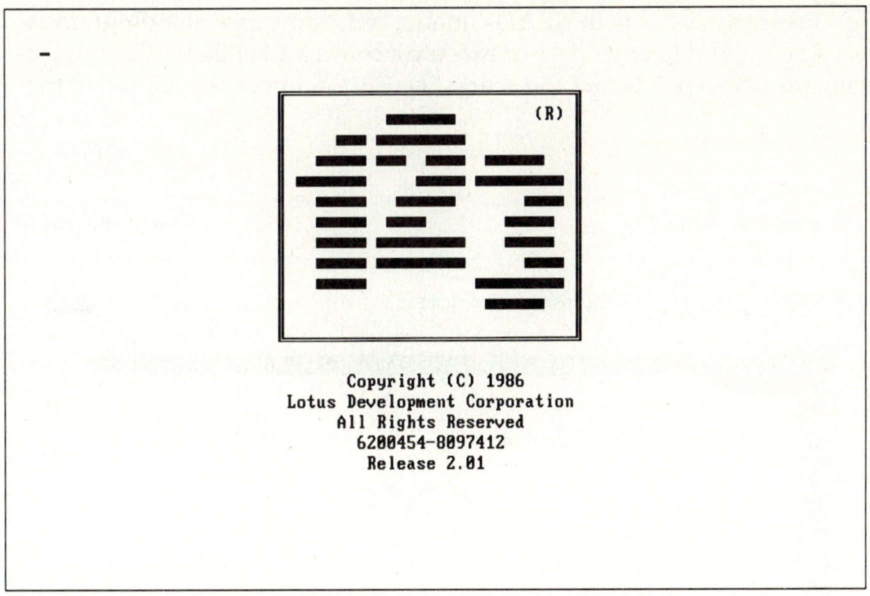


**Figure 9.2 The 1-2-3 Copyright Screen**

Whether you use the Lotus Access System or start 1-2-3 directly, this screen appears for a moment.

## THE 1-2-3 SCREEN

*Enter data, activate menus, execute commands*

After the copyright notice disappears, 1-2-3 displays a screen that, among other items, contains a blank worksheet. Here you can enter data, activate menus, and execute commands. Before we go on to the specifics of actually using 1-2-3, let's take a look at how the screen is organized.

## The Blank Worksheet

*256 columns and 8192 rows*

Figure 9.3 shows the blank worksheet screen 1-2-3 displays after the copyright notice disappears. We've added some notes to identify each part of the screen. Although this screen shows only 8 columns and 20 rows, Release 2.01 of 1-2-3 can address 256 columns and 8192 rows. The rest of the rows and columns extend past the right and bottom edges of the screen.

Like most spreadsheet programs, 1-2-3 labels columns with letters and rows with numbers. The first 26 columns are labeled A through Z. The next 26 are labeled AA through AZ, the next labeled BA through BZ, and so on up to IV. The rows are simply numbered 1 through 8192. Even though 1-2-3 can address 2,097,152 cells (256 columns times 8192 rows), the actual number of cells you can fill with data ultimately depends on the amount of memory installed in your computer.

The cell pointer, currently at cell A1, is indicated by a reverse-video bar. The three lines just above the column border are called the *control panel*. This area displays pertinent information, menus, and prompts. Figure 9.3 shows only two items in the control panel: the current cell address and the mode indicator. The A1: indicates the address of the active cell, the one at the current cell pointer position. The contents of the active cell are also shown in the control panel, just after the current cell address. Since the worksheet is still empty, nothing is displayed in the control panel for the contents of the current cell. The mode indicator is the highlighted block in the upper-right corner of the control panel. This tells you what 1-2-3 is currently doing. Presently, 1-2-3 is in READY mode, indicating that the program is ready and waiting for you to enter data or execute a command. Finally, the current date and time are displayed below the worksheet in the lower-left corner of the screen.

**Figure 9.3 The Blank 1-2-3 Worksheet Screen**

After the copyright notice disappears, a blank worksheet appears on your display. The notes have been added to point out important parts of the screen.

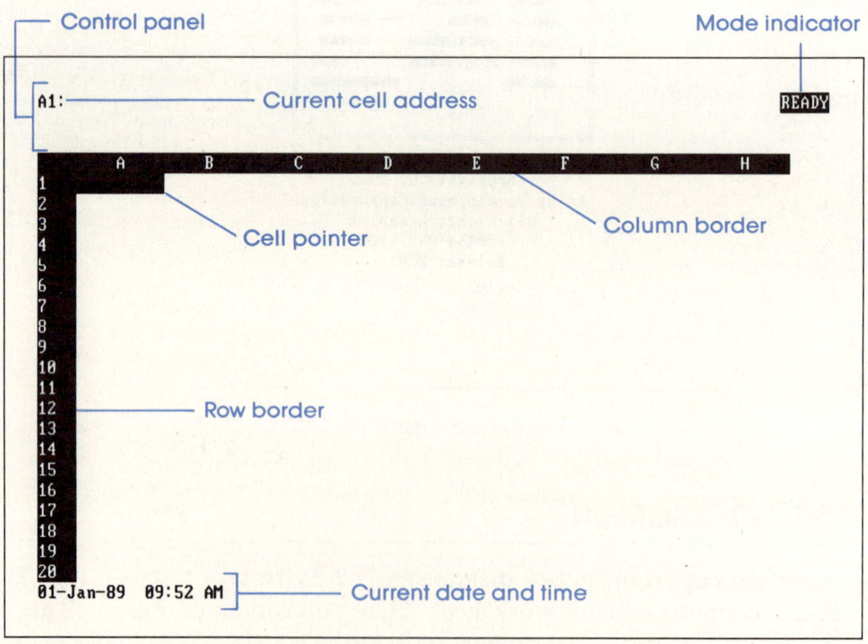

## Menus

*Selecting commands*

To accomplish many tasks in 1-2-3, you select commands from menus that appear in the control panel. When 1-2-3 is in READY mode, as in Figure 9.3, no menu appears in the control panel. You need to press the forward slash (/) key to activate the Main menu. Figure 9.4 shows what 1-2-3 displays when you press this key. Notice that the mode indicator now says MENU. The second line of the control panel shows the commands that are available in the Main menu. Right now, Worksheet is highlighted. The third line of the control panel displays a submenu or a description of the highlighted command. A **submenu** is simply another menu that is activated by selecting an option from a higher-level menu. In this case, if you choose the Worksheet command, the submenu you see directly below it will be activated.

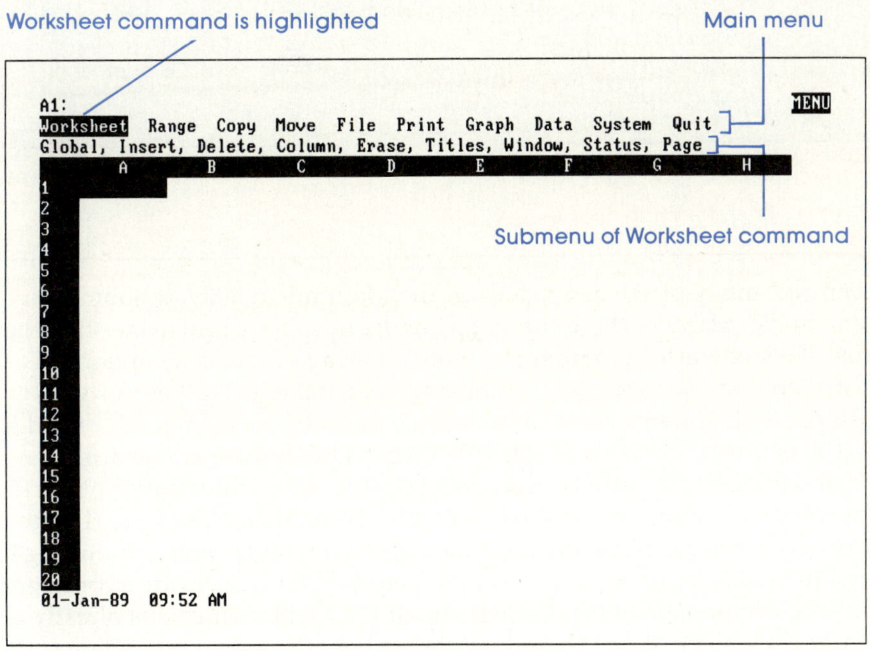


**Figure 9.4 The Main Menu**
After you press / (forward slash), the Main menu appears in the control panel. Notes have been added.

There are two ways to select an option from any 1-2-3 menu. The first is to highlight the option and press the **Enter** key. You can move the highlight bar from one option to the next by pressing the Left Arrow or Right Arrow keys. For example, if you press the Right Arrow key, the highlight will move from Worksheet to Range. The other way to select a command from a 1-2-3 menu is to type the command's first letter. Every item in a 1-2-3 menu begins with a different letter. To select the File command, for instance, all you have to do is type **F**. Many people prefer the latter method because it often involves fewer keystrokes.

Menus are the means by which you select and execute 1-2-3 commands. Commands let you edit, format, and otherwise manipulate data, as well as control the appearance, disk storage, and output of 1-2-3 worksheets. Although we cannot cover every 1-2-3 command in detail, we will describe several of the most important in this chapter. In addition, Table 9.1 lists each command in the Main menu, along with a brief description.

**Table 9.1 Lotus 1-2-3 Main Menu Commands**

| COMMAND | ACTION |
|---|---|
| Worksheet | Activates a submenu of commands that let you control the overall appearance of the worksheet, make major changes to its contents, control 1-2-3's overall work methods, and change some disk directory and printer settings. |
| Range | Activates a submenu of commands that let you perform operations on a rectangular block of one or more cells. |
| Copy | Allows you to copy a range of one or more cells. |
| Move | Allows you to move a range of one or more cells. |
| File | Activates a submenu of commands that let you manage your worksheet files. |
| Print | Allows you to send all or part of your worksheet to a printer or a file. |
| Graph | Activates a submenu of commands that let you graph your data. |
| Data | Activates a submenu of commands that let you enter and analyze data in a worksheet. |
| System | Allows you to temporarily suspend 1-2-3, perform a DOS operation, and return to 1-2-3. |
| Quit | Ends your session with 1-2-3 and returns to DOS. |

## Help

*Learning more about 1-2-3*

As you can see, many of the commands in the Main menu activate submenus of other commands. Many of these submenu commands, in turn, activate still other submenus. This powerful program has quite an array of available options. Few people learn how to use every 1-2-3 command. Fortunately, 1-2-3 comes with excellent tutorial and reference manuals to teach you about the commands. In addition, 1-2-3 has a very good on-line help facility. This feature is like a reference manual that automatically opens to the correct page to reveal information about the particular command or area of the program with which you are working. The help facility can also further explain any error messages you might receive for trying to perform an invalid activity. Let's see how the help facility can provide information about the 1-2-3 commands in the Main menu. If the Main menu is not already on the screen, type / to bring it up. To find out more about this menu, simply press the **F1** function key. Your work is temporarily suspended and 1-2-3 displays the screen you see in Figure 9.5.

Each help screen includes a menu of topics about which you can get further information. In Figure 9.5, for example, the topic /Worksheet is highlighted. To find out more about this topic, press the **Enter** key. To select another topic, move the highlight with the arrow keys and then press the **Enter** key. When you are finished with the help facility, simply keep pressing the **Escape** key until you return to the worksheet screen.

# ENTERING AND EDITING DATA

*Constructing a worksheet*

One of the advantages of using 1-2-3 is that the program makes it easy to enter and edit data. At the simplest level, this involves moving the cell pointer, typing entries, editing cells, inserting and deleting rows and columns, and copying and moving data.

```
A1:                                                                      HELP
Worksheet  Range  Copy  Move  File  Print  Graph  Data  System  Quit
Global, Insert, Delete, Column, Erase, Titles, Window, Status, Page
--------------------------------------------------------------------------------
1-2-3 Commands

Select a command from the menu on the second line of the control panel or
press [ESCAPE] to return to READY mode.

1-2-3 commands establish overall procedures; copy, move, and delete data in
the worksheet; change numeric formats; transfer data to and from disk storage;
print your work; draw graphs; handle databases; and let you leave 1-2-3:

/Worksheet          /Move          /Graph          /Quit
/Range              /File          /Data
/Copy               /Print         /System


To cancel a command and back up one step, press [ESCAPE].

To cancel a command and return to READY mode, press [BREAK].

--------------------------------------------------------------------------------
Command Menus            Help Index
01-Jan-89  09:52 AM
```

**Figure 9.5 Help Screen**
Press **F1** to bring up the help facility and reveal more information about your current activity.

## Moving the Cell Pointer

*Many ways to move in the worksheet*

The easiest way to move the cell pointer is to use the arrow keys. Pressing the Up Arrow key moves the cell pointer to the row directly above, pressing the Right Arrow key moves the cell pointer to the next column to the right, pressing the Down Arrow key moves the cell pointer to the row directly below, and pressing the Left Arrow key moves the cell pointer to the previous column to the left. To scroll the worksheet beyond the 8 columns or 20 rows initially on the screen, simply continue moving the cell pointer once you reach the edge of the screen. For example, to scroll the worksheet to the right, press the **Right Arrow** key until the cell pointer is in column H. Then press the **Right Arrow** key again; column A disappears off the left side of the screen and column I appears on the right side.

Although you can move the cell pointer quite rapidly by holding down an arrow key to repeat keystrokes, the 1-2-3 worksheet is very large. Fortunately, 1-2-3 has even quicker methods of moving the cell pointer to different parts of the worksheet. Pressing the Home key always returns the cell pointer to cell A1. The Page Up (PgUp) and Page Down (PgDn) keys move the cell pointer up or down one whole screen at a time. Holding down the Control (Ctrl) key and pressing the Right Arrow key moves the cell pointer one whole screen to the right, and holding down the Control key and pressing the Left Arrow key moves the cell pointer one whole screen to the left.

There are even ways to immediately move to one particular edge of your worksheet. For example, to move to the bottom edge of your worksheet, press the **End** key, release it, and then press the **Down Arrow** key. If the worksheet is completely empty, this moves the cell pointer to row 8192. If you have data in your worksheet, this action moves the cell pointer to the last row in which you have data, assuming that the cell pointer started out in a row above this last one. Similarly, pressing and releasing the **End** key before pressing one of the other arrow keys moves the cell pointer to that edge of your worksheet.

Finally, 1-2-3 also provides a way to move to any particular cell in the worksheet. For example, let's say that the cell pointer is currently at A1 and you want to move to H10. Press the **F5** function key, which the 1-2-3 manuals call the GOTO key, and you are prompted with:

```
Enter address to go to: A1
```

The default destination is the current location of the cell pointer, A1. In other words, if you just press the Enter key, 1-2-3 will not move the cell pointer. To move to cell H10, type **H10** (which will erase the A1) and press the **Enter** key.

## Typing Entries

*How to enter data*

Once you move the cell pointer to the cell where you want a piece of data to go, you simply begin typing. Each character you type appears in the second line of the control panel. Just as in a word processor, a blinking underscore cursor indicates where the next character you type will appear. Any mistakes you make can be corrected by backspacing and retyping. The item you type isn't actually inserted into the worksheet until you complete the entry either by pressing the Enter key or by moving the cell pointer, perhaps with one of the arrow keys. No 1-2-3 data entry may be longer than 240 characters. As we said in the previous chapter, a worksheet cell holds one of three types of data: numbers, labels, or formulas.

### Numbers

*Quantities*

Numbers are the most common type of data found in most worksheets. The 1-2-3 program considers any entry that begins with one of the following characters to be a number:

```
0 1 2 3 4 5 6 7 8 9 . + - $ (
```

When typing a number, you should not include spaces, commas, or more than one decimal point. Numbers may begin with a currency symbol ($), end with a % to indicate a percentage, or be entered in scientific format. For example, 2.16E+05 may be entered instead of 216000.

### Labels

*Headings and notes*

Labels are text used for headings and explanations. Any entry that 1-2-3 determines is not a number or a formula is considered a label. If a label starts with a character normally associated with numbers or formulas, it must be preceded with a **label prefix character**. This is a special character that tells 1-2-3 the item that follows is a label and not a number or formula. Label prefix characters also tell 1-2-3 how to align labels within cells or if a character is to be repeated within a cell. There are four label prefix characters in 1-2-3:

- ' Aligns the label at the left edge of a cell.
- ^ Centers the label within a cell.
- " Aligns the label at the right edge of a cell.
- \ Repeats the following character within a cell.

Figure 9.6 illustrates the use of these four label prefix characters.

### Formulas

*Performing calculations*

In 1-2-3, a formula is an instruction to calculate or otherwise manipulate numbers or text. It can contain numbers (such as 100), operators (such as +), labels enclosed in double quotes (such as "Result"), and cell references (such as B10). To be recognized as such, a formula must begin with one of the following characters:

```
0 1 2 3 4 5 6 7 8 9 . + - ( @ # $
```

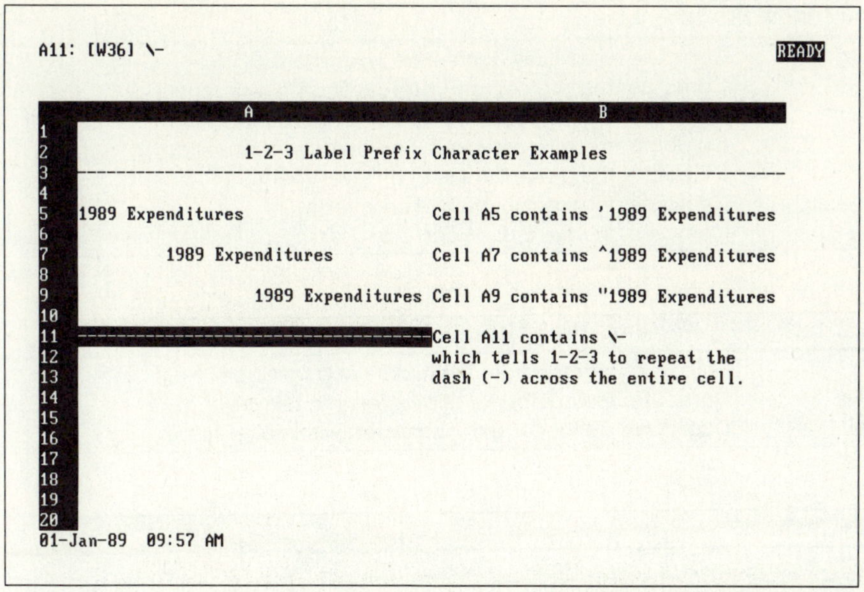


**Figure 9.6 Label Prefix Characters**
This worksheet demonstrates the use of 1-2-3's label prefix characters.

If the first part of a formula is a cell reference, it should be preceded with a plus sign, like this: +A1-B2. This simple formula subtracts the contents of cell B2 from the contents of cell A1.

In addition to numbers, operators, and cell references, formulas also can contain functions. You'll recall that a function is a built-in procedure that performs tedious, complex, or frequently used computations and other data manipulations. More than 80 functions are available in 1-2-3. All of them have names that begin with the @ character. This special character tells 1-2-3 that the characters that follow represent the name of a function and not a label. Table 9.2 lists some of the most commonly used 1-2-3 functions.

**Table 9.2 Commonly Used 1-2-3 Functions**

| MATHEMATICAL FUNCTIONS | |
|---|---|
| @ABS | Computes the absolute value of a number. |
| @INT | Returns the integer (whole number) part of a number. |
| @MOD | Computes the remainder (modulus) of a division operation. |
| @RAND | Gives a random number between 0 and 1. |
| @ROUND | Rounds a value to a given number of decimal places. |
| @SQRT | Computes the square root of a number. |

| STATISTICAL FUNCTIONS | |
|---|---|
| @AVG | Computes the average of a list of values. |
| @COUNT | Computes the number of entries in a list of values. |
| @MAX | Returns the largest value in a list of values. |
| @MIN | Returns the smallest value in a list of values. |
| @STD | Computes the standard deviation of a list of values. |
| @SUM | Computes the sum of a list of values. |
| @VAR | Computes the variance of a list of values. |

| FINANCIAL FUNCTIONS | |
|---|---|
| @FV | Computes the future value of an investment. |
| @IRR | Computes the internal rate of return of an investment. |
| @NPV | Computes the net present value of an investment. |
| @PMT | Computes the payment on a loan per payment period. |
| @PV | Computes the present value of an investment. |
| @RATE | Computes the rate of return of an investment. |
| @TERM | Computes the number of loan payments. |

| TEXT FUNCTIONS | |
|---|---|
| @MID | Extracts characters from the middle of a text label. |
| @LENGTH | Computes the number of characters in a text label. |
| @REPEAT | Duplicates a sequence of characters within a text label. |

| LOGICAL FUNCTIONS | |
|---|---|
| @IF | Returns one number if a condition is true, another if false. |
| @ISERR | Returns TRUE (the number 1) if a calculation error occurred. |

| DATE AND TIME FUNCTIONS | |
|---|---|
| @DATE | Returns a code number representing the given date. |
| @TIME | Returns a code number representing the given time of day. |
| @NOW | Returns a code number representing the current date and time. |

| TRIGONOMETRIC FUNCTIONS | |
|---|---|
| @COS | Computes the cosine of an angle. |
| @SIN | Computes the sine of an angle. |
| @TAN | Computes the tangent of an angle. |
| @PI | Returns the value of $\pi$ (approximately 3.1415926). |

| LOGARITHMIC FUNCTIONS | |
|---|---|
| @EXP | Computes the value of the constant e raised to a given power. |
| @LN | Computes the natural (base e) logarithm of a value. |
| @LOG | Computes the base 10 logarithm of a value. |

## Editing Cells

*Changing a cell's contents*

There are two basic ways to change the existing contents of a cell. You can move the cell pointer back to that cell and re-enter its entire contents, or you can edit the cell. The latter method can save you time if you need to change a small portion of a long label or formula. With the cell pointer on the cell you want to change, press the **F2** function key. This puts 1-2-3 into EDIT mode and displays the current cell contents on the second line of the control panel. The cursor is placed just past the end of the entry in the control panel. When you are in EDIT mode, 1-2-3 lets you move the cursor within the current entry and make changes. The Left Arrow and

Right Arrow keys are used to move the cursor one character at a time. The Home key moves the cursor to the first character in the entry and the End key moves the cursor just past the last character in the entry. By default, 1-2-3 inserts any characters you type into the existing cell contents at the current cursor position. You can switch between overwriting and inserting by pressing the Insert key. The Backspace key erases the character to the immediate left of the cursor, while the Delete key erases the character at the current cursor position. You can even erase the entire entry by pressing the Escape key. When you are finished editing, you press the Enter key to actually put what you've edited into the current cell.

## Inserting and Deleting Rows and Columns

*Adding new data and removing old data*

One of the reasons word processors are superior to typewriters is that they make it very easy to add and remove text anywhere in a document. Similarly, spreadsheet programs make it easy to insert and delete rows and columns of cells anywhere in a worksheet. To perform these operations in 1-2-3, you use the Insert and Delete commands from the Worksheet submenu. For example, let's say that you want to insert a new row between rows 3 and 4 in the worksheet in Figure 9.7(a). First you move the cell pointer to a cell in row 4. Then you type a / (slash) to activate the Main menu, a **W** to activate the Worksheet submenu, an **I** to select the Insert command, and an **R** to choose the Row option. As Figure 9.7(b) shows, 1-2-3 prompts you to enter the row insert range, and it suggests A4..A4. This means that unless you specify otherwise, 1-2-3 will insert only one row after row 3. To insert more than one row, you could enter a new range. For instance, entering A4..A5 would insert two rows. To insert just one row, all you have to do is press the **Enter** key to select the range A4..A4 initially suggested by 1-2-3. The contents of row 4 and any rows below row 4 are shifted down one row, and a new blank row is inserted after row 3. Figure 9.7(c) illustrates the final effect of this command.

As you can see, the contents of rows 4 and 5 have been shifted down to rows 5 and 6, respectively. Spreadsheets, however, generally do more than just shift data when rows are inserted. Before the insertion, cell A5 contained the formula @SUM(A1..A4). The A1 and A4 in this formula are relative cell references. As we said in the previous chapter, relative cell references are automatically adjusted to account for any changes in position whenever cells are inserted, deleted, moved, or copied. After the new row was inserted between rows 3 and 4, the formula was moved to cell A6, but it was not merely copied. Cell A6 now contains the formula @SUM(A1..A5). The 1-2-3 program automatically adjusted the second cell reference in the formula to account for the inserted row. Although relative cell references are the most common in worksheet formulas, 1-2-3 also allows absolute and mixed cell references. These are indicated by preceding the column and row designations with a dollar sign, as we described in the previous chapter.

Inserting a column is almost the same as inserting a row, except that you type **C** to choose the Column option after typing **/WI** to invoke the Worksheet Insert command. Deleting rows or columns is also very similar. To delete column B, for example, move the cell pointer to a cell in column B, type **/WDC**, and press the **Enter** key. This executes the Worksheet Delete Column command, removing the column currently occupied by the cell pointer. The contents of all columns to the right of the cell pointer are shifted one column to the left. Any formulas containing relative cell references are adjusted as needed.

(a)

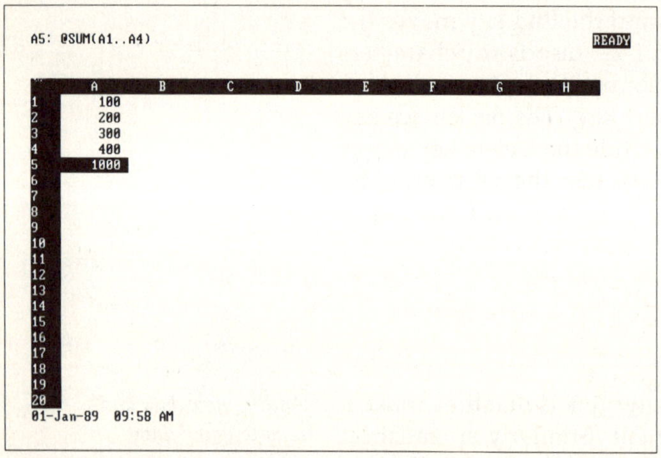


(b)

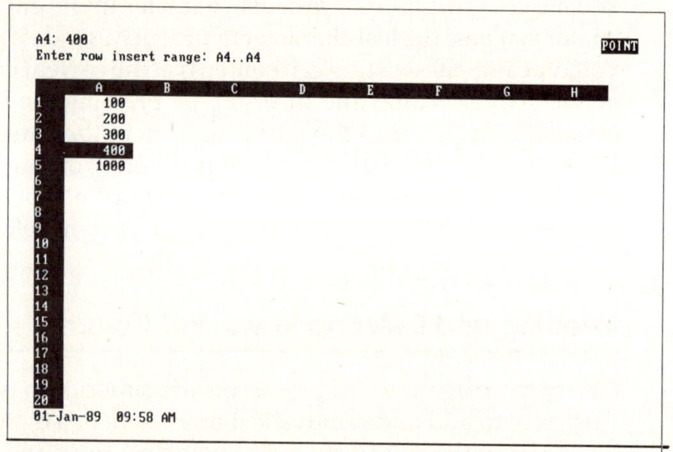


(c)

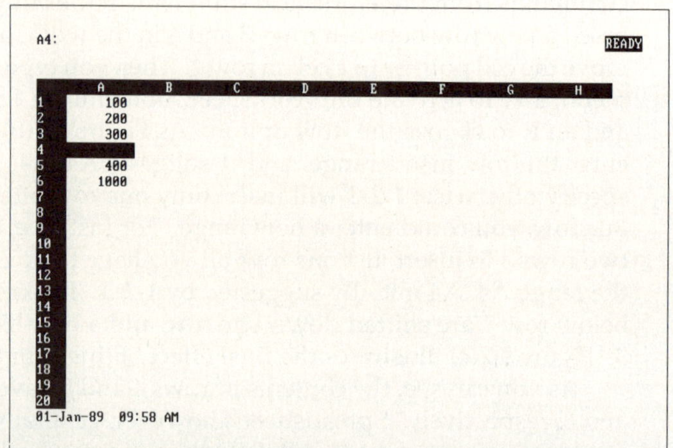


**Figure 9.7 Inserting a Row**

(a) The original worksheet.

(b) Position the cell pointer and type **/WIR** to execute the Worksheet Insert Row command. The program suggests A4..A4 as the insert range.

(c) Press **Enter** and 1-2-3 inserts a new blank row.

## Moving and Copying Data

*"Cutting and pasting" data*

Like most spreadsheets, 1-2-3 can also move and copy data. For example, let's take the data in the worksheet in Figure 9.7(a) and move it to a different location. First place the cell pointer in the upper-left corner of the range of cells to be moved. Then type **/M** to execute the Move command from the Main menu. Figure 9.8(a) shows that 1-2-3 then prompts you for the range of cells you want to move. Notice that the mode indicator says POINT, just as it did in Figure 9.7(b). With many 1-2-3 commands, there are two ways to select a range. One way is to simply type the range and press the **Enter** key. In this example, 1-2-3 initially suggests that A1..A1 is the range of cells you want to move. You could type A1..A5 and press the Enter key to tell 1-2-3 which cells you want to move, but in POINT mode you can also specify a range by highlighting it. In this case, simply press the **Down Arrow** key four times to highlight cells A1 through A5, and then press the **Enter** key. As shown in Figure 9.8(b), 1-2-3 then prompts you to indicate the cell to which you want to move the selected range. You can either type a cell address, or move the cell pointer with the arrow keys to the cell where you want to move the selected range. To move the selected range to cell D1, for example, you can either type **D1** and press the **Enter** key, or press the **Right Arrow** key three times and then press the **Enter** key. Figure 9.8(c) shows the result.

(a)

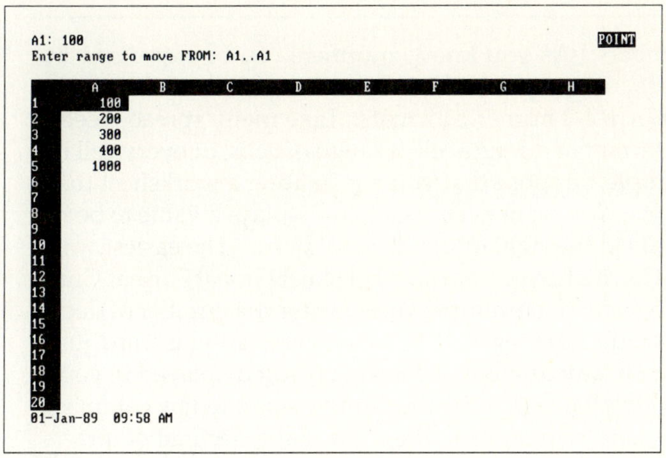


(b)

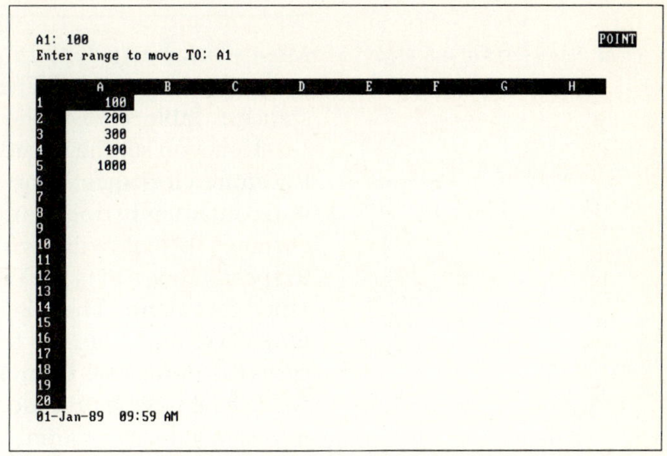


(c)

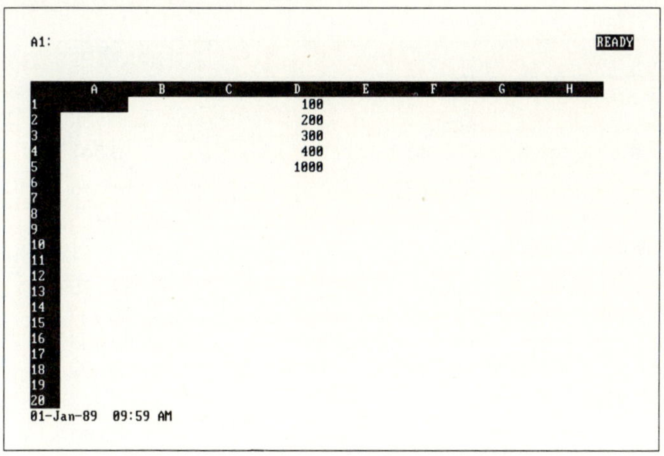


**Figure 9.8 Moving Data**

(a) Position the cell pointer and type **/M** to execute the Move command from the Main menu.

(b) Press the **Down Arrow** key four times and press the **Enter** key to select cells A1 through A5. Then 1-2-3 asks for the range to which you want to move the selected data.

(c) Either type **D1** and press **Enter**, or press the **Right Arrow** key three times and press **Enter** to move the data to column D.

Copying data in a 1-2-3 worksheet is very similar to moving data. All you do is enter **/C** to execute the Copy command instead of entering /M to execute the Move command. You specify the range of cells to be copied and then indicate where you want the copy to be placed. The only difference between the two commands is that the Copy command leaves the original range of cells intact, whereas the Move command does not. Both the Move and the Copy commands automatically adjust relative cell references in formulas as necessary.

## FORMATTING DATA

*Controlling the worksheet's appearance*

Spreadsheet programs help you organize, calculate, display, and print tables of numeric and textual data. An important part of performing these activities is being able to format your data. Formatting allows you to control the data's appearance, thereby letting you make the worksheets easy to use and read. Lotus 1-2-3 has commands for specifying numeric formats, column widths, alignment, and the display of formulas.

## Numeric Formats

*The many faces of numbers*

Most worksheets contain numbers. As you know, numbers can be expressed in many different ways. The particular expression you use depends on the circumstances. Table 9.3 lists the major 1-2-3 numeric formats. Like many spreadsheets, 1-2-3 lets you set the numeric format of a single cell, a range of cells, or every cell in the entire worksheet. For example, suppose that you are creating a worksheet that will contain only dollar amounts. You want every cell that displays a value to be in currency format, with two digits to the right of the decimal point. The easiest way to specify this is to type **/WGFC**, which executes the Worksheet Global Format Currency command. The 1-2-3 program then prompts you to enter the number of decimal places and suggests the default number of 2. Since this is what you want, just press the **Enter** key. From now on, any number or formula result displayed in your worksheet will be preceded by a dollar sign, with thousands separated by commas, negative values in parentheses, and two digits to the right of the decimal point.

**Table 9.3 Lotus 1-2-3 Numeric Formats**

| FORMAT | DESCRIPTION | EXAMPLES |
|---|---|---|
| Fixed | Numbers expressed with no commas, no dollar signs. You can specify the number of digits to the right of the decimal point (0 to 15). | 13<br>-542.798<br>0.361 |
| Scientific | Numbers expressed in exponential notation. You can specify the number of digits to the right of the point (0 to 15). | 5.7E+02<br>-5.789E+55<br>4.26E-21 |
| Currency | ($) sign appears before each entry; commas separate thousands; negative values are enclosed in parentheses. You can specify the number of digits to the right of the decimal point (0 to 15). | $25.75<br>($5.21)<br>$9,854<br>$0.52 |
| (comma) | Commas separate thousands; negative values are enclosed in parentheses. You can specify the number of digits to the right of the decimal point (0 to 15). | 9,854.00<br>(12,000)<br>0.52 |
| General | This is the default format used unless otherwise specified. Trailing zeros are suppressed, decimal places are used as necessary, and very large and very small numbers appear in scientific format. | 21.568<br>0.72<br>-5.64<br>2.14E+14<br>3E-09 |
| Percent | Numbers expressed as a percentage, that is the value times 100 followed by a percent (%) sign. You can specify the number of digits to the right of the decimal point (0 to 15). | 1324.5%<br>-8.25% |

The format command we just described is called *global* because it applies to every cell in the entire worksheet. In many instances, however, you need different numeric formats in the same worksheet. For example, let's say that cells A1 through A20 are to contain numbers that aren't dollar amounts. Perhaps these cells will be used to simply number the items in the worksheet. Cells B1 through B20, on the other hand, will contain dollar amounts. Since the default global format in 1-2-3 is General, the easiest thing to do is change the numeric format of cells B1 through B20 to Currency. Type **/RFC** and pressing the **Enter** key to execute the Range Format Currency command with two decimal places. The 1-2-3 program then prompts you to enter the range to format; you type **B1..B20** and press the **Enter** key. By offering the various formats listed in Table 9.3, Lotus 1-2-3 gives you a great deal of flexibility in the display of numeric values in your worksheets.

## Column Widths

*Make room for data*

The default column width in Lotus 1-2-3 is nine characters, but as we said in the last chapter, you may have to increase or decrease this width. Somewhat like numeric formats, column widths can be changed for a single column or for the entire worksheet. For example, look again at the worksheet in Figure 9.6. Before the data in this worksheet was entered, the widths of columns A and B were changed from the default value of nine characters to 36 characters. This was done by first moving the cell pointer to column A. Then the Worksheet Column Set-Width command was executed by typing **/WCS**. When you do this, 1-2-3 prompts you to enter a column width between 1 and 240. In this case, **36** was entered. Column A widened accordingly and the notation [W36] appeared in the control panel after the current cell address to indicate the new column width. This process was repeated for column B.

The command we've just described is generally used to set the width of individual columns. To change the width of every column in the entire worksheet, you use the Worksheet Global Column-Width command. For instance, let's say that you want to decrease the global column width to 5 because you know that all your numbers will be small and you want to fit more columns on the screen. You type **/WGC** and 1-2-3 prompts you to enter the global column width, as shown in Figure 9.9(a). Then you type **5** and press the **Enter** key (see Figure 9.9(b)). Figure 9.9(c) shows the result: all columns are now five characters wide and now 14 columns, A through N, fit on the screen.

## Alignment

*Justifying data*

Like most spreadsheets, Lotus 1-2-3 left-justifies labels and right-justifies numeric values by default. We've already discussed the use of label prefix characters to explicitly control the alignment of labels (see Figure 9.6). Unfortunately, Lotus 1-2-3 Release 2.01 does not allow you to alter the alignment of numeric values; all numbers and formula results are automatically right-justified within their cells. You can, however, change the default global alignment of labels from left-justified to right-justified or centered. For example, let's say that you want all labels in your worksheet to be automatically centered instead of left-justified. Before you begin entering labels, you must change the global label prefix. This is done by typing **/WGLC**, which executes the Worksheet Global Label-Prefix Center command. After you do this, all labels subsequently entered without a label-prefix character are automatically centered.

In addition to changing the global label prefix, you also can alter the alignment of an existing range of labels. This is done by using the Range Label command. Let's say that you have already entered labels in cells A1 through A10. Furthermore, suppose these labels are left-justified because you didn't change the default global label prefix. Now you decide that you want these labels to be centered. To center just the labels in cells A1 through A10, you type **/RLC** to execute the Range Label Center command. The program prompts you for the range of labels; you enter **A1..A10**. All labels within these cells are immediately centered.

(a)

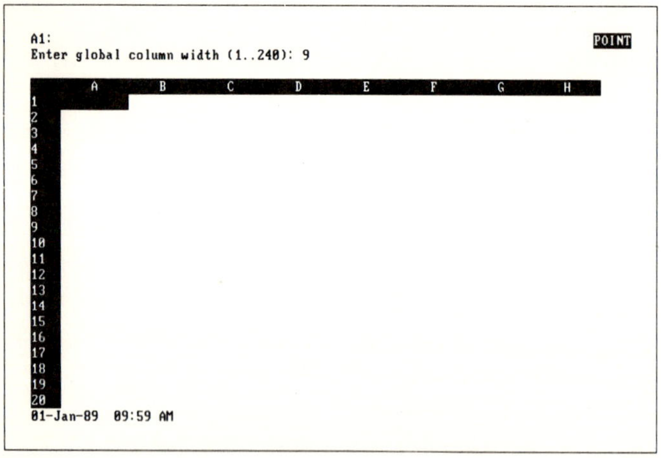


(b)

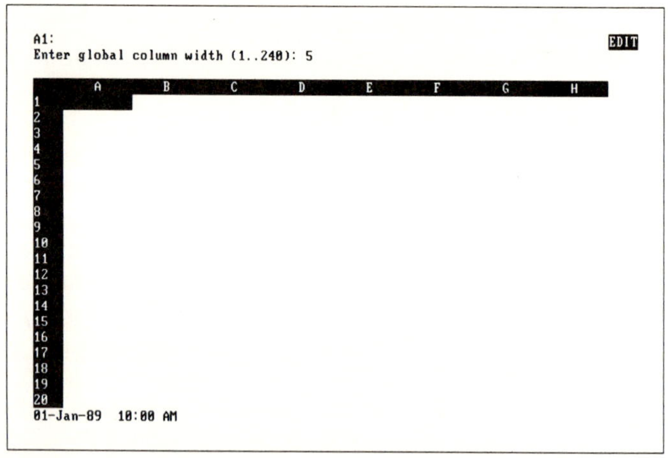


(c)

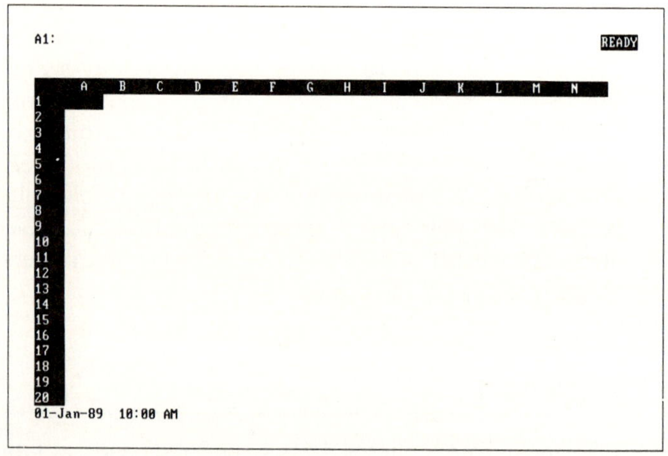


**Figure 9.9 Setting Global Column Width**

(a) First you type **/WGC** to invoke the Worksheet Global Column-Width command, and 1-2-3 prompts you with this message.

(b) Then you type **5** and press **Enter** to set the new global column width.

(c) The final result is a worksheet in which all columns are 5 characters wide.

## Displaying Formulas

*Seeing exactly what you entered*

As we said in Chapter 8, worksheets normally display formatted numbers and formula results. If you want to see the actual contents of a cell, you can move the cell pointer to that cell. The control panel shows the exact number or formula entered into that cell. Although this method of determining a cell's true contents works well for a single cell at a time, it is not very useful for looking at several cells at once. Displaying numbers and formulas as entered in their own cells can be very helpful when checking the accuracy of a complex worksheet. Fortunately, 1-2-3 lets you do this. You can display formulas in a range of cells by using the Range Format Text command. For example, to display any formulas in cells A1 to H20, you type **/RFT** and then enter **A1..H20**. Depending on the length of your formulas and the current width of your columns, you might also have to widen your columns.

## CALCULATING RESULTS

*Evaluating formulas*

The primary use of spreadsheets is to calculate the results of formulas that refer to data stored in worksheet cells. In fact, spreadsheets are so convenient for doing these calculations that many people use them without knowing exactly how they work. Simple worksheets with simple formulas are generally quite straightforward and calculations proceed just as you would expect. In some cases, however, it helps to know a little more about how your particular spreadsheet program calculates formula results.

### Formulas and Operators

*Symbols that tell formulas what to do*

As we have said, a formula is simply an expression entered into a cell that performs a calculation or some other data manipulation. You've already seen a few examples of formulas, but many more can be constructed with 1-2-3. Because of the flexibility with which you can construct formulas, 1-2-3 has the ability to perform an almost endless variety of tasks. Nevertheless, there are just three basic types of formulas:

- *Arithmetic.* These formulas manipulate numeric values and produce a numeric result.
- *Text.* These formulas manipulate labels and usually produce a label as a result.
- *Logical.* These formulas compare numeric values or labels and produce either TRUE (symbolized by a value of 1) or FALSE (symbolized by a value of 0).

An *operator* is a symbol that indicates a certain operation to be performed in a formula. Just as there are three basic types of formulas in 1-2-3, there are three types of operators:

- *Arithmetic.* These operators symbolize the most common mathematical procedures:

| | | | |
|---|---|---|---|
| + | (addition) | - | (subtraction or negative value) |
| * | (multiplication) | / | (division) |
| ^ | (exponentiation) | | |

  Exponentiation, you'll recall, means raising a number to a power. For example, 2^5 means 2 to the fifth power, which equals 32.

- *Text.* Only one operator in 1-2-3 manipulates labels. It is the text combination operator (&), which joins together two labels. For example, the formula "One"&" Hundred" produces "One Hundred".
- *Logical.* These operators produce a value of TRUE (1) or FALSE (0):

| | |
|---|---|
| = | (TRUE if two items are equal) |
| <> | (TRUE if two items are not equal) |
| > | (TRUE if first item is greater than the second) |
| < | (TRUE if first item is less than the second) |
| >= | (TRUE if first item is greater than or equal) |
| <= | (TRUE if first item is less than or equal) |
| #NOT# | (changes FALSE to TRUE and TRUE to FALSE) |
| #AND# | (produces TRUE only if both items are TRUE) |
| #OR# | (produces FALSE only if both items are FALSE) |

## Order of Operations

*How formulas are computed*

As you've seen, 1-2-3 has several operators that can be used in formulas. Frequently, more than one operator is used in a single formula. This brings up the question of the order in which operations are performed in a formula. For example, the formula 100+200/100 yields a different result depending on which operator you evaluate first. If you do the addition first, the result is 3; if you do the division first, the result is 102. Fortunately, there are well-defined rules that determine the order in which operations take place. Assuming there are no parentheses in an expression, operations proceed in the following order:

1. All exponentiations are performed, proceeding from left to right.
2. Values preceded by a unary minus sign are converted to negative.
3. All multiplications and divisions are performed, proceeding from left to right.
4. All additions and subtractions are performed, proceeding from left to right.
5. All of the following logical operations are performed, proceeding from left to right: =, <>, >, <, >=, <=.
6. All #NOT# operations are performed, proceeding from left to right.
7. All #AND# operations are performed, proceeding from left to right.
8. All #OR# operations are performed, proceeding from left to right.
9. All & (text combination) operations are performed, proceeding from left to right.

According to these rules, the correct result of the formula 100+200/100 is 102, because the division is performed before the addition. This default order of operations, however, can be altered by using parentheses. Any expressions enclosed in parentheses are to be evaluated first. If sets of parentheses are nested inside one another, the expression within the innermost set is evaluated first, and evaluation proceeds successively outward. So, the formula (100+200)/100 yields 3, because the expression enclosed in parentheses is evaluated first. In general, it's a good idea to use parentheses if you are not sure about the order in which operations will be performed. Besides eliminating uncertainty in your own mind, using parentheses makes your formulas more understandable to any other people who might also use your worksheet.

## Recalculation

*How calculations proceed*

In the previous chapter, we discussed some ways in which spreadsheet programs recalculate formulas when you change the contents of a worksheet cell. Like most advanced spreadsheets, Lotus 1-2-3 gives you some control over when, in what order, and how many times formulas are recalculated. By default, 1-2-3 uses automatic natural recalculation. This means that every time you change the contents of a cell, all formulas in the worksheet are automatically recalculated. Furthermore, before recalculating a particular formula, all other values on which it depends are recalculated first. Also by default, iterative recalculation is turned off, so that any circular references encountered in a formula are only attempted once. If a circular reference is found, 1-2-3 simply displays 0 in that cell and displays CIRC in reverse video at the bottom of the screen beneath the worksheet.

The Worksheet Global Recalculation command lets you change these default settings. Figure 9.10 shows the submenu that 1-2-3 displays when you type **/WGR** to execute this command. As you can see, there are five options: Natural, Columnwise, Rowwise, Automatic, Manual, and Iteration.

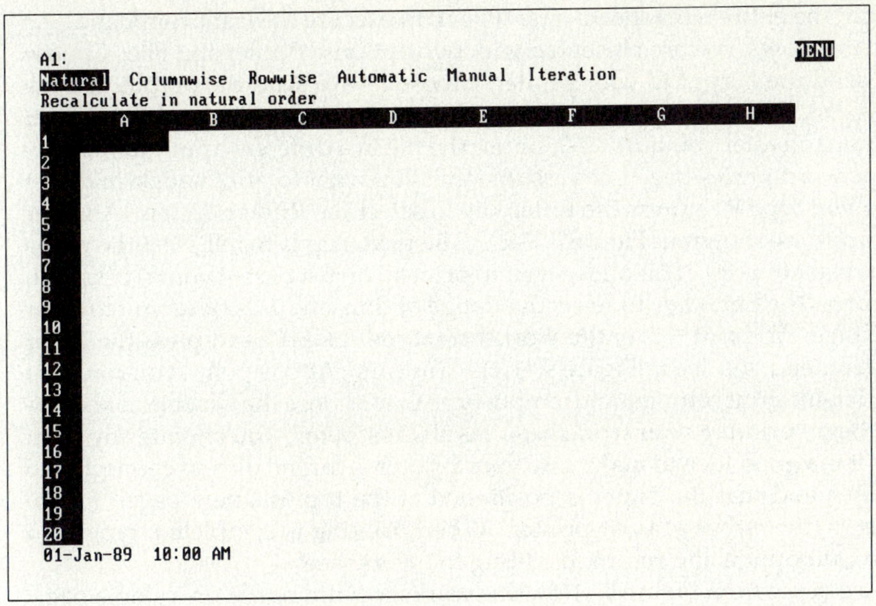


**Figure 9.10 Worksheet Global Recalculation**
This screen shows the Worksheet Global Recalculation submenu, which lets you change the way in which formulas are recalculated.

To change the *order* of recalculation, you choose either Natural, Columnwise, or Rowwise. As we said in Chapter 8, column-wise recalculation begins with cell A1, proceeds down column A, and then does the remaining columns in order; row-wise recalculation also begins with cell A1, but proceeds across row 1, then row 2, and so on. In most cases, the default setting of natural recalculation is preferable.

To change *when* recalculation occurs, you choose either Automatic or Manual. If you choose Manual, the worksheet will be recalculated only when you press the F9 function key. This allows you to enter data into a large or complex worksheet without having to wait for the program to update every cell. Unfortunately, Lotus 1-2-3 Release 2.01 does not have smart recalculation, so your only choices are Automatic and Manual.

Finally, to change *how many times* recalculation occurs, you use the Iteration option, which allows you to set the number of iterations from 1 to 50. If the order of recalculation is column-wise or row-wise, this number determines how many times the worksheet will be recalculated. If natural recalculation is in effect, this number determines how many times the worksheet will be recalculated when a circular reference occurs.

## PRINTING THE WORKSHEET

*Producing a hard copy*

Most worksheets are eventually printed on paper so that they can be distributed to other people. Lotus 1-2-3 allows you to print any part of a worksheet at any time while you are working on it. Several options are provided that give you some measure of control over the appearance of the final output. Let's use the Parkridge

Condominium Association budget we presented in the previous chapter to illustrate how to print a worksheet with 1-2-3. Assume that you have already entered, edited, and formatted the worksheet. Figure 9.11(a) shows what your screen would look like.

Because the screen is limited to a width of 80 characters, you cannot see the row totals, which are beyond the right edge in column H. Nevertheless, you can still tell 1-2-3 to print the entire worksheet. First type **/P** to execute the Print command. As Figure 9.11(b) shows, you are presented with two options: Printer and File. Choose Printer to send the output to your printer; choose File to send the output to a file saved on a disk. The File option lets you print the worksheet later with the DOS PRINT command after you quit 1-2-3, or use the file in a different application package, such as word processing. Let's assume that you want to print your worksheet directly, so you type **P** or press the **Enter** key to select the Printer option. Another submenu appears, shown in Figure 9.11(c). The next step is to tell 1-2-3 the range of cells you want to print. This allows you to print all or just part of your worksheet. Type **R** or press the **Enter** key to select the Range option, and 1-2-3 asks you to enter the print range. To print this entire worksheet, type **A1..H17** and press the **Enter** key. The submenu you see in Figure 9.11(c) reappears. At this point, you can elect to use the default print settings, and simply type **G** to choose the Go option and immediately begin printing your worksheet. As always, before you execute any print command it is a good idea to make sure your printer is turned on and connected to the computer, and that the paper is positioned at the top of a new page. Figure 9.11(d) shows the output of your printer. When printing is completed, type **Q** to choose the Quit option and return to editing the worksheet.

As you can see from Figure 9.11(d), this worksheet did not fit on a single page. The last column was put on a new page because 1-2-3 uses a default line length of 72 characters. Although Lotus 1-2-3 Release 2.01 cannot print worksheets sideways on a page, it can "compress" characters or print on wider paper, working with certain printers. The Options command you see in the submenu in Figure 9.11(c) activates another submenu that lets you do the following:

- Specify a header line to be printed at the top of every page.
- Specify a footer line to be printed at the bottom of every page.
- Set the left, right, top, and bottom margins of printed pages.
- Print the row border (1, 2, 3, etc.) along the left side of the worksheet.
- Print the column border (A, B, C, etc.) along the top of the worksheet.
- Specify a **printer setup string**—a group of special control codes directing the printer to turn on such options as compressed print.
- Specify the number of lines per page.
- Print a listing of the actual contents of each nonempty cell in the print range, one cell per line. For each cell, this listing shows what appears on the first line of the control panel when the cell pointer is on that cell. This option can be useful for checking the accuracy of a complex worksheet or producing a listing that describes exactly how to create an entire worksheet.
- Print the worksheet unformatted—without page breaks, headers, and footers.

## SAVING AND RETRIEVING WORKSHEETS

*Keeping worksheet files*

The ability to save and retrieve worksheets on disks is an important benefit of using a spreadsheet program. You can maintain, revise, update, and experiment with worksheets, like word-processed documents. You can save a partial worksheet

**Figure 9.11 Printing a Worksheet**

(a) This is the worksheet to be printed.

(b) Type **/P** to execute the Print command, and 1-2-3 presents two options: Printer and File.

(c) After you select Printer, another submenu appears. Type **R** and enter **A1..H17** for the range to print, and type **G** to execute the Go command.

(d) The printed copy of the worksheet on two pages.

(a)

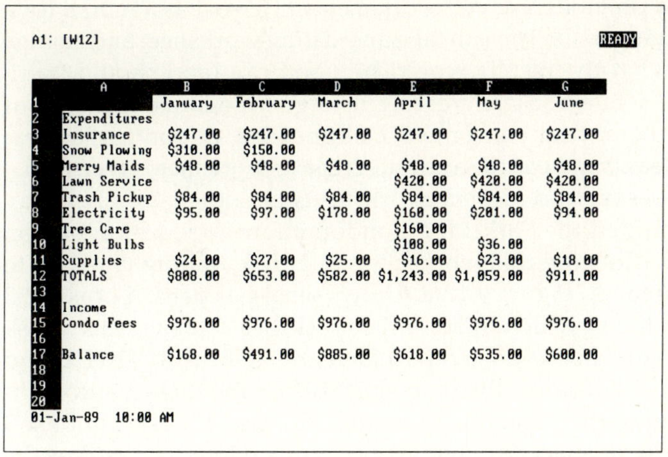

A1: [W12] READY

| | A | B | C | D | E | F | G |
|---|---|---|---|---|---|---|---|
| 1 | | January | February | March | April | May | June |
| 2 | Expenditures | | | | | | |
| 3 | Insurance | $247.00 | $247.00 | $247.00 | $247.00 | $247.00 | $247.00 |
| 4 | Snow Plowing | $310.00 | $150.00 | | | | |
| 5 | Merry Maids | $48.00 | $48.00 | $48.00 | $48.00 | $48.00 | $48.00 |
| 6 | Lawn Service | | | | $420.00 | $420.00 | $420.00 |
| 7 | Trash Pickup | $84.00 | $84.00 | $84.00 | $84.00 | $84.00 | $84.00 |
| 8 | Electricity | $95.00 | $97.00 | $178.00 | $160.00 | $201.00 | $94.00 |
| 9 | Tree Care | | | | $160.00 | | |
| 10 | Light Bulbs | | | | $108.00 | $36.00 | |
| 11 | Supplies | $24.00 | $27.00 | $25.00 | $16.00 | $23.00 | $18.00 |
| 12 | TOTALS | $808.00 | $653.00 | $582.00 | $1,243.00 | $1,059.00 | $911.00 |
| 13 | | | | | | | |
| 14 | Income | | | | | | |
| 15 | Condo Fees | $976.00 | $976.00 | $976.00 | $976.00 | $976.00 | $976.00 |
| 16 | | | | | | | |
| 17 | Balance | $168.00 | $491.00 | $885.00 | $618.00 | $535.00 | $600.00 |
| 18 | | | | | | | |
| 19 | | | | | | | |
| 20 | | | | | | | |

01-Jan-89 10:00 AM

(b)

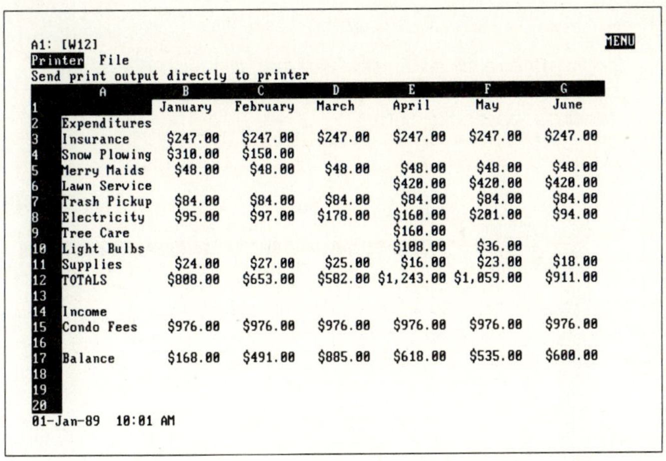

A1: [W12] MENU

Printer File

Send print output directly to printer

| | A | B | C | D | E | F | G |
|---|---|---|---|---|---|---|---|
| 1 | | January | February | March | April | May | June |
| 2 | Expenditures | | | | | | |
| 3 | Insurance | $247.00 | $247.00 | $247.00 | $247.00 | $247.00 | $247.00 |
| 4 | Snow Plowing | $310.00 | $150.00 | | | | |
| 5 | Merry Maids | $48.00 | $48.00 | $48.00 | $48.00 | $48.00 | $48.00 |
| 6 | Lawn Service | | | | $420.00 | $420.00 | $420.00 |
| 7 | Trash Pickup | $84.00 | $84.00 | $84.00 | $84.00 | $84.00 | $84.00 |
| 8 | Electricity | $95.00 | $97.00 | $178.00 | $160.00 | $201.00 | $94.00 |
| 9 | Tree Care | | | | $160.00 | | |
| 10 | Light Bulbs | | | | $108.00 | $36.00 | |
| 11 | Supplies | $24.00 | $27.00 | $25.00 | $16.00 | $23.00 | $18.00 |
| 12 | TOTALS | $808.00 | $653.00 | $582.00 | $1,243.00 | $1,059.00 | $911.00 |
| 13 | | | | | | | |
| 14 | Income | | | | | | |
| 15 | Condo Fees | $976.00 | $976.00 | $976.00 | $976.00 | $976.00 | $976.00 |
| 16 | | | | | | | |
| 17 | Balance | $168.00 | $491.00 | $885.00 | $618.00 | $535.00 | $600.00 |
| 18 | | | | | | | |
| 19 | | | | | | | |
| 20 | | | | | | | |

01-Jan-89 10:01 AM

(c)

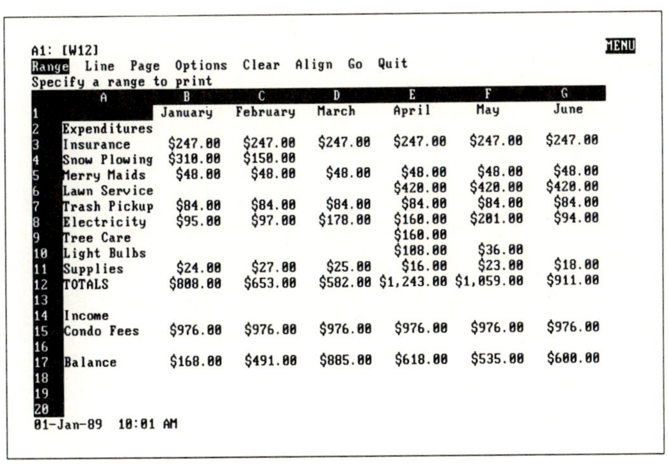

A1: [W12] MENU

Range Line Page Options Clear Align Go Quit

Specify a range to print

| | A | B | C | D | E | F | G |
|---|---|---|---|---|---|---|---|
| 1 | | January | February | March | April | May | June |
| 2 | Expenditures | | | | | | |
| 3 | Insurance | $247.00 | $247.00 | $247.00 | $247.00 | $247.00 | $247.00 |
| 4 | Snow Plowing | $310.00 | $150.00 | | | | |
| 5 | Merry Maids | $48.00 | $48.00 | $48.00 | $48.00 | $48.00 | $48.00 |
| 6 | Lawn Service | | | | $420.00 | $420.00 | $420.00 |
| 7 | Trash Pickup | $84.00 | $84.00 | $84.00 | $84.00 | $84.00 | $84.00 |
| 8 | Electricity | $95.00 | $97.00 | $178.00 | $160.00 | $201.00 | $94.00 |
| 9 | Tree Care | | | | $160.00 | | |
| 10 | Light Bulbs | | | | $108.00 | $36.00 | |
| 11 | Supplies | $24.00 | $27.00 | $25.00 | $16.00 | $23.00 | $18.00 |
| 12 | TOTALS | $808.00 | $653.00 | $582.00 | $1,243.00 | $1,059.00 | $911.00 |
| 13 | | | | | | | |
| 14 | Income | | | | | | |
| 15 | Condo Fees | $976.00 | $976.00 | $976.00 | $976.00 | $976.00 | $976.00 |
| 16 | | | | | | | |
| 17 | Balance | $168.00 | $491.00 | $885.00 | $618.00 | $535.00 | $600.00 |
| 18 | | | | | | | |
| 19 | | | | | | | |
| 20 | | | | | | | |

01-Jan-89 10:01 AM

(d)

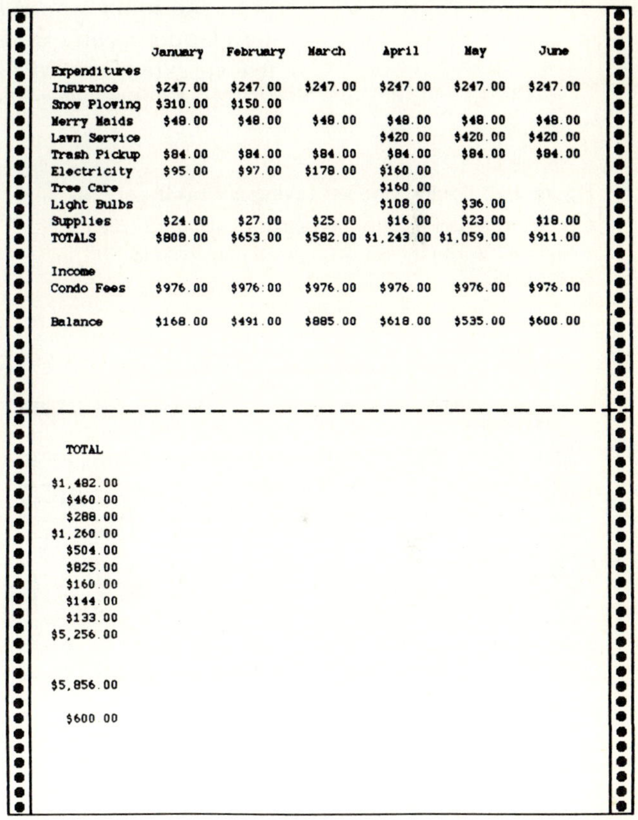

| | January | February | March | April | May | June |
|---|---|---|---|---|---|---|
| Expenditures | | | | | | |
| Insurance | $247.00 | $247.00 | $247.00 | $247.00 | $247.00 | $247.00 |
| Snow Plowing | $310.00 | $150.00 | | | | |
| Merry Maids | $48.00 | $48.00 | $48.00 | $48.00 | $48.00 | $48.00 |
| Lawn Service | | | | $420.00 | $420.00 | $420.00 |
| Trash Pickup | $84.00 | $84.00 | $84.00 | $84.00 | $84.00 | $84.00 |
| Electricity | $95.00 | $97.00 | $178.00 | $160.00 | | |
| Tree Care | | | | $160.00 | | |
| Light Bulbs | | | | $108.00 | $36.00 | |
| Supplies | $24.00 | $27.00 | $25.00 | $16.00 | $23.00 | $18.00 |
| TOTALS | $808.00 | $653.00 | $582.00 | $1,243.00 | $1,059.00 | $911.00 |
| | | | | | | |
| Income | | | | | | |
| Condo Fees | $976.00 | $976.00 | $976.00 | $976.00 | $976.00 | $976.00 |
| | | | | | | |
| Balance | $168.00 | $491.00 | $885.00 | $618.00 | $535.00 | $600.00 |

| TOTAL |
|---|
| |
| $1,482.00 |
| $460.00 |
| $288.00 |
| $1,260.00 |
| $504.00 |
| $825.00 |
| $160.00 |
| $144.00 |
| $133.00 |
| $5,256.00 |
| |
| |
| $5,856.00 |
| |
| $600.00 |

before you are finished creating it, retrieve it at some later time, and complete your entries. You can retrieve a previously saved worksheet and use it as a model for a new one by slightly modifying it. Or you can take an existing worksheet and change some figures just to see what the results would be. You can (and should) periodically save a worksheet while you are creating it to guard against losing your work if a power failure occurs, your equipment malfunctions, or you make some drastic error. Obviously, learning how to save and retrieve worksheets is critical.

Fortunately, it's easy to save and retrieve worksheets in Lotus 1-2-3. Let's say that you've created and printed the Parkridge Condominium Association budget depicted in Figure 9.11(a). To store this worksheet on a disk, simply type **/FS** to execute the File Save command. Figure 9.12(a) shows what happens. Lotus 1-2-3 prompts you to name the file in which to store the worksheet. It suggests a disk drive and directory, so all you have to do is type a filename, such as **BUDGET**, and press the **Enter** key. When 1-2-3 stores the worksheet file on the disk, it automatically appends an extension to the filename you enter. Release 2 versions of 1-2-3 use the extension *.WK1* for worksheet files, while previous versions use *.WKS* as the filename extension.

**Figure 9.12 Saving and Retrieving a Worksheet File**

(a) To save your current worksheet, first type **/FS** to execute the File Save command, and then enter a filename.

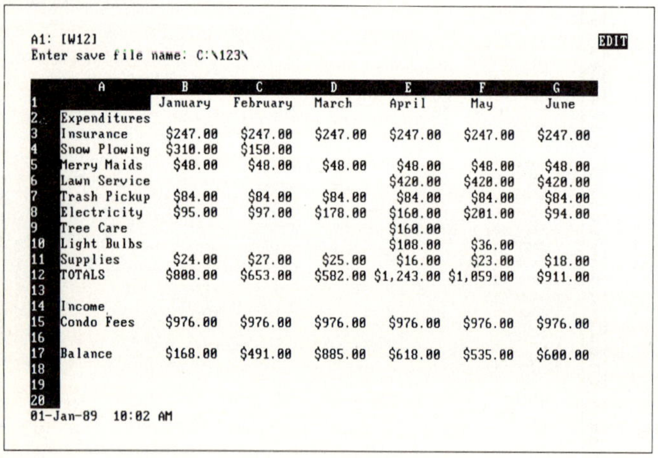


| | A | B | C | D | E | F | G |
|---|---|---|---|---|---|---|---|
| 1 | | January | February | March | April | May | June |
| 2 | Expenditures | | | | | | |
| 3 | Insurance | $247.00 | $247.00 | $247.00 | $247.00 | $247.00 | $247.00 |
| 4 | Snow Plowing | $310.00 | $150.00 | | | | |
| 5 | Merry Maids | $48.00 | $48.00 | $48.00 | $48.00 | $48.00 | $48.00 |
| 6 | Lawn Service | | | | $420.00 | $420.00 | $420.00 |
| 7 | Trash Pickup | $84.00 | $84.00 | $84.00 | $84.00 | $84.00 | $84.00 |
| 8 | Electricity | $95.00 | $97.00 | $178.00 | $160.00 | $201.00 | $94.00 |
| 9 | Tree Care | | | | $160.00 | | |
| 10 | Light Bulbs | | | | $108.00 | $36.00 | |
| 11 | Supplies | $24.00 | $27.00 | $25.00 | $16.00 | $23.00 | $18.00 |
| 12 | TOTALS | $808.00 | $653.00 | $582.00 | $1,243.00 | $1,059.00 | $911.00 |
| 13 | | | | | | | |
| 14 | Income | | | | | | |
| 15 | Condo Fees | $976.00 | $976.00 | $976.00 | $976.00 | $976.00 | $976.00 |
| 16 | | | | | | | |
| 17 | Balance | $168.00 | $491.00 | $885.00 | $618.00 | $535.00 | $600.00 |
| 18 | | | | | | | |
| 19 | | | | | | | |
| 20 | | | | | | | |

(b) To retrieve an existing worksheet, first type **/FR** to execute the File Retrieve command, highlight the filename, and press **Enter**.

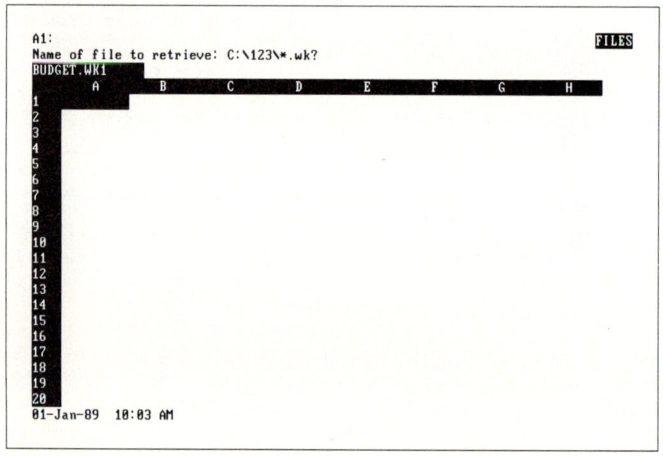


The disk drive and directory path C:\123\ you see in Figure 9.12(a) is called the **startup directory**. This is the disk drive and directory 1-2-3 automatically uses to store and retrieve your worksheet files unless you specify otherwise. When you first install 1-2-3, the program sets the startup directory to A:\, the root directory of the floppy disk in drive A. This can be changed by typing **/WGDD** to execute the Worksheet Global Default Directory command. For example, if you are using 1-2-3 on a computer with a hard disk, and you installed the program in a subdirectory named 123, you might want to set the startup directory to C:\123\. This is what we did prior to executing the File Save command in Figure 9.12(a). Once you set the startup directory, you don't have to specify it again unless you want to change it, since the 1-2-3 program remembers the startup directory from session to session.

If you want to save or retrieve a file in a disk drive directory different from the startup directory, you have to press the Escape key and then enter the whole path—disk drive, directory, and filename.

Retrieving an existing file from the startup directory is even easier than saving one. Suppose that you just started 1-2-3 and you want to work on the BUDGET worksheet you previously saved. Your worksheet is initially blank. To load the BUDGET worksheet from the disk into memory, you type **/FR** to execute the File Retrieve command. The 1-2-3 program displays the list of worksheet files stored in your startup directory and highlights the first one, as shown in Figure 9.12(b). In this case, BUDGET is the only file present. It is already highlighted, so all you have to do is press the **Enter** key. The worksheet is loaded into memory and your screen will look like Figure 9.11(a) again.

## ADDITIONAL FEATURES

*More capabilities*

Many more features are included in Lotus 1-2-3 besides the basics we've just covered. Some are used more than others. Graphing and data management, the "2" and the "3" of 1-2-3, are perhaps the most prominent. In addition, 1-2-3 also lets you specify macros, set up templates, hide and protect cells, split the screen into two windows, combine worksheets, and translate data between applications.

### Graphing

*Five ways to draw your data*

Lotus 1-2-3 was one of the first packages to integrate graphics with a spreadsheet. Release 2.01 can create five basic types of graphs, illustrated in Figure 9.13:

- *Line Graph.* Each value is represented by a point at an appropriate distance above the horizontal axis. Related points are designated by the same symbol and connected by line segments. Line graphs are useful for plotting values that change over time, such as monthly dollar sales.
- *Bar Graph.* Each value is represented by a vertical bar. Bar graphs are useful for comparing different sets of data, such as the unit sales of three different products.
- *X-Y Graph.* Also called a scatterplot, an X-Y graph shows the relationship between two or more different data items. For example, an X-Y graph can be used to show the relationship between the price of a product and the number of units sold.
- *Stacked Bar Graph.* This variation of the basic bar graph shows components and total amounts for each category. For example, a stacked bar graph might show the unit sales of three different products both in the United States and abroad.
- *Pie Chart.* Each value is represented as a wedge of a circle. Pie charts are used to show proportionally how the individual components that comprise a single set of data are related. For example, pie charts are often used to depict the breakdown of total expenditures into various categories.

As an example, let's do a bar graph of the Parkridge Condominium Association's bank balances for the months of January through June, as we did in Chapter 8 in Figure 8.12. You can only do this, however, if your IBM-compatible microcomputer has a graphics adapter and monitor, and the 1-2-3 program has been installed to take advantage of this equipment. The first step in creating the bar graph is to execute the Graph command by typing **/G**. Figure 9.14(a) shows the sub-

**Figure 9.13 The Five Types of 1-2-3 Graphs**
Examples of the five types of graphs that can be produced with Lotus 1-2-3 Release 2.01.

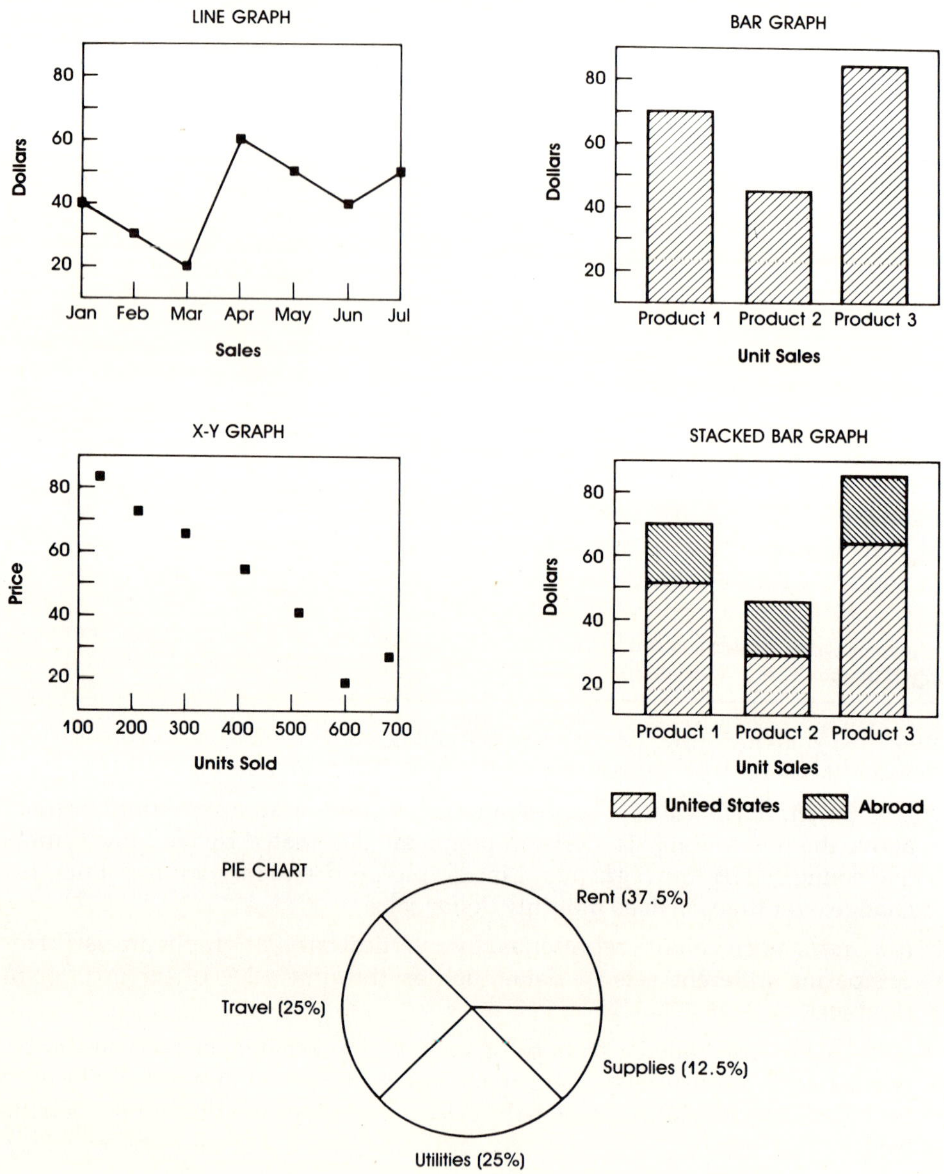


menu 1-2-3 displays on your screen. Next you have to tell 1-2-3 what type of graph you want to create, so you type **T** to select the Type option. The program displays another submenu listing the five types of graphs we've just described. You type **B** to select the Bar graph option, and 1-2-3 returns to the Graph submenu shown in Figure 9.14(a). Now type **X** to specify the horizontal axis and then enter **B1..G1**. This will put the names of the months along the horizontal axis when the graph is drawn. The Graph submenu is displayed again and this time you type **A** and then enter **B17..G17** to specify the range representing the balance figures you want to graph. Finally, you type **V** to select the View option; 1-2-3 clears the screen and displays the bar graph you see in Figure 9.14(b). When you are finished viewing the

**Figure 9.14 Creating a Bar Graph**

(a) The Graph submenu.

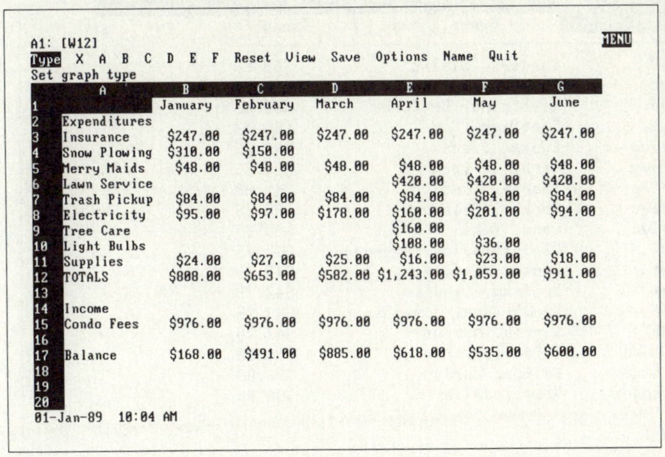


(b) The finished bar graph displayed on the screen.

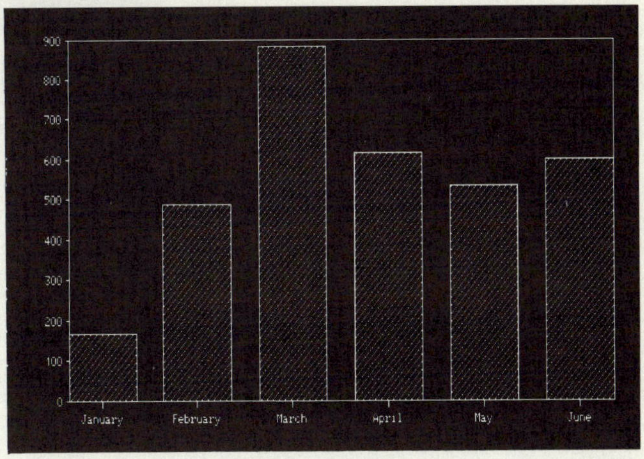


graph, press the **Escape** key to return to the Graph submenu. Although you cannot directly print a graph from within Lotus 1-2-3 Release 2.01, you can save it with the Graph Save command. Then, after you exit 1-2-3, you can print it later with the PrintGraph program.

## Data Management

*Rearranging and searching data tables*

As we said in Chapter 8, spreadsheet programs can be used to store simple tables of data. Lotus 1-2-3 provides several specialized commands for dealing with such data tables. For example, Figure 9.15 shows a table of apartment addresses, owner names, and condominium fees for the Parkridge Condominium Association. The submenu that you see in the control panel was activated by typing **/D** to execute the Data command. This submenu lists those specialized commands that let you enter, manipulate, and analyze data in a worksheet.

Sort and Query are two of the most frequently used commands from this submenu. Sort lets you rearrange rows based on the contents of one or two columns. For example, the rows you see in Figure 9.15 are now sorted in ascending order by apartment address. With the Data Sort command, you could sort the rows of this table alphabetically on the basis of the names in column B. You could even sort them by condominium fee.

This table is fairly small, so it wouldn't take you long to visually scan through the rows to find a particular apartment or owner. If the table had hundreds or even thousands of rows, finding a particular row would be considerably more difficult. The Data Query command lets you tell 1-2-3 to search for a particular row and highlight it. This command also lets you copy the row you find to another part of the worksheet or remove it from the table entirely.

**Figure 9.15 Data Management with 1-2-3**

This screen shows a data table of addresses, names, and condominium fees. The control panel reveals the submenu that appears after typing **/D** to execute the Data command.

```
A1: [W25] ^Apartment Address                                          MENU
Fill  Table  Sort  Query  Distribution  Matrix  Regression  Parse
Fill a range with numbers
              A                          B                   C          D
1     Apartment Address          Owner's Name          Condo Fee
2  -------------------------------------------------------------
3  5925 Pomona Blvd.          Sanders, Elaine            $69.53
4  5927 Pomona Blvd.          Engels, Fred               $55.22
5  5929 Pomona Blvd.          Harbision, Betty           $69.53
6  5931 Pomona Blvd.          Santiago, Tom              $55.22
7  6722 Lincoln Drive         Lyons, Diane               $45.25
8  6724 Lincoln Drive         Mack, Jeffrey              $38.25
9  6726 Lincoln Drive         Thorpe, Todd               $45.00
10 6728 Lincoln Drive         Archer, Ellen              $38.25
11 6730 Lincoln Drive         Chou, Yuki                 $45.00
12 7241 Easy Street           Christopoulos, Anthony     $42.75
13 7243 Easy Street           Scott, Montgomery          $49.25
14 7245 Easy Street           Brodsky, Candice           $42.75
15 7247 Easy Street           Trowbridge, Jonathan       $49.25
16 7249 Easy Street           Garcia, Marcos             $42.75
17 8118 Long Lake Lane        Jefferson, Henry           $96.00
18 8120 Long Lake Lane        Fulton, Wendy              $96.00
19 8122 Long Lake Lane        Kruse, Julie               $96.00
20
01-Jan-89  10:18 AM
```

## Macros

*Saving and replaying keystrokes*

As we said in the previous chapter, a spreadsheet macro lets you define and store a sequence of keystrokes and replay this sequence later by pressing a single combination of keys. Macros can reduce repetitive typing and help automate the entry of complex sequences of keystrokes. They are frequently included in templates for novices. Macros, one of 1-2-3's most advanced features, can be quite complex. Our aim here is to provide a very simple example to show what 1-2-3 macros can do and how they are defined.

Suppose that you want to create a macro that will enter the names of the months of the year across the columns. This could be useful if you need to repeat these labels several times in a worksheet. In 1-2-3, a macro definition is stored in a single column range of cells in an unused part of a worksheet. Each cell in this range describes one or more steps in the sequence of keystrokes and cell entries that you want to perform. Figure 9.16 shows the definition of a macro that enters labels for the months of the year in the next twelve columns, beginning with the current cell pointer position. This macro definition is placed in cells A100 through A112, far below any rows we plan to use for the actual worksheet. The entries enclosed in braces, such as {right}, designate movements of the cell pointer. The last entry, {end}{left}, moves the cell pointer back to the left edge of the worksheet.

Before this macro can be used, the range of cells that hold it must be given a name. A macro name must consist of a backslash (\) followed by a letter from A to Z. For example, this macro could be named \M to remind you that it enters month labels. The Range Name Create command is used to assign the name \M to the range A100..A112. After you have assigned a name to the macro, you can invoke it by holding down the Alternate key and pressing the single letter that names the macro. For example, to insert the month names in cells A2 through L2, you move the cell pointer to A2, hold down the **Alternate** key, and type **M**. The program automatically performs the steps you listed in the macro definition, just as if you did them yourself: *January* is entered and the cell pointer moves to the right, *February* is entered and the cell pointer moves to the right, and so on. After *December* is entered, the macro moves the cell pointer back to A2.

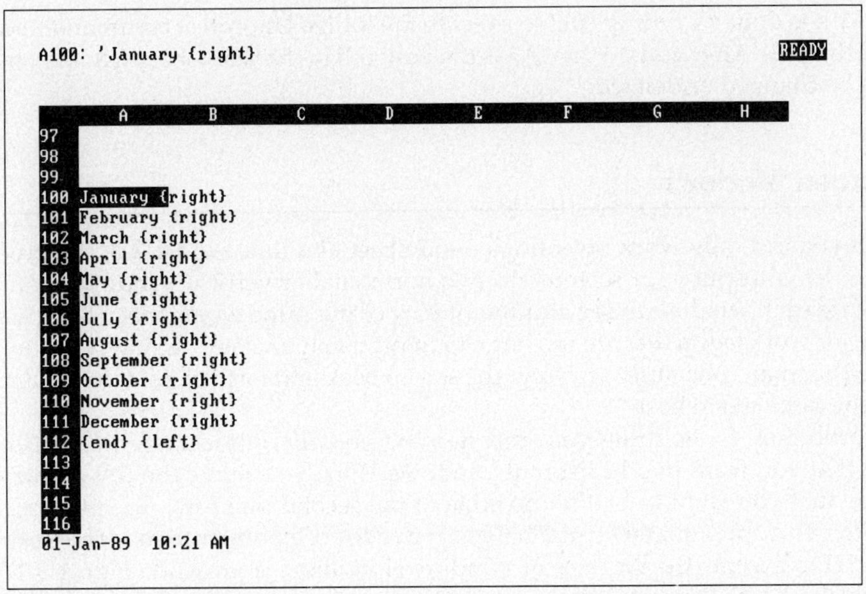


**Figure 9.16 Creating a Macro**
This screen shows the definition of a macro that enters labels for the months of the year in the next twelve columns, beginning with the current cell pointer position.

## Templates

*Fill-in-the-blank worksheets*

Like most spreadsheets, 1-2-3 can be used to set up templates. As we said in Chapter 8, a template is simply a ready-made, general-purpose worksheet somewhat like a blank form. It contains the necessary labels, constants, and formulas, but the user fills in the key variables. Since 1-2-3 is such a popular program, many templates are available for it. People who create templates may distribute them freely to the general public, publish them in books, sell them on disks as stand-alone products, or reserve them for use within a particular organization or company. There are 1-2-3 templates on the market for all kinds of tasks, from tax preparation and accounting chores to games and tutorials.

## Hiding and Protecting Cells

*Safeguarding your data*

Lotus 1-2-3 can hide and protect cells, features that come in handy for creating templates or for any worksheets that might be used by others.

Although you cannot hide individual cells, 1-2-3 does let you hide entire columns. All you do is type **/WCH** to execute the Worksheet Column Hide command. The program prompts you for the column you want to hide. When a column is hidden, its data is still there but the column doesn't appear on the screen. To "unhide" a previously hidden column, you type **/WCD** to execute the Worksheet Column Display command.

The process for protecting cells is somewhat different. When cells are protected, they are still visible but they cannot be changed or deleted. Let's say that you have created a template with only one number for the user to enter. You want to protect every cell in the worksheet except the one cell that is to contain this number. Let's say that the cell you want to leave unprotected is A5. The first step is to turn on the protection of all cells in the worksheet. This is done by typing **/WGPE** to execute the Worksheet Global Protection Enable command. Next you selectively unprotect cell A5. This is done by typing **/RU** to execute the Range Unprotect command and then entering **A5**. After you do this, A5 is the only cell in the worksheet whose contents can be changed or deleted.

## Split-Screen Windows

*Two views of the same worksheet*

Although you can only work on a single worksheet at a time with 1-2-3, the program does let you split your screen into two horizontal or vertical windows. You can then use each window to see a different part of the same worksheet. This can be handy for worksheets that are too large to fit on a single screen. Using two windows is easier than constantly scrolling the screen back and forth to see two distant parts of the same worksheet.

The procedure for splitting your screen into two windows is straightforward. Let's say that you want two horizontal windows. First you move the cell pointer to the row that you want to be the top edge of the second window. To split your screen into two approximately equal halves, move the cell pointer to row 11. Next, type **/WWH** to execute the Worksheet Window Horizontal command. Figure 9.17 shows the result. At this point the top window is active, and the cell pointer only moves within this portion. You must press the **F6** function key to switch to the other window. The two windows can be used to view one part of a worksheet while you edit another part of the same worksheet.

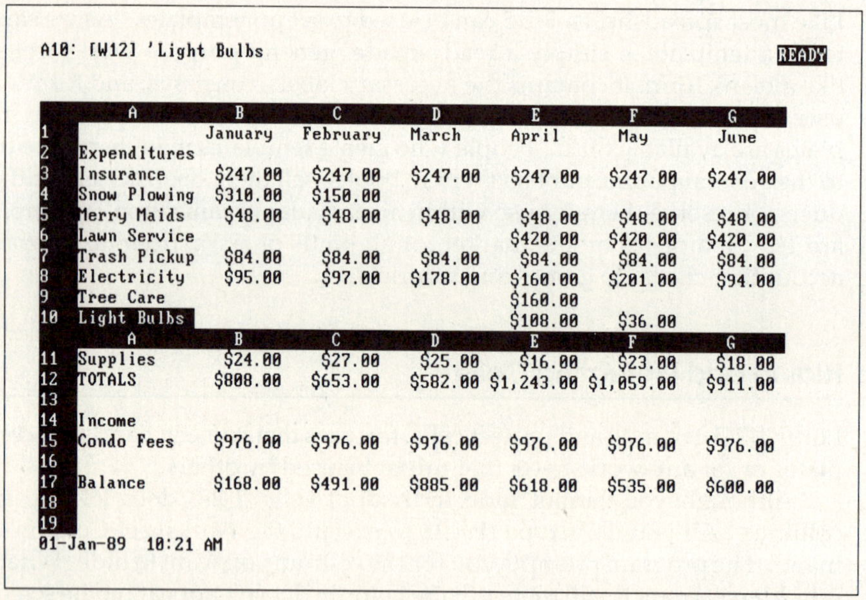
A10: [W12] 'Light Bulbs READY

| | A | B | C | D | E | F | G |
|---|---|---|---|---|---|---|---|
| 1 | | January | February | March | April | May | June |
| 2 | Expenditures | | | | | | |
| 3 | Insurance | $247.00 | $247.00 | $247.00 | $247.00 | $247.00 | $247.00 |
| 4 | Snow Plowing | $310.00 | $150.00 | | | | |
| 5 | Merry Maids | $48.00 | $48.00 | $48.00 | $48.00 | $48.00 | $48.00 |
| 6 | Lawn Service | | | | $420.00 | $420.00 | $420.00 |
| 7 | Trash Pickup | $84.00 | $84.00 | $84.00 | $84.00 | $84.00 | $84.00 |
| 8 | Electricity | $95.00 | $97.00 | $178.00 | $160.00 | $201.00 | $94.00 |
| 9 | Tree Care | | | | $160.00 | | |
| 10 | Light Bulbs | | | | $108.00 | $36.00 | |
| | A | B | C | D | E | F | G |
| 11 | Supplies | $24.00 | $27.00 | $25.00 | $16.00 | $23.00 | $18.00 |
| 12 | TOTALS | $808.00 | $653.00 | $582.00 | $1,243.00 | $1,059.00 | $911.00 |
| 13 | | | | | | | |
| 14 | Income | | | | | | |
| 15 | Condo Fees | $976.00 | $976.00 | $976.00 | $976.00 | $976.00 | $976.00 |
| 16 | | | | | | | |
| 17 | Balance | $168.00 | $491.00 | $885.00 | $618.00 | $535.00 | $600.00 |
| 18 | | | | | | | |
| 19 | | | | | | | |

01-Jan-89 10:21 AM

**Figure 9.17 Split Screen Windows**
To split your screen into two horizontal windows, move the cell pointer to where you want the split to occur, and type **/WWH** to execute the Worksheet Window Horizontal command.

## Combining Worksheets

*Merging files*

The 1-2-3 program also can merge worksheets, a process Lotus calls combining files. A different worksheet can be merely copied over the currently active worksheet, or its contents can be added to or subtracted from entries in corresponding cells. For example, suppose that you have a different BUDGET worksheet file for each of the two previous years: BUDGET1.WK1 and BUDGET2.WK1, and you want to combine both of these into a single worksheet. First you start 1-2-3 and retrieve one of the worksheets, say BUDGET2. With the cell pointer in cell A1, you type **/FCAE** to execute the File Combine Add Entire-file command. The program prompts you for the name of the file to combine, and you enter **BUDGET1**. Incoming values from BUDGET1 are then added to the corresponding values in the current worksheet, BUDGET2.

## Translating Data between Applications

*Working with other programs*

We've already mentioned one way that 1-2-3 can produce data for use in another program. You can "print" a worksheet to a file. This produces an ordinary text file that can be used by some word processors, data base managers, and other applications. In addition to this technique, Lotus provides a separate utility program with 1-2-3 called Translate, which allows you to exchange data files between 1-2-3 and a few other programs. These programs include the various releases of 1-2-3 and a selected set of popular data base managers and other spreadsheets. You simply enter **TRANS** from the DOS prompt to execute the Translate program. Translate displays a menu of programs from which you can translate and asks you to select one of these programs. Then you are shown a menu of programs to which you can translate and you are again asked to select one of these programs. Translate goes on to give you special instructions about the exchange you are attempting. Then it asks you for the name of the file you want to translate and the name of the new file you want to produce. If there are no problems, the program proceeds with the translation. When Translate is finished, you end up with a file from another application package you can retrieve as a worksheet within 1-2-3, or a file from 1-2-3 you can use with your other application package.

### The Real World

## Temporaries Trained to Use Lotus 1-2-3

Kelly Services, one of the largest agencies of temporary workers in the United States, now provides employees who are spreadsheet literate. Because of the increase in the number of requests for temporary workers with spreadsheet skills, the agency has instituted a nationwide program to teach and certify its qualified employees in the use of programs such as Lotus 1-2-3.

"Depending on the mix of skills identified by our branch offices, we train to meet those needs," explained Carolyn Fryar, senior vice president of Kelly Services. "Software skills include setting the column width and cell display, retrieving a spreadsheet, activating calculations, sending to print, and storing a spreadsheet."

This program, the Kelly PC-Pro System for spreadsheet training, is now available in all 700 Kelly offices in the United States. Trainees receive detailed reference guides for selected spreadsheet programs and a toll-free hotline that they can call to get on-the-job help. Kelly temporaries who qualify for spreadsheet training include those who already have secretarial and word processing skills, or ledger and bookkeeping experience.

As more businesses and organizations acquire microcomputers and spreadsheet programs, their need for skilled employees grows. It seems that familiarity with spreadsheet programs is almost a necessity in today's business world.

Source: "Kelly Trains Temps to Use Spreadsheets" by Daniel Sommer, *InfoWorld*, September 28, 1987, p. 48.

## Summary

- *How to start 1-2-3.* To start 1-2-3, using the Lotus Access System, enter **LOTUS** and then press the **Enter** key to select 1-2-3; execute 1-2-3 directly by entering **123** from the DOS prompt.
- *The various components of the 1-2-3 display screen.* The 1-2-3 display screen consists of the control panel at the top and an array of labeled columns and numbered rows beneath. You press the / (forward slash) key to bring up the Main menu.
- *How to enter new data into a worksheet and change existing data.* The cell pointer, which marks the cell where an entry is to be made or changed, is moved by using the arrow keys, Page Up, Page Down, Home, End, and the F5 function key. Numbers, labels, and formulas are simply typed into the active cell. To edit the existing contents of a cell, move the cell pointer to that cell and press the **F2** function key. New rows and columns can be inserted with the Worksheet Insert command, and existing rows and columns can be deleted with the Worksheet Delete command. Ranges of cells can be moved with the Move command and copied with the Copy command.
- *How to control the appearance of a worksheet.* Various numeric formats are available to specify how numbers and numeric formula results are displayed in a worksheet. Individual columns, or every column, can be set to any width from 1 to 240 characters. Although all numeric values are automatically right-justified, you can set the default global alignment of labels to be left-justified, centered, or right-justified.
- *The way in which 1-2-3 calculates formula results.* Formulas are constructed with various arithmetic, text, and logical operators, which are evaluated in a specific order. By default, 1-2-3 uses automatic natural recalculation with iteration turned off, but these settings can be changed.
- *How to print a worksheet.* The 1-2-3 Print command lets you print all or part of your worksheet, either directly on your printer, or to a file for printing later or for use in another program.
- *How to save and retrieve a worksheet.* The File Save command is used to store a worksheet on a disk for later use. An existing worksheet can be loaded into 1-2-3 with the File Retrieve command.
- *Some additional features included in Lotus 1-2-3.* Using data from your worksheets, 1-2-3 can display and print five different types of graphs. Data management commands allow you to sort and search through tables of data. In addition, 1-2-3 lets you specify macros, set up templates, hide and protect cells, split the screen into two windows, combine worksheets, and translate data between 1-2-3 and other applications.

# Command Summary

The following table summarizes Lotus 1-2-3 Release 2.01 keypresses.

| KEYPRESS | DESCRIPTION |
|---|---|
| / | Activates the Main menu. |
| Enter | Completes an entry. |
| Backspace | Erases preceding character. |
| Delete | Deletes character at cursor. |
| Insert | Switches from INSERT to OVERWRITE mode, and vice versa. |
| Escape | Exit from a menu; erases entry in control panel. |
| Home | Moves to cell A1. |
| Left Arrow | Moves left one cell. |
| Right Arrow | Moves right one cell. |
| Up Arrow | Moves up one cell. |
| Down Arrow | Moves down one cell. |
| Ctrl-Left Arrow | Moves left one screen. |
| Shift-Tab | Moves left one screen. |
| Ctrl-Right Arrow | Moves right one screen. |
| Tab | Moves right one screen. |
| Page Up | Moves up one screen. |
| Page Down | Moves down one screen. |
| End | When followed by an arrow key, moves to worksheet edge. |
| F1 | Activates the help facility. |
| F2 | Changes to EDIT mode. |
| F3 | Displays a menu of range names. |
| F4 | Changes the type of cell addressing. |
| F5 | Moves to a particular cell address. |
| F6 | Switches to other split-screen window. |
| F7 | Repeats most recent Data Query command. |
| F8 | Repeats most recent Data Table command. |
| F9 | Recalculates all worksheet formulas. |
| F10 | Displays the most recently specified graph. |

The following table summarizes the first two levels of Lotus 1-2-3 Release 2.01 menu commands.

| COMMAND | DESCRIPTION |
|---|---|
| /WG | Worksheet Global:<br>Specifies the default settings applied to all cells for items such as numeric format, label alignment, column width, recalculation method, cell protection, and the display of zero values. |
| /WI | Worksheet Insert:<br>Adds blank rows or columns to an existing worksheet. |
| /WD | Worksheet Delete:<br>Removes rows or columns from an existing worksheet. |
| /WC | Worksheet Column:<br>Specifies settings for column width and column hiding. |
| /WE | Worksheet Erase:<br>Completely erases the entire worksheet. |
| /WT | Worksheet Titles:<br>"Freezes" rows or columns so they can always be seen. |
| /WW | Worksheet Window:<br>Allows use of two horizontal or vertical windows. |

| COMMAND | DESCRIPTION |
|---|---|
| /WS | Worksheet Status:<br>Displays information about memory, global settings, and hardware. |
| /WP | Worksheet Page:<br>Inserts a printer page break into the worksheet. |
| /RF | Range Format:<br>Sets the numeric format for a range of cells. |
| /RL | Range Label:<br>Aligns existing labels in a range of cells. |
| /RE | Range Erase:<br>Removes the contents of a range of cells. |
| /RN | Range Name:<br>Allows naming of a range of cells. |
| /RJ | Range Justify:<br>Rearranges words in a column to fit within a specified width. |
| /RP | Range Protect:<br>Prevents changes and deletions to a range of cells. |
| /RU | Range Unprotect:<br>Allows changes and deletions to a range of cells. |
| /RI | Range Input:<br>Restricts cell pointer movement to unprotected cells. |
| /RV | Range Value:<br>Converts formulas to their computed values in a range of cells. |
| /RT | Range Transpose:<br>Reorders a range of cells, switching rows and columns. |
| /C | Copy:<br>Creates a copy of existing cell contents. |
| /M | Move:<br>Moves a range of cells to another place in the worksheet. |
| /FR | File Retrieve:<br>Loads a worksheet from a disk into memory. |
| /FS | File Save:<br>Copies a worksheet from memory to a disk file. |
| /FC | File Combine:<br>Copies, adds, or subtracts values from one worksheet to another. |
| /FX | File Xtract:<br>Extracts and saves part of one worksheet in another file. |
| /FE | File Erase:<br>Removes one or more files from a disk. |
| /FL | File List:<br>Displays the names of files on a disk. |
| /FI | File Import:<br>Imports data from a text file into the worksheet. |
| /FD | File Directory:<br>Changes the current disk drive directory. |
| /PP | Print Printer:<br>Sends a worksheet directly to the printer. |
| /PF | Print File:<br>Sends a worksheet to a file to be printed later. |
| /GT | Graph Type:<br>Specifies the type of graph to be created. |
| /GX | Graph X:<br>Specifies the range of cells for the X-axis labels. |
| /GA | Graph A:<br>Specifies the first range of cells to be used as data for the graph.<br>/GB through /GF are used to specify additional data ranges. |

| COMMAND | DESCRIPTION |
|---|---|
| /GR | Graph Reset:<br>Cancels graph settings. |
| /GV | Graph View:<br>Displays the current graph on the screen. |
| /GS | Graph Save:<br>Stores the current graph in a disk file so it can be printed later. |
| /GO | Graph Options:<br>Specifies various options for enhancing a graph's appearance. |
| /GN | Graph Name:<br>Creates, uses, deletes, or resets a graph name. |
| /GQ | Graph Quit:<br>Exits from the Graph submenu. |
| /DF | Data Fill:<br>Enters a sequence of numbers into a range of cells. |
| /DT | Data Table:<br>Tabulates the effects of changing values in formulas. |
| /DS | Data Sort:<br>Rearranges rows of cells in a specified order. |
| /DQ | Data Query:<br>Searches for, copies, extracts, or removes specified rows of cells. |
| /DD | Data Distribution:<br>Creates a frequency distribution of the values in a range of cells. |
| /DM | Data Matrix:<br>Multiplies and inverts matrices of cells. |
| /DR | Data Regression:<br>Fits a line to a set of data points. |
| /DP | Data Parse:<br>Breaks up long labels into individual cell entries. |
| /S | System:<br>Allows the use of DOS commands while working with 1-2-3. |
| /Q | Quit:<br>Ends 1-2-3 and returns to DOS. |

## Key Terms

As an extra review of this chapter, try defining the following terms. If you have trouble with any of them, refer to the page number listed.

label prefix character (320)
Lotus Access System (313)
printer setup string (332)
startup directory (334)
submenu (317)

## Review Questions

1. List four programs other than 1-2-3 itself that come with the Lotus 1-2-3 package.
2. On a computer with a hard disk, how do you begin working with 1-2-3?
3. How does 1-2-3 designate columns and rows?
4. How do you activate the Main menu?

5. What are the two methods of choosing an option from a 1-2-3 menu?
6. How do you activate the 1-2-3 help facility?
7. How do you move the cell pointer to a particular cell address in the worksheet?
8. Which label prefix character would you use to center a label within a cell?
9. Why do 1-2-3 formulas often begin with a plus sign (+)?
10. What do all 1-2-3 function names have in common?
11. One way to change the existing contents of a cell is to retype the entire entry. Describe a different way to change the contents of a cell.
12. What happens when you delete a column with the Worksheet Delete Column command?
13. How would you change every cell in a worksheet to currency format?
14. What is the default column width in 1-2-3? What is the range of permissible column widths?
15. How would 1-2-3 compute the result of the formula 1+2/1?
16. Why might you want to "print" a worksheet to a file, instead of sending it directly to the printer?
17. How do you store a worksheet on a disk?
18. What type of graph would you use to depict the breakdown of total expenditures into various categories?
19. What 1-2-3 command would you use to rearrange a table of data?
20. What command would you use to split the 1-2-3 screen into two horizontal windows?

## Multiple Choice

1. After you have switched to the proper disk drive directory, which of the following commands will execute the Lotus 1-2-3 program directly, without first activating the Lotus Access System?
   (a) LOTUS (b) 123
   (c) 1-2-3 (d) TRANS
2. The second 26 columns of a 1-2-3 worksheet are labeled
   (a) A through Z. (b) AA through AZ.
   (c) BA through BZ. (d) A through IV.
3. Lotus 1-2-3 Release 2.01 can address 2,097,152 cells, but the actual number of cells you can fill with data depends on the
   (a) amount of memory installed in the computer. (b) size of the graphics display screen.
   (c) width of the printer carriage. (d) speed of the microprocessor.
4. The area of the 1-2-3 screen that displays menus and prompts is called the
   (a) cell pointer. (b) message line.
   (c) control panel. (d) help facility.

5. Which key do you press to activate 1-2-3's Main menu?
   (a) **F1** (b) **Enter**
   (c) **Escape** (d) / (forward slash)
6. What is the fastest way to execute the File command from 1-2-3's Main menu?
   (a) Highlight the option and press **Enter**. (b) Use the Lotus Access System.
   (c) Press F. (d) Use the System command.
7. In 1-2-3, pressing F1 activates the
   (a) function key menu. (b) translate utility.
   (c) help facility. (d) Main menu.
8. Which key would you press to move immediately to cell A1?
   (a) Home (b) Escape
   (c) Enter (d) Page Up
9. Which of the following is not a type of data that can be placed in a worksheet cell?
   (a) number (b) label
   (c) formula (d) graph
10. Which of the following entries will appear centered within its cell?
    (a) 'Expenses (b) "Expenses
    (c) ^Expenses (d) \Expenses
11. Which 1-2-3 function would you use to add the contents of cells A1 through A100?
    (a) @SUM (b) @COUNT
    (c) @MAX (d) @MOD
12. Which of the following programs would you use to produce a 1-2-3 graph on paper?
    (a) View (b) Translate
    (c) Install (d) PrintGraph
13. Which of the following is a valid 1-2-3 macro name?
    (a) @M (b) \M
    (c) MACRO.WK1 (d) {macro}
14. Which command would you use to add the corresponding cells of two separate worksheets?
    (a) File Combine Add (b) Worksheet Insert Add
    (c) Range Copy Add (d) Data Merge
15. Which of the following programs included with Lotus 1-2-3 would you use to exchange data with a popular data base management package?
    (a) PrintGraph (b) Install
    (c) View (d) Translate

## On-line Exercises

1. If you are not already running 1-2-3, change to the proper disk drive directory and enter **123**. In cell A1, type **100** and press the **Down Arrow** key. In cell A2, type **200** and press the **Down Arrow** key. In cell A3, type **A1+A2** and press the **Enter** key. You want cell A3 to display the sum of the contents of cells A1 and A2. What did you do wrong? Determine how you can correct the error and do so.
2. Use the Worksheet Insert Row command to insert two new rows between cells A2 and A3. (Remember that you press / to bring up the Main menu.) Enter **300** into cell A3 and **400** into cell A4.
3. Move the cell pointer to cell A5 and press **F2** to invoke 1-2-3's EDIT mode. Modify the formula so that it reads @SUM(A1..A4).
4. Use the Move command to move the contents of cells A1 through A5 to cells B2 through B6.
5. Use the Worksheet Global Format command to change the worksheet's default numeric format to currency, with two places to the right of decimal points. (Asterisks appear in cell B6 because the cell is no longer wide enough to display the result of the formula in currency format. Exercise 6 will show how to increase the cell width.)
6. Use the Worksheet Column Set-Width command to change the widths of both columns A and B to 12 characters. Cell B6 should now display $1,000.00.
7. Enter **^EXPENSE** into cell A1 and **^AMOUNT** into cell B1. Now enter **"Supplies** into cell B2, **"Utilities** into cell B3, **"Insurance** into cell B4, **"Rent** into cell B5, and **"TOTAL** into cell B6. Explain the difference between the ^ and the " label-prefix characters.
8. If you have a printer attached to your computer, try printing your worksheet. First execute the Print Printer Range command and enter **A1..B6** as the range of cells to be printed. Make sure that the printer is turned on, its on-line indicator is lit, and paper is loaded and positioned at the top of a new page. Then type **G** to execute the Go option. After the worksheet has finished printing, execute the Quit option to leave the Print submenu.
9. Execute the File Save command and enter **EXPENSES** to store this worksheet in a disk file named EXPENSES.WK1.
10. Use the Worksheet Erase Yes command to clear the contents of your screen.
11. Execute the File Retrieve command, use the **Right Arrow** key to highlight EXPENSES.WK1, and press the **Enter** key to load the EXPENSES worksheet from the disk into memory.
12. If your computer is equipped with a graphics adapter and monitor, produce a pie chart from the EXPENSES worksheet. First, execute the Graph Type Pie command. Type **X** and enter **A2..A5** as the range of cells that contains the pie wedge labels. Type **A** and enter **B2..B5** as the range of cells containing the values that 1-2-3 will represent as wedges of the pie. Execute the Options Titles First command and enter **EXPENSES** as the title of the pie chart. Press **Q** for Quit to leave the Options submenu and return to the Graph submenu. Now invoke the View option to see the pie chart on your screen. When you are finished viewing the pie chart, press the **Escape** key and use the Quit option to leave the Graph submenu.

13. Rearrange your expenses in alphabetical order. Execute the Data Sort Data-Range command and enter **A2..B5** as the range of cells to be sorted. Next, invoke the Primary-Key option and enter **A2** to indicate that the labels in the EXPENSE column will be the basis for the sort. The program will then prompt you for the sort order. Enter **A** for ascending order, which is the same as alphabetical order when sorting on the basis of text labels. Finally, type **G** (for Go) to actually perform the sort operation.

14. We are finished with the EXPENSES worksheet, so let's remove it from the disk. In fact, you should only do this if you are sure that you want to permanently discard the worksheet. Execute the File Erase Worksheet command. Use the **Right Arrow** key to highlight EXPENSES if it is not already highlighted, and press **Enter**. Type **Y** for yes to confirm that you want to erase this file. Now use the Worksheet Erase Yes command to remove the worksheet from the screen and give you a new blank worksheet.

15. Suppose that you've just opened an Individual Retirement Account (IRA). The account pays 8% interest, compounded annually and paid on the last day of each year. You plan to deposit $2000 on the last day of every year. How much will your IRA hold after 30 years? You can use 1-2-3's @FV function, which computes the future value of an investment, to find out. First, use the Worksheet Global Column-Width command to increase the default column width to 15, and execute the Worksheet Global Format Currency command. Enter **@FV(2000,8%,30)** into any cell. The first number inside the parentheses is the annual payment, the second number is the annual interest rate, and the third number is the number of years. The worksheet cell displays the computed result of the formula. To see the advantages of compounded interest, compare this result to $60,000, which is the value of $2000 saved for 30 years without any interest. Use the **F2** key to edit the values and experiment with the formula. For example, try only $1000 per year and an interest rate of 7%.

## Projects

1. Use 1-2-3 to create a worksheet that lists your major expenditures for the past 12 months. Include items like rent, room and board, or mortgage payments; tuition; power bills; telephone bills; health, automobile, and property insurance; travel expenses; credit card purchases; and so on. Be sure to compute both the row and column totals. Try to use the Copy command to reduce repetitive typing. Use appropriate labels and numeric formatting to improve the clarity and appearance of your worksheet.

2. Balancing your checkbook is fairly easy if you use the form many banks print on the back of your monthly statement. Use 1-2-3 to create a template that replicates the following form in a worksheet, so that you can get the computer to help you balance your checkbook. Remember that a template is simply a worksheet that has all the labels and formulas, but some cells are left empty to be filled in later.

CHECKS OUTSTANDING
(written but not yet
shown on this statement)

| Check Number | Amount |
|---|---|
| | |
| Total | |

ACCOUNT BALANCE.......... $__________
(shown this statement)

ADD DEPOSITS..................... $__________
(made but not
yet shown on
this statement)

TOTAL...................................... $__________

SUBTRACT
---> OUTSTANDING CHECKS.... $__________

BALANCE............................... $__________
(should agree with
your checkbook)

3. Use 1-2-3 to create a loan payment worksheet similar to the one in Figure 8.15. Remember that the @PMT function computes the monthly payment on a loan given the amount of the loan (principal), monthly interest rate, and term in months. Note that the @PMT function works slightly differently in 1-2-3 than it does in Microsoft Excel, which we used for the worksheet in Figure 8.15. For example, if the principal is $8500, the annual interest rate is 12% (1% per month), and the term is 48 months, the 1-2-3 formula that computes the monthly payment is @PMT(8500,0.01,48). In your worksheet, construct the formula to use cell references instead of actual numbers so that you can more easily see the results of changing the values of the principal, interest rate, and term.

4. Use 1-2-3 to generate a table of squares and square roots of the whole numbers from 1 to 25. List each number in column A, its square in column B, and its square root in column C. Use appropriate labels for column headings; use the Copy command wherever you can.

# Part 5

# DATA BASE MANAGEMENT

The very first electronic digital computers were designed to perform time-consuming and complex calculations, such as computing the trajectories of artillery shells. Primary and secondary storage was very limited and expensive. No one even considered using these sophisticated devices for mundane tasks like record keeping. But through the last forty years, technology has advanced to make computers much less expensive and much faster, while storage capacity has dramatically increased. This trend is continuing. Today, people routinely use computers to store, update, and retrieve huge quantities of all kinds of information. Data base management systems are the software that helps people perform these tasks.

Part 5 examines the record-keeping software many individuals, businesses, and organizations simply cannot do without. Chapter 10 introduces microcomputer data base management systems in general. Chapter 11 covers dBASE III PLUS, one of the world's most popular microcomputer data base management systems.

# 10

# Data Base Management Concepts

## In This Chapter

## PREVIEW

Why do *you* have to learn to use a data base management system? Chances are good that if you work in government, education, research, business, or almost any other profession, you will use computers. Workers in a variety of settings are using computers now to help them on the job. For example, at the Carra Donna Provision Company of Boston, dock workers use IBM microcomputers to enter inventory data as frozen foods are unloaded from trucks. Since so many people use computers to deal with large quantities of information, it is very likely that at some point you will use data base management software. This can no longer be delegated solely to expert programmers. To function in our information age, we'll all have to manage our own data bases. This chapter begins your training by introducing the basic concepts of data base management systems.

After studying this chapter, you will understand

- the different types of data base managers.
- how to create a data base.
- how to find information in a data base.
- how to keep a data base up-to-date.
- how to rearrange a data base.
- how to produce printed data base reports.
- some of the additional features offered by data base management systems.
- three popular data base managers for microcomputers.

## TYPES OF DATA BASE MANAGERS

As we said in Chapter 3, a *data base* is a collection of one or more files of related data, generally organized for quick access, such as a magazine publisher's mailing list, a department store's inventory, or a library's card catalog. Many people combine *data* and *base* into the single word *database*. That term is also used to describe programs that deal with data bases. In this book, we use *data base* to refer to one or more data files, and *data base manager* or *data base management system* to describe programs that work with those files. A *file*, as you know by now, is simply data that is kept together in secondary storage. Word processors, for example, store documents in files, and spreadsheet programs store worksheets in files. Each file has its own unique name and can be treated as a single entity, even though it is comprised of individual data items. The data stored in files, and hence data bases, basically consists of numbers and text. So, a data base can contain anything that can be expressed in numbers or text. This broad definition means that several different types of programs can be classified as data base managers. For example, there are spreadsheet, flat-file, free-form, relational, and programmable data base managers.

### Spreadsheet Data Base Managers

*Used for short, simple lists*

Although spreadsheet programs are primarily number processors, most can be used as simple data managers. Remember, worksheets store both numbers and text. As we said in the previous two chapters, most spreadsheet programs include special commands for data management. These commands help you create, view, update, rearrange, and print collections of data. Many people who already use a spread-

**Insight**

## Do Data Bases Jeopardize Personal Privacy?

In one corner is the individual's right to privacy. In the other is the need for government and business to keep tax, census, billing, and credit records. Round after round, they keep slugging it out. It's going to be a long fight.

The fight between individual privacy and the need to keep records will go on and on, because there are two legitimate sides to the issue.

Whenever information is kept in a centralized form, whether manually or on a computer, it is subject to potential abuse. The capabilities of a computerized data base merely increase the potential for abuse and invasion of privacy.

However, it doesn't make sense to outlaw data bases. The problem is not the data base or the computer, but the use and misuse of the information. The realization of this has led to a series of federal statutes and court decisions that strictly limit who may collect data and who may use it, and the right to challenge the contents of the data base is reserved for the individual.

sheet can avoid having to purchase and learn a different program for data management. Spreadsheets are quite adequate for tracking expenses, inventories, addresses, phone numbers, and other relatively short and simple lists. They also have the advantage of being able to perform all kinds of calculations and analysis on your data.

There are two main disadvantages to using a spreadsheet program as a data manager, however. The first is that spreadsheet programs are not as flexible or powerful as other types of data managers for entering and manipulating data. The second disadvantage is that spreadsheet software can handle far less data than most other types of data managers. For example, a spreadsheet program with 8192 rows can maintain a mailing list of at most 8192 addresses. In comparison, some of the most powerful data base management systems for microcomputers can theoretically handle a mailing list of one or two *billion* addresses.

### Flat-File Data Base Managers

*One file at a time*

A **flat-file data base manager** is a program that works with one file of structured data at a time. In other words, this type of program is designed to handle single files that are conveniently organized into regular-sized pieces of data, such as names, addresses, phone numbers, and price listings. Flat-file managers are generally simple, easy-to-use, and modestly priced. They are designed to do one basic job very well—accepting, reorganizing, and reporting information. Consequently, many professionals and small businesses find that a flat-file manager is more than adequate for their simple needs. Doctors, lawyers, accountants, print shops, carpet cleaners, and even pizza parlors are just a few examples of those successfully using flat-file data base managers. Flat-file managers are ideal for maintaining mailing lists, addresses and phone numbers, personnel files, product price lists, and property inventories. Almost any sequential list of information can be kept with a flat-file manager. This type of program is often used as an electronic index or like a set of computerized Rolodex cards.

# Using Microcomputer Hardware

Advances in microprocessor technology are a primary reason for the growing role microcomputers now play in our society. Hardware determines the software that can be run, and hence profoundly influences how computers are used. You needn't become a computer engineer, but it is important to have a basic understanding of the hardware components that make up a typical system. In this section, we examine the physical parts of a microcomputer and see how they work. We discuss what makes the newest microprocessors so powerful. Memory, disk drives, displays, keyboards, mice, expansion boards, printers, and modems are all covered. Learning about these devices will help you realize what computers can do, given the right software. Once you become familiar with the hardware of microcomputer systems, you can then concentrate on the software that puts it to work.

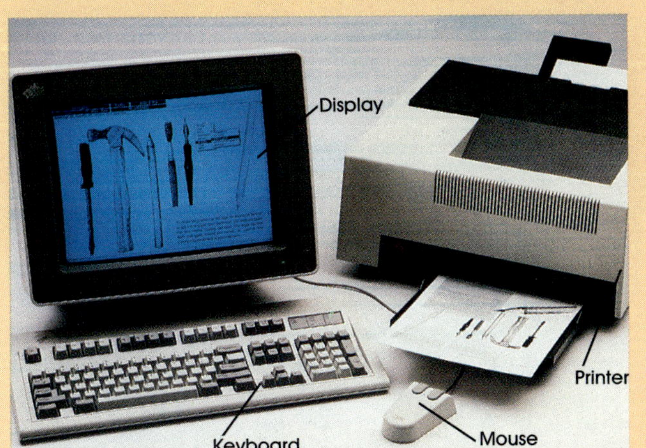


The four basic hardware components of a microcomputer system are the display, system unit, keyboard, and printer. The display is a screen to present text and graphics. The system unit contains the central processing unit (CPU), control circuitry, memory, and disk drives. The keyboard is the primary device for entering commands and data, but many microcomputers also use a mouse. Finally, the auxiliary printer is used to produce text and graphics on paper. *(IBM)*

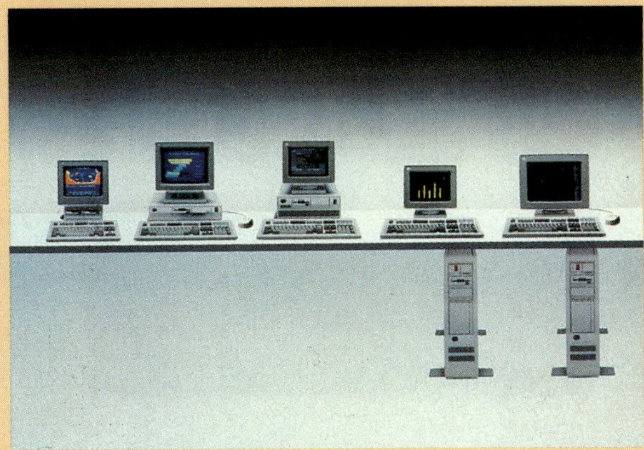

IBM's PS/2 family. *(IBM)*

The Macintosh. *(Apple Computer, Inc.)*

The Mac II. *(Apple Computer, Inc.)*

Lap-top and portable computers offer portability and power in a package that can weigh less than 10 pounds. *(Toshiba, below; Compaq, right)*

(a) The Intel 4004 microprocessor. (b) The Intel 80286 chip. (c) The Intel 80386 chip. *(Intel Corp.)*

(b)

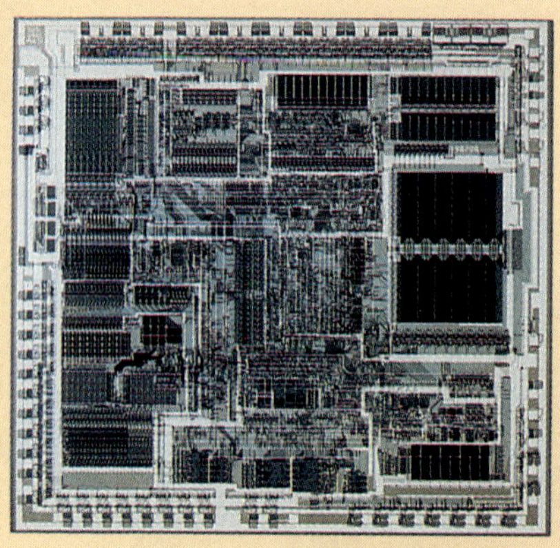

(a)

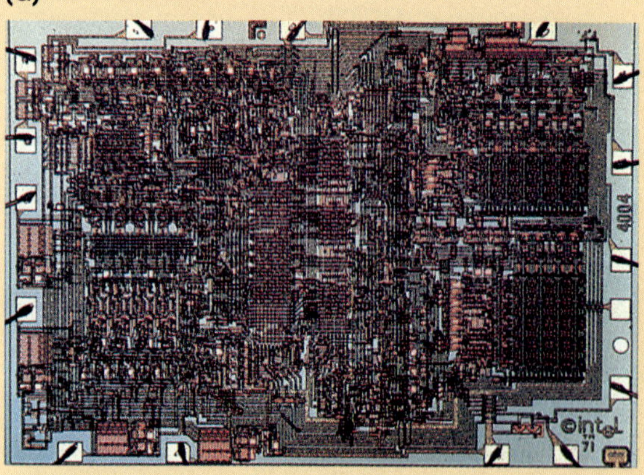

(c)

(a) This photograph shows the system unit of an IBM Personal System 12 Model 50 broken down into its major components. *(Thom O'Connor)*
(b) Here is a closeup of the motherboard or system board. *(IBM)*

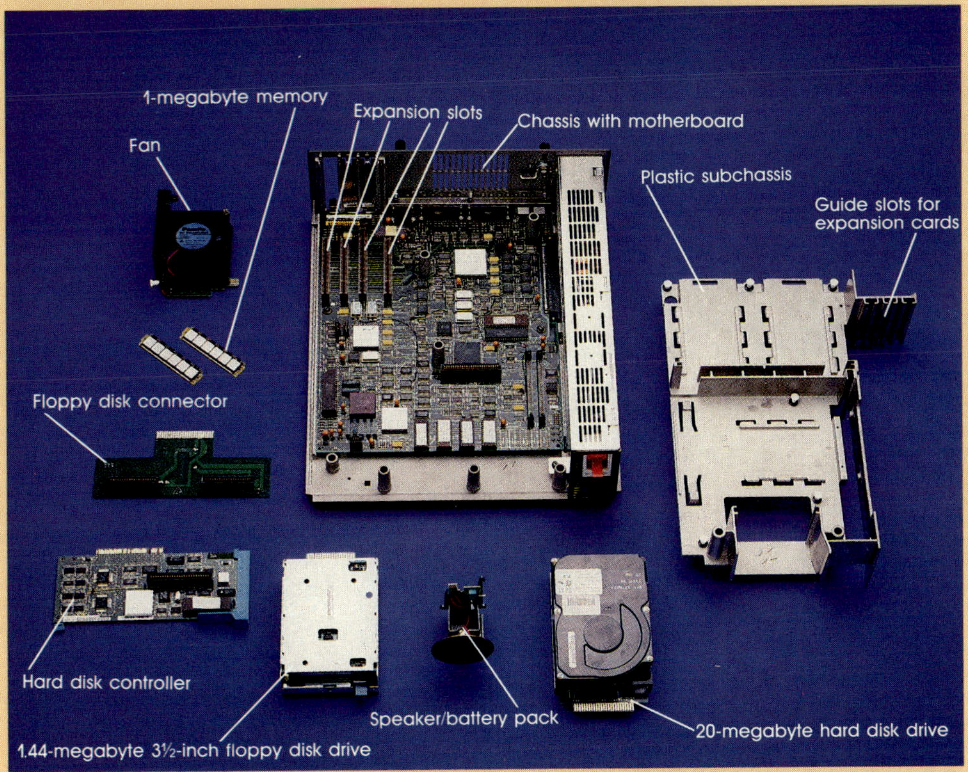


(a)

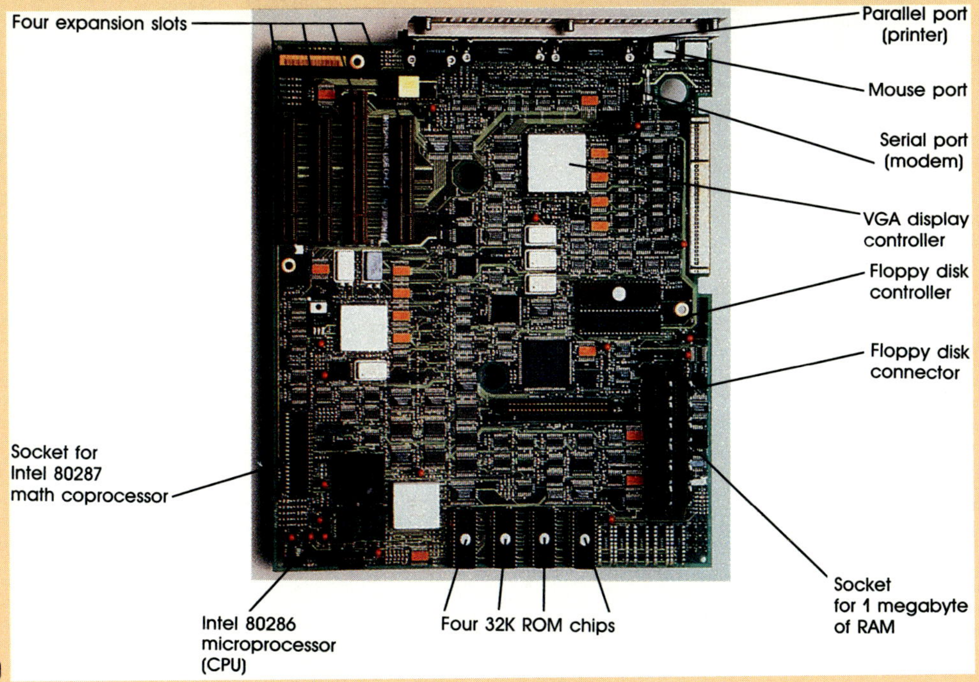


(b)

The floppy disk is a commonly used medium for storing computer program and data. The two most commonly used sizes are (left) 5¼-inch and (right) 3½-inch disks. *(IBM)*

Seagate Technology hard disk drive. *(Seagate Technology)*

A page scanner turns artwork and photographs into digital images. The images can be enlarged, enhanced, and cropped by computer and later incorporated directly into printed output. *(Hewlett Packard)*

Hitachi's 4¼-inch audio compact disc and compact disc player. *(Hitachi)*

The Laser Jet Series II printer from Hewlett-Packard offers publication quality printing for the office environment. This fast, quiet, high-quality office printer can merge text and graphics for desktop publishing needs. *(Hewlett Packard)*

A direct-connect modem can send information at up to 19,200 bits per second by using data compression techniques. *(Hayes Microcomputer)*

# Using Lotus 1-2-3

Spreadsheet packages help users store, manipulate, analyze, and present data, most often numeric data. Many different kinds of tasks can be performed with a spreadsheet program. To give you an idea of what it's like to use this type of application software, in this section we'll create a simple income statement for an imaginary small business with Lotus 1-2-3, which is by far the most popular microcomputer spreadsheet package. An *income statement* is simply a report that lists the sources of income and expenses of a business over a given time period. The *bottom line* of an income statement shows the net profit earned, calculated by subtracting the total expenses from the total income. After we set up the income statement with Lotus 1-2-3, we will make a bar graph that shows the income for each quarter of the year.

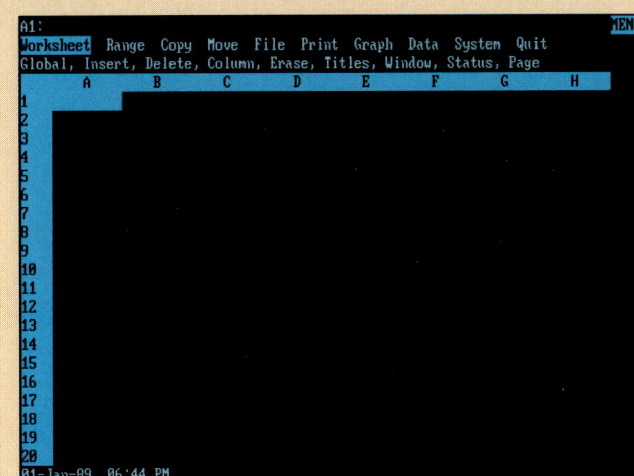


1. Lotus 1-2-3, blank worksheet.

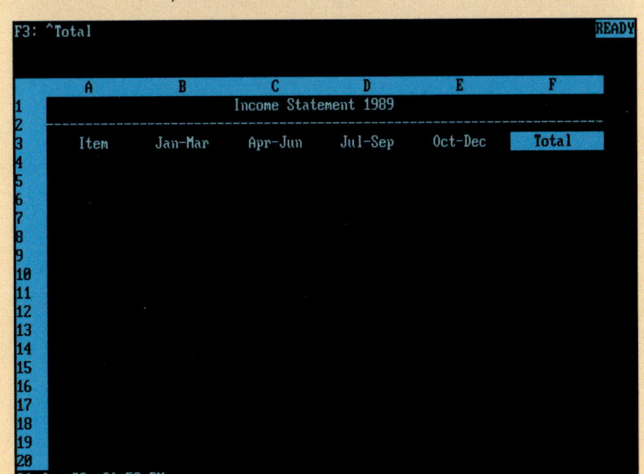


2. Most people begin by entering the text labels that will annotate the contents.

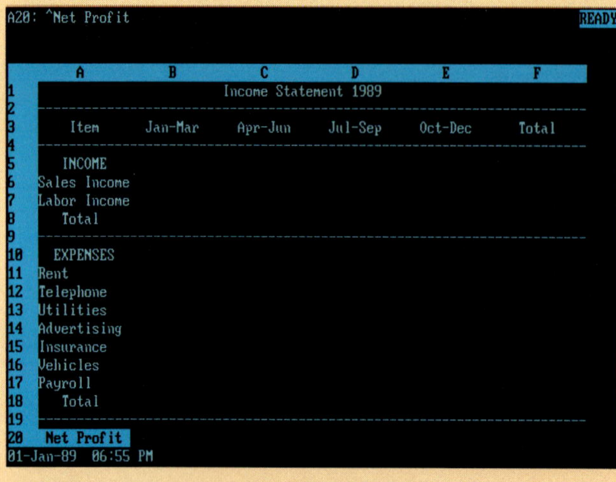


3. After you're finished entering all of the labels, the worksheet looks like this.

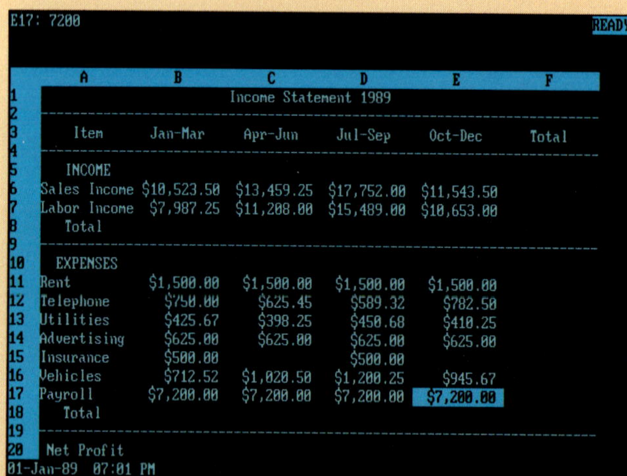


4. The next step is to enter the actual data, the numbers that represent the various income and expense figures for the four quarters of 1989.

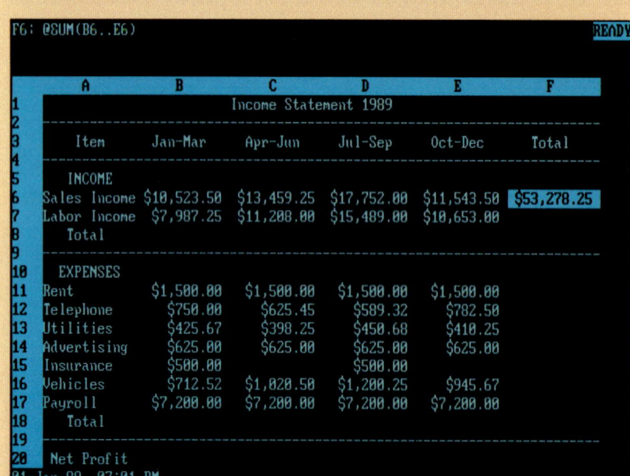


5. Once the data values are entered, you can put in the formulas that will compute totals and the net profit.

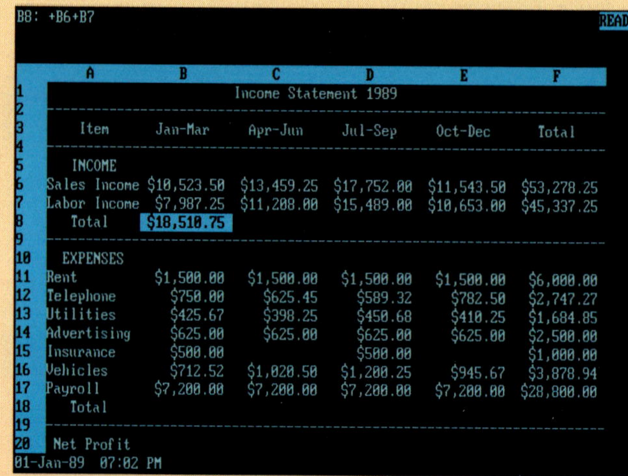


6. The next set of formulas you must enter will sum the two income figures for each quarter.

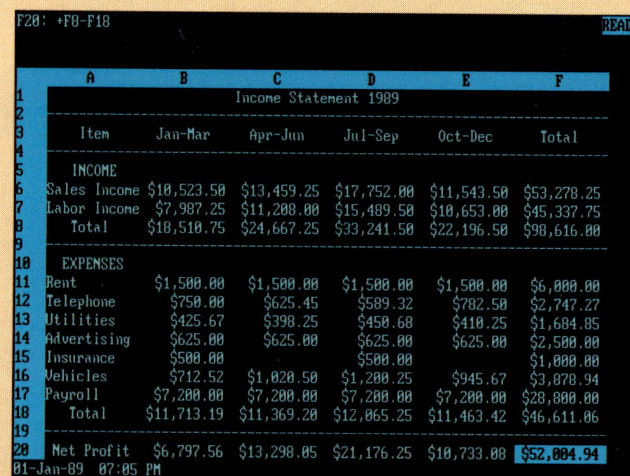


7. When you are finished with all of the formulas, the worksheet looks like this.

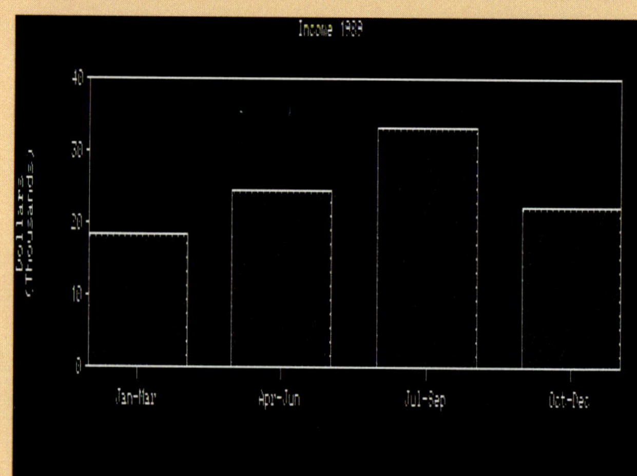


8. As a final sample of what you can do with a spreadsheet program, we've made a bar graph of the totals.

# Using dBASE III PLUS

Data base management packages basically let users create, add to, delete from, update, sort, rearrange, select from, print out, and otherwise manipulate data files. Since managing data is one of the most common tasks performed by computers, especially in businesses, data base management packages are an extremely important type of application software. To give you an idea of what it's like to use this type of software, in this section we'll create a simple parts inventory data base for an imaginary small business with dBASE III PLUS, the most popular microcomputer data base management package.

1. dBASE III PLUS presents its Assistant menu system with the Set Up menu initially selected.

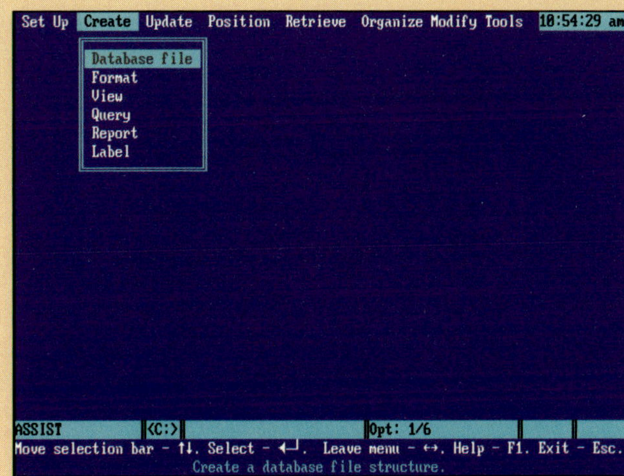


2. To go from the Set Up menu to the Create menu, you can either press the right arrow key once, or type C.

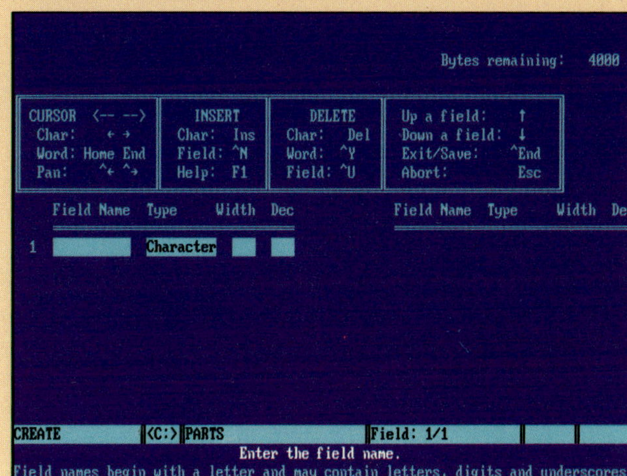


3. After you enter an acceptable name, dBASE displays an empty data base file structure table on your screen.

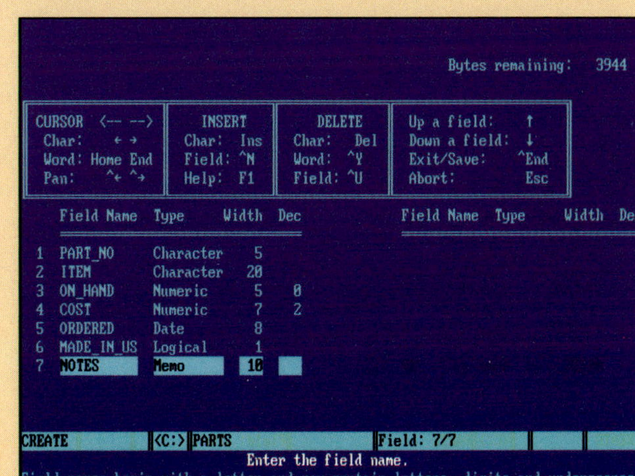


4. Here is the completed record structure table for our example PARTS data base file.

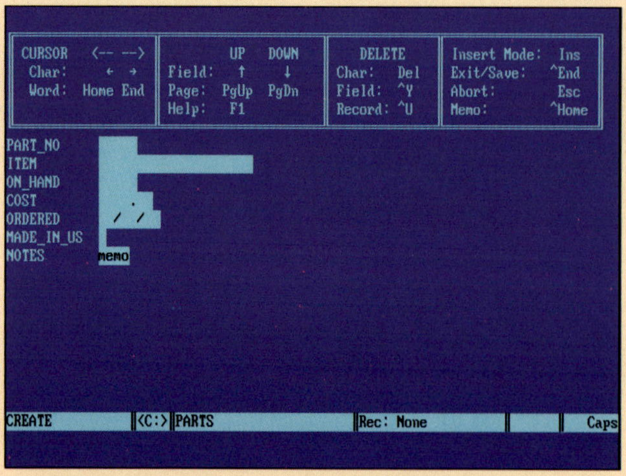


5. After telling dBASE you want to go ahead and enter your records, the program displays a blank data entry form on your screen.

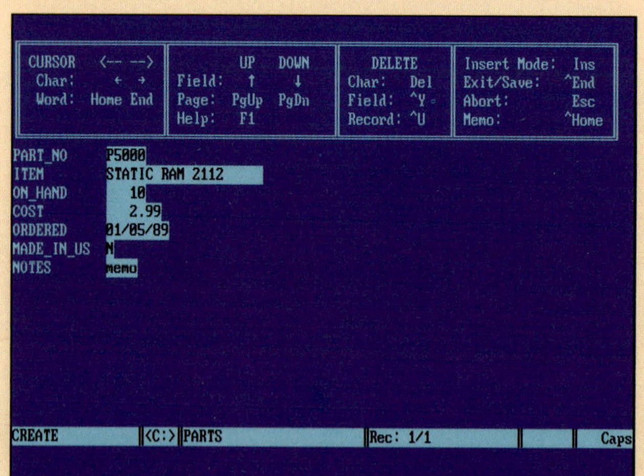


6. You simply enter the data for each field in a record, like this.

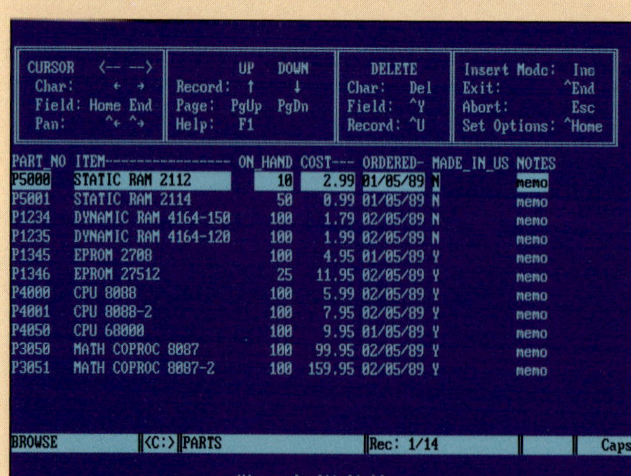


7. The first 11 records of the PARTS data base file are displayed on the screen in a table format.

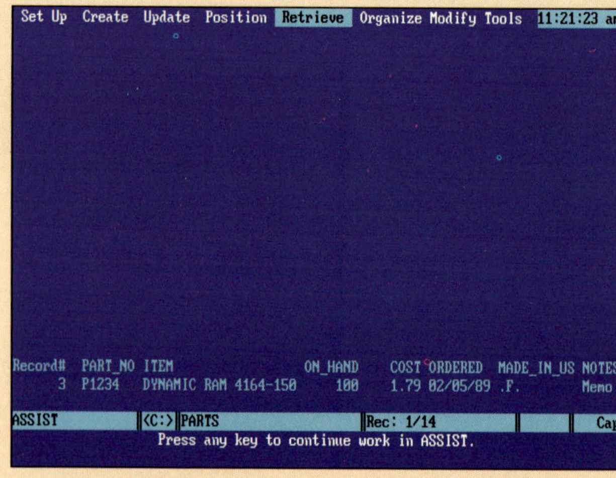


8. Here is the dBASE screen that results from a simple query.

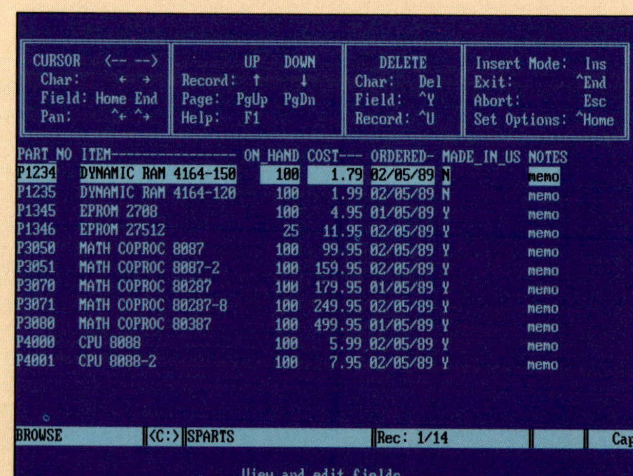


9. Once you set up a report layout, you use the Report option from the Retrieve menu to actually send the formatted listing to your printer.

# Using WordPerfect

The most common word-processing system consists of a general-purpose microcomputer running a word-processing application package. Simply stated, a word-processing package helps you enter, store, modify, format, copy, and print text. Most contemporary word-processing software goes beyond these basic functions to offer features such as a built-in spelling checker, an on-line thesaurus, and the ability to incorporate graphics in a document. To give you an idea of what it's like to use a modern word-processing program, in this section we'll create a simple report about the U.S. space shuttle, using WordPerfect 5.0 on an IBM-compatible microcomputer. We cannot, of course, demonstrate every feature of this popular, powerful program. Nevertheless, we can go through the basic procedure of creating, editing, formatting, and printing a document that includes both text and graphics. Although WordPerfect is not a page layout program, it can be used for simple desktop publishing applications in which previously created charts, drawings, or diagrams appear inside documents.

1. The WordPerfect document editing screen.

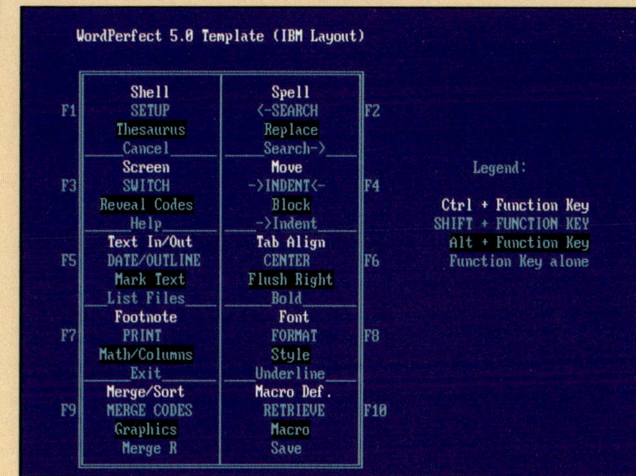


2. On-screen version of WordPerfect's keyboard template.

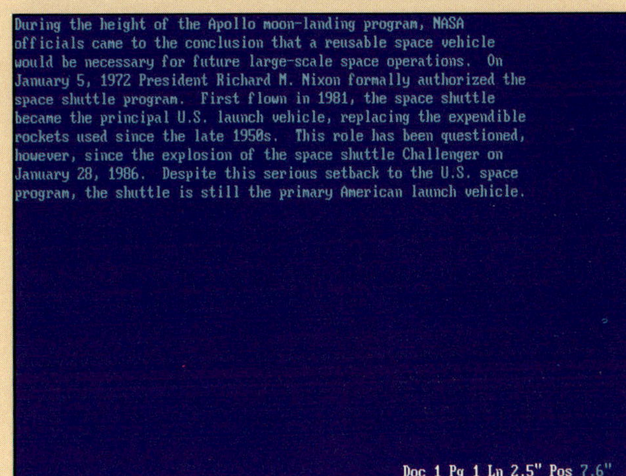


3. It's actually very easy to use WordPerfect. Once you start up the program, you can simply begin typing.

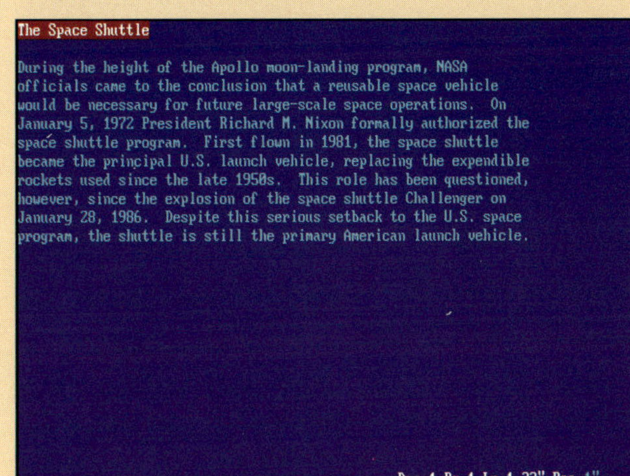


4. With a word processor, it's easy to go back and insert text at any place in an existing document.

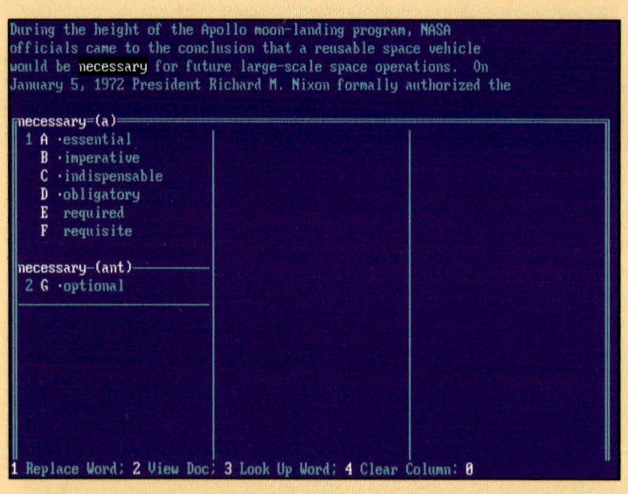


5. The WordPerfect thesaurus.

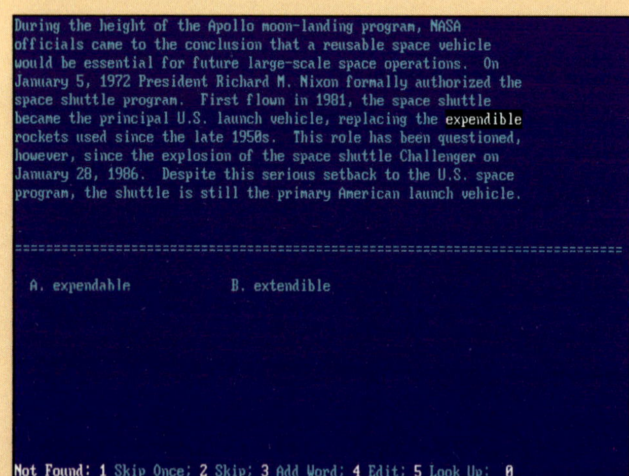


6. The WordPerfect spelling checker.

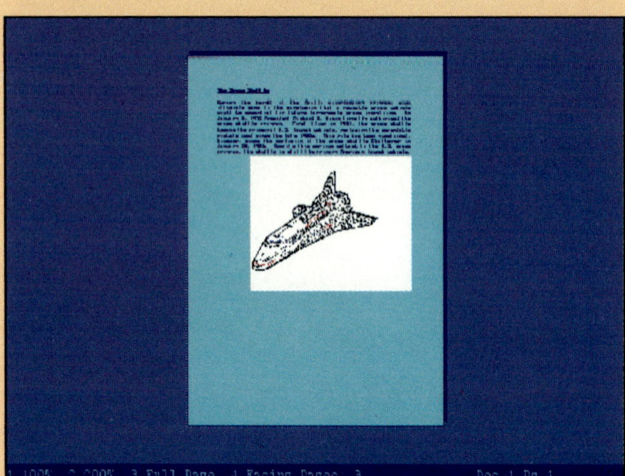


7. WordPerfect 5.0 is one of the best word-processing packages for mixing text and graphics together, without having to use a page layout program.

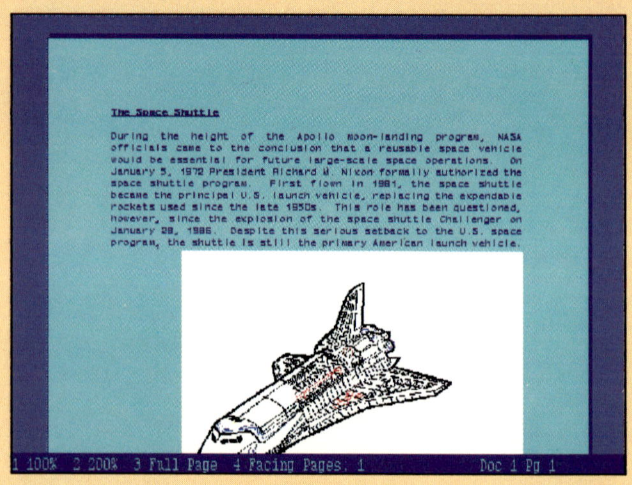


8. You can see an actual-size view of your document.

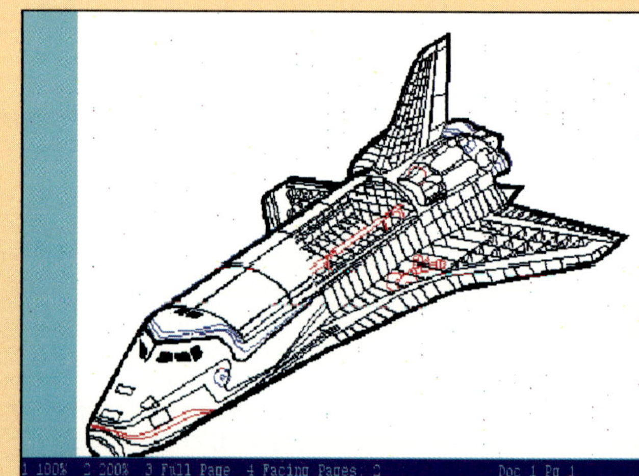


9. You can also zoom in to see a 200% view.

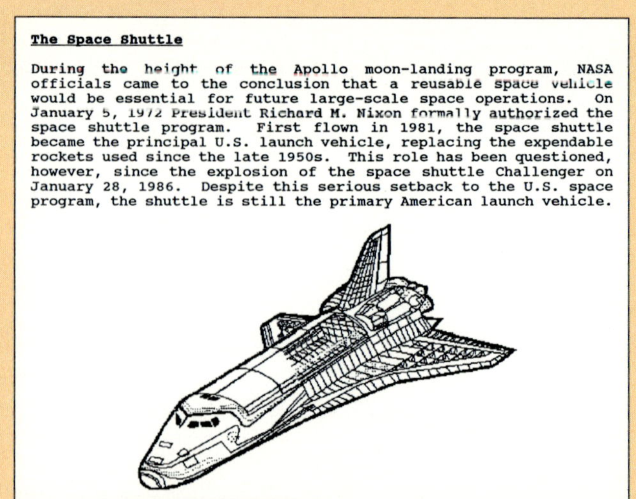


10. If you are satisfied with the way your document looks, you can proceed to print it.

# Using Microcomputers

The most striking feature of our time is not so much the wonderful scientific and technological advances that have occurred, but the rate at which they continue to occur and the profound impact they have on our lives. These photos show some remarkable ways to use microcomputers.

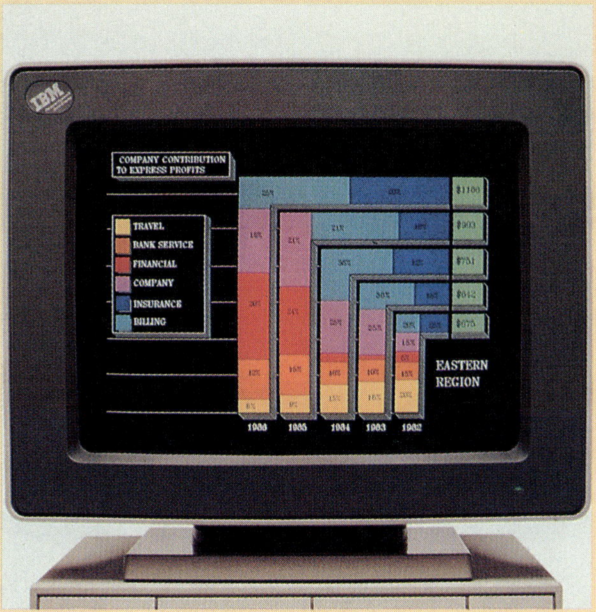


Graphics software is increasingly used in the automated office environment to produce all types of graphs, charts, and drawings. *(IBM)*

Secretary of the Interior Donald Hodel used an Apple Macintosh II microcomputer and a program called Hypercard to present his 1989 budget proposal. This is an example of presentation graphics.

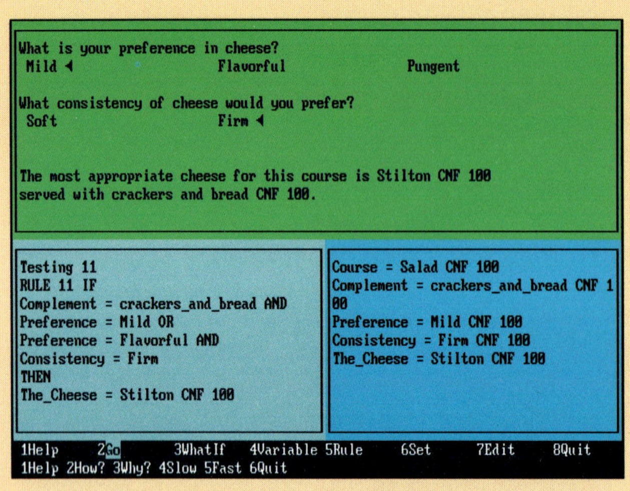


An expert system is a computer program that gives advice, emulating certain aspects of human problem-solving abilities.

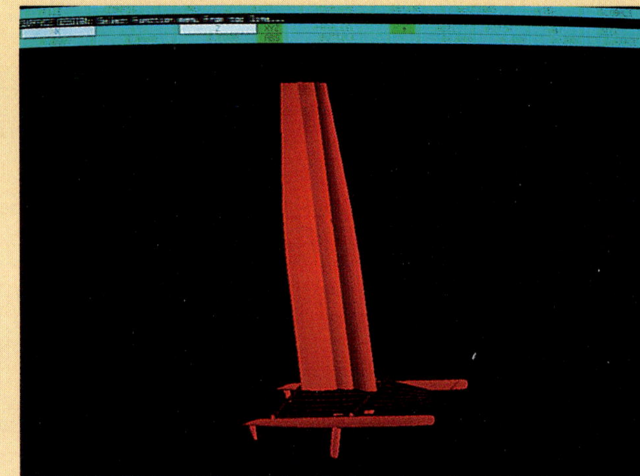

A computer-aided design (CAD) software package called *Fast Yacht* was used to design last year's winning America's Cup yacht. *(Dan Nerney/Dot)*

At the University of Illinois, computers enable students to simulate mixing dangerous chemicals without the danger of real injury. *(Stan Smith, Univ. of Ill.)*

Computer enhanced musicianship, with the aid of a microcomputer-based system. *(IBM)*

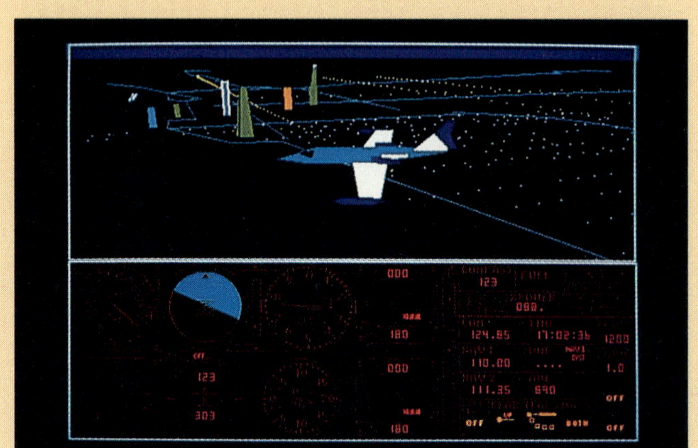

Microcomputers are often used to play games and pursue other entertaining activities. This screen shows Microsoft Corporation's popular Flight Simulator.

## Free-Form Data Base Managers

*For unstructured text, notes, memos*

In some cases, the information we want to organize with a computer cannot be conveniently broken down into regular-sized pieces of data. A **free-form data base manager** is a program designed to handle narrative text and irregular pieces of data, such as paragraphs, pages, articles, notes, discussions, and instructions. Many authors, educators, journalists, and researchers rely on free-form data base managers. These programs generally let you organize and index information by choosing key words to locate sections of text. Some free-form data base managers allow you to search through all of your text for occurrences of any words or phrases. For example, if you use a free-form data base manager to organize recipes, you can attach key words such as *salad*, *entree*, *beverage*, and *dessert* to your recipes. Then you can obtain a listing of all your salad recipes. Or, if the program searches through all your data for a specific word or phrase, such as *banana*, you can find all the recipes that include bananas. Free-form data base managers are usually relatively simple, easy-to-use, and inexpensive. They are used for such things as maintaining bibliographies, research observations, periodical abstracts, law listings, and even for random, unrelated notes.

## Relational Data Base Managers

*Linking separate files*

Like a flat-file manager, a **relational data base manager** also allows you to create, maintain, reorganize, and print structured data. But it has the added ability to work with more than one file at a time. This sophisticated software can connect or *relate* data from two or more different files. For example, suppose that you are the manager of a supermarket and you have a personnel data base that consists of two files. One file contains each employee's name, social security number, address, and phone number. To help keep sensitive information private, the other file contains just the employees' social security numbers, current salaries, and performance evaluations. A relational data base management system can draw on both files at the same time to produce a report listing each employee's name and current salary, even though these two pieces of data reside in different files.

Relational data base managers are generally quite sophisticated and expensive. They may not be as easy to use as other types of data managers, but they are more flexible and more powerful. In general, a relational data base manager can do everything that a flat-file or spreadsheet data base manager can do, but it is usually not very well adapted to the kinds of tasks done by a free-form data manager. Nevertheless, many businesses and organizations find that a relational data base management system is best for their needs.

## Programmable Data Base Managers

*Customize and automate*

A **programmable data base manager** is a relational or flat-file data base manager that includes its own programming language or works with a standard programming language such as BASIC, C, COBOL, FORTRAN, or Pascal. Although most average users never attempt programming a data base manager, the added feature gives experts the ability to customize the operation of the package for their own particular needs. For example, suppose that a mail-order company uses a programmable data base manager to keep track of all of the products it sells. At the end of every day, employees enter how many of each product were sold that day. Every Friday evening, a summary report is printed that lists the quantities of each product sold for the entire week. With a simple menu system that can be set up for employees' ease of use, the programmable data base manager automates some activities and makes others easier to handle. Programmable data base management systems generally are the most sophisticated, powerful, and expensive types of data base managers.

## CREATING A DATA BASE

Unfortunately, computers and software cannot do all the work in managing data. Although they can help a great deal, you must still plan your data base and collect the information that is to be stored. One way or another, data must be entered into the computer before it can be organized and stored on a disk. The three basic steps to creating a data base are defining its structure, entering the data, and saving the files.

### Defining the Structure

*Using files, records, fields*

Except for free-form programs, data base managers all require data to be structured in some orderly manner out of files, records, and fields. Figure 10.1, for example, illustrates the structure of a data base for the fictional Parkridge Condominium Association. The data base is made up of two files: the OWNERS file, which contains data about each condominium unit owner, and the FEES file, which contains the association's monthly condominium fee for each unit.

Each file in a data base is a collection of individual records. A **record** contains all the data about a particular person or object. For example, each record in the OWNERS file contains all the data about a particular condominium unit's owner. Similarly, each record in the FEES file contains all the data about a particular unit's monthly condominium fee.

As Figure 10.1 shows, records are subdivided into fields. A **field** is simply a single data item, such as a number, character, word, or phrase. For example, the records of the OWNERS file are made up of six fields: Last Name, First Name, Address, City, State, and ZIP. A field has two basic attributes: its length (in characters or bytes), and the type of data it can hold (such as numeric or text).

Generally, all the records in the same file have the same structure. In other words, the number, lengths, and data types of fields is the same for every record in a particular file. Different files in the same data base can have different record structures, however. The structure of the OWNERS file, for example, is clearly different from the FEES file, yet they are both in the Parkridge Condominium Association data base. These two different files do have one thing in common—they both contain an ADDRESS field with the same attributes. Since both of these files have a field in common, together they form a **relational data base**. Each file in a relational data base contains at least one field that is also present in another file in that data base.

Why not just put all the fields in the same file? Different files are usually formed for convenience, organization, and security. For example, the Parkridge Condominium Association keeps owners' names and condominium fees in separate files so that when a unit is sold, all the information that must be updated is in one place. Condominium fees stay the same regardless of the owner, but the owners must be changed when a unit is sold. The addresses in both files also stay the same because in this particular condominium association, owners must reside in their units (no renters are allowed). If possible, it is better to keep logically unrelated data in separate files. Keeping owner names and condominium fees in separate files helps reduce the likelihood of accidentally changing a condominium fee while updating an owner's name, or vice versa.

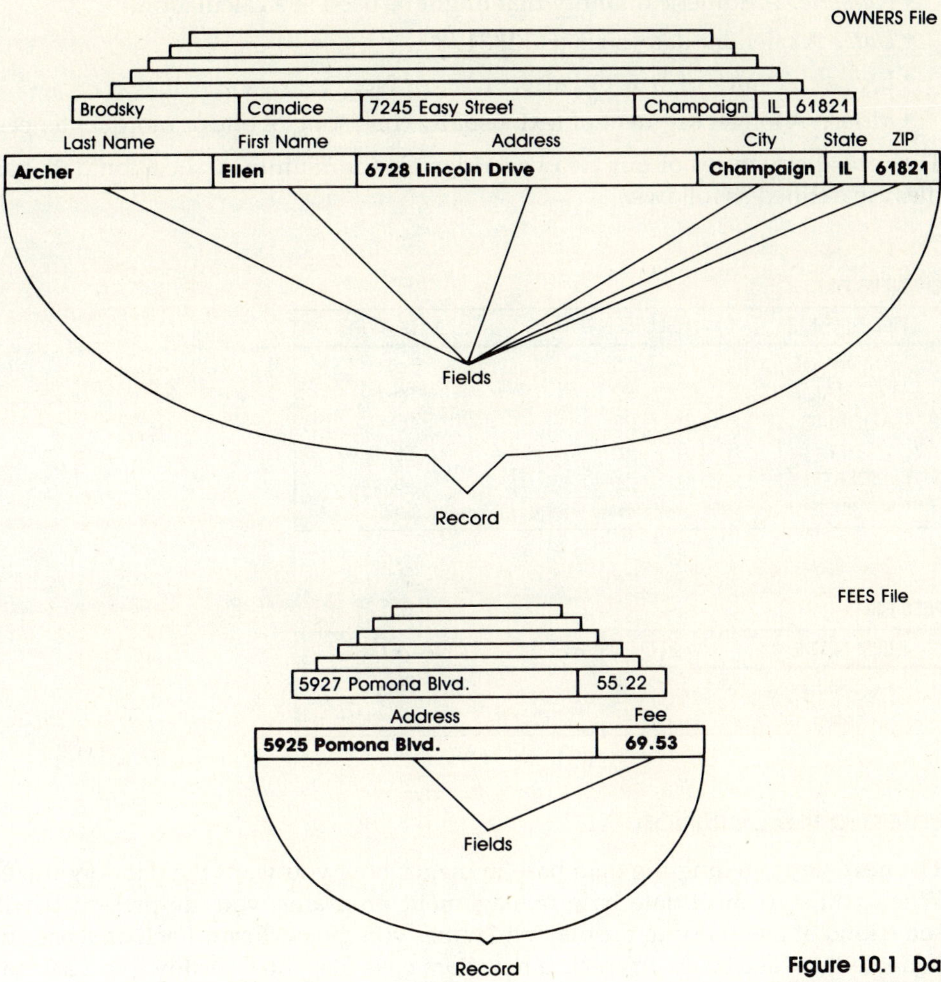


**Figure 10.1 Data Base Structure**
The Parkridge Condominium Association data base is made up of two files: OWNERS and FEES. Each file is a collection of records, which are made up of fields.

## Planning the Structure

*Decide what to include*

Before you can begin to enter records into a data base file, you must plan the record structure, which is the way the data will be organized. Remember, all records in a file consist of the same fields in the same order. Each field in the record structure must be given a name, length, and data type. The name of a field is usually a one or two word description of the contents of that field, such as LAST NAME or ADDRESS. The length of a field is the maximum number of characters it can hold. For example, the length of the STATE field in the Parkridge Condominium Association OWNERS file is 2 characters. The data type specifies the kind of information that can be stored in a field. Most data base managers, for instance, can handle at least the following types of data:

- *Text.* Any sequence of letters, digits, punctuation marks, and other symbols—often a single word or phrase. Sequences of digits that don't represent quantities, like addresses and ZIP codes, are also usually defined as text.

- *Numeric.* A numeric quantity that might be used in a calculation.
- *Date.* A calendar date, such as 12/31/89.
- *Logical.* A value of True or False, or Yes or No.
- *Memo.* A longer segment of text, usually consisting of one or more sentences.

The record structures of our two Parkridge Condominium Association data base files are defined as follows:

**OWNERS File**

| FIELD NAME | FIELD LENGTH | DATA TYPE |
|---|---|---|
| LAST NAME | 15 | Text |
| FIRST NAME | 10 | Text |
| ADDRESS | 25 | Text |
| CITY | 10 | Text |
| STATE | 2 | Text |
| ZIP | 5 | Text |

**FEES File**

| FIELD NAME | FIELD LENGTH | DATA TYPE |
|---|---|---|
| ADDRESS | 25 | Text |
| FEE | 7 | Numeric |

## Entering the Definition

*Tell the data base manager*

The next step is telling the data base manager how you want the data organized. When you start most data base management programs, you are presented with some kind of menu listing the major activities you can perform. Each data base file is created one at a time. To create a new data base file, you typically select a Create or New command, and the program asks you to supply a name for your file. In the case of Reflex Plus, a popular data base manager for the Apple Macintosh, you select the New command from the File menu to create a new data base file. As Figure 10.2(a) shows, Reflex Plus then prompts you for the file name, which we have entered as "Owners." Next, you must specify the structure of the file. Some programs prompt you for each record field, one at a time, or you may be asked to fill in an empty table that specifies the record structure. In either case, every field in the record must have a name, length, and data type. Some data base programs assume default values for the length and data type of each field, so you may not have to explicitly specify these attributes. Reflex Plus, for example, initially assumes that all fields are text and that they are eighteen characters long. If these assumptions are not adequate for your record structure, then you can explicitly set the length and data type of each field. If these assumptions are acceptable, however, then simply enter each field's name into the empty box shown in Figure 10.2(b). Figure 10.2(c) shows the Reflex Plus screen after entering the definition of the Parkridge Condominium Association OWNERS data base file.

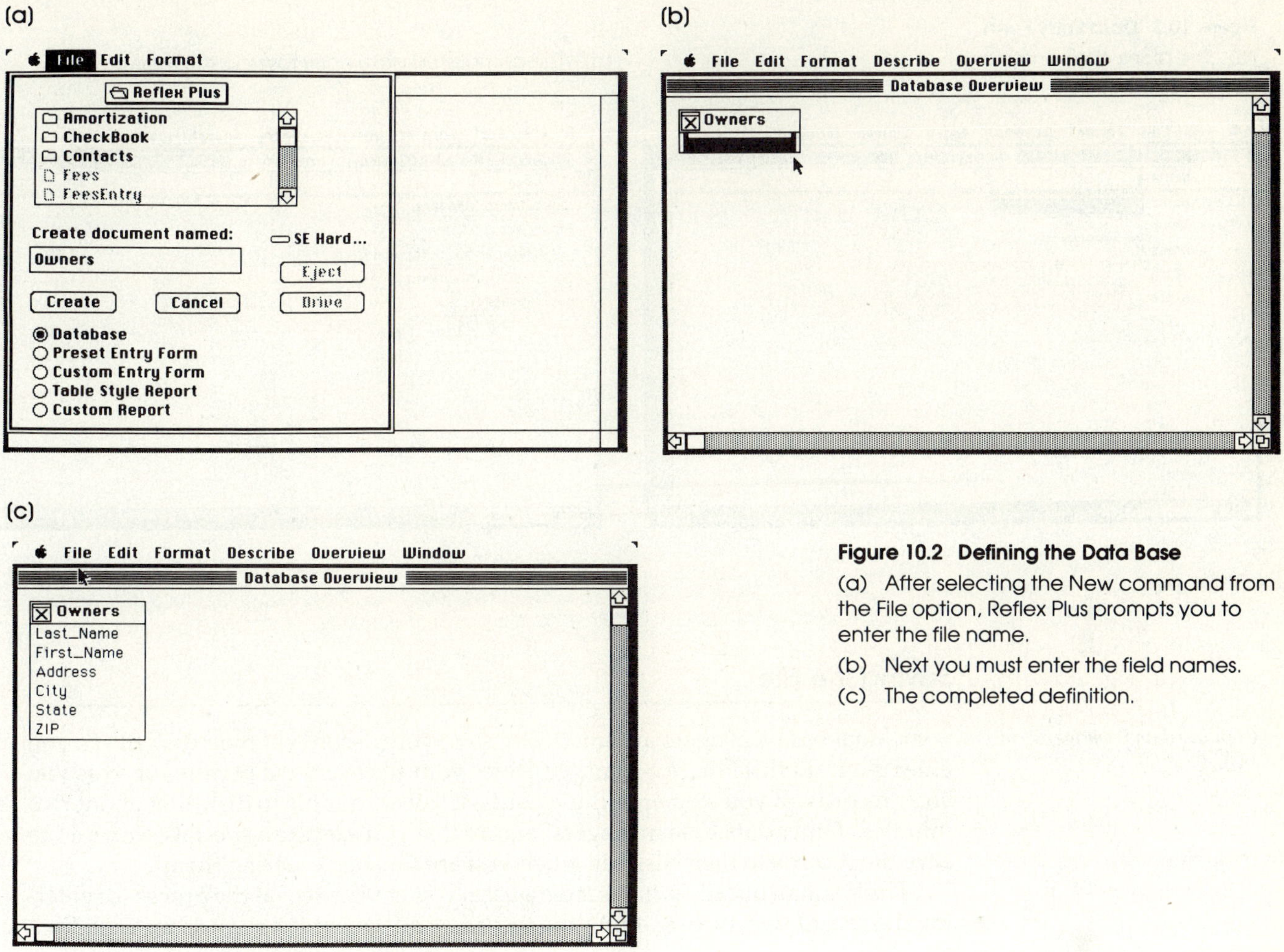


**Figure 10.2 Defining the Data Base**

(a) After selecting the New command from the File option, Reflex Plus prompts you to enter the file name.

(b) Next you must enter the field names.

(c) The completed definition.

## Entering Records

*Where you add your data*

Once the structure of your data base file has been defined, you can actually begin entering data. This involves typing the contents of each record's fields into your file. For each new record, the data base program presents you with a blank **data entry form**, which may look something like Figure 10.3(a). As the figure shows, this form lists each field you've defined and provides an empty box for its contents. The size of the box indicates how much room you have by depicting the maximum length of that field. You usually begin typing with the first character of the first field. A cursor or insertion point is usually present to show where you type characters. All you do is key in the entries for the fields in this record, pressing the **Enter** key after each one. You can correct mistakes by using the backspace key or by inserting and deleting selected characters within a field. Figure 10.3(b) shows the completed data entry form for the first record in the Parkridge Condominium Associations OWNERS file. When you are finished typing the last field of a record, the data base program may automatically go on to the next new record, or it may ask you if you want to enter a new record. After you have finished entering all of the records, you usually have to execute a command to tell the program to stop presenting new data entry forms and to return to the main menu.

**Figure 10.3 Data Entry Form**

(a) The blank data entry form. (b) The completed data entry form for the first record.

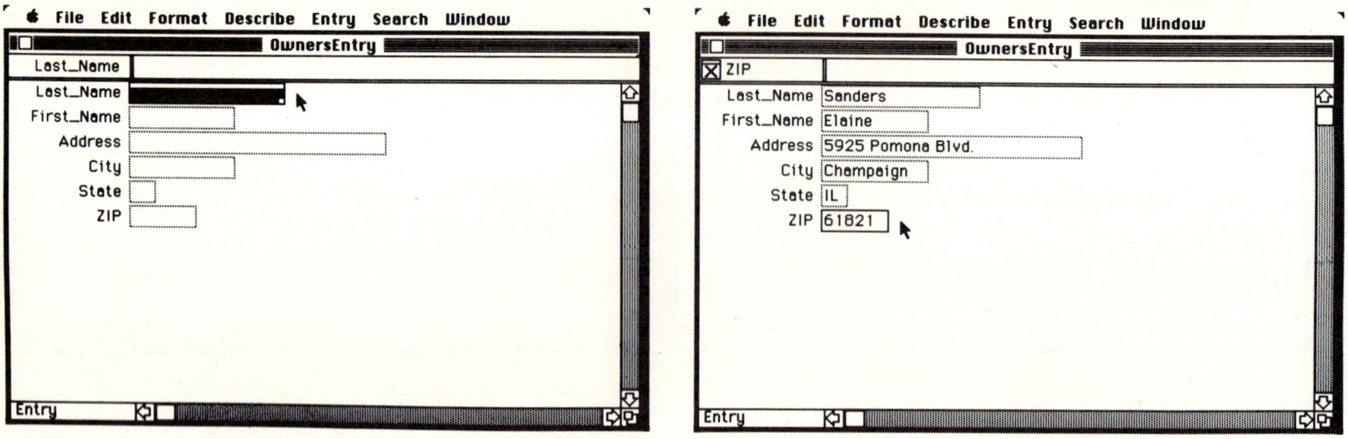


## Saving the File

*Copying data from memory to disk*

Some data base managers automatically save your records in their disk file as you enter them. Reflex Plus, for example, saves your file every ten minutes or so as you enter records. If you stop entering records, it saves your file to disk after about two minutes. Other data base managers require that you execute a special command to save the records to their disk file when you are finished entering them.

If more than one file is in your data base, you have to repeat the process of entering the record structure, entering the records, and saving the records for each file.

# VIEWING A DATA BASE

Let's assume that you have created and saved a data base. Now what do you do with it? Well, there are many reasons for keeping a data base, but the simplest is to store information so you can look it up later. Perhaps the most common data base operation is viewing what has already been stored.

## Retrieving the File

*Copying data from disk to memory*

Before you can view the contents of a data base file, you must retrieve it. This involves starting your data base manager program if you are not already running it and executing a command or selecting a menu option that loads the data base file from disk into memory. For example, to load the OWNERS data base file we've just created in Reflex Plus, you simply pull down the File menu, select the Open option, and then select OWNERS from the list of existing files. The program displays the filled data-entry form for the first record in the OWNERS file.

## Browsing

*Scanning the records*

If your data base file is small and you are not looking for one particular record, the easiest way to view your data is to **browse**. This allows you to casually go through and view the records in your data base file. Typically, the data base manager lets you start with the first or last record in the file, or with some record in between. It may present just one record on the screen in a filled data entry form, or it may display several records in a table format, with one record per row. In Reflex Plus, for example, when you retrieve a data base file from disk, the program displays the first record on the screen. To see other records, you pull down the Search menu (see Figure 10.4). The options in this menu let you display the first record in the file, the last record in the file, or the record just before or just after the one currently on the screen. Starting at the beginning, for instance, you can browse forward through the records in a file by repeatedly selecting the Next Record option from the Search menu. Similarly, if you select the Last Record option and then repeatedly select the Prior option from the Search menu, you can browse backward through the file.

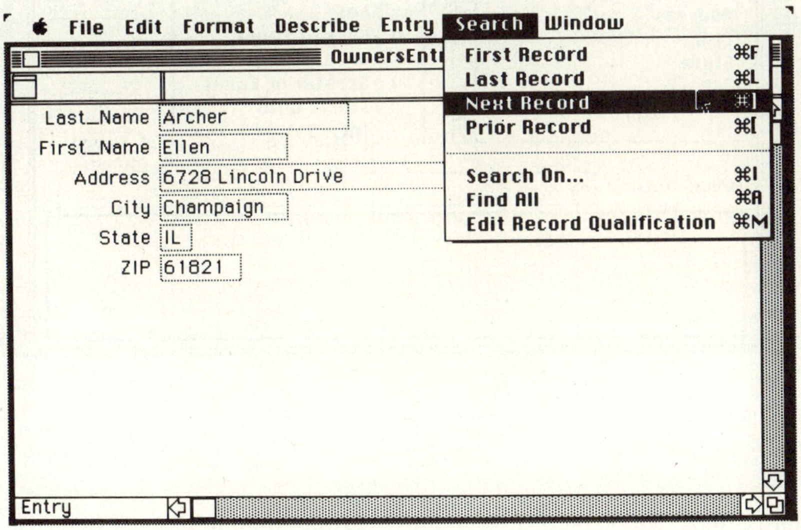


**Figure 10.4 Browsing with the Search Menu**
In Reflex Plus, you can browse through a data base file by using the Search menu.

## Finding Records

*Looking for particular items*

Browsing is fine for examining short data base files, but it becomes impractical for files with many records. In other cases you may want to look at only one specific record or a selected set of records, not the entire data base. Data base management systems generally have several different ways to help you find the records you want to see. These programs let you search for only those records that meet one or more specific criteria. This is sometimes called **querying** a data base. The simplest type of query asks for only those records that contain a particular entry in one of their fields. For example, let's say that you want to see Henry Jefferson's record. You query the data base for the record that has *Jefferson* in its LAST NAME field. In the Parkridge Condominium Association data base, only one record meets this simple criterion. In other data bases, such as a telephone book, several or even dozens of records may meet this criterion. You may have to further narrow down the search by also specifying the contents of another field. Querying a data base for records that have *Jefferson* in the LAST NAME field and *Henry* in the FIRST NAME field should yield fewer matches. With complex data bases, you may have to narrow down the search even further by specifying still more criteria, such as CITY, STATE, or ZIP code.

Let's illustrate the process of finding a specific record in our Parkridge Condominium Association OWNERS file with Reflex Plus. You want to find Henry Jefferson's record. The first step is to choose the Search On... option from the Search menu. This displays the screen you see in Figure 10.5. After entering *Jefferson* as the value to find in the LAST NAME field, the program finds Jefferson's record and presents in on the screen in a filled data entry form, similar to the one in Figure 10.3(b).

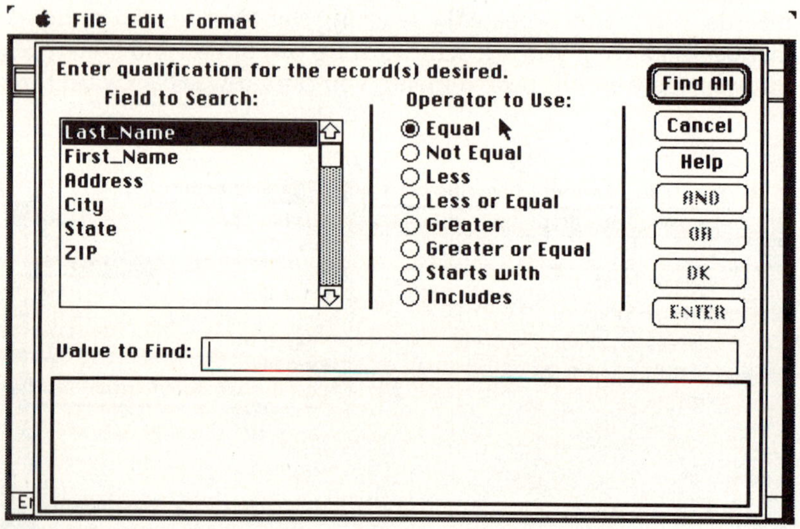


**Figure 10.5 Finding a Specific Record**
To find Henry Jefferson's record, you would enter *Jefferson* into the box labeled *Value to Find.*

Finding Henry Jefferson's record is a very simple search operation. You searched only one field for only one value. It is common, however, to formulate more complex queries. This involves searching one or more additional fields for other values. For example, you could search for those records with LAST_NAME equal to *Jefferson* and FIRST_NAME equal to *Henry* and CITY equal to *Champaign*. Another example might be all those records with CITY equal to *Champaign* or CITY equal to *Urbana*. By stringing together search operations in this manner with AND and OR, you can construct very specific queries. This is especially helpful with very large data bases.

## UPDATING A DATA BASE

Most data bases must be changed over time. Some data bases may be changed regularly, as often as several times a day. For example, supermarkets must frequently alter their prices, which are stored in data bases tied into the checkout registers. Other data bases may very seldom need changing. The government's census records, for instance, would not have to be changed under normal circumstances, except possibly to correct data entry errors. One of the major functions of a data base management system is allowing you to keep your data bases up-to-date and accurate. This involves letting you add, delete, and modify records, as well as letting you change the existing structure of a data base.

## Adding Records

*Expanding the data base*

New records often must be added to many data bases. A mail-order company's mailing list, for example, is expanded as new customers are acquired. The process of adding a new record to an existing data base file is very similar to entering records in a new file. To add records, typically, you select an option from a menu or execute a command that presents a new blank data entry form on the screen. In Reflex Plus, for example, you do this by selecting the Blank Record option from the Entry menu. Data is typed into the blank fields and the new record is added to the data base file. If several new records are to be added, the process is simply repeated. If the records must be kept in some particular order, say alphabetized by last name, you also may have to rearrange the data base file after you are finished adding records. We'll discuss how you do this later in the chapter in the section on sorting and indexing.

## Deleting Records

*Discarding unneeded information*

It is also necessary to be able to remove records from a data base. A mail-order company, for example, may decide not to send a new catalog to previous customers who placed their last order more than three years ago. This company needs to go through its data base periodically and delete the records of inactive customers. The first step is to find the record to be removed. In this case you search the data base for a record with an order date more than three years ago. Then you select an option from a menu or execute a command, often called Delete, that removes the selected record from the data base file. In some data base programs, this removal is not finalized until you confirm your deletion or execute still another command. For example, in Reflex Plus you delete a record by selecting the Delete Record option from the Entry menu. Before the record is actually removed, the program gives you a chance to change your mind by asking you if you really want to delete this record.

Sometimes you only need to delete records from a data base one at a time. For example, if you know the names of five people who no longer want catalogs, you would want to remove their names from your data base. You search for each person's record and delete it from the data base. In other cases, you might want to remove from the entire data base all records that meet certain criteria. A good example is the mail-order company we just mentioned that no longer wants to send catalogs to customers who haven't placed an order in three years. This company needs to search its entire mailing list for such customers and remove their records. Although this can be accomplished by simply repeating the same search and delete process over and over until the entire file has been done, virtually all data base managers give you the option of a **global delete**. With a global delete option or command, the mail-order company can remove all the records of inactive customers in just one or two steps. Reflex Plus, for example, lets you use a global delete by first finding the records you want to delete, as in Figure 10.5, and then selecting the Delete Qualified Records option from the Entry menu. Every record that matches the specified criteria is then deleted from the file.

### Modifying Records

*Changing existing contents*

Entirely removing a record from a data base is somewhat drastic. In many cases all you need to do is modify a record by changing the contents of selected fields. For example, if a customer moves, the mail-order company wants to update the address, not remove the customer's record. All data base management systems let you update existing records without removing them. In Reflex Plus, for example, you first find the record you want to change. Its filled data entry form is presented on the screen. You can use the mouse to move the insertion point and insert, delete, or overwrite characters anywhere within the fields. For making small changes, modifying a record is much quicker than deleting it and adding a new one.

For changing several records at once, some data base managers also have a **global modify** command. Sometimes called **global search and replace**, these operations let you modify all the records in a data base that meet certain criteria. For example, let's say that you've created a data base file that contains the addresses of many people who live in Champagne, Illinois. You discover later that you've made a common mistake—the city is not *Champagne* (after a region in northeast France noted for its effervescent white wine), but rather *Champaign* (meaning flat, open country). With a global modify command, you can easily change every *Champagne* to *Champaign* in just one or two steps.

### Changing the Structure

*Redesigning records*

Adding, deleting, and modifying records are all common data base operations. Changing the existing structure of a data base is done less frequently. Nevertheless, you must occasionally change the name, length, or data type of a field; add new fields; or delete existing fields. Most data base managers let you perform all of these modifications.

For example, let's say that you decide to use the extended nine-digit ZIP codes in your mailing list data base. Unfortunately, you only allocated five spaces for ZIP codes when you defined and entered the record structure of your mailing list data base. To convert to nine-digit ZIP codes, you first have to change the length of the ZIP field from 5 to 9. That is the easy part. Then you have to modify every record in your data base to add the remaining four digits onto the ZIP codes.

Although it is occasionally unavoidable, changing the structure of a huge data base is not to be taken lightly. As you can see, it sometimes involves quite a bit of effort. You may wind up having to modify many records, especially if you add new fields. For this reason, it is important that you carefully consider the structure of your data base in the very beginning, before you enter any records. That initial plan is critical to the maintenance of your data base in the future. It pays to take the time to think ahead and try to anticipate your future data storage needs.

## REARRANGING A DATA BASE

In general, data must be kept in some predictable order if it is to be useful. This becomes increasingly true the more data you have. Imagine trying to find one particular word in a dictionary if all words weren't alphabetized. The task would be so daunting that dictionaries would be practically useless. Keeping records organized is one of the most important jobs of a data base management system. As new records are added and old records deleted, a data base may have to be reorganized.

You also might want to rearrange your data to see or use it in a different way. Instead of ordering your mailing list by last name, for example, you might want to temporarily rearrange records into ZIP code order. By printing mailing labels for your catalogs in ZIP code order, you can take advantage of special discounts from the post office. Many data base managers offer two basic ways of rearranging records: sorting and indexing.

## Sorting

*Putting records in order*

The term sorting is generally used to mean arranging the actual records of a data base into some particular order. Some data base management systems create a completely new file when records are sorted. The records in this new file are the same as the records in the original file, but they are arranged in a different order. Other data base management systems don't actually create a new file, they just rearrange the records in the original file. Either way, sorting results in a file with all records in a predictable order.

Before you can sort a data base you have to decide which field will be the **key**. This is the field used as the basis for the sort. If you want to alphabetically sort the records of a mailing list by last name, then the field that contains last names is the key. If you want to sort by ZIP code, then the field that contains ZIP codes is the key.

In some cases, you want to sort records on the basis of more than one key. For example, let's say that you want to sort your mailing list first by ZIP code and then alphabetically by last name. In other words, records are to be alphabetized by last name within each ZIP code. The ZIP code field is the **primary key** and the last name field is the **secondary key**. The primary key is the field you sort on first and the secondary key is the field you sort on second. Virtually all data base management systems can sort on the basis of at least two keys. Many data base programs let you have as many keys as there are fields in a record.

Another decision you must make before sorting a data base is the order. There are two orders in which records can be sorted: **ascending order** and **descending order**. If the sort key contains numeric values, then sorting in ascending order arranges the numbers from smallest to largest. If the sort key contains text, then sorting in ascending order arranges records alphabetically, from A to Z. Descending order goes from largest to smallest for numbers and from Z to A for text. By default, most data base managers assume that you want ascending order unless you specify otherwise.

In Reflex Plus, sorting a data base file is quite simple. When you define the structure of a data base file, you are required to indicate at least one key field. For example, in our Parkridge Condominium Association OWNERS file the key field we chose was LAST_NAME. This is the field that uniquely identifies each record in this particular data base file. Reflex Plus automatically keeps files sorted on the basis of the key fields indicated when the data base structure was defined. So, if you add or delete records, the file is always kept sorted.

If you have ever tried to alphabetize a card catalog or even arrange your canceled checks in numerical order, you know that sorting can be a time-consuming process. The more items there are to sort, the longer it takes. While computers are much faster than people, partly because they don't physically shuffle papers, sorting is still relatively time consuming compared to other types of data processing. In fact, sorting is one of the most time-consuming jobs for computers to do. Although conceptually quite simple, the process of rearranging many data records quickly is no easy task. Many computer scientists have devoted their entire careers to developing efficient methods of sorting.

Besides being a relatively slow process, sorting also can take up disk space. As we said, some data base programs create a completely new file every time you sort an existing file. If the file is large, sorting it can consume a great deal of additional storage space. There may be occasions in which you need to keep the same data arranged differently for different purposes. For example, you might want one version of your mailing list always alphabetized by last name, and another version always arranged by ZIP code. Every time you sort the original file to create a different arrangement, you create a new file that duplicates all records, only in a different order. Whenever you update this data base, you have to make the same changes in both files. This duplication of effort is also time-consuming and can introduce errors. Fortunately, there is another way to rearrange records in a data base.

## Indexing

*Listing record numbers in order*

**Indexing** is a way to reorder the records of a data base without actually duplicating the data in a new file or rearranging the actual records in the original file. Every time you enter a record into a new data base file or add a record to an existing file, that record is assigned a unique **record number**. This number is used by the data base management system to identify each record. By indexing a data base file, you create an **index file** that contains only record numbers, listed in a particular order. An index file represents a different arrangement of the original file, without duplicating any of the data. For example, let's say that you have the mailing list file of Figure 10.6(a). The records in this file were entered in no particular order. Instead of sorting that mailing list to alphabetize it by last name, you can index it instead. The resulting index file is shown in Figure 10.6(b). When you index a data base file, you don't change the order of the records and the record numbers in the original file. Instead you create an index file that just lists the record numbers in the new order. With large data bases, the index file is usually much smaller than the data base file from which it was created. You can keep several different index files and use much less disk space than if you had performed several different sorts of the original file. Because indexing a file eliminates the need to copy or rearrange all of the data stored in the original file, it is also much quicker than sorting.

**Figure 10.6 Indexing**

(a) Parkridge Condominium Association OWNERS file.

(b) INDEX file of the OWNERS file, indexed by owner's last names.

(a)

| | | | | | | |
|---|---|---|---|---|---|---|
| 1 | Sanders | Elaine | 5925 Pomona Blvd. | Champaign | IL | 61821 |
| 2 | Engels | Fred | 5927 Pomona Blvd. | Champaign | IL | 61821 |
| 3 | Harbison | Betty | 5929 Pomona Blvd. | Champaign | IL | 61821 |
| 4 | Santiago | Tom | 5931 Pomona Blvd. | Champaign | IL | 61821 |
| 5 | Lyons | Diane | 6722 Lincoln Drive | Champaign | IL | 61821 |
| 6 | Mack | Jeffrey | 6724 Lincoln Drive | Champaign | IL | 61821 |
| 7 | Thorpe | Todd | 6726 Lincoln Drive | Champaign | IL | 61821 |
| 8 | Archer | Ellen | 6728 Lincoln Drive | Champaign | IL | 61821 |
| 9 | Chou | Yuki | 6730 Lincoln Drive | Champaign | IL | 61821 |
| 10 | Christopoulos | Anthony | 7241 Easy Street | Champaign | IL | 61821 |
| 11 | Scott | Montgomery | 7243 Easy Street | Champaign | IL | 61821 |
| 12 | Brodsky | Candice | 7245 Easy Street | Champaign | IL | 61821 |
| 13 | Trowbridge | Jonathan | 7247 Easy Street | Champaign | IL | 61821 |
| 14 | Garcia | Marcos | 7249 Easy Street | Champaign | IL | 61821 |
| 15 | Jefferson | Henry | 8118 Long Lake Lane | Champaign | IL | 61821 |
| 16 | Fulton | Wendy | 8120 Long Lake Lane | Champaign | IL | 61821 |
| 17 | Kruse | Julie | 8122 Long Lake Lane | Champaign | IL | 61821 |

(b)

| |
|---|
| 8 |
| 12 |
| 9 |
| 10 |
| 2 |
| 16 |
| 14 |
| 3 |
| 15 |
| 17 |
| 5 |
| 6 |
| 1 |
| 4 |
| 11 |
| 7 |
| 13 |

As an analogy, think of a library as a data base. Each book on the shelf is like a record in the data base. Each book has its own unique catalog number, just like a record number. To sort this library by book title, you would have to physically rearrange all of the books. To index this library by book title, you would create an index file. In most libraries, this is known as the card catalog. Which would you rather rearrange: the books themselves or the cards in the card catalog? What if you needed books arranged by author's name and subject as well? It is much easier, cheaper, and more compact to keep three card catalogs and one set of books than to have three duplicate sets of books arranged by title, author, and subject.

The process of telling the data base manager to index a file is similar to sorting it. You have to decide which field will be the key, or which fields for multiple keys. You also have to decide on the order, either ascending or descending. The major difference is that you execute an Index command instead of a Sort command. Unfortunately, Reflex Plus doesn't allow you to index files as we've described in this section. This program only lets you sort the original file. If you want to rearrange your data in a different order, you must sort them. In the next chapter, however, we will give details on both how to sort and index files using the dBASE III PLUS data base management system.

## GENERATING DATA BASE REPORTS

*Hard-copy data output*

Like word processors and spreadsheets, data base management systems are frequently used to produce printed output. A data base **report** is simply a printed collection of record fields, usually formatted in some manner. Most data base managers give you a good deal of flexibility in specifying the layout of reports. You can indicate the fields to be included, the order in which they are to appear, their positions on the page, their headings, and whether to sum numeric fields. Margins, line spacing, page length, and page numbering also can be specified. Once you set up a report layout, many data base programs let you save this layout in a disk file so that you can use it again in the future without having to respecify all of the format settings.

As an example, let's use Reflex Plus to generate a simple data base report of the OWNERS file. Since we know that every building in the Parkridge Condominium Association has the same city, state, and ZIP code, there is no need to print these items. We want a table listing first name, last name, and then the street address in three columns across the page with appropriate headings. Fortunately, this is an easy report to produce. First you select the New option from the File menu. This allows you to open and name a new report file. Reflex Plus calls the type of report we want to produce a *table style report*. After you tell Reflex Plus what kind of report you want to produce, you choose the data base file from which to produce it. In this case, the data base file is OWNERS. Once you do this, Reflex Plus presents a screen that lists all of the fields in this data base file and then asks you to select the fields you want to include in your report. You select FIRST_NAME, LAST_NAME, and ADDRESS in that order. Another screen appears that lets you formulate a search condition to indicate which records are to be included in the report. This is a valuable feature that lets you generate reports that list only those records fulfilling certain criteria. You also can select the default option, which includes every record in the report. Since you want to see all of the owners names and addresses, you choose Find All, the default option. Finally, Reflex Plus presents the report on the screen. You can print the report by selecting the Print option from the File menu. Figure 10.7 shows the final result.

**Figure 10.7 Printed OWNERS File Report**
Here is the printed report of the owners names and addresses.

| First_Name | Last_Name | Address |
|---|---|---|
| Ellen | Archer | 6728 Lincoln Drive |
| Candice | Brodsky | 7245 Easy Street |
| Yuki | Chou | 6730 Lincoln Drive |
| Anthony | Christopoulos | 7241 Easy Street |
| Fred | Engels | 5927 Pomona Blvd. |
| Wendy | Fulton | 8120 Long Lake Lane |
| Marcos | Garcia | 7249 Easy Street |
| Betty | Harbison | 5929 Pomona Blvd. |
| Henry | Jefferson | 8118 Long Lake Lane |
| Julie | Kruse | 8122 Long Lake Lane |
| Diane | Lyons | 6722 Lincoln Drive |
| Jeffrey | Mack | 6724 Lincoln Drive |
| Elaine | Sanders | 5925 Pomona Blvd. |
| Tom | Santiago | 5931 Pomona Blvd. |
| Montgomery | Scott | 7243 Easy Street |
| Todd | Thorpe | 6726 Lincoln Drive |
| Jonathan | Trowbridge | 7247 Easy Street |

## ADDITIONAL FEATURES

Data base management systems are among the most complex and powerful of all microcomputer software. They are used extensively by businesses and organizations to perform all kinds of data storage, retrieval, and processing chores. So far, we've covered just the basics of data base management. There are many advanced capabilities that are beyond the scope of this book. Nevertheless, several additional features are especially noteworthy.

### Custom Data Entry Forms

*Create your own forms*

When you add records to a new or existing file, the data base manager presents you with a simple data entry form based on the record structure. Fields are presented as named, in the order in which they were defined, with no additional instructions on the screen. Although this entry form may be sufficient for the sophisticated user who designed the data base, other users may need more assistance. Data bases are often updated by data entry personnel who are not computer experts. They may not know all the intricacies of operating the data base manager and the simple data entry form used by default may leave them confused about what to do. In some cases, it may be desirable to present a data entry form similar to an existing paper form already used in the organization, so that input errors can be minimized. Fortunately, many data base management systems let you design your own custom data entry forms.

In Reflex Plus, for example, you can use the Entry Design feature to create a customized data entry form. This feature allows you to change both the appearance and structure of an existing data entry form. Specifically, you can

- change field lengths.
- move fields to different screen positions.
- add, change, and delete field labels.

- change the font size and style of field labels and contents.
- add graphics to the entry form.
- add and delete fields.
- add fields to calculate formulas using other numeric fields.
- create a single form for related data base files.

Figure 10.8 shows a somewhat more attractive data entry form for the OWNERS data base file, which was created with the Reflex Plus Entry Design feature.

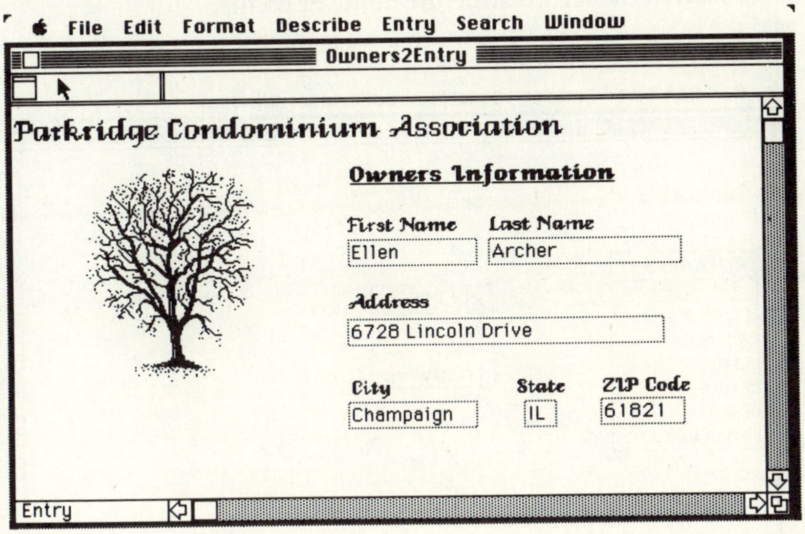


**Figure 10.8 Custom Data Entry Form**
Reflex Plus lets you easily create almost any kind of data entry form.

## Mailing Labels

*Automated addressing*

As you know, data base management systems are frequently used to maintain large mailing lists. One of the primary reasons for doing this is that data base managers can be used to generate mailing labels automatically. Records can be formatted so that names and addresses print directly on envelopes or on standard sheets of detachable mailing labels, saving time and labor and reducing errors.

While some data base managers have built-in options specifically designed for printing mailing labels, other packages require that you set up a specially formatted report. Reflex Plus, for example, has no menu option reserved for printing labels, but it does include a sample data base with several report formats already set up for a number of printers. These samples can be easily modified to print mailing labels from your own data bases.

## Relating Multiple Files

*Interconnecting data*

As we have said, most powerful data base management systems sold for microcomputers these days are relational. This means that they let you relate data in one file to data in another file, provided these two files have a field in common or are connected in some other way. In our Parkridge Condominium Association data base, for example, the two different files have a common field (see Figure 10.1). Both the

OWNERS file and the FEES file have a field that contains each unit's address. Let's say that you want to generate a report that lists each name along with the owner's monthly condominium fee. Since these two data items reside in different files, you have to relate the two files to generate the report. Different data base management systems have different procedures for relating multiple files. Reflex Plus, for example, lets you do this by adding **link fields**, special fields that connect records in different data bases. A link is symbolized by a line connecting the two link fields in the data base structures of different files. Figure 10.9 shows how Reflex Plus depicts our Parkridge Condominium Association data base, with a link connecting the TO_FEES link field in the record structure of the OWNERS file to the TO_OWNERS link field in the record structure of the FEES file.

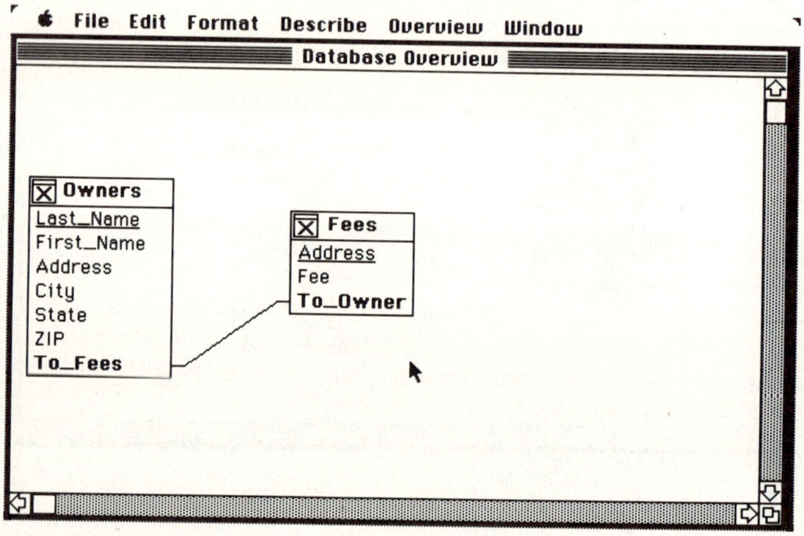


**Figure 10.9 Linked Files**
The OWNERS and FEES files have been linked by connecting the special fields TO_FEES and TO_OWNER.

There are three possible ways to link the records of a multiple file data base: one-to-one, one-to-many, and many-to-many. The connection between the OWNERS and FEES files shown in Figure 10.9 is the simplest, a **one-to-one link**. This type of link connects a single record in one file to a single record in another file. A **one-to-many link** connects a single record in one file to multiple records in one or more other files. For example, you could use one-to-many links in a data base that connects a file of college instructors to one or more files of class assignments. In other words, an instructor can teach more than one class, but each class has only one instructor. Finally, a **many-to-many link** connects multiple records to other multiple records in data base files. A data base connecting students to instructors might use many-to-many links. Each student has several instructors in different classes, and each instructor has many students.

After you have linked files with a relational data base management system, you can perform many useful operations on them. In Reflex Plus, for example, you can create a data entry form that lets you enter records for several files using the same form. Such a multiple-file entry form makes it easy to see which records are linked and it allows data from different linked files to appear on the same form. These forms are frequently used as invoices. You can also create reports that display data from multiple linked files. In this way, relational data base managers help you keep your records well-organized in separate files and still give you a great deal of flexibility in finding and printing your data.

## Query Languages

*Standard commands to extract data*

Some data base managers have their own unique commands for such operations as finding records and relating multiple files. Others offer a more standardized method of executing common data base operations. A **query language**, for example, is a specialized set of commands for rearranging or extracting data from data bases. It provides a way to directly interrogate a data base management package about the contents of a data base. Many query languages have been used in sophisticated data base management systems over the years. Today, two major rivals have become standards in the industry: SQL, or Structured Query Language, and QBE, or Query-by-Example. In addition, there has been a considerable amount of effort directed at using subsets of natural languages (such as ordinary English) as relational data base query languages.

### Structured Query Language

*Used in many relational systems*

**Structured Query Language (SQL)** was developed to express certain basic operations on relational data bases. The language evolved from work done by Dr. Edgar F. Codd, an IBM Fellow who developed the basic theory behind relational data bases in 1969. SQL is primarily used as an interactive language for extracting information from a data base. In some ways, SQL resembles a general-purpose high-level programming language such as COBOL. The American National Standards Institute (ANSI) accepted SQL as a standard query language for relational data base systems in 1986. Today, SQL is being adopted, or at least considered for use, by most major relational data base management system developers for use in their products. Several popular microcomputer data base management packages now use SQL. The Extended Edition of IBM's OS/2 operating system includes an SQL data base management system, and dBASE IV from Ashton-Tate is also an SQL package.

### Query-by-Example

*Easy-to-use, interactive*

**Query-by-Example (QBE)** is another one of IBM's data base contributions. This query language grew out of work done by M. M. Zloof at IBM's Research Laboratory in Yorktown Heights, New York in 1977. QBE was designed from the start to be a highly interactive, easy way to extract information from a data base. The user at a terminal or microcomputer runs a special screen editor to tell the system what to do. This screen editor displays a visual image of a single-row data base table, with one space for every field in the data base. The user simply moves the cursor across the screen and leaves check marks in the fields where answers are desired (see Figure 10.10). Paradox, from Ansa Software, is an example of a popular data base management package for microcomputers that uses QBE.

### Natural Query Language

*Queries in English*

Some query languages are designed to be as close as possible to ordinary natural languages such as English. In reality, these so-called natural language interfaces generally have rather small vocabularies, and you may have to "teach" the system the English words that refer to your particular data base in order to subsequently query it in English. For example, Q&A from Symantec is a file manager that in-

**Figure 10.10 Querie-by-Example**
This screen shows Querie-by-Example being used to search a parts inventory data base.

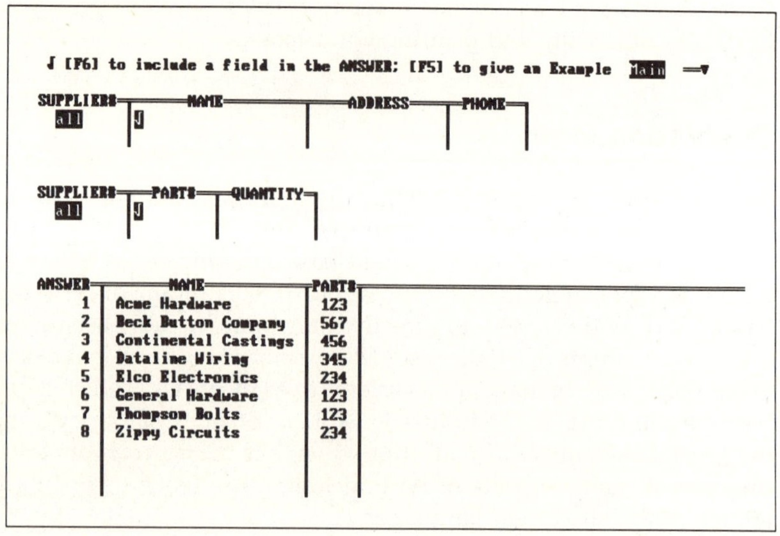


cludes what it calls the Intelligent Assistant. The Intelligent Assistant comes with a built-in vocabulary of 400 words and it automatically "knows" the words you use to name the fields in your file. You can personalize the Intelligent Assistant, but you have to give it certain lessons before you ask it any questions. During these lessons, you enter the words you want to use to refer to the different fields and data values in your file. Figure 10.11 shows a sample screen from Q&A that describes its natural query language. Although there are more sophisticated natural query languages used in a few mainframe computer data base management systems, this type of query language does not approach the popularity of SQL and QBE.

## Protecting Data

*Reducing accidents and snooping*

The simplest way to protect the information stored in a data base is to prevent someone from accidentally changing it. Many data base programs can help prevent such accidents by letting you designate record fields as **read-only** or **display-only fields**. After you enter data into a field, you can give it display-only status so that it cannot be altered until the display-only feature is turned off. Reflex Plus, for example, lets you designate fields to be display-only. Data stored in display-only fields are shown in entry forms, but they cannot be changed.

Sometimes merely protecting data from accidental alteration is not enough. Data bases are often used to store sensitive information. Salary figures, course grades, medical histories, disciplinary reports, performance evaluations, and police records are but a few of the different kinds of private data kept by computers. Some data base management systems provide advanced security measures for preventing unauthorized access to sensitive data. One method, known as **data encryption**, encodes information so that it can be read and changed only by authorized people who know the special password. When a data base is encrypted, data is scrambled in a way that makes no sense to anyone trying to read it. The only way that the data can be unscrambled is by entering the password, specified when the file was originally encrypted.

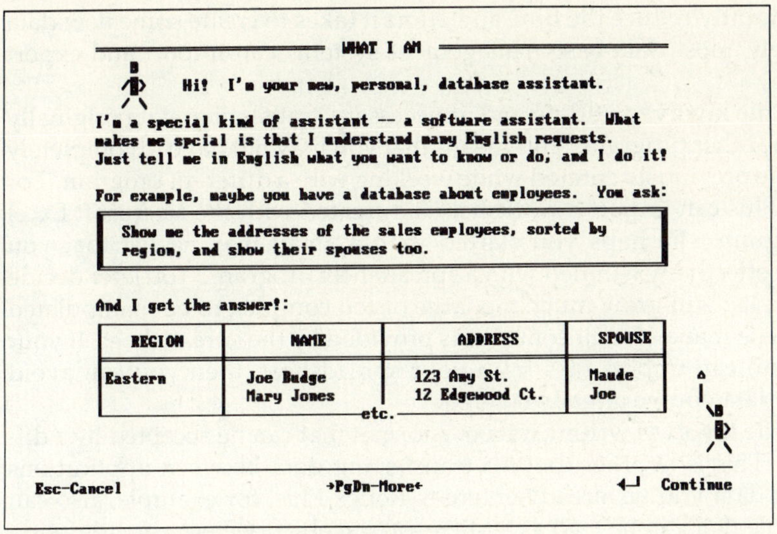


**Figure 10.11 Natural Query Language**
The help screen from Symantec's Q&A, a microcomputer file manager that uses a natural query language called the Intelligent Assistant.

## Data Base Programming

*Customizing and automating*

As we have said, some sophisticated data base management systems include their own programming language or can be made to work with a standard programming language like BASIC, C, COBOL, FORTRAN, or Pascal. This gives expert users the ability to customize and automate the way that the data base management system works in specific instances. Generally, data base programming is done to make it easier for novice users to accomplish frequently performed activities. Like all programs, a data base program is simply an explicit list of instructions that tells the computer how to perform one or more tasks. A program is typed into the computer and stored in a disk file so that the same set of instructions can be retrieved and executed over and over.

A common use of data base programming is to set up a simple menu system that can be more easily understood by data entry personnel and other casual users. Instead of directly executing individual commands and options of the data base manager, the user simply runs the prepared program, makes choices from the menu, and follows the instructions that appear on the screen. This alleviates the need for all users to become experts in running the data base management system.

## Importing and Exporting Files

*Swapping data with other programs*

Data base management packages must often exchange data with other application packages. Since creating a large data base generally means spending a great deal of time entering many records, it is important to be able to use that data with other programs. In addition, being able to use data originally entered through other programs can significantly reduce the time and effort it takes to create some new data bases. Fortunately, most data base management systems can import and export files.

**Importing** a file involves reading and, if necessary, translating, data originally created with some other program. This means that you may not have to completely retype data you've previously entered while working with a different program. For example, Reflex Plus can import a worksheet file created with the Microsoft Excel spreadsheet program. Perhaps you started with a small mailing list that you thought could be effectively handled with a spreadsheet program. You later decide that your mailing list will grow much too large or too complex to be manipulated with the simple data management commands provided by the spreadsheet. If your data base program can import files from your spreadsheet, then you can avoid having to retype data you've already entered.

**Exporting** a file involves writing data in a format that can be accepted by a different program. This is another tool for transferring data between applications without retyping data you've already entered. Reflex Plus, for example, also can export data to a file that can be read as a Microsoft Excel worksheet.

## Network Data Bases

*Simultaneous sharing*

Back in Chapter 2 we said that a *local area network* or *LAN* links two or more microcomputers to exchange messages and share hardware, software, and data. We'll have more to say about networks in Chapter 12, but it is important here to realize that they can create certain problems for data base management systems. Not all data base programs can run correctly on a network. A special (usually more expensive) version may be necessary to handle the various potential conflicts that can arise when two or more people are using the same data base management system and sharing the same data files. For example, what happens if two users working on different computers try to simultaneously update the same data file? One user may be trying to delete the very same record that another user is trying to modify. If the data base software is not designed to operate on a network, serious problems can occur. One user may cancel another user's changes, data may be lost, and in extreme cases the conflict can cause the software controlling the network to "crash" and bring all connected computers to a grinding halt.

Fortunately, many of the most popular data base management systems do come in versions that operate on local area networks. They typically handle potential conflicts between users with two techniques: file locking and record locking. **File locking** prevents anyone from gaining access to a file currently in use by another person on the same network. **Record locking** is similar, but not as drastic. It prevents someone from deleting or modifying an individual record currently being used by another person. Record locking does not, however, prevent two users from viewing and updating different records of the same file.

In addition to file and record locking, network data base management systems often include still more features for ensuring the security and privacy of sensitive data. Access to files may be limited to only authorized users who must provide a secret password in order to run the data base manager. Different users may be granted different priorities and privileges that determine both file access and who gets precedence when files or records are locked. While network data bases can be quite valuable in many instances, they also are necessarily more complex to set up and operate.

## POPULAR DATA BASE MANAGERS

*Big names in data bases*

Many popular data base packages are currently available, from simple flat-file programs to fully programmable relational systems. Like Lotus 1-2-3 in the spreadsheet market, dBASE is the clear leader in the data base market. Singling out other data base packages is somewhat arbitrary, but R:base and Reflex are two of the most frequently used competitors to dBASE.

### dBASE

In the minds of many people, *dBASE* is synonymous with data base management. Sold by Ashton-Tate, dBASE is the most popular programmable relational data base management system for IBM-compatible computers. It is a very powerful, fast, feature-laden package that is the standard against which all other high-end data base managers are compared. Like other programs with a long history, various versions of dBASE have been released and the system has been consistently improved with each new version. Although dBASE has not always been known for user-friendliness, it is the program of choice for people who need power, speed, flexibility, and programmability in a data base management system. The two most recent versions of dBASE for IBM-compatibles, dBASE III PLUS and dBASE IV, come with a menu system that makes them much easier to use than earlier, command-oriented versions. In 1987, Ashton-Tate released an Apple Macintosh version, called dBASE Mac, that combines the power of the IBM-compatible dBASE with the ease of use and graphics ability of the Macintosh.

### R:base

The R:base series of data base management systems, from Microrim Incorporated, has been one of the strongest competitors with the various versions of dBASE for IBM-compatible computers. R:base is a programmable relational data base management system that has just as many, if not more, features than dBASE. Some people think that R:base is significantly easier to use, even if it is somewhat slower, than dBASE. While dBASE seems more oriented to programmers who develop data base applications for other users, R:base caters more to end users who need to occasionally customize data base applications.

### Reflex

Reflex is the name given to a number of different products sold by Borland International. There are versions of Reflex for both IBM-compatible and Apple Macintosh computers. On both types of computer, Reflex is a powerful, easy-to-use, yet relatively inexpensive relational data base management system. It offers a good deal of flexibility in creating data bases, gaining access to information, and generating reports. Reflex Plus, the popular Macintosh version, can even store graphic images and produce reports incorporating figures and various typefaces. In addition, Reflex has more features for calculating than many data base managers. By providing number crunching abilities similar to spreadsheets, Reflex is a versatile tool for manipulating numerical data bases.

## The Real World

### Challenger

It was a grim and demanding task. The remains of the space shuttle Challenger lay scattered about the ocean floor off the coast of Florida.

The salvage company Eastport International was faced with the job of cataloging the hundreds of pieces of wreckage, which would help investigators determine the cause of the crash. The shuttle exploded shortly after launching in January 1986.

Eastport International officials decided that, rather than laboriously recording the location of each piece by hand, they would have their workers use data base management software to keep track of the information. The data base manager let them quickly check the sea-floor location of the parts, which provided major clues in determining the cause of the tragedy.

Many businesses and organizations now find that they can no longer do without data base management software. In our rapidly changing world, gathering and utilizing accurate information is a prerequisite for effective competition. Virtually all businesses and organizations must juggle an ever-increasing collection of data. Computers and data base software have become essential in bearing up under information overload.

"There are hundreds of reasons why people should use a data base, and there are thousands of ways that data bases are already being used," according to Edward M. Esber, chief executive officer of Ashton-Tate. Esber's company makes dBASE III PLUS, the best-selling microcomputer data base management system.

Data base software helps people effectively manage information. "To store it, update it, manipulate it," says Esber, "this is, quite simply, what a data base product does."

Source: "Why You Need a Data Base," Edward M. Esber, *Personal Computing*, Oct., 1986, p. 296.

## Summary

- *The different types of data base managers.* There are spreadsheet, flat-file, free-form, relational, and programmable data base managers.
- *How to create a data base.* Plan the record structure of each file; specify the name, length, and data type of each field in a record; enter the contents of each record; and save the completed file on a disk.
- *How to find information in u dala base.* Once you retricvc a data base file from disk, you can casually browse through all the records or submit queries to find specific records.
- *How to keep a data base up-to-date.* An existing data base file can be updated by adding new records, deleting old records, modifying the contents of records, and changing the record structure.
- *How to rearrange a data base.* Sorting rearranges the actual records into numerical or alphabetical order on the basis of the contents of one or more key fields. Indexing produces an index file that merely lists record numbers in the specified order, without actually rearranging the data records themselves.
- *How to produce printed data base reports.* You select the individual fields and records to be included in a formatted data listing that can be displayed on the screen or sent to the printer.
- *Some of the additional features offered by data base management systems.* Many data base management systems let you create customized data entry forms; produce printed mailing labels; relate or link data from multiple files; include query lan-

guages such as SQL, QBE, or natural query language; protect sensitive data from unauthorized access and alteration; create programs to customize and automate the way the system works; transfer files to and from other application packages; and work with shared data bases on local area networks.

- *Three popular data base managers for microcomputers.* The various versions of dBASE, R:base, and Reflex are popular programmable relational data base management systems for microcomputers.

## Key Terms

As an extra review of this chapter, try defining the following terms. If you have trouble with any of them, refer to the page number listed.

ascending order (365)
browse (361)
data encryption (372)
data entry form (359)
descending order (365)
exporting (374)
field (356)
file locking (374)
flat-file data base manager (354)
free-form data base manager (355)
global delete (363)
global modify (global search and replace) (364)
importing (374)
index file (366)
indexing (366)
key (365)
link fields (370)
many-to-many link (370)
one-to-many link (370)
one-to-one link (370)
primary key (365)
programmable data base manager (355)
query language (371)
Query-by-Example (QBE) (371)
querying (361)
read-only (display-only) fields (372)
record (356)
record locking (374)
record number (366)
relational data base (356)
relational data base manager (355)
report (367)
secondary key (365)
Structured Query Language (SQL) (371)

## Review Questions

1. Which type of data base manager would be best suited to storing magazine article and book summaries?
2. What are two main disadvantages to using a spreadsheet program as a data base manager?
3. What is the major difference between a flat-file and relational data base manager?
4. What are the two basic attributes of a record field?
5. List five data types supported by most data base managers.
6. What is the easiest way to view a small data base if you aren't looking for a particular record?
7. What is the simplest type of query?
8. What kind of option or command would you use to remove from an entire file all those records that meet a specified set of criteria?

9. Why is it important to carefully design the record structure of a data base file before you enter any records?
10. What term describes a field used as the basis for sorting records in a data base file?
11. What are the two orders in which records can be sorted or indexed?
12. What is contained in an index file?
13. Why would you want to save a report layout in a file?
14. Why might you want to create a custom data entry form?
15. List three possible ways to connect the records of a multiple file data base.
16. List two ways to help protect information stored in data bases.
17. What is a common use of data base programming?
18. What do importing and exporting allow you to do with data files?
19. What are two techniques used by network data base management systems to handle potential conflicts between users trying to gain access to the same data at the same time?
20. List three popular data base managers.

## Multiple Choice

1. Which of the following is not a type of data base manager?
   (a) flat-file (b) free-form
   (c) relational (d) multi-dimensional
2. Which type of data base manager can work with more than one file at the same time?
   (a) flat-file (b) free-form
   (c) relational (d) multi-dimensional
3. Which of the following is not a component of a data base?
   (a) field (b) record
   (c) file (d) worksheet
4. What are the two basic attributes of a field?
   (a) length and data type (b) filename and extension
   (c) magnitude and sign (d) number of dimensions and character set
5. Which of the following is not a type of data handled by most data base managers?
   (a) text (b) algebraic
   (c) numeric (d) date
6. Adding a record to a data base involves typing the contents of each field into a(n)
   (a) data entry form. (b) worksheet template.
   (c) report generator. (d) index file.

7. If your data base is small and you are not looking for one particular record, the easiest way to view your data is to
   (a) query.
   (b) extrapolate.
   (c) browse.
   (d) global search.
8. Two ways to rearrange the order of records in a data base are
   (a) searching and replacing.
   (b) sorting and indexing.
   (c) browsing and querying.
   (d) modifying and updating.
9. Input errors can often be minimized by using a
   (a) worksheet.
   (b) data encryption scheme.
   (c) query language.
   (d) custom data entry form.
10. Which of the following is not a way to link the records of a multiple file data base?
    (a) one-to-none
    (b) one-to-one
    (c) one-to-many
    (d) many-to-many
11. Which query language was accepted by the American National Standards Institute (ANSI) in 1986 as a standard for relational data base systems?
    (a) Reflex
    (b) Structured Query Language (SQL)
    (c) Query-by-Example (QBE)
    (d) natural query language
12. Two ways to protect a data base are
    (a) lock and key fields.
    (b) display-only fields and data encryption.
    (c) global search and replace.
    (d) data entry forms and query languages.
13. Which of the following terms describes reading, and if necessary translating, data originally created with some other program?
    (a) sorting
    (b) indexing
    (c) exporting
    (d) importing
14. Two techniques that handle potential conflicts between users of network data base systems are
    (a) record locking and file locking.
    (b) importing and exporting.
    (c) searching and replacing.
    (d) sorting and indexing.
15. Which is the most popular series of microcomputer data base management systems?
    (a) dBASE
    (b) R:base
    (c) Reflex
    (d) Paradox

## Projects

1. In this chapter we have briefly described some of the basic and advanced features offered by today's data base management systems. Try to find a few other features we have not mentioned and write a paragraph describing each one. Magazines like *PC Magazine*, *BYTE*, *MacWorld*, *Mac User*, and *InfoWorld* often publish comparative reviews and surveys that list software features.
2. We've mentioned only three popular data base management packages in this chapter, but many others are on the market. Research three additional data base

management systems and write a paragraph or two about each one. Again, computer periodicals are a good source of information. Try to find issues that contain product reviews of data base management software.

3. Do you think that you could use a data base manager at school, work, or home? For what specific tasks would you use one? Based on the descriptions we've given and the research you have done for the previous question, which type and brand of data base package would you choose? Why?

4. Try to find a real-world example of a business or organization that routinely uses a microcomputer data base management system. Perhaps such a system is used where you, a friend, or a relative works. A department or office at school might use a data base manager. If you cannot find any organization you have access to, then research magazine and newspaper articles. Write a paragraph or two describing how a real business or organization uses data base management software in its daily activities.

# 11

# Data Base Management Details: dBase III PLUS

## In This Chapter

**Insight**

## Large Data Base Packages vs. File Management Programs

It's like using an elephant gun to kill a flea. Hauling out dBASE III PLUS to solve a simple problem just isn't worth the time or effort.

Anyone who has worked with large-scale data base programs realizes they aren't particularly easy to use. To solve elaborate problems, dBASE III PLUS requires that you develop actual programs in the dBASE language. These programs are as complex as programs written in BASIC, COBOL, or Pascal.

For simple applications, dBASE III PLUS may be more powerful than necessary, especially considering the work in putting together the dBASE program system. Experienced users ignore dBASE III PLUS, first, when the problem needs only one file that is not linked to any other files and, second, when the computations are simple and limited to such things as taking the sum of some fields or deriving a new field based on simple calculations on other fields in the data base.

A number of flat-file manager programs can provide excellent solutions for situations such as this. Unlike dBASE III PLUS, flat-file manager programs can't link the fields in different files. All the information has to be in a single file. Simple address or customer lists and client billing files are examples.

Two typical file managers that meet these needs are PFS:FILE and Nutshell. Each allows the user to define simple file structures, produce report forms, perform search and record selection, and do simple computations, without the complex and time-consuming programming required by large data base packages.

### PREVIEW

In January 1981, a new company called Ashton-Tate introduced its first product, dBASE II. There was no dBASE I, there was no Ashton, and co-founder George Tate didn't develop the program. Nevertheless, Tate and his partner, Hal Lashlee, along with Los Angeles advertising man Hal Pawluk, are credited with the merchandising flair that helped make *dBASE* synonymous with *data base management*. It was Pawluk who coined the name Ashton-Tate, simply because he liked the way it sounded.

The original program was called *Vulcan*, named after the home planet of *Star Trek's* Mr. Spock. It was developed for CP/M microcomputers by Wayne Ratliff, an engineer then working for NASA's Jet Propulsion Laboratory. Vulcan was a very versatile data base management program, but Ratliff only sold fifty copies the first year from an ad in the back of *Byte* magazine. Tate and Lashlee heard about the program, contacted Ratliff, and signed him to an exclusive contract. The sales of that program, renamed dBASE II, and of its successors, would ultimately make all three of them multimillionaires.

The original dBASE II program ran on CP/M systems and the Apple II family of microcomputers. A version for the IBM Personal Computer soon followed and by 1983 dBASE II had sold more than 200,000 copies. In May 1984, Ashton-Tate released dBASE III, a more powerful successor to dBASE II designed especially for

16-bit computers like the IBM PC family. A year and a half later, dBASE III PLUS was introduced, offering a friendlier menu-driven user interface and local area network support for IBM-compatible microcomputers. An extremely powerful and easy-to-use version for the Apple Macintosh computer, called dBASE Mac, was released in 1987. Despite increased competition from other software packages, dBASE remains the leading programmable relational data base management system against which all others are compared. This chapter examines how dBASE III PLUS for IBM-compatibles helps manage data bases.

After studying this chapter, you will understand

- how to begin working with dBASE III PLUS.
- the operation of dBASE menus and commands.
- how to create a data base with dBASE.
- how to examine an existing data base with dBASE.
- how to keep a data base up-to-date with dBASE.
- how to organize a data base with dBASE.
- how to display and print dBASE reports.
- some of the advanced features included in dBASE.

## WORKING WITH dBASE III PLUS

*A sophisticated package*

In this chapter we examine dBASE III PLUS Version 1.1 for IBM-compatible microcomputers. The dBASE III PLUS system is large, expensive, and quite sophisticated. When you purchase this package, which lists for $695, you get two thick manuals of about 500 pages each, a booklet on installing and starting the program, a quick reference guide, and seven 5 1/4-inch diskettes. One of the manuals covers learning and using dBASE, while the other one concentrates on programming with dBASE. In Appendix C we discuss how to install dBASE III PLUS on your computer. For this chapter, we'll assume that you already have dBASE III PLUS installed on your computer.

Although it is technically possible to use dBASE on a microcomputer with only floppy disk drives, the vast majority of people use dBASE on a system with a hard disk. The dBASE package takes up considerable disk space and you need a hard disk to store large data bases anyway. Usually, dBASE is installed in a hard disk subdirectory named DBASE.

### Starting the Program

*Running dBASE III PLUS from a hard disk*

Once dBASE III PLUS has been installed (see Appendix C), starting it is easy. First you turn on your computer and boot DOS, as in Chapter 5. Then you switch to the DBASE subdirectory on the hard disk by typing **CD C:\DBASE** and pressing the **Enter** key. To actually run the program you type **DBASE** and press the **Enter** key. The program takes a few moments to load from disk into memory. Figure 11.1 shows what appears on your screen—the copyright notice and license agreement. After you've read this start-up screen, you press the **Enter** key to actually begin working with dBASE. If you don't press the **Enter** key, the program simply goes on after a minute or so anyway.

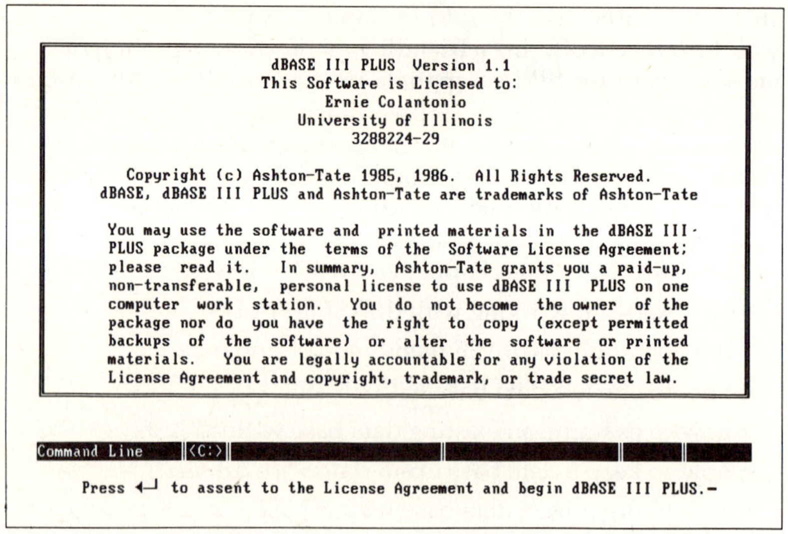


**Figure 11.1 dBASE III PLUS Startup Screen**
This screen appears for a few moments when you begin dBASE III PLUS.

## THE dBASE ASSISTANT

*Menu system*

The original dBASE II program was strictly a command-driven system. In other words, there were no menus; you told it what to do by entering commands, just as you do with DOS. As we said in Chapter 3, a command-driven user interface is quick and powerful, but it requires that you memorize commands or constantly look them up in a reference manual if you cannot remember them. When Ashton-Tate released dBASE III, it included a simple menu system called Assist that could be invoked as an option. For dBASE III PLUS, this menu system was expanded, improved, and renamed **The Assistant**. Although you can still use commands, as with dBASE II and dBASE III, you also have an easy-to-use menu system that is automatically invoked whenever you start dBASE III PLUS. The dBASE III PLUS package gives you the advantages of both commands and menus, although most people stick to The Assistant menu system when they first start out.

### Menus

*How you select your options*

After the initial copyright and license notice disappears from your screen, dBASE III PLUS displays The Assistant main menu, as shown in Figure 11.2. Although it looks different from that of Lotus 1-2-3, this menu system operates similarly. Eight main options are listed in the menu bar across the top of the screen: Set Up, Create, Update, Position, Retrieve, Organize, Modify, and Tools. When selected, each of these main options presents a menu of additional options. In Figure 11.2, the Set Up option is selected, indicated by its reverse-video highlight and the menu that appears in the box below. To select an option within a menu, you press the **Up Arrow** or **Down Arrow** key to move the menu highlight bar and then press the **Enter** key. For example, the menu highlight bar is now on the Database File option within the Setup menu. To quit dBASE III PLUS and return to DOS, you press the **Down Arrow** key five times to highlight the Quit dBASE III PLUS option, and then press the **Enter** key.

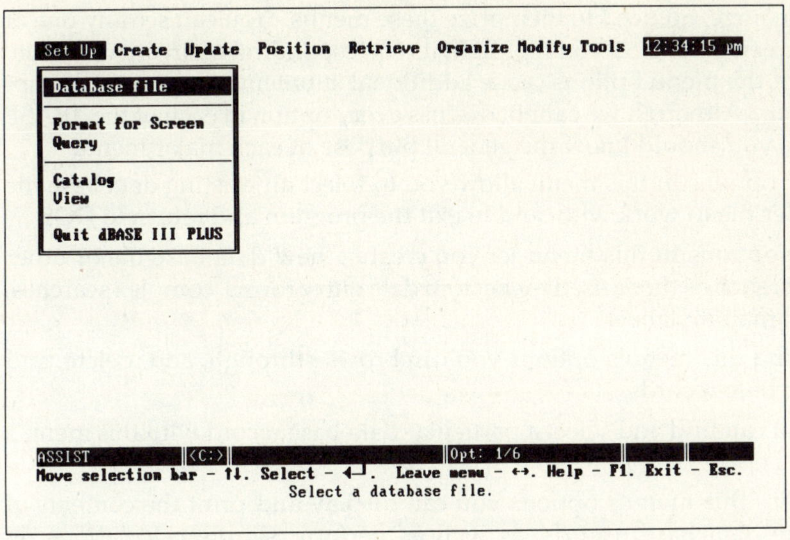


**Figure 11.2 The Assistant Menu System**
The dBASE III PLUS program automatically displays its Assistant menu system.

The Up and Down Arrow keys are the only means to move the highlight bar within a menu, but there are two ways to select a different main menu option. Just as with Lotus 1-2-3, you can either press the **Left Arrow** or **Right Arrow** keys, or you can type the first letter of the name of the main menu option you want to select. For example, to select the Tools option and display its menu, you can press the **Right Arrow** key seven times, or simply type **T**. Since the highlight bar "wraps around," you can also press the **Left Arrow** key once to move from Set Up to Tools. Figure 11.3 shows all of The Assistant's menus, but remember that only one menu at a time can actually be selected and displayed on your screen.

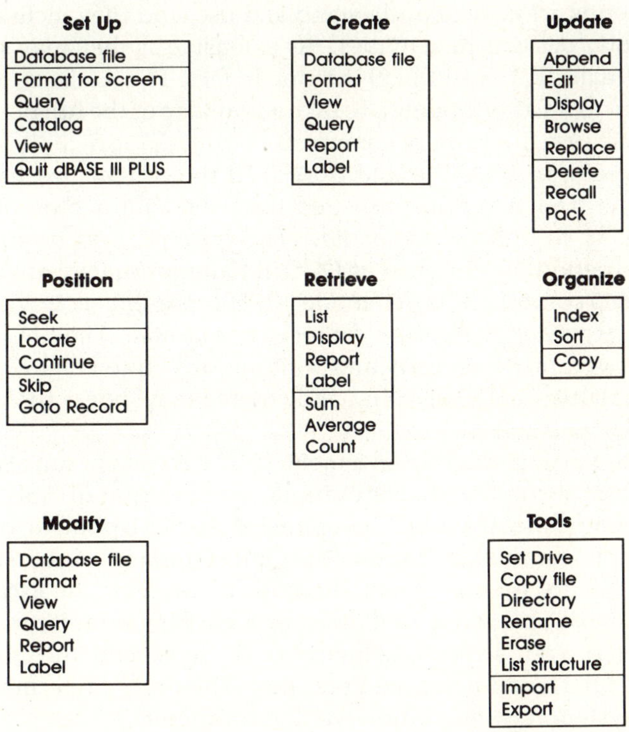


**Figure 11.3 The Assistant Menus**
Here are all of the major dBASE III PLUS menus.

There is, of course, no need to memorize these menus. You can see any one of them on your screen whenever you highlight its corresponding main menu option. Besides, many of the menu options cause additional submenus or prompts to appear on the screen. Although we cannot discuss every option in each of the dBASE III PLUS menus, you should know the general purpose of each major menu:

*The major menus*

- *Set Up*. The options in this menu allow you to select an existing data base file or some other file to work with, and to exit the program and return to DOS.
- *Create*. The options in this menu let you create a new data base file or other types of files, such as those used for custom data entry forms, complex searches, reports, and mailing labels.
- *Update*. Using this menu's options you can browse through, add, delete, and change data base records.
- *Position*. You can find and select a particular data base record with this menu's options.
- *Retrieve*. With this menu's options you can display and print the contents of one or more data base records, as well as perform simple calculations on numeric fields in those records.
- *Organize*. The options in this menu allow you to index and sort a data base file, as well as copy selected fields from an existing file to form a new file.
- *Modify*. This menu's options let you change the structure of an existing data base file, as well as change data entry forms, search specifications, report formats, and mailing labels.
- *Tools*. With the options in this menu you can switch disk drives and directories; copy, rename, and erase files; show the structure of an existing data base; and import and export files.

## Dot Prompt Commands

*Bypassing the menus*

The Assistant menus are easy to understand and use, and they include options for the most frequently performed activities. As extensive as they may seem, they do not represent all that dBASE III PLUS can do. In fact, The Assistant menu system was added almost as an afterthought. To take advantage of the full power of dBASE III PLUS, you must use dot prompt commands.

As we have said, in dBASE II and dBASE III the primary user interface was command-driven. The program presented the user with a prompt and simply waited for the user to enter a command. The prompt used by dBASE is very simple—a single period, or dot. Just as DOS initially presents you with A> or C> as its prompt, in its command-driven mode, dBASE presents you with a dot. This gave rise to the terms *dot prompt* and *dot prompt command*. The **dot prompt** is the way dBASE tells you that it is ready and waiting for you to enter a command. A **dot prompt command** is a dBASE command entered in response to the dot prompt and not selected from a menu.

Every activity you can select from a menu of The Assistant can also be done by entering a dot prompt command. For example, you can quit dBASE and return to DOS by using the Quit dBASE III PLUS option of the Set Up menu, or by entering the Quit dot prompt command. To enter the Quit command, you first switch from The Assistant to the dot prompt command mode by pressing the **Escape** key. This erases the menu and displays a dot followed by a blinking underscore cursor in the lower left portion of your screen (see Figure 11.4). To execute the Quit command, you simply type **QUIT** and press the **Enter** key. The program terminates and the DOS operating system regains control over the computer.

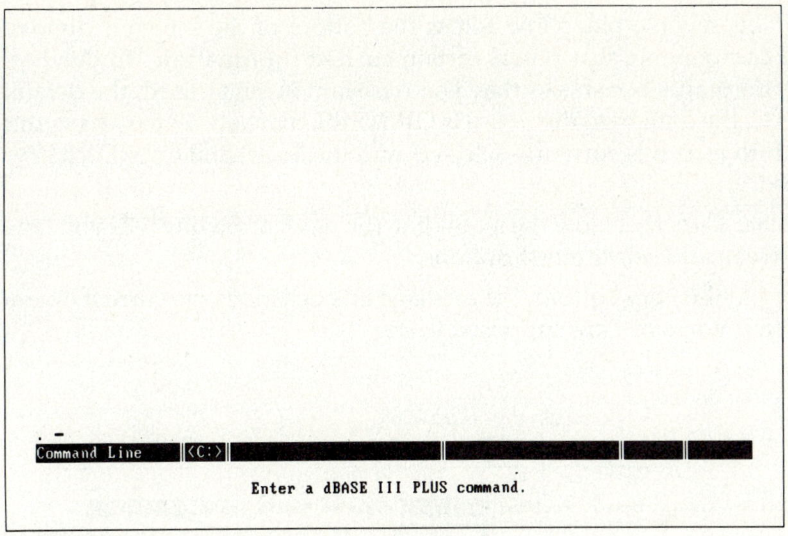


**Figure 11.4 The Dot Prompt**

You can press the **Escape** key from The Assistant to switch to the dBASE III PLUS dot prompt. Any operation that can be performed with The Assistant can also be performed by entering the appropriate dot prompt command.

Although every menu option has an equivalent dot prompt command, not every dot prompt command has an equivalent menu option. In other words, you can do many things with dot prompt commands that you cannot do from The Assistant. Nevertheless, the most common dBASE activities are represented by menu options. In most instances, a beginner can get by without having to use dot prompt commands. For most of this chapter, we use only The Assistant. Many people, however, prefer dot prompt commands once they become more proficient with dBASE because they find that entering commands is often quicker than selecting menu options. Expert users and data base programmers generally find that they must use dot prompt commands, at least some of the time.

## The Assistant Screen

*Information and feedback*

Let's turn our attention back to The Assistant, since that is where we will spend most of our time. Besides the main menu options and menus, The Assistant displays other important items on the screen. These are illustrated in Figure 11.5. This figure shows what the screen might look like during the process of telling dBASE to display the contents of a data base file. Note the following items:

- *Menus.* See how the Display option of the Retrieve menu has its own submenu. Furthermore, the Specify Scope option of the Display menu also has its own submenu.
- *Current Time.* The current time of day is displayed in the upper right corner of the screen.
- *Action Line.* This line, directly above the reverse video status bar, displays the dot prompt command equivalent to the current sequence of menu selections. By carefully watching the action line while using The Assistant, you can learn more about dot prompt commands.

- *Status Bar.* This reverse-video line across the bottom of the screen is divided into several components that reveal certain current information. In this particular case, the status bar shows that The Assistant is being used, the default disk drive is C, the data base file in use is OWNERS, there are 17 records in this file and the fifth record is currently selected, and the Insert and Caps Lock keys are depressed.
- *Navigation Line.* Directly below the status bar, the navigation line tells you how to move between and select menu options.
- *Message Line.* At the very bottom, the message line describes the current operation or tells you what you are supposed to do.

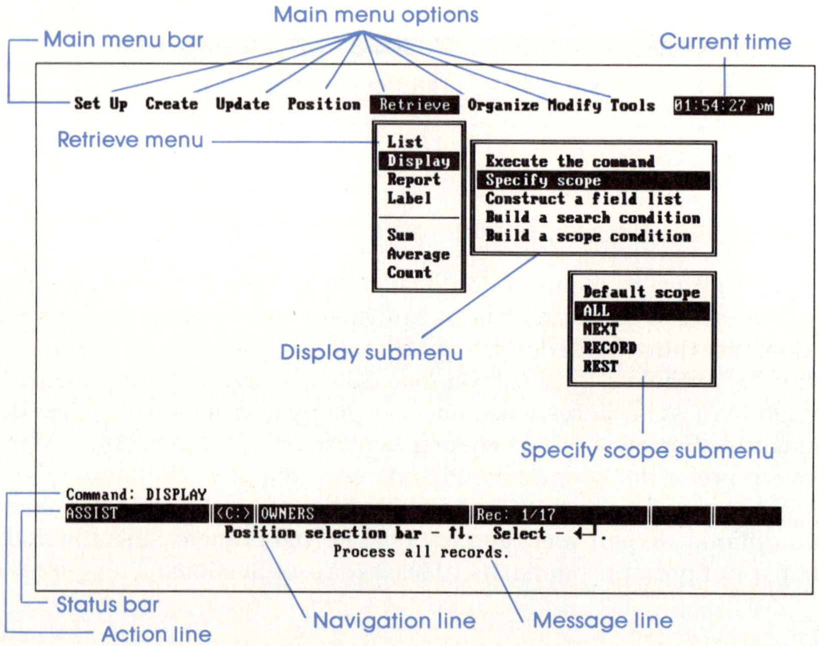


**Figure 11.5 Typical Assistant Screen**
Here are the components of a typical Assistant screen.

## Help

*Finding out more about dBASE commands*

Besides the excellent dBASE III PLUS manuals and the on-disk tutorial program provided by Ashton-Tate, The Assistant menus and the message line themselves give you some information about the various options available. You can get even more information by using the on-line help facility. All you have to do is press the help key, which is the **F1** function key. This presents a more detailed description of the currently highlighted menu option. For example, Figure 11.6 shows the result of pressing the **F1** key when the Quit option of the Set Up menu is highlighted. When you are finished reading the help screen, you simply press any key to continue working where you left off.

# CREATING A DATA BASE

Before you can use a data base, you must create it. There are several steps to creating a data base in dBASE III PLUS. The Parkridge Condominium Association data base we used in the previous chapter will serve as the example for this chapter as well. You'll recall that this data base consists of two files: an OWNERS file, which

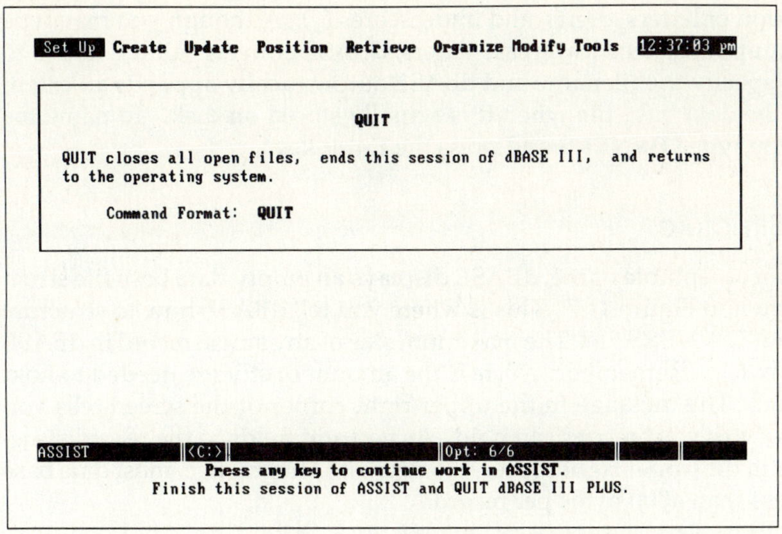


**Figure 11.6 Help Screen for Quit**
Press the F1 function key to obtain further information from dBASE III PLUS about the currently selected menu option.

holds the names and addresses of unit owners, and a FEES file, which holds the condominium fee for each apartment. Each file must be created separately. We'll only go through the steps of creating the OWNERS file; the same process would have to be repeated to also create the FEES file.

## Defining the Structure

When you start dBASE, the first option in the main menu bar, Set Up, is highlighted. You have to move the highlight to the Create option to create a new data base file. Press the **Right Arrow** key once or type **C**. The Set Up menu disappears and the Create menu appears on the screen. The first option in the Create menu, which is Database File, is automatically highlighted. Simply press the **Enter** key to invoke this option.

### Choosing the Disk Drive

Next, dBASE pops up a small submenu containing a list of possible disk drive letters. If you are working off a copy of dBASE in floppy drive A, the A: option is initially highlighted. If you are working off a hard disk copy of dBASE, the C: option is highlighted. To change to some other drive, you press the **Up Arrow** or **Down Arrow** key to move the submenu highlight bar. The drive you select is where dBASE will store your data base file after you create it. If you are using a computer with a hard disk, you probably want to store your data base on drive C. In some situations, however, you might want to store your files on a floppy disk in drive A or B. Once you have highlighted the drive you want, you press the **Enter** key to select it.

### Naming the File

The next step is to name your data base file. After you select the drive, dBASE prompts you to enter a name. The name you choose can have no more than eight characters. The first character should be a letter, but the remaining characters can be any combination of letters, digits, and underscores (_). Although you may type your filename in uppercase or lowercase letters, dBASE converts all the letters to uppercase. You specify the filename and dBASE automatically appends an extension of .DBF to the data base file when it is actually stored on disk. To name the OWNERS file, you type **OWNERS** and press the **Enter** key.

## Planning the Structure

After you enter an acceptable name, dBASE displays an empty data base file structure table, as shown in Figure 11.7. This is where you tell dBASE how to structure the records of your OWNERS file. The maximum size of any single record in dBASE III PLUS is 4000 bytes. (Remember: a *byte* is the amount of storage needed to hold a single character.) The message in the upper right corner of the screen tells you how many more bytes your record can hold. As you add fields to the record structure, the number in the upper right corner will decrease. In practice, most data base files use much less than 4000 bytes per record.

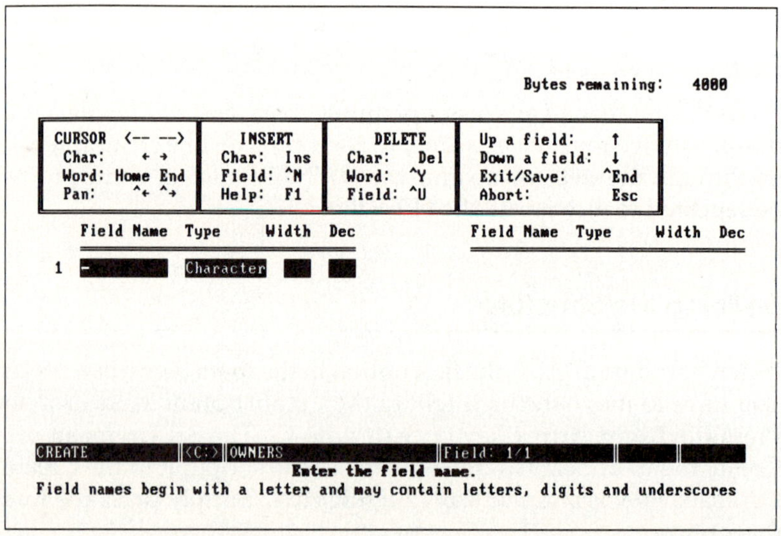


**Figure 11.7 Empty Data Base File Structure Table**

Here is where you enter each field's name, data type, and width. For numeric fields, you also have to specify the number of places to the right of the decimal point.

*Record size*

The boxed-in area beneath the bytes-remaining message is a help menu that tells you how to move about the screen, enter specifications, and edit what you've already entered. The caret ( ^ ) character is shorthand for the Control key. For example, if you enter a field name and you change your mind, you can hold down the **Control** key and type **U** to erase the entire field name.

Beneath the help menu is the empty table where you enter the name, data type, and width of each field in a record. First you must decide what fields to include in each record of your file; then you have to enter the name, data type, and width in characters of each field. If the field is to contain a numeric value, you also must enter the number of digits to appear to the right of the decimal point. This is put in the structure table under the column labeled *Dec.*

As we said in Chapter 10, there are six fields in each record of the OWNERS file: LAST NAME, FIRST NAME, ADDRESS, CITY, STATE, and ZIP code. It is a good idea to name fields after their contents. In dBASE, a field name can be up to ten characters long, it must begin with a letter, and can contain only letters, numbers, and underscores. Names cannot contain embedded blanks. So, good names for the six fields of the records in the OWNERS file would be: LAST_NAME, FIRST_NAME, ADDRESS, CITY, STATE, and ZIP. You can type field names in uppercase or lowercase letters, but dBASE converts them to uppercase.

Deciding on the data type for each field is also fairly straightforward. The dBASE III PLUS program allows five different data types:

*dBASE data types*

- *Character*. Any string of up to 254 letters, digits, and symbols, usually a single word, name, phrase, or some closely related group of words and digits, such as an address.
- *Numeric*. Numbers to be used as quantities or in calculations.
- *Date*. A calendar date, such as 12/31/89.
- *Logical*. A value of True or False, or Yes or No. For example, you may want a field in a personnel file named MARRIED, to indicate whether the employee is married or not. The data type of this field would be logical, because all it need contain is a simple yes or no answer.
- *Memo*. Free-form text, up to 4000 characters, generally used for notes, memos, references, or observations.

Unless you specify otherwise, dBASE assumes a field's data type to be character. This is because the most commonly used data type is character. For example, all of the fields in the OWNERS data base are character fields.

*Determining field widths*

Field width is probably the most difficult determination in planning the structure of a record. If you choose a width that is too large, disk space will be wasted. This waste can be significant in files that contain many hundreds or thousands of records. On the other hand, if you choose a width that is too small, you will have to go back and alter the structure of a data base file—not impossible, but somewhat inconvenient. Clearly, you want to choose your field widths carefully. Here again are the widths we've chosen for the fields of the OWNERS file:

| FIELD NAME | FIELD WIDTH |
|---|---|
| LAST_NAME | 15 |
| FIRST_NAME | 10 |
| ADDRESS | 25 |
| CITY | 10 |
| STATE | 2 |
| ZIP | 5 |

## Entering the Structure

Once you have planned your structure, you need to enter it into the empty table displayed on your screen (see Figure 11.7). The cursor starts out at the first character of the name of the first field. You simply type the name of the first field, **LAST_NAME**, and then press the **Enter** key. The cursor jumps to the data type column. In this case, since Character is the data type you want, you simply press the **Enter** key. If you want to change to a different data type, all you need to do is type one letter: **C** for character, **N** for numeric, **D** for date, **L** for logical, and **M** for memo. After entering the data type, you type the field width, which is **15** for LAST_NAME, and then press the **Enter** key. The specification for the LAST_NAME field is completed, so the highlight and cursor drop down to the next field. Then you enter the name, data type, and width for the remaining record fields. If you make mistakes, the help box tells you how to go back and correct your work. When you are finished with the record structure, your screen looks like Figure 11.8. If you are sure that everything is correct, you hold down the **Control** key and press the **End** key. This tells dBASE that you are finished defining the structure of your data base file. The program asks you to press the **Enter** key to confirm that you are finished. When you do this, dBASE saves your file structure and asks you if you want to go ahead and enter your records now. In our case, this is exactly what you want to do, so you type **Y** for yes. If instead you type **N** for no, dBASE returns to the Create menu of The Assistant.

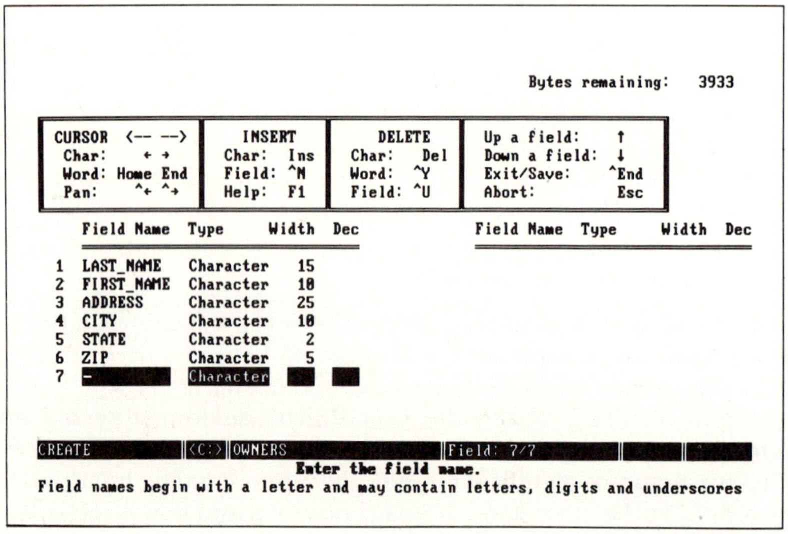


**Figure 11.8 Completed Data Base File Structure Table**

All of the fields for the Parkridge Condominium Association OWNERS file have been specified. The empty columns on the right side of the screen just continue the same table, and provide room for entering more than eight fields.

## Entering Records

So far, all you've done is define the structure of the file. No data has been entered. The most tedious task of creating a data base is entering the records. For huge data bases, this can involve a significant amount of time and effort. Fortunately, our OWNERS file has only seventeen records.

After telling dBASE you want to go ahead and enter your records, the program displays a blank data entry form on your screen, as shown in Figure 11.9. The boxed-in area at the top is a help menu like the one you saw while creating the record structure. It lists the keys you need to press to move about, enter, and correct record fields. Below the help menu on the left side of the screen is a list of the names of the fields in each record of this file. The reverse-video block to the right of each field name is where you enter the data for that field. The width of the block indicates the field width you specified when you created the record structure. The cursor is initially placed at the first character of the first field in the first record.

*Enter records in any order*

Since you can later sort or index the file, records can be entered in any order. The first record you enter into the OWNERS file, for example, might be that of Elaine Sanders. To fill the first field, simply type **Sanders** and press the **Enter** key. Then enter **Elaine** into the FIRST_NAME field, **5925 Pomona Blvd.** into the ADDRESS field, **Champaign** into the CITY field, **IL** into the STATE field, and **61821** into the ZIP field. Since the STATE and ZIP fields are always completely filled by their contents, dBASE automatically beeps and advances to the next field before you get a

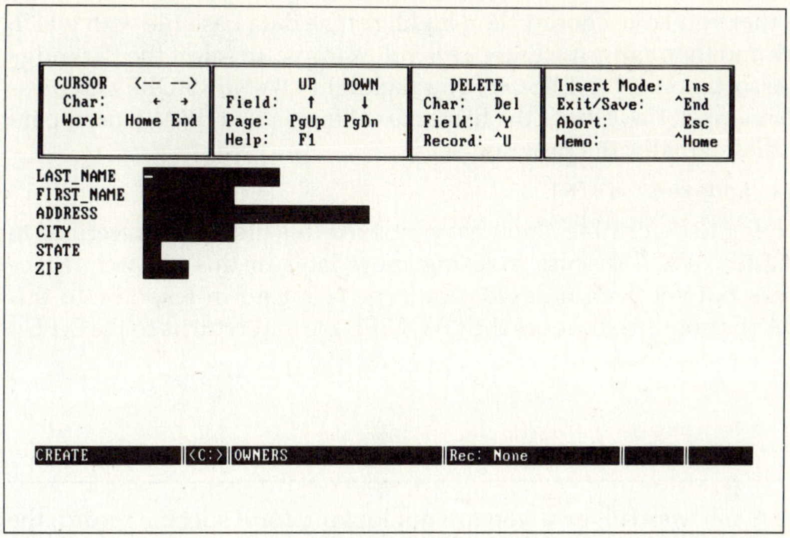


**Figure 11.9 Blank Data Entry Form**
Here is where you enter the data for a record.

chance to press the **Enter** key. When you finish with one record, dBASE automatically advances to the next record, putting a new blank data entry form on your screen.

### Saving the File

*Copying data from memory onto disk*

Once you have entered all the records in a file, it is a good idea to go back and recheck them for accuracy. This can be done by using the **Page Up** and **Page Down** keys to move through the records and make any needed corrections. When you are sure that all records are correct, you hold down the **Control** key and press the **End** key to save your data base file. The dBASE program returns to the Database File option of the Create menu.

## VIEWING A DATA BASE

One of the primary advantages of using a data base program is the flexibility with which you can retrieve previously stored information. Most programs let you view records on the screen as well as produce formatted data base reports. You can examine several records presented in a table or just look at one record at a time.

### Retrieving the File

*Copying data from disk into memory*

The first thing you must do before viewing an existing data base file is to tell the dBASE program to retrieve the file from its disk. This is accomplished via the Set Up menu. You simply highlight the Database File option of the Set Up menu and press the **Enter** key. The program then displays a submenu of disk drive letters. You highlight the disk drive where your file is stored and press the **Enter** key. Another submenu is displayed that lists the data base files currently stored on the disk in the drive that you have chosen. You highlight the data base file with which you want to work and then press the Enter key. For example, to select the Parkridge Condominium Association OWNERS file, you highlight OWNERS.DBF and press the **Enter** key. Remember, the .DBF is the filename extension that dBASE uses to indicate data base files. Finally, the program asks

```
Is the file indexed? [Y/N]
```

Here dBASE is trying to determine if you have indexed this file, as we described in the previous chapter. We'll discuss indexing more later in this chapter. Since OWNERS.DBF has not yet been indexed, you type **N** for no in response to this prompt. The dBASE program retrieves the OWNERS file and returns to the Set Up menu.

## Browsing

*Scanning the records*

If your data base is fairly small, or if you are not looking for a specific record, the easiest way to view the contents of a file is to browse. First activate the Update menu by typing **U**. Then highlight the Browse option and press the **Enter** key. Figure 11.10 shows the result. The first 11 records of the OWNERS data base file are displayed in a table format. The first record in the file is highlighted. You can see additional records by repeatedly pressing the **Down Arrow** key to move the highlight bar down. When you reach the bottom of the screen the records scroll up, revealing the next record. Another way to see more records is to press the **Page Down** key. This reveals the next whole page of records. To see previous records, you use the **Up Arrow** key or the **Page Up** key. When you are finished looking at the file, you hold down the **Control** key and press the **End** key, or simply press the **Escape** key. This returns the program to the Update menu.

**Figure 11.10 Browsing**

The Browse option of the Update menu allows you to see eleven records on the screen at the same time.

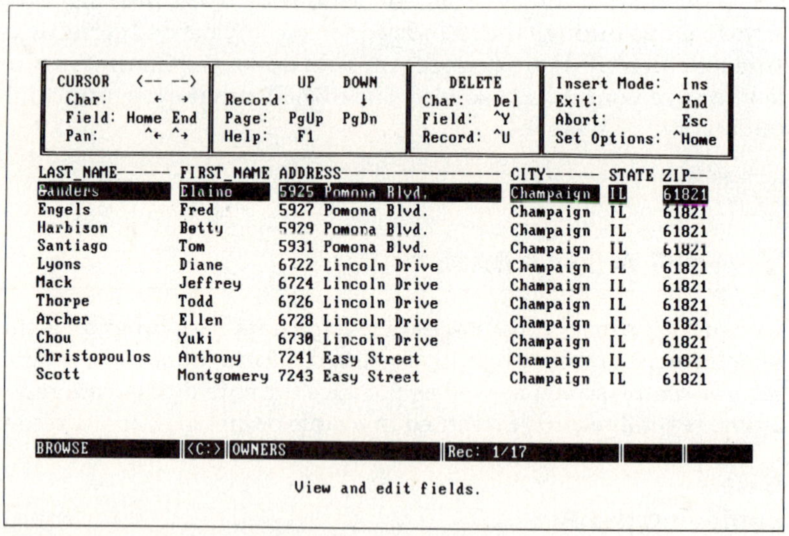

## Finding Records

Browsing is fine for casually examining the contents of a small data base, but it isn't a very efficient method of locating one or more specific records in a large file. It is just too time consuming to scroll or page through a long file in search of a particular record. Besides, people cannot perform such tedious tasks very accurately. Although the record you want to see could be near the beginning of the file, it is just as likely that it is closer to the end. You might have to look through thousands of records to find the one you want. Fortunately, like all data base management systems, dBASE provides a better method of finding specific records.

*Searching for particular data*

As we said in Chapter 10, a *query* is a request for information. A simple query would be asking to see Ellen Archer's record. A more complex query would be asking to see the records of all people whose last names begin with *S* and who live in Champaign, Illinois. As you can imagine, the greater the number of fields and records in a data base, the more complex your queries can be. Sophisticated data base programs like dBASE III PLUS provide may ways to search for records.

As an example, let's do that simple query we just mentioned and ask to see Ellen Archer's record from the Parkridge Condominium Association OWNERS file. Although this seems like a simple operation, there are several menus and a prompt you must traverse to complete your task. As shown in Figure 11.11(a), here are the steps you follow to find and display Ellen Archer's record:

1. Activate the Retrieve menu by typing **R**.
2. Select the Display option by highlighting it and pressing the **Enter** key.
3. Select Specify Scope.
4. Select ALL.
5. Select Build a Search Condition.
6. Select LAST_NAME.
7. Select = Equal To.
8. Enter the last name you want to find: **Archer**.
9. Select No More Conditions.
10. Select Execute the Command.

Figure 11.11(b) shows the dBASE screen that results from these actions.

*Searching with a dot prompt command*

As we said before, everything you can do from dBASE menus can also be performed by entering a dot prompt command. Just before you do step 10 from the above list, the action line on the screen holds the following command:

```
DISPLAY ALL FOR LAST_NAME = 'Archer'
```

This is the dot prompt command equivalent to all of those menu selections. If you press the **Escape** key to switch to the dot prompt and enter the above command, dBASE will also find and display Ellen Archer's record, just as if you had done the ten steps from The Assistant. After some experience with dBASE, many people find that they would rather enter a dot prompt command than go through many menu selections. Let's say that you do use a dot prompt command. When you are finished with a particular operation, you'll probably want to return to using The Assistant menu system. To reactivate The Assistant, you must type **ASSIST** and press the **Enter** key.

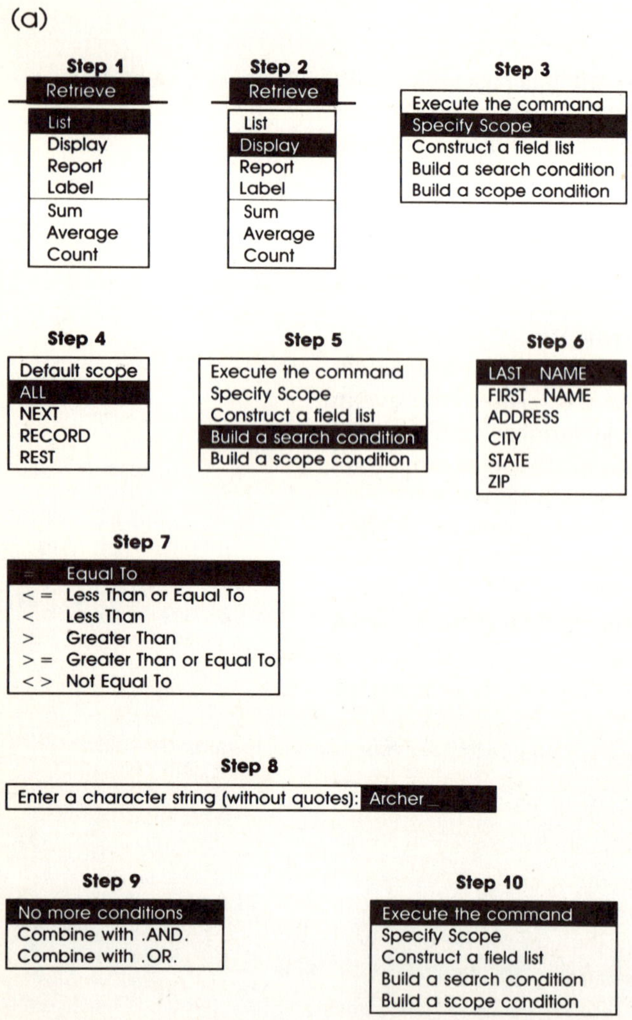


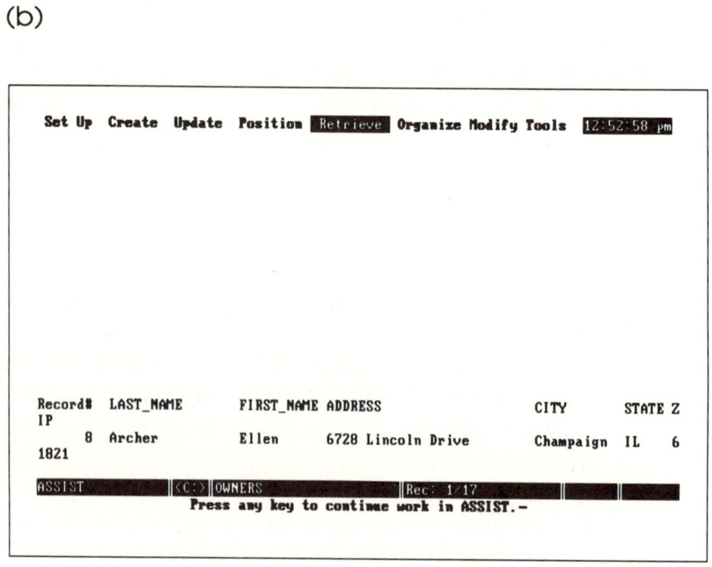


**Figure 11.11 Finding a Record**

(a) Here are the steps in searching for Ellen Archer's record.

(b) Here is the screen that displays her record.

The operation we've just described is the simplest kind of query—looking for a record that has a particular value in just one field. In our short OWNERS file there is only one record with *Archer* in the LAST_NAME field. If our data base were much larger, there might be several people whose last names were Archer. The query we've just described would display all of their records. If you want to single out just Ellen Archer's record, you have to build a more complex search condition. This consists of looking for a record in which the LAST_NAME field equals *Archer* and the FIRST_NAME field equals *Ellen*. If you use The Assistant, this query requires repeating several steps to also specify *Ellen* as the first name for which to search. The corresponding dot prompt command is

```
DISPLAY ALL FOR LAST_NAME = 'Archer' .AND. FIRST_NAME = 'Ellen'
```

Very complex search conditions can be built in this manner to find records that fulfill multiple criteria. For example, you could find all those records of people whose last names begin with a particular letter and who live in a particular city, state, or ZIP code. As you can see, data base queries let you easily locate records that might otherwise be both difficult and time consuming to find by browsing.

## UPDATING A DATA BASE

Almost all data bases must be occasionally, if not regularly, updated. One of the primary reasons computers are used to store information is that data base management systems make it relatively easy to keep that information current. Data bases are updated by adding new records, deleting existing records, modifying existing records, and changing the structure of records.

### Adding Records

*Adding new data*

Perhaps the most common type of update is the addition of new records to a data base. Organizations that keep mailing lists, for example, are almost constantly adding names and addresses to their data bases as they get new members. Ease of adding new records to files is therefore an essential function of any data base management system.

The process of adding a new record to an existing file with dBASE III PLUS is almost identical to adding a new record to a new file. The first step is to select the file to which you want to add records. As we have said before, this is done by executing the Database File option from the Set Up menu and selecting the disk drive and data base file with which you want to work. Then you activate the Update menu by typing **U**. The first option in this menu, called Append, is highlighted. Since this is the option you use to add new records to the current file, the next step is to simply press the **Enter** key. A blank data entry form is displayed on your screen. If you were adding a new record to the Parkridge Condominium Association OWNERS file, this blank data entry form would look just like the one shown in Figure 11.9, except that the status bar across the screen bottom would list EOF/17 as the current record instead of 1/1. This means that you have 17 records already in the OWNERS file and you are about to add number 18 to the end of the file (EOF). All you do is enter the appropriate new item into each blank field. After you enter the contents of the last field, the new record is added to the end of the current data base file. The program then assumes that you want to add more records and displays another blank data entry form on your screen. When you are finished adding new records, you hold down the **Control** key and press the **End** key. The file is updated and dBASE returns to The Assistant.

### Deleting Records

*Discarding old data*

Just as new records must be added to existing files, sometimes old records must be removed. For example, people who cancel their subscriptions must have their records removed from a magazine's mailing list. Every data base management system has some provision for purging unused records from existing files.

The first step is to locate the record you want to delete. Unless you already know it, you have to find the exact record number of the record you want to delete. The process of locating a record you want to delete is similar to finding a particular record to display its contents on the screen. The major difference is that to delete, you use the Locate option of the Position menu, instead of the Display option of the Retrieve menu.

For example, let's say that you want to remove Ellen Archer's record from the OWNERS file. First you type **P** to activate the Position menu, highlight the Locate option, and press the **Enter** key. Then you go through the same ten steps we outlined in Figure 11.11(a), except that for Step 4 you choose the Default Scope option.

Locating Ellen Archer's record also can be done by executing this dot prompt command:

```
LOCATE FOR LAST_NAME = 'Archer'
```

Whichever of these two methods you choose, the program merely reports that 8 is the record number located. In other words, Ellen Archer's record is record number 8. Once you locate a record in this manner, dBASE remembers the record number. This record becomes the current record, on which you will perform some subsequent action.

In this case, the action to be performed is a deletion. From The Assistant, you type **U** to activate the Update menu, highlight the Delete option, and press the **Enter** key. A submenu just like the one shown in Step 3 of Figure 11.11(a) appears on the screen, and you press **Enter** to select the highlighted option, which is Execute the Command. You are informed that the record has been deleted and told to press any key to return to The Assistant.

Any time you delete something—single records as well as entire data files—you should be careful. It is usually much easier to erase data than it is to re-enter that data. Fortunately, dBASE has a built-in safety feature that helps reduce the likelihood of mistakenly deleting needed data. Even after you execute the Delete option of the Update menu, the deleted record is not actually removed from your file until you execute still another command. Because of the way records are stored by dBASE, deleting a record does not immediately remove it from storage. A deleted record is only invisibly marked as such. You can reinstate deleted records by executing the Recall option of the Update menu (see Figure 11.3 again). To permanently remove all deleted records, you must execute the Pack option of the Update menu. This operation removes all records marked for deletion and renumbers the remaining records. Once you execute a Pack operation, you can no longer reinstate deleted records. So, be sure that you really want to remove your deleted records before you select the Pack option.

## Modifying Records

*Changing existing data*

Sometimes records just have to be changed and not completely removed from a file. For example, magazine subscribers who move must have their records modified to reflect their new mailing address. There are two basic ways to modify existing records with dBASE III PLUS. The first method involves using the Browse option of the Update menu. As we said, browsing is a good way to examine records if a file is short. In dBASE, you can also modify records while browsing. Look again at Figure 11.10, which illustrates browsing through the Parkridge Condominium Association OWNERS file. Notice that the message line says, "View and edit fields." Also notice that the first record on the screen is highlighted in reverse video and there is a cursor beneath the first character of the first field. To modify the contents of this record, all you have to do is simply move the cursor and insert, delete, or overwrite characters in any field. You can modify any record in the file by moving the highlight with the Up Arrow, Down Arrow, Page Up, or Page Down keys.

We've already said that browsing is fine for short files, but it is inefficient and time-consuming for long files. In these cases, there is a better way to modify records. The first step is to locate the record to be changed with the Locate option of the Position menu, just as we described for deleting a record. Then you use the Edit option of the Update menu. This displays a filled data entry form on the screen within which you can move the cursor and alter the existing contents of fields. When you are finished making your modifications, you hold down the **Control** key and press the **End** key to return to The Assistant.

### Changing the Structure

*Redefining the record*

Occasionally, you need to change the record structure of an existing data base file. Although such a change is not to be taken lightly, it is sometimes unavoidable. For example, you might have to change the name, data type, or width of a field; add a new field to the records in a file; or delete an existing field from the records in a file. Fortunately, dBASE III PLUS can perform all of these operations.

For example, suppose that you've decided to use the extended nine-digit ZIP codes in the Parkridge Condominium Association OWNERS file. When you defined the structure of this file, you only allotted five characters for the ZIP code field. To increase the width of this field, you need to activate The Assistant's Modify menu and select the Database File option. The program displays a filled record structure table, just like the one shown in Figure 11.8. You can change any of the items in this table. Changing the length of the ZIP field is done by using the **Down Arrow key** to highlight this field and pressing the **End** key twice to move the cursor to the width column. Then you simply type a **9** and press the **Enter** key. In this manner you can change the name, data type, and width of any field in this record structure. You can even add new fields and delete existing ones. When you are finished with your modifications, you hold down the **Control** key and press the **End** key. The program asks

```
Should data be COPIED from backup for all fields? [Y/N]
```

Most of the time you will want to answer this question with a **Y** for yes. Whenever you change the structure of a data base file, the program makes a temporary copy of the whole file. If you answer no to this question, the contents of any fields you've changed won't be copied from the temporary file. In the case of changing the width of the ZIP field, answering no to this question will effectively tell dBASE to discard every ZIP code in the file. Instead of going back and adding just the four extended digits, you would then have to enter all of the ZIP codes. If you have added any completely new fields, you also will have to go back and modify each record to insert a value into each of the new fields.

## REARRANGING A DATA BASE

A data base is virtually worthless if you cannot quickly and conveniently retrieve records from it. One of the best ways to facilitate the retrieval of records is to keep them arranged in some predictable order. Besides helping you find items in long lists, it is often necessary to order data for presentation on the screen and in printed reports. There are two distinct methods of rearranging records with dBASE: sorting and indexing.

### Sorting

*A new copy in rearranged order*

As we have said before, *sorting* is the process of arranging items in a particular order. Numbers are sorted by arranging them from smallest to largest (ascending order), or from largest to smallest (descending order). Text items are sorted by arranging them alphabetically from A to Z (also ascending order), or backwards from Z to A (descending order). In dBASE, sorting creates a new copy of an existing data base file with the records in this new file rearranged on the basis of one or more keys. A *key* is simply a field that is used to order the records in a file. In a mailing list arranged alphabetically by last name, for example, the field containing last names is the key. Sometimes more than one key is used to rearrange records. The data base manager does this by successively rearranging records on the basis of each specified key. So you could also sort a data base by ZIP code (the primary key) and then by last name (the secondary key). Note that when using The Assistant, dBASE automatically assumes that you want to do an ascending sort.

As an example, let's use dBASE to sort the Parkridge Condominium Association OWNERS file. The records of this file were originally entered according to the building in which each owner lives. For some purposes, this might be a perfectly adequate arrangement of the records. You might, however, want to alphabetize the records by last name instead. The first step is to make the OWNERS file your current data base file if you have not already done so. Remember, this is done by selecting the Database File option from the Set Up menu, indicating the disk drive, and then choosing the name OWNERS.DBF. Next you type **O** to activate the Organize menu, highlight the Sort option, and press the **Enter** key. A submenu listing the fields appears on your screen, just like the one shown in Step 6 of Figure 11.11(a). The LAST_NAME field is already highlighted and this is the field on which you want to sort, so all you do is press the **Enter** key. LAST_NAME becomes your primary key. If you want to specify additional keys, you would also highlight them and press the **Enter** key. In our simple example, LAST_NAME is the only key we want. To stop selecting keys and go on, you press the **Right Arrow** or **Left Arrow** key. The program then displays a submenu of disk drive letters, and you select the drive where you want to put the sorted file. Finally, dBASE asks you to supply a name for the new sorted file. You enter a valid filename, say **BY_NAME**, and dBASE performs the sort, indicates how many records were sorted, and tells you to press any key to go back to The Assistant. There are now two complete versions of the OWNERS data base file on your disk: OWNERS.DBF and BY_NAME.DBF.

To see the new file you've created, you need to activate the Set Up menu again, select the Database File option, indicate the disk drive, and this time choose BY_NAME.DBF. If you then select the Browse option from the Update menu, Figure 11.12 shows what your screen will look like. Notice that the records in BY_NAME.DBF are in ascending order by last name, in contrast with the records in the original OWNERS.DBF, shown in Figure 11.10.

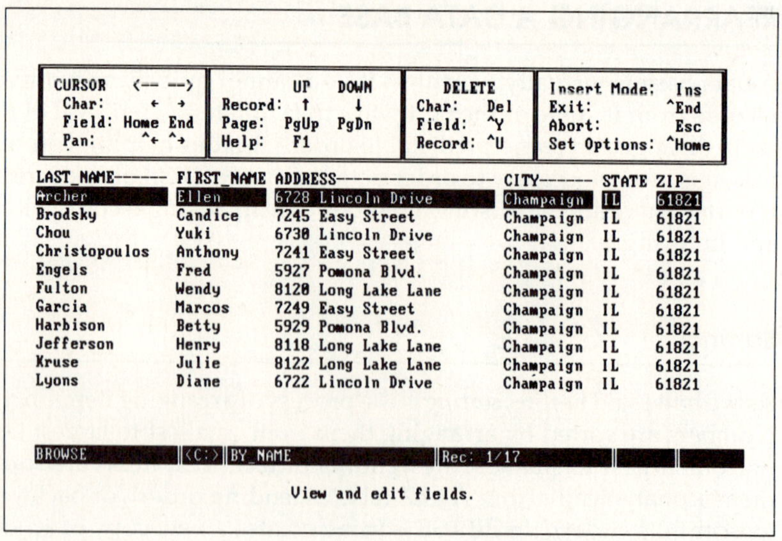


**Figure 11.12 Sorting**
Here is the data base file sorted by last name.

## Indexing

*A new file of only record numbers*

Large data bases with many fields and records can take a long time to sort. Besides, every time you sort a file in dBASE a completely new copy of the file is created. The newly sorted copy is the same size as the original. If you have several versions of the same data base file, each sorted in a different way, they can take up a great deal of disk space. Indexing reduces these problems.

When you index a data base file, you don't create a completely new copy. As we showed in the last chapter in Figure 10.6, a new file is created, but it contains only record numbers, not complete records. Instead of rearranging records, indexing rearranges only record numbers. This is generally faster and consumes less disk space than sorting. Let's go back and rearrange the Parkridge Condominium Association OWNERS file, but this time let's index the file instead of sorting it.

After you have selected the data base file you want to index, the next step is to choose the Index option from the Organize menu. The program asks you to enter the index key. Similar to a sort key, an index key is the field to be used as the basis for rearranging the record numbers. Files are usually indexed on only one key. In this case we want records alphabetized by last name, so the index key you enter is **LAST_NAME**. A submenu of disk drive letters appears to let you choose the drive on which you want to store the index file. Then you are asked to supply a filename for the new index file. You can enter just a primary filename, say BY_NAME, and dBASE will automatically attach the extension used for index files, which is .NDX. Next, the indexing is performed, dBASE indicates how many records were indexed and tells you to press any key to return to The Assistant.

Now you have the original data base file OWNERS.DBF and an index file called BY_NAME.NDX. Remember that the OWNERS file itself is not sorted by name. You can, however, tell dBASE to use the index file you've created in conjunction with the OWNERS file. Once you've done this, records can be displayed and printed according to the order specified by the index file and not by the original data base file. To establish this association, you have to return to the Set Up menu again. Then you select the Database File option, indicate the disk drive, and choose OWNERS.DBF. This time, however, you answer **Y** for yes to the question

```
Is the file indexed? [Y/N]
```

You are then presented with a list of index files from which to choose. Simply highlight BY_NAME.NDX and press the **Enter** key. This file is now considered to be the **master index file**. All records will be displayed according to the order of this index file unless you specify otherwise. Although only the master index file actively determines the order in which records are presented, up to six other index files can also be selected if you have them. Then if you make any changes to the records in the data base file, the master index file and any additional inactive index files you've selected will also be automatically updated. When you are finished selecting index files, you press the **Left Arrow** or **Right Arrow** key to return to The Assistant menu.

To see the consequence of indexing the OWNERS file on the basis of the LAST_NAME field, you can select the Browse option from the Update menu. The resulting screen looks very similar to Figure 11.12, with records displayed in alphabetical order by last name. The only difference is that you are viewing the OWNERS data base file arranged in the order dictated by the BY_NAME index file.

## GENERATING DATA BASE REPORTS

*Printed output*

You have seen how to use the Browse option of the Update menu and the Display option of the Retrieve menu to view one or more data base records on the screen. It's very common, however, to want printed listings of all or part of a data base. These listings, usually called *reports*, can be generated by dBASE according to instructions that you provide. The program gives you a great deal of flexibility in specifying report layouts. You can indicate the fields to include, the order in which they are to appear, where to put them on the page, what their headings should be, and whether to sum the contents of numeric fields. Once you set up a report layout, you can save it in a disk file and use it again in later dBASE sessions without having to respecify the format settings.

Let's say that you want a report that lists the names and addresses of the Parkridge Condominium Association owners. Only first names, last names, and street addresses need to be included since all Parkridge buildings are in the same city, state, and ZIP code. Furthermore, you want the names listed in alphabetical order by last name. There should be a title at the top of the page and appropriate headings over the three columns. The dBASE program automatically puts the date and page number in the upper left corner of each page.

The first step is to select the version of the OWNERS file that is sorted by last name, or select the OWNERS file and index it by last name. Then you activate the Create menu and select the Report option. The program displays a list of disk drives and you select the one where you want to store the file that is to contain the report layout. Then dBASE asks you to provide a name for the report layout file. The program will automatically append an extension of .FRM (for report FoRMat) to the filename you enter, so using OWNERS is perfectly acceptable. Figure 11.13 shows what dBASE displays on your screen.

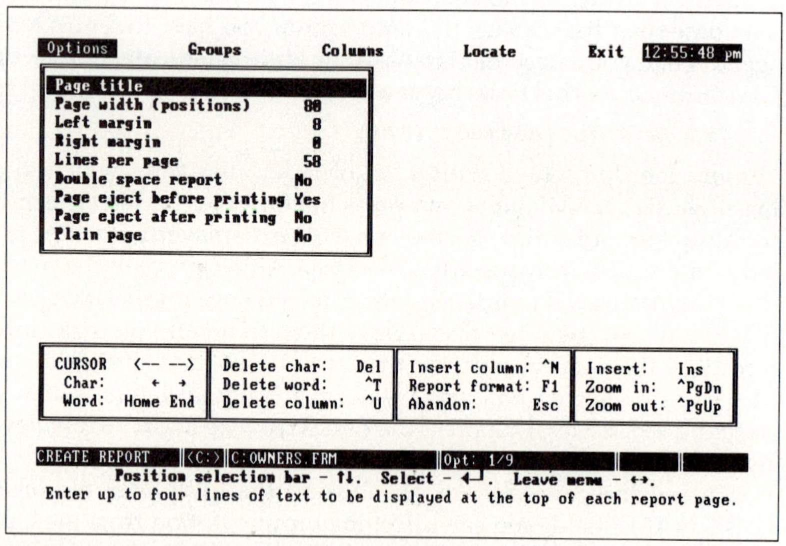


**Figure 11.13 Generating the Report Layout**
Here is where you specify the format of your printed data base report.

This screen is where you specify the layout for each page of your report. As you can see, dBASE has already supplied default entries for most of the format settings in the Options menu. At this point, you press the **Enter** key to specify the report's title. A box pops up on the right side of the screen within which you can type up to four lines of text to be printed at the top of each report page. In this case, a good title would be **Parkridge Condominium Association Owners**. After you type the title, you hold down the **Control** key and press the **End** key to go on. The rest of the settings you see in Figure 11.13 under the Options menu are fine for this report.

The next step is to activate the Columns submenu by typing **C**. This is where you specify each field to be included in the report along with its column heading. You press the **Enter** key and then enter **FIRST_NAME** to specify the first column's contents. Then you press the **Down Arrow** key to highlight the Heading option, press the **Enter** key, type **First Name**, and press **Ctrl-End** to specify the first column's heading. You press the **Page Down** key to repeat the process for the next column, which lists the last names, and again to do the final column, which lists the street addresses. The widths of these columns are already specified by default, and dBASE will automatically leave one space between field columns. You can change these settings if you wish, but they are fine for this report. When you are finished specifying columns, you type **E** to activate the Exit menu and then press the **Enter** key to save this report layout in the file named OWNERS.FRM. The program returns to The Assistant's main menu.

The final step is to print the report. You type **R** to activate the Retrieve menu, highlight the Report option, and press the **Enter** key. Then you select the disk drive and the report layout file, which in this case is OWNERS.FRM. You press the **Enter** key again to execute the command and dBASE asks

```
Direct the output to the printer? [Y/N]
```

If you type **Y** for yes, the report will be printed; if you type **N** for no, the report will instead be displayed on your screen. Figure 11.14 shows the final printed report.

Page No. 1
01/01/89

Parkridge Condominium Association Owners

| First Name | Last Name | Address |
|---|---|---|
| Ellen | Archer | 6728 Lincoln Drive |
| Candice | Brodsky | 7245 Easy Street |
| Yuki | Chou | 6730 Lincoln Drive |
| Anthony | Christopoulos | 7241 Easy Street |
| Fred | Engels | 5927 Pomona Blvd. |
| Wendy | Fulton | 8120 Long Lake Lane |
| Marcos | Garcia | 7249 Easy Street |
| Betty | Harbison | 5929 Pomona Blvd. |
| Henry | Jefferson | 8118 Long Lake Lane |
| Julie | Kruse | 8122 Long Lake Lane |
| Diane | Lyons | 6722 Lincoln Drive |
| Jeffrey | Mack | 6724 Lincoln Drive |
| Elaine | Sanders | 5925 Pomona Blvd. |
| Tom | Santiago | 5931 Pomona Blvd. |
| Montgomery | Scott | 7243 Easy Street |
| Todd | Thorpe | 6726 Lincoln Drive |
| Jonathan | Trowbridge | 7247 Easy Street |

**Figure 11.14 Printed Owners Report**
This is what the report looks like when it is printed.

## ADDITIONAL FEATURES

The dBASE III PLUS package is very sophisticated software with many complex features. So far, we've introduced its most basic data base management operations. The two user manuals that come with dBASE III PLUS together consist of more than 1000 pages of documentation. Obviously, we cannot cover the subject in the same depth. Nevertheless, there are a few more features that you should know about.

### Custom Data Entry Forms

*Painting your own data input screens*

When you add records to a new or existing data base file, by default dBASE presents you with a simple data entry form. This form shows the name and length of each field in the record structure, which you defined when you created the data base file. Although using this default data entry form is easier for the data base designer, it might not be so easy to use for those who must enter records on a day-to-day basis. People who aren't data base experts benefit from more descriptive field labels, instructions, and editing constraints that help prevent errors. Just having an entry form that is more pleasing to look at also can help reduce fatigue and typographical errors.

Like many data base management systems, dBASE provides a way for you to design your own custom data entry forms. This feature, called the **Screen Painter**, allows you to build forms that resemble the printed forms commonly used in many offices. It also lets you select which fields are to be included in the entry form so that you can prevent data entry personnel from seeing and altering certain other fields. The dBASE program can be instructed to automatically use a particular custom entry form whenever you add or modify records.

To create a custom data entry form, you use the Format option from The Assistant's Create menu. After choosing a disk drive and filename for the entry form, the Screen Painter's menu bar appears on the screen. This menu contains options that display submenus to let you set up a new form, modify an existing form, add lines and boxes to a form, and save a form to disk and return to The Assistant menu. We won't go through all the necessary steps, but Figure 11.15 shows an example of the kind of custom data entry form you can create with dBASE III PLUS.

**Figure 11.15 Custom Data Entry Form**
With the Screen Painter, you can create your own data entry forms.

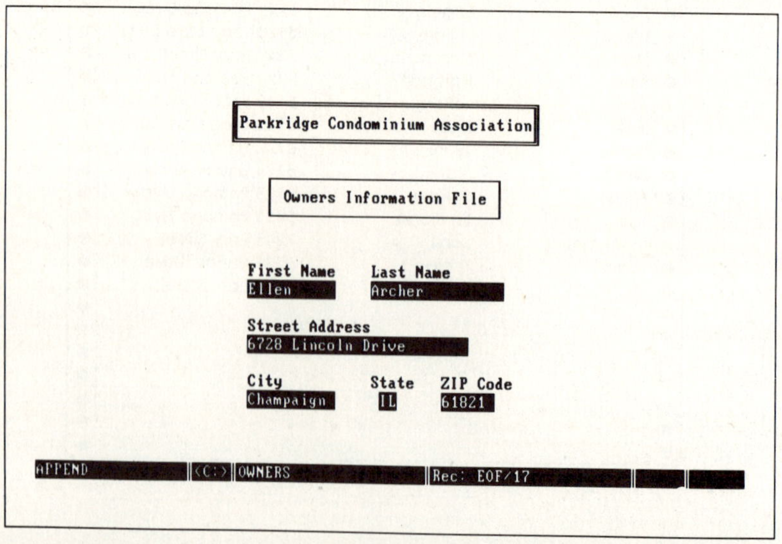

## Mailing Labels

*Automated addressing*

One of the most common uses of data base packages is maintaining mailing lists. A handy feature is the ability to print mailing labels. This can dramatically decrease the time and effort it takes to address envelopes while increasing the accuracy. Because the process is so frequently done, dBASE III PLUS has a special menu option just for producing mailing labels.

As an example, let's use dBASE to produce mailing labels from the Parkridge Condominium Association OWNERS file. We'll use a popular type of mailing label for computer printers. These standard labels, 3 1/2 x 15/16–inch size, come three across an 8 1/2 x 11–inch page of fan-fold computer paper. After they are printed, these pre-gummed labels are simply peeled from the paper backing and affixed to envelopes.

The first step is to activate the Set Up menu and select the Database File option. You indicate the proper drive and select OWNERS.DBF, the file from which you want to generate labels. Then you activate the Create menu and select the Label option. The program asks you for the disk drive and name of the file that will be used to store your label format. You could use a name like OWNLABEL for the label format file. After you select a name, dBASE presents the Label menu, shown in Figure 11.16(a). A number of commonly used label formats are already built into the program. Initially, the program assumes that you want to print 3 1/2 x 15/16–inch labels, which are only one across each page. Press the **Enter** key twice, and the predefined size changes to 3 1/2 x 15/16 x 3, which is the type of labels we have. If instead you have non-standard sized labels, dBASE lets you individually change the settings you see in the Options menu.

The next step is to tell dBASE what fields you want to print on the labels. This is done by pressing the right arrow key to activate the Contents submenu. Then you type the following entries onto lines 2, 3, and 4 of the label format:

```
FIRST_NAME,LAST_NAME
ADDRESS
CITY,", ",STATE," ",ZIP
```

Press the **Enter** key when you are finished typing these lines, press the **Right Arrow** key to activate the Exit submenu, and press the **Enter** key to save this label format file.

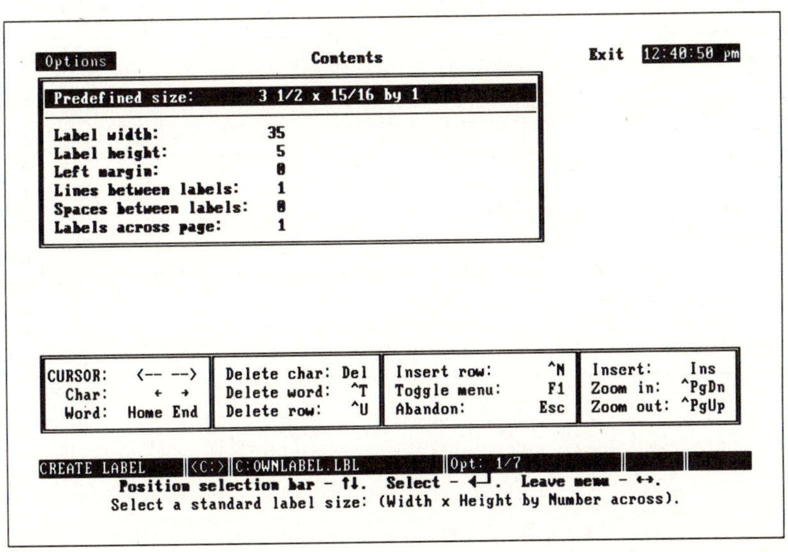


**Figure 11.16 Mailing Labels**
(a) Specifying the mailing label format.

To actually print the mailing labels, you use The Assistant's Retrieve menu. Select the Label option, indicate the disk drive, and choose OWNLABEL.LBL, the label format file you've just created. You press the **Enter** key again to execute the command and the program asks

```
Direct the output to the printer? [Y/N]
```

Assuming that you already have the mailing label pages loaded into your printer, you type **Y** for yes and the program prints your labels, which should look like Figure 11.16(b).

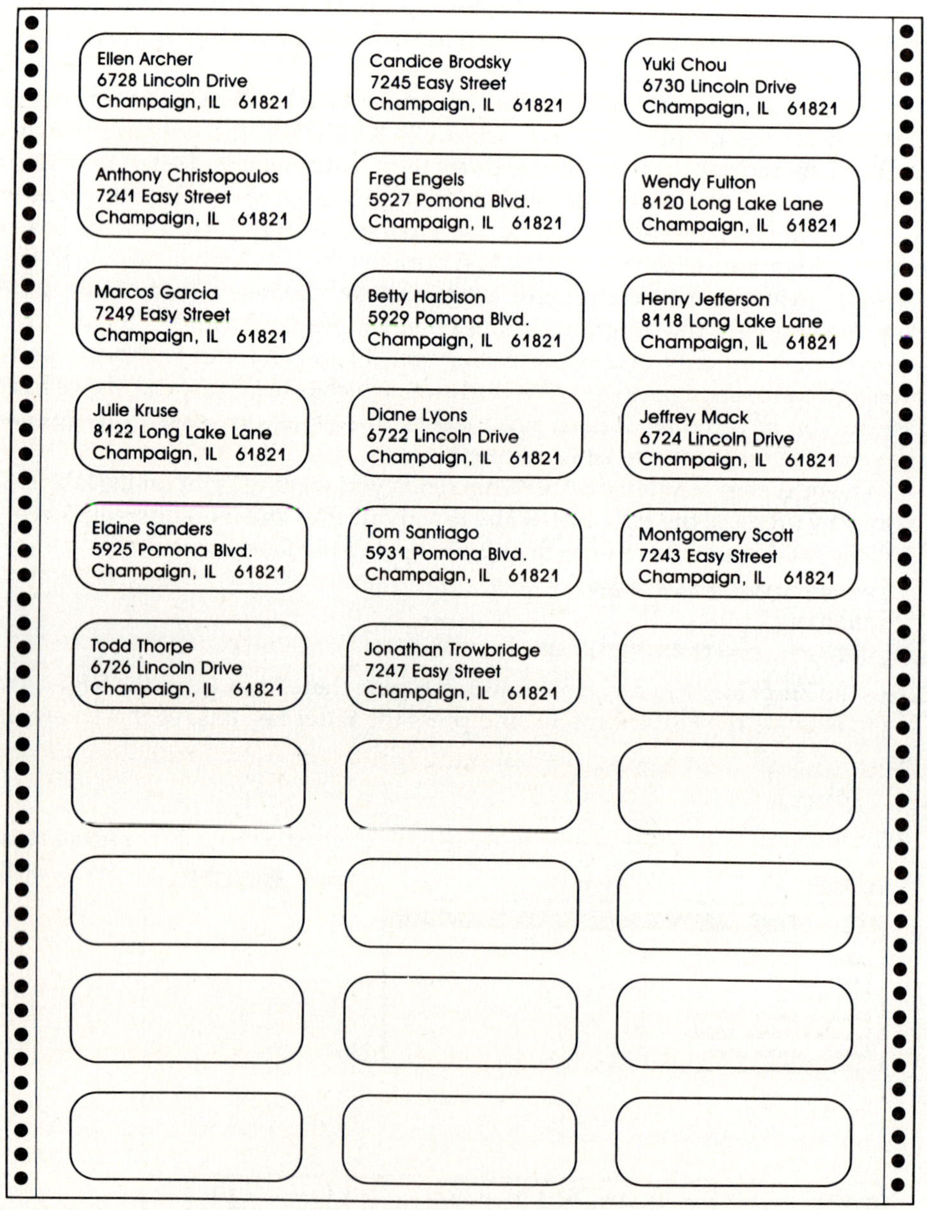


**Figure 11.16**
(b) The printed mailing labels.

## Relating Multiple Files

*Displaying and printing connected data*

As we have said, a relational data base manager allows you to use more than one file at a time by establishing relationships between files. In dBASE III PLUS, you can relate multiple files by means of a common field included in each file. Our Parkridge Condominium Association data base, for example, has two files with just such a common field. Both the OWNERS and the FEES file have an identical ADDRESS field. Let's say that you want to display or print a listing of the owners' names and their condo fees. Since this data resides in different files, you have to relate the OWNERS and FEES files before you can produce such a listing.

One way to accomplish this task is to create a **view file** that links the two data bases. A view file enables you to look at two or more data base files from a particular perspective. It tells dBASE the particular fields and files you want to display, update, or print. To create the view file, you select the View option from the Create menu. Then you select a disk drive and a name, say **OWNERFEE**, for the view file you are creating. The next step is to select the data base files along with any index files to be included in the view. In our case, the data base files would be OWNERS.DBF and FEES.DBF. Note that all of the data base files included in a view must be indexed. Remember that we indexed the OWNERS file on the basis of the LAST_NAME field earlier in this chapter. The FEES file should be indexed according to ADDRESS before attempting to create the view file.

After selecting the data base files along with their respective index files, the next step is to select the common field that will relate the data base files. The common field in the OWNERS and FEES file is ADDRESS. Remember that to be a common field, a field must have the same name, data type, and length in both files.

Once you select the common field, you can select those fields from both data base files that you want displayed from the view file. These fields need not include the common field. For example, in our view file we only want the FIRST_NAME and LAST_NAME fields from the OWNERS file, and the FEE field from the FEES file. After these fields are selected, the view file is saved and dBASE returns to The Assistant's main menu.

To activate the view file, you must return to the Set Up menu, select the View option, indicate the disk drive, and choose OWNERFEE.VUE, the view file you've just created. As Figure 11.17 shows, now when you browse through the records, you see the last names, first names, and condo fees. At this point you can also generate a report in the desired format listing just the owners' names and their condo fees.

## Protecting Data

*Preventing accidental erasure and unauthorized snooping*

There are several ways to protect data in dBASE III PLUS. The simplest is to designate a field to be display-only. As we described in the previous chapter, the contents of a field designated as display-only can be viewed, but not changed. In dBASE, this is done by using the Action option of the Modify menu of the Screen Painter while designing a custom data entry form.

Also included with dBASE III PLUS is a separate utility program called PROTECT. This program creates a security system that can be used to prevent the unauthorized access of sensitive, private, or otherwise classified data. PROTECT is primarily intended for use with dBASE systems installed on local area networks,

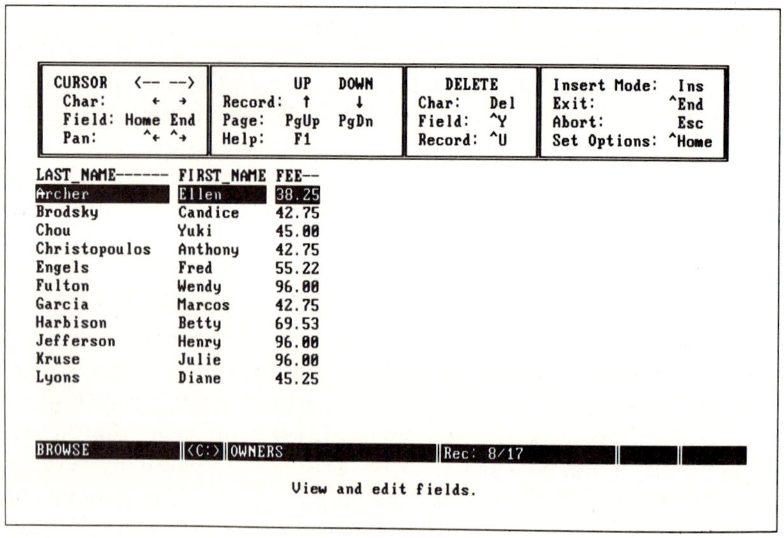


**Figure 11.17 Browsing the View File**
The OWNERFEE view file lets you relate the OWNERS and FEES data base files.

which we'll be discussing shortly. The program provides three types of data base protection:

- *Log-in Security.* Each user is required to **log-in** by entering his or her assigned group name, user name, and password. These three items uniquely identify each authorized user of the data base system. Users get three chances to enter the correct log-in information; if they fail, dBASE immediately returns to DOS without granting them access to any files.
- *File and Field Access Security.* Certain files and fields within files can be protected by allowing access only to users who have been granted special permission. Various privilege levels can be assigned that restrict the types of changes that can be made to data bases.
- *Data Encryption.* Data bases are automatically kept encoded or scrambled in an unreadable form. Encrypted data bases cannot be read unless a proper group name, user name, and password are supplied.

## Data Base Programming

*Automated sequences of saved dot prompt commands*

One of the greatest strengths of dBASE is its programmability. This data base management system includes its own sophisticated programming language that can be used by experts to create programs that control every aspect of how users work with their data. The dBASE programming language has become practically a standard in the data base management market. As a result, many other data base packages have been designed so that they can execute programs written in the dBASE programming language. Although most users don't write their own data base programs, they can benefit from programs created by others.

In its simplest form, a dBASE program consists of a sequence of dot prompt commands stored in a disk file. Instead of entering each individual command whenever you want to execute this particular sequence, you simply tell dBASE to run the previously stored program file. So, dBASE programs are basically used to perform frequently executed sequences of commands. For example, here is a simple dBASE program:

```
USE C:OWNERS INDEX BY_NAME
LIST LAST_NAME, ADDRESS FOR SUBST(ADDRESS,6,6) = 'Pomona'
RETURN
```

This program, which consists of dot prompt commands, is typed into a file named POMONA.PRG and saved on disk. To run it, you start dBASE, press the **Escape** key to get into dot prompt mode, and enter **DO POMONA.** The program lists on the screen the last names and addresses of all those Parkridge Condominium Association owners who live on Pomona Boulevard. If this were a task that you frequently performed, running the POMONA program would be much easier and quicker than using The Assistant menus or repeatedly entering the equivalent dot prompt commands.

This example program is very simple; there is much more that you can do with the dBASE programming language. You can design your own menus and display screens; you can have dBASE ask questions and accept responses from users; you can calculate formulas based on the contents of record fields; you can make decisions based on data or user input; and you can repeat sequences of dBASE commands. The combination of a full-fledged programming language along with a powerful data base management system makes dBASE III PLUS one of the most versatile types of software, applicable to a wide range of jobs and used by all kinds of organizations.

## Importing and Exporting Files

*Transferring data to and from other packages*

As we said in Chapter 10, it is especially important for data base managers to be able to import and export data. Fortunately, dBASE III PLUS can easily transfer data to and from many popular application packages. There are six basic file formats that dBASE can use to transfer data:

- *ASCII.* The **American Standard Code for Information Interchange (ASCII,** pronounced as-key) is an international method of representing characters (see Appendix A). Most microcomputers use this code for ordinary text files—files that contain only letters, numbers, punctuation, and a few control codes like carriage returns and form feeds.
- *Delimited.* Delimited format files are ASCII files that contain records in which the fields are surrounded by quotation marks and are separated from other fields by commas. Each record occupies its own line and is terminated by a carriage return.
- *SDF.* System Data Format files are also ASCII files that store each record on its own line, but fields are not enclosed in quotes or separated by commas. Instead each field is assigned a fixed number of spaces, regardless of the actual size of the entry in that field.
- *SYLK.* SYmbolic LinK files follow a format developed by Microsoft Corporation as a means of transferring data between their software products, such as Microsoft Chart (graphics), Multiplan (spreadsheet), and File (data base manager).
- *DIF.* The Document Interchange Format was originally developed for VisiCalc, the first spreadsheet, as a means of sharing files with a wide assortment of other programs. Internally DIF files somewhat resemble Delimited format files.

- *WKS.* You might remember that WKS is the filename extension used by Lotus Corporation for worksheet files produced with their early versions of Lotus 1-2-3. The dBASE program can also work with the WK1 worksheet files produced by later versions of Lotus 1-2-3.

Although there is an Import and an Export option in The Assistant's Tools menu, these two commands only transfer data between dBASE and one other file manager program, Software Publishing Corporation's PFS:File. Why Ashton-Tate chose this particular file manager as the only one represented in The Assistant menu is not clear. If you want to import or export a file from some other software package, you have to use the APPEND FROM or COPY TO dot prompt commands.

For example, let's say that you have a Lotus 1-2-3 worksheet file named WORKDATA.WK1 that contains data you want to import into a dBASE data base file. In a worksheet, a record corresponds to a single row and its fields correspond to columns. First you have to create a data base structure in dBASE that matches the worksheet's column layout in terms of the number and lengths of fields. Then you press the **Escape** key to activate dot prompt mode and enter the following command:

```
APPEND FROM WORKDATA.WK1 WKS
```

This tells dBASE to read the contents of the WORKDATA worksheet using the WKS file format and to add those contents to your current data base file.

Similarly, to export your current dBASE data base file to create a 1-2-3 worksheet file named WORKDATA.WK1, you would use this dot prompt command:

```
COPY TO WORKDATA.WK1 WKS
```

## Network Data Bases

*Sharing data files among users*

There is no doubt that dBASE III PLUS is a sophisticated, powerful, and expensive data base management system. One of the reasons is that the program can be installed and used on a local area network. You'll recall that a network is a hardware and software arrangement that connects several microcomputers. A primary purpose for installing a network is to be able to share data bases between several users. Although local area networks offer many advantages to organizations that need to share hardware, software, and data, they are also somewhat more complex to set up and maintain than single-user systems. Installing and administering dBASE III PLUS on a local area network can be complicated. Not only does data base security become an important issue when files are shared between many potential users, but networks pose some additional challenges for those who attempt data base programming. Nevertheless, as long as you don't have to install or maintain it, a network data base management system is not really more difficult to use.

The way you start dBASE on a network varies. You may have to log into the system, as we described in the section on protecting data. The exact procedure varies among organizations, depending on the particular application and the way dBASE has been installed. For example, you may have to enter **ACCESS** instead of **DBASE** to start the dBASE program from DOS when working on a network. Or you may be required to run a special start-up batch file designated by the data base administrator at your organization. With these few exceptions, however, the average user will find that running dBASE on a local area network is much the same as on a stand-alone computer. The added benefit is that data bases can be shared with other users.

## The Real World

### The dBASE Plunge

Ed Bowen owns the Freedom Guitar music store in Hollywood, California and he took the dBASE plunge. With virtually no hands-on computer experience, Bowen decided that he needed to learn to use a relational data base management system to help him run his business.

He bought an IBM Personal Computer along with Ashton-Tate's dBASE III. It took him three months before he could use the program to manage his payroll, expenses, and other routine business data, but after the first year, Bowen was also using his data base system to track sales commissions and calculate total sales tax.

At first, it was sometimes difficult to master the program's intricacies. Bowen considered going to a consultant for help, but decided that he didn't want to become dependent on someone else every time he wanted to change the way he used the program. He persevered. Soon Bowen found that the more he worked with dBASE, the more he enjoyed it. Altogether, he has written more than thirty customized data base programs in the dBASE programming language to handle all kinds of business tasks, including general ledger, accounts receivable, monthly statements, and overdue balance reports.

For Bowen, the fruit of his labors is more control over the daily operation of his business and an increased ability to serve his customers. Besides, dBASE saves him a great deal of time. "I can't compare it to anything else," Bowen admits. "I used file folders for fourteen years and it would take three or four hours just to figure out what I owed in sales tax. On the computer it takes less than a minute."

Source: "Everybody Started Somewhere," David Needle, *Personal Computing*, Dec. 1985, pp. 103-109.

## Summary

- *How to begin working with dBASE III PLUS.* To run the program, you switch to the DBASE subdirectory, type **DBASE**, and press the **Enter** key.
- *The operation of dBASE menus and commands.* The dBASE III PLUS package includes an easy-to-use menu system known as The Assistant. Operations also can be performed by using dot prompt commands.
- *How to create a data base with dBASE.* You select the Database File option of the Create menu; choose the disk drive, name the file, and specify the record structure; give each field a name, data type, and length; and then enter the data and save the file on a disk.
- *How to examine an existing data base with dBASE.* First retrieve from disk the data base file that you want to view. Then you can either browse through the records or submit a query to find one or more records that meet a specified set of criteria.
- *How to keep a data base up-to-date with dBASE.* New records are added with the Append option of the Update menu. Old records are tentatively removed with the Delete option and permanently removed with Pack option. Existing records can be modified with the Browse option or the Edit option. An existing record structure can be changed by using the Database File option of the Modify menu.
- *How to organize a data base with dBASE.* A data base file can be sorted with the Sort option, or indexed with the Index option.

- *How to display and print dBASE reports.* Data base reports are generated with the Report option of the Create menu.
- *Some of the additional features included in dBASE.* Additional features allow you to create custom data entry forms, create mailing labels, relate multiple files, protect data, develop data base programs, import and export files from other programs, and use data bases on a network.

## Command Summary

The following table summarizes the actions of the dBASE III PLUS Assistant menu options.

| MENU | OPTION | DESCRIPTION |
|---|---|---|
| *Set Up* | *Database File* | Loads an existing data base file into memory. |
| *Set Up* | *Format for Screen* | Loads an existing data entry form. |
| *Set Up* | *Query* | Loads an existing search specification. |
| *Set Up* | *Catalog* | Loads a catalog of files into memory. |
| *Set Up* | *View* | Loads an existing view file into memory. |
| *Set Up* | *Quit dBASE III PLUS* | Closes all files, ends dBASE, returns to DOS. |
| *Create* | *Database File* | Designs the structure of a data base file. |
| *Create* | *Format* | Designs a custom data entry form. |
| *Create* | *View* | Relates multiple data base files. |
| *Create* | *Query* | Creates and saves a search specification. |
| *Create* | *Report* | Designs a report layout. |
| *Create* | *Label* | Designs mailing labels. |
| *Update* | *Append* | Adds new records to a data base file. |
| *Update* | *Edit* | Changes record contents. |
| *Update* | *Display* | Displays the contents of a record. |
| *Update* | *Browse* | Displays and edits entire screens of records. |
| *Update* | *Replace* | Modifies a record without displaying it. |
| *Update* | *Delete* | Marks records for removal. |
| *Update* | *Recall* | Reinstates records marked for removal. |
| *Update* | *Pack* | Permanently removes deleted records. |
| *Position* | *Seek* | Searches an indexed data base file. |
| *Position* | *Locate* | Searches a data base file. |
| *Position* | *Continue* | Resumes a search started by *Locate*. |
| *Position* | *Skip* | Moves the current record pointer. |
| *Position* | *Goto Record* | Moves the pointer to a specific record. |
| *Retrieve* | *List* | Lists specified records and fields. |
| *Retrieve* | *Display* | Displays a screen of records and fields. |
| *Retrieve* | *Report* | Produces a printed report. |
| *Retrieve* | *Label* | Produces printed mailing labels. |
| *Retrieve* | *Sum* | Computes total of selected numeric fields. |
| *Retrieve* | *Average* | Computes mean of selected numeric fields. |
| *Retrieve* | *Count* | Computes the number of selected records. |
| *Organize* | *Index* | Creates and opens an index file |
| *Organize* | *Sort* | Creates a reordered copy of a data base file. |
| *Organize* | *Copy* | Duplicates all or part of a data base file. |

| MENU | OPTION | DESCRIPTION |
|---|---|---|
| *Modify* | *Database File* | Changes the structure of a data base file. |
| *Modify* | *Format* | Changes an existing data entry form. |
| *Modify* | *View* | Changes an existing view file. |
| *Modify* | *Query* | Changes an existing search specification. |
| *Modify* | *Report* | Changes an existing report layout. |
| *Modify* | *Label* | Changes an existing mailing label format. |
| *Tools* | *Set Drive* | Changes the default disk drive. |
| *Tools* | *Copy File* | Duplicates any file. |
| *Tools* | *Directory* | Displays a disk drive directory. |
| *Tools* | *Rename* | Changes a file's name. |
| *Tools* | *Erase* | Deletes a file from a disk. |
| *Tools* | *List Structure* | Displays the structure of a data base file. |
| *Tools* | *Import* | Reads data from a PFS File data base. |
| *Tools* | *Export* | Creates a PFS File data base. |

## Key Terms

As an extra review of this chapter, try defining the following terms. If you have trouble with any of them, refer to the page number listed.

American Standard Code for Information Interchange (ASCII) (409)
dot prompt (386)
dot prompt command (386)
log-in (408)
master index file (401)
Screen Painter (404)
The Assistant (384)
view file (407)

## Review Questions

1. Why is dBASE almost always used on hard disk systems?
2. How do you select a main menu option in The Assistant?
3. How do you select an option within a menu?
4. Why might you use a dot prompt command instead of a menu selection?
5. How do you get on-line help in dBASE?
6. What three attributes must you specify for every field in a data base file's record structure?
7. List the five different data types of dBASE fields.
8. What can you do with the Browse option of the Update menu?
9. How do you add new records to an existing data base?
10. What option do you use to get back an accidentally deleted record?
11. How do you change the structure of an existing data base file?
12. Why does sorting a file in dBASE consume more disk space than indexing it?
13. How do you produce a report layout file?
14. What would you create if you select the Format option of the Create menu?
15. How do you use dBASE to print mailing labels?

16. What does dBASE use to link two data base files?
17. List the three types of security provided by the PROTECT utility program.
18. What makes up a program written in the dBASE programming language?
19. List the six basic file formats that dBASE can use to transfer data to and from other application packages.
20. What is the primary reason for installing dBASE on a local area network?

## Multiple Choice

1. Which dBASE menu is used to select an existing data base file with which to work?
   (a) Set Up (b) Create
   (c) Update (d) Retrieve
2. Every activity you can select from The Assistant can also be done with a
   (a) function key. (b) escape sequence.
   (c) dot prompt command. (d) DOS command.
3. Where is the dot prompt command equivalent to your current sequence of menu selections displayed on The Assistant's screen?
   (a) Action Line (b) Status Bar
   (c) Navigation Line (d) Message Line
4. The dBASE help key is
   (a) F1. (b) F2.
   (c) H. (d) Esc.
5. Which extension does dBASE use for data base files?
   (a) .FRM (b) .DBF
   (c) .FMT (d) .NDX
6. The maximum size of any single record in dBASE III PLUS is
   (a) 2000 bytes. (b) 3000 bytes.
   (c) 4000 bytes. (d) 5000 bytes.
7. Which of the following data types is not available in dBASE III PLUS?
   (a) character (b) numeric
   (c) logical (d) time
8. One way to search for records is to use the Browse option of the Update menu. A more efficient way to search for a specific record in a large data base is to use the
   (a) View option of the Create menu. (b) Display option of the Retrieve menu.
   (c) Recall option of the Update menu. (d) Directory option of the Tools menu.
9. To permanently remove all deleted records from a dBASE database file, you must execute the
   (a) Pack option of the Update menu. (b) Erase option of the Tools menu.
   (c) Delete option of the Update menu. (d) Quit option of the Set Up menu.

10. One way to modify a record in dBASE is to use the Edit option of the Update menu. Another way is to
    (a) use the Database File option of the Modify menu.
    (b) use the Erase option of the Tools menu.
    (c) use the Browse option of the Update menu.
    (d) use the Query option of the Create menu.
11. Which method of rearranging a file creates a new copy of that file?
    (a) sorting
    (b) indexing
    (c) updating
    (d) browsing
12. You relate multiple files in dBASE by creating
    (a) an index file.
    (b) a view file.
    (c) a report format file.
    (d) a label format file.
13. Which of the following types of data security is not provided by dBASE?
    (a) log-in security
    (b) file and field access security
    (c) data encryption
    (d) lock and key security
14. You might want to import and export files in order to use
    (a) dBASE files from other countries.
    (b) dBASE files from other users.
    (c) files from other application packages.
    (d) files from other disks.
15. What is a benefit of running dBASE on a local area network?
    (a) less expense
    (b) data bases can be shared
    (c) input errors are reduced
    (d) easier installation

## On-line Exercises

1. You can use dBASE III PLUS to store information about your personal checks. For example, most checkbooks let you record the check number, the date, the recipient, the amount, and whether the expenditure is tax deductible. Create a data base file named CHKBOOK with the following structure:

| FIELD NAME | TYPE | WIDTH | DEC |
|---|---|---|---|
| CHECK_NO | Character | 3 | |
| DATE | Date | 8 | |
| PAYEE | Character | 25 | |
| AMOUNT | Numeric | 7 | 2 |
| DEDUCTIBLE | Logical | 1 | |

2. Now enter the following records into your CHKBOOK data base file:

| CHECK_NO | DATE | PAYEE | AMOUNT | DEDUCTIBLE |
|---|---|---|---|---|
| 212 | 05/14/89 | American Express | 47.26 | Yes |
| 201 | 05/01/89 | Heartland Federal | 428.92 | Yes |
| 206 | 05/07/89 | Jerry's IGA | 34.21 | No |
| 207 | 05/08/89 | Amoco Oil Company | 19.00 | Yes |
| 202 | 05/03/89 | C-U Communications | 14.95 | No |
| 210 | 05/11/89 | Illinois Bell | 103.25 | No |
| 208 | 05/08/89 | Discover Card | 41.91 | No |
| 203 | 05/03/89 | Illinois Power | 75.18 | No |
| 211 | 05/12/89 | Parkridge Condo | 49.53 | No |
| 205 | 05/06/89 | Dental Clinic | 36.00 | No |
| 209 | 05/10/89 | State Farm | 225.56 | No |
| 204 | 05/05/89 | VISA | 99.15 | No |

3. Use the Browse option of the Update menu to view your checkbook data base.
4. Use the Display option of the Retrieve menu to view the record for check number 210.
5. Add the following two records to your existing CHKBOOK data base file:

| CHECK_NO | DATE | PAYEE | AMOUNT | DEDUCTIBLE |
|---|---|---|---|---|
| 213 | 05/15/89 | Domino's Pizza | 11.53 | No |
| 214 | 05/16/89 | PC Magazine | 34.97 | Yes |

6. Delete any two records from your CHKBOOK data base file. (Don't use the Pack option of the Update menu.)
7. Reinstate the two deleted records.
8. Modify check 208 by making it tax deductible.
9. Modify the structure of the CHKBOOK data base file by adding the following field to categorize your expenditures:

| FIELD NAME | TYPE | WIDTH |
|---|---|---|
| CATEGORY | Character | 15 |

10. Enter the following values into the new CATEGORY field of each record:

| CHECK_NO | CATEGORY |
|---|---|
| 212 | Travel |
| 201 | Mortgage |
| 206 | Food |
| 207 | Automobile |
| 202 | Cable TV |
| 210 | Telephone |
| 208 | Clothing |
| 203 | Utilities |
| 211 | Utilities |
| 205 | Health |
| 209 | Insurance |
| 204 | Clothing |
| 213 | Food |
| 214 | Publications |

11. Sort the CHKBOOK data base file in ascending order on the basis of check number.

12. When you sort a file using The Assistant, records are automatically arranged in ascending order. If you want to sort in descending order, you must use the SORT dot prompt command. For example, sort the CHKBOOK data base file in descending order on the basis of date with this dot prompt command:

    ```
    SORT ON DATE/D TO CHKBOOK3.DBF
    ```

    *DATE* is the key, */D* indicates descending order, and *CHKBOOK3.DBF* is the name of the new sorted data base file that will be created.

13. Index the CHKBOOK data base file in ascending order on the basis of amount.

14. Generate a data base report of the CHKBOOK file, with records arranged in ascending order on the basis of record number. Print the report on paper.

15. Generate the same report as in On-Line Exercise 14, but this time display the report on the screen instead of printing it on paper.

## Projects

1. The dBASE III PLUS program can store a fairly large block of text (up to 4000 characters) for each record in a memo field. This feature is ideal for creating a data base to store book and magazine references. Choose some subject that interests you or one required for a term paper. Design and create a data base of at least twenty of your reference sources. Be sure to include fields for author, title, publisher, copyright data, and notes. Use a memo data type for this final field and include in it descriptions and critical notes relating the subject matter of the work.

2. Create an "electronic Rolodex." Build a data base to hold the information you keep in your personal address book. Be sure to include fields for name, address, city, state, ZIP code, and phone number. If you like, also include fields for work address and phone, birthdays, anniversaries, and any other information you ordinarily keep. You might even include a memo field for more detailed personal notes.

3. A dBASE application that might be useful to you for many years after you graduate is a data base that contains information on all of the courses you've taken throughout your college career. Create a data base that includes fields for course title, course number, semester or quarter and year taken, hours or credits earned, grade, instructor, and school (if you've attended more than one). For extra credit, see if you can get dBASE to compute your grade point average.

4. Traveling business people must keep careful records of their expenses in order to be reimbursed by their employers or to claim them as deductions on their income tax forms. Airline tickets, car rental, mileage, meals, lodging, and supplies are a few of the possible expense categories. Design, create, and enter at least twenty records for a travel expenses data base.

Part

# 6

# SPECIAL APPLICATIONS

Operating systems, word processors, spreadsheets, and data base management systems are clearly the most commonly used microcomputer software, especially in the business world. But these are by no means the only kinds of programs run on today's computer systems. In fact, there is a wealth of additional software to choose from. We now turn our attention to some other important types of microcomputer application software. Chapter 12 explores the ways microcomputers can gain access to other computers both near and far. The creation and presentation of visual images on microcomputers is the topic of Chapter 13. Combining aspects of both word processing and graphics, Chapter 14 presents the fundamentals of desktop publishing. Chapter 15 turns to the business world by discussing accounting software. Finally, Chapter 16 briefly presents a variety of other notable types of microcomputer software.

# 12

# Communications and Networking

## In This Chapter

## PREVIEW

As humans, we need to communicate with each other almost as much as we need water, food, and shelter. Ever since the beginning of time, we have sought ways to improve communications. Our distant ancestors adorned cave walls with magnificent paintings depicting hunting expeditions and religious ceremonies. The Babylonians used wedge-shaped symbols impressed in portable clay tablets to record historic events, business dealings, personal correspondence, and even recipes. Written communication advanced much further with the invention of papyrus, parchment, and paper. As society became increasingly more complex, better and faster methods of communication were developed. The electromechanical telegraphs of the nineteenth century could transmit messages over long distances at speeds of about two characters per second. Thanks to electronics, lasers, computers, and satellites, some of today's phone systems are capable of transmitting the equivalent of more than one hundred *million* characters per second. Anyone with a phone can now almost instantly converse with anyone else with a phone almost anywhere on this planet.

Even by itself, a computer is an amazing device. But equip it with a few relatively inexpensive enhancements, and a computer can communicate through the world-wide telephone network to any other similarly equipped computer. An almost infinite supply of information becomes instantly available. This is the potential of microcomputer communications. On a smaller scale, local area networks bring the benefits of program, data, and equipment sharing to closely knit groups of interconnected computers. We'll now turn to the world of computer communications and networking.

After studying this chapter, you will understand

- the basic hardware of microcomputer communications.
- the primary functions of communications software.
- the various software settings that govern microcomputer communications.
- how to call a mainframe computer with a microcomputer.
- how to use an electronic mail facility.
- how to use an on-line information service.
- how to call one microcomputer from another.
- the fundamental components and uses of local area networks.

## COMMUNICATIONS HARDWARE

For most of this chapter, we'll be discussing the connection of a microcomputer to some other computer via a telephone line. The hardware and software of local area networks are different and will be covered in the last major section of this chapter. At the most basic level, four primary hardware components are necessary for microcomputer communications:

- a microcomputer.
- a serial interface.
- a modem.
- a telephone line.

*Parts needed to go on line*

Figure 12.1 illustrates the typical arrangement of a microcomputer communications system. By now, you should have a pretty good idea what a microcomputer is. As we said back in Chapter 2, a *serial interface* is circuitry used to connect a variety of input/output devices to a computer. One bit of data at a time is transmitted through a serial interface. The most common type of serial interface is the RS-232 standard, which terminates in a socket with 25 tiny holes or a plug with 25 pins. As we explained in Chapter 2, a *modem* is a device that converts digital computer data (zeros and ones) into analog electrical signals (continuous voltage levels) that can be transmitted over telephone lines originally designed to carry voices. It also converts analog signals from phone lines back into digital computer data. Finally, a telephone line is necessary to connect the computer to the outside world. In most cases, you'll need a line that terminates in a **modular phone jack**, a socket that accepts the little plastic plug on the end of a telephone cord. At the other end of the telephone line there must be a modem and a computer to answer your call and complete the circuit. The computer you are calling is usually referred to as the **host computer**. Although the host computer may also be a microcomputer, it is frequently a larger, more powerful computer.

**Figure 12.1 Typical Microcomputer Communications System**
The typical system consists of a microcomputer and modem connected to a host computer and modem over a telephone line.

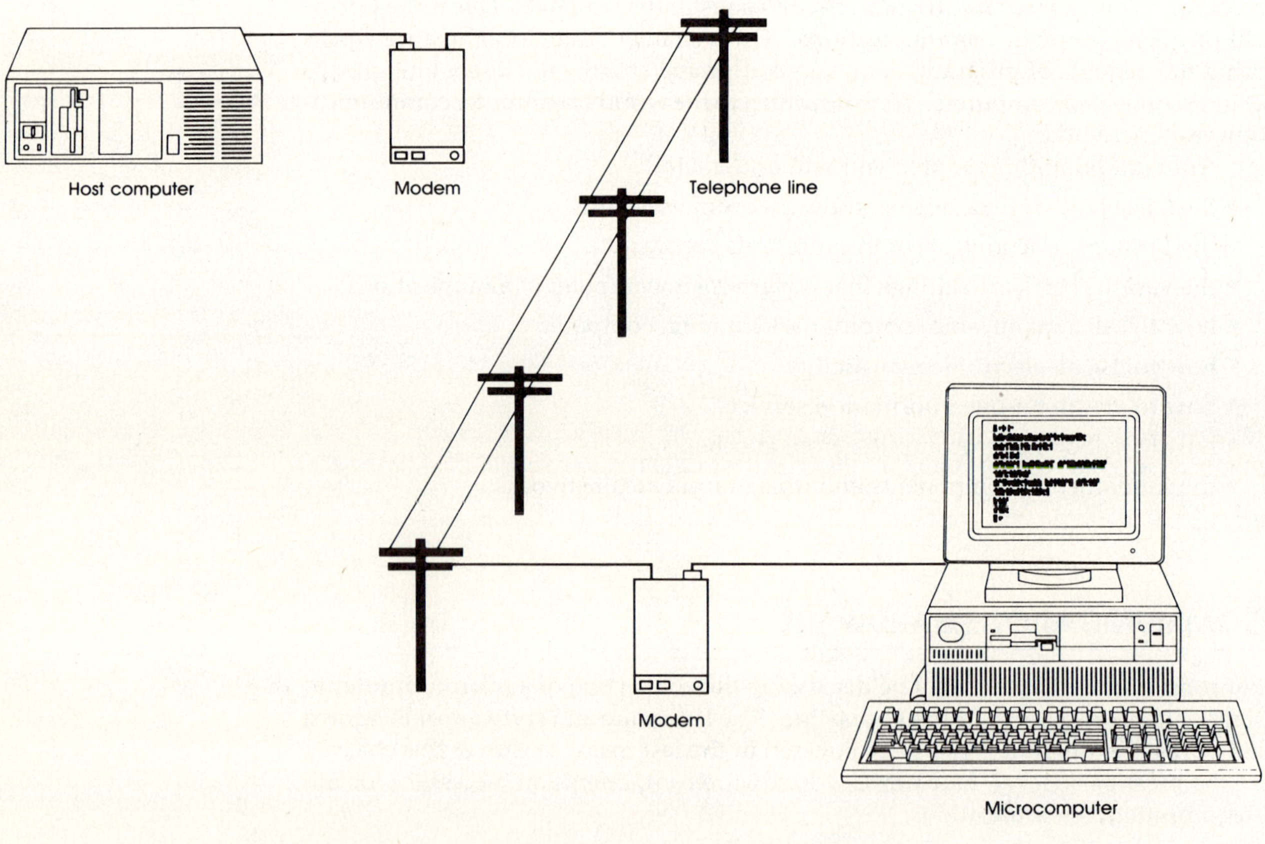


Most microcomputer communications systems consist of a microcomputer, a serial interface, a modem, and a telephone line. There are two common modem arrangements, however: the internal modem system and the external modem system.

## Insight

### Unauthorized Hackers: A Serious Problem?

Hackers are the cat burglars of the information age.

When they break into a computer system, however, it's probably because someone left the door open just a crack. Unauthorized access usually is the fault of careless managers who don't see the need for computer security until it's too late.

Any system that uses telephone lines is vulnerable to hackers; one only needs to know a computer system's telephone number to slip into the system. From there, it's only a matter of sneaking past the system's initial security measures.

Invading demonstration accounts is a favorite hacker strategy. Demonstration accounts are used to show potential users the features of a system. From within a demonstration account, it may be possible to gain access to files containing information on working accounts. This can become a problem if the computer administrator has not controlled access to the password and to account files.

Another way to penetrate a system is through the special accounts and passwords that were used when the original system was sent from the computer manufacturer. If the computer system administrator doesn't change or remove them, they can be the keys the hacker is looking for.

Hackers also have been known to steal a legitimate password or account. They may read a password on a screen that someone forgot to clear, or they may see it written down near a terminal. Sometimes, hackers have been able to trick a public network or data base administrator into issuing them a password even though they have unverified credentials.

Unauthorized access to a computer can be a serious problem if computer center administrators ignore the security available to them.

### Internal Modem System

*Modem on an expansion board*

An internal modem combines the modem and serial interface components on a single circuit board (see Figure 12.2(a)). With most microcomputers, an internal modem is an optional device mounted on a circuit board that must be plugged into an expansion slot. Remember, an expansion slot is just a connection inside the computer's system unit into which an additional circuit board can be inserted to increase the computer's capabilities. The internal modem expansion board fits inside the computer, and at the back of the board are one or two modular phone jacks accessible to the outside. If there is only one modular phone jack at the back of the board, a single phone cord goes from the wall jack to the modem. If there are two jacks, one phone cord goes from the wall jack to one of the jacks on the back of the internal modem board, and another cord goes from the other modem jack to a telephone. This arrangement enables you to still use a telephone on the line when you are not using the modem. Figure 12.2(b) illustrates the internal modem system.

There are both advantages and disadvantages to such an internal modem system. Internal modems are slightly less expensive than external modems because they draw their electrical power right from the computer and require no separate housing. Furthermore, internal modems are especially convenient because they do not take up any additional desk space or electrical sockets. Except for the phone cords, there are no external power or serial interface cables. Two disadvantages to internal modems, however, are that they require an expansion slot and they are computer-specific, so that, for example, an internal modem for an IBM-compatible computer cannot be used in an Apple Macintosh.

**Figure 12.2 Internal Modem**

(a) An internal modem adapter card.

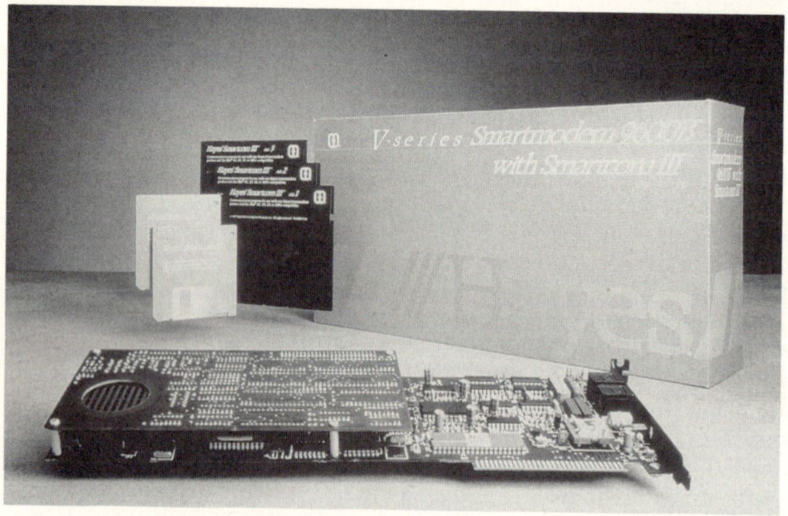


(b) Diagram of internal modem connections.

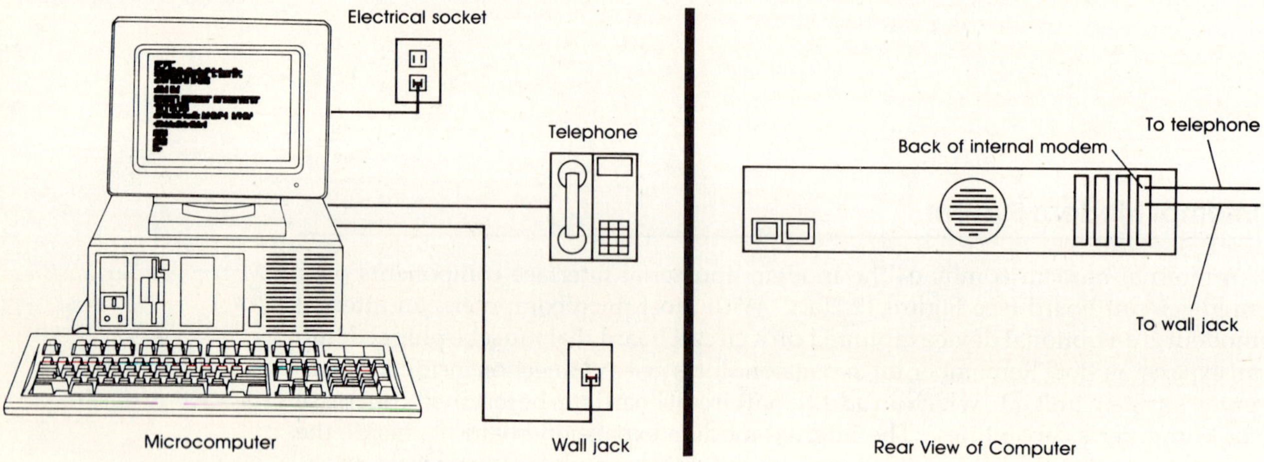


## External Modem System

*Modem in its own housing*

An external modem is built into a box about the size of a paperback book (see Figure 12.3(a)). It usually requires a separate power supply, consisting of a small adapter to be plugged into an electrical socket. The computer must have a serial interface, either built onto the motherboard or on an expansion board. Also required is a special **modem cable** to connect the external modem to the serial interface socket at the back of the computer. In many cases, the modem cable is computer-specific.

Just like an internal modem, an external modem also has one or two modular phone jacks in back. If there are two jacks, one is used for a cord from the wall phone jack and the other is used for a cord to the telephone. Figure 12.3(b) illustrates an external modem system.

**Figure 12.3 External Modem**

(a) An external modem.

(b) Diagram of external modem connections.

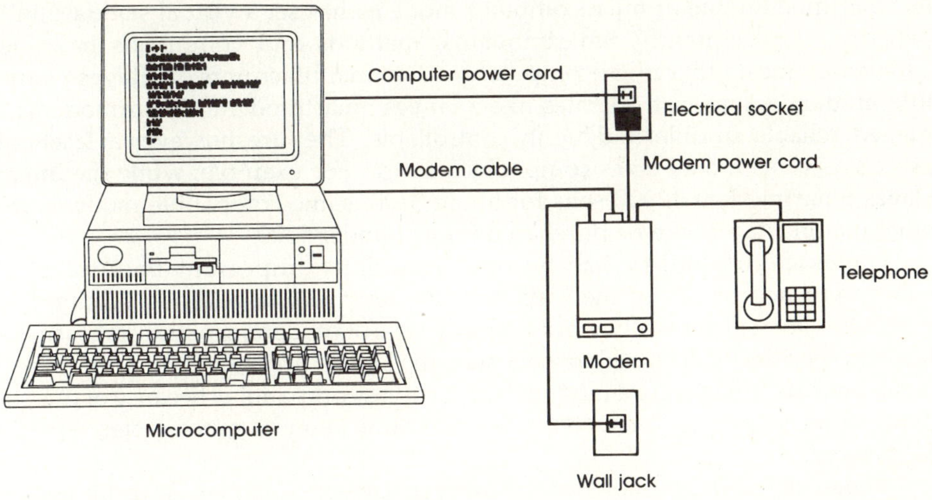


External modems have their advantages and disadvantages, too. The main advantage is that an external modem generally can be used with any computer that has a serial interface. This can save you money, for example, if you have both an IBM and an Apple Macintosh computer. Although two different modem cables may be required, it's less expensive to buy two cables and one external modem than an internal modem for each of two different types of computers. Nevertheless, external modems are slightly more expensive than internal modems, they take up desk space, they require an additional electrical socket, and they use an external serial interface cable and power cord. For these reasons, people who only have one computer usually opt for an internal modem.

## Other Modem Considerations

In addition to the factors we have just mentioned, there are two other major considerations in the selection of a modem: speed and Hayes compatibility.

### Speed

*Data transmission rate*

Modems are rated by the speed at which they can transmit and receive data over telephone lines. As we said in Chapter 2, this speed is usually expressed in terms of bits per second (bps). Virtually all modern microcomputer modems can transmit data at speeds of at least 300 bps, or about 30 characters per second. Most popular models can achieve speeds of 1200 bps, and many 2400-bps modems also are sold. Typically, faster modems also can transmit and receive data at slower speeds too. For example, a 2400-bps modem also can transmit and receive at speeds of 1200 and 300 bps. Microcomputer modems faster than 2400 bps are on the market, but these are significantly more expensive and may not work with all telephone lines and computers.

### Hayes Compatibility

*Industry standard*

The largest microcomputer modem manufacturer in the world is Hayes Microcomputer Products Inc. This company sells over half of all the 1200 bps modems sold. Its Smartmodem line of microcomputer modems has set a virtual standard in the industry. Consequently, Smartmodems' methods and commands have been adopted by most other microcomputer modem manufacturers. A **Hayes-compatible modem** is one that operates like a Hayes Smartmodem. Smartmodems are rugged, reliable, flexible, and highly controllable. They are, however, at least twice as expensive as most Hayes-compatible clones. For example, while the internal Hayes Smartmodem 1200B sells for about $300, some compatible modems from other manufacturers can be purchased for just under $100.

Hayes compatibility has become especially important because of the widespread acceptance of the way Smartmodems work. Although communications software will generally work with any type of modem, most packages include features specifically designed to work with the Hayes Smartmodem. Thus there are many benefits to selecting a modem that is Hayes compatible. Because of this standardization, setting up microcomputer communications is much easier, especially for novices.

The so-called Hayes standard is, however, subject to change. As technology advances, modem manufacturers have added new features and commands, so that varying degrees of Hayes compatibility now exist among modems from other manufacturers. Some modems recognize only the most basic Hayes modem commands. Others elaborately mimic virtually every feature of the standard Hayes Smartmodem. For most people, the safest bet is to select a modem that is as Hayes-compatible as possible.

## COMMUNICATIONS SOFTWARE

*Make the connection and transfer data*

Even with a microcomputer, serial interface, modem, and telephone line, you still cannot call up other computers unless you also have communications software. This is a program that performs a variety of essential and convenient communications tasks. It lets you set up your serial interface and modem to work with the host computer you want to call. Then the software lets you dial the host computer's phone number. Once a connection is made, the communications program acts as a vehicle through which you work with the host computer. It provides ways for you to transmit and receive data to and from the host computer. Many communications programs have programmable features that let you automate frequently performed tasks. When you are finished working with the host computer, the communications program lets you terminate the session, hang up the phone, and return to the operating system.

As it is with most types of software, many communications programs are on the market, each with its own "personality." Some of the most popular communications programs are offered free or for a very nominal cost from hobbyist programmers. There are also quite a few commercial communications packages that provide a wide range of features. One of the best-selling commercial communications programs is CROSSTALK from Microstuf, Inc. There are versions of CROSSTALK for most microcomputers that run the CP/M and DOS operating systems. As an example, throughout this chapter we'll use CROSSTALK XVI for IBM-compatibles to illustrate some of the important concepts and operations of microcomputer communications. CROSSTALK, and indeed all communications software, performs two basic functions for the user: terminal emulation and file transfer.

### Terminal Emulation

*Mimicking a computer terminal*

**Terminal emulation** is a feature of communications software that lets you use a microcomputer as a computer terminal. In Chapter 4 we discussed some aspects of multi-user operating systems, which typically allow many people access to the same computer on a time-sharing basis. The type of computer used in this manner is usually a medium-sized minicomputer or a large mainframe computer. Individual users work at their own terminals, which are input/output stations consisting of a keyboard and a display. Terminals may be directly connected to the central computer by a serial interface cable or connected via a modem and telephone line.

A number of popular models of computer terminals manufactured by various companies are on the market. In most cases, different types of terminals can be connected to the same computer. Terminals differ from microcomputers in that they generally don't offer much in the way of computing ability or storage capacity. They basically display incoming characters on the screen and send characters typed at the keyboard to the central computer. The central computer interprets what is typed and acts accordingly. There may, however, be slight differences in the keyboards of different terminals or in the signals that they send to the central computer. Terminal emulation also involves making a microcomputer act just like some particular model of terminal.

For example, one of the most popular types of computer terminal is the DEC VT100, made by Digital Equipment Corporation. By default, CROSSTALK will direct a microcomputer to act like a generic terminal and only use signals common to all computer terminals. You can, however, tell CROSSTALK to make your microcomputer mimic a DEC VT100. Once you do this, your microcomputer will appear just like a DEC VT100 to the host computer you call. Besides the DEC VT100, CROSSTALK can also emulate several other popular terminals.

## File Transfer

*Download to your computer, upload to the host*

Terminal emulation is useful, but it only allows your microcomputer to act as a computer terminal. If you already have a microcomputer and need to use other computers, terminal emulation saves you from having to purchase a separate computer terminal. Nevertheless, all you can do is send commands to the host computer and see the results on your screen. The ability to transfer files between computers is what really makes a microcomputer and communications software more useful than a simple computer terminal.

By using CROSSTALK on a microcomputer, you can **capture** incoming data from the host computer and save it in a disk file. This is especially useful if you want to keep a record of part or all of your session with the host computer. In addition, you can tell the host computer to display a particular file on your screen, capture that data, and create an identical file on your microcomputer's hard or floppy disk. Communications programs also may let you directly transfer files from the host computer to your computer without displaying them on your screen. With either method, transferring a file from a host computer to your microcomputer is called **downloading** (see Figure 12.4(a)). This process allows you to get programs and data from other computers to use with your own microcomputer. Since you can store the downloaded data on your own disk, you are free to edit and manipulate this data in any manner you wish with your own word processor, spreadsheet, data base manager, or other application package.

Similarly, communications programs like CROSSTALK also allow you to transfer files from your microcomputer's secondary storage to the host computer. This is called **uploading** (see Figure 12.4(b)). There are many reasons for uploading files. For example, depending on the particular circumstances, there may be significant costs involved in using a host computer. Educational institutions and commercial organizations typically charge by the minute for use of their computers. By preparing files on your own microcomputer before you connect to the host computer, you can save both time and money. Besides, if you had to retype everything you wanted to send to another computer, it would be too tedious and time-consuming to transfer long files.

When you use a communications program like CROSSTALK, you usually can transfer files between any computers that are compatible with that program. The other computer doesn't have to be the same type of computer, nor does it need to be running the same operating system. You don't have to worry about any of the hardware and operating system incompatibilities between the two computers. Ordinary text files consisting of ASCII character codes can almost always be sent between any two computers. Special file transfer techniques are available to correctly send programs between computers, but you can only use downloaded programs that have been designed for your particular microcomputer. For example, there is no problem downloading a text file from an Apple Macintosh to an IBM microcomputer. Nevertheless, although it is technically possible to download a Macintosh program, like MacWrite, from a Macintosh to an IBM computer, that program would not run on the IBM. We'll have more to say about the details of transferring various types of files in the following sections. Right now, let's start up CROSSTALK and see what happens.

**Figure 12.4 Transferring Files**

(a) Downloading. (b) Uploading.

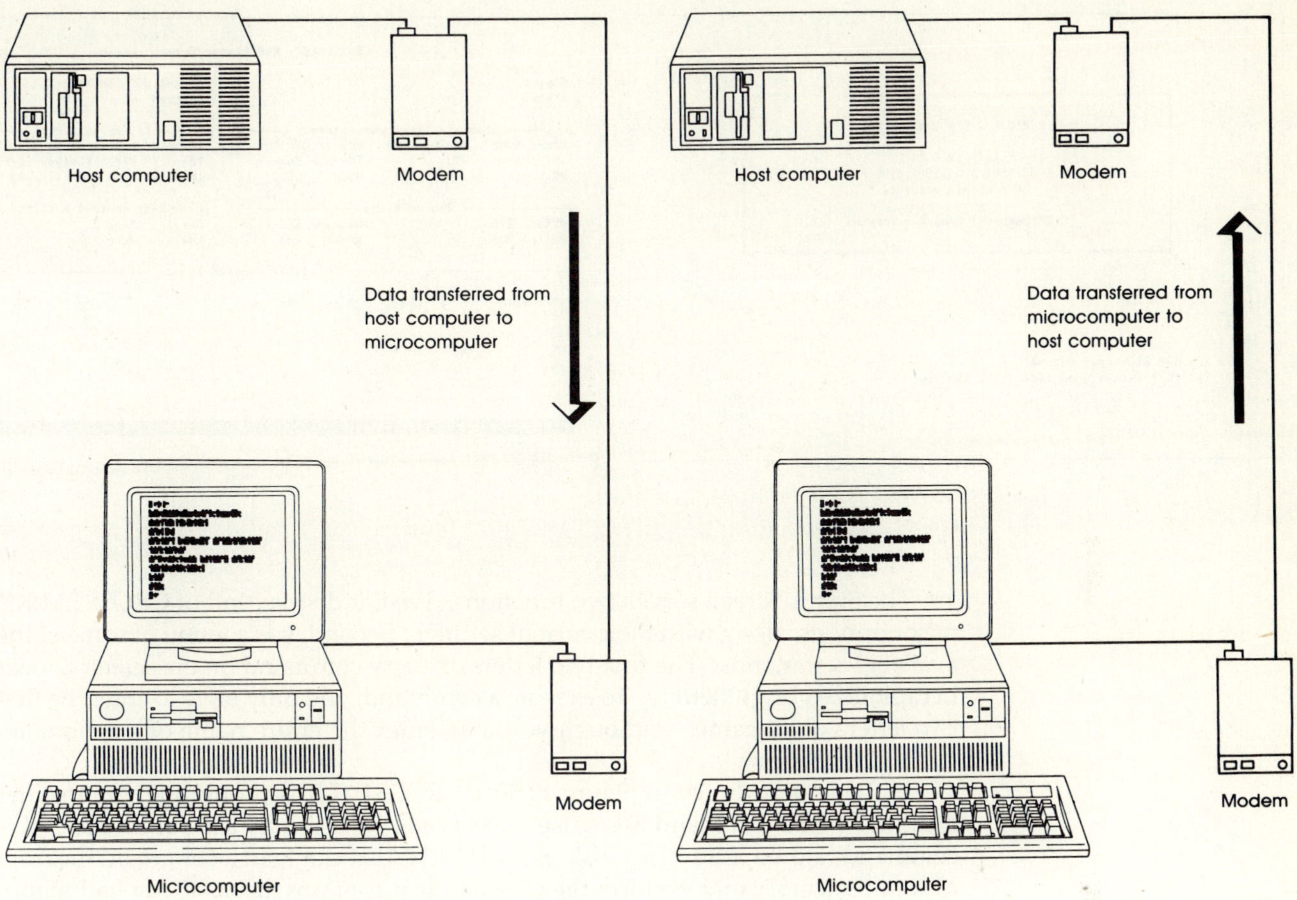


## Introducing CROSSTALK

*How to run CROSSTALK*

For all of the examples and figures in this chapter, we'll be using CROSSTALK XVI Version 3.61 for IBM-compatible microcomputers. This popular program comes on a single diskette with a concise printed manual of about 170 pages. The manual suggests that immediately after purchasing the package you should make a copy of the original CROSSTALK diskette for your daily use. You also can create a subdirectory on your hard disk for CROSSTALK and simply copy the files from the original diskette to this subdirectory. Once you have your working copy and have switched to the proper disk drive or subdirectory, you simply type **XTALK** and press the **Enter** key to start the CROSSTALK program. The initial copyright message pops up on your screen, followed by any one of a number of possible humorous sayings (see Figure 12.5(a)). After a few seconds wait to let you appreciate its authors' wit, CROSSTALK displays the Status Screen you see in Figure 12.5(b).

**Figure 12.5 Running CROSSTALK**

(a) CROSSTALK copyright screen.

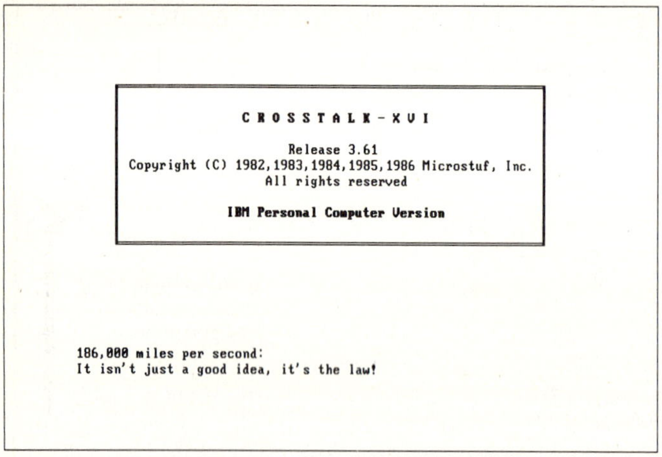


(b) CROSSTALK status screen.

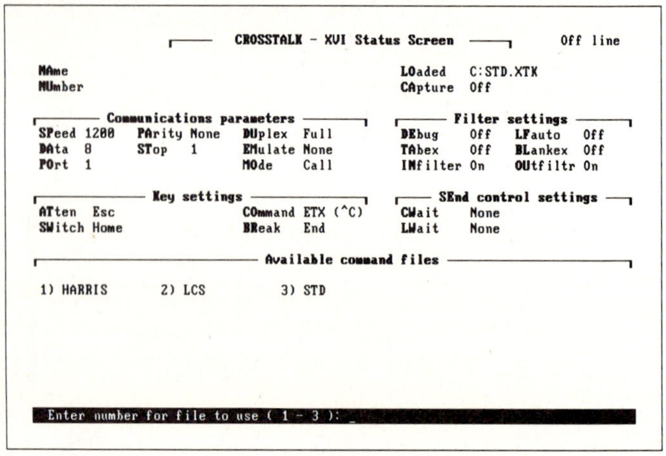


The Status Screen serves two functions. First, it displays all of CROSSTALK's major options, along with their current settings. Second, it is a menu of some of the available commands. The first two letters of every command on the screen appear in capitalized bright letters. To execute a command, you only have to enter the first two letters of its name. Although you may enter the entire name of a command, this isn't necessary.

In the screen shown in Figure 12.5(b), CROSSTALK is prompting you to enter the number of a command file to use. A *command file* is simply a list of CROSSTALK commands stored as text in a disk file. CROSSTALK can load a command file from disk into memory and perform the commands it contains just as if you had manually entered those commands from the keyboard. Command files are handy for performing frequently used sequences of commands. For example, if you often call a particular host computer, you can set up a command file to automate the specific operations necessary to make the connection. Several ready-made command files are provided by Microstuf along with CROSSTALK. By default, the one named STD.XTK is automatically loaded into memory and executed whenever you start CROSSTALK. This command file initializes all of CROSSTALK's default settings. Since these default settings are sufficient for now and we don't want to load any other command files, in response to the prompt to enter the number of a file to use, you can just press the **Enter** key.

After you do this, CROSSTALK displays the prompt Command? in the reverse video bar across the bottom of the screen. This is called the *command line*, and it is where you enter CROSSTALK commands. Whenever you see the command line at the bottom of the screen, you know that you can enter a CROSSTALK command. The command line is not present on the screen when you are interacting with a host computer.

Right now, you are not connected to a host computer and the command line is on your screen, so you are free to enter a CROSSTALK command. Although it is not present in the status screen menu, QUit is the command to end CROSSTALK and return to DOS. You can type either **QU** or **QUIT** and then press the **Enter** key to terminate your CROSSTALK session.

## COMMUNICATIONS PARAMETERS

*Specifying technical details*

As you can see from Figure 12.5(b), the CROSSTALK status screen has many options. The most important are listed beneath the heading **Communications parameters.** These are the settings that specify the technical details of how your microcomputer will communicate with another computer. In one way or another, most communications programs let you specify these settings. Since they are so important, let's go through each of these items one at a time.

### Speed

*How fast*

The Speed option indicates the bits-per-second rate at which the modem will transmit and receive data over the telephone line. Since most modems have a range of possible speeds, a communications program must let you specify the transmission rate. The initial default speed for CROSSTALK is 1200 bps. Depending upon the host computer, you may occasionally have to change the speed before you make a connection. While almost all host computers can use 1200 bps, in some instances it may be less expensive to use 300 bps. Faster speeds, however, are more convenient and generally less frustrating. CROSSTALK can operate at speeds of 110, 300, 600, 1200, 2400, 4800, and 9600 bps. The actual speeds you can use depend on your modem and the telephone line. In addition, even faster data transfer rates are available in the latest versions of CROSSTALK for special systems that use very high-speed modems or with computers directly connected with cables. These speeds include 19,200 bps, 38,400 bps, 57,600 bps, and 115,200 bps.

### Data

*Character length*

The Data option indicates the number of data bits used by the host computer to represent a single character. This value is sometimes called the *word length* or *character length* of the host computer. There are only two possible values, 7 and 8. The initial default number of data bits is 8. The value you use depends upon the computer you are calling.

### Port

*Which serial interface*

Many microcomputers can have more than one serial interface, also called a serial port. Serial ports connect a variety of input/output devices to computers, including modems, some printers, plotters, mice, trackballs, scanners, and graphics tablets. If more than one serial interface is present, the communications program must be told to which port the modem is connected. Serial ports are usually numbered 1, 2, and so on. By default, CROSSTALK assumes that your modem is plugged into serial port 1.

### Parity

*Error checking*

**Parity** is a method of error checking used to help ensure that all of the data bits of a character were received correctly after a transmission. Without going into technical details, there are two types of parity: *even* and *odd*. In addition, the parity parameter can also be set to *none*, which shuts off parity error checking. The parity setting you use depends on the computer you are calling. In practice, parity is almost always set to *none*, but a few host computers require even or odd parity.

## Stop

*Ending bits*

The Stop option indicates the number of stop bits used in the transmission of a single character. **Stop bits** mark the end of an individual data character. Again, this depends on the computer you are calling, but as a general rule, one stop bit is used at speeds of 300 bps and greater, and two stop bits are used at 110 bps. Consequently, the Stop option is almost always set to 1.

## Duplex

*Character echoing*

When you use a modem and communications program, your microcomputer acts as a terminal to a host computer. Once the connection is made, the characters you type at your keyboard are sent directly to the host computer. If the host computer operates in **full-duplex** mode, the characters you type are also sent back and echoed on your screen. If the host computer operates in **half-duplex** mode, the characters you type are not echoed back to your screen. The most common setting is full-duplex and so this is what CROSSTALK has as the default. The duplex setting you use also depends on the computer you are calling. If you don't know beforehand whether to use full- or half-duplex, there is an easy way to tell after you make a connection. If you cannot see the characters you are typing, the host computer is probably not echoing your data. In this case, you should set the duplex option to **half**. On the other hand, if you see two of every character you type, the duplex setting should be changed to **full**.

## Emulate

*Which terminal to mimic*

The Emulate option lets you tell CROSSTALK to mimic a particular type of computer terminal. This is needed only if the computer you are calling sends special codes to position the cursor and clear the screen. Unless you specify otherwise, most host computers do not assume that you are using a particular model of terminal and so they do not send any machine-specific screen formatting codes. Only standard formatting codes like backspaces, carriage returns, and line feeds will be used. In this case, your microcomputer doesn't need to emulate any particular terminal. So, the default and most commonly used setting for the Emulate option is **none**.

## Mode

*Call or answer?*

The Mode option lets you tell CROSSTALK to prepare your modem to either call another computer or wait for a call from another computer. Whenever you call a host computer, there is a modem at the other end of the telephone line that answers your call, as shown in Figure 12.1. Most people only use their modems to call other computers. To do this, set CROSSTALK's Mode option to **Call**, which is the default setting. You can, however, set up your modem and computer to receive calls from other computers. In this case, set CROSSTALK's Mode option to **Answer**. Once in Answer mode, CROSSTALK simply waits for a call rather than dialing a phone number. With your modem set up to answer calls, your microcomputer can be a host computer. You might use the Answer mode to receive data directly from an associate's computer. Answer mode is also used by people to set up their own computer bulletin board systems, about which we'll have more to say later in this chapter.

## CALLING A MAINFRAME COMPUTER

*Linking to a big computer*

Computer communications can be a somewhat technical subject, with many special terms to describe various options and settings. We could fill this entire book and not cover all the details of transferring information between computers. A better approach is to show you examples of some of the most common uses of microcomputer communications. One of the simplest and most popular microcomputer uses is that of calling a mainframe host computer.

Many businesses, organizations, and schools have their own mainframe computers. At large universities, it's common for individual departments to have their own large computer. The psychology department at the University of Illinois at Urbana-Champaign, for example, has its own Harris H800 mainframe computer. This computer is used by the psychology faculty, staff, and students for many different purposes, including word processing, statistical analyses, programming, administrative duties, and for sending internal memos. Many department members have microcomputers at home or in their offices, but they also need to use the Harris mainframe for some of their work. To give you a fairly representative example, let's go through the process of using CROSSTALK on an IBM-compatible microcomputer to call up this Harris mainframe.

### Determine and Set the Parameters

*Making the call*

The first step is to gather the information you need to call your particular host computer. In this case, you need to know the phone number, speed, number of data bits, type of parity, and number of stop bits. The Harris computer can communicate at 1200 bps with 8 data bits, no parity, and 1 stop bit. Fortunately, these settings are already the current CROSSTALK default communications parameters. You just have to tell the program the proper phone number and instruct it to make the call. First, make sure CROSSTALK is ready to receive commands by pressing the **Escape** key. To set the phone number, you type the command **NU** followed by a space and then enter the phone number of the computer you want to call. All you have to do to tell CROSSTALK to actually place the call is type **GO** and press the **Enter** key. Assuming your modem is turned on and correctly connected to your microcomputer, CROSSTALK automatically dials the number. You should hear the tones or pulses through the modem's speaker as CROSSTALK dials the phone number and waits for a connection. On the other end of the line, the modem connected to the Harris mainframe answers the call with a special tone. Once the connection has been established, CROSSTALK tells you to proceed.

## Log On to the Mainframe

*Passwords and codes*

At this point, you need to follow the procedures for logging onto the particular computer you have called. The exact procedures vary from computer to computer. In the case of this particular Harris mainframe computer, the first thing you do is hold down the **Control** key and type a **G**. Then the Harris prompts you to enter your sign-on, which is a special code number followed by your social security number. Next you are prompted to enter your password. When you type a password, most computers don't display the characters on the screen. This is a security measure to help prevent an unauthorized person from looking over your shoulder and seeing your password as you type it. Sign-on numbers are generally assigned by the person who manages the host computer system. Passwords may also be assigned, or you may be able to choose your own password the first time you log on to the computer. Once you have a password for a particular computer, it's important not to forget it. After your sign-on identification and password have been accepted, the computer system greets you and perhaps tells you about any messages or news that await you. Figure 12.6 shows the microcomputer screen after logging onto the Harris mainframe.

**Figure 12.6 Calling a Mainframe**
This shows the screen after logging onto the Harris mainframe.

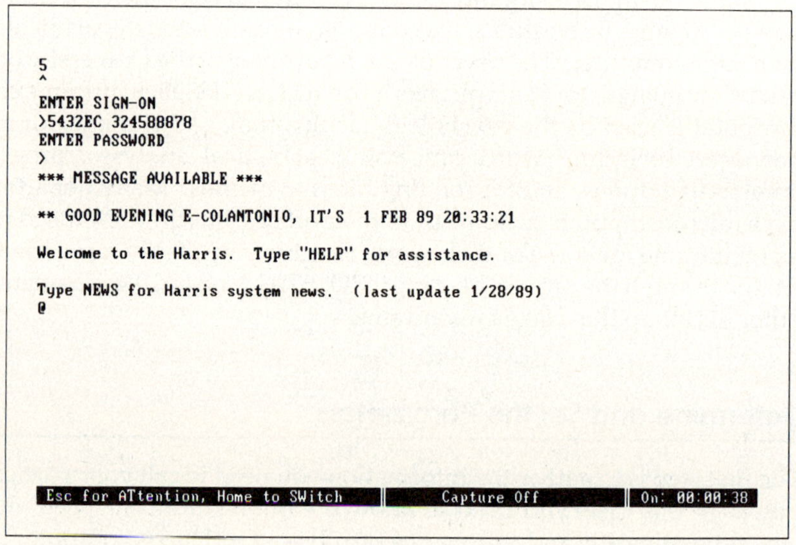


## Use the Mainframe

*Just like a terminal*

The @ character you see on the screen in Figure 12.6 is the Harris computer prompt. The mainframe is simply waiting for you to tell it what to do. The reverse-video line at the bottom of the screen is displayed by CROSSTALK and not the host computer. Since you are now connected to the Harris computer just as if you were using a terminal, the characters you type are sent to the Harris computer and its responses appear on your screen. For example, to get on-line help about the Harris computer, you type **HELP** and press the **Enter** key. Figure 12.7 shows the result.

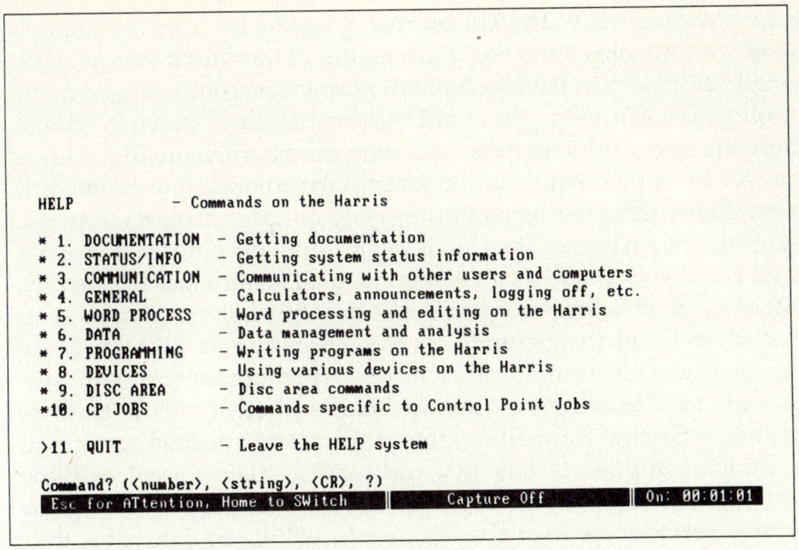


**Figure 12.7 Using a Mainframe**
This screen shows the Harris HELP system.

Of course, our purpose here is not to teach you how to use a particular mainframe computer operated by the psychology department at the University of Illinois. You wouldn't be calling such a computer unless you were authorized and had specific tasks to perform. You would have to read the documentation or perhaps take a special class to learn how to use such a computer. Our purpose has been to use this particular example to illustrate the general process of calling a mainframe computer. Although there are differences between computers, the steps you must take to call most mainframes are similar to those we just outlined.

### Disconnect

*Signing off*

When you are finished working with the mainframe computer, you must sign off, break the connection, and return to CROSSTALK. Most timesharing host computers have a command such as BYE, QUIT, or END that you enter to terminate your current session. When you do this, CROSSTALK senses that the connection has been broken and "hangs up" the phone line. The program then waits for further instructions from you. You can execute other commands, make another call, or enter **QUIT** to stop running CROSSTALK and return to DOS.

## SENDING AND RECEIVING ELECTRONIC MAIL

*Instant electronic letters*

**Electronic mail** or **E-Mail** is a way to send and receive messages with a computer. It is one of the most useful and most popular applications of computers and communications and is widely used in many businesses today. Basically, electronic mail allows you to send text messages to any other user participating in the system. Messages are saved in private "mailboxes" until users get a chance to call up the system and read their mail. In many cases, you can either enter your messages directly into the electronic mail facility, or upload a text file previously prepared with a word processing package. Messages are sent almost instantaneously. Your correspondents can often read your messages and reply in a matter of minutes if they are currently using the mail facility. Even if a correspondent is not presently logged on to the system, electronic mail can help you avoid the frustration of playing "phone tag," since messages are saved in mailboxes until they can be conveniently read.

Electronic mail can be implemented on almost any computer system or network with multiple users. Many timesharing computer systems have internal electronic mail facilities just for their own users. The Harris mainframe computer system used as an example earlier in this chapter has an electronic mail facility that lets faculty, students, and staff of the psychology department at the University of Illinois send messages to one another. Local area networks, which we discuss later in this chapter, also may have their own electronic mail facilities. Although these private systems are widely used and extremely popular, there is another whole class of electronic mail facilities. Several companies offer public electronic mail services to anyone who has a microcomputer or terminal and modem. These services allow subscribers to exchange messages by calling a central computer system. Because public electronic mail services are available to anyone willing to subscribe, they greatly enhance your ability to communicate with other computer users all over the world. Many of these public electronic mail services also offer ways to print messages on paper and send them to nonsubscribers via the U.S. Mail, express mail companies, or telegrams. Some can even print paper letters on registered letterheads with reproduced signatures.

One of the most popular public electronic mail services is MCI Mail, offered by MCI Telecommunications Corporation. This particular service has more than 140,000 subscribers. Subscribers pay an initial registration fee of $18 and a mailbox fee of $18 per year. Additional charges are based on the number of minutes spent connected to the system and the lengths of the messages sent. For example, sending an instant electronic message between 500 and 7500 characters in length costs $1.00. Using advanced services and sending printed mail to nonsubscribers also require paying additional fees. Although MCI Mail is somewhat more expensive than the U.S. Postal Service for ordinary letters, it is quicker, more reliable, and it has the advantages of a well-established public electronic mail service that is both easy to use and offers access to a large number of subscribers. To give you an example of electronic mail, let's use CROSSTALK to call MCI Mail to send and receive a message.

## Log On to the System

It's a simple matter to subscribe to a service like MCI Mail. All you do is call their toll-free number, and provide your name, address, and credit card number. MCI sends you your user name, user identification number, password, and a starter kit containing instructional manuals and other helpful materials.

*Avoiding long-distance charges*

After you become a subscriber, you are able to call the MCI Mail system and send and receive messages. This assumes, of course, that there are other subscribers with whom you plan to correspond routinely. The first step in using the MCI Mail service is to call up and log on to the system. MCI Mail has local telephone numbers in more than 50 U.S. cities. They also have a WATS (800) number you can call, but this costs an additional $.10 per minute. Many subscribers call MCI Mail through a public data network such as TYMNET. In brief, a **public data network** is a way to call a distant communications service, such as MCI Mail, from a local telephone number. The terms **packet-switching network** and **value-added network** are also used to describe these facilities. In most cases there are additional connect charges, from $2 to $10 per hour. Nevertheless, using a public data network is still usually less expensive than placing direct long distance calls. TYMNET, operated by McDonnell-Douglas Corporation, is one of the world's largest public data networks with local phone number access to more than 750 U.S. and Canadian cities and more than 70 foreign countries. All you do is call your local TYMNET number with a communications program such as CROSSTALK and tell TYMNET that you want to use MCI Mail.

For example, let's say that you are in Champaign, Illinois, and you want to use MCI Mail. The local TYMNET phone number is 359-1163, which the people at MCI tell you when you subscribe. The default CROSSTALK settings of 1200 bps, 8 data bits, 1 stop bit, and no parity are fine for calling MCI Mail. After starting CROSSTALK and pressing the **Escape** key to get to the command line, you enter **NU 359-1163** to set the phone number and **GO** to dial the number. CROSSTALK makes the connection and then some random characters appear on the screen while TYMNET senses and matches your communications settings. When these characters stop, you type an **A** to start TYMNET. The public data network responds with:

```
please log in:
```

Now you have to tell TYMNET that you want to use MCI Mail, so you type **MCI-MAIL** and press the **Enter** key. TYMNET then connects you with MCI Mail, which asks you to:

```
Please enter your user name:
```

Here you type your first initial immediately followed by your last name, with no spaces or periods, and then press the **Enter** key. MCI Mail then asks for your password, which was assigned to you when you subscribed. After you enter your correct password, MCI Mail greets you, tells you if you have any messages, gives a few brief news headlines, and tells you to press the **Enter** key to continue (see Figure 12.8(a)). The news headlines are courtesy of Dow Jones/News Retrieval Service, which is also offered through MCI Mail. After you press the Enter key, the main menu appears, as shown in Figure 12.8(b).

**Figure 12.8 Calling MCI Mail**

(a) MCI Mail log on.

```
5
x¦¦x`~¦xxx<`xx`xx<`x`x<~xx@~x<`x`xx@xxxx<~x`x<~xx<`xxx¦xx@xxxx`¦xx`xx@xx<`x<`xx<
-5414-000-
please log in: MCIMAIL
MCI IS ON LINE
Please enter your user name:  ECOLANTONIO
Password:

Welcome to MCI Mail!

Today's Headlines at 4:30 pm EST:

--January Retail Sales 'Poor';
    Slow Pace Seen For Early 1988
--Chrysler's Net Below Expectations
    * Special Report On Earnings *

Type //BUSINESS on Dow Jones for details.

MCI Mail Version 4.0

    Your INBOX has 1 message

Press <RETURN> to continue
 Esc for ATtention, Home to SWitch |      Capture Off      | On: 00:00:41
```

(b) MCI Mail main menu.

```
You may enter:

SCAN        for a summary of your mail
READ        to READ messages or LISTS
PRINT       to display messages nonstop
CREATE      to write an MCI Letter
CREATE LIST to make a distribution list
DOWJONES    to Dow Jones News/Retrieval
ACCOUNT     to adjust terminal display
HELP        for assistance

Command (or MENU or EXIT):
 Esc for ATtention, Home to SWitch |      Capture Off      | On: 00:01:36
```

## Send a Message

*Address, type, and mail a letter*

As you can see, MCI Mail's basic menu is quite simple. More information about the various commands can be obtained by entering **HELP**. To send a message to someone, first you enter the **CREATE** command. Messages have the format of an office memo. MCI Mail prompts you with TO:, and you enter the name or identification number of the person to whom you want to send the message. Then you are prompted with another TO:, which lets you send the same message to another person. If you don't want to send the message to anyone else, you just press the **Enter** key. Next, MCI Mail prompts you with CC:, which lets you send a courtesy copy of the message to others who should also see it. If you don't want to send any courtesy copies, you just press the **Enter** key. The computer then asks for a SUBJECT: and you can enter a few words that describe the topic of your message. Finally, you enter the text of the message itself. Simple mistakes can be corrected with the backspace key and new lines are started by pressing the Enter key. When you're finished typing the message, you enter a single / (forward slash) at the beginning of a new line. Figure 12.9 shows the screen after entering a sample message.

**Figure 12.9 Typing a Mail Message**
In MCI Mail, you use the CREATE command to type a new message.

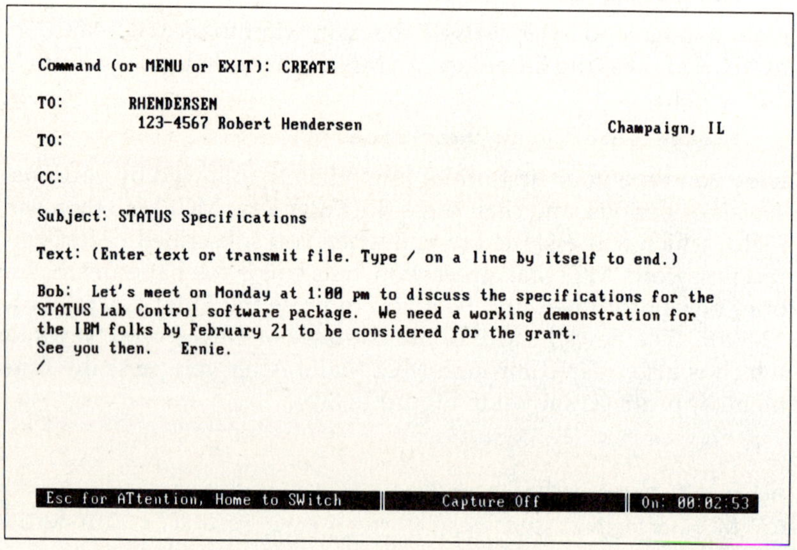


When you're finished, MCI Mail presents a menu of choices for the first draft of your newly created message (see Figure 12.10). You can enter **READ** to review your draft before you send it. **EDIT** invokes a built-in text editor that lets you modify the draft. To actually send the message, you enter the **SEND** command. If the recipient is an MCI Mail subscriber, the message is sent as an instant electronic letter. MCI Mail confirms the date and time your message was posted, puts a copy of the message in your "OUTBOX," and returns to the main menu.

```
You may enter:

READ       to review your letter
READ PAPER to review your letter for paper
EDIT       to correct your letter
SEND       Postal delivery for paper; instant electronic delivery
SEND ONITE OVERNIGHT courier for paper; PRIORITY electronic delivery
HELP       for assistance

Command (or MENU or EXIT):
 Esc for ATtention, Home to SWitch |  Capture Off  | On: 00:03:07
```

**Figure 12.10 Sending a Message**
After you enter a message, MCI Mail presents a menu of options.

## Read a Message

*The computer inbox, outbox, and desk*

Reading a message that someone has sent to you is even easier than sending a message. When you first log on to MCI Mail, the computer tells you if you have any messages in your "INBOX" (see Figure 12.8(a)). The **SCAN** command lets you see a list of all of your messages. To see messages one by one, you enter the **READ** command from the main menu. This presents the menu shown at the bottom of Figure 12.11(a). You enter **INBOX** to see any messages that you haven't read yet from other subscribers. Figure 12.11(b), for example, shows the result of reading an INBOX message. **OUTBOX** displays any messages that you have already sent to others. **DESK** lets you reread messages from others that you have already seen. After you read each new message, MCI Mail gives you a chance to answer the message immediately or simply go on to read the next message.

**Figure 12.11 Reading a Message**

(a) Using the READ command.

```
You may enter:

SCAN        for a summary of your mail
READ        to READ messages or LISTS
PRINT       to display messages nonstop
CREATE      to write an MCI Letter
CREATE LIST to make a distribution list
DOWJONES    to Dow Jones News/Retrieval
ACCOUNT     to adjust terminal display
HELP        for assistance

Command (or MENU or EXIT): READ

You may enter:

INBOX     to READ your unread messages
OUTBOX    to READ messages you sent
DESK      to READ messages read before
DRAFT     to READ your draft message
ALL       to READ ALL your messages
LIST      to READ a LIST
HELP      for assistance

Command (or MENU or EXIT): INBOX
 Esc for ATtention, Home to SWitch |  Capture Off  | On: 00:04:36
```

(b) Using the INBOX command.

```
Date:     Thu Feb 04, 1988 11:03 pm  EST
From:     Robert Hendersen / MCI ID: 123-4567

TO:     * Ernest Colantonio / MCI ID: 348-7392
Subject:  STATUS Meeting

Fine with me, Ernie.  I'll see you in my office at 1:00 pm on Monday.
I'm anxious to hear your ideas for the user interface of the input/output
configuration.  We REALLY could use that grant from IBM! --- Bob.

Press <RETURN> to continue

You may enter:

READ       to READ this message again
ANS        to ANSWER the message sender
ANS EACH   to ANSWER the message sender and each recipient
NEXT       to go on to the NEXT message
HELP       for assistance

Command (or MENU or EXIT):
 Esc for ATtention, Home to SWitch |  Capture Off  | On: 00:04:51
```

By turning on CROSSTALK's CAPTURE command just before you read your mail, you can download messages from MCI Mail to a disk file on your microcomputer. These messages can be used with word processing software or printed after you quit CROSSTALK. If you like, you can use CROSSTALK's PRINTER command instead to print your messages directly as they are being displayed on your screen. Simply press the **Escape** key to switch to CROSSTALK's command line and enter the command **PRINTER ON** to duplicate on your printer any text subsequently displayed on your screen. The command **PRINTER OFF** stops sending incoming data to your printer. Many people find that using an electronic mail service from a microcomputer this way helps them manage, organize, and significantly speed up much of their routine correspondence.

## USING AN ON-LINE INFORMATION SERVICE

*Expand your computer horizons*

A commercial electronic mail facility like MCI Mail is just one of a broad range of on-line communications services available to microcomputer users. There are at least 3000 of these services in the United States alone. Most are specialized on-line data bases aimed primarily at business, academic, and scientific researchers. Others are targeted at more general educational and home markets. These multi-purpose on-line information services support a wide variety of data base, news, electronic mail, shopping, entertainment, and other miscellaneous facilities. To subscribe, all you need is a microcomputer, a modem, a telephone, and usually a credit card. Without even leaving your home or office, these have-it-all information services let you work, learn, shop, and play. Here are just a few of the capabilities provided by the major on-line information services:

- Gain access to electronic versions of popular encyclopedias.
- Search *Books in Print* and the *Reader's Guide to Periodical Literature.*
- Check the latest weather report for almost any place in the world.
- Read up-to-the-minute news from major wire services.
- Obtain stock quotes and buy and sell stocks.
- Plan your vacation, review airline schedules, and book your tickets.
- Exchange electronic mail.
- "Converse" with other on-line subscribers.
- Obtain free software.
- Get answers to questions about computer hardware and software from other subscribers.
- Browse through electronic shopping malls.
- Read reviews of the latest books, movies, and records.
- Play computer games.
- Join special interest groups.
- Participate in electronic forums.

CompuServe, from the Columbus, Ohio-based company of the same name, is the premier on-line information service. Established in 1969, CompuServe has been in existence at least ten years longer than its closest competitor, The Source. With more than 380,000 subscribers, CompuServe also has at least twice as many customers and four times as many features as The Source. There is an almost dizzying array of individual activities offered by CompuServe, but the major topics include communications and bulletin boards; news, weather, and sports; travel; electronic shopping; money matters and markets; entertainment and games; home, health, and family; reference and education; computers and technology; and business and other interests. CompuServe even has its own magazine for subscribers called *Online Today*, which is published daily in electronic form and monthly in printed form. All this is far from free, however, because CompuServe has a $39.95 one-time registration fee, and it charges $6.00 per hour for using a speed of 300 bps and $12.50 per hour for 1200 bps. If you use the TYMNET public data network to call CompuServe from a local telephone number, there are additional charges of $10 per hour during "prime time"—regular business hours, and $2 per hour during "standard time"—evenings and weekends. Many of the better services, like the on-line Grolier's *Academic American Encyclopedia*, also have additional surcharges or subscription fees. Nevertheless, on-line information services like CompuServe offer a unique way to greatly expand the potential of your microcomputer.

As a good example of using an on-line information service, let's call CompuServe with CROSSTALK and try a couple of its features. Obviously, we cannot cover every aspect of this abundant resource. Entire books have been written about CompuServe's many possibilities. We'll have to content ourselves with logging on, reading some news, and looking up a topic in the on-line encyclopedia.

## Log On to the System

*Calling CompuServe through TYMNET*

Subscribing and logging on to CompuServe is similar to gaining access to MCI Mail. After you call to subscribe, CompuServe sends you a starter kit that includes your user identification number, password, a manual, and some other handy reference guides. In most major cities, you can reach CompuServe directly with a local phone call through the CompuServe Network for a nominal surcharge of $0.25 per hour. In many other communities, you can reach CompuServe through a public data network such as TYMNET. For example, to call CompuServe via TYMNET, you start with the procedure we outlined in our discussion of logging on to MCI Mail. When you get the *please log in* message from TYMNET, however, you respond with **CIS02** to access CompuServe. As Figure 12.12(a) shows, CompuServe then asks for your user identification number and password. CompuServe welcomes you on-line and usually displays some recent news about the system or ads for special services. Eventually, the main or TOP menu appears on your screen, as shown in Figure 12.12(b).

**Figure 12.12 Calling CompuServe**

(a) Logging on.

```
5
x!!x`~!xxx<`xx<`x,~~`xxx~xx<@`xxxxx@xxx<~x`x<~xx<`xxx!xxx`xx<`xx@!xx<`x<`xx
-5414-001-
please log in: CIS02

host:  WELCOME TO COMPUSERVE  1133

User ID: 76314,3625
Password:


CompuServe Information Service
 19:15 CST Friday 05-Feb-88

Last access: 10:13 05-Feb-88

    Copyright (C) 1988
  CompuServe Incorporated
    All Rights Reserved



 Esc for ATtention, Home to SWitch |      Capture Off      | On: 00:01:24
```

(b) The main or TOP menu.

```
CompuServe                    TOP

 1 Subscriber Assistance
 2 Find a Topic
 3 Communications/Bulletin Bds.
 4 News/Weather/Sports
 5 Travel
 6 The Electronic MALL/Shopping
 7 Money Matters/Markets
 8 Entertainment/Games
 9 Home/Health/Family
10 Reference/Education
11 Computers/Technology
12 Business/Other Interests


Enter choice number !4
 Esc for ATtention, Home to SWitch |      Capture Off      | On: 00:01:24
```

CompuServe uses a combination of menus and direct commands to give you access to its many varied services. The menus are especially nice for beginners because they can be used with very little instruction. There is also an on-line tutorial that teaches new subscribers the basics of navigating through CompuServe's menus. After a while, however, the menus can become tiresome. It begins to seem like most of your time (and money) is spent waiting for menus to scroll across your screen. Since CompuServe has many levels of menus, just reaching the service you want to use can take several minutes. Fortunately, CompuServe also lets you jump directly to any service with the **GO** command, which can save you a great deal of time if you know exactly which feature you want to use. An index of services and "**GO** commands" is given in the CompuServe documentation and is periodically updated in the *Online Today* magazine sent to all subscribers.

## Read the News

*See news, weather, sports*

Some of the most popular on-line features offered by CompuServe present the latest news in various forms. As you can see from CompuServe's Top menu in Figure 12.12(b), item 4 corresponds to news, weather, and sports. Selecting this option brings up the News menu shown in Figure 12.13(a). The second item in this list, NewsGrid, is a feature that compiles dispatches from some of the world's largest wire services, including United Press International and The Associated Press. Each news story that arrives in the NewsGrid service—about one every two minutes—is evaluated by professional editors and reporters. The top stories are selected and presented in a list of brief headlines. You can select any one of these headlines to see the actual story. For example, Figures 12.13(b) through 12.13(d) illustrate the process of selecting and reading a NewsGrid story. First you choose the NewsGrid option from the News menu, then you select the type of headlines you want to see, and finally you pick the headline whose story you want to read. When you're finished, you can select other headlines or return to CompuServe's main menu by entering the **TOP** command.

**Figure 12.13 Using NewsGrid**

(a) The NEWS menu.

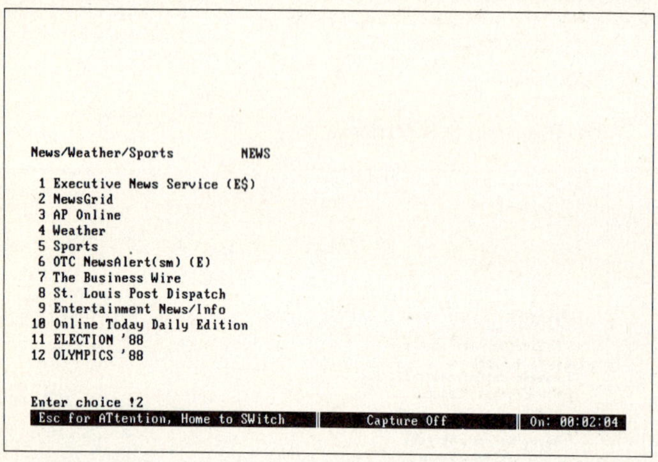


(b) The NewsGrid menu.

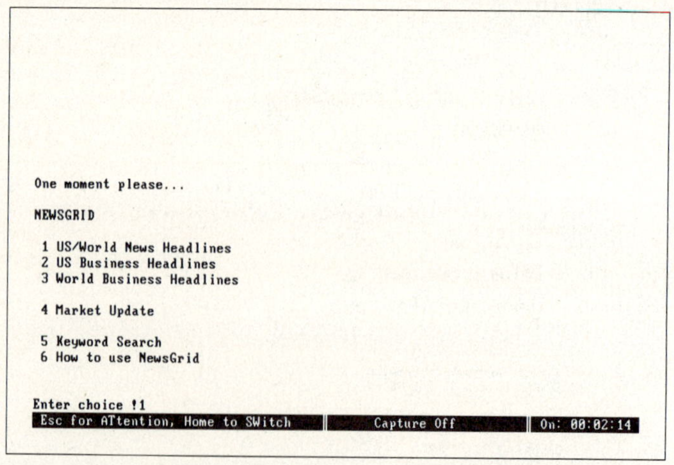

(c) NewsGrid headlines.

```
NEWSGRID         US/World News Headlines

 1  02/05 1754  CONGRESSIONAL LEADERS ACCUSE REAGAN OF "COVERUP" ...
 2  02/05 1228  LEBANESE RADIO STATION SAYS CAPTORS HAVE KILLED TERRY WAITE
 3  02/05 1706  TWO U.N. RELIEF WORKERS KIDNAPPED IN LEBANON
 4  02/05 1919  EFFORTS BEING MADE TO FREE U.N. WORKERS KIDNAPPED ...
 5  02/05 1430  NICARAGUAN CONTRA LEADER RESIGNS OVER COSTA RICA'S ...
 6  02/05 1622  U.S. HOUSE DEMOCRATS MAY PROPOSE ALTERNATIVE ...
 7  02/05 1634  PANAMANIAN RULER NORIEGA CALLS U.S. INDICTMENT "A JOKE"
 8  02/05 1213  IRANIAN GUNBOAT ATTACKS PANAMANIAN-REGISTERED GULF TANKER
 9  02/05 1124  EUROPEAN ALLIES URGE U.S. TO RATIFY NUCLEAR MISSLE TREATY
10  02/05 1119  PLO OFFICIAL CRITICIZES NEW U.S. MIDEAST PEACE PROPOSAL
11  02/05 1531  PALESTINIANS, ISRAELI SETTLERS CLASH IN WEST BANK
12  02/05 1320  EGYPTIAN PRESIDENT MUBARAK IN TURKEY TO DISCUSS ...
13  02/05 1203  BRITISH POLICE ARREST SIKH SUSPECT IN 1985 ...
14  02/05 1335  U.N. ENVOY CONTINUES AFGHAN PEACE MISSION
15  02/05 1246  W. GERMAN LEADERS DISCUSS CHEMICAL WEAPONS BAN ...
16  02/05 1723  TWENTY SOVIETS EXECUTED UNDER STALIN REHABILITATED ...
17  02/05 1655  U.S. PRESIDENTIAL HOPEFULS DROP N.H. CAMPAIGNS TO ...
18  02/05 2003  THE ARIZONA HOUSE TENTATIVELY VOTES TO IMPEACH ...


Enter choice !15
 Esc for ATtention, Home to SWitch |     Capture Off     | On: 00:03:30
```

(d) NewsGrid story.

```
NEWSGRID        US/World News Headlines

02/05 1246  W. GERMAN LEADERS DISCUSS CHEMICAL WEAPONS BAN ...

CHEMICAL WEAPONS
   BONN, West Germany (FEB. 5) AP - West German leaders Friday emphasized the
need for a worldwide ban on chemical weapons during talks with U.S. Defense
Secretary Frank Carlucci, officials said.
   Carlucci, on the third stop of a European tour, met with Chancellor Helmut
Kohl and Defense Minister Manfred Woerner.
   Bonn officials said Kohl and Woerner focused on the need for an East-West
agreement to ban chemical weapons and to reduce the Warsaw Pact's superiority
over NATO in conventional arms.
 "We are discussing the course of NATO strategy and which steps should be taken
toward disarmament now that the medium-range missile accord has been signed by
the superpowers," said Defense Ministry spokesman Peter Monte.
   He was referring to the accord signed in December by President Reagan and
Soviet leader Mikhail S. Gorbachev that will eliminate the superpowers'
intermediate-range missiles in Europe.
   "We hope the U.S. side is in agreement that while strategic issues take
priority for the superpowers, the issue of chemical weapons and the (East-West)
imbalance in conventional weapons must be speedily addressed, said another

Press <CR> for more !
 Esc for ATtention, Home to SWitch |     Capture Off     | On: 00:05:22
```

## Research an Encyclopedia

*On-line encyclopedia*

It's 2:30 A.M. and you have a term paper due tomorrow in your first class. The school library has been closed for hours. If you're a CompuServe subscriber, all is not lost. Besides, the TYMNET surcharges are less at night. Just boot up the computer, turn on the modem, start CROSSTALK, and call CompuServe. You can probably find something about your topic in the on-line edition of Grolier's *Academic American Encyclopedia*. Updated and revised four times each year, this is one of the most current encyclopedic references you're likely to find. It has more than 32,000 articles, fact boxes, bibliographies, and tables. Although there is an additional subscription charge ($7.50 for one month, $29.95 for six months, and $49.95 for one year), many CompuServe subscribers gladly pay to use the Grolier's encyclopedia for help with research, homework, speeches, travel plans, trivia answers, and other reference needs.

As an example, let's look up the word *modem* in the on-line encyclopedia. From CompuServe's Top menu, the quickest way to use the *Academic American Encyclopedia* is to enter the command **GO AAE**. Figure 12.14(a) shows the menu that appears on your screen. Assuming that you have already subscribed to the encyclopedia service, you select item 2 to look up a topic. CompuServe gives you some brief instructions and then prompts you for the *search term*, as shown in Figure 12.14(b). This is where you enter the topic that you want to research. To look up *modem*, simply type the word **modem** and press the **Enter** key. Figure 12.14(c) shows the result.

# CALLING ANOTHER MICROCOMPUTER

*Transfer files between micros*

Electronic mail and on-line information services can be helpful, educational, and fun. Unfortunately, they also can be expensive. You don't have to call up mainframe computers or subscribe to on-line services, however, to make use of microcomputer communications. There are some relatively inexpensive ways to connect one microcomputer to another using a communications program such as CROSSTALK.

**Figure 12.14 Using an On-line Encyclopedia**

(a) CompuServe's *Academic American Encyclopedia* menu.

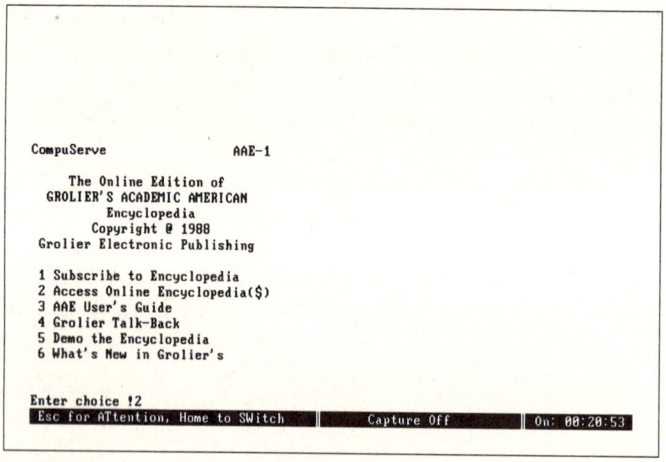


(b) Entering the search term.

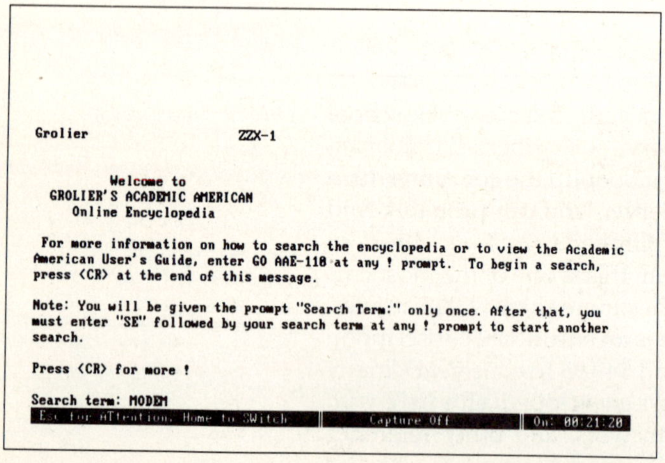


(c) The article on *modem*.

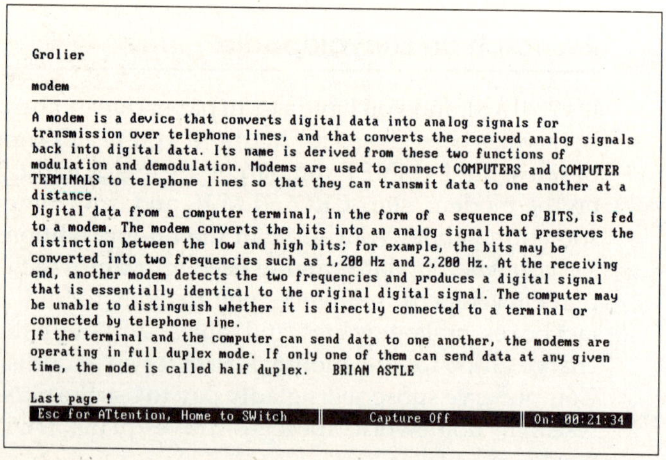


For example, you can directly connect two microcomputers without modems or telephone lines. A special cable, called a **null-modem cable**, can be used to connect the serial ports of the two computers. This cable makes each computer "think" that it is hooked up to a modem, when it is really directly connected to another computer. A communications program, such as CROSSTALK, is necessary to transfer files between the two computers. Obviously, connecting two computers with a null-modem cable is usually restricted to computers in the same room or building. This arrangement is sometimes used with two different types of microcomputers, such as an IBM-compatible and an Apple Macintosh, to transfer files between them.

For more distant microcomputers, you can use modems and the telephone network. Although you can connect different computers running different communications software, the simplest arrangement is to use one microcomputer to call another microcomputer of the same type, with both machines running their own copies of the same communications program. Let's say that you want to send a text file named DOCUMENT.TXT to an associate who lives in another town. You both have IBM-compatible microcomputers and you both have CROSSTALK. First, you call up your associate, agree on which communication parameters to use, and tell her to get her equipment ready to receive a call from your computer. You both say goodbye and hang up your telephones. Your colleague boots up her computer, turns on her modem, starts CROSSTALK, and sets the agreed-upon parameters. Then she puts CROSSTALK into ANSWER mode by entering the command **MODE ANSWER**. CROSSTALK, the modem, and her computer simply wait.

In the meantime, you boot up your computer, start CROSSTALK, and set your communications parameters. By default, CROSSTALK puts your modem and computer into CALL mode. You enter your associate's phone number with the **NU** command and dial the number with **GO**. Your computer calls her computer and her computer answers. To transmit the file DOCUMENT.TXT, you enter the CROSSTALK command **XMIT DOCUMENT.TXT**. Your screen will look something like Figure 12.15. As you can see from Figure 12.15, CROSSTALK reports the progress of the file transfer. At the other end of the line, the other copy of CROSSTALK displays a similar screen so your associate can also see the progress of the file transfer. CROSSTALK tells you when the transfer is complete, at which point you can transfer other files, or use the **BYE** command to hang up the phone and break the connection.

```
              CROSSTALK - XVI Status Screen                 Local

NAme   CROSSTALK defaults                 LOaded   C:STD.XTK
NUmber 555-1234                           CApture  Off

   Communications parameters                 Filter settings
SPeed 1200  PArity None  DUplex  Full     DEbug    Off  LFauto   Off
DAta  8     STop   1     EMulate None     TAbex    Off  BLankex  Off
POrt  1                  MOde    Call     INfilter On   OUtfiltr On

         Key settings                        SEnd control settings
ATten  Esc               COmmand ETX (^C) CWait    None
SWitch Home              BReak   End      LWait    None

                       Transmitting DOCUMENT.TXT

        | Block # | % complete | Consec. errors | Total errors |
        |   1_    |     25     |      none      |     none     |

         PROTOCOL TRANSFER UNDERWAY -- Press Esc to cancel
```

**Figure 12.15 Transmitting a File with CROSSTALK**

With the sending computer in CALL mode and the receiving computer in ANSWER mode, you can transmit a file with the XMIT command. This screen shows how CROSSTALK reports the progress of the transmission.

If your computer is calling another computer with CROSSTALK, you can also use the RQUEST command to download files. Note that the computer in CALL mode is always in control. The person on the answering end basically just sets up the system and waits for the file transfers.

## LOCAL AREA NETWORKS

*Share hardware, software, and data*

Connecting one microcomputer to another as we have just described is fine for an occasional transfer of files. This procedure is not suitable, however, in situations that require several microcomputers to routinely share data files, programs, and expensive hardware devices such as laser printers, hard disks, and scanners. In these cases, a local area network or LAN is a much better arrangement. As we said in

Chapter 2, a local area network allows you to directly connect two or more microcomputers together. Special hardware components and cables are used to link the machines, which are usually located in the same building. Special software is used to control the exchange of files, the execution of shared software, and access to shared hardware devices.

There are many benefits to installing a local area network. Most of these are related to the concept of sharing. Transferring files from one computer to another becomes as easy as copying files between disk drives on the same computer. Even networks that connect different types of computers can easily transfer files. Several users can simultaneously tap into the same data base, which can be kept on a single disk drive. The ability to share data in this manner is a major reason many organizations install networks. If the computers connected to the network are all compatible, software also can be shared. For example, instead of ten copies of dBASE for ten users, a single copy of the network version of dBASE can be run by all users on a network. Although special versions or multi-user licenses may be legally required by the manufacturers of commercial software to be used on a network, this makes distributing updates and installing new packages much simpler. Internal electronic mail is yet another benefit offered by local area networks. This can be a real communications boon to organizations that occupy several offices on different floors of a building. Finally, another major reason for installing a LAN is to share expensive peripheral equipment. For example, a single high-speed, high-quality laser printer can be connected to a network and used by several individuals, who get their documents printed on a first-come, first-served basis. A shared laser printer is certainly more economical than a separate one for each user, even if it does take a little longer to get everyone's documents printed.

There are also some disadvantages to local area networks. Each microcomputer may have to be equipped with a special expansion board to be connected to a network. For example, although Apple Macintosh computers come with network circuitry built in, IBM microcomputers require the purchase of an additional network adapter board. Special connection hardware and cables must be purchased and installed in the building. Network software and special versions of application packages may add to the expense. Additional peripheral devices and a high-speed microcomputer to help control the network also may be required. In other words, local area networks can be expensive. The average cost is about $1000 to connect a microcomputer to a network, not including the cost of the microcomputer and any peripheral devices such as printers. Besides the expense involved, networks also can be difficult to set up and maintain. A network expert, skilled in hardware and software installation, is often needed to get the equipment running reliably. In general, networks are much more complex than single-user systems. Finally, installing a local area network can introduce some potential security problems. Special care must be taken to make sure that sensitive data is not shared with unauthorized users.

## Hardware

*Network physical components*

Local area networks consist of several physical components. The key pieces of network hardware include workstations, servers, media, and interfaces. Let's examine each of these.

### Workstations

*Microcomputers*

In most cases, a **network workstation** is an ordinary microcomputer used to run software, transfer files, and send messages. Some companies sell less expensive microcomputers uniquely adapted to be network workstations. These specialized terminals have a microprocessor and memory to run microcomputer software, but they lack the disk drives, serial interfaces, and parallel interfaces needed for stand-alone computing. The actual number of workstations that can be linked together depends on the specific hardware and software, but it can be as few as two, as many as several hundred, or more than 1000 workstations per network.

### Servers

*Specialized workstations*

A **network server** is a workstation that handles special chores. For example, a **file server** is used to store shared program and data files on a large-capacity, high-speed hard disk; a **print server** is used to control a printer shared by other workstations on a network; and a **communications server** lets network users communicate with computers outside the network via serial ports and a high-speed modem. Sometimes a workstation is reserved solely for one or more of these chores, in which case it is called a **dedicated server**. Small networks may have only one server, while large networks may have many servers.

### Media

*Connecting cables*

The **network media** connects the various workstations. Usually, the media is either twisted-pair wire, coaxial cable, or fiber-optic cable. **Twisted-pair wire**, which makes up ordinary telephone lines, consists of two wires that have been partially wrapped around each other. Twisted-pair wire is easy to install and inexpensive, but it cannot transmit data as fast as other media. **Coaxial cable**, also used for cable television, consists of a center conductor surrounded by a shield or wire braid. It's faster than twisted-pair wire, but harder to work with and more expensive. Finally, **fiber-optic cable** transmits data in the form of extremely rapid pulses of light generated by lasers. It's expensive and difficult to install, but is capable of very high-speed data transmission.

### Interfaces

*Network circuit boards*

Each workstation is linked to the network by a **network interface**. In most cases, this is a network adapter with a connector for the appropriate media. As we said in Chapter 2, a network adapter is usually a circuit board that fits into one of the computer's expansion slots. In addition to the connector, the network adapter has a specialized microprocessor and other integrated circuits that perform communications and data processing tasks.

## Topology

*Geometric configuration of networks*

The way that hardware components are arranged in a network is called the **topology**. The three fundamental network topologies are the bus, the ring, and the star. Figure 12.16 shows an example of each of these arrangements. In a bus network, each workstation is connected to a single cable running past all the workstations. A ring network is similar to a bus network, except that the two ends of the central cable are hooked together. The star network has an individual cable run from a central server to each workstation.

The topology of a network affects its efficiency, reliability, maintenance, and cost. For example, a bus network requires less wiring than a star network, so it costs less. A star network, however, is easier to troubleshoot if a problem occurs. You

**Figure 12.16 Network Topology**

(a) Bus network.

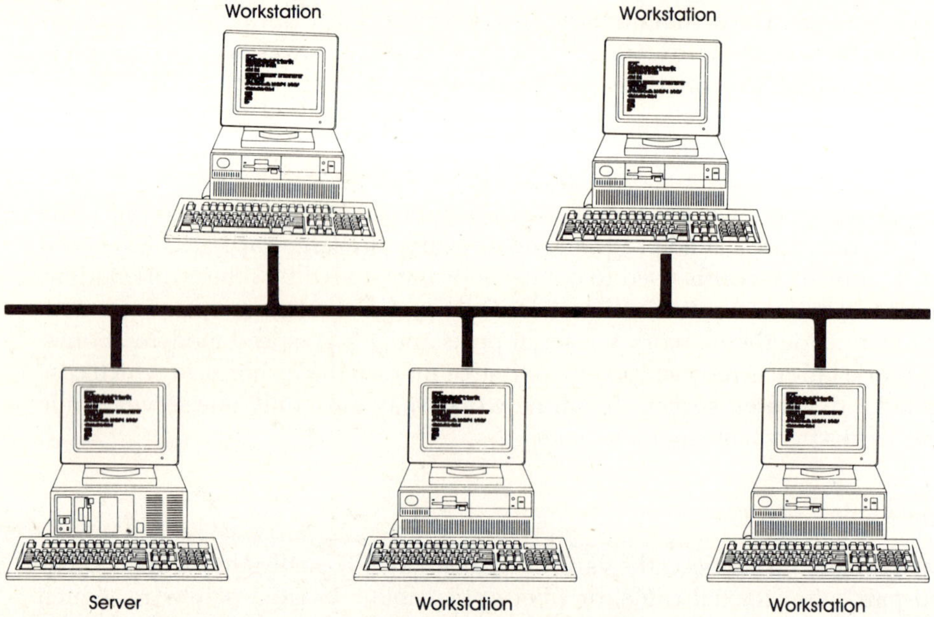


(b) Ring network.

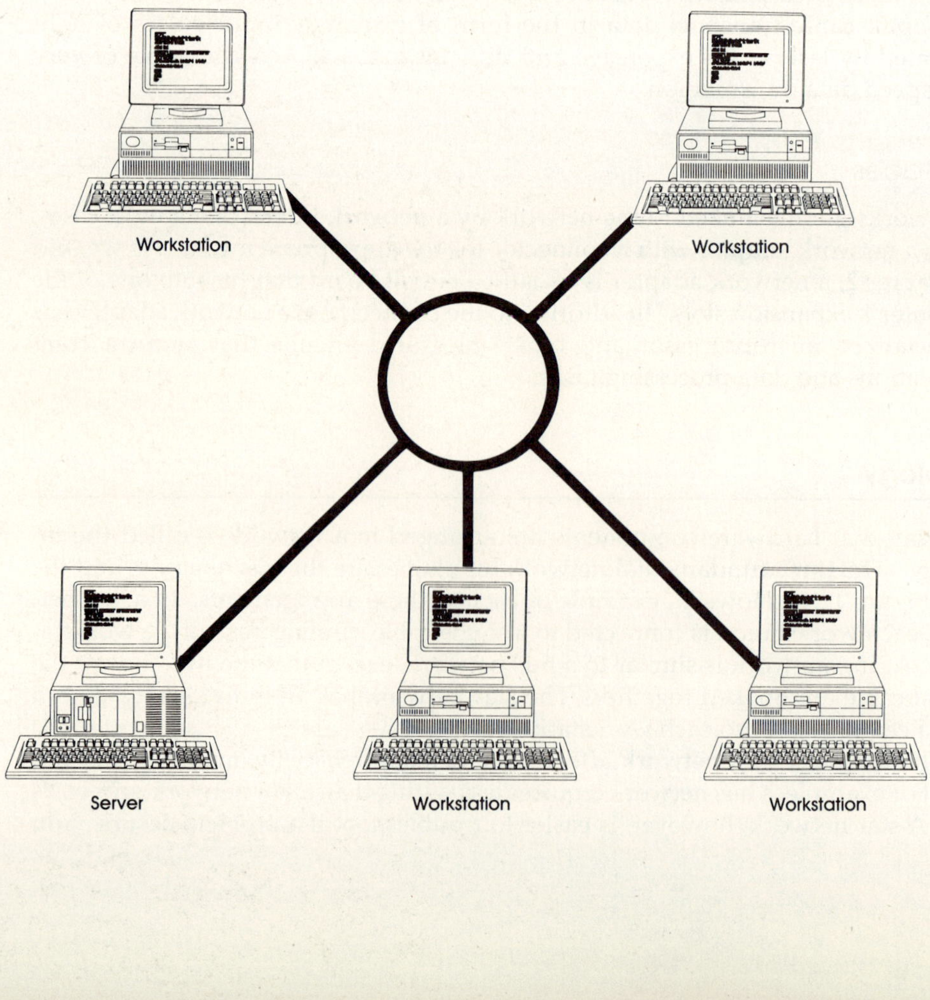

(c) Star network.

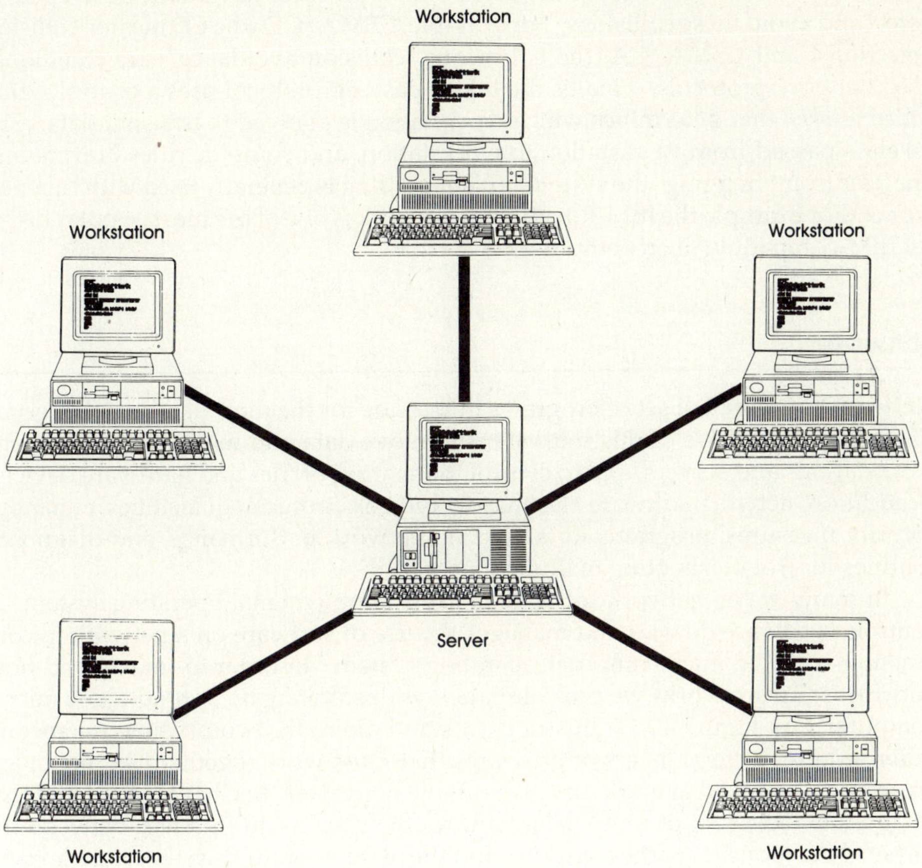


can simply unplug each workstation in a star network to see which one is causing the problem. On the other hand, ring networks are more reliable than star networks. If the central server in a star network breaks down, the whole network is disabled. If any one of the workstations in a ring network breaks down, however, the remaining functional workstations can still communicate.

## Protocols

*Rules for sharing on a network*

A **protocol** is a set of rules that govern how computers communicate. Various schemes are in common use. For the most part, you need not be too concerned with network protocols, unless you are an engineer designing a network. Nevertheless, protocols are often mentioned in books and articles about networking, and it helps to know the meaning of these terms.

The most commonly used protocols in local area networks are polling, carrier sense multiple access, and token-passing. With **polling,** a controlling workstation sends messages to the other workstations on the network, asking each one in turn if it has any messages or data to transmit. In contrast, the **carrier sense multiple access (CSMA)** protocol requires each workstation to listen before sending messages. Like people on a party-line telephone, workstations using CSMA only transmit messages or data if they sense that the line is clear. Since two workstations can potentially begin transmitting at the same instant, their messages may "collide" and become garbled. Variations of the basic CSMA protocol have been developed to detect and avoid these collisions. For example, CSMA/CD (the *CD* means "collision detection") and CSMA/CA (the *CA* means "collision avoidance") are commonly used network protocols. Finally, the **token-passing** protocol uses a control signal called a *token* that determines which workstation is allowed to transmit data. The token is passed from workstation to workstation, and complex rules prevent any one user from "hogging" the system. Token-passing is generally used with ring networks. For example the IBM Token-Ring Network is one of the most popular LANs for IBM-compatible microcomputers.

## Software

*Programs that control the network*

**Network software** is a set of programs that reside for the most part on a file server. The primary purpose of this software is to move data and messages between the workstations and servers, and to control the sharing of files and hardware devices. In addition, network software also may include electronic mail facilities, enhanced security measures, programs for analyzing network performance, and diagnostic routines for troubleshooting malfunctions.

In many ways, network software is like a supplemental operating system. It controls hardware devices and manages the use of software on a network in conjunction with the microcomputer operating system. In order to understand how network software works we can compare it with software on a stand-alone microcomputer. As Figure 12.17 illustrates, a stand-alone IBM-compatible microcomputer requires several layers of programs that must work together. At the lowest level are programs that work directly with the hardware. In Chapter 4 we said that these BIOS (Basic Input Output System) routines act as an interface between the physical components of the computer and the other operating system software and application packages. The next layer consists of the disk operating system (DOS) software that performs more complex activities, such as the logical storage of programs and data in disk files. Finally, the highest level of stand-alone software consists of the application packages used for word processing, spreadsheets, data base management, and other tasks. In each of these layers, software is basically designed for use on a single computer at a time.

Network software on a file server has the same fundamental layers as on a stand-alone machine, but a few more programs and layers are added (see Figure 12.18). **NETBIOS (NETwork Basic Input/Output System)** routines are added at the lowest level to send and receive data to and from the network adapter board, just as ordinary BIOS routines control the serial and parallel interfaces. Working beside DOS at the next higher level, network server software allows workstations to share disks and peripheral devices, as well as communicate with other workstations. Above DOS and the server software is the **redirector** layer. This software acts as a traffic controller for the data and messages transmitted over the network. Network utilities, menu systems, and security programs make up the next layer of software. These are programs that users can call upon to set up workstations to run on the network, send messages to other workstations, send files to the print server to be printed, gain access to disks and directories on file servers, and see network status reports. Finally, at the top level are application packages like word processors, spreadsheets, and data base managers.

## Using a Network

*Like using a stand-alone computer, only better*

Fortunately, using a local area network is much easier than setting one up or understanding exactly how it works. Network media, interfaces, topologies, protocols, and software layers are generally transparent to the end user. He or she has little or nothing to do with them. Most operating system commands work exactly the same as on a stand-alone computer, except that the user has access to additional disk drives and peripheral devices on a network. For example, a shared hard disk on a file server in a network of IBM-compatible microcomputers is assigned a letter just like the A, B, and C disk drives on a stand-alone machine. The only difference is that shared network hard disks are assigned letters beyond C, such as D, E, F, and so on. So even though your workstation may have only two floppy drives, A and B, it may also have access to hard disk E in one of the file servers. To switch drives, copy files, or run software from the file server, you treat hard disk E just as if it were installed in your own computer. In some cases you may have to use net-

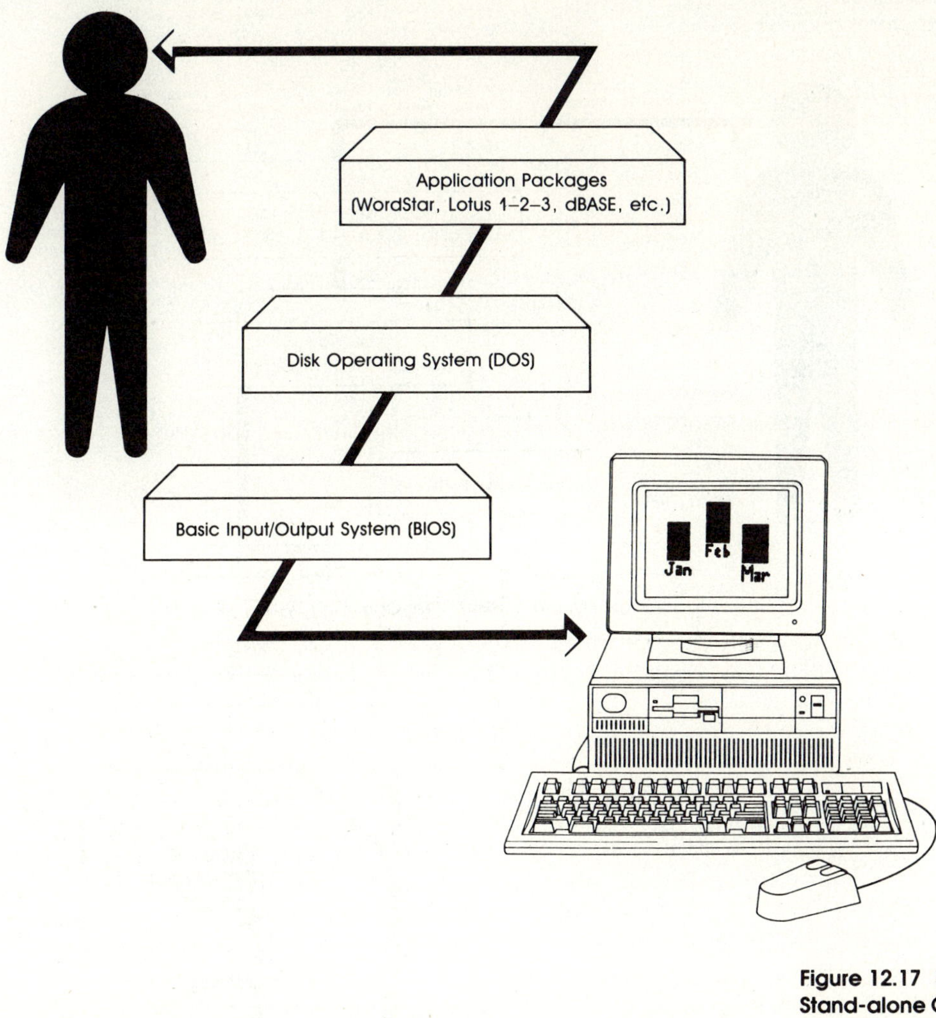


**Figure 12.17 Software Layers on a Stand-alone Computer**

An IBM-compatible microcomputer requires several layers of programs that must work together.

work versions of DOS commands, but they work similarly to ordinary DOS commands. IBM networks, for instance, require you to use the NET PRINT command instead of the regular PRINT command. The NET PRINT command allows you to send a file to a printer that is shared with other network users.

Running application packages on a network is also similar to running them on a stand-alone computer. If users don't share their data files, no special features or procedures are needed to run programs on a network. It doesn't matter whether programs and data are stored on a user's own disk or on a file server's disk. Software manufacturers may require special licenses for multiple workstations to run the same copy of a program at the same time legally. Nevertheless, even non-network versions of programs like WordStar and Lotus 1-2-3 run well on a network as long as users work with only their own data files. If two users on a network try to edit the same document with WordStar, for example, the work of one of them can be lost. The last person to save the document to the disk will destroy any previous copy saved by someone else.

**Figure 12.18 Software Layers on a Network Server**

Network software is like a supplemental operating system, adding more programs and layers.

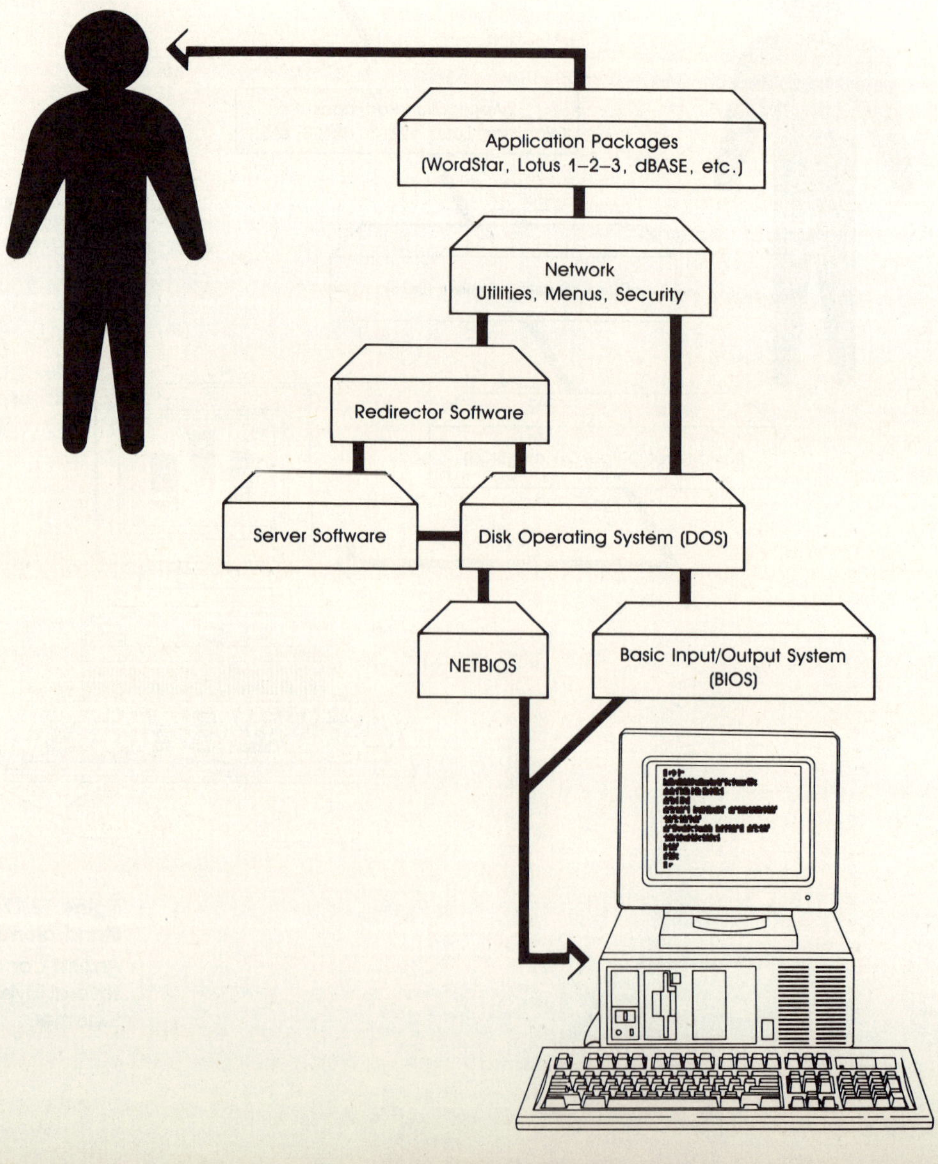

One of the best reasons for installing a network, however, is to let users share the same data files. Special network versions of software packages are required to let users successfully gain access to the same data files at the same time with no mishaps. As we said in Chapters 10 and 11, many data base management systems, such as dBASE III PLUS, are designed to run on networks. These programs employ a variety of file locking, record locking, and security measures to prevent users from destroying each other's data.

## The Real World

### An On-line Cornucopia

Peggy Berk, a Manhattan communications consultant, starts her day by turning on her modem-equipped computer, dialing into the GTE Telemail network, and reading on her screen any overnight telexes from her clients. Tapping a few keys, she scans the electronic version of *USA Today* before switching to another network, the Source, and perusing the A.P. and U.P.I. news wires. "I can get along without my morning toast and coffee," she says, "but I can't leave home without going on-line first."

Preparing to take a vacation in Jamaica, systems analyst Haig Hovanees logs on to CompuServe, another computer network, calls up Travel Forum, and reads all about the political situation on the Caribbean island. He switches to the electronic *Official Airline Guide*, checks Jamaica flights for departure times, fares, and availability of seats, and makes his plans. Then, turning to his investment portfolio, he taps into the Value Line Database to flick through quarterly results, Standard & Poor's to see earnings forecasts, and Disclosure II to read official reports to the Securities and Exchange Commission. "The system gives me all the information I need to make strategic decisions," says Hovanees. "It's replaced a file cabinet stuffed with newspaper clips."

Across the country, more and more Americans are logging on to computer information and service networks and discovering an ever-enlarging cornucopia at their fingertips. Today anybody with a computer, a modem, and a deep line of credit can buy an airline ticket to Cleveland, rent a Hertz car at the airport, book a room at the Sheraton, buy a novel from Waldenbooks, check the closing prices on Wall Street, and purchase 100 shares of IBM—without ever getting up from the computer.

Source: "Calling Up an On-Line Cornucopia," by Philip Elmer-DeWitt, *Time*, April 7, 1986, p. 69.

## Summary

- *The basic hardware of microcomputer communications.* Four primary components are necessary for communications: a microcomputer, serial interface, modem, and telephone line. Two other considerations in the selection of a modem are speed and Hayes compatibility.
- *The primary functions of communications software.* In addition to letting you set up your equipment to call other computers, communications software performs terminal emulation and allows you to download and upload files.
- *The various software settings that govern microcomputer communications.* Several parameters specify the technical details of how your microcomputer will communicate with other computers: speed, number of data bits, which serial port to use, type of parity, number of stop bits, type of duplex, which type of terminal emulation, and whether to call or answer.
- *How to call a mainframe computer with a microcomputer.* First, find out the settings required by the mainframe and, if necessary, change the communications parameters to match. Call the mainframe and enter your sign-on and password. Use the mainframe's facilities; terminate the call when finished.

- *How to use an electronic mail facility.* After subscribing, calling, and logging on to the system, you can send messages to other subscribers and read messages that have been sent to you. Simple menus guide you through addressing your messages, entering the text, and sending them.
- *How to use an on-line information service.* Once you subscribe, many services are at your disposal. After calling and logging on to the system, you can select items from menus or directly enter commands to read the most recent news, research a topic in an on-line encyclopedia, and so on.
- *How to call one microcomputer from another.* Match the communications parameters on both machines. One computer is put into CALL mode and the other into ANSWER mode. The user of the calling computer then dials the answering computer's phone number. The calling computer can then download and upload files from the answering computer.
- *The fundamental components and uses of local area networks.* Networks consist of workstations, servers, media, and interfaces. They allow you to connect two or more microcomputers to share programs, data, and peripheral equipment.

## Key Terms

As an extra review of this chapter, try defining the following terms. If you have trouble with any of them, refer to the page number listed.

bus network (447)
capture (428)
carrier sense multiple access (CSMA) (449)
coaxial cable (447)
communications parameters (431)
communications server (447)
dedicated server (447)
downloading (428)
electronic mail (E-mail) (435)
fiber-optic cable (447)
file server (447)
full-duplex (432)
half-duplex (432)
Hayes-compatible modem (426)
host computer (422)
modem cable (424)
modular phone jack (422)
NETBIOS (Network Basic Input/Output System) (452)
network interface (447)
network media (447)
network server (447)
network software (450)
network workstation (446)
null-modem cable (444)
parity (431)
polling (449)
print server (447)
protocol (449)
public data network (packet-switching network, value-added network) (436)
redirector (452)
ring network (447)
star network (447)
stop bits (432)
terminal emulation (427)
token-passing (450)
topology (447)
twisted-pair wire (447)
uploading (428)

## Review Questions

1. List the four basic components of a microcomputer communications system.
2. How is the transmission speed of a modem usually expressed?
3. Why is Hayes compatibility so important in a modem?
4. What are two basic functions performed by all communications software?

5. What is the difference between uploading and downloading?
6. Name one popular communications package for CP/M and DOS microcomputers.
7. List eight communications parameters you can set with most communications software.
8. Why might you want to call a mainframe computer with your microcomputer?
9. On what type of computer system can electronic mail be implemented?
10. Which CROSSTALK command can you use to send incoming characters presented on your screen to a printer?
11. What happens when you send an electronic mail message to a fellow subscriber who isn't currently using the system?
12. Why might you use a public data network such as TYMNET to call a communications service such as MCI Mail?
13. List five activities you can do with a major on-line information service.
14. What is the oldest and largest on-line information service?
15. Give two reasons why you might use an on-line encyclopedia such as Grolier's *Academic American Encyclopedia* instead of a printed edition at your local library.
16. List two ways to connect two microcomputers that are not on a local area network.
17. Give three benefits to installing a local area network.
18. What distinguishes a network server from an ordinary network workstation?
19. What is the purpose of a communication protocol?
20. What is the primary purpose of network software?

## Multiple Choice

1. Which of the following components is not necessary for distant microcomputer communications?
   (a) serial interface (b) modem
   (c) printer (d) telephone line
2. A disadvantage of internal modems is that they
   (a) are more expensive than external modems.
   (b) draw their electrical power from the computer.
   (c) require no external cables.
   (d) are computer specific.
3. Two basic functions of all communications software are
   (a) terminal emulation and file transfer.
   (b) error detection and file correction.
   (c) data base management and file security.
   (d) hardware and software sharing.
4. Transferring a file from a host computer to your microcomputer is called
   (a) uploading. (b) downloading.
   (c) polling. (d) emulating.

5. Which of the following is not a communications parameter?
   (a) speed (b) modem
   (c) port (d) parity
6. If you see two of every character you type when using a communications program, which setting should you change?
   (a) duplex (b) port
   (c) speed (d) parity
7. Which of the following is a security measure that helps prevent unauthorized access to a mainframe computer?
   (a) parity (b) duplex
   (c) password (d) stop bits
8. Which of the following is a popular way to send and receive messages with a computer?
   (a) uploading (b) downloading
   (c) terminal emulation (d) electronic mail
9. A public data network such as TYMNET is often used to call a distant communications service because
   (a) it is more convenient than calling directly.
   (b) it is less expensive than calling long distance.
   (c) it is faster than calling directly.
   (d) it is more accurate than calling long distance.
10. Which of the following is the most popular multi-purpose on-line information service?
    (a) CompuServe (b) The Source
    (c) MCI Mail (d) Dow Jones/News Retrieval Service
11. Which of the following CompuServe commands is a way to bypass intermediate menus and jump directly to the feature you want to use?
    (a) TOP (b) MENU
    (c) BYE (d) GO
12. Which of the following is an inexpensive way to connect two microcomputers?
    (a) local area network (b) on-line information service
    (c) null-modem cable (d) fiber-optic cable
13. Which of the following arrangements is the best way to link several microcomputers for the purpose of sharing data files, programs, and peripheral devices?
    (a) null-modem cable (b) local area network
    (c) modems and the telephone network (d) on-line information service
14. Which of the following is not a key piece of network hardware?
    (a) network workstation (b) network server
    (c) network media (d) network mouse
15. Which of the following is not a commonly used network protocol?
    (a) polling (b) parity
    (c) carrier sense multiple access (d) token-passing

## Projects

1. At 1200 bps, a modem transmits approximately 120 characters per second over the telephone line. A typical single-spaced page of text consists of 50 lines of 60 characters each. How long does it take to transmit one page of text at 1200 bps? Not including figures, each chapter in this book, on average, is equivalent to about 30 single-spaced typewritten pages. How long would it take to transmit one chapter over the phone line at 1200 bps? Finally, there are 16 chapters in this book. About how long would it take to send all 16 chapters at 1200 bps? Now repeat these calculations with 300 bps and 2400 bps.

2. In this chapter we briefly introduced the CROSSTALK communications package. Do some research to find out more about this type of application software. Compare CROSSTALK with other popular communications programs on the market. Write a short report summarizing what you learn. *PC Magazine*, *BYTE* magazine, *InfoWorld*, and other computer periodicals are good sources of information and product reviews.

3. Find out more about on-line information services. Compare the features and facilities offered by CompuServe and The Source. Write a brief report with your findings. Which service do you think you would prefer? Why?

4. Does your school, office, or company use a local area network? If you don't personally know of a local area network being used by some organization with which you come in contact, find a magazine or newspaper article about one. Write a brief report describing this "real world" use of a local area network. What kind of a local area network is it? How many workstations are connected together? Why did the organization decide to install the network? How well has the network worked out so far? How much did it cost? Try to answer some of these questions or any others you think are important to get a good understanding of how networks are being put to use in our society.

# 13

# Graphics

## In This Chapter

## PREVIEW

Computer graphics used to be the domain of scientists and engineers, laboring in their high-tech world of expensive and unwieldy equipment. But now, virtually all modern microcomputers have the potential to produce stunning visual displays. Hardware and software advancements have made computer graphics affordable, effective, easy to use, and even fun. Whether you're a student, artist, author, or executive, computer graphics can help you create pictures to get your point across.

Drawing graphs, charts, and plots by hand is quickly becoming a thing of the past. If you've ever plotted a curve for a science class, drawn a graph for a math class, or constructed a bar chart for a business class, you know the tedium of manual graphics. With the right combination of microcomputer hardware and software, however, you can generally perform such tasks faster, easier, and more accurately than you could by hand. Unless you're a graphic artist, using a computer also produces much more attractive results—on the screen, on paper, on slides, and on overhead transparencies.

Graphs, charts, and plots are structured pictures derived from numerical data. Computer graphics can also help you produce all kinds of free-hand figures and illustrations. For example, some graphics packages let you use a mouse to "draw" or "paint" pictures on the display screen. These programs provide a wide range of sketching, shading, and editing tools. Completed pictures can be saved in disks files and printed or plotted. With a little practice, almost anyone can produce figures, diagrams, and other illustrations for reports, presentations, articles, and books. Besides software for drawing and painting, more specialized graphics packages are available for technical drafting and for producing "slide shows" that run on a computer screen. In this chapter, first we will examine the hardware and then the software of computer graphics systems.

After studying this chapter, you will understand

- the hardware of microcomputer graphics.
- the basic types of microcomputer graphics software.
- how to use a charting program.
- how to use a painting program.
- how to use a drawing program.
- how to use a computer-aided design program.
- how to use a computer slide show program.

## GRAPHICS HARDWARE

*Parts needed to make images*

Before you can run any graphics software, you must have a computer system that includes several key components. Some computers, such as the Apple Macintosh Plus and Macintosh SE, come complete with all you need to work with graphics. These systems are easy to purchase and set up because they don't require the selection of individual graphics hardware components. In most cases, however, owners must choose from a range of different hardware options to equip their computers for graphics. This is especially true for IBM-compatible microcomputers. Although many different options are available, four basic hardware components are necessary, along with a computer, for a complete graphics system: a display adapter, monitor, input device, and hard-copy output device (see Figure 13.1). Let's examine each of these in detail.

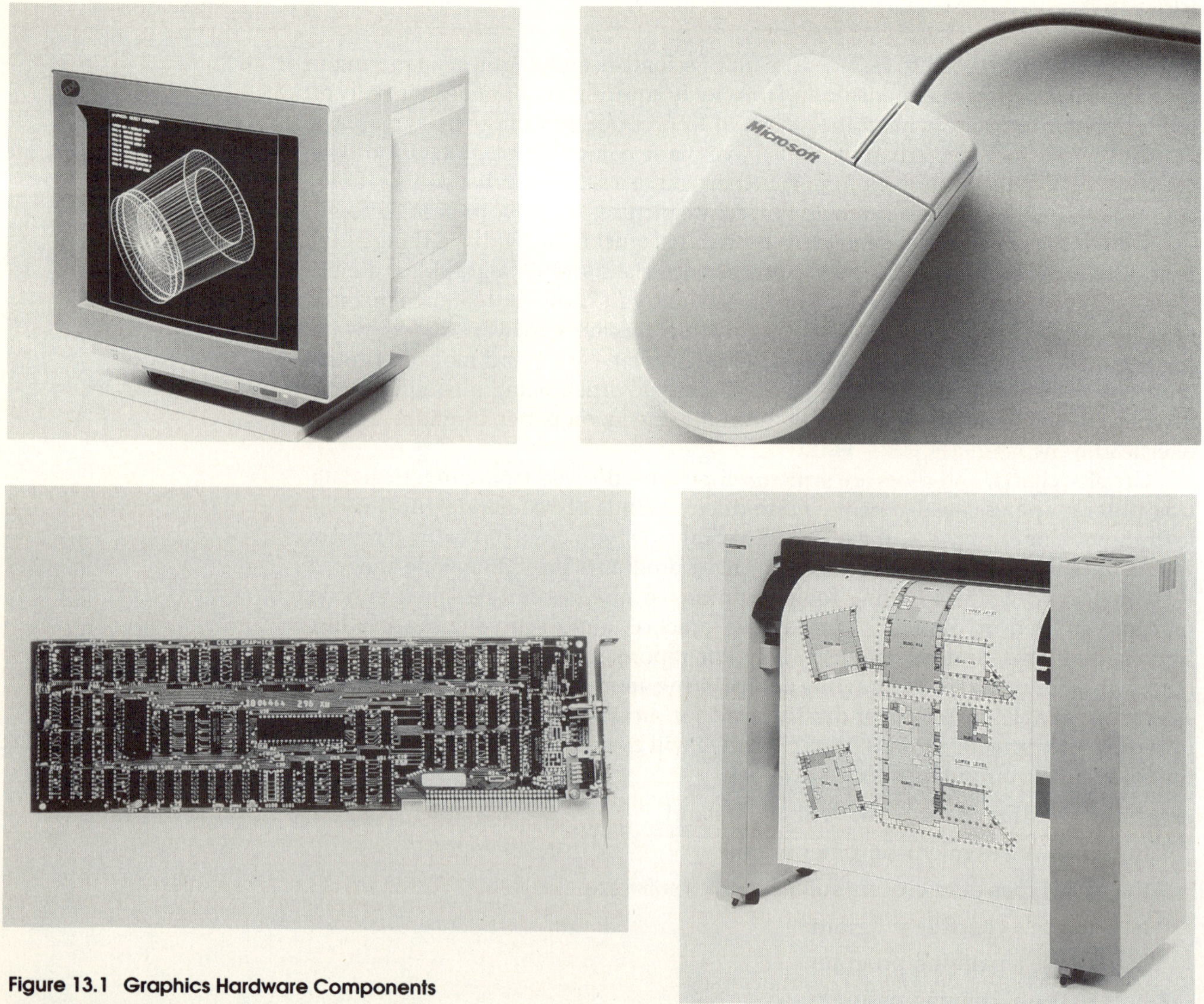


**Figure 13.1 Graphics Hardware Components**
Along with a computer, a complete graphics system must have a display adapter, monitor, input device such as a mouse, and a hard-copy output device such as a printer or plotter.

## Display Adapter

*Circuit board controls the screen*

The single most important part of any graphics system is the display adapter. A display adapter that is capable of producing graphics is sometimes called a **graphics adapter**. As we said in Chapter 2, this is the circuit board that controls the monitor. Sometimes, the display adapter is built onto the computer's motherboard. This is the case in the Apple Macintosh Plus, the Apple Macintosh SE, and the IBM Personal System/2 microcomputers. In many other computers, the display adapter is a completely separate expansion board that fits into one of the expansion slots (see Figure 13.2). Most of these computers can be equipped with any one of a number of different display adapters. Even computers with a display adapter built onto the motherboard sometimes can be fitted with an optional circuit board to enhance or upgrade the graphics capability.

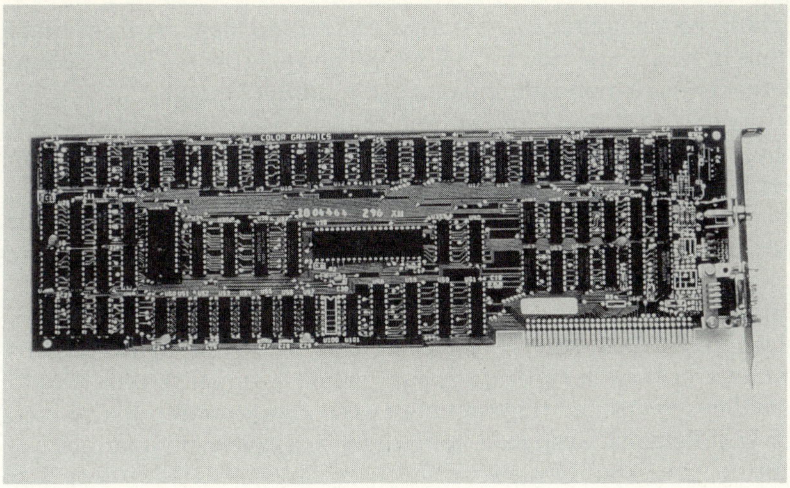


**Figure 13.2 Graphics Adapter**
The graphics adapter contains the circuitry that controls the monitor.

Your display adapter determines the video modes that can be used by your software, as well as the type of monitor that you can connect to your system. As we said in Chapter 2, a *video mode* specifies the screen resolution and the colors that can be displayed on the monitor. Screen resolution determines the sharpness and clarity of the images you see. Virtually all microcomputer displays present a matrix of tiny dots, or *pixels,* that are turned off and on in various colors to make pictures. Resolution is expressed in terms of the total number of horizontal and vertical pixels that can be displayed on the screen. Color capability is usually described by the number of different colors that can be on the screen at one time, along with the total number of possible colors to choose from. Some display adapters have only one video mode. The built-in Apple Macintosh SE display adapter, for example, has a screen resolution of 512 horizontal by 342 vertical pixels and just two "colors," black and white. Most display adapters, however, can operate in a number of different video modes. As Table 13.1 (p. 462) shows, IBM microcomputer owners have a choice of several different graphics display adapters, most of which can operate in several different video modes.

## Monitor

*Displaying your images*

The display adapter and monitor must be perfectly matched to work correctly. Nevertheless, in many instances there are various acceptable combinations. Some display adapters work with a number of different monitors. For example, the IBM Enhanced Graphics Adapter (EGA) can be connected to an IBM Monochrome Display, an IBM Color Display, or an IBM Enhanced Color Display. Some monitors can be connected to a number of different display adapters. These **multiscan monitors** work by changing their resolution to match the display adapter. The NEC MultiSync monitor, for example, can be connected to most of IBM's display adapters as well as the Apple Macintosh II display adapter. Many compatible display adapters and monitors made by other manufacturers can be connected in various combinations. The most important aspect of selecting a monitor is making sure that it works correctly with your display adapter.

Besides matching your monitor to your display adapter, there are three other basic considerations in selecting a monitor: color, size, and sharpness. The first consideration is whether to use a monochrome or a color graphics monitor. Some display adapters can accept either kind. For example, the Video Graphics Array (VGA) display adapter built into the IBM Personal System/2 Models 50, 60, 70, and 80 can be connected to either a black and white monochrome monitor or a color monitor. The monochrome monitor costs around $250—less than half as much as the color monitor. It is the same size and just as sharp, but uses shades of gray to simulate different colors.

Another monitor consideration is the screen size. Measured diagonally, the most common sizes are 9, 12, 14, 16, and 19 inches. In general, the smaller screens appear sharper but present smaller characters and pictures. Larger screens tend to cost more than smaller screens, but this isn't always so. For example, the 12-inch color monitor for IBM Personal System/2 computers costs $90 more than the 14-inch color monitor.

**Table 13.1 IBM Graphics Video Modes and Adapters**

| MODE | RESOLUTION[a] | DISPLAY ADAPTER[b] | DISPLAY COLORS[c] |
|---|---|---|---|
| 4, 5 | 320 x 200 | CGA | 4 out of 16 |
| | | EGA | 4 out of 64 |
| | | MCGA | 4 out of 262,144 |
| | | VGA | 4 out of 262,144 |
| 6 | 640 x 200 | CGA | 2 out of 16 |
| | | EGA | 2 out of 64 |
| | | MCGA | 2 out of 262,144 |
| | | VGA | 2 out of 262,144 |
| 13 | 320 x 200 | EGA | 16 out of 64 |
| | | VGA | 16 out of 262,144 |
| 14 | 640 x 200 | EGA | 16 out of 64 |
| | | VGA | 16 out of 262,144 |
| 15 | 640 x 350 | ECA | Monochrome |
| | | VGA | Monochrome |
| 16 | 640 x 350 | EGA | 16 out of 64 |
| | | VGA | 16 out of 262,144 |
| 17 | 640 x 480 | MCGA | 2 out of 262,144 |
| | | VGA | 2 out of 262,144 |
| 18 | 640 x 480 | VGA | 16 out of 262,144 |
| 19 | 320 x 200 | MCGA | 256 out of 262,144 |
| | | VGA | 256 out of 262,144 |

[a]The Resolution column expresses the total number of horizontal by vertical pixels on the screen.
[b]Display Adapter column abbreviations: CGA=Color Graphics Array; EGA=Enhanced Graphics Adapter; MCGA=Multicolor Graphics Array; VGA=Video Graphics Array.
[c]The Colors column shows the number of different colors that can simultaneously appear on the screen out of the total number of possible different colors.

The main reason for this cost difference is the third basic monitor consideration: sharpness. **Dot pitch** is another, more technical term for the sharpness of a monitor. Usually expressed in millimeters, this is the distance between the illuminated centers of any two adjacent dots. The smaller the dot pitch, the sharper the image. The 12-inch IBM color monitor for the Personal System/2 computers costs more because it has a dot pitch of 0.28 mm, while the 14-inch monitor has a dot pitch of 0.41 mm. This makes the images on the larger display somewhat more grainy.

**Insight**

## Professional Artists and Microcomputers

Their art may not be destined to grace the galleries of the Louvre, but artists today are producing an astonishing variety of work with microcomputers.

For many years, a good computer graphics system cost more than $20,000 per terminal, not including the hefty price of the mainframe that drove the graphics terminals. The arrival of the microcomputer, with its substantial graphics capabilities, has changed all that. There has been a surge of interest in using the computer for design and even to create drawings and paintings.

Today, many students who are majoring in art and industrial design use computer-aided design (CAD) packages such as AUTOCAD. With a good CAD package, it's possible to develop the design of any complex object by working on smaller subassemblies.

A computer-aided design package is to an artist and designer what the spreadsheet is to the accountant.

### Input Device

*Pointing and drawing*

Besides the keyboard, many graphics programs require the use of an additional graphics input device. Although the mouse is by far the most common, other types of input devices, such as the trackball and graphics tablet, are also used. As we said in Chapter 2, these input devices allow you to easily move a cursor or pointer anywhere on the screen. A mouse, trackball, or graphics tablet is practically essential for drawing and manipulating objects. Some computers, such as the Apple Macintosh, come with a mouse as standard equipment. With many others, a mouse is an option that must be purchased separately. The mouse plugs into a serial interface, into its own special expansion board, or directly into the motherboard. The mouse and similar input devices are basically used to draw and manipulate objects by hand, one at a time.

Another type of input device, the *scanner,* takes a different approach (see Figure 13.3). As we said in Chapter 2, a page scanner reads in a whole page of text and graphics. The images that are scanned are converted into dots that can be displayed on the screen, manipulated by graphics programs, stored in files, and printed. In addition to full page scanners, some less expensive, hand-held scanners are also now on the market that let you read images in strips two or three inches wide. Scanners are becoming increasingly popular as their prices decrease and as people use graphics and desktop publishing packages more and more. This method of entering graphical data into computers is suitable for reproducing many different types of images, including photographs, drawings, charts, signatures, and even ordinary text. Although the vast majority of scanners can only copy in black and white, and perhaps some gray tones, there are a few very expensive models that can reproduce color images.

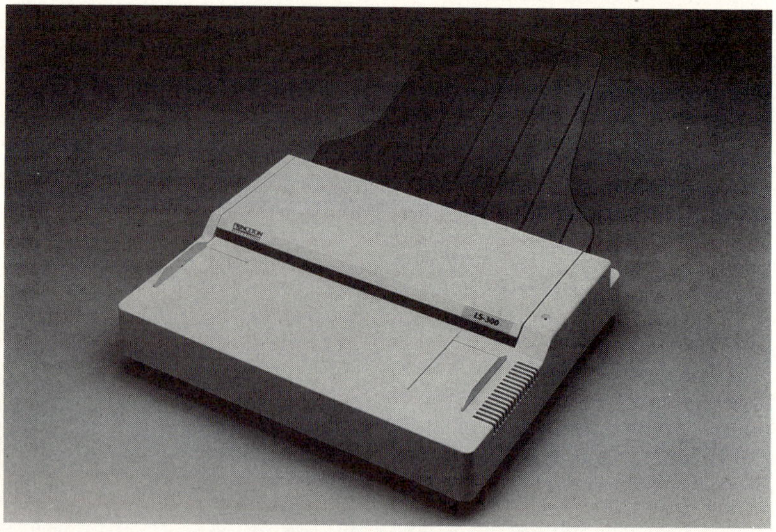

**Figure 13.3 Optical Scanner**
A scanner enables a computer to read existing text and graphics from a printed page.

## Hard-Copy Output Device

*Preserving your images*

Admittedly, some programs use graphics only to present images on a display screen. Computer game, simulation, and slide-show programs are a few examples of this type of software. Nevertheless, most graphics programs are much more useful if they can produce some permanent record of the images they display. So, a hard-copy output device such as a printer, plotter, or film recorder is usually considered an essential component of a complete graphics system.

The most common hard-copy output device for graphics is the ordinary printer. As we said in Chapter 2, the most common type of printer used with microcomputers is the *dot-matrix printer.* This output device is reliable, relatively inexpensive, and easy to operate. Furthermore, dot-matrix printers produce their output on an inexpensive medium—paper. Since all dot matrix printers by definition use dots to create text, most of them have no trouble at all also producing graphics. Some dot-matrix printers can even use multi-color ribbons to produce color pictures. In many cases, the images made by dot-matrix printers are superior to those presented on the display screen, because printers typically have a higher maximum resolution than most monitors. For example, the standard built-in Apple Macintosh display screen has a maximum resolution of 72 dots per inch. The Apple Imagewriter II printer often used with this computer can easily achieve a resolution of 144 dots per inch.

Besides dot-matrix printers, *laser printers* are also frequently used for graphics output. Laser printers are sophisticated devices that can achieve resolutions of at least 300 dots per inch. Besides producing high-quality images, laser printers are also quiet and fast. With a few expensive exceptions, however, laser printers can only print in one color, usually black.

Another fairly common graphics output device is the *ink-jet printer,* which sprays tiny drops of ink on paper to produce images. This less expensive alternative to the laser printer is also quiet and fairly quick. Some of the newest ink-jet printers now on the market can rival laser printers with resolutions of nearly 300 dots per inch. Unlike laser printers, many ink-jet printers can also produce output in several colors.

*Plotters* use pens instead of a printing mechanism to produce hard-copy output. As a result, they are generally better suited to drafting and map-drawing applications. In addition, most plotters can produce pictures in different colors with different pens. They can even be used to draw on sheets of acetate plastic for use with overhead projectors. Plotters are, however, generally slower than printers.

A more specialized output device used in some graphics systems is the **film recorder** (see Figure 13.4). Basically, a film recorder turns screen images into 35-mm slides, which can then be shown with an ordinary slide projector. Slides are often more convenient for presenting graphics to large audiences. The film recorder is usually plugged into the computer's display adapter or serial interface. It works by reproducing computer screen images on its own internal screen at one end of an enclosed box. This screen is then photographed with a 35-mm camera mounted on the other end of the box. Generally, film recorders can create images at a higher resolution and with a greater variety of colors than is possible on a computer monitor. The slides produced by film recorders are usually sharper, more detailed, and more colorful. Once the pictures have been taken, the film must be processed at a film lab just like any other 35-mm slides. Costing at least $2,000, film recorders are somewhat expensive, but they are well suited to producing high-quality slides for use in presentations and publications.

**Figure 13.4 Film Recorder**
A film recorder, such as the Polaroid Palette Plus, turns screen images into 35-mm slides.

## GRAPHICS SOFTWARE

*Programs that make the images*

Unless you're a programmer, a computer equipped with graphics hardware is of little use without graphics software too. Instead of writing your own programs, you'll probably use commercial software packages to create, display, and print charts, pictures, figures, diagrams, and computerized slide shows. Fortunately, an abundance of excellent software is available to help you use your computer as a graphics tool.

Many different kinds of graphics packages are on the market, and new types of programs are being devised all the time. The distinctions between different types of graphics software are sometimes blurred because developers frequently include many diverse features in the same package. Nevertheless, most commonly used microcomputer graphics programs primarily fall into one of the following categories: charting, painting, drawing, computer-aided design, and slide show.

For the rest of this chapter, we will examine each one of these categories of graphics software in greater detail. In each case, we will give a specific example of a popular commercial package used on either IBM-compatible or Apple Macintosh computers.

## CHARTING PROGRAMS

*Enter or import data*

It's practically impossible to go through a day without seeing at least one chart, graph, or plot. These graphics are very common in newspapers, magazines, books, and television. Countless speakers at presentations, meetings, press conferences, and lectures use charts to help them get their messages across quickly, clearly, and concisely. Graphs have always been valuable for depicting numbers in a more understandable and memorable visual format. Now one of the reasons charts are used so often is the ease with which they can be generated on a computer. All you need is the appropriate graphics hardware and a charting program. A **charting program** produces graphs, plots, and charts from data you enter directly or import from a spreadsheet or data base file. Charting programs typically provide a wide range of different kinds of charts and give you a great deal of control over the charts' final appearance.

### Types of Charting Programs

*Popular charting programs*

Many types of application packages are capable of producing charts. A few of the most popular kinds of charting programs include:

- *Spreadsheet Enhancement.* In Chapters 8 and 9 we said that many spreadsheet programs can display and print various graphs. Although some have more advanced features, spreadsheet programs generally are limited to a few different types of graphs and give the user little control over their final format. For many people, this is enough. Other computer users require more elaborate output. Some programs on the market are specifically designed to spruce up the graphs of a particular spreadsheet. For example, 3D-Graphics from Intex Solutions is a program that lets you add depth, instead of just width and height, to Lotus 1-2-3 charts. Spreadsheet enhancement charting programs such as 3D-Graphics can help you easily improve the appearance of your spreadsheet charts at a relatively low cost.
- *Data Base Charting.* Unlike spreadsheets, most data base management systems don't have built-in graphics capabilities. Some graphics packages, however, are designed to work with particular data base systems. DB Graphics from Microrim, for instance, is a charting program specifically for users of dBASE and R:base. This program reads data base files directly to let you create eight different types of color graphs. A data base charting program such as DB Graphics may be the easiest solution for people who need to routinely create graphs from a particular data base management system.
- *Map Making.* Some popular charting programs specialize in generating maps to present data. For example, Atlas Graphics from Strategic Locations Planning is a program for IBM-compatible computers that creates only maps (see Figure 13.5). Instead of displaying data in bar graphs or pie charts, Atlas Graphics presents information in a map format that can reveal complex geographic relationships. A well-conceived map chart is often better than other graphs for data such as market potential, regional sales performance, and other popula-

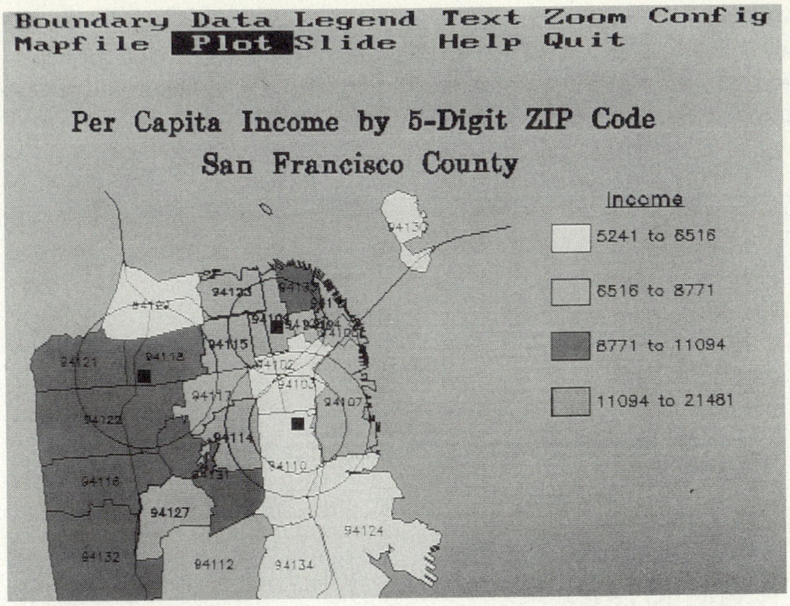


**Figure 13.5 Map-making Program**
Some charting programs specialize in making maps, such as Atlas Graphics from Strategic Locations Planning.

tion statistics. You can enter your own map outlines or purchase additional files that contain regional boundaries for many countries, states, counties, zip codes, census tracts, and communities.

- *Dedicated Charting.* Most charting programs on the market offer a wide range of different types of graphs as well as a good deal of control over the graphs' final appearance. These programs are often called *dedicated charting* programs to distinguish them from graphics packages that are integrated with spreadsheets or data base managers. Dedicated charting programs need no other packages to create graphs. Although they can usually accept data files from word processors, spreadsheets, and data base managers, they also take data entered directly from the user. Dedicated charting packages are one of the most popular types of application software, especially in business, government, education, and journalism.

## Introducing EnerGraphics

*Charting package for IBM-compatibles*

EnerGraphics is a good example of a typical dedicated charting program. Made by Enertronics Research Inc., this popular program was one of the first full-featured charting packages developed for IBM-compatible microcomputers. Despite its many fine competitors, EnerGraphics is still considered to be a top-notch product, especially well-suited to creating business graphics. For data analysis, you can create simple pie charts, bar graphs, several types of line plots, and statistical graphs. In addition, EnerGraphics lets you do two- and three-dimensional drawings. This drawing capability can be used to design organizational charts, flowcharts, electrical circuits, mechanical parts, and architectural plans. EnerGraphics also can present your charts in the form of a simple slide show. Let's stick to the basics, however, and see what it's like to use EnerGraphics (version 2.2) to produce a couple of charts.

Installing and running EnerGraphics is quite simple. Most users put the program on a hard disk. After switching to the appropriate disk drive directory, you simply enter **ENG** from DOS to begin. Figure 13.6 shows the Main menu that appears on your screen.

**Figure 13.6 EnerGraphics Main Menu**
This screen shows the Main menu of the EnerGraphics charting program for IBM-compatible microcomputers.

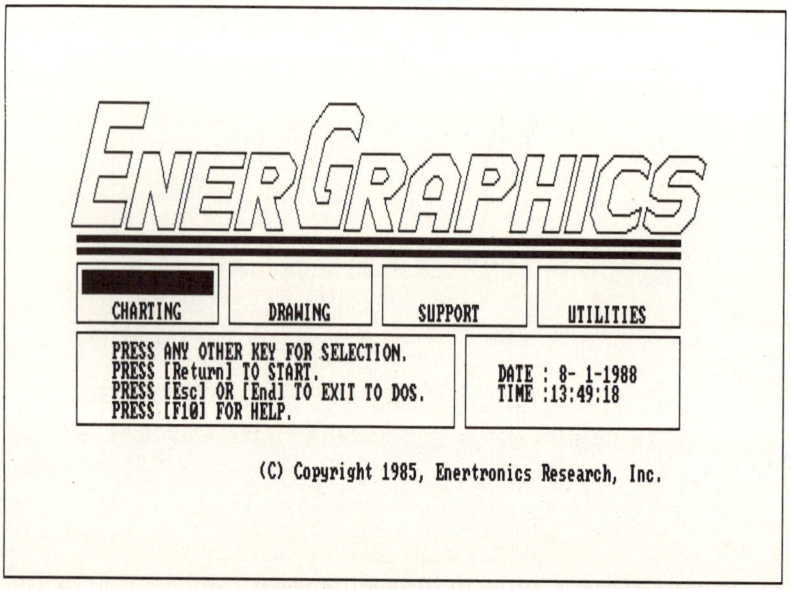


## Creating a Pie Chart

*Show cost breakdown*

Let's say that you want to create a pie chart showing the cost breakdown of goods manufactured at a cookie factory. There are three components to this cost:

1. Materials = $80 million
2. Labor = $20 million
3. Overhead = $10 million

The first step is to select the Charting option from the Main menu. Since this is the default option, all you have to do is press the **Enter** key. EnerGraphics then displays its Chart menu, shown in Figure 13.7(a). The available options are listed in the upper right box. To select an option, you can either press the function key that precedes it, or use the arrow keys to position the highlight bar upon it and then press the **Enter** key. For example, you press the **F3** function key to select the Create/Edit Chart option.

The Edit menu then appears on your screen (see Figure 13.7(b)). Now you select the Create/Edit Data option by pressing the **F1** function key. Next EnerGraphics asks you to specify the type of chart to be created. You can choose a Pie, Bar, Line, or Text chart. Simply type **P** to create a pie chart.

EnerGraphics then presents a screen in which you enter the data and formatting instructions for the pie chart. Figure 13.7(c) shows this screen after all the information for your pie chart has been entered. For each slice in the pie, you enter its numeric value, its color, its fill pattern, and a number between 0 and 9 that specifies how far the slice should be pulled out, or *offset,* from the rest of the pie. For example, the Overhead slice has a value of 10 ($10 million) and it is to be displayed in color 3 (white or yellow) with pattern 3 (solidly filled in). For emphasis, this slice is given an offset value of 2 so that it will be pulled out from the pie a little more than the other slices.

When you're finished specifying the pie chart slices, you press the **End** key. EnerGraphics then lets you enter a title for the chart, such as **Cost of Goods Manufactured**. Press the **End** key to return to the Edit menu, and then press **F9** to return to the Chart menu. Now press **F1** to draw the chart. Another screen appears with options for changing certain aspects of the chart's final appearance. For example, you can specify the chart's background color, make the chart three dimensional, or select a frame (border) for the chart. Usually, the default display parameters are fine. EnerGraphics asks if you want to use the default display parameters, and you can answer yes by simply pressing the **Enter** key. Figure 13.7(d) shows the pie chart that appears on your screen.

When you are finished viewing the chart, you can press any key to return to the Chart menu. At this point, you can print your chart and save it in a disk file. The Chart menu also provides options for loading previously saved charts so that you can view or modify them, and deleting existing charts that are no longer needed.

**Figure 13.7 Creating a Pie Chart**

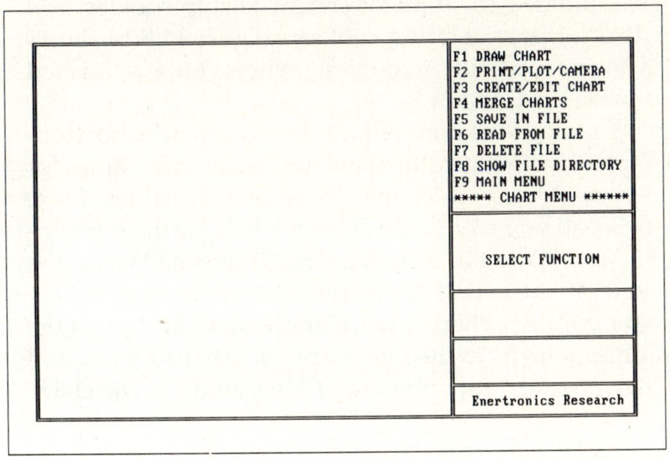


(a) The Chart menu.

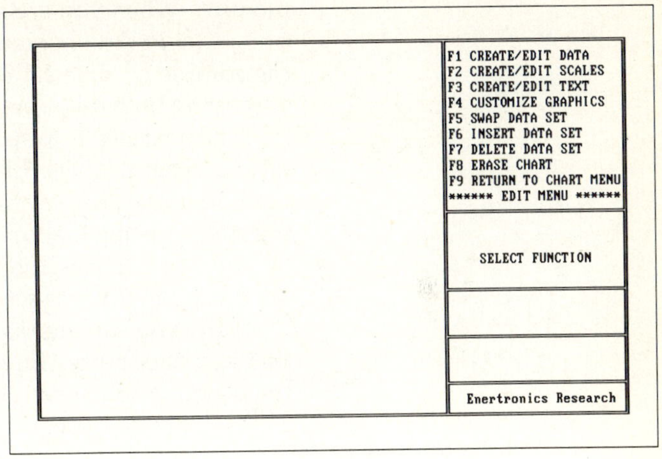


(b) The Edit menu.

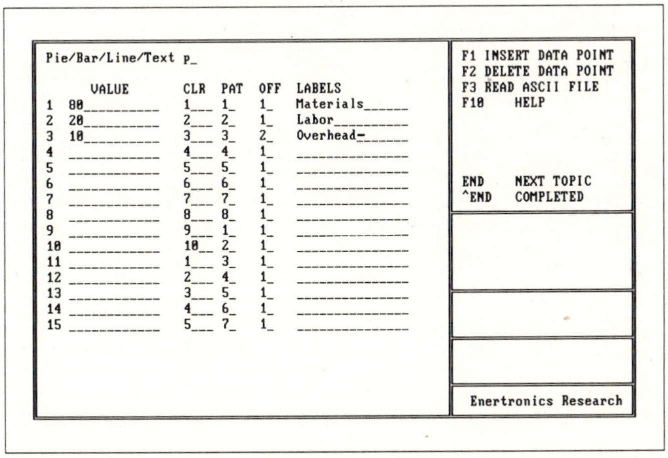


(c) The completed pie chart data table.

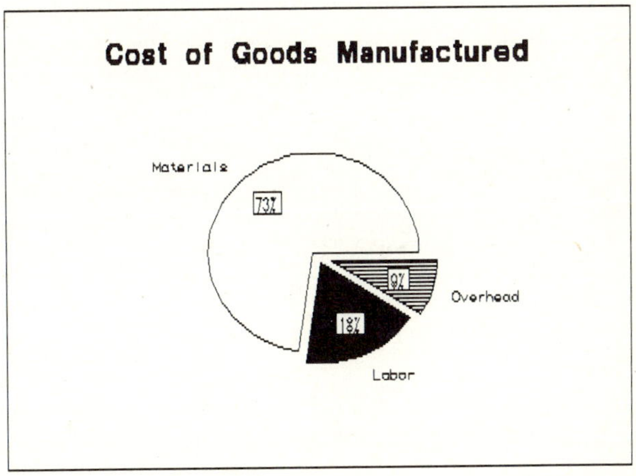


(d) The completed pie chart.

## Creating a Bar Graph

*Compare sales*

As we said in Chapter 9, bar graphs are useful for comparing different sets of data. For example, you could use a bar graph to show the unit sales of two different products, say chocolate chip cookies and peanut butter cookies, for the first six months of the year. In such a graph, the value of the units sold of each cookie for each month is represented by a bar, where the length of the bar corresponds to the magnitude of the value. The bars of each cookie are distinguished by filling them in with different patterns or colors. Let's use EnerGraphics to produce a simple bar graph like the one we've just described.

The first few steps are the same as creating a pie chart. You choose Charting from the Main menu, Create/Edit Chart from the Chart menu, and Create/Edit Data from the Edit menu. When EnerGraphics prompts you for the kind of chart, however, you type **B** for bar chart. The program then allows you to choose from several different types of bar charts. *Normal* is the default type of bar chart, which you can select by pressing the **Enter** key. EnerGraphics then presents a screen in which you enter information about your first data set. Figure 13.8(a) shows the completed screen for your first data set, which contains the data for chocolate chip cookies. The Legend Entry identifies these bars as representing chocolate chip cookie sales. The Color and Pattern entries specify the appearance of the bars. The Values are the sales figures for each month, and the Labels indicate the names of the months. When you are finished entering the data for chocolate chip cookies, you press **Ctrl-PgDn** to enter the data for peanut butter cookies. Figure 13.8(b) shows the completed data set screen for peanut butter cookies. When you are finished specifying both data sets, you press the **End** key.

The next step is to specify the scale of the horizontal axis and enter the horizontal and vertical labels. EnerGraphics automatically calculates reasonable values for the horizontal axis scaling. Although you can change these default values if you like, they are fine for our chart. So, all you have to do is enter labels for the horizontal and vertical axes. Figure 13.8(c) shows the completed Scale screen. When you are finished with this screen, you press the **End** key again.

Now you can enter a title for your bar chart. Type **Cookie Sales** and press the **End** key once more. EnerGraphics returns to the Edit menu. Press the **F9** key and the program returns to the Chart menu. Now press the **F1** key to draw the chart.

**Figure 13.8 Creating a Bar Chart**

(a) The completed data set table for chocolate chip cookie sales.

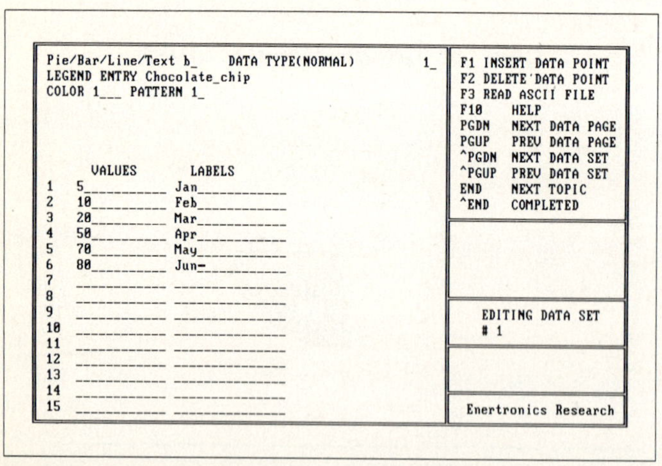


(b) The completed data set table for peanut butter cookie sales.

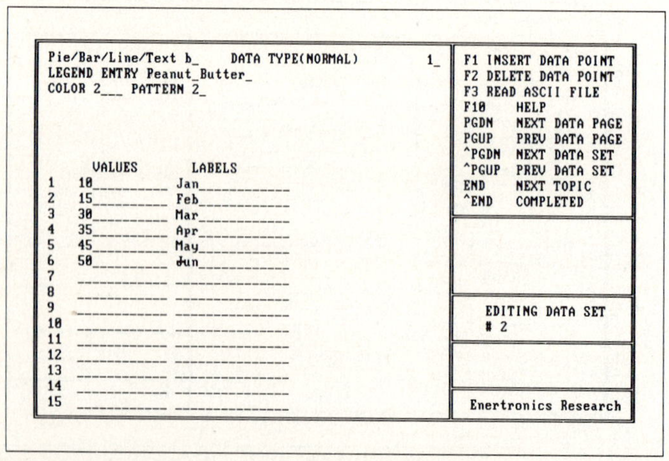

(c) Specifying the scaling and axis labels.

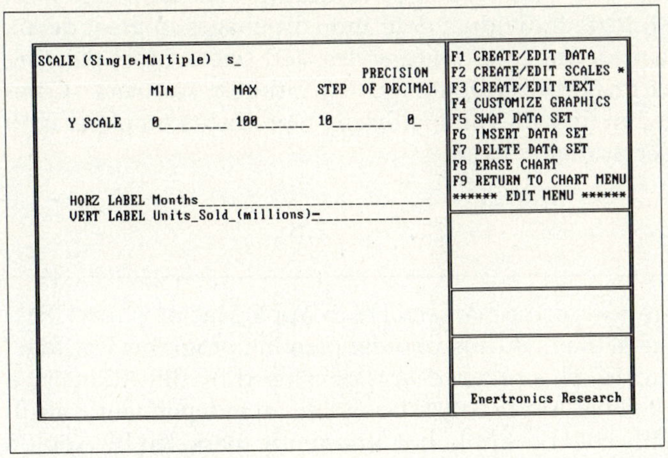


(d) The completed bar chart.

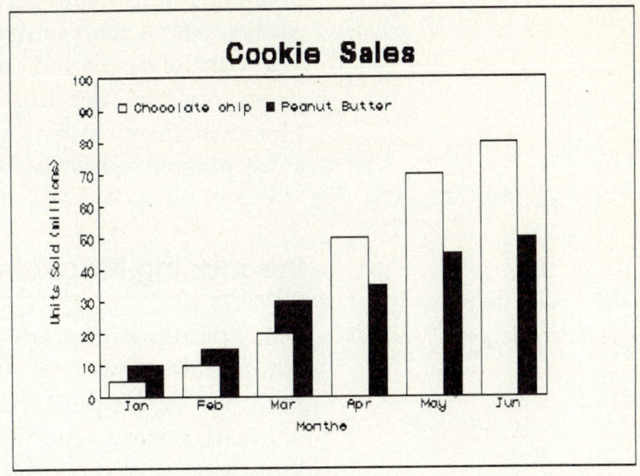


EnerGraphics presents a screen of options that let you alter certain aspects of the chart's appearance. The default values are fine for this graph, so all you have to do is press the **Enter** key. Figure 13.8(d) shows the chart that appears on your screen.

After viewing the chart, you can press any key to return to the Chart menu. Just like the pie chart, the bar chart can be printed, saved in a disk file, modified, and deleted. When you are finished with EnerGraphics, you can press the **F9** key to return to the Main menu, and then press the **Esc** key to return to DOS.

EnerGraphics, like most dedicated charting programs, can do much more than the two simple graphs we've shown in this section. A wide variety of charts can be made with such programs. Their main purpose, however, is to graphically depict data. For more creative images, there are other programs better suited to painting, drawing, designing, and presenting slide shows.

## PAINTING PROGRAMS

*Best suited to freehand painting*

Painting programs make it easy to produce on your computer screen almost any kind of picture you can imagine. These packages are often described as **pixel-based** or **bit-mapped** because they give you ultimate control over every single dot on the screen. Although early painting programs were considered to be little more than toys, many current versions are impressive design and illustration tools. Artists can use painting programs as another vehicle of expression; the rest of us can use them to produce figures neater and more accurate than we could ever create by hand. For example, some of the figures in this book were first sketched by the author with a painting program before they were redrawn by a professional artist.

Although almost any kind of chart, diagram, figure, and illustration can be produced with a painting program, this type of graphics software is perhaps best suited to free-hand drawing. Several predefined objects like lines, rectangles, and ovals can be incorporated in your creations, but you are by no means limited to these. You can draw your own shapes and use a variety of shading patterns. Many painting programs let you fully utilize the color capabilities of your display adapter and monitor. Sections of the screen and individual objects can be moved, copied, deleted, rotated, and flipped over horizontally or vertically. You can zoom in on parts of the screen to manipulate individual dots and edit images in great detail. Text can be displayed in a wide range of fonts, styles, and sizes. Most painting programs can even import images from full-page or hand-held scanners. Completed pictures can be saved in disk files and faithfully reproduced on paper with a dot-matrix, ink-jet, or laser printer.

## Introducing MacPaint

*A popular Macintosh painter*

Many painting programs are now on the market for both Apple Macintosh and IBM-compatible computers. One of the first truly popular painting programs was MacPaint for the Apple Macintosh. This program was developed by Bill Atkinson, a software wizard who worked for Apple before becoming an independent consultant. MacPaint was originally sold by Apple, but is currently marketed by Apple's software spinoff, a company named Claris. Originally, a copy of MacPaint was included with every Macintosh at no extra charge. This software, available since the introduction of the Macintosh back in 1984, was probably a major reason many early customers purchased Apple's newest computer in the first place. MacPaint has been continually upgraded and is still one of the most popular of all Macintosh programs, even though you no longer get a free copy with every new computer (it now costs $125).

In many ways, MacPaint is the perfect example of a painting program. It has all the basic features found in most painting programs, yet is well-designed and simple to use. In fact, MacPaint is so self-explanatory that most users rarely feel the need to consult the manual, which is only thirty-two pages long (for version 1.5). By experimentation, beginners quickly learn the drawing skills they need to produce pictures. Yet despite its simplicity, MacPaint is a highly flexible program with an impressive set of powerful features. In skilled hands, it can produce striking illustrations like the one you see in Figure 13.9. As an example of a painting program, let's explore MacPaint and see what it can do.

**Figure 13.9 MacPaint: A Painting Program**
MacPaint is one of the most popular painting programs for Apple Macintosh computers.

## The MacPaint Screen

*Computer easel*

On the Macintosh, you start a program by moving the pointer to its icon and **double clicking** (pressing the mouse button twice in rapid succession). Like most painting programs, MacPaint requires a mouse or some other graphics input device such as a trackball or tablet. After the program is loaded into memory, MacPaint presents the screen you see in Figure 13.10. Although there are differences in various painting programs, most of them present a screen similar to this one. The MacPaint screen has five distinct sections:

- *Pull-Down Menus.* With their titles listed across the top of the screen, these menus contain commands for manipulating all or part of your picture. You open a menu by pointing to its title with the mouse and then holding down the mouse button. A menu option is selected by highlighting it with the mouse button held down and then releasing the button.
- *Tool Palette.* At the left side of the screen is a group of boxes filled with symbols. This **tool palette** contains icons that represent tools you can use to draw, add text, move to different parts of the page, and select parts of your picture. The tool shown in reverse video (white on black) is the one currently selected.
- *Border Palette.* Just below the tools, in the lower left corner of the screen, is a group of short line segments. These show the types of lines you can use in your picture. This **border palette** is where you select the thickness MacPaint will use to draw lines and outline shapes. The segment with the check mark beside it shows the current width selection.
- *Pattern Palette.* Along the bottom of the screen is an area known as the **pattern palette**. This shows the patterns you can use with the tools to draw objects and fill in enclosed areas on the screen. The larger box at the left end of the pattern palette shows the pattern that is the current selection.
- *Drawing Window.* This is the large empty area in the center of the screen, the "canvas" where you actually "paint" your picture. The striped bar across the top of the drawing window shows the name of the current picture, which MacPaint refers to as a *document*. Until you specify a name, the picture document is simply labeled *untitled*.

## The MacPaint Pointer

*Mastering mouse techniques*

Another important item to note on the MacPaint screen is the pointer. Right now, the pointer is that black dot in the upper left corner of the drawing window in Figure 13.10. It takes on different shapes, depending on which tool you're using. When the pointer is outside the drawing window, it looks like an arrow and is used to make menu, tool, and palette selections. When the pointer is inside the drawing window, it's used to draw and select portions of the picture for manipulation on the screen.

To use a painting program, you must master three basic mouse techniques. The first is simply **moving** the pointer, which is accomplished by rolling the mouse across the desktop in the direction you want to go. The second technique, known as **clicking**, is used to select tools, line widths, and patterns. This involves moving the mouse pointer on top of the item you want to select, and then briefly pressing and releasing the mouse button. **Dragging** is the third mouse action, which is used to pull down menus, outline parts of the picture, move selections, and "stretch" objects. All you do is position the pointer and hold down the mouse button while you

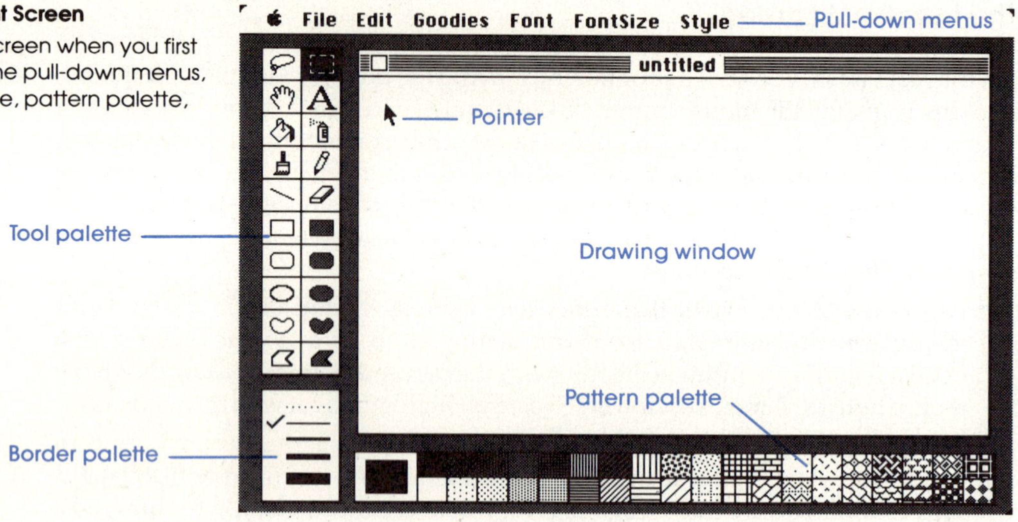


**Figure 13.10 The MacPaint Screen**
This shows the MacPaint screen when you first start the program. Note the pull-down menus, tool palette, border palette, pattern palette, and drawing window.

move the mouse. When you've reached the final position, you then release the mouse button. These three mouse pointer actions are used over and over when working with a painting program such as MacPaint.

## The MacPaint Tools

*The artist's arsenal*

The twenty tools you see on the screen in Figure 13.10 are typical features you find in most painting programs. These tools, used in conjunction with the patterns, border widths, and a few menu commands, give you the potential to produce almost any kind of picture you can imagine. There is an endless array of visual effects you can achieve by combining the various MacPaint options. Unfortunately, it still takes skill and patience to create truly artistic work. Nevertheless, the tools provide a way for any user to produce accurate shapes and neat lettering. Before we go on to actually create a picture with MacPaint, let's briefly describe each of the tools, starting with the upper-left corner in Figure 13.10:

- *Lasso.* Looking like a cowboy's lariat, the lasso is used to encircle irregularly shaped objects and select them to be moved, deleted, or changed in some manner.
- *Selection Rectangle.* This dashed rectangle is stretched to enclose rectangular areas to be manipulated in some fashion.
- *Grabber.* This hand-shaped tool is used to shift the picture document under the drawing window so you can use an entire 8-by-10-inch page.
- *Text.* The letter A symbolizes the tool that is used to enter text into a picture. The font, size, and style of the characters can be chosen from the corresponding pull-down menus.
- *Paint Bucket.* This tool is used to fill an enclosed area with the currently selected pattern.
- *Spray Paint Can.* Simulating the effect of spray painting, this tool is used to gradually shade areas with the currently selected pattern.

- *Paintbrush.* As you move the mouse with the button held down, this tool leaves behind a brush stroke in the currently selected pattern. You can change the shape, size, and slant of the simulated paintbrush by choosing the Brush Shape option from the Goodies menu.
- *Pencil.* This tool draws a thin freehand line—black on white backgrounds and white on black backgrounds.
- *Line.* Symbolized by a diagonal line, this tool draws a straight black line in any direction you drag the mouse pointer.
- *Eraser.* Like a magical gum eraser, this tool wipes away anything in its path.
- *Rectangles.* These tools are used to draw sharp-cornered squares and rectangles. The empty one produces just a hollow outline, while the darker tool automatically fills the rectangle with the current pattern.
- *Rounded Rectangles.* These tools draw hollow and filled rectangles with slightly rounded corners.
- *Ovals.* These two tools are used to draw hollow and filled circles and ovals.
- *Freehand Shapes.* The heart-shaped tools are used to create hollow and filled freehand shapes.
- *Polygons.* The last two tools are used to create hollow and filled geometric shapes with multiple straight-line sides.

## Designing a Logo with MacPaint

*Steps in logo design*

No painting program will make an artist out of you, but a package such as MacPaint can help you create simple, good-looking figures, even if you have little artistic talent. A typical use for MacPaint might be to design a company's logo. Once it's finished, the logo can be saved in a file and used over and over again in other illustrations, charts, diagrams, and letterheads. Let's use MacPaint to create a logo for a fictional software company called E Z Systems.

The logo we have in mind is simple. The name of the company will be displayed in a slightly shaded circle, which is superimposed on a stripe-filled rectangle. The image will be displayed against a drop shadow to give it a three-dimensional look.

The first step is to choose the fill pattern for the rectangle. How about the one with narrow horizontal stripes? To select this pattern, you position the pointer on top of it and click the mouse button. Now you can choose the filled rectangle tool by pointing to its icon in the tools palette and clicking the mouse button. The pointer takes on a plus sign shape when you move it to the drawing window. To create the rectangle, first position the pointer where you want its upper left corner to be. Then hold down the mouse button and drag the mouse diagonally toward the lower right. This opens and "stretches" the rectangle as you drag. Keeping the mouse button pressed down, you can create a rectangle of the desired size. In our case, the rectangle should be about two inches wide and one inch high (see Figure 13.11(a)).

Next you need to create the circle. The easiest thing to do is to make the circle above, below, or beside the rectangle and then move it on top of the rectangle later. First, you choose the fill pattern for the circle. This time, how about a lightly dotted pattern? Then you select the filled oval tool. Finally, the circle is created like the rectangle—by holding down the mouse button and dragging to open and stretch the shape. The circle should be about 1.5 inches in diameter. Figure 13.11(b) shows the screen so far.

To move the circle on top of the rectangle, you must first lasso the circle. This is done by selecting the lasso tool and using it to completely enclose the circle. Once you do this, the lasso shrinks to fit the outline of the circle, squeezing out any empty space around the border. The edge of the circle flashes to indicate that it is currently selected. To move it, you position the pointer inside the circle, hold down the mouse button, and drag. The circle should be superimposed over the center of the rectangle, as shown in Figure 13.11(c).

The drop shadow is next. First you duplicate the circle-rectangle combination by lassoing it, holding down the **Option** key, and moving the new copy aside. Then you select a gray pattern from the pattern pallet and choose the Fill option from the Edit menu. Your screen now looks like Figure 13.11(d). This time lasso the original circle-rectangle and move it on top of the gray shadow, with a slight offset. Figure 13.11(e) shows the result.

Finally, you need to type the company name and put it inside the circle. You have a wide range of fonts, sizes, and styles of type to choose from in the Font, Font-Size, and Style menus. How about a Geneva font, with a 12-point size, using boldface and shadow styles? Using the Align Middle option also from the Style menu will help to center your text. Select the text tool, move the pointer to an empty spot, and click the mouse button. Now type **E Z SYSTEMS**, pressing the **Return** key after the Z. Lasso the text and move it inside the circle. The completed logo is shown in Figure 13.11(f). The logo can be saved in a disk file with the Save option and printed with the Print option, both of which are in the File menu.

## DRAWING PROGRAMS

*Making precise, scaled drawings*

Drawing programs differ from painting programs in several important respects. First of all, drawing programs are **object-oriented**, not pixel-based. This means that they let you create and manipulate images comprised of only discrete geometric objects such as lines, curves, rectangles, ovals, irregular outlines, polygons, and text. Drawing programs generally do not include freehand pixel painting features such as brush strokes, paint buckets, spray painting, and erasers. Instead, their features facilitate making very precise scaled drawings. In addition, drawing programs usually take better advantage of high-resolution, hard-copy output devices. For example, although MacPaint reproduces screen images on paper very well, these images have a resolution of only 72 dots per inch, even on a laser printer capable of 300 dots per inch. Drawing programs typically produce sharper output on paper with both dot-matrix and laser printers. Hence they are better suited than most painting programs for architectural renderings, layouts, blueprints, diagrams, charts, maps, mechanical drawings, and other technical illustrations.

In short, drawing programs are good for making structured figures. They are easy-to-use tools for simple drafting applications. Drawing programs let you define on-screen rulers and accurately scale objects to metric or English measurements. Objects keep their individual identities, even if they are partially or completely obscured by other objects. Shapes can be selected, moved, stretched, duplicated, and deleted as needed. An on-screen **grid**, like the squares on graph paper, can be used to keep objects lined up with each other. Many drawing programs can create figures much larger than a single 8-by-10-inch page. Reduction, enlargement, and scrolling features make it easier to work on drawings that are very detailed or too big to fit within a single screen. Although drawing programs don't let you erase parts of an object or edit individual pixels, they do let you change the way objects look by moving them, resizing them, and altering their border and fill patterns.

**Figure 13.11 Designing a Logo with MacPaint**

(a) Create a rectangle with horizontal stripes.

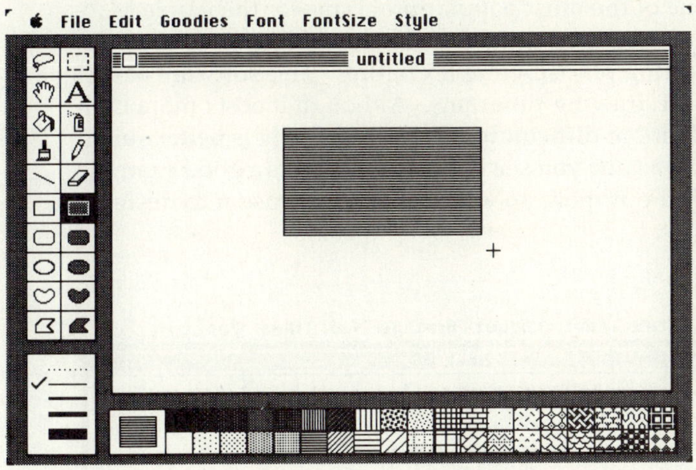


(b) Create a circle filled with a lightly dotted pattern.

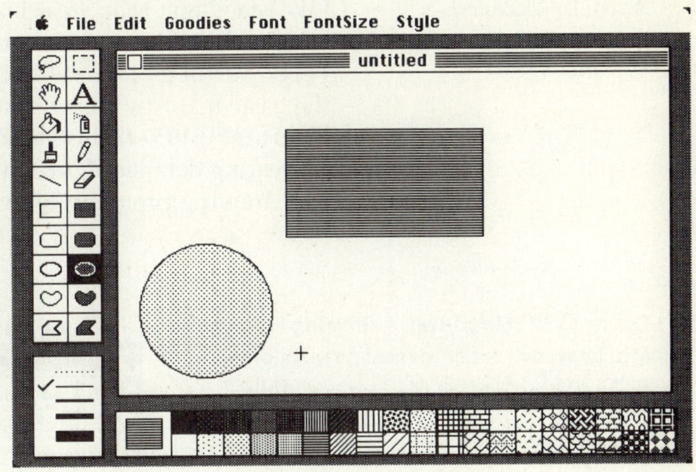


(c) Lasso the circle and move it on top of the rectangle.

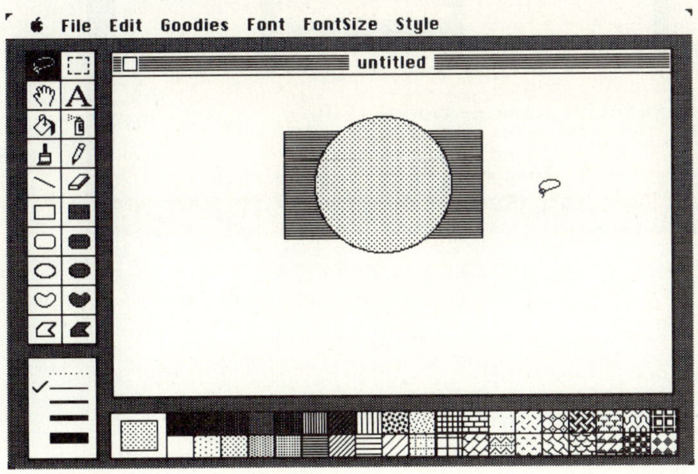


(d) Lasso the circle and rectangle, duplicate them, and select the gray pattern to create the drop shadow.

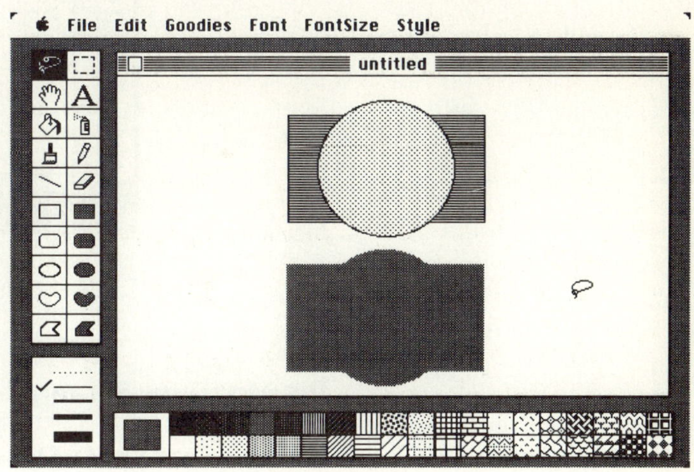


(e) Move the circle and rectangle on top of the drop shadow.

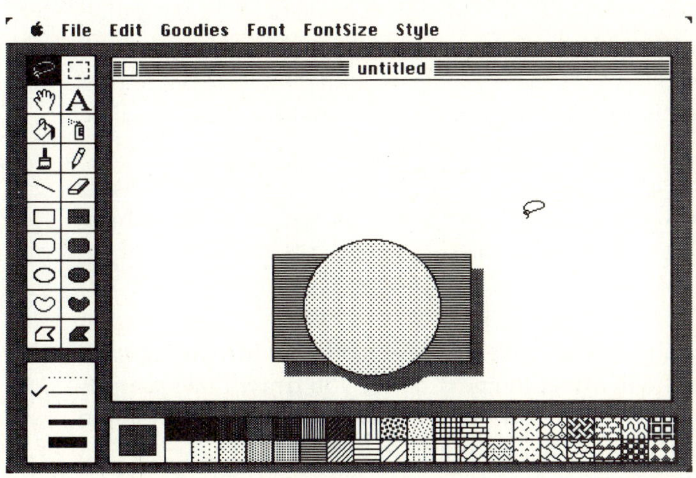


(f) Select the font, size, and style and then enter the text to complete the logo.

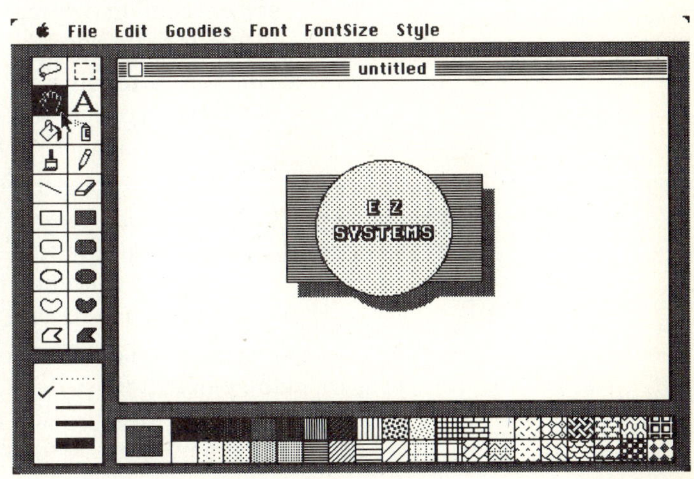

## Introducing MacDraw

*A popular Macintosh drawing program*

Like MacPaint, MacDraw is one of the most popular programs for the Apple Macintosh. Other drawing programs may offer more features, but MacDraw is a simple, yet powerful tool for easily creating precise, complex figures. This software has all the basic features found in most drawing programs. Although it costs more than MacPaint ($195) and is slightly more difficult to master, MacDraw is better suited to creating detailed figures like the one you see in Figure 13.12. As a good example of a drawing program, let's find out more about MacDraw and use it to design a figure.

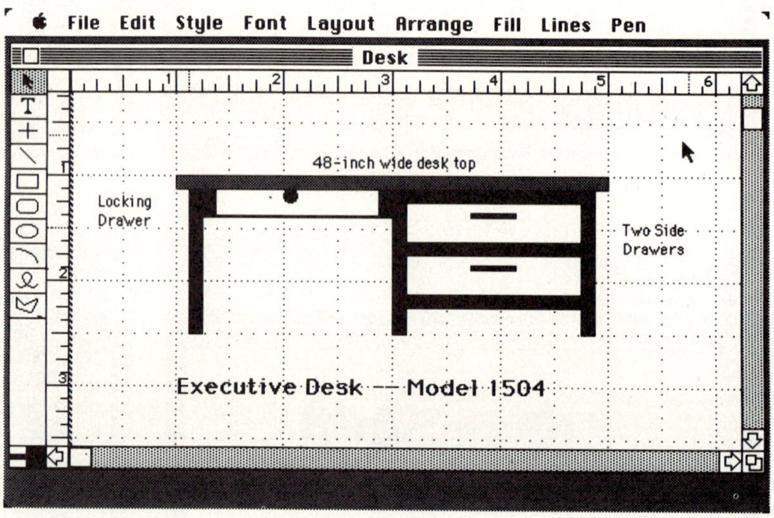


**Figure 13.12 MacDraw: A Drawing Program**
MacDraw is one of the most popular drawing programs for Apple Macintosh computers.

## The MacDraw Screen

*Computer drafting table*

When you start up MacDraw, the program presents a screen like the one you see in Figure 13.13. It looks a little like the MacPaint screen, but there are some important differences. Figure 13.13 labels the key items, which include:

- *Pull-Down Menus.* These menus, with their titles listed across the top of the screen, contain commands for controlling how the tools work and manipulating your drawings.
- *Title Bar.* Extending across the top of the drawing window, the title bar shows the name of the current document, and on the left side contains the Close Box, which you can click on to close the current drawing file.
- *Tool Palette.* Along the left side of the screen are the icons that represent your drawing tools. Except for the top one, the selection tool, each of these tools creates a single graphic object. Remember: a graphic object is an individual entity and not a collection of pixels, as is a MacPaint shape. The currently selected tool is shown in reverse video.
- *Line/Pattern Box.* This area shows the currently selected line width along with the pen and fill pattern that will affect the next object you draw. The *pen pattern* is the design used to draw lines and borders, while the *fill pattern* is the design used inside solid objects such as rectangles and ovals.

- *Scroll Bars.* As we said in Chapter 6, scroll bars are used to move within a document. These MacDraw scroll bars let you see different parts of your drawing by moving it up, down, and sideways behind the window.
- *Size Box.* This little box at the intersection of the scroll bars can be dragged to change the size of your drawing window.
- *Drawing Window.* This is the "drafting table" where you create your drawings. Note the dotted ruler lines that are turned on by default to help you precisely size and align your objects.

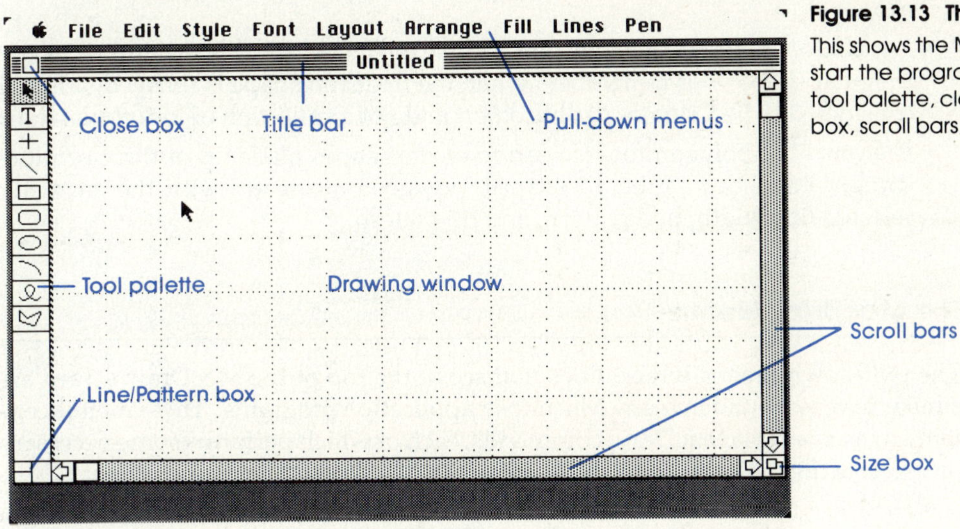


**Figure 13.13 The MacDraw Screen**
This shows the MacDraw screen when you first start the program. Note the pull-down menus, tool palette, close box, title bar, line/pattern box, scroll bars, size box, and drawing window.

## The MacDraw Tools

*Create or modify geometric objects*

As you can see from Figure 13.13, there are fewer MacDraw tools than there are MacPaint tools. These tools are typical of the ones found in many drawing programs. With the exception of the first, all the tools are used to create or modify a particular type of geometric object. To select a particular tool, you simply move the pointer on top of its icon and click the mouse button. The currently selected tool is shown in reverse video. Starting from the top of the tool palette, the MacDraw tools include:

- *Selection.* The selection tool, whose icon is shaped like an arrow, allows you to select, move, and resize objects that have already been drawn.
- *Text.* You can create captions, labels, and even entire paragraphs by selecting the text tool, clicking anywhere within the drawing window, and typing. Various character fonts, sizes, and styles can be selected from the Font and Style menus.
- *Perpendicular Line.* This tool allows you to create only perfectly straight horizontal and vertical lines. The lines are drawn with the currently selected line width and pen pattern, as are all lines drawn with any of the tools that create graphic objects.
- *Diagonal Line.* A line can be drawn at any angle with this tool. Although the diagonal line tool can draw perfectly straight horizontal and vertical lines too, this is easier to do with the perpendicular line tool.

- *Rectangle.* This tool lets you create sharp-cornered rectangles and squares. The shapes are made with the currently selected line width, pen pattern, and fill pattern.
- *Round-Cornered Rectangle.* This is just like the previous tool, except that it draws rectangles with rounded corners.
- *Oval.* The oval tool is used to draw ellipses and circles with the currently selected line width, pen pattern, and fill pattern.
- *Arc.* This tool lets you make 90-degree arcs; in other words, quarter circles and ovals.
- *Freehand Shape.* With this tool, you can use the mouse to trace the outline of any irregular shape. But remember: when the freehand shape is finished, it is still considered to be a single graphic object and not a collection of individual dots.
- *Polygon.* The polygon tool is used to create shapes made up of three or more straight-line sides. Like all shapes, polygons are made with the currently selected line width, pen pattern, and fill pattern.

## The MacDraw Menus

*MacDraw commands*

The pull-down menus whose titles you see at the top of the MacDraw screen are similar to those found in many Macintosh application programs. These menus contain all the available MacDraw commands, each of which performs some necessary or useful action. Figure 13.14 shows all of the MacDraw menus, including:

- *File.* The commands in this menu allow you to create a new drawing, begin work on an existing drawing, discard the current drawing, save the current drawing in a file, print the current drawing, and quit the MacDraw program.
- *Edit.* This menu contains editing commands that allow you to undo the most recent action; cut, copy, and paste objects from one place to another; and reshape, smooth, and round the outlines of some objects.
- *Style.* The commands in the Style menu allow you to set the character style, alignment, line spacing, and capitalization of text in a caption or paragraph.
- *Font.* This menu allows you to set the typeface and size of characters created with the text tool.
- *Layout.* The Layout menu contains commands for setting up on-screen rulers and grids, as well as enlarging and reducing parts of a drawing.
- *Arrange.* This menu allows you to control the way objects are stacked up, grouped together, and aligned in a drawing. It also contains commands to rotate and create mirror images of existing objects.
- *Fill.* This menu offers thirty-six patterns you can select to fill your shapes and use as the background of captions and paragraphs. A special pattern, called "None," lets you make an object into an empty frame, allowing objects behind it to show through.
- *Lines.* This menu allows you to select the appearance of lines and the borders of all objects except text.
- *Pen.* The Pen menu offers the same thirty-six patterns as the Fill menu, but it just operates on lines and the borders of objects.

**Figure 13.14 The MacDraw Menus**
Here are all of MacDraw's pull-down menus.

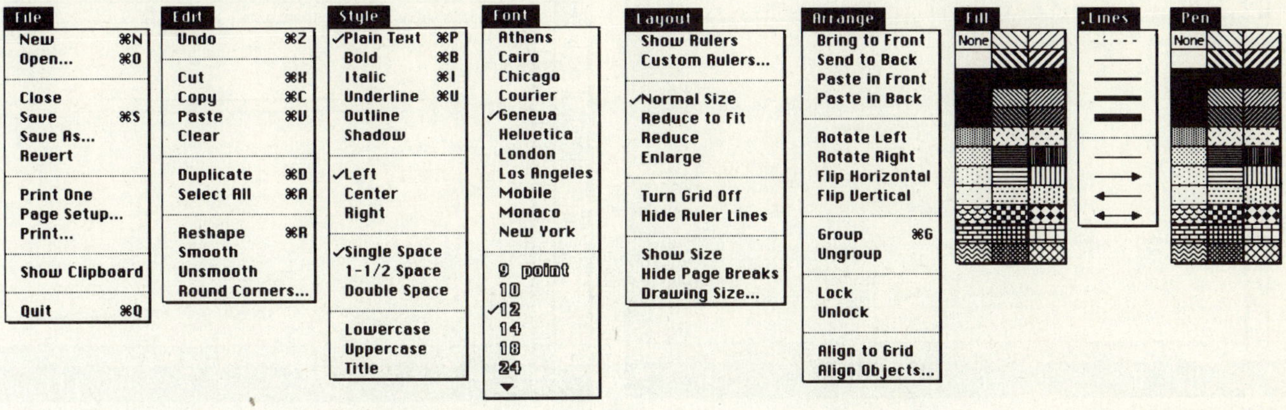


## Designing a Desk with MacDraw

*Using MacDraw*

Suppose that you work at an office furniture design company, and your task is to sketch the plans for a new desk model. Since the desk plans must be precisely scaled and will be made up of relatively simple shapes, you decide to use MacDraw to create your design. After starting up the program, the first step is to turn on the display of rulers along the top and left sides of the drawing window (see Figure 13.15(a)). This is done by selecting the Show Rulers option from the Layout menu. By default, the ruler scale is in inches, but you can use the metric system or create your own custom rulers instead. In your case, inches are just fine because you decide that one inch in the drawing will represent one foot in the actual desk. To keep this example simple, we'll just do the front view of the desk.

The desk top is to be four feet wide, so you can represent it in your drawing by a thin rectangle four inches wide. You select the rectangle tool and move the mouse pointer to a convenient starting position, say one inch from the top and one inch from the left. As you move the pointer with the rulers turned on, your exact position in the drawing is precisely indicated by a dotted line in each ruler. Once the pointer is at the desired upper left corner, you hold down the mouse button and drag open the rectangle. After you stretch the rectangle so that it's four inches wide, you release the mouse button. It's easy to do this with accuracy, because objects are automatically aligned to the grid in the drawing window. At this point, your screen looks like Figure 13.15(b).

*Options for manipulating your drawing*

Each of the six little black squares you see on the boundary of the rectangle is called a **handle**. When an existing object is selected, you can drag any of its handles to resize it. Handles only appear when an object is selected and do not show up when it is printed. To move an entire object, all you have to do is position the selection tool pointer within the object and drag it anywhere on the screen.

Now you can use rectangles, lines, and any other shapes you need to finish the desk design. Fill patterns can be selected to fill in the shapes. Labels and measurements can be added to annotate the plans. When you're finished, your screen might look something like Figure 13.15(c). At this point, the drawing can be saved on a disk and printed by using options from the File menu. When it is printed, the drawing will not display any rulers, grid lines, or handles. The lines and text will be as sharp as the printer can manage. On a laser printer, this will look very nice. But even on a dot-matrix printer, drawing programs generally produce crisper output than painting programs.

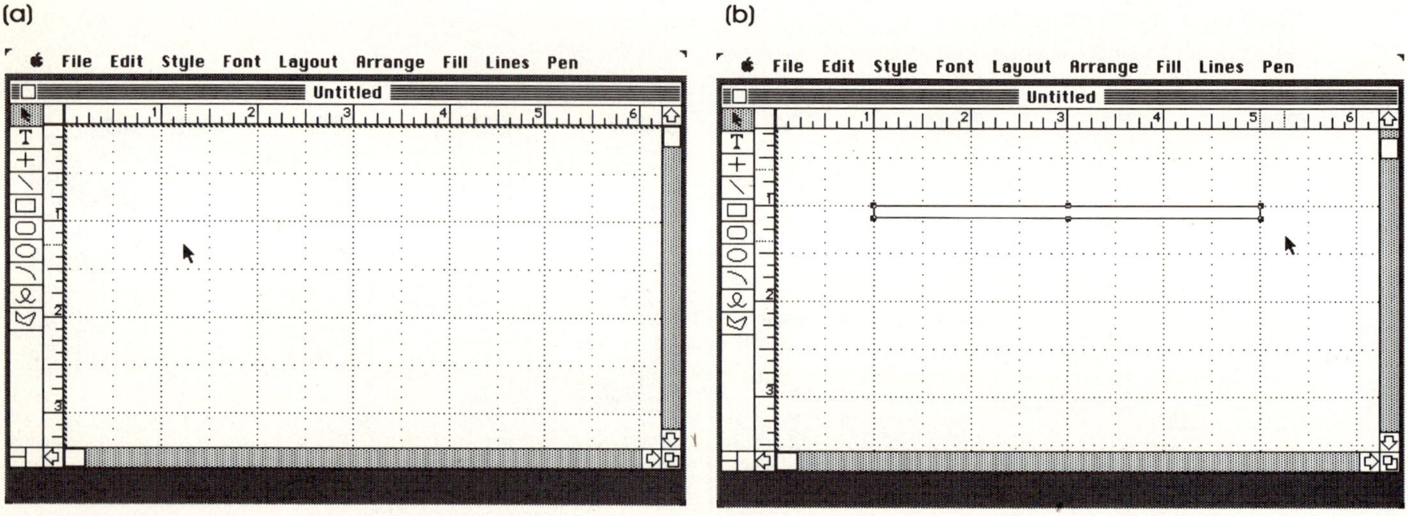


**Figure 13.15 Designing a Desk with MacDraw**
(a) Turn on the display of rulers.
(b) Create the desktop with the rectangle tool.
(c) Use rectangles, lines, and other shapes and fill patterns to finish the desk design.

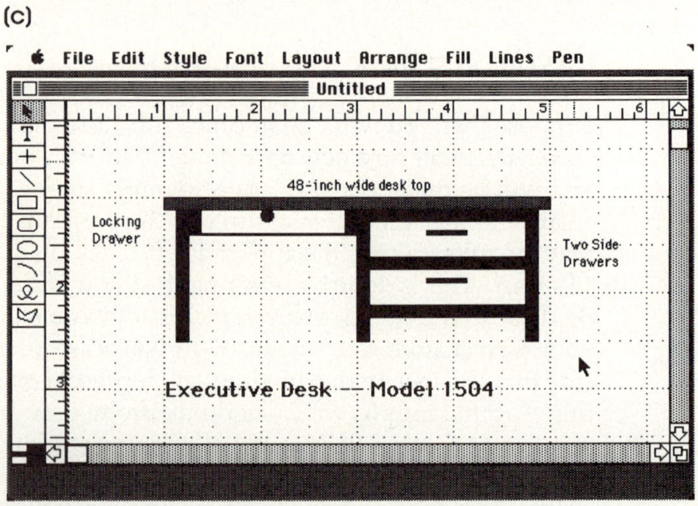


## COMPUTER-AIDED DESIGN PROGRAMS

*Sophisticated drafting packages*

Drawing programs such as MacDraw are fine for relatively simple plans, diagrams, and blueprints. Although drawing programs can be used to produce detailed figures, they are not powerful enough for many engineering, architectural, and technical illustrations. For truly complex drafting applications, **computer-aided design**, or **CAD**, packages are much better. They are typically used for drafting plans, blueprints, models, schematics, and other detailed drawings of parts, mechanisms, and buildings. These programs have been used for years on large computer systems, and have become increasingly popular on microcomputers. Thanks to recent technological advances, microcomputer CAD systems now can do many things that mainframe CAD systems can do, only at a fraction of the cost.

Although CAD programs are generally more difficult to learn how to use than are painting and drawing programs, they still have a wide range of potential users. Mechanical engineers, architects, circuit board designers, civil engineers, surveyors, interior planners, and graphic artists are just a few examples of the many diverse professionals who are using CAD packages. Almost anyone who routinely makes complex, detailed drawings can be helped by a CAD package. Consequently, tens of thousands of CAD hardware and software systems are installed every year.

Besides being more difficult to learn, CAD programs are usually significantly more expensive than painting and drawing programs. For example, while many good painting and drawing programs can be purchased for around $100, most full-featured microcomputer CAD packages cost more than $2000. Although this might seem like a hefty price tag, microcomputer CAD packages are quite a bargain compared to the cost of similar CAD systems for larger computers.

Finally, CAD programs also require more sophisticated hardware components than most painting and drawing programs. To make the best use of a CAD package, you need a powerful microcomputer, a high-resolution color display adapter and monitor, a good mouse or graphics tablet, and a color printer or plotter. Despite their steep learning curve, cost, and hardware requirements, CAD programs are still popular because of their unparalleled ability to create extremely detailed drawings.

## CAD Features

*Advanced options for technical illustration*

Like drawing programs, CAD software is object-oriented. This means that a complicated set of drawing and editing capabilities is used to create and manipulate individual graphic objects, which are sometimes called primitives, elements, or entities. These objects typically include points, lines, curves, arcs, circles, ellipses, rectangles, squares, polygons, and free-form shapes. Some programs also let you draw three-dimensional solids.

You can usually locate objects on the drawing in several different ways. Exact coordinates can be entered at the keyboard, or a mouse or tablet can be used to indicate where objects are to be put. Because precise scaling is so important in most drafting and design applications, good CAD programs let you work in almost any measurement system. For example, when drafting a small mechanical part you can use a centimeter scale, but then switch to feet for an architectural blueprint.

Most CAD packages offer grid and snap features. Like the squares on graph paper, a **grid** is a visual aid for placing objects in the drawing. **Snap** is a feature that automatically aligns objects to the nearest grid lines. Still other drawing aids place axes on the screen, display the current cursor coordinates, and constrain movement to horizontal and vertical directions. You can *zoom in* on objects to get a closer look and *zoom out* to see the big picture. A **pan** feature is usually available to let you move the viewing window up, down, left, or right.

Once objects have been drawn, they must often be edited in various ways. Two CAD editing commands commonly used in drafting are fillet and chamfer. **Fillet** joins two lines to create a rounded corner, while **chamfer** joins two lines with another straight line. Other editing features let you move, copy, erase, rotate, reverse, resize, trim, and fill objects.

For especially complex figures, many CAD programs let you create drawings made up of several layers or levels. A **layer** is like a transparent overlay sheet on a chart: you can create it separately and then superimpose it on top of other layers. Individual layers can be pulled out, viewed, and printed by themselves. Since most CAD programs can also draw in several colors, this layering ability makes them ideal for designing electronic schematics, architectural plans, and other engineering diagrams.

Finally, CAD programs let you save your drawings in disk files and produce accurate reproductions on paper. They typically support a wide range of printers and plotters. Some even work with film recorders to make 35-mm slides directly from the screen.

## Introducing AutoCAD

*The most popular micro CAD package*

AutoCAD, from Autodesk Incorporated, is the single most popular microcomputer CAD package on the market today. With more than 100,000 copies sold, this software is used in some 44 percent of all microcomputer-based CAD installations. Like Lotus 1-2-3 and dBASE, AutoCAD has become a *de facto* standard in the industry. More third-party books, programs, and hardware devices are available for AutoCAD than for any other CAD package. It's a powerful, flexible program against which all other CAD packages are measured.

Originally, AutoCAD was designed for IBM-compatible computers under the DOS operating system, but a version is now available for the Apple Macintosh, too. The package supports an unusually wide range of display adapters, graphics input devices, printers, and plotters. This comprehensive package is one of the most sophisticated graphics applications you can find on a microcomputer. Expensive and time-consuming to fully master, AutoCAD is clearly not for everyone. Nevertheless, if you have to do detailed drafting projects, like the one you see in Figure 13.16, then AutoCAD may be just what you need.

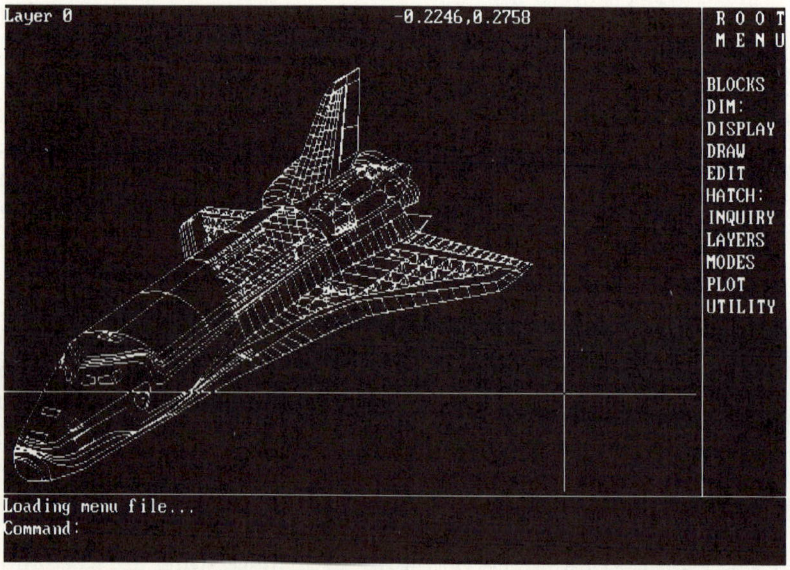


**Figure 13.16 AutoCAD**
AutoCAD is a sophisticated computer-aided design package for creating detailed diagrams.

## Designing a Floor Plan with AutoCAD

As we have said, AutoCAD is a sophisticated software package that is not particularly easy to master. The program has many advanced features and it works quite differently than painting and drawing programs. Although we cannot possibly demonstrate all of AutoCAD's powerful capabilities, we can illustrate a few of its features with a simple example. Since AutoCAD is well-suited to many architectural applications, let's use it on an IBM-compatible computer to design the floor plan of a two-bedroom condominium.

*Starting AutoCAD*

Once you turn on your computer, boot DOS, and switch to the proper subdirectory, you start AutoCAD by typing **ACAD** and pressing the **Enter** key. The program then presents its Main menu, which is shown in Figure 13.17(a). After you enter **1** to begin a new drawing, AutoCAD asks you to supply a name for your drawing.

Then the program switches to graphics mode and presents the screen you see in Figure 13.17(b).

Here is where you create your drawing. The top line on the screen presents status information that indicates you're working on layer 0 and your current cursor coordinates are (0,0). The Root menu, listed along the right side of the screen, displays several options, most of which call up additional submenus. You tell AutoCAD what to do by selecting menu options and entering commands at the keyboard. The three lines at the bottom of the screen are where you enter commands and view AutoCAD's responses to your commands. Finally, the two long lines that intersect on the screen are the **crosshair**; this indicates your current cursor position. Although the crosshair can be moved with arrow keys, it's usually manipulated by using a pointing device such as a mouse, trackball, or graphics tablet. The pointing device is also used to highlight and select menu options.

One of the advantages of using a CAD package is the ease with which you can precisely scale your drawings. For working on large objects, such as buildings, you can tell AutoCAD to use architectural units of measurement. This allows you to work directly in feet and inches. You can also specify how much horizontal and vertical space you need to fit on your screen. Furthermore, you can turn on the grid and snap features to accurately line up your objects. Finally, you can have AutoCAD continuously display your current cursor coordinates in feet and inches at the top of the screen. For example, to specify all of these settings, this is what you do:

*Specify settings*

1. Select the Utility option from the Root menu, the Units option from the Utility submenu, and the Architectural option from the Units submenu. This tells AutoCAD to measure objects in feet and inches.
2. Select the Limits option from the Root menu and set the lower left corner coordinates to (0′,0′) and the upper-right corner coordinates to (60′,40′). This gives you 40 vertical feet and at least 60 horizontal feet of space on your screen.
3. Select the Display option, then Zoom, and then All. This ensures that your screen is zoomed out all the way to show the full 60-by-40 feet.
4. Select the Modes option, then the Grid option, and then enter **1′**. This turns on a 1-by-1-foot grid.
5. Select the Modes option, then the Snap option, and then enter **1′**. This "snaps" objects to the 1-by-1-foot grid.
6. Hold down the **Control** key and type **D** to turn on the continuous digital readout of your current crosshair position in feet and inches.

After setting up AutoCAD in this manner, your screen looks like Figure 13.17(c). Now you can begin drawing your floor plan. Switch to the Draw submenu and select the Trace command. Basically, Trace lets you draw a series of connected fat lines—perfect for floor plan walls. AutoCAD asks for the thickness of the line you want to draw and you can also indicate whether the line is to be filled in or left empty like a thin rectangle. The walls in this plan are 6 inches thick. Solid walls are filled in while window sections are left empty. AutoCAD asks you for a starting point and ending point for each line you draw. You can type coordinates or move the crosshair and press the mouse button to indicate each line's endpoints. The grid and crosshair digital readout help you construct rooms that are the right size. Besides the Trace command, you can also use the Line command to draw thin lines, and the Text command to enter labels. Figure 13.17(d) shows the completed floor plan with the grid turned off.

**Figure 13.17 Designing a Floor Plan with AutoCAD**

(a) The Main menu.

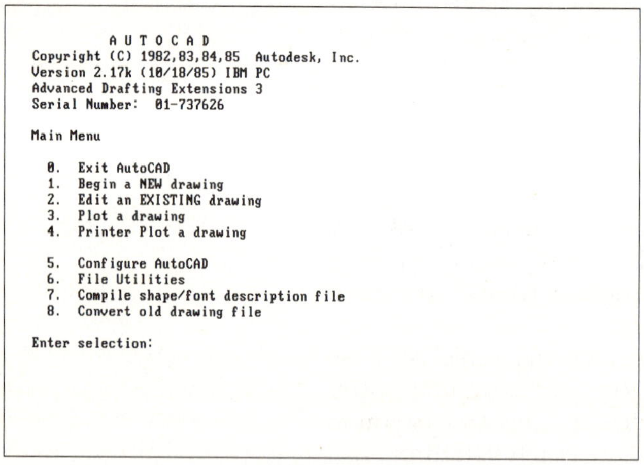


(b) The AutoCAD drawing screen.

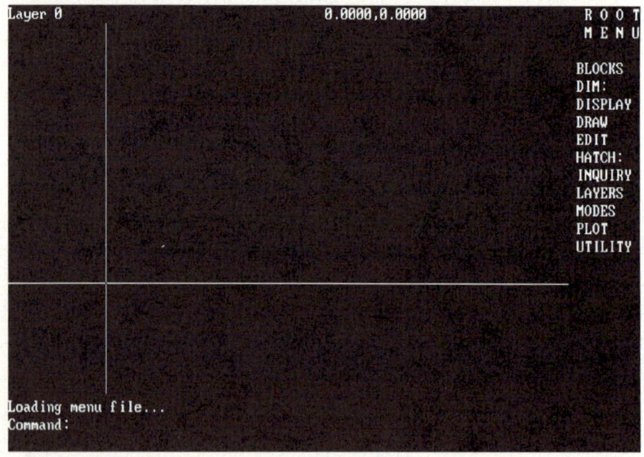


(c) Turning on the Grid and Snap features.

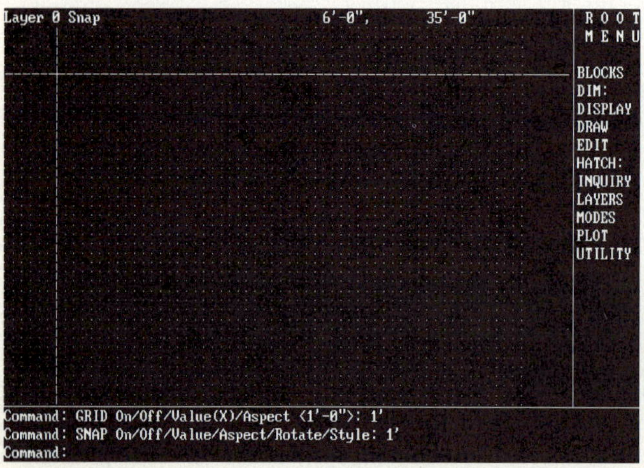


(d) The completed floor plan.

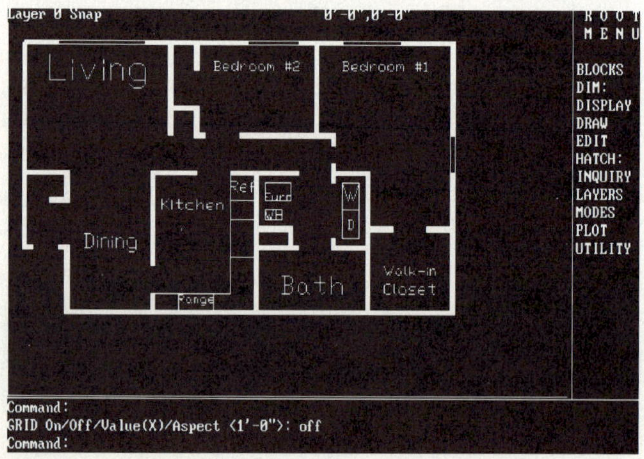


At this point, you can save your drawing in a disk file by returning to the Root menu, selecting the Utility option, and executing the Save command. You also can produce a hard copy on a printer or plotter by using the Plot command from the Root menu or the Main menu.

## SLIDE SHOW PROGRAMS

*Making your point through pictures*

Graphics software is of little use unless you can show the pictures you make to other people. That's why charting, painting, drawing, and CAD programs all let you print or plot your figures. With a film recorder, some of them can also produce 35-mm photographic slides directly from your screen images. Our final category of graphics software takes a different approach to let you produce simulated slide shows on your computer display. A **slide show program** allows you to present a sequence of pictures on your computer screen, either automatically timed to go from picture to picture, or directly controlled by you. These pictures are imported from other graphics programs or produced within the slide show program itself.

A slide show program lets you assemble a series of computer-generated pictures and control the manner in which they are played back on your monitor. For example, the individual pictures can be obtained from other graphics software or produced within the slide show program itself. Once the pictures have been made, you then use the slide show program to specify the order in which you want them to be displayed, as well as how long the computer is to pause before switching slides or whether it is to simply wait for a particular keypress before continuing. A host of special effects can be included to vary the visual transition from one slide to the next. For example, instead of instantly flipping from one picture to another, you can have the computer slowly "dissolve" the image and fade into the next slide. Slide show programs typically allow you to make full use of your computer display's color capabilities. Some packages can even do simple animations.

Computer slide shows have proven to be an effective, inexpensive, and interesting way to present information. Text, numbers, graphs, charts, and freehand drawings can be combined in stunning visual displays. What's more, you don't need a darkened room, and you don't have to wait and pay for photographic film processing. This makes computer slide shows ideal for business presentations, educational demonstrations, tutorial lessons, traffic-stopping advertising pitches, and product descriptions. You see them used in boardrooms, schools, museums, shopping malls, and airports. Computer slide shows can even be presented to large audiences by connecting the controlling computer to a big-screen projection monitor.

## Introducing PC Storyboard

*A popular IBM-compatible slide show generator*

IBM's PC Storyboard is one of the oldest and most popular slide show packages for IBM-compatible microcomputers. Originally introduced in 1985, PC Storyboard is straightforward and easy to use. The package actually consists of four separate programs:

- *Picture Taker.* This is a memory-resident program used to "capture" images from other graphics programs. Once Picture Taker is installed, the Print Screen key works like the shutter button on a camera. You simply hold down the **Shift** key and press the **Print Screen** key to "snap" a picture of your current graphics screen and store it in a disk file. Later, this picture file can be included in a slide show.
- *Picture Maker.* This is a simple graphics editor, somewhat like a primitive painting program. You can use Picture Maker to generate slides for your slide show. It's a command-driven program that lets you draw points, lines, boxes, circles, and text. Picture Maker can also create simple bar graphs, pie charts, and line graphs.
- *Story Editor.* This is the program you use to describe the sequence of pictures in your slide show, how they will be displayed, and how to make the transitions from picture to picture.
- *Story Teller.* This is the program you use to run slide shows previously created with the Story Editor program.

To give you an idea of what it's like to use a slide show package, let's create a simple tutorial with PC Storyboard. This lesson will consist of just three slides that explain how to boot DOS.

## Creating the Pictures

*Making each slide*

The first step is to generate the individual slides that will make up the lesson. If you like, you can install the Picture Taker program and then use your favorite painting program to create each picture. For our simple example, however, the Picture Maker graphics editor will be sufficient. To start the program, you enter **PM** from the DOS prompt. After the IBM copyright notice appears and you press any key to continue, the Picture Maker presents a blank screen with a crosshair cursor in the middle. You move this cursor about by pressing the arrow keys; the current version of the program does not support a mouse. All commands in the Picture Maker are executed by typing a particular key on the keyboard. For example, you can get on-line help by pressing the **F1** key.

Unfortunately, drawing freehand figures with the Picture Maker is not as easy as using a mouse-controlled painting program such as MacPaint. There is, however, a picture library of clip art you can select from and use in your own slides. You press the **F2** function key to bring up the picture library and to page through it. If you find a figure that you like, you can use the C command to copy it from the library and then use the P command to paste it into your own picture. Text can be entered with the T command and positioned by moving the cursor. Colors can be changed with the function keys and areas of the screen filled in with the F command. Figure 13.18(a) shows the first slide of the lesson, created with just these few commands. Once you're finished with the slide, you use the O command to copy it into a disk file, which you might name something like SLIDE1. Then you press **Alt-E** to erase the screen and begin your next slide. The two other slides in our simple lesson, named SLIDE2 and SLIDE3, are shown in Figures 13.18(b) and (c).

There are around 35 Picture Maker commands in all, so we won't go through the rest. They aren't difficult to learn, but you will probably need to read the manual to fully master them. When you've finished creating slides, you press **Alt-Q** to quit the Picture Maker program and return to the operating system.

## Editing the Slide Show

*Putting the slides together*

Story Editor is the PC Storyboard program that lets you make a slide show out of your previously created pictures. Unlike Picture Maker, Story Editor is very easy to use. You start the program by entering **SE** from the DOS prompt. After you press any key to clear the IBM copyright notice screen, you enter a new file name, say LESSON1, to create a new slide show. Story Editor then presents the form you see in Figure 13.19(a). You specify how your slide show will progress by entering information into the columns of this story table. Each line in the table represents one step in your slide show.

Figure 13.19(b) reveals the completed story table for our simple slide show. Examine the row for Slide1. The display method is Diagonal, which means that the picture will appear by sweeping diagonally across the screen. The direction is Down, so the diagonal sweep will proceed from top to bottom. The Line setting is None, which means that there will not be a line sweeping across the screen as the new picture appears. The Time setting of 1 indicates that it will take one second to complete the diagonal sweep as the picture appears. This picture will stay on the screen until a key is pressed, as indicated in the column labeled *Then wait for*. The *Pal* column indicates the color *palette,* which is the set of all foreground colors that can be on the screen at the same time. LCMW stands for low-intensity cyan, magenta, and white. The background color is black. The Area setting is Full, which means that the entire screen will be used.

Once you complete the story table, you can press the **F4** function key to try out the show. If you're not satisfied, you can simply go back and change the table to

(a)

(b)

(c)

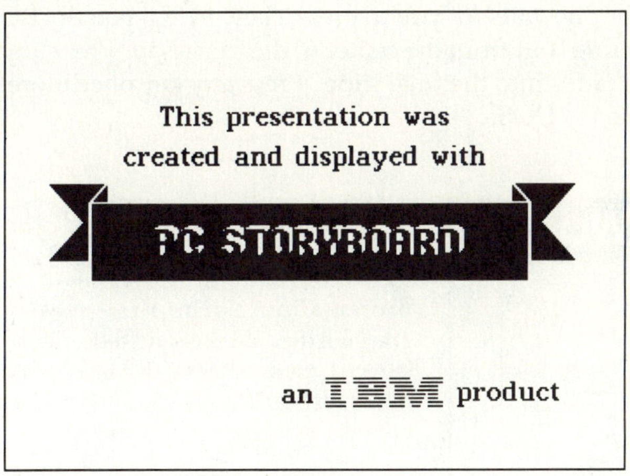


**Figure 13.18 Creating Slides**
These are the three pictures or "slides" of our simple, computer-simulated slide show.
(a) Slide 1
(b) Slide 2
(c) Slide 3

**Figure 13.19 Editing the Story**
(a) This table is where you specify how your slide show will progress.

PC STORYBOARD Story Editor
Edit the Story

Story Name LESSON1

| Label | Picture Name or Command | Display picture using: Method | Dir | Line | Time | Then wait for | Set Color Pal | Back | Area |
|---|---|---|---|---|---|---|---|---|---|
| | | REPLACE | UP | CYN | FAST | KEY | LCMW | BLK | FULL |

FUNCTION KEYS F1 Help F2 Editing Keys | F3 Step Story F4 Run Story F5 View Picture | F6 Save Story sF6 Save & Quit F7 Print Story | F8 Select Story sF8 Quit (NO Save) F9/10 Rotate

(b) The completed slide show table.

PC STORYBOARD Story Editor
Edit the Story

Story Name LESSON1

| Label | Picture Name or Command | Display picture using: Method | Dir | Line | Time | Then wait for | Set Color Pal | Back | Area |
|---|---|---|---|---|---|---|---|---|---|
| | slide1 | DIAGONAL | DOWN | NONE | 1 | KEY | LCMW | BLK | FULL |
| | slide2 | EXPLODE | OUT-H | NONE | 1 | KEY | | | |
| | slide3 | FADE | OUT-H | NONE | 1 | KEY | | | |

FUNCTION KEYS F1 Help F2 Editing Keys | F3 Step Story F4 Run Story F5 View Picture | F6 Save Story sF6 Save & Quit F7 Print Story | F8 Select Story sF8 Quit (NO Save) F9/10 Rotate try different options. When you're finished with the slide show, you hold down the **Shift** key and press **F6** to save it on your disk, quit Story Editor, and return to DOS.

## Presenting the Slide Show

*Running Story Teller*

Although you can use Story Editor to view your slide show as you develop it, the Story Teller program is what you normally use to run a completed slide show. IBM allows you to copy and distribute Story Teller along with your pictures, provided each diskette is appropriately labeled to acknowledge IBM's copyright on the program. This makes PC Storyboard handy for making demonstrations and tutorials that will be sold or given away to others.

Running Story Teller is easy. To start our example slide show, simply enter **ST LESSON1**. Story Teller's one drawback is that you get IBM's logo and copyright notice at the beginning of every show. After you press any key, however, this notice disappears and the slide show proceeds. In our example, the screen clears and an invisible diagonal line sweeps across it from top left to lower right, revealing the first slide. Then the program simply waits for you to press a key. When you do, the second slide appears by "exploding" out from the center of the first slide. Press any key again, and the second slide fades into the final slide. Press any key once more, and Story Teller ends and returns to DOS.

### The Real World

## Graphics Gain a Foothold

Managers can be 43 percent more effective if they use computer-generated graphics in their presentations, researcher Gary W. Dickson believes.

Dickson, who is a member of the Minnesota Managerial Graphics Project at the University of Minnesota School of Management, bases his conclusion on more than fifteen experiments with 1500 subjects. "There is tremendous oral and written support of communication using graphics," he said.

Mark Carroll, assistant to the president of Southwestern Bell, produces monthly graphs of customer complaints on his personal computer and updates them daily to quickly spot trends. He converts the graphs into color handouts and overhead transparencies when it's time to present his findings to upper management. "I can paint my message better in pictures than I can in words," he says.

Virginia Johnson, marketing development and training manager at 3M's Audio Visual Division, a sponsor of the Minnesota Project, believes that the creative use of computer graphics makes managers more productive by making meetings more effective. Since managers can spend around 40 percent of their time in meetings, the increased productivity is significant.

Presentation graphics—computer graphics converted to overhead transparencies, color slides, or hard copy with an ink-jet printer, dot-matrix printer, or plotter—is not the only tool that businesses use today. Desktop video is rapidly gaining popularity. Combining the technologies of microcomputer and video, desktop video produces low-cost, high-resolution graphic shows that look as if they were produced in a studio.

Ernst & Whinney, a Hartford, Connecticut-based accounting firm, uses the new desktop video technology to pep up its client presentations. The firm uses graphics that dissolve and fade, titles that dance across the screen, and strobe-like effects. "We're presenting the same information," according to L. Ward Holdridge, "but now we're drawing rave reviews."

International Data Corporation reports that U.S. companies will spend $536.4 million a year on business graphics for microcomputers by 1990, which is up from $215.6 million in 1985. Advances in hardware, such as the laser printer, is one reason for the growth. The high expectations of a visually oriented society is another.

Sources:

"Computer Graphics: Seeing Is Believing," by June Rogoznica, *Newsweek Special Advertising Supplement on Business Technology*, November 2, 1987, p. S-10.

"Graphics Come of Age," by Karen Berney, *Nation's Business*, June, 1987, pp. 53-55.

"Now Playing at an Office Near You—Desktop Videos," by Jeffrey Rotfeder, *Business Week*, June 1, 1987, pp. 85-86.

## Summary

- *The hardware of microcomputer graphics.* In addition to the computer, four primary components are necessary: a graphics display adapter, a graphics monitor, a graphics input device, and a hard-copy output device.
- *The basic types of microcomputer graphics software.* Although many packages use graphics, the most popular categories are charting, painting, drawing, computer-aided design, and slide show programs.
- *How to use a charting program.* Charting programs, such as EnerGraphics, let you enter or import data to create all kinds of pie charts, bar graphs, line plots, and statistical graphs.
- *How to use a painting program.* Painting programs, such as MacPaint, are pixel-based tools for creating freehand illustrations.
- *How to use a drawing program.* Drawing programs, such as MacDraw, are object-oriented tools for creating structured figures made up of geometric shapes and text.
- *How to use a computer-aided design program.* CAD programs, such as AutoCAD, are sophisticated drafting tools useful for engineering, architectural, and technical illustrations.
- *How to use a slide show program.* Slide show programs, such as PC Storyboard, let you assemble sequences of computer-generated pictures and control the manner in which they are played back on your screen.

## Key Terms

As an extra review of this chapter, try defining the following terms. If you have trouble with any of them, refer to the page number listed.

border palette (473)
chamfer (483)
charting program (466)
clicking (473)
computer-aided design (CAD) (482)
crosshair (485)
dot pitch (463)
double clicking (473)
dragging (473)
fillet (483)
film recorder (465)
graphics adapter (460)
grid (476)
handle (481)
ink-jet printer (464)
layer (483)
multiscan monitor (461)
object-oriented (476)
painting program (471)
pan (483)
pattern palette (473)
pixel-based (bit-mapped) (471)
slide show program (486)
snap (483)
tool palette (473)

## Review Questions

1. What hardware component determines the video modes that can be used by your software as well as the type of monitor that you can connect to your system?
2. List three basic considerations in choosing a monitor.
3. What is by far the most common graphics input device?

4. What hard-copy output device would you use to reproduce screen images on 35-mm slides?
5. List five basic types of graphics software commonly used on microcomputers.
6. List the most popular kinds of charting programs.
7. What types of graphs can you make with most charting programs?
8. What is the basic difference between painting and drawing programs?
9. What is probably the most popular painting program for the Apple Macintosh?
10. What three basic mouse techniques must you master in order to use most painting and drawing programs?
11. List five MacPaint tools and briefly describe their functions.
12. After you create a picture with a painting program, what can you do with it?
13. Why are drawing programs better than painting programs for architectural renderings, layouts, blueprints, diagrams, charts, maps, mechanical drawings, and other technical illustrations?
14. List and briefly describe five of MacDraw's tools.
15. How do you turn on MacDraw's on-screen rulers for precisely measuring objects?
16. How are computer-aided design programs different than drawing programs?
17. List five common CAD features.
18. What is the most popular microcomputer CAD package on the market?
19. Where do the "slides" come from in a computer-generated slide show?
20. List the four component programs of IBM's PC Storyboard package.

## Multiple Choice

1. Many modern microcomputers have their display adapter
   (a) built into the monitor. (b) built onto the motherboard.
   (c) plugged into the serial port. (d) connected to a laser printer.
2. Microcomputer displays present a matrix of
   (a) pixels. (b) objects.
   (c) video modes. (d) resolutions.
3. Which of the following is not a consideration in selecting a monitor?
   (a) screen colors (b) screen size
   (c) dot pitch (d) pixel weight
4. Which type of output device turns screen images into 35-mm slides?
   (a) laser printer (b) scanner
   (c) film recorder (d) plotter
5. Which type of charting program would you use to spruce up a graph made with Lotus 1-2-3?
   (a) spreadsheet enhancement (b) data base charting
   (c) map-making (d) dedicated charting

6. Which type of chart would you use to show a cost breakdown?
   (a) pie (b) bar
   (c) line (d) text
7. Which type of chart would you use to compare the sales of two products?
   (a) pie (b) bar
   (c) line (d) text
8. Painting programs are
   (a) bit-mapped. (b) object-oriented.
   (c) dedicated. (d) animated.
9. Which of the following is NOT a commonly used mouse technique?
   (a) clicking (b) double clicking
   (c) skipping (d) dragging
10. Which MacPaint tool would you use to select an irregularly shaped object?
    (a) lasso (b) selection rectangle
    (c) grabber (d) paint bucket
11. Drawing programs are
    (a) bit-mapped. (b) object-oriented.
    (c) dedicated. (d) animated.
12. Which MacDraw menu would you use to cut, copy, and paste objects from one place to another?
    (a) File (b) Edit
    (c) Layout (d) Arrange
13. Which type of graphics package is best for creating very complex engineering, architectural, and technical illustrations?
    (a) charting (b) painting
    (c) drawing (d) computer-aided design (CAD)
14. CAD programs are
    (a) bit-mapped. (b) object-oriented.
    (c) dedicated. (d) animated.
15. Which type of graphics package is best for presenting a sequence of computer-generated pictures?
    (a) charting (b) painting
    (c) CAD (d) slide show

## Projects

1. Write a brief report comparing the hardware graphics capabilities of IBM-compatible and Apple Macintosh computers. Be sure to note the resolution and number of colors offered by the various graphics adapters and displays available for each type of computer. Cost is another important consideration. Computer books, magazines, and newspapers are good sources of information.

2. In this chapter, we have presented one particular example of a commercial program for each of the following categories of graphics software: charting, painting, drawing, CAD, and slide show. Find another example of a package in each of these categories and briefly describe the programs you pick in a short report. Try to choose popular programs that run on computers different from our selections. For example, EnerGraphics runs on IBM-compatible computers. Research some other popular charting program that runs on the Apple Macintosh.

3. If you have access to a charting program, use it to reproduce some graph that you've seen in a newspaper, magazine, or textbook. See how many graphs you can find in publications such as USA Today, Newsweek, Time, the Wall Street Journal, and Business Week.

4. If you have access to a painting, drawing, or computer-aided design package, use it to produce some illustration of your own choosing. You could do the floor plan of your house or apartment, design clothing, sketch something you're planning to build, or just make a creative drawing or abstract design.

# 14

# Desktop Publishing

## In This Chapter

## PREVIEW

Few advances in computer technology have enchanted users like the recent phenomenon of desktop publishing. Perhaps it's because desktop publishing promises to give you total control over your document's final appearance. Now, it seems, you can do without professional typesetters and graphic artists. You can write and edit your own text, draw figures, incorporate photos, design page layouts, and print completed documents on a high-resolution laser printer. Compared to traditional typesetting and printing, desktop publishing is flexible, quick, and inexpensive.

Unfortunately, desktop publishing is also not quite as wonderful as it sounds. First, a substantial hardware investment is necessary. Although a $5000 to $10,000 microcomputer system is much less expensive than full-fledged typesetting equipment, the price tag is still too steep for many potential users. Desktop publishing packages do offer a great deal of flexibility in document design, but you must first learn how to use the software and this can take time. Even if you have the hardware and software for desktop publishing, attractive results are not guaranteed. It also takes talent and skill to design and lay out pages that look good. Professional typesetters and graphic artists can still produce better results than most desktop publishers.

Nevertheless, desktop publishing does fill a very real need for many individuals, businesses, and organizations. There is a huge market for hardware and software that can produce documents that look better than typewritten pages, even if they're not quite as good as true typeset printing. For example, in 1986 an estimated 4000 desktop publishing systems were sold. According to DataQuest, a San Jose, California, market research firm, the 1990 projected sales figure for desktop publishing systems is around 400,000. Even if desktop publishing isn't used at your school or office, it probably will be in the near future. This chapter is a good place to start exploring the dynamic new field of microcomputer desktop publishing.

After studying this chapter, you will understand

- why desktop publishing is so useful and popular.
- the applications of desktop publishing.
- the basic hardware and software components of a desktop publishing system.
- the principles of good page design.
- how to use a desktop publishing system to produce a newsletter.

## WHY DESKTOP PUBLISHING?

*Cut costs, reduce delays, add control*

As Figure 14.1 shows, on the continuum of document composition, desktop publishing lies somewhere between typewriting and professional publishing. You'll recall from Chapter 6 that a font or typeface is a set of letters, numbers, punctuation marks, and other symbols with a consistent appearance. Desktop publishing goes beyond typewriting and word processing to offer multiple fonts, proportionally spaced characters, graphics integration, and page layout features. Desktop publishing cannot, however, produce documents that look as sharp as those created by traditional typesetting methods. Nevertheless, desktop publishing provides capabilities that were prohibitively expensive for most microcomputer users just a few years ago.

**Figure 14.1 Document Composition Continuum**
The quality of all four types of document composition is constantly being improved by new hardware and software technology.

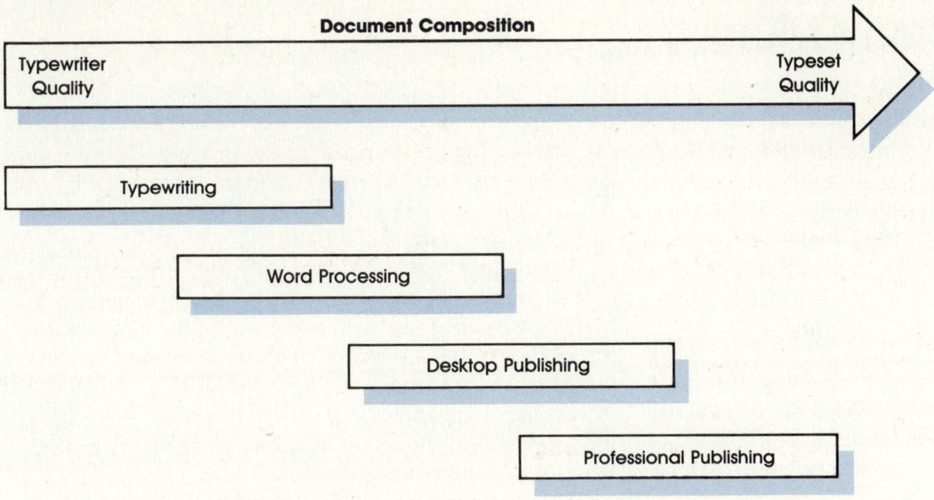


In the previous chapter, we pointed out the fact that ours is a visually oriented society. Attractive printed materials are an essential component of personal, academic, and business communications. More simply put, the better a document looks, the more likely it is to inform, persuade, or interest the reader. The ability to combine text and graphics in an appealing printed format provides a powerful communications tool.

In a nutshell, desktop publishing is useful and popular because it can cut the costs and reduce the delays associated with producing attractive documents. This is especially true if you have to create near-typeset-quality materials on a regular basis. You may not need to have your work redone by an expensive professional typesetter every time you make minor changes to your text or graphics. In many cases, you can save money and finish quicker by doing the word processing, graphics, page design, page layouts, and printing yourself. Thanks to these savings of time and money, desktop publishing often lets you tackle projects you otherwise couldn't afford to do. For example, limited-distribution newsletters and brochures that would be too expensive to produce by traditional typesetting methods may be economically feasible if done with an in-house desktop publishing system.

Desktop publishing also gives you added control and the freedom to experiment with your document designs. With patience and practice, you can master the skills to entirely produce your own newsletters, brochures, and even books. You can do everything with your own computer without being dependent on others to translate your ideas into finished documents. Many users find it easier to meet deadlines and fine-tune their presentations by doing all the work themselves. By eliminating many tedious and time-consuming page layout chores, desktop publishing allows you to devote more attention to the creative aspects of document design and production.

**Insight**

## How Can Desktop Publishing Save a Company Money?

In business, time means money and money means you stay in business. Let's see how desktop publishing fits in.

Imagine that Harry J. Hoodwink owns a small company called Illusions Inc. that makes magicians' supplies. He wants to put out a low-cost yet attractive catalogue of his products. He has two choices in how to produce the catalogue: the conventional typesetting process or desktop publishing.

Using the conventional method, the catalogue's text must be written and edited first. Next, the designer must decide how the catalogue should look. What typeface should be used for the text and headlines? Where should the artwork go?

The designer produces the initial layout by blocking out text and illustrations on a piece of paper, creating a dummy of the material. When the design is complete, the text and headings are set in the typeface chosen. Then the final art must be completed. Finally, the material is pasted together and photographed to produce the negative that will be used to create the printing plate.

If any changes must be made, the text may have to be reset or the art changed in size or scale. The whole process is tedious, expensive, and time consuming. In fact, putting a catalogue together can be prohibitively expensive for a small company.

Using desktop publishing, however, a word processor or part of the desktop publishing system is used to generate the text. Instead of setting type, the graphics capability of the computer translates the text from the word processor into any desired typestyle. Since the text is then in graphics form, it can be moved anywhere on the screen. Line art can also be created with a mouse and moved anywhere as well.

The designed pages are sent to a high-resolution laser printer, and the output is used to produce the printing plates. Revising the catalogue requires simply editing the pages just as you would with a word processor.

Using desktop publishing, Illusion Inc.'s 30-page catalogue can be put together in about a week. If you were Harry J. Hoodwink, which system would you choose?

## DESKTOP PUBLISHING APPLICATIONS

*The many uses of desktop publishing*

Newsletters and brochures are probably the first applications that come to mind when you mention desktop publishing to most people. In fact, desktop publishing can be used for almost any printed material that must look good and be produced on time and at minimal cost. Students, consultants, entrepreneurs, retailers, executives, authors, editors, business people, and other professionals use desktop publishing for all kinds of documents. For example, here's a list of just a few common desktop publishing applications:

- Advertisements
- Annual reports
- Books
- Brochures
- Business cards
- Business plans
- Catalogs
- Magazines
- Newsletters
- Newspapers
- Posters
- Presentations
- Product descriptions
- Proposals
- Resumes
- Signs
- Software documentation
- Training guides
- User manuals
- Workbooks

## COMPONENTS OF A DESKTOP PUBLISHING SYSTEM

*Hardware and software required*

Desktop publishing generally requires a combination of fairly sophisticated hardware and software components. Several of the devices used in desktop publishing are the same as those needed for microcomputer graphics. A powerful microcomputer, a graphics display adapter and monitor, a mouse, and a printer are the minimum necessary equipment. Most desktop publishing systems use laser printers and many include a scanner. Besides word processing and graphics packages, you also need special **page layout software** to enable you to arrange text and graphics on your pages before they are printed. Figure 14.2 shows a typical desktop publishing system.

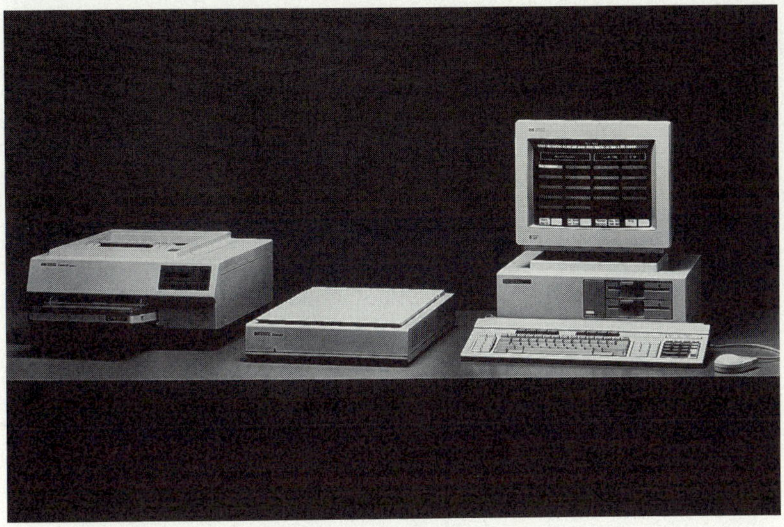

**Figure 14.2 A Typical Desktop Publishing System**
The hardware of a typical desktop publishing system consists of a powerful microcomputer, graphics display, mouse, and laser printer. Some systems also have a scanner. The software needed for desktop publishing includes a word processing package, graphics packages, and a page layout package.

### Powerful Microcomputer

*Fast, with lots of memory and disk storage*

Desktop publishing involves manipulating both text and graphics on the display screen at the same time. This works best if you have a computer with a fast, powerful microprocessor, and plenty of primary memory and secondary storage. Computers such as the high-end Apple Macintoshes, the IBM Personal Computer AT, and IBM Personal System/2 Models 50, 60, 70, and 80 are a few of the most commonly used desktop publishing machines (see Figure 14.3). Usually equipped with at least 1 megabyte of memory and a hard disk with a minimum capacity of 20 megabytes, these computers have both the speed and storage necessary for desktop publishing. Many other computers with similar capabilities from various manufacturers are also used.

### Graphics Display

*High-resolution display adapter and screen*

True desktop publishing is impossible without a high-resolution graphics display adapter and monitor. To be more specific, this means an Apple Macintosh or an IBM-compatible equipped with an Enhanced Graphics Adapter, a Video Graphics Array, a Multicolor Graphics Array, or some other high-resolution graphics adapter.

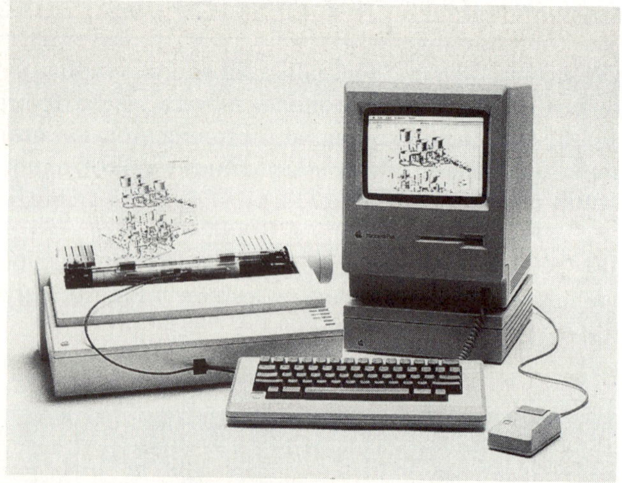

**Figure 14.3 Microcomputers Used for Desktop Publishing**

Desktop publishing requires a microcomputer with a fast, powerful microprocessor, and plenty of primary and secondary storage. Microcomputers commonly used for desktop publishing include the IBM Personal Computer AT, the IBM Personal System/2 Model 50 (or Model 60, 70, or 80), the Apple Macintosh SE, and the Apple Macintosh II.

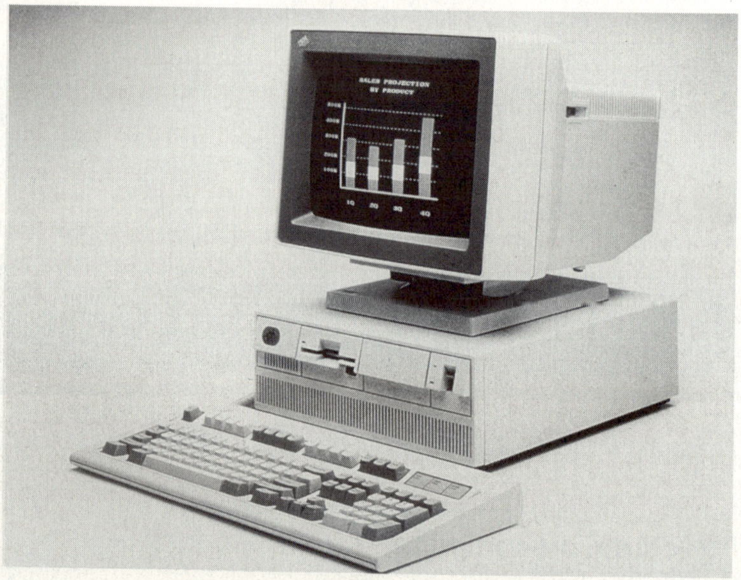

Color capability is not really essential, at least not yet, since only a few high-resolution printers can produce near-typeset-quality output in color. Although desktop publishing is possible on small-screen monitors, many users opt for large-screen models that can legibly display one or two entire pages at once (see Figure 14.4).

## Mouse

*Mouse for pointing, moving, and drawing*

Virtually all desktop publishing systems use a mouse or some other graphics input device such as a trackball or graphics tablet; a mouse is by far the most common device. It's used within the desktop publishing software to precisely place text and graphics on each page, and also to draw simple objects like lines, boxes, and ovals.

**Figure 14.4 Large-Screen Display**
Although desktop publishing is often done on microcomputers with small display screens such as the Apple Macintosh SE, a large-screen display is much more convenient because it can show one or two entire pages.

## Laser Printer

*High-resolution hard-copy output device*

Although dot-matrix or ink-jet printers are sometimes used, the laser printer is the predominant hard-copy output device for desktop publishing. These quick, quiet printers use photocopier technology to produce text and graphics at resolutions of at least 300 dots per inch. A few color models are now available, but the vast majority of laser printers can produce only black and white output. Typical speeds range from six to twelve pages per minute, for pages that contain only text. Printing graphics is significantly slower. Some laser printers, for example, take more than five minutes to print a page that contains graphics. The three most common types of laser printers used with microcomputers are Hewlett-Packard LaserJets (and their compatible printers), PostScript printers, and QuickDraw printers (see Figure 14.5).

Hewlett-Packard LaserJets and compatible printers made by other companies are relatively inexpensive laser printers that start at about $1500. They can print both text and graphics at 300 dots per inch and are primarily used with IBM-compatible computers. LaserJet printers can produce various fonts, which must be loaded into the printer's memory from plug-in font cartridges or downloaded from disk files. Each font cartridge contains regular, boldface, and italic letters and symbols in two or three sizes. Font cartridges are convenient, but offer only a limited number of different fonts. For more fonts, you have to buy additional cartridges. Equipping a LaserJet with many fonts can be expensive.

**PostScript** is a page description language for high-resolution printers and typesetters. Basically, a **page description language** is a specialized computer programming language for defining the size, format, and position of text and graphic elements on a printed page. In other words, a page description language tells a printer how to reproduce a page on paper. PostScript, developed and licensed by Adobe Systems, is one of the most popular page description languages. It's encoded into the hardware of several popular laser printers, including the Apple LaserWriter and IBM's Personal Pageprinter. Starting at around $4000, PostScript printers are rather expensive, but they often include many fonts and provide a great

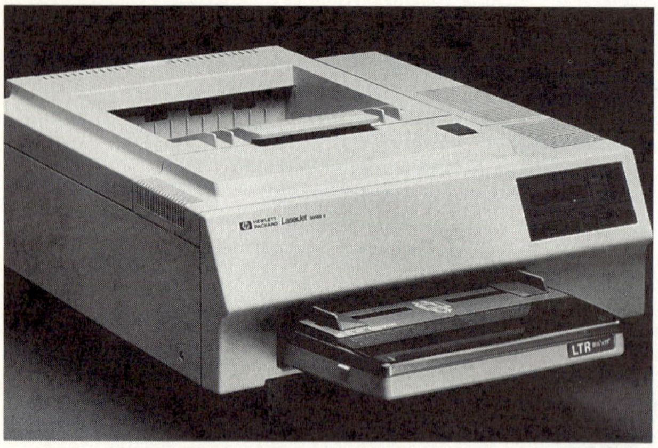

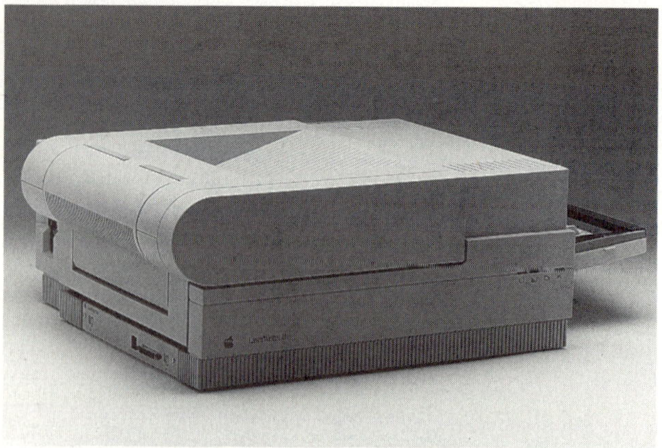

**Figure 14.5 Laser Printers**

The three types of laser printers most commonly used with microcomputers for desktop publishing are Hewlett-Packard LaserJets (and compatible printers from other manufacturers), Postscript printers, and QuickDraw printers. Here we show the Hewlett-Packard LaserJet II, the Apple LaserWriter IINTX Postscript printer, and the General Computer Corporation Personal LaserPrinter, which is a QuickDraw printer.

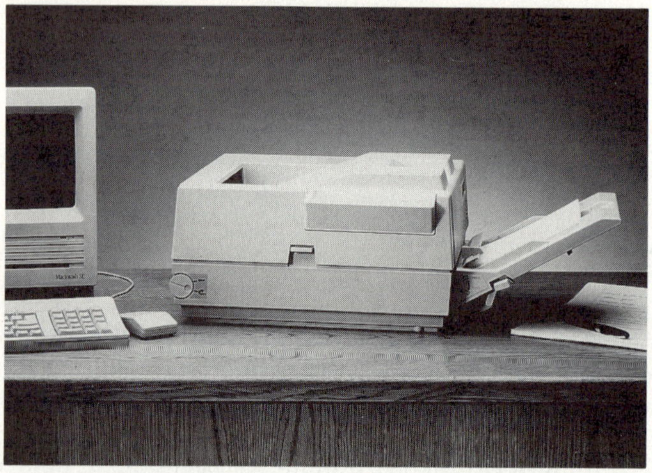

deal of flexibility in the size, shape, and orientation of printed objects. Since PostScript is a *device-independent* language, you can design a document on one system and print it later on another system at a higher resolution. For example, you can rough out your document on a Macintosh and print a draft on a 300-dots-per-inch LaserWriter. When you are finished, you can have your final version printed on an Allied Linotype Linotronic 100 typesetter. This impressive machine, which costs around $35,000, uses the PostScript language to produce output on photographic paper at a resolution of 1270 dots per inch. PostScript laser printers and typesetters can be used with many different types of computers.

**QuickDraw laser printers** are designed especially for Apple Macintosh computers as lower-cost alternatives to PostScript printers. They are named after the QuickDraw graphics routines built into the hardware of Apple Macintosh computers. Instead of using the PostScript language to specify page layouts, QuickDraw printers use the same built-in system software the Macintosh uses to draw text and graphics on the screen. Two of the most popular QuickDraw printers for the Macintosh are Apple's own LaserWriter IISC and General Computer Corporation's Personal Laser Printer. QuickDraw laser printers have a resolution of 300 dots per inch and typically cost between $1800 and $3000.

## Scanner

*Reading in photos and line art*

Although a scanner isn't strictly necessary, it's a popular option in many desktop publishing systems (see Figure 14.6). As we said in Chapter 2, this device lets you convert photographs and line drawings into computer-readable form. While some scanners can also read text, in desktop publishing systems they're most often used for pictures. Once pictures are stored in disk files, they can be edited with graphics software or inserted directly into page layouts. Many scanners can read 300 dots per inch, matching the output resolution of most laser printers. While this resolution is adequate for many applications, it's still quite grainy when compared to the photographs you see in typeset magazines and books.

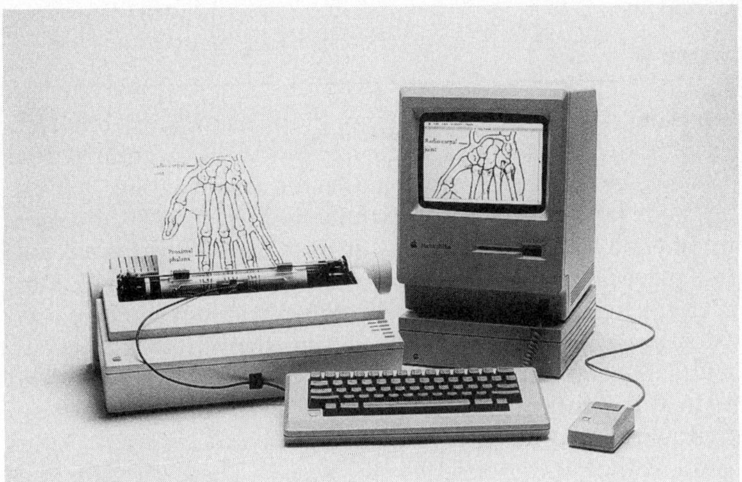

**Figure 14.6 ThunderScan**
Most scanners are stand-alone desktop models that can cost more than $1000. ThunderScan, on the other hand, is a popular low-price ($249) scanner for the Apple Macintosh that fits into an Apple ImageWriter dot-matrix printer in place of the ribbon cartridge.

## Word Processing Software

*Writing and editing document text*

A word processing program is an essential component of any desktop publishing system. Page layout software does let you enter titles, headers, footers, captions and other incidental text items. Nevertheless, a word processor is still necessary for entering most of the text into a document. Almost any word processor can be used in a desktop publishing system, but it's best to use a program with good formatting abilities. If your page designs are simple, you may be able to get by with the desktop publishing features of a high-end word processor. As we said in Chapter 6, several what-you-see-is-what-you-get (WYSIWYG) word processing programs can incorporate graphics and snaking and parallel columns. Some use a mouse and a graphics interface, and all can produce near-typeset-quality output on a laser printer. WordPerfect and Microsoft Word are two examples of powerful word processors that can produce final results similar to that of page layout software. If your documents are not elaborate, one of these advanced word processors may be all you need. If your documents are elaborate, however, you'll probably need a page layout program to combine your text and graphics.

### Graphics Software

*Creating and enhancing pictures*

Another component of most desktop publishing systems is some kind of graphics software. After all, one of the major reasons for using a desktop publishing system is to include drawings, diagrams, charts, and photographs in your documents. In some cases, these graphics can be captured by scanning existing images already on paper. With special equipment, it's even possible to capture and store live images from an ordinary video camera. Many of the figures to be included in documents can be produced from graphics software, however. Charting, painting, drawing, and computer-aided design programs can all be used to generate images for desktop publishing. In addition, painting programs can be used to enhance or otherwise manipulate scanned or captured images. Once you store your images, page layout software lets you insert them into your documents.

### Page Layout Software

*Arranging text and graphics on each page*

A page layout program is neither word processing nor graphics package, but it lets you integrate products of both of these into a single document. An accurate visual representation of one or two entire pages is depicted on the screen at once. Unlike many word processors, page layout programs generally have WYSIWYG displays. You can specify the number and width of columns on each page. Text from word-processed documents is placed on a page and can be easily arranged into columns. Empty blocks can be left for figures, and previously stored graphics can be placed within these spaces. Most page layout programs let you crop (trim), stretch, or compress graphics to fit within the blank spaces you've reserved. Headings, labels, and captions can be added in any number of fonts, styles, and sizes. Imported text can also be reformatted and rearranged from within the page layout program. **Rules** can be placed to separate columns and offset blocks of text. These dividing lines can be drawn anywhere on a page in a number of different styles and thicknesses. Most page layout programs also can add boxes, ovals, shaded backgrounds, and reversed (white on black) text. Finally, page layout programs are generally not limited to standard letter- or legal-size paper. You can work with documents of almost any size—from small business cards to large 17-by-22-inch newspaper pages. Once your pages have been designed, you can send them directly to your printer from within the page layout program.

## PRINCIPLES OF PAGE DESIGN

*How to make your pages look good*

Before we see how desktop publishing is used, let's examine the principles that must be your guide. It's easy to get carried away with powerful page layout software. Many beginners make the mistake of employing exotic features just because they're there. Simply having a page layout program won't make you a master of page design. But you don't have to graduate from a school of design to produce attractive pages that communicate clearly. Remember that your goal is to convey a message and not distract the reader. Here are a few basic principles of page design that can help you achieve this goal:

- *Use plenty of white space.* Don't clutter the page. The reader's eye needs a break between text and graphic elements. This is the primary principle of good page design, but it's probably one of the most violated. Just because there's empty space on a page doesn't mean you have to fill it. Be sure to leave adequate margins on all four sides, too.

- *Keep objects lined up.* It's important not to let the items in your document wander all over the page. Most page layout packages have horizontal and vertical guides you can use to help keep your objects precisely aligned. Professional page designers use grids to ensure the consistent alignment of margins, columns, and headings.
- *Use graphics sparingly.* Beginners are often so enchanted by their newfound ability to add pictures to their text that they put them everywhere. Don't incorporate figures with abandon just because you like the way they look. It's better to use graphics only when they directly relate to the text. And when you do use pictures, keep them small and simple.
- *Use fonts sparingly.* Here is another case in which more is not better. Although you may have many different fonts available, it's best to restrain your creative urges. Professional designers generally stick to just two typefaces in most simple documents: a sans serif font for headings, and a serif font for the rest of the text. **Serif** typefaces, such as the font used for the body text in this book, have lines crossing and finishing off the main strokes of the characters. **Sans serif** typefaces, like the font used for the headings in this book, are plainer, literally without serifs.
- *Use rules.* Use rules to differentiate parts of a page, but use them sparingly. These dividing lines can make a page appear more inviting and easier to read.
- *Keep your text lines short.* There's a reason why magazines, newspapers, and books often print text in two or three columns across a page. It's difficult for the eye to follow long lines of text, especially if the characters are small. Unless you're using a typeface size larger than 12 points, you should probably use at least two columns, each no wider than four or five inches.
- *Plan your page design first.* Don't jump right into your page layout program without thinking about how you want your final document to look. If you're not a professional page designer, you might try using some existing publication as a model.

## INTRODUCING PageMaker

*The most widely used desktop publishing package*

In July 1985, Aldus Corporation released a page layout program called PageMaker for the Apple Macintosh and LaserWriter printer. Available since 1987 for IBM-compatibles too, PageMaker has sold more than twice as many copies as any of its competitors. Many experts consider the availability of this program to mark the real birth of desktop publishing. This software truly sets the standard for desktop publishing features, including simple pull-down menus, WYSIWYG page displays, the ability to incorporate text and graphics from many other programs, and support for popular high-resolution laser printers and typesetters.

PageMaker is the most popular page layout program, perhaps because it is powerful, easy to learn, and simple to use. Another plus is the fact that PageMaker looks and "feels" almost exactly the same on both Apple Macintoshes and IBM-compatibles. If you learn to use PageMaker on one of these types of computers, you'll have no trouble running it on the other as well. You can even trade PageMaker documents back and forth between Macintoshes and IBM- compatibles. For the rest of this chapter, we'll be using PageMaker for the Macintosh to illustrate some of the principles of desktop publishing.

## PRODUCING A NEWSLETTER

*Producing a newsletter*

The best way to learn about desktop publishing is to see it in action. Perhaps the most common application of desktop publishing is producing newsletters. As an example, let's create a newsletter for a small business. Our fictional business is Paddle and Portage Canoe Outfitters, which rents canoes and camping equipment to people who want to explore the wilderness waters that border Minnesota and Canada. Owned and operated by Becky and Bob Johnson, Paddle and Portage Canoe Outfitters also sells supplies, mainly trail food, and operates an overnight bunkhouse for outgoing and incoming campers. Since canoe outfitting is a seasonal business, the Johnsons send out a newsletter every winter in a subtle effort to get customers to make early reservations. Figure 14.7 shows the final product—the front and back of the single-sheet newsletter we will produce with PageMaker.

**Figure 14.7 The Finished Newsletter**
This is the newsletter we will produce with PageMaker.

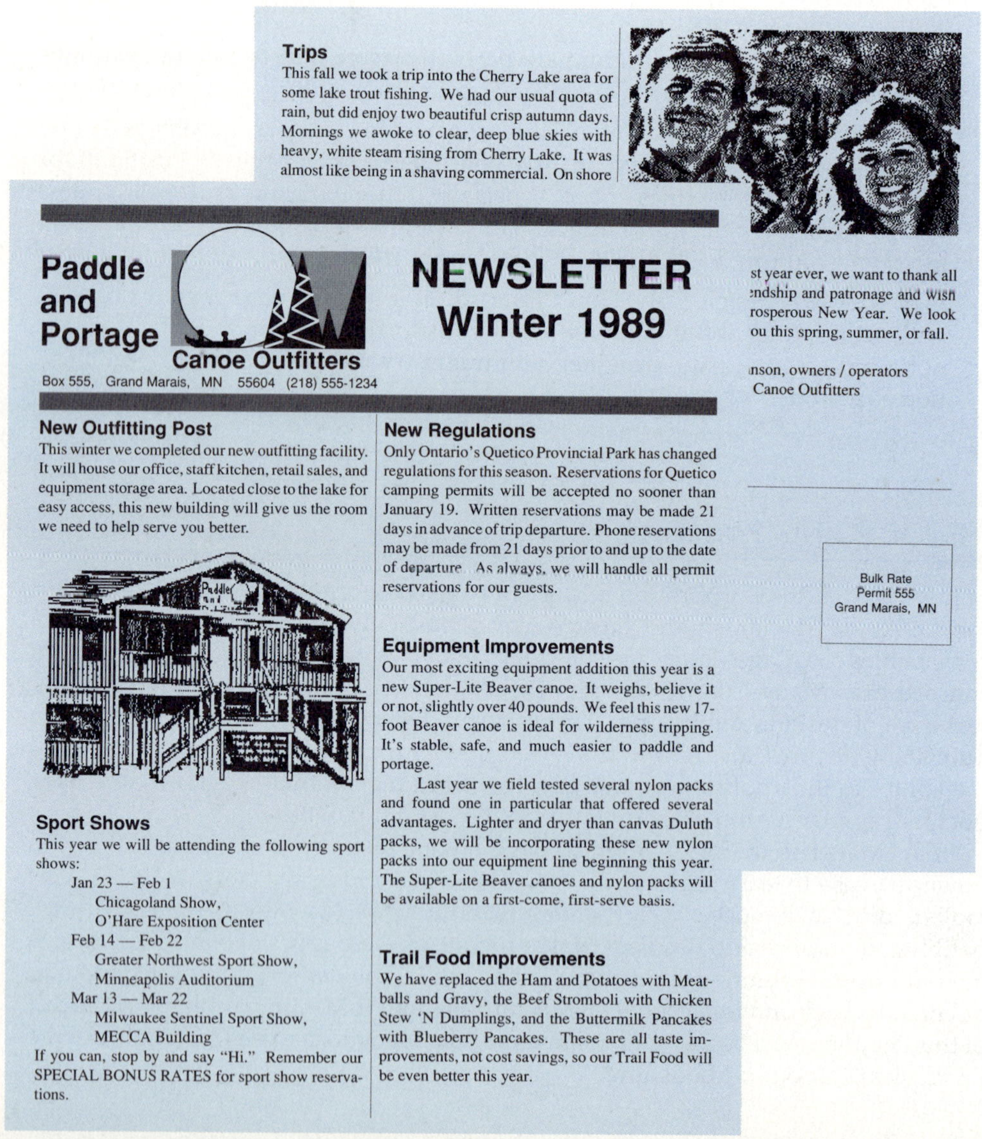

**Trips**
This fall we took a trip into the Cherry Lake area for some lake trout fishing. We had our usual quota of rain, but did enjoy two beautiful crisp autumn days. Mornings we awoke to clear, deep blue skies with heavy, white steam rising from Cherry Lake. It was almost like being in a shaving commercial. On shore

st year ever, we want to thank all
ndship and patronage and wish
rosperous New Year. We look
ou this spring, summer, or fall.

nson, owners / operators
Canoe Outfitters

Bulk Rate
Permit 555
Grand Marais, MN

**Paddle and Portage Canoe Outfitters**
Box 555, Grand Marais, MN 55604 (218) 555-1234

**NEWSLETTER**
**Winter 1989**

**New Outfitting Post**
This winter we completed our new outfitting facility. It will house our office, staff kitchen, retail sales, and equipment storage area. Located close to the lake for easy access, this new building will give us the room we need to help serve you better.

**Sport Shows**
This year we will be attending the following sport shows:
Jan 23 — Feb 1
Chicagoland Show,
O'Hare Exposition Center
Feb 14 — Feb 22
Greater Northwest Sport Show,
Minneapolis Auditorium
Mar 13 — Mar 22
Milwaukee Sentinel Sport Show,
MECCA Building
If you can, stop by and say "Hi." Remember our SPECIAL BONUS RATES for sport show reservations.

**New Regulations**
Only Ontario's Quetico Provincial Park has changed regulations for this season. Reservations for Quetico camping permits will be accepted no sooner than January 19. Written reservations may be made 21 days in advance of trip departure. Phone reservations may be made from 21 days prior to and up to the date of departure. As always, we will handle all permit reservations for our guests.

**Equipment Improvements**
Our most exciting equipment addition this year is a new Super-Lite Beaver canoe. It weighs, believe it or not, slightly over 40 pounds. We feel this new 17-foot Beaver canoe is ideal for wilderness tripping. It's stable, safe, and much easier to paddle and portage.

Last year we field tested several nylon packs and found one in particular that offered several advantages. Lighter and dryer than canvas Duluth packs, we will be incorporating these new nylon packs into our equipment line beginning this year. The Super-Lite Beaver canoes and nylon packs will be available on a first-come, first-serve basis.

**Trail Food Improvements**
We have replaced the Ham and Potatoes with Meatballs and Gravy, the Beef Stromboli with Chicken Stew 'N Dumplings, and the Buttermilk Pancakes with Blueberry Pancakes. These are all taste improvements, not cost savings, so our Trail Food will be even better this year.

There are five basic steps to creating most documents with a desktop publishing system: writing and editing the text, creating or scanning the artwork, laying out the pages, printing the document, and making multiple copies. Let's go through each of these steps, one by one, for the Paddle and Portage newsletter.

## Writing and Editing the Text

*Preparing the body copy*

PageMaker does let you enter and edit text, but it's not really adequate for typing entire documents. For this you still need a word processing program. Almost any word processing package will do, but it's better to use one specifically endorsed by PageMaker, such as MacWrite or Microsoft Word. If you use a word processor not endorsed by PageMaker, you can only import plain text (without embellishments such as multiple character fonts, styles, and sizes). You'll then have to format all of your text within PageMaker. It's generally easier to set formatting options such as paragraph alignment and character fonts within your word processor, if this is possible. Since MacWrite is fully supported by PageMaker, we'll use it for our newsletter example.

To start MacWrite, you simply position the mouse pointer on the MacWrite icon (pictorial symbol) and press the mouse button. Next, you need to select the formatting options you want to use. In newsletters, paragraphs are usually single-spaced and justified between the left and right margins. You don't have to worry about the exact margins because the paragraphs will be automatically reformed when you place them into their columns later with PageMaker. Single-spacing is already the default line spacing in MacWrite, but you'll have to turn on paragraph justification. This is done by clicking the mouse pointer on the page icon that shows all lines of equal length (see Figure 14.8).

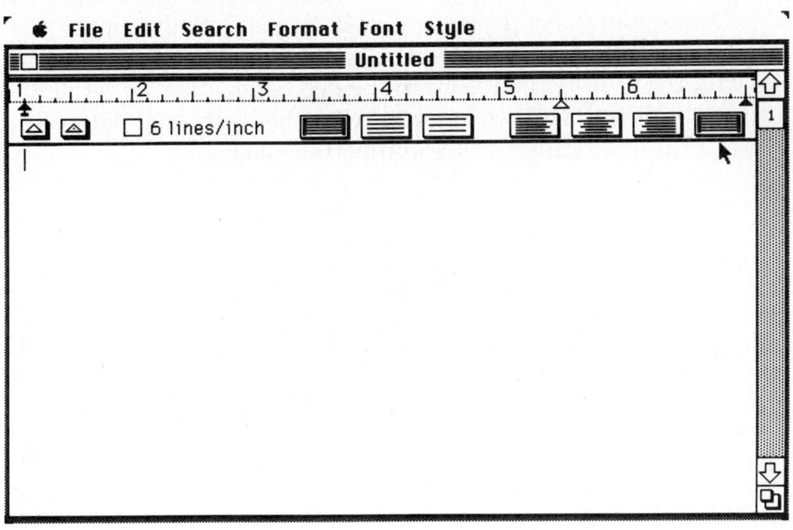


**Figure 14.8 Formatting Options in MacWrite**
The icons that let you set formatting options are located above the text area in the MacWrite word processing package.

You also need to decide which character fonts, styles, and sizes to use. Although there are a number of possible choices, it's best to keep things simple. The newsletter will consist of several small sections, with a short headline above each one. How about using 14-point boldface Helvetica type for the headlines, and 12-point plain Times type for the paragraphs themselves? These are commonly used fonts that look nice when printed with the LaserWriter. To select a font, you simply pull down

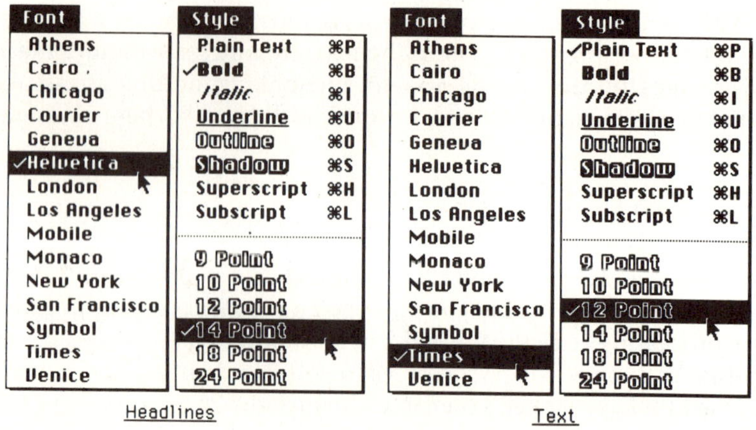


**Figure 14.9 Character Formatting Settings for Headlines and Text**

Select the 14-point Helvetica font for the headlines and the 12-point Times font for the text in our newlsletter.

the Font menu, highlight the one you want, and release the mouse button. Similarly, character style and size options are selected from the Style menu. These MacWrite menu selections are shown in Figure 14.9. You'll have to switch fonts, styles, and sizes several times as you enter titles and then the paragraphs themselves.

Once you've decided on the basic formatting conventions, you simply enter the newsletter's text as shown in Figure 14.10. Don't worry about the exact final form of the newsletter and don't leave space for figures. All that will be done within PageMaker. When you've finished entering the text, you should go back, check it for errors, and edit it if necessary. Although you don't have to print the document from within MacWrite, you can do so if you find it easier to check over a printed copy for errors. Once you're sure it's correct, the completed document must be saved in a disk file with the Save command from the File menu. You might name it something like NEWSLETTER TEXT. When you're finished with MacWrite, you exit the program by selecting the Quit command from the File menu.

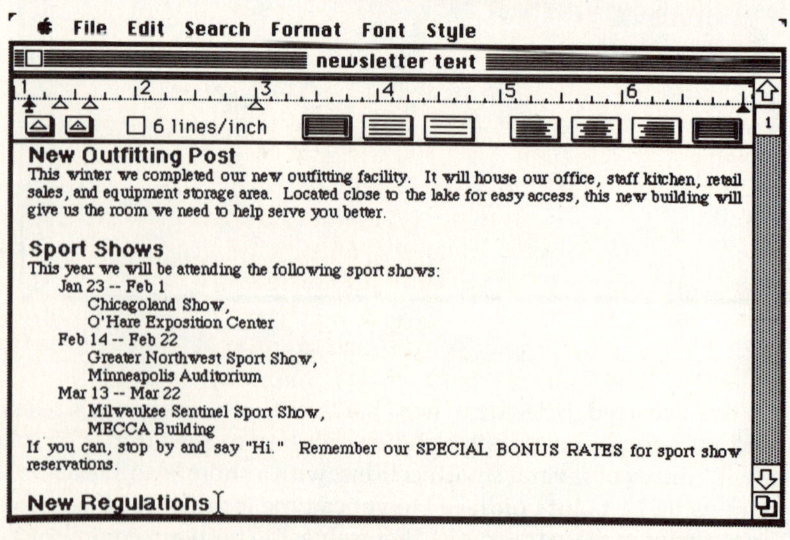


**Figure 14.10 Entering the Newsletter Text with MacWrite**

This screen shows the text of the newsletter being created with MacWrite

## Creating or Scanning the Artwork

*Preparing the pictures*

Most newsletters contain artwork of some kind, even if it's only a company logo. As you can see from Figure 14.7, our particular newsletter contains three different graphics: the Paddle and Portage logo, a sketch of the new outfitting building, and a photograph of Becky and Bob Johnson.

The logo, shown in Figure 14.11, was created with MacDraw. This fairly simple logo is made up of just a few shapes, lines, and words. Using a drawing program such as MacDraw is preferable to using a painting program such as MacPaint because the logo can be produced on the laser printer at a higher resolution than you can see on the computer screen. As we said in the previous chapter, drawing programs generally take better advantage of high-resolution printers. After the logo is finished, it's stored in its own MacDraw document file named LOGO.

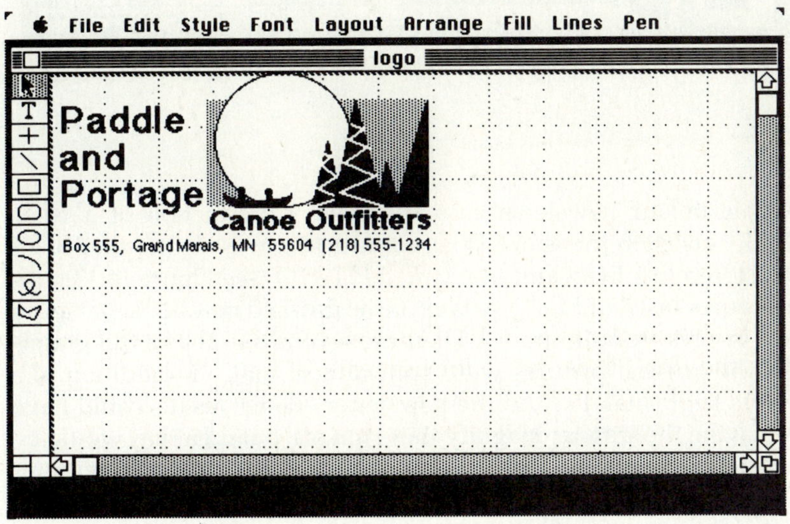


**Figure 14.11 Creating the Logo with MacDraw** This screen shows the Paddle and Portage logo being created with MacDraw.

The sketch of the new outfitting post was originally done by an artist with pen and paper. It was copied with a scanner and enhanced with MacPaint (see Figure 14.12). The scanner we used is ThunderScan, from Thunderware Incorporated. This inexpensive device is a full-featured scanner that replaces the printer ribbon cartridge in an Apple Imagewriter dot-matrix printer. It's list price is only $249, yet ThunderScan produces images that rival stand-alone scanners costing ten times as much. ThunderScan's main disadvantages are that it's somewhat slow and it only scans pages that can be fed through the ImageWriter printer. Once ThunderScan has been installed in an ImageWriter, all you do to scan a picture is insert the original into the printer and run the ThunderScan software. The resulting picture can be adjusted for brightness and contrast, and stored in a number of different graphics file formats. In this particular case, the image was stored in a MacPaint file named BUILDING.

**Figure 14.12 The Scanned Building Sketch in MacPaint**

The sketch of the building was scanned with ThunderScan and stored in MacPaint format.

The last graphic in our newsletter is a digitized reproduction of a color photograph of Becky and Bob Johnson. This reproduction was also created with ThunderScan and stored in a MacPaint file named PHOTO (see Figure 14.13). As you can see from Figures 14.12 and 14.13, as well as the finished newsletter in Figure 14.7, these scanned images are quite grainy. There are several reasons for this graininess. First of all, the original pictures were both rather small. In addition, the scanned copies were kept small to fit in the newsletter. Better results could have been obtained by having the scanner magnify the originals, but then they would be too big for the newsletter. The original photo of Becky and Bob was in color without much contrast. It had to be photocopied to be fed through ThunderScan, which somewhat degraded the image. In addition, storing the images in MacPaint format limits their resolution to 72 dots per inch, even though ThunderScan and the LaserWriter printer can resolve 300 dots per inch.

**Figure 14.13 The Scanned Photo in MacPaint**

The photograph of Becky and Bob Johnson was scanned with ThunderScan and stored in MacPaint format.

Without going into technical details, there are ways to improve the results of scanning sketches and photographs, but they involve using advanced techniques and require more storage. For example, images can be saved by ThunderScan in **Encapsulated PostScript (EPS) files**. These are large files containing gray-shade information that can be imported and printed by page layout programs, such as PageMaker, which use the PostScript language. Encapsulated PostScript images are printed in a manner that simulates the gray tones you see in an original black and white photograph. Although EPS files produce better results than MacPaint files, they cannot be easily edited on the screen, since the resolution of most displays is only around 72 dots per inch. Few painting and drawing programs can work with EPS files, so the only way to see your results is to print them on a LaserWriter from your scanner software or from PageMaker. Nevertheless, with patience and the right combination of hardware and software, you can produce scanned images much better than ours that are adequate for many applications.

## Laying Out the Pages

The basic text and graphics of the newsletter are finished. The next step is to merge them with PageMaker and add the finishing touches. Starting PageMaker is just like starting MacWrite, except that you click the mouse pointer on the PageMaker icon. The program then presents the screen you see in Figure 14.14.

**Figure 14.14 PageMaker Startup Screen**
This screen appears after you click the mouse button on the PageMaker icon to start up the page layout program.

### Setting Up the Pages

*Specifying page and margin size*

Since you are creating a new PageMaker document, you first need to pull down the File menu and execute the New command. PageMaker presents the Page Setup screen, as shown in Figure 14.15. Here's where you tell PageMaker the size, orientation, and margins of your pages. Our newsletter will be printed on the front and back of a single 8.5-by-11-inch piece of paper. Since we don't need to leave extra space on the inside margin for binding, you should change the inside margin to 0.75-inch, just like the other margins. Furthermore, you should also turn off the Double Sided option because our newsletter will not have facing pages like a bound booklet. This is done by simply clicking on the box beside the Double Sided option. When you do this, the X disappears from the box and the Facing Pages option automatically shuts off too. Finally, you should set the number of pages to 2—one page for the front and one page for the back. When you're finished with the page setup specifications, simply click on the OK box.

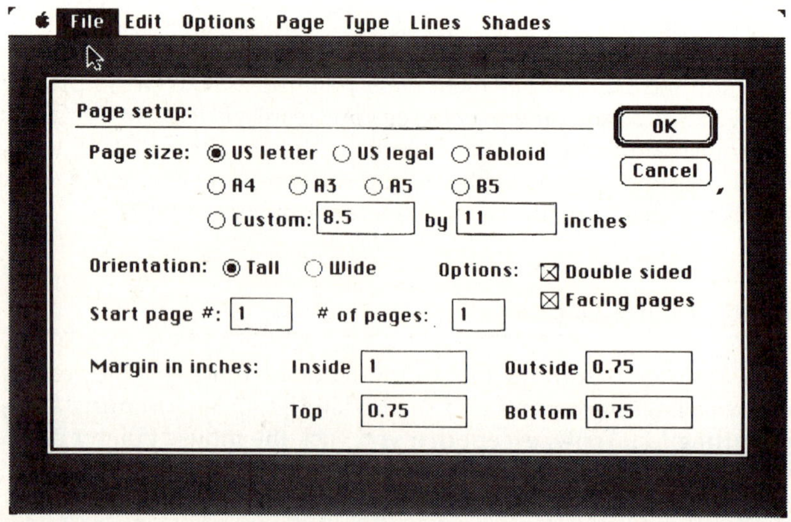


**Figure 14.15 Page Setup Screen**
Here is where you specify page formatting options.

## Turning on Rulers and Column Guides

*Precise measurements and double columns*

After you finish with the Page Setup screen, PageMaker presents the first blank page of your document, as shown in Figure 14.16(a). The dotted lines indicate your margins. This particular view is compressed to entirely fit on the screen. PageMaker also can present pages in actual size as well as half as large, three-quarters as large, and twice as large as actual size. The best way to precisely lay out your pages is to activate the on-screen rulers. This is done by selecting the Rulers command from the Options menu.

At this point you should also tell PageMaker how many columns you want on your pages. By default, there is only one column showing, but we want two columns in our newsletter. To change the number of columns on a page, you select the Column Guides command from the Options menu and enter **2** for the number of columns. The default space between columns is 0.167 inches, which you can also change if you like, but this distance is fine for our newsletter. After you turn on rulers and specify two columns, your screen looks like Figure 14.16(b).

## Placing the Letterhead Logo

*Importing graphics*

The PageMaker screen is like a typesetter's paste-up board, but much more flexible. You use the computer to arrange your pages instead of manually cutting and pasting text and graphics with razor blades, a T-square, and rubber cement. Since the work is done electronically, it's much easier to perfectly align items horizontally and vertically on the page.

The Paddle and Portage logo, which we created with MacDraw, will appear at the top left of the first page of our newsletter. To do this, you select the Place com-

**Figure 14.16 Specifying the Columns**

(a) This screen shows the first blank page, which initially has no columns.

(b) This screen shows the page after the ruler and column guides have been turned on.

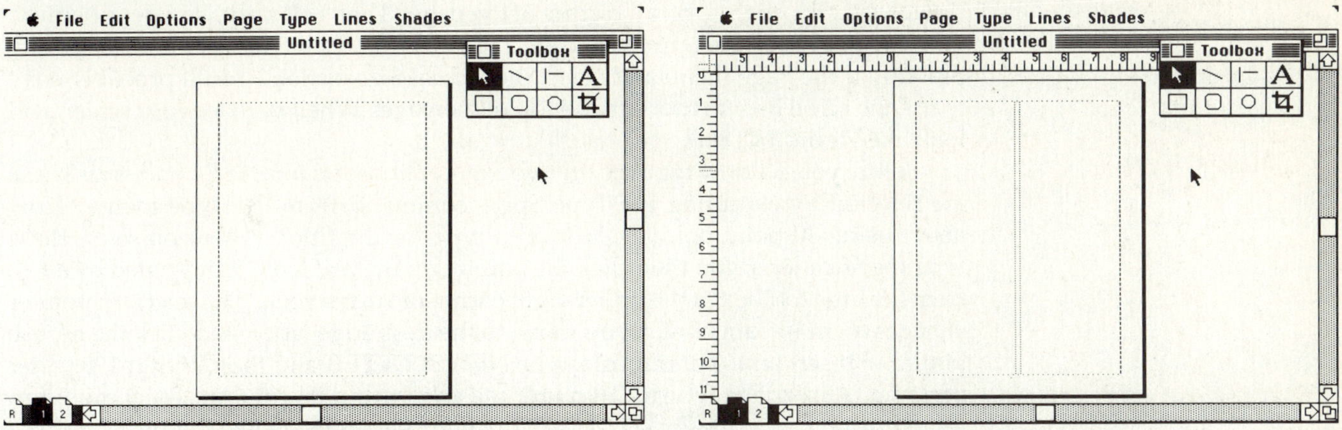


mand from the File menu. PageMaker presents a list of both text and graphics documents, and you pick one of these to place on your page. You may have to switch to a different folder or disk to find the document you need. In our case, the MacDraw document is named LOGO. After you select the LOGO document, PageMaker returns to the page screen, but now the mouse pointer has changed to a corner symbol that contains a drawing pen (see Figure 14.17(a)). This icon represents the logo you just imported. To place it on the page, simply move the icon to the desired location and click the mouse button. The logo can be moved later if you like, but for now let's put it at the upper left corner of the page. As you move close to the corner where the top and left margins meet, the icon "snaps" into place. This is a handy PageMaker feature that helps you precisely align text and graphics to guide lines. After you press the mouse button to place the logo, your screen looks like Figure 14.17(b).

**Figure 14.17 Placing the Logo on the Page**

(a) This screen shows the Draw icon, a symbol used to position a drawing on the page.

(b) After you place the Draw icon and press the mouse button, the Draw icon disappears and the actual logo appears.

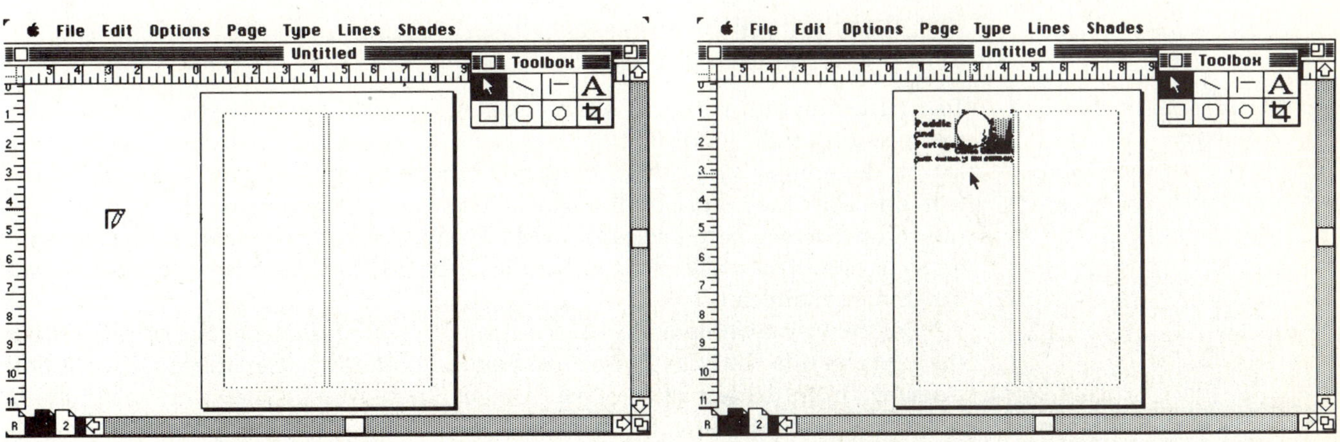

## Typing the Newsletter Title

*Adding the title*

Now let's add a title to the newsletter beside the logo. At this point, it's a good idea to switch to a full-size view of the page. This will make it easier to see details, although you'll lose the overall picture of the page. That's all right, however, because you can go back to the miniature view at any time. To switch to actual size, simply pull down the Page menu and select the Actual Size option. You'll probably have to use the scroll bars to move to the top of the page. When you do, your screen will look like Figure 14.18(a).

Before you actually type the title, you must choose its font, style, and size. These are selected by executing the Type Specs command from the Type menu. How about using 30-point boldface Helvetica type for the title? After you select these type specifications, you then click the pointer on the text icon, represented by an A, from the little toolbox in the upper-right corner of your screen. The selection pointer changes to an I-beam, which you move to the desired location and click the mouse button to insert text. For our title, type **NEWSLETTER** and then **Winter 1989** after pressing the carriage return. To center the title within its column, select the Align Center option from the Type menu. Now your screen looks like Figure 14.18(b).

**Figure 14.18 Typing the Newsletter Title**

(a) It's easier to see details if you switch to the actual-size view of the page.

(b) This screen shows the top of the page after the headline has been entered.

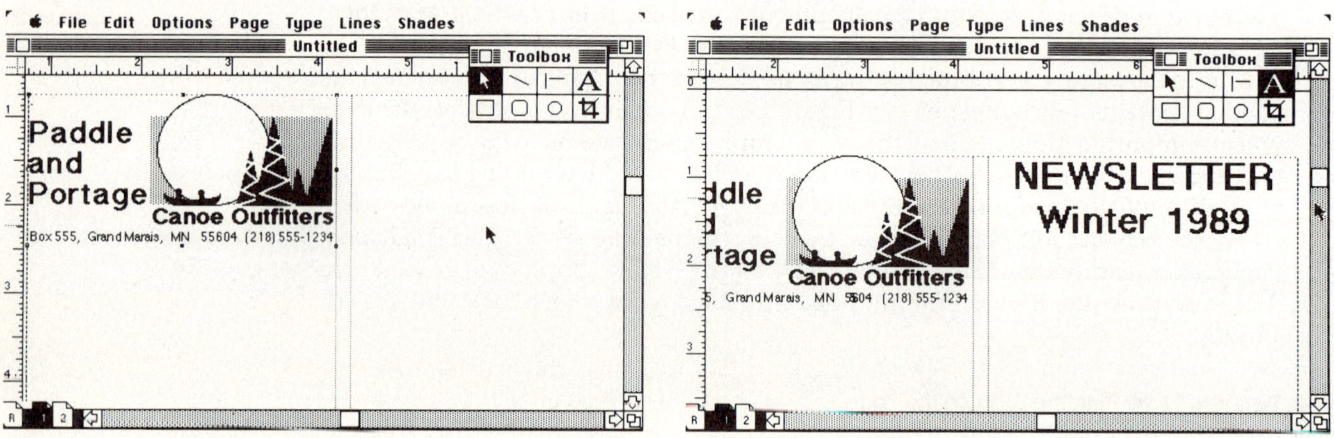


## Finishing Off the Heading

*Moving objects and drawing shaded bars*

To spruce things up a little, let's offset our logo and title with two shaded bars. First, we need to shift the logo and title down a bit. Go back to the selection tool by clicking on the pointer icon from the toolbox. Move the pointer anywhere within the logo and click the mouse button again. Handles appear around the logo just like they do when an object is selected in MacDraw. You can now drag the logo around or even resize it by "pulling" on its handles. The title can also be selected and moved in a similar manner.

Before we move them, however, let's use a **ruler guide** to help precisely align the logo and title. This is a dotted line you can pull down from the top ruler or pull sideways from the left ruler. Like margins, these dotted lines won't actually be printed; they just help you keep text and graphics lined up on your pages. PageMaker lets you have up to 40 of these vertical and horizontal alignment guides. Figure 14.19(a) shows your page after using a horizontal ruler guide to align the text of the logo and title.

Now let's put a shaded bar above and below the logo and title. For this you need to select the box icon from the toolbox, which is used just like the MacDraw rectangle tool. Place the crosshair cursor at the intersection of the top and left margins, and drag open a thin rectangle all the way over to the right margin. Select the 40 percent shading from the Shades menu to fill in the rectangle, and select the None option from the Lines menu to shut off the rectangle's outline. After you have this one bar made, you can use the Cut and Paste commands from the Edit menu to create a copy and place it below the logo and title. Once you do this, your screen looks like Figure 14.19(b).

**Figure 14.19 Finishing Off the Heading**

(a) You can use a ruler guide to precisely align the logo and headline.

(b) You can add shaded bars above and below the heading.

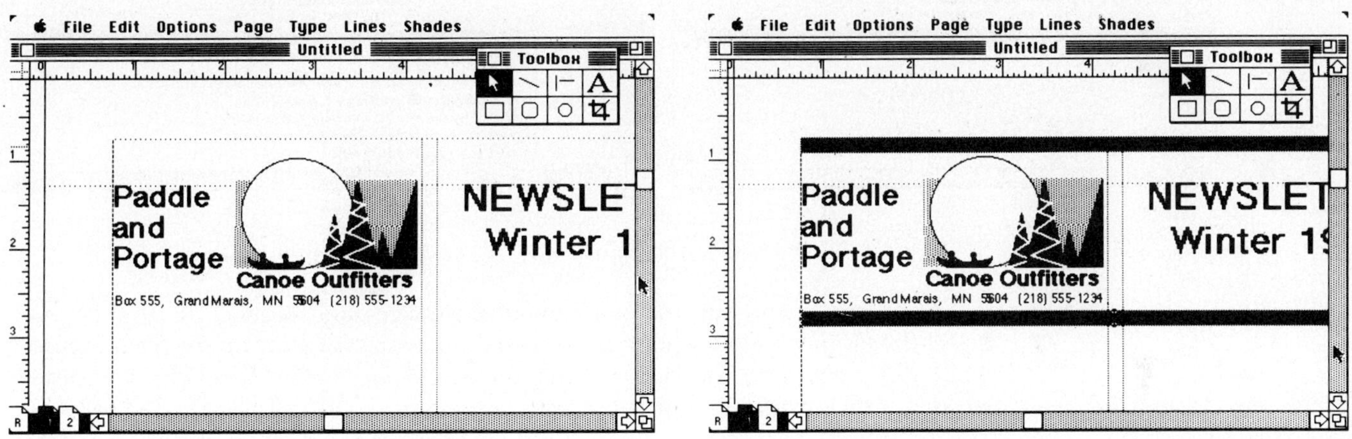


If you look closely at this figure, you can see that the zip code in the logo is a bit squashed and all the letters appear somewhat jagged. Although PageMaker is considered a WYSIWYG program, there will always be slight discrepancies between what appears on the screen and what appears on the final LaserWriter output. This is because the Macintosh screen has a resolution of only 72 dots per inch while the LaserWriter can print at 300 dots per inch. If you look back at Figure 14.7, which shows the final printed newsletter, you can see the differences. Characters are much sharper and their spacing is much better. The combination of PageMaker and the LaserWriter produces attractive results, but you may have to experiment a little to work out the very fine details that cannot be resolved on the screen.

## Placing the Text

*Importing text*

The next step is to get the actual text of the newsletter and place it on the page. Again execute the Place command from the File menu, but this time select NEWSLETTER TEXT, the MacWrite document we created previously. When you select a word processed document file, PageMaker's pointer turns into a symbol that looks like a tiny page (see Figure 14.20(a)). Simply place this symbol at the upper-left corner of the area where you want the text to be placed and click the mouse button. The text expands to fill the column, as shown in Figure 14.20(b). Because MacWrite is fully supported by PageMaker, the formatting conventions you selected when you entered the text are preserved on the page.

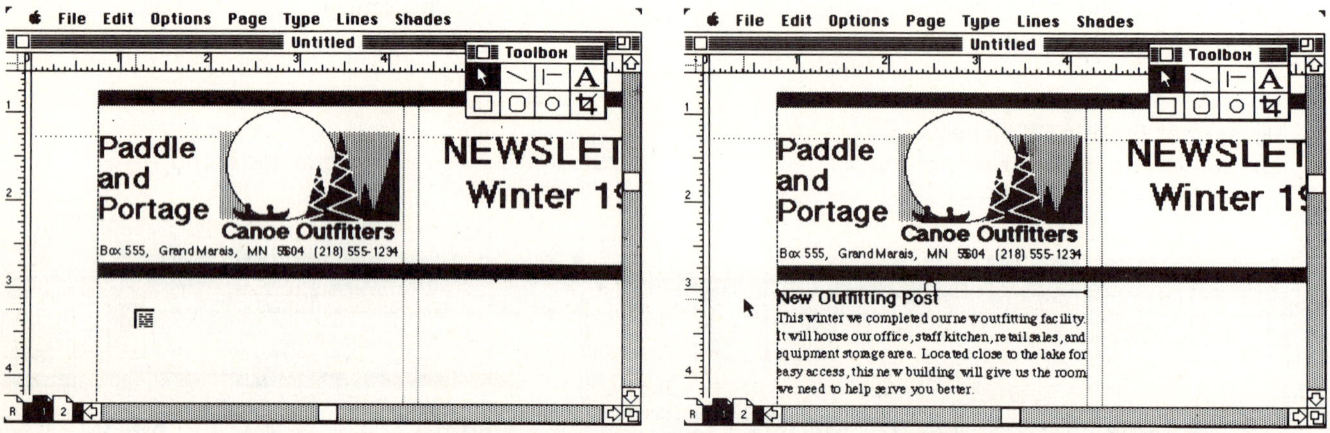


**Figure 14.20 Placing the Newsletter Text**

(a) This screen shows the Text icon, a symbol used to position text on the page. and the actual text appears.

(b) After you place the Text icon and press the mouse button, the Text icon disappears

Now let's "zoom out" to get a view of the entire page at once. To do this you select the Fit in Window option from the Page menu. As you can see from Figure 14.21, this gives you a good idea of what the whole page looks like, even if you can't make out the details. In particular, lines of text are represented by shaded bars instead of the actual characters, which would be too small to distinguish. Converting text to these symbolic bars is called **greeking**; it is done to show the position of text on the screen.

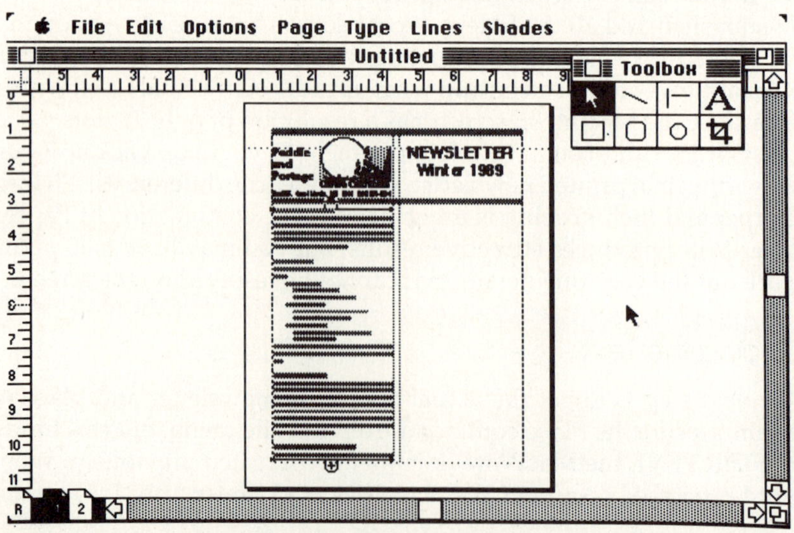


**Figure 14.21 Full-Page View Showing Text Greeking**

You can "zoom out" to get a view of the full page, but text becomes too small to read. Page layout programs use greeking to represent text as shaded bars. Greeking allows you to see the position of text on the page, although you can't make out the details.

Notice that the top of the text block is indicated by a horizontal line with a loop sticking up from the center (see Figure 14.21). The bottom of the text block has a similar line, but the loop protrudes down and has a plus sign (+) inside. This plus sign indicates that there is more text in the file waiting to be placed. The loops are like the loops on a window shade—you can "pull" them up or down with the mouse pointer to open up spaces for artwork. For example, the first paragraph of our newsletter text describes the new Paddle and Portage outfitting building. The building sketch is to be inserted after this paragraph, so we need to leave room for it. Simply move the pointer to the bottom loop, hold down the mouse button, and drag the bottom edge of the text block up to a point just below the end of the first paragraph. Then click the mouse pointer on the plus sign in the bottom loop to continue placing text. A little text page icon appears, just like the one that appeared when you began placing text. Move the text icon along the left margin a couple of inches or so below the first paragraph and click the mouse button. As Figure 14.22 shows, an empty space remains and the text continues below it to the bottom of the column.

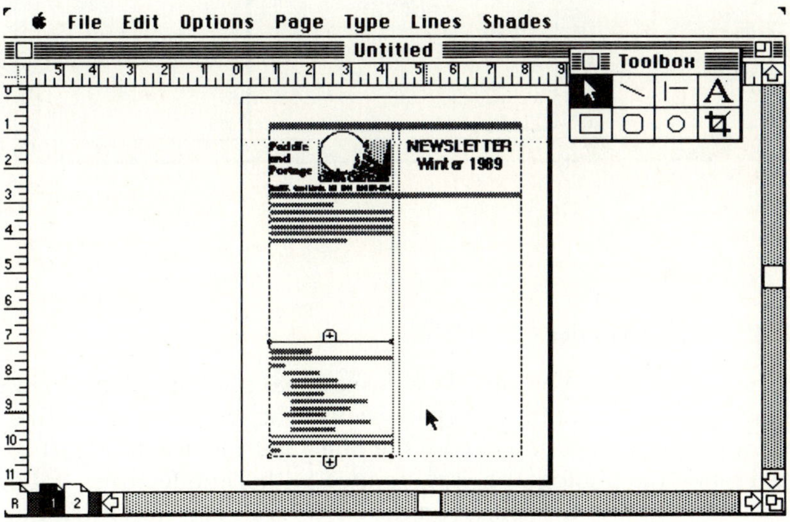


**Figure 14.22 Making Room for the Building Sketch**

You can move the little loops at the top and bottom of a text block to open up a "hole" for a picture. This screen shows the space created for the sketch of the new outfitting building.

Unlike some page layout programs, PageMaker (Macintosh version 2.0) does not automatically continue text in the next column and on the next page. This can make it tedious to use for long documents, such as books, but it does give you a great deal of control over text placement. To finish placing the rest of the text in our newsletter, click on the bottom plus sign again and move the page icon up to the top of the right-hand column. Click the mouse button again, and the text fills the column. The plus sign at the bottom of the right-hand column indicates that there is still more text to be placed, and it will have to be placed on the second page.

To switch to the next page, you simply click the pointer on the page symbol with the 2 inside at the lower-left corner of the screen. You'll have to use the Column Guides command from the Options menu to set up two columns on this page too. Then go back to the first page and click on the plus sign in the loop at the bottom of the right-hand column. Switch back to the second page again and now place the text at the top of the left-hand column. The number sign (#) at the bottom of the text block indicates that you finally have all the text placed on the pages. The bottom half of this second page, however, will be reserved for the mailing label. So, move the last text paragraph over to the right-hand column, leaving space above it for our scanned photograph of Becky and Bob. Your second page should now look like Figure 14.23.

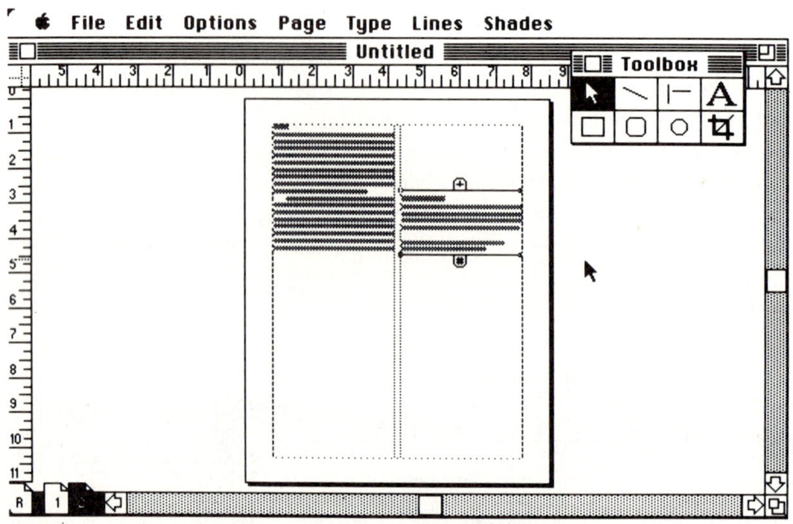


**Figure 14.23 The Second Page of the Newsletter**

This screen shows the full-page view of the second page of the newsletter after placing the text.

## Placing the Sketch and Photo

*Importing more graphics*

While you're on the second page, you can place the scanned photograph of Becky and Bob in the space you left above the final paragraph. The procedure is just like placing the MacDraw logo, except you choose the MacPaint file named PHOTO, which was created when the photograph was scanned with ThunderScan. If the photo is a little too big to fit into the space you have left for it, you can shrink the photo by dragging its lower-right handle toward the upper left. The second page now looks like Figure 14.24(b).

To place the scanned sketch of the new outfitting building, go back to the first page. Again, execute the Place command from the File menu, but this time pick the MacPaint document named BUILDING. Move the paint icon into the empty space below the first paragraph in the left-hand column, and press the mouse button to expand the sketch. Again, you may have to slightly adjust the size of the sketch to fit into the space by dragging its lower-right handle toward the upper left. The resulting screen should look like Figure 14.24(a).

## Creating the Mailer

*Resizing graphics and drawing lines*

At this point, you're almost finished with the page layout. As we said before, this simple newsletter will be put onto a single sheet of paper. The paper will be folded in half and stapled or taped shut. So, the bottom half of the second page must display the mailing information. This consists of the return address in the upper-left corner and the bulk rate mailing permit in the upper-right corner where the postage stamp would normally go. The actual customer addresses will be printed on gummed labels and affixed to the finished newsletters after they are printed.

**Figure 14.24 Placing the Graphics**

(a) This screen shows the full-page view after the building sketch has been placed on the first page

(b) This screen shows the full-page view after the photo has been placed on the second page.

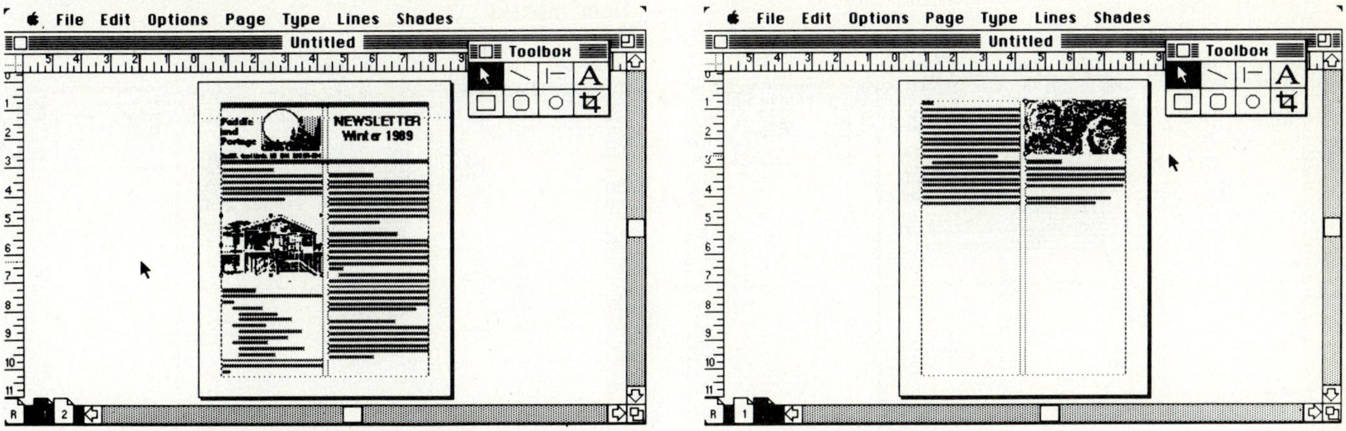


First, you need to draw a horizontal rule across the middle of the second page to indicate where the newsletter is to be folded. Pull down the Lines menu and select the Hairline option. Then select the horizontal and vertical line icon from the toolbox; this is the one to the immediate left of the A text icon. This tool is just like the perpendicular line tool in MacDraw. Move the crosshair cursor to the left page margin, 5.5 inches from the top of the page, as indicated by the vertical ruler. To draw the rule, simply hold down the mouse button, drag open the line all the way to the right margin, and release the button. While you're at it, you might also want to draw vertical hairline rules separating the columns on both pages. At this point, your second page looks like Figure 14.25(a).

For the return address, we'll use the Paddle and Portage logo. Again execute the Place command from the File menu to put another copy of the logo at the upper-left side of the bottom of the page. This time, however, let's scale it down a little and make it smaller than the logo on the first page. To do this, simply drag the lower-right handle of the logo toward the upper left. The figure will be correspondingly reduced in size.

Finally, you can use the box tool and the text tool to create the bulk rate permit stamp in the upper-right corner of the bottom half of the page. You'll need to switch to an actual-size view of the page to see what you're doing. Feel free to use a ruler guide to help you align the logo and permit on the page. When you're finished, the overall view of the second page should look like Figure 14.25(b).

## Final Adjustments

*Adjusting alignments*

At this point, your newsletter is basically complete. You might, however, want to make some minor adjustments to precisely align text and figures on your pages. Switch to actual-size view or even two times actual size to get a more detailed picture of each page. Feel free to move items around a little. Use ruler guides wherever they might help you align the items. You might even want to use PageMaker's text tool to insert carriage returns and spaces here and there in your text to improve its overall appearance. The time you spend on these details can greatly enhance the final product.

**Figure 14.25 Finishing the Second Page**

(a) This screen shows the second page after drawing the horizontal and vertical hairline rules.

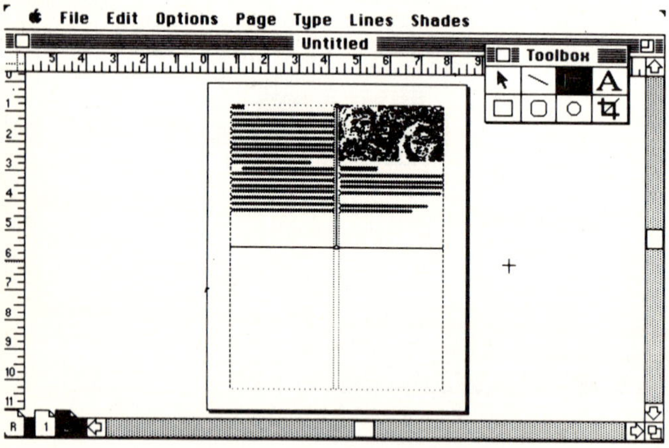


(b) This screen shows the completed second page, after the mailing label has been created and the return address logo has been placed.

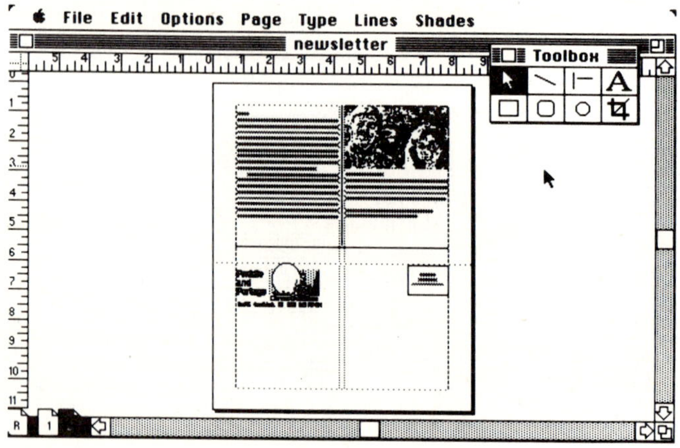


## Printing the Document

*Making a hard copy*

When you're satisfied with the way your pages look, it's time to print them. You'll obtain the best results by using a laser printer or a true typesetter. We used the Apple LaserWriter Plus to produce the final copy of our newsletter, which you see in Figure 14.7. All you do to print your document from within PageMaker is to execute the Print command from the File menu. Assuming you have a LaserWriter Plus connected to your Macintosh, PageMaker will display the screen you see in Figure 14.26. As this screen shows, several options are available for printing on the LaserWriter. For our newsletter, we just used the default options, which are highlighted in black.

## Making Multiple Copies

*Reproducing your product*

The term publishing generally refers to preparing and disseminating a document to the public. In most cases, this means making multiple copies of your printed document. If you need just a few copies, say four or five, you can simply have PageMaker print them on the LaserWriter. All you do is enter the number you want in the Copies box when you execute the Print command from the File menu (see Figure 14.26). If you need lots of copies, it's faster and more economical to use a good plain paper copier or an offset printer. Professional offset printing is probably best for more than a few hundred copies, and it yields better results than an ordinary office copy machine. Print shops that specialize in offset printing can also collate, fold, and bind your documents if necessary.

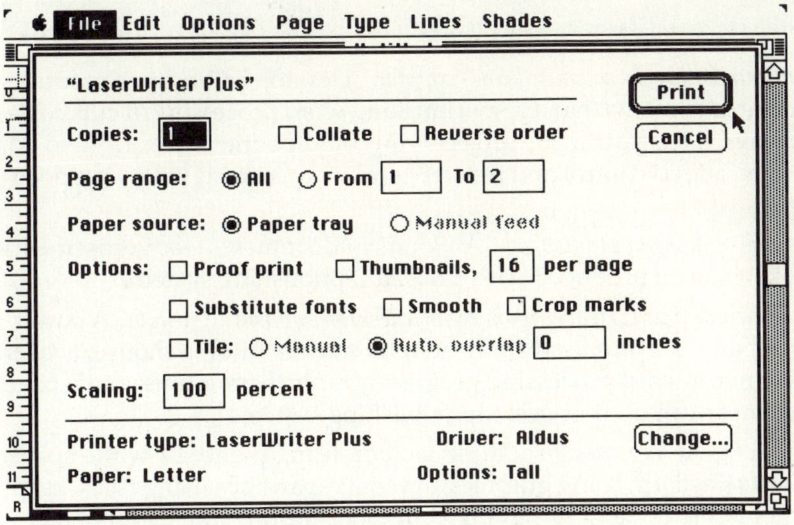


**Figure 14.26 Printing the Newsletter on the Apple LaserWriter Plus**

This is the screen you see after selecting the Print command from PageMaker's File menu, if you have an Apple LaserWriter Plus Printer.

## The Real World

### Desktop Publishing Looks Ahead

"Ultimately, the desktop publishing revolution will have as much impact on business as the telephone and photocopier did in their day."

This bold prediction was made in an industry newsletter editorial by John Sculley, chairman and chief executive officer of Apple Computer, Inc. Sculley's company has a big stake in the desktop publishing market, but he's not the only one who feels this way.

Consider this: U.S. corporations produce more pages a year than all book, magazine, and newspaper publishers combined. More than 80,000 companies in the United States produce technical documentation, and many more put out newsletters, brochures, and sales documents. According to a Bell Laboratories study, technical documentation alone will increase at a rate of 500,000 pages per minute worldwide. That's a big potential market.

With desktop publishing technology, businesses can slash their typesetting, camerawork, layout, and pasteup costs, save time, and produce attractive products as well.

GTE Government Systems Corporation in Westborough, Massachusetts, produces about 400,000 pages a year. Using desktop publishing, the company spends about $1.33 per page, which is less expensive than what they could do with a typewriter, according to company officials.

But desktop publishing is not limited to the conventional page. The New York design firm of Carbone-Smolan Associates used desktop publishing to develop informational and directional signs for the Louvre Museum in Paris. Using an Apple Macintosh and LaserWriter printer, the firm prepared models of how the signs would look. As a result, they produced professional-looking documents within a tight time frame.

"It would never have been possible without the Mac," said Key Carbone, a partner in the firm.

Sources:

"Desktop Publishing Moves Into the Mainstream," by Alex Kozlov, *Newsweek Special Advertising Supplement on Business Technology*, November 2, 1987, p. S18.

"How Desktop Publishing and LANs Work Together," by Mike Higgins, *The Office*, December, 1987, p. 32.

## Summary

- *Why desktop publishing is so useful and popular.* Desktop publishing produces more attractive documents than typewriting and word processing, it cuts costs, it reduces delays, it lets you tackle projects you couldn't otherwise afford to do, and it gives you added control and the freedom to experiment with your document designs.
- *The applications of desktop publishing.* All kinds of documents—advertisements to workbooks—can be produced with a desktop publishing system.
- *The basic hardware and software components of a desktop publishing system.* A powerful microcomputer, a graphics display adapter and monitor, a mouse, a laser printer, a scanner, a word processing program, graphics programs, and a page layout program are all used in desktop publishing systems.
- *The principles of good page design.* These include using plenty of white space, keeping objects lined up, using graphics and fonts sparingly, using rules, keeping your text lines short, and designing your pages before you lay them out.
- *How to use a desktop publishing system to produce a newsletter.* The five basic steps to creating a document with a desktop publishing system are writing and editing the text, creating or scanning the artwork, laying out the pages, printing the document, and making multiple copies.

## Key Terms

As an extra review of this chapter, try defining the following terms. If you have trouble with any of them, refer to the page number listed.

Encapsulated PostScript (EPS) file (511)
greeking (516)
page description language (501)
page layout software (499)
PostScript (501)
QuickDraw laser printer (502)
ruler guide (514)
rules (504)
sans serif (505)
serif (505)

## Review Questions

1. What makes desktop publishing an attractive alternative to professional publishing?
2. List five applications of desktop publishing.
3. List the major hardware components of a typical desktop publishing system.
4. What software packages are needed for desktop publishing?
5. What are the three basic laser printer standards used in desktop publishing systems?
6. List five capabilities of page layout software.
7. Which page layout program sells twice as many copies as its competitors?
8. What are the five basic steps to producing a document with a desktop publishing system?
9. Why is it best to use a word processing package explicitly endorsed by your page layout program?

10. Why is a drawing program such as MacDraw better than a painting program such as MacPaint for producing simple graphics to be incorporated into a document and printed on a laser printer?
11. What device would you use to reproduce a photograph or line art for inclusion in a document?
12. Which PageMaker command do you use to import and position text and graphics on a page?
13. What PageMaker feature can be used to help you precisely align text and graphics on your pages?
14. Why is there a slight discrepancy between what you see on your screen and what is ultimately printed on the laser printer?
15. Why is greeking used in full page displays?
16. How do you compress a graphic in PageMaker?
17. How do you draw a rule in PageMaker?
18. How do you print a document in PageMaker?
19. What are two common methods of producing many copies of a document produced with a desktop publishing system?
20. List seven principles of good page design.

## Multiple Choice

1. Desktop publishing lies on a continuum between
   (a) file management and data base management.
   (b) charting and computer-aided design.
   (c) typewriting and typesetting.
   (d) word processing and spreadsheets.
2. Which of the following computer components is not strictly necessary for desktop publishing?
   (a) powerful microcomputer
   (b) graphics display adapter and monitor
   (c) high-resolution printer
   (d) modem
3. Which of the following is a device-independent page description language commonly used in laser printers and typesetters?
   (a) PostScript (b) LaserJet
   (c) QuickDraw (d) Modula-2
4. Which of the following devices might you use to convert photographs and line drawings into computer-readable form?
   (a) laser printer (b) scanner
   (c) mouse (d) keyboard
5. Page layout software lets you combine the output of
   (a) spreadsheet and data base management packages.
   (b) communications and networking packages.
   (c) word processing and graphics packages.
   (d) project management and accounting packages.

6. Which of the following is *not* a principle of good page design?
   (a) Use plenty of fonts. (b) Use plenty of white space.
   (c) Use graphics sparingly. (d) Use rules.
7. The first step to creating a desktop published document is usually
   (a) laying out the pages. (b) printing the document.
   (c) making multiple copies. (d) writing and editing the text.
8. Which of the following types of files contains gray- shade information about a scanned picture?
   (a) ASCII file (b) Encapsulated PostScript (EPS) file
   (c) binary file (d) EXE file
9. Which of the following techniques is used to represent lines of text that are too small to distinguish individual characters?
   (a) greeking (b) zooming
   (c) clicking (d) justification
10. Page layout programs help you align text and graphics through the use of
    (a) fonts. (b) menus.
    (c) ruler guides. (d) handles.
11. Which of the following PageMaker commands do you use to put text on a page?
    (a) Column Guides command from the Options menu
    (b) Cut command from the Edit menu
    (c) Fit in Window command from the Page menu
    (d) Place command from the File menu
12. Which of the following PageMaker commands do you use to put graphics on a page?
    (a) Column Guides command from the Options menu
    (b) Cut command from the Edit menu
    (c) Fit in Window command from the Page menu
    (d) Place command from the File menu
13. Which of the following output devices achieves the highest resolution?
    (a) dot-matrix printer (b) ink-jet printer
    (c) laser printer (d) typesetter
14. What kind of typeface is commonly used for headings?
    (a) serif (b) sans serif
    (c) pica (d) elite
15. Laser printers produce output at resolutions of at least
    (a) 300 dots per inch. (b) 600 dots per inch.
    (c) 900 dots per inch. (d) 1200 dots per inch.

## Projects

1. In this chapter we have used PageMaker to illustrate some principles of desktop publishing. A number of other page layout programs are also used on both Apple Macintosh and IBM-compatible microcomputers. Write a brief report that compares one or two of these other programs to PageMaker. Examine features, cost, and support for hardware and software products from other companies. Product reviews in computer magazines and newspapers are a good source of information.

2. What use would you have for a desktop publishing system at school or work? Specifically, what kinds of documents would you produce and why do you think desktop publishing would be better than typewriting or word processing? Do you think these uses would justify the added expense? Write a brief report explaining your position.

3. Is desktop publishing used at your school or office? Try to find an example of an actual desktop publishing system currently used by an individual, business, or organization that you know about and write a brief report about this system. If you don't personally know of anyone using desktop publishing, try to find an example described in a newspaper or computer magazine such as *Personal Computing*. What kind of computer, word processor, graphics software, page layout program, and printer do they use? What kinds of documents do they produce? Why did they decide a desktop publishing system was necessary? Do they use a scanner? And are they satisfied with their system?

4. If you have access to a desktop publishing system, use it to prepare a document of your choice. You could do an ad, brochure, newsletter, resume, or informal report for one of your classes. If you don't have access to a system, just plan and sketch out your page designs on paper. Be sure to say what your margins would be, how many columns you would have, which fonts you would use, and what kinds of graphics you would include.

# 15

# Accounting

## In This Chapter

## PREVIEW

In one sense, this entire textbook is about business software. Every type of application package we have mentioned is used extensively in businesses and organizations of all types. This is especially true of word processing, spreadsheet, and data base management packages, which are general productivity tools applicable to a wide range of tasks. Another type of software, however, is geared more toward the daily bookkeeping tasks needed to run a business. Accounting is the process of recording, analyzing, and reporting business transactions. Accounting information, provided it's accurate and timely, is often the key to success in business, since good decision-making is simply impossible without a systematic record of business transactions. The most efficient way to maintain, manage, and summarize these records is with accounting software. Consequently, if you work in business or any organization that receives and makes payments, you'll probably be exposed to accounting software. These accounting programs are the topic of this chapter.

Accounting software, one of the very first commercial uses of computers, has become indispensable in our economy. Virtually all large businesses and many small businesses use computers to help with their bookkeeping. To understand accounting software and what it can do for a business, you must become familiar with the basic principles and terminology of accounting. After a brief introduction to accounting, we will take a popular accounting package as an example and see how it can be used to set up and maintain a bookkeeping system for a fictional small business.

After studying this chapter, you will understand

- some basic terminology and principles of accounting.
- one specific example of a microcomputer accounting package.
- how to set up a microcomputer accounting system.
- how a microcomputer system is routinely used by a small business.

## AN ACCOUNTING PRIMER

Without even knowing it, you already use some accounting principles in your everyday life. After all, everyone receives and spends money. When you get paid, you probably deposit the money in your checking account and record the transaction in your checkbook. When you pay bills or make purchases, you write checks, use credit cards, or pay cash. In most cases, you or your bank records your transactions. The purpose of accounting is to simply and precisely track income and expenditures in a systematic way.

### The Double Entry System

*Balancing the books*

The basic method used by all modern accounting systems is **double entry accounting**. First described in the fifteenth century by a monk named Luca Paccioli, double entry accounting requires that "for every debit there is a corresponding credit." More simply put, every time you apply money to some payment or purchase, that exact amount of money must come from some source. A **debit** is an application of money, and a **credit** is a source of money. For example, let's say that you go to the store and write a check to buy $25 worth of groceries. As shown in Figure 15.1, your checking account is the source of money and the purchase of groceries is the application of that money. The $25 entered on the left side of this T-shaped chart is a debit and is *added* to the previous balance on that side. The $25 entered on the right side is a credit, and is *subtracted* from the previous balance on that side. With each transaction, there is always an application and source of money. By definition, the application (debit) must always equal the source (credit). Unless something has been incorrectly computed, debits and credits *must* balance.

**Figure 15.1 Double Entry Accounting**
The "T" chart shows that each debit must have a corresponding and equal credit to keep accounts properly balanced.

| APPLICATION | | SOURCE | |
|---|---|---|---|
| **Groceries Account** | | **Checking Account** | |
| Previous Balance | 432.00 | Previous Balance | 550.00 |
| Today's Purchase | 25.00 | Groceries Payment | 25.00 |
| Current Balance | 457.00 | Current Balance | 525.00 |
| **Total Debits = $25.00** | | **Total Credits = $25.00** | |

## Insight

# Should a Small Business Computerize Its Accounting?

You're walking down the street past an electronics store when you see it—the stereo system you've always wanted. It's right there in the window, and it's on sale.

You curb your impulse to elbow other shoppers aside, run in, and fling your money on the counter because you realize that some thought processes should be involved. Instead, you ask yourself two questions: Do I really need it? Can I afford it?

Managers considering whether to computerize their company's accounting have to ask the same two questions.

Some companies have very elaborate accounting procedures, particularly to manage payroll. Many banks and accounting firms, though, provide payroll-check writing and accounting services at a price per check that's hard to beat. How can computers help with other tasks, such as accounts payable, accounts receivable, or inventory management?

Some businesses might have very little activity in one area and more in another, depending on how much they purchase or sell. These busier areas—inventory management or accounts receivable—are prime candidates for computerized accounting.

But first, management must analyze how accounting is done now. If the manual accounting system gives the necessary results in the right form and on time, there may be no need to computerize accounting. On the other hand, if the current system is unsatisfactory, then a computerized accounting system should be considered. If the system is working badly because it is managed badly, the business will just be replacing one set of problems with another by going to computers.

Looking at the cost factor is a little less complicated. Most small businesses should spend no more than 1–2 percent of gross revenues to computerize their accounting. On that basis, gross revenues of $200,000 to $400,000 would justify buying a computer and accounting software system for $4,000. This scenario describes many small businesses.

When the cost of the computer and accounting software is amortized, or spread out over the useful life of the system, only the smallest businesses are unable to justify buying a computer.

Remember: a computer can be useful for many tasks, such as word processing and spreadsheets. A data base system can be used as the basis for the accounting system, or a modular accounting package can be selected. Other accounting modules, such as payables or inventory, can be purchased as they are needed.

## Accounts

*Recording and classifying financial data*

Figure 15.1 shows two accounts: one for groceries and one for checking. In accounting, an **account** is simply a file of financial information about what you own, owe, earn, or pay out. Each record in an account is called an **entry**. Applications and sources of money are recorded as entries in different accounts. You can keep as many accounts as necessary to provide the level of detail you need. For example, you have separate accounts for checking and savings at a bank so that you can maintain an independent balance for each one. If your finances are simple and you make few transactions per month, you may need only a few accounts. On the other hand, if your financial situation is more complex and you make a variety of different types of transactions, you might use many accounts. The ultimate purpose of keeping accounts is to have clear, accurate, and timely sources of information about your financial status.

When many accounts are used, they are often grouped into families. This is done to provide organization and summarize information. Let's take Paddle and Portage Canoe Outfitters, the small business we discussed in Chapter 14, as an example for this chapter as well. They have five major accounts, each of which is divided into subsidiary accounts, as shown in Figure 15.2. The major accounts include:

- *Assets*. Money and property owned by the business are called **assets**. Typical assets include cash, land, buildings, equipment, supplies, and merchandise inventory.
- *Liabilities*. Amounts of money owed to others are called **liabilities**. These include purchases not yet paid for, taxes, mortgages, and loans.
- *Capital*. Also called **owners' equity**, **capital** reflects the owners' stake in the business and includes their initial investment along with any net earnings they have left in the business.
- *Revenues*. **Revenues** are the payments or promises to pay received from sales, rentals, interest, or other investments. Revenues are basically any money coming into the business.
- *Expenses*. The monies paid out for the normal operation of the business are known as **expenses**. These include the cost of materials and items resold as well as rent, payroll, utilities, office supplies, maintenance, and insurance. Expenses are basically any money going out of the business.

As you can see from Figure 15.2, each of these five "parent" accounts—assets, liabilities, capital, revenues, and expenses—has two or more "children" accounts, some of which have their own "children" accounts, too. This allows a business to organize complex accounts at a manageable level of detail. In accounting, the total listing of parents, children, grandchildren, and so on is called the **chart of accounts**. This chart is invaluable for classifying all of the financial information of a business.

Note: Figure 15.2 has two acronyms, FICA and FUTA, as children of the Payroll account. FICA stands for Federal Insurance Contributions Act, also known as Social Security tax. FUTA stands for Federal Unemployment Tax Act; it is the taxes some employers are required to pay for unemployment compensation.

## Financial Reports

*Printed summaries*

Accounting systems are used to prepare several types of financial reports that reveal useful information about a business. The most basic type of financial report is the **journal**. This is a chronological listing of transactions, recording all relevant ap-

**Figure 15.2 Chart of Accounts**
This is a diagram of Paddle and Portage Canoe Outfitters' chart of accounts.

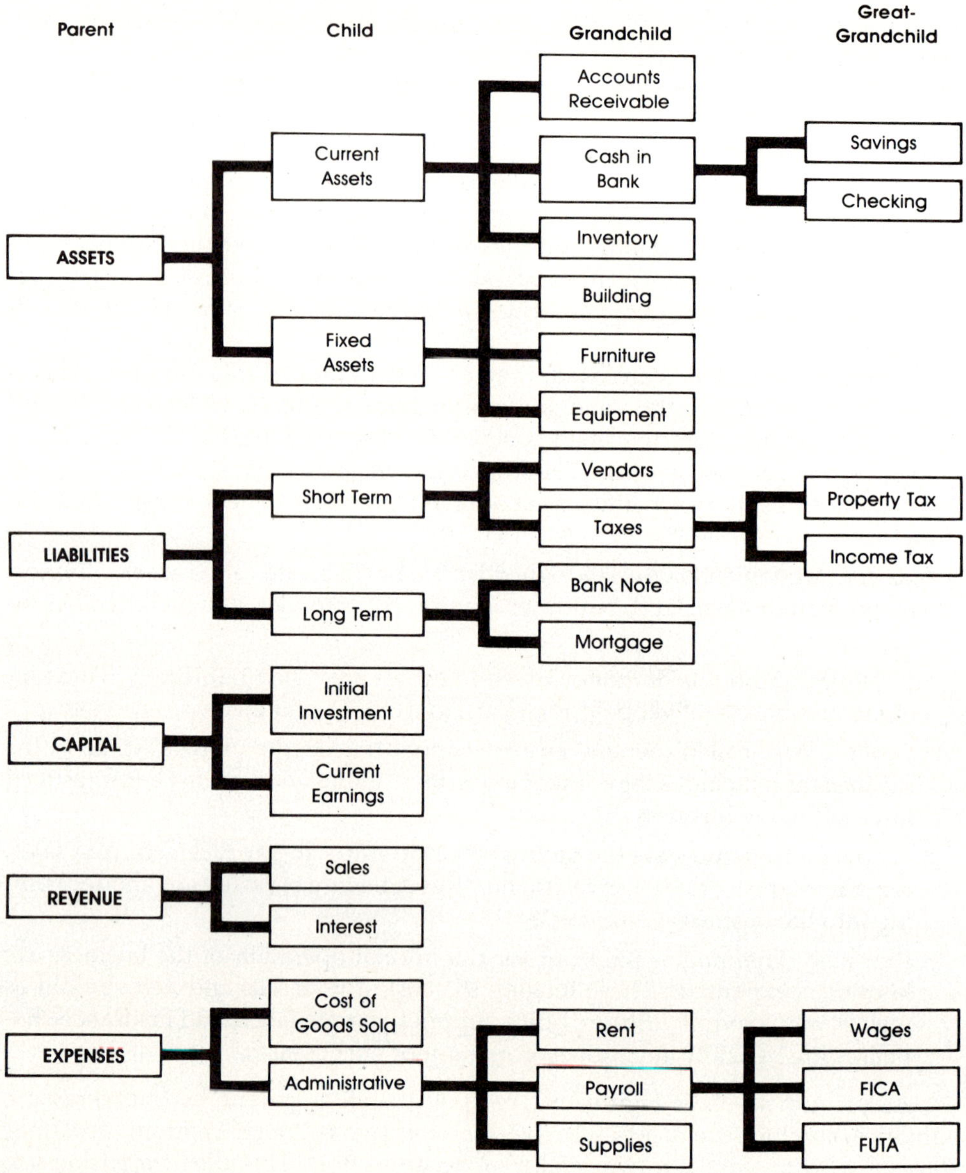


plications and sources of money (see Figure 15.3). A journal that automatically records the date, time, debit, and credit of every transaction is also called an **audit trail**. Maintaining such journals is a sound practice in any accounting system because it helps you track down errors more easily. Some companies keep a different journal for each type of transaction. For example, you might have separate journals for sales, rentals, and purchases. By helping you trace errors and group transactions by their origins, journals give you a way to maintain a record of all the events that affect the finances of a business.

**Figure 15.3 Journal Report**

Here is an example of a typical journal report, which chronologically lists business transactions.

Date : 03/31/89
Time : 10:31 AM

Paddle and Portage Canoe Outfitters
Post Office Box 555
Grand Marais, MN 55604
Phone (218) 555-1234

Page no. 1

General Ledger Journal Report

| Journal Trans.# | Date | Acct. # | Account Name | Description | Debits | Credits | Posted? |
|---|---|---|---|---|---|---|---|
| AP 0329 | 03/29/88 | 2101 | Accts Payable-Module | Payments Summ.-AP Post | 525.00 | | NO |
| | | 11021 | Checking Account | Mountain House F-000001 | | 100.00 | NO |
| | | 11021 | Checking Account | Mountain House F-000002 | | 425.00 | NO |
| | | | | TOTAL TRANSACTION : | 525.00 | 525.00 | |
| AR 0330 | 03/30/88 | 11021 | Checking Account | Payments Summ.-AR Post | 108.00 | | NO |
| | | 11051 | Accts Rec'ble Module | Payments Summ.-AR Post | | 108.00 | NO |
| | | | | TOTAL TRANSACTION : | 108.00 | 108.00 | |
| GJ 0001 | 03/30/88 | 11023 | Savings Account | Transfer from Savings | 1000.00 | | NO |
| | | 11021 | Checking Account | Transfer from Savings | | 1000.00 | NO |
| | | | | TOTAL TRANSACTION : | 1000.00 | 1000.00 | |
| PY 0330 | 03/30/88 | 520112 | Hourly | PAYROLL POST SUMMARY | 1200.00 | | NO |
| | | 520131 | Fica Employer | PAYROLL POST SUMMARY | 85.80 | | NO |
| | | 520132 | Futa | PAYROLL POST SUMMARY | 74.40 | | NO |
| | | 11022 | Payroll Account | PAYROLL POST SUMMARY | | 905.48 | NO |
| | | 210411 | Federal Income W/H | PAYROLL POST SUMMARY | | 167.88 | NO |
| | | 210412 | Fica W/H Employee | PAYROLL POST SUMMARY | | 85.80 | NO |
| | | 210413 | Fica W/H Employer | PAYROLL POST SUMMARY | | 85.80 | NO |
| | | 210414 | Futa | PAYROLL POST SUMMARY | | 74.40 | NO |
| | | 210416 | State Income W/H | PAYROLL POST SUMMARY | | 40.84 | NO |
| | | | | TOTAL TRANSACTION : | 1360.20 | 1360.20 | |
| SU 0325 | 03/25/88 | 11071 | Inventory - Module | Summ. Products Setup | 304.75 | | YES |
| | | D | Journal Difference | Summ. Products Setup | | 304.75 | YES |
| | | | | TOTAL TRANSACTION : | 304.75 | 304.75 | |
| SU 0330 | 03/30/88 | 11071 | Inventory - Module | Summ. Products Setup | -690.00 | | YES |
| | | D | Journal Difference | Summ. Products Setup | | -690.00 | YES |
| | | | | TOTAL TRANSACTION : | -690.00 | -690.00 | |
| | | | | TOTAL TRANSACTION : | 2607.95 | 2607.95 | |

# OF ENTRIES PRINTED : 20

Although journals are essential for keeping complete records of transactions, they don't present a good picture of the current financial status or overall condition of a business. To do this you need to summarize the large quantities of data recorded in journals. Two of the most common reports that present a general view of the financial health of a business are the balance sheet and the income statement.

A **balance sheet** summarizes the assets, liabilities, and capital of a business. In a compact form, it lists the current balances in the accounts that reflect an enterprise's financial condition. As the simplified example in Figure 15.4 shows, a balance sheet lists the assets, liabilities, and capital accounts in separate sections and presents the current totals of each of these. It's called a balance sheet because the sum of liabilities and capital must *always* equal total assets. In simple terms, the current "worth" of your business consists of how much you have minus how much you owe, as shown in this formula:

ASSETS – LIABILITIES = CAPITAL

If you rearrange this formula, you get the fundamental **accounting equation** that summarizes the financial condition of a business:

ASSETS = LIABILITIES + CAPITAL

The balance sheet is just a more detailed expression of the components that make up this equation. It always presents the status of a business on the date the balance sheet was created. Since liabilities and assets can change from day to day, a balance sheet is like an individual snapshot of a business frozen in time. A balance sheet is most meaningful when it's compared with past balance sheets.

**Figure 15.4 Balance Sheet**
A balance sheet lists the assets, liabilities, and capital accounts, and presents their totals.

```
Date: 03/31/89      Paddle and Portage Canoe Outfitters         Page no. 1
Time: 10:35 AM             Post Office Box 555
                         Grand Marais, MN  55604
                           Phone (218) 555-1234

                              BALANCE SHEET


ASSETS
Current Assets                      14132.55
Fixed Assets                        88714.30
                                  ----------
Total Assets                       102846.85
                                  ==========


LIABILITIES
Accounts Payable                     2451.62
Notes Payable                        5000.00
                                  ----------
Total Liabilities                    7451.62
                                  ==========


CAPITAL
Initial Investment                  80000.00
Profit                              15395.23
                                  ----------
Total Capital                       95395.23
                                  ==========
Total Liabilities and Capital      102846.85
```

An **income statement** summarizes the revenues and expenses of a business for a given period of time (see Figure 15.5). Its main purpose is to show the profit of a business over a particular month, quarter, or year. **Profit** is defined as the difference between revenues and expenses, as shown by this equation:

PROFIT = REVENUES – EXPENSES

If revenues are greater than expenses, then the difference is positive and the company has made a profit. If the resulting value is negative, then the business has suffered a **loss**. For this reason, income statements are sometimes called *profit and loss statements*. They reflect the operating results of running a business, and can be used with balance sheets to get a more complete view of the overall status and operational performance of a business. For example, we can expand the accounting equation to include profit as another component of total assets:

ASSETS = LIABILITIES + CAPITAL + REVENUES – EXPENSES

Here again, the main point to remember is that the amount on the left *must* balance the amounts on the right side of the equal sign. By definition, double entry accounting systems are always in balance. If they are not, an error has been made that must be corrected.

**Figure 15.5 Income Statement**
An income statement summarizes the revenues and expenses of a business for a given period of time.

```
Date: 03/31/89      Paddle and Portage Canoe Outfitters        Page no. 1
Time: 10:36 AM               Post Office Box 555
                          Grand Marais, MN  55604
                            Phone (218) 555-1234


                              INCOME STATEMENT

                    For the Year Ending December 31 of 1988


Sales                               103124.25
Cost of Goods Sold                   21391.30
                                   ----------
Gross Margin                         81732.95

General Expenses                     63179.97
                                   ----------
Profit from Operations               18552.98
Taxes                                 3157.75
                                   ----------
Net Profit                           15395.23
                                   ==========
```

## Primary Accounting Functions

*Basic accounting system components*

Traditionally, accounting systems are divided into several subsystems, each of which has a particular function (see Figure 15.6). These subsystems interact with one another to help you enter, classify, store, analyze, summarize, and report the essential financial data of your business. In a computerized accounting system, the

**Figure 15.6 Accounting Subsystems**
This diagram illustrates how the accounting subsystems are related.

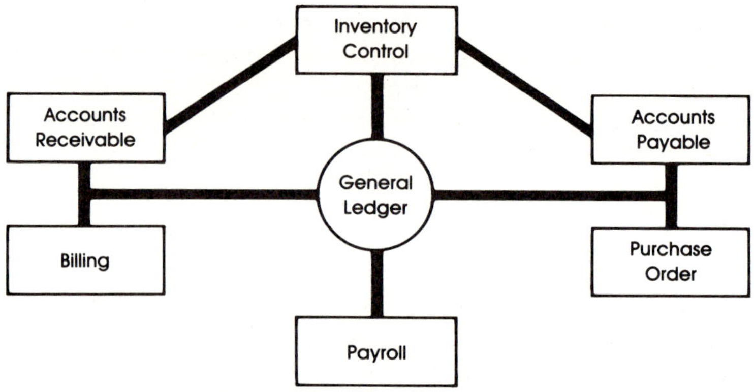


subsystems are either separate programs or separate modules within the same program. Specifically, most accounting systems include several subsystems.

## General Ledger

*The heart of an accounting system*

This subsystem is the heart of any accounting system. Basically, the **general ledger** is the main storehouse of information about the accounts of a business. As we said before, business transactions are recorded in journals. At the end of an accounting period, say a month for example, the totals for each journal are copied or **posted** to the corresponding accounts in the general ledger. In a computerized system, the general ledger is automatically and continuously updated. The general ledger lets you set up your chart of accounts and constantly monitor all business activities. It gathers data from the other accounting modules and lets you summarize the data in reports such as balance sheets and income statements.

## Accounts Receivable

*Keeping track of sales*

The **accounts receivable** subsystem records all sales of goods and services to customers. It also keeps track of customer credit, payments, and balances. The accounts receivable entries are used to issue statements to customers summarizing their transactions, the total amount owed as of that date, and how long the money has been due. These entries are also used to generate **aged accounts receivable reports** that indicate how much money each customer owes and how long it has been outstanding.

## Accounts Payable

*Keeping track of purchases*

The **accounts payable** subsystem records the purchases of goods and services from each **vendor**, that is, from a person or company that sells you something. Besides keeping track of the money due to each vendor, the accounts payable system is also used to generate checks and project the cash balances needed to make the necessary payments. By helping a business pay its bills on time, the accounts payable system makes it easier to take advantage of cash discounts offered by vendors. It also helps monitor and control the cash flow of a business.

## Inventory Control

*Keeping track of products*

Every business that sells goods must keep running counts of its products and materials on hand. The **inventory control** subsystem helps to track these items, which are continuously being purchased and sold. It also interacts with the general ledger, accounts receivable, and accounts payable systems to keep essential business information up to date. By generating inventory status reports, the inventory control system signals when additional materials should be purchased and helps identify slow-moving products.

### Purchase Order

*Keeping track of orders*

Virtually every business purchases products, materials, and services. In many cases, **purchase orders** must be completed before products and services can be bought. These are printed forms sent to vendors and kept on file to prevent duplicate purchases. The purchase order subsystem can save a great deal of time and help automate the process of acquiring the materials and services needed to run a business. Obviously, the purchase order subsystem must work very closely with the accounts payable subsystem.

### Billing

*Keeping track of invoices*

Many businesses that sell goods or services send bills to their customers informing them of the money they owe for their purchases. These bills, called **invoices**, list each item shipped along with its price and any other terms of the sale. By printing these invoices, the **billing** subsystem provides proof of payment for customers, controls sales taxes, increases cash flow, helps in the packing and shipping of products, and maintains records of each customer's buying history. As you might expect, the billing subsystem is tied in with the accounts receivable system.

### Payroll

*Keeping track of paychecks*

Any business with employees can use a payroll system; businesses with many employees simply cannot do without one. Basically, the **payroll** system maintains personnel and pay rate information; generates employee paychecks; computes withholdings and deductions; produces tax reports for federal, state, and local governments; and creates summary reports of employee earnings.

## INTRODUCING DAC-EASY ACCOUNTING AND PAYROLL

*The most popular package*

For the rest of this chapter we're going to illustrate the use of an actual accounting package for IBM-compatible microcomputers. The specific programs we'll discuss are Dac-Easy Accounting (Version 2.0) and Dac-Easy Payroll (Version 2.0), from Dac Software, Incorporated. Originally released in 1985, Dac-Easy Accounting has become the world's best-selling accounting package. According to Ken Howe, president of Dac Software, the program sells around 25,000 copies each month. This is probably due to the program's functionality, its ease of use, and its low retail list price of around $100. Dac-Easy Accounting combines the basic general ledger, accounts receivable, accounts payable, purchase order, billing, and inventory control modules, along with a system for budgeting and forecasting. Although it doesn't include a payroll system, this function is available for around $70 from Dac Software in a separate program called Dac-Easy Payroll. The subsystems all work together and share data to minimize having to make repetitive entries. Furthermore, the programs are menu-driven and include an on-line help facility. In short, Dac-Easy Accounting and Dac-Easy Payroll are ideal for introducing the concepts of microcomputer accounting software.

## SETTING UP THE ACCOUNTING SYSTEM

*Potentially difficult task*

The most difficult part of using a computerized accounting system is initially setting it up. First, all of your business records must be entered into the computer, a time-consuming and tedious process. Nevertheless, most businesses find that accounting software eventually saves them a significant amount of time and money while helping them better manage their finances.

As an example, we're going to use the Dac-Easy software to set up a computerized accounting system for our imaginary small business, Paddle and Portage Canoe Outfitters. Let's assume the software has already been installed on a computer with a hard disk. The Dac-Easy Accounting package is kept in a subdirectory named DEA, and Dac-Easy Payroll is in a subdirectory named DEP.

### Defining the Accounting Files

*Making room for accounting data*

Before you begin entering your business records, you must tell the Dac-Easy Accounting program where to put your files. You also have to answer some questions that allow the program to estimate the size of your files and reserve space on the disk. To do these things you start the program by switching to the DEA subdirectory and entering **DEA**. After the program presents its initial copyright screen, you press any key to begin. Dac-Easy Accounting then asks you to specify the subdirectory for your business files. By default, the program will create a subdirectory named FILES under your DEA subdirectory. This is fine for our example, so all you have to do is press the **Enter** key.

In the next screen, Dac-Easy Accounting asks if you want to use the sample chart of accounts included with the package. This chart of accounts, which we'll be discussing shortly, is quite comprehensive and could be used as is by many businesses. Using the sample chart of accounts is easiest because it saves you the trouble of creating your own. If necessary, you can modify the sample chart of accounts later to meet your own specific needs. To use the sample chart of accounts, simply type **Y** for yes and press the **Enter** key.

To help Dac-Easy Accounting estimate the size of your business files, you must answer the five questions you now see on the screen in Figure 15.7. The first one is answered automatically if you choose the sample chart of accounts. The remaining questions must be answered with your estimates on the number of customers, vendors, products and services, and daily invoices you have. As the screen message says, you don't have to be exact. The Dac-Easy Accounting reference manual suggests that you enter numbers that reflect your current status, plus 20 percent for growth. After you answer these questions, the program calculates the approximate number of bytes of disk space required by your accounting system. It then asks if you want to start creating your files now, and you can enter **Y** for yes.

### Entering the Accounting Records

*Creating the files*

After you define your files and tell the program that you want to start creating them, Dac-Easy Accounting displays its Main menu, shown in Figure 15.8. The definition of files we've just described needs to be done only once. Once you perform these operations, Dac-Easy Accounting goes directly from the initial copyright screen to the Main menu whenever you start the program.

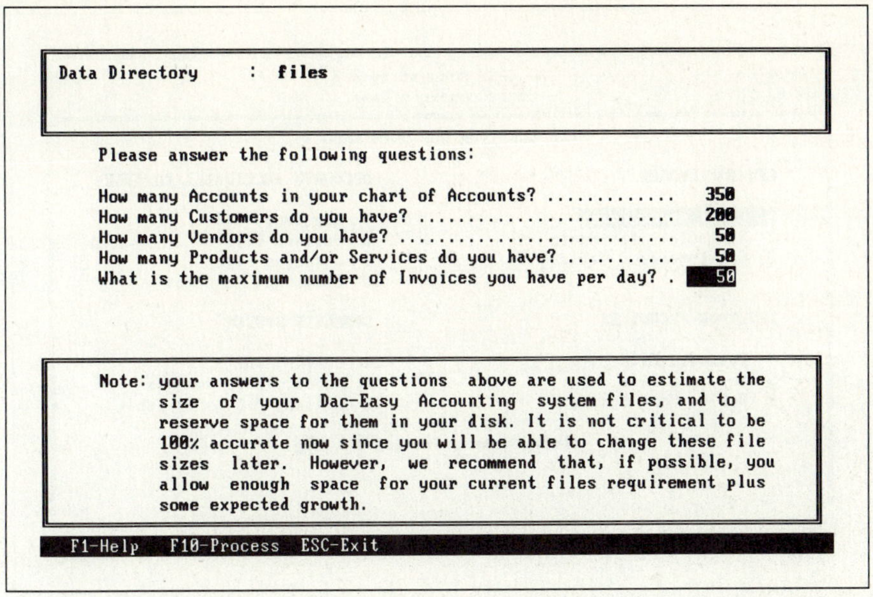


**Figure 15.7 Defining the Files**
Dac-Easy Accounting asks these questions to estimate the size of your business files.

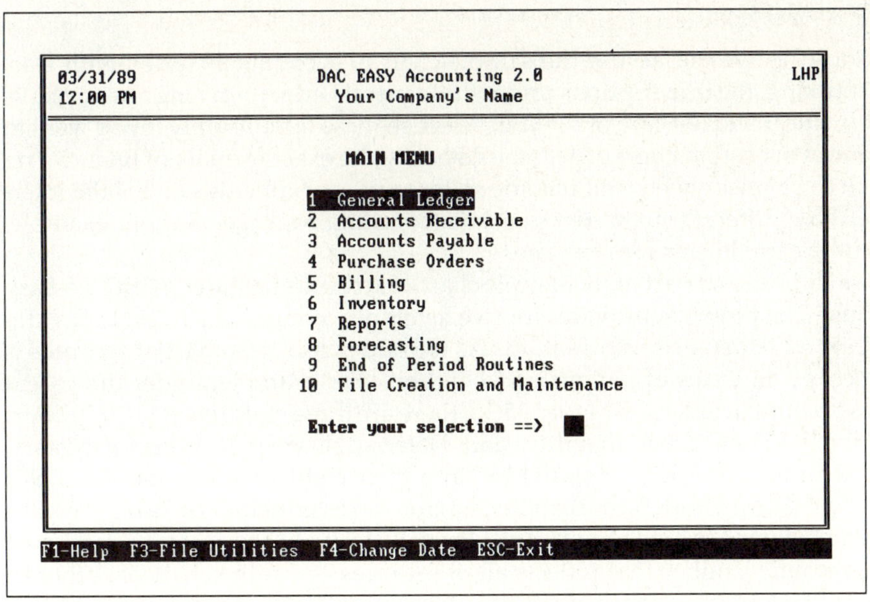


**Figure 15.8 Dac-Easy Accounting Main Menu**
This screen shows the Dac-Easy Accounting (Version 2.0) Main menu.

As you can see, among other items, the Main menu lists all of the major accounting subsystems that we discussed previously, except for payroll, which is a separate program. Before you can use any of them, however, first you must create the necessary data files. To do this, you select option 10, File Creation and Maintenance from the Main menu. Figure 15.9 shows the new menu that appears on your screen. This File Creation and Maintenance menu displays several headings with options for creating various accounting files. Fortunately, you don't have to create all of the files in this menu. We'll go through only the most important ones.

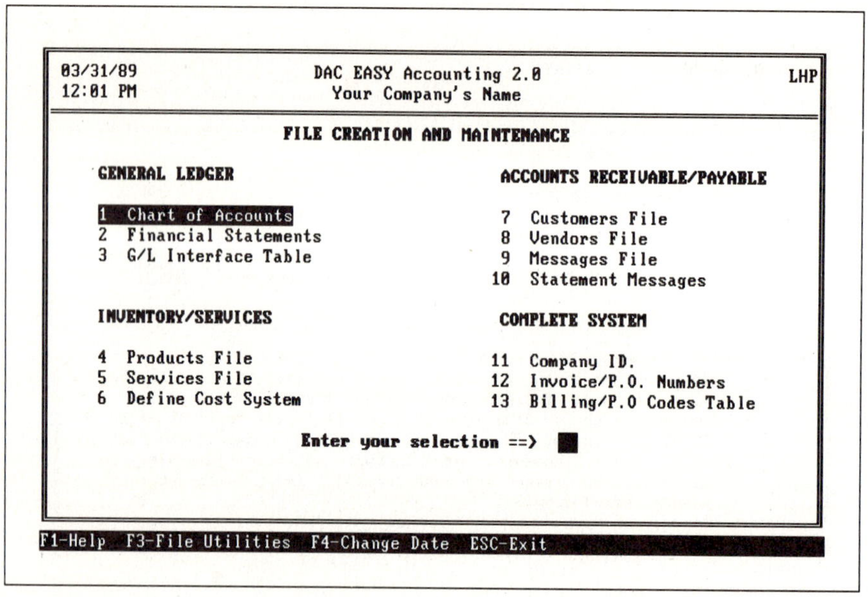


**Figure 15.9 File Creation and Maintenance Menu**
The File Creation and Maintenance menu is used to set up the data files before you enter the actual data.

## General Ledger

*Specifying the accounts*

If you choose, as we did, to use the sample chart of accounts included with Dac-Easy Accounting, the three options under the General Ledger heading already have been automatically taken care of for you. You use these options only if you want to create your own custom chart of accounts, specify the exact formats of financial reports such as balance sheets and income statements, or explicitly control the interaction between different subsystems of the accounting package. For our example, the default general ledger files are fine.

Figure 15.10 shows part of the sample chart of accounts included with Dac-Easy Accounting. The program provides for five levels of accounts. Each level provides successively more detailed information. As we said before, the chart of accounts is often described in terms of parents and children. For example, under the parent Liabilities account at level 1 in Figure 15.10, there are three children at level 2: Short Term Liability, Long Term Liability, and Deferred Liability. When necessary, children accounts are further subdivided into their children accounts. So, Taxes Payable is a child of Short Term Liability, Payroll Taxes is a child of Taxes Payable, and Federal Income Withheld is a child of Payroll Taxes. Every account is assigned a unique account number that reflects all of its ancestors in the chart of accounts. Accounts at the lowest level are called **detail accounts**. These are the accounts that actually record credit and debit transactions. All other accounts are called **general accounts**. These are the accounts that automatically receive data from the accounts below. This multilevel account structure allows you to flexibly organize your financial data.

## Inventory/Services

Once you have your general ledger set up, you can begin entering the data for your product and services inventory. This is necessary before you can use the purchase order and billing systems.

First, let's enter the product inventory. Select option 4 from the File Creation and Maintenance menu to create the products file. A form appears on the screen for you to enter information about each particular product. Figure 15.11 shows a

**Figure 15.10 Sample Chart of Accounts**
This is a partial listing of the Dac-Easy Accounting sample chart of accounts.

| Acct. # | Account Name | Acct. Type | Level | Type | General |
|---|---|---|---|---|---|
| 2 | Liabilities | LIAB. | 1 | GENERAL | |
| 21 | Short Term Liability | LIAB. | 2 | GENERAL | 2 |
| 2101 | Accounts Payable-Module | LIAB. | 3 | DETAIL | 21 |
| 2102 | Notes Payable | LIAB. | 3 | DETAIL | 21 |
| 2103 | Accrued Payable | LIAB. | 3 | DETAIL | 21 |
| 2104 | Taxes Payable | LIAB. | 3 | GENERAL | 21 |
| 21041 | Payroll Taxes | LIAB. | 4 | GENERAL | 2104 |
| 210411 | Federal Income Withheld | LIAB. | 5 | DETAIL | 21041 |
| 210412 | FICA Withheld Employee | LIAB. | 5 | DETAIL | 21041 |
| 210413 | FICA Withheld Employer | LIAB. | 5 | DETAIL | 21041 |
| 210414 | FUTA | LIAB. | 5 | DETAIL | 21041 |
| 210415 | SUTA | LIAB. | 5 | DETAIL | 21041 |
| 210416 | State Income Withheld | LIAB. | 5 | DETAIL | 21041 |
| 210417 | City Income Withheld | LIAB. | 5 | DETAIL | 21041 |
| 210418 | Disability Insurance | LIAB. | 5 | DETAIL | 21041 |
| 21042 | Sales Tax Payable | LIAB. | 4 | DETAIL | 2104 |
| 21043 | Property Tax | LIAB. | 4 | DETAIL | 2104 |
| 21044 | Franchise Tax | LIAB. | 4 | DETAIL | 2104 |
| 21045 | Foreign Tax | LIAB. | 4 | DETAIL | 2104 |
| 21046 | Income Tax Payable | LIAB. | 4 | GENERAL | 2104 |
| 210461 | Federal Income Tax | LIAB. | 5 | DETAIL | 21046 |
| 210462 | State Income Tax | LIAB. | 5 | DETAIL | 21046 |
| 210463 | City Income Tax | LIAB. | 5 | DETAIL | 21046 |
| 21047 | Other Tax Payable | LIAB. | 4 | DETAIL | 2104 |
| 2105 | Other Payroll Payable | LIAB. | 3 | GENERAL | 21 |
| 21051 | Union Dues | LIAB. | 4 | DETAIL | 2105 |
| 21052 | Employee Charity | LIAB. | 4 | DETAIL | 2105 |
| 21053 | Christmas Fund Accrued | LIAB. | 4 | DETAIL | 2105 |
| 2106 | Dividends Payable | LIAB. | 3 | DETAIL | 21 |
| 2107 | Other Payable | LIAB. | 3 | DETAIL | 21 |
| 22 | Long Term Liability | LIAB. | 2 | GENERAL | 2 |
| 2201 | Mortgages Payable | LIAB. | 3 | DETAIL | 22 |
| 2202 | Notes Payable | LIAB. | 3 | DETAIL | 22 |
| 2203 | Current Long Term Liability | LIAB. | 3 | DETAIL | 22 |
| 2204 | Other Long Term Liability | LIAB. | 3 | DETAIL | 22 |
| 23 | Deferred Liability | LIAB. | 2 | GENERAL | 2 |
| 2301 | Commit & Contingency | LIAB. | 3 | DETAIL | 23 |
| 2302 | Deferred Income | LIAB. | 3 | DETAIL | 23 |
| 2303 | Profit/Installment Sales | LIAB. | 3 | DETAIL | 23 |
| 2304 | Unearned Interest | LIAB. | 3 | DETAIL | 23 |

partially completed form for a packaged trail-food dinner sold by Paddle and Portage Canoe Outfitters. As you can see, you need to enter several items of information about each product, including its product code, description, unit of measure, department, sales price, bin (storage location), minimum number you want to keep on hand, optimum number to reorder, and vendor code. After you enter these data, you should press the **F7** function key to specify your current stock. A small window pops up on your screen requesting you to enter the number of units you have on hand, and your per unit cost. When you're finished, you press the **F10** function key to save the data for that item. You can then go on to enter the inventory information about the next product. This process is repeated for each product sold by the business. When you're finished with all of the products, you press the **Escape** key to return to the File Creation and Maintenance menu.

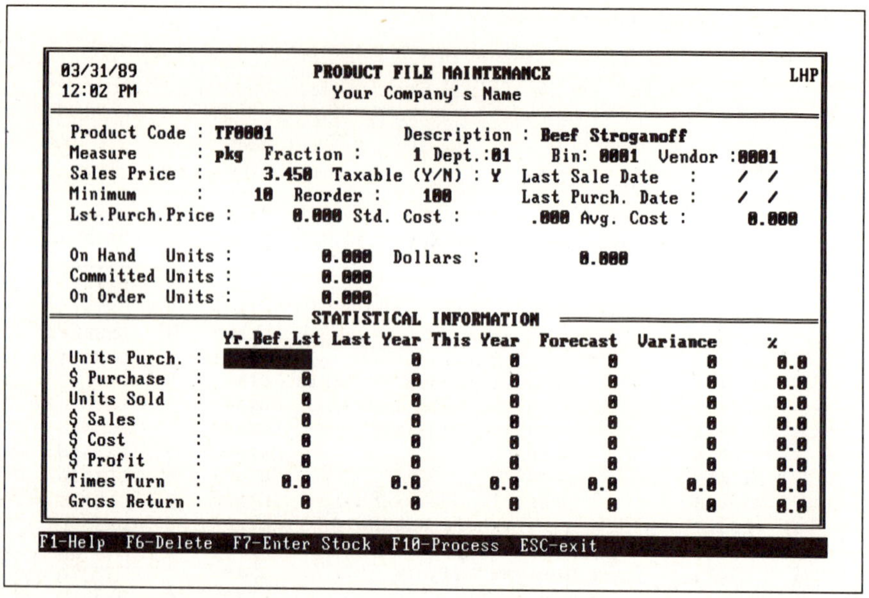


**Figure 15.11 Creating the Product File**
Here you enter data about each product sold by the company.

*Entering the products and services*

Dac-Easy Accounting can be used by businesses that offer both products and services. Since Paddle and Portage Canoe Outfitters rents a variety of equipment, they also need to keep track of services. This can be done by selecting option 5 from the File Creation and Maintenance menu to create a service file. The process is similar to creating a product file. A blank form appears on the screen for entering data about a particular service. You simply fill in the blanks for service code number, description, unit of service measurement, department code, price, and whether the service is taxable. Figure 15.12 shows a completed form for the daily canoe rental service. When you're finished specifying a service, you press the **F10** function key to save the specification and go on to the next service. Again, when you're finished with all the records, you press the **Escape** key to return to the File Creation and Maintenance menu.

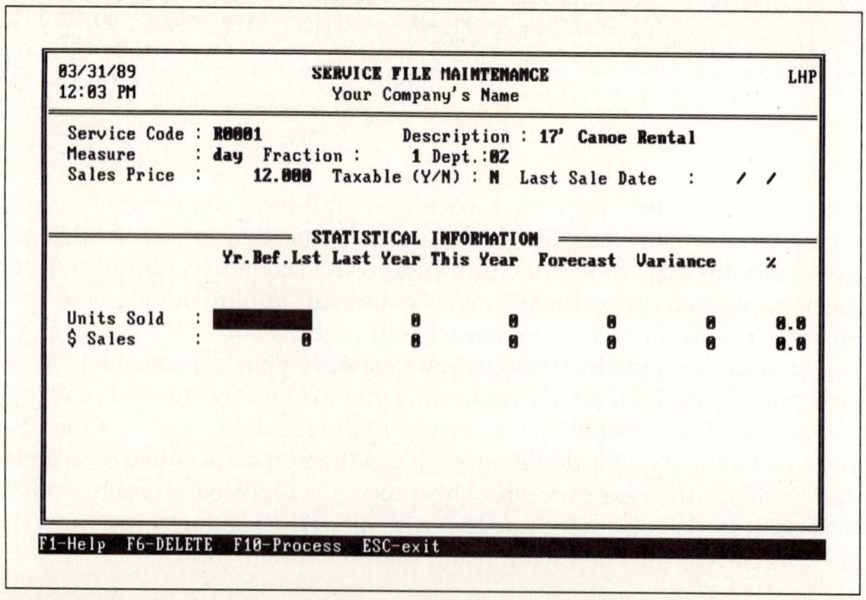


**Figure 15.12 Creating the Service File**
Here is where you enter data about each service offered by the company.

## Accounts Receivable/Payable

*Entering customers and vendors*

In order to use the accounts receivable and accounts payable systems, first you need to enter data about your customers and vendors. To set up a customer file, you select option 7 from the File Creation and Maintenance menu. A blank form then appears on your screen and you simply fill in the relevant fields about your first customer (see Figure 15.13). Besides identification code, name, address, and telephone number, you also can maintain credit and balance information about each customer. When you're finished entering a customer's data, you press the **F10** key to save them and go on to the next customer. Pressing the **Escape** key returns you to the File Creation and Maintenance menu.

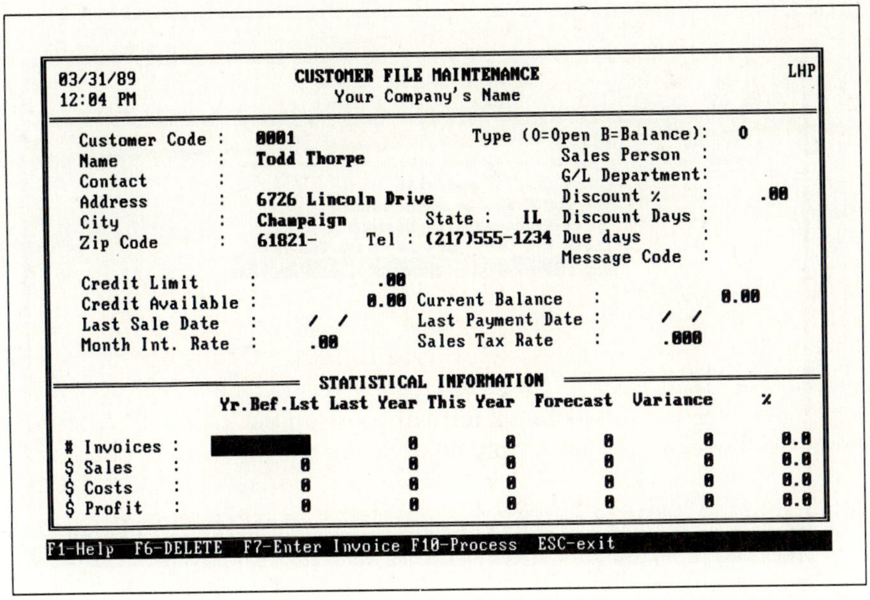


**Figure 15.13 Creating the Customer File**
Here you enter data about each customer.

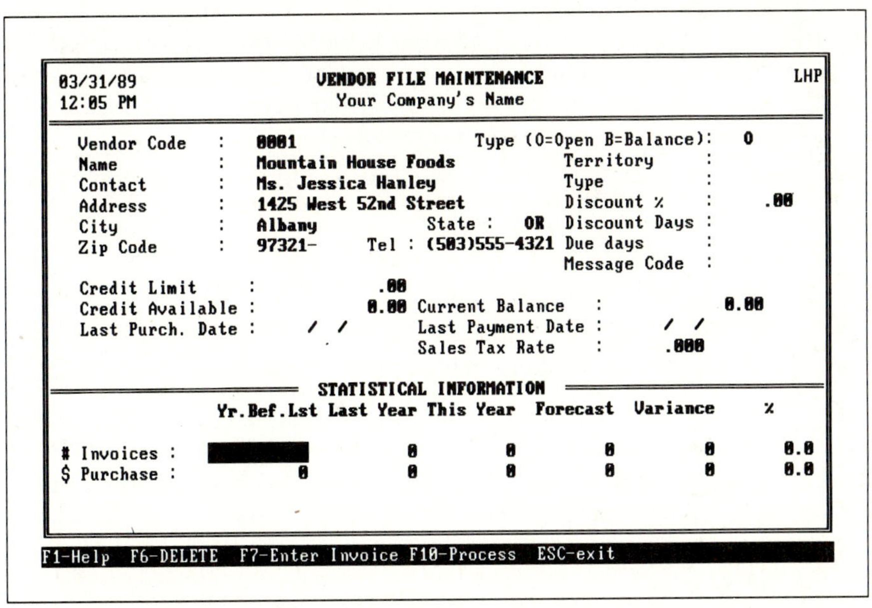


**Figure 15.14 Creating the Vendor File**
Here you enter data about each vendor from which the company buys goods or services.

The process is essentially the same for creating a file of vendors, except that you choose option 8 from the File Creation and Maintenance menu. Figure 15.14, for example, shows the form you complete for each business or organization from which you buy goods and services.

The final two selections under the Accounts Receivable/Payable heading of the File Creation and Maintenance menu are strictly optional. Nevertheless, they can come in handy. Option 9 lets you create a messages file for up to 40 different messages. Any one of these messages can be assigned to a customer or vendor account and displayed on the screen whenever that account is called up. These messages also can be printed on purchase orders and invoices. Figure 15.15 shows a few sample messages.

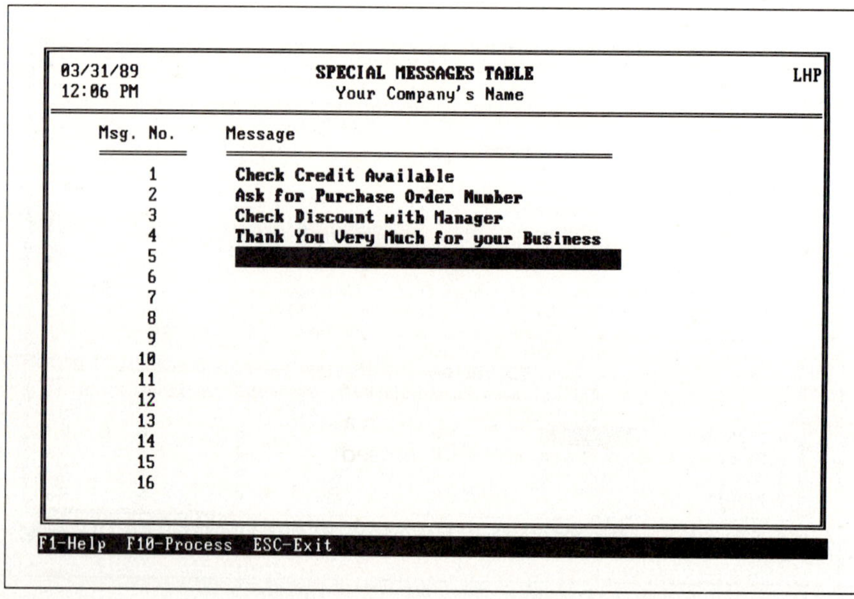


**Figure 15.15 Creating the Messages File**
You can enter and assign messages to customers and vendors that will be displayed whenever their accounts are called up, or can be printed on purchase orders and invoices.

*Entering messages*

Option 10 lets you enter various messages to be automatically printed on monthly statements sent to customers. These messages are based on the customers' current balances and whether they are past due on their payments. There are five different situations for which you can create a message:

- *Inactive.* The customer has not made a purchase during that month and has no balance.
- *Current Balance.* The customer has made his or her payment on time.
- *Due 1-30 Days.* The customer's balance has been delinquent from 1 to 30 days.
- *Due 31-60 Days.* The customer's balance has been delinquent from 31 to 60 days.
- *Due Over 60.* The customer's balance has been delinquent more than 60 days.

Figure 15.16 shows sample messages you might print on statements to either thank customers or urge them to make their payments. Customized statement messages such as these can help customers feel appreciated when they pay on time or perhaps guilty enough to make their payments if they are past due.

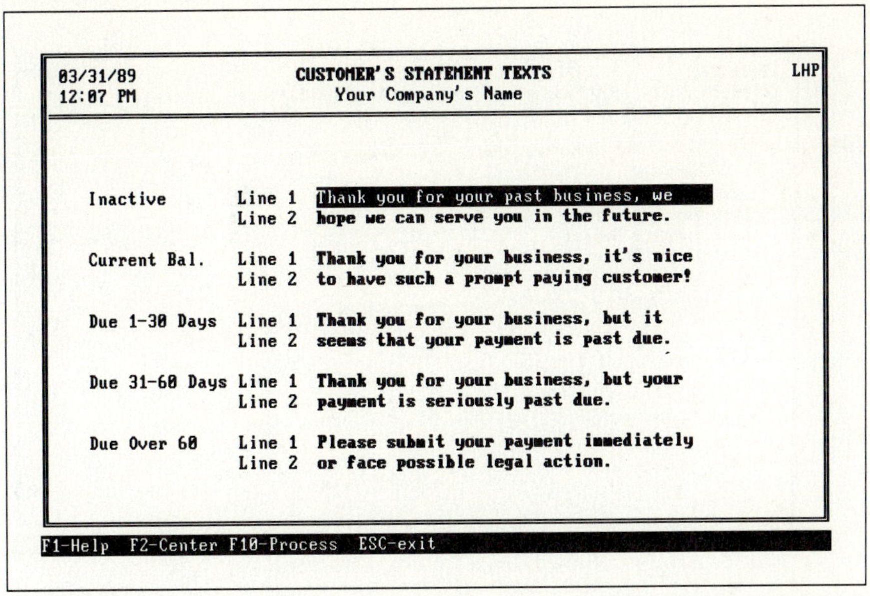


**Figure 15.16 Creating Statement Messages**
You can create messages to be printed on statements sent to customers.

## Complete System

*Specifying the company and its numbering scheme*

The final heading of the File Creation and Maintenance menu is labeled Complete System (see Figure 15.9). The three options under this heading are miscellaneous functions for completing the set up of an accounting system.

The first option, Company ID, is used to tell Dac-Easy Accounting the name, address, and phone number of your business. As Figure 15.17 shows, after executing option 11 from the File Creation and Maintenance menu, the program allows you to enter four lines of information about your business. Once you do this, Dac-Easy Accounting will print these lines at the top of every report. In addition, the first line will appear at the top of most screen displays, instead of the "Your Company's Name" label you see in several of this chapter's figures.

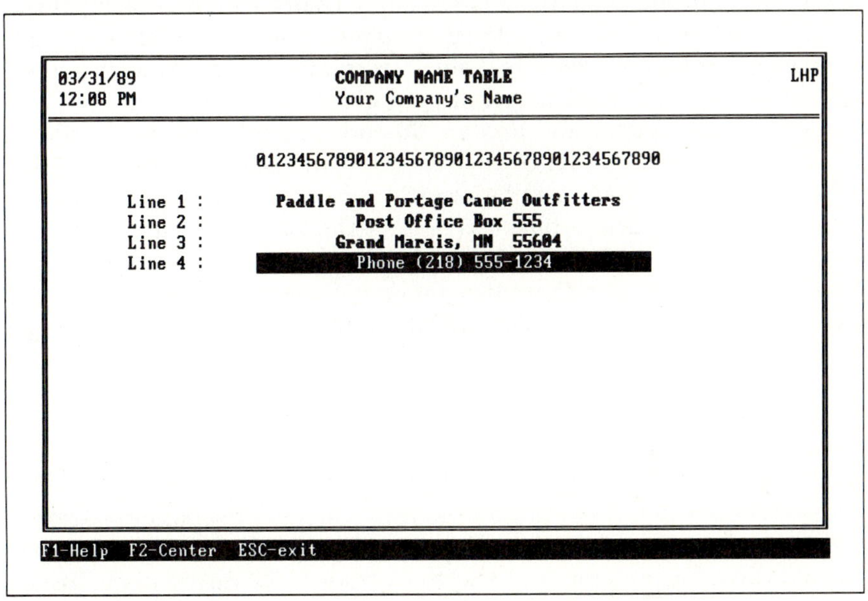


**Figure 15.17 Entering the Company ID**
Here you enter the name, address, and phone number of the company.

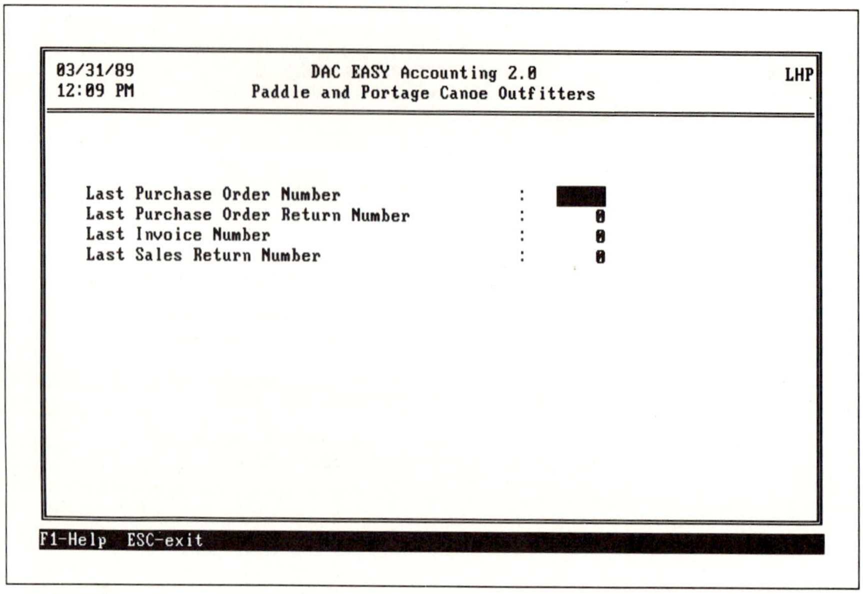


**Figure 15.18 Entering Invoice/P.O. Numbers**
Here you tell the program how to begin numbering invoices and purchase orders.

The second option under the Complete System heading is used for setting up the automatic numbering of invoices and purchase orders. In most cases, invoices and purchase orders have unique, sequential numbers printed on them, just like personal checks. When switching from a manual to a computerized accounting system, you may want to maintain the same numbering of invoices and purchase orders. Unless you invoke the Invoice/P.O. Numbers option, Dac-Easy Accounting will begin numbering invoices and purchase orders with 00001. As Figure 15.18 shows, when you execute option 12 from the File Creation and Maintenance menu, you can tell the program to begin numbering your invoices and purchase orders wherever your manual accounting system left off—with numbers other than 00001.

Finally, the last option under the Complete System heading is used to set up a table of code numbers for classifying miscellaneous items purchased and sold. Typically, these are items that are not listed in your product and service inventory files. For example, your business might need to buy insurance, advertising, furniture, and other products not directly related to manufacturing or reselling. In addition, your business might sell items that aren't its primary products, such as used equipment and furniture. Dac-Easy Accounting gives you 20 different codes for miscellaneous purchase orders and another 20 codes for miscellaneous billing. When you execute option 13 under the File Creation and Maintenance menu, the program displays the table you see in Figure 15.19. You can use this table as is or modify it for your own particular business needs. The table associates these miscellaneous purchase order and billing codes with the corresponding accounts that will receive the debit or credit in the general ledger. Once this table is set up, you can use these codes in the purchase order and billing systems and the general ledger will be automatically updated.

## Defining the Payroll Files

*Making room for payroll data*

With Dac-Easy software, the accounting and payroll systems are separate programs. Consequently, in order to set up the payroll system you must first exit Dac-Easy Accounting. This is done by pressing the **Escape** key from the Main menu. To invoke

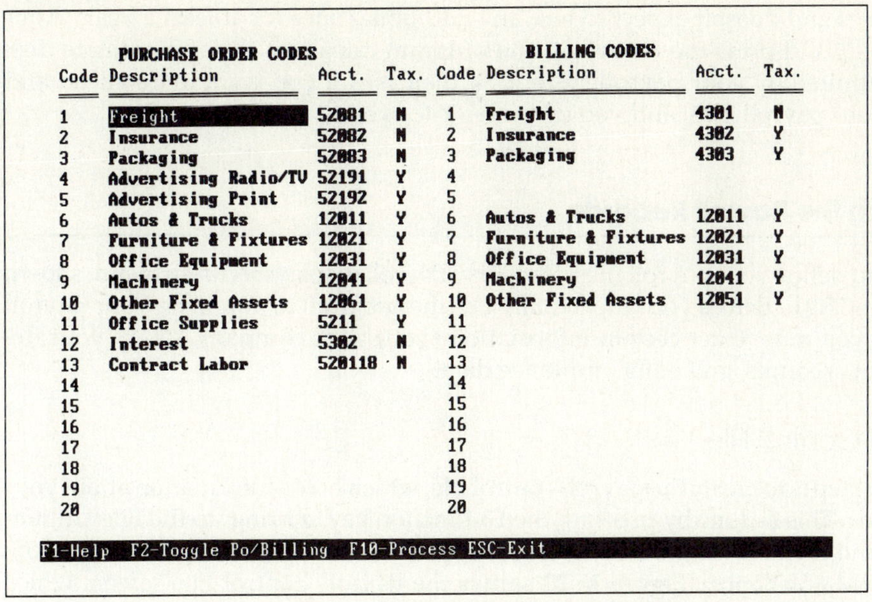

| | PURCHASE ORDER CODES | | | | BILLING CODES | | |
|---|---|---|---|---|---|---|---|
| Code | Description | Acct. | Tax. | Code | Description | Acct. | Tax. |
| 1 | Freight | 52001 | N | 1 | Freight | 4301 | N |
| 2 | Insurance | 52002 | N | 2 | Insurance | 4302 | Y |
| 3 | Packaging | 52003 | N | 3 | Packaging | 4303 | Y |
| 4 | Advertising Radio/TV | 52191 | Y | 4 | | | |
| 5 | Advertising Print | 52192 | Y | 5 | | | |
| 6 | Autos & Trucks | 12011 | Y | 6 | Autos & Trucks | 12011 | Y |
| 7 | Furniture & Fixtures | 12021 | Y | 7 | Furniture & Fixtures | 12021 | Y |
| 8 | Office Equipment | 12031 | Y | 8 | Office Equipment | 12031 | Y |
| 9 | Machinery | 12041 | Y | 9 | Machinery | 12041 | Y |
| 10 | Other Fixed Assets | 12061 | Y | 10 | Other Fixed Assets | 12051 | Y |
| 11 | Office Supplies | 5211 | Y | 11 | | | |
| 12 | Interest | 5302 | N | 12 | | | |
| 13 | Contract Labor | 520110 | N | 13 | | | |
| 14 | | | | 14 | | | |
| 15 | | | | 15 | | | |
| 16 | | | | 16 | | | |
| 17 | | | | 17 | | | |
| 18 | | | | 18 | | | |
| 19 | | | | 19 | | | |
| 20 | | | | 20 | | | |

F1-Help F2-Toggle Po/Billing F10-Process ESC-Exit

**Figure 15.19 Billing/P.O. Table**
Here you can set up miscellaneous purchase order and billing codes.

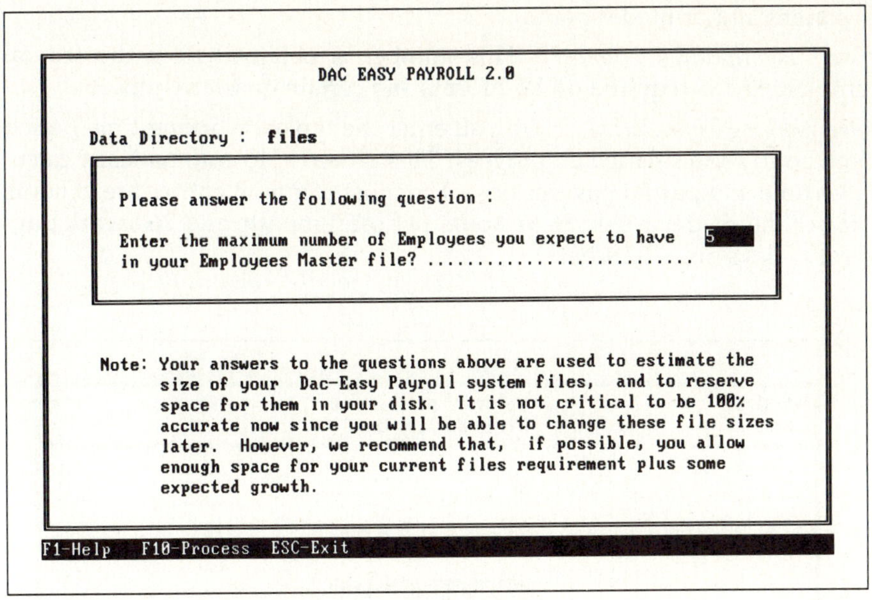


**Figure 15.20 Defining Payroll files**
Here you tell Dac-Easy Payroll the number of employees.

the payroll system, you enter **DEP** from DOS after switching to the *DEP* subdirectory with **CD \DEP**. The initial copyright message then appears on your screen.

After pressing any key to continue, Dac-Easy Payroll asks for the directory where you want to store your data files. The program suggests a subdirectory named FILES under the C:\DEP directory. This is fine for our example, so all you have to do is press the **Enter** key here.

As Figure 15.20 shows, Dac-Easy Payroll now asks you to estimate your total number of employees. Paddle and Portage Canoe Outfitters has only five employees and doesn't expect to hire any additional ones for at least a year. After you type **5** and press the **Enter** key, the program calculates the approximate disk space required by your payroll system. It then asks if you want to go ahead and create your payroll files, and you can enter **Y** for yes.

## Entering the Payroll Records

*Automating the payroll*

Once you define your payroll files, Dac-Easy Payroll displays its Main menu, shown in Figure 15.21. Before you can actually use the program to automate your payroll system, you must enter certain information about your company, set up your department accounts, and enter employee data.

### Payroll Control File

*General payroll specifications*

The first step is to create the payroll control file, which holds information about your company. This is done by pressing the **F3** function key to bring up the File Utilities menu, and then pressing the **Enter** key to select the first option in that menu: Control File Maintenance. Figure 15.22 shows the Payroll Control File screen, which must be filled out completely for proper payroll processing. Specifically, you must enter:

- *Company Identification.* The name and address of your business will appear on most screens and printed reports.
- *Employer Identification Number.* This number is obtained from the federal government and is required on W-2 forms and certain quarterly reports.
- *Regular Working Time Period.* Here you enter the typical working time period for both hourly and salaried employees. This is needed to automatically calculate overtime and partial pay periods. The most common entries are: 8 hours per day, 40 hours per week, 86.67 hours per semi-month, and 260 work days per year (5 days times 52 weeks).

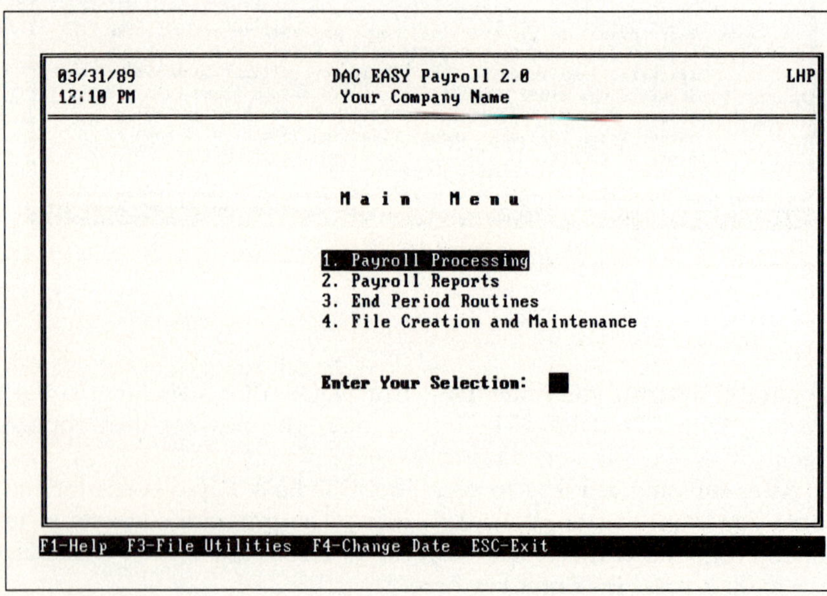


**Figure 15.21 Payroll Main Menu**
This screen shows the Dac-Easy Payroll (Version 2.0) Main menu.

- *FICA Percent and Limit.* Under the Federal Insurance Contributions Act (FICA), most employers are required to withhold and pay employees' shares of their social security taxes. The current tax rate is 7.15% and the wages subject to these taxes are limited to the first $43,800. Since tax laws frequently change, Dac-Easy Payroll allows you to enter these values explicitly.
- *FUTA Percent and Limit.* Under the Federal Unemployment Tax Act (FUTA), some employers are required to pay taxes to provide unemployment compensation to workers who have lost their jobs. Assuming your state has no unemployment tax (SUTA) of its own, the current FUTA rate is 6.2% and the wages subject to these taxes are limited to the first $7,000. Again, the laws can change and the FUTA rate is less if your state also has unemployment taxes, so Dac-Easy Payroll lets you manually enter these values.
- *Check Register.* Dac-Easy Payroll will automatically erase records of cleared checks after they are posted to the general ledger if you answer Y for yes to the question: "Erase check file after Post Process?" If you answer N for no, then the payroll program will maintain its register of issued checks.
- *Accounting Interface.* Dac-Easy Payroll can automatically send transactions to Dac-Easy Accounting, if you have both programs. To link the two programs, you need to answer Y for yes and supply the subdirectory path of your accounting data files.

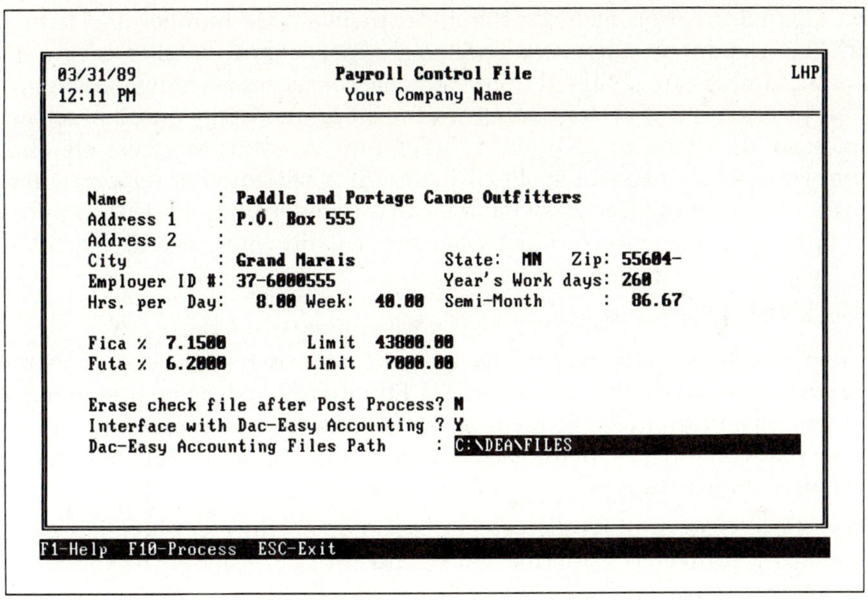


**Figure 15.22 Creating the Payroll Control File**

Here you enter information concerning the company payroll.

## Departments and Codes

*Classifying payroll transactions*

The next step is to set up your departments so that Dac-Easy Payroll can automatically generate categories of earnings and deductions and post these results to Dac-Easy Accounting. Since Paddle and Portage Canoe Outfitters is a small business, you need to set up only one department. To do this, select option 4 from the Dac-Easy Payroll Main menu to display the File Creation and Maintenance menu shown in Figure 15.23. From this menu you select the Departments and Codes option, which will then display a screen that allows you to enter information about a de-

**Figure 15.23 File Creation and Maintenance Menu**

This menu allows you to set up your payroll files.

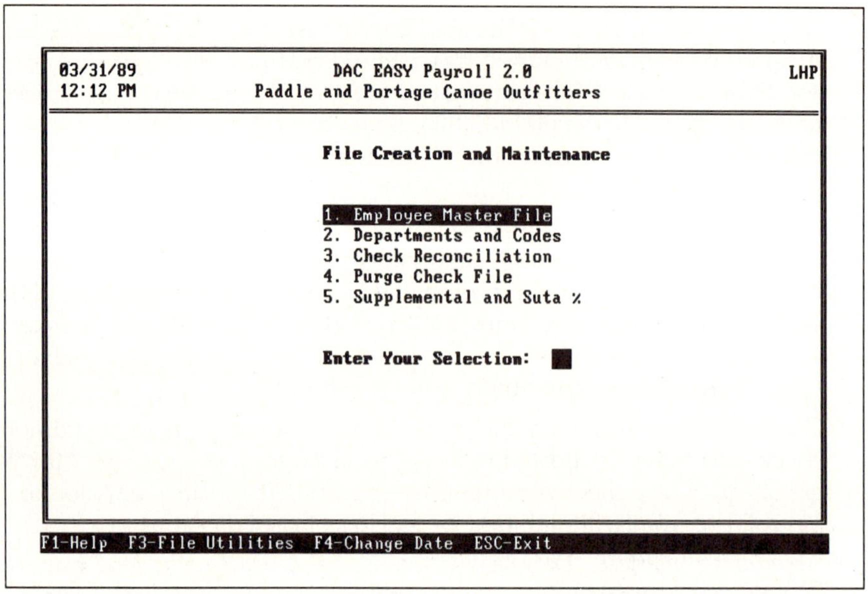


partment. This information includes the department's code number and name, along with the account numbers for checking, expense, and liability accounts. These account numbers are obtained from your chart of accounts listing (see Figure 15.10). After you enter these account numbers, the program displays another screen where you enter the earnings accounts. Again, these account numbers are also copied from your chart of accounts. Finally, you fill in still another screen for the deductions accounts. Now Dac-Easy Payroll can automatically update the appropriate accounts in Dac-Easy Accounting whenever you do your payroll.

## Employee Master File

*Entering personnel data*

The final step in setting up the payroll system is to enter each employee's personnel and payroll data. To do this you select the Employee Master File option from the File Creation and Maintenance menu. Dac-Easy Payroll then presents a form on the screen that you must fill in for each employee (see Figure 15.24). In particular, the following information may be entered:

- *Employee Data.* The employee's code number, name, address, phone number, social security number, sex, marital status, and ethnic origin may be entered.
- *Dates.* Here you enter the employee's date of birth, date of hire, of expected raise, of expected evaluation review. You can indicate whether the employee is currently on a leave of absence, or if the employment has been terminated.
- *Payment Information.* These fields are for the employee's department and classification code numbers; whether the employee is paid hourly or salaried; how frequently paid; and, for salaried employees, the amount of the base salary.
- *Hourly Rates.* For hourly workers, you can enter their normal hourly rate and up to two overtime rates: perhaps time-and-a-half for working more than 40 hours a week and double-time for working holidays.
- *Tax Information.* These fields hold various items used to compute the employee's taxes and withholdings—whether he or she is single, married and filing separately, or married and filing jointly; whether the employee is exempt

from social security or unemployment taxes; the number of allowances declared on the W4 form; state tax exemptions; and any city, county, or local withholding taxes.

- *Withholdings Added.* Some employees elect to have additional amounts withheld from their earnings to make up for other income not subject to automatic withholding. Here is where you enter these additional withholdings.
- *Vacations.* Here you enter the date vacation time will be due to the employee, the hours accrued, and the vacation time actually used.
- *Sick Time.* Similar to vacation data, here you enter the sick time that will be due to the employee, the hours accrued, and the sick time actually used.
- *Earnings.* Here is where you enter information about additional earnings paid to the employee besides normal wages or salary, such as a car allowance.
- *Deductions.* These fields are used for any automatic deductions other than standard withholdings, such as life insurance premiums or contributions to a company retirement plan.

Even after you enter all of these data, you're still not finished if you are starting your payroll system in mid-year. In this case, you also have to enter the employee's accumulated earnings and deductions so far for that year. To do this, you press the **Page Down** key to reveal another form where you enter the employee's data. When you're finished entering these accumulated earnings and deductions, you press the **F10** function key to store the data for that employee. Then you repeat the whole process for each of your remaining employees.

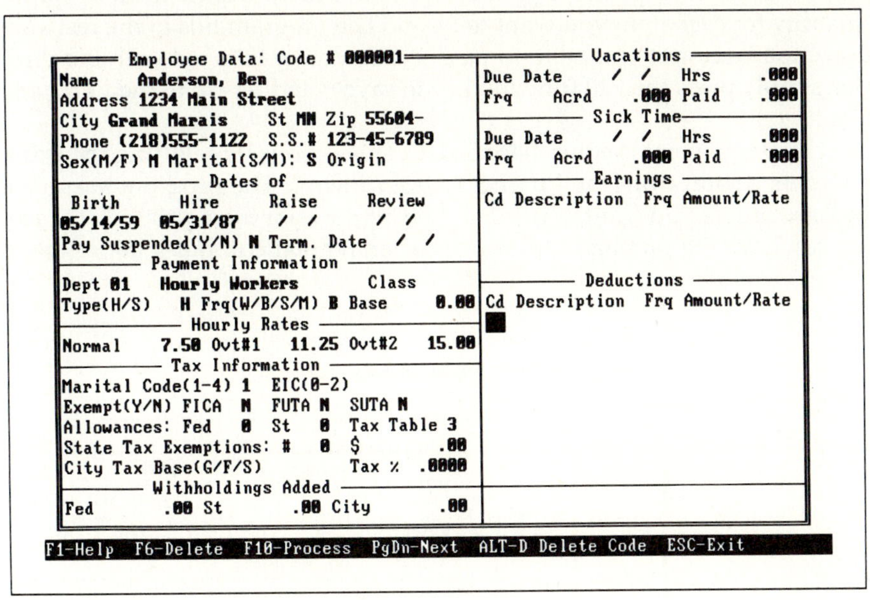


**Figure 15.24 Creating the Employee Master File**
Here you enter data about each employee.

## USING THE ACCOUNTING SYSTEM

*Daily bookkeeping chores*

Now let's see how an accounting system is actually put to use by a business such as Paddle and Portage Canoe Outfitters. Fortunately, using an accounting system for routine bookkeeping tasks is easier than setting up the system in the first place.

Once the initial hurdle of entering all of the data has been cleared, business transactions can be managed much more efficiently. Some of the daily chores performed by accounting systems include ordering purchases, paying for purchases, billing customers, collecting payments, taking inventory, updating the general ledger, and generating the payroll.

## Ordering Purchases

*Printing and posting purchase orders*

Paddle and Portage Canoe Outfitters purchases various types of freeze-dried trail food that they resell to their customers. One of their major vendors of trail food is Mountain House Foods. Whenever inventory gets low on certain items, Paddle and Portage prepares a purchase order for those items, which is then mailed to Mountain House Foods.

The first step is to activate the *Purchase Orders* option from the Main menu of the Dac-Easy Accounting program. This brings up the Purchase Order menu, shown in Figure 15.25(a). From this menu you choose the Enter Purchase Order option to actually create the purchase order. Dac-Easy Accounting then displays a blank purchase order form on your screen. As you can see from Figure 15.25(b), this screen allows you to enter information such as the purchase order number, vendor code number, shipping instructions, and the item numbers and quantities of the products you want to order. The program helps wherever it can by filling in information it already has. For example, when you enter the vendor code, Dac-Easy Accounting automatically fills in the vendor's name, contact person, and address. Similarly, when you enter an item number, the program goes to your product file to copy the description and price for you. All you have to do is enter the item number and quantity for each item you want to order. The program fills in the rest and computes the total amount you have to pay. When you're finished with the purchase order, simply press the **F10** function key to save it and return to the Purchase Order menu.

The next step is to print the purchase order. This is done by selecting the Print Purchase Orders option from the Purchase Order menu. The program asks you which purchase orders you want to print and how you want them printed. For example, you can have the purchase order printed on regular computer paper or on

**Figure 15.25 Ordering Purchases**

(a) The Purchasing Order Menu

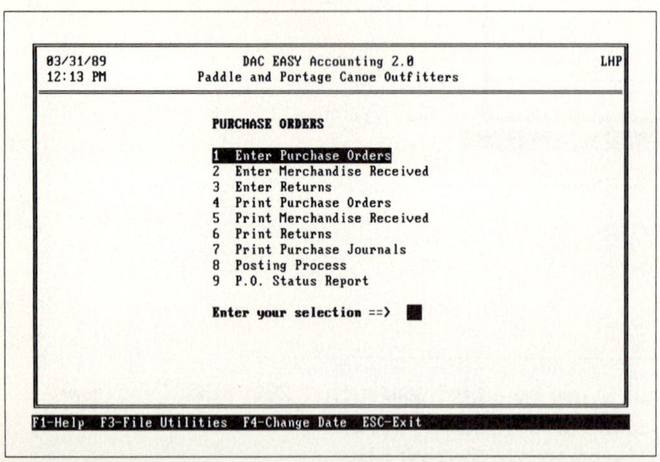


(b) The Purchase Order Form

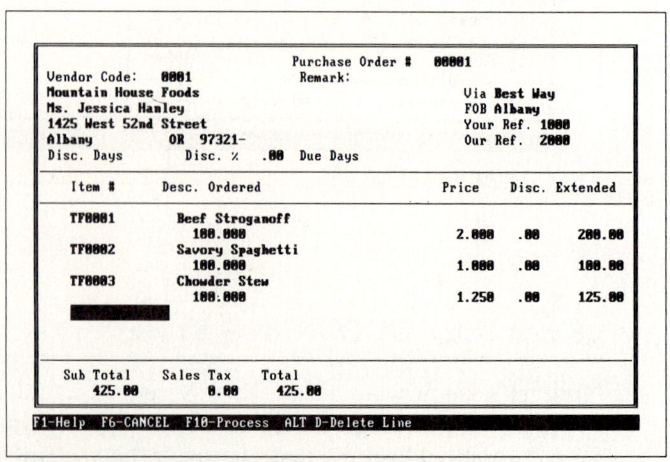

one of several different types of pre-printed forms sold by Dac Software. Many businesses opt for pre-printed forms with their logos and addresses already on them because they have a professional appearance. Once the purchase order is printed, it can be mailed to the vendor.

The accounting program keeps a record of the purchase order, which you can periodically review by printing a purchase order status report. This report is generated by selecting option 9 from the Purchase Order menu. It shows purchase orders that are still open; that is, those that have been sent out, but whose merchandise hasn't been received yet.

When products are received from the vendor, the accounting system must be updated by executing the Enter Merchandise Received option from the Purchase Order menu. This option lets you indicate purchase orders that have been filled. The final step each day is to run the Purchase Order Posting process, which is option 8 in the Purchase Order menu. This updates the product file by indicating the new items received, the vendor file by maintaining new balances and other historical data, and the purchase order file by recording the products received and on back order. The purchase order posting process also updates the general ledger transaction file to reflect debits and credits to the appropriate accounts.

## Paying for Purchases

*Updating accounts payable and printing checks*

Managing payments effectively is essential for any business. Timely payments contribute to a good credit image and help avoid disastrous cash flow problems. Dac-Easy Accounting provides many features for generating and recording payments for purchases.

Once merchandise has been received from a vendor, it's entered and posted through the Purchase Order menu, as we described in the previous section. Dac-Easy Accounting automatically updates the vendor's open invoice file with the new liability. The next step is to pay part or all of the outstanding balance by sending a check to the vendor.

Go back to the Main menu and select option 3, Accounts Payable. Figure 15.26(a) shows the Accounts Payable menu that will be displayed on your screen. From this menu you choose the Enter Payments option. After you enter a vendor's code number, the program displays all outstanding invoices from that vendor with

**Figure 15.26 Paying for Purchases**

(a) The Accounts Payable Menu

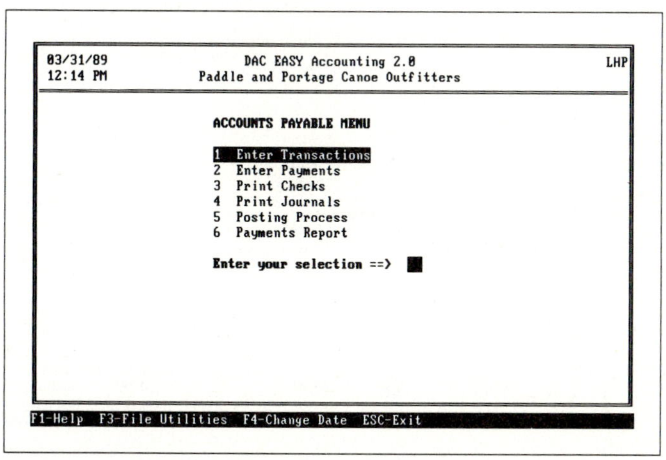


(b) Entering Payments

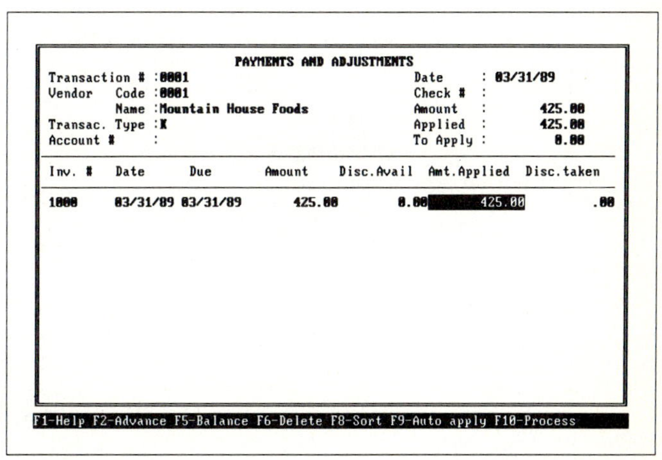

up-to-the-minute balances (see Figure 15.26(b)). All you have to do is enter the payment amounts you want to apply to each invoice. When you're finished, you press the **F10** function key to save a record of the payments. If you have other purchases to pay for, you can then enter payments to other vendors, too. When you're finished entering all of your payments, press the **Escape** key to return to the Accounts Payable menu.

The next step is to have the program print checks to the vendors. This is done by executing the Print Checks option from the Accounts Payable menu. After answering a few questions about how to date the checks and which account number to use, you align your blank pre-printed check forms in your printer and tell the program to proceed. You can then mail these printed checks to your vendors.

The final step is to execute the Posting Process option from the Accounts Payable menu. This tells Dac-Easy Accounting to update the vendor balances, the checking accounts, and the general ledger. After you're done with the posting process, you press the **Escape** key to return to the Main menu.

## Billing Customers

*Printing and posting customer invoices*

The objective of any business is to sell enough goods or services to yield a profit. Consequently, customers must be sent bills charging them for their purchases. Dac-Easy Accounting allows you to prepare invoices to be printed and either presented or mailed to customers. These invoices list the products or services purchased, their individual prices, any sales taxes, and the total amount owed. Invoices are prepared by selecting the Billing option from the Dac-Easy Accounting Main menu. This activates the Billing menu, shown in Figure 15.27(a). To actually create an invoice, you choose the first option, Enter Invoices.

The program then displays a blank invoice form on your screen. Here you press the **Enter** key to assign the next available invoice number and then enter the code number of the customer to be billed. As Figure 15.27(b) shows, the program fills in the rest of the information about the customer. You then go on to fill in the item numbers of the products or services, along with how many the customer purchased. Dac-Easy Accounting automatically computes the sub-total and lets you enter any applicable sales taxes. Then you enter the amount of any payment already made by the customer, and the program shows how much money still has to be paid.

**Figure 15.27 Billing Customers**

(a) The Billing Menu

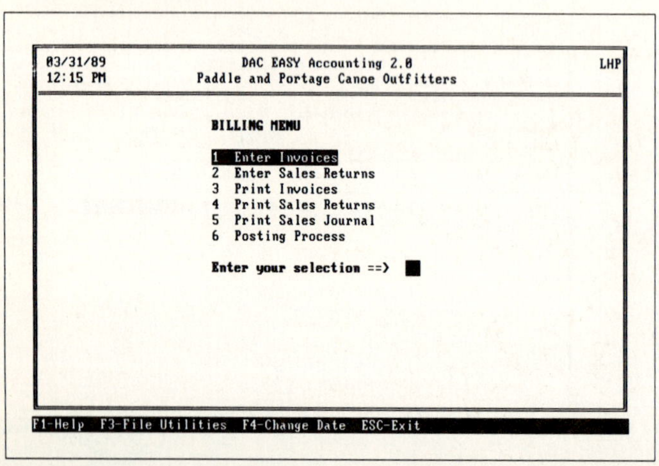


(b) Entering Invoices

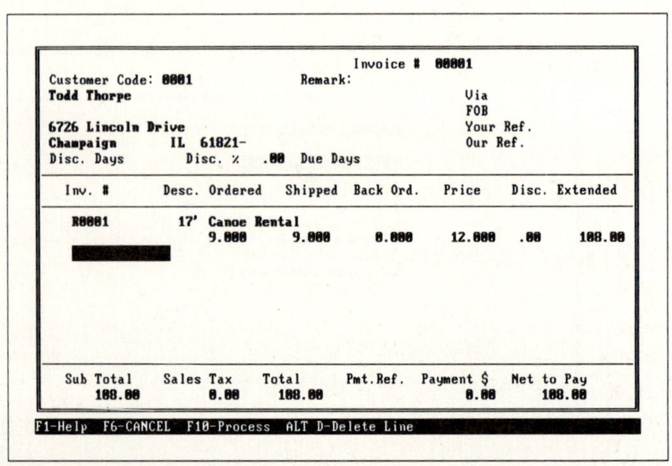

When you're finished entering the invoice, you can print it immediately by pressing the **F7** function key. The program gives you a choice of using a pre-printed invoice form or just plain computer paper. After the invoice has been printed, you press the **F10** function key to save a record of the invoice. At this point, you can create additional invoices for other customers or press the **Escape** key to return to the Billing menu. Now you should select the Posting Process option, which will update the product file, customer file, and general ledger. To return to the Dac-Easy Accounting Main menu, you simply press the **Escape** key again.

## Collecting Payments

*Updating accounts receivable*

Hopefully, customers will pay their bills promptly. When they do, you must enter each payment received into the accounting system. This is done by selecting the Accounts Receivable option from the Dac-Easy Accounting Main menu. As Figure 15.28(a) shows, the program then displays the Accounts Receivable menu. To record a customer's payment, you select the Enter Cash Receipts option from this menu. The program will display a form where you enter information about the payment (see Figure 15.28(b)).

**Figure 15.28 Collecting Payments**

(a) The Accounts Receivable Menu (b) Entering Receipts

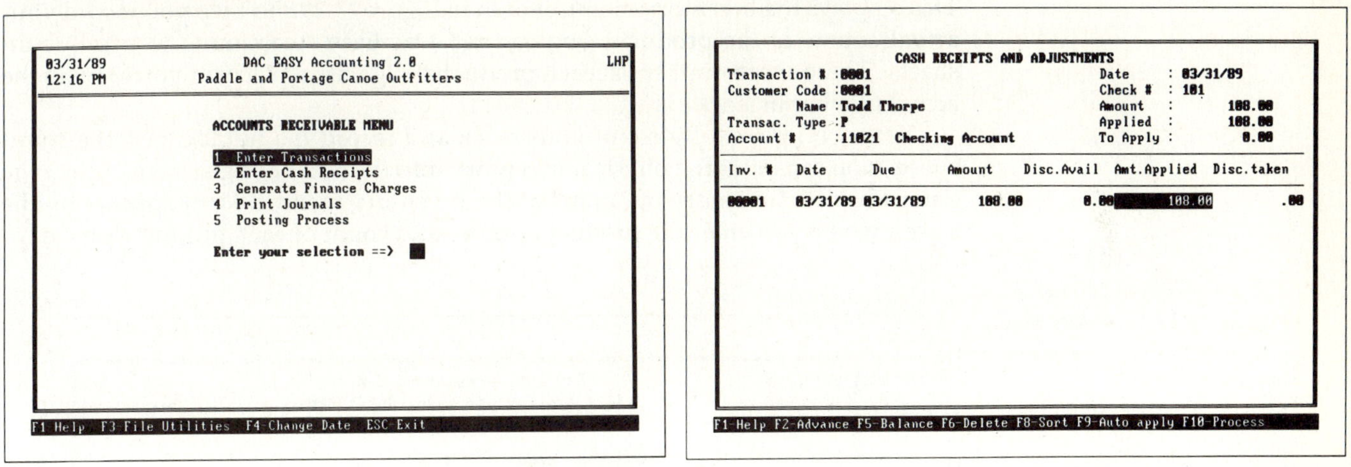


Press the **Enter** key in the Transaction # field and Dac-Easy Accounting will assign the next available transaction number. After you enter the customer's code number, the program will automatically display the customer's name. Then enter **P** for payment into the Transaction Type field, and the account number in which the payment is to be deposited into the Account # field. If the customer has paid with a check, the check number goes into the Check # field. If the customer has paid with cash, then simply enter the word **CASH** into this field. Finally, you enter the amount the customer has paid and how much of that payment is to be applied to the current invoice balance. The To Apply field shows the difference between the Amount and Applied fields, and represents the payment amount still to be applied to other invoices. This lets you apply a single large payment to several outstanding invoices.

When you're finished entering a payment, you press the **F10** function key to save it. At this point you can go on to enter any other customer payments you have received. When you're finished recording all of your customers' payments, you press the **Escape** key to return to the Accounts Receivable menu. As always, the final step is to execute the Posting Process option, which will post the transactions you've entered to the customer file and the general ledger.

## Taking Inventory

*Counting the stock*

Any business that sells products must know how many products it has on hand to sell. We've seen that an accounting system can automatically update inventory files whenever products are bought and sold. It's also necessary, however, to physically count items in stock at least once a year. Many businesses must take inventory more frequently than once a year. There are various reasons why the actual physical inventory might not correspond to the inventory records maintained by the accounting system: theft, carelessness, or failure to follow established accounting procedures. In order to protect sales flow and maintain proper purchasing, inventory records must be periodically updated to reflect the actual physical inventory. Fortunately, accounting programs such as Dac-Easy Accounting can help with this process.

Let's say that Paddle and Portage Canoe Outfitters wants to take inventory. First, you select the Inventory option from the Dac-Easy Accounting Main menu. This displays the Inventory menu, shown in Figure 15.29. To help you record your actual counts of the products, you can tell Dac-Easy Accounting to print count sheets. These sheets simply list each product along with a place for you to fill in the actual number in stock.

After you physically count your stock and record the numbers on the count sheets, you can enter the physical inventory into the accounting system. Select the Enter Physical Inventory option from the Inventory menu; a form appears on the screen where you enter the product number and count of each product you carry.

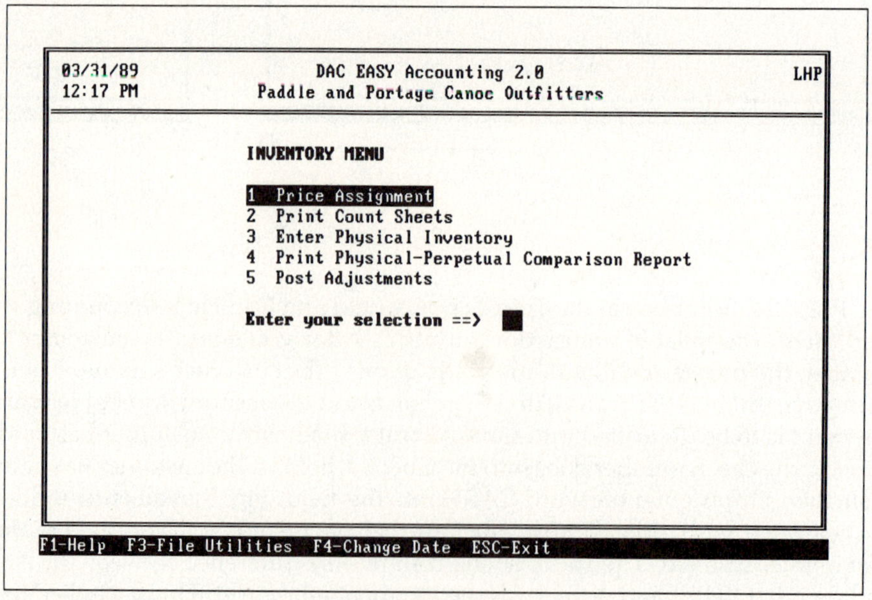


**Figure 15.29 Inventory Menu**
This screen shows the menu of the inventory subsystem.

**Figure 15.30 Physical-Perpetual Comparison Report**
This report compares the physical counts of products on the shelf with the counts kept by the accounting system.

```
Date: 03/31/89                    Paddle and Portage Canoe Outfitters                    Page no. 1
Time: 04:53 PM                             Post Office Box 555
                                        Grand Marais, MN  55604
                                          Phone (218) 555-1234

Sorted by: Inventory #              Physical-Perpetual Comparison Report          Ranked by: Inventory #

                                                                     Perpetual  Physical   Difference
   Inventory #   Description          Unit Frac Dept  Bin  Vendor Units Frac Units Frac Units Frac      Remarks
   ------------  -------------------- ---- ---- ----- ---- ------ ---------- ---------- ----------  -----------------
   TF0001        Beef Stroganoff      pkg  1    01    0001 0001       83.000     83.000      0.000  _________________
   TF0002        Savory Spaghetti     pkg  1    01    0002 0001       48.000     47.000      1.000  _________________
   TF0003        Chowder Stew         pkg  1    01    0003 0001       29.000     29.000      0.000  _________________
   TF0004        Lumberjack Pancakes  pkg  1    01    0004 0001       62.000     63.000     -1.000  _________________
   TF0005        Eggs and Bacon       pkg  1    01    0005 0001       55.000     55.000      0.000  _________________

                 Total Products : 5 records
```

Now comes the "moment of truth." The next step is to print a report comparing the actual physical counts of products on the shelf with the counts your accounting system says you should have. This is done by selecting the Print Physical-Perpetual Comparison Report option from the Inventory menu. Figure 15.30 shows an abbreviated example of such a report. In this case, the counts correspond pretty closely, so there is really no need for concern. If there were any large discrepancies in the counts, however, you would have to investigate why there seemed to be too few or too many units of a product.

The final step in taking inventory is to update your accounting records to reflect your actual physical inventory. This is done by executing the Post Adjustments option from the Inventory menu. The product file will be updated to contain the new counts and a transaction will be posted to the general ledger to show the new inventory balance.

## Updating the General Ledger

*Handling miscellaneous transactions*

In the previous sections we described several routine accounting activities common to a small business. All of them update certain general ledger accounts whenever their transactions are posted. A number of transactions, however, are not covered by the purchase order, accounts payable, billing, accounts receivable, or inventory control systems. As we said before, a business can maintain any number of different accounts. The general ledger module of an accounting system is used to update these accounts and produce various summary reports.

For example, Paddle and Portage Canoe Outfitters has both a savings and a checking account at the local bank. The general ledger system of Dac-Easy Accounting can be used to record such transactions as transferring $1000 from the savings to the checking account. First you call up the General Ledger menu by selecting the General Ledger option from the Dac-Easy Accounting Main menu (see Figure 15.31(a)). Next you select the Enter Transactions option from the General Ledger menu. After entering the journal code (GJ stands for General Journal) and the transaction number, you then specify the actual transaction, as shown in Figure 15.31(b). In this case, the $1000 from the savings account is the credit, and the $1000 put into the checking account is the debit. Remember: a credit is a source of funds and a

**Figure 15.31 Updating the General Ledger**

(a) The General Ledger Menu (b) Entering Transactions

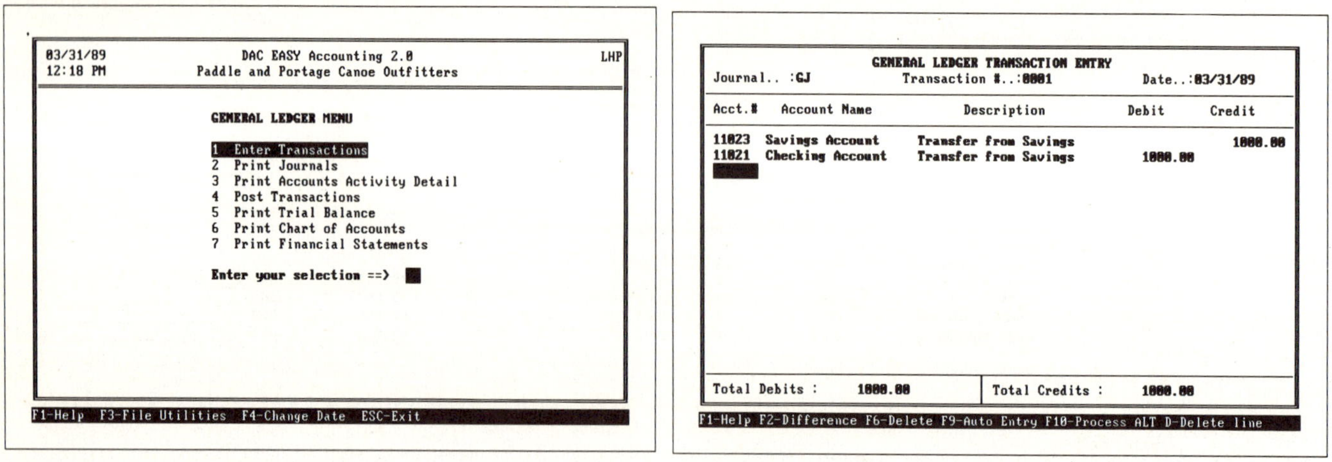


debit is an application of funds. As the figure shows, total debits must equal total credits. When you're finished entering a transaction, you press the **F10** function key to save it and continue with the next transaction. Pressing the **Escape** key returns you to the General Ledger menu, where you select the Post Transactions option to update the general ledger account balances with the entries just recorded in the transaction file.

As the menu in Figure 15.31(a) shows, you can do more than just enter transactions with the general ledger module of Dac-Easy Accounting. Specifically, you can also:

- *Print General Ledger Journals.* Recall that a journal is simply a chronological listing of transactions. All journals are maintained by the general ledger system. If you need to see an audit trail to track down an erroneous entry, printing all or part of one or more journals can provide such an audit trail.
- *Print Account Activity Detail Reports.* An **account activity detail report** is one of the most valuable reports produced by an accounting system. It lists each account's transactions during a particular month, showing the beginning balance, each debit and credit, and the current balance. You can produce a report for a single account, several accounts, or all accounts. You can also print this report for a single day, a range of days, or all the days in a month.
- *Print Trial Balance.* The trial balance report lists the current balance in each of your general ledger accounts.
- *Print Chart of Accounts.* As we said before, the chart of accounts is a hierarchical listing of the titles of all the accounts in the general ledger.
- *Print Financial Statements.* This option lets you print balance sheets, income statements, and reports that show changes in the financial condition of your business.

## Generating the Payroll

*Preparing the paychecks*

One of the most important business activities is paying employees—accurately and on time, while maintaining all necessary records. Once you set up your payroll system, as we described earlier in this chapter, generating the payroll is quite straightforward.

The first step is to exit the Dac-Easy Accounting program, switch to the DEP subdirectory, and start the Dac-Easy Payroll program. Then you select the first option from the Main menu: Payroll Processing. This, of course, displays the Payroll Processing menu, shown in Figure 15.32. In most cases, you can use the Automatic Payroll Generation option to compute all regular earnings and deductions. All you need to do is enter any exceptions to the normal payroll, such as overtime hours or special deductions.

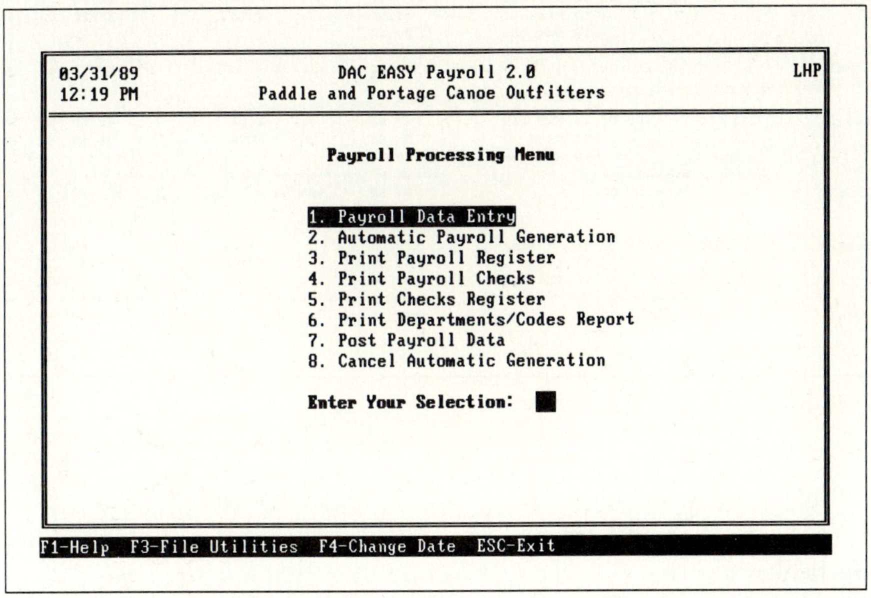


**Figure 15.32 Payroll Processing Menu** This screen shows the menu used to process the payroll.

After the payroll has been computed, you return to the Payroll Processing menu. Now you should execute the Print Payroll Register option for auditing purposes. As Figure 15.33 shows, this report lists all employees along with their hours, earnings, and deductions. It also totals the hours, earnings, and deductions for the entire company. The payroll register report is essential for verifying the accuracy of the payroll computations *before* employee paychecks are printed.

After printing and reviewing the payroll register, you are now ready to print the checks. Along with its other business forms, Dac Software offers a line of preprinted blank checks and earning statements you can load into your printer. Computer supply stores also sell blank payroll check forms designed for use in printers. All you do is feed the check forms into the printer and select the Print Payroll Checks option from the Payroll Processing menu. The program then prompts you for the employees who are to be paid, and you can enter just one employee, just hourly or just salaried workers, an entire department, or all the employees in the company. It also asks you for the starting check number and the date to be printed on the checks. Once all this information is supplied, Dac-Easy Payroll automatically prints the paychecks and earning statements for your employees.

The next step is to select the Print Checks Register option from the Payroll Processing menu. This generates a summary report of your payroll that lists all check numbers, dates, and employees, along with their earnings, deductions, and

**Figure 15.33 Payroll Register Report**
This report lists information about Paddle and Portage Canoe Outfitters' hourly workers.

Date : 03/30/89
Time : 11:12 PM

Paddle and Portage Canoe Outfitters
P.O. Box 555

Grand Marais, MN 55604

BI-WEEKLY PAYROLL REGISTER : HOURLY

Page no. 1

| Code | Employee Name | Earnings Cd | Earnings Description | Earnings Number | Earnings Amount | Deductions Cd | Deductions Description | Deductions Amount | Net to Pay | Liabilities Description | Liabilities Amount |
|---|---|---|---|---|---|---|---|---|---|---|---|
| 000001 | Anderson, Ben | 2 | Hourly | 80.000 | 600.00 | 16 | FWH Tax | 83.94 | | FICA | 42.90 |
| | | | | | | 17 | Fica | 42.90 | | FUTA | 37.20 |
| | | | | | | 18 | SWH Tax | 20.42 | | | |
| | | | Total | | 600.00 | | | 147.26 | 452.74 | | 80.10 |
| 000002 | Thomas, Becky | 2 | Hourly | 80.000 | 600.00 | 16 | FWH Tax | 83.94 | | FICA | 42.90 |
| | | | | | | 17 | Fica | 42.90 | | FUTA | 37.20 |
| | | | | | | 18 | SWH Tax | 20.42 | | | |
| | | | Total | | 600.00 | | | 147.26 | 452.74 | | 80.10 |
| | Total 1 Hourly Workers | 2 | Hourly | 160.000 | 1200.00 | 16 | FWH Tax | 167.88 | | FICA | 85.80 |
| | | | | | | 17 | Fica | 85.80 | | FUTA | 74.40 |
| | | | | | | 18 | SWH Tax | 40.84 | | | |
| | | | Total | | 1200.00 | | | 294.52 | 905.48 | | 160.20 |
| | Company Totals | 2 | Hourly | 160.000 | 1200.00 | 16 | FWH Tax | 167.88 | | FICA | 85.80 |
| | | | | | | 17 | Fica | 85.80 | | FUTA | 74.40 |
| | | | | | | 18 | SWH Tax | 40.84 | | | |
| | | | Total | | 1200.00 | | | 294.52 | 905.48 | | 160.20 |

net pay. The checks register is often used to verify that all of the checks issued have cleared the bank.

Finally, like all accounting procedures, the payroll must be posted to the general ledger. This is done by selecting the Post Payroll Data option from the Payroll Processing menu. Dac-Easy Payroll then updates the employee master file as well as the Dac-Easy Accounting general ledger and prints a brief summary of these journal transactions.

## Other Activities

*Closing the books and printing reports*

Even though we've covered quite a few accounting activities, most packages, including Dac-Easy Accounting and Dac-Easy Payroll, can do much more. For example, a whole range of financial statements and summary reports can be generated to yield more information about the general ledger, accounts receivable, accounts payable, inventory, and payroll systems. There are also procedures that are followed to *close the books* at the end of each month and each year. The purpose of these closing procedures is to clean out the transaction files, update historical data, and compute current balances. Finally, Dac-Easy Accounting also includes programs to automatically forecast future inventory usage, sales quotas, purchasing levels, and financial budgets. Although we haven't covered every feature available in today's microcomputer accounting packages, you should now have a pretty clear idea of what they can do to help run a small business.

## The Real World

### Let Your Computer Do the Accounts

On the surface, Charkit Chemical seemed to be sitting pretty. A Darien, Connecticut-based importer of specialty chemicals, it had soared in three and a half years from a start-up selling a half-dozen items to a $2.5 million-a-year business marketing more than 70 products.

To Charkit's astute sales manager, Linda Crosby, this was just the calm before the storm, however. "I recognized that because the business was growing so rapidly, our manual accounting and administrative procedures would soon be inadequate and might even stunt our sales growth," Crosby said. "For example, a clerk was supposed to record a filled order in the inventory records by hand, reducing the quantity in stock by the appropriate amount. But with so many transactions to record, the clerk would occasionally forget to reduce the inventory figure. Then when a customer ordered 15 bags of chemical A and we found that contrary to the inventory log there were only 10 in stock, it was panic time."

"The point is that when we were a smaller company with fewer items in inventory, we could keep a mental balance. But those days are long gone. And every mistake in the inventory accounting costs us money and good will. For this and other reasons, we decided to computerize our accounting procedures."

This decision is an increasingly common one at thousands of small companies because computerized accounting can offer a business three critical benefits: speed, accuracy, and a rich lode of management information.

Source: "Let Your Computer Do the Accounts," by Mark Stevens, *Working Woman*, April 1986, pp. 102-104.

## Summary


- *Some basic terminology and principles of accounting.* Accounting is the process of recording, analyzing, and reporting business transactions. Modern accounting systems use the double entry method in which every debit, or application of funds, has a corresponding and equal credit, or source of funds. Accounts are files of financial data about assets, liabilities, capital, revenues, and expenses. Accounting systems are used to generate a variety of reports, such as journals, balance sheets, and income statements. The basic accounting subsystems are general ledger, accounts receivable, accounts payable, inventory control, purchase order, billing, and payroll.
- *One specific example of a microcomputer accounting package.* Originally released in 1985 for IBM-compatible microcomputers, Dac-Easy Accounting is the world's best-selling accounting package. It can be used in conjunction with the separate Dac-Easy Payroll program.
- *How to set up a microcomputer accounting system.* Setting up an accounting system entails installing the programs, defining the data files, and entering the records required by the various subsystems.
- *How a microcomputer system is routinely used by a small business.* Everyday activities include creating purchase orders, issuing checks for purchases, printing customer invoices, recording customer payments, taking inventory, updating general ledger accounts, and generating the payroll.

## Key Terms

As an extra review of this chapter, try defining the following terms. If you have trouble with any of them, refer to the page number listed.

account (529)
account activity detail report (556)
accounting equation (532)
accounts payable (534)
accounts receivable (534)
aged accounts receivable reports (534)
assets (529)
audit trail (530)
balance sheet (532)
billing (535)
capital (owners' equity) (529)
chart of accounts (529)
credit (527)
debit (527)
detail accounts (538)
double entry accounting (527)
entry (529)
expenses (529)
general accounts (538)
general ledger (534)
income statement (533)
inventory control (534)
invoices (535)
journal (529)
liabilities (529)
loss (533)
payroll (535)
posted (534)
profit (533)
purchase order (535)
revenues (529)
vendor (534)

## Review Questions

1. What is the main purpose of accounting?
2. In what situation would debits not balance with credits?
3. What are the five major types of accounts?
4. Why is it a good idea to maintain audit trails?
5. What is the basic difference between a balance sheet and an income statement?
6. List the major component modules of most accounting systems.
7. Why are the Dac-Easy Accounting and Dac-Easy Payroll programs so popular?
8. Why is setting up a computerized accounting system more difficult than actually using it?
9. Why might you use the sample chart of accounts provided with an accounting package?
10. What are the only accounts that can actually record credit and debit transactions?
11. Which files must you create before you can use the purchase order and billing systems?
12. Which files must you create before you can use the accounts receivable and accounts payable systems?
13. Which files must you create before you can automatically generate the payroll?
14. List some of the daily business chores you can perform with an accounting system.
15. Which system do you use to record payments from customers?
16. Why is it important to always post transactions after you enter them?

17. What kind of report would you generate to see if the actual inventory corresponds with the inventory reflected by your accounting records?
18. What can you do with the general ledger module of Dac-Easy Accounting other than enter miscellaneous transactions?
19. Why might you print a checks register report?
20. Why are closing procedures followed at the end of each month and year?

## Multiple Choice

1. A debit is a(n)
   (a) application of money. (b) source of money.
   (c) group of 8 bits. (d) type of currency.
2. A file of financial information about what you own, owe, earn, or pay out is called a(n)
   (a) entry. (b) account.
   (c) credit. (d) debit.
3. Money and property owned by a business are called
   (a) capital. (b) liabilities.
   (c) assets. (d) revenues.
4. Payments or promises to pay from sales, rentals, interest, or other investments are called
   (a) capital. (b) liabilities.
   (c) assets. (d) revenues.
5. A chart of accounts lists accounts in terms of
   (a) credits and debits. (b) "parents" and "children."
   (c) bits and bytes. (d) principal and interest.
6. A financial report that chronologically lists transactions is called a(n)
   (a) balance sheet. (b) income statement.
   (c) journal. (d) profit and loss statement.
7. Which equation summarizes the financial condition of a business?
   (a) PROFIT = REVENUES / EXPENSES
   (b) ASSETS = LIABILITIES + CAPITAL
   (c) CAPITAL = INCOME + REVENUES
   (d) EXPENSES = LIABILITIES – REVENUES
8. Which accounting subsystem records all sales of goods and services to customers?
   (a) general ledger (b) accounts receivable
   (c) accounts payable (d) inventory control
9. Which accounting subsystem prepares customer invoices?
   (a) inventory control (b) purchase order
   (c) payroll (d) billing
10. In the Dac-Easy Accounting sample chart of accounts, the accounts at the lowest level that actually record credit and debit transactions are called
    (a) detail accounts. (b) general accounts.
    (c) parent accounts. (d) liability accounts.

11. Which accounting subsystem would Paddle and Portage Canoe Outfitters use to buy trail food from Mountain House Foods?
    (a) purchase order (b) accounts payable
    (c) billing (d) accounts receivable
12. After the trail food has been received, which accounting subsystem would be used to pay for it?
    (a) purchase order (b) accounts payable
    (c) billing (d) accounts receivable
13. Which accounting subsystem would be used to determine how much, if any, merchandise and materials is being stolen?
    (a) general ledger (b) billing
    (c) purchase order (d) inventory
14. Which accounting subsystem would be used to record the transfer of funds from a company savings account to a checking account?
    (a) general ledger (b) billing
    (c) purchase order (d) inventory
15. A summary report that lists all the check numbers, pay dates, and employees, along with their earnings, deductions, and net pay is called a
    (a) general ledger. (b) account activity detail report.
    (c) checks register. (d) aged accounts receivable report.

## Projects

1. In this chapter we have used Dac-Easy Accounting and Dac-Easy Payroll to illustrate some principles of microcomputer accounting systems. There are a great many other packages available for use on both IBM-compatible and Apple Macintosh computers. Write a brief report comparing one or two of these competitors with the Dac-Easy software. Examine features, ease of use, and cost. Product reviews in computer periodicals such as *InfoWorld*, *PC Magazine*, and *Mac User* are good sources of detailed information.
2. At what point should a small business consider installing a computerized accounting system? Research computer and business books and magazines for some experts' guidelines on when it becomes worthwhile for a business to automate its bookkeeping. Write a brief report summarizing your findings.
3. Is a microcomputer accounting package used at any business or organization with which you are familiar, perhaps at work or at school? If so, try to find out which package is being used and why it was selected. If you don't personally know of any organization that uses a microcomputer accounting system, find a case study of such a company in a book or magazine. Write a brief report about your example.
4. We've mentioned a few of the most commonly used business reports generated by accounting software. Compile a more comprehensive list of reports that can be created with today's popular accounting packages, and briefly describe the specific use of each of these reports.

# 16

# Software Sidelights

## In This Chapter

## PREVIEW

As Paul Harvey says in his syndicated radio show, "Now it's time for the rest of the story." This chapter covers some of the other important types of microcomputer software on the market today. There is, of course, no way that we can discuss every significant program. Nevertheless, we will introduce many specific examples of popular microcomputer software products, and we hope this will give you an appreciation for the truly amazing variety of microcomputer software packages at your disposal.

After studying this chapter, you will understand

- the advantages and disadvantages of integrated software.
- how a windowing environment can enhance an operating system.
- how a DOS shell can make DOS more user friendly.
- the various types of utility programs available for microcomputers.
- which desk accessories are handy software options.
- that on-line references can save time and effort.
- the availability of statistical and math software for microcomputers.
- how project management software is used as a valuable organizational tool.
- how personal finance and tax programs can help manage your money matters.
- the range of educational software packages available for microcomputers.
- the vast array of entertaining computer games, simulators, and music programs.
- how hypertext is used to tap into vast stores of information.
- the practical uses of artificial intelligence and expert systems.

## INTEGRATED SOFTWARE

*Several applications in one package*

As you know, most people who work with microcomputers use several different types of application software. The most commonly used packages are word processors, spreadsheets, data base managers, communications programs, and graphics programs. In this book we've discussed several different programs in each of these categories, but many more programs are on the market. Consumers are presented with a truly bewildering array of software options. Why haven't developers come up with packages that include all five of these major applications? Well, they have, with packages called **integrated software**.

### Advantages of Integrated Software

*Consistent interface, superior data transfer, less expense*

Using integrated software is like one-stop shopping—you can get almost everything you need under one roof. The most important advantage of integrated software is that you learn a single set of consistent menus and commands for a wide range of tasks. In other words, the user interfaces of all included applications are very similar. It generally takes a good deal of time and effort to master any sophisticated application package. But because of its uniform approach to menus and commands, integrated software is usually much easier to learn and use than several separate application programs.

Another advantage of integrated software is its superior ability to transfer data internally among its own individual components. Users can effortlessly share data among the word processing, spreadsheet, data base, communications, and graphics modules. If you were a salesperson, for example, you could download some sales figures from the regional office with the communications program, use the figures to update your data base, transfer the figures to the spreadsheet to generate next quarter's sales projections, produce a bar graph, and insert this graph into a report being prepared with the word processor. All of this can be done in a very straightforward manner with the same integrated package. Although many separate application packages can import and export data to other applications, the procedures are often complicated. By integrating the applications into a single package and using consistent formats for data files, integrated software makes it much easier to manipulate and present data in various ways.

Besides the advantages of consistency and data sharing, integrated software is almost always less expensive than a combination of several individual programs. For example, while an integrated software package may cost $700 or $800, five separate applications might cost $200 to $500 each, for a total of $1000 to $2500.

**Insight**

## The Future of Software Packages

The crystal ball is cloudy today. The future is a little hard to see.

The truth is that no one knows who will invent the next Wordstar, Lotus 1-2-3, or dBASE III PLUS, or what the next breakthroughs will be. The development of microcomputers that are faster, have more memory, and use almost unlimited disk storage has lifted a lot of the constraints on their use already.

One of the most promising areas currently under development is an application of artificial intelligence known as the expert system. An expert system mimics the behavior of a person solving a problem. For example, if the light on your desk isn't lit, you probably go through a series of questions like this:

- Is the light switch on?
- Is the lamp plugged in?
- Is the house fuse blown?
- Is the power out?
- Is the light burned out?
- Is the lamp itself broken, and should it be replaced?

Each of these questions can be answered yes or no. If an answer is yes, there is an action to be taken, such as replacing the bulb or turning on the switch. If the answer is no, you ask another question.

The choice of which question to ask first may be important. Experience suggests that it is fairly unlikely that the lamp itself is broken or that the power is off in the house. It's more likely that the lamp is not plugged in, the switch is off, or the bulb is burned out.

An expert system needs software to produce logical inferences and a large knowledge base to support the particular application. The inference engine needs a fast processor and a large memory, while the knowledge base can require a large disk-storage device. With the powerful new generation of microcomputers, we may have a computerized consultant right at our fingertips.

## Disadvantages of Integrated Software

*Limited choice, large memory requirement*

When integrated software was first introduced in the early 1980s, expectations for it were high, but sales have not quite lived up to those expectations. Many users were simply unwilling to give up their familiar stand-alone applications. Although integrated packages are an important software category and are gaining favor in many organizations, they do have two major disadvantages. First, integrated software hampers your ability to choose applications for their individual strengths. For example, while you may really like the spreadsheet in a particular integrated package, you may really dislike the word processor or data base manager. Unfortunately, you're stuck with the entire package, even if you don't need or like certain individual components.

The other main disadvantage to integrated software packages is that they tend to be complex programs that require a good deal of primary memory. Furthermore, some integrated packages are a little slower than smaller stand-alone applications.

## Popular Integrated Software Packages

*Integrated software examples*

The term *integrated software* has been applied to many packages that include more than one basic application. For example, Lotus 1-2-3 has often been categorized as integrated software because it includes spreadsheet, data base, and graphics capabilities. These days, however, an integrated software package has come to mean one that includes at least word processing, spreadsheet, data base, communications, and graphics capabilities. In addition, integrated software generally includes some programmability, ranging from keyboard macros to a full-fledged, high-level programming language. Several integrated software packages on the market fulfill these requirements, but here are a few of the most popular:

- *Enable.* This package, from The Software Group, is often compared with both Symphony and Framework as one of the leaders in integrated software for IBM-compatible microcomputers (see Figure 16.1). Of the three, Enable is the most well-balanced package, with an especially powerful data base manager. All of its components are comprehensive and functional.

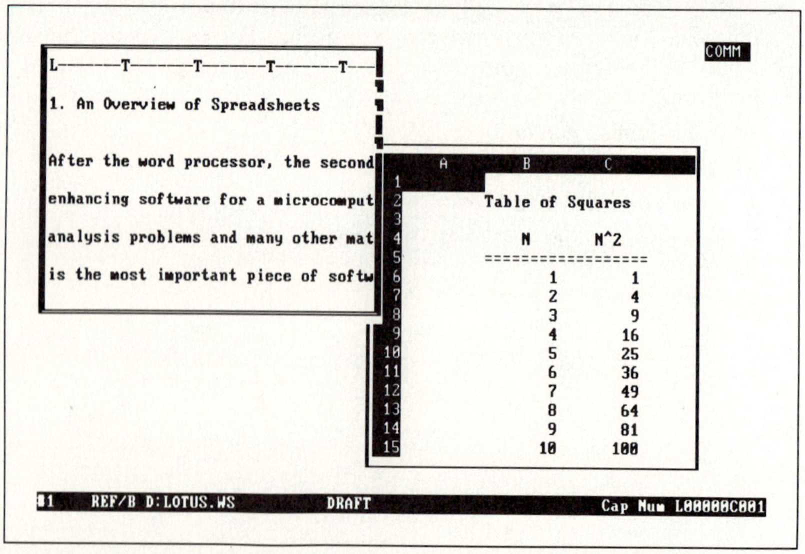


**Figure 16.1 Enable**
Enable, from The Software Group, is a well-balanced integrated software package.

- *Symphony.* Lotus Development Corporation, maker of 1-2-3, also sells this integrated software package for IBM-compatibles (see Figure 16.2). As you might expect, Symphony's spreadsheet is one of the best in the business, building on the strong tradition started with Lotus 1-2-3. It also has powerful built-in programming capabilities.

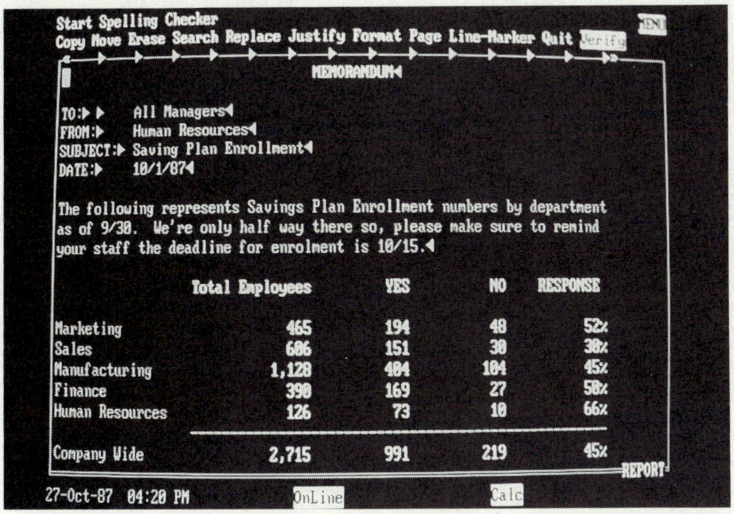


**Figure 16.2 Symphony**
Symphony, from Lotus Development Corporation, is an integrated software package with especially good spreadsheet capabilities.

- *Framework II.* Ashton-Tate developed this integrated software package for IBM-compatibles (see Figure 16.3). Although you might expect that the developer of dBASE would include an especially powerful data base manager with Framework II, this isn't so. Framework II does shine, however, in its word processing capabilities, which are among the best of all those to be found in integrated software packages. Framework II includes its own powerful programming language, called FRED, and it also has one of the best communications modules available. Like both Enable and Symphony, Framework sells for around $700.
- *Microsoft Works.* This integrated software package, with versions available for both Apple Macintosh and IBM-compatible computers, is aimed at novice users (see Figure 16.4). It includes simple word processing, spreadsheet with charting, data base, and communications functions. Although Works cannot boast all of the features found in Enable, Symphony, and Framework, the Apple Macintosh version is extremely popular. The IBM version of Works sells for around $200, while the Macintosh version sells for $300.

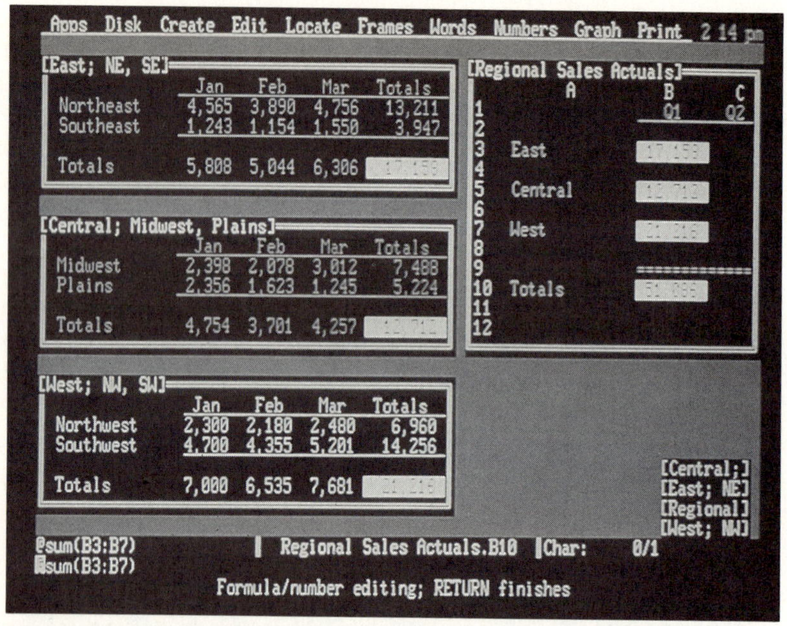


**Figure 16.3 Framework II**

Framework II, from Ashton-Tate, is an integrated software package with especially good word processing capabilities.

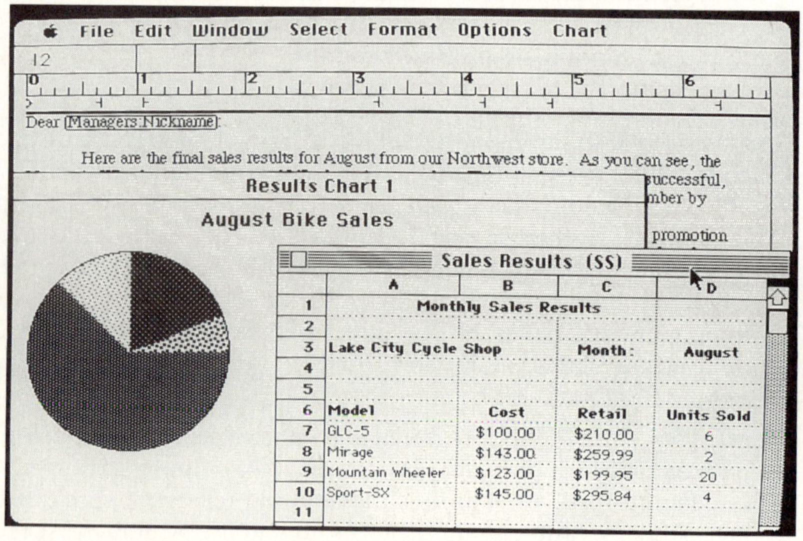


**Figure 16.4 Microsoft Works**

Microsoft Works is a popular, relatively low-cost integrated software package aimed at novices.

## WINDOWING ENVIRONMENTS

*Several applications on the same screen*

Integrated software provides several applications with a consistent user interface and an easy way to share data. Another way to achieve these objectives is to use a **windowing environment**. This is a special type of software that works very closely with the operating system. It allows you to divide your screen into a number of different boxes, or *windows*, and run a separate program in each one (see Figure 16.5). Since Apple Macintosh computers are by definition window-oriented, the term *windowing environment* is most often used to describe software that enhances or replaces DOS for IBM-compatible computers.

With a windowing environment, you can rapidly switch from one application to the next and easily transfer data among them. Furthermore, you aren't required to abandon your favorite application packages for new ones because most windowing environments generally work with existing software. As a particular windowing environment becomes accepted, however, software developers create special versions of their programs that abide by certain rules specified by that windowing system. Eventually, the windowing environment may lead many independent software developers to adopt a more uniform user interface for their programs. Thus, a windowing environment can provide most of the advantages of integrated software, without forcing you to buy and learn new application packages.

## Types of Windowing Environments

*Classify by multitasking, text and graphics*

In many ways, the capabilities of windowing environments far surpass those of integrated software. First of all, a windowing environment lets you have several programs on your screen at the same time; the actual number of programs may be limited only by the number of windows you can fit on your screen and the amount of memory installed in your computer. You can run almost any program within any window—not just a word processor, spreadsheet, data base manager, communications program, or graphics program. You can even have the same program running separately in two or more different windows. For example, you could create two different windows on your screen, run your word processor separately in each window, and simultaneously edit two different documents. Furthermore, windowing environments often let you cut or copy material from one window and paste it into another window, thereby providing an easy way to transfer data between applications.

If you think this sounds like the single-user, multitasking operating system we described in Chapter 4, you're absolutely right. In fact, many windowing environments are multitasking, which means you can run several programs concurrently. For example, you could print a document from a word processor in one window, at the same time as a large and complicated spreadsheet recalculates in another window, while you draw a chart with a graphics program in yet another window. This is true multitasking.

A few windowing environments, however, are not truly multitasking. These simpler systems allow you to switch between several windows on the screen, but only the program in your current active window is actually running. Each of the other programs on the screen is held in a kind of suspended animation, only to be revived when you switch to that window. So, one way to classify windowing environments is according to whether they are truly multitasking.

The other major distinction between windowing systems is whether they are text-based or graphics-based. The simpler **text-based windowing environment** uses only the standard character set built into the computer. Windows are enclosed in boxes constructed of special line characters. This type of system cannot display graphics within its windows.

A **graphics-based windowing environment**, on the other hand, allows you to run programs that deal with pictures and characters of all different sizes, styles, and fonts. It uses a bit-mapped display similar to what you see on an Apple Macintosh screen. Microsoft Windows, shown in Figure 16.5, is a graphics-based windowing environment. Graphics-based windowing systems are more flexible, yet also more complex, than text-based systems. Consequently, they work best when used on computers that have a powerful microprocessor along with a good deal of memory.

## Popular Windowing Environments

A major advantage of a windowing environment is that it offers a way to run a number of different programs on the screen at the same time while allowing you to easily transport data among them. Furthermore, the user interface of a windowing environment is generally menu-based and much easier to learn than ordinary operating system commands. Many windowing environments use graphics and a mouse, both of which help novices as well as experts.

*Noteworthy examples*

Because of these advantages, there is a definite trend toward windowing and away from the DOS style command line in the operating systems of most mid- to high-end microcomputers. It's likely that in the near future most of these machines will come with an operating system that has a built-in windowing environment, such as the Presentation Manager of OS/2, which we mentioned back in Chapter 4. In the meantime, however, several popular windowing environments on the market enhance existing operating systems. These include:

- *Microsoft Windows.* There is no doubt that Microsoft Windows leads the pack of windowing environments for IBM-compatibles. As Figure 16.5 shows, this software lets you run several different programs at the same time on the screen in overlapping windows. Microsoft Windows is a true multitasking, graphics-based windowing environment that uses a mouse and several features also found on Macintosh screens, such as icons and scroll bars.

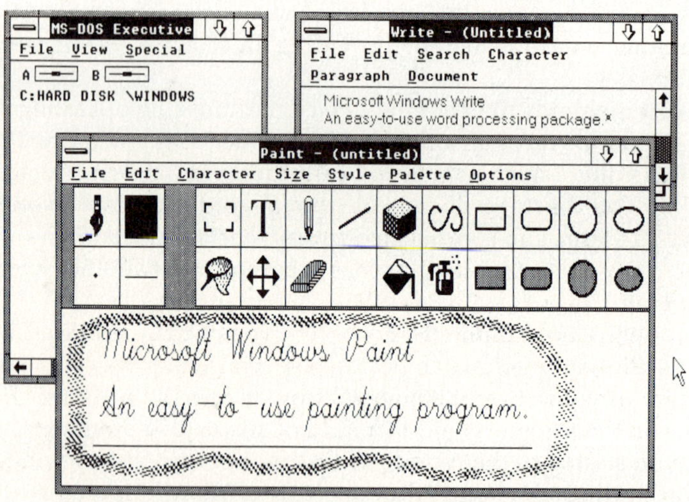


**Figure 16.5 Microsoft Windows**
Microsoft Windows lets you run several different programs at the same time.

- *DESQview.* This program from Quarterdeck Office Systems is a true multitasking windowing environment for all IBM-compatible computers (see Figure 16.6). Originally a strictly text-based environment, DESQview can now run most graphics programs in its windows. Unlike Microsoft Windows,

DESQview doesn't simulate a desktop with little icons like the Apple Macintosh. Using DESQview is similar to using DOS, except that you can open up several windows on your screen and run a different program in each one. In fact, DESQview can theoretically run up to 255 programs at the same time. Many experts consider DESQview the most elegant windowing environment for DOS computers and claim that its multitasking abilities are superior to those of Microsoft Windows.

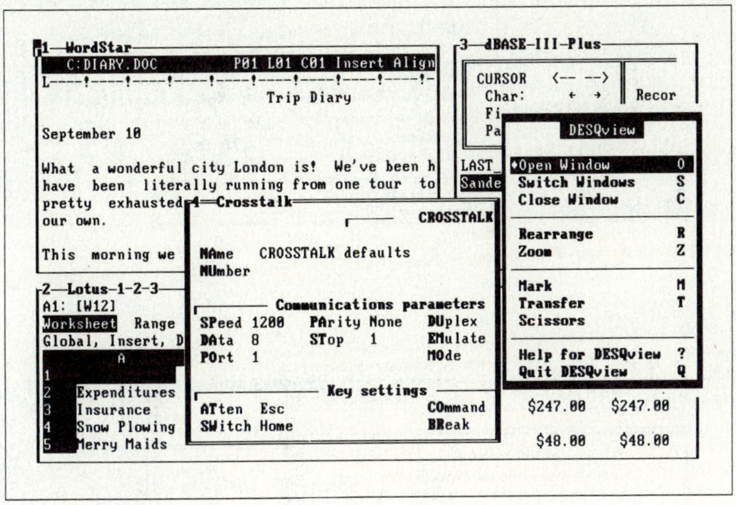


**Figure 16.6 DESQview**
Quarterdeck Office Systems' DESQview is a powerful multitasking windowing environment for IBM-compatible microcomputers.

- *TopView.* In 1985 IBM released TopView, a true multitasking, text-based windowing environment for its line of personal computers (see Figure 16.7). TopView was one of the first systems from a big-name manufacturer to let you run several programs concurrently on the same IBM-compatible computer. Although the system successfully handles multitasking, windowing, and switching among applications, TopView is somewhat cumbersome and not particularly easy to use. With the improvements of IBM's new OS/2 multitasking operating system, TopView is probably doomed to quietly fade away.
- *MultiFinder.* The MultiFinder, from Apple Computer, is an enhancement to the Macintosh operating system that adds some multiwindow, multitasking capabilities (see Figure 16.8). Despite its name, the MultiFinder is not totally multitasking. It does allow you to open up several windows with a different program in each one, but only the program in the currently selected window is fully active. Certain specially designed programs can run in the background, however, and perform unattended, time-consuming tasks such as printing documents, backing up disks, downloading files, recalculating spreadsheets, and sorting data bases. The major advantages of the MultiFinder are that it lets you have several windows open on the screen at the same time and rapidly switch between the programs in these windows.

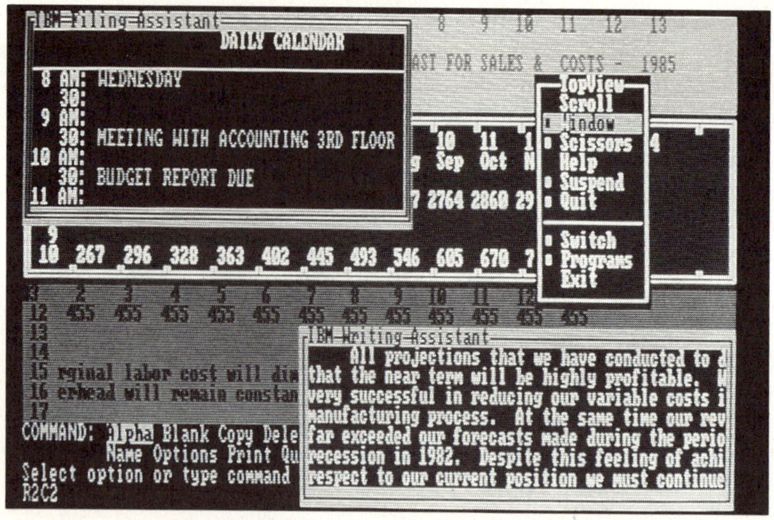


**Figure 16.7 TopView**
TopView is a text-based windowing system offered by IBM.

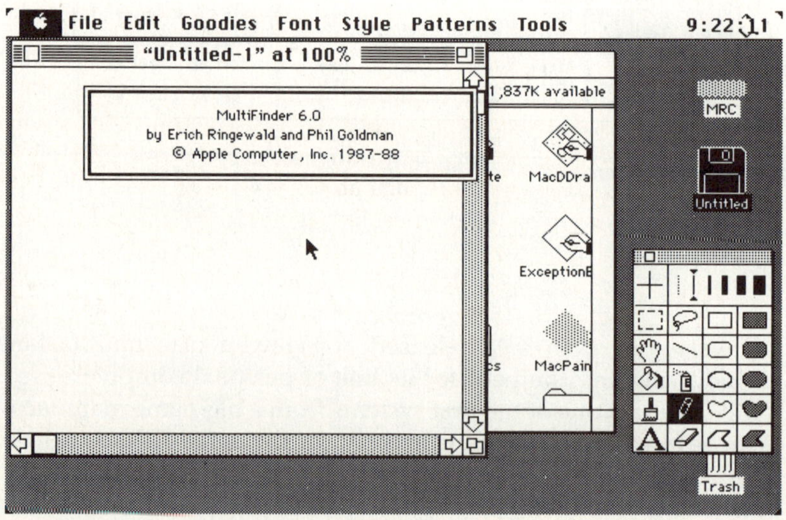


**Figure 16.8 MultiFinder**
MultiFinder is part of the Apple Macintosh operating system that allows some multitasking capabilities.

## DOS SHELLS

*Put on a user friendly face*

A windowing environment is sophisticated software that lets you have several different applications on the screen at the same time. It also can make the underlying operating system easier to use. Microsoft Windows, for example, makes the rather cryptic DOS look and feel somewhat like the user-friendly Apple Macintosh operating system. In a sense, the windowing environment surrounds the operating system with a software shell that enhances the operating system's user interface. Another popular class of software specializes in this type of enhancement for DOS computers. Such programs are called DOS shells. Basically, a **DOS shell** is a menu-driven addition to DOS that helps you manage your disk files and directories (see Figures 16.9 and 16.10). Unlike a windowing environment, a DOS shell generally does not provide multitasking or the ability to transfer data among applications.

The unadorned DOS for IBM-compatible microcomputers is a command-oriented operating system. After booting up, you are faced with a prompt and a blinking cursor that may look like this:

```
A>_
```

The screen provides absolutely no hint as to what you should do next. If you're a novice, this barren prompt can be quite intimidating. Even experts have trouble remembering all of the sometimes inconsistent commands for performing various system functions. A DOS shell provides a way to execute most DOS operations from an easy-to-understand menu, instead of forcing you to memorize or look up cryptic commands in a reference manual. It simplifies the task of setting up and moving between disk directories. Most DOS shells also include advanced features that let you view and edit the contents of your files, build your own custom menus for running application packages, set up security systems for computers that are used by different people at different times, and help you manage the immense storage capacity of hard disks. To top it off, most DOS shells are relatively inexpensive, with prices ranging from around $40 to $120.

As we discussed in Chapter 5, IBM began including its own DOS shell with DOS, starting with version 4.0. In addition, several DOS shells are currently on the market from other software developers. They all attempt to make DOS easier to use and help you manage your disk files. Besides IBM's DOS Shell, two of the most popular DOS shells sold today are:

*Popular DOS shells*

- *Xtree Pro.* This is a revamped version of one of the most popular DOS shells on the market to date, Xtree from Executive Systems (see Figure 16.9). The screen it presents shows a chart of all your directories, the first 12 file names in the currently selected directory, statistics about your disk, and a menu of available commands. Xtree Pro lets you easily manipulate files and directories in ways that are difficult if not impossible with DOS alone. The program comes with a text editor similar to WordStar and it allows you to customize the appearance of your Xtree menus. Xtree Pro also has extensive help facilities and a more comprehensive array of features than most DOS shells.

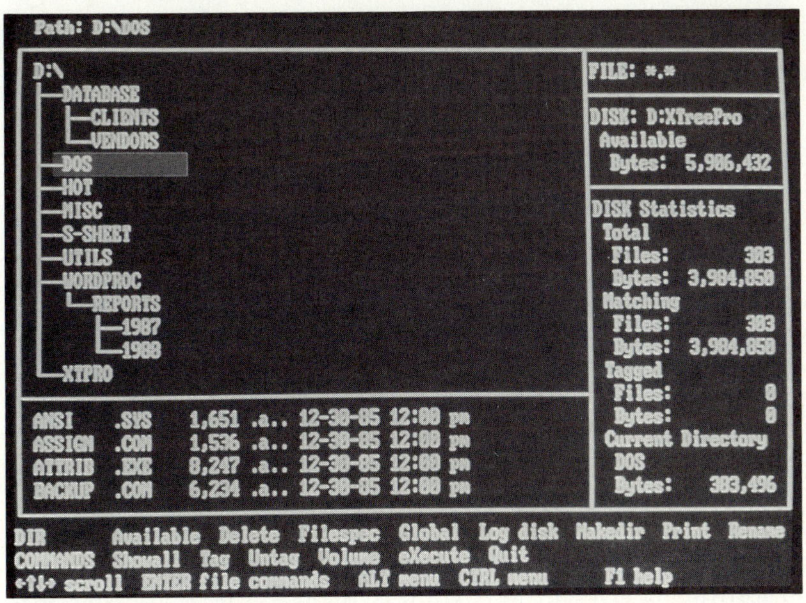


**Figure 16.9 Xtree Pro**

Xtree Pro, from Executive Systems, is a popular DOS shell with extensive help facilities.

- *Norton Commander*. While the Norton Commander doesn't have every feature found in more comprehensive DOS shells like Xtree Pro, it does its job extremely well. This no-frills DOS shell from Peter Norton Computing is, above all, designed for speed and efficiency (see Figure 16.10). The program is easy to learn and easy to use, working in ways most people find intuitively obvious. Standard DOS operations are invoked by pressing function keys, which are listed in a menu across the bottom of the screen. The Norton Commander gives you a great deal of flexibility in listing file names on your screen; you can even see the contents of two different directories simultaneously, side-by-side. It has a built-in file viewer and editor that lets you examine and alter the contents of any type of file. Finally, the Norton Commander allows you to easily design your own pop-up menu of up to 20 frequently used programs. To execute any application from this list, you simply select its option.

**Figure 16.10 Norton Commander**
The Norton Commander is a DOS shell from Peter Norton Computing designed for speed and efficiency.

## UTILITIES

*Software supplements*

Windowing environments and DOS shells are developed to address perceived deficiencies in existing operating systems. Even the best operating system, however, cannot possibly provide all the functions its imaginative users can dream up. Utilities help fill in the gaps. As we said back in Chapter 3, these are generally small, relatively inexpensive programs designed to perform one or more very specific tasks. Some utilities are included or actually built into the operating system, others are purchased separately to perform tasks that are difficult or impossible to do within a given operating system or application package.

DOS, for example, has no built-in command to recover or "unerase" an accidentally deleted file. To their dismay, many users find they occasionally need just such a facility. Clever software developers have come to the rescue and now there are quite a few utilities available that let you recover deleted files.

Here's another example that relates to an unmet need in a particular type of application package. Many spreadsheet programs, including the first two major releases of Lotus 1-2-3, cannot print spreadsheets sideways across several pages of paper. This capability is handy for printing extra-wide spreadsheets, which are commonly used for budgets, income statements, and all kinds of worksheets with many columns. Without the ability to print sideways, the spreadsheet program prints several vertical "stripes" which you must tear apart and tape together horizontally. Fortunately, it didn't take software developers long to invent utilities that let you directly print spreadsheets sideways across several pages. One such program, Sideways, from Funk Software, is shown in Figure 16.11.

**Figure 16.11 Sideways**
Sideways, from Funk Software, is a popular utility that lets you print worksheets across several pages.

There are literally hundreds, if not thousands, of utility programs available for popular microcomputers such as IBM-compatibles and Apple Macintoshes. These handy little programs address all kinds of problems, deficiencies, and omissions of both operating systems and application software. Some utilities simply provide clever shortcuts and enhancements to help you work faster, better, and smarter. Others are practically necessities that no regular computer user should do without. Although we can't list every type of utility on the market, three of the most popular categories are disk and file utilities, printer utilities, and keyboard utilities.

## Disk and File Utilities

*Handy programs for secondary storage*

Disk and file utilities are programs that help you manipulate, organize, and use your disks and files more easily and efficiently. Within this category alone are many subsets. **File recovery utilities**, such as the Norton Utilities, from Peter Norton Computing, let you reinstate accidentally erased files and restore accidentally reformatted hard disks (see Figure 16.12). Most of these utilities also include many other handy options for helping you use your computer, including procedures to rearrange your directories, view and edit the contents of files, test disks, report file statistics, and locate files and individual sections of text within files.

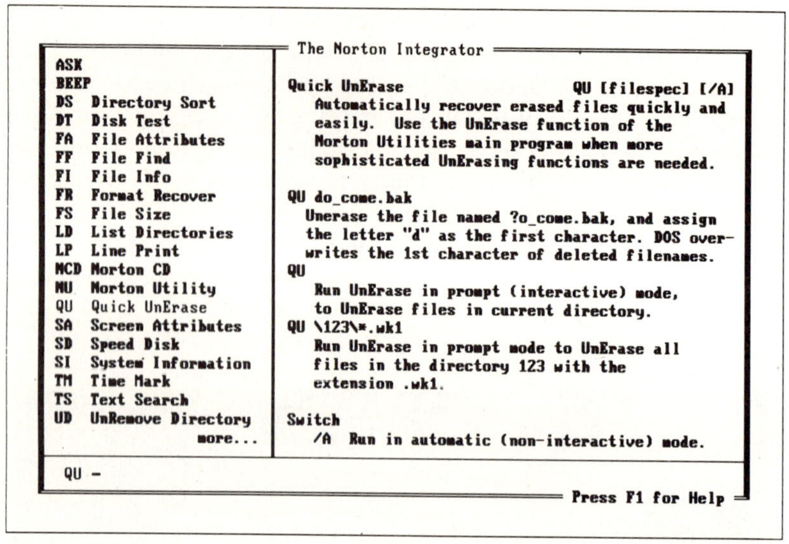


**Figure 16.12 Norton Utilities**
The Norton Utilities let you recover accidentally erased files and include a host of other handy options.

**File compression utilities** let you squeeze your files into less disk space by eliminating waste and redundant data. SQZ! Plus, from Turner Hall Publishing, for example, compacts spreadsheet files to about 10 percent of their original size. In other words, SQZ! Plus can pack 10 times more spreadsheet data onto any disk. There are also file compression utilities that work on all kinds of data files, but their space savings are usually not as dramatic as those programs that specialize in one particular type of data file. Even more general file compression utilities, such as NEWSPACE, from Isogon Corporation, can effectively double the data storage capacity of a hard disk.

**File transfer utilities** let you move data among different types of computers. MacLink Plus from DataViz is a program that can transfer data files between an IBM-compatible and an Apple Macintosh connected with a special cable. Other file transfer utilities can move files between computers that are basically compatible, except for different disk drive formats. Brooklyn Bridge, from White Crane Systems, for instance, lets you transfer files between IBM-compatible computers with incompatible disk drives, such as an IBM Personal Computer that uses 5 1/4-inch floppies and an IBM Personal System/2 Model 50 that uses 3 1/2-inch floppies.

There are also **file conversion utilities** that can modify files from one application so that they can be used by another application. Software Bridge, from Systems Compatibility Corporation, for example, lets you convert documents among nine different word processing programs without losing formatting features such as underlining, boldfacing, and italics.

**Disk copying utilities** specialize in duplicating files and disks, especially those that are copy protected. Programs such as Copy II PC for IBM-compatibles and Copy II Mac for the Apple Macintosh from Central Point Software provide file and disk copying procedures that are more efficient and more versatile than those included with the microcomputers' operating systems.

Both DOS and the Macintosh operating system let you make a backup copy of the contents of your hard disk on floppy disks. Periodically making such backup copies is extremely important for preserving your programs and data in case the hard disk malfunctions. These operating system backup procedures, however, are relatively slow and awkward to use, and they typically require a large number of floppy disks. **Disk backup utilities**, such as Fastback, from Fifth Generation Systems, are generally faster, more efficient, easier to use, and require fewer floppy disks than the backup procedures of most operating systems. This particular program is available in different versions for IBM-compatibles and the Apple Macintosh.

Computers spend much of their time reading and writing programs and data on disks. If you hasten these disk accesses, you can significantly decrease the amount of time you spend on certain types of tasks. A host of **disk optimizing utilities** have been developed to help make secondary storage devices operate more efficiently. Some of these utilities, such as Disk Optimizer, from SoftLogic Solutions, reorganize the contents of a disk to achieve maximum performance. As you use a disk, you delete or modify old files and add new files. Pieces of files invariably get broken up and scattered across the disk as the operating system fits new data into whatever unused space it can find. While the operating system always keeps track of these pieces so that your files are kept logically intact, finding the dispersed file segments takes more time. Disk optimizing utilities simply rewrite your file segments in sequence next to each other on the disk so that they can be reached more quickly.

Other utilities, called **disk caching utilities**, take a different approach to speeding up program and data retrieval. Programs such as Lightning, from Personal Computer Support Group, reserve part of primary memory as an intermediary storage place or **cache** for frequently used software and data. By having your programs automatically use this RAM cache whenever possible, a disk caching utility reduces the number of times your software must directly gain access to disk drives. Since RAM is much quicker than any disk drive, disk caching utilities can noticeably speed up your work.

## Printer Utilities

*Use all of your printer's abilities*

A vast array of different computer printers are on the market. Thanks to standardized parallel and serial interfaces, most printers can be connected to most microcomputers. This can make life difficult for software manufacturers who must develop programs that support many different printers. It's often impossible for any single program, such as a word processor, to take advantage of every feature of every printer. This is especially true of laser printers, which tend to be more complex than other types of printers. As a result, several software developers have come up with printer utilities to help you more fully utilize your printer's potential. SoftStyle's Printworks for Lasers, for example, specializes in letting you use the advanced features of Hewlett-Packard Laserjets and compatible printers with IBM-compatible computers. This program lets you choose fonts, set margins and page lengths, specify how many copies to print, and control many other aspects of page formatting. SoftStyle also sells Printworks for the Mac, a comprehensive control system for Macintosh dot-matrix printers.

Some printer utilities are more specific and attempt to fulfill one particular need, such as printing wide worksheets sideways across one or more pages.

Another type of printer utility reduces or eliminates the wait for your printer to produce documents. A **print spooler** works in the background, sending characters to the printer whenever there's a free moment, while you continue running your application software as usual. Print spooling may slightly slow down the computer, but printing while you work can save a great deal of time in the long run. PrintQ, from Software Directions, is a good example of a printer spooler for IBM-compatible computers. This program intercepts documents bound for the printer, temporarily redirects them to disk storage, and then prints them piecemeal whenever the computer isn't busy doing something else. PrintQ lets you submit any number of documents to be printed without having to wait until the previous print job is finished. You can also print documents in order of priority, print multiple copies of a document, monitor the status of your print jobs, and manage two printers.

### Keyboard Utilities

*Stand-alone keyboard macro facilities*

In Chapter 6 we introduced the concept of keyboard macros as they are used in advanced word processors. In Chapter 8 we showed that most spreadsheet programs have similar macro capabilities. These macro features allow you to assign frequently used command sequences and long strings of characters to just one or two keypresses. Keyboard utilities, also called *keyboard enhancers*, are utility programs like stand-alone keyboard macro facilities. For example, SuperKey from Borland International, is an IBM-compatible keyboard enhancer that you can use from DOS or within almost any application program (see Figure 16.13). With this program, commands, names, sentences, paragraphs, and even cursor movements can be recorded and replayed at will by pressing just one or two keys. Since commands and data are often repetitive, many people find that a keyboard utility such as SuperKey can save them a significant amount of typing time and effort.

**Figure 16.13 SuperKey**
Keyboard enhancers, such as SuperKey from Borland International, can help you reduce repetitive typing.

## DESK ACCESSORIES

*Handy pop-up mini-programs*

Microcomputers have become high-tech, simulated desktops. We have said before that the Apple Macintosh operating system has taken this concept quite literally, using a desktop image on its screen. The user interfaces of other types of computers are also helping to simulate the activities performed at a desktop. To appreciate the range of activities available, think about how you typically work at a desk. You might be writing a report and suddenly pick up a hand-held calculator to compute some figures. Throughout the day you probably check your clock and calendar, jot down some notes, look up addresses, call associates on the phone, and send memos. There are quite a few utilities on the market that let you do all of these tasks and many more with your computer. They are called **desk accessories, desktop organizers**, or simply **pop-up utilities**.

The Apple Macintosh operating system was specifically designed to let you temporarily interrupt your work and use desk accessories. In fact, several desk accessories come built into the operating system. There is an alarm clock, a calculator, a note pad, a graphics scrapbook, and various other operating system utilities. These accessories are available at any time from the Apple menu at the far left side of the menu bar across the top of most Macintosh applications. All you have to do is pull down the Apple menu and select a desk accessory from the list. Your original task is put on hold until you're finished with the desk accessory. Besides those that come with the Macintosh, you can buy additional or enhanced ones from independent software developers. SideKick, from Borland International, for example, is a comprehensive set of desk accessories for the Macintosh that includes a note pad, calculator, communications package, phone directory, automatic phone dialer, appointment scheduler, alarm clock, outline editor, and mini-spreadsheet (see Figure 16.14).

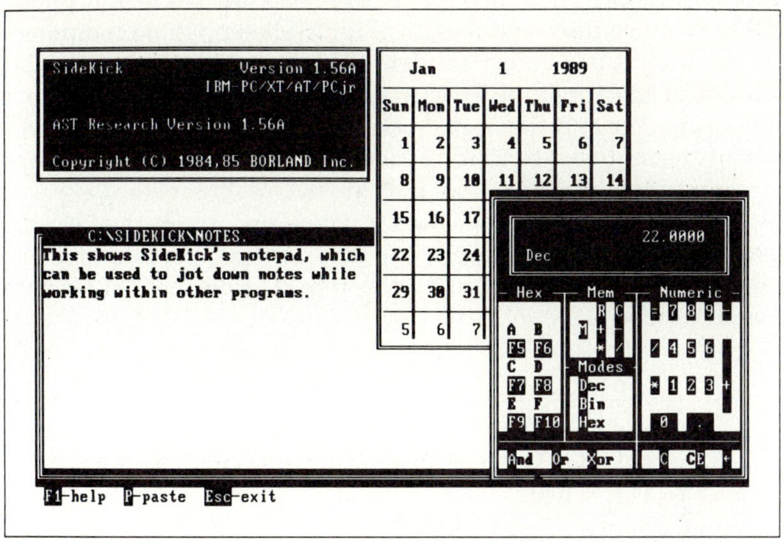


**Figure 16.14 SideKick**
SideKick, from Borland International, is one of the most popular sets of desk accessories for both IBM-compatibles and the Apple Macintosh.

Desk accessories (including SideKick) are also available for IBM-compatible computers, although they work somewhat differently from the Apple Macintosh packages. DOS requires that such utilities be memory-resident programs. As we said in Chapter 4, a memory-resident program is initially loaded into RAM but remains dormant until it is activated by pressing a special combination of keys. When this is done, your current program is suspended and the computer immediately switches to the memory-resident routine. When you are finished with the memory-resident utility, it becomes dormant again and you return to your original program.

Many memory-resident utilities have been developed for IBM-compatible computers. Unlike most Macintosh desk accessories, which are stored on a disk until needed, memory-resident programs must be kept in memory if you want to use them. This means that they also consume memory that would otherwise be used for programs and data. DOS was not originally designed to switch rapidly between programs on a routine basis. Unfortunately, confusion and incompatibilities sometimes occur when you try to load and use several different memory-resident programs on the same computer at the same time. Despite the difficulties, clever software developers have created some amazing and very popular memory-resident desk accessories for IBM-compatible computers.

## ON-LINE REFERENCES

*Instant access to references*

Most modern application packages have on-line help facilities that can almost instantly provide, at the touch of a key, more information about how they work. Most modern word processors now include a spelling checker and many come with an on-line thesaurus. Software developers have expanded and generalized these features to provide a host of stand-alone, on-line reference materials. For example, Webster's New World Combo, from Simon & Schuster Software, is a memory-resident spelling checker, word counter, and thesaurus for IBM-compatible computers (see Figure 16.15). Because it is memory-resident, Webster's New World Combo can be used within almost any application package. If your word processor doesn't have its own spelling checker and thesaurus, you can use Webster's New World Combo. You can also use these facilities inside your spreadsheet, data base manager, and communications package. Not only are the on-line spelling checker and thesaurus fast and convenient, they also cover impressive numbers of words. The Combo's spelling checker, for example, contains 114,000 words, while the thesaurus has 330,000 synonyms for 20,000 root words. The current list price of Webster's New World Combo is around $90.

**Figure 16.15 Webster's New World Combo**
Webster's New Word Combo includes a spelling checker, word counter, and thesaurus.

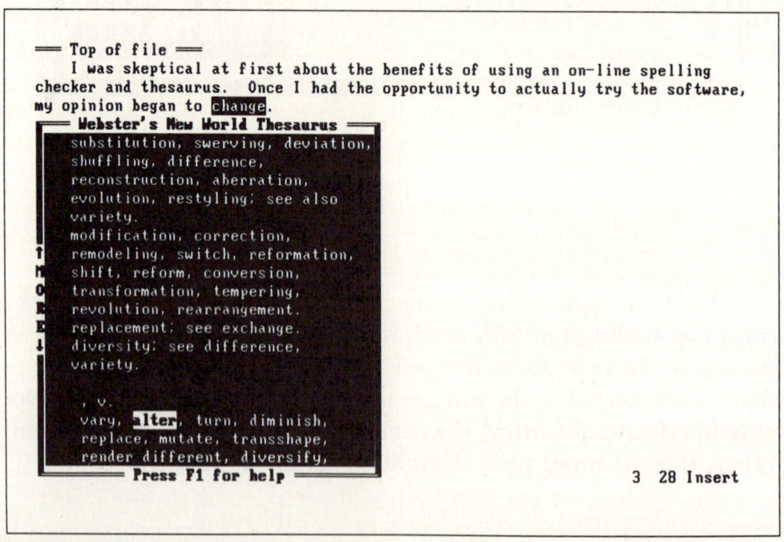

Some software developers have gone beyond the now-common spelling checker and thesaurus to offer many other more sophisticated on-line references. Some of these are quite specific and only cover particular operating systems, programming languages, or application packages. Others are aimed at a more general audience. The Micro Library Series, from Inductel, for example, is a comprehensive set of on-line reference works for IBM-compatibles. Here's what is included in the series:

- Funk & Wagnall's Standard Desk Dictionary
- Lyle Stuart's Concise Dictionary of 26 Languages
- McGraw-Hill's Dictionary of Computers
- Dictionary of Electrical & Electronic Engineering
- Dictionary of Physics
- Dictionary of Chemical Terms
- Dictionary of Biology
- Dictionary of Mechanical & Design Engineering
- US Post Office 5-Digit ZIP Code Directory

The dictionaries are not mere spelling checkers, but rather abbreviated versions of the original reference works that actually contain definitions. The Micro Library Series comes with Inductel's Knowledge Acquisition System software, which allows rapid information retrieval—much more rapid and flexible than a manual search of the actual printed books. These reference works can be purchased individually at prices ranging from roughly $50 to $100. They do, however, consume a great deal of disk space. For instance, the Funk & Wagnall's Dictionary and the Concise Dictionary of 26 Languages come together on 21 floppy disks and require 7.2 megabytes of disk storage. For this reason, some on-line references, such as Microsoft's Bookshelf, come on CD-ROM disks. Although these optical disks can hold more than 500 megabytes of information, they require special disk drives that can cost up to $1000.

## STATISTICAL AND MATH PACKAGES

*Analyze numerical data*

With all that computers do, it's easy to forget what they do best: work with numbers. Professionals use computers to analyze all kinds of numerical data, from regional sales figures in business reports to rat reaction times in psychological experiments. Statistics is the branch of mathematics concerned with the collection, analysis, interpretation, and presentation of numerical data. Statistical analysis is a critical tool in a variety of fields: the Census Bureau monitors economic and social change, manufacturers maintain product quality controls, public health officials track infectious diseases, agricultural scientists study crop yields, actuaries set insurance premiums, and poll takers gauge public opinion. In fact, the list of those who need statistics is almost endless.

If everyone who needed to do a statistical analysis had to write his or her own software, however, very few analyses would get done. Fortunately, a number of statistical packages that can do these analyses for you are on the market. All you have to do is supply the data, select the particular statistical procedure, and wait for the results. SYSTAT, from the company of the same name, is one example of a popular statistical package for both Apple Macintosh and IBM-compatible microcomputers (see Figure 16.16). This particular program was modeled after

SAS, a major statistical package for mainframe computers. SYSTAT excels at handling large data bases with many different variables. Originally developed by a psychology professor at the University of Illinois, SYSTAT is especially well suited to the advanced statistical techniques used in the behavioral and social sciences.

**Figure 16.16 SYSTAT**
SYSTAT is a popular statistical package for both Apple Macintosh and IBM-compatible microcomputers.

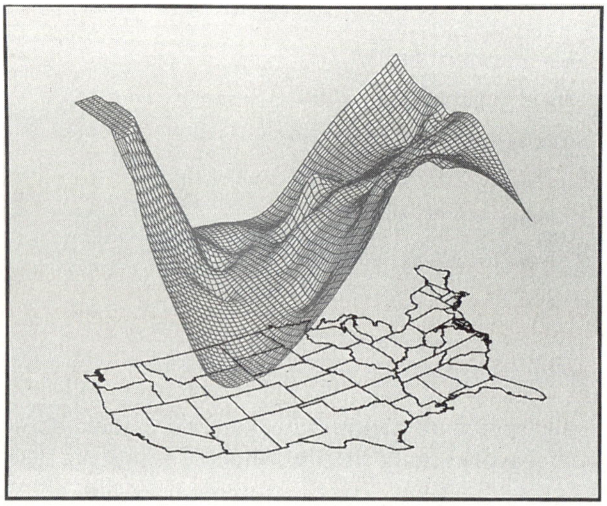

*Other mathematical software*

Besides statistical packages, other types of mathematical software are commonly used by scientists, engineers, and business people. Eureka, from Borland International, for example, is an algebraic equation solver with versions available for both Apple Macintosh and IBM-compatible computers (see Figure 16.17). This easy-to-use program is a good educational tool for almost any field involving mathematics. Eureka allows you to automatically solve sets of equations and graph the results. For instance, let's say that you have the following set of equations and you want to solve them for $x$ and $y$:

$$y = x - 1$$

$$x = 2y$$

You simply type these expressions into Eureka's equation window and activate the Solve command. Eureka combines and rearranges the equations to conclude that $y = 1$ and $x = 2$. Furthermore, you could have Eureka plot these two equations and actually see the solution—where the two lines intersect at coordinates (2,1).

## PROJECT MANAGEMENT SOFTWARE

*Computerized planning*

More and more, computers are being used as organizational tools. All kinds of programs are now available for helping you outline, schedule, and chart your thoughts and activities. **Project management software** is one of the most popular and advanced categories of these various organizational programs. The purpose of a project management package is to help you formally plan and control complex undertakings, such as the construction of a new office building, the development of a new product, or the installation of a large computer system. The project management

**Figure 16.17 Eureka**
Borland International's Eureka is an algebraic equation solver.

software lets you identify the individual tasks necessary to complete a project and calculate the time, money, and other resources each of these tasks will require.

Modern project management procedures are based on the Critical Path Method (CPM) and Program Evaluation and Review Technique (PERT). The **Critical Path Method (CPM)** is a scheduling method that focuses on the sequence of critical activities that must be performed to complete a project. Critical activities are ones that must start after others are finished, and must be completed before subsequent activities can begin. This sequence of activities is known as the *critical path*.

*CPM and PERT*

The **Program Evaluation and Review Technique (PERT)** was originally developed to schedule projects in which the completion times of individual tasks were difficult to estimate. Project schedules were generated for three possible scenarios: pessimistic, optimistic, and most likely. Today, CPM and PERT have become practically synonymous. The term *PERT* is generally used to describe a chart that graphically depicts a project as a network of interconnected activities (see Figure 16.18). The critical path through this network of activities is usually highlighted in some manner. Virtually all microcomputer project management packages use the critical path method for scheduling and PERT charts to display the relationships between tasks.

The **Gantt chart** is another important tool of project management. Named for Henry L. Gantt, who developed it while working as a consulting engineer for the U.S. government during World War I, the Gantt chart is a horizontal bar graph that shows the major tasks of a project, when each task must be performed, and how long each task will take (see Figure 16.19). By displaying activities on a time line, a Gantt chart reveals how the duration of individual tasks affects the final completion date of a project. All project management packages produce Gantt charts and many of them use the Gantt chart as their main component.

**Figure 16.18 PERT Chart**
This screen shows a PERT chart produced with Microsoft Project.

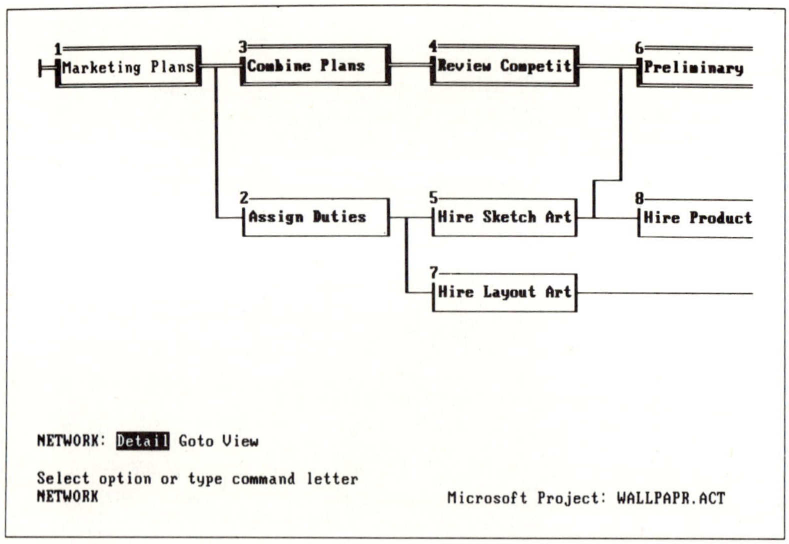


**Figure 16.19 Gantt Chart**
This screen shows a Gantt chart produced with Microsoft Project.

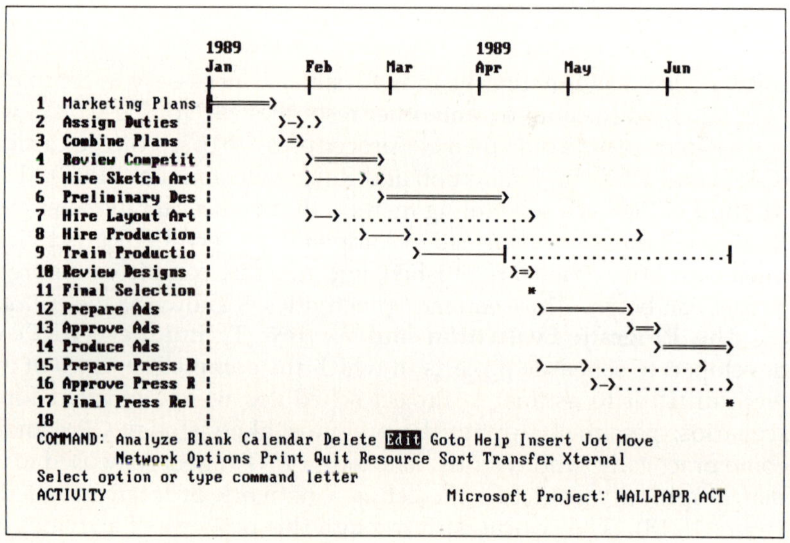


Almost any undertaking can be better organized through the use of project management techniques. The result can be greater efficiency, higher productivity, better-kept schedules, and significant savings. Realizing the benefits, the U.S. Navy first computerized its project management of the Polaris missile system in the late 1950s. By the 1960s, project management software for mainframe computers was being commercially marketed at prices as high as $200,000. Today, more than a hundred project management programs are available for microcomputers, ranging in price from around $35 to nearly $8000.

One of the most popular microcomputer project management packages is Microsoft Project (see Figures 16.19 and 16.20). This $400, IBM-compatible program is especially well-suited to organizing small- to medium-sized projects. Microsoft Project has powerful, yet easy-to-use Gantt charting features. The program also lets you create simple PERT charts to show the overall structure of a project. A wide range of customized reports can be printed with Microsoft Project, and data can be exported to popular spreadsheet programs such as Lotus 1-2-3. Although it lacks the fancy features found in more expensive programs, Microsoft Project is a capable and straightforward project management system.

## PERSONAL FINANCE AND TAX PROGRAMS

*Your own accountant*

For more personal needs, microcomputer software can help you organize your own finances, too. Some of the best-selling packages for home computers are personal financial-management programs. Whether you're struggling to balance your checkbook or trying to leverage your investments, a personal finance program can be a useful addition to your software library. One of the most popular, easy to use, and powerful personal financial managers on the market is Andrew Tobias' Managing Your Money, from MECA Ventures (see Figure 16.20). This program, which sells for about $220, contains financial advice and personal accounting procedures developed by the author of the best-selling book *The Only Investment Guide You'll Ever Need.*

**Figure 16.20 Managing Your Money**
Andrew Tobias' Managing Your Money is one of the most popular personal finance packages.

The core of Managing Your Money is a computerized checkbook register to help pay your bills. You can enter details about your checks after writing them, have the program print your checks directly, or use a modem to call Chase Manhattan Bank and have the bank print and mail your checks. But Managing Your Money can do much more than just keep your checkbook balanced. As you enter all of your income and payment records into the program, Managing Your Money automatically updates your budget and tax forms; you can print out budget summaries and sample tax forms at any time. With the Portfolio Manager, you can also keep track of almost any kind of investment, from common stocks to tax-free municipal bonds.

On-line help screens provide information about how various types of investment records should be maintained. Your net worth and tax records are automatically updated as you buy and sell investments. With Managing the Market, an $80 add-in option, you have direct access to the Dow Jones News Retrieval service for current stock prices. One of the most useful features of Managing Your Money is the Net Worth section, which automatically maintains a breakdown of your net worth by extracting current data from your bank accounts, investments, loans, equity, real estate, insurance, pension plans, and any other holdings. In addition to all of these features, Managing Your Money also includes a simple word processor, a financial calculator, a retirement planner, and sections to help you determine your taxes and insurance needs.

Although personal finance programs can help you estimate your taxes, most cannot produce actual tax forms and schedules for IRS submittal. For that you need more specialized tax-preparation software. Since the federal Tax Reform Act of 1986, this type of software has exploded into widespread use as confused taxpayers search for help. One of the best tax-preparation programs is Macintax Taxview (Federal Version), from Softview. This program, which comes in different versions for both the Apple Macintosh and IBM-compatible computers, is easy to use, straightforward, yet surprisingly sophisticated. Macintax Taxview not only follows the structure of IRS tax forms, it exactly duplicates them on your computer screen (see Figure 16.21). Instead of writing your entries on paper forms, you type them right on the screen. If you need help or want to see the IRS instructions for an entry, you simply point to it and double-click a mouse button. All worksheets, forms, and schedules are automatically linked to each other and the main 1040 form. The $119 program includes support for 30 different forms and schedules and nine worksheets. Furthermore, the IRS has approved all of the forms produced by Macintax for direct submission. So, when you are finished filling out the necessary forms, all you have to do is print them on a dot-matrix or laser printer, sign them, attach your earnings statement and possibly a check, and mail them to the IRS. It almost makes doing your taxes fun.

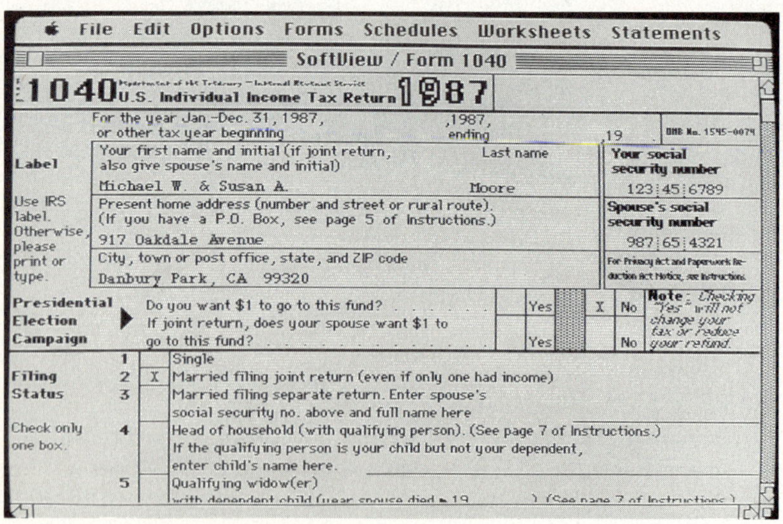


**Figure 16.21 Macintax**

Tax preparation software, such as Macintax from Softview, lets you fill out tax forms with your computer.

## EDUCATIONAL SOFTWARE

*Computerized instruction*

Besides helping you with specific tasks like managing your finances and preparing your taxes, microcomputers also can teach you various subjects and skills. Educational software packages for microcomputers covering almost every topic imaginable are available. At one end of the spectrum are programs for young children, such as Alphabet Blocks, from Bright Star Technology. This Macintosh program presents an on-screen elf who teaches prereaders the letters and sounds of the alphabet with a clear, digitized voice. At a more advanced level, Broderbund Software's Sensei Physics is a well-designed study aid that covers topics such as vectors, thermodynamics, and the nature of light (see Figure 16.22). Students learn concepts of physics by designing their own animated experiments. Educational packages such as these are quite effective because they combine graphics, sound, and student participation to make learning both interesting and fun.

Some of the best selling educational packages are those that train specific skills such as typing, math, and foreign languages. The computer's "infinite patience" allows students to work at their own pace until they have reached their desired level of competence. Type!, also from Broderbund Software, is a keyboard training program designed for both classroom and individual use. A special tutorial uses animated hands to show the proper placement of fingers on the keys (see Figure 16.23). The program is based on extensive research about how people learn to type. Furthermore, Type! provides ample feedback by displaying bar graphs showing speed and accuracy by letter, finger, and hand.

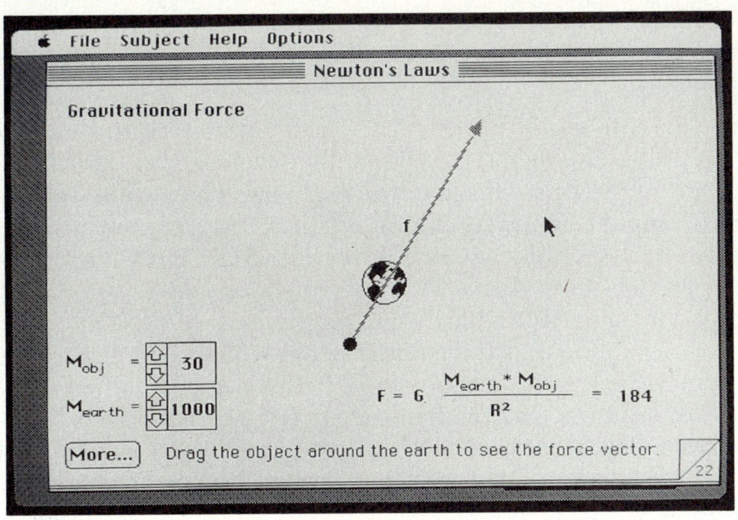


**Figure 16.22 Sensei Physics**
Broderbund Software's Sensei Physics is one example of a well-designed, computerized study aid.

## ENTERTAINMENT SOFTWARE

*Fun and games*

Microcomputers can be fun, even if you don't learn anything. An amazing variety of software has been developed with the primary intention of merely providing entertainment. Typically priced below $100, these entertainment packages range from simple childhood diversions such as Tic-Tac-Toe to sophisticated real-life simulations. There are adventure games, strategy games, card games, board games, sports games, parlor games, game show games, pinball games, and arcade "shoot-em-up" games. There are submarine simulators, race car simulators, airplane simulators,

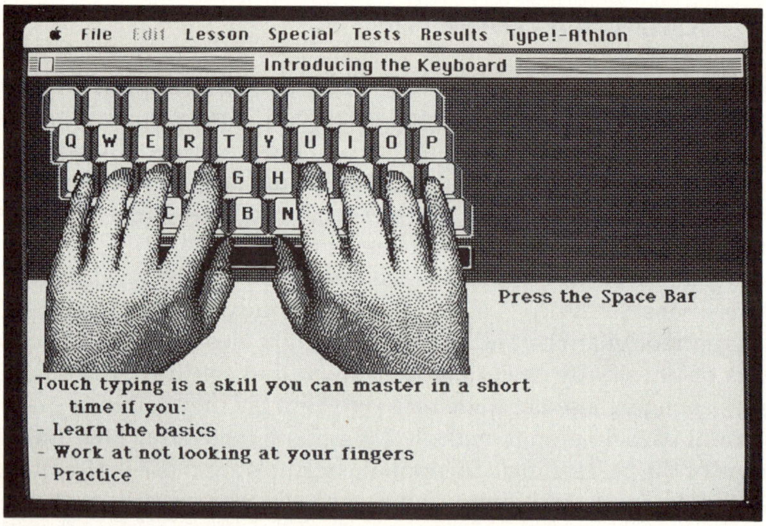


**Figure 16.23 Type!**
Also from Broderbund Software, Type! is a keyboard training program.

jet simulators, and spaceship simulators. There are even musical programs that range from simple computerized pianos to multi-instrument studio synthesizers and professional music composition tools. As impressive as this seems, it's only a brief list of some of the entertainment software you can run on a microcomputer. With the diversity of programs available, it's difficult to single out a few specific products above all others. Nevertheless, and at the risk of offending those whose favorites we don't mention, here are three examples of popular entertainment packages for microcomputers:

*Popular entertainment packages*

- *Flight Simulator*. This $50 "game" is one of the most popular microcomputer programs ever sold (see Figure 16.24). Originally developed by SubLOGIC Corporation in 1979 for the Apple II computer, Flight Simulator is also sold by Microsoft for IBM-compatibles and Apple Macintoshes. The program has been constantly updated and versions have been developed for most microcomputers, including models from Apple, Atari, Commodore, IBM, and Tandy. With realism approaching that of a $100,000 aircraft simulator, Flight Simulator includes full instrumentation and three-dimensional window displays. The program features more than eighty airports and detailed scenery maps of many U.S. landmarks. For example, you can fly your aircraft past the Statue of Liberty and even between the twin towers of the World Trade Center in New York City. There also is a World War I Ace aerial battle game included for more action-packed fun.
- *Dark Castle*. For the Apple Macintosh, this $40 game is second only to Flight Simulator in popularity. Developed by Silicon Beach Software, Dark Castle is a game in which you are a medieval warrior who has volunteered to go after the Black Knight (see Figure 16.25). This is no easy task, for you must travel through several treacherous rooms in the Dark Castle. Awaiting you are plague-ridden bats and rats, knife-throwing guards, boulder-rolling and whip-wielding henchmen, vultures, mutants, gargoyles, dragons, the Burning Eye, and magic brooms. Your only defenses are running, jumping, ducking, throwing rocks, and acquiring elixir, the Shield, and the Fireball. You can defeat the Black Knight only by toppling his throne. Dark Castle is a captivating adventure thanks to its exceptional animation and realistic sound effects.

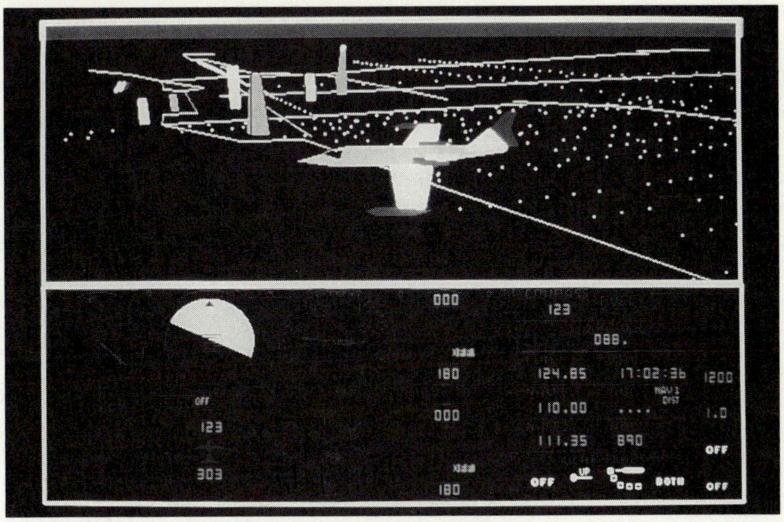


**Figure 16.24 Flight Simulator**
Flight Simulator, which lets you see what it's like to fly a small aircraft, is one of the most popular microcomputer programs ever sold.

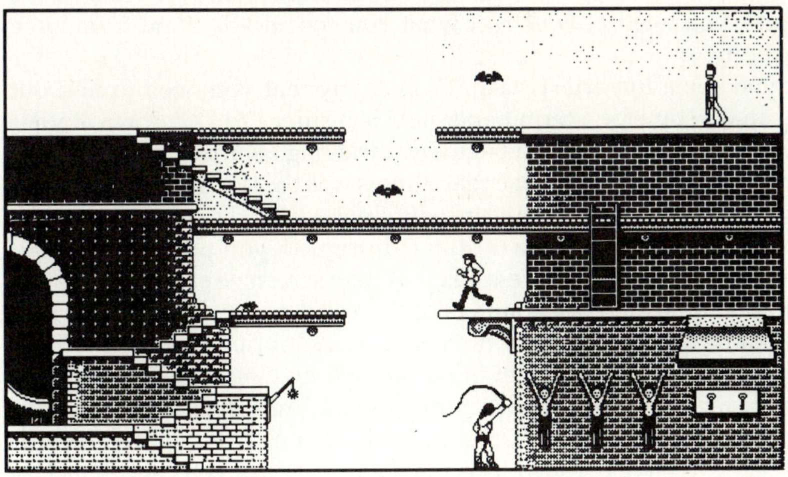

**Figure 16.25 Dark Castle**
Silicon Beach Software's Dark Castle is a popular adventure game for the Apple Macintosh.

- *Studio Session*. This $90 program, from Bogas Productions, is not nearly as popular as Flight Simulator and Dark Castle. Nevertheless, Studio Session is an excellent example of a music composition package for the Apple Macintosh. It consists of two programs, an Editor and a Player. The Editor allows you to create new songs or modify existing ones, including the 21 sample songs that come with the package. Music for 91 different instruments can be written on as many as six staffs. Each staff is like a separate track of a multi-channel tape deck. The Player plays the music you've written, allowing you to adjust the tempo control and simulated sound meters for the volume level of each track. Although Studio Session can be a serious music composition tool, it is also entertaining and educational.

## HYPERTEXT PROGRAMS

*Unique approach to information access*

In 1963 Ted Nelson was working on a satellite navigation system for the National Aeronautics and Space Administration (NASA). He and his project team needed information about a series of landmarks that would be easy to spot from space. One of the landmarks they chose was Islote Pelado, a small island off the coast of Peru. Although Nelson searched for detailed information about this island, such as how its size changed with the tides, what its color was, and whether its vegetation changed with the seasons, he had little success until a librarian at Stanford's Department of Systematic Biology finally suggested a book called *Birds of the Americas*. Sure enough, a passage in this unlikely book indirectly revealed everything Nelson needed to know about Islote Pelado. It was a classic example of an unstructured approach to information retrieval. These events made an impression on Nelson as he pondered better ways of using computers for information retrieval. In 1965 Nelson coined the term **hypertext** to describe the nonsequential organization and presentation of information with a computer. Today, the word *hypermedia* is sometimes used as a more encompassing term than *hypertext*. **Hypermedia**, like hypertext, refers to the nonsequential organization and presentation of information, but it also includes graphics, audio, and video. Theoretically, a true hypermedia system would allow you to randomly jump from topic to related topic, tapping into any kind of information the computer can digitize and store. Since you can bypass intermediate topics, you need only extract what you specifically want from huge stores of information.

How might you use a hypertext system? Let's say that you need to find out when Illinois became a state for a term paper in U.S. history. You sit down at your computer with hypertext software and begin by retrieving an article about Illinois history. It doesn't take long to determine that Illinois was the twenty-first state and it entered the union on December 3, 1818. In a different part of the same article, you read that the state bird of Illinois is the cardinal. Intrigued, you point to the word *cardinal* and click a mouse button or press a key. A new screen pops up, giving you a choice between several different meanings of the word *cardinal*. You don't particularly want to know about cardinal numbers or officials appointed by the Pope to his council, so you select the option entitled *A Bright-red American Songbird*. Yet another screen appears with an article describing the cardinal. This screen also has options for seeing a full-color picture of the bird and listening to a digitized recording of its call. When you have finished learning about the bird, you can go back to review cardinal numbers, return to Illinois history, or randomly jump to any other topic currently on the screen.

For 20 years or so, computer scientists dabbled with the concepts of hypertext. Then in the mid 1980s, several companies released limited hypertext programs for microcomputers. Today, two of the most noteworthy microcomputer hypertext programs are:

*Noteworthy hypertext programs*

- *Guide*. This program from OWL International was originally created for the Apple Macintosh in 1985, but was adapted in 1987 for IBM-compatibles as well. Although Guide is limited to text and graphics, it does allow you to create your own hypertext documents called Guidelines (see Figure 16.26). Certain words, phrases, and graphic objects can be designated as "buttons" that provide links to other hidden text and graphics. Priced at less than $200, Guide is a highly functional program that effectively incorporates the basic concepts of hypertext.

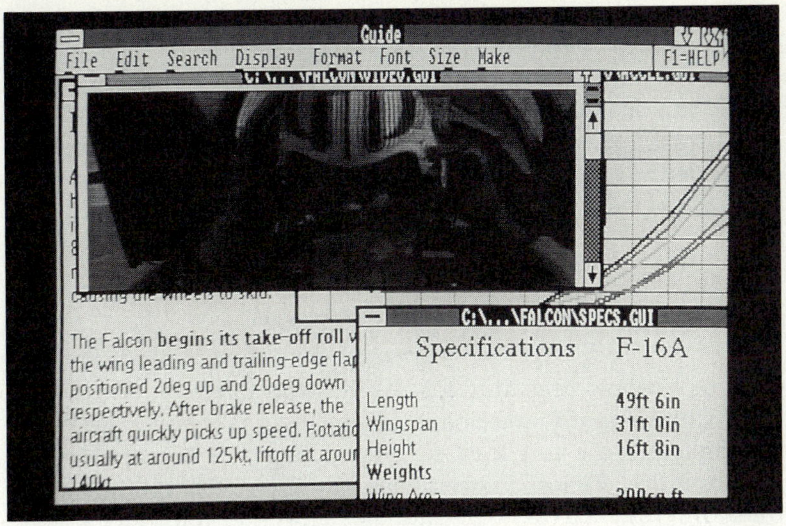


**Figure 16.26 Guide**
OWL International's Guide is a basic hypertext package available for both Apple Macintosh and IBM-compatible microcomputers.

- *Hypercard*. This \$50 program from Apple Computer for the Macintosh is by far the most well-known hypertext product on the market (see Figure 16.27). Developed by Bill Atkinson, author of MacPaint, and introduced in August 1987, Hypercard lets you store information on computerized index cards. This information can be in the form of text, graphics, animations, sounds, or digitized voices. Individual index cards are grouped into stacks, usually reflecting some common theme. These stacks can be linked in many different ways, allowing the extremely rapid information retrieval characteristic of hypertext systems. Each index card can hold up to 32 kilobytes of information; the theoretical maximum size of each stack is 500 megabytes. Atkinson estimates that stacks as large as 20 megabytes can be searched in about two seconds. As an even more exciting feature, Hypercard includes its own programming language, called Hypertalk, which is designed especially for nonprogrammers.

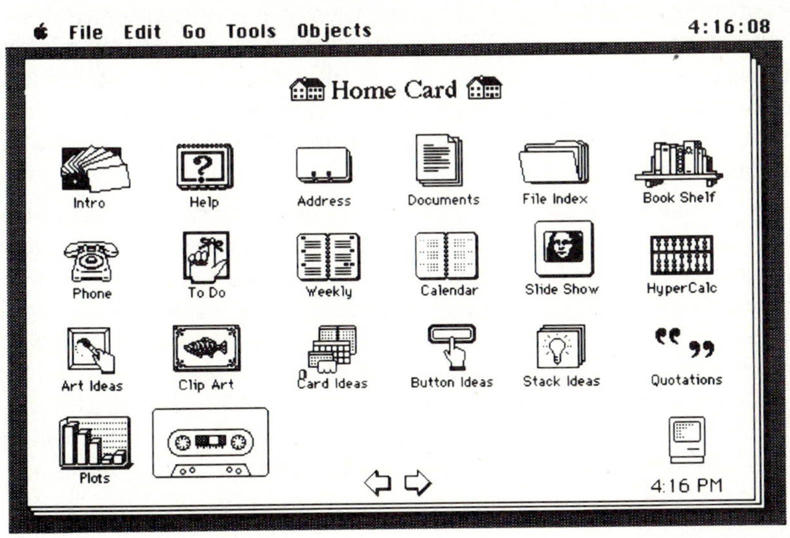


**Figure 16.27 Hypercard**
Apple's Hypercard is the leading hypertext package for Macintoshes.

Using Hypertalk, even novices can build their own customized information systems, called **stackware**. Thousands of stacks have been developed and are currently available commercially and in the public domain. They cover almost every application imaginable, from address books and other traditional data storage facilities, to animated games, illustrated mini-encyclopedias, and educational tutorials.

## ARTIFICIAL INTELLIGENCE AND EXPERT SYSTEMS

*Mimic human decision making*

We've all seen computers, robots, and androids on television and in movies that behave just like people. Unfortunately, or perhaps fortunately, this is pure fantasy and it's likely to remain fantasy, at the very least, for a long, long time. Computers and other machines cannot think. Period. Nevertheless, there is an intriguing field of study called **artificial intelligence (AI)** that combines aspects of computer science, mathematics, philosophy, psychology, and linguistics. Since psychologists don't even know for sure what "natural" intelligence is, it's unlikely that computer scientists can develop it artificially. Nevertheless, the main goal of artificial intelligence is to enable computers to mimic certain aspects of human learning and decision making. Artificial intelligence programming techniques have been developed that are now successfully used in a variety of systems, including the following:

*Artificial intelligence systems*

- *Natural Language Processors.* Much work is being done to enable computers to understand portions of ordinary human languages such as English. This **natural language processing** has many potential uses, especially in the querying of large data bases. By eliminating the need for users to learn rigid, complex programming languages, natural language processors make computers significantly more accessible. Thanks to artificial intelligence, many natural language systems are currently in use, especially on large mainframe computers.
- *Robots.* A **robot** is a computer-controlled machine that performs mechanical tasks. Techniques of artificial intelligence, including machine learning and automated vision, are currently used in many of today's sophisticated robots. **Machine learning** is a method by which computers can program themselves, through trial and error, to accomplish a particular task. **Automated vision** software allows a computer to distinguish and interpret images from optical sensors, and is widely used to inspect manufactured items and to guide the actions of robot arms. Robots are now used to manufacture all kinds of products, from automobiles to computers.
- *Expert Systems.* An **expert system** or **knowledge-based system**, is a computer program that contains a collection of facts and a list of rules for making inferences about those facts. The facts and rules usually concern one particular field and are generally contributed by experts in that field. Expert systems use those facts and rules to advise, analyze, categorize, diagnose, explain, identify, interpret, and teach. They attempt to address problems traditionally solved by human experts. A few of the many expert systems now in use are MYCIN, which helps doctors to diagnose infections; PROSPECTOR, which aids geologists in evaluating mineral sites; and TAXADVISOR, which gives estate-planning advice.

*Expert system shells*

Expert systems are among the most useful and marketable products of artificial intelligence. The examples we've just mentioned are quite specific, and many expert systems run only on minicomputers or mainframes. Special artificial intelligence programming languages, such as LISP and PROLOG, are frequently used to develop proprietary expert systems. There is, however, a relatively new class of software that runs on microcomputers and lets nonprogrammers set up their own expert systems. These programs are called expert system shells.

An **expert system shell** greatly simplifies the process of developing an expert system. You supply the facts to create the *knowledge base* and the rules to create the *rule base*. The expert system shell contains the *inference engine*, which actually uses your facts and rules to try and answer questions asked by end users, sometimes called clients. If necessary, the inference engine replies with further questions to get additional information. The inference engine then uses simple logic to draw conclusions from the details of a particular situation. Many expert system shells can also explain, with text and graphics, exactly how their conclusions have been reached.

One of the most popular expert system shells for microcomputers is VP-Expert, from Paperback Software International (see Figure 16.28). At about $100, VP-Expert provides an economical way to develop simple expert systems. The program takes you through all the steps needed to create an expert system, from entering the knowledge base to specifying the details of a typical consultation session with a client. Once you enter the facts that comprise the knowledge base, VP-Expert analyzes the data and automatically derives a preliminary set of rules to govern those data. You can examine this rule base and modify or supplement it as needed. Then the program lets you test the expert system by seeing how it behaves when a client asks a question. Multiple windows take you through a simulated consultation session. One window displays the rules as they are being tested. Another window shows the conclusions that have been reached so far. A third window lists the questions that the client would be asked for more information. In an actual session, the client would have to answer those questions. When the simulated consultation session is finished, VP-Expert displays a graphical tree that shows the complete reasoning path that was followed to reach the conclusions. VP-Expert also lets you assign a *confidence factor* from 0 to 100 to an answer if it's not simply yes or no. Once the expert system has been thoroughly tested in this manner, it is ready for consultation by clients.

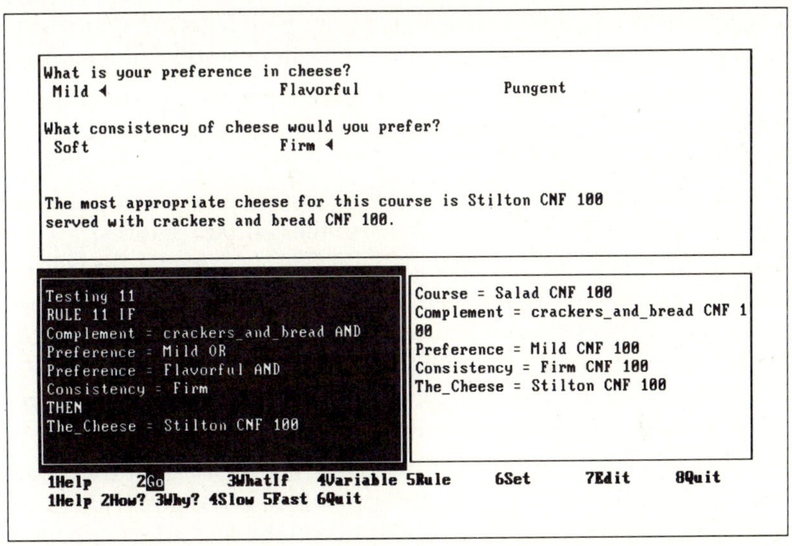


**Figure 16.28 VP-Expert**

This screen shows a session from a simple expert system designed with VP-Expert that helps you select cheeses for different courses of a meal.

## The Real World

### Breaking the Rules

Ask a dozen people what Hypercard is and you'll probably get a dozen different answers.

One keeps an address book and to-do list in it, one uses it to organize clip art for a newsletter, another runs a personal finance program. One wrote a program that spells out words when his daughter clicks the mouse. Hypercard, it seems, breaks all the rules.

Its producer, Apple, calls it system software, a "personal toolkit that gives users the power to use, customize, and create new information using text, graphics, video, music, voice, and animation."

Hypercard lets people with no programming experience create "stacks" of information that are like stacks of index cards. Each of the cards in the stack can contain text, sounds, and graphics. Using a stack about fishing, a user could get facts about trout and even cause the image of a trout to appear on the screen.

Apple's Chief Executive Officer, John Sculley, believes that Hypercard makes the process of organizing and gaining access to information completely natural and intuitive. "You can discover the contrasts between different subjects that may have no other relationship than your own curiosity," he said.

Hypercard is only the first of a generation of software that defies traditional descriptions. One program, Lotus's Agenda, has been called a "spreadsheet for words," a kind of personal secretary that makes sense of the notes you scribble to yourself on the keyboard. A user can ask to see only items about "Bob" and "butterflies." If Bob collects butterflies, Agenda can link the topics.

Sources:

"Yes, But What Does It Do," by John Schwartz, *Newsweek*, December 14, 1987, p. 68.

"Hypercard," by Gregg Williams, *Byte*, December, 1987, p. 109.

"Out to Change the World: A Conversation with John Sculley," by Keith Ferrell and Selby Bateman, *Compute!*, December, 1987, pp. 18-22.

## Summary

- *The advantages and disadvantages of integrated software.* The advantages of integrated software include the convenience of having a single set of consistent menus and commands, increased ease in transferring data among applications, and less expense in acquiring all the applications. Disadvantages include the inability to choose alternate applications, the requirement for a lot of memory, and possibly slower execution time than with stand-alone applications.
- *How a windowing environment can enhance an operating system.* A windowing environment allows you to have several applications running on your screen at the same time in different windows.
- *How a DOS shell can make DOS more user friendly.* A DOS shell is a menu-driven addition to DOS that helps you manage your disk files and directories.
- *The various types of utility programs available for microcomputers.* Utility programs include disk and file utilities for file recovery, compression, transfer, conversion; as well as disk copying, backup, optimizing, and caching. There are printer utilities for supporting various printers' features, printing spreadsheets sideways, and print spooling. Also, keyboard utilities (keyboard enhancers) provide stand-alone keyboard macro facilities.
- *Which desk accessories are handy software options.* Desk accessories to provide all kinds of useful aids while you are using an application package include calculators, clocks, calendars, note pads, scrapbooks, phone and address books, phone dialers, appointment schedulers, outline editors, and mini-spreadsheets.

- *That on-line references can save time and effort.* Using stand-alone on-line references such as spelling checkers, thesauruses, and other dictionaries is often faster and more convenient than using conventional printed books.
- *The availability of statistical and math software for microcomputers.* Statistical packages help users analyze, interpret, and present numerical data. Other types of math software perform tasks such as automatically solving algebraic equations.
- *How project management software is used as a valuable organizational tool.* Project management packages help users formally plan and control complex undertakings.
- *How personal finance and tax programs can help manage your money matters.* Personal finance packages contain valuable financial advice and personal accounting procedures. Tax software helps users fill out and print tax forms.
- *The range of educational software packages available for microcomputers.* Packages are available on almost every subject imaginable for young children and adults. Training packages teach specific skills such as typing, math, and foreign languages.
- *The vast array of entertaining computer games, simulators, and music programs.* There are adventure, strategy, card, board, sports, parlor, game show, pinball, and arcade games. There are simulators for different types of vehicles. There are computer programs that synthesize sounds from musical instruments and help you compose music.
- *How hypertext is used to tap into vast stores of information.* Hypertext is a nonsequential method of organizing and presenting information with a computer. The term *hypermedia* is sometimes used to describe hypertext systems that include text, graphics, audio, and video.
- *The practical uses of artificial intelligence and expert systems.* The purpose of artificial intelligence is to endow computers with the ability to mimic certain aspects of human learning and decision making. It is used in natural language processors, robots, and expert systems. Expert systems are computer programs that contain facts and rules, which can be consulted for the answers to specific types of questions.

## Key Terms

As an extra review of this chapter, try defining the following terms. If you have trouble with any of them, refer to the page number listed.

artificial intelligence (AI) (592)
automated vision (592)
cache (577)
critical path method (CPM) (583)
desk accessories (desktop organizers, pop-up utilities) (579)
disk backup utilities (577)
disk caching utilities (577)
disk copying utilities (576)
disk optimizing utilities (577)
DOS shell (572)
expert system (knowledge-based system) (592)
expert system shell (593)
file compression utilities (576)
file conversion utilities (576)
file recovery utilities (575)
file transfer utilities (576)
Gantt chart (583)
graphics-based windowing environment (569)
hypermedia (590)
hypertext (590)
integrated software (564)
machine learning (592)
natural language processing (592)
print spooler (577)

program evaluation and review technique (PERT) (583)
project management software (582)
robot (592)
stackware (592)
text-based windowing environment (569)
windowing environment (568)

## Review Questions

1. What are the advantages to using an integrated software package?
2. What five applications are usually included in an integrated software package?
3. What can a windowing environment do that an integrated software package cannot do?
4. Name two ways to classify windowing environments.
5. What distinguishes a DOS shell from a windowing environment?
6. List eight types of disk and file utilities.
7. What type of utility lets you print documents while you continue working within an application package?
8. What type of utility lets you assign frequently used command sequences and long strings of characters to just one or two keypresses?
9. List a few examples of commonly used desk accessories.
10. What are the advantages to using a stand-alone spelling checker and thesaurus?
11. Who might be likely to use a statistical package?
12. Name the two types of charts produced by virtually all project management packages.
13. Describe the potential benefits of using project management techniques.
14. What tasks can be performed with a personal finance package?
15. What techniques do many educational packages employ to make learning both interesting and fun?
16. List three basic categories of entertainment software.
17. What type of software allows you to randomly jump from topic to topic, finding any kind of information the computer can store?
18. What kinds of information can be stored with Hypercard?
19. What is the primary goal of artificial intelligence?
20. What type of software lets nonprogrammers set up their own expert systems?

## Multiple Choice

1. Which of the following applications is not usually included in integrated software packages?
   (a) word processing
   (b) spreadsheet
   (c) accounting
   (d) data base management

2. Which type of software lets you run several different application packages at the same time, with each one in a separate area on the screen?
   (a) integrated software (b) windowing environment
   (c) DOS shell (d) utility

3. Like some advanced operating systems, some windowing environments are
   (a) multiprocessing. (b) multitasking.
   (c) multi-user. (d) networking.

4. A menu-driven addition to DOS that helps you manage your disk files and directories is called a
   (a) DOS shell. (b) DOS utility.
   (c) DOS routine. (d) DOS command.

5. A small program to help you recover an accidentally deleted file is usually classified as a(n)
   (a) operating system. (b) application package.
   (c) programming language. (d) utility.

6. What type of utility might you use to try to fit more files on an existing disk?
   (a) file recovery (b) file compression
   (c) file transfer (d) file conversion

7. What type of utility reduces or eliminates the wait as a printer produces documents?
   (a) print spooler (b) print caching
   (c) print optimizing (d) print backup

8. On IBM-compatible computers running DOS, desk accessories are usually implemented as
   (a) multitasking programs. (b) multiprocessing programs.
   (c) multi-user programs. (d) memory-resident programs.

9. One disadvantage of most on-line reference programs is that they
   (a) are difficult to use. (b) are very slow.
   (c) consume a great deal of disk space. (d) contain few references.

10. Which type of chart graphically depicts a project as a network of interconnected activities?
    (a) pie chart (b) PERT chart
    (c) Gantt chart (d) X-Y chart

11. Which type of chart shows the major tasks of a project, when each task must be performed, and how long each task will take?
    (a) pie chart (b) PERT chart
    (c) Gantt chart (d) X-Y chart

12. Which type of software package would you use to balance your checkbook, maintain a budget, estimate your taxes, and track investments?
    (a) word processing (b) data base management
    (c) personal finance (d) hypertext

13. The term *stackware* is usually associated with which particular program?
    (a) Guide (b) Hypercard
    (c) Lotus 1-2-3 (d) WordStar

14. What type of software is among the most useful and marketable products of artificial intelligence?
    (a) word processing (b) spreadsheet
    (c) expert system (d) data base management

15. *Knowledge base, rule base,* and *inference engine* are terms that normally refer to what kind of software?
    (a) hypertext (b) data base management
    (c) spreadsheet (d) expert system shell

## Projects

1. We've listed several types of utilities you can buy to supplement the capabilities of an operating system or application package. Try to find five kinds of utility programs not mentioned in this chapter and give a specific example of each one. Computer periodicals such as *PC Magazine, Byte, PC World, InfoWorld, Macworld,* and *MacUser* are good sources of information.

2. Does your school or workplace use any educational software packages? If so, briefly describe the packages and how they are used to instruct students or train workers. If not, try to find two or three specific packages that you think could be used at your school or workplace. List them along with a brief description of their features.

3. A large number of stacks is currently available for Apple's Hypercard program. Research computer periodicals, such as *Macworld* and *MacUser,* to find ten specific examples of commercial or public domain stackware. List them along with a brief description of what they do. Can you think of any other potential uses for hypertext systems?

4. In this chapter we've given a few examples of expert systems that are actually being used. What are some other potential uses of expert systems? What kinds of situations can be broken down into facts and rules? List two or three of your suggested uses and explain how expert systems would be used for these.

# Appendix A

## Data Representation

The CPU in a microcomputer deals only with the zeros and ones of the binary system, which correspond to the on and off states of an electronic switch. People, however, find data more readable when it is presented as **alphanumeric characters** (letters, numbers, and punctuation marks). This difference raises the problem of how to get from the alphanumeric representations that are convenient for people to the binary ones and zeros that are necessary for computers.

Various number systems and coding schemes have been employed to address this problem. Let's examine the most common ones in use today.

### BINARY NUMBERS

The number system we are most familiar with, the decimal system, uses 10 symbols (the digits 0 through 9) to represent numerical quantities; single digits represent quantities smaller than 10, and groups of two or more digits represent quantities larger than 9. A digit's position in a numeral and its value contribute to the overall value of the numeral. Since each position stands for a certain power of 10, the decimal system is said to have a *base* of 10.

The binary system, with a base of 2, uses the symbols 0 and 1 to represent values less than 2, in the same way that the decimal system uses 0 through 9 for values less than 10. Quantities larger than 1 are represented by groups of zeros and ones. The digit positions in these groups represent successive powers of 2, rather than powers of 10. For example, in the decimal system, the number 57 is a short-hand expression meaning

```
5   7
|   └──────────────────────> (7 x 10^0) = 7 x  1 =  7
└──────────────────────────> (5 x 10^1) = 5 x 10 = 50 +
                                                   ──
                                                   57
```

In the binary system, the decimal number 57 is expressed as 111001:

```
1   1   1   0   0   1
|   |   |   |   |   └──────────> (1 x 2^0) = 1 x  1 =  1
|   |   |   |   └──────────────> (0 x 2^1) = 0 x  2 =  0
|   |   |   └──────────────────> (0 x 2^2) = 0 x  4 =  0
|   |   └──────────────────────> (1 x 2^3) = 1 x  8 =  8
|   └──────────────────────────> (1 x 2^4) = 1 x 16 = 16
└──────────────────────────────> (1 x 2^5) = 1 x 32 = 32 +
                                                     ──
                                                     57
```

**Table A.1 Powers of 2**

Just as the decimal number system uses successive powers of 10 (that is, 1, 10, 100, 1000, ...), the binary number system uses successive powers of 2. Some of these powers and their decimal equivalents are listed here.

| Power | | Value | Power | | Value |
|---|---|---|---|---|---|
| $2^0$ | = | 1 | $2^9$ | = | 512 |
| $2^1$ | = | 2 | $2^{10}$ | = | 1024 |
| $2^2$ | = | 4 | $2^{11}$ | = | 2048 |
| $2^3$ | = | 8 | $2^{12}$ | = | 4096 |
| $2^4$ | = | 16 | $2^{13}$ | = | 8192 |
| $2^5$ | = | 32 | $2^{14}$ | = | 16,384 |
| $2^6$ | = | 64 | $2^{15}$ | = | 32,768 |
| $2^7$ | = | 128 | $2^{16}$ | = | 64,536 |
| $2^8$ | = | 256 | | | |

Table A.1 lists the decimal values of the powers of 2. People who work around computers intimately, such as assembly language programmers, soon become as familiar with these as with the powers of 10. Note that a 10-digit decimal number can represent any of 10 billion values (from 0,000,000,000 through 9,999,999,999), while a 10-digit binary number can only represent 1024 different values (0000000000 through 1111111111). It may clarify this to note that 9,999,999,999 is 1 less than 10,000,000,000 and similarly, 1111111111 is 1 less than 10000000000 (which is $2^{10}$, or 1024). It is customary, by the way, to use no commas or spaces when writing binary numbers. Binary numbers can be used to represent fractions and mixed numbers as well as whole numbers (integers). For example, let's examine the decimal number 43.75. Its whole number or integer part is 43; the period is called the decimal point; its fractional part is 75. Here is how 43.75 breaks down in the decimal system:

4 3 . 7 5

| | | | | |
|---|---|---|---|---|
| 5 | → ($5 \times 10^{-2}$) | = 5 x 1/100 | = | 0.05 |
| 7 | → ($7 \times 10^{-1}$) | = 7 x 1/10 | = | 0.70 |
| 3 | → ($3 \times 10^{0}$) | = 3 x 1 | = | 3.00 |
| 4 | → ($4 \times 10^{2}$) | = 4 x 10 | = | 40.00 + |
| | | | | 43.75 |

This shows how 43.75 breaks down in the binary system:

1 0 1 0 1 1 . 1 1

| | | | | |
|---|---|---|---|---|
| 1 | → ($1 \times 2^{-2}$) | = 1 x 1/4 | = | 0.25 |
| 1 | → ($1 \times 2^{-1}$) | = 1 x 1/2 | = | 0.50 |
| 1 | → ($1 \times 2^{0}$) | = 1 x 1 | = | 1.00 |
| 1 | → ($1 \times 2^{1}$) | = 1 x 2 | = | 2.00 |
| 0 | → ($0 \times 2^{2}$) | = 0 x 4 | = | 0.00 |
| 1 | → ($1 \times 2^{3}$) | = 1 x 8 | = | 8.00 |
| 0 | → ($0 \times 2^{4}$) | = 0 x 16 | = | 0.00 |
| 1 | → ($1 \times 2^{5}$) | = 1 x 32 | = | 32.00 + |
| | | | | 43.75 |

In the second case, the period is called the **binary point** (instead of the decimal point). The binary digits to the left of it represent positive powers of 2, and the binary digits to the right of it represent negative powers of 2.

## FIXED-POINT AND FLOATING-POINT NUMBERS

Computers can handle two main types of numbers: fixed-point numbers and floating-point numbers. A **fixed-point number** is one whose point (decimal or binary) is in a fixed place in relation to the digits. For example, both integers and fractions can be represented as fixed-point numbers. For integers, the point is fixed at the extreme right; for fractions, the point is fixed at the extreme left. Since the point position is fixed and predefined, it does not have to be stored in memory with the value. A **floating-point number**, also called a **real number**, is one in which the position of the point can vary from number to number. Floating-point numbers can be used to represent quantities that contain both an integer part and a fractional part. You may already be familiar with this concept, which is similar to *scientific notation*. One number is used for the fractional part, called the *mantissa*, and another number is used for the power of the base, or the *exponent*. For example, the number 43.75, which can't be stored as a fixed-point number because it has both an integer part and a fractional part, can be stored as a floating-point number like this:

| Mantissa | Exponent |
|---|---|
| 4375 | 2 |
| ↑ Decimal point is assumed to be here. | |

The decimal point in the mantissa is assumed to be at the extreme left, and thus is not explicitly stored. The exponent indicates that the mantissa (.4375) is to be multiplied by $10^2$ to get the actual value ($.4375 \times 10^2 = 43.75$). Most of the time, it is best to have the mantissa shifted all the way to the left, that is, to have a mantissa with no leading zeros. A floating-point number stored in this way is said to be *normalized*.

Fixed-point binary numbers can express either integers or fractions. The binary point is assumed to be at the extreme right in the case of an integer, and at the extreme left in the case of a fraction. Here is the decimal number 43.75 expressed as a fixed-point binary integer and fixed-point binary fraction:

| Fixed-point integer 43 | Fixed-point fraction 0.75 |
|---|---|
| 00101011 | 11000000 |
| ↑ Binary point is assumed to be here | ↑ Binary point is assumed to be here. |

Here is the floating-point number 43.75 (101011.11 in binary) expressed as a mantissa and exponent:

| Mantissa | Exponent |
|---|---|
| 10101111 | 00000110 |
| ↑ Binary point is assumed to be here. | Integer value only. |

## OCTAL AND HEXADECIMAL NUMBERS

You've probably realized from the few examples given here how unsuited people are to the routine handling of binary numbers. Their length (six digits to represent the decimal value 43) and their monotony (nothing but zeros and ones) make dealing with them tedious and error-prone for humans. Two compromises between binary and decimal—the **octal system** (base 8) and the **hexadecimal system** (base 16)—are often used by programmers and other users who work with low-level details of a computer (see Table A.2).

**Table A.2 Powers of 8 and 16**

Octal numbers are based on successive powers of 8.

| | | |
|---|---|---|
| $8^0$ | = | 1 |
| $8^1$ | = | 8 |
| $8^2$ | = | 64 |
| $8^3$ | = | 512 |
| $8^4$ | = | 4,096 |
| $8^5$ | = | 32,768 |

Hexadecimal numbers are based on successive powers of 16.

| | | |
|---|---|---|
| $16^0$ | = | 1 |
| $16^1$ | = | 16 |
| $16^2$ | = | 256 |
| $16^3$ | = | 4,096 |
| $16^4$ | = | 65,536 |
| $16^5$ | = | 1,048,576 |

The octal system uses eight symbols: 0, 1, 2, 3, 4, 5, 6, and 7. Since $2^3$ is equal to 8, the octal system is a convenient shorthand for binary; each octal digit is equivalent to three binary digits. This is illustrated more graphically in the following diagram, which shows how each digit of an octal number can stand for three binary digits:

7 2 5 0 (base 8)

$(0 \times 8^0) = 0 \times 0 = 0$

$(5 \times 8^1) = 5 \times 8 = 40$

$(2 \times 8^2) = 2 \times 64 = 128$

$(7 \times 8^3) = 7 \times 512 = 3584 +$

3752 (base 10)

| 1 1 1 | 0 1 0 | 1 0 1 | 0 0 0 | ← Base 2 |
|---|---|---|---|---|
| 7 | 2 | 5 | 0 | ← Base 8 |

| BASE 16 | BASE 10 |
|---|---|
| 0 | 0 |
| 1 | 1 |
| 2 | 2 |
| 3 | 3 |
| 4 | 4 |
| 5 | 5 |
| 6 | 6 |
| 7 | 7 |
| 8 | 8 |
| 9 | 9 |
| A | 10 |
| B | 11 |
| C | 12 |
| D | 13 |
| E | 14 |
| F | 15 |

**Table A.4 Hexadecimal Digits**

Because it must represent values from 10 through 15 with single characters, the hexadecimal number system uses six letters as "digits."

The hexadecimal number system uses 16 symbols, which are listed in Table A.4 with their decimal system equivalents. Although using letters as numbers might seem strange, it is necessary in order to have a single character to represent each value from 10 to 15. Since each hexadecimal digit is equivalent to four binary digits ($2^4$ is equal to 16), the hexadecimal system is also a shorthand way to express binary numbers, as illustrated here:

```
E   A   8   (base 16)
|   |   |
|   |   +------------> ( 8 x 16^0) =  8 x   1 =    8
|   +----------------> (10 x 16^1) = 10 x  16 =  160
+--------------------> (14 x 16^2) = 14 x 256 = 3584 +
                                                ----
                                                3752 (base 10)

              1 1 1 0   1 0 1 0   1 0 0 0  <--- Base 2
                 E         A         8     <--- Base 16
```

## THE ASCII CODING SYSTEM

Generally, computers use the binary number system to store and manipulate numeric data. In order to store and represent text in a computer, some scheme must be employed to convert letters, punctuation marks, and special characters to binary numbers. In fact, one way to think of octal numbers is as a set of 3-bit codes that represent the characters 0 through 7. Similarly, the hexadecimal system can be thought of as a 4-bit system for representing the characters 0 through 9 and A through F. These codes can only represent decimal and binary values, however. To represent more than 16 characters, some scheme is required that uses codes of more than 4 bits. Various coding systems have been developed over the years using 6-bit, 7-bit, and 8-bit codes. Of these, the ASCII system is by far the most common.

**ASCII (American Standard Code for Information Interchange)** is a 7-bit code cooperatively developed by several computer manufacturers whose objective was to produce a standard code for all computers. Their objective has been fulfilled, at least for microcomputers—virtually every such machine marketed today uses some variant of the ASCII code. Although ASCII is officially a 7-bit code (see Table A.5) with 128 different characters and control codes, there is an 8-bit version dubbed ASCII-8. In practice, some manufacturers such as IBM also extend standard 7-bit ASCII with another bit to include 127 additional special-purpose characters (see Figure A.1).

Table A.5 shows the 128 standard ASCII codes. The first column shows the character itself or an abbreviation of a control code. The second column gives the ASCII code for that character or control code in decimal (base 10). The third column gives the same ASCII code in hexadecimal (base 16) and the fourth column gives it in binary (base 2). In some computers, ASCII codes from 0 to 31 are not actually characters that can appear on the screen or be printed. They are control codes for actions such as carriage return, backspace, line feed, form feed, and other signals for coordinating communication between a computer and a display screen, printer, modem, or some other input/output device.

**Figure A.1 IBM Extended ASCII Codes**

This screen shows the extended ASCII code system used by IBM-compatible microcomputers, which includes special characters that appear on the screen for the first 32 ASCII codes, and an additional 128 characters that are encoded by using the eighth (leftmost) bit in an 8-bit byte (normally unused in standard 7-bit ASCII). In this figure, the decimal ASCII codes appear in black numbers and the characters themselves are white.

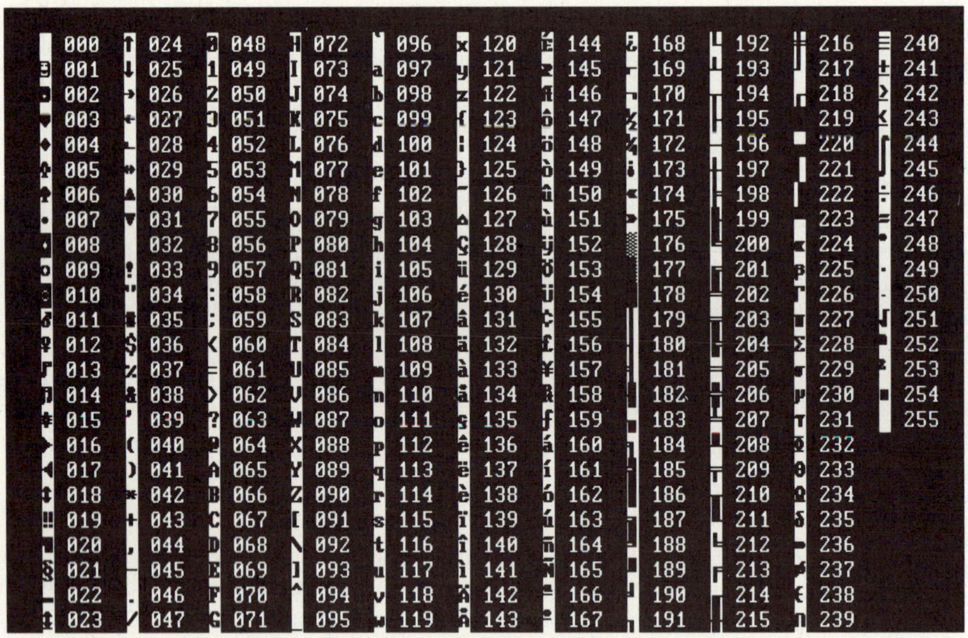

**Table A.5 Standard ASCII Codes**

| CHAR | DEC | HEX | BINARY | CHAR | DEC | HEX | BINARY | CHAR | DEC | HEX | BINARY |
|---|---|---|---|---|---|---|---|---|---|---|---|
| NUL | 0 | 00 | 00000000 | + | 43 | 2B | 00101011 | V | 86 | 56 | 01010110 |
| SOH | 1 | 01 | 00000001 | , | 44 | 2C | 00101100 | W | 87 | 57 | 01010111 |
| STX | 2 | 02 | 00000010 | - | 45 | 2D | 00101101 | X | 88 | 58 | 01011000 |
| ETX | 3 | 03 | 00000011 | " | 46 | 2E | 00101110 | Y | 89 | 59 | 01011001 |
| EOT | 4 | 04 | 00000100 | / | 47 | 2F | 00101111 | Z | 90 | 5A | 01011010 |
| ENQ | 5 | 05 | 00000101 | 0 | 48 | 30 | 00110000 | ( | 91 | 5B | 01011011 |
| ACK | 6 | 06 | 00000110 | 1 | 49 | 31 | 00110001 | \ | 92 | 5C | 01011100 |
| BEL | 7 | 07 | 00000111 | 2 | 50 | 32 | 00110010 | ) | 93 | 5D | 01011101 |
| BS | 8 | 08 | 00001000 | 3 | 51 | 33 | 00110011 | ^ | 94 | 5E | 01011110 |
| HT | 9 | 09 | 00001001 | 4 | 52 | 34 | 00110100 | _ | 95 | 5F | 01011111 |
| LF | 10 | 0A | 00001010 | 5 | 53 | 35 | 00110101 | ` | 96 | 60 | 01100000 |
| VT | 11 | 0B | 00001011 | 6 | 54 | 36 | 00110110 | a | 97 | 61 | 01100001 |
| FF | 12 | 0C | 00001100 | 7 | 55 | 37 | 00110111 | b | 98 | 62 | 01100010 |
| CR | 13 | 0D | 00001101 | 8 | 56 | 38 | 00111000 | c | 99 | 63 | 01100011 |
| SO | 14 | 0E | 00001110 | 9 | 57 | 39 | 00111001 | d | 100 | 64 | 01100100 |
| SI | 15 | 0F | 00001111 | : | 58 | 3A | 00111010 | e | 101 | 65 | 01100101 |
| DLE | 16 | 10 | 00010000 | ; | 59 | 3B | 00111011 | f | 102 | 66 | 01100110 |
| DC1 | 17 | 11 | 00010001 | < | 60 | 3C | 00111100 | g | 103 | 67 | 01100111 |
| DC2 | 18 | 12 | 00010010 | = | 61 | 3D | 00111101 | h | 104 | 68 | 01101000 |
| DC3 | 19 | 13 | 00010011 | > | 62 | 3E | 00111110 | i | 105 | 69 | 01101001 |
| DC4 | 20 | 14 | 00010100 | ? | 63 | 3F | 00111111 | j | 106 | 6A | 01101010 |
| NAK | 21 | 15 | 00010101 | @ | 64 | 40 | 01000000 | k | 107 | 6B | 01101011 |
| SYN | 22 | 16 | 00010110 | A | 65 | 41 | 01000001 | l | 108 | 6C | 01101100 |
| ETB | 23 | 17 | 00010111 | B | 66 | 42 | 01000010 | m | 109 | 6D | 01101101 |
| CAN | 24 | 18 | 00011000 | C | 67 | 43 | 01000011 | n | 110 | 6E | 01101110 |
| EM | 25 | 19 | 00011001 | D | 68 | 44 | 01000100 | o | 111 | 6F | 01101111 |
| SUB | 26 | 1A | 00011010 | E | 69 | 45 | 01000101 | p | 112 | 70 | 01110000 |
| ESC | 27 | 1B | 00011011 | F | 70 | 46 | 01000110 | q | 113 | 71 | 01110001 |
| FS | 28 | 1C | 00011100 | G | 71 | 47 | 01000111 | r | 114 | 72 | 01110010 |
| GS | 29 | 1D | 00011101 | H | 72 | 48 | 01001000 | s | 115 | 73 | 01110011 |
| RS | 30 | 1E | 00011110 | I | 73 | 49 | 01001001 | t | 116 | 74 | 01110100 |
| US | 31 | 1F | 00011111 | J | 74 | 4A | 01001010 | u | 117 | 75 | 01110101 |
|  | 32 | 20 | 00100000 | K | 75 | 4B | 01001011 | v | 118 | 76 | 01110110 |
| ! | 33 | 21 | 00100001 | L | 76 | 4C | 01001100 | w | 119 | 77 | 01110111 |
| " | 34 | 22 | 00100010 | M | 77 | 4D | 01001101 | x | 120 | 78 | 01111000 |
| # | 35 | 23 | 00100011 | N | 78 | 4E | 01001110 | y | 121 | 79 | 01111001 |
| $ | 36 | 24 | 00100100 | O | 79 | 4F | 01001111 | z | 122 | 7A | 01111010 |
| % | 37 | 25 | 00100101 | P | 80 | 50 | 01010000 | { | 123 | 7B | 01111011 |
| & | 38 | 26 | 00100110 | Q | 81 | 51 | 01010001 | \| | 124 | 7C | 01111100 |
| ' | 39 | 27 | 00100111 | R | 82 | 52 | 01010010 | } | 125 | 7D | 01111101 |
| ( | 40 | 28 | 00101000 | S | 83 | 53 | 01010011 | ~ | 126 | 7E | 01111110 |
| ) | 41 | 29 | 00101001 | T | 84 | 54 | 01010100 |  | 127 | 7F | 01111111 |
| * | 42 | 2A | 00101010 | U | 85 | 55 | 01010101 |  |  |  |  |

# Appendix B

# Selecting a System

More and more people are buying microcomputers for business and home use. Most companies already have at least one microcomputer, and they are continually acquiring more. Schools at all levels have been purchasing microcomputers for both students and faculty. It's been estimated that at least 20% of all U.S. households will ultimately have some type of microcomputer. Just as most of you will eventually purchase stereo systems, video systems, other high-tech home appliances, and automobiles, it's likely that in the near future you may be investing in a computer system, too. Perhaps you won't be buying a computer for your home, but you might still be involved in the process of selecting a system for your school or work. This chapter offers some guidelines that can help both individuals and organizations in their process of computerization.

Computers are complicated equipment. Although their prices have been steadily dropping, computers still represent a substantial investment for most people. With so many different computer models and an overwhelming array of software packages on the market, unless you're wealthy or are already a computer expert, purchasing a system is no trivial task. The choices you make can have profound effects on the quantity and quality of work you will accomplish with your computer. To make good choices, you need to have a plan.

Selecting a computer system is somewhat like selecting a stereo system or automobile. If you buy on irrational impulses, you risk regretting your decision for years to come. If, on the other hand, you follow a well-thought-out, step-by-step selection process, chances are good that you'll end up with an economical labor-saving system. One such approach involves six basic steps:

1. Learn about computers.
2. Define your needs.
3. Select the software.
4. Select the hardware.
5. Purchase the system.
6. Install the system.

## STEP 1: LEARN ABOUT COMPUTERS

You need not be a computer scientist to effectively select and use computers. Some basic knowledge, however, can help a great deal. The first step in selecting a system is to become familiar with the capabilities and limitations of computers. In other words, you need to know what computers can and cannot do for you. The chapters in this book are designed to provide you with an understanding of the capabilities and limitations of microcomputers.

Of course, this book can by no means cover all relevant microcomputer topics. Although learning more is not absolutely required, the more you do know the better prepared you'll be to take advantage of what computers have to offer. Fortunately, there are many opportunities for you to learn more about computers. Some of the possibilities books, periodicals, organizations, shows, courses, conferences, and workshops.

## Books

An astonishing number of computer books are available in local bookstores, libraries, and computer stores. Some are quite technical, but many others have been written especially for novices. Some of the most common books you'll find are "How to" books that cover specific computer models or software packages. Others teach programming in certain languages or deal with the philosophical and sociological aspects of using computers. You can even buy books that discuss how to select a computer system.

## Periodicals

In 1975, only two magazines were devoted solely to microcomputers. Today, hundreds of microcomputer newspapers, newsletters, and magazines are available. Although books can cover topics in great detail, they're usually somewhat out of date by the time they actually hit the shelves. Newspapers, newsletters, and magazines reveal what's happening in the marketplace *now.* They frequently contain reviews and in-depth evaluations of hardware and software products. Periodicals also contain informative articles and columns that answer questions and provide tips from other computer users. They are crammed with ads from manufacturers, retailers, and mail-order outfits. Many owners have at least one subscription to a microcomputer periodical. Some of the more popular publications include *A+*, *Byte*, *Infoworld*, *Macworld*, and *PC Magazine.*

In addition to traditional periodicals printed on paper, *disk magazines* have been gaining popularity recently. These publications are issued on floppy disks and are aimed at users of particular computer models. They uniquely provide subscribers with tested programs for business, education, entertainment, and home use.

## Organizations

Computer users, it seems, are a very sociable lot. At regular intervals, thousands of folks gather in societies, clubs, and user groups to share computer experiences, help solve each others' problems, and trade software. Although most people don't join such organizations until after they purchase a computer system, joining before buying can be advantageous. Many user groups are centered around a particular computer model or type of popular software. Group members can usually offer advice on where to get the best deals. Joining a computer organization may even qualify you for certain group discounts off the retail prices of selected hardware and software products. Once you have your system, a computer organization can put you in contact with people who have the same hardware and software. These colleagues can be an invaluable source of information because it's likely that they've already solved problems you might be having as a beginning user.

Computer organizations offer fellowship, support, general information, and answers to those tricky questions not answered in any manuals. Many groups have been established since the advent of microcomputers in the mid-1970s. For example, more than 850 groups in the United States serve Apple computer users. Some groups have remained local, small, and dedicated to one particular type of computer, like the Champaign-Urbana, Illinois Apple II Users Group with its 40 or so members. Other groups have grown immense and wield a good deal of influence over the microcomputer industry. The Boston Computer Society, for instance, was founded in 1977 by Jonathan Rotenberg when he was thirteen years old. Today, with about 24,000 members, it's perhaps the nation's largest microcomputer users group. The Boston Computer Society has its own magazine, *Computer Update*, sponsors around 100 monthly events, and has approximately 40 special-interest subgroups, each of which publishes its own newsletter.

## Shows

Every year, computer shows are held in various cities across the United States. These events may be sponsored by individual entrepreneurs, manufacturers, retail stores, magazine publishers, or other associations that deal with computers. Although many shows specifically target manufacturers and retailers, others are open to the general computer-buying public. They are typically held in large exhibit halls, with booth space rented to hardware manufacturers, software manufacturers, dealers, distributors, retailers, computer clubs, publishers, and any other organizations that want to sell products or advertise. Admission is often charged. Besides exhibiting new products and services, many shows also offer short talks, seminars, and classes for attendees, frequently given by well-known computer personalities. These shows may last several days and attract thousands of people who come from all over the country.

Computer shows can offer the following opportunities:

- *See new products.* Manufacturers often introduce products at computer shows, so it may be an early chance to see what's new in the market. Furthermore, most shows exhibit a wider variety of products than you can usually find in the typical computer store. It's easy to collect all kinds of brochures, product descriptions, advertisements, and other handouts.
- *Try out products.* Many computer show exhibits are specifically designed to let you "test drive" hardware and software products. This may be your only chance to get hands-on experience with an item before you actually buy it.
- *Buy products.* Frequently, computer shows allow exhibitors to sell their products directly to consumers. At some shows, you can buy anything from a single diskette to an entire microcomputer system. Prices are generally less than retail and it's possible to get some good bargains at computer shows, especially as closing time nears.
- *Learn more.* As we mentioned before, many computer shows sponsor lectures and seminars. Subjects may include very specific topics, such as how to use a particular feature of a software package, or more general matters, such as the role of microcomputers in our society.
- *Meet people.* Computer shows offer excellent opportunities to come into contact with other people who have similar interests. You may meet just one person at a booth looking for the same product, or you may discover an entire users group that you want to join. The people you meet can offer advice, answer questions, and share some of their computer experiences with you.

- *Talk to manufacturers.* Since many hardware and software manufacturers send representatives to computer shows, you may get an opportunity to ask questions, get more information, or even complain about a particular product.

### Courses

For people who seek a more structured approach to learning about computers, a wide variety of formal courses is offered to both students and the general public. Traditional educational institutions, like high schools, community colleges, and universities, hold classes aimed primarily at those seeking diplomas. Many community colleges and university continuing education and extension services also offer computer courses for non-degree students. Classes range from simple, non-technical introductions for novices, to in-depth studies for those pursuing computer careers. Alternative learning centers, such as those affiliated with local churches, libraries, and park districts, often conduct classes taught by computer experts in their spare time. Although such courses may be less academic than those run by traditional educational institutions, they may be more accessible to the general public. Computer stores often teach courses about particular hardware and software products, but these courses may be limited to customers. Several proprietary (for-profit) schools also offer computer-related coursework. Many accredited home study schools as well as colleges and universities have correspondence courses that teach computer subjects by mail. Finally, some private individuals offer computer courses, too. Before you enroll in any course, however, be sure to investigate it thoroughly to determine just what is being offered and how much it will cost.

### Conferences and Workshops

Many organizations offer conferences and workshops covering particular computer topics. Some of these events are expensive, intensive training sessions aimed specifically at computer professionals. Others are less technical and attract novice computer users. They typically last from several hours to several days, and are held in various cities across the country.

## STEP 2: DEFINE YOUR NEEDS

Once you have a general picture of what microcomputers can do, you can begin to examine how you might use one. It's important to carefully consider exactly what you want to do with a computer before you purchase anything. Of course, you probably can't anticipate every possible use you'll find for your computer once you get it, but you should have some clearly stated, specific reasons for investing in a system. A good approach is to make a list. Write down, in order of importance, all of the uses you expect to have for a computer. At this stage, try not to think too much about costs, but keep your ideas realistic. As a sample, your list might look something like this:

1. *Word Processing.* For term papers, reports, class notes, and letters.
2. *Record Keeping.* For addresses, phone numbers, personal property inventory, bank account numbers, credit cards, and tax-deductible expenses.
3. *Calculating.* For bills, budgets, and income taxes.

4. *Education.* For math review, foreign language study, college entrance test review, and learning about computer programming.
5. *Entertainment.* For fun with computer games and simulations.

This list is probably fairly typical of the uses a student or other individual might have for a computer at home or school. A business, however, might have a more specific list of computer needs, especially if it is computerizing for the first time, or perhaps considering replacing an existing system. A small business, for example, might have the following uses for a microcomputer system:

1. *General Ledger.* To keep track of financial records and produce reports, such as balance sheets and profit and loss statements, that summarize the financial status of the firm.
2. *Accounts Receivable.* To keep track of the money owed to the company and when payments are due.
3. *Accounts Payable.* To keep track of money the company owes to its suppliers.
4. *Payroll.* To calculate each employee's gross pay, withhold taxes, subtract deductions, print paychecks, and maintain necessary payroll records.
5. *Inventory.* To monitor the goods on hand and make sure enough are in stock for production and customer requests.
6. *Mailing List.* To prepare direct mailing of ads and notices.
7. *Word Processing.* To create letters, reports, newsletters, and memos.
8. *Personnel Files.* To hold information for insurance, retirement, and governmental regulations.

## STEP 3: SELECT THE SOFTWARE

Now comes perhaps the most difficult step in acquiring a computer system: selecting the software. First of all, from the user's standpoint, software is much more important than hardware. Software is what makes the computer accomplish useful work. Without programs, computer hardware is utterly worthless. It's likely that you'll pay much more for all the software you'll eventually buy than the hardware. If you have a stereo system, this probably doesn't surprise you, since most people have more money invested in records, tapes, or compact disks than they originally paid for the stereo components. Shopping for software is also more difficult than shopping for hardware, because there is so much more software on the market than hardware. Some software companies sell only by mail, so it may be difficult to obtain information about their programs. A thorough evaluation of software requires using it in your own particular situation for a substantial amount of time. This may be difficult, if not impossible, to do by running a program at a single sitting in your local computer store. Finally, because software usually has a smaller profit margin than hardware, computer salespeople may not be as enthusiastic or helpful about selling a program as they would an entire computer system.

All those difficulties aside, it really is possible, even for novices, to make good software selections. First, go back to your list of computer uses. For each item, come up with at least three different software packages. Here you'll need some of those learning resources we talked about previously. Perhaps the best source of possible selections may be people you know from school, work, clubs, user groups, or computer shows. See if you can arrange to try a potential software selection for an extended period of time. Perhaps a friend or relative has a computer and software you can use. If your school has a computer lab, you may be able to use it at times when classes aren't in session. Many school labs have software you can check out and run on a computer at your own pace.

Probably the best source of information comparing various software packages are computer magazines. Most have reviews of new software products; some even devote entire issues to comparing all the major competitors in a particular application. The publications extensively test each package by using it for a predetermined set of activities, and then quantitatively rate how each one does. Often, the reviewers will conclude with one or more "editor's choices," and give their reasons for selecting these packages as the best of the lot. Scanning the magazine stands and going through back issues in the library are excellent ways to find out more about specific application packages.

As you begin to compile your list of potential software selections, make your own evaluations and rank order the packages, if possible. As you talk to people and read product reviews, note the following characteristics of good software:

- *Competent.* Capable of performing an important job well.
- *Easy to Learn.* Can be mastered with moderate effort in a reasonable amount of time.
- *Easy to Use.* Intrudes as little as possible between the user and getting the job done.
- *Tolerant.* Gently and sensibly handles errors made by the user.
- *Layered.* Simple and self-evident on the outside for beginners, and progressively more complex and powerful as internal features are mastered.
- *Flexible.* Can be adapted to handle variations in its basic task.
- *Compatible.* Works well with other software by using standard conventions and being able to share files.
- *Well-Documented.* Comes with clearly written, correct instruction and reference manuals designed with both novices and experts in mind.
- *Supported.* Backed by its manufacturer, which conscientiously fixes errors, provides updated versions, and answers users' questions.
- *Reasonably-Priced.* Provides value comparable to its cost.

Once you complete this process, you'll have a list of computer uses ordered according to your priorities, within which will be sublists of potential software packages ranked by preference. You're not ready to buy anything yet, and you haven't singled out the exact packages you'll eventually get, but you have a pretty good idea of the field of contenders.

## STEP 4: SELECT THE HARDWARE

By seriously considering software first, the selection of hardware is much easier. The idea is to choose hardware that can run the software packages you've selected. This helps you put together a system that really matches your needs.

## Computer

Some of the software packages you've selected have versions that run on different computers, but many will only work on a single machine. This is where you begin to determine the most important hardware decision facing you: which computer to get. Although there are hundreds of different companies making microcomputers, the great majority of machines fit into one of just a few categories. Today, these categories are IBM and IBM-compatible computers, Apple Macintoshes, Apple II computers, and all others. This is not to belittle all those "other" computers. There are quite a few great machines with large numbers of devoted users. However, there's no doubt that microcomputers in the first three categories far outnumber all the rest, especially in businesses, offices, and schools.

### IBM and IBM-Compatible Computers

IBM is the recognized leader in the microcomputer industry. They sell far more microcomputers than any other single manufacturer. People who prefer other computers may not concede that IBM sells the "best" computers, but the fact remains that they sell the most. Although IBM no longer manufactures members of its original Personal Computer line (PC Jrs, PCs, PC Portables, XTs, and ATs), millions of these machines remain in use and some dealers are still selling new ones. The current IBM Personal System/2 line of computers improves on the previous models while still being able to run all the old software. IBM computers tend to be solidly-built, reliable machines that have been traditionally popular in the business world. Even though IBM computers might be a bit more expensive than comparable machines from other manufacturers, they have been getting more price-competitive lately. It's been said that "No manager ever got fired for buying IBM."

A true **IBM-compatible** computer is one that can run all the software and accept all the expansion boards and peripheral units that IBM microcomputers can use. Because IBM chose standard parts, published detailed design descriptions in technical references, and used an operating system designed and also sold by Microsoft, it was relatively easy for other manufacturers to produce compatible computers. Although there may still be some exceptions, most IBM-compatibles produced today do a very good job of mimicking the way IBM computers work. Many such "clones" offer more advanced features at a significantly lower price than IBM computers. Some IBM-compatible manufacturers, such as COMPAQ, have become highly-respected microcomputer industry leaders in their own right. Many well-established computer and electronic companies, like Tandy-Radio Shack and Zenith, have expanded their lines to include IBM-compatible machines. In addition, quite a few mail-order firms sell IBM-compatibles that they construct themselves from standard components. In fact, many more IBM-compatibles are sold today than IBM microcomputers.

Although IBMs and IBM-compatibles have their critics, selecting such computers has many advantages. American businesses have over $80 billion invested in IBM and IBM- compatible computers. This includes over 72 million software and hardware products, and hundreds of millions of hours of training. Books, magazines, and user groups devoted solely to IBM-compatible computers abound. Chances are good that you can find experts nearby to help you if you have problems. Most IBM and IBM-compatible systems can be easily expanded if you need to add more capabilities later.

### Apple Macintosh Computers

In the early days of IBM microcomputers, many people considered them to be powerful and expandable, but not particularly easy to set up and use. Apple, building on their great success with the Apple II line, decided to address these concerns and build a computer "for the rest of us." In 1984, Apple introduced the Macintosh. Easy to learn and fun to use, the Macintosh has changed the way people perceive computers. Today's models preserve the philosophy of simplicity, yet have become more powerful and expandable. The Macintosh is becoming increasingly popular in businesses, especially for word processing, graphics, and desktop publishing applications. Many individuals and schools are also purchasing Macintoshes in ever greater numbers. Hundreds of software packages and a variety of optional peripherals are now available for this machine.

### Apple II Computers

The original Apple II computer was introduced in 1977. Since then, several million of the Apple II family (including the Apple II+, Apple IIe, Apple III, Apple IIc, and Apple IIGS) have been sold. These computers have done very well in elementary and secondary schools. The Apple II's share of sales in this market is currently around 50%, although some schools are turning more toward Macintoshes and low-cost IBM-compatibles. Apple II computers have also been quite popular as home computers and were common in businesses before the introduction of the IBM Personal Computers. At least 10,000 software packages run on Apple II computers and a wide variety of expansion devices and peripherals are available. Although this family of computers is not as powerful and fast as Macintoshes and IBM-compatibles, they are still viable machines with a large number of devoted users.

## Memory

In the early days of microcomputers, RAM was expensive and most machines could have no more than 64K. This situation has changed dramatically. Many microcomputers now have the potential to contain up to 16 megabytes of RAM, and memory chips are less expensive. For many people, the memory that comes with the computer will be sufficient for most of their needs. For example, most IBM microcomputers now come with at least 640K standard and all Macintoshes come with at least one megabyte installed. On other machines, you'll have to make sure you get enough memory to run the application packages you've selected. Since most software manufacturers state how much memory is required for their programs, figuring out how much memory to buy should be fairly simple. If you can, try to choose a computer system that can accept more RAM than you may initially need. Then if you later purchase software that requires more memory, you can add more RAM to upgrade your system.

## Disk Drives

When it comes to secondary storage, you have several choices to make. The first one is whether you need the high capacity and rapid data access of a hard disk. This depends on the types of applications you'll run and the quantity of data you'll be working with. Some application packages require a hard disk. Others don't actually require one, but would work much better and faster with a hard disk. If the application programs you run and the data files you'll work with won't each fit on a single floppy disk, you probably need a hard disk. If you're not sure if you want to invest the extra few hundred dollars in a hard disk, make sure that you get a computer system that can accommodate a hard disk if you decide to add one later.

The other most common secondary storage decisions involve what kind and how many floppy drives to get. The 5 1/4- inch diskette drives are still more common, less expensive, and use less expensive floppies than 3 1/2-inch drives. However, many computers, like the Macintosh and IBM Personal System/2 computers, come with only 3 1/2-inch disk drives standard. Most software is now distributed on either type of disk. Each type of floppy drive has its advantages, but your major concern should be whether you can trade diskettes with colleagues, coworkers, and friends. It's best to get the same type of diskette drives as any other people with whom you'll be frequently exchanging programs and data. If you do get a hard disk, one floppy drive will probably be sufficient. However, if you often need to copy entire diskettes, it might be worth investing in two drives. In systems without hard disks, having two floppy drives is the most practical arrangement.

## Display

With some computers, you have no choice as to what kind of display to get. The lower-end Apple Macintoshes, for example, all come with a built-in 9-inch monochrome graphics display. On most other computers, you have a choice among several alternatives. Older and less-expensive computers give you a choice between monochrome text, monochrome graphics, and color graphics monitors. Many newer microcomputers, like the IBM Personal System/2 series, only come with graphics monitors, but you do have a choice between monochrome and color. To complicate matters more, many computers can accept several different display adapters, each of which may support several video modes.

To resolve your display dilemma, first look to your software selections. If you want to run software that uses graphics, you'll need a graphics display. On the other hand, if you're *positive* that you'll only be working with text, you may want to opt for a less expensive monochrome text monitor. Although in most cases color is not absolutely necessary, many people find that color monitors are more pleasant to work with, despite the added expense. If you are planning to use software that manipulates detailed graphics, you'll need a high-resolution display. As with most hardware selections, try to choose a system that can be upgraded later, if possible. Your needs may expand and prices may fall to a point where you would like to invest in a more sophisticated display. It's much easier and less expensive to replace a display adapter and monitor than an entire computer system.

## Printer

Literally hundreds of microcomputer printers are on the market. Before you choose a particular model, you must first decide on what type of printer you need. Most microcomputer users have 9-pin dot-matrix printers. These printers can do graphics and can print fairly rapidly in draft mode, yet also have a more attractive, but much slower, near-letter-quality mode. If you will be printing letters on bond or letterhead paper, be sure to look for models that can easily accept single sheets as well as the fan-fold, pin-feed computer paper most dot-matrix printers use. For true letter quality, you might want to get a daisy-wheel printer. These printers produce text that looks just like that from typewriters, but they are quite slow. Applications that produce very high-quality text and graphics may require a 24-pin dot-matrix printer or perhaps even an expensive laser printer. Before you make your final decision on any printer, be sure to see samples of the text and graphics (if any) it can produce. Also consider the cost of supplies like paper, ribbons, toner cartridges (for laser printers) and additional typefaces.

## Other Peripherals

As you learned in Chapter 2, a wide range of optional peripheral devices can be connected to a microcomputer. In your selection of a system, you should try to choose initially only those devices that will be absolutely necessary. You can always add more peripherals later, provided that you've chosen a system that can be expanded. If you'll be calling remote computers, you'll need to select a modem. Many graphics applications require the use of a mouse. Some computer games use joysticks or trackballs. Examine your software selections carefully to make sure that you understand exactly what hardware devices are necessary.

## Specifications and Benchmarks

In the preceding sections, we've briefly described the hardware you need to select. But, how do you pick the exact models to buy? Just as in making software selections, one method is to look carefully at what people around you have purchased. Some experts have even suggested that you get a system exactly like another one you have access to, perhaps at school, work, or a friend's. This way, you can become familiar with the components before you buy, and after you get your system, you have an exact duplicate available in case your system isn't working. Although it definitely helps to have access to a similar system, if you only buy what someone else has, you're depending a great deal on their judgment, which may or may not be better than your own.

Another method of selecting hardware is to read reviews published in computer and consumer magazines. Just like software reviews, hardware reviews compare and evaluate actual products. For computers, hardware reviews can provide in-depth information about how they are constructed and how they work. For devices like displays, printers, and modems, reviews can compare models quantitatively and tabulate their features. Be forewarned, however, that these reviews are often saturated with specifications and benchmarks.

**Specifications** are a detailed list of the exact components, options, and capabilities of a particular hardware device. Microcomputer specifications typically list the manufacturer, exact size, microprocessor, coprocessors, system clock speed, amount of standard RAM, total possible RAM, amount of ROM, disk drives and capacities, number and type of expansion slots, number and type of interfaces, retail list price, and many other details. Sometimes, specifications include measures of performance. For example, many printer specifications include the number of characters printed per second. Although specifications can be one way to compare different devices, they may be misleading. Performance measurements are often made under ideal conditions. So, a printer advertised at 200 characters per second, may not actually be that fast when printing a document from your word processor, especially if it contains underlining, boldface, and italics.

A **benchmark** is an objective, reproducible measure of hardware or software performance, typically the amount of time it takes to run a standard program or process a particular set of data. Just like specifications, benchmarks are one way to compare hardware, but they can also be misleading. For example, a common benchmark for computer performance is one cycle of a calculation known as the *Sieve of Eratosthenes*. This is a method of finding prime numbers (numbers only evenly divisible by themselves and 1) that has been adapted to computers. Although benchmarks such as these may be useful for measuring the time required for certain very specific kinds of computer operations, they provide little or no information about ease of use, reliability, maintainability, the amount of manufacturer support for a product, or other equally important attributes. Sometimes, magazines like *Byte* and *PC Magazine* develop their own benchmarks for reviewing products. Although these benchmarks are designed to measure performance under typical conditions, they may still not reflect how fast your software will run on your machine. Benchmark results, like specifications, should be taken with a grain of salt.

## STEP 5: PURCHASE THE SYSTEM

After selecting your hardware, you may have to go back and modify your list of software packages so that you have ones that will all run on the machine you've chosen. Before you even think of buying anything, you should have a fairly complete list of the exact software and hardware products you'll need. Since most product reviews and ads contain prices, you should also have a good notion of how much all this will cost. This is the time to look at your budget and make some realistic choices. You may not be able to afford all the software packages and optional peripherals you want to get. Fortunately, some of these purchases can be postponed. If you've listed your selections by priority, you can initially buy only those most essential items.

### When to Buy

For many people, the most disconcerting circumstances of microcomputer shopping are the rate at which technology advances and how quickly prices can drop. Computer newspapers and magazines are filled with rumors, educated guesses, and pre-release previews about new products and upgrades to existing ones. Most manufacturers, it would seem, are constantly on the verge of releasing a computer, peripheral, or software package that will render every preceding product hopelessly obsolete. Even worse, what you pay $4,000 for this year may cost less than $1,000 two years from now. This perpetual anticipation can immobilize some potential computer shoppers.

Unfortunately, you must simply accept the facts that whichever hardware and software you choose, prices will drop and new versions will be released. There may be some prudence in waiting one or two months if a product is about to be released that will truly meet your needs. However, production often lags behind the demand for new products and it's sometimes best not to be one of the first owners of a brand new piece of hardware or software. New technology, such as automobiles, stereos, hardware, and software, frequently has unsuspected flaws. It's nearly impossible to detect all of the potential problems in a complex product that's being rushed out of the factory into a highly competitive marketplace. Although it's tempting to be one of the first to get the latest hardware or software, you may wind up as a guinea pig whose complaints contribute to the design of Version 2.0.

In most cases, the time to buy is *now.* If you truly need a computer, you probably can't afford to wait months for the release and delivery of a brand new product.

A great deal of hardware and software is currently available that will provide years of valuable service, even if new versions are released after your purchase. Assuming you've done your homework and selected a system that fulfills your requirements, it shouldn't matter that less expensive, more powerful alternatives will eventually be released. Even if your computing needs grow, you can most likely expand your current system later. Someday, you may even want to select a completely new system, but in the meantime you will have a computer that can help you now.

## Where to Buy

Nowadays, computer hardware and software can be purchased from a variety of sources. The outlet you select often depends upon such factors as how much you know about computers, how much money you want to save, how soon you need a system, whether you're buying a well-established brand name product, and whether you're buying hardware or software. You can purchase a computer system from computer stores, department stores, school stores, manufacturers, mail-order firms, and used equipment dealers.

### Computer Stores

Local retail outlets that specialize in computers, such as Computerland and Radio Shack Computer Centers, are the traditional source of hardware and software products for many shoppers, especially novices. Sales people are usually knowledgeable and can help a great deal in putting together a system that meets your needs. Most computer stores can also service your hardware should it need repair after the purchase. Many items are in stock or can be ordered and obtained in a few days. Unfortunately, many computer stores sell only a few brands. Although the brands tend to be from a select group of well-established manufacturers, your choices may be somewhat limited at a computer store. Items are usually sold at retail list prices, but there may be occasional sales or discounts given to certain groups of people. It may cost a bit more to buy a computer or peripheral device at a computer store, but dealers are nearby, accessible, and stand behind the hardware they sell.

Despite the additional cost, it often makes sense to buy hardware from a computer store. There is less advantage, however, to buying brand-name software from a computer store. Software doesn't break down in the sense that hardware does, so a computer store technician can't repair a program. For most software packages, any problems or questions you might have must usually be taken directly to the manufacturer. Although computer store salespeople may be able to answer some of your software questions, they simply can't be experts on every program they sell. In many cases, brand-name software can be purchased for less from other sources.

### Department Stores

Sometimes, retail department stores like Sears, Target, and Service Merchandise sell computers and software. List prices are usually discounted and you can get items immediately, if they are in stock. Unfortunately, department store salespeople may not be very knowledgeable about computers. Furthermore, each store typically only carries a single computer brand. In most cases, service after the sale may only be obtained from the original manufacturer. However, if you're fairly knowledgeable about computers and a local department store has exactly what you want, you may be able to get a good bargain.

### School Stores

If you're a student, faculty, or staff member of a college or university and in the market for a computer system, you may be in luck. Many schools have special deals with computer hardware and software manufacturers enabling them to offer products to qualified buyers at substantial savings. Hardware and software may be sold through a university bookstore, student union, educational consortium, or local computer center at discounts of up to 50% for students, faculty, and staff. Computer manufacturers like Apple, IBM, Hewlett-Packard, and Zenith often make deals with schools to sell their equipment at very low prices. In many cases, sales agents are knowledgeable and schools may also have their own service centers.

### Manufacturers

Sometimes, there's no dealer in the area that sells the computer you want. Or, you may qualify for a volume discount by wanting to purchase a number of systems all at once. In such situations it may be advantageous to go directly to the manufacturer of a particular hardware or software product. Unless you're purchasing in volume, you'll probably pay the list price and it may take several days or weeks for the item to be shipped to you. However, at least you know that you're going directly to the source and eliminating the middleman. Some large manufacturers like IBM, may even have a local office through which you can purchase products and get equipment serviced after the sale.

### Mail-Order Firms

In the past, computer mail-order firms have had a somewhat less than prestigious reputation. With very few exceptions, that reputation is no longer justified. In fact, the seventh largest domestic microcomputer manufacturer, Dell Computer Corporation, is strictly a mail-order firm. This particular company even offers an optional next-day, on-site service contract for most major metropolitan areas and unlimited access to technicians over toll-free phone lines. Although most mail-order firms may not be this accommodating, a great many individuals, schools, and businesses buy computer hardware and software through the mail. Mail-order buying can save you money, and, in this day of overnight package delivery, can also be very convenient.

Still, the rule is "let the buyer beware" when it comes to mail-order purchasing. Ordering hardware over the phone can be daunting to computer novices. Many mail-order firms put together their own computers from standard components. These computers can be fantastic machines, but unless you know exactly what you're doing, it's probably best to stick to established brand-names. Although, as we said, some mail-order firms offer repair service, most of them don't. Many advertise technical support over the phone, but it can sometimes be difficult to get through and have your questions answered politely, quickly, and accurately. Make sure that any mail-order firm you do choose has been in business for awhile.

Buying brand-name software through the mail, however, offers several advantages. Discounts are usually substantial and the package you get in the mail is identical to what you would get from your local computer store or directly from the manufacturer. Large mail-order firms may have many items in stock and can often deliver them the next day via an overnight carrier, for a modest extra charge.

### Used Equipment Dealers

A recent market study showed that most people buying new computers have owned at least one computer before. What's happening to all those computers that are being replaced? Some are winding up at used computer dealers. As the microcomputer industry ages, more and more used computer stores are opening. Sometimes you can find real bargains at such stores but, like buying a used car, purchasing a pre-owned computer or hardware component can be somewhat risky. Many of the machines in used computer stores are obsolete. They may still be quite useful, but it might be difficult to get parts, service, and software for computers no longer in production. If, on the other hand, a used computer is being sold because its owner simply upgraded to a more powerful system, there may be no reason not to buy it as long as it's been thoroughly tested and guaranteed by the dealer.

## STEP 6: INSTALL THE SYSTEM

You've chosen and purchased your software and hardware. The system was delivered today and now it's at home still in the boxes. What do you do? Well, first open all the boxes and get out the instructions. Make sure all the components, cables, disks, and other items are there. Follow the directions and set up the machine. Some computers come with tutorial programs you can run to teach you the basics of using the hardware and running the operating system. Besides being entertaining, these tutorials are usually quite informative and well worth the time. Once you feel comfortable with the fundamentals, you can follow the instructions to install your software on your computer. Don't be surprised if you have problems or if things don't work exactly as the tutorials and manuals indicate. Reread the instructions and try again. If you're still having problems, call your dealer or the manufacturer's customer service department. If you still can't get your system running, you may have an honest-to-goodness defect and will have to return your system.

Once you do get your system up and running, try out all of the hardware and software components as soon as possible. Read your warranties and mail in the cards that register you with the manufacturers as a new owner. Not only will this validate your warranties, it will also put you on mailing lists so that you can get information about new versions and upgrades. At this time you might be thinking about insurance and service contracts. If your computer system represents a substantial investment to you, and you come to need it on a daily basis, you'll want to make sure that it's insured and that you can get it repaired if it breaks down.

Finally, consider the surroundings in which you set up your system. A sturdy, roomy table or desktop and a well-designed, comfortable chair are musts if you expect to use your computer system for hours at a time. Keep your system clean and free from dust, spills, food crumbs, and other foreign materials. Try to keep any cooling vents unobstructed so that your system won't overheat. Unplug your hardware when not in use and try not to run it during electrical storms. Computer equipment, like other electronic devices, can be easily damaged or even destroyed by electrical surges caused by lightning or other power line disturbances. It might be prudent to plug all of your equipment into a **surge protector**. This is a relatively inexpensive device with a main switch, several electrical sockets, and circuitry to rapidly cut off power when a voltage surge occurs. Careful installation of your computer system can help ensure its reliability and usefulness for years to come.

# Appendix C

## Software Installation

Most operating systems and application packages must be **installed** on your computer before you can use them. This typically involves running a special installation or setup program included with the software. Installation programs often create a new subdirectory on your hard disk, copy the files from the floppy disks included with the package to that subdirectory, and let you specify what kind of hardware you have. At most school microcomputer labs, this has already been done for you by the attendants. If you own a computer, however, you will probably have to install any new software you purchase yourself. The documentation that comes with the software should explain, step-by-step, how to run the installation program and answer any questions that may be asked about your hardware and software. Let's briefly go over the steps necessary to install the software we discussed in Chapters 5, 7, 9, and 11: DOS, WordStar, Lotus 1-2-3, and dBASE III PLUS.

### IBM DOS Version 4.00

The DOS 4.00 package comes with two short manuals entitled *Getting Started with Disk Operating System Version 4.00* and *Using Disk Operating System Version 4.00.* The first one contains the instructions for installing the system. The package can be purchased on either 3 1/2-inch, 720K floppy disks or 5 1/4-inch, 360K floppy disks. You should get the package with disks that match your floppy drive A. The 3 1/2-inch package comes with two disks, one labeled *Install* and the other *Operating*. The 5 1/4-inch package comes with five disks labeled *Install, Select, Operating 1, Operating 2,* and *Operating 3.*

Although DOS 4.00 can be installed on floppy disks to boot up the computer from drive A, most people install the operating system on their hard disk C, if they have one. To install DOS 4.00 on a hard disk, follow these steps:

1. Insert the DOS 4.00 *Install* disk into drive A.
2. Turn on the computer. If it is already on, press **Ctrl-Alt-Del** to reboot.
3. After the copyright screen appears, press **Enter** and follow the instructions given by the installation program, which is called *Select.*
4. When you are finished with the installation program, remove the DOS floppy disk from drive A, store all your DOS disks in a safe place, and press **Ctrl-Alt-Del** to reboot your computer from the hard disk with DOS 4.00.

### WordStar Professional Release 5

When you purchase WordStar Professional Release 5, you get a reference manual in a three-ring binder. Also included are various keyboard guides and a quick reference card. The 5 1/4-inch package includes 12 disks:

- *Program.* This disk contains the uninstalled WordStar program and some sample documents.
- *Installation Customization.* This disk contains the WINSTALL program for setting up WordStar, and the WSCHANGE program for modifying WordStar after it has already been installed.
- *Advanced Page Preview.* This disk contains programs for the Advanced Page Preview feature that lets you see what your pages will look like before they are actually printed.
- *Printer Data 1* and *Printer Data 2.* These disks contain files that tell WordStar how to use many different printers.
- *PostScript Files Font Utility.* This disk contains files for laser printers that use the PostScript page description language.
- *Spelling Dictionary Thesaurus.* This disk contains WordStar's on-line spelling checker and thesaurus.
- *Definitions.* This disk contains word definitions for the thesaurus.
- *ProFinder.* This disk contains a separate program called ProFinder™ that helps you keep your files and programs organized.
- *MailList TelMerge PC-Outline.* This disk contains the MailList program for working with mailing lists, the TelMerge program for communications, and the PC-Outline program for using outlines to help create your documents.
- *Advanced Customization.* This disk contains WordStar's README file and programs and data for modifying WordStar.
- *Tutors.* This disk contains the onscreen tutorial program.

To install WordStar 5 on a hard disk, follow these steps:

1. Turn on your computer.
2. Type **MD \WS5** and press **Enter** to create a new subdirectory named WS5 on your hard disk.
3. Type **CD \WS5** and press **Enter** to switch to the subdirectory you've just created.
4. Insert the *Program* disk into drive A.
5. Type **COPY A:*.*** and press **Enter**.
6. After the contents of the floppy disk have been copied into the WS5 subdirectory, remove the disk from drive A.
7. Repeat Steps 4 through 6 for the remaining floppy disks included with the package. (You don't have to copy the *Tutors* disk unless you want to run the on-line tutorial program.)
8. Type **WINSTALL WS** and press **Enter**.
9. The WINSTALL program displays the Main Installation menu on the screen. You should select each option from this menu and follow the directions to choose your monitor, printer, default printer, and operating system and disk drives, and to specify the location of the dictionary files and whether you want to use the new pull-down menus or WordStar's old classic menus. Press **?** for more help with any of the menu options.
10. Press **X** when you are finished with the WINSTALL program and press **Y** when the program asks if you are finished making changes. When you see the DOS prompt again, reboot your computer by pressing **Ctrl-Alt-Del**.
11. Put your original WordStar floppy disks away in a safe place.

## Lotus 1-2-3 Release 2.01

When you purchase Lotus 1-2-3 Release 2.01, you get three softcover manuals entitled *Getting Started, Tutorial,* and *Reference.* Also included are various keyboard guides and a quick reference card. The 5 1/4-inch package contains six floppy disks:

- *System Disk.* This disk holds the actual 1-2-3 program, along with a program called *Lotus* that lets you switch between 1-2-3 and the other programs included with it.
- *PrintGraph.* This disk holds a separate program called *PrintGraph* that allows you to print your 1-2-3 graphs. Depending on your printer's ability, this program lets you control colors, fonts, and the layout of your graphs.
- *Utility Disk.* This disk contains the *Install* program that lets you set up 1-2-3 to use a printer and display graphs, and the *Translate* program that lets you transfer data between 1-2-3 and other application packages.
- *Install Library Disk.* This disk contains files used by the Install program to set up 1-2-3 to run with various monitors and printers.
- *A View of 1-2-3.* This disk holds *View,* an onscreen tutorial program to help you learn about 1-2-3.
- *Backup System Disk.* This is simply a backup copy of the *System Disk,* in case you damage or lose the original.

To install Lotus 1-2-3 on a hard disk, follow these steps:

1. Turn on your computer.
2. Type **MD \123** and press **Enter** to create a new subdirectory named 123 on your hard disk.
3. Type **CD \123** and press **Enter** to switch to the subdirectory you've just created.
4. Insert the *System Disk* into drive A.
5. Type **COPY A:*.*** and press **Enter**.
6. After the contents of the floppy disk have been copied into the 123 subdirectory, remove the disk from drive A.
7. Repeat Steps 4 through 6 for all the remaining floppy disks included with the package, except the *Backup System Disk.*
8. Type **INSTALL** and press **Enter**.
9. Press **Enter** after reading the introductory screen.
10. The INSTALL program displays the Main menu on the screen. Press **Enter** to select the First-Time Installation option from the menu and follow the directions to answer questions about your monitor and printer.
11. When you finish the First-Time Installation, select the Exit Install option.
12. Put your original Lotus 1-2-3 floppy disks away in a safe place.

## dBASE III PLUS Version 1.1

When you purchase dBASE III PLUS Version 1.1, you get two thick manuals in three-ring binders entitled *Learning and Using dBASE III Plus* and *Programming with dBASE III PLUS.* You also get two small booklets named *Getting Started with dBASE*

*III PLUS* and *Applications Generator dBASE III PLUS* and a small quick reference guide. The 5 1/4-inch package contains seven floppy disks:

- *System Disk #1* and *System Disk #2.* These disks contain the actual dBASE III PLUS program.
- *Administrator #1* and *Administrator #2.* These disks are used to set up and run dBASE III PLUS on a local area network.
- *Applications Generator.* This disk contains programs that let you create customized menu systems within dBASE III PLUS.
- *Sample Programs & Utilities.* This disk contains data bases and programs used as examples in the manuals, and a utility program for converting dBASE II files to dBASE III PLUS format.
- *On-Disk Tutorial.* This disk contains a program that teaches you about dBASE III PLUS.

To install dBASE III PLUS on a hard disk, follow these steps:

1. Turn on your computer.
2. Type **MD \DBASE** and press **Enter** to create a new subdirectory named DBASE on your hard disk.
3. Type **CD \DBASE** and press **Enter** to switch to the subdirectory you've just created.
4. Insert *System Disk #1* into drive A.
5. Type **A:** and press **Enter**.
6. Type **INSTALL C:** and press **Enter**.
7. Follow the directions that appear on the screen.
8. Remove the dBASE disk from drive A, and put all of your original dBASE floppy disks away in a safe place.
9. Reboot your computer by pressing **Ctrl-Alt-Del**.

# Appendix D

## Spreadsheet Details: SuperCalc 5.0

### In This Appendix

## PREVIEW

SuperCalc, from Computer Associates International, is one of a rare breed of spreadsheet programs that existed *before* Lotus 1-2-3 and still thrives today. The original version was written for early microcomputers that ran the CP/M operating system. In 1981, SuperCalc was adapted to run on the then new IBM Personal Computer. Lotus 1-2-3 was not released until January 1982, but it made better use of the power of the new IBM microcomputers and it had a then unprecedented $4 million advertising budget. While Lotus 1-2-3 got most of the attention over the next few years, Computer Associates International was steadily improving SuperCalc. Today, SuperCalc has evolved into a powerful, well-designed program that compares favorably with any of the high-end spreadsheet programs for IBM-compatible microcomputers.

After studying this appendix, you will understand

- how to start SuperCalc.
- the various components of the SuperCalc display screen.
- how to enter new data into a worksheet and change existing data.
- how to control the appearance of a worksheet.
- the way in which SuperCalc calculates formula results.
- how to print a worksheet.
- how to save and retrieve a worksheet.
- some additional features included in SuperCalc.

## WORKING WITH SuperCalc

As you might expect, there have been several releases of SuperCalc since its introduction. For the examples in this appendix, we'll be using SuperCalc 5.0 for IBM and IBM-compatible microcomputers. Nevertheless, much of what we cover also applies to earlier SuperCalc releases. We'll assume that SuperCalc has been installed on a hard disk in a subdirectory named CALC. To run the program, you must first switch to this subdirectory by entering **CD \CALC**. Then you enter **SC5** to actually start SuperCalc 5.0 The copyright notice appears on your screen, as shown in Figure D.1. When you are finished reading the screen, press any key to continue.

*On a hard disk, in subdirectory \CALC*

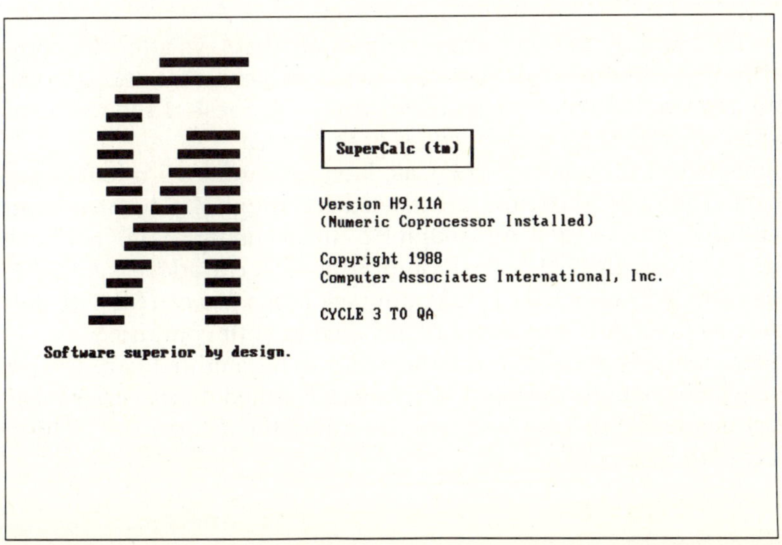


**Figure D.1 The SuperCalc Copyright Screen**
After you start SuperCalc, this screen appears until you press a key.

**Insight**

## How Can I Avoid Errors in My Spreadsheets?

Consider the sad case of the controller of James A. Cummings, Inc., a Florida construction company.

The controller was assembling a spreadsheet model to bid on a $3 million office complex when he realized he forgot to include a $254,000 overhead cost item. Probably with great relief, he inserted it at the top of a column. Unfortunately, his entry was in the wrong place and was not included in the final totals. James A. Cummings Inc. underbid by (and effectively lost) $254,000.

Fortunately, errors such as this are uncommon in the spreadsheet world. However, less stupifying mistakes are everywhere. Thank goodness there are ways to minimize them.

First, every spreadsheet should be carefully checked. Larry Nippon, president of New York clothing manufacturer Albert Nippon, caught a $1.5 million error this way. The culprit was a mix-up in designating two cell addresses to be multiplied.

It's important to test any model. Some spreadsheet users insert a 1 for every data entry, so that in a simple column total the sum will equal the number of rows in the column. Others add extra blank rows in @SUM formulas to avoid error ranges. Some executives graph their results to see if they look logical.

One common mistake is making incorrect assumptions in spreadsheet formulas. No amount of checking will catch these.

Other often painful mistakes include mixing up formulas, creating macros and then forgetting what they are, losing track of a spreadsheet's underlying assumptions, and forgetting to save your work to disk. Keeping spreadsheets small will eliminate many problems. But there's no substitute for careful construction.

Source:
Steve Ditlea, "Spreadsheets Can Be Hazardous to Your Health," *Personal Computing*, January, 1987, pp. 60-69.

## THE SuperCalc SCREEN

*Enter data, activate menus, execute commands*

After the copyright notice disappears, SuperCalc displays a screen that, among other items, contains a blank worksheet. This is where you enter data, activate menus, and execute commands. Before we go on to the specifics of actually using SuperCalc, let's take a look at how the screen is organized.

### The Blank Worksheet

*255 columns and 9999 rows*

Figure D.2 shows the blank worksheet screen SuperCalc displays after the copyright notice disappears. Although this screen shows only 8 columns and 20 rows, SuperCalc 5.0 can address 255 columns and 9999 rows. The rest of the rows and columns extend past the right and bottom edges of the screen.

Like most spreadsheet programs, SuperCalc labels columns with letters and rows with numbers. The first 26 columns are labeled A through Z. The next 26 are labeled AA through AZ, the next 26 BA through BZ, and so on up to IU. The rows are simply numbered 1 through 9999. Even though SuperCalc can address 2,549,745 cells (255 columns times 9999 rows), the actual number of cells you can fill with data ultimately depends on the amount of memory installed in your computer.

The cell pointer, currently at cell A1, is indicated by a highlighted bar. The top part of the screen, which contains the blank worksheet, is called the *display window*. The four lines just below the display window are called the *dialog panel*. This is where you interact with SuperCalc.

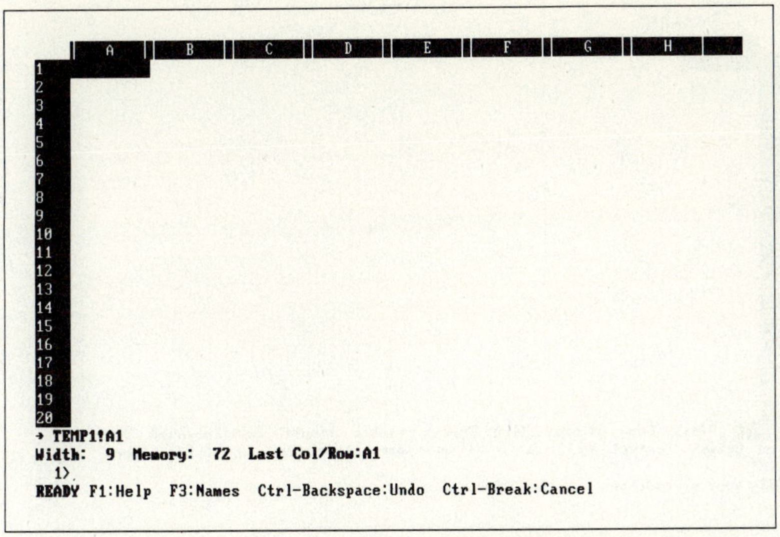


**Figure D.2 The Blank SuperCalc Worksheet Screen**

After the copyright notice disappears, this is what you see on your display.

The first line of the dialog panel is the *status line,* which shows the current file name, cell address, commands, options, and error messages. For example, the TEMP1 you see in the status line of Figure D.2 is the temporary name given to a worksheet you have not yet named and the A1 indicates that your current position is at cell A1.

The *prompt line* is directly below the status line. It shows various size indicators, such as the current column width, available memory, and the bottom right cell in your active worksheet. In Figure D.2, the prompt line shows that the column width is 9, the memory available is 72K, and the bottom right cell is A1 (even though it contains no data yet). When a menu is active, the prompt line lists the available options.

The third line of the dialog panel is the *entry line,* which displays whatever you type. This is where you enter data, formulas, commands, options, and cell ranges.

The bottom line is the *help line,* which displays the mode indicator, help messages, and reminders. The mode indicator, presented in the lower-left corner of the screen, tells you what SuperCalc is doing at the moment. Figure D.2, for example, shows that SuperCalc is in READY mode, indicating that the program is simply waiting for you to enter data or execute a command.

## Menus

*Selecting commands*

Many SuperCalc tasks are performed by selecting commands from menus that appear in the dialog panel. When SuperCalc is in READY mode, no menu appears in the dialog panel. The main command menu is activated by pressing the forward slash (/) key. Figure D.3 shows what SuperCalc displays when you press this key. Notice that the mode indicator now says MENU. The status and prompt lines of the dialog panel show the commands that are available in the main menu. Right now, Arrange is highlighted. The help line of the dialog panel displays a description of the highlighted command.

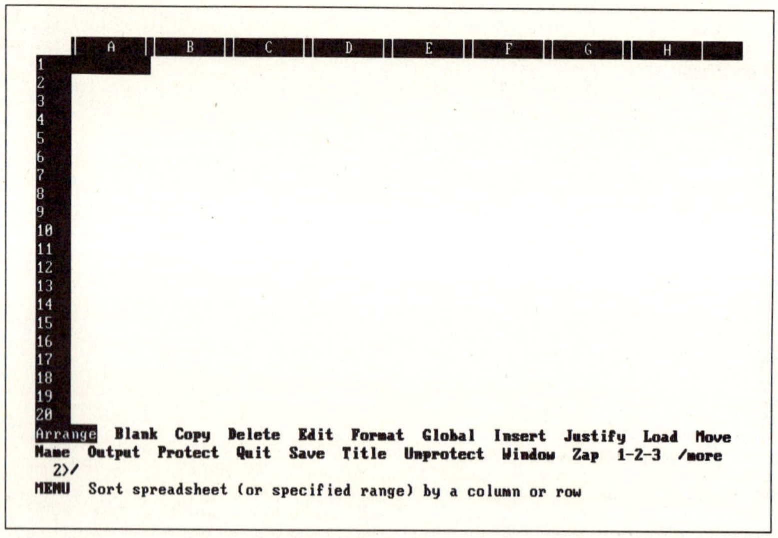


**Figure D.3 The Main Menu**

After you press / (forward slash), the main menu appears in the dialog panel.

There are two ways to select an option from any SuperCalc menu. The first way is to highlight the option and press the **Enter** key. You can move the highlight bar from one option to the next by pressing the **Left Arrow** or **Right Arrow** keys. For example, if you press the Right Arrow key, the highlight will move from Arrange to Blank. The other way to select a command is to type the command's first letter. Every item in a SuperCalc menu begins with a different letter. To select the Quit command, for instance, all you have to do is type **Q**. Many people prefer the latter method because it often involves fewer keystrokes.

**Table D.1 SuperCalc Main Menu Commands**

| COMMAND | ACTION |
|---|---|
| Arrange | Sorts the contents of a block of cells into ascending or descending order. |
| Blank | Erases the contents of one or more cells and resets default formatting. |
| Copy | Allows you to duplicate a range of one or more cells. |
| Delete | Erases a range of cells or a disk file. |
| Edit | Allows you to modify an existing cell's contents and put the result into another cell. |
| Format | Controls the appearance of the screen and printed output. |
| Global | Establishes settings that apply to the entire worksheet. |
| Insert | Adds a new row, column, or block of cells to a worksheet. |
| Justify | Aligns text entries to the left, center, or right. |
| Load | Copies all or part of a worksheet from a disk file into the display window. |
| Move | Allows you to move a range of one or more cells. |
| Name | Lets you assign a name to a range of cells. |
| Output | Sends all or part of a worksheet to the printer or a disk file. |
| Protect | Prevents any changes to specified cells. |
| Quit | Exits SuperCalc. |
| Save | Copies all or part of a worksheet from the display window to a disk file. |
| Title | Keeps specified columns and/or rows in the display window even if the worksheet is scrolled. |
| Unprotect | Allows changes again to protected cells. |
| Window | Splits the display window into two parts. |
| Zap | Completely erases an entire worksheet from the display window. |
| 1-2-3 | Executes the following command as a Lotus 1-2-3 command. |
| /more | Activates another menu of SuperCalc commands. |

Menus are the means by which you select and execute SuperCalc commands. Commands let you edit, format, and otherwise manipulate data, as well as control the appearance, disk storage, and output of SuperCalc worksheets. Although we cannot cover every SuperCalc command in detail, we will describe several of the most important in this appendix. In addition, Table D.1 lists each command in the main menu, along with a brief description.

## Help

*Learning more about SuperCalc*

As you can see, the main menu contains many commands. Some of these commands activate still other menus. This powerful program has quite an array of available options. Although few people learn how to use every SuperCalc command, fortunately SuperCalc comes with excellent tutorial and reference manuals to teach you about them. In addition, SuperCalc has a very good on-line help facility. This feature is like a reference manual that automatically opens to the correct page to reveal information about the particular command or area of the program with which you are working. The help facility can also further explain any error messages you might receive for trying to perform some invalid activity. Let's see how the help facility can provide information about the SuperCalc commands in the main menu. If the menu is not already on the screen, press / to bring it up. To find out more about this menu, simply press the **F1** function key. Your work is temporarily suspended and SuperCalc displays the screen you see in Figure D.4.

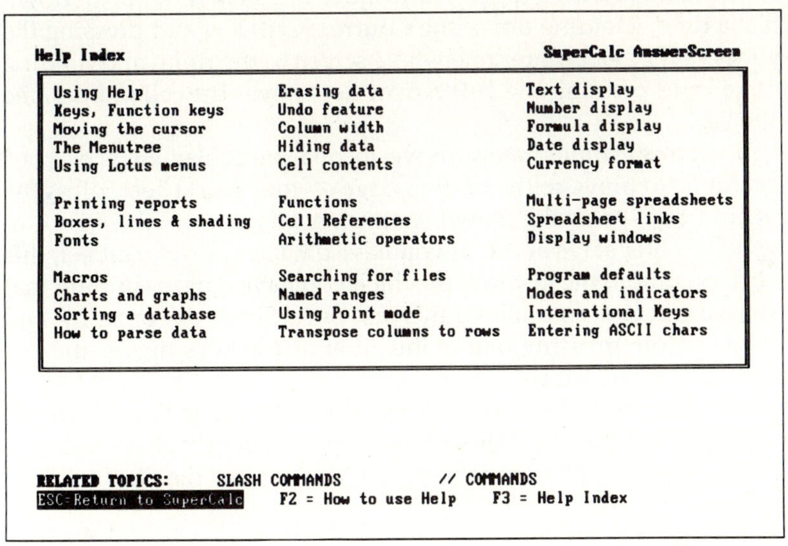


**Figure D.4 Help Screen**
Press **F1** to bring up the help facility and reveal more information about your current activity.

Each help screen includes a menu of topics about which you can get further information. To find out more about a topic, you simply highlight it and press the **Enter** key. To select another topic, you move the highlight with the arrow keys and then press the **Enter** key. When you are finished with the help facility, keep pressing the **Escape** key until you return to the worksheet screen.

## ENTERING AND EDITING DATA

*Constructing a worksheet*

One of the advantages of using SuperCalc is that the program makes it easy to enter and edit data. At the simplest level, this involves moving the cell pointer, typing entries, editing cells, inserting and deleting rows and columns, and copying and moving data.

### Moving the Cell Pointer

*Many ways to move in the worksheet*

The easiest way to move the cell pointer is to use the arrow keys. Pressing the **Up Arrow** key moves the cell pointer to the row directly above; pressing the **Right Arrow** key moves the cell pointer to the next column to the right; pressing the **Down Arrow** key moves the cell pointer to the row directly below; and pressing the **Left Arrow** key moves the cell pointer to the previous column to the left. To scroll the worksheet beyond the 8 columns or 20 rows initially on the screen, continue moving the cell pointer once you reach the edge of the screen. For example, to scroll the worksheet to the right, press the **Right Arrow** key until the cell pointer is in column H. Then press the **Right Arrow** key again; column A disappears off the left side of the screen and column I appears on the right side.

Although you can move the cell pointer quite rapidly by holding down an arrow key to repeat keystrokes, the SuperCalc worksheet is very large. Fortunately, SuperCalc has even quicker methods of moving the cell pointer to different parts of the worksheet. Pressing the **Home** key always returns the cell pointer to cell A1. The **Page Up** (PgUp) and **Page Down** (PgDn) keys move the cell pointer up or down one whole screen at a time. Holding down the **Control** (Ctrl) key and pressing the **Right Arrow** key moves the cell pointer one whole screen to the right, and holding down the **Control** key and pressing the **Left Arrow** key moves the cell pointer one whole screen to the left.

There are even ways to immediately move to one particular edge of your worksheet. For example, to move to the bottom edge of your worksheet, press the **End** key, release it, and then press the **Down Arrow** key. If the worksheet is completely empty, the cell pointer stays at A1. If you have data in your worksheet, this action moves the cell pointer to the last row in which you have data, assuming that the cell pointer started out in a row above this last one. Similarly, pressing and releasing the **End** key before pressing one of the other arrow keys moves the cell pointer to that edge of your worksheet.

Finally, SuperCalc also provides a way to move to any particular cell in the worksheet. For example, let's say that the cell pointer is currently at A1 and you want to move to H10. Press the **F5** function key, which executes the Go To operation, and you are prompted with

```
Enter cell to jump to.
```

The default destination is the current location of the cell pointer, A1. In other words, if you just press the Enter key, SuperCalc will not move the cell pointer. To move to cell H10, simply type **H10** (which will erase the A1) and press the **Enter** key.

### Typing Entries

*How to enter data*

Once you move the cell pointer where you want a piece of data to go, you simply begin typing. Each character you type appears in the entry line of the dialog panel. Just like in a word processor, a blinking underscore cursor indicates where the next character you type will appear. Any mistakes you make can be corrected by backspacing and retyping. The item you type isn't actually inserted into the worksheet until you complete the entry by pressing the Enter key or moving the cell pointer, say with one of the arrow keys. No SuperCalc data entry may be longer than 127 characters. As we said in Chapter 8, a worksheet cell holds one of three basic types of data: numbers, labels, or formulas.

## Numbers

*Quantities*

Numbers are the most common type of data found in most worksheets. SuperCalc considers any entry that begins with one of the following characters to be a number:

`0 1 2 3 4 5 6 7 8 9 . + - $ (`

When typing a number, you should not include spaces, commas, or more than one decimal point. Numbers may begin with a currency symbol ($), end with a % to indicate a percentage, or be entered in scientific format. For example, 2.16E+05 may be entered instead of 216000.

## Labels

*Headings and notes*

Labels are text used for headings and explanations. SuperCalc considers a label to be any entry that does not begin with a number or one of these characters:

`/ = ! ? ; & |`

If you want a label to begin with a number (such as a date like 10/15/89) or one of these characters, you must precede it with a double quote (").

SuperCalc also has a special type of label known as repeating text. **Repeating text** consists of one or more characters preceded by an apostrophe ('). SuperCalc repeats those characters across adjacent columns until they reach an occupied cell. For example, if you enter '- into a cell, SuperCalc will repeat a - until it reaches another apostrophe or data in a cell to the right.

## Formulas

*Performing calculations*

In SuperCalc, a formula is an instruction to calculate or otherwise manipulate numbers or text. It can contain numbers (such as 100), operators (such as +), labels enclosed in double quotes (such as "Result"), and cell references (such as B10).

In addition to numbers, operators, and cell references, formulas also can contain functions. You'll recall that a *function* is a built-in procedure that performs tedious, complex, or frequently used computations and other data manipulations. More than 140 functions are available in SuperCalc. Formulas are entered like text; you don't have to precede them with a special character such as @, which is required in Lotus 1-2-3. Table D.2 lists some of the most commonly used SuperCalc functions.

**Table D.2 Commonly Used SuperCalc Functions**

| MATHEMATICAL FUNCTIONS | |
|---|---|
| ABS | Computes the absolute value of a number. |
| INT | Returns the integer (whole number) part of a number. |
| MOD | Computes the remainder (modulus) of a division operation. |
| RAND | Gives a random number between 0 and 1 |
| ROUND | Rounds a value to a given number of decimal places. |
| SQRT | Computes the square root of a number. |

| STATISTICAL FUNCTIONS | |
|---|---|
| AVG | Computes the average of a list of values. |
| COUNT | Computes the number of entries in a list of values. |
| MAX | Returns the largest value in a list of values. |
| MIN | Returns the smallest value in a list of values. |
| STD | Computes the standard deviation of a list of values. |
| SUM | Computes the sum of a list of values. |
| VAR | Computes the variance of a list of values. |

| FINANCIAL FUNCTIONS | |
|---|---|
| FV | Computes the future value of an investment. |
| IRR | Computes the internal rate of return of an investment. |
| NPV | Computes the net present value of an investment. |
| PMT | Computes the payment on a loan per payment period. |
| PV | Computes the present value of an investment. |
| RATE | Computes the rate of return of an investment. |
| TERM | Computes the number of loan payments. |

| TEXT FUNCTIONS | |
|---|---|
| MID | Extracts characters from the middle of a text label. |
| LENGTH | Computes the number of characters in a text label. |
| REPEAT | Duplicates a sequence of characters within a text label. |

| LOGICAL FUNCTIONS | |
|---|---|
| NOT | Changes TRUE to FALSE and FALSE to TRUE. |
| AND | Returns TRUE if all values are TRUE; otherwise FALSE. |
| OR | Returns TRUE if any value is TRUE; otherwise FALSE. |
| IF | Returns one number if a condition is TRUE, another if FALSE. |
| I SERR | Returns TRUE (the number 1) if a calculation error occurred. |

| DATE AND TIME FUNCTIONS | |
|---|---|
| DATE | Returns a code number representing the given date. |
| TIME | Returns a code number representing the given time of day. |
| NOW | Returns a code number representing the current date and time. |

| TRIGONOMETRIC FUNCTIONS | |
|---|---|
| COS | Computes the cosine of an angle. |
| SIN | Computes the sine of an angle. |
| TAN | Computes the tangent of an angle. |
| PI | Returns the value of $\pi$ (approximately 3.1415926). |

| LOGARITHMIC FUNCTIONS | |
|---|---|
| EXP | Computes the value of the constant e raised to a given power. |
| LN | Computes the natural (base e) logarithm of a value. |
| LOG | Computes the base 10 logarithm of a value. |

## Editing Cells

*Changing a cell's contents*

The existing contents of a cell can be changed in two ways. You can move the cell pointer back to that cell and reenter its entire contents or you can edit the cell. The latter method can save you time if you need to change a small portion of a long label or formula. With the cell pointer on the cell you want to change, press the **F2** function key or type **/E** to execute the Edit command. This brings the contents of the cell down to the entry line and puts the cursor just past the end. SuperCalc lets you move the cursor within the current entry and make changes. The Left Arrow and Right Arrow keys are used to move the cursor one character at a time. The Home key moves the cursor to the first character in the entry and the End key moves the cursor just past the last character in the entry. By default, SuperCalc inserts any characters you type into the existing cell contents at the current cursor position. You can switch between overwriting and inserting by pressing the Insert key. The Backspace key erases the character to the immediate left of the cursor, while the Delete key erases the character at the current cursor position. You can even erase the entire entry by pressing the Escape key. When you are finished editing, you press the **Enter** key to actually put what you've edited back into the current cell.

## Inserting and Deleting Rows and Columns

*Adding new data and removing old data*

One of the reasons word processors are superior to typewriters is that they make it very easy to add and remove text anywhere in a document. Similarly, spreadsheet programs make it easy to insert and delete rows and columns of cells anywhere in a worksheet. To perform these operations in SuperCalc, you use the Insert and Delete commands. For example, let's say that you want to insert a new row between rows 3 and 4 in the worksheet in Figure D.5(a). First you move the cell pointer to a cell in row 4. Then you type **/I** to select the Insert command and **R** to choose the Row option. As Figure D.5(b) shows, SuperCalc prompts you to enter the row range, and it suggests row 4. This means that unless you specify otherwise, SuperCalc will insert only one row after row 3. To insert more than one row, you could enter a new range. For instance, entering **4:5** would insert two rows. To insert just one row, all you have to do is press the **Enter** key to select the row range of 4 initially suggested by SuperCalc. The contents of row 4 and any rows below row 4 are shifted down one row, and a new blank row is inserted after row 3. Figure D.5(c) illustrates the final effect of this command.

As you can see, the contents of rows 4 and 5 have been shifted down to rows 5 and 6, respectively. Spreadsheet programs, however, generally do more than just shift data when rows are inserted. Before the insertion, cell A5 contained the formula SUM(A1:A4). The A1 and A4 in this formula are relative cell references. As we said in Chapter 8, relative cell references are automatically adjusted to account for any changes in position whenever cells are inserted, deleted, moved, or copied. After the new row was inserted between rows 3 and 4, the formula was moved to cell A6, but it was not merely copied. Cell A6 now contains the formula SUM(A1:A5). SuperCalc automatically adjusted the second cell reference in the formula to account for the inserted row. Although relative cell references are the most common in worksheet formulas, SuperCalc also allows absolute and mixed cell references. These are indicated by preceding the column and row designations with a dollar sign, as we described in Chapter 8.

Inserting a column is almost the same as inserting a row, except you type **C** to choose the Column option after typing **/I** to invoke the Insert command. Deleting rows or columns is also very similar. To delete column B, for example, you move

(a)

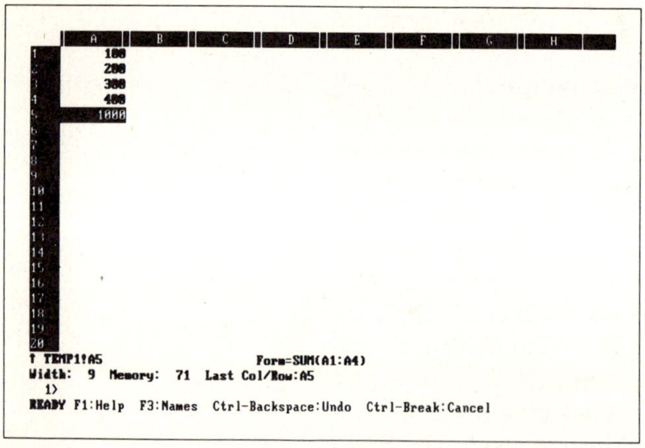


(b)

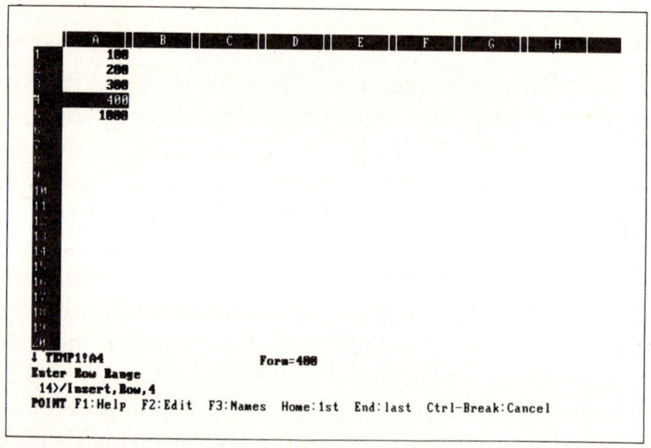


**Figure D.5 Inserting a Row**

(a) The original worksheet.

(b) Position the cell pointer and type **/IR** to execute the Insert Row command. The program suggests row 4.

(c) Press **Enter** and SuperCalc inserts a new blank row.

(c)

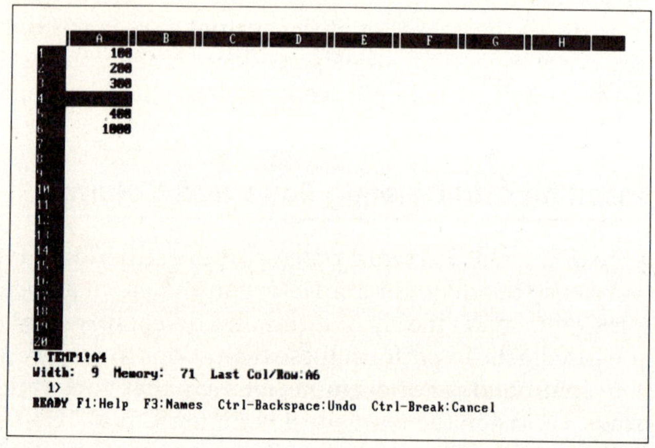


the cell pointer to a cell in column B, type **/DC**, and press the **Enter** key. This executes the Delete Column command, removing the column currently occupied by the cell pointer. The contents of all columns to the right of the cell pointer are shifted one column to the left. Any formulas containing relative cell references are adjusted as needed.

## Moving and Copying Data

*Cutting and pasting data*

Like most spreadsheets, SuperCalc can also move and copy data. For example, let's take the data in the worksheet in Figure D.5(a) and move it to a different location. First place the cell pointer in the upper-left corner of the range of cells to be moved, then type **/MB** to execute the Move Block command. Figure D.6(a) shows that SuperCalc then prompts you to enter the range of cells you want to move. Notice that the mode indicator says POINT, just like it did in Figure D.5(b). With many SuperCalc commands, there are two ways to select a range. One way is to simply type the range and press the **Enter** key. In this example, SuperCalc initially suggests that A1 is the range of cells you want to move. You could type **A1:A5** and press the **Enter** key to tell SuperCalc which cells you want to move, but in POINT mode you can also specify a range by highlighting it. In this case, you first press the **Period** (.) key to anchor the highlighting block, then the **Down Arrow** key four times to highlight cells A1 through A5, and then the **Enter** key. As shown in Figure D.6(b), SuperCalc then prompts you to indicate the cell to which you want to move the selected range. You can either type a cell address, or move the cell pointer with the arrow keys to the cell where you want to move the selected range. To move the selected range to cell D1, for example, you can either type **D1** and press the **Enter** key, or press the **Right Arrow** key three times and press the **Enter** key. Figure D.6(c) shows what happens.

(a)

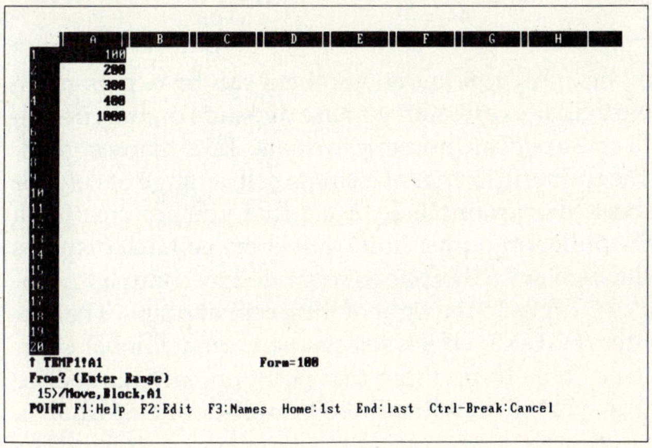


(b)

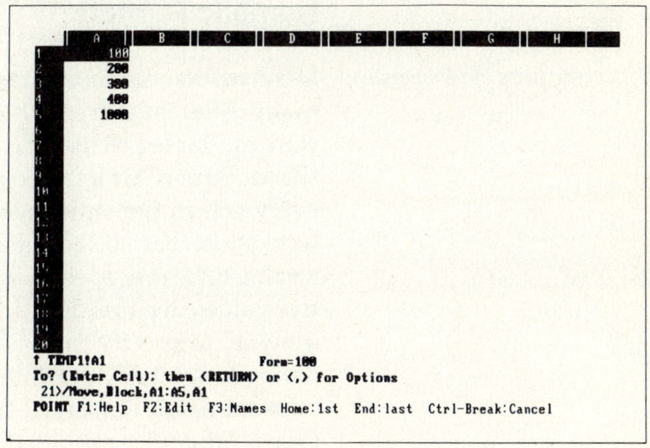


(c)

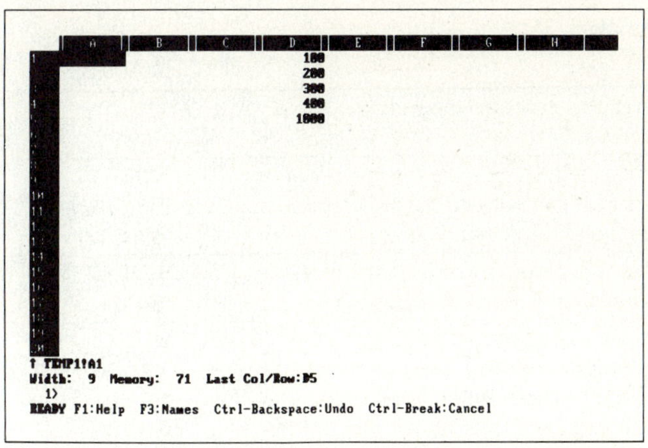


**Figure D.6 Moving Data**

(a) Position the cell pointer and type **/M** to execute the Move command from the main menu.

(b) Press **Period** (.) and the **Down Arrow** key four times and press the **Enter** key to select cells A1 through A5. Then SuperCalc asks for the range to which you want to move the selected data.

(c) Either type **D1** and press **Enter**, or press the **Right Arrow** key three times and press **Enter** to move the data to column D.

Copying data in a SuperCalc worksheet is very similar to moving data. All you do is enter **/C** to execute the Copy command instead of entering **/M** to execute the Move command. You specify the range of cells to be copied and then indicate where you want the copy to be placed. The only difference between the Move command and the Copy command is that the Copy command leaves the original range of cells intact. Both the Move and the Copy commands automatically adjust relative cell references in formulas as necessary.

## FORMATTING DATA

*Controlling the worksheet's appearance*

Spreadsheet programs help you organize, calculate, display, and print tables of numeric and textual data. An important part of performing these activities is being able to format your data. Formatting allows you to control the appearance of data, thereby making worksheets easier to use and read. SuperCalc has commands for specifying numeric formats, column widths, alignment, and the display of formulas.

### Numeric Formats

*The many faces of numbers*

Most worksheets contain numbers. As you know, numbers can be expressed in many different ways. Which particular expression you use depends on the circumstances. Table D.3 lists the built-in SuperCalc numeric formats. Like many spreadsheets, SuperCalc lets you set the numeric format of a single cell, a range of cells, or every cell in the entire worksheet. For example, let's say that you are creating a worksheet that will contain only dollar amounts. You want every cell that displays a value to be preceded by a dollar sign, with thousands separated by commas, negative values in parentheses, and two digits to the right of the decimal point. The easiest way to specify this is to enter **/FGUN3**, which selects the Format Global User-defined Number 3 command (see Table D.3). From that point on, any number or formula result displayed in your worksheet will adhere to user-defined format 3, unless otherwise specified.

**Table D.3 SuperCalc Numeric Formats**

| FORMAT | DESCRIPTION | EXAMPLES |
|---|---|---|
| Integer | Numbers are rounded to the nearest whole number value. | 13<br>-1024 |
| General | Numbers are displayed as entered—either as integers or numbers with as many decimal places as the column width allows. | 14<br>21.567821<br>-5.648127 |
| Exponential | Numbers are expressed in scientific notation as a mantissa, an E, and an exponent. | 5.78E-02<br>-5.78E+55 |
| $ Currency | Numbers are expressed with 2 digits to the right of the decimal point, with no dollar sign or commas used. If you want a dollar sign or commas, you must select one of the user-defined formats (see below). | 25.75<br>1000.00<br>.50<br>1.00<br>-10.00 |
| User-defined Format<br>1 | These are 8 predefined number formats that are more specialized than the ones above:<br><br>$-11,111,111.11<br>Currency sign, commas separating thousands, negative values preceded by minus sign. | $1453.14<br>$-100.25<br>$.00 |
| 2 | $-11,111,111.11<br>Currency sign, commas separating thousands, negative values preceded by minus sign, values of zero appear as blank. | $1453.14<br>$-100.25 |
| 3 | ($11,111,111.11)<br>Currency sign, commas separating thousands, negative values enclosed in parentheses. | $1453.14<br>($100.25)<br>$.00 |

| FORMAT | DESCRIPTION | EXAMPLES |
|---|---|---|
| 4 | ($11,111,111.11)<br>Currency sign, commas separating thousands, negative values enclosed in parentheses, values of zero appear as blank. | $1453.14<br>($100.25) |
| 5 | $-11111111<br>Currency sign, no commas, values rounded to the nearest whole number, negative values preceded by minus sign. | $1453<br>$-100 |
| 6 | -11,111,111<br>No currency sign, commas separating thousands, values rounded to the nearest whole number, negative values preceded by minus. | $1453<br>$-100 |
| 7 | (11,111,111)<br>No currency sign, commas separating thousands, values rounded to the nearest whole number, negative values in parentheses. | $1453<br>($-100) |
| 8 | -1111111111.11%<br>Percentage formatting with no commas, 2 places to the right of the decimal point, negative values preceded by minus, and percent sign at the end. | 50.00%<br>1000.25%<br>.02%<br>-25.00% |

The format command we just described is called *global* because it applies to every cell in the entire worksheet. In many instances, however, you need different numeric formats in the same worksheet. For example, let's say that cells A1 through A20 are to contain numbers that aren't dollar amounts. Perhaps these cells will be used to simply number the items in the worksheet. Cells B1 through B20, on the other hand, will contain dollar amounts. Since the default global format in SuperCalc is General, the easiest thing to do is to change column B to User-defined Number 3 format. This can be done by entering **/FC** to execute the Format Column command. SuperCalc then prompts you to enter the column range and you enter **B**. Then you enter **UN3** to select User-defined Number 3 format. By offering the various formats listed in Table D.3, SuperCalc gives you a great deal of flexibility in the display of numeric values in your worksheets.

## Column Widths

*Make room for data*

The default column width in SuperCalc is nine characters, but you frequently have to increase or decrease this width. Somewhat like numeric formats, column widths can be changed for a single column or for the entire worksheet. For example, to change the width of every column in the entire worksheet, you use the Format Global Width command. Suppose that you want to decrease the global column width to 5 because you know that all your numbers will be small and you want to fit more columns on the screen. You type **/FGW** and SuperCalc prompts you to enter the global column width, as shown in Figure D.7(a). Then you type **5** and press the **Enter** key. Figure D.7(b) shows the result: all columns are now five characters wide and 15 columns, A through O, now fit on the screen.

**Figure D.7 Setting the Global Column Width**

(a) First you type **/FGW** to invoke the Format Global Width command, and SuperCalc prompts you with this message.

(b) Then you type **5** and press **Enter** to set the new global column width. The final result is a worksheet in which all columns are 5 characters wide.

(a)

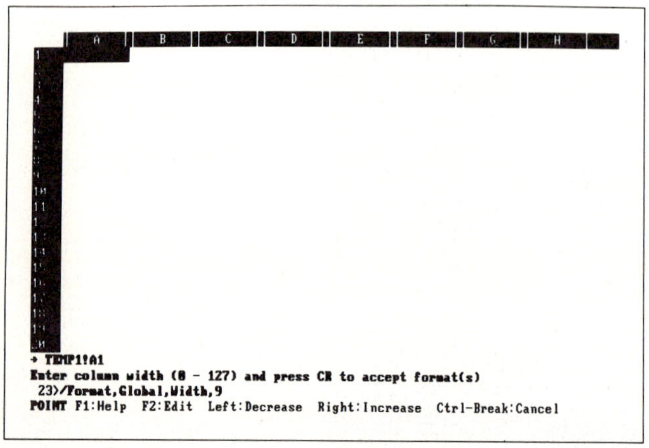


(b)

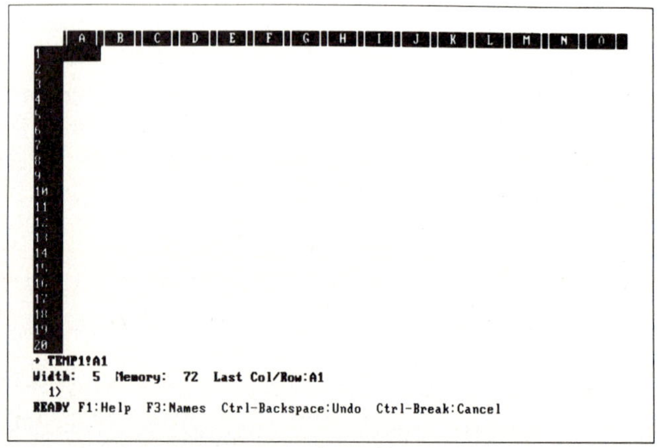


## Alignment

*Justifying data*

Like most spreadsheet programs, SuperCalc left-justifies labels and right-justifies numeric values by default. You can, however, change the alignment of both labels and numbers to be right-justified, centered, or left-justified for a cell, row, column, block, or entire worksheet. For example, suppose that you want all labels in your worksheet to be centered automatically instead of left-justified. All you have to do is enter **/FGTC**, which executes the Format Global Text Center command. After you do this, all labels are automatically centered, unless you specify otherwise.

The procedure is very similar for changing the alignment of numbers. Suppose that you also want all numeric values to be centered within their cells instead of being right-justified. Simply enter **/FGC** to execute the Format Global Center command.

## Displaying Formulas

*Seeing exactly what you entered*

As we said in Chapter 8, worksheets normally display formatted numbers and formula results. If you want to see the actual contents of a cell, you can move the cell pointer to that cell and look in the dialog panel, which shows the exact number or formula you entered into that cell. Although this method of determining a cell's true contents works well for a single cell at a time, it is not very efficient for looking at several cells at once. The ability to display numbers and formulas as entered in their own cells can be very helpful for checking the accuracy of a complex worksheet. Fortunately, SuperCalc lets you do this; you can display formulas instead of formula results on the screen by typing **/GF** to execute the Global Formulas command. Type **/GF** again to change back to displaying formula results.

## CALCULATING RESULTS

*Evaluating formulas*

The primary use of spreadsheet software is to calculate the results of formulas that refer to data stored in worksheet cells. In fact, spreadsheet packages are so convenient for doing these calculations that many people use them without knowing exactly how they work. Simple worksheets with simple formulas are generally quite straightforward and calculations proceed just as you would expect. In some cases, however, it helps to know a little more about how your particular spreadsheet program calculates formula results.

### Formulas and Operators

*Symbols that tell formulas what to do*

As we have said, a formula is simply an expression entered into a cell that performs a calculation or some other data manipulation. You've already seen a few examples of formulas, but these barely scratch the surface of what you can do with a spreadsheet program like SuperCalc. Because of the flexibility with which you can construct formulas, SuperCalc has the ability to perform an almost endless variety of tasks. Nevertheless, there are just three basic types of formulas:

- *Arithmetic.* These formulas manipulate numeric values and produce a numeric result.
- *Text.* These formulas manipulate labels and usually produce a label as a result.
- *Logical.* These formulas compare numeric values or labels and produce either TRUE (symbolized by a value of 1) or FALSE (symbolized by a value of 0).

An *operator* is a symbol that indicates a certain operation to be performed in a formula. Just as there are three basic types of formulas in SuperCalc, there are three types of operators:

- *Arithmetic.* These operators symbolize the most common mathematical procedures:

  + (addition)<br>
  - (subtraction or negative value)<br>
  * (multiplication)<br>
  / (division)<br>
  ^ (exponentiation)

  Exponentiation, you'll recall, means raising a number to a power. For example, 2^5 means 2 to the fifth power, which equals 32.

- *Text.* Only one operator in SuperCalc manipulates labels. It is the text combination operator (&), which joins together two labels. For example, the formula "One"&" Hundred" produces "One Hundred".
- *Logical.* These operators produce a value of TRUE (1) or FALSE (0):

  = (TRUE if two items are equal)<br>
  <> (TRUE if two items are not equal)<br>
  > (TRUE if first item is greater than the second)<br>
  < (TRUE if first item is less than the second)<br>
  >= (TRUE if first item is greater than or equal to the second)<br>
  <= (TRUE if first item is less than or equal to the second)

## Order of Operations

*How formulas are computed*

As you've seen, SuperCalc has several operators that can be used in formulas. Frequently, more than one operator is used in a single formula. This brings up the question of the order in which operations are performed in a formula. For example, the formula 100+200/100 yields a different result depending on which operator you evaluate first. If you do the addition first, the result is 3; if you do the division first, the result is 102. Fortunately, well-defined rules determine the order in which operations take place. Assuming an expression contains no parentheses, operations proceed in the following order:

1. Values preceded by a unary minus sign are converted to negative.
2. All exponentiations are performed, proceeding from left to right.
3. All multiplications and divisions are performed, proceeding from left to right.
4. All additions and subtractions are performed, proceeding from left to right.
5. All of the following logical operations are performed, proceeding from left to right: =, <>, >, <, >=, <=.
6. All & (text combination) operations are performed, proceeding from left to right.

According to these rules, the correct result of the formula 100+200/100 is 102, because the division is performed before the addition. This default order of operations, however, can be altered by using parentheses. Any expressions enclosed in parentheses are evaluated first. If sets of parentheses are nested inside one another, the expression within the innermost set is evaluated first, and evaluation proceeds successively outward. So, the formula (100+200)/100 yields 3, because the expression enclosed in parentheses is evaluated first. In general, it's a good idea to use parentheses if you are not sure about the order in which operations will be performed. Besides eliminating uncertainty in your own mind, using parentheses makes your formulas more understandable to any other people who might also use your worksheet.

## Recalculation

*How calculations proceed*

In Chapter 8, we discussed several aspects of the way in which spreadsheet programs recalculate formulas when you change the contents of a worksheet cell. Like most advanced spreadsheet programs, SuperCalc gives you some control over when, in what order, and how many times formulas are recalculated. By default, SuperCalc uses automatic natural (or dependent) recalculation. This means that every time you change the contents of a cell, all formulas in the worksheet are automatically recalculated. Furthermore, before recalculating a particular formula, all other values on which it depends are recalculated first. If a circular reference is found, SuperCalc displays CIR in the lower right corner of the screen and attempts to resolve it. If no final solution is achieved, the formula keeps recalculating until you press Ctrl-Break to tell SuperCalc to stop.

The Global Evaluation command lets you change these default settings. Figure D.8 shows the menu that SuperCalc displays when you type **/GE** to execute this command. As you can see, there are five options: Quit, Order, When, Iteration-control, and Range.

To change the *order* of recalculation, you choose the Order option and then select either Dependent, Row, or Column. Dependent recalculation is the same as natural recalculation, the default setting. Formula results are calculated by determining the results of all dependent formulas first. As we said in Chapter 8, column (or column-wise) recalculation begins with cell A1, proceeds down column A, and then does the remaining columns in order; row (or row-wise) recalculation also begins with cell A1, but proceeds across row 1, then row 2, and so on. In most cases, the default setting of Dependent recalculation is preferable.

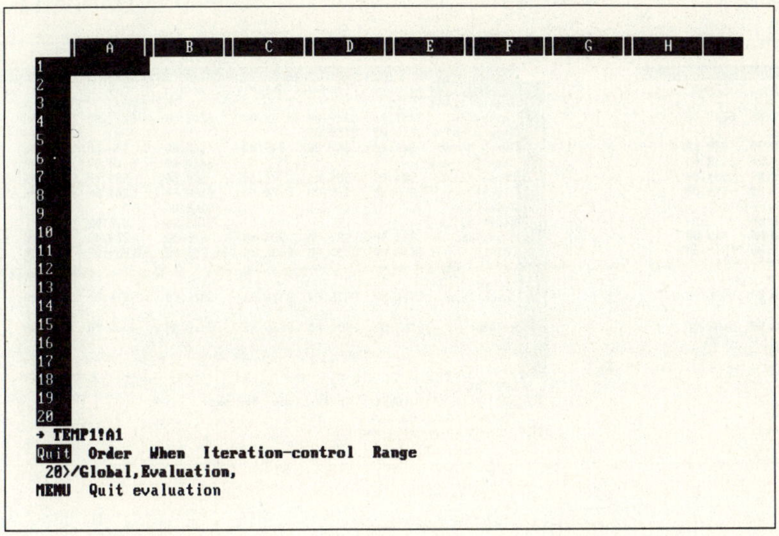


**Figure D.8 Global Evaluation**
This screen shows the Global Evaluation menu, which lets you change the way in which formulas are recalculated.

To change *when* recalculation occurs, you choose either Auto or Manual. If you choose Manual, the worksheet will be recalculated only when you press the F7 function key. This allows you to enter data into a large or complex worksheet without having to wait several seconds for the spreadsheet program to update every cell.

To change *how many times* recalculation occurs, you choose the Iteration-control option. This allows you to set the maximum number of iterations or let SuperCalc continue until circular references are resolved to a specified degree of precision.

The Range option of the Global Evaluation menu allows you to specify a range of cells to be recalculated, instead of the entire worksheet.

Finally, the Quit option simply returns you to the Global menu.

## PRINTING THE WORKSHEET

*Producing a hard copy*

Most worksheets are eventually printed on paper so that they can be included in reports or distributed as is to other people. SuperCalc allows you to print any part of a worksheet at any time while you are working on it. Several options are provided that give you some measure of control over the appearance of the final output. Let's use the Parkridge Condominium Association budget we presented in Chapter 8 to illustrate how to print a worksheet with SuperCalc. Assume that you have already entered, edited, and formatted the worksheet. Figure D.9(a) shows what your screen would look like.

Because the screen is limited to 80 characters across, you cannot see the row totals, which are beyond the right edge in column H. Nevertheless, you can still tell

**Figure D.9 Printing a Worksheet**

(a) This is the worksheet to be printed.

(b) Type **/P** to execute the Print command and SuperCalc presents two options: Printer and File.

(c) After you select Printer, another menu appears. Type **R** and enter **A1:H17** for the range to print, and type **G** to execute the Go command.

(d) The printed copy of the worksheet on two pages.

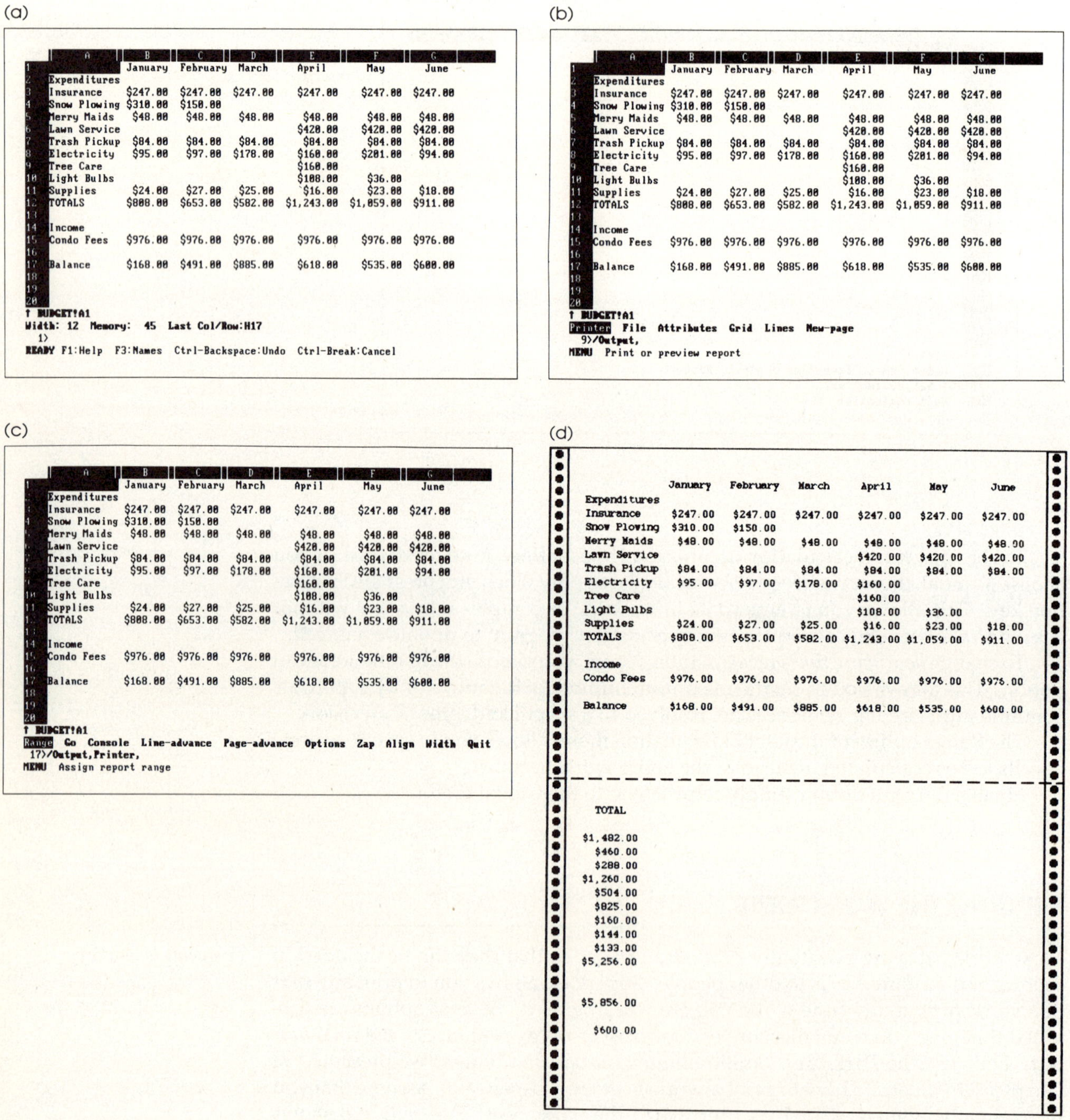

SuperCalc to print the entire worksheet. First type **/O** to execute the Output command. As Figure D.9(b) shows, you are presented with several options, two of which are Printer and File. If you choose Printer, SuperCalc sends the output to your printer; if you choose File, SuperCalc sends the output to a file saved on a disk. "Printing" to a file lets you print the worksheet later with the DOS PRINT command after you quit SuperCalc, or use a program called SIDEWAYS, which is included with SuperCalc, to print the worksheet across the long edge of the pages. Let's assume that you want to print your worksheet directly, so you type **P** to select the Printer option. Another submenu appears, shown in Figure D.9(c). The next step is to tell SuperCalc the range of cells you want to print. This allows you to print all or just part of your worksheet. Type **R** to select the Range option, and SuperCalc asks you to enter the print range. To print this entire worksheet, enter **A1:H17**. The submenu you see in Figure D.9(c) reappears. At this point, you can elect to use the default print settings, and simply type **G** to choose the Go option and immediately begin printing your worksheet. As always, before you execute any print command it is a good idea to make sure your printer is turned on and connected to the computer, and that the paper is positioned at the top of a new page. Figure D.9(d) shows what emerges from your printer. When printing is completed, you type **Q** to choose the Quit option and return to editing the worksheet.

As you can see from Figure D.9(d), this worksheet did not fit on a single page. The last column was put on a new page because SuperCalc uses a default page width of 80 characters. Although SuperCalc cannot directly print worksheets sideways on a page, it does come with a separate program that will let you do this. The Options command you see in the menu in Figure D.9(c) activates another menu with options that let you do the following:

- Format the output to indicate page breaks, show formulas instead of formula results, and include special codes for the printer.
- Adjust the page length, page width, and margins.
- Control paper handling and line spacing.
- Print the column border (A, B, C, etc.) and/or row border (1, 2, 3, etc.).
- Repeat title text to appear above columns or to the left of rows on each page.
- Specify the number of copies to be printed.
- Specify up to four lines of text each for headers and footers.
- Specify a **printer setup string**, which is a group of special control codes sent to the printer that turns on options such as compressed print.

## SAVING AND RETRIEVING WORKSHEETS

*Keeping worksheet files*

One of the most important benefits of using a spreadsheet program is being able to save worksheets on disks and retrieve them later. Worksheets, like word processed documents, need not be static entities. They are frequently maintained, revised, updated, and experimented with. You can save a partial worksheet before you are finished creating it, retrieve it at some later time, and complete your entries. You can retrieve a previously saved worksheet and use it as a model for a new one by slightly modifying it. You can take an existing worksheet and change some figures just to see what the results would be. You can (and should) periodically save a worksheet while you are creating it to guard against losing your work if a power failure occurs, your equipment malfunctions, or you make some drastic error. Obviously, learning how to save and retrieve worksheets is critical.

**Figure D.10 Saving and Retrieving a Worksheet File**

(a) To save your current worksheet, first type **/S** to execute the Save command, and then enter a filename.

(b) To retrieve an existing worksheet, first type **/L** to execute the Load command, press **F3** to display a file list, highlight the filename you want, and press **Enter**.

(a)

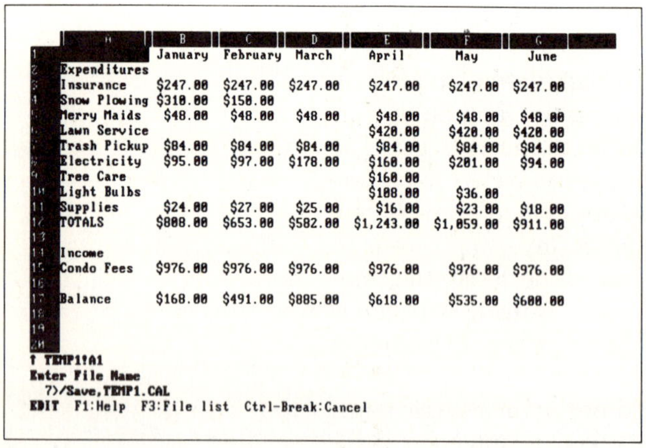


(b)

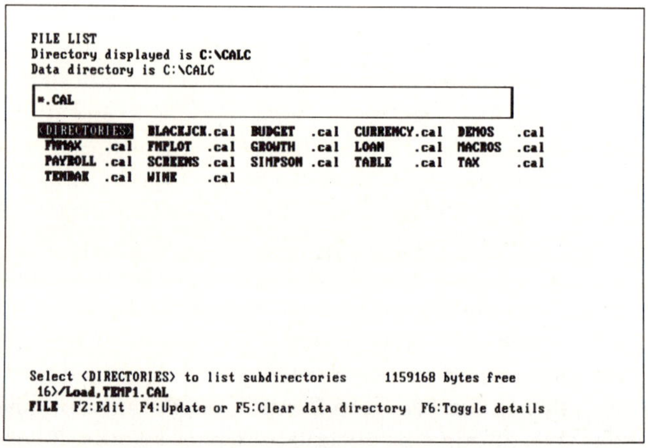


Fortunately, it's easy to save and retrieve worksheets in SuperCalc. Let's say that you've created and printed the Parkridge Condominium Association budget depicted in Figure D.9(a). To store this worksheet on a disk, simply type **/S** to execute the Save command. Figure D.10(a) shows what happens. SuperCalc prompts you to name the file in which to store the worksheet and suggests the name of the current worksheet, which will be TEMP1 for a new worksheet. If this isn't the name you want to use, all you have to do is type a different filename, such as **BUDGET**, and press the **Enter** key. When SuperCalc stores the worksheet file on the disk, it automatically appends an extension of .CAL to the filename you enter. After you enter the filename, type **A** to save all of the data.

Retrieving an existing file from the startup directory is even easier than saving one. Suppose that you just started SuperCalc and you want to work on the BUDGET worksheet you previously saved. Your worksheet is initially blank. To load the BUDGET worksheet from the disk into memory, you type **/L** to execute the Load command and then press **F3** to see a list of worksheet files in your current directory, as shown in Figure D.10(b). Use the arrow keys to highlight the .CAL file you want to load, say BUDGET, and then press **Enter**. The worksheet is loaded into memory and your screen will look like Figure D.9(a) again.

## ADDITIONAL FEATURES

*More capabilities*

Many more features are included in SuperCalc besides the basics we've just covered. Some are used more than others. Graphing and data management are perhaps the most prominent. In addition, SuperCalc also lets you specify macros, set up templates, hide and protect cells, split the screen into two windows, combine worksheets, and translate data between applications.

## Graphing

*Ways to draw your data*

SuperCalc lets you easily produce professional-looking charts for reports and presentations. The program can create eight basic types of graphs, the five most common of which are illustrated in Figure D.11:

- *Line Graph.* Each value is represented by a point at an appropriate distance above the horizontal axis. Related points are designated by the same symbol and connected by line segments. Line graphs are useful for plotting values that change over time, such as monthly dollar sales.
- *Bar Graph.* Each value is represented by a vertical bar. Bar graphs are useful for comparing different sets of data, such as the unit sales of three different products.
- *X-Y Graph.* Also called scatterplots, X-Y graphs show the relationship between two or more different data items. For example, an X-Y graph can be used to show the relationship between the price of a product and how many units are sold.
- *Stacked Bar Graph.* This variation of the basic bar graph shows components and total amounts of each set of data. For example, a stacked bar graph could be used to show the unit sales of three different products both in the United States and abroad.
- *Pie Chart.* Each value is represented as a wedge of a circle. Pie charts are used to show the relative amounts of components that comprise a single set of data. For example, pie charts are often used to depict the breakdown of total expenditures into various categories.

As an example, let's do a bar graph of the Parkridge Condominium Association's bank balances for the months of January through June, as we did in Chapter 8 in Figure 8.12. You can do this, however, only if your IBM-compatible

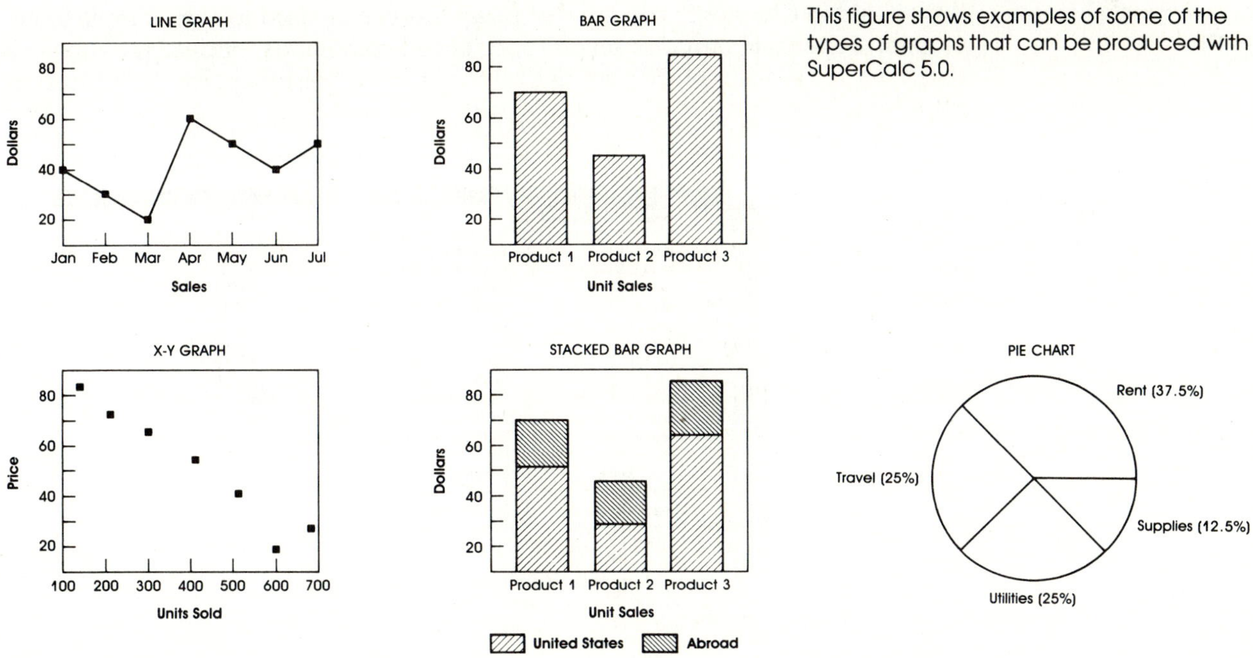


**Figure D.11 SuperCalc Graphs**
This figure shows examples of some of the types of graphs that can be produced with SuperCalc 5.0.

**Figure D.12 A SuperCalc Bar Graph**
Here is the bar graph of Parkridge Condominium Association balances displayed on the screen.

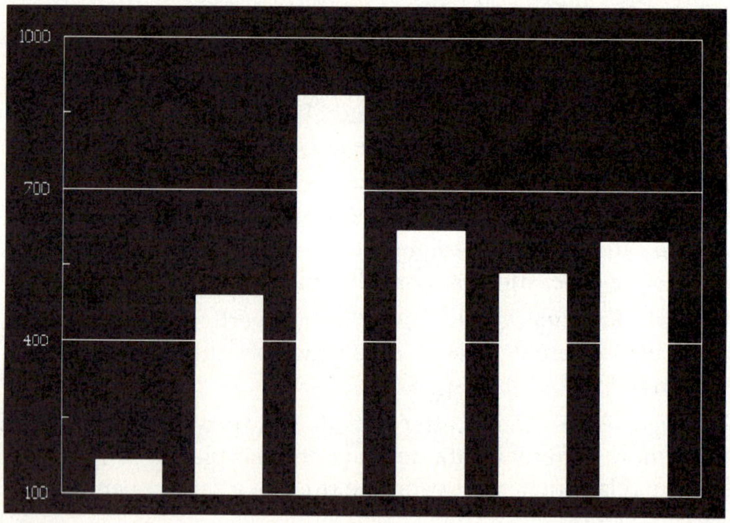


microcomputer has a graphics adapter and monitor, and SuperCalc has been installed to take advantage of this equipment. The first step in creating the bar graph is to execute the Graph command by typing **//G**. Then you enter a name for your graph, say **BALANCE**. A bar graph is the default type of graph, so we can go directly to specify the data by typing **D**. Enter the range of cells to be included in the bar graph, **B17:G17**. Finally, press **F10** to display the graph. Figure D.12 shows how the screen looks. When you are finished viewing the graph, press **Escape**. Other options in the //Graph menu let you embellish your graph by selecting different colors and adding titles, labels, and legends.

## Data Management

*Rearranging and searching data tables*

As we said in Chapter 8, spreadsheet programs can be used to store simple tables of data. SuperCalc provides several specialized commands for dealing with such data tables. For example, Figure D.13 shows a data table of apartment addresses,

**Figure D.13 Data Management with SuperCalc**
This screen shows a data table of addresses, names, and condominium fees. The control panel reveals the menu that appears after typing **//D** to execute the Data command.

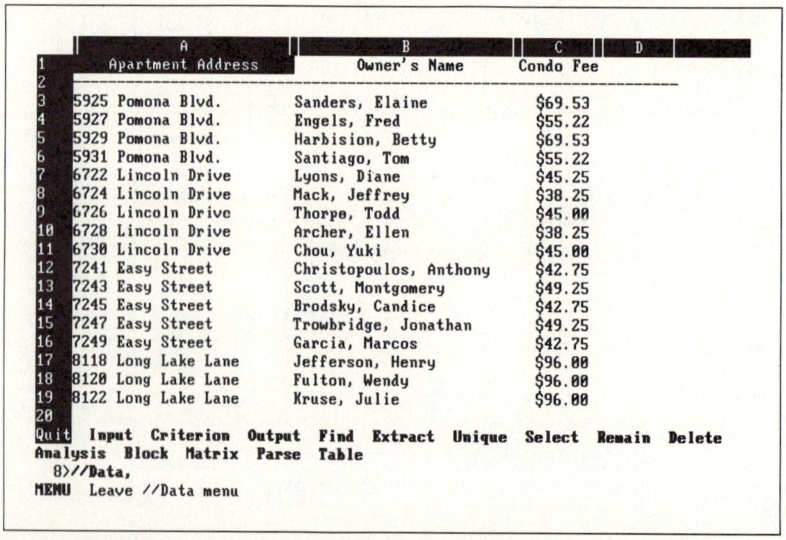

| | A | B | C | D |
|---|---|---|---|---|
| 1 | Apartment Address | Owner's Name | Condo Fee | |
| 2 | | | | |
| 3 | 5925 Pomona Blvd. | Sanders, Elaine | $69.53 | |
| 4 | 5927 Pomona Blvd. | Engels, Fred | $55.22 | |
| 5 | 5929 Pomona Blvd. | Harbision, Betty | $69.53 | |
| 6 | 5931 Pomona Blvd. | Santiago, Tom | $55.22 | |
| 7 | 6722 Lincoln Drive | Lyons, Diane | $45.25 | |
| 8 | 6724 Lincoln Drive | Mack, Jeffrey | $38.25 | |
| 9 | 6726 Lincoln Drive | Thorpe, Todd | $45.00 | |
| 10 | 6728 Lincoln Drive | Archer, Ellen | $38.25 | |
| 11 | 6730 Lincoln Drive | Chou, Yuki | $45.00 | |
| 12 | 7241 Easy Street | Christopoulos, Anthony | $42.75 | |
| 13 | 7243 Easy Street | Scott, Montgomery | $49.25 | |
| 14 | 7245 Easy Street | Brodsky, Candice | $42.75 | |
| 15 | 7247 Easy Street | Trowbridge, Jonathan | $49.25 | |
| 16 | 7249 Easy Street | Garcia, Marcos | $42.75 | |
| 17 | 8118 Long Lake Lane | Jefferson, Henry | $96.00 | |
| 18 | 8120 Long Lake Lane | Fulton, Wendy | $96.00 | |
| 19 | 8122 Long Lake Lane | Kruse, Julie | $96.00 | |
| 20 | | | | |

Quit Input Criterion Output Find Extract Unique Select Remain Delete
Analysis Block Matrix Parse Table
8>//Data,
MENU Leave //Data menu

owner names, and condominium fees for the Parkridge Condominium Association. The submenu that you see in the control panel was activated by typing **//D** to execute the Data command. This menu lists those specialized commands that let you enter, manipulate, and analyze data in a worksheet.

One of the most frequently used data management commands, however, is in the main menu. The Arrange command lets you sort the contents of a block of cells into ascending or descending order, with or without adjusting cell references. You can even have more than one sort key. For example, the rows you see in Figure D.13 are now sorted in ascending order by apartment address. With the Arrange command, you could sort the rows of this table alphabetically on the basis of the names in column B. You could even sort them by condominium fee.

This table is fairly small, so it wouldn't take you long to visually scan through the rows to find a particular apartment or owner. If the table had hundreds or even thousands of rows, finding a particular row would be considerably more difficult. The //Data Find command lets you tell SuperCalc to search for a particular row and highlight it. You could then copy the row you find to another part of the worksheet or remove it from the table entirely.

## Macros

*Saving and replaying keystrokes*

As we said in Chapter 8, a spreadsheet macro lets you define and store a sequence of keystrokes and replay this sequence later by pressing a single combination of keys. Macros are handy for reducing repetitive typing and automating the entry of complex sequences of keystrokes. They are also frequently included in templates to make them easier for novices to use. Macros are one of SuperCalc's most advanced features and they can be quite complex. Our aim here is to provide a very simple example just to give you an idea of what SuperCalc macros can do and how they are defined.

Let's say that you want to create a macro that will enter the names of the months of the year across the columns. This could be useful if you need to repeat these labels several times in a worksheet. Figure D.14 shows the definition of a macro

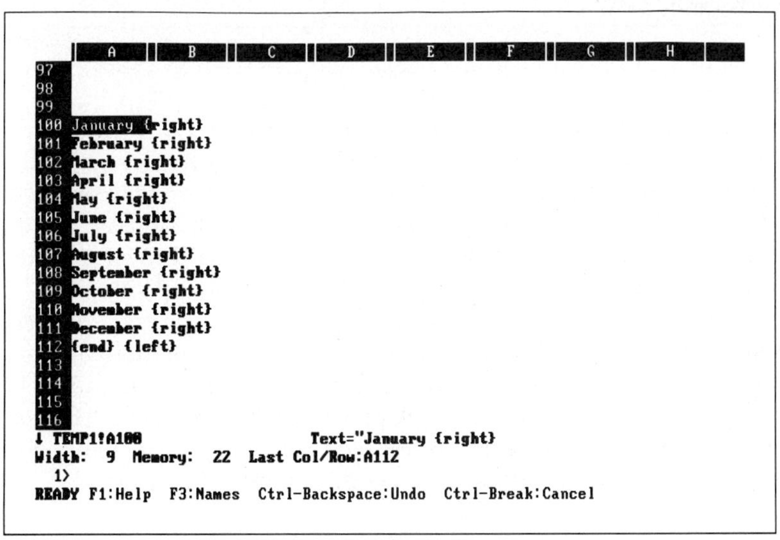


**Figure D.14 Creating a Macro**
This screen shows the definition of a macro that enters labels for the months of the year in the next twelve columns, beginning with the current cell pointer position.

that enters labels for the months of the year in the next twelve columns, beginning with the current cell pointer position. This macro definition is placed in cells A100 through A112, far below any rows we plan to use for the actual worksheet. The entries enclosed in braces, such as {right}, designate movements of the cell pointer. The last entry, {end} {left}, moves the cell pointer back to the left edge of the worksheet.

Before this macro can be used, the range of cells that hold it must be given a name. A macro name must consist of a backslash (\) followed by a letter from A to Z. For example, this macro could be named \M to remind you that it enters month labels. The Name Create command is used to assign the name \M to the range A100:A112. After you do this, you invoke the macro by holding down the Alternate key and pressing the single letter that names the macro. For example, to insert the month names in cells A2 through M2, you move the cell pointer to A2, hold down the **Alternate** key, and type **M**. The program automatically performs the steps you listed in the macro definition, just as if you did them yourself: *January* is entered and the cell pointer moves to the right, *February* is entered and the cell pointer moves to the right, and so on. After *December* is entered, the macro moves the cell pointer back to A2.

## Templates

*Fill-in-the-blank worksheets*

Like most spreadsheets, SuperCalc can be used to set up templates. As we said in Chapter 8, a template is simply a ready-made, general-purpose worksheet somewhat like a blank form. It contains the necessary labels, constants, and formulas, but the user fills in the key variables. Since SuperCalc is such a popular program, many templates are available for it. People who create templates may distribute them freely to the general public, publish them in books, sell them on disks as stand-alone products, or reserve them for use within a particular organization or company. There are SuperCalc templates on the market for all kinds of tasks, from tax preparation and accounting chores to games and tutorials.

## Hiding and Protecting Cells

*Safeguarding your data*

SuperCalc has the ability to hide and protect cells, features used in creating templates or worksheets that might be used by others.

Suppose you want to hide the contents of column A because it contains sensitive data like employee salaries. To do this you type **/FH** to execute the Format Hide-column command, type **A** to indicate column A, and then type **Y** for yes to proceed. When a column is hidden, its data is still there but the column doesn't appear on the screen. To "unhide" a previously hidden column, you type **/FH** to execute the Format Hide-column command, type the column letter, and then type **N** for no.

The process for protecting cells is somewhat different. When cells are protected, they are still visible but they cannot be changed or deleted. Let's say that you have created a template that contains a critical number or formula that should never be changed. Simply move the cell pointer to that cell and enter **/P** to execute the Protect command. After you do this, the protected cell can be viewed but not changed or deleted. To change or delete the cell, you must use the Unprotect command.

## Split Screen Windows

*Two views of the same worksheet*

SuperCalc lets you split your screen into two horizontal or vertical windows. You can then use each window to see a different part of the same worksheet, which can be handy for worksheets that are too large to fit on a single screen. Using two windows is easier than constantly scrolling the screen back and forth to see two distant parts of the same worksheet.

The procedure for splitting your screen into two windows is straightforward. If you want two horizontal windows, first you move the cell pointer to the row that you want to be the top edge of the second window. To split your screen into two approximately equal halves, this would be row 11. Next you type **/WH** to execute the Window Horizontal command. Figure D.15 shows the result. At this point the bottom window is active, and the cell pointer only moves within this portion. You must press the **F6** function key to switch to the other window. The two windows can be used to view one part of a worksheet while you edit another part of the same worksheet.

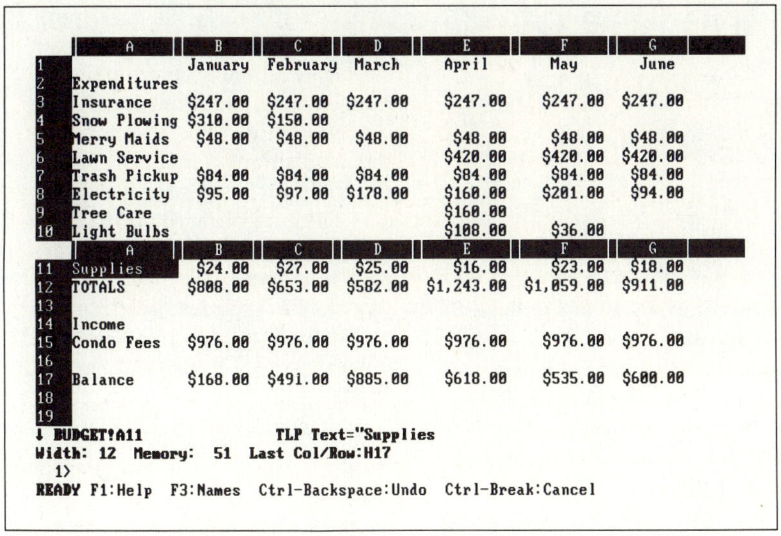


**Figure D.15 Split Screen Windows**
To split your screen into two horizontal windows, move the cell pointer to where you want the split to occur, and type **/WH** to execute the Window Horizontal command.

## Linking Worksheets

*Multiple worksheets in memory*

In Chapter 8 we said that some spreadsheet programs let you link cells in different worksheets. With SuperCalc 5.0, you can load and view more than one worksheet, use formulas to link the current worksheet with other worksheets both in memory and disk files, and create multipage worksheets to more easily handle related data.

For example, to have more than one worksheet in memory at the same time, press **Ctrl-Enter** to create a new blank worksheet. Then you can load an existing file into this worksheet or build a new one from scratch. Once you have two or more worksheets in memory, you can move among them by pressing the following keys:

- *Ctrl-Plus* (+ on the numeric keypad). Moves to the next worksheet in memory.
- *Ctrl-Minus* (- on the numeric keypad). Moves to the previous worksheet in memory.

- *Ctrl-Equal* (=). Lets you enter the name of the worksheet you want to see.
- *Tab-Ctrl-Home.* Moves to the first worksheet in memory.
- *Tab-Ctrl-End.* Moves to the last worksheet in memory.

You also can copy and move data between the different worksheets in memory. A cell in one worksheet can be referenced from within another worksheet to create links. For example, if you want to use the contents of cell A1 from worksheet BUDGET in another worksheet, you reference this cell as BUDGET!A1. You can even display up to three worksheets on the screen at the same time with the //Spreadsheets Display command. These capabilities make SuperCalc 5.0 an extremely powerful spreadsheet package.

## The Real World

### The Rise of Computer Associates

Computer Associates, producer of SuperCalc 5.0 spreadsheet software, didn't get to the top of the software industry by creating new products.

Most companies start with an idea and then develop it into a software product. Computer Associates, based in Garden City, New York, grew by taking over other software companies. The strategy has been phenomenally successful. Between 1982 and 1988, Computer Associates acquired 16 software houses, making it the world's largest independent software company. It employs 4500 people, has offices in 22 countries, and was expecting to pull in $900 million in revenues in the 1988-89 fiscal year.

SuperCalc 5.0 is one of about 200 software items that the company sells. These products run on everything from mainframes to personal computers of every make and configuration. Most of Computer Associates' profits and revenues come from systems software that makes huge data centers run smoothly, however.

The company began with just one man: Charles Wang (pronounced *Wong*). Wang and his family came to the United States from Shanghai in 1952 when he was just a child. After studying math and physics at Queens College in New York, he became a programmer and then peddled software for a New York computer service bureau. Then his break came. He won a contract to distribute a program called CA-SORT, which was a smash hit. Joined by his brother, a Wall Street lawyer, Wang was on his way.

Wang's strategy has remained the same through the years. He wants to develop an efficient and effective sales and service network and to acquire and develop new products to satisfy his customers. About half of Computer Associates' 1000 programmers update existing programs, while the other half write new programs. But the acquisitions remain the key to the company's success.

The goal Wang set in 1977—to be the biggest and best software and services company in the world—has largely come true. He was named the best chief executive officer in the software industry in 1983.

Sources:

Katherine M. Hafner, "How Computer Associates Climbed to No. 1 in Software," *Business Week*, July 11, 1988, pp. 77-79.

Theresa Barry, "Bringing Up His Own 'Little Family,'" *Datamation*, March 1, 1987, p. 106.

"Charles Wang and His Thundering Nerds," *Forbes*, July 11, 1988, pp. 118-124.

## Translating Data Between Applications

*SuperCalc works well with others*

We've already mentioned one way that SuperCalc can produce data for use in another program: you can "print" a worksheet to a file. This produces an ordinary text file that might be used by word processors, data base managers, or other applications. In addition, SuperCalc can directly load and save data in Lotus 1-2-3 and dBASE III PLUS files. The //Import command converts files from other programs to SuperCalc files and the //Export command converts SuperCalc files so that they can be used by other programs.

## Summary

- *How to start SuperCalc.* To start SuperCalc, you switch to the proper subdirectory and enter **SC5**.
- *The various components of the SuperCalc display screen.* The SuperCalc display screen consists of the display window with labeled columns and numbered rows on top, and the dialog panel below with the status, prompt, entry, and help lines. You press the / (forward slash) key to bring up the main menu.
- *How to enter new data into a worksheet and change existing data.* The cell pointer, which marks the cell where an entry is to be made or changed, is moved by using the arrow keys, Page Up, Page Down, Home, End, and the F5 function key. Numbers, labels, and formulas are simply typed into the active cell. To edit the existing contents of a cell, move the cell pointer to that cell and press the F2 function key. New rows and columns can be inserted with the Insert command, and existing rows and columns can be deleted with the Delete command. Ranges of cells can be moved with the Move command and copied with the Copy command.
- *How to control the appearance of a worksheet.* Various numeric formats are available to specify how numbers and numeric formula results are displayed in a worksheet. The width of individual columns or every column in a worksheet can be set. You can set the default global alignment of both labels and numbers to be left-justified, centered, or right-justified.
- *The way in which SuperCalc calculates formula results.* Formulas are constructed with various arithmetic, text, and logical operators, which are evaluated in a specific order. By default, SuperCalc uses automatic natural (dependent) recalculation with iteration turned on, but these settings can be changed.
- *How to print a worksheet.* The SuperCalc Print command lets you print all or part of your worksheet, either directly on your printer, or to a file for printing later or for use in another program.
- *How to save and retrieve a worksheet.* The Save command is used to store a worksheet on a disk for later use. An existing worksheet can be loaded into SuperCalc with the Load command.
- *Some additional features included in SuperCalc.* Using data from your worksheets, SuperCalc can display and print various types of graphs. Data management commands allow you to sort and search through tables of data. In addition, SuperCalc lets you specify macros, set up templates, hide and protect cells, split the screen into two windows, link worksheets, and translate data between SuperCalc and other applications.

## Command Summary

The following table summarizes SuperCalc keypresses.

| KEYPRESS | DESCRIPTION |
|---|---|
| / | Activates the main menu. |
| // | Activates a menu of more commands. |
| Enter | Completes an entry. |
| Backspace | Erases preceding character. |
| Delete | Deletes character at cursor. |
| Insert | Switches from insert to overwrite mode, and vice versa. |
| Escape | Exit from a menu; erases entry in dialog panel. |
| Home | Moves to cell A1. |
| Left Arrow | Moves left one cell. |
| Right Arrow | Moves right one cell. |
| Up Arrow | Moves up one cell. |
| Down Arrow | Moves down one cell. |
| Ctrl-Left Arrow | Moves left one screen. |
| Ctrl-Right Arrow | Moves right one screen. |
| Page Up | Moves up one screen. |
| Page Down | Moves down one screen. |
| End | When followed by an arrow key, moves to worksheet edge. |
| F1 | Activates the help facility. |
| F2 | Changes to EDIT mode. |
| F3 | Displays a menu of range names. |
| F4 | Changes the type of cell addressing. |
| F5 | Moves to a particular cell address. |
| F6 | Switches to other split screen window. |
| F7 | Recalculates worksheet. |
| F8 | Resumes macro execution. |
| F9 | Plots a graph. |
| F10 | Displays the most recently specified graph. |

The following table summarizes the first two levels of SuperCalc menu commands.

| COMMAND | DESCRIPTION |
|---|---|
| /AC | Sorts contents of a column of cells. |
| /AR | Sorts contents of a row of cells. |
| /AM | Sorts a column or row with one to three sort keys. |
| /B | Erases contents current cell. |
| /BR | Erases contents of a range of cells. |
| /BG | Erases one or more graphs. |
| /C | Duplicates contents of one or more cells. |
| /DR | Deletes contents of a row of cells. |
| /DC | Deletes contents of a column of cells. |
| /DB | Deletes contents of a block of cells. |
| /DF | Deletes a file. |
| /E | Edits the contents of a cell. |
| /FG | Specifies global formats. |
| /FC | Specifies formats for a column of cells. |
| /FR | Specifies formats for a row of cells. |
| /FE | Specifies formats for selected cells. |
| /FU | Specifies user-defined formats. |
| /FH | Hides one or more columns of cells. |

| COMMAND | DESCRIPTION |
|---|---|
| /GO | Displays menus of default values. |
| /GK | Keeps the current default settings in a disk file. |
| /GS | Displays menus of hardware options. |
| /GE | Controls recalculation method. |
| /GV | Displays status screen of global settings. |
| /G1 | Turns on and off the global Lotus 1-2-3 mode. |
| /GF | Turns on and off the display of formulas. |
| /G" | Turns on and off the leading double quote requirement. |
| /GL | Turns on and off the display of range names in formulas. |
| /GP | Temporarily turns on and off cell protection. |
| /GB | Turns on and off the display of column and row borders. |
| /GN | Turns on and off cursor auto-advance. |
| /GT | Turns on and off cursor lockout option. |
| /GZ | Switches between standard and expanded screen views. |
| /IR | Inserts one or more blank rows. |
| /IC | Inserts one or more blank columns. |
| /IB | Inserts a blank block of cells. |
| /JS | Justifies text in a column. |
| /JM | Justifies text broken up by a non-text cell or row. |
| /JW | Turns on word wrap. |
| /L | Reads a worksheet from its disk file into memory. |
| /MB | Moves a block of cells. |
| /MR | Moves a row of cells. |
| /MC | Moves a column of cells. |
| /NC | Creates a named range of cells. |
| /ND | Deletes a name from a range of cells. |
| /NL | Extracts a series of names from a range of cells. |
| /NT | Creates a table of names and associated ranges. |
| /NZ | Deletes all range names. |
| /OP | Sends worksheet output to a printer. |
| /OF | Sends worksheet output to a file. |
| /OA | Lets you define lines, boxes, and shading in a report. |
| /ON | Places a page break in a worksheet report. |
| /OG | Draws horizontal and vertical lines in the report. |
| /P | Prevents any changes to a range of cells. |
| /QN | Cancels Quit command. |
| /QY | Exits SuperCalc and returns to DOS. |
| /QT | Exits SuperCalc and executes some other program. |
| /QS | Temporarily suspends SuperCalc to run a DOS command. |
| /S | Copies current worksheet to a disk file. |
| /TH | Locks the current row and all above it on the screen. |
| /TV | Locks the current column and all to the left of it on the screen. |
| /TB | Locks the current row and column on the screen. |
| /TC | Removes any title locks. |
| /WH | Splits screen horizontally. |
| /WV | Splits screen vertically. |
| /WC | Removes the split screen. |
| /WS | Causes both windows to scroll simultaneously. |
| /WU | Causes each window to scroll independently. |
| /ZN | Cancels Zap command and returns to the worksheet. |
| /ZY | Erases entire worksheet and invokes all default settings. |
| /ZC | Erases entire worksheet but retains user-defined formats. |
| /1 | Executes the following command as a Lotus 1-2-3 command. |
| //AA | Attaches an add-in application. |
| //AD | Removes an add-in application. |
| //AI | Invokes an add-in program. |
| //AQ | Returns to worksheet from add-in application. |

| COMMAND | DESCRIPTION |
|---|---|
| //DQ | Cancels data management command; returns to READY mode. |
| //DI | Specifies data management input. |
| //DC | Specifies data management criteria. |
| //DO | Specifies data management output. |
| //DF | Searches input for data that matches criteria. |
| //DE | Extracts requested data. |
| //DU | Extracts unique data. |
| //DS | Selectively extracts data. |
| //DR | Retains cursor position when you leave data management menu. |
| //DD | Removes records that match criteria. |
| //DA | Performs regression or frequency distribution analysis. |
| //DB | Generates a range of ascending or descending numbers. |
| //DM | Performs matrix multiplication. |
| //DP | Extracts a set of fields out of a column of data. |
| //DT | Allows you to create a table of values to be tested in formulas. |
| //E1 | Exports worksheet in Lotus 1-2-3 format. |
| //EX | Exports worksheet in Extended Data Interchange format. |
| //ED | Exports worksheet in Data Interchange Format. |
| //EC | Exports worksheet in Comma Separated Values format. |
| //EB | Exports worksheet in dBASE III format. |
| //FG | Lets you specify a path for loading files for the entire session. |
| //FS | Lets you specify a path for a single worksheet. |
| //G | Lets you create and view graphs. |
| //I1 | Imports Lotus 1-2-3 file. |
| //IX | Imports Extended Data Interchange Format file. |
| //ID | Imports Data Interchange Format file. |
| //IC | Imports Comma Separated Values file. |
| //IN | Imports numeric format file. |
| //IT | Imports an ASCII text file. |
| //IV | Imports a VisiCalc file. |
| //IB | Imports dBase III file. |
| //ML | Captures your keystrokes into a macro. |
| //MR | Reads a macro from a disk file. |
| //MW | Writes a macro to a disk file. |
| //MX | Executes a macro. |
| //MT | Traces the execution of a macro. |
| //MB | Sets breakpoints in a macro. |
| //MA | Analyzes the structure of a macro. |
| //MC | Converts a Lotus 1-2-3 macro to SuperCalc format. |
| //ND | Displays network directory. |
| //NL | Protects files from alteration by a network user. |
| //NU | Unprotects files on a network. |
| //NO | Lets you choose printer on a network. |
| //O | Optimizes use of memory. |
| //PG | Lets you define directory path for a SuperCalc session. |
| //PS | Lets you define directory path for a worksheet. |
| //R | Restricts data input to a specified range. |

## Key Terms

As an extra review of this appendix, try defining the following terms. If you have trouble with any of them, refer to the page number listed.

printer setup string (A45)

repeating text (A33)

## Review Questions

1. On a computer with a hard disk, how do you begin working with SuperCalc?
2. If the maximum number of columns is 255 and the maximum number of rows is 9999, how many cells can SuperCalc address?
3. How does SuperCalc designate columns and rows?
4. How do you activate the main menu?
5. What are the two methods of choosing an option from a SuperCalc menu?
6. How do you activate the SuperCalc help facility?
7. How do you move the cell pointer to a particular cell address in the worksheet?
8. Which command would you use to center all labels within their cells?
9. How do SuperCalc formulas differ from Lotus 1-2-3 formulas?
10. Which SuperCalc function would you use to compute the square root of a number?
11. One way to change the existing contents of a cell is to retype the entire entry. Describe a different way to change a cell without having to retype the entire entry.
12. What happens when you delete a column with the Delete Column command?
13. How would you change every cell in a worksheet to integer format?
14. What is the default column width in SuperCalc?
15. How would SuperCalc compute the result of the formula 1+2/2?
16. Why might you want to "print" a worksheet to a file, instead of sending it directly to the printer?
17. How do you store a worksheet on a disk?
18. What type of graph would you use to depict the breakdown of total expenditures into various categories?
19. What SuperCalc command would you use to rearrange a table of data?
20. What command would you use to split the SuperCalc screen into two horizontal windows?

## Multiple Choice

1. After you have switched to the proper disk drive directory, which of the following commands will execute SuperCalc 5.0?
   (a) CALC (b) SC5
   (c) SuperCalc (d) 123
2. The second 26 columns of a SuperCalc worksheet are labeled
   (a) A through Z. (b) AA through AZ.
   (c) BA through BZ. (d) A through IU.
3. SuperCalc can address a great many cells, but the actual number of cells you can fill with data depends on the
   (a) amount of memory installed in the computer. (b) size of the graphics display screen.
   (c) width of the printer carriage. (d) speed of the microprocessor.

4. The area of the SuperCalc screen that displays menus and prompts is called the
   (a) cell pointer. (b) border.
   (c) dialog panel. (d) help facility.
5. Which key do you press to activate SuperCalc's main menu?
   (a) F1 (b) Enter
   (c) Escape (d) / (forward slash)
6. What is the fastest way to execute the Save command from SuperCalc's main menu?
   (a) Highlight the option and press **Enter**. (b) Use the Access System.
   (c) Press **S**. (d) Use the System command.
7. In SuperCalc, pressing **F1** activates the
   (a) function key menu. (b) translate utility.
   (c) help facility. (d) main menu.
8. Which key would you press to move immediately to cell A1?
   (a) Home (b) Escape
   (c) Enter (d) Page Up
9. Which of the following is not a type of data that can be placed in a worksheet cell?
   (a) number (b) label
   (c) formula (d) graph
10. Which of the following commands would you use to prevent any changes to a cell?
    (a) Edit (b) Justify
    (c) Protect (d) Delete
11. Which SuperCalc function would you use to add the contents of cells A1 through A100?
    (a) SUM (b) COUNT
    (c) MAX (d) MOD
12. Which of the following commands would you use to produce a worksheet on paper?
    (a) View (b) Translate
    (c) Install (d) Print
13. Which of the following is a valid SuperCalc macro name?
    (a) M (b) \M
    (c) MACRO.WK1 (d) {macro}
14. Which command would you use to cut and paste a range of cells?
    (a) Copy (b) Move
    (c) Insert (d) Delete
15. Which operation is performed first?
    (a) Division (b) Subtraction
    (c) Addition (d) Exponentiation

## On-line Exercises

1. If you are not already running SuperCalc, change to the proper disk drive directory and enter **SC5**. In cell A1, type **100** and press the **Down Arrow** key. In cell A2, type **200** and press the **Down Arrow** key. In cell A3, type **A1+A2** and press the **Enter** key.

2. Use the Insert Row command to insert two new rows between cells A2 and A3. (Remember that you press / to bring up the main menu.) Enter **300** into cell A3 and **400** into cell A4.

3. Move the cell pointer to cell A5 and press **F2** to invoke SuperCalc's EDIT mode. Modify the formula so that it reads SUM(A1:A4).

4. Use the Move command to move the contents of cells A1 through A5 to cells B2 through B6.

5. Use the Format Global User-defined Number 3 command to change the worksheet's default numeric format to currency format, with two places to the right of decimal points. The > symbols appear in cell B6 because the cell is no longer wide enough to display the result of the formula in currency format. (This will be corrected in the next exercise.)

6. Use the Format Column Width command to change the widths of both columns A and B to 12 characters. Cell B6 should now display $1000.00.

7. Enter **EXPENSE** into cell A1 and **AMOUNT** into cell B1. Now enter **Supplies** into cell B2, **Utilities** into cell B3, **Insurance** into cell B4, **Rent** into cell B5, and **TOTAL** into cell B6.

8. If you have a printer attached to your computer, try printing your worksheet. First execute the Output Printer Range command and enter **A1:B6** as the range of cells to be printed. Make sure that the printer is turned on, its on-line indicator is lit, and paper is loaded and positioned at the top of a new page. Then type **G** to execute the Go option. After the worksheet has finished printing, execute the **Quit** option to leave the Output Printer menu.

9. Execute the Save command and enter **EXPENSES** to store this worksheet in a disk file named EXPENSES.CAL.

10. Use the Zap Yes command to clear the contents of your screen.

11. Execute the Load command, press **F3**, use the **Right Arrow** key to highlight EXPENSES.CAL, and press the **Enter** key to load the EXPENSES worksheet from the disk into memory.

12. If your computer is equipped with a graphics adapter and monitor, produce a pie chart from the EXPENSES worksheet.

13. Sort your expenses in alphabetical order with the Arrange command.

14. We are finished with the EXPENSES worksheet, so let's remove it from the disk. In fact, you should do this only if you are sure that you want to permanently discard the worksheet. Execute the Delete File command and then press **F3**. Use the **Right Arrow** key to highlight EXPENSES if it is not already highlighted, and press **Enter**. Type **Y** for yes to confirm that you want to erase this file. Now use the Zap Yes command to remove the worksheet from the screen and give you a new blank worksheet.

15. Suppose that you've just opened an Individual Retirement Account (IRA). The account pays 8% interest, compounded annually and paid on the last day of

each year. You plan to deposit $2000 on the last day of every year. How much will your IRA hold after 30 years? You can use SuperCalc's FV function, which computes the future value of an investment, to find out. First, use the Format Global Width command to increase the default column width to 15, and execute the Format Global User-defined Number 3 command. Enter **FV(2000,8%,30)** into any cell. The first number inside the parentheses is the annual payment, the second number is the annual interest rate, and the third number is the number of years. The worksheet cell displays the computed result of the formula. To realize the advantages of compounded interest, compare this result to $60,000, which would be the value of $2000 saved for 30 years without any interest. Use the **F2** key to edit the values and experiment with the formula. For example, try only $1000 per year and an interest rate of 7%.

## Projects

1. Use SuperCalc to create a worksheet that lists your major expenditures for the past 12 months. Include items like rent, room and board, or mortgage payments; tuition; power bills; telephone bills; health, automobile, and property insurance; travel expenses; credit card purchases; and so on. Be sure to compute both the row and column totals. Try to use the Copy command to reduce repetitive typing. Use appropriate labels and numeric formatting to improve the clarity and appearance of your worksheet.

2. Balancing your checkbook is fairly easy if you use the form many banks print on the back of your monthly statement. Use SuperCalc to create a template that replicates the following form in a worksheet, so that you can get the computer to help you balance your checkbook. Remember that a template is simply a worksheet that has all the labels and formulas, but some cells are left empty for you to fill in values later.

CHECKS OUTSTANDING
(written but not yet
shown on this statement)

| Check Number | Amount |
|---|---|
| | |
| | |
| | |
| | |
| | |
| Total | |

ACCOUNT BALANCE.......... $________
(shown this statement)

ADD DEPOSITS ..................... $________
(made but not
yet shown on
this statement)

TOTAL..................................... $________

SUBTRACT
---> OUTSTANDING CHECKS.... $________

BALANCE .............................. $________
(should agree with
your checkbook)

3. Use SuperCalc to create a loan payment worksheet similar to the one we did in Figure 8.15 of Chapter 8. Remember that the PMT function computes the monthly payment on a loan given the amount of the loan (principal), monthly

interest rate, and term in months. Note that the PMT function works slightly differently in SuperCalc than it does in Microsoft Excel, which we used for the worksheet in Figure 8.15. For example, if the principal is $8500, the annual interest rate is 12% (1% per month), and the term is 48 months, the SuperCalc formula that computes the monthly payment is PMT(8500,0.01,48). In your worksheet, construct the formula to use cell references instead of actual numbers so that you can more easily see the results of changing the values of the principal, interest rate, and term.

4. Use SuperCalc to generate a table of squares and square roots of the whole numbers from 1 to 25. List each number in column A, its square in column B, and its square root in column C. Use appropriate labels for column headings, and be sure to use the Copy command wherever you can.

# Appendix E

## Word Processing Details: WordPerfect 5.0

### In This Appendix

## PREVIEW

WordPerfect is the leader in microcomputer word processing software. Since its introduction in October 1982, the package has generally received high praise from both reviewers and users. WordPerfect Corporation has significantly enhanced its product with every new release. Although WordPerfect is considered one of the most feature-laden word processing packages on the market, it is also known for its simple, well-designed user interface.

After studying this chapter, you will understand

- how to start WordPerfect.
- how to create a new document.
- how to edit a new or existing document.
- how to format characters, lines, and pages.
- how to save and print a document.
- how to manage document files.
- how to use some additional features included in WordPerfect.

## WORKING WITH WordPerfect

*Powerful word processing package*

In this appendix, we take a closer look at WordPerfect 5.0, a powerful word processing package made by WordPerfect Corporation for IBM and IBM-compatible microcomputers.

Like many powerful application packages, WordPerfect must first be installed on your system before you can use the program. If your computer has a hard disk, this process typically involves creating a subdirectory on the hard disk, copying files from the original diskettes to this subdirectory, and then running the program to tell it what kind of printer you have. For the examples in this appendix, WordPerfect 5.0 has been installed on a hard disk in a subdirectory named WP5.

Once WordPerfect has been installed, running it is easy. First, you change to the WP5 subdirectory by typing **CD C:\WP5** and pressing the **Enter** key. To start WordPerfect, you then type **WP** and press the **Enter** key. The copyright notice shown in Figure E.1 then appears on the screen for a few moments.

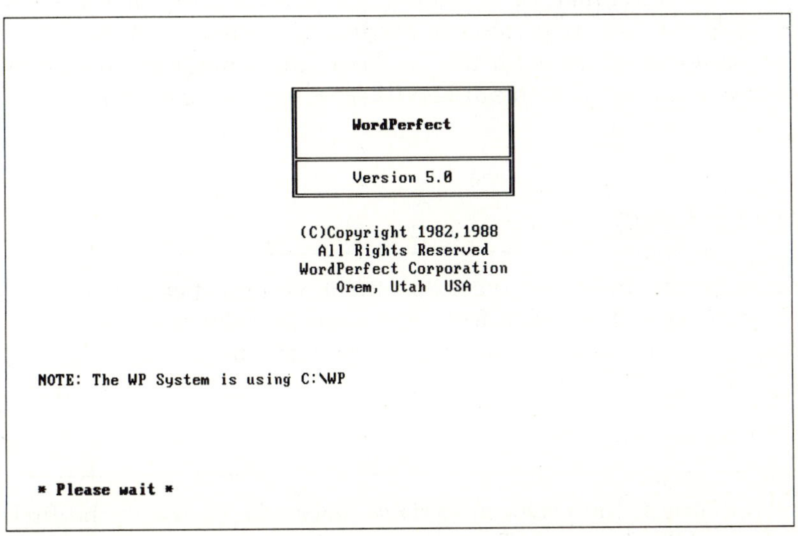


**Figure E.1 WordPerfect Copyright Screen**
This screen appears for a moment after you start WordPerfect.

*WordPerfect's clean screen*

After the copyright notice disappears, WordPerfect displays the almost empty screen shown in Figure E.2. The cursor, which marks your current position, initially appears in the upper left corner of the screen. The *status line*, shown at the bottom of the screen, displays messages and warnings from WordPerfect. Right now, the status line indicates that you are working on document one (of a possible two) and that your position within the document is one inch from the left edge and one inch from the top edge of page one. WordPerfect already has default margins, tab stops, and line spacing set up. All you have to do is type.

**Figure E.2 Editing Screen**
WordPerfect's initial editing screen is almost blank, with only a brief status line indicating your current document and cursor position.

Most WordPerfect commands and menus, as we will be discussing throughout this appendix, are invoked by pressing a function key, either by itself, or along with a Shift, Control, or Alternate key. For example, to quit WordPerfect and return to DOS, you press **F7**, which the software and documentation refer to as the Exit key. When you purchase the software package, you get a *keyboard template* that lists the most common WordPerfect commands. This plastic guide fits over or near the function keys on the keyboard and is invaluable for beginning users. Although a keyboard template is not included with this textbook, the more comprehensive Command Summary near the end of this appendix serves the same purpose.

## CREATING DOCUMENTS

*A sample letter*

Before you can edit, format, print, or save a document, you must create it. Let's create a sample document with WordPerfect. This particular document will be a letter from the secretary of a condominium association to the unit owners.

### Typing Text

*Automatic word wrap*

After you start WordPerfect, the program initially places the cursor in the first column of the first line of the first page. To create a new document, you simply type the words and punctuation. WordPerfect has automatic word wrap, so that whenever you type a word that extends into the right margin, WordPerfect moves that word down to the next line. This is known as a **soft return**. If you explicitly want to begin a new line or start a new paragraph, just press the **Enter** key, which inserts a **hard return** into your document. Figure E.3 shows the screen after some of the text of the letter has been typed.

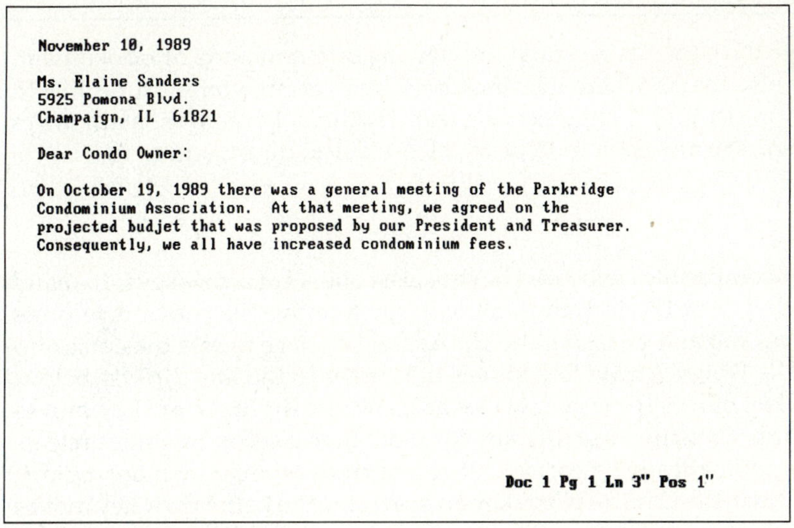
```
November 10, 1989

Ms. Elaine Sanders
5925 Pomona Blvd.
Champaign, IL  61821

Dear Condo Owner:

On October 19, 1989 there was a general meeting of the Parkridge
Condominium Association.  At that meeting, we agreed on the
projected budjet that was proposed by our President and Treasurer.
Consequently, we all have increased condominium fees.

                                       Doc 1 Pg 1 Ln 3" Pos 1"
```

**Figure E.3 Editing Screen with LETTER.DOC**
Some of the text of the LETTER.DOC document has been entered.

## Insight

### What is the Secret to WordPerfect's Success?

Even though you've read and reread the manual, pressed every key combination you can think of, and asked all your friends, your new word processing software is laughing at you. You haven't even managed to set it up, much less write your term paper. What do you do now?

WordPerfect Corporation, maker of WordPerfect word processing software, has an answer: lifetime, toll-free support for everyone who buys its products. The company has a fleet of support operators on the payroll who answer phoned-in questions Monday through Friday from 7 a.m. to 6 p.m. and Saturday from 8 a.m. to noon, Mountain Standard Time. The monthly telephone tab for this service tops $300,000.

"It's truly unlimited support," says Stan Mackay, head of WordPerfect's support group. "We don't even ask for user numbers. We want to help them, unhassled."

Each support worker specializes in either installation; features; printers; the company's other software, including DataPerfect, Library, and PlanPerfect; the Amiga and Atari versions; the Apple Macintosh version; or general questions. Callers hear three levels of recordings, and the goal is to answer the phone in two minutes and never to let anyone languish on hold for more than 45 minutes. That's not exactly lightning fast, but apparently OK to the people who make the 80,000 calls that come in every month.

Of course, no system is perfect. When WordPerfect 5.0 and WordPerfect for the Macintosh were released within days of one another, so many people called in that all toll-free lines into Utah were knocked out, disabling the telemarketing centers for American Express, Delta Air Lines, and others.

This extensive customer support is a major reason for the astonishing success of the Orem, Utah-based company. Other reasons are its marketing savvy and, as is often the case with software stars, a measure of good timing.

Sources:
Christine Strehlo, "What's So Special About WordPerfect?" *Personal Computing*, March, 1988, pp. 100-116.

Daniel J. Rosenbaum, "Evolutionary Strategy Pays Off for WordPerfect," *PC World*, December, 1988, pp. 82-86.

## EDITING DOCUMENTS

*Viewing and changing files*

To edit a document, you look at existing text and make changes if necessary. WordPerfect, like all word processing software, provides many ways to examine and modify documents. Let's look at the WordPerfect editing process more closely.

### Moving the Cursor

*Going places*

Learning to move the cursor is essential for viewing different parts of a document. Since the cursor also marks where modifications are to occur, you must be able to move the cursor precisely to change existing text. Fortunately, there are many ways to move the cursor, the most common of which are quick, direct, and easy.

#### Arrow Keys

*Up, down, left, and right*

All IBM and IBM-compatible keyboards have at least one set of arrow keys. In many programs, including WordPerfect, the simplest way to move the cursor is to press an arrow key. Pressing and releasing the **Up Arrow** key once moves the cursor up one line, while the **Down Arrow** key moves the cursor to the line directly below. The **Left Arrow** key moves the cursor backward, and the **Right Arrow** key moves the cursor forward. Pressing an arrow key for more than a second without releasing it causes it to automatically repeat, so that you can move the cursor more rapidly. Finally, holding down the **Control (Ctrl)** key and pressing the **Left Arrow** key moves the cursor to the beginning of the word to the left. Similarly, holding down the **Control** key and pressing the **Right Arrow** key moves the cursor to the beginning of the word to the immediate right.

#### Scrolling and Paging

*Moving within long documents*

Most documents are too long to fit completely on the display at once. Scrolling and paging commands let you change the part of your document displayed on the screen. One simple way to scroll the screen is to press the **Up Arrow** or **Down Arrow** key even after the cursor reaches the top or bottom edge of the text area. If there are more lines above or below, WordPerfect scrolls the screen and moves the cursor to the next line.

The **Grey Plus (+)** and **Grey Minus (-)** keys on the numeric keypad are used to move the cursor an entire screen at a time. Pressing the **Grey Minus** key moves the cursor up to the first line of the current screen, and pressing it again moves the cursor up through the previous screen. Similarly, pressing the **Grey Plus** key moves the cursor down to the last line of the current screen, and pressing it again moves the cursor down through the next screen.

Paging is like scrolling an entire page at a time. If your document has several pages, pressing the **Page Up** key moves the cursor to the first line of the previous page, and pressing the **Page Down** key moves the cursor to the first line of the next page.

#### End and Home

*More ways to move the cursor*

End and Home are the two other cursor movement keys on all IBM-compatible keyboards. In WordPerfect, pressing **End** moves the cursor to the end of the current line.

**Home** is pressed and released followed by other keypresses to perform various cursor movements. For example, you press **Home** and then press **Right Arrow** to move the cursor to the right edge of the current screen. **Home** followed by **Left Arrow** moves the cursor to the left edge of the current screen. Pressing and releasing **Home** twice and then pressing **Up Arrow** moves the cursor to the beginning of the document, and **Home** twice followed by **Down Arrow** moves the cursor to the end of the document.

### The Go To Command

*Jump to a particular page*

Another sequence of keypresses lets you move to a particular page number in a WordPerfect document. Hold down the **Control** key and press the **Home** key, and WordPerfect will prompt you with "Go to." Then type the page number to which you want to go and press **Enter**. WordPerfect moves the cursor to the top of that page.

## Inserting and Overwriting

*Adding new text*

WordPerfect, like most word processing software, has two basic typing modes: insert and overwrite. By default, WordPerfect has insert mode turned on when you open a document. This means that to insert new material into a document, you just move the cursor to the location where you want the insertion to occur, then simply type. For example, you can move the cursor just past the end of the last sentence of the document in Figure E.3 and insert the rest of the letter (see Figure E.4). The new characters you type push any existing characters to the right.

```
November 10, 1989

Ms. Elaine Sanders
5925 Pomona Blvd.
Champaign, IL  61821

Dear Condo Owner:

On October 19, 1989 there was a general meeting of the Parkridge
Condominium Association.  At that meeting, we agreed on the
projected budjet that was proposed by our President and Treasurer.
Consequently, we all have increased condominium fees.  The monthly
fee for your unit is now $69.53.  If you have not already sent this
amount for the month of November, we would appreciate it if you
could send the balance as soon as possible.

Sincerely,

David Franklin
Secretary



                                     Doc 1 Pg 1 Ln 4.33" Pos 1"
```

**Figure E.4 Inserting the Rest of the Letter**
This screen shows the completed LETTER.DOC document.

To switch typing modes, you simply press the **Insert** key. If insert mode is already on, WordPerfect changes to overwrite mode; if overwrite mode is on, pressing the **Insert** key switches back to insert mode. When you change to overwrite mode, WordPerfect displays the word *Typeover* in the status line. When overwrite mode is turned on, characters you type replace existing characters in the same positions. Although overwrite mode is handy for correcting small mistakes, insert mode is necessary for adding new material to existing text.

## Deleting Text

*Erasing characters, words, and lines*

One of the most common editing operations is deleting text. WordPerfect has commands for erasing individual characters, words, and lines. As with most word processing packages, the **Backspace** key erases the character to the left of the cursor, and the **Delete** key erases the character at the current cursor position.

WordPerfect also makes it easy to erase an entire word or line of text. To delete a word, place the cursor on the first character in the word and press **Ctrl-Backspace**. To delete a line, place the cursor at the beginning of the line and press **Ctrl-End**. WordPerfect has several other commands for deleting text, but Backspace, Delete, Ctrl-Backspace, and Ctrl-End are the ones most frequently used.

## Working with Blocks of Text

*Sections of text*

In addition to individual characters, words, and lines, most word processing packages let you specify and manipulate blocks of text. In WordPerfect, a **block** is a piece of text that can be of any size—from a single character to an entire document. Once a block is designated, or marked, it can be deleted, copied, or moved.

### Marking a Block

*Highlighting a section of text*

The first step in working with a block of text is to mark where it begins and ends. To mark the beginning of a block, you move the cursor to the first character in that block, hold down the **Alternate** key, and then press the **F4** function key. The message "Block on" flashes on and off in the status line. Then you move the cursor to the last character to be included in the block. As the cursor moves, the text in the block changes to reverse video (dark characters against a light background, as in Figure E.5). You can increase or reduce the size of the marked block by simply moving the cursor.

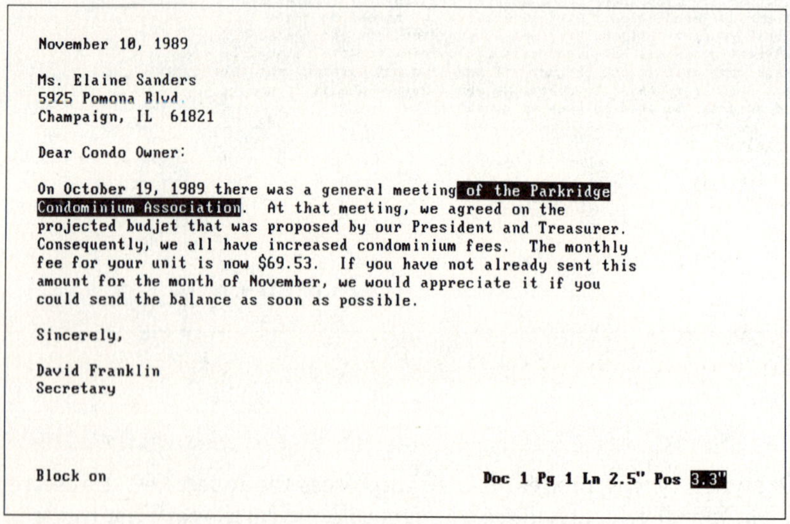

November 10, 1989

Ms. Elaine Sanders
5925 Pomona Blvd
Champaign, IL 61821

Dear Condo Owner:

On October 19, 1989 there was a general meeting of the Parkridge Condominium Association. At that meeting, we agreed on the projected budjet that was proposed by our President and Treasurer. Consequently, we all have increased condominium fees. The monthly fee for your unit is now $69.53. If you have not already sent this amount for the month of November, we would appreciate it if you could send the balance as soon as possible.

Sincerely,

David Franklin
Secretary

Block on Doc 1 Pg 1 Ln 2.5" Pos 3.3"

**Figure E.5 Marked Block**
This screen shows a marked block on the screen in reverse video.

## Deleting a Block

*Removing a section of text*

Using a block is a handy way to delete several words, several lines, or some other irregular portion of text. Examine Figure E.4 again. Suppose that you want to delete the phrase *of the Parkridge Condominium Association* from the end of the first sentence. Simply mark the phrase as a block and press the **Delete** key. WordPerfect will then ask

```
Delete block? (Y/N) No
```

If you are sure you want to delete the marked block, you type **Y** for yes.

## Moving or Copying a Block

*Relocating or duplicating a section of text*

WordPerfect's Move command lets you cut a section of text from one place and paste it into another place. First you mark the block to be moved and then press **Ctrl-F4**. Figure E.6(a) shows the Move menu that WordPerfect displays at the bottom of the screen. To move the marked block, select the first option by typing **1**. Another menu appears, shown in Figure E.6(b). Type **1** again, then move the cursor to the place where you want the block to go and press **Enter**. The block is deleted from its original position and inserted in the new location.

To copy a block, you type **2** to select the Copy option from the second menu.

**Figure E.6 Moving a Block**

(a) The Move menu. (b) The Move Block submenu.

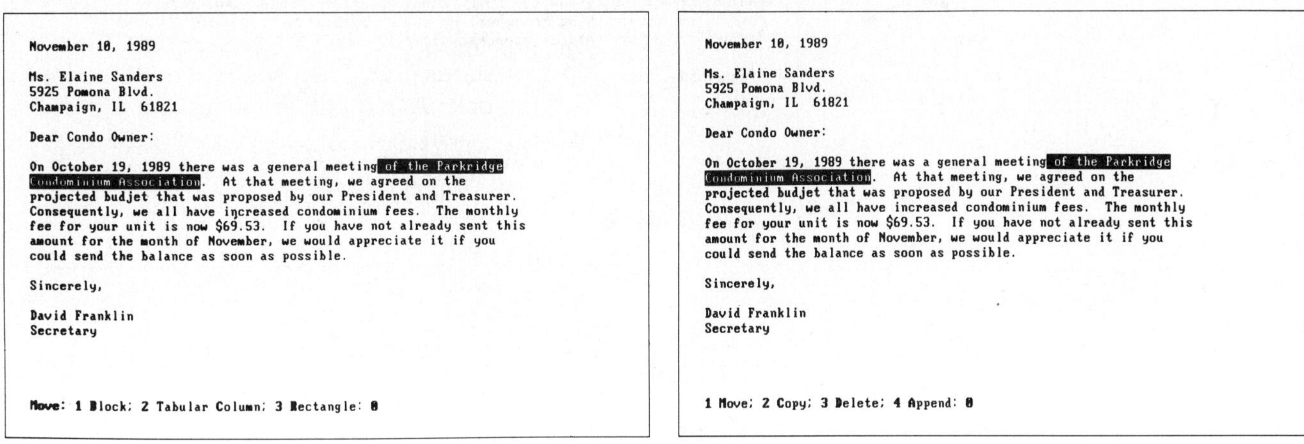

(a)

November 10, 1989

Ms. Elaine Sanders
5925 Pomona Blvd.
Champaign, IL 61821

Dear Condo Owner:

On October 19, 1989 there was a general meeting of the Parkridge Condominium Association. At that meeting, we agreed on the projected budjet that was proposed by our President and Treasurer. Consequently, we all have increased condominium fees. The monthly fee for your unit is now $69.53. If you have not already sent this amount for the month of November, we would appreciate it if you could send the balance as soon as possible.

Sincerely,

David Franklin
Secretary

Move: 1 Block; 2 Tabular Column; 3 Rectangle: 0

(b)

November 10, 1989

Ms. Elaine Sanders
5925 Pomona Blvd.
Champaign, IL 61821

Dear Condo Owner:

On October 19, 1989 there was a general meeting of the Parkridge Condominium Association. At that meeting, we agreed on the projected budjet that was proposed by our President and Treasurer. Consequently, we all have increased condominium fees. The monthly fee for your unit is now $69.53. If you have not already sent this amount for the month of November, we would appreciate it if you could send the balance as soon as possible.

Sincerely,

David Franklin
Secretary

1 Move; 2 Copy; 3 Delete; 4 Append: 0

## Searching and Replacing

*Finding and substituting text*

The letter to condominium owners we've been using as an example document is quite short; it wouldn't be difficult to find and fix an error consistent throughout the entire document. With longer documents, however, manually searching and replacing can be tedious. WordPerfect, like most word processing packages, can automatically seek out and substitute text.

Sometimes you don't want to replace text, but just want to see where a certain word or phrase is mentioned. WordPerfect's Search command can quickly locate any piece of text. Suppose that you want to find every occurrence of the word *President* in a document. First you move the cursor to the beginning of the document. Then you press the **F2** function key, type **President**, and press **F2** again. WordPerfect advances the cursor to the next location of the word *President*. If it can't find the word, WordPerfect displays "* Not Found *" in the status line.

If the word you want to find is repeated throughout the document, you can tell WordPerfect to find the next occurrence, without having to redo the Search command and retype the word. Pressing **F2** twice automatically repeats the previous search and advances the cursor to the next location of the word.

To search and replace, you use a different command. Let's say that you want to change *President* to *Director*. First, press **Alt-F2** to execute the Replace command. Figure E.7 shows the message that appears in the status line. Type **Y** for yes if you want to confirm or cancel each replacement. If you type **N** or just press **Enter**, WordPerfect will automatically replace every occurrence of the text without confirmation. (This is known as a *global search and replace.*) Next, you type the text you want to replace (in this case, **President**) and press **F2**, and then type its replacement (**Director**) and press **F2** again. WordPerfect executes the replace operation throughout the entire document, stopping for confirmation if you told it to do so.

**Figure E.7 Global Search and Replace**
WordPerfect asks you to confirm the replace operation.

```
November 10, 1989

Ms. Elaine Sanders
5925 Pomona Blvd.
Champaign, IL  61821

Dear Condo Owner:

On October 19, 1989 there was a general meeting of the Parkridge
Condominium Association.  At that meeting, we agreed on the
projected budjet that was proposed by our President and Treasurer.
Consequently, we all have increased condominium fees.  The monthly
fee for your unit is now $69.53.  If you have not already sent this
amount for the month of November, we would appreciate it if you
could send the balance as soon as possible.

Sincerely,

David Franklin
Secretary


w/Confirm? (Y/N) No
```

## Canceling Mistakes

*Restoring deletions*

At one time or another, everyone who uses a word processing package mistakenly initiates some command or operation, but wishes to cancel it before it reaches completion. WordPerfect has a Cancel command that can stop an executing command or restore accidentally erased text. This command, which is invoked by pressing the **F1** function key, can do the following:

- Return from a WordPerfect menu or cancel your response to a WordPerfect prompt before the response is final.
- Turn off the Block feature.
- Restore any of the three most recently deleted text items.

Whenever you erase text, be it a single character or an entire block, WordPerfect temporarily stores this text in a special area of memory. Up to three deletions are saved, allowing you to reverse an erroneous delete command. For example, suppose you accidentally deleted the phrase *of the Parkridge Condominium Association*, and you now want to retrieve this text. First, move the cursor to the place where you want to insert the restored text. Press **F1** to display WordPerfect's Undelete menu (see Figure E.8). Finally, type **1** to restore the highlighted text (which is the most recently deleted item) at the current cursor location. The deleted text is then reinstated. To restore a previously deleted item, you would type **2** to select Show Previous Deletion, until the text you want to restore is displayed.

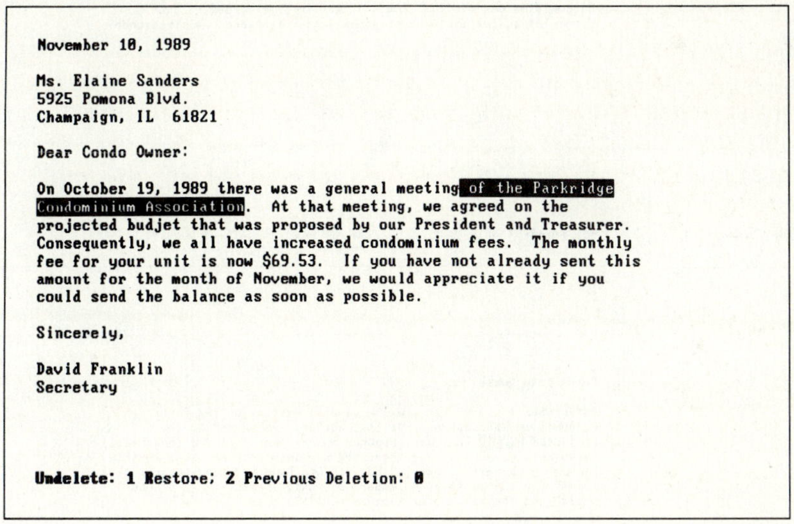
November 18, 1989

Ms. Elaine Sanders
5925 Pomona Blvd.
Champaign, IL 61821

Dear Condo Owner:

On October 19, 1989 there was a general meeting of the Parkridge Condominium Association. At that meeting, we agreed on the projected budjet that was proposed by our President and Treasurer. Consequently, we all have increased condominium fees. The monthly fee for your unit is now $69.53. If you have not already sent this amount for the month of November, we would appreciate it if you could send the balance as soon as possible.

Sincerely,

David Franklin
Secretary

Undelete: 1 Restore; 2 Previous Deletion: 0

**Figure E.8 Canceling Mistakes**
Pressing F1 after a deletion activates WordPerfect's Undelete menu.

## Checking Spelling

*Proofreading*

WordPerfect, like many word processing packages, includes a dictionary that can help you find and correct misspellings and typographical errors. You can check the spelling of a word, block, page, or entire document. As an example, let's check the spelling of the letter you see in Figure E.4. First, be sure the cursor is at the beginning of the document. Then, press **Ctrl-F2** to display the Speller menu (see Figure E.9(a)), and type **3** to check the entire document. When it finds a word it doesn't recognize, WordPerfect highlights the word, suggests possible replacements, and displays the Not Found menu at the bottom of the screen.

As you can see from Figure E.9(b), the first unknown word in this letter is *Pomona*. This word isn't misspelled; it's a proper name not found in the dictionary. WordPerfect has no suggestions on what this word might be. At this point you can tell WordPerfect to skip the word just once, skip it permanently, or put it into your personal supplementary dictionary. The personal supplementary dictionary feature allows you to compile your own list of names or technical terms not normally found in ordinary dictionaries. Any word you add to your personal dictionary will be recognized in the future and not singled out as a potential misspelling. If you choose not to add *Pomona* to your personal dictionary, type **2** to tell WordPerfect to skip this word and to continue checking the rest of the words. Similarly, WordPerfect will go on to question the word *Parkridge*. Since this word is correct, just not in the dictionary, press **2** again to tell WordPerfect to skip it too. Finally, WordPerfect will come to the word *budjet*. This word really is misspelled, and WordPerfect suggests two possible corrections (see Figure E.9(c)). *Budget* is the correct choice. To automatically replace an error with a suggested correction, simply type the letter of the correction. In this case *budget* is preceded by A, so type **A** to have WordPerfect replace *budjet* with *budget*. WordPerfect then checks the rest of the words in the letter, tells you that 94 words were counted, and asks you to press any key to continue.

(a)

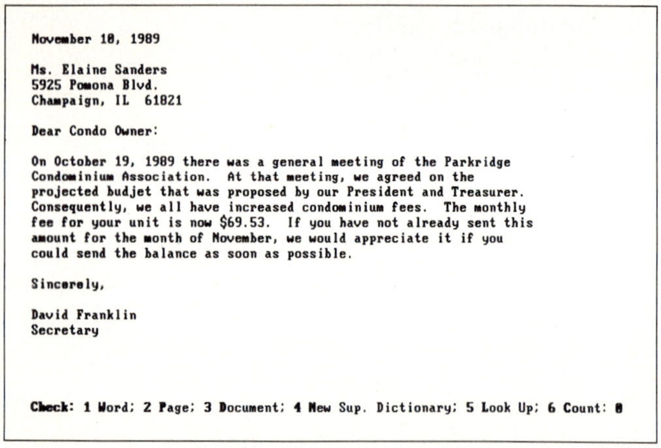


(b)

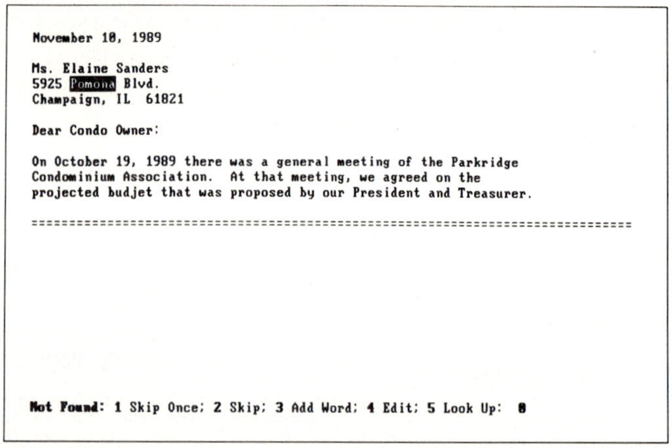


**Figure E.9 Checking Spelling**

(a) The Speller menu.

(b) Pomona is the first term questioned by the WordPerfect spelling checker.

(c) The word *budjet* really is misspelled and WordPerfect suggests two possible corrections.

(c)

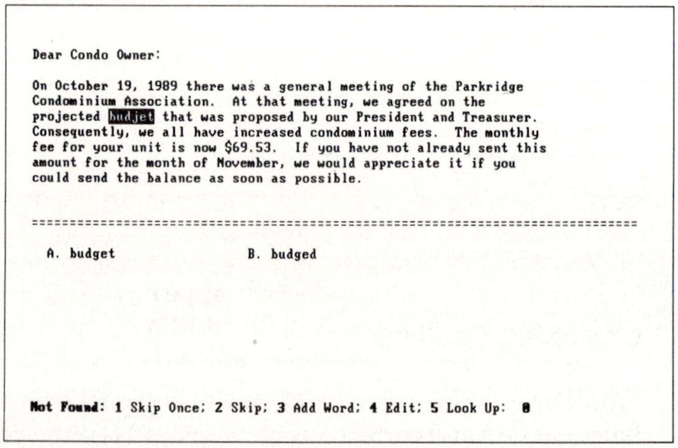


## FORMATTING DOCUMENTS

*Specifying document appearance*

Formatting a document means specifying how it will look when it is eventually printed. True what-you-see-is-what-you-get (WYSIWYG) word processing software has an exact correspondence between the screen and the printed page. WordPerfect is not a WYSIWYG word processing package; some formatting specifications show up on the display screen, but others only become evident when the document is viewed with the View Document feature (which we will discuss later in this appendix) or is committed to paper. WordPerfect has several levels of formatting, including character, line, and page levels.

### Character Formatting

*Boldface and underlining*

WordPerfect offers several options that let you change the appearance of characters in a document. For example, let's say that you want to underline the word *increased* in the condominium association letter. First you mark this word as a block with **Alt-F4** and then press **F8** to turn on underlining. The marked text is underlined, highlighted, or presented on the screen in a different color, depending on the type of monitor you have (see Figure E.10). When the document is printed, however, the word *increased* will be underlined.

```
November 10, 1989

Ms. Elaine Sanders
5925 Pomona Blvd.
Champaign, IL  61821

Dear Condo Owner:

On October 19, 1989 there was a general meeting of the Parkridge
Condominium Association.  At that meeting, we agreed on the
projected budget that was proposed by our President and Treasurer.
Consequently, we all have increased condominium fees.  The monthly
fee for your unit is now $69.53.  If you have not already sent this
amount for the month of November, we would appreciate it if you
could send the balance as soon as possible.

Sincerely,

David Franklin
Secretary


                                        Doc 1 Pg 1 Ln 2.83" Pos 4.5"
```

**Figure E.10 Underlining**
The word *increased* has been underlined by marking it as a block and then pressing F8.

To type new underlined text, first press **F8** to turn on underlining, type the text, and then press **F8** again to turn off underlining. Boldface works similarly, except you press the F6 key instead of the F8 key.

Boldface and underlining are the two most commonly used character formats, but WordPerfect also provides other options. Press **Ctrl-F8** to activate the Font menu and then type **2** to select the appearance option. The menu shown in Figure E.11 will appear on the screen. In addition to boldface and underlining, this menu also gives you double underline, italics, outline, shadow, small capitals, redline, and strikeout character formats.

```
November 10, 1989

Ms. Elaine Sanders
5925 Pomona Blvd.
Champaign, IL  61821

Dear Condo Owner:

On October 19, 1989 there was a general meeting of the Parkridge
Condominium Association.  At that meeting, we agreed on the
projected budget that was proposed by our President and Treasurer.
Consequently, we all have increased condominium fees.  The monthly
fee for your unit is now $69.53.  If you have not already sent this
amount for the month of November, we would appreciate it if you
could send the balance as soon as possible.

Sincerely,

David Franklin
Secretary


1 Bold 2 Undrln 3 Dbl Und 4 Italc 5 Outln 6 Shadw 7 Sm Cap 8 Redln 9 Stkout: 0
```

**Figure E.11 The Font Appearance Menu**
This menu shows the character formats available in WordPerfect.

## Line Formatting

*Controlling lines of text*

Like most word processing packages, WordPerfect has a number of features that control the appearance of lines, paragraphs, and other sections of text. The most common formatting operations allow you to change margins, set tab stops, turn justification on or off, turn hyphenation on or off, set line spacing, set line height, and center text.

### Margins

*Document edges*

WordPerfect initially sets both the left and right margins of a document at one inch from the edge of the paper. Although these margins will be adequate for most documents, you may need to change them for some documents. To set the left and right margins, first move the cursor to where you want the new margins to begin. Then press **Shift-F8** to display the Format menu, shown in Figure E.12(a). Type **1** to display the Line Format menu (see Figure E.12(b)) and then enter the new left and right margin measurements. Press **F7**, the WordPerfect Exit key, to return to the document. The new margins will be in effect in your document from that point forward, unless you change them again.

**Figure E.12 Setting Margins**

(a) The Format menu.

```
Format

     1 - Line
              Hyphenation                      Line Spacing
              Justification                    Margins Left/Right
              Line Height                      Tab Set
              Line Numbering                   Widow/Orphan Protection

     2 - Page
              Center Page (top to bottom)      New Page Number
              Force Odd/Even Page              Page Numbering
              Headers and Footers              Paper Size/Type
              Margins Top/Bottom               Suppress

     3 - Document
              Display Pitch                    Redline Method
              Initial Codes/Font               Summary

     4 - Other
              Advance                          Overstrike
              Conditional End of Page          Printer Functions
              Decimal Characters               Underline Spaces/Tabs
              Language

Selection: 0
```

(b) The Line Format submenu.

```
Format: Line

     1 - Hyphenation                         Off

     2 - Hyphenation Zone - Left             10%
                            Right            4%

     3 - Justification                       Yes

     4 - Line Height                         Auto

     5 - Line Numbering                      No

     6 - Line Spacing                        1

     7 - Margins - Left                      1"
                   Right                     1"

     8 - Tab Set                             0", every 0.5"

     9 - Widow/Orphan Protection             No


Selection: 0
```

### Tab Stops

*Using the Tab key*

Computer keyboards, just like typewriters, have at least one Tab key. When this key is pressed, the cursor advances immediately to some preset location. By default, WordPerfect initially sets tab stops at half-inch intervals. To move the cursor to the next tab stop, just press the **Tab** key. If insert mode is turned on, pressing the Tab key pushes any existing characters to the right; if overwrite mode is turned on, the Tab key just moves the cursor over existing text.

To change the current tab settings, press **Shift-F8** to activate the Format menu (see Figure E.12(a)), type **1** to select the Line Format menu (see Figure E.12(b)), and then type **8** to display the Tab Set menu (see Figure E.13). The dotted line at the bottom of the screen is a *ruler line* showing the current tab stops. Each L denotes a left-justified tab stop. You can use the Left Arrow and Right Arrow keys to move the cursor within the ruler line, and then delete existing tab stops with the Delete key. You can add a new tab stop at any position by typing one of the following characters:

*L* Inserts a left-justified tab stop, which aligns text along the left side at the tab stop.

*C* Inserts a centered tab stop, which centers text at the tab stop.

*R* Inserts a right-justified tab stop, which aligns text along the right side at the tab stop.

*D* Inserts a decimal tab stop, which aligns numbers by their decimal points at the tab stop.

If you like, you can also delete every existing tab stop in the ruler line by pressing Ctrl-End, and then insert all new tab stops. When you are finished setting tab stops, press **F7** twice to return to the document.

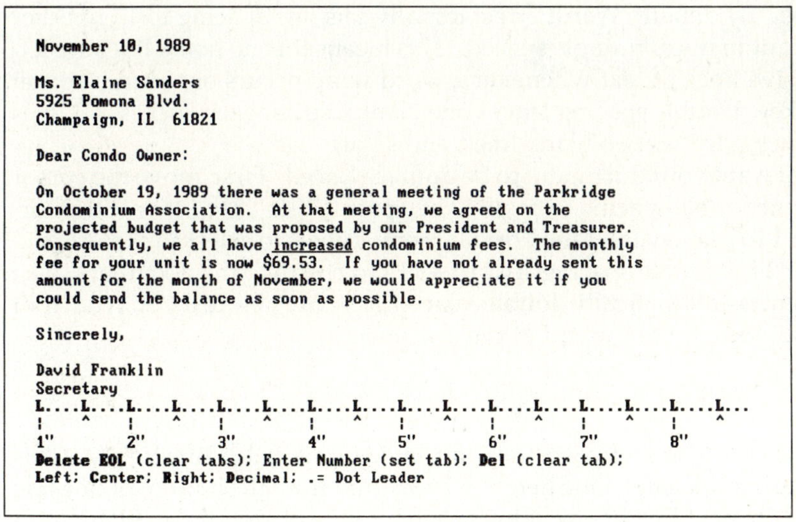

```
November 10, 1989

Ms. Elaine Sanders
5925 Pomona Blvd.
Champaign, IL  61821

Dear Condo Owner:

On October 19, 1989 there was a general meeting of the Parkridge
Condominium Association.  At that meeting, we agreed on the
projected budget that was proposed by our President and Treasurer.
Consequently, we all have increased condominium fees.  The monthly
fee for your unit is now $69.53.  If you have not already sent this
amount for the month of November, we would appreciate it if you
could send the balance as soon as possible.

Sincerely,

David Franklin
Secretary
L....L....L....L....L....L....L....L....L....L....L....L....L....L....L....L...
¦    ^    ¦    ^    ¦    ^    ¦    ^    ¦    ^    ¦    ^    ¦    ^    ¦    ^
1"        2"        3"        4"        5"        6"        7"        8"
Delete EOL (clear tabs); Enter Number (set tab); Del (clear tab);
Left; Center; Right; Decimal; .= Dot Leader
```

**Figure E.13 Setting Tab Stops**

The Tab Set menu displays the current ruler line and lets you change the tab stops.

## Justification

*Turning justification off or on*

When a document is justified, text is aligned exactly to both the left and right margins. If necessary, spaces are automatically inserted here and there to give the text a block look. By default, WordPerfect initially has the justification feature turned on, but this does not appear on the screen. Justification only becomes evident when the document is examined with the View Document feature (which we will discuss later in this appendix) or when it is printed. Justified text can look professionally typeset when it is produced by a printer that can do proportional spacing. As we said in Chapter 6, proportional spacing allots different amounts of space for different characters. The combination of justification and proportional spacing produces text that looks like the typeset material in this book.

With printers that cannot do proportional spacing, it's often better to turn off justification. The resulting text will have a ragged right margin similar to that of typewritten text. To turn off justification, move the cursor to the desired location, press **Shift-F8** to activate the Format menu, type **1** to display the Line Format menu, type **3** to select the Justification option, type **N** to turn it off, and press **F7** to return to the document. Justification will then be turned off from the cursor position to the end of the document.

## Hyphenation

*Turning hyphenation on or off*

WordPerfect, like many word processing packages, can automatically hyphenate words to more evenly fill out lines of text. The hyphenation feature, however, is initially turned off by default. To turn on automatic hyphenation, move the cursor to the place where you want hyphenation to begin, press **Shift-F8** to activate the Format menu, type **1** to display the Line Format menu, type **1** to select the Hyphenation option, type **3** to select the Automatic option, and press **F7** to return to the document.

## Line Spacing

*Blank lines between lines of text*

Most typewriters have a lever that controls the space that is left between lines when you press the carriage return. Word processing packages give you similar control over line spacing. By default, WordPerfect initially sets line spacing to 1. In other words, lines are automatically single spaced. This means that no blank lines are left between successive lines of text whenever a word wrap occurs or whenever you press the Enter key. Double spacing leaves one blank line between successive lines of text, triple spacing leaves two blank lines, and so on.

Suppose you want your document to be double-spaced. First, move the cursor to where you want double spacing to begin. Then press **Shift-F8** to activate the Format menu, type **1** to display the Line Format menu, type **6** to select the Line Spacing option, enter **2** for double spacing, and press **F7** to return to the document. The existing document is automatically double-spaced, as is any new text you type from the current cursor location to the end of the document.

## Line Height

*Distance between lines of text*

In WordPerfect, the distance between lines of printed text is called **line height**. This is not the same as line spacing. Line height is measured from the bottom of one line to the bottom of the next line below. Line spacing refers to how many blank lines are left between successive lines of text. In practice, line height is seldom changed. WordPerfect's default line height yields 6 lines of text per vertical inch, which is the standard line height of most typewriters. To change line height, you press **Shift-F8** to activate the Format menu, type **1** to display the Line Format menu, type **4** to select the Line Height option, type **2** to select the Fixed option, enter a new line height measurement, and press **F7** to return to the document.

## Centering Text

*Placing text in the center*

Many documents require certain headings or other text to be centered between the left and right margins. To do this manually, you have to count the number of characters in the heading, subtract it from the line length, divide the result by two, and then press the space bar that many times before typing the heading. Another method is to go to the center of the line and backspace once for every two characters in the heading. Fortunately, word processing packages generally let you avoid all this and automatically center text.

To center a new line of text with WordPerfect, move the cursor to the left margin, press **Shift-F6** to move the cursor to the center of the line, type the text, and press **Enter**. You can also center an existing line of text by moving the cursor to the beginning of the line, pressing **Shift-F6**, and then pressing the **Down Arrow** key. The line must end with a hard return, however, to be centered correctly.

## Page Formatting

*Laying out pages*

Page formatting features affect entire pages of text. WordPerfect has several commands that let you specify how pages are laid out. Some of these commands control page size, top and bottom margins, page breaks, page numbering, and headers and footers.

### Paper Size and Type

*What kind of paper?*

Standard letter-size paper is 8 1/2 inches wide and 11 inches long. Given a standard line height of 6 lines per inch, the number of lines on letter-size paper is 6 times 11, or 66. WordPerfect's default paper size is 8 1/2 by 11 inches, but this can be changed: Press **Shift-F8** to activate the Format menu, type **2** to display the Page Format menu (see Figure E.14(a)), type **8** to display the Paper Size menu (see Figure E.14(b)), select a paper size, and press **F7**. Then the Paper Type menu appears, as shown in Figure E.14(c). Select a paper type and press **F7** twice to return to the document.

(a)

```
Format: Page

     1 - Center Page (top to bottom)    No

     2 - Force Odd/Even Page

     3 - Headers

     4 - Footers

     5 - Margins - Top                  1"
                   Bottom               1"

     6 - New Page Number                1
           (example: 3 or iii)

     7 - Page Numbering                 No page numbering

     8 - Paper Size                     8.5" x 11"
               Type                     Standard

     9 - Suppress (this page only)

Selection: 8
```

(b)

```
Format: Paper Size

     1 - Standard                  (8.5" x 11")

     2 - Standard Landscape        (11" x 8.5")

     3 - Legal                     (8.5" x 14")

     4 - Legal Landscape           (14" x 8.5")

     5 - Envelope                  (9.5" x 4")

     6 - Half Sheet                (5.5" x 8.5")

     7 - US Government             (8" x 11")

     8 - A4                        (210mm x 297mm)

     9 - A4 Landscape              (297mm x 210mm)

     0 - Other

Selection: 1
```

(c)

```
Format: Paper Type

     1 - Standard

     2 - Bond

     3 - Letterhead

     4 - Labels

     5 - Envelope

     6 - Transparency

     7 - Cardstock

     8 - Other

Selection: 1
```

**Figure E.14 Setting the Paper Size and Type**
(a) The Page Format menu.
(b) The Paper Size menu.
(c) The Paper Type menu.

## Top and Bottom Margins

*Leaving space top and bottom*

Most documents are printed with some blank space at the top and bottom of every page. By default, WordPerfect leaves one inch top and bottom margins. To change these settings, press **Shift-F8** to activate the Format menu, type **2** to display the Page Format menu, and type **5** to select the Margins, Top and Bottom option. Then enter the new top and bottom margin measurements and press **F7** to return to the document.

## Page Breaks

*Starting a new page*

The actual number of lines of text printed on a page depends on the factors we've been discussing. For example, WordPerfect's default page format has a line height of 1/6th of an inch, a page length of 11 inches, a top margin of 1 inch, and a bottom margin of 1 inch. That leaves 66 minus 12, or 54, as the number of lines of text actually printed on a page.

As you type text with WordPerfect, the word wrap feature automatically starts new lines. Similarly, assuming the default page-format settings are in effect, WordPerfect automatically starts a new page by inserting a soft page break after every 54 lines you type. A **soft page break** is a division between two pages automatically generated by the word processing software. It is symbolized on the screen by a horizontal line of dashes (see Figure E.15). This line is not actually printed on paper, it just shows you on the screen where a new page will begin.

**Figure E.15 Page Breaks**
WordPerfect's default settings generate an automatic page break into your document every 54 lines, but you can enter a hard page break by pressing **Ctrl-Enter.**

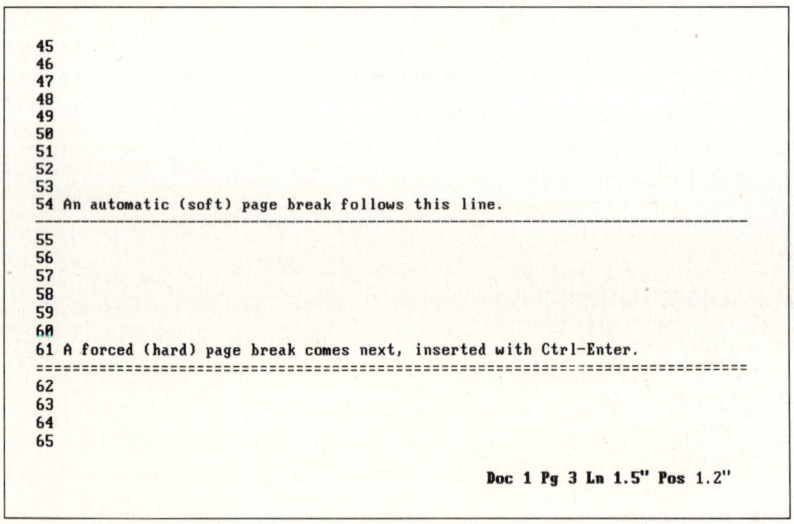


Although WordPerfect's automatic page break feature is nice for typing long sections of text, you may want to begin a new page at some point other than every 54 lines. In these cases a new page can be *forced* by pressing **Ctrl-Enter** to insert a **hard page break**. This is a division between two pages manually generated by the user. It is symbolized on the screen by a horizontal line of equal signs (see Figure E.15). You can begin a new page at any point within a document simply by pressing Ctrl-Enter. A hard page break can be removed from a document with the Delete or Backspace key.

## Page Numbering

*Controlling page numbers*

WordPerfect automatically keeps track of page numbers while you work on a document and displays the current page number that is preceded by the letters *Pg* in the status line. By default, however, WordPerfect does not print page numbers. To turn on printed page numbers, you must press **Shift-F8** to activate the Format menu, type **2** to display the Page Format menu, and type **7** to select the Page Numbering option. The Page Number Position menu then appears on your screen as shown in Figure E.16. Select a page numbering option and press **F7** to return to the document. For example, if you want a page number to appear in the top right corner of every page, you type **3** and then press **F7**.

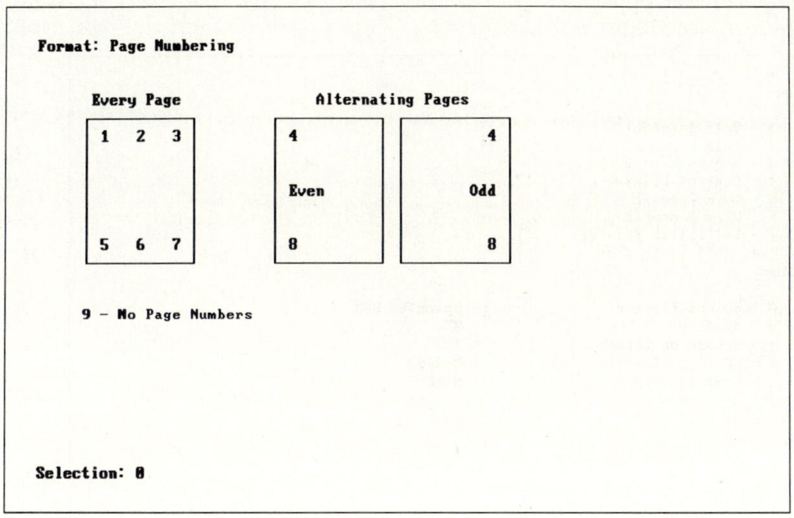


**Figure E.16 Page Numbering**
The Page Number Position menu lets you select where page numbers are to appear, or have page numbering shut off completely.

## Headers and Footers

*Text in the top and bottom margins*

In WordPerfect, a **header** is one or more lines of text printed in the top margin of every page A **footer** is like a header, except it is printed in the bottom margin of every page. You can have a header or footer printed at the top or bottom of every page, odd pages, or even pages. You can also create up to two headers (Header A and Header B) and two footers (Footer A and Footer B) in a document.

For example, suppose you want to print the header *The Great American Novel* at the top of every page. Move the cursor to the beginning of the document, press **Shift-F8** to activate the Format menu, type **2** to display the Page Format menu, and type **3** to select the Headers option. Then type **1** to define Header A, type **2** to print the header at the top of every page, type **The Great American Novel**, and press **F7**. The header will appear when the document is printed or examined with the View Document feature.

## SAVING AND PRINTING DOCUMENTS

*Storing your work and getting a hard copy*

With all you've learned about WordPerfect so far, you would have little trouble creating, editing, and formatting most documents. The next step, of course, is printing. Let's print the condominium association letter we've been using as an example.

Once the text is formatted, proofread, and corrected if necessary, it should be saved before it's printed. You can do this by pressing the **F10** function key. WordPerfect will ask for the name of the document to be saved and you should enter a valid DOS filename that describes your document, such as **LETTER.DOC**. Check your printer to make sure it's turned on and connected to your computer. Then call up the Print menu by pressing **Shift-F7** (see Figure E.17) and type **1** to print the entire document.

**Figure E.17 Printing**

The Print menu lets you specify how your document is to be printed.

```
Print

     1 - Full Document
     2 - Page
     3 - Document on Disk
     4 - Control Printer
     5 - Type Through
     6 - View Document
     7 - Initialize Printer

Options

     S - Select Printer                        Epson LQ 800
     B - Binding                               0"
     N - Number of Copies                      1
     G - Graphics Quality                      Medium
     T - Text Quality                          High


Selection: 0
```

## MANAGING DOCUMENTS

*Organizing files*

A document is almost always kept in a disk file even after it is printed. Consequently, document files tend to accumulate on disks. WordPerfect has several commands that let you maintain and organize your documents. These commands are available through the List Files menu, which is activated when you press the **F5** function key and then the **Enter** key to select the current directory (see Figure E.18). Besides showing you the files in your current directory, the List Files menu contains options that let you retrieve, delete, rename, and copy files, as well as change disk drive directories.

### Retrieving Files

*Loading existing documents*

One way to load an existing document is to type its name after the WP when you begin WordPerfect from DOS. For example, to start WordPerfect and edit the existing document LETTER.DOC, you could enter the following command at the DOS prompt:

**WP LETTER.DOC**

Another way to load an existing document is to retrieve it from within WordPerfect. Press **F5** and then **Enter** to activate the List Files menu, highlight the name of the desired file with the arrow keys, and type **1** to select the Retrieve option. The selected file is then loaded at the current cursor location. If the screen is not blank, WordPerfect will ask for confirmation before retrieving the selected file, and will push any existing text down to make room for the incoming file.

You can also retrieve an existing document file by pressing **Shift-F10** and then entering the document's name.

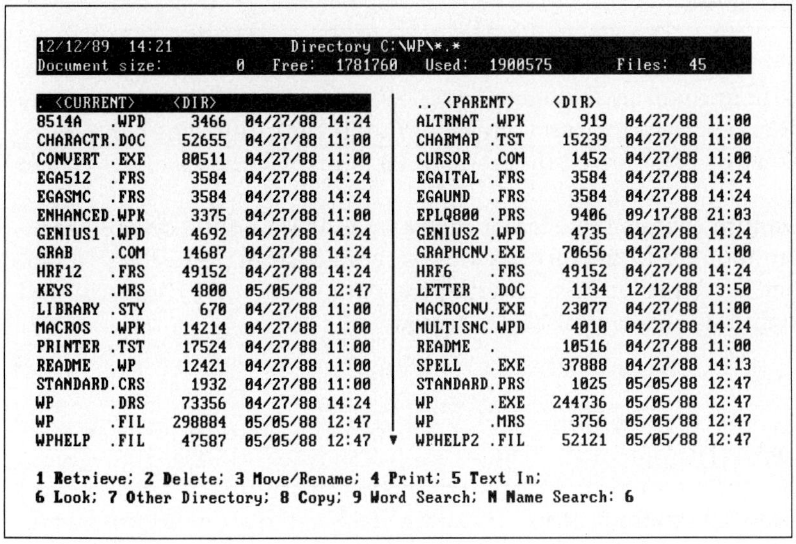


**Figure E.18 The List Files Menu**
The List Files menu shows the files in your current directory and presents various options for managing these files.

## Deleting Files

*Discarding documents*

WordPerfect duplicates the function of the DOS DEL (or ERASE) command by letting you delete files from the List Files menu. First, activate the List Files menu by pressing **F5**. Then use the arrow keys to highlight the file you want to delete and type **2** to select the Delete option. WordPerfect will ask for confirmation before deleting the file. If you type **Y** for yes, the file will be removed from the disk.

## Renaming Files

*Changing file names*

When you save a new document for the first time, WordPerfect asks you to supply a file name. This name need not be permanent. Just as DOS lets you rename existing files with the RENAME command, WordPerfect also allows you to change file names. It's often more convenient to change a file name from within WordPerfect rather than exit WordPerfect, change the file name with the DOS RENAME command, and then restart WordPerfect. To rename a file, press **F5** to activate the List Files menu, highlight the file you want to rename, type **3** to select the Move/Rename option, and enter the new file name.

### Copying Files

*Duplicating documents*

Sometimes you want to reproduce an existing document so that you can make a slightly different version. In other cases, you might want to copy a document from one disk or directory to another for backup purposes. Although you can use the DOS COPY command, the Copy option from WordPerfect's List Files menu may be more convenient. First, press **F5** to display the List Files menu. Then, highlight the source file to be copied, type **8** to select the Copy option, and enter the name of the target file. The target may be a new file or an existing file.

### Changing Directories

*Using a different disk or directory*

In WordPerfect, the default disk drive directory is the one you're currently working in, and initially is the one you are in when you start WordPerfect. Unless you specify otherwise, WordPerfect looks for and stores files in this directory. The contents of the current directory can be viewed by pressing **F5** to display the List Files screen (see Figure E.18).

You might want to change the current directory to work with a document on another disk or in another subdirectory. Do this by typing **7** from the List Files menu to select the Other Directory option, entering the path of the new directory, and pressing **Enter** to display the new List Files screen.

## ADDITIONAL FEATURES

*Handy options*

WordPerfect Version 5.0's many features make it a state-of-the-art word processing package. Some of these features are used quite often, others only in special situations. Besides the features we've already discussed, the most recent version of WordPerfect includes on-line help, a thesaurus, sorting, mail-merge, keyboard macros, multiple windows, and View Document. Let's briefly examine each of these.

### On-line Help

*Instant reference manual*

WordPerfect has an on-line help facility that can answer many questions about using the package without your having to refer to the manual. To invoke the help facility, press the **F3** function key; WordPerfect will present the screen shown in Figure E.19(a). If you press **F3** again, WordPerfect will display the function key template shown in Figure E.19(b). Since WordPerfect makes extensive use of the function keys in conjunction with the Control, Alternate, and Shift keys, this keyboard template can be very helpful. While the help facility is active, you can get additional information about any function key simply by pressing the key. For example, Figure E.19(c) shows the help screen presented when you press the Exit key, F7. You can also get an alphabetical list of WordPerfect features by pressing any letter. In other words, if you press **B**, the WordPerfect help facility will list the features whose names begin with the letter B. When you are finished with the help facility, press the **Enter** key or the **Space Bar** to return to your document.

(a)

```
Help                                               WP 5.0   05/05/88

     Press any letter to get an alphabetical list of features.

          The list will include the features that start with that letter,
          along with the name of the key where the feature is found.  You
          can then press that key to get a description of how the feature
          works.

     Press any function key to get information about the use of the key.

          Some keys may let you choose from a menu to get more information
          about various options.  Press HELP again to display the template.

     Press Enter or Space bar to exit Help.
```

(b)

WordPerfect 5.0 Template (IBM Layout)

| | | | |
|---|---|---|---|
| F1 | Shell<br>SETUP<br>Thesaurus<br>Cancel | Spell<br><-SEARCH<br>Replace<br>Search-> | F2 |
| F3 | Screen<br>SWITCH<br>Reveal Codes<br>Help | Move<br>->INDENT<-<br>Block<br>->Indent | F4 |
| F5 | Text In/Out<br>DATE/OUTLINE<br>Mark Text<br>List Files | Tab Align<br>CENTER<br>Flush Right<br>Bold | F6 |
| F7 | Footnote<br>PRINT<br>Math/Columns<br>Exit | Font<br>FORMAT<br>Style<br>Underline | F8 |
| F9 | Merge/Sort<br>MERGE CODES<br>Graphics<br>Merge R | Macro Def.<br>RETRIEVE<br>Macro<br>Save | F10 |

Legend:

Ctrl + Function Key
SHIFT + FUNCTION KEY
Alt + Function Key
Function Key alone

(c)

```
Exit

     Gives you the option to save your document and then allows you to either
     exit WordPerfect or clear the screen.

     It is also used to exit from editing headers, styles, footnotes, etc.

     When you are in screens other than editing screens, it is used to leave
     menus and will normally take you back to the editing screen.
```

**Figure E.19 On-Line Help**

(a) Pressing F3 displays this help screen.

(b) Pressing F3 again displays the keyboard template.

(c) Pressing a function key after F3 presents more information about that key.

## Thesaurus

*Finding synonyms*

WordPerfect Version 5.0 has a built-in thesaurus that makes it very easy to look up synonyms while you work on a document. Suppose that you want to see synonyms of the word *meeting* in the condominium association letter we've been working on. First, you move the cursor anywhere within *meeting* and then press **Alt-F1**. Figure E.20 shows the result. At this point, you can replace *meeting* with one of the synonyms by typing **1** to select the Replace Word option and then typing the letter that's in front of the synonym you want. Alternatively, you can simply press **F7** to return to the document without changing anything. You can also have the thesaurus display synonyms of these synonyms or look up another word you enter with the Look Up Word option.

## Sorting

*Rearranging lines of text*

As we said in Chapter 6, sorting is arranging items in some particular order. WordPerfect Version 5.0 makes it very easy to sort lines of text into alphabetic or numeric order. For example, suppose you have lines of text or numbers that you want sorted. These may be names, addresses, zip codes, or simply individual words that you

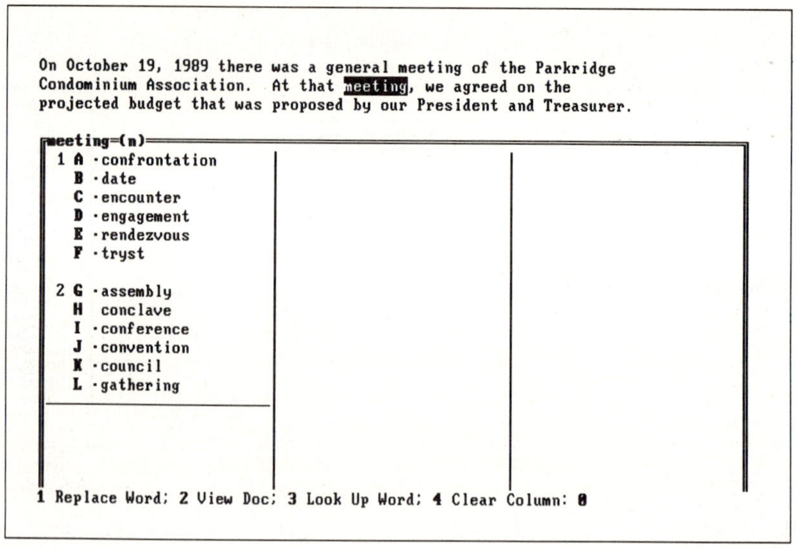


**Figure E.20 Thesaurus**
WordPerfect's thesaurus is handy for finding synonyms.

(a)

(b)

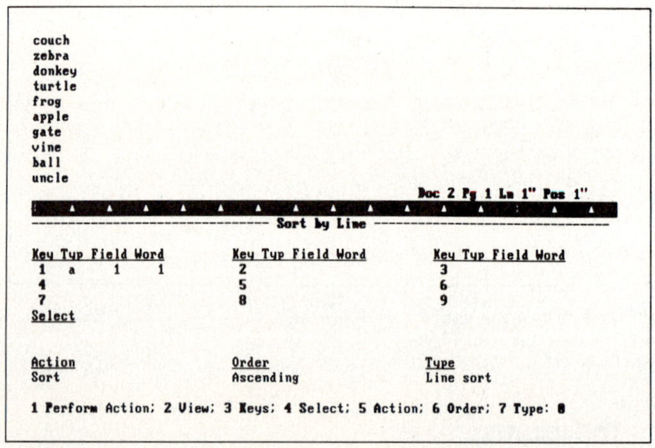


**Figure E.21 Sorting**
(a) Lines of text must be marked as a block before they can be sorted into ascending or descending order.
(b) The Sort menu.
(c) The words have been sorted into ascending order.

(c)

want to alphabetize. The first step is to mark as a block the items to be sorted, as shown in Figure E.21(a). To actually sort the lines of text, press **Ctrl-F9** to activate the Sort menu (see Figure E.21(b)), and then type **1** to select the Perform Action option. By default, WordPerfect sorts the lines into ascending (alphabetical) order. The result is shown in Figure E.21(c).

## Mail-Merge

*Creating form letters*

Mail-merge allows you to print form letters or other personalized text by combining a document with a data file. This is very useful to businesses and organizations that send letters or bills to various individuals. WordPerfect's mail-merge facility is quite good and relatively easy to use. To show you how it works, let's make our condominium association document into a form letter.

The first step is to create a data file containing the variable information. In our example, this variable data consists of the names and addresses of the condominium unit owners. Suppose there are just four owners. The data file consists of one record for each owner. Each record consists of five fields: the name, street address, city, state, and zip code. Each field is typed on its own line and is terminated when you press **F9**. A record is terminated when you press **Shift-F9** and then **E**. In our example, the data file, named OWNERS, looks like Figure E.22(a). The ^R and ^E are *merge codes* generated when you press F9 or Shift-F9; the codes are used by the WordPerfect mail-merge feature.

Once the data file is finished, you can create the *primary file*. This is the text of the form letter along with some special commands. In our case, we can simply modify the condominium association letter to include a centered letterhead in boldface and the commands that merge the names and addresses. For example, instead of an explicit condominium owner's name, you press **Shift-F9** and then type **F1** to create the ^F1^ merge code. This tells WordPerfect where to put the contents of the first data field. Similarly, the street address, city, state, and zip code fields are represented by the ^F2^, ^F3^, ^F4^, and ^F5^ merge codes, respectively. Figure E.22(b) shows the document after the letterhead and merge codes have been added. It is saved with a different name, FORM.DOC, to leave the original LETTER.DOC document intact.

The data file and letter are now complete. When they are merged, WordPerfect will substitute items from the data file for the ^F1^ through ^F5^ merge codes in the letter. A new document will be created containing four separate letters, each one addressed to a different condominium owner. To perform the merge procedure, press **Ctrl-F9** and type **1** to select the Merge option. WordPerfect prompts you to enter the *primary file*, which in this case is the letter, **FORM.DOC**. Next you are prompted for the *secondary file*, which is the **OWNERS** data file. WordPerfect merges the two files to create the four letters, one of which is shown in Figure E.22(c). At this point, you can save the new document or simply print it to get each of the four letters on its own page.

## Keyboard Macros

*Recording and replaying keystrokes*

WordPerfect has a keyboard macro feature that allows you to replace a long series of keystrokes with just two: holding down the Alternate key and typing a letter from A to Z. In essence, you can "record" a sequence of keystrokes and "replay"

(a)

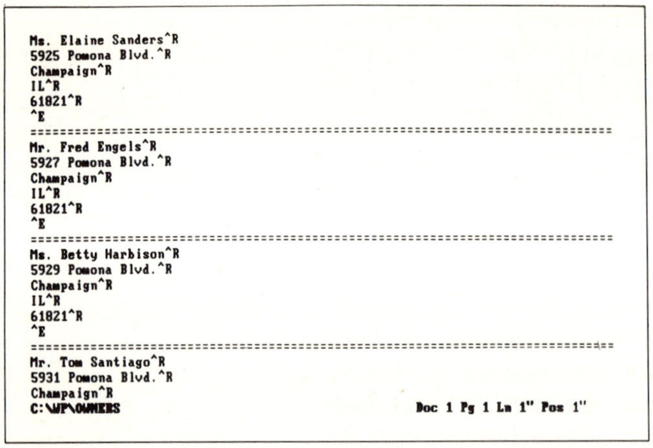

```
Ms. Elaine Sanders^R
5925 Pomona Blvd.^R
Champaign^R
IL^R
61821^R
^E
================================================================================
Mr. Fred Engels^R
5927 Pomona Blvd.^R
Champaign^R
IL^R
61821^R
^E
================================================================================
Ms. Betty Harbison^R
5929 Pomona Blvd.^R
Champaign^R
IL^R
61821^R
^E
================================================================================
Mr. Tom Santiago^R
5931 Pomona Blvd.^R
Champaign^R
C:\WP\OWNERS                                     Doc 1 Pg 1 Ln 1" Pos 1"
```

(b)

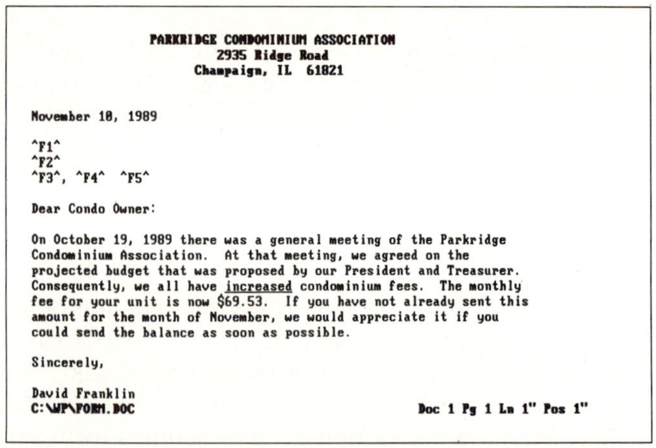

```
                    PARKRIDGE CONDOMINIUM ASSOCIATION
                            2935 Ridge Road
                         Champaign, IL  61821


November 10, 1989

^F1^
^F2^
^F3^, ^F4^  ^F5^

Dear Condo Owner:

On October 19, 1989 there was a general meeting of the Parkridge
Condominium Association.  At that meeting, we agreed on the
projected budget that was proposed by our President and Treasurer.
Consequently, we all have increased condominium fees.  The monthly
fee for your unit is now $69.53.  If you have not already sent this
amount for the month of November, we would appreciate it if you
could send the balance as soon as possible.

Sincerely,

David Franklin
C:\WP\FORM.DOC                                  Doc 1 Pg 1 Ln 1" Pos 1"
```

**Figure E.22 Mail-Merge**

(a) The data file contains names and addresses and merge codes to separate the fields and records.

(b) The form letter, or *primary file*, contains the text and merge codes indicating where the names and addresses go.

(c) Here is one of the four generated form letters.

(c)

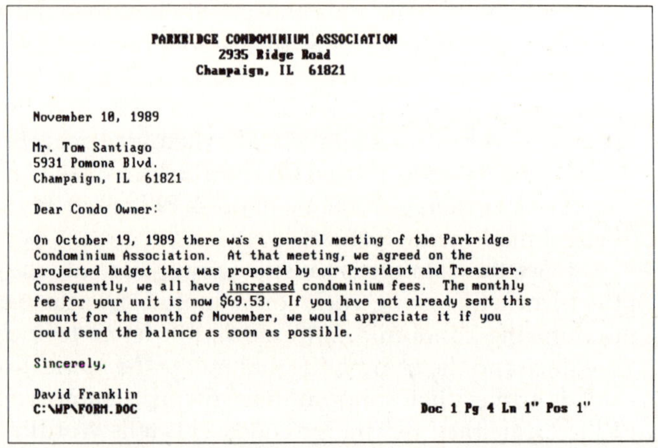

```
                    PARKRIDGE CONDOMINIUM ASSOCIATION
                            2935 Ridge Road
                         Champaign, IL  61821


November 10, 1989

Mr. Tom Santiago
5931 Pomona Blvd.
Champaign, IL  61821

Dear Condo Owner:

On October 19, 1989 there was a general meeting of the Parkridge
Condominium Association.  At that meeting, we agreed on the
projected budget that was proposed by our President and Treasurer.
Consequently, we all have increased condominium fees.  The monthly
fee for your unit is now $69.53.  If you have not already sent this
amount for the month of November, we would appreciate it if you
could send the balance as soon as possible.

Sincerely,

David Franklin
C:\WP\FORM.DOC                                  Doc 1 Pg 4 Ln 1" Pos 1"
```

them at any time. These keystrokes may include function keys, menu selections, and ordinary text. For example, suppose you are working on a document in which you must frequently type *Parkridge Condominium Association*. WordPerfect lets you assign this whole phrase to an abbreviated command, such as Alt-P. Once you do this, instead of typing *Parkridge Condominium Association* over and over, you can simply hold down the **Alternate** key and then type **P**. WordPerfect automatically inserts the entire phrase at the current cursor location.

To define a keyboard macro, press **Ctrl-F10**. WordPerfect prompts you with

```
Define macro:
```

This is where you choose a name for your macro. You can enter a name up to eight characters long, press Enter to have WordPerfect choose a name for you, or hold down the Alternate key and type any letter from A to Z. The last method is the easiest to use, but you get only a single letter with which to name your macro. Let's name our macro Alt-P, for Parkridge Condominium Association. To do this, hold down the **Alternate** key and type **P**.

WordPerfect then prompts you for a macro description, which is an explanation of what your macro does. This is optional; a description can be helpful for complex macros, but our simple example hardly requires a comment. Press the **Enter** key to leave the description blank.

Next you must enter the macro definition itself—the keystrokes that will be activated when you press Alt-P. To specify the definition of our simple macro, type **Parkridge Condominium Association** and press **Ctrl-F10**. After you do this, you need only press Alt-P to insert the entire phrase *Parkridge Condominium Association* anywhere in your document.

## Multiple Windows

*Two views*

WordPerfect Version 5.0 lets you have two windows on your screen to look simultaneously at two different documents or two parts of the same document. For example, suppose you are editing FORM.DOC and you want to see the OWNERS file. To open a new window, press **Ctrl-F3** to activate the Screen menu and type **1** to select the Window option. WordPerfect then prompts you for the number of lines you want in the top window. With most displays, you would enter **12**, to split the screen approximately in half horizontally. You can also press the **Up Arrow** and **Down Arrow** keys to move the reverse-video bar that divides the two windows, and press **Enter** when it is in the desired position. Press **Shift-F3** to move from one window to the other; each window can be treated as a separate editing session. You can use the List Files menu to load a file into the new window, as shown in Figure E.23. To close a window, press **Ctrl-F3** to activate the Screen menu, type **1** to select the Window option, and enter **0** as the number of lines in this window.

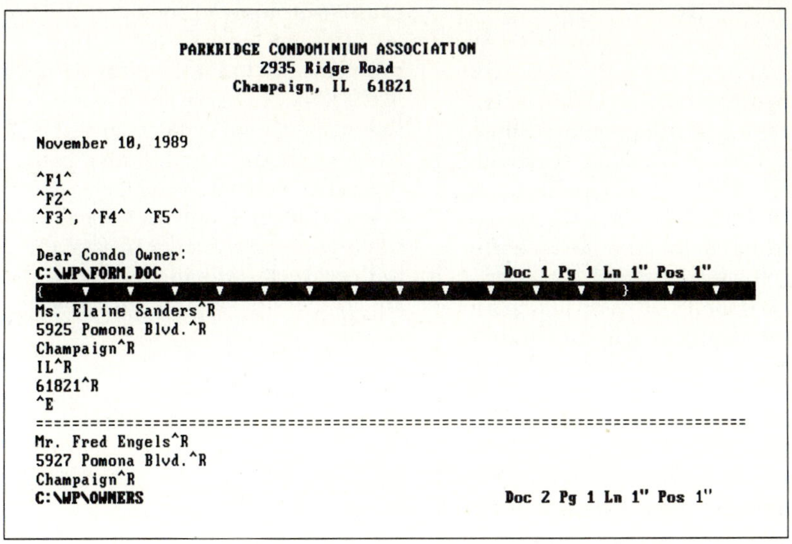

```
                 PARKRIDGE CONDOMINIUM ASSOCIATION
                          2935 Ridge Road
                       Champaign, IL  61821

November 10, 1989

^F1^
^F2^
^F3^, ^F4^  ^F5^

Dear Condo Owner:
C:\WP\FORM.DOC                                 Doc 1 Pg 1 Ln 1" Pos 1"
{  ▼  ▼  ▼  ▼  ▼  ▼  ▼  ▼  ▼  ▼  ▼  ▼  ▼  }  ▼  ▼
Ms. Elaine Sanders^R
5925 Pomona Blvd.^R
Champaign^R
IL^R
61821^R
^E
==========================================================================
Mr. Fred Engels^R
5927 Pomona Blvd.^R
Champaign^R
C:\WP\OWNERS                                   Doc 2 Pg 1 Ln 1" Pos 1"
```

**Figure E.23 Multiple Windows**
The screen is split into two windows, with FORM.DOC on top and OWNERS on the bottom.

## View Document

*Depicting the printout on your screen*

WordPerfect Version 5.0 includes a feature called View Document that lets you see on your screen how your document will look when it is printed. This page preview feature fairly accurately depicts character, line, and page formatting, but it only works well if your computer is equipped with a graphics monitor. To use it, press

**Shift-F7** to activate the Print menu (see Figure E.17) and then type **6** to select the View Document option.

Initially, View Document presents a full-page view on the screen. This is handy for seeing the overall appearance of text on the page, even if most of it is too small to read. To examine the text more closely, you can type **1** to select the 100% option, which will present an actual-size view of the document on the screen, or type **2** to select the 200% option, which will show the document at twice its normal size. With these options, you can use the arrow keys to scroll the document and see the parts that don't fit on the screen. A Facing Pages option is also available for viewing documents that have different formats for even and odd pages (like those in a book).

When you are finished with the View Document feature, press **F7** to return to the WordPerfect editing screen.

## The Real World

### The Men Behind WordPerfect

Alan Ashton was so happy with his company's profits in 1987 that he took everyone—the whole company—to Hawaii for a week.

Ashton's goal was that his WordPerfect Corporation would make $100 million in profits, double the 1986 figure. On December 22, 1987, the figure stood at $100.3 million in sales. What's more, the company he cofounded has achieved record sales and profits every year since it was created in 1980.

Its success in large part is due to the success of its WordPerfect word processing software. WordPerfect is currently the world's best-selling word processing program. The White House, Congress, and law offices all over the world use it.

Who are the people who took a company to such dizzying heights in just seven years?

Ashton, president and chief executive officer, owns 49.9 percent of the stock in this private company. A former Brigham Young University professor, he is a Mormon who brings strong values and a sense of family to work with him. He is, according to employees, a father figure so down-to-earth that he recently only reluctantly traded in his pickup truck for a Cadillac. But he's a father figure with incredible drive—a tough combination to beat.

Bruce Bastian founded the company along with Ashton and is now an equal partner with him. Also a Mormon and a former college professor, Bastian now serves as chairman of the board and president of WordPerfect's highly successful international division.

The man who holds the tie-breaking 0.2 percent of the company stock is Pete Peterson. Back when the company was called Satellite Software International, Peterson was hired to keep the books. He quit the next day because there were no books.

There were also other problems, including no business license and very sketchy records. But when Ashton and Bastian realized that this man with a psychology degree knew what he was doing, they hired him back. Peterson uses a South American saying to describe the situation: "In the land of the blind, the one-eyed man is king."

Source: Christine Strehlo, "What's So Special About WordPerfect?" *Personal Computing*, March, 1988, pp. 100-116.

## Summary

- *How to start WordPerfect.* After WordPerfect has been installed, you switch to the proper subdirectory and enter **WP**.
- *How to create a new document.* Simply type the words and punctuation; WordPerfect has automatic word wrap.
- *How to edit a new or existing document.* View the existing text using the arrow keys, scrolling, paging, End, Home, and the Go To command. Change existing text by inserting, overwriting, and deleting characters; marking, deleting,

moving, and copying blocks; searching for and replacing text; canceling mistakes; and checking spelling.

- *How to format characters, lines, and pages.* Boldface, underlining, italics, and other options can be used to change the appearance of characters. Lines can be formatted by setting margins, tab stops, justification, hyphenation, line spacing, line height, and centering. Pages can be formatted by setting the paper size and type, top and bottom margins, page breaks, page numbering, headers, and footers.
- *How to save and print a document.* Press **F10** to save the current document in a disk file. Press **Shift-F7** to activate the Print menu and type **1** to print the entire document.
- *How to manage document files.* Press **F5** to activate the List Files menu, which lets you change directories and retrieve, delete, rename, and copy files.
- *How to use some additional features included in WordPerfect.* Version 5.0 also lets you get on-line help, use a built-in thesaurus, sort text, create form letters, create keyboard macros, use two windows, and display page previews.

## Command Summary

The following table summarizes commonly used WordPerfect Version 5.0 keypresses and commands.

| KEYPRESS | DESCRIPTION |
|---|---|
| | Cursor Movement |
| Up Arrow | Moves up one line. |
| Down Arrow | Moves down one line. |
| Left Arrow | Moves left one space. |
| Right Arrow | Moves right one space. |
| Ctrl-Left Arrow | Moves left one word. |
| Ctrl-Right Arrow | Moves right one word. |
| Tab | Moves to the next tab stop. |
| Home | Moves to the top of the current screen. |
| End | Moves to the bottom of the current screen. |
| Grey Minus (num. keypad) | Moves up one screen. |
| Grey Plus (num. keypad) | Moves down one screen. |
| Page Up | Moves up one page. |
| Page Down | Moves down one page. |
| Home, Right Arrow | Moves to the right edge of the screen. |
| Home, Left Arrow | Moves to the left edge of the screen. |
| Home, Home, Up Arrow | Moves to the beginning of the document. |
| Home, Home, Down Arrow | Moves to the end of the document. |
| Ctrl-Home | Moves to specified page number (Go To command). |
| | Inserting and Deleting |
| Insert | Turns insert typing mode on or off. |
| Enter | Inserts a hard return. |
| Ctrl-Enter | Inserts a page break. |
| Delete | Deletes the character at the cursor or a marked block. |
| Backspace | Deletes the character to the left of the cursor. |
| Ctrl-Backspace | Deletes the word at the cursor. |
| Ctrl-End | Deletes to the end of the line. |
| Ctrl-PgDn | Deletes to the end of the page. |

| | Function Key Commands |
|---|---|
| F1 | Cancels the last command or recovers deleted text. |
| Ctrl-F1 | Temporarily returns to DOS. |
| Shift-F1 | Invokes the Setup menu. |
| Alt-F1 | Invokes the thesaurus. |
| F2 | Searches forward for text. |
| Ctrl-F2 | Invokes the spelling checker. |
| Shift-F2 | Searches backward for text. |
| Alt-F2 | Performs a global search and replace. |
| F3 | Invokes the Help facility. |
| Ctrl-F3 | Reformats screen, splits screen, or draws lines. |
| Shift-F3 | Switches to the other window. |
| Alt-F3 | Reveals hidden formatting codes. |
| F4 | Indents entire paragraph from left margin. |
| Ctrl-F4 | Moves, copies, or deletes a section of text. |
| Shift-F4 | Indents entire paragraph equally from both margins. |
| Alt-F4 | Turns on block marking. |
| F5 | Invokes the List Files menu. |
| Ctrl-F5 | Saves or loads an ASCII text file. |
| Shift-F5 | Invokes the Date/Outline menu. |
| Alt-F5 | Invokes the Mark Text menu. |
| F6 | Boldfaces new or existing text. |
| Ctrl-F6 | Aligns text or numbers to a tab stop. |
| Shift-F6 | Centers new or existing text. |
| Alt-F6 | Aligns text flush against the right margin. |
| F7 | Exits a menu, document, or WordPerfect. |
| Ctrl-F7 | Creates, edits, or deletes footnotes and endnotes. |
| Shift-F7 | Invokes the Print menu. |
| Alt-F7 | Invokes the Math/Columns menu. |
| F8 | Underlines new or existing text. |
| Ctrl-F8 | Changes the font and/or appearance of printed text. |
| Shift-F8 | Invokes the Format menu. |
| Alt-F8 | Invokes the Style menu. |
| F9 | Inserts an end-of-field merge code (^R). |
| Ctrl-F9 | Invokes the Merge/Sort menu. |
| Shift-F9 | Invokes the Merge Codes menu. |
| Alt-F9 | Incorporates graphics into a document. |
| F10 | Saves the current document in a disk file. |
| Ctrl-F10 | Defines a new keyboard macro. |
| Shift-F10 | Retrieves an existing document. |
| Alt-F10 | Invokes a macro named by WordPerfect. |

## Key Terms

As an extra review of this chapter, try defining the following terms. If you have trouble with any of them, refer to the page number listed.

block (A68)
footer (A79)
hard page break (A78)
hard return (A65)
header (A79)
line height (A76)
soft page break (A78)
soft return (A65)

## Review Questions

1. After you have changed to the WordPerfect subdirectory, what command do you enter at the DOS prompt to start WordPerfect?
2. Where does WordPerfect display messages and warnings while you are entering or editing text?
3. When WordPerfect performs a word wrap, is a hard return or a soft return inserted into the document?
4. Which key(s) would you press to move the cursor to the first line of the next page?
5. How do you switch from insert mode to overwrite mode?
6. List two different ways to remove a single character from a document.
7. Once a block is marked, how do you delete it?
8. Which WordPerfect key would you press to retrieve text removed by a previous erase operation?
9. How would you check the spelling of every word in a document?
10. Is WordPerfect Version 5.0 a WYSIWYG word processing package?
11. How do you underline an existing word in a WordPerfect document?
12. What is the difference between line spacing and line height?
13. What is the easiest way to center a heading in WordPerfect?
14. How do you tell WordPerfect to begin a new page?
15. How do you tell WordPerfect to save a document?
16. How do you tell WordPerfect to print a document?
17. List three ways to retrieve a WordPerfect document.
18. How would you display on your screen help information about the F7 function key?
19. How do you look up a word with WordPerfect's thesaurus?
20. What are the two types of files needed to print mail-merge letters?

## Multiple Choice

1. Which command do you enter from DOS to begin WordPerfect?

   (a) WORD (b) WP
   (c) WS (d) PERF

2. When you first start WordPerfect, the only item on the screen is the

   (a) Opening Menu. (b) default document.
   (c) status line. (d) ruler line.

3. Many WordPerfect commands and menus are invoked by pressing Control, Alternate, or Shift along with a

   (a) function key. (b) number key.
   (c) letter key. (d) arrow key.

4. The word wrap feature automatically starts a new line when you reach the right margin. Which key do you press to start a new paragraph?
   (a) F1 (b) Right Arrow
   (c) Insert (d) Enter

5. Which sequence of keys do you press to move the cursor to the end of the current document?
   (a) Home, End (b) Control, Page Down
   (c) Home, Home, Up Arrow (d) Home, Home, Down Arrow

6. To mark a block of text, move the cursor to the first character to be included, then
   (a) press Home, and exit WordPerfect.
   (b) press Alt-F4, and move to the end of the block.
   (c) press Num Lock, and then Ctrl-End.
   (d) press both Shift keys, and invoke the Print menu.

7. Which of the following functions is not performed by pressing F1, the Cancel key?
   (a) Return from a menu. (b) Delete a block.
   (c) Turn off block marking. (d) Restore the most recently deleted text.

8. What is the first step in checking the spelling of an entire document?
   (a) Press Ctrl-F2 to display the Speller menu.
   (b) Check the document with the Thesaurus.
   (c) Move the cursor to the beginning of the document.
   (d) Create a personal supplementary dictionary.

9. Which two character formats can each be invoked by pressing a single function key?
   (a) italics and double underlining (b) superscript and subscript
   (c) boldface and underlining (d) redline and strikeout

10. Which type of tab stop would you most likely use to align numbers?
    (a) left-justified (b) centered
    (c) right-justified (d) decimal

11. One or more lines of text printed in the top margin of every page is called a
    (a) page offset. (b) flag.
    (c) header. (d) footer.

12. Which key is pressed to get on-line help?
    (a) F3 (b) F10
    (c) Escape (d) Page Up

13. Before you can look up a word with the thesaurus, you must
    (a) check the spelling of your document.
    (b) mark the word as a block of text.
    (c) move the cursor anywhere within the word.
    (d) load the thesaurus as a document file.

14. Which feature would you use to look at two different documents on your screen at the same time?
    (a) the Window option from the Screen menu
    (b) the Shell command
    (c) the Look option from the List Files menu
    (d) the Page option from the Format menu

15. If your computer has a graphics monitor, which WordPerfect Version 5.0 feature would you use to see how your document will look when it is printed?
    (a) Graphics
    (b) List Files
    (c) View Document
    (d) Merge/Sort

## On-line Exercises

1. If you are not already running WordPerfect, change to the proper disk drive directory and enter **WP**. Type the following text, pressing the **Enter** key only once after the last line:

```
The next meeting of the Parkridge Condominium Association
Board of Managers will be held at 7:00 P.M. on November 19,
1989 in Room 217 of Champaign Federal Savings.  This is an
important meeting, so please try to attend.
```

2. Move the cursor to the top of the document and type the following lines, pressing **Enter** after each one:

```
To:   Board of Managers
From:   David Franklin, Secretary
Re:   Next meeting
```

3. Press the **Enter** key again to leave a blank line before the paragraph. Move the cursor to the top of the document, type **M E M O**, and press **Enter**. Boldface, underline, and center this title.
4. Move the cursor to the last line of the memo and delete it by pressing **Ctrl-End**. Restore the text you've deleted with the Cancel command.
5. Mark *Parkridge Condominium Association* as a block of text and copy it in front of the *Board of Managers* after the *To:*.
6. Move the cursor to the top of the file. Use the search and replace command to change *Managers* to *Directors* throughout the entire document.
7. Move the cursor to the beginning of the document and set the left and right margins to 1 1/2 inches.
8. Change the tab stops so that they occur at 1-inch intervals.
9. Turn off justification for this memo.
10. Go back and double-space the entire document (use the Line Spacing option from the Line Format menu).
11. Save the document in a disk file named MEMO.DOC, but don't exit WordPerfect.
12. If your computer is equipped with a printer, make sure it is turned on and online, and print this memo.

13. Use WordPerfect's on-line help facility to get a list of all features that begin with B. Select a different letter and try it again. Now try learning more about the function keys.
14. With MEMO.DOC displayed on your screen, highlight a word and invoke WordPerfect's thesaurus. Try using the options that appear in the Thesaurus screen to see additional synonyms.
15. If your computer is equipped with a graphics monitor, use the View Document feature to examine MEMO.DOC. Does the screen view accurately depict the actual printout? Try the 100% and 200% options from the View Document menu. You can shift the display to see other parts of your document by pressing the arrow keys.

## Projects

1. Use WordPerfect to print your academic schedule for this semester. List days, times, classes, buildings, rooms, and instructors.
2. Look in a newspaper or placement office listing for job ads. Select a position in line with your experience and goals. Use WordPerfect to prepare a résumé and cover letter for this job. Be sure to use underlining and boldface where appropriate.
3. Use WordPerfect to create a quick reference guide to WordPerfect. List the menu commands and other keystrokes you think are especially important to remember. Feel free to use WordPerfect's on-line help facility to get information about the various commands.
4. Use WordPerfect to create a mail-merge form letter to be sent to the following software companies requesting information about the word processing packages they sell:

   WordPerfect
   WordPerfect Corporation
   288 W. Center St.
   Orem, UT 84057

   WordStar
   MicroPro International Corporation
   33 San Pablo Ave.
   San Rafael, CA 94903

   Microsoft Word
   Microsoft Corporation
   N.E. 36th Way
   Redmond, WA 98073

Appendix F

# Word Processing Details: WordPerfect 4.2

## Learning Objectives

After reading this chapter, you should be able to do the following:

- Start WordPerfect
- Understand the editing screen
- Execute commands and get help
- Enter text into a document
- Move the cursor
- Insert new text
- Overwrite mistakes
- Delete mistakes
- Search for and replace text within a document
- Save a document in a disk file
- Check spelling
- Mark, move, copy, and delete blocks of text
- Cancel commands and restore deletions
- Underline, boldface, and otherwise format characters
- Set margins, tab stops, justification, and line height
- Center text
- Format pages
- Print a document
- Edit an existing document
- Exit WordPerfect

---

## Introduction

A word processor is a computer system that helps you type, edit, store, and print documents. Memos, letters, term papers, reports, contracts, articles, and book chapters are all examples of documents that can be produced with a word processing package. The typical word processor consists of a microcomputer, a printer, and a word processing software package. Systems of this type are very common today and are helping all kinds of people with their daily writing chores. Students, educators, authors, scientists, businesspeople, professionals, and office workers are just some of the people who use word processing systems. **Word processing packages**, also called word processors, are perhaps the most popular type of software used on microcomputers.

WordPerfect is the leader in microcomputer word processing software. Since its introduction in October 1982, the package has generally received high praise from reviewers and users. WordPerfect Corporation has significantly enhanced its product with every new release. Although WordPerfect is considered one of the most feature-laden word processing packages on the market, it is also known for its simple, well-designed user interface.

## General Features of WordPerfect

WordPerfect can be used for documents ranging from simple memos to long books. Although it has many powerful and complex features, we'll concentrate on WordPerfect's most commonly used basic features. The kinds of operations you can perform with WordPerfect include the following:

- **Executing Commands** Most WordPerfect commands are initiated by pressing a function key—either by itself or with Control, Shift, or Alternate.
- **Getting Help** By pressing the Help key, you can get more information about specific features and commands.
- **Entering Text** Documents are created by entering text with the keyboard.
- **Moving the Cursor** WordPerfect uses the cursor movement keys (Up Arrow, Down Arrow, Left Arrow, Right Arrow, Page Up, Page Down, Home, and End) to move the cursor around in a document.
- **Inserting Text** Words or characters can be inserted into a document when the Insert mode is on.
- **Overwriting Mistakes** Typing errors can be overwritten when the Typeover mode is on.
- **Deleting Mistakes** Errors, from single characters to entire lines, can be easily erased.
- **Searching for and Replacing Text** A word or phrase anywhere within a document can either be found or be found and automatically replaced.
- **Saving a Document** Documents can be saved in disk files.
- **Checking Spelling** Documents can be checked for spelling accuracy.
- **Working with Blocks of Text** Entire blocks of text can be marked, moved, copied, or deleted.
- **Canceling Commands** Commands can be canceled, and deleted text can be restored.
- **Formatting Characters** Text can be underlined, boldfaced, or emphasized in other ways.
- **Formatting Lines** Margins, tab stops, justification, and line height can be set. Lines of text can be centered.
- **Formatting Pages** The size and type of paper, top and bottom margins, page breaks, and page numbering can be specified.
- **Printing Document** If your system includes a printer, WordPerfect can print a document.
- **Editing an Existing Document** A previously created document can be retrieved and examined, corrected, updated, or otherwise modified.

## Getting Started

Although WordPerfect is a large and sophisticated software package, it is not difficult to learn how to use for basic word processing tasks. There are several different ways WordPerfect might be set up at your particular computer installation. You're most likely to use the package in one of the following arrangements:

1. On a microcomputer with two floppy drives and WordPerfect installed on a diskette.

2. On a microcomputer with a hard disk and WordPerfect installed in a subdirectory name WP.
3. On a microcomputer connected to a local area network with WordPerfect installed on the network disk server.

Although you may need some additional directions from your instructor on how to start WordPerfect, once WordPerfect is loaded you should be able to do the following lessons as they are described.

## Lesson 1: Running WordPerfect

You're all ready to start word processing. The first thing to do is execute the WordPerfect program.

### Step 1: Boot Up DOS

If your computer has two floppy drives, put your DOS disk in drive A, close the door or latch, and turn on the system unit. If your computer has a hard disk or is connected to a local area network, just turn it on. Turn on your monitor, and if your system includes a printer turn it on, too. Enter the date and time, as described in Lesson 1 of Chapter 2, to complete the DOS boot-up process.

### Step 2: Insert the WordPerfect Diskette or Switch to the WordPerfect Subdirectory

If you have a system with only two floppy drives, remove the DOS disk from drive A and replace it with the WordPerfect diskette. Type **a:** and press **Enter** to switch to drive A.

If you have a microcomputer with a hard disk or one that is connected to a local area network, you may have to follow some other directions from your instructor before actually starting the WordPerfect program. For example, on a hard disk system, you may have to switch to the WordPerfect subdirectory by entering **cd c:\wp**.

### Step 3: Invoke WordPerfect

Once you are in the proper disk drive directory, running WordPerfect is easy. Type **wp** and press **Enter**. It will take a few seconds for WordPerfect to be loaded from the disk into memory. Then you'll see Figure 1(a) appear on your screen. This screen displays information about the special training version of WordPerfect 4.2 that we will be using in this chapter. Read the screen, and press any key to continue.

Next, WordPerfect will display the initial help screen you see in Figure 1(b). Read this screen, too, and press any key to continue.

## Lesson 2: The Editing Screen

Your screen should now look like Figure 2. This is WordPerfect's editing screen, where you enter, view, and modify text.

**Figure 1 (a) The WordPerfect Information Screen**

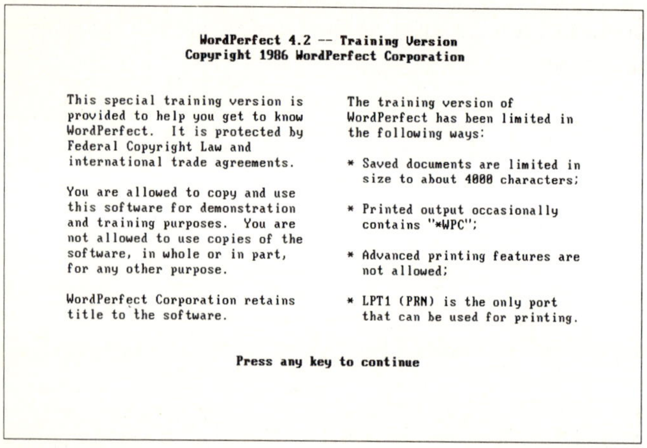


**(b) The Initial Help Screen**

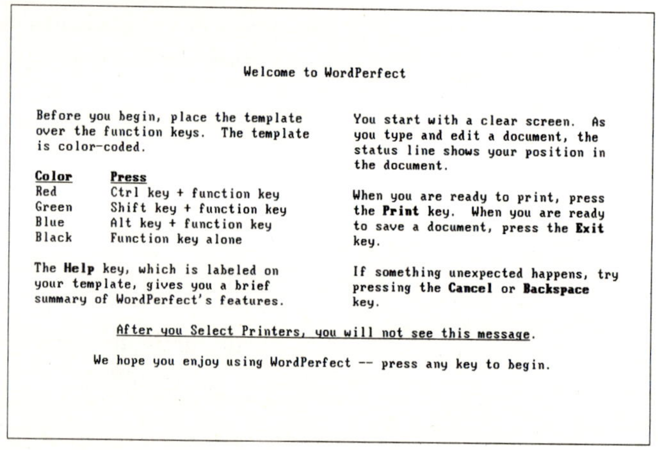


**Figure 2 The Editing Screen**

### Step 1: Examine the Cursor

Look at the upper left corner of the screen. You should see a blinking underscore, known as the cursor, which marks your current position within the document. The cursor indicates the place where text will be inserted, deleted, or changed in some way..

### Step 2: Examine the Status Line

The *status line*, shown at the bottom of the screen, displays messages from WordPerfect. Right now, the status line indicates you are working on document 1 (of a possible two), page 1, and your position within the document is 10 characters from the left edge of the page on the first line. WordPerfect already has default margins, tab stops, and line spacing set up. To create a document, all you have to do is begin typing.

### Step 3: Examine the Text Area

The rest of the screen, from the cursor down to the status line, is the text area. This is the space in which you will enter text and perform editing functions on your document.

## Lesson 3: Executing Commands and Getting Help

Most WordPerfect commands and menus are executed either by pressing a function key alone, or by pressing a function key and the Shift, Control, or Alternate key.

### Step 1: Invoke the Help Command

As an example, let's execute the Help command. WordPerfect has an on-line help facility. You can find the answer to many questions about WordPerfect without having to refer to the manual. To invoke the Help command, press the **F3** function key. WordPerfect will present the screen shown in Figure 3.

**Figure 3 The Help Screen**

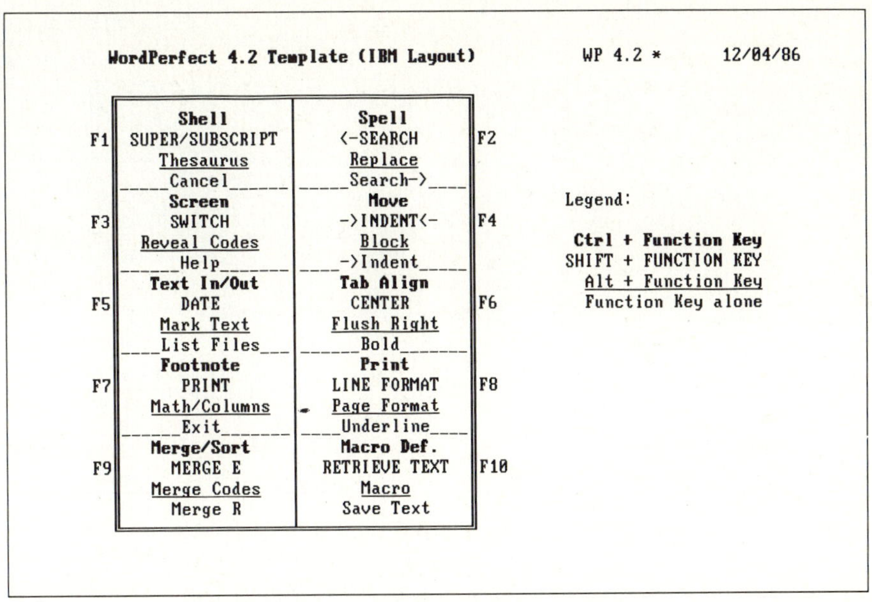


This is the only help screen provided with the educational version of WordPerfect 4.2. It shows the on-screen keyboard template that lists the most common commands.

### Step 2: Return to the Editing Screen

When you are finished examining the function key template, press **Enter** to return to the editing screen.

## Lesson 4: Entering Text

The actual process of entering text with a word processor is similar to typing with a typewriter. There are, however, a few important differences that make using a word processor much easier. To illustrate how to use WordPerfect, let's create a memo. This memo, from the personnel department of a company to its employees, will explain company policy on employee sick leave.

### Step 1: Type the Heading

As we said before, WordPerfect initially places the cursor in the first line of the first page. To create a new document, simply type the words and punctuation. Don't be too concerned if you make some typing errors. We'll show you how to fix mistakes later. Type the following three lines, pressing **Enter** at the end of each one:

**To: All Employees**
**From: Personnel Department**
**Re: Sick Leave**

At this point, your screen should look like Figure 4.

**Figure 4 Memo Heading**

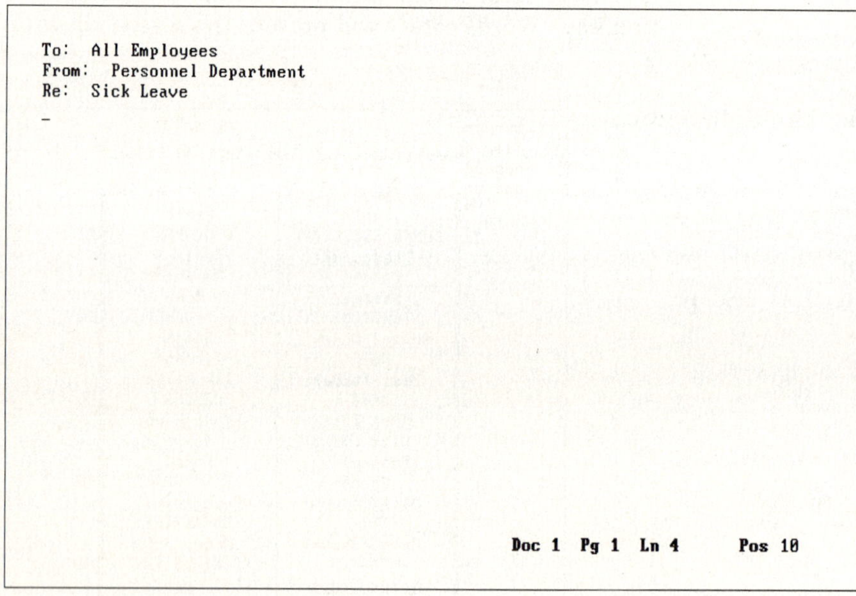


### Step 2: Type the Body of the Memo

If you had to press Enter at the end of every line typed with a word processor, it wouldn't be all that much better than typing text with an electric typewriter. Virtually all word processing programs, however, have a feature called **word wrap** that eliminates having to press Enter after each line. The word processing program detects when you are approaching the right margin. If you type a word that extends beyond the right margin, that word is automatically shifted, or wrapped around, to the beginning of the next line. In other words, the word processing program inserts a **soft return** just before the wrapped word. You continue typing on the new line without having to press the Enter key. Word wrap significantly speeds up typing because it eliminates the need to constantly check the screen to be sure you don't overrun the right margin. You need only press the Enter key when you want to insert a **hard return**, which forces a new line or begins a new paragraph.

To see how word wrap works, press **Enter** once to space down a line from the heading of the memo. Then type the rest of the memo. Do not press Enter at the end of each line.

> Full-time employees are entitled to twelve working days of sick leave each year. Time taken off is charged against these twelve days and at the end of the year the unused balance is carried forward. Sick leave should only be used for an employee's illness or doctor's appointments. It is essential that accurate records are kept because employees are entitled to payment for one-half of their unused sick days when they resign or retire.

When you have finished typing, your screen should look like Figure 5.

**Figure 5 Word Wrap Automatically Begins New Lines**

```
To:  All Employees
From:  Personnel Department
Re:  Sick Leave

Full-time employees are entitled to twelve working days of sick
leave each year.  Time taken off is charged against these twelve
days and at the end of the year the unused balance is carried
forward.  Sick leave should only be used for an employee's
illness or doctor's appointments.  It is essential that accurate
records are kept because employees are entitled to payment for
one-half of their unused sick days when they resign or retire._










                                      Doc 1  Pg 1  Ln 11     Pos 72
```

## Lesson 5: Moving the Cursor

You must be able to move the cursor to see different parts of a document. Since the cursor marks where modifications are to occur, you must also be able to move the cursor to change existing text. Fortunately, there are many ways to move the cursor. The most common ways are quick, direct, and easy.

### Step 1: Use the Arrow Keys

All IBM and IBM-compatible keyboards have at least one set of arrow keys. In many programs, including WordPerfect, the simplest way to move the cursor is to press an arrow key. Try the following key presses:

- Press the **Up Arrow** key to move the cursor to the line directly above.
- Press the **Down Arrow** key to move the cursor to the line directly below.
- Press the **Left Arrow** key to move the cursor backward.
- Press the **Right Arrow** key to move the cursor forward.
- Press and hold an arrow key to automatically repeat the key press and move the cursor more rapidly.
- Hold down the **Control** key and press the **Left Arrow** key to move the cursor to the beginning of the word to the left.
- Hold down the **Control** key and press the **Right Arrow** key to move the cursor to the beginning of the word to the right.

### Step 2: Use Scrolling and Paging

Your document is quite short, but many documents are too long to fit entirely on the screen. Strolling and paging commands let you change the part of your document displayed on the screen. One way to scroll the screen is to continue pressing the Up Arrow or Down Arrow key after the cursor reaches the top or bottom edge of the text area. This won't work on the memo because all of it fits on a single screen. If there were more lines than can fit on the screen, however, pressing the Up Arrow or Down Arrow key after reaching the edge would scroll the screen and move the cursor to the next line.

The **Grey+** and **Grey–** keys on the numeric keypad are used to move the cursor an entire screen at a time. Press the **Grey+** key to move the cursor down to the last line of the current screen. If your document were too long to fit on the screen, pressing the Grey+ key again would move the cursor down through the next screen. Now press the **Grey–** key to move the cursor up to the first line of the current screen. If you had more text above your current screen, pressing the Grey– key again would move the cursor up to the previous screen.

Paging is like scrolling an entire page at a time. Press the **Page Down** key to move the cursor to the first line of the next page. Since your document has only one page, this simply moves the cursor to the end of the document. Press the **Page Up** key to move the cursor to the first line of the previous page. Again, since your document has only one page, this moves the cursor to the beginning of the document.

### Step 3: Use the End and Home Keys

End and Home are the two other cursor movement keys on all IBM-compatible keyboards. Press **End** to move the cursor to the end of the current line. In WordPerfect, the Home key is used with other keypresses to perform various cursor movements. For example, press and release **Home**, then press **Left Arrow** to move the cursor to the left edge of the current screen—in other words, the beginning of the current line. Press and release **Home**, then press **Right Arrow** to move the cursor to the right edge of the current line. Press and release **Home** twice, then press **Down Arrow** to move the cursor to the end of your document. Finally, press and release **Home** twice, then press **Up Arrow** to move the cursor to the beginning of your document.

### Step 4: Use the Go To Command

Another sequence of keypresses lets you move to a particular page number in a WordPerfect document. Since your current document fits entirely on a single page, the Go To command is of little use. Nevertheless, you can still try it. Hold down the **Control** key and press the **Home** key. WordPerfect will display the prompt "Go To" on the status line. Type the page number to which you want to go, in this case **1**, and press **Enter**. WordPerfect moves the cursor to the top of that page.

## Lesson 6: Inserting Text

WordPerfect, like most word processing software, has two basic typing modes: **insert** and **typeover**. By default, when you open a WordPerfect document Insert mode is on. To insert new material into a document, you simply move the cursor to the location where you want the insertion to occur and begin typing. The new characters you type push any existing characters to the right. As an example, let's insert some text into the memo you have typed.

### Step 1: Move the Cursor

Suppose you want to insert the word *cumulative* between the words *twelve* and *working* in the first line of the memo. Use any of the cursor movement keys described in Lesson 5 to position the cursor beneath the *w* in the word *working*.

### Step 2: Type the New Text

Since the WordPerfect default is Insert mode, all you have to do is type the text to be inserted. Type **cumulative**, then press the **Space Bar**. Press the **Up Arrow** key to see how WordPerfect automatically reformats the paragraph and wraps words to fit within the margins when you move the cursor. Your screen should now look like Figure 6.

**Figure 6 Text Inserted in a Document**

```
To:  All Employees
From:  Personnel Department
Re:  Sick Leave

Full-time employees are entitled to twelve cumulative working
days of sick leave each year.  Time taken off is charged against
these twelve days and at the end of the year the unused balance
is carried forward.  Sick leave should only be used for an
employee's illness or doctor's appointments.  It is essential
that accurate records are kept because employees are entitled to
payment for one-half of their unused sick days when they resign
or retire.

                                   Doc 1  Pg 1  Ln 4      Pos 10
```

## Lesson 7: Overwriting Mistakes

One of the benefits of using a word processor is the ease with which you can make corrections. Since no one is perfect, typing errors are bound to occur—as you may have already discovered. In addition, you may want to change a word or phrase that has already been entered. One way to make corrections is by typing over existing text.

### Step 1: Move the Cursor

Suppose that employees are only entitled to eleven days of sick leave. You must change the word *twelve* to *eleven* in the memo. Using any of the cursor movement keys described in Lesson 5, position the cursor beneath the *t* in the first *twelve*.

### Step 2: Change to Typeover Mode

To switch, or toggle, between Insert and Typeover, press the **Insert** key. Since Insert mode is the default, WordPerfect changes to Typeover mode. If Typeover mode were on, pressing the Insert key would switch back to Insert mode. When you change to Typeover mode, WordPerfect displays the word "Typeover" on the status line. In this mode, any characters you type will replace existing characters in the same positions.

### Step 3: Make the Correction

With the cursor at the beginning of the world *twelve* type **eleven**. Your screen should now look like Figure 7.

**Figure 7 Word Corrected in Typeover Mode**

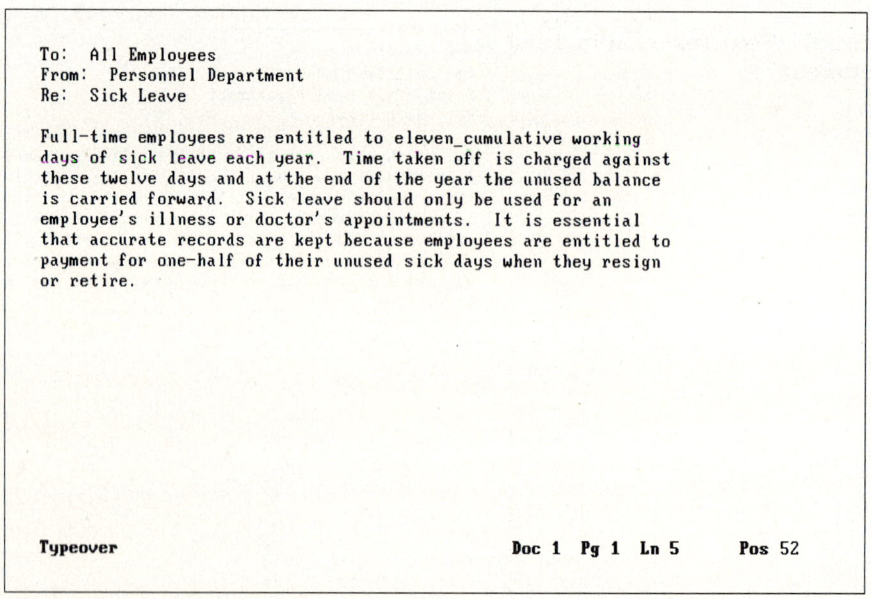

To: All Employees
From: Personnel Department
Re: Sick Leave

Full-time employees are entitled to eleven_cumulative working
days of sick leave each year. Time taken off is charged against
these twelve days and at the end of the year the unused balance
is carried forward. Sick leave should only be used for an
employee's illness or doctor's appointments. It is essential
that accurate records are kept because employees are entitled to
payment for one-half of their unused sick days when they resign
or retire.

Typeover Doc 1 Pg 1 Ln 5 Pos 52

## Lesson 8: Deleting Mistakes

Another way to make corrections and modification is to delete text.

### Step 1: Move the Cursor

Before any text can be deleted, the cursor must be moved to the first character to be erased. Let's change the eleven sick days to just ten. The first three letters of *eleven* can simply be overwritten with **ten**. Move the cursor to the first *e* in *eleven* and type **ten**. The cursor should now be at the *v*. Press the **Insert** key to turn on Insert mode again.

### Step 2: Use the Delete Key

The Delete (Del) key removes the character at the cursor and shifts all characters to the right of the cursor one space to the left. To remove the characters *ven*, press **Delete** three times. Your screen should now look like Figure 8.

**Figure 8 Characters Erased with Delete Key**

```
To:  All Employees
From:  Personnel Department
Re:  Sick Leave

Full-time employees are entitled to ten_cumulative working
days of sick leave each year.  Time taken off is charged against
these twelve days and at the end of the year the unused balance
is carried forward.  Sick leave should only be used for an
employee's illness or doctor's appointments.  It is essential
that accurate records are kept because employees are entitled to
payment for one-half of their unused sick days when they resign
or retire.

                                   Doc 1  Pg 1  Ln 5      Pos 49
```

### Step 3: Use the Backspace Key

The Delete key removes the character at the current cursor location. Another way to erase text is to use the Backspace key. This key removes the character to the immediate left of the cursor. Press **Backspace** three times to erase the *ten*.

Now, make sure Insert mode is turned on, and type **twelve** to restore the memo to its original wording.

### Step 4: Delete an Entire Word

WordPerfect also makes it easy to erase an entire word. Position the cursor on the first character of the word *twelve*. Press **Ctrl-Backspace**, that is, hold down the

**Control** key and press the **Backspace** key. The entire word will disappear, along with the space that followed it.

With Insert mode turned on, type **twelve** and press the **Space Bar** to replace the word.

### Step 5: Delete an Entire Line

WordPerfect also has a command that lets you erase an entire line of text. Move the cursor up to the beginning of the third line in the memo, the one that reads *Re: Sick Leave*. Press **Ctrl-End**. All the text from the cursor to the end of the line will be deleted. Press **Delete** to erase the hard return, and the lines of text below will move up to fill in the empty space (see Figure 9).

**Figure 9 An Entire Line Deleted**

```
To:  All Employees
From:  Personnel Department

Full-time employees are entitled to twelve cumulative working
days of sick leave each year.  Time taken off is charged against
these twelve days and at the end of the year the unused balance
is carried forward.  Sick leave should only be used for an
employee's illness or doctor's appointments.  It is essential
that accurate records are kept because employees are entitled to
payment for one-half of their unused sick days when they resign
or retire.

                                        Doc 1  Pg 1  Ln 3      Pos 10
```

Needless to say, Ctrl-End should be used carefully. Unfortunately, we need the deleted line for the remaining lessons, so retype **Re: Sick Leave** and press **Enter**.

Although WordPerfect has several other commands for deleting text, Delete, Backspace, Ctrl-Backspace, and Ctrl-End are the most frequently used.

## Lesson 9: Searching and Replacing

The memo you've typed is fairly short, so making corrections throughout the entire document would not be difficult. But you may have to modify much longer documents. In some cases, the same mistake is made in several places throughout the document. Most word processors have features that help you locate specific portions of text and change them if necessary.

### Step 1: Find Text

You may have noticed that the word *twelve* is used twice in the memo. If you found out that employees were really entitled to only eleven days of sick leave, you would have to change both instances of *twelve* to *eleven*. In this case, you could simply look through the memo to make sure there are no more occurrences of *twelve*. If the document were much longer, however, you would have to scan through many pages of text, and it's likely you would miss one or more occurrences of *twelve*. Fortunately, WordPerfect has a search command that can find text quickly and accurately. This feature can be used to make corrections or merely to locate each occurrence of a certain word or phrase.

Press **Home** twice, then press **Up Arrow** to move the cursor to the beginning of the document. Then press the **F2** function key, type **twelve**, and press **F2** again. WordPerfect will advance the cursor just past the first occurrence of the word *twelve*. If it cannot find the word you tell it to search for, WordPerfect will display "* Not Found *" on the status line.

### Step 2: Modify the Text

In many cases, you search for a piece of text because you want to change it or some text around it. Now that you've found *twelve*, use **Backspace** to erase it, then type **eleven**.

### Step 3: Repeat the Search

Particular words or phrases are often repeated, especially in a long document. You can search for the next occurrence of the word or phrase without having to redo the entire search command. Press **F2** twice to repeat the previous search operation. The cursor will advance to the next occurrence of the word *twelve*. Press **Backspace** six times and type **eleven** here, too.

### Step 4: Find and Replace Text

Since it is often necessary to find and then change a word or phrase, WordPerfect can do both at once. Move the cursor to the beginning of your memo by pressing **Home** twice, then **Up Arrow**. To find each occurrence of *eleven* and change it to *twelve*, execute the Replace command by pressing **Alt-F2**. Figure 10 shows the message that appears on the status line. Type **N** or press **Enter** to have WordPerfect automatically replace every occurrence of the text without confirmation. This is known as a *global search and replace*. (If you want to confirm each replacement, you would type Y for yes.) Next, type **eleven** as the text you want to replace. Then press **F2**. Type **twelve** as the replacement text, and press **F2** again. WordPerfect will execute the search and replace operation throughout the entire document, without stopping for confirmation.

## Lesson 10: Saving the Document

Word processing programs are useful not only because they make it easier to enter and edit text, but also because they let you save documents on disks. While you are editing a document, it is kept in the computer's primary memory. This gives the software quick access, but the contents of primary memory are lost when the computer is turned off. You should periodically save a document as you work on it, even if it is not finished yet. This guards against losing all of your work if the power should fail or if you make some drastic mistake. By saving a document in a disk file, you get a more permanent copy of your work that can be stored for future

**Figure 10 Prompt to Confirm Each Replacement**

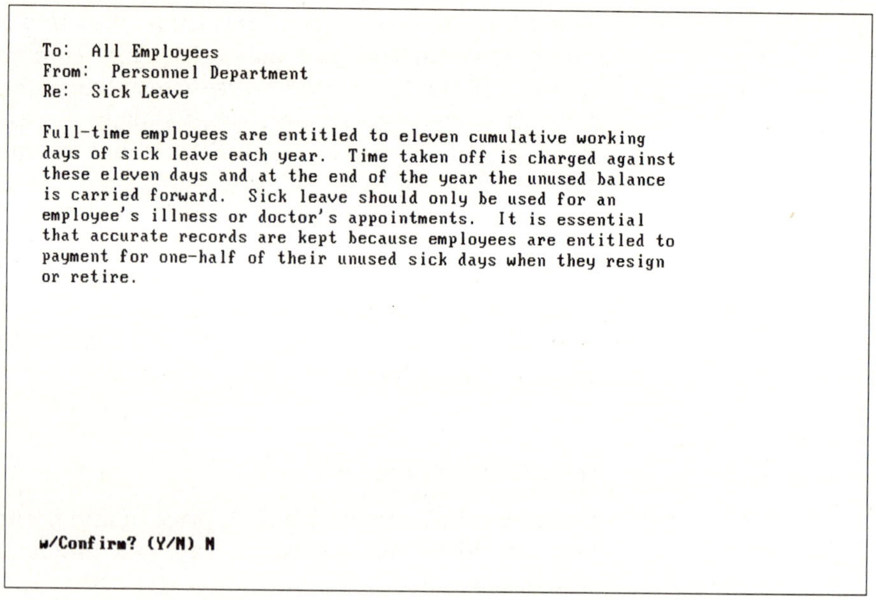

```
To:  All Employees
From:  Personnel Department
Re:  Sick Leave

Full-time employees are entitled to eleven cumulative working
days of sick leave each year.  Time taken off is charged against
these eleven days and at the end of the year the unused balance
is carried forward.  Sick leave should only be used for an
employee's illness or doctor's appointments.  It is essential
that accurate records are kept because employees are entitled to
payment for one-half of their unused sick days when they resign
or retire.

w/Confirm? (Y/N) N
```

reference, printed out, or retrieved and modified. A long document, such as an article or a book chapter, can be created and edited a little at a time. Corrections, updates, and new versions can be made without having to retype everything. So, before we go on, let's save our memo in a disk file.

### Step 1: Invoke the Save Command

Press **F10** to execute WordPerfect's Save command. This will allow you to copy the memo to a disk file, yet continue working on it. If you are using a computer with two floppy drives and no hard disk, you may want to store your document file on a separate diskette. In that case, insert a formatted floppy disk into drive B.

### Step 2: Enter the File Name

WordPerfect will prompt you for the name of the document to be saved (see Figure 11). You can enter any valid DOS file name. If you are working on a hard disk and want to save the memo in your current directory, type **memo.doc**. If you are using a computer with two floppy drives and want to save your document in a file on the diskette in drive B, type **b:memo.doc**. The document will then be copied to the disk under the name MEMO.DOC and WordPerfect will return to the editing screen. Notice that the left side of the status line now displays the path and name of your document file.

## Lesson 11: Checking Spelling

One of WordPerfect's most useful features is its spelling checker. Let's put a misspelled word in the memo to use as an example. Go to the first line and remove an *e* from the word *Employees*.

**Figure 11 Name the Document to Be Saved**

```
To:  All Employees
From:  Personnel Department
Re:  Sick Leave

Full-time employees are entitled to twelve cumulative working
days of sick leave each year.  Time taken off is charged against
these twelve days and at the end of the year the unused balance
is carried forward.  Sick leave should only be used for an
employee's illness or doctor's appointments.  It is essential
that accurate records are kept because employees are entitled to
payment for one-half of their unused sick days when they resign
or retire.

Document to be Saved:
```

### Step 1: Move the Cursor

Press **Home** twice, then press **Up Arrow** to move the cursor to the beginning of the document.

### Step 2: Invoke the Spelling Checker

Press **Ctrl-F2** to invoke the spelling checker. WordPerfect will present the menu shown in Figure 12. Press **3** to check the entire memo. After the dictionary has been loaded from the disk into memory, the spelling checker begins to examine each word in your document to see if it is in the dictionary.

**Figure 12 The Spelling Checker Menu**

```
To:  All Employes
From:  Personnel Department
Re:  Sick Leave

Full-time employees are entitled to twelve cumulative working
days of sick leave each year.  Time taken off is charged against
these twelve days and at the end of the year the unused balance
is carried forward.  Sick leave should only be used for an
employee's illness or doctor's appointments.  It is essential
that accurate records are kept because employees are entitled to
payment for one-half of their unused sick days when they resign
or retire.

Check: 1 Word; 2 Page; 3 Document; 4 Change Dictionary; 5 Look Up; 6 Count
```

### Step 3: Correct Spelling Mistakes

When WordPerfect finds a word it doesn't recognize, it highlights the word, suggests possible replacements, and displays the Not Found menu at the bottom of the screen (see Figure 13). Press **4** to Edit the word, press **Right Arrow** six times, and type **e** to add the missing letter. Press **Enter** to go on. Because this is the educational version of WordPerfect, the spelling checker includes only a very small dictionary. It does not contain most of the words in your document. So, keep pressing **1** to skip words until the program gives you a word count. Press any key to continue.

**Figure 13 The Not Found Menu**

```
To:  All Employes
From:  Personnel Department
Re:  Sick Leave

Full-time employees are entitled to twelve cumulative working
days of sick leave each year.  Time taken off is charged against
these twelve days and at the end of the year the unused balance
is carried forward.  Sick leave should only be used for an
employee's illness or doctor's appointments.  It is essential
that accurate records are kept because employees are entitled to
payment for one-half of their unused sick days when they resign

================================================================================

Not Found!  Select Word or Menu Option (0=Continue): 0
1 Skip Once; 2 Skip; 3 Add Word; 4 Edit; 5 Look Up; 6 Phonetic
```

## Lesson 12: Working with Blocks of Text

In addition to individual characters, words, and lines, most word processing packages let you define and manipulate blocks of text. In WordPerfect, a **block** is a portion of text of any size–from a single character to an entire document. Once a block is defined, or marked, it can be moved, copied, or deleted.

### Step 1: Mark a Block

To better illustrate WordPerfect's block commands, let's add more text to the memo. Press **Home** twice, then press **Down Arrow** to move the cursor to the end of the document. Press **Enter** twice to leave a blank line after the first paragraph. Then type this second paragraph:

> Full-time employees earn twenty-four working days of vacation per year. These are in addition to official company holidays and must be used by the end of each year. Accurate records of vacation leave taken must be kept because employees will be paid for their unused days when they resign or retire.

Press **Enter** twice to leave a blank line at the end of the document. The paragraph you just typed is the block you're going to work with. To mark the block, move the cursor to the first character in the paragraph. Press **Alt-F4**. The flashing message "Block on" will appear on the status line. Move the cursor to the last character to be included in the block, in this case, the end of the document. As the cursor moves, the text in the block will change to reverse video (dark characters against a light background) as shown in Figure 14. You can change the size of the marked block by simply moving the cursor.

**Figure 14 A Marked Block**

```
To:  All Employees
From:  Personnel Department
Re:  Sick Leave

Full-time employees are entitled to twelve cumulative working
days of sick leave each year.  Time taken off is charged against
these twelve days and at the end of the year the unused balance
is carried forward.  Sick leave should only be used for an
employee's illness or doctor's appointments.  It is essential
that accurate records are kept because employees are entitled to
payment for one-half of their unused sick days when they resign
or retire.

Full-time employees earn twenty-four working days of vacation per
year.  These are in addition to official company holidays and
must be used by the end of each year.  Accurate records of
vacation leave taken must be kept because employees will be paid
for their unused days when they resign or retire.



Block on                                  Doc 1  Pg 1  Ln 20     Pos 10
```

### Step 2: Move a Block

Once a block has been marked, it's easy to move it to another position in the document. Suppose you want to put the vacation leave paragraph before the sick leave paragraph. Press **Ctrl-F4** to activate the Move menu (see Figure 15). Press **1** to select the Cut Block option. Move the cursor to the first character of the sick leave paragraph. Press **Ctrl-F4** to activate the Move menu again. Press **5** to select the Text option. The cut block is inserted in the new location.

### Step 3: Copy a Block

Sometimes it's useful to copy text from one location to another. You might need an exact duplicate or a version that's only slightly different. Instead of retyping the text in a new location, you can mark a block, copy the text, then make any modifications if necessary. This can save time when you are working on documents that frequently repeat sections of text. Just for practice, make a copy of the vacation leave paragraph and put it at the end of the memo. Although the duplicate paragraphs won't make sense in your particular document, the exercise will effectively demonstrate how to copy a block.

**Figure 15 The Move Menu**

```
To:  All Employees
From:  Personnel Department
Re:  Sick Leave

Full-time employees are entitled to twelve cumulative working
days of sick leave each year.  Time taken off is charged against
these twelve days and at the end of the year the unused balance
is carried forward.  Sick leave should only be used for an
employee's illness or doctor's appointments.  It is essential
that accurate records are kept because employees are entitled to
payment for one-half of their unused sick days when they resign
or retire.

Full-time employees earn twenty-four working days of vacation per
year.  These are in addition to official company holidays and
must be used by the end of each year.  Accurate records of
vacation leave taken must be kept because employees will be paid
for their unused days when they resign or retire.




1 Cut Block; 2 Copy Block; 3 Append; 4 Cut/Copy Column; 5 Cut/Copy Rectangle: 0
```

First, mark the block to be copied, in this case the first paragraph: move the cursor to the first character, press **Alt-F4**, and press **Down Arrow** six times. Then press **Ctrl-F4** to activate the Move menu. Press **2** to select the Copy Block option. Move the cursor to the end of the document. Press **Ctrl-F4** to activate the Move menu again. Press **5** to select the Text option. WordPerfect then duplicates the vacation leave paragraph at the end of the document (see Figure 16).

**Figure 16 First Paragraph Copied at End of Document**

```
To:  All Employees
From:  Personnel Department
Re:  Sick Leave

Full-time employees earn twenty-four working days of vacation per
year.  These are in addition to official company holidays and
must be used by the end of each year.  Accurate records of
vacation leave taken must be kept because employees will be paid
for their unused days when they resign or retire.

Full-time employees are entitled to twelve cumulative working
days of sick leave each year.  Time taken off is charged against
these twelve days and at the end of the year the unused balance
is carried forward.  Sick leave should only be used for an
employee's illness or doctor's appointments.  It is essential
that accurate records are kept because employees are entitled to
payment for one-half of their unused sick days when they resign
or retire.

Full-time employees earn twenty-four working days of vacation per
year.  These are in addition to official company holidays and
must be used by the end of each year.  Accurate records of
vacation leave taken must be kept because employees will be paid
for their unused days when they resign or retire.
B:\MEMO.DOC                                Doc 1  Pg 1  Ln 20    Pos 10
```

### Step 4: Delete a Block

You now have two copies of the vacation leave paragraph, but you only need one for this memo. This is a good opportunity to try deleting a block. Instead of deleting every character, word, or line in a paragraph, you can erase the whole thing at once. For example, mark the first vacation leave paragraph with **Alt-F4**, then press **Delete**. WordPerfect will display the prompt

```
Delete block? (Y/N) No
```

You are sure that you want to delete the marked block, so type **Y** for yes. Figure 17 shows the result.

**Figure 17  Paragraph Deleted**

```
To:  All Employees
From:  Personnel Department
Re:  Sick Leave

Full-time employees are entitled to twelve cumulative working
days of sick leave each year.  Time taken off is charged against
these twelve days and at the end of the year the unused balance
is carried forward.  Sick leave should only be used for an
employee's illness or doctor's appointments.  It is essential
that accurate records are kept because employees are entitled to
payment for one-half of their unused sick days when they resign
or retire.

Full-time employees earn twenty-four working days of vacation per
year.  These are in addition to official company holidays and
must be used by the end of each year.  Accurate records of
vacation leave taken must be kept because employees will be paid
for their unused days when they resign or retire.



B:\MEMO.DOC                              Doc 1  Pg 1  Ln 5     Pos 10
```

## Lesson 13: Canceling Commands

At some time or another, everyone who uses a word processing package initiates some command or operation and wants to cancel it before it reaches completion. WordPerfect has a Cancel command that can halt a command or restore erased text. This command, which is invoked by pressing F1, can do the following:

- Return from a WordPerfect menu, or cancel your response to a WordPerfect prompt before the response is final.
- Turn off, or unmark, a marked block.
- Restore any of the three most recently deleted text items.

Whenever you erase text, whether a single character or an entire block, WordPerfect temporarily stores that text in a special area of memory. Up to three deletions are saved, allowing you to reverse a delete command. For example, suppose you accidentally deleted the vacation leave paragraph at the beginning of the document, and now you want it back.

#### Step 1: Move the Cursor

First, position the cursor at the place you want to insert the restored text. For this example, press **Home** twice, then press **Down Arrow** to move the cursor to the end of the document.

#### Step 2: Invoke the Cancel Command

Press **F1** to display WordPerfect's Undelete menu (see Figure 18). Type **1** to restore the deleted text at the current cursor location. The deleted text, which is highlighted on the screen, is reinstated. To restore a previously deleted item, you would type 2 until the text you want to restore is displayed. Then you would type 1 to restore the highlighted text.

**Figure 18 The Undelete Menu**

```
Re:  Sick Leave

Full-time employees are entitled to twelve cumulative working
days of sick leave each year.  Time taken off is charged against
these twelve days and at the end of the year the unused balance
is carried forward.  Sick leave should only be used for an
employee's illness or doctor's appointments.  It is essential
that accurate records are kept because employees are entitled to
payment for one-half of their unused sick days when they resign
or retire.

Full-time employees earn twenty-four working days of vacation per
year.  These are in addition to official company holidays and
must be used by the end of each year.  Accurate records of
vacation leave taken must be kept because employees will be paid
for their unused days when they resign or retire.

Full-time employees earn twenty-four working days of vacation per
year.  These are in addition to official company holidays and
must be used by the end of each year.  Accurate records of
vacation leave taken must be kept because employees will be paid
for their unused days when they resign or retire.


Undelete: 1 Restore; 2 Show Previous Deletion: 0
```

Since we really do not want this duplicate vacation leave paragraph in the memo, mark it and delete it again, as you did in Step 4 of Lesson 12.

## Lesson 14: Formatting Characters

Formatting a document means specifying how it will look when it is printed. True what-you-see-is-what-you-get (WYSIWYG) word processing software has an exact correspondence between the screen and the printed page. WordPerfect is not a WYSIWYG word processing package; some formatting specifications show up on the display screen, but others only become evident when the document is printed. WordPerfect has many features that let you format characters, lines, and entire pages. We will start with the character formatting options.

#### Step 1: Underline Text

WordPerfect offers several ways to emphasize characters in a document. Let's add a heading before the sick leave paragraph and underline it. First, make sure Insert mode is turned on. Move the cursor to the first character of the sick leave paragraph. Type **Sick Leave**, then press **Enter** twice. Next, mark this heading as a block with **Alt-F4**. Press **F8** to turn on underlining. The marked text is underlined, highlighted, or presented on the screen in a different color, depending on the type of monitor you have and how WordPerfect has been set up (see Figure 19). When the document is printed, however, the heading *Sick Leave* will be underlined.

**Figure 19 Underlined Text**

```
To:  All Employees
From:  Personnel Department
Re:  Sick Leave

Sick Leave

Full-time employees are entitled to twelve cumulative working
days of sick leave each year.  Time taken off is charged against
these twelve days and at the end of the year the unused balance
is carried forward.  Sick leave should only be used for an
employee's illness or doctor's appointments.  It is essential
that accurate records are kept because employees are entitled to
payment for one-half of their unused sick days when they resign
or retire.

Full-time employees earn twenty-four working days of vacation per
year.  These are in addition to official company holidays and
must be used by the end of each year.  Accurate records of
vacation leave taken must be kept because employees will be paid
for their unused days when they resign or retire.



B:\MEMO.DOC                                  Doc 1  Pg 1  Ln 5      Pos 20
```

### Step 2: Boldface Text

WordPerfect makes it just as easy to boldface text. Type the heading **Vacation Leave** before the second paragraph of the memo. Mark the heading as a block with **Alt-F4**, then press **F6** to boldface it. The heading will be presented on the screen in brighter characters, in a different color, or in reverse video, depending on your monitor and the way in which WordPerfect has been set up (see Figure 20). When the document is printed, however, the heading *Vacation Leave* will appear in boldface.

## Lesson 15: Formatting Lines

Like most word processing packages, WordPerfect has a number of features that control the appearance of lines, paragraphs, and other sections of text. The most frequently used formatting operations allow you to change margins, set tab stops, turn justification on or off, set line spacing, set line height, and center text.

**Figure 20 Boldfaced Text**

```
To:  All Employees
From:  Personnel Department
Re:  Sick Leave

Sick Leave

Full-time employees are entitled to twelve cumulative working
days of sick leave each year.  Time taken off is charged against
these twelve days and at the end of the year the unused balance
is carried forward.  Sick leave should only be used for an
employee's illness or doctor's appointments.  It is essential
that accurate records are kept because employees are entitled to
payment for one-half of their unused sick days when they resign
or retire.

Vacation Leave

Full-time employees earn twenty-four working days of vacation per
year.  These are in addition to official company holidays and
must be used by the end of each year.  Accurate records of
vacation leave taken must be kept because employees will be paid
for their unused days when they resign or retire.

B:\MEMO.DOC                               Doc 1  Pg 1  Ln 16    Pos 25
```

### Step 1: Change Margins

WordPerfect initially sets both the left and right margins of a document at one inch from the edge of the paper. Although these margins are usually adequate, you may need to change them for some documents. Let's change the left and right margins of the memo. First, move the cursor to the beginning of the document, where you want the new margins to begin. Then press **Shift-F8** to display the Line Format menu (see Figure 21(a)). Press **3** to select the Margins option. Enter **12** for the new left margin (in columns). Enter **72** for the new right margin. The new margins are now in effect (see Figure 21(b)). They will remain in effect in this document unless you change them again.

**Figure 21 (a) The Line Format Menu**

```
To:  All Employees
From:  Personnel Department
Re:  Sick Leave

Sick Leave

Full-time employees are entitled to twelve cumulative working
days of sick leave each year.  Time taken off is charged against
these twelve days and at the end of the year the unused balance
is carried forward.  Sick leave should only be used for an
employee's illness or doctor's appointments.  It is essential
that accurate records are kept because employees are entitled to
payment for one-half of their unused sick days when they resign
or retire.

Vacation Leave

Full-time employees earn twenty-four working days of vacation per
year.  These are in addition to official company holidays and
must be used by the end of each year.  Accurate records of
vacation leave taken must be kept because employees will be paid
for their unused days when they resign or retire.

1 2 Tabs; 3 Margins; 4 Spacing; 5 Hyphenation; 6 Align Char: 0
```

**(b) Sick Leave Memo with New Margins**

```
To:  All Employees
From:  Personnel Department
Re:  Sick Leave

Sick Leave

Full-time employees are entitled to twelve cumulative working
days of sick leave each year.  Time taken off is charged
against these twelve days and at the end of the year the
unused balance is carried forward.  Sick leave should only be
used for an employee's illness or doctor's appointments.  It
is essential that accurate records are kept because employees
are entitled to payment for one-half of their unused sick
days when they resign or retire.

Vacation Leave

Full-time employees earn twenty-four working days of vacation
per year.  These are in addition to official company holidays
and must be used by the end of each year.  Accurate records
of vacation leave taken must be kept because employees will
be paid for their unused days when they resign or retire.

B:\MEMO.DOC                          Doc 1  Pg 1  Ln 1    Pos 12
```

### Step 2: Set Tab Stops

Like typewriters, computer keyboards have at least one Tab key. When this key is pressed, the cursor advances to some preset location. By default, WordPerfect initially sets tab stops at half-inch intervals. To move the cursor to the next tab stop, simply press the **Tab** key. If Insert mode is on, pressing the Tab key pushes any existing characters to the right; if Typeover mode is on, the Tab key moves the cursor over existing text. (If Insert mode was on when you pressed Tab, press **Backspace** now to remove the Tab.)

To view or change the current tab settings, press **Shift-F8** to activate the Format menu. Type **1** to select the Tabs option (see Figure 22). The dotted line near the bottom of the screen is a *ruler line* showing the current tab stops. Each *L* denotes a left-justified tab stop. You can use the Left Arrow and Right Arrow keys to move the cursor to a tab stop within the ruler line, then delete existing tab stops with the Delete key. You can add a new tab stop at any position by typing one of the following letters:

- *L* inserts a left-justified tab stop, which aligns text along the left side at the tab stop.
- *C* inserts a centered tab stop, which centers text at the tab stop.
- *R* inserts a right-justified tab stop, which aligns text along the right side at the tab stop.
- *D* inserts a decimal tab stop, which aligns numbers by their decimal points at the tab stop.

You can also delete all existing tab stops in the ruler line by pressing Ctrl-End. For now, leave the tab stops as they are and press **F7** to return to the document.

**Figure 22 The Tabs Option of the Line Format Menu**

```
To:  All Employees
From:  Personnel Department
Re:  Sick Leave

                         Sick Leave

Full-time employees are entitled to twelve cumulative working
days of sick leave each year.  Time taken off is charged
against these twelve days and at the end of the year the
unused balance is carried forward.  Sick leave should only be
used for an employee's illness or doctor's appointments.  It
is essential that accurate records are kept because employees
are entitled to payment for one-half of their unused sick
days when they resign or retire.

                       Vacation Leave

Full-time employees earn twenty-four working days of vacation
per year.  These are in addition to official company holidays
and must be used by the end of each year.  Accurate records
...L....L....L....L....L....L....L....L....L....L....L....L....L....L....L....L
2345678901234567890123456789012345678901234567890123456789012345678901234567890
       20        30        40        50        60        70        80        99
Delete EOL (clear tabs); Enter number (set tab); Del (clear tab);
Left; Center; Right; Decimal; .= Dot leader; Press EXIT when done.
```

### Step 3: Turn Off Justification

When a document is justified, text is aligned exactly to both the left and right margins. If necessary, **soft spaces** are automatically inserted by the word processor to give the text a block look. (**Hard spaces** are inserted only when you press the

Space Bar.) By default, WordPerfect initially has the justification feature turned on, but the on-screen text is not displayed as justified. Justification becomes evident only when the document is printed. Justified text looks best when it is produced by a printer that can do proportional spacing, which allots different amounts of space for different characters. The combination of justification and proportional spacing produces text similar to the typeset material in this book.

If your printer cannot do proportional spacing, it's better to turn off justification. The resulting text will have a ragged right margin similar to that of typewritten text. To turn off justification for our memo, move the cursor to the beginning of the document, and press **Ctrl-F8** to activate the Print Format menu (see Figure 23). Press **3** to turn off justification. Press **F7** to return to the document. Justification will be turned off from the cursor position to the end of the document, but the appearance of on-screen text will not change.

**Figure 23 The Print Format Menu**

```
Print Format

     1 - Pitch                          10
         Font                           1

     2 - Lines per Inch                 6

    Right Justification                 On
     3 - Turn off
     4 - Turn on

    Underline Style                     5
     5 - Non-continuous Single
     6 - Non-continuous Double
     7 - Continuous Single
     8 - Continuous Double

     9 - Sheet Feeder Bin Number        1

     A - Insert Printer Command

     B - Line Numbering                 Off

Selection: 0
```

### Step 4: Set Line Spacing

Word processing packages allow you to determine the line spacing for documents. By default, WordPerfect initially sets line spacing to 1. In other words, lines are automatically single-spaced. This means no blank lines are left between successive lines of text whenever a word wrap occurs or whenever you press the Enter key. Double spacing leaves one blank line between successive lines of text, triple spacing leaves two blank lines, and so on.

Suppose you want your document to be double-spaced. First, move the cursor to where you want double spacing to begin. For this example, press **Home** twice and then **Up Arrow** to position the cursor at the beginning of the memo. Then press **Shift-F8** to activate the Line Format menu. Type **4** to select the Spacing option and enter **2** for double spacing. The memo is now double-spaced, as shown in Figure 24. Any new text you type from the current cursor location to the end of the document will also be double-spaced.

Since memos are usually single-spaced, change the line spacing from 2 back to 1.

**Figure 24 Double-spaced Text on the Screen**

```
To:  All Employees

From:  Personnel Department

Re:  Sick Leave


Sick Leave


Full-time employees are entitled to twelve cumulative working

days of sick leave each year.  Time taken off is charged

against these twelve days and at the end of the year the

unused balance is carried forward.  Sick leave should only be

used for an employee's illness or doctor's appointments.  It

is essential that accurate records are kept because employees
B:\MEMO.DOC                                Doc 1  Pg 1  Ln 1      Pos 10
```

### Step 5: Center Text

Many documents require certain headings or other text to be centered between the left and right margins. To do this manually is a tedious process. Fortunately, WordPerfect, like most word processing packages, has a feature to automatically center text.

Let's center the headings above the two paragraphs in our memo. First, move the cursor to the beginning of the line with the heading *Sick Leave*. Press **Shift-F6**, then the **Down Arrow** key. The line is automatically centered. Now repeat the above process for the *Vacation Leave* heading. Your screen should look like Figure 25.

**Figure 25 Centered Headings**

```
To:  All Employees
From:  Personnel Department
Re:  Sick Leave

                         Sick Leave

Full-time employees are entitled to twelve cumulative working
days of sick leave each year.  Time taken off is charged
against these twelve days and at the end of the year the
unused balance is carried forward.  Sick leave should only be
used for an employee's illness or doctor's appointments.  It
is essential that accurate records are kept because employees
are entitled to payment for one-half of their unused sick
days when they resign or retire.

                       Vacation Leave

Full-time employees earn twenty-four working days of vacation
per year.  These are in addition to official company holidays
and must be used by the end of each year.  Accurate records
of vacation leave taken must be kept because employees will
be paid for their unused days when they resign or retire.


B:\MEMO.DOC                                Doc 1  Pg 1  Ln 17     Pos 12
```

You can also center a new line of text with WordPerfect. You would simply move the cursor to the left margin of the new line, press **Shift-F6** to move the cursor to the center of the line, type the text, and press **Enter**.

## Lesson 16: Formatting Pages

Page formatting features affect entire pages of text. WordPerfect has several commands that let you specify how pages are laid out. Although you don't need to change any of the default page format settings for our simple memo, you may need to change them for other documents. Let's go through the commands that control page length, top and bottom margins, page breaks, and page numbering.

### Step 1: Set the Page Length

Standard letter-size paper is 8½ inches wide and 11 inches long. Given a standard line height of 6 lines per inch, the number of lines on letter-size paper is 6 times 11, or 66. WordPerfect's default paper size is 8½ by 11 inches, but this can be changed. Press **Alt-F8** to activate the Page Format menu (see Figure 26(a)). Press **4** to activate the Page Length menu (see Figure 26(b)). Here is where you could change the page length. Let's just leave the page length set to letter-size paper. Press **F7** twice to return to the editing screen.

**Figure 26 (a) The Page Format Menu**

```
Page Format

     1 - Page Number Position

     2 - New Page Number

     3 - Center Page Top to Bottom

     4 - Page Length

     5 - Top Margin

     6 - Headers or Footers

     7 - Page Number Column Positions

     8 - Suppress for Current page only

     9 - Conditional End of Page

     A - Widow/Orphan

Selection: 0
```

**(b) The Page Length Menu**

```
Page Length

     1 - Letter Size Paper: Form Length = 66 lines (11 inches)
         Single Spaced Text lines = 54 (This includes lines
         used for Headers, Footers and/or page numbers.)

     2 - Legal Size Paper: Form Length = 84 lines (14 inches)
         Single Spaced Text Lines = 72 (This includes lines
         used for Headers, Footers and/or page numbers.)

     3 - Other (Maximum page length = 108 lines.)

Current Settings

     Form Length in Lines (6 per inch): 66

     Number of Single Spaced Text Lines: 54

Selection: 0
```

### Step 2: Set the Top Margin

Most documents are printed with some blank space at the top and bottom of every page. By default, WordPerfect leaves one-inch top and bottom margins. To change these settings, press **Alt-F8** to activate the Page Format menu. Press **5** to set the top margin. The bottom margin cannot be set directly. Its size depends on the page length and the top margin. Let's just leave the top margin set to one inch, so press **F7** twice to return to the editing screen.

### Step 3: Start a New Page

The actual number of lines of text printed on a page depends on several factors. For example, WordPerfect's default line height is 1/6-inch. The default page length is 11 inches (66 lines), with a top margin of 1 inch (6 lines) and a bottom margin of 1 inch (6 lines). The default for number of lines of text printed on a page, therefore, is 66 minus 12, or 54.

As you type text with WordPerfect, the word wrap feature automatically starts new lines. WordPerfect also automatically starts new pages. Assuming the default page-format settings are in effect, a soft page break is inserted after every 54 lines you type. A **soft page break** is a division between two pages that is automatically generated by the word processing software. It is displayed on the screen as a horizontal line of dashes. This line is not actually printed on paper, it is simply displayed on-screen to indicate where a new page will begin.

Although WordPerfect's automatic page-break feature is convenient, you may sometimes want to have a page with fewer than 54 lines. A new page can be forced by pressing Ctrl-Enter to insert a **hard page break**. This is a division between two pages that is manually generated by the user. It is displayed on the screen as a horizontal line of equal signs. You can begin a new page at any point within a document simply by pressing Ctrl-Enter. For example, let's insert a hard page break between the two paragraphs in the memo. Move the cursor to the beginning of the line just above the *Vacation Leave* heading and press **Ctrl-Enter**. Your screen should look like Figure 27. If this document were printed, the text below the line of equal signs would begin on a new page.

**Figure 27 A Hard Page Break**

```
To:  All Employees
From:  Personnel Department
Re:  Sick Leave

                         Sick Leave

Full-time employees are entitled to twelve cumulative working
days of sick leave each year.  Time taken off is charged
against these twelve days and at the end of the year the
unused balance is carried forward.  Sick leave should only be
used for an employee's illness or doctor's appointments.  It
is essential that accurate records are kept because employees
are entitled to payment for one-half of their unused sick
days when they resign or retire.

==============================================================================

                         Vacation Leave

Full-time employees earn twenty-four working days of vacation
per year.  These are in addition to official company holidays
and must be used by the end of each year.  Accurate records
of vacation leave taken must be kept because employees will
be paid for their unused days when they resign or retire.
A:\MEMO.DOC                                  Doc 1 Pg 2 Ln 1      Pos 12
```

A hard page break can be removed from a document with the Delete or Backspace key. Remove the hard page break you just inserted by moving the cursor to the beginning of the line above the *Vacation Leave* heading and pressing **Backspace**. The page break will disappear.

### Step 4: Set the Page Numbering

WordPerfect automatically keeps track of page numbers while you work on a document and displays the current page number at the bottom of the screen on the status line (see Figure 27). But WordPerfect does not print page numbers unless you tell it to do so. Although we don't need a page number on our single-page memo, let's see how you would turn on printed page numbering. Press **Alt-F8** to activate the Page Format menu. Type **1** to activate the Page Number Position menu (see Figure 28). The options in this menu let you choose the type of page numbering to appear on your printed document. We don't want page numbers, so press **F7** twice.

**Figure 28 The Page Number Position Menu**

```
Position of Page Number on Page

     0 - No page numbers

     1 - Top left of every page

     2 - Top center of every page

     3 - Top right of every page

     4 - Top alternating left & right

     5 - Bottom left of every page

     6 - Bottom center of every page

     7 - Bottom right of every page

     8 - Bottom alternating left & right


Selection: 0
```

## Lesson 17: Printing a Document

You've entered, formatted, proofread, and corrected your document. You're satisfied with your work, and now it's time to produce the final product. You need to print your document on paper.

### Step 1: Save the Document

It is a good idea to save your document before printing. As we described in Lesson 10, you do this by pressing **F10**. If you have previously saved the document you are editing, WordPerfect will suggest the file name you already entered. You do not need to type the file name again unless you want to save the document to a file with a different name. Just press **Enter**. Next, WordPerfect will ask if you want to replace the existing file with your latest version. Type **Y** for yes.

### Step 2: Turn On the Printer

Be sure the printer is connected to the computer and turned on. Also, check to be sure paper is loaded and aligned to the top of a new page. Finally, make sure that the printer's On Line light is lit. (If it isn't, press the On Line button.)

### Step 3: Invoke the Print Command

Press **Shift-F7** to activate the Print menu (see Figure 29). Then type **1** to print the entire document. When WordPerfect is finished printing the document, it will return to the editing screen.

**Figure 29  The Print Menu**

```
To:  All Employees
From:  Personnel Department
Re:  Sick Leave

                         Sick Leave

Full-time employees are entitled to twelve cumulative working
days of sick leave each year.  Time taken off is charged
against these twelve days and at the end of the year the
unused balance is carried forward.  Sick leave should only be
used for an employee's illness or doctor's appointments.  It
is essential that accurate records are kept because employees
are entitled to payment for one-half of their unused sick
days when they resign or retire.

                       Vacation Leave

Full-time employees earn twenty-four working days of vacation
per year.  These are in addition to official company holidays
and must be used by the end of each year.  Accurate records
of vacation leave taken must be kept because employees will
be paid for their unused days when they resign or retire.


1 Full Text; 2 Page; 3 Options; 4 Printer Control; 5 Type-thru; 6 Preview: 0
```

## Lesson 18: Returning to DOS

When you are finished working with WordPerfect, you will exit the program and return to DOS.

### Step 1: Invoke the Exit Command

From the editing screen, press **F7**, the Exit key, to tell WordPerfect that you either want to work on a different document or return to DOS.

### Step 2: Save the Document

WordPerfect will ask if you want to save the document. Unless you are just viewing a document that you have not changed, you should type **Y** for yes. If you have never saved this document before, you must enter a file name. If you have saved this document before, as we have done twice in this chapter, WordPerfect will suggest the current name. Press **Enter** to choose this name. You can, however, type a new name if you want to save the document to a different file. If you choose the same name, WordPerfect will ask if you want to replace the existing document file with the version on the screen. Type **Y** for yes.

### Step 3: Confirm the Exit

WordPerfect will copy the document to the disk and display the prompt

```
Exit WP? (Y/N) No          (Cancel to return to document)
```

Here the program is asking if you really want to return to DOS, and it assumes you do not. If you press F1, the Cancel key, you will return to your current document. If you type N or press Enter, you can begin a new document. Type **Y** to exit WordPerfect. You should see the DOS prompt on your screen.

## Lesson 19: Editing an Existing Document

Word processors make it so easy to store documents in disk files, editing an existing document is a very common procedure. Any time you want to examine, modify, or update a previously stored document, all you have to do is tell WordPerfect to retrieve the file.

### Step 1: Specify the Document When Loading WordPerfect

At this point you should be at the DOS prompt because you exited WordPerfect at the end of the last lesson. Before you can edit an existing document, you must first make sure its file is stored on an accessible disk. The location of the document file depends on your default directory or the name you chose when you last saved the document. Your document may be on the diskette in drive B, on your hard disk C, or on a network file server disk.

If you know the name and location of the document file you want to edit, you can start WordPerfect and load the document at the same time. If you are using a computer with a hard disk, from DOS, type **wp memo.doc** and press **Enter**. If you are running WordPerfect on a computer with two floppy drives and you saved the memo on the diskette in drive B, enter **wp b:memo.doc**. Your document will be loaded into memory along with WordPerfect and you can view or edit it after you press any key twice to get past the initial information and help screens of the WordPerfect 4.2 educational version.

### Step 2: Use the List Files Menu

Another way to edit an existing document is to retrieve the file from within WordPerfect. Exit WordPerfect and return to DOS. Start WordPerfect again by entering **wp** from the DOS prompt. Press any key twice to get past the initial information and help screens. Press **F5** to activate the List Files menu. WordPerfect will suggest your current drive and directory. If you are working from a hard disk and your document is stored in the default directory, just press **Enter**. If your document is on the diskette in drive B, type **b:** and press **Enter**. A screen like the one in Figure 30 will appear. This screen shows the files in the specified directory and presents the List Files menu. Your screen may have different files, or, if you specified drive B, perhaps only one file will be listed.

To load an existing document, use the arrow keys to move the reverse video highlight bar to the appropriate file name. For this example, locate MEMO.DOC, highlight it, and press **1** to retrieve it. WordPerfect will load the file into memory and present the memo on the editing screen.

**Figure 30 The List Files Menu**

```
01/03/89  15:08              Directory B:\*.*
Document Size:         0                               Free Disk Space:    75776

. <CURRENT>     <DIR>                    | .. <PARENT>     <DIR>
LEX       .WP        8535  12/16/86 03:01 | MEMO      .DOC      1109  02/16/89 15:01
README    .WP        1304  12/03/86 10:08 | TH        .WP       2051  12/03/86 09:44
WP        .EXE     264113  12/04/86 15:09 | WPHELP    .FIL      1508  12/04/86 15:09
{WP}      .BV1          0  02/16/89 15:08 | {WP}      .CHK         0  02/16/89 15:08
{WP}      .SPC       4096  02/16/89 15:08 | {WP}      .TV1         0  02/16/89 15:08

1 Retrieve; 2 Delete; 3 Rename; 4 Print; 5 Text In;
6 Look; 7 Change Directory; 8 Copy; 9 Word Search; 0 Exit: 6
```

### Step 3: Edit the Document

Sometimes you load an existing document file just to read it. Other times you actually want to correct, update, or modify the contents. Let's make a couple of additions to our sample memo. With the cursor at the first character of the first line, press **Enter** to add a blank line and press **Up Arrow** to move the cursor back up. Type **Date:**, then type today's date. Now move the cursor to the end of the line that reads *Re: Sick Leave*. Press the **Space Bar** and type the phrase **and Vacation Leave**. Except for the date, your screen should look like Figure 31.

**Figure 31 The Completed Memo**

```
Date:  January 3, 1989
To:  All Employees
From:  Personnel Department
Re:  Sick Leave and Vacation Leave_

                         Sick Leave

Full-time employees are entitled to twelve cumulative working
days of sick leave each year.  Time taken off is charged
against these twelve days and at the end of the year the
unused balance is carried forward.  Sick leave should only be
used for an employee's illness or doctor's appointments.  It
is essential that accurate records are kept because employees
are entitled to payment for one-half of their unused sick
days when they resign or retire.

                       Vacation Leave

Full-time employees earn twenty-four working days of vacation
per year.  These are in addition to official company holidays
and must be used by the end of each year.  Accurate records
of vacation leave taken must be kept because employees will
be paid for their unused days when they resign or retire.

A:\MEMO.DOC                              Doc 1  Pg 1  Ln 4      Pos 46
```

### Step 4: Save the File and Exit WordPerfect

Press **F7, Y, Enter, Y,** and **Y** again to invoke the Exit command, save the updated memo, and return to DOS.

## Conclusion

In this chapter we have covered the basics of using WordPerfect 4.2. Although we have not discussed every feature of this powerful and versatile package, you should have no trouble entering, editing, formatting, and printing documents on your own. Feel free to experiment and try some of the commands that we haven't covered. The WordPerfect help facility can provide much of the information you need. In addition, you may want to read the *WordPerfect* reference manual (from WordPerfect Corporation) or an ancillary book on the subject.

## Exercises

### Multiple Choice

Choose the best selection to complete each statement.

______ 1. When you start WordPerfect without loading a document, the only thing on the editing screen, except for the cursor, is the
(a) Start Up menu (c) status line
(b) ruler line (d) Help facility

______ 2. Which keys would you press to see an on-screen version of the WordPerfect function key template?
(a) F1 (c) F7
(b) F3 (d) Alt-F3

______ 3. What is inserted into your document when you press the Enter key?
(a) hard return (c) hard page break
(b) soft return (d) soft page break

______ 4. What feature eliminates having to press Enter at the end of every line?
(a) justification (c) word-wrap
(b) proportional spacing (d) auto-hyphenation

______ 5. Which keys would you press to move the cursor to the beginning of the next word to the right?
(a) Right Arrow (c) Ctrl-Right Arrow
(b) Shift-Right Arrow (d) Home-Right Arrow

______ 6. You can move the cursor to the beginning of a document by pressing
(a) Ctrl-End (c) Ctrl-PgDn
(b) End, End, then Down Arrow (d) Home, Home, then Up Arrow

______ 7. Pressing the Insert key toggles the
(a) delete mode (c) line spacing
(b) Insert mode (d) tab settings

______ 8. Pressing the Delete key deletes the character
(a) at the current cursor location (c) to the immediate left of the cursor
(b) to the immediate right of the cursor (d) farthest from the cursor

_______ 9. Pressing Ctrl-Backspace
(a) deletes the word to the right of the cursor
(b) deletes the word at the cursor
(c) moves the cursor to the beginning of the line
(d) moves the cursor to the end of the line

_______ 10. One operation that WordPerfect cannot do to a marked block is
(a) copy it
(b) lock it
(c) delete it
(d) move it

_______ 11. Which keys would you press to repeat the previous search operation?
(a) F2, F2
(b) Alt-R
(c) F3, F3
(d) Ctrl-R

_______ 12. To insert a new page break, you must press
(a) Alt-P
(b) Ctrl-Enter
(c) Ctrl-PgDn
(d) Alt-End

_______ 13. Power failures, voltage fluctuations, system crashes, and unknown system bugs are all good reasons to periodically
(a) print your document
(b) edit your document
(c) retrieve your document
(d) save your document

_______ 14. When starting WordPerfect, including a file name after the command **wp**
(a) prints that file
(b) automatically loads that file
(c) periodically saves that file
(d) deletes that file

_______ 15. Which key(s) would you press to restore the most recently deleted word or phrase?
(a) Ctrl-U
(b) F1
(c) Ctrl-End
(d) Escape

_______ 16. Which two character formatting options can each be used by pressing a single function key?
(a) italics and outline
(b) shadow and strikeout
(c) underline and boldface
(d) double underline and small capitals

_______ 17. What are the default WordPerfect settings for left and right margins?
(a) 10 and 74
(b) 12 and 72
(c) 10 and 68
(d) 0 and 74

_______ 18. How many blank lines are left between double-spaced lines?
(a) 0
(b) 1
(c) 2
(d) 3

_______ 19. What keys do you press to activate the Print menu?
(a) Shift-F7
(b) Ctrl-P
(c) Ctrl-F1
(d) Shift-PrtSc

_______ 20. What key do you use to exit WordPerfect and return to DOS?
(a) F1
(b) F3
(c) F5
(d) F7

### Fill-In

1. To start WordPerfect, you type _______________ and press Enter.

2. The line at the bottom of the WordPerfect editing screen is called the _______________.

3. Pressing _______________ and then _______________ moves the cursor to the left edge of the screen.

4. Pressing F3 brings up WordPerfect's ______________ facility.

5. ______________ is the key you press to move the cursor to the end of the current line.

6. When a document is formatted such that all of the lines line up at the right margin, it is ______________.

7. Word processors have a feature called ______________ that eliminates having to press Enter at the end of each line.

8. Pressing Enter generates what's known as a ______________ return.

9. The ______________ keys include the Home, End, Page Up, Page Down, and arrow keys.

10. If Insert mode is on, pressing the Insert key switches to ______________ mode.

11. To overwrite mistakes, you must first turn Insert mode ______________.

12. Backspace, Delete, Ctrl-Backspace, and Ctrl-End are all examples of commands that ______________ text.

13. Existing text can be centered between the left and right margins by pressing ______________.

14. A ______________ is any section of text, from a single character to a whole document, that can be marked and treated as a single entity.

15. A global ______________ and ______________ operation is used to automatically change every occurrence of a word or phrase.

16. By default, WordPerfect sets both the top and bottom page margins to ______________.

17. When justification is not used, you get a ______________ right margin.

18. If the spelling checker stops on a word that is not misspelled, you can use the ______________ or ______________ option to continue.

19. When you ______________ a document, WordPerfect copies it from primary memory to a disk file.

20. In WordPerfect, page numbering is turned ______________ by default.

### Short Problems

1. If you are not already running WordPerfect, change to the proper disk drive directory and type **WP**. Type the following text. Press **Enter** only once, after the last line.

   **The next meeting of the EZ Systems Board of Managers will be held at 7:00 P.M. on November 19, 1989, in Room 217 of Champaign Federal Savings. This is an important meeting, so please try to attend.**

2. Move the cursor to the top of the document and type the following lines. Press **Enter** after each one.

   **To: Board of Managers**
   **From: David Franklin, Secretary**
   **Re: Next meeting**

3. Press the **Enter** key again to leave a blank line before the paragraph. Move the cursor to the top of the document, type **M E M O**, and press **Enter**. Boldface, underline, and center this title.

4. Move the cursor to the last line of the memo and delete it by pressing **Ctrl-End**. Restore the text you've deleted with the Cancel command.

5. Mark *EZ Systems* in the first line of text as a block. Copy the block, putting it in front of *Board of Managers* after the *To:*.

6. Move the cursor to the top of the file. Use the search and replace command to change *Managers* to *Directors* throughout the entire document.

7. Move the cursor to the beginning of the document and set the left and right margins to 1.5 inches.

8. Change the tab stops so that they occur at 1-inch intervals.

9. Turn off justification for this memo.

10. Double-space the entire document.

11. Without exiting WordPerfect, save the document in a disk file named MEETING.DOC.

12. If your computer is equipped with a printer, make sure it is turned on and on-line. Print the EZ Systems memo.

### Long Problems

1. Use WordPerfect to create a letter to be sent to three different software companies requesting information about the word processor they sell. Use the same basic letter, but tailor it to each company and its product. Save each version in its own disk file and print out all three. If you have no word processors in mind, use these three:

| WordPerfect | WordStar | Microsoft Word |
|---|---|---|
| WordPerfect Corp. | MicroPro International Corp. | Microsoft Corp. |
| 288 W. Center St. | 33 San Pablo Ave. | 16011 N.E. 36th |
| Orem, UT 84057 | San Rafael, CA 94903 | Box 97017 |
| | | Redmond, WA 98073 |

2. Use WordPerfect to write a paper for one of your classes or a report for your company. Be sure to follow any format guidelines specified.

3. Look in a newspaper or placement office listing for a position you might apply for. Prepare a realistic resume and cover letter for this job with WordPerfect. Use underlining and boldface where appropriate.

4. Investigate three different word processing programs. Use WordPerfect to prepare a report that compares their features.

5. Use WordPerfect to create your academic schedule for this semester. List the days, times, classes, buildings, rooms, and instructors.

6. Create a weekly appointment calendar with WordPerfect. Print out several copies for the next few weeks.

7. Write a letter with WordPerfect to a company, praising or criticizing their product or service.

8. Use WordPerfect to write a letter to WordPerfect Corp. detailing some of the things you like or dislike about their word processing package. You can use the address given in Problem 1.

9. Create an address and phone listing of your friends and acquaintances using WordPerfect.

10. Use what you learned in Chapter 2 to create a quick reference guide to DOS with WordPerfect. In other words, list each DOS command along with a brief description of what it does and how to invoke it.

11. Use WordPerfect to create a quick reference guide to WordPerfect. List the commands and operations that you think are most important to remember.

12. Take a week's worth of notes from a class you are taking and redo them with WordPerfect. Try to do more than just transcribe them. Organize, rearrange, and reword the material as appropriate. How could using a word processor improve your notes?

13. As you redo your notes for Problem 12, keep in mind any possible questions you might have about the material. Write a letter to your professor in which you outline your questions.

14. Suppose you have some item, such as a musical instrument, bicycle, car, couch, television, stereo, or computer, that you would like to sell through a newspaper ad. Or suppose you are looking for a roommate or have an apartment to sublet. Use WordPerfect to design a classified ad to place in your school or town newspaper.

15. Choose some current event or local news item that interests you and use WordPerfect to write a letter expressing your views to the editor of your school or town newspaper.

# Glossary

**absolute cell reference** a cell address that does not change when it is moved or copied (Ch. 8)
**access arm** a mechanical extension in a disk drive that moves the read-write head toward or away from the center of the disk (Ch. 2)
**account** a file containing financial information (Ch. 15)
**account activity detail report** a listing of each account's transactions during a particular month (Ch. 15)
**accounting equation** the formula that summarizes the financial condition of a business (Ch. 15)
**accounting package** software that manages an organization's finances (Ch. 1)
**accounts payable** the accounting subsystem that records the purchases of goods and services from each vendor (Ch. 15)
**accounts receivable** the accounting subsystem that records all sales of goods and services (Ch. 15)
**active cell** see *current cell* (Ch. 8)
**Ada** a powerful, comprehensive high-level programming language applicable to a wide range of problems (Ch. 3)
**adapter** see *expansion board* (Ch. 2)
**address** a unique identifying number for a storage location in memory (Ch. 2)
**aged accounts receivable report** a report that indicates how much money each customer owes and how long the amount has been outstanding (Ch. 15)
**alphanumeric characters** letters, numbers, and punctuation marks (Appendix A)
**alternate operating environment** see *windowing environment* (Ch. 3)
**American Standard Code for Information Interchange (ASCII)** the code used by most microcomputers for representing text in binary form (Ch. 11 and Appendix A)
**application** see *application software* (Ch. 1)
**application generator** see *fourth generation language* (Ch. 3)
**application package** see *application software* (Ch. 1)
**application software** a program or set of programs that applies the computer to useful tasks like helping you write letters, figure taxes, maintain mailing lists, and draw charts (Ch. 1)
**artificial intelligence (AI)** a field of study combining aspects of computer science, mathematics, philosophy, psychology, and linguistics whose main goal is to mimic human learning and decision making (Ch. 16)
**ascending order** the arrangement of numbers from smallest to largest, and of text alphabetically from A to Z (Ch. 10)
**assembler** a program that translates assembly language instructions into the binary numbers of machine language (Ch. 3)
**assembly language** a programming language that substitutes meaningful abbreviations for the numerically coded instructions of a machine language (Ch. 3)
**assets** money and property owned by a business (Ch. 15)
**audit trail** a journal that automatically records the date, time, debit, and credit of every transaction (Ch. 15)
**auto-hyphenation** a word processing feature that automatically hyphenates words at the ends of lines when necessary (Ch. 7)
**automated vision** a type of software that allows computers to distinguish and interpret images from optical sensors (Ch. 16)
**automatic recalculation** the ability of a spreadsheet program to immediately update the entire worksheet whenever the contents of a cell are changed (Ch. 8)
**backup** an extra copy of vital programs or data; to make such a copy (Ch. 2)
**balance sheet** a report that summarizes the assets, liabilities, and capital of a business (Ch. 15)

**BASIC** a simple, interactive programming language originally designed to teach students about computer programming (Ch. 3)

**Basic Input/Output System (BIOS)** on some computers, the hardware interface that controls physical components such as disk drives, monitor, keyboard, and printer (Ch. 4)

**batch file** a text file that lists operating system commands to be performed automatically when the name of the batch file is entered (Ch. 4)

**batch processing** using batch files to reduce several frequently used operating system commands to just one command to save time and effort (Ch. 4)

**benchmark** an objective, reproducible measure of hardware or software performance (Appendix B)

**Bernoulli box** see *Bernoulli disk drive* (Ch. 2)

**Bernoulli disk drive** a secondary storage device that combines the advantages of both floppy and hard disk drives (Ch. 2)

**billing** the accounting subsystem that prepares and records invoices (Ch. 15)

**binary point** the period that separates the whole part from the fractional part of a mixed binary number (Appendix A)

**bit** the basic unit of data processing; a single binary digit, 0 or 1, off or on (Ch. 2)

**bit-mapped** see *pixel-based* (Ch. 13)

**bits per second (bps)** unit of modem transmission speed (Ch. 2)

**block** a contiguous section of text—can consist of a single character up to an entire document (Ch. 7)

**booting up** initially loading and executing the operating system (Ch. 5)

**border palette** a menu of line thicknesses used to draw lines and outline shapes (Ch. 13)

**briefcase computer** see *laptop computer* (Ch. 1)

**browse** to casually scan the records of a data base (Ch. 10)

**bug** an error or problem in a computer program

**built-in dictionary** an automatic proofreading feature that looks for spelling errors (Ch. 6)

**bus** a set of wires and connectors that link the CPU to memory and other computer components (Ch. 2)

**bus network** a topology in which each workstation is connected to a single cable running past all the workstations (Ch. 12)

**byte** a contiguous group of eight bits; the amount of memory it takes to store a single character (Ch. 2)

**C** a concise, yet powerful programming language frequently used for the development of system software and application packages (Ch. 3)

**cache** an intermediary storage place (Ch. 16)

**capital** an owner's stake in a business (Ch. 15)

**capture** to gather incoming data from a host computer and save it in a disk file (Ch. 12)

**carrier sense multiple access (CSMA)** a protocol that requires each network workstation to listen before sending messages or data (Ch. 12)

**cathode ray tube (CRT)** a display that uses an electronic gun to paint images on a phosphor-coated glass screen (Ch. 2)

**cell** the box at the intersection of a row and a column in a worksheet (Ch. 8)

**cell address** a designation that specifies a cell's exact location within a worksheet (Ch. 8)

**cell pointer** the highlighted cell that marks the current location in a worksheet (Ch. 8)

**central processing unit (CPU)** the part of a computer that performs calculations, logic, and control operations (Ch. 1)

**chamfer** a CAD feature that joins two lines with another straight line (Ch. 13)

**character formatting** specifying the way individual letters or words are presented (Ch. 6)

**charting program** a program that produces graphs, plots, and charts from data entered directly or imported from a spreadsheet or data base file (Ch. 13)

**chart of accounts** a hierarchical listing of all accounts, invaluable for classifying all of the financial information of a business (Ch. 15)

**chassis** a metal and plastic frame that houses all of the internal components of a computer (Ch. 2)

**chip** see *integrated circuit chip* (Ch. 2)

**circular reference** the result of a formula in a cell being either directly or indirectly dependent on the value in that very same cell (Ch. 8)

**clicking** moving the mouse pointer on top of an item to be selected and briefly pressing and releasing the mouse button (Ch. 13)
**clipboard** a temporary storage area for copying data (Ch. 8)
**clone** a computer that works just like, or very similar to, another computer (Ch. 1)
**coaxial cable** a center conductor surrounded by a shield or wire braid, used for cable television and local area networks (Ch. 12)
**COBOL** a high-level programming language introduced in 1960 especially for business data processing (Ch. 3)
**color graphics monitor** a monitor that can display both text and graphics in more than one color (Ch. 2)
**column-wise recalculation** the order of worksheet recalculation that begins with cell A1 and proceeds down column A, goes on to cell B1 and proceeds down column B, and so on (Ch. 8)
**combining** see *merging* (Ch. 8)
**command** a directive that is issued to a program (Ch. 3)
**communications package** software that lets a computer transfer messages, programs, and data to other computers (Ch. 1)
**communications parameters** the settings that specify the technical details of how a computer will communicate with another computer (Ch. 12)
**communications server** a network workstation that lets users communicate with computers outside the network via serial ports and a high-speed modem (Ch. 12)
**compact disk read-only memory (CD-ROM)** an optical disk drive that allows access to previously recorded data, but not storage of any new data (Ch. 2)
**compiler** a program that translates high-level language instructions into machine language (Ch. 3)
**computer** an electronic device that performs calculations and processes data into information
**computer-aided design (CAD)** a type of software package for drafting complex plans, blueprints, models, schematics, and other detailed drawings of parts, mechanisms, and buildings (Ch. 13)
**computer graphics** the presentation of images such as figures, charts, graphs, maps, diagrams, and other pictures on a display screen (Ch. 2)
**context-sensitive** the ability of a help facility to display information specifically relevant to the current activity (Ch. 6)
**coprocessor** integrated circuit chip designed to perform a specialized task for the main microprocessor (Ch. 2)
**copy-and-paste** a word processing operation in which a section of text is reproduced in another location (Ch. 6)
**copy-protection** a way to prepare diskettes so that it is difficult or impossible to copy them with ordinary operating system commands (Ch. 5)
**CP/M** a single-user, single-tasking generic microcomputer operating system sold by Digital Research (Ch. 4)
**credit** a source of money (Ch. 15)
**Critical Path Method (CPM)** a scheduling method that focuses on the sequence of critical activities that must be performed to complete a project (Ch. 16)
**crosshair** two lines that intersect on the screen to indicate the current cursor position (Ch. 13)
**current cell** the cell marked by the cell pointer, where you can enter data or initiate commands (Ch. 8)
**cursor** a small, blinking underscore or box that marks the position where characters will appear on the screen when typed
**cursor diamond** in WordStar, an arrangement of letter keys used in conjunction with the Control key for moving the cursor (Ch. 7)
**cut-and-paste** a word processing operation in which a section of text is moved from one location to another (Ch. 6)
**daisy-wheel printer** a printer with solid, raised characters embossed on the ends of little arms arranged like the spokes of a wheel, for producing slow, but letter-quality output (Ch. 2)
**data** numbers, text, pictures,and sounds that are to be processed into information (Ch. 1)
**data base** an organized collection of one or more files of related data (Ch. 1)

**data base management package** software that lets you organize large quantities of information, such as mailing lists and inventories (Ch. 1)
**data bus** the pathway connecting the microprocessor to memory (Ch. 2)
**data encryption** a security method that encodes information so that it can be read and changed only by authorized users who know the password (Ch. 10)
**data entry form** a listing of each field in a record, accompanied by an empty box for each field's contents (Ch. 10)
**debit** an application of money (Ch. 15)
**debug** to remove the errors from a computer program
**debugger** a program that helps to detect errors in software under development (Ch. 4)
**dedicated server** a network workstation reserved solely as a file, printer, or communications server (Ch. 12)
**dedicated word processor** a microcomputer system expressly designed and solely used to prepare, store, and print documents (Ch. 6)
***de facto* standard** a standard that emerges from many manufacturers voluntarily making products that will work together (Ch. 1)
**default** predefined settings for certain features (margins, line spacing, column widths, etc.) that a software package uses automatically if the user does not explicitly establish settings
**default drive** the disk drive where DOS will look for programs and data files unless otherwise specified (Ch. 5)
**delete** to remove, erase, or destroy one or more pieces of information
**delimiter** a space, comma, semicolon, equal sign, or tab (Ch. 5)
**descending order** the arrangement of numbers from largest to smallest, and of text alphabetically from Z to A (Ch. 10)
**desk accessory** a utility program that provides commonly used desk functions such as a calculator, calendar, or address book (Ch. 16)
**desktop computer** the most common type of microcomputer, small enough to fit on top of a table or desk (Ch. 1)
**desktop organizer** see *desk accessory* (Ch. 16)
**desktop publishing** using a computer and laser printer to produce near-typeset-quality documents
**desktop publishing package** software that combines the results of word processing and graphics to produce near-typeset-quality documents (Ch. 1)
**detail accounts** the accounts that actually record credit and debit transactions (Ch. 15)
**device controller** a set of chips or a circuit board that operates a piece of computer equipment such as a disk drive, display, keyboard, mouse, or printer (Ch. 2)
**digitizer** see *graphics tablet* (Ch. 2)
**direct access medium** storage medium, such as magnetic disk, that allows data items to be retrieved in any order (Ch. 2)
**direct-connect modem** see *external modem* (Ch. 2)
**directory** a list of the files stored on a disk; another term for subdirectory
**disk** a medium used by computers to store information, consisting of one or more flat surfaces on which bits are recorded magnetically or optically
**disk backup utility** a program that facilitates making backup copies of a hard disk on floppy disks (Ch. 16)
**disk caching utility** a program that reserves part of memory as an intermediary storage place to speed up the retrieval of frequently used software and data (Ch. 16)
**disk copying utility** a program that specializes in duplicating files and disks, especially those that are copy protected (Ch. 16)
**disk drive** a computer system component that reads and writes programs and data on disks (Ch. 1)
**diskette** see *floppy disk* (Ch. 1)
**disk optimizing utility** a program that makes secondary storage devices operate more efficiently (Ch. 16)
**display** output screen on which the computer presents text and graphic images (Ch. 1)
**display adapter** a circuit board or set of chips that controls a monitor (Ch. 2)
**display-only field** see *read-only field* (Ch. 10)
**document** the paper output of a word processor

**documentation** the user manual or technical information about a computer or software package
**document file** a collection of text created by a word processing program in such a way that the text includes embedded formatting codes
**DOS** a generic name for PC-DOS and MS-DOS (Ch. 4)
**DOS prompt** a symbol that identifies the current default drive and indicates that DOS is waiting for a command (Ch. 5)
**DOS shell** a menu-driven addition to DOS that helps manage disk files and directories (Ch. 16)
**dot command** in WordStar, a command that begins with a period in column one and is stored with a document (Ch. 7)
**dot-matrix printer** a common type of printer that constructs character images by repeatedly striking pins against the ribbon and paper (Ch. 2)
**dot pitch** the distance between the illuminated centers of any two adjacent dots on a display screen (Ch. 13)
**dot prompt** the period used by dBASE to indicate that it is waiting for a command (Ch. 11)
**dot prompt command** a dBASE command entered in response to the dot prompt and not selected from a menu (Ch. 11)
**double-clicking** pressing and releasing a mouse button twice in rapid succession (Ch. 13)
**double entry accounting** the basic method used by all modern accounting systems, which requires a corresponding credit for every debit (Ch. 15)
**downloading** transferring a file from a host computer to your computer (Ch. 12)
**draft mode** the fastest print mode in which low-quality characters are formed by a single pass of the printhead (Ch. 2)
**dragging** holding down the mouse button while moving the mouse—used to pull down menus, outline parts of a picture, move selections, and stretch objects (Ch. 13)
**drive specifier** a disk drive letter immediately followed by a colon (Ch. 5)
**edit** to make changes in a file
**electronic mail (E-mail)** a way to send and receive messages with a computer (Ch. 12)
**electronic typewriter** an electric typewriter with a built- in microprocessor (Ch. 6)
**Encapsulated PostScript (EPS) file** a graphics file containing gray-shade information that can be imported and printed by page layout programs that use the PostScript language (Ch. 14)
**end user** see *user* (Ch. 1)
**entry** a record in an account (Ch. 15)
**expansion board** a circuit board that plugs into an expansion slot (Ch. 2)
**expansion card** see *expansion board* (Ch. 2)
**expansion slot** an internal connector that allows you to plug an additional circuit board into the motherboard; an extension of the bus (Ch. 2)
**expenses** monies paid out for the normal operation of a business (Ch. 15)
**expert** an experienced computer user (Ch. 1)
**expert system** a computer program that contains both a collection of facts and a list of rules for making inferences about those facts (Ch. 16)
**expert system shell** microcomputer software that contains an inference engine and lets nonprogrammers set up expert systems by supplying (1) their own facts to create knowledge bases and (2) rules to create rule bases (Ch. 16)
**exporting** writing data in a format that can be accepted by a different program (Ch. 10)
**extension** the second part of a DOS file's name (Ch. 5)
**external command** a DOS command that is kept in disk storage and temporarily loaded into memory only when needed or specifically requested (Ch. 5)
**external modem** a modem built into its own separate housing (Ch. 2)
**fiber-optic cable** glass filaments that transmit data in the form of extremely rapid pulses of light generated by lasers, used for high-speed local area networks (Ch. 12)
**field** a group of related characters in a data base record; a single data item, such as a number, character, word, or phrase (Ch. 10)
**file** a collection of information kept in secondary storage and loaded into primary memory when needed by a program; in a data base, a group of related records (Ch. 3)
**file compression utility** a program that squeezes files into less disk space by eliminating waste and redundant data (Ch. 16)

**file conversion utility** a program that modifies files from one application so that they can be used by another application (Ch. 16)

**file locking** preventing access to a file currently in use by another person on the same network (Ch. 10)

**filename** the primary part of a DOS file's name (Ch. 5)

**file recovery utility** a program that can reinstate accidentally erased files, restore reformatted hard disks, or perform other useful file operations (Ch. 16)

**file server** a network workstation used to store shared program and data files on a large-capacity, high-speed hard disk (Ch. 12)

**file specification** the combination of a disk drive specifier, a filename, and an extension (Ch. 5)

**file transfer utility** a program that can move data among different types of computers (Ch. 16)

**fillet** a CAD feature that joins two lines to create a rounded corner (Ch. 13)

**film recorder** a graphics output device that turns screen images into 35-mm slides (Ch. 13)

**Finder** a part of the Apple Macintosh operating system that allows users to run application programs, set up disks, and organize, copy, and delete files (Ch. 4)

**firmware** low-level, system software stored in ROM chips, such as the BIOS (Ch. 4)

**fixed currency format** a worksheet format in which two places are to the right of the decimal point, thousands are separated by commas, and each number is preceded by a dollar sign (Ch. 8)

**fixed disk drive** see *hard disk drive* (Ch. 2)

**fixed-point number** a number whose decimal or binary point is in a fixed place in relation to the digits (Appendix A)

**flag** in WordStar, a special character displayed at the end of each line on the screen (Ch. 7)

**flag column** in WordStar, the column along the right side of the screen that displays a character revealing something about each line of text (Ch. 7)

**flat-file data base manager** a program that works with one file of structured data at a time (Ch. 10)

**floating-point number** a number in which the position of the decimal or binary point can vary (Appendix A)

**floor model** a powerful, expensive microcomputer with a system unit larger than that of the typical desktop computer and designed to accommodate more add-in hardware components (Ch. 1)

**floppy disk** an inexpensive, flexible magnetic medium for storing computer programs and data, and that can be removed from the disk drive when not in use (Ch. 1)

**floppy disk drive** a disk drive that accepts floppy disks (Ch. 2)

**font** a set of letters, numbers, punctuation marks, and other symbols with a consistent appearance (Ch. 6)

**footer** one or more lines of text printed in the bottom margin of every page (Ch. 7)

**form** see *template* (Ch. 8)

**formatting** initializing a disk so that files can be stored on it (Ch. 4)

**formula** an expression that instructs a spreadsheet program to perform calculations or other manipulations on numbers, labels, or the contents of cells (Ch. 8)

**FORTRAN** one of the first high-level programming languages, designed to fulfill the computational needs of scientists, engineers, and mathematicians (Ch. 3)

**fourth generation language (4GL)** the most abstract type of programming language, designed to make it as easy as possible for users to tell a computer what to do (Ch. 3)

**free-form data base manager** a program designed to handle narrative text and irregular pieces of data, such as paragraphs, pages, articles, notes, discussions, and instructions (Ch. 10)

**full-duplex** a communications mode in which the characters sent to the host computer are echoed back to the terminal's screen (Ch. 12)

**function** a ready-made procedure that performs tedious, complex, or often-used computations or other manipulations in a worksheet (Ch. 8)

**function keys** on an IBM-compatible computer, the keys on the left side or top of the keyboard labeled F1 through F10 or F12, used to perform common operations

**game adapter** a circuit board or set of chips that allows the use of joysticks or trackballs (Ch. 2)

**Gantt chart** a horizontal bar graph that shows the major tasks of a project, when each task must be performed, and how long each task will take to perform (Ch. 16)
**general accounts** the accounts that automatically receive data from lower-level accounts (Ch. 15)
**general ledger** the main listing of the accounts of a business (Ch. 15)
**generic operating system** an operating system that can be adapted to almost any type of computer (Ch. 4)
**gigabyte (G)** 1,073,741,824 bytes (Ch. 2)
**global** pertaining to or acting upon an entire document, spreadsheet, or data base file
**global delete** the ability to remove all those records that meet certain criteria (Ch. 10)
**global filename characters** the characters * and ?, which can be used in DOS file specifications to indicate names with one or more characters in common (Ch. 5)
**global modify** the ability to change all those records that meet certain criteria (Ch. 10)
**global search and replace** see *global modify* (Ch. 10)
**graphics** any kind of graphs, plots, drawings, and other images not restricted to text characters (Ch. 1)
**graphics adapter** a display adapter that can produce graphics (Ch. 13)
**graphics-based windowing environment** a windowing environment that can work with programs that display pictures and characters of all different sizes, styles, and fonts (Ch. 16)
**graphics package** software that can produce graphs, plots, drawings, pictures, or charts (Ch. 1)
**graphics tablet** a flat surface on which the user draws with a stylus, pen, or some other pointing device (Ch. 2)
**greeking** representing text too small to be distinguished by shaded bars in order to show its position on a page (Ch. 14)
**grid** criss-crossed lines used to keep objects lined up with each other on the screen; a visual aid for placing objects in a drawing (Ch. 13)
**half-duplex** a communications mode in which the characters sent to the host computer are not echoed back to the terminal's screen (Ch. 12)
**hand-held computer** the smallest type of microcomputer, smaller than a paperback book and weighing less than a pound (Ch. 1)
**handle** a little black square on the boundary of a selected object, used to drag or resize the object (Ch. 13)
**hard disk** a circular platter of rigid aluminum covered with a thin magnetic coating for storing computer programs and data (Ch. 2)
**hard disk drive** a disk drive that contains one or more hard disks (Ch. 2)
**hard hyphen** a hyphen created by pressing the - key (Ch. 7)
**hard return** a carriage return created by pressing the Enter key (Ch. 7)
**hard space** blank created by pressing the Space Bar (Ch. 7)
**hardware** the physical components of a computer system (Ch. 1)
**Hayes-compatible modem** a modem that operates like a Hayes Smartmodem (Ch. 12)
**head crash** the result of a disk drive's read-write head colliding with a minute obstruction or hitting the surface of the disk (Ch. 2)
**header** one or more lines of text printed in the top margin of every page (Ch. 7)
**help level** in WordStar, the number that determines which menus and prompts are displayed (Ch. 7)
**hexadecimal system** base 16 number system (Appendix A)
**hidden column** a worksheet column that exists and contains data, but is not displayed or printed (Ch. 8)
**hierarchical** a method of organizing files into rank-ordered groups (Ch. 4)
**high-level language** an abstract programming language that facilitates the expression of complex data processing operations (Ch. 3)
**host computer** the computer being called by another computer (Ch. 12)
**hypermedia** the nonsequential organization and presentation of information, including graphics, audio, and video (Ch. 16)
**hypertext** the nonsequential organization and presentation of information with a computer (Ch. 16)

**IBM-compatible** a microcomputer that works just like, or in some ways better than, an IBM microcomputer, and can run the same software (Ch. 1)
**icon** a small pictorial symbol that represents some file, file folder, action to be performed, or program to be run (Ch. 1 and Ch. 4)
**importing** reading and, if necessary, translating data originally created with some other program (Ch. 10)
**income statement** a report that summarizes the revenues and expenses of a business for a given period of time (Ch. 15)
**index file** a file that contains only record numbers listed in a particular order (Ch. 10)
**indexing** a way to reorder the records of a data base without actually duplicating the data in a new file or rearranging the actual records in the original file (Ch. 10)
**information** a more organized and useful form of input data (Ch. 1)
**ink-jet printer** a printer with a mechanism for squirting tiny droplets of ink to form text and graphics on paper (Ch. 2)
**input** any data or information entered into a computer (Ch. 1)
**insertion point** another term for *cursor;* where text is inserted with a word processing package (Ch. 6)
**insert mode** a typing mode in which all characters typed at the current cursor location push aside existing text to the right (Ch. 6)
**installed** when a software package is copied to a hard or floppy disk and set up to be run (Appendix C)
**instruction set** a limited collection of low-level tasks a computer can do with a single instruction. (Ch. 3)
**integrated circuit chip** a thin slice of semiconductor material, such as pure silicon crystal, impregnated with carefully selected impurities, commonly used in computers and many other electronic devices (Ch. 2)
**integrated software** a software package that includes word processing, spreadsheet, data base, graphics, and communications capabilities (Ch. 16)
**intelligent recalculation** see *smart recalculation* (Ch. 8)
**interface** a connection between a computer's CPU and an external device operated under its control (Ch. 2)
**internal command** an essential or frequently used DOS command that is kept in memory (Ch. 5)
**internal modem** a modem built onto an expansion board or directly onto the motherboard (Ch. 2)
**interpreter** a program that translates and runs one high-level language instruction at a time as it is entered into a computer (Ch. 3)
**interrupt** a signal that suspends the current program to tell the CPU that some critical event has occurred (Ch. 4)
**inventory control** the accounting subsystem that tracks products and materials on hand (Ch. 15)
**invoice** a bill sent to a customer (Ch. 15)
**iteration** see *iterative recalculation* (Ch. 8)
**iterative recalculation** a way to obtain an approximate result to an indirect circular reference in a worksheet by recomputing the formulas a number of times (Ch. 8)
**journal** a chronological listing of transactions (Ch. 15)
**joystick** a vertical lever that can be tilted in any direction to control a cursor or steer a simulated vehicle (Ch. 2)
**justified** a type of text alignment in which text is flush to both the left and right margins (Ch. 6)
**key** a field used to sort or index the records of a data base (Ch. 10)
**keyboard** the primary input device with which you enter data and tell a computer what to do (Ch. 1)
**keyboard macro** a timesaving feature for abbreviating a sequence of commands or a line of text (Ch. 6)
**kilobyte (K)** 1,024 bytes (Ch. 2)
**knowledge-based system** see *expert system* (Ch. 16)
**label** a heading, title, or other note in a worksheet cell (Ch. 8)

**label prefix character** in Lotus 1-2-3, a special character (', ^, ", \) that tells the program that the following item is a label and not a number or formula, and indicates how to align labels within cells or if a character is to be repeated within a cell (Ch. 9)
**laptop computer** a full-fledged microcomputer squeezed into a 4- to 15-pound housing smaller than most briefcases (Ch. 1)
**laser printer** a high-quality printer that uses tightly focused beams of light to transfer images to paper (Ch. 2)
**layer** a CAD feature like a transparent overlay sheet that can be created separately and superimposed on top of other layers (Ch. 13)
**learn mode** an easy-to-use method of defining a macro by recording keystrokes (Ch. 8)
**letter-quality** like the output of a good electric typewriter (Ch. 2)
**liabilities** amounts of money owed to others (Ch. 15)
**light pen** a rod used to point at or draw on a computer display screen (Ch. 2)
**line editor** a simple program that can only work with a single line of text at a time (Ch. 4)
**line height** in WordStar, the distance between lines of printed text (Ch. 7)
**link fields** special fields that connect records in different data bases (Ch. 10)
**linker** a program that combines the output files of programming language translators into a single executable program file (Ch. 4)
**liquid crystal display (LCD)** a flat-panel screen that presents black characters against a grey background, commonly used in watches, clocks, calculators, and hand-held and laptop microcomputers (Ch. 1 and Ch. 2)
**load** to copy a program or data file from disk into memory
**local area network (LAN)** several microcomputers connected together within the same building, or nearby buildings, to share hardware, software, and data (Ch. 2)
**locked cell** see *protected cell* (Ch. 8)
**logged** the current disk drive or directory (Ch. 7)
**log-in** to enter the assigned group name, user name, and password to gain access to a system (Ch. 11)
**loss** negative profit (Ch. 15)
**Lotus Access System** a program called Lotus that lets you start 1-2-3 or any of the other programs that come with the Lotus 1-2-3 package (Ch. 9)
**machine language** the only programming language that can be directly used by a computer, consisting of binary number that represent CPU instructions, memory addresses, and data (Ch. 3)
**machine learning** a method by which computers can program themselves, through trial and error, to accomplish a particular task (Ch. 16)
**macro** a sequence of keystrokes that can be entered, named and replayed
**magnetic disk** a semipermanent storage medium that can be erased and written over and over again (Ch. 1)
**magnetic tape** a long strip of thin plastic covered with a magnetic coating (Ch. 2)
**magnetic tape drive** a secondary storage device that uses magnetic tape to hold programs and data (Ch. 2)
**mail-merge** combining a master document with a data file of names and addresses to create personalized form letters (Ch. 6)
**mainframe** a big, powerful, fast, expensive computer (Ch. 1)
**manual recalculation** a feature that causes the formulas in a worksheet to be recalculated only when explicitly directed to do so (Ch. 8)
**many-to-many link** a type of link that connects multiple records to other multiple records in data base files (Ch. 10)
**master document** a document containing text and special commands to be mail-merged with a data file (Ch. 7)
**master index file** the index file that specifies the order in which all records will be displayed unless otherwise specified (Ch. 11)
**megabyte (M)** 1,048,576 bytes (Ch. 2)
**megahertz (MHz)** a unit of frequency that equals one million cycles per second (Ch. 2)
**memory** a computer's internal storage for temporarily holding programs and data (Ch. 1)
**memory-resident** a type of program that allows a user to temporarily suspend an activity and switch to another one under a single-tasking operating system such as DOS (Ch. 4)
**menu** a list showing options available in a program (Ch. 1)

**menu bar** a list of the names of pull-down menus across the top of the screen (Ch. 7)
**merging** combining two worksheets into one (Ch. 8)
**Micro Channel Architecture** the high-performance bus (underlying circuit) design of IBM's Personal System/2 Models 50 through 80 microcomputers (Ch. 1)
**microcomputer** a small computer that uses a single microprocessor chip as its central processing unit (Ch 1)
**microcomputer standard** a generally accepted set of rules by which hardware and software operate (Ch. 1)
**microjustification** spreading the white space of a line between words and letters so that no large gaps appear (Ch. 7)
**microprocessor** a central processing unit made up of a single integrated circuit chip (Ch. 1)
**million instructions per second (MIPS)** a unit of computer performance that represents the execution of computer instructions (Ch. 1)
**minicomputer** a medium-sized computer that simultaneously serves several users or controls complex equipment (Ch. 1)
**mixed cell reference** a cell address that is half-relative and half-absolute, in which either a row or column is absolute, but not both (Ch. 8)
**mnemonic** an easy-to-remember abbreviation for a computer operation, such as ADD (Ch. 3)
**modem** a device that allows a computer to transmit and receive programs and data over ordinary phone lines (Ch. 2)
**modem cable** a cable that connects an external modem to a serial interface socket at the back of a computer (Ch. 12)
**modular phone jack** a socket that accepts the little plastic plug on the end of a telephone cord (Ch. 12)
**monitor** a computer display screen (see *display*) (Ch. 1)
**monochrome graphics monitor** a single-color screen that can display both text and graphics (Ch. 2)
**monochrome text monitor** a single-color screen that displays sharply-defined characters, but no graphics (Ch. 2)
**motherboard** the main circuit board of a computer (Ch. 2)
**mouse** an input device consisting of a small box with one or more buttons that is slid across the table top to manipulate objects on the screen and to select menu options (Ch. 1)
**MS-DOS** see *PC-DOS* (Ch. 4)
**multidimensional spreadsheet** a spreadsheet program that allows every cell in a worksheet to be connected to corresponding cells in other worksheets (Ch. 8)
**MultiFinder** an addition to the Apple Macintosh operating system that allows some multitasking capabilities and lets users run application programs, set up disks, and organize, copy, and delete files (Ch. 4)
**multifunction board** an expansion board that includes several add-on options, such as memory, a real-time clock, a game adapter, a display adapter, and serial and parallel interfaces (Ch. 2)
**multiprocessing** the ability to run several programs simultaneously by using more than one processing unit (Ch. 4)
**multiscan monitor** a monitor that can change its resolution to match a number of different display adapters (Ch. 13)
**multitasking** the ability to run more than one program concurrently (Ch. 4)
**natural language processing** getting computers to understand portions of ordinary human languages such as English (Ch. 16)
**natural recalculation** the order of worksheet recalculation that updates a cell only after evaluating any cells on which it depends (Ch. 8)
**near letter-quality (NLQ)** a dot-matrix print mode that produces attractive output by having the printhead make two or more passes over each character (Ch. 2)
**NETBIOS (Network Basic Input/Output System)** low-level programs that send and receive data to and from the network adapter (Ch. 12)
**network** computers connected to share hardware, software, and data (Ch. 1)
**network adapter** a sophisticated expansion board that connects a microcomputer to a local area network (Ch. 2)
**network interface** the adapter and connector that link a workstation to a network (Ch. 12)

**network media** the cables that connect network workstations (Ch. 12)
**network server** a network workstation that handles special chores (Ch. 12)
**network software** a set of programs, mostly on the file server, that moves data and messages between the workstations and servers, and controls the sharing of files and hardware devices (Ch. 12)
**network workstation** an ordinary microcomputer used to run software, transfer files, and send messages on a network (Ch. 12)
**newspaper-style columns** see *snaking columns* (Ch. 6)
**nondocument file** in WordStar, a file that contains only text and no formatting codes (Ch. 7)
**nonprocedural language** see *fourth generation language* (Ch. 3)
**novice** a beginning computer user (Ch. 1)
**null-modem cable** a cable for directly connecting the serial ports of two computers (Ch. 12)
**numeric keypad** on an IBM-compatible computer, the area on the right side of the keyboard arranged like the number keys on a calculator
**object code** software that has been translated into machine language (Ch. 3)
**object-oriented** a package that lets you create and manipulate images made up of only discrete geometric objects such as lines, curves, rectangles, ovals, irregular outlines, polygons, and text (Ch. 13)
**octal system** base 8 number system (Appendix A)
**one-to-many link** a type of link that connects a single record in one file to multiple records in one or more other files (Ch. 10)
**one-to-one link** a type of link that connects a single record in one file to a single record in another file (Ch. 10)
**on-line** connected to and controlled by the computer
**on-line help** information about how a program works that you can display on the screen, without your having to look it up in a printed reference manual (Ch. 6)
**on-line information service** a service that allows computers equipped with a modem to retrieve vast quantities of information and communicate with other users (Ch. 1)
**on-line reference** a program such as a spelling checker, thesaurus, or user manual that you can use while running another program
**operand** a number on which an operation is to be performed (Ch. 3)
**operating system** a set of programs that controls a computer's hardware and manages the use of software (Ch. 3)
**operation code (opcode)** the part of a machine language instruction that indicates which operation is to be performed (Ch. 3)
**optical disk drive** a secondary storage device that uses a laser to read or write data on a plastic disk (Ch. 2)
**OS/2** a single-user, multitasking operating system, developed by IBM and Microsoft, for IBM and IBM-compatible microcomputers that use the Intel 80286 or Intel 80386 microprocessor (Ch. 4)
**output** any information produced by the computer; the computer's responses to your input (Ch. 1)
**overwrite mode** a typing mode in which characters typed at the current cursor location replace existing characters (Ch. 6)
**owner's equity** see *capital* (Ch. 15)
**packet-switching network** see *public data network* (Ch. 12)
**page break** a division between two pages (Ch. 7)
**page description language** a specialized computer programming language for defining the size, format, and position of text and graphic elements on a printed page (Ch. 14)
**page formatting** specifying the general organization of an entire page of text (Ch. 6)
**page layout software** a package for arranging text and graphics on pages before they are printed (Ch. 14)
**page offset** in WordStar, the space between the left edge of the paper and the left margin (Ch. 7)
**painting program** a pixel-based program for producing pictures on a computer screen (Ch. 13)
**palette** the total number of colors to choose from in a particular video mode (Ch. 2)
**pan** a CAD feature that lets you move the viewing window up, down, left, or right (Ch. 13)

**paragraph formatting** specifying the appearance of individual blocks of text (Ch. 6)
**parallel columns** columns of text that continue on another page, instead of on the same page in the next column to the right (Ch. 6)
**parallel interface** a connection that transmits data, an entire byte at a time, between a computer and an external device, such as a printer (Ch. 2)
**parallel port** see *parallel interface* (Ch. 2)
**parameter** an entry that designates possible alternate actions (Ch. 5)
**parity** a method of error checking used to help ensure that all of the data bits of a character were received correctly after a transmission (Ch. 12)
**Pascal** a general-purpose, high-level language originally designed to teach students the principles of good programming (Ch. 3)
**path** a drive specifier followed by a list of subdirectory names, separated by backslashes, that describes the route to a particular subdirectory (Ch. 5)
**pattern palette** a menu of patterns that can be used with drawing tools to create objects and to fill in enclosed areas on the screen (Ch. 13)
**payroll** the accounting subsystem that maintains personnel information, generates paychecks, computes tax withholdings, and creates summary reports of employee earnings (Ch. 15)
**PC-DOS** a single-user, single-tasking operating system developed by Microsoft for IBM microcomputers (Ch. 4)
**pel** see *pixel* (Ch. 2)
**personal computer** see *microcomputer* (Ch. 1)
**pixel** picture element; a tiny dot on a computer display (Ch. 2)
**pixel-based** a package that has control over every dot on the screen (Ch. 13)
**plotter** an output device that uses one or more pens to draw on paper (Ch. 2)
**point** a typographical measure equal to $^1/_{72}$ of an inch (Ch. 6)
**polling** a protocol in which a controlling workstation sends messages to other workstations on the network, asking each one in turn if it has any messages or data to transmit (Ch. 12)
**pop-up menu** a list of options that appears on the screen only when a user issues a special command (Ch. 3)
**pop-up utility** see *desk accessory* (Ch. 16)
**portable computer** a microcomputer about the size of a small suitcase, designed to be moved, but not used in transit (Ch. 1)
**posted** when the totals for each journal are copied to the corresponding accounts in the general ledger (Ch. 15)
**PostScript** a page description language for high-resolution printers and typesetters (Ch. 14)
**power supply** a refined source of electrical power for a computer that contains a transformer to lower and regulate the voltage level (Ch. 2)
**power user** see *expert* (Ch. 1)
**primary key** the field on which records are sorted first (Ch. 10)
**primary storage** a computer's internal memory (Ch. 2)
**print buffering** see *print spooling* (Ch. 6)
**printer** a device for producing permanent copies of computer output on paper (Ch. 1)
**printer setup string** a group of special control codes directing the printer to turn on such options as compressed print (Ch. 9)
**print queuing** the ability to specify a list of documents to be printed (Ch. 6)
**print server** a network workstation used to control a printer shared by other workstations on a network (Ch. 12)
**print spooler** a utility program that reduces or eliminates waiting for a printer to produce documents (Ch. 16)
**print spooling** the ability to print one document while working on another (Ch. 6)
**procedure file** see *batch file* (Ch. 4)
**ProDOS** a single-user, single-tasking proprietary operating system for the Apple II family of microcomputers (Ch. 4)
**profit** the difference between revenues and expenses (Ch. 15)
**program** a sequence of step-by-step instructions that tell a computer what to do (Ch. 1)
**Program Evaluation and Review Technique (PERT)** a scheduling method for tasks whose completion times are difficult to estimate (Ch. 16)

**programmable data base manager** a relational or flat-file data base manager that includes its own programming language or works with a standard programming language such as BASIC, C, COBOL, FORTRAN, or Pascal (Ch. 10)
**programmer** a person who creates computer programs (Ch. 1)
**programming language** a set of symbols and rules that direct the operations of a computer (Ch. 1)
**project management software** a package that helps to formally plan and control complex undertakings (Ch. 16)
**prompt** a symbol or statement that indicates the computer is waiting for a response from the user (Ch. 3)
**proportional spacing** allotting different amounts of space for different characters (Ch. 6)
**proprietary** hardware or software, with tightly controlled patents or copyrights, that cannot be legally duplicated without being licensed by the originator (Ch. 1)
**proprietary operating system** an operating system designed specifically for a single model or line of computers (Ch. 4)
**protected cell** a cell that cannot be altered, deleted, or moved unless its protection is first turned off (Ch. 8)
**protocol** a set of rules that govern how computers communicate (Ch. 12)
**public data network** a way to call a distant communications service from a local telephone number (Ch. 12)
**pull-down menu** a list of options that appears when the list's title or symbol is selected from the top of the screen (Ch. 3)
**purchase order** a printed form for buying products and services (Ch. 15)
**Query-by-Example (QBE)** a highly interactive query language that makes it easy for a user to extract information from a data base (Ch. 10)
**querying** searching for only those data base records that meet one or more specific criteria (Ch. 10)
**query language** a specialized set of commands for rearranging or extracting data from data bases (Ch. 10)
**QuickDraw laser printer** a laser printer designed especially for Apple Macintosh computers as a lower-cost alternative to PostScript printers (Ch. 14)
**RAM cache** a part of memory specially reserved for data that must be frequently retrieved (Ch. 4)
**RAM disk** an area of memory that is set up to simulate a disk drive (Ch. 4)
**RAM resident** see *memory resident* (Ch. 4)
**random access memory (RAM)** storage in which all addresses are equally accessible; the portion of a computer's primary storage used to hold programs and data temporarily (Ch. 2)
**range** a series of adjacent cells in a worksheet (Ch. 8)
**read-only field** a data base field whose contents can be viewed but not altered (Ch. 10)
**read-only memory (ROM)** permanent primary storage that is encoded with programs and data at the factory, retains its contents when the power is turned of, and can be read and used but never erased, changed, or augmented (Ch. 2)
**read-write head** a tiny electromagnet on a disk drive's access arm that can create or erase minuscule magnetic spots on the disk directly below (Ch. 2)
**real number** see *floating-point number* (Appendix A)
**real-time clock** a built-in clock that keeps the date and time- of-day for a computer (Ch. 2)
**record** an array of related fields that contains all the data about a particular person or object (Ch. 10)
**record locking** preventing the deletion or modification of an individual record currently being used by another person on the same network (Ch. 10)
**record number** a unique number assigned to each record in a data base file (Ch. 10)
**redirector** a layer of software that acts as a traffic controller for the data and messages transmitted over a network (Ch. 12)
**reformatting** erasing and reinitializing a previously formatted disk (Ch. 4)
**register** a storage compartment inside the CPU for temporarily holding numbers that are currently being manipulated (Ch. 2)
**relational data base** two or more files that contain at least one field in common (Ch. 10)

**relational data base manager** a program that allows you to create, maintain, reorganize, and print structured data from more than one file at a time (Ch. 10)
**relative cell reference** a cell address that pertains to a cell's position rather than to the cell itself (Ch. 8)
**repeating text** in SuperCalc, one or more characters preceded by an apostrophe (') (Appendix D)
**replace** a word processing feature used to automatically substitute one word or phrase for another throughout a document (Ch. 6)
**report** with a data base program, a printed collection of record fields, usually formatted in some manner (Ch. 10)
**resident routine** see *internal command* (Ch. 5)
**resolution** the sharpness of a display screen (Ch. 2)
**revenues** payments or promises to pay received from sales, rentals, interest, or other investments (Ch. 15)
**ring network** a topology in which each workstation is connected to a single cable that runs past all of the workstations, with the two ends of the central cable hooked together (Ch. 12)
**robot** a computer-controlled machine that performs mechanical tasks (Ch. 16)
**root directory** the main directory on every DOS disk (Ch. 5)
**row-wise recalculation** the order of worksheet recalculation that begins with cell A1 and proceeds across row 1, then row 2, and so on (Ch. 8)
**ruler guide** in a page layout program, a dotted line that helps keep text and graphics aligned (Ch. 14)
**ruler line** a line that shows the positions of the margins and tab stops (Ch. 7)
**rules** dividing lines placed to separate columns and offset blocks of text (Ch. 14)
**running head** the same title printed on every page (Ch. 6)
**sans serif** a kind of plain typeface without serifs (Ch. 14)
**scanner** an input device that can read text and/or graphics from paper and enter it directly into the computer (Ch. 2)
**Screen Painter** the dBASE III PLUS feature that lets you build forms that resemble the printed forms commonly used in many offices (Ch. 11)
**scroll bar** an on-screen tool used to allow movement within a document, usually found in word processing packages with graphics interfaces (Ch. 6)
**scrolling** the upward movement of text on a display screen (Ch. 5)
**search** a word processing feature used to locate a name or topic within a document (Ch. 6)
**secondary key** the field on which records are sorted second, after the primary key (Ch. 10)
**secondary storage** storage that supplements primary storage by providing a place to keep programs and data when they are not needed (Ch. 2)
**semiconductor** a substance that conducts electricity poorly at low temperatures, but well at high temperatures, and is used to make integrated circuit chips (Ch. 2)
**sequential access medium** storage medium, such as magnetic tape, on which data items can be retrieved only in the order in which they were recorded (Ch. 2)
**serial interface** a connection that transmits bytes of data, one bit at a time, between a computer and an external device, such as a modem (Ch. 2)
**serial port** see *serial interface* (Ch. 2)
**serif** a kind of typeface that has lines crossing and finishing off the main strokes of the characters (Ch. 14)
**service program** low-level program in the BIOS that can be invoked by other software to perform hardware-related tasks (Ch. 4)
**shared word processor** a word processing system on a large, multiuser computer (Ch. 6)
**single-tasking** the simplest type of operating system that accommodates a single user and runs a single program at a time (Ch. 4)
**slide show program** a program that allows you to present a sequence of pictures on a computer screen, either automatically timed or directly controlled (Ch. 13)
**Small Computer System Interface (SCSI)** a connection that provides high-speed access to peripheral devices such as hard disks (Ch. 2)
**smart recalculation** the ability of a spreadsheet program to automatically update only those cells, if any, that are affected when a new entry is made (Ch. 8)

**snaking columns** text that continues from the bottom of one column to the top of the next column to the right (Ch. 6)
**snap** a CAD feature that automatically aligns objects to the nearest grid lines (Ch. 13)
**soft hyphen** a hyphen generated by the auto-hyphenation feature (Ch. 7)
**soft return** a carriage return generated by the word wrap feature (Ch. 7)
**soft space** an extra blank generated by a word processing program to justify text (Ch. 7)
**software** a program or set of programs that tells a computer system what to do (Ch. 1)
**sorting** arranging items in some particular order (Ch. 6)
**source code** software in an assembly language or a high-level language before it is translated into machine language (Ch. 3)
**specifications** a detailed list of the exact components, options, and capabilities of a particular hardware device (Appendix B)
**speech synthesizer** an output device that either mimics human speech or constructs it out of prerecorded sounds (Ch. 2)
**spelling checker** see *built-in dictionary* (Ch. 6)
**spreadsheet** see *worksheet* (Ch. 3)
**spreadsheet package** software that helps you manipulate tables of numbers (Ch. 1)
**stackware** information systems created with the Hypertalk language of Apple's Hypercard program (Ch. 16)
**star network** a topology in which an individual cable is run from a central server to each workstation (Ch. 12)
**startup directory** in Lotus 1-2-3, the disk drive and directory automatically used to store and retrieve worksheet files unless otherwise specified (Ch. 9)
**static menu** a list of options that usually remains on the screen in a fixed position (Ch. 3)
**status line** in WordStar, the top line of the screen that displays the current disk drive and the file name of the document (Ch. 7)
**stop bits** bits that mark the end of an individual data character transmission (Ch. 12)
**Structured Query Language (SQL)** a standardized language for extracting information from a relational data base (Ch. 10)
**style sheet** a collection of formatting instructions that can be saved in a file and applied to different documents (Ch. 6)
**subdirectory** a group of files on a disk organized under a single name (Ch. 4)
**submenu** a menu that is activated by selecting an option from a higher-level menu (Ch. 9)
**supercomputer** an extremely fast mainframe (Ch. 1)
**supermicro** see *workstation* (Ch. 1)
**supermini** a powerful minicomputer with capabilities similar to those of some mainframes (Ch. 1)
**surge protector** a device that rapidly cuts off the electricity when a voltage surge occurs (Appendix B)
**symbolic addressing** the assignment of meaningful names, such as TOTAL, to computer memory locations (Ch. 3)
**system board** see *motherboard* (Ch. 2)
**system call** see *service program* (Ch. 4)
**system clock** a crystal, oscillating several million times per second, that synchronizes the internal operations of the microprocessor and other computer components (Ch. 2)
**system prompt** see *DOS prompt* (Ch. 5)
**system software** the software that handles the many details of managing a computer system (Ch. 1)
**system unit** in many microcomputers, the box that houses the central processing unit, control circuitry, expansion boards, memory, and disk drives (Ch. 1)
**telecommute** to work at home using a microcomputer or a terminal connected to a computer at the office (Ch. 2)
**teleconference** an electronic forum that allows computer users who share special interests to communicate and hold on-line meetings (Ch. 1)
**template** a general-purpose, ready-made worksheet in which the user fills in the blanks or changes selected entries (Ch. 8)
**terminal** a computer input/output station consisting of a keyboard and a display (Ch. 4)
**terminal emulation** a communications software feature that lets you use a microcomputer as a computer terminal (Ch. 12)

**text-based windowing environment** a windowing environment that uses only the standard character set built into the computer and that cannot work with graphics programs (Ch. 16)

**The Assistant** the menu system of dBASE III PLUS (Ch. 11)

**time-sharing** an operating system that rapidly switches among several users at fixed intervals of time (Ch. 4)

**token-passing** a protocol that uses a control signal called a token that determines which workstation is allowed to transmit messages or data (Ch. 12)

**tool palette** a menu of icons for drawing, adding text, moving about, and selecting parts of a picture created with a painting or drawing program (Ch. 13)

**topology** the way hardware components are arranged in a network (Ch. 12)

**touch screen** an input device built into or over a display screen that uses infrared light beams or an electrically conductive surface to identify the position of a finger as it points to the screen (Ch. 2)

**trackball** a box that contains a protruding ball that can be freely rotated in any direction and is often used as an alternative to a mouse (Ch. 2)

**transient routine** see *external command* (Ch. 5)

**Transputer** a special microprocessor that can be connected with other Transputers to construct a fast, powerful multiprocessing computer (Ch. 4)

**twisted-pair wire** two wires that have been partially wrapped around each other, used for ordinary telephone lines and inexpensive local area networks (Ch. 12)

**typeface** see *font* (Ch. 6)

**undo** a feature that lets you cancel your most recently performed operation (Ch. 6)

**UNIX** a multiuser, multitasking generic operating system originally developed at AT&T's Bell Laboratories (Ch. 4)

**uploading** transferring a file from your computer to a host computer (Ch. 12)

**upwardly compatible** the ability of a new software product to handle every official command that worked with previous versions of it (Ch. 5)

**user** a person who runs software on a computer to accomplish some task (Ch. 1)

**user friendly** easy-to-learn; can be used by people who don't have a lot of computer experience (Ch. 1)

**user interface** how a user directs the actions of software and how the software responds to these requests (Ch. 3)

**utility** a small, specific program that adds handy features to a particular operating system or application package (Ch. 3)

**value-added network** see *public data network* (Ch. 12)

**vendor** a person or company that sells something (Ch. 15)

**very high level language** see *fourth generation language* (Ch. 3)

**video mode** a combination of screen resolution and number of colors that can be used at one time (Ch. 2)

**view file** in dBASE III PLUS, a file that lets you look at two or more data base files from a particular perspective (Ch. 11)

**voice recognition system** an input device that can recognize a finite number of isolated sounds, words, and phrases (Ch. 2)

**what-you-see-is-what-you-get (WYSIWYG)** a feature in which a document is printed on paper exactly as it appears on the screen (Ch. 6)

**window** a boxed-in area on the screen that shows the activity of a particular software program (Ch. 1)

**windowing environment** system software that lets you divide your screen into a number of different boxes and run a separate program in each one (Ch. 3 and Ch. 16)

**word processing** a common computer application that allows you to produce documents, such as letters and reports, with a computer (Ch. 1)

**word processing package** a software package used to create, enter, edit, format, store, and print documents

**word wrap** a word processing feature that automatically begins new lines when necessary without the user having to press the Enter key (carriage return) (Ch. 6)

**worksheet** a table of columns and rows of numbers, text labels, and formulas used in an electronic spreadsheet package for the manipulation of numerical, financial, and accounting data (Ch. 3 and Ch. 8)

**workstation** a small, yet powerful computer generally used by only one person at a time, traditionally used by scientists and engineers for drafting, design, and map-making (Ch. 1)

**write once, read many (times) (WORM)** an optical disk drive that allows users to record data once, and then only read it thereafter (Ch. 2)

**write-protection** a diskette feature that can be used to prevent the contents from being erased or altered (Ch. 5)

**write-protect notch** a small rectangle cut out of one side of a 5.25-inch diskette that can be covered with a gummed tab to write-protect the disk (Ch. 5)

**write-protect switch** a tab on a 3.5-inch diskette that can be slid to open a little hole in the disk's plastic case, thereby write-protecting the disk (Ch. 5)

# Photo Credits

## Chapter 1

1.1 IBM; 1.2 Northwestern Life Insurance; 1.3 WordPerfect Corp; 1.4 University of Illinois; 1.12 (a) IBM (b) Apple Computer, Inc., (c) Toshiba America, Inc.; 1.13 Memorex; 1.14 Tandy Corp; 1.15 NEC America, Inc.; 1.16 Compaq Computer Corp.; 1.17 IBM; 1.18 IBM; 1.19 Apple Computer, Inc; 1.20 IBM; 1.21 IBM; 1.22 Apple Computer, Inc.; 1.23 Sun Microsystems, Inc.; 1.24 Digital Equipment Corp.; 1.25 IBM; 1.26 Cray Research, Inc.

## Chapter 2

2.1 Thom O'Connor; 2.2 IBM; 2.3 Intel Corp.; 2.6 BASF; 2.7 TEAC Corp. of America; 2.9 Seagate Technology; 2.11 Tallgrass Technologies; 2.12 IOMEGA Corp.; 2.14 SONY Corp. of America; 2.15 IBM; 2.16 Apple Computer, Inc.; 2.17 IBM; 2.18 Apple Computer, Inc.; 2.19 AST Research, Inc.; 2.20(b) IBM; 2.21(b) Brother International Corp.; 2.22(b) Hewlett-Packard Co.; 2.23(b) Hewlett-Packard Co.; 2.24 Hewlett-Packard Co.; 2.25 Hayes Microcomputer Products, Inc.; 2.26 Apple Computer, Inc.; 2.27 Wico Corp.; 2.28 IBM; 2.29 IBM; 2.30 CalComp; 2.31 Princeton Graphic Systems.

## Chapter 4

4.17 Microsoft Corp.; 4.19 Apple Computer, Inc.

## Chapter 5

5.9 IBM.

## Chapter 6

6.1 Smith Corona; 6.2 Raytheon; 6.3 Hewlett-Packard Co.; 6.4 IBM.

## Chapter 12

12.2(a) Hayes Microcomputer Products, Inc.; 12.3(a) Hayes Microcomputer Products, Inc.

## Chapter 13

13.1(a) IBM, (b) Microsoft Corp., (c) Hewlett-Packard Co.; 13.2 IBM; 13.3 Princeton Graphic Systems; 13.4 Polaroid Corp.; 13.5 Strategic Locations Planning, Inc.

## Chapter 14

14.2 Hewlett-Packard Co.; 14.3(a&b) Apple Computer, Inc., (c) IBM; 14.4 Sigma Designs, Inc.; 14.5(a) GCC Technologies, (b) Apple Computer, Inc., (c) Hewlett-Packard Co.; 14.6 Thunderware, Inc.

## Chapter 16

16.2 Lotus Development Corp.; 16.3 Ashton-Tate; 16.4 Microsoft Corp.; 16.7 IBM; 16.9 XTREE Co.; 16.10 Peter Norton Computing, Inc.; 16.11 Funk Software, Inc.; 16.13 Borland International; 16.16 Systat, Inc.; 16.17 Borland International; 16.20 MECA Ventures, Inc.; 16.21 SoftView, Inc.; 16.22 Broderbund Software, Inc.; 16.23 Broderbund Software, Inc.; 16.24 Microsoft Corp.; 16.26 OWL International, Inc.

# Index

# School Software Direct Order Form

☐ Ship to student ☐ Ship to reseller (replacement stock)

Qualifying teachers, as well as college, university, and other post-secondary students, can now purchase WordPerfect Corporation (WPCORP) software directly from WPCORP at a reduced price. To qualify, a participant must be a full-time teacher/administrator or currently enrolled as a full-time post-secondary student, and must agree in writing not to resell or transfer any package purchased under this program.

If you satisfy these qualifying conditions and would like to purchase software directly from WPCORP under the School Software Program, complete the following six steps and sign at the bottom of the form.

**Step 1.** From the list below, select the appropriate software and disk size for your computer (please note that you are limited to *one* package of each program) and mark an "x" in the corresponding box(es).

| Product | Price* | Disk Size | |
|---|---|---|---|
| ☐ WordPerfect 5.0—IBM Personal Computers | $135.00 | ☐ 3½" | ☐ 5¼" |
| ☐ WordPerfect 4.2—IBM PC & Compatibles | 125.00 | ☐ 3½" | ☐ 5¼" |
| ☐ WordPerfect—Apple IIe/IIc | 59.00 | ☐ 3½" & 5¼" | |
| ☐ WordPerfect—Apple IIGS | 59.00 | ☐ 3½" | |
| ☐ WordPerfect—Amiga | 99.00 | ☐ 3½" | |
| ☐ WordPerfect—Atari ST | 99.00 | ☐ 3½" | |
| ☐ WordPerfect—Macintosh | 99.00 | ☐ 3½" | |
| ☐ PlanPerfect—IBM PC & Compatibles | 99.00 | ☐ 3½" | ☐ 5¼" |
| ☐ DataPerfect—IBM PC & Compatibles | 150.00 | ☐ 3½" & 5¼" | |
| ☐ WordPerfect Library—IBM PC & Compatibles | 59.00 | ☐ 3½" & 5¼" | |
| ☐ WordPerfect Library—Amiga | 59.00 | ☐ 3½" | |
| ☐ WordPerfect Executive—IBM PC & Compatibles | 79.00 | ☐ 3½" & 5¼" | |
| ☐ Junior WordPerfect—IBM PC & Compatibles | 35.00 | | ☐ 5¼" |
| ☐ WordPerfect, Foreign Versions—IBM PC & Compatibles<br>Language ______________ | 175.00 | ☐ 3½" | ☐ 5¼" |
| ☐ WordPerfect Speller, Foreign Versions—IBM PC & Compatibles<br>Language ______________ | 40.00 | ☐ 3½" | ☐ 5¼" |

**No changes or additions can be made to this list.*

**Step 2.** Make a photocopy of your current Student ID or Faculty card *and* a photocopy of some well known form of identification displaying your social security number, such as your Driver License or Social Security Card. (WPCORP will hold this information strictly confidential and use it only to guard against duplicate purchases.) Your school ID must show current enrollment. (If it does not show a date, you must send verification of current enrollment.) If you have serious reservations about providing a social security number, call the Education Division at (801) 227-7131 to establish clearance to purchase any of the above software products at these special prices.

**Step 3.** Enter your social security number: ___ ___ ___ – ___ ___ – ___ ___ ___ ___ .

**Step 4.** Enclose payment for the total cost of the package(s) ordered with personal check, money order, Visa, or MasterCard.

Account # ______________________ Expiration Date ________ ☐ VISA ☐ MasterCard

(Make check or money order payable to WordPerfect Corporation.)

**Step 5.** List your shipping address and the address of your local computer store (dealer) in the space provided:

Ship To ______________________ Designated Dealer ______________________

______________________ D.C. Heath and Company, College Div.

______________________ 125 Spring St., Lexington, MA 02173

Phone ______________________ Phone (800) 235-3565

**Step 6.** Enclose this signed and completed form, the photocopies of your identification cards, and your signed check or money order (or Visa or MasterCard account number and expiration date) in an envelope and mail to School Software Program, WordPerfect Corporation, 1555 N. Technology Way, Orem, UT 84057.

The information provided herein is correct and accurate, and I will abide by the restricting conditions outlined by WPCORP in this document. I understand that at its sole discretion, WPCORP may refuse any order for any reason.

Signature ______________________ Date ______________________

*Utah residents add 6.25% sales tax. Prices are quoted in U.S. dollars and apply to U.S. delivery for U.S. customers *only.*